R. L. WILSON

THE OFFICIAL® PRICE GUIDE TO

GUN COLLECTING

D0572170

R. L. WILSON

THE OFFICIAL® PRICE GUIDE TO GUN COLLECTING

THIRD EDITION

HOUSE OF COLLECTIBLES
The Crown Publishing Group • New York

Important Notice. All of the information, including valuations, in this book has been compiled from the most reliable sources, and every effort has been made to eliminate errors and questionable data. Nevertheless, the possibility of error, in a work of such immense scope, always exists. The publisher will not be held responsible for losses that may occur in the purchase, sale, or other transaction of items because of information contained herein. Readers who feel they have discovered errors are invited to *write* and inform us, so they may be corrected in subsequent editions. Those seeking further information on the topics covered in this book are advised to refer to the complete line of *Official Price Guides* published by the House of Collectibles.

Copyright © 2000 by R. L. Wilson

All rights reserved. No part of this book may be reproduced or transmitted in any form or by any means, electronic or mechanical, including photocopying, recording, or by any information storage and retrieval system, without permission in writing from the publisher.

House of Collectibles and the HC colophon are trademarks of Random House, Inc.

Published by: House of Collectibles
The Crown Publishing Group
New York, NY

Distributed by The Crown Publishing Group, a division of Random House, Inc., New York, and simultaneously in Canada by Random House of Canada Limited, Toronto.

www.randomhouse.com

Manufactured in the United States of America

ISSN: 1096-3960

ISBN: 0-676-60153-7

10 9 8 7 6 5 4 3 2 1

Third Edition: December 2000

Dedicated with Respect and Affection
to
William B. Ruger Sr.
Chairman of the Board and Founder
Sturm, Ruger & Co., Inc.
Inventor, Gun Designer, Gunmaker,
and Arms Collector

For the Pleasure He Has Brought
to
Millions of Sportsmen, Target and Recreational Shooters,
and Gun Collectors
Through His Unique Line
of
Fine Guns
and Advocacy of the Shooting and Outdoor Life
*****
In the 51st Year of His Corporation
and in Commemoration
of His 84th Birthday
June 21, 2000

The author with William B. Ruger and editor Paul D. McCarthy at the launch of Ruger & His Guns *at Holland & Holland, Ltd., New York, November 1996.*

Contents

Acknowledgments

The third edition of *The Official Price Guide to Gun Collecting* called into play a more international entourage of advisers than the first edition. The author gratefully acknowledges the cooperation of the many who have helped make this publication possible. My thanks go to:

Wm. "Pete" Harvey, for sharing his expertise and experience in fine-tuning the massive array of technical and evaluation information presented in the database. The breadth and scope of this data is so extensive that only a person with the comprehensive knowledge of Pete Harvey would prove instrumental in assuring a useful and up-to-date array of data and prices.

Martin J. Lane, for innumerable favors and assistance, for several crucial insights into his own experience in the firearms field, for assistance in collecting photographs, and for numerous crucial assists over the years on this book and other projects. And to his staff at United Protective Security Systems and his Martin Lane Historical Americana Gallery, New York City, particularly Phil, Mary, Josh, Ruben, Deborah, and Karen.

My gifted and innovative agent, Peter Riva, and his wife and colleague Sandy, for their mastery of the publishing world, and for guiding the author's career to publishers the likes of Crown, Random House, Simon & Schuster, and Abbeville Press.

Robert M. Lee, founder and President, Hunting World, Inc., for his inspiration, cooperation, and assistance. His dedicated connoisseurship continues to play a vital role in setting a new standard of excellence in the arms field. To Anne Brockinton, Scott Bergan, and the Hunting World and Deeside Trading Co. staffs, for their help, support, and interest.

Alvin A. White for his ongoing education of the author (from 1961) in the rarefied realm of the arms engraver, and—as he so uniquely knows—the world of the all-around craftsman in decorative arts. And to Andrew Bourbon and Daniel Cullity for the insights on the gunmaking arts they have shared with the author.

William B. Ruger Sr., and the talented staff at Sturm, Ruger & Co., Inc., for the wisdom unique to their firm, which has impacted significantly all the writer's work during and following completion of *Ruger & His Guns.*

Ugo Gussalli Beretta, President, Fabbrica d'Armi Pietro Beretta SpA, Gardone, Italy, for the generous promotion of the author's *The World of Beretta: An International Legend.*

John R. Woods Jr., former NRA Foundation President, and to Wilson Phillips and H. Wayne Sheets, National Rifle Association of America, for their dedication to public education on firearms subjects, for their support of the author's projects over the years, and for their roles in creating the R. L. Wilson Educational Endowment of the NRA Foundation.

Greg and Petra Martin, and Greta, for their cordiality while the author was sequestered in San Francisco, completing this tome. To the staff of Butterfield & Butterfield, especially Katja S. Kaiser, Department Manager, Arms & Armor, for assistance with information and illustrations.

Peter Buxtun, not only for his hospitality while the author was escaping from his office in Connecticut, in order to complete the manuscript for this book, but for his own insights and extensive files shedding light on the captivating universe of firearms.

Jackie Autry, Monte and Joanne Hale, Executive Director John L. Gray, James and Mary Ellen Hennessey Nottage, and to the staff of the Autry Museum of Western Heritage, for their devoted and imaginative presentation of the "Buffalo Bill's Wild West" exhibition, on loan from the Michael Del Castello, Buffalo Bill Museum (Buffalo Bill Historical Center), and Greg Martin collections, which opened March 2, 2000.

Guy Wilson, Director, Royal Armouries Museum (Leeds) and Master of the Armouries, H.M. Tower of London, and to Graeme Rimer, Keeper of Weapons, for organizing the "Buffalo Bill's Wild West" loan exhibition, first opening in Leeds in May 1999. The show ran through the summer and proved to be the most spectacular exhibit of Buffalo Bill material presented in a traveling venue.

Ian D. Skennerton, Arms & Militaria Press, Australia, for numerous suggestions, additions, and comments on the British military section. His continuing advice and assistance on that material have proven most helpful and enlightening. His periodical, *International Arms & Militaria Collector,* is a highly recommended source of information and illustrations.

Special appreciation to the following officials of Colt Industries, Colt Firearms Division, and to the present Colt's Mfg. Co., Inc.: Donald Zilkha, Chairman of the Board, General William Keyes, President, Al DeJohn, Kathleen Hoyt (Historian), the late R. H. Wagner, M. S. Huber and Beverly Jean Rhodes.

Peter Hawkins, Howard Dixon, Christopher Austyn, and Natasha Hanscomb, of Christie's Arms and Armour and Gun departments, London, and to Conor Fitzgerald, of Christie's Western Americana Department, New York.

Gary Reynolds, whose Hamburg Cove emporium continues to serve as a point of rejuvenation and inspiration for the author, for his assistance in collecting firearms and illustrations.

The many additional collectors, dealers, museum curators, engravers, and others who generously have supplied the author with literally thousands of photographs and reams of information on American and European arms.

A myriad of dealers and collectors, all friends of the author, some dating back to the 1950s: Robert E. Petersen, William H. Tilley, Herb Glass and Herb Glass Jr., Claude Blair, William Reid, John Gangel, Fred Sweeney, George S. Lewis Jr., Michael Zomber, David Condon, Richard Ellis, Mike Clark, Tom Wibberley, Bernard Braverman, Norm Flayderman, Jack Malloy, Monte Whitley, John Jones (CAI Investments), Buck Stevens, Richard P. Mellon, Walter B. Ford III, Mrs. John B. Solley III, Jerry D. Berger, David S. Woloch, Rene Delcour, John Amicucci, John Hovaness Hintlian, Donald Stika, Buddy Hackett, Michael V. Korda, Don Wilkerson, Albert Brichaux, A. T. Seymour III, Horace Greeley IV, R. B. Berryman, Charles Ruger, Alexander Vogel, Carolyn R. Vogel, Craddock Goins, John G. Hamilton, George L. Deal, Sr. and Jr., Dr. Chester P. Bonoff, Roy G. Jinks, Mrs. James E. Serven, Mrs. L. C. Jackson, Thomas Haas, Jonathan M. Peck, John S. duMont, David Winks, William H. Myers, N. Brigham and Louise Pemberton, Glode M. Requa, Joseph G. Rosa, Charles Schreiner III, Larry Sheerin, Andrew Singer, G. Maxwell Longfield, MD, George Taylor, Dennis LeVett, Chris deGuigne IV, Ira Weinstein, William Hosley, Karen Blanchfield, Bernard Osher and John Gallo of Butterfield's, and that master finder of fine guns and fellow vintage automobile racer *extraordinaire,* Hans W. Schemke.

A special tribute to the memory of the following, now deceased, who played a role in the evolution of the author's gun collecting career over the years: Gene Autry, Hans Barthel, Johnie Bassett, Howard L. Blackmore, James U. Blanchard III, Charles L. Bricker, Arnold M. Chernoff, Dr. Robert G. Cox, C. C. Cunningham, Gaines deGraffenried, Stanley Diefenthal, Jack Dutton, Hugh J. Fitzgerald, Gerald G. Fox, Glenn Gierhart, William H. Goldbach, Karl Glahn, Stephen V. Grancsay, Barry Gray, Herbert E. Green, Robert E. Hable, Jim Hoiby, Benjamin F. Hubbell, Lew Hutcheson, L. C. Jackson, Harry C. Knode, Sid Latham, Merrill K. Lindsay, John Jarvis, Mr. and Mrs. William M. Locke, Dr. Richard C. Marohn, Miss E. B. McCormick, A. I. McCroskie, Mrs. William D. Maver, Henry P. Maynard, Dr. R. L. Moore Jr., Ronald A. Ogan, John E. Parsons, Harold L. Peterson, Philip R. Phillips, H. A. Redfield, Fred A. Roff Jr., James E. Serven, Clare F. Short, William E. Simon Sr., Samuel E. Smith, John B. Solley III, William Otis Sweet, Dr. Leonid Tarassuk, Thomas A. Thornber, Arno Werner, Hermann Warner Williams Jr., and Dr. John M. Wilson Sr.

My thanks to the following photographers, and a salute to their artistry, imagination, patience, and skills:

Peter Beard, Tom Beiswenger, E. Irving Blomstrann, G. Allan Brown, Susan Einstein, Richard Ellis, Roger Fuhr (Roland Design), Paul Goodwin, Harrington-Olson, Gus Johnson, Meyers Studio, Inc., Rick Oltmans, Mauro Pezzotta, Louise Pemberton, Bruce Pendleton, Beau Pierce, Ed Prentiss, Douglas Sandberg, Phil Spangenberger, S. P. Stevens, David Wesbrook, and Christopher T. Wilson.

Mark K. Benenson and the members of the board of the National Foundation for Firearms Education, headquartered in New York City, for their role in public education on firearms matters.

Marketing whiz Jeffrey Starr, and his energetic and perceptive wife Carolyn, for their encouragement of the author over the years, and for inspired insights on the fine art of selling books and other products.

Judi Glover, the author's secretary and assistant, who patiently deals with countless details, deadlines, double- and triple-checking, follow-ups, emergencies, the seemingly endless wrapping and shipping of books by the gross, and making sure nothing goes undone.

The staff at House of Collectibles, Crown Books (a division of Random House), particularly: Laura Paczosa, editor, her assistant Liz Matthews, and Cindy Berman, senior production editor.

And finally, special thanks to the author's loyal and patient family: Heidi and Neal (and their son Nicholas Arno), Heather and Peter (and their daughter Brier Rose), Christopher and Stephen, all of them keen on firearms, and all but the grandchildren knowing the joy of a day in the field or at the range, or hours at home, in museums, and art and auction galleries, admiring the creations of the dedicated craftsmen who have made—and are making—the firearms we all enjoy.

R. L. Wilson
Castle View
Hadlyme, Connecticut

Preface to the Third Edition

The multifaceted world of collecting offers endless themes for the enthusiast: paintings, drawings, prints, and other two-dimensional art and artifacts, and the vast domain of the three-dimensional: sculpture, decorative arts, the world of "kitsch," matchbooks, ashtrays, *ad infinitum.* Devoted to these specialties are collectors' clubs, buy-sell-trade meets and shows, magazines, newspapers, and even TV shows (like the increasingly popular *Antiques Road Show* on PBS), mail-order companies, and the relatively new medium available to millions: the Internet. When a mainstream magazine like *Forbes* has its own collectors' column, when *Time* magazine gives the world of collecting cover stories and prices soar, then you know this extraordinary universe has truly arrived.

The author contends that the realm of the arms collector easily ranks at or certainly near the pinnacle of the most fascinating of all fields of collecting. Arms enthusiasts cover the complete history of man, from the beginning. Weapons were crucial for survival in the Stone Age, and although not universally essential for survival in modern times, they bring immense pleasure to countless millions. Going beyond the world of the arms collector, firearms also encompass satellite interests, as expressed in the author's dedication to the NRA Foundation, in the book *Steel Canvas:*

> Collectors, curators, historians, antiquarians, sport-, target-, and silhouette-handgun shooters, local club marksmen through Olympic-level international competitors, gunsmiths, engravers, trap-, skeet-, and sporting clay-shotgun shooters, historical reenactors, muzzle loading devotees, air-gun and pellet shooters, handloaders and cartridge enthusiasts

Any person from those satellites might experience the transition to becoming a collector, loosely translated as one who accumulates with a purpose, and—usually—a passion. An arms collector is usually born, that is, he (or she) started off collecting something; in the author's case, it was coins, accrued at first from payments collected from customers on his *Minneapolis Star and Tribune* paper route. Somehow that collecting instinct led to firearms.

The collecting appeal of firearms objects is multifaceted, and more comprehensive than in any other field of collecting: artistry and craftsmanship, history, mechanics, performance, and romance. As an indication of this deep and abiding interest, consider the fact that as of this date the existing literature on firearms numbers approximately 10,000 books, and countless issues of magazines—with more coming out on a regular basis.

Still another factor to consider: the scale of guns. Unlike cars, or many other subjects of collector passions, a gun is generally of a size that allows handling, transporting, taking apart, and otherwise enjoying. Unlike a car, which requires a garage, and a large collection a warehouse, a large gun collection can be kept in a safe, or in a closet, or under a bed!

THE MAKING AND MAKEUP OF AN ARMS COLLECTOR

Many times a collector has come from the ranks of active shooters, such as hunters. One of the Mellon banking family became a keen arms collector, but his first interest was sparked by hunting. Young Mellon was led to the antiquarian world under the astute guidance of legendary shotgun-shooting champion Rudy Etchen and pistol-shooting champion and antique-arms dealer Herb Glass.

As the collector becomes increasingly consumed by his fascination of firearms, he begins to branch out. Needing to research a particular item, he often becomes a bibliophile. Documenting an arm not only means poring through books, but often the world of photographs, and sometimes paintings, drawings, or other art work. To learn about a particular historical figure may require investigating genealogies and other unpublished sources. If the historical figure was involved in the Revolutionary War, the Mountain Man period, or in the Wild West of Jesse James, Wyatt Earp, and Doc Holliday, or in any number of other eras, themes, or events, the collector soon becomes knowledgeable in those subjects as well.

Perhaps due to a special exhibit at his or her home or office, the collector will become familiar with methods of displaying artifacts, with lighting, with fabrics, with design and presentation. Sometimes collectors are more up-to-date with advanced techniques, like fiber-optics, than professionals in the museum field. The exhibit or research trail may well lead to the world of autograph collecting, to the history of photography, to the circus and Wild West shows (e.g. Buffalo Bill and Annie Oakley), to memorabilia, costumes, badges, and any number of other interests. In the author's own research for special exhibitions, for writing books, or for ferreting out detailed data on particular arms, there is barely a field of collectible that he has not examined. In fact, he enjoys attending a book fair, or visiting an autograph dealer, or browsing through a general antique show, even touring a country house, almost as much as one of his favorite enthusiasms: attending a show dedicated to arms collecting.

The author's explorations and detours through the universe of art and antiques always returns to his pivotal dedication to the field of firearms. Janet Zapata, formerly Archivist, Tiffany & Co., and an expert in antique silver, has said that of all the different types of collectors she has met over the years, the arms collectors have been consistently the most interesting—and more likely able to speak with authority on a broader range of subjects than collectors from any other specialty. My old friend Norm Flayderman, a dealer in arms for nearly fifty years, is probably as knowledgeable on any subject as any person one could meet in a lifetime. His primary consuming passion, of course, is firearms. And when Norm suffered from a brain tumor in his sixties, his love of life and of his collecting passions were instrumental in his complete recovery!

Thus, the firearms field is not only totally captivating, but it is invigorating and stimulating. Having made a comfortable living from a dedication to the field of arms collecting for nearly forty years, the author can honestly say that he feels he has never "worked" a day in his life—it's been fun all the way, and he wouldn't trade places with anyone on earth. He has no intention of ever retiring, and likes to quote gunmaker, inventor, designer, arms, art, and automobile collector William B. Ruger's erudite observation: "When you rest, you rust."

CELEBRITY ARMS ENTHUSIASTS

Far more people are keen on firearms and their responsible uses than is generally thought, even by analysts in the arms field. This immense fraternity of men and women comes from all walks of life, and from virtually every sphere of human interest and lifestyle. From bankers, lawyers, doctors, and politicians to film, TV, and rock stars, to priests and other clerics, to secretaries and insurance salesmen—from the lowliest of voters and nonvoters to (sometimes, but sadly *not* just now) presidents of the United States—and from the most leftwing of liberals to the most rightwing of conservatives, *ad infinitum.* Gun collectors may be screaming leftwing liberals, moderates, or rightwingers. But what they are generally not is of the socialist bent—capitalism is definitely the drumbeat to which nearly all arms collectors march.

Consider this list of enthusiasts, some shooters, some collectors, some hunters, some just plinkers, some keen on the craftsmanship, or the mechanics, or the artistry, the performance, or even the precise discipline of handloading or target shooting: Ronald Lauder (younger son of cosmetics tycoon Estee Lauder), John Entwhistle (bass guitarist, The Who), actresses Cybil Shepherd and Sharon Stone, financier Henry Kravis, Arnold Schwarzenegger, Sylvester Stallone, the British royal family, race driver Jackie Stewart, Roger Waters (Pink Floyd), Mark Knopfler (Dire Straits), Jerry Lewis, Dan Aykroyd, Bruce Willis, *ad infinitum.* For still more names, see the chapter titled "A Noble Tradition: A History of Arms Collecting."

Gun collecting is a crucial element in the seemingly endless battle against those misguided and uninformed souls who dismiss all guns as simply "made to kill" and "without socially redeeming value." Gun collectors represent a relatively small group in number, but form potentially the most powerful of all firearms groups in terms of access and influence where it counts. Further, gun collectors present the reality of scholarship, of careful, dedicated, and enthusiastic studies of the art and craftsmanship, history, mechanics, and romance of fine guns.

Pete Harvey with the author, each enjoying a rare Winchester. At left, a Model 1873 Saddle Ring Carbine number 143216, engraved and signed by John Ulrich, and presented to the winner of a live pigeon shoot in South America, c. 1884; one from a set of nine, two of which have been found by Martin Lane as of this writing. At right, the magnificent Model 1886 Takedown Sporting Rifle, number 129666, a new design in 1900 by John Ulrich, for the cover of the new "Highly Finished Arms" catalogue. Exquisitely engraved, and inlaid with platinum and gold. Both Winchesters fully documented in the factory ledgers.

WM. "PETE" HARVEY AND THE VALUES IN THIS BOOK

One of the best-known figures in firearms, Wm. "Pete" Harvey has been active in the field since 1944, first as a collector, and later as a collector/dealer, and then as president of one of the world's leading auction houses specializing in all types of firearms. A member of numerous arms collectors' organizations, Pete was instrumental in setting up the auction for the first NRA Gun Collectors Show and Conference, in Nashville, 1996. Operation of the Wm. "Pete" Harvey Auction Service, Inc., began full-time in 1993. Prior to that Pete had been in partnership with another New England auction house since 1987, and still prior had worked with the Richard Bourne Co., auctioneers, from the mid-1970s.

An experienced sportsman, collector, and well-rounded widely recognized expert, having handled virtually every type of firearm known to collectors, shooters, and enthusiasts in general, Pete is uniquely qualified to play a key role in corroboration of the values presented in the *Price Guide,* and will continue to do so as the book continues to be refined in future editions.

The author has known Pete Harvey since the early 1960s, and when taking on the contract to do the *Price Guide*, immediately thought of calling on his expertise. Certainly an important part of the pleasure of doing this complex project has been to work with a professional of the stature of Wm. "Pete" Harvey.

A WONDERFUL OPPORTUNITY

The *Official Price Guide to Gun Collecting* has offered a wonderful opportunity to the writer. Because the work not only provides values and identifications for a broad range of firearms, it is also designed to introduce readers to the incredible world of guns—and designed to do so in a way that will appeal, we fervently wish, not only to the novices but to the old-timers who think that, perhaps, they've "been there and done that" in this field.

This book will be in a state of evolution throughout its lifetime. The subject of collectors firearms is too vast for the work to evolve in any other way. Each year's edition, therefore, will present a fresh "The Season in Review" section. Each edition will have added information in a variety of sections and on a variety of subjects as dealers, collector/dealers, and collectors help with more material, and as the author continues his never-ending quest for fresh data and illustrations. Updated values, of course, will continue to be a paramount feature of each of these new editions.

So, look for the 2002 edition to appear in the fall of 2001, with more than enough new facts, observations, and illustrations to satisfy the most demanding of gun devotees. The author looks upon each new *Official Price Guide to Gun Collecting* as if it were a totally new book—and will be striving to make each and every edition full of surprises, and the most exciting and informative new book in the world of gun collecting every year. We feel strongly that to have a first-class and basic firearms library, the collector, dealer, collector/dealer, historian, gun crank, or whatever, should at the least have in his library: *Flayderman's Guide to Antique American Firearms and Their Values,* S. P. Fjestad's *Blue Book of Gun Values,*[1] Stoeger's *The Shooter's Bible*, Ned Schwing's *Standard Catalogue of Firearms, The Gun Digest,* and (of course) the author's *Official Price Guide to Gun Collecting*. To go beyond these basic titles, the author's further suggestions are in the detailed bibliography on page 454.

As a freelance writer and antiquarian, and one fortunate enough to travel extensively, the author has had the opportunity to meet thousands upon thousands of people from a great many different locations, cultures, and spheres of influence. It is no understatement that in virtually every such sphere there are persons keen on firearms. One thing a professional in the arms-collecting world quickly realizes nearly every day is that this business is so vast that no one knows it all, or has done it all! All that's part of the excitement, adventure, and appeal of the world of guns. I cannot wait to get started every day, and all-night sessions on a manuscript or other project are not unusual—sometimes it's hard to put on the brakes and stop for some rest!

I am honored to be a part of this international fraternity of dedicated enthusiasts. In every single article and book ever written on arms in my forty-nine years in this field (the first piece was on King Henry VIII's "gonne shields" in the National Muzzle Loading Rifle Association's *Muzzle Blasts* magazine), my excitement for this incredible subject has remained keen.

Good collecting, and remember, you can never have too many good guns!

[1] See a column done by the author for Steven Fjestad, for the 20th anniversary edition: "Gun Collecting."

Introduction: The Season in Review, 1999–2000

Even more than its predecessor season, that of 1999–2000 proved to be an extraordinary period to digest. Gun auctions and gun shows continued to evolve and to be refined, publications continued to flow, and prices and values (at times superior in gains to the extraordinary stock market) generally continued to escalate. Many collectors' arms increased in scarcity and in desirability. But the gun continued to be a convenient target for inept politicians who used the issue as a scapegoat for their failures at dealing with the root causes of crime. "Gun Shows" have become new buzzwords with President Clinton, desperate for any "legacy" but that of lies—for which he will probably most be remembered, at least by the majority of gun owners, and certainly by gun collectors.

The modern gun business was given a spurt of growth, as the politicians took aim at guns and gun owners. When these opportunists and the press attack gun shows, gun owners, and the NRA, they send a message to the public, which is, in effect: buy your guns now because next year they may be illegal.

The likelihood of the next president being a Republican suggests that draconian gun control legislation should not be a factor for at least the next four or eight years. Unfortunately, the generally liberal press still has not understood that passing more gun laws will not reduce crime. They should read Professor John Lott's book, *More Guns Less Crime,* and recognize that the antigun activists have a real problem with the truth.

Charlton Heston has continued to carry the firearms banner. His reign as president of the NRA was scheduled to end with the May 2000 election, during the Annual Meetings, in Charlotte, North Carolina. However, a special arrangement was made through the NRA Board of Directors, allowing Heston to be reelected for his third year. The long-popular star's charisma, access, and convincing rhetoric have proven instrumental in helping the cause of gun ownership at a most crucial time. Despite the hysteria following the murders by the two crazed students at Columbine High School and all the pressure from politicians and the misguided, misled media for severe gun legislation, no major federal antigun bills were passed.

The battle lines have indeed been drawn. But try as he has, and assisted by the media (which has often been hostile to him), Clinton failed miserably to crush the "gun culture." If the media were to cover other areas of social concern with the same ignorance and bigotry, the injured constituents would be in a continuous chorus of uproar.

On the subject of firearms laws and regulations, the reader should see the author's remarks in the Introduction to the 1996–97 and 1998–99 season, which has information that need not be repeated for the present, third edition. Further, see the comments of Mark K. Benenson, on page 20.

COMPETITION BETWEEN AUCTION HOUSES AND DEALERS

Auctions continue to be a strong presence in the arms collecting trade. However, gun shows are still very much a presence—although in some instances the material offered is recycled from an auction, having been freshly purchased by a dealer who may have had difficulty obtaining stock through other means. The trade is also carried on via magazines and journals like *Shotgun News, Gun List,* and *Gun Journal,* and the ever-increasing activity on the Internet. Despite claims that those sales are being conducted illegally, delivery is strictly forbidden without obeying firearms laws of national, state, and local jurisdictions. The powerhouse of on-line auctions, eBay, has a stated policy of obeying these laws, and has the guidance of its recently purchased Butterfield's, whose expertise in the area of gun sales at auction is world-renowned.

The resulting competition among dealers and auction houses has enlivened the business, helping to place firearms among the hottest collectibles of the 1990s and the commencement of the 21st century. Many of the new auction houses in the arms field have been opened by dealers who realized that auctions are presently dominating the field and started their own galleries as a way to cultivate the phenomenon.

Judging from the author's ever-increasing collection of catalogues by auctioneers and dealers, plus the consistent increase in prices and values, the field of collectors firearms has never been healthier than at present. Martin Lane, the guiding executive at Bannerman's, observes:

> Bannerman's intends to pick up where the mainstream auction houses have dropped the ball—specializing in best quality antique firearms and related items. We have reasonable commission rates, an expert vetting committee, and objects absolutely guaranteed as described—or money refunded. Like the original Bannerman's, our house is a source for arms and accessories.
>
> The New York auction houses have put arms

and armor on a back seat, preferring to sell "politically correct" items.* We specialize in the arms field exclusively, so the subject is first and foremost in everything that we do. We feel that nothing is more American—or politically correct—than these treasures of our history.

Furthermore, ours is the only auction house exclusively offering these items in the world capital of art and antiques—New York.

BUTTERFIELD'S CONTINUES TO LEAD THE WAY

There is no denying that in the United States at present, Butterfield's (formerly Butterfield & Butterfield) continues to occupy the dominant position in arms collectors auctions. The firm's position was strengthened by its purchase in 1999 by the multibillion-dollar firm of eBay. Directed by Greg Martin, who is generally recognized as the leading auction figure and dealer in the arms business today (and one of the top collectors as well), the San Francisco–based firm continues to capture prime collections. Among its 1999 offerings were three particularly distinguished sales: *Antique European and American Firearms, Edged Weapons, Bayonets and Militaria* (February 22–23); *Fine American and European Antique Arms and Sporting Guns* (May 24–25); and *The Millennium Sale* (November 15–16, 1999). The new millennium began with the *Fine Arms and Western Americana* sale of February 28–29, featuring the estate of Montie Montana.

In 1999, Butterfield's sold more than $10 million in collectors' firearms, with the department maintaining its stature as the largest grossing and the most profitable of all of the firm's departments.

OTHER AUCTION HOUSES IN THE UNITED STATES

Other auction houses, however, firmly held their own: Little John's (John Gangel) held several sales, among them the spectacular Robert B. Berryman Collection.† Jeff Faintich held his sales, while Rock Island Auction Co. and Brad Witherell's held theirs, Jim Supica held his, and the Eastern contingent of David Condon, Inc., J. C. Devine, Inc., Wm. "Pete" Harvey, and James D. Julia, Inc., held their sales, to name but a few of the most active. The point is: there has been plenty of business for everyone.

The color section of *The Official Price Guide,* third edition, pictures some of the 1999–2000 catalogues. The quality of these publications generally continues to be on an extremely high level, presenting a most impressive image for the world of firearms and collecting.

* Estimated to total $4 billion annually.

† Little John's predict the firm will surpass Butterfield's.

EUROPEAN AND BRITISH AUCTION HOUSES AND DEALERS

Meanwhile, in England, Sotheby's, Christie's, Bonham's, Wallis & Wallis, and Weller & Dufty carried on with their own departments in antique arms and armor, as well as in vintage and modern sporting arms. The arms collecting world has yet to settle down after the ill-advised confiscation by the British government of approximately one million handguns. It has been established that gun crime increased by about 15 percent *after* the drastic legislation, while the government expended something on the order of £85,000,000 buying up guns from law-abiding citizens!

The color catalogues of Peter Finer are spectacular, scholarly, and brimming with rarities. They span weaponry and armor of several centuries, and rival or surpass the vast majority of heavily illustrated books on collectors firearms. The published collection is offered for sale and clients can contact Finer via e-mail, or can view the items on his Internet web page: http://www.peterfiner.com.

DEALERS REMAIN ACTIVE

As also reflected by lists of auction houses, the list of dealers presented in the Appendix is evidence of the fact that there remains a wealth of business for those who wish to work at the collectible firearms business. Any one of these professionals can attest to the fact that the business is healthier now than it has ever been. Although good guns are increasingly hard to find, the number of keen collectors continues to increase. There will always be the turnover of pieces from collectors whose estates need to be settled through sales, or whose guns are to be sold due to divorce, debt, or simply to move on to another subject of collecting (recycling, as it were).

Among the extraordinary pieces sold through dealers in this past season were a cased Belt Model Paterson formerly in the collection of the Duke of Orleans (heir to the French throne) and a Model 1866 Winchester carbine that had been presented to Buffalo Bill Cody as a champion buffalo hunter. Some spectacular firearms were displayed, with many sold, at Wallace Beinfeld's Antique Arms Shows, particularly at the winter show at the Riviera Hotel, Las Vegas—the world's finest gun show.

PRIVACY AN ISSUE

In completing the manuscript for the new, two-volume *The Colt Engraving Book,* the author was offered the opportunity to reflect on his previous editions, of 1974 and 1982.

In those days, collectors were far more inclined to allow owners' credits to accompany publication of pictures of their firearms. The collectors who did not wish to be identified in these credits were few and far between, one in particular being Philip R. Phillips (a Phillips Petroleum Co. heir). At this writing the opposite is true: most of the credits are to "Private Collection." Admittedly, a few of these are due to the fact that the author was no longer aware of the collection in which a particular gun resided. That brings up yet another issue: as I've researched and written about firearms for some forty years, one might think that if I don't know where all the fine guns are, who does? The fact is, *no one does!*

This sense of privacy plays a role in the marketing of firearms. Some collectors today will not deal directly with more than one source, such as a dealer or a dealer/collector. Some will buy only at auction, usually either through an agent or private curator, or by telephone bidding.

The author is so frequently asked to keep confidences that he is ever on the alert to follow the dictum: a closed mouth captures no flies! Because of the importance of confidentiality and privacy, historical letters by this writer, which originally were addressed directly to the name of the owner of the subject firearm, are generally given a title that details important features of the subject and are never addressed to a particular person, unless specifically requested.

CHARLTON HESTON AND THE NRA[1]

The election of Charlton Heston as president of the National Rifle Association at the annual meetings early in May 1998 was a historic step for the organization. For the first time in decades, the Association had elected as its leader a national figure—to whom the media could not deny access.

Heston has since made numerous public appearances. He has proven a skilled spokesman on the issue of firearms ownership and its relationship to freedom. Although the mainstream press has not always been kind to Heston, they cannot ignore him.

Further, it is important that the NRA not be perceived as a right-wing organization—which it decidedly *is not.* Rather, the NRA needs to be recognized as a group believing strongly in the importance of the right of law-abiding citizens to own firearms in a free society. Gun ownership is not a political issue, it is a freedom issue. Heston's election as president has proven instrumental in broadcasting the beliefs and views of the NRA to a much wider public, and has proven to be the most important and positive step forward for the Association in the past forty years.

For too long our words and deeds have either been ridiculed, or we have been "singing to the choir." Of course, the other side in the great gun debate—and "cultural Civil War" (to quote Heston)—is doing its best to crucify him. Truth is not a word with which these demagogues are at all comfortable.

Heston's column in the February 2000 issue of *The American Rifleman, The American Hunter,* and *The Guardian* was a classic, with the same piercing logic and understanding displayed in his address at the Harvard Law School Forum, February 16, 1999 (quoted in *The Official Price Guide to Gun Collecting,* second edition).

To quote in part from the February 2000 column:

> The Second Amendment guarantees us the absolute ability to defend ourselves from anyone who would take away our liberties or our lives, whether it be King George's Redcoats or today's criminal predators. It is the one natural right that allows "rights" to exist at all. If that freedom is ever lost, the rest of our freedoms are sure to follow.

"TALES OF THE GUN" THE CONTINUING SAGA OF TALES OF THE GUN

Following broadcast of the A&E special *The Story of the Gun* Parts I and II, July 21, 1996, the owners of A&E and the History Channel soon determined that the "gun culture" was a loyal constituency. Considering the fact that the total of fifty-two hour-long programs that have followed now have such distinguished sponsors as the Cadillac Division of General Motors, obviously these shows have been drawing stellar reviews.

A media source has told the author that the network does very little to advertise the firearms-related programming. But management finds that all that is needed is to list the shows in various programming guides, and word-of-mouth advertising takes care of the rest. The firearms programming on the History Channel receives the highest ratings of any of their shows. Further, viewers are not satisfied to watch the shows once, twice, or even three times—they watch them repeatedly. As a result, the audience grows every time a program is aired and has been estimated to be as high as *two million* for an episode.

Consequently, *Tales of the Gun* has the prime slot for Sunday evening viewing, and the total of programs done to date is impressive. Listed by series, with code numbers, these are as follows:

First Series:
- 3601: The Tommy Gun
- 3602: Infamous Guns
- 3603: The Guns of Colt
- 3604: Dueling Pistols
- 3605: Early Machine Guns
- 3606: M16 (Arms Race #1)
- 3607: AK47 (Arms Race #2)
- 3608: German Small Arms WWII
- 3609: The Making of a Gun

[1] See also chapter entitled "National Rifle Association of America."

3610: Early Guns
3611: Winchester
3612: Guns of the Civil War
3613: Girls and Guns

Second Series:

3614: Big Guns
3615: Gangster Guns of the 1920s & '30s
3616: The Luger
3617: Shotguns
3618: Guns of Browning
3619: Guns of Infantry, Pt. 2
3620: U.S. Guns of World War II
3621: Guns of the Bizarre
3622: Automatic Pistols
3623: Guns of the U.S. Mounted Cavalry
3624: Revolvers of Europe
3625: Guns of the Movies
3626: Japanese Guns of World War II

Third Series:

3627: Super Guns of Today and Tomorrow
3628: Guns of Remington
3629: Million Dollar Guns
3630: Naval Guns
3631: Guns of Mauser
3632: Guns of the Famous
3633: Bullets and Ammunition
3634: Guns of the Revolution
3635: Guns of the Sky
3636: Police Guns
3637: Guns of the Russian Military
3638: Guns of Smith & Wesson
3639: Guns of Infamy, Pt. 3

The recently slated fourth series programs are as follows:

3640: Rapid Firepower
3641: Guns of Valor
3642: The Gunslingers
3643: Guns of the British Military
3644: Guns of the Commandos
3645: The Rifle
3646: Sharpshooters & Long Range Weapons
3647: Guns of Beretta
3648: Guns of Israel
3649: Rockets, Mortars, and Missiles
3650: Guns of the Orient
3651: Guns That Changed the World
3652: Magnificent Failures

The author has had the pleasure of appearing in several of these programs. As one who attends a fair number of gun shows each year, he has been impressed by the fact that more comments are made on his television appearances than on his various books and magazine articles. A matter of further amazement is that a number of these shows have been syndicated in foreign countries. While I was having lunch with Peter Hawkins of Christie's, near the firm's London headquarters, someone at a nearby table recognized me from *Tales of the Gun*! And it was while proofing the new *The Colt Engraving Book,* the designer's accountant said that he had seen me on the History Channel, and on A&E! On yet another occasion, I was approached at a country club in Nashville, Tennessee, by a keen fan of the series.

What we are observing is a remarkable phenomenon: these programs help the public to understand what firearms are all about. Further, I am sure that the producers recognize if they broadcast an inaccurate, biased show about gun control, as was done by the Discovery Channel late in the 1990s, the ratings are not only poor, but after-broadcast sales of such a bigoted videotape are *dismal*. However, if a "gun control" program were to be done with integrity, accurately presenting the arguments, video sales would be excellent, because such a program would discount the ravings of the real gun nuts (those who hate guns and want to outlaw them) and celebrate the pro-gun point of view.

THE ROYAL ARMOURIES MUSEUM'S "BUFFALO BILL'S WILD WEST" LOAN EXHIBITION—AT THE AUTRY MUSEUM OF WESTERN HERITAGE[1]

Sure to draw positive public attention to firearms in American history, the Royal Armouries Museum's "blockbuster" traveling exhibition "Buffalo Bill's Wild West" opened March 2, 2000, at the Autry Museum of Western Heritage, Los Angeles, to rave reviews. The exhibition was inspired by the book *Buffalo Bill's Wild West: An American Legend*, and was brilliantly executed, drawing particularly from the collection of Michael Del Castello, with material from the Greg Martin collection, from the Buffalo Bill Museum, Buffalo Bill Historical Center, Cody, Wyoming, and private collectors.

Many of the objects pictured in the *Buffalo Bill's Wild West* book are shown in the exhibition, providing a rare opportunity to see some of the most fascinating historical artifacts associated with the West. Several important firearms, accoutrements, saddles, holsters, photographs, and numerous objects of memorabilia will be seen publicly for the first time in the United States.

From the Autry Museum, the show traveled to the Tennessee State Museum (Nashville), for approximately three months in the fall of 2000. The tour will be completed at The Colorado Historical Society for a run of approximately three months, beginning in the spring of 2001.

Featuring one of our greatest national heroes and a number of his "pards," the exhibitions are sure to draw a tremendous amount of public attention to these colorful characters and to their guns, without which they could not have plied their trade or survived the dangers of the West.

[1]See *The Official Price Guide to Gun Collecting*, second edition, page 6.

HAYS SPIRIT OF THE COWBOY COLLECTION

The Desert Caballeros Western Museum, "Arizona's Most Western Museum," in Wickenburg, an hour northwest of Phoenix, has the Abe Hays Western Americana Collection on long-term loan. Hays, owner of Arizona West Galleries, Scottsdale, is a veteran collector of Western Americana and an authority on the art, artifacts, and literature of the American West.

While visiting in the Phoenix–Scottsdale area, the author enjoyed a stop at the Arizona West Galleries, meeting Hays and his son Greg. It was almost impossible to leave the gallery, there were so many fascinating objects and beautiful, often historic, art and photographs on display, accompanied by unfailingly engaging conversation, symptomatic of the captivating subject of the great American West.

The illustration shows a selection of objects from the Abe Hays Collection. Quoting from the promotional piece on the display:

> Take a step back in time to the days when "cowboying" was a way of life. See the leather worn shiny with use and age, the patina of well loved silver, and the reatas used to corral wild mavericks of the range. Dating from the 1870's to recent times, *Hays Spirit of the Cowboy Collection* is one of the largest and finest selections of early working cowboy, wild west, rodeo, prison made, movie, and parade gear, ever opened to public view. The more than 500 artifacts are on long-term loan to the Desert Caballeros Western Museum from the Western Americana Collections of Abe Hays, owner of Arizona West Galleries, Scottsdale.

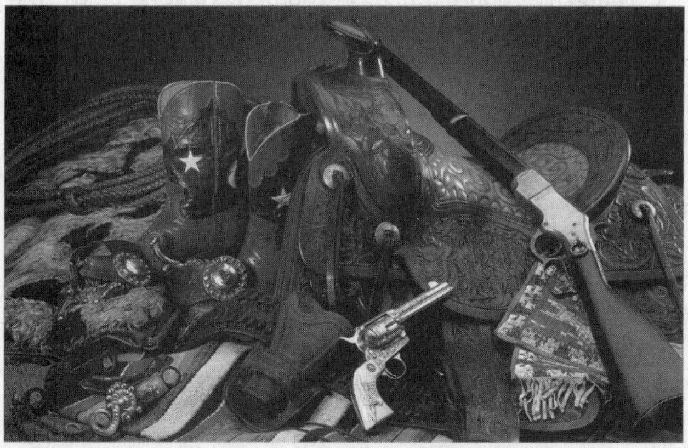

Selections from the Abe Hays Western Americana Collection, on display at the Desert Caballeros Western Museum: Frank Hamer .45 Colt Single Action Army revolver rests on 1928 Hamley World Championship Rodeo trophy saddle, with Model 1866 Winchester saddle ring carbine adjacent to Sioux quill and beaded wild West gauntlets. At lower center, *F. A. Meanea cartridge and money belt rig for Colt Single Action. G. S. Garcia silver snake pattern spade bit at* lower left, below *Visalia silver and gold snake pattern spurs. Handsomely stitched and embellished cowgirl rodeo boots done in red, white, and blue. The spotted woolly chaps are by Al Furstnow and the rawhide reata is by Louis B. Orgega.*

For further information, call Arizona West Galleries (480) 994-3752, or the Desert Caballeros Western Museum (520) 684-2272.

SIMEON STODDARD APPOINTED CURATOR, CODY FIREARMS MUSEUM

In a press release dated February 7, 2000, the Buffalo Bill Historical Center, Cody, Wyoming, announced the selection of Simeon Stoddard as curator of the Cody Firearms Museum. A history major at Brigham Young University (1993), Stoddard joined the Buffalo Bill Historical Center in 1994, as curatorial assistant at the CFM, and archival assistant with the McCracken Research Library. He had been serving as interim curator of the CFM, succeeding Curator Howard Madaus, who had resigned in 1999.

To quote Deputy Director for Collections and Education Dr. Robert Pickering:

> We're excited to turn over the Cody Firearms Museum's collection to Simeon Stoddard's care. He is an enthusiastic student of the history of firearms who has become intimately acquainted with our entire collection. He has the vision to guide the Cody Firearms Museum in the decades ahead and to contribute to development of the entire Buffalo Bill Historical Center.

As a member of the CFM's Advisory Board, the author has had the chance to meet with Curator Stoddard, and enjoyed some time with him and other members of the BBHC entourage at the Royal Armouries Museum, Leeds, during the opening ceremonies of the Buffalo Bill's Wild West exhibition in June 1999.

As one of the great arms collections in the world, the Cody Firearms Museum offers a considerable challenge to any curator. The competition for the appointment was keen, and Simeon Stoddard is more than qualified to undertake the responsibility. The position is particularly important, since over 300,000 visitors pour through the museum annually, and in many instances, what they see and experience heavily influences their understanding and appreciation of the incredible world of firearms.

NRA WHITTINGTON CENTER

While on a trip to New Mexico, the author made his first visit to the NRA Whittington Center, a pilgrimage worthwhile for any enthusiast of firearms and shooting. This unique institution was founded in 1973, and is comprised of an astounding fifty-two square miles of countryside. It is the largest and most comprehensive shooting and training facility in the world.

Available for members and public use is an extraordinary panorama of fully-equipped range facilities, recreational and camping sites, and hunting opportunities. In a lengthy interview with Mike Ballew, executive director, the author had the opportunity to comprehend the special role played by the Center in fostering the enjoyment, understanding, and appreciation of the shooting sports.

The firing ranges encompass high power and smallbore rifle, benchrest, metallic silhouette, pistol (including action shooting), black powder, hunter sighting-in, skeet, trap, and sporting clays. The ranges are spread over considerable amounts of land, not too distant from the entrance off Interstate Highway 25 (on the Santa Fe Trail, and the route from Santa Fe to Denver). Safety is emphasized at each and every station.

The Whittington Center brochure notes "Safety as a Priority" and states that:

> Firearms training makes up an important part of the activities. . . . Nationally-known instructors regularly conduct training in all shooting disciplines. Marksmanship and competition are strongly promoted, with the guiding principle the safe handling of firearms.

Under the heading "Trophy Class," the Center's brochure further notes:

> The game rich Whittington Center offers hunting opportunities for deer, elk, turkey, antelope, black bear and mountain lion. Through effective wildlife management, consistently high success rates are achieved for all species at the Center. . . . the finest hunting country in the Rockies. Everything you need to create the hunting and recreation adventure of a lifetime is available.

Facilities for visitors are impressive. There is a broad range of housing and other facilities for large and small groups, as well as individuals and families. Among the lodging options are modern housing, rustic cabins, campground with RV hook-ups, and primitive camping. Gift shop and other services are also available.

Many events at the Center for the year 2000 were listed, including competitions in every discipline, such as the Coors Annual International Schuetzenfest, the Silhouette National Championships in the NRA Hunter Pistol, NRA B.P.C.R., NRA High Power Rifle, and NRA Smallbore Rifle competitions, and the Old West Shootists Association National Shoot-Out.

Annually, approximately 200,000 visitors enjoy the programs of the Center, funded by donations from patrons, and by thousands who may not use the services but understand its key role in the preservation of the American heritage of firearms ownership, hunting, and the shooting sports. For further information on the NRA Whittington Center, write to P.O. Box 30-06, Raton, New Mexico 87740. Donations are tax-deductible, and that support plays a vital role in continuing the Center's unique array of services.

NEW BOOKS

Among the new titles that joined the ever-growing bibliography on firearms were:

British Gun Engraving, Douglas Tate

Douglas Tate's new work was highly sought-after at the Safari Club International convention in Reno, January 2000. Only a handful of copies were present, and all were coveted by the many attendees who were keen on fine guns. Tate collaborated with photographer David Grant to provide what U.S. publisher Safari Press has termed "the most opulent examples of British gun engraving in existence, from the greatest private collections in Europe and the USA." Safari Press further describes the book as follows:

> This book traces the traditions of British gun engraving from the end of the eighteenth century to today, and . . . [shows] how national styles, both English and Scottish, changed over time—from the conservative Victorian era when London's 'best' firms developed subtly different patterns to distinguish themselves from their competitors to the twentieth century when game scenes evolved to become hyper-realistic. . . . chronicles Celtic engraving as practiced chiefly by Scottish makers, the influence of the Arts and Crafts movement, and the significance the Indian maharajas had on British gun ornamentation. . . . 300 pages; large, oblong format; limited edition of 500 copies, signed, numbered and slip-cased.

This strikingly handsome book will sell out very quickly, and is a must title for any enthusiast of embellished firearms.

Custom Rifles in Black & White, Steven Dodd Hughes

This 186-page soft-cover book presents in handsome black-and-white photographs the work of twenty-nine master gunmakers and engravers, in bolt and lever action and single shot rifles. The work extends from the period of 1989 through 1999, and the pictures were taken by the author, himself a master stockmaker and metalworker, trained at the gunsmithing program of Trinidad State College, Trinidad, Colorado. To quote from the author's introduction:

> Through these photographs, I have attempted to illustrate the complexity and nuances of the individual details that combine to make a complete custom rifle. Most of the rifles are presented with a full-length view so the reader can see the whole and appreciate the overall lines as well. Where possible, I have included views showing the transition areas: metal to wood fit, how the comb nose blends into the grip, the melding of the action area through the grip into the buttstock and cheekpiece, and how the checkering enhances these transitions.

Hughes's admirable work will not only give anyone keen on fine gunmaking an understanding of the merit of contemporary craftsmen, it will also inspire present and future custom gunmakers and engravers. Too often arms collectors think only in terms of what was made in the past and are unaware of the intense quality and beauty of what is being made today.

The Colt Engraving Book, R. L. Wilson

The author's *The Colt Engraving Book* finally appeared in the fall of 2000, after having been delayed by nearly three years, because of the outrageous ineptitude of some bungling employee of one of the better-known shippers. Designed to be the matching volume to *The Book of Colt Firearms,* the new work totals more than 900 pages and contains over 1,100 illustrations, most of them in color. In order for the work to be more easily handled, it was issued in two volumes: volume one goes from the Paterson through the end of the Helfricht period (c. 1832–1921), and volume two from the Kornbrath and Glahn period through modern times (c. 1919–2000).

A most agreeable reason the new tome was delayed was the opportunity to do *Fine Colts: The Dr. Joseph A. Murphy Collection.* This 264-page volume, with over 220 color and more than 45 black-and-white illustrations, appeared in the fall of 1999. The book is, in effect, an additional volume of *The Colt Engraving Book.* The quality of Dr. Murphy's collection is exemplary, with numerous magnificent rarities, even an extraordinary cased set of modern Third Model Dragoons, inspired by the Sultan of Turkey revolver on display in the Arms and Armor Galleries of The Metropolitan Museum of Art, New York. The printer, Kwong Fat of Hong Kong, outdid itself in every respect, producing a book that sets a high standard for design and manufacture.

The Art of Miniature Firearms Centuries of Craftsmanship, Miniature Arms Society.

This lavish, color-illustrated 336-page *magnum opus* is a tribute to the jewel-like world of miniature gunmakers. A joint work of enthusiasts Arthur Brown, Joel Morrow, and David Hall, the book has a giant 9″ × 12.5″ vertical format, and is organized by contemporary, twentieth-century, makers, followed by historical makers of past centuries, as well as sections on knives and accessories.

As explained in the work's Dedication:

> For hobbyists, the making and collecting of miniature arms came into full flower in the middle of this century, a flowering sparked by Aldo Uberti, and culminating in the founding of the Miniature Arms Collectors/Makers Society in 1973.
>
> Aldo Uberti, one of the world's most respected manufacturers of replica and miniature firearms, is undoubtedly responsible for almost single-handedly prompting the current world-wide interest in miniature arms. Beginning as an apprentice for the Beretta company, Uberti began his own business in 1959 and almost immediately was on his way to becoming one of Italy's most respected gunsmiths. As a sideline to his renowned replica full-sized firearms, Uberti began to produce miniature

> replica guns. There is no question that the Uberti Company has produced more miniature firearms than any individual or company in the world. . . .

With the large format, many of the guns pictured are near to their actual size.

Appropriately, the work is dedicated to the memory of Aldo Uberti, and to the Miniature Arms Collectors/Makers Society, "with the knowledge that the work of both has had far-reaching results in the furtherance of the enjoyment and pleasure of the artistry, workmanship, and beauty of miniature arms."

Cottar: The Exception Was the Rule, by Charles Cottar

This fascinating book, in a limited edition of 1,000 copies, numbered and signed by Pat Cottar, is 350 pages of action and adventure, with 130 illustrations, in an 8.5″ × 11″ format. The work is one of several in the series of big game and adventure first-person works from Trophy Room Books of Agoura, California.

Cottar tells the story—in his own words—of Charles, patriarch of the Cottar family. Having been inspired by the writings of Theodore Roosevelt in *African Game Trails,* Cottar emigrated to Kenya from Texas and Oklahoma in 1909, to take up a life of big game hunting. A superb horseman and rifle shot, Cottar devoted the rest of his life to the pursuit of big game, surviving several maulings, and carrying out much of his career with one eye and one good leg! His death was in a manner to be expected: he was gored by a rhinocerous.

The author has hunted with one of Cottar's great-grandchildren, Calvin Cottar, while on the 1985 Tanzanian expedition that resulted in the film *In the Blood,* directed by George Butler (maker of Arnold Schwarzenegger's fame through the film *Pumping Iron*). Charles Cottar's grandson Glen was a guide on William B. Ruger's two expeditions to East Africa, in 1959 and 1961. The family endures to this day, in the fourth generation.

This captivating book helps to explain the fascination big game hunting and the guns used on safari hold for readers around the world, many of whom will never come close to having the opportunity to hunt the big five and other game of Africa, except through the wonders of books like *Cottar: The Exception Was the Rule.*

Beyond the Wild Bunch: The Fast-Growing Sport of Cowboy Action Shooting, by Gary Kieft, Dillon Precision Products, Inc.

Well on its way to becoming one of the most visible and talked-about hobbies within the vast spectrum of arms collecting, Cowboy Action Shooting is handsomely celebrated in this beautiful book, a copy of which the author stumbled onto while spending some time in New Mexico. The Single Action Shooting Society has given many Wild West devotees the opportunity to shoot an array of firearms in competitions that simulate actual events from our frontier past. SASS can be reached at www.SASSnet.com and at 1938 North Batavia Street, Suite M., Orange, CA 92865, (714) 998-1899.

The Introduction to *Beyond the Wild Bunch* explains what this fascinating new world is all about:

> Cowboy Action Shooting uses metal reactive targets, electronic timers and presents shooting problems in a scenario for the individual to solve. Unlike other shooting sports, Cowboy Action Shooting calls for the use of single-action revolvers, pistol-caliber lever-action rifles and either double-barrel or exposed-hammer pump shotguns.
>
> There are three classes of firearms: Modern, which means a pistol having adjustable sights such as a Ruger Blackhawk or a Colt New Frontier; Traditional, which is either an original or a reproduction of a pistol with fixed sights such as a Colt Bisley or a Uberti reproduction of the Colt Single Action Army revolver; and Black Powder, which utilizes either a cap-and-ball revolver like a Colt 1860 Army . . . or a Traditional-class cartridge revolver using black powder for propellant. Black Powder class also requires that the shooter use black powder loads in the rifle and shotgun as well. The type of pistol and propellant determine the class in which you participate. . . . Most stages involve the use of two or more firearms in combination. . . . The shooter starts standing in a doorway, pistol in hand. (No quick-draw techniques are allowed.) . . . Dress is an important part of Cowboy Action Shooting, as competitors MUST dress in vintage costumes. . . . The primary purpose of Cowboy Action Shooting is to have fun. . . . Some matches encourage family participation by having male-female or parent-child team states, and all matches have classes for women, junior and senior shooters.

Many of the striking color pictures in this captivating book could have been shot on movie sets; some even look as if they could have been taken in the real Old West.

When acquiring *Beyond the Wild Bunch,* I was also introduced to a two-hour video by Bar H Productions, *A Complete Guide & Introduction to the Exciting Sport of Cowboy Action Shooting,* and *The Top Shooters Guide to Cowboy Action Shooting, Part II, Quicken the Pace.* Sponsors the likes of Black Hills Ammunition and Uberti USA helped underwrite the costs of the production of these videos, which were designed to "save the buyer a lot of money and headache . . . [focusing] on equipment such as the pistols, rifles, and shotguns used most in the sport. . . . [as well as] authentic clothing, and accessories that will give you a terrific looking outfit!" "Bounty Hunter" (the alias of

Hunter Scott Anderson) narrates both videos, as well as producing, directing, and starring, in action that has earned him over 200 awards in competitions around the United States.

The book and videos can be purchased directly from Bar H Productions; see also the website: www.cowboyactionshooting.com.

100 Guns from the J. M. Davis Arms & Historical Museum the Largest Gun Collection in the World. An Interactive Multimedia CD-ROM, PC-compatible.

Something relatively new to the arms field was sent to the writer for review, from Douglas Henderson, Multimedia of Tulsa, Oklahoma (www.douglashenderson.com). The accompanying press release noted as follows:

> The most interesting guns from the J. M. Davis Arms & Historical Museum . . . are now showcased on an interactive multimedia, PC-compatible CD-ROM. The museum, located in Claremore, Oklahoma, is home to more than 20,000 guns.
>
> This interactive CD-ROM is filled with full-color photos, video clips, sound-bytes, animation, interviews, facts, legends and lies. It also contains a history of the biggest, oldest, smallest, most valuable and oddest guns in the world. Categories covered include Modern Military, Sporting, Odd, Ancient, Civil War, Frontier, and more. Lavishly photographed and beautifully illustrated, the "100 Guns" CD-ROM also contains cross-sectional diagrams that display the interior mechanical workings of technologically significant guns, including successful advances as well as colossal failures.
>
> This user-friendly, fully interactive CD-ROM will run on Windows 95, 98 and NT platforms. It is not Mac compatible. No browser is necessary and the CD-ROM installs nothing on hard drives. This CD-ROM can be ordered for $24.95 from the Web site [see above] or by direct mail from the J. M. Davis Arms & Historical Museum, 333 North Lynn Riggs Blvd., Claremore, OK 74017.

HIGH-END FIREARMS IN NEW YORK CITY

New York City can boast the finest museums, restaurants, clubs, architecture, entertainment, and any number of other "the bests." But, due to draconian firearms laws, the "Big Apple" has had a dearth of best quality arms-related stores and activity since the passage of the Sullivan Law some ninety years ago. Of first-rate firearms stores, only Griffin & Howe (est. 1921) and Beretta (est. 1995) existed, accompanied by only a handful of more conventional gun stores, in this highly restricted climate. Tiffany & Co. resumed the manufacture of super-grade embellished firearms in the early 1980s, averaging only about one deluxe gun a year, and at a minimum price of $25,000!

As of May 1996, the ranks of high-end arms dealers in New York City increased with the opening of the elegant Holland & Holland store on East 57th Street. At about the same time, Asprey & Co., Ltd, began marketing best quality sporting arms through their New York store (now known as Asprey & Garrard, Ltd), on Fifth Avenue. In 1999, another legendary British firm, James Purdey & Sons, opened its gallery on Madison Avenue.

Unlike the flagship store of the renowned retailer and trend-setter Ralph Lauren, these shops go one step further: you'll find shotguns and rifles at Griffin & Howe, Beretta, Holland & Holland, Asprey and Purdey.

These are not just any shotguns and rifles, but sporting arms of the most exquisite style and quality, often beautifully engraved, and of such distinction that the British shops are under royal warrants from various members of the British Royal Family (H.M. the Queen, the Duke of Edinburgh, and the Prince of Wales). Beretta even has a stock of handguns, although New York law forbids showing these arms to clients without proper firearms licenses.

Although not marketing firearms, among the high-end shops in New York City that sell hunting and shooting gear are Hunting World, Orvis, Eddie Bauer, L. L. Bean and Abercrombie & Fitch. Even Ralph Lauren offers clothing that could easily be worn in the field, and some of the firm's stores have British-made brassbound leather cartridge cases, stuffed big game heads, and mounted horns as part of the décor.

Christie's, Sotheby's, and the new auction house, Bannerman's, also offer historical arms and armor, although the bulk of Christie's sales remain in London. Former Butterfield arms expert Conor Fitzgerald is involved in both arms and armor and Western Americana weaponry and memorabilia, in his post at Christie's East. Martin Lane and associates are in the midst of creating Bannerman's, specializing in the world of arms and armor, and related memorabilia and accessories. Further, the Martin Lane Gallery of Historical Americana, at 205 West Houston Street, is a mecca for collectors in the firearms field. Distinguished art dealer Peter Tillou, who from time to time handles exquisite antique arms, has opened a new gallery near The Metropolitan Museum of Art.

One must also not forget the magnificent arms and armor collections at The Metropolitan Museum of Art—unrivaled anywhere in the Western Hemisphere. Although the displays present nothing after c. 1900, the workmanship and craftsman evident have served to inspire generations of engravers, metalsmiths, and stockmakers in contemporary gunmaking.

Closely supportive of the Metropolitan's Arms and Armor Galleries over the decades, is The Armor and Arms Club of New York, founded in 1921 by the museum's first curator of Arms and Armor, Dr. Bashford Dean.

Among other New York clubs that boast members keen

on firearms and shooting are Tiro a Segno, the oldest Italian club in America (founded in 1887), the New York Athletic Club, the Leach Club, the Racquet and Tennis Club, and The Explorers Club. In addition to these, the Boone & Crockett Club (founded in New York City by New Yorker Theodore Roosevelt and other like-minded friends) and The Camp Fire Club of America in nearby Chappaqua boast a number of New York members. Over fifty shooting ranges are in New York City, many of them private, including that in the lower reaches of The Metropolitan Museum of Art!

These museums, galleries, and clubs would not exist if there were not a substantial patronage existing in New York City for fine guns and the shooting sports. Rattling off a list of New Yorkers keen on firearms is like reciting a who's who of the city, something that the writer plans to do in his forthcoming book, *The Guns of Manhattan.* As an example of the strength of the market in New York City, Beretta's Vice President, Retail, Peter L. Horn II, does a land-office business with a very high-end clientele, keenly devoted to fine guns, from his courtly headquarters at the Beretta Gallery on Madison Avenue.

To those who love guns and the shooting sports, New York City has been considered "enemy territory" for over thirty-five years. Too often, the New York–based media, particularly papers like *The New York Times,* have trashed firearms and hunting, treating our world as if it was populated exclusively by rednecks and murderers. They have virtually ignored the original purpose of many of the extraordinary arms displayed at The Metropolitan Museum of Art, as well as ignoring the thousands of New Yorkers—like Theodore Roosevelt—who have been patrons of gunmakers, and whose dedication to shooting pioneered the most successful conservation efforts in history. Pity those ignorant men and women who visit the American Museum of Natural History, many no doubt thinking all those specimens of mounted wildlife were picked up having died a natural death, instead of collected by hunters the likes of TR, TR Jr., brother Kermit, taxidermist-explorer Carl Akeley, and sportsmen like Russell Barnett Aitken.

The exquisite showrooms of the gunmaking firms present a statement that cannot be ignored by the gun-haters and the animal rights fanatics: guns and shooting and the responsible pursuit thereof, are *here to stay and cannot be summarily dismissed as the interests of criminals or nuts.* It is interesting to note that rarely have any pickets marched in front of these firms, though when Beretta was picketed, the company did excellent business, among the best single-day sales volume in its existence to date!

One can walk into any of the New York emporiums as a misguided city person, ignorant of country ways and the appeal of firearms and the shooting sports, and walk out a dedicated shooter and sportsman or sportswoman. These galleries can change a person's life, and are among the most important pro-gun and pro-hunting establishments in the world today.

The entire shooting community owes a debt of gratitude to these companies, the private clubs, even the Metropolitan Museum's Arms and Armor Department, each subtly and elegantly promoting the incredible world of firearms and the shooting sports.

FIREARMS MUSEUMS

Since boyhood, the author has been captivated by museums, visiting them whenever possible, studying their contents, and libraries, and dreaming about someday having seen them all. A comprehensive work, *Museums of Arms and Armour of the World,* is being assembled with coauthor Brooke Chilvers. The research for this volume is nearly complete, and our listings are too expansive to fit in the present volume. However, the following represents a selected list of institutions that have firearms collections worth visiting. Organization is by state and city, some with a brief commentary. Since hours of attendance change from time to time with some sites, it is best to call before heading off for a visit. As a general matter, most museums and historical sites are closed on Mondays and major holidays.

Arizona
Seligman
Museum of the Old West

Tombstone
Birdcage Theater, 6th and Allen Streets

Tombstone Courthouse State Monument

Tucson
Arizona Pioneers' Historical Society

Arkansas
Berryville
Saunders Memorial Museum

California
Buena Park
Knott's Berry Farm

Los Angeles
Los Angeles County Museum
Exposition Park
Impressive general collection of firearms, particularly reflecting history of the West.

Autry Museum of Western Heritage
Griffith Park
Extraordinary collection of firearms associated with the American West—guns of Buffalo Bill, Annie Oakley, Theodore Roosevelt, Ned Buntline, and much, much more—plus the Colt Industries and George A. Strichman Colt collections.

San Francisco
Wells Fargo Bank History Room
Although few firearms are on display, those that are merit a visit, including the extraordinary presentation Henry Rifle, from the express company to a valiant employee, who despatched some outlaws in a pitched gun battle.

Colorado
Denver
Colorado State Historical Museum
14th Avenue at Sherman Street
General collection, relating to the history of firearms, and more specifically to their use in the West.

Fort Garland
A branch of the Colorado State Museum; with firearms of the types as used in the Fort.

Connecticut
Hartford
Wadsworth Atheneum
25 Atheneum Square North, and Main Street
Samuel Colt's own collection of firearms and related material. Not presently on display, but may return to exhibit soon.

Raymond Baldwin Museum of Connecticut History
Connecticut State Library
231 Capitol Avenue
The arms collection of the Colt factory, donated to the state of Connecticut by the Colt company in 1957. Several hundred firearms on display, including the Serial No. 1 Colt revolver, and the celebrated cased pair of Texas Paterson Colt revolvers. Although the collection numbers approximately 1,000 pieces, approximately two-thirds of this number remain in storage.

The Connecticut Historical Society
1 Elizabeth Street
The most important collection of original Colt papers, from the lifetime of Colonel Samuel Colt, plus unique Model 1851 Navy revolver, presented by the inventor to the Historical Society.

Florida
St. Augustine
St. Augustine Historical Society
22 Saint Francis Street
General collection, dealing with early history of the area.

Georgia
Fort Oglethorpe
Chickamauga National Military Park
Claud E. Fuller Collection of U.S. military and Confederate firearms. One of the most striking collections on public view in the world.

Illinois
Chicago
Art Institute of Chicago
George F. Harding Collection of arms and armor, including many firearms. Augmented by the donation of Raymond Wielgus, master engraver and designer of embellished arms.

The Chicago Historical Society
North Avenue and Clark Street
Excellent general collection, with several pieces of regional historical importance.

Rock Island
John M. Browning Museum
Wide collection of military arms, as well as rare group of firearms captured during the Indian Wars.

Indiana
La Porte
La Porte County Museum, Court House
W. A. Jones Collection, of about 850 firearms.

Kansas
Topeka
Kansas State Historical Society
Kansas State Museum
Collection reflects the gun in Kansas, and features the extraordinary Winchester Model 1873 embellished and presented to Town Marshal, former sidekick of Billy the Kid, Henry Brown, who was later killed by a lynch mob after having been captured following a bank robbery.

Louisiana
New Orleans
Louisiana Historical Association
929 Camp Street
Mainly Civil War arms, but also a group from the War of 1812.

Louisiana State Museum
The Cabildo, Jackson Square
Cross-section, featuring Civil War and War of 1812, with some World War I, and other arms.

Maryland
Aberdeen
Ordnance Museum, Aberdeen Proving Ground
Important and large collection, military-related, mainly 20th-century, but strong on earlier periods as well.

Annapolis
U.S. Naval Academy Museum
Important collection, reflecting armaments of the U.S. Navy and Marines.

Baltimore
Fort McHenry National Monument and Historic Site
E. Berkley Bowie Collection featured, with several American arms, including particularly U.S. military and Confederate pieces.

Massachusetts
Boston
First Corps Cadet Armory
105 Arlington Street
Military arms, as well as early Colonial pieces.

Plymouth
Pilgrim Hall
Court and Chilton Streets
Reflecting arms of the Pilgrims and early Massachusetts history.

Salem
Essex Institute
Colonial, Revolutionary and Civil War arms featured.

Springfield
Springfield Armory National Historic Site
The original Springfield Armory Museum, housed in the headquarters building. One of the most important arms collections in the world.

Connecticut Valley Historical Museum
The Smith & Wesson factory donated the bulk of its arms collection, dating back to the company's origins in 1852, to the Museum Center. This is the world's finest collection of S & W arms, and includes rare decorated pieces by Tiffany & Co., many rare experimentals, and pieces representing the evolution of the company's products, and some by competitors.

Sturbridge
Old Sturbridge Village
Harrington Gun Shop with representative display of percussion and flintlock firearms, figuring in the period of the Village, the early and mid-19th century.

Taunton
Old Colony Historical Society
66 Church Green
Small but worthwhile collection, particularly of colonial pieces.

Worcester
John Woodman Higgins Armory
Primarily an armor collection, but does exhibit some fine examples of firearms through the mid-19th century.

Michigan
Dearborn
Henry Ford Museum
Airport Drive and Oakwood Boulevard
Reconstructed John Brown gunshop; plus miscellaneous American and European firearms.

Missouri
St. Louis
City Art Museum
Forest Park
Primarily European arms, with artistic merit.

Missouri Historical Society
Jefferson Memorial Building
Strong on the 19th century, reflecting the city's importance in the fur trade and as a gateway to the West.

Nebraska
Chadron
Museum of the Fur Trade
Best collection reflecting the fur trade; an important museum for any enthusiast of the early American West.

Lincoln
Nebraska State Historical Society Museum
1500 R Street
Walter Charnley Collection, approximately 800 firearms, selections from which are displayed, representing the history of guns.

New Jersey
Morristown
Morristown National Historical Site
Revolutionary War firearms, with the most important a Ferguson rifle breechloader.

New York
Fort Ticonderoga
Fort Ticonderoga Museum
Firearms of the period, particularly Colonial and the Revolutionary War. Kentucky Rifles also displayed.

New York City
The Metropolitan Museum of Art
Fifth Avenue and 82nd Street
One of the world's most distinguished collections, dating up through the late 19th century.

The New York Historical Society
170 Central Park West
Important New York related arms, including some rare Paterson Colt revolvers, donated by John E. Parsons.

Newburgh
Washington's Headquarters
Revolutionary War arms, as well as other firearms with local historical interest.

West Point
West Point Museum
U.S. Military Academy
Important and broad-based collection, covering all periods in American military history. The reference collection, in storage for special research and for cadet study purposes, is large and extraordinary. Historic pair of flintlock pistols of George Washington a featured display.

North Carolina
Raleigh
North Carolina Division of Archives and History
Firearms of state manufacture, as well as Confederate arms.

Ohio
Cleveland
The Cleveland Museum of Art
John Long Severance Collection, both arms and armor, displayed for their decorative, artistic qualities.

Columbus
Ohio Historical Society
Ohio State Museum
Selections from the museum's collections on display; representing the history of firearms manufacture, and use, in the state.

Oklahoma
Bartlesville
The Woolaroc Museum
Featuring the Philip R. Phillips Colt Collection, the finest display of Paterson Colt firearms in the world, as well as one of the finest Colt Collections to be seen anywhere. Other firearms also on display, including a large number of Winchesters and frontier-related guns.

Claremore
J. M. Davis Gun Museum
Formerly housed in Mr. Davis's Mason Hotel, this is billed as "the largest collections of firearms in the world." A wide mix of arms from all periods, but particularly 19th and 20th centuries.

Lawton
Fort Sill Artillery Museum
Frontier displays, as well as artillery material.

Oklahoma City
National Cowboy Hall of Fame and Western Heritage Center
Representing arms of the cowboy and rancher, including and up to contemporary times. John Wayne display, and guns of other historical figures also represented. Historic gun shop recreation, from a period cowtown.

Pennsylvania
Doylestown
Bucks County Historical Society
Pine and Ashland Streets
Kentucky rifles featured, as well as a general arms collection.

Harrisburg
Pennsylvania Historical & Museum Commission
General collection, including some impressive Kentucky Rifles.

Philadelphia
The Philadelphia Museum of Art
The Carl Otto Von Kienbusch Collection of Arms and Armor, an extraordinary array of European, and some American, arms and armor, all worthy of an art museum. The last great private collection to be assembled by an American in this extremely select field.

Valley Forge National Historical Park
Featuring the George C. Neumann Collection of Colonial and Revolutionary War Firearms

Pittsburgh
Historical Society of Western Pennsylvania
General arms collection, as well as pieces made by regional gunmakers.

South Carolina
Charleston
Confederate Museum
Market and Meeting Streets
Includes important Confederate arms, though a relatively small collection.

Texas
Austin
Texas Memorial Museum
San Jacinto Boulevard at 24th Street
General collection, a highlight of which is a pair of Texas Paterson Colt revolvers, and other Colts.

Canyon
Panhandle-Plains Historical Museum
Representative grouping of cowboy, rancher, and Indian firearms.

College Station
Memorial Student Center
Texas A & M College
The Carl Metzger Collection, one of the best Colt displays anywhere, with many rare and important examples.

Houston
San Jacinto Battlefield Museum
State Route 134
Firearms of Texas and regional interest.

San Antonio
The Alamo
Relatively small group of arms, most with Alamo significance.

Witte Museum
3801 Broadway
Indian arms and arms of the West, particularly Texas.

Waco
Texas Ranger Museum and Hall of Fame
Greatest collection of Texas Ranger firearms in existence, plus general arms collection, featuring that of museum founder Gaines de Graffenried.

Virginia
Fairfax
National Firearms Museum
11250 Waples Mill Road
The arms collection formed by the National Rifle Association of America. NRA members are encouraged to support the museum, and are kept up-to-date in the fund-raising for this $6 million exhibit and reference complex. Over 2,000 guns on display, in superbly designed galleries, by Lucian Leone, formerly of the Metropolitan Museum of Art.

Fredericksburg
Fredericksburg National Battlefield Site
Civil War firearms, with some Confederate items.

Lexington
The Virginia Military Institute Museum's featured arms collection displays selected pieces assembled by Henry M. Stewart, a bequest to the institution from one of America's foremost arms experts.

Newport News
The War Memorial Museum of Virginia
9285 Warwick Road
Huntington Park
World Wars I and II well represented, as well as arms from earlier conflicts.

Quantico
U.S. Marine Corps Museum
Marine Corps arms, with emphasis on the 20th century.

Richmond
American Historical Foundation Museum
Both antique and modern arms, including replicas made by the company, which specializes in commemorative firearms issues for collectors.

Confederate Museum
12th and Clay Streets
In a building next door to the White House of the Confederacy, the finest and most important collection of Confederate arms in existence.

Virginia Historical Society
428 North Boulevard
The distinguished Richard D. Steuart Collection of Confederate firearms is featured, in the Society's Battle Abbey exhibit complex.

Williamsburg
Colonial Williamsburg
The Gun Shop is well worth visiting, to see how firearms of the period were made. Also to see, the Powder Magazine.

Washington, DC
National Museum of American History
The Mall, A Division of the Smithsonian Institution
Important and general arms collection, as the subject relates to American history. Some of the most historic, and often beautiful, firearms in America.

West Virginia
Huntington
Huntington Galleries
Featuring the Herman P. Dean Collection, strong on the Kentucky Rifle and on the evolution of firearms.

Wisconsin
Janesville
Lincoln-Tallman Museum
440 North Jackson Street
General collection of firearms.

Madison
Wisconsin State Historical Society
816 State Street
Worthwhile collection concentrating on Wisconsin history, but also of national interest.

Milwaukee
Milwaukee Public Museum
Wisconsin Avenue and 8th/9th Streets

Rudolph J. Nunnemacher Collection, formed in the late 19th and early 20th centuries, well worth viewing, broad in scope and often high in quality.

Wyoming
Cody
Cody Firearms Museum
Buffalo Bill Historical Center
The premier firearms research center and museum in the Western Hemisphere, actively supported by arms collectors, and by the firearms industry. Over 6,000 guns are in this collection, the exhibition of which features themes such as the evolution of firearms, a stagecoach stop, a period gun shop, a period gun factory, the art of the gun, a hunting encampment, the National Collection of Heads and Horns (with cooperation of the Boone & Crockett Club), specialized exhibits of significant manufacturers, and still another floor housing the reference collection.

CANADA
Ontario
Kingston
Fort Henry
Period of the collection from War of 1812 through mid-19th century. Includes demonstrations of guard drill with firearms.

Murney Redoubt
Macdonald Park
Tower dating from 1846–1851, with collection of firearms, featuring pieces from that of Mexican President Porfirio Diaz.

Royal Military College Museum
Extraordinary collection of Porfirio Diaz.

Toronto
Royal Ontario Museum
A relatively small collection, but with fine examples, mainly of European arms and interesting mechanisms.

Quebec
Quebec
The Citadel
Small arms, with artillery.

Saskatchewan
Regina
The Royal Canadian Mounted Police Museum
Firearms of the RCMP, from its beginning, in 1873. Includes Winchester Model 1876 lever-actions, and various revolvers, including the New Service Colt.

EUROPE
Austria
Graz
Steiermärkisches Landesmuseum Joanneum, Landeszeughaus
Armory dating from 1642–44, with unique arsenal of arms and armor, many of the firearms of the 16th and 17th centuries.

Vienna
Heeresgeschichtliches Museum
Huge collection, detailing the military history of Austria, with firearms over the centuries.

Kunsthistorisches Museum
Considered generally as the greatest collection in the world of arms and armor. Assembled originally by the Hapsburg dynasty; many of the pieces have specific histories, and most are in remarkable condition. The same museum also houses the legendary Benvenuto Cellini Salt Cellar.

Belgium
Brussels
Musée Royal de l'Armée et d'Histoire Militaire
Belgian Army arms, primarily from the 18th century, but up to and including World Wars I and II, and other conflicts in which the Belgian military has played a role.

Musée Royal d'Armes et d'Armures
Porte de Hal
Gates to the city have been adapted to displaying arms and armor general collection, along with cannon.

Liège
Musée d'Armes de Liège
Housed in the palace used by Napoleon's brother when he ruled in Belgium, during the Napoleonic Wars; general collection, featuring the wide spectrum of Belgian gunmakers, including an array of Browning firearms.

Denmark
Copenhagen
De Danske Kongers Kronologiske Samling Po Rosenborg
Danish Royal Family arms collection; limited to about 200 items, but of exquisite quality.

Tøjhusmuseet
Exhibited in an amazing, huge and comfortably laid out arsenal, the displays represent the full spectrum of the history of firearms, and number thousands of guns, accessories, and cannon.

France
Paris
Musée de l'Armée
In the heart of Paris, at the Hotel des Invalides, the collection is one of the greatest in the world. Some galleries are not open at all times, so it is possible that a visitor might not see a specific category of special interest. Features primarily French historical material, but the collection is extensive, and even has some important American arms.

Musée de la Chasse
Town house turned into impressive hunting museum; with selected guns representing primarily European hunters, but also those from the Western Hemisphere.

Germany
Dresden
One of the world's great armories, with numerous magnificent firearms, primarily of the 16th, 17th and 18th centuries.

Emden
Rustkammer der Stadt Emden
Arsenal of more than 1,000 firearms, dating primarily from the 15th to 17th centuries.

Nuremberg
Germanisches Nationalmuseum
Firearms with German historical connections.

GREAT BRITAIN
England
London
Royal Armouries, H.M. Tower of London
Although the bulk of the collection has moved to the spectacular multistory complex at the Royal Armouries Museum, Leeds, there are still many objects of firearms, and armor, displayed in the White Tower, traditional site of England's oldest museum (1,000 years). The display was redone and reinstalled, planned for completion in 1997.

The Victoria and Albert Museum
The Department of Metalwork has a relatively small, but distinguished collection, of fine arms, armor, and accessories. The objects date through the late 19th century.

The Wallace Collection
Manchester Square
This art museum includes an historic armory, with many magnificent firearms, armor, and accoutrements.

Leeds
Royal Armouries Museum
Formally opened by H.M. The Queen, March 15, 1996, this museum is the crown jewel of all arms and armor museums, with displays that are truly dazzling, computer interactive systems, a media room, demonstrations by trained specialists, and a craftsmen's courtyard where arms are made and repaired. Outside is a tilt yard, presenting demonstrations that help to bring the exciting world of arms and armor alive.

Woolwich
The Rotunda
Royal Artillery Institution collection of cannon and small arms, representing a broad spectrum of firearms.

Scotland
Edinburgh
The National Museum of Antiquities of Scotland
Superior collection of Scottish arms through the mid-19th century.

The Scottish United Services Museum
Edinburgh Castle
Scottish armed forces collections.

Glasgow
Glasgow Art Gallery and Museum
R. L. Scott, A. Martin, and C. E. Whitelaw collections, concentrating primarily on Scottish arms.

Italy
Brescia
The Luigi Marzoli Collection and general collection in the Castle; 500 weapons and pieces of armor.

Gardone (major gunmaking center, west of Brescia)
Beretta Museum, at Beretta Factory; open by appointment.

Naples
Museo e Gallerie Nazionale di Capodimonte
Arms and armor, with several fine Italian firearms, including air guns, and continuing up through the mid-19th century.

Rome
Museo Nazionale di Castel S. Angelo
Broad based collection, from small arms to artillery; the firearms mainly of Italian use or origin.

Odescalchi Collection, Museo di Palazzo Venezia
Important collection assembled by the Odescalchi family, primarily composed of a great many wheel locks and flintlocks, many of them Italian manufacture.

Turin
Museo Storico Nazionale d'Artiglieria
Firearms over the centuries, accompanied by artillery.

Armeria Reale
One of Europe's most distinguished arms collections. Several outstanding embellished arms.

Netherlands
Delft
Het Nederlands Leger en Wapenmuseum "Generaal Hoefer"
Dutch army collection, over the centuries.

Norway
Oslo
Haermuseet
Norwegian military arms, over the last 400 years.

Portugal
Lisbon
Museu Militar do Porto
Cannon and small arms from the 14th century, up to the period of World War I.

Russia
Moscow
The Kremlin Museum

St. Petersburg
The Hermitage Museum
Extraordinary arms and armor, the imperial collection formed by the Czars, and featuring magnificent arms by Boutet and other renowned artisans, and approximately sixteen presentation Colt revolvers, three of them magnificently gold inlaid, to Czars Nicholas I and Alexander II, and two brothers of Alexander.

The Artillery Museum
Massive museum with substantial collections of military arms, from small arms to large cannon.

Spain
Madrid
Museo de la Real Armeria
Although particularly rich in armor, this museum has some extraordinary firearms as well. Covers the history of arms, into the 19th century.

Museo del Ejército Español
Small arms and artillery of the Spanish military, some important American arms included.

Sweden
Skokloster
Skokloster Castle
Dating from the 17th into the 19th centuries, the arms collection is nearly intact.

Stockholm
Hallwylska Museet
European, and some oriental arms; about 300 objects, including armor; covering primarily the 16th and 17th centuries.

Kungliga Armémuseum
General arms and armor collection; one of Europe's best.

Kungliga Livrustikammaren
The Royal Armory collection, exhibiting arms from the Royal Family of Sweden.

Switzerland
Basel
Historisches Museum Basel
Broad array of arms covering the period from the origins of firearms, through the 19th century.

Bern
Bernisches Historisches Museum
Collection of arms and armor, of a general nature; considered best in Switzerland.

Geneva
Musée d'Art et d'Histoire
As an art museum, the pieces are displayed for their decorative and design qualities; general grouping, dating through the mid-19th century.

Solothurn
Museum Altes Zeughaus
General collection, through modern times.

Zurich
Schweizerisches Landesmuseum
Large collection, artillery and small arms, associated with the history of Switzerland.

DEATH TAKES ITS TOLL

Mercifully, 1999 and early 2000 have not been as devastating as 1998 and early 1999 were in deaths within the arms and armor community. Most notably the field lost Howard Blackmore and Ronald Ogan.

Howard L. Blackmore; 1917 to November 24, 1999

Author of innumerable articles and several major books, Howard Loftus Blackmore was hailed by authority Claude Blair as "the leading authority on the history of firearms in Britain and on London gunmakers." Since his days as a schoolboy Blackmore had been fascinated by arms and armor, though born the son of a clerk with the Southern Railway company. A native of Wallington, Surrey, he had the equivalent of a high school education, but never went on to receive a college degree. Blackmore's career began not in the arms field, but with the Inland Revenue service (the IRS of England).

During World War II he served with the Pioneer Corps (beginning in 1940), and as an Armorer Sergeant, the Pay Corps of London, as well as briefly with the Royal Artillery. In 1946 he joined Customs and Excise, rising over the years to the position of Purchase Tax Officer.

Claude Blair's tribute to Blackmore, published in the *Independent* (December 1, 1999) noted:

> It is characteristic of Blackmore that, finding himself at a disadvantage when dealing with members of the jewellery trade there over technical matters, he should have studied in his spare time to acquire the professional qualification of a Fellowship of the Gemmological Association, which he did in 1957, the year in which he also became a Fellow of the Society of Antiquaries of London.

Following World War II the explosion of interest in arms collecting in the United States had its counterpart in the United Kingdom, and Blackmore was in the midst of it all. One of eight founders of the Arms and Armour Society (1950), he soon became its president, and served in that capacity for over twenty years. His leadership was instrumental in establishing the organization as one of the foremost of its kind in the world. The Society's *Journal* is recognized the world over for its scholarship and professionalism. Blackmore himself authored a number of the articles the *Journal* published.

Blackmore's researches in original manuscript records, including work done at the British Museum Library and the Guildhall Library, and with such sources as the Board of Ordnance records, at the Public Record Office, Chancery Lane, led to his landmark work, *British Military Firearms* (1961). The result of his research was to revolutionize the study and collecting of those firearms.

In 1967 Master of the Armouries A. R. Dufty was instrumental in arranging the transfer of Blackmore from Customs and Excise to the Tower of London Armouries staff. He would become Assistant Master of the Armouries, and later Deputy Master, retiring in 1981.

Besides *British Military Firearms* and scores of articles in a myriad of periodicals, his major published works were *Hunting Weapons* (1971), *Royal Sporting Guns at Windsor* (1968), *The Armouries of the Tower of London—Ordnance* (1976), *A Dictionary of London Gunmakers 1350–1850* (1986), *Supplement to a Dictionary of London Gunmakers* (1999), and the paperbacks *Firearms* (1964) and *Arms and Armor* (1965). Both *British Military Firearms* and the *Dictionary* were monumental undertakings, and signal works, either of which would have been remarkable lifetime achievements for any researcher and author.

Among honors extended to Blackmore were the medal of the Arms and Armour Society (1984), Honorary Member of the American Society of Arms Collectors and of the Canadian Guild of Antique Arms Collectors, special guest lecturer to the Australian Antique Arms Society, a research fellowship at the Winchester Gun Museum (now the Cody Firearms Museum), and Honorary President of the Arms and Armour Society (1972, when retiring from his position as president).

In 1960, while an intern at the Armouries, H.M. Tower of London, the author had the privilege of meeting Blackmore. He was still with Customs and Excise at the time, and had come in out of the raw London fall weather. I well recall his genuine friendliness, and gentlemanly nature, and how he unceremoniously stuffed his hat into his worn leather briefcase. I was keenly already aware of his work, from a highly detailed article on Colt's London factory, published in an early issue of *The Gun Digest*.

While I was in the midst of completing photography for *The Peacemakers* book, Howard was visiting in Connecticut. He was then on a three-week tour made possible through a grant from the Armor and Arms Club, of which the author was then president. Peter Beard was on hand laying out some of the photographs, and Howard graciously joined to assist, providing notes on some of the more complex illustrations, and frequently lending the benefit of his expertise. We also paid a visit to artist-engraver Alvin White, and traveled into New York to see the Arms and Armor galleries at The Metropolitan Museum of Art. He was a wonderful traveling companion, often making unforgettable, sometimes hilarious, observations.

In nearly forty years of friendship, he never failed to offer good advice and the benefit of that special brand of humor. One of his favorite stories was of standing guard during World War II, when what appeared to be a rainfall began a pattering on his helmet; it was an officer relieving himself from a balcony above! Howard could also do an impersonation of the colorful comments of a former Armouries employee, who had the misfortune to have been splattered upon by a bird, while en route to the Tower in his sports car. Yet another of his favorites was from the opening ceremonies of the Sporting Arms gallery at the Armouries, when he and Master of the Armouries Dufty were giving a tour to H.R.H. Prince Philip, Duke of Edinburgh. A friendly exchange followed having to do with the nature of damascus gun barrels. This pitted His Grace up against the experts Dufty and Blackmore; on checking the facts in the Armouries Library, Prince Philip was found to be correct!

Howard kindly accompanied the author and his son Peter on visits to museums and country houses, among them the famous shooting estate, Holkenham Hall. He kindly arranged for us to see the Gun Room, normally not shown to visitors. We even went on a shoot together in Yorkshire, for driven pheasant—a form of shooting that he had not previously enjoyed. His sometimes pithy observations were delivered with the style of as good a straight man as one could imagine on the performing stage. And when he saw that I had cut some pictures out of his paperback book *Firearms* (for engraving source used by Alvin White), his inscription to me was: *To that mutilator of books!*

Anyone with the honor of knowing Howard Blackmore will forever remember him as not only one of the finest of figures in the history of the study and collecting of arms and armor, but also among the most productive, influential, and prolific.

Ronald A. Ogan; April 15, 1936 to December 19, 1999

For over twenty-six years one of America's foremost dealers in collector's firearms, and a widely published author in the field, Ron Ogan died at the age of sixty-three, following more than fourteen years of battling leukemia. From 1959 to 1969, Ron had been a policeman in Chicago, during which time he lived through adventures that rivaled those of not a few of the original owners of the antique guns he offered and sold to an enthusiastic following of collectors.

The most violent and testing of those Chicago Police Department adventures came while he was serving as an undercover narcotics agent. Three drug dealers had discovered the true identity of Ron and his partner. After executing Ron's partner, the dealers shot Ron and beat him savagely. It was only because of a backup pistol that Ron was able to survive, killing one thug and wounding another with a handgun that had been in an ankle holster. Among other exploits, he served during the rioting at the Democratic convention of 1968, in the street around the clock for nearly the entire three days. These were but two of many encounters in the line of duty.

If one visited widely-known dealer and collector Arnold Marcus Chernoff in the 1950s and 1960s, chances were you would also meet Arnold's protégé, boyhood friend and later C.P.D. Officer Ron Ogan. The two had been friends since they were thirteen years old. Ron remembers throwing snowballs at Arnold, a form of music criticism, since he was such an unpolished tuba player in the high school band. While visiting the Chernoff household in 1965, Ron told the author of his wish to join the fraternity of arms dealers. As a regular at Arnold's house, Ron's knowledge rapidly developed from one of the best dealers in the antique arms business.

In 1973, Ron took the big step and became a full-time professional dealer. Until Arnold's death in 1985, Ron remained the robust dealer's favorite pupil. In time, one of Ron's intended literary efforts was to be the life story of Arnold Chernoff, a rotund personality who remains high in the ranks of the most colorful figures in the history of arms collecting. Ron's photographs and files on that celebrity have been kindly passed on to the author.

Although specializing in Colts and guns of the West, Ron was likely to handle almost any kind of collector's firearms. Among these were General Jimmy Doolittle's Winchester Model 21 shotgun, the Prototype Serial No. 4 Colt Fluted Cylinder Dragoon, and historic guns from Chicago gangsters, movie stars, cowboy actor and Wild West show figures, and even modern decorated Colts by masters like Alvin A. White and Rudolph Kornbrath.

Over the years Ron's love of guns and of writing resulted in dozens of articles for a variety of periodicals. From October 1976 to February 1983, he authored a regular column for *The Gun Report*. These pieces were often highly detailed, and presented information that was often unavailable in any other publication. In addition to researching the Chernoff biography, Ron wrote a novel based on the experiences of himself and his acquaintances within the Chicago Police Department. The work totaled a massive 785 manuscript pages. Had there not been such a proliferation of police- and crime-oriented books at the time, the tome could well have become a bestseller, according to a talented editor who read the manuscript.

Besides handling several important collections and numerous significant collectible firearms, and continuing with various writing projects, Ron was active in promoting collecting through support of the NRA, of the Collectors and Dealers Association (CADA, of which he was a founding member), of the Colt Collectors Association, and numerous organizations nationwide. It was Ron who turned the CCA black-and-white newsletter into a full-fledged magazine. He changed the format, expanded the content, added color illustrations, and created the basis of *The Rampant Colt* as it is today—ranked among the best of all arms collectors publications.

In all of these pursuits, Ron's sense of humor, his skill at story-telling, and his optimistic outlook on life contributed to his widespread popularity. The camaraderie, friendly rivalry, and swapping of guns and information were things every participant looked forward to at shows, across the country. Few traveled to as many of these events as did Ron Ogan.

One of Ron's old friends, collector/dealer Martin Lane, summed up his life with the observation that "Ron Ogan represented a period in gun collecting that is now a part of history. Thanks mainly to the encroachment by slippery politicians into gun collectors' shows, what might be called the 'Ron Ogan Days' are rapidly becoming experiences of the past. Blaming 'gun shows' for inner-city crime is just another way to escape responsibility of failures by mayors like Daly of Chicago. We will miss Ron's knowledge, experience and above all his friendship in the unique fraternity of gun collecting—the last frontier in America, as Norm Flayderman has so incisively observed."

Ronald A. Ogan is survived by his beloved wife Robin and his son Brandon.

The family requests that memorial contributions be made to the NRA Foundation, specifically to the fund now being established: The Ronald A. Ogan Educational Endowment.

GUN OWNERSHIP AS WE ENTER THE MILLENNIUM—COMMENTARY BY MARK K. BENENSON[2]

As we enter 2000, the sustained assault on gun ownership continues in full force. At this time last year, four cities had sued gunmakers and dealers. The number is now up to approximately thirty, and the Clinton administration is thinking of joining in. In about all the cases motions to dismiss or for summary judgment were made and as they reached the point of the judges deciding these motions the cases were, with the exception of Chicago, so far dismissed. Of course, all the dismissals are being appealed. As I said in this space last year (second edition, pages 8–9), the legal theories upon which this litigation is based are weak.

With the Columbine and other school killings and, a few days before I write this, the shooting of a six-year-old girl by another child, the pressure on Congress and state legislatures is high. For the first time in my recollection, both contestants for the Democratic presidential nomination, Messrs. Gore and Bradley, want to register handguns. Such a plan will thus almost certainly be included in that party's platform in November. The dangers posed are obvious and manifest: one of our two political parties is about to become, formally and officially, antigun, a development without precedent in American history.

There are some favorable developments. About twenty states have passed laws preventing local governments from suing gunmakers and it is likely that this number will increase. Similarly, there is still impetus for the passage of preemption laws, which block local governments from making their own stricter-than-state gun ownership laws. The drive to pass right-to-carry laws seems to have slowed, notwithstanding the clear evidence that such regulations do not increase, and probably reduce, the incidence of violent crime.

Overall, I am not happy. The long-term demographic and sociological trend is against us. There are fewer places to shoot, a smaller and smaller proportion of youngsters are being brought up with sporting guns in the household, and the media have long since decided that the prevalence of gun ownership in the United States is one of the principal flaws in our culture.

This direction could easily and immediately be reversed, and gun owners would triumph, if we would only get off our behinds and vote our convictions, especially in primary elections. There are now nearly four million NRA members, enough to decide many elections, and an estimated *eighty million gun owners*—enough to control the country. But most shooters are as politically inactive as their other countrymen.

And we are divided. The shotgun target shooters, a particularly powerful group socially, are indifferent to handgun ownership and positively shrink from those of us who like modern military-style firearms. Little do they realize that after the self-loaders and handguns are gone, their over-and-unders will be next. It happened in England and if present trends continue, it will happen here.

CONCLUSION

The author just returned from a five-day visit to Beretta's Italian factories, in the company of three leading NRA officials: Craig Sandler, Executive Director of Operations, H. Wayne Sheets, Director, NRA Foundation Endowments, and Whit Fentem, Director, National Firearms Museum. It was heartening to learn from Craig Sandler that he felt there were clear signs that the block of firearms owners and shooters would emerge from the battle with Clinton and

Chuck Yeager and the author, admiring his new Bertuzzi over-and-under shotgun, made for limited-edition issue by U.S. Historical Society (now America Remembers/ U.S. Society of Arms and Armour). The legendary pilot is a keen hunter, sportsman, and gun buff.

[2]President, National Foundation for Firearms Education, and partner, Benenson & Kates, attorneys-at-law, specializing primarily in firearms matters.

his minions more powerful than ever. The NRA's confidence is so high that a recent television advertisement was run in the Washington, DC, area—immediately receiving national attention—in which Charlton Heston directly attacked the dishonesty of Clinton and his opportunist regime on the firearms issue (it would take a week's program to deal with Clinton's dishonesty on numerous other issues). The firestorm surrounding the exchange that followed is still reverberating in the press, and promises to help keep gun ownership as a hot issue in the 2000 elections.

A fresh voice in the gun control arena is none other than superstar Bruce Willis. The internationally known actor was quoted in the February 11–13, 2000, issue of *USA Weekend*, in a profile by writer Mary Roach, with his views on the firearms debate:

> "Everyone has a right to bear arms. If you take guns away from legal gun owners, then the only people who have guns are the bad guys." Even a pacifist, he insists, would get violent if someone were trying to kill her. "You would fight for your life. You'd use a rock or tear one of these chairs out of the floor."

With each fresh edition of *The Official Price Guide to Gun Collecting,* the author and publisher aim to add new material, new images, and to expand the domain of the publication. Having the opportunity of reviewing events of the previous season, one cannot help but conclude that the world of arms collecting continues to grow, recruiting new enthusiasts, and adding more fine guns to the list of collectibles.

Having completed preparation of the 1999–2000 season volume, we now look forward with great pleasure to that of 2000–2001, our fourth edition, work on which has already begun. We invite readers to send us information, pictures, and snapshots taken at gun shows or other collecting events and books for review and listing in the bibliography. This will help to make *The Official Price Guide to Gun Collecting* progressively bigger and better.

A Noble Tradition: A History of Arms Collecting[1]

Due to their history, artistry, craftsmanship, mechanics, romance, and performance, arms and related collectibles have been coveted for centuries. Never a dull or uninteresting pursuit, the passion for these objects is as old as civilization. With the cultural explosion that was a hallmark of the European Renaissance, the collecting of arms became a popular pastime of royalty. No royal house or aristocratic family in Europe lacked a treasury made up of art, artifacts, and arms and armor. Some of these were objects in use; others were ancestral, preserved as trophies or as pieces used in historic events, booty of war, and so forth.

EARLY RULERS AND FINE GUNS

Among the earliest houses actively conserving arms and armor was that of the German Emperor Frederick III (ruled 1440–93),[2] and his son and successor Maximilian (1493–1519). Maximilian was a keen admirer of the art of the armorer and gave these craftsmen privileged positions in his vast domains, as well as enriching the Hapsburg arms collections with a great many striking masterpieces. Both of Maximilian's grandsons and heirs, Charles V and Ferdinand, followed his lead, each in his own way. The dukes of Brabant, in Brussels, made up still another royal house amassing a major armory.

While the period of c. 1400 through 1550 was one of major achievement in the production of armor, hand-held firearms remained relatively unsophisticated implements, used mainly by foot soldiers. Among the several inventors attempting to replace primitive matchlocks with improved systems of ignition was the artistic and scientific genius Leonardo da Vinci (1452–1519). An enthusiast of firearms, he designed (in the *Codex Atlanticus*) a wheelock, the earliest mechanism of automatic ignition.

By 1550, practical application of this revolutionary invention had dramatically advanced the role of hand firearms in military, political, economic, and social evolution. The wheelock made it possible to introduce pistols and light arquebuses for cavalry. It gave birth to superior guns and to combination devices requiring instant automatic ignition, and was further responsible for the rapidly expanding role of firearms for hunting.

From clumsy tools of the infantry, guns quickly developed into expensive weapons of princes and select military units. And since the privileged and wealthy appreciated firearms and proved to be generous patrons of gunmakers, engravers, and stockmakers, every care was taken to produce weapons that were looked upon both as mechanical marvels and as works of art, worthy of being treasured and collected by the elite.

A successor to arms connoisseur Maximilian I was Charles V (1519–58), German emperor and Spanish king, in whose personal armories were several dozen elaborately decorated wheelock pistols and carbines. Many of these firearms have been preserved at the Royal Armory established in Madrid by Charles' son, King Philip II of Spain (1556–98), and a few pieces can be seen in other famous arms collections, among them the magnificent holdings of the Metropolitan Museum of Art, New York.

Maximilian's second grandson, Ferdinand (1558–64), Archduke of Austria, who became king of Bohemia and Hungary, and finally German emperor, was particularly fond of collecting historic armor, weapons, and militaria. He and his son, the archduke of Tyrol, made valuable additions to the Hapsburg hereditary armories by creating a Hall of Heroes with a splendid array of arms and armor that had belonged to the dynasty's members and to famous military leaders. Regarded by many as the greatest arms and armor collection in the world, these magnificent works of artistry, craftsmanship, and mechanical ingenuity are housed at the Kunsthistorisches Museum, Vienna.

KING HENRY VIII

A renowned contemporary and ally of these German rulers, King Henry VIII of England (1509–47) had several personal armories in royal palaces and paid special attention to such novelties of his time as wheelocks, breechloaders, and combination weapons. The King's armories were later assembled at the Tower of London, which still houses portions of one of the world's premier arms collections (most of the balance redisplayed in 1996 at the Royal Armouries Museum, Leeds).

SAXON RULERS

Prince-Elector August of Saxony (1553–86) was a connoisseur fortunate to have inherited large family collections of artistic and historic treasures. He took care to separate from

[1]This chapter was adapted and revised from articles by Dr. Leonid Tarassuk and the author for *Man at Arms* and *American Rifleman* magazines.
[2]Except where stated otherwise, dates for royalty indicate period of rule.

them all militaria, actually establishing Saxony's historic collection of arms and armor in special galleries with their own attendants. His successors, Christian I (1586–91) and Christian II (1591–1611), great patrons of armorers and artists, erected a new armory building and generously expanded the hereditary treasures with a number of pieces of exquisite artistic and technical quality. Another powerful prince of the time, Duke Julius of Brunswick (1568–89), had a predilection for spectacularly decorated all-metal wheelock firearms, which he collected in considerable numbers in his armory.

FIREARMS IMPROVEMENTS AND LOUIS XIII

By the 1630s, new and significant improvements in hand firearms appeared in Europe. More and more smoothbore longarms, rifles, pistols, and even revolvers were being provided with flintlocks of different construction, which gradually superseded the complicated and expensive wheelock. The most efficient design of flintlock, to be used for over two hundred years, was introduced in France, whose King Louis XIII (1610–43) enjoyed a well-deserved reputation as a connoisseur of firearms and shooting.

Starting at the age of ten, the king soon assembled an important arms collection, his famous *Cabinet d'armes*. Some of His Majesty's striking array of deluxe and military firearms were specifically rendered in a remarkable portrait by an artist from the school of Rubens. The king was so fond of his collection that he would spend long hours in the privacy of his *Cabinet*, dismounting, cleaning, assembling, and admiring his favorite pieces. A contemporary expert claimed that the king's knowledge and skills could even allow him to make firearms with his own hands. From over 650 weapons and armors collected by Louis XIII, nearly 500 were firearms, both contemporary and antique. Louis XIV being the Sun King, his father Louis XIII could be termed the "Gun King."[3]

Louis XIII of France, the "Gun King," with selected pieces from his exquisite arms and armor collection, begun when he was a boy. (School of Rubens, reproduced by permission of The Royal Armouries Museum)

RUSSIAN IMPERIAL COLLECTORS

Far away from France, another passionate lover of firearms and shooting came to supreme power soon after Louis XIII's death. Alexy Mikhailovich, Czar of Muscovy (1645–76), was a somewhat unusual figure among Russian rulers of the period. Keen on knowledge, he was dedicated to the arts, theater, heraldry, fine arms, and the chase. From his predecessors he inherited the Kremlin Armories with vast stores and workshops employing many first-class craftsmen and artists, both Russian and foreign. During his long reign, Czar Alexy ordered hundreds of guns of various designs for his private use and for his collection, which has remained nearly intact in the museums of Moscow.

His son, Peter the Great (1682–1725), also favored firearms and was responsible for establishing a new imperial factory, in Tula, which soon gained world renown. Peter was a gifted craftsman of no little talent.

In addition to the Kremlin Armories, another distinguished Russian family, that of Sheremetev (later counts), had traditionally deposited personal weapons and armors at their ancestral armory, formed before the 18th century. This custom was carried on throughout the centuries. Still another collection, that of the Boyars, numbered some 1,400 items (including approximately 600 antique firearms). The 1917 Revolution led to confiscation by the Soviets of all private arms collections in Russia and in other lands under Communist domination, and some museum-held cartridge firearms were drilled through the breech to prevent their being fired by enemies of the state!

POLISH COLLECTORS

Russia's neighbors and rivals also demonstrated a keen enthusiasm for arms collecting. The Polish-Lithuanian princes Czartoryski and Radziwill established family armories, with the earliest pieces dating back to the 16th century. August the Strong (1694–1733), King of Poland and Prince Elector of Saxony, especially favored luxurious

[3]The renowned royal property of Versailles was originally built as a hunting estate.

hunting firearms and added a sumptuous "Gun Gallery" to the Saxon hereditary armory in Dresden. His successor, August III (1733–63), augmented the gallery with splendid pieces he collected for pleasure, and for his elaborate hunting parties. Despite unfortunate losses over the years, the Saxon arms collection still boasts over 10,000 pieces, about a third of them deluxe firearms.

SCANDINAVIAN COLLECTIONS

A small but precious historic arms collection was founded by King Frederick III of Denmark (1648–70) at Rosenborg Castle, where he assembled armor, weapons, costumes, and regalia of Danish rulers. Another treasury of antique weapons in Scandinavia was put together at Skokloster Castle, Sweden, by the great collector Field Marshal Count Carl Gustaf Wrangel (1613–76). Through the marriage of his daughter, the Wrangel Armory fortunately came into possession of the arms and armor of the Counts Brahe, who were passionate and active arms collectors themselves. Both armories at Skokloster eventually became a public museum.

King Charles XV of Sweden and Norway was still another dedicated collector. His holdings were handsomely enriched by regally embellished and cased gifts from President Abraham Lincoln and Samuel Remington. Many of Charles' arms are on view at the Royal Armory, Stockholm. But his magnificent cased pair of Colt Model 1860 Army revolvers, gold inlaid and engraved by Gustave Young, and presented by Lincoln, were stolen in the 1960s and have yet to be recovered.

ARTISTS AS ARMS COLLECTORS

Many great artists were lovers of fine arms. Among them, Rembrandt van Rijn (1606–69) had an arms collection, some of which he used in his paintings. Flemish painter David Teniers Jr. (1610–90) showed his profound knowledge of weapons, especially firearms, in several canvases showing military scenes. A number of pieces were painted with almost photographic accuracy.

NOBLE RUSSIAN LADIES, AND GRANDSONS

Nor were some noble ladies strangers to the related passions of hunting and arms collecting. Peter the Great's daughter Empress Elizabeth of Russia (1741–62) earnestly patronized the Tula gunmakers, who produced for her hunting pavilions dozens of magnificent garnitures of fowling pieces, rifles, and paired pistols. Empress Catherine the Great (1762–96) followed suit, adding still more fine firearms to the imperial gun rooms. To please her beloved grandsons, Grand Princes Alexander and Constantine, the empress presented them working miniatures of pistols, revolvers, and longarms made to her order by Tula's finest armorers and artists. Ironically, not these boys but their two brothers, born shortly after their grandmother's death, were to become especially active arms collectors.

RUSSIAN CZARIST COLLECTORS

Grand Prince Nicholas (b. 1796, d. 1855) started collecting arms and armor, as well as militaria, while still a boy. By the date of his accession to the Russian throne (1825) he had already assembled so many items that they required special premises for proper display. To accommodate this collection, a new palace, known as Tsarskoseliskii Arsenal, was built near the capital city of St. Petersburg. As czar, Nicholas I had many opportunities to enlarge his collection.

Antique and rare arms and armor were brought in from old state armories and imperial palaces, acquired abroad and at home, seized at captured armories during foreign wars, and donated by relatives and others. Firearms were often presented to the czar by gunmakers and manufacturers. The most prominent of these foreign donors was Colonel Samuel Colt, who personally presented Nicholas I a spectacular set of three gold-inlaid percussion revolvers. The fact that Nicholas was an arms collector undoubtedly served to encourage Colt's own collecting interests.

The czar's youngest brother, Grand Prince Michael (1798–1849), shared this love for fine weapons and patiently put together his own impressive arms collection, which he bequeathed to Nicholas. The next Russian ruler, Alexander II (1855–81), was a dedicated hunter with a special passion for collecting contemporary high-quality firearms. He too received a splendid set of rifles and revolvers from Colonel Colt. Alexander II significantly enlarged the imperial arms collection, which is now preserved at the Hermitage Museum in St. Petersburg. The Grand Duke Alexis, on a visit to the United States in 1871–72, was presented a gold-inlaid and engraved revolver by Smith & Wesson, which His Highness proceeded to use while buffalo hunting on the plains. His enthusiastic guides were Lieutenant Colonel George Armstrong Custer and William F. "Buffalo Bill" Cody. Alexis' buffalo hunts were the highlight of his extended visit to the New World. The whereabouts of the grand duke's elaborate revolver is unknown at this writing—a treasure perhaps awaiting a lucky collector or dealer at some future date.

NAPOLEON BONAPARTE, IMPERIAL COLLECTOR

To Napoleon, Emperor of France (1801–14), arms collectors owe the existence of some of the finest firearms produced in the 19th century. A patron and protector of all the arts, Napoleon particularly favored gunmakers and arms decorators. Their choice pieces came into the emperor's personal possession or were reserved by him for presentation to dignitaries and for awards honoring distinguished military service.

His nephew, Emperor Napoleon III (1852–70), also patronized producers of deluxe firearms and proved to be an eager collector of arms and armor, as well as an active hunter—and a remarkably talented shot. Displayed in the formidable medieval castle of Pierrofonds, the imperial collection later joined the Musée de l'Armée in Paris, which also preserves certain key segments of the arms collections assembled by King Louis XIII, the princes de Conde, and the dukes de Bouillon. Count de Nieuwerkerke, Superintendent of Fine Arms and Director of the Louvre Museum, and the French architect and antiquarian Viollet-le-Duc were two other distinguished French connoisseurs.

BRITISH ARISTOCRATIC ENTHUSIASTS

Among the most prominent connoisseurs and collectors of firearms in the 19th century, mention should be made of the Prince Regent, who became King George IV (1811–30), as well as Prince Albert (b. 1819, d. 1861; consort to Queen Victoria) and King George V (1910–36). The British public was favored by a generous bequest, in 1897, of art collections formed by the Wallace family. Included were about 2,400 pieces of armor and weapons, with many beautiful and fine antique firearms. Most important in this group were items assembled by Sir Richard Wallace, who had been lucky enough to acquire the distinguished collections of arms and armor of Sir Samuel Rush Meyrick and Count de Nieuwerkerke. Today the Wallace Collection is displayed in the family's London mansion, known as Hertford House.

A fascinating series of historical connections began with the arms and armor gallery at British author Horace Walpole's Strawberry Hill estate. Walpole's armory served as the inspirational setting for the first of the "gothic" novels, his *Castle of Otranto* (1764). Early-19th-century author Sir Walter Scott is considered to have patterned his own country house and armory, Abbotsford, on the model of Walpole's. And Sir Samuel Rush Meyrick (1783–1848), a contemporary of Scott, became the first serious scholar in the study of arms and armor. Scott's novels, especially *Ivanhoe* and *The Tales of the Crusaders*, had a profound influence on the interests of British antiquarians and collectors.

Scott's romantic period novels and Meyrick's studies reflected an interest that became almost a Victorian epidemic—armories or, at the least, arms and armor displays in the grand mansions of aristocrats and the new rich. When the Meyrick-Wallace collection opened as a British national museum in June 1900, the ceremonies were distinguished by the presence of an avid shooter and gun enthusiast, Edward, Prince of Wales (later King Edward VII).

For many years, the largest and most fascinating private collection of quality arms extant was that of the English connoisseur and author W. Keith Neal. These amazing treasures were preserved for years in a special building on the Neal estate on the Island of Guernsey. The Neal Collection was reminiscent of princely ancestral armories, and his reputation as an arms specialist was of regal proportions. Much of the collection remains intact, in the hands of his heirs.

In the Soviet Union of 1917 to 1991, arms collecting was not specifically prohibited by law, but the keeping by private citizens of firearms and edged weapons of any kind and of any date was punishable by confiscation of such property and mandatory imprisonment of the owner. Exempt from these prohibitions were members of state-controlled hunting clubs (allowed to have registered shotguns only) and professional hunters catering to state trade institutions (who could own licensed rifles and ammunition). Certainly there were a few passionate lovers of antique weapons in Russia who attempted to collect despite the risk of heavy civil penalties. Understandably, they tried to keep their collections secret—as far as possible.

Since the collapse of the Soviet Union, another problem exists for contemporary collectors in Russia: the fear of theft in the present crime wave, resulting from the chaos of a country emerging from centuries of czars and dictators. One thing is certain: There are collectors in Russia, and always will be.

Among those with the privilege to collect firearms in Soviet times, and who could afford to do so—modern guns included—was the late Field Marshal G. Zhukov (1896–1974). His was the largest private collection of firearms in the U.S.S.R., composed of about 1,000 pieces, mostly "war trophies" from private mansions and castles (taken during World War II). After Zhukov's death, the collection quietly passed into the hands of the state, with a number of his firearms going to Moscow's state museums.

Another important collection of firearms, mainly modern deluxe presentations, was owned by the secretary general of the Soviet Union's Communist Party, Leonid Brezhnev, who was also the U.S.S.R.'s commander in chief. The secretary's favorite hobbies were, reportedly, the collecting of firearms and exotic foreign cars.

RENOWNED ENGLISH, AMERICAN, AND CONTINENTAL COLLECTORS

The Wallace Collection was a vital link in the evolution of arms and armor as a fashionable hobby, and Sir Richard's collection set the fashion of private art galleries for American collectors in the late 19th and early 20th centuries. Among the prominent U.S. patrons of the arts who were influenced were J. Pierpont Morgan, Clarence H. Mackay, and William Randolph Hearst. And among the Europeans who became dedicated collectors were Baron Ferdinand de Rothschild, Sir Ralph Payne-Gallwey, and Henry H. Harrod (of the London department-store family).

In Italy, by the late 19th century, Prince Ladislas

Odescalchi had collected some 1,200 items of fine arms, which were later acquired by the state and established as a national arms museum in Rome. Another connoisseur of art, Federigo Stibbert, put together extensive collections, strong in European and Oriental arms and armor. In 1908, the Stibbert collections were willed to the city of Florence, and are now on display in his richly appointed villa.

MEXICAN AND SOUTH AMERICAN DEVOTEES

Surely one of the keenest arms collectors in history was Porfirio Diaz, president of Mexico for most of the years 1877 to 1911. Although he was a dictator who ruled with an iron hand, Diaz took the time to not only assemble a remarkable collection, but to have custom-made arms built—sometimes to his own order. These pieces are primarily at the Royal Military College Museum, Kingston, Ontario, Canada, and are so extraordinary that the author has traveled to Kingston specifically to admire them.

Peru boasts the phenomenal collection of Miguel Musica Gallo, one of the most impressive groups of arms assembled privately in the history of the Western Hemisphere. Gallo, better known for his museum of gold, built his varied arms group at his home base of Lima, but enjoyed hunting to the extent that his display of animal heads and horns is one of the finest privately owned. A monograph was published on the Gallo collection, revealing a great many rare, embellished, and historic pieces.

Judging from the numbers of exquisite arms sold to clients south of the border, there are numbers of wealthy families in Mexico and in Central and South America who have been keenly interested in possessing fine arms. However, most of these would be regarded not so much as collectors, but as enthusiasts of high-grade arms, many of them used for hunting.

CONTEMPORARY COLLECTORS IN EUROPE

The ranks of contemporary collectors of arms in Europe no longer include many of the ancestral estates, due to the ravages of war and taxation. The majority of treasured family collections have been split up under the auctioneer's hammer, while others have gone directly into public museums. In any case, it seems a higher proportion of arms and armor collectors can remain anonymous, because the best-quality of objects seldom are publicly sold—and the relatively small scale of firearms makes them less a challenge (and less costly) to move from place to place.

The number of arms auctions of quality pieces are relatively few in comparison to fine furniture, silver, or even Impressionist paintings. And even private sales are few and far between, so much of the exceptional specimens of armor having long been in public collections, and the same becoming increasingly so with arms. The sale by Christie's in London, November 18, 1981, set what was then the all-time record price at auction for an object of arms and armor when the duke of Brunswick suit of Greenwich armor went for $790,000. However, just a few years later Sotheby's sold a suit of armor of the French King Francis I at $3.5 million! Today both armors are worth noticeably more.

Major firms like Holland & Holland, Ltd., based in London, are promoting arms collecting, with exquisitely appointed shops in Paris and New York and elegantly designed advertising in fashionable publications, and by catering to extremely wealthy clients. Firms like Holland & Holland and J. Purdey & Sons are instrumental in promoting arms collecting as a fashionable, indeed chic, collecting pursuit.

Despite the trend toward privacy in modern circles of arms and armor collectors of distinction, the identities of a few individuals are known. It appears that among them, and certainly the most distinguished, is H.R.H. Prince Philip, the Duke of Edinburgh. The degree of dedication of His Grace to arms collecting is not publicly known, but at the least it is enough to find him appearing on television discussing arms subjects with obvious knowledge, relish, and insight, and to have been the honored guest at the dedication of the new firearms galleries at The Armouries, H.M. Tower of London, in 1974.

Prince Philip is also quite knowledgeable on the subject of modern gunmaking, and his patronage of such firms as Holland & Holland and Purdey is well known. Aristotle Onassis, though he was not an arms collector *per se*, did enjoy shotgun shooting and appreciated the craftsmanship of fine arms. A photograph of Onassis in quarters aboard his yacht *Christina* reveals a deluxe pair of Napoleonic-period flintlock pistols displayed on the wall in the background.

MIDDLE EASTERN OIL POTENTATES AND CONTINENTAL COLLECTORS

Now residing in Paris is an Iranian prince, half brother to the late shah, who is an active sportsman and prizes quality rifles and shotguns: Prince Abdorezza. Several prominent industrialists in Switzerland, Holland, Italy, France, and Germany are keen arms collectors, among them Ugo Gussalli Beretta, patriarch of the world-famous gunmakers.

But these fanciers of fine arms are faced with increasing competition from Middle Eastern sheiks and princes, whose oil wealth allows an indulgence on a scale that harks back to the grand aristocrats of the 17th and 18th centuries and the age of Napoleon. And according to an article in *The New Yorker* magazine, the world's richest man, the Sultan of Brunei, is a collector of fine Colt revolvers.

Generally leaning toward large quantities of shooting guns, Middle Eastern collectors have a special affection for deluxe gold-mounted and inlaid modern arms. The best known of arms enthusiasts from that part of the world is the late King Hussein I of Jordan. Several members of the Saudi Arabian royal family are known to be keen collectors. An entire new special category in rare arms has been created by Swiss jeweler and watchmaker Ives St. Blaize, whose line of deluxe modern arms features diamond-encrusted grips of 18-karat gold and other exotica. Considering the international fascination with the American West, it would not be surprising to see a craving develop among the Middle Eastern collecting fraternity for Americana, especially Colts and Winchesters.

Jewelers the likes of Asprey & Co., Ltd, in London and New York–based Tiffany & Co. have made some of the most deluxe firearms in history, the former even setting up its own gunmaking operation. Tiffany's creations in this challenging area began in the 1850s, and today the firm concentrates on exquisite Colt and S&W revolvers, wholly designed to exclusive custom orders.

Although the stately collectors merit envy in their private possessions, a tradition has been established since the French Revolution (and particularly strong in the 20th century) of the very finest specimens of antique arms gradually going into museums. Already much of the best of European arms and armor has gone into public hands, with the result that these exquisite objects are available for the public to see and appreciate. With the passage of time the same pattern is evolving in America, aided by beneficial circumstances of tax laws and an increasing public awareness of museums and their prominent role in American culture.

AMERICAN COLLECTORS

The American experience with firearms is unique. British historian Thomas Carlyle classified the "three great elements of modern civilization" as "gunpowder, printing, and the Protestant religion." In no nation have these elements proven to be of such profound significance as in our own. Without firearms, our pioneer civilization would never have survived, and in our nearly 500-year history, no object has played a more vital role.

America does indeed have a "gun culture," and one in which we can take considerable and justifiable pride. Our myriad of gun-related businesses, hobbies, and sports, including the collecting of arms, are wholly understandable.

The origins of arms collecting in America are somewhat akin to those of Europe. The "ruling families" in the New World, like their European counterparts, assembled ancestral arms holdings, accumulated over years of shooting and hunting. Families here did not have the opportunities or wealth for large collections on the European scale, at least not until the late 19th and early 20th centuries. But by American standards, fine early collections were formed, one of which was that of the "father of his country," George Washington.

GEORGE WASHINGTON, A KEEN COLLECTOR

Writer Ashley Halsey's research on Washington's favorite guns (*American Rifleman*, February 1968) documented that the first president "may have owned 50 firearms," of which about ten are known to collectors and museums today. Private diary entries and other sources show that Washington appreciated firearms for their artistic, mechanical, and functional excellence, and that he had a predilection for English-made flintlock pistols and fowling pieces of quality. As an active and enthusiastic shooter, Washington appreciated the importance of fine design and craftsmanship, and to quote Halsey, he was "a sportsman hunter of the first rank."

In common with many an American "aristocrat," Washington frequently rode to the hounds on fox hunts and went afield with gun in hand after duck, hare, deer, and other game. Halsey proves that Washington was not only an avid sportsman, but one who knew guns and had great affection for them. Evidence of his appreciation of quality is found in such arms as his silver-mounted pair of gentleman's pistols from Hawkins, London.

That his contemporaries shared a similar appreciation for guns and shooting is shown by Washington's gifts of firearms to relatives, friends, and fellow soldiers, not the least of whom was General the Marquis de Lafayette. Our first president also received gifts of arms, and among those of record were two pairs of flintlock pistols that he described in letters to the donors as "very elegant." Unfortunately, the Washington collection was split up over the years, and thus the few pieces known today are as far afield as the Mount Vernon historic site, near Alexandria, Virginia, and a private collection in the western United States.

THOMAS JEFFERSON—ARMS COLLECTOR AND INNOVATOR

Surely the most enlightened gun and shooting enthusiast in the early years of arms collecting in America was Thomas Jefferson. His brilliant mind and cultured, artistic eye attracted Jefferson to a wide range of interests, indeed passions, encompassing art and architecture, music, literature, science, guns and shooting, the world of ideas, and affairs of state. It was Jefferson who wrote some time-honored advice to his nephew, Peter Carr:

> A strong body makes the mind strong. As to the species of exercise, I advise the gun. While this gives a moderate exercise to the body, it gives boldness, enterprise, and independence to the mind. . . . Let your gun therefore be the constant companion of your walks.

Jefferson was recognized as an aristocrat but also a man of freedom, and a liberal in the classic sense. His views on gun use and ownership ring true today. In 1776, in a draft for the constitution of Virginia, he wrote: "No freeman shall ever be debarred the use of arms." He also wrote to George Washington that "one loves to possess arms." Ashley Halsey's article "Jefferson's Beloved Guns" (*American Rifleman*, November 1969) concludes, "To this cultural genius . . . few things surpassed the delight that he derived from shooting."

As with Washington, Jefferson's account books and other papers bear frequent reference to the purchase, repair, and even restocking of pistols, fowling pieces, and muskets. However, only two pistols have survived that can be accepted as his; they are a pair of brass screw-barrel flintlocks by Dealtry, London, on display at Monticello.

Jefferson's main love for guns was for field shooting, but one of the most significant results of his knowledge and experience with arms was in introducing the idea of parts interchangeability to U.S. industry. While ambassador to France, Jefferson had been introduced to the pioneering work of Blanc in producing gun locks on a theory of parts interchangeability. Jefferson saw the potential in Blanc's work and wrote of it in some detail to American officials. Although that correspondence served to introduce the concept to American industry, it remained for Eli Whitney and, more important, such creative industrialists as Simeon North and Robbins & Lawrence to make practical application of these ideas in the United States.

OTHER DEVOTEES OF ARMS

Washington and Jefferson shared their love for guns and shooting with the majority of their male contemporaries. America has been a virtual paradise for the gun enthusiast and shooter since the arrival of the original colonists and explorers. A relatively limited body of information has been ferreted out by researchers on the degree of private enjoyment of gun ownership by the better-known of our pioneer citizen-shooters. This is inevitable, since when a scholar pursues the likes of the governing class, he is generally in pursuit of information specific to subjects for which the individuals are best known.

But to consider only U.S. presidents prior to 1900, those who had gun and shooting interests far outnumber those likely to have had no practical experience or interest. In the former category, standouts would be, in addition to Washington and Jefferson, James Madison, Andrew Jackson, William Henry Harrison, James K. Polk, Zachary Taylor, Franklin Pierce, Abraham Lincoln, Ulysses S. Grant, and Grover Cleveland (an active bird shooter).

In a modern sense we would not term these gentlemen pure collectors; rather, they were shooters who enjoyed guns. However, as in the cases of Washington and Jefferson, who both had quite a few arms during their lifespans, at least one could use the terminology "informed accumulator."

Washington even owned trophies of war, such as a pair of flintlock pistols believed to have been presented to him by Lafayette and carried by him in the Revolutionary War; another pistol is traditionally considered to have been a gift from General Edward Braddock, who had carried it during the French and Indian War.

Relics or trophies of war have spawned many an arms collection over the years. And it is safe to say that such was the origin of most pioneer U.S. arms collections of the 19th century. But the two most important private arms groups of the pre–1900 period in America originated from quite another inspiration—the Industrial Revolution.

SAMUEL COLT AND OLIVER WINCHESTER

Both Samuel Colt and Oliver Winchester were able to deduce to some extent their historic impact on industry, technology, contemporary history, and the field of gun making. As early as 1853, Colt's collecting intent was implied in a letter that announced to the gunmaker that a shipment of curious guns representative of the Turkish empire had been dispatched to him. In 1856 Commodore Matthew Perry wrote that he understood Colt had already assembled a "number of . . . arms" and would "establish a museum of arms well worthy of the commendable object he had in mind." And a Colt journal of 1861 records the existence of a museum room, with its contents valued at $3,245.75.

Colt collected arms because he had a genuine passion for them, but also in order to provide reference specimens for design work, to dramatize his own role in firearms history, and to keep abreast of his own production and that of rivals. That he had a good working knowledge of the evolution of repeating firearms is apparent from the paper he delivered to the Institution of Civil Engineers, London, in 1851. The plates in the article and Colt's published expertise lead one to believe that his serious collecting began at least as early as 1850.

On the colonel's death in 1862, the collection was divided into two sections, with about 100 pieces at his home, Armsmear, and several hundred at the factory. The Armsmear group was bequeathed by his widow to the Wadsworth Atheneum, Hartford, in 1905, and the factory collection was generously presented to the State of Connecticut by the Colt firm in 1957. Sharing a known origin estimated at least as early as 1850, these two arms groups represent, to the author's knowledge, the oldest formal American arms collection privately assembled and still existing.

Oliver Winchester was a manufacturer, not a keen gun fancier, who created in the Winchester Repeating Arms Co. one of the giant private armories of the 19th century. His industrial background had been as a shirtmaker in New Haven. But it would appear that Winchester became quite infatuated with firearms and was very much aware of the contributions of his firm to American industry and our emergence as a world power. A letter from Winchester to manufacturer B. S. Lawrence documents that Winchester had an arms collection by 1871; he was delighted to have acquired from Lawrence a Jennings rifle, which he correctly termed "a connecting link in the history of our gun."

The Winchester factory collection was a gift to the Buffalo Bill Historical Center, Cody, Wyoming, in 1975, and is displayed in one of the most impressive installations of any of the world's arms museums. The collection today is in its own specially constructed wing of the Historical Center, and is termed the Cody Firearms Museum.

OTHER U.S. GUNMAKERS

Other U.S. gunmakers also put together collections, and among the earliest were Remington and Smith & Wesson. The Remington firm was founded in 1816, but no records exist that date the arms collection exactly. An estimate of its likely origins can be gleaned from specimen guns. By the mid- to late 1860s, the firm was on a course that called for maintaining a display collection of experimental and production models. The Remington Gun Museum in Ilion, New York, was reopened to the public in August 1980, after an ambitious program of development and fresh displays.

Smith & Wesson's collection can also be dated by study of surviving specimens and by considering the firm's antiquity. Founded in 1852, the company was producing its first Model .22 rimfire revolver by 1860. S&W Volcanic lever-action pistols in the factory museum suggest that the owners were gun collectors before 1860.

It is important for every firearms manufacturer to have reference collections, and one of the most modern of the former, Sturm, Ruger & Co., has its own impressive holdings. William B. Ruger himself launched the firm's collecting, which is devoted to as wide a spread of makes and types as are relevant to the broad range of Ruger's own product interests and that of the company. Bill Ruger's outlook on a company collection and mastery of gun knowledge (historical and otherwise) closely parallels the approach of Sam Colt.

Surely rivaling Ruger in gun savvy and experience, and akin to Colonel Colt, was the late Samuel Cummings, the American munitions magnate whose firm, Interarms, was headquartered in Europe. As founder and president, Cummings established major offices around the world. His gun enthusiasms, and those of Interarms, were broad, covering the complete history of firearms, and particularly the military armaments of the 20th century. The collection was housed in Manchester, England, but, like that of Sturm, Ruger & Co., it was not on public display.

Other major U.S. gun manufacturers with important collections include Browning in Morgan, Utah, and Navy Arms in Ridgefield, New Jersey.

Older than all of the collections, even that of Colt, is the Springfield Armory Museum. Established by Congress in 1795, the Armory began accumulating guns immediately, and its formal collecting may well have predated 1850. This public assemblage numbering into the thousands of small arms is now maintained by the National Park Service on the original site in Springfield, Massachusetts.

FAMILY AND PRIVATE COLLECTIONS

As one might expect, the collections of the manufacturers have a continuity lacking in the American collections of private individuals or families, in contrast to the great ancestral holdings of the royal houses and private estates of Europe.

Since collecting in many fields of antiquities, firearms included, has often been done quietly, the author has no doubt that at least a few old-time, pre-1900 arms groups are still together at this writing. Some of the prominent private U.S. collections from before 1900 that survived into the 20th century should be noted.

Though not well known himself, A. E. Brooks of Hartford began as a collector in the post–Civil War period. His was a large and general collection of antiques, featuring U.S. arms, and concentrating on Colts more than any other maker. At about the turn of the century the U.S. Cartridge Co. bought the Brooks Collection, and then published the items in book form. Brooks himself had published his own *Illustrated Catalogue of The A.E. Brooks Collection* (1899). Brooks–U.S. Cartridge Co. pieces are of special appeal to modern-day collectors, and specimens are usually marked with catalogue reference numbers. In the mid-1940s Robbins Ritter of East Hartford, Connecticut, sold the Brooks–U.S. Cartridge collection.

A contemporary of Brooks who was a celebrity in his day and a keen Colt enthusiast was Major John R. Hegeman Jr., scion of an old Massachusetts and New York family. Son of the first president of the Metropolitan Life Insurance Company, Hegeman was a friend of William F. "Buffalo Bill" Cody and General Nelson A. Miles. Thanks partly to close connections with the Colt company, Hegeman was able to put together an exceptional array of specimens, from the Paterson up to self-loading pistols; more than half a dozen of the latter bore serial number 1. The Hegeman collection was broken up around 1947, sold largely by the old-time arms dealership of W.G.C. Kimball, Woburn, Massachusetts.

GUN COLLECTING INTO THE 21TH CENTURY

Brooks and Hegeman are representative of pioneer private arms collectors. Their interest in guns paralleled that of collectors in other fields, a serious pursuit largely limited to persons with both money and time. Collecting art and antiques had been a tradition among the wealthy in Europe since the Renaissance. But in America, the passion did not become infectious until toward the end of the 19th century.

Our public museums blossomed as the nation's wealth, leisure time, and national and local consciousness and pride rapidly developed—aided in the 20th century by laws covering tax-deductible donations. Wealthy Americans on the "Grand Tour" of Europe often purchased liberally of art and antiques, seeming to be acquiring status and culture in the process. Observing the magnificent European collections in public and private hands powerfully influenced the evolution of collecting in America.

Samuel Colt was one of the first Americans to frequent Europe, and the influence of the regal wealth he saw there is evident in his lavish estate, Armsmear. The mansion house was an Italianate villa, the centerpiece of a massive landscaped park along the lines of fashionable English country estates. A Cabinet of Memorials, featuring guns, paintings, and sundry antiquities and sculpture, was displayed in an upper gallery of substantial proportions. The gallery was developed mainly by Mrs. Colt as tribute to her late husband's genius. Also part of establishing a respectable position among the wealthy, the arms collection, documents, and memorabilia would be bequeathed to Hartford museums on Mrs. Colt's death.

Large estates with mansion houses, like Colt's Armsmear, were springing up almost like mushrooms in Victorian America. As a shooter's paradise, the great West drew like a magnet not a few scions of wealthy Eastern families. At the same time, the South was returning to a position of power, and pockets of wealth in real estate, minerals, ranching, oil, industry, and finance were rapidly developing in the West and the Midwest. America discovered it was truly rich. And the leisure time that sometimes accompanies fortune coincided with an ever-growing interest in and appreciation of collecting.

William F. "Buffalo Bill" Cody, gun collector, holding one of his favorites, the Winchester Model 1873 Sporting Rifle.

The welcome new epidemic offered a variety of specialties—paintings, bronzes, antiques, decorative art—and, of the latter, arms and armor had a definite, and very native, appeal. Buffalo Bill's Wild West show and its successors traveled America and Europe from 1883 until 1916. Not only was Cody himself a crack shot and dedicated hunter, but he had an arms collection made up of several types and makes of guns. John R. Hegeman's gun interest was partially sparked by his friendship with Buffalo Bill. Furthermore, millions of Americans and Europeans saw firearms in romantic settings, as they enjoyed the extravaganzas of Buffalo Bill and his troupe.

Theodore Roosevelt, whose social and political credentials were impeccable, was a lover of fine arms and of hunting, and was already a regular customer of outfitter-dealer Schuyler, Hartley and Graham, and of Winchester, by the mid-1880s. More than fifty guns belonging to Roosevelt have been identified, and TR was the most gun-oriented and knowledgeable president since Thomas Jefferson. Roosevelt had a keen love of custom-made Winchesters, and two of his Colts were deluxe engraved and plated Single Action Armies. No president before or since contributed more to wildlife and habitat conservation and to a national appreciation of marksmanship and gun sports.

DISTINGUISHED COLLECTORS AND MUSEUMS

Hegeman and Brooks were contemporaries of TR, and among other active arms collectors of the Victorian period were the Nash and Williams families of Boston, the Bryants of central Connecticut, Lieutenant Colonel George Armstrong Custer, Annie Oakley, Doc Carver, and, as noted, Buffalo Bill himself. Cody was also a collector of art and patronized contemporaries the likes of Frederic Remington, Rosa Bonheur, and Charles Schreyvogel. A corporate collector of note, whose museum was begun by an officer in the 1920s, is the Wells Fargo Bank of San Francisco. Its arms collection rates high marks for color and history.

A most fascinating development in arms collecting in the U.S. took place under the inspiration of the first Curator of Arms and Armor at the Metropolitan Museum of Art in New York City, Dr. Bashford Dean. Dean was Curator of Reptiles and Fish at the American Museum of Natural History when the Metropolitan Museum acquired the splendid collection of the Duke de Dino in 1904. The purchase immediately established the Metropolitan as the major institution with arms and armor holdings in the United States. Dean was pressed into service to set up the collection, simultaneously continuing his duties at the Museum of Natural History.

In 1912 Dean was appointed Curator of Arms and Armor at the Metropolitan. From the early 20th century until his death in 1928, this scholarly and innovative gentleman was the central figure in a circle of enthusiastic collectors, which at times numbered financier J. Pierpont Morgan, banker William H. Riggs, social scion Rutherford Stuyvesant, silver heir Clarence H. Mackay (Irving Berlin was his son-in-law), financier Edward Hubbard Litchfield, Francis P. Garvan (a generous benefactor of Yale University), Howard Mansfield (a lawyer friend of artist James Abbott McNeill Whistler), George Cameron Stone (friend of Rudyard Kipling and a prominent metallurgist), C. O. von Kienbusch (tobacco merchant of note who gave his armory to the Philadelphia Museum of Art), Alexander McMillan Welch (N.Y.C. architect who married Bashford Dean's sister), George F. Harding (Chicago realtor who set up a museum by bequest, later absorbed by the Art Institute of Chicago), John Woodman Higgins (who founded Worcester Pressed Steel and established a museum at the company site), John Long Severance (a benefactor of the Cleveland Museum of Art), and George A. Douglass (whose wife was an heiress to the Helm tobacco fortune). Most of the above were members of the Armor and Arms Club of New York. Founded in 1921, it was the first organization of its kind in America. Its president was, of course, Bashford Dean.

WILLIAM RANDOLPH HEARST AND OTHERS

A friend of Dean's and a most active arms and armor collector was publishing giant William Randolph Hearst. But so distinguished and exclusive was the New York Club that Hearst was never allowed membership! He nevertheless maintained an acquaintance with Dr. Dean and lived in baronial style at residences like the fabulous San Simeon and, though he spent relatively little time there, St. Donat's Castle in Wales. European arms and armor were among the favorites in Hearst's broad collecting interests. Among other celebrity arms collectors contemporary with Hearst were Henry Ford, Tom Mix, William S. Hart, Josiah K. Lilly, William K. Vanderbilt II, Stephen Van Rensselaer, Henry du Pont, and distinguished artist Maxfield Parrish (also a dedicated machinist, with a first-rate machine shop).

A later member of the Armor and Arms Club was John E. Parsons: Yale graduate, law clerk to U.S. Supreme Court Chief Justice William Howard Taft (1928–29), Wall Street lawyer, author, trustee of the New-York Historical Society, and active Colt collector and authority. Parsons almost single-handedly created a reference library on American arms collecting in the 1950s, doing books and articles on Colt, Winchester, Smith & Wesson, and derringers. He was a fly-fishing friend of Nelson Rockefeller's, and it was through Rockefeller that Parsons met Colt aficionado Philip R. Phillips of the prominent Oklahoma oil family. Parsons' death in 1976 signaled the end of an era in American arms collecting.

Film legend Ceil B. DeMille, proudly wielding the pair of Colt Single Action Army .45 revolvers presented to him by the Colt company in the 1950s. A client of James E. Serven, DeMille had a general collection, ranging from Western guns, like Colts, to European duelers.

A NEW ERA OF ARMS COLLECTING IN AMERICA

In the 1950s and '60s, as the airplane made gun-collecting shows more accessible and gun values were skyrocketing, some of the moneyed-celebrity collectors slowed down or eliminated their attendance at collector meetings. The rapid pace of modern life has also led some enthusiasts to forgo the gun-show circuit, preferring instead to enjoy their firearms in the privacy of home or apartment, or by occasional private visits to bank vaults or museums where their pieces are on loan display.

The Armor and Arms Club of New York is still active. Among its post-1950 members were *The New Yorker* cartoonist Charles Addams, Dr. John Lattimer (author of a celebrated book on the Lincoln and Kennedy assassinations), Richard H. Randall Jr. (for many years director of the Walters Art Gallery, Baltimore), P. R. Phillips (father and uncle founded Phillips 66), Clay P. Bedford (president of Kaiser Aerospace & Electronics, and builder of the Hoover Dam), and Russell B. Aitken (one of the world's most experienced big-game hunters and bird shots). With the threat of crime in New York City, and the city's long-term negative attitude toward firearms, attendance at club meetings is not what one would wish it to be, but the historic arms and armor organization is still active.

JOHN B. SOLLEY AND TODAY'S COLLECTING FRATERNITY

A New Yorker who never belonged to the Armor and Arms Club and who had no interest in attending shows or belonging to any gun organization (except the National Rifle Association) was the late John B. Solley III. A grandson of Evan Lilly and an heir to the Lilly pharmaceutical fortune, Solley launched his collection when he was four years old and a family friend gave him a flintlock pistol. At his death in 1979, John Solley had, gun for gun, the finest collection of American antique arms in the world. His favorites were Colts, and he had the Serial No. 1 pre-Paterson Colt revolver, a pair of Lieutenant Colonel Custer's Navy Colts, five pairs of Dragoon Colts, *the* cased Walker Colt, *the* cased pair of Texas Patersons, several presentations from Colonel Colt (one of them to President Franklin Pierce), and the sensational forty-six-gun display board of Colt jobbers and New York dealers Hartley & Graham. The entire Solley collection was sold in 1979, and some of the most important pieces became part of the Colt Collection of the Raymond Baldwin Museum of Connecticut History. John Solley represented a modern species of collector to whom privacy is paramount.

In terms of numbers of collectors, values, and demand, the period since World War II has seen a rapidly expanding boom for arms collecting in America. Among the better-known collectors active in that period: members of the Ford, Mellon, Lilly, du Pont, Phillips, Olin, Donnolley, Woolworth, and Tufts families; entertainers Buddy Hackett, John Wayne, Johnny Cash, Hank Williams Jr., Mel Torme, Steve Cropper (of Booker T and the MGs), John Entwhistle (of The Who), Sammy Davis Jr., Clark Gable, Elvis Presley, Robert Conrad, Robert Fuller, Erik Estrada, Charlie Callas, Johnny Depp, Steve McQueen, Steven Segal, Sylvester Stallone, Ernie Kovacs, Ted Nugent, and Jerry Lewis. Others include author and editor Michael V. Korda, New York radio commentator Barry Gray (originator of the talk-show format), novelist-screenwriter-playwright Dan Greenburg, screenwriter-playwright David Mamet, Calhoun Norton (whose father endowed the Norton Gallery of Art, Palm Beach, Florida), film producer-director Blake Edwards, director-writer John Milius, oilmen Jay P. Altmayer and John Mecom, athlete Kareem Abdul Jabbar, YO Ranch owner and developer Charles Schreiner III, magazine publisher Robert E. Petersen, George Strichman (for over twenty years chairman of the board of Colt Industries), and several very, very prominent giants of American contemporary business who would prefer to remain anonymous—among them the president of a major philanthropic and educational organization; the founder and president of a luxury luggage, clothing, and accessories company; and an heir to a major cosmetics concern.

From Henry VIII to the Fords and Mellons, what a rich heritage arms collectors share—both in the objects collected and in the pedigrees of past and present collectors of note. All have found captivating the unique attraction of arms, their history, mechanics, artistry, and function. What other collectibles can equal this rich and fascinating heritage, and what objects can boast of a more significant role in history's past 500 years?

At left, Aldo Uberti, one of the 20th century's most innovative and artisic gunmakers, his daughter Maria, and the author. Taken at the Uberti factory, Val Trompia, Italy, September 1997.

How to Find Guns and Buy Them

Bearing in mind that injudicious advertising might invite a thief to your home or place of business, there are many ways to find collectors firearms. Basically these divide up into the following sources, all of which require hard work and developing a network of contacts.

THE GUN-SHOW CIRCUIT, LETTERHEADS, AND CARDS

A great deal will be said about gun shows in the present discourse; suffice it to say that much of the trading, buying, and selling in arms takes place at these events. This is the arena in which the skills of the trader come out, and there is a show ethic that must be observed: e.g., if you are scouting the show looking for treasures, and you see someone else already negotiating for a particular item, it is considered unethical to barge in and try to buy the item(s) out from under the person already trying to make a deal. However, having observed that a sale or trade did not take place, you may well wish to approach the seller, and inquire if the object still remains available.

If you know certain dealers and collectors are the source of the kinds of guns you seek, there is nothing wrong with advising them of your interest. A sample card that could solicit pieces is as follows:

J. D. Jones
Collector-Dealer
Seeking Fine Derringer Pistols
1100 Main Street
Any Town, CT 06999 U.S.A.
(860) 666-6666
Fax: (860) 666-6667

An appropriate letterhead could also be designed. In the author's case he has a half dozen different letterheads, some that are more personal and have nothing commercial on them whatever, and others that are quite commercial.

Cards and letterheads show that one is serious and active in a field, and not a tire-kicker, who could turn into a "time-sponge" and end up wasting time and energy on the part of those who are contacted.

The writer began collecting business cards when in his early twenties, and now has in excess of 6,000 of them. One thing that is clearly evident in this mass of material is that some cards are rather elegant, while others are on the cheap side—most are somewhat average. Any and all, however, are clear declarations that the party is serious about his gun collecting, and is willing to pay to purchase in the field of his desires.

GUN SHOPS

Every gun shop has potential as a source of items for the collector. And many such shops already carry in stock pieces that are more suited for the collector than for the shooter. Granted most of these are secondhand guns, but all the guns we collect were once "secondhand." If you are a traveler, like most Americans, and you find out the locations of gun shops that might have the goods, it might pay to call on them. On the other hand, most such shops already have someone, usually local, who is seeking objects, and might very well give that regular client first refusal on the good stuff. Being aware that many shops already have a loyalty to a dealer or friendly collector, sometimes it is not worth the effort to call on gun shops at all.

AUCTIONS

The business of collectors firearms seems to run in cycles. In the pioneering days of arms collecting, auction houses and dealers were an important source of material, with the dealers doing a lot of the action. These were such pre–World War II operations as the American Art Association, which later became Parke-Bernet (still later bought out by Sotheby's); one of the old-time dealers was Stephen Van Rensselaer, and still another was Sumner Healey. In the early days of collecting in New York City, Bashford Dean, first Curator of Arms and Armor for the Metropolitan Museum of Art, was a key source of fine items to the upper crust of collectors. Today, of course, that kind of commercialism would not be permitted by museum officials.

In the post–World War II era, much of the business in the United States was among dealers and collectors who were part-time dealers ("collector/dealers"). But in the 1980s the auction houses really came on with a vengeance, particularly Christie's and Sotheby's, and for several years Richard Bourne Co.; next, in a very big way (and still dominating the field), arose Butterfield's. There are presently several other very active firms handling quite a bit of merchandise. Names and addresses of the leading auctioneers now presenting arms auctions are listed in Appendix 3.

Buying at auctions allows the client the opportunity to examine his purchases, or at the least to discuss the items beforehand with the experts who handle the material and operate the sales. Viewing days preceding the sales present the objects under ideal conditions. The client should handle whatever is of interest, and decide on a limit to which he or she will bid for each piece. Though this requires a good deal of willpower, it is best to establish limits, thus avoiding the inevitable urge to keep on bidding and sometimes ending up paying more than the object might be worth.

You will also see other experts, besides those employed by the auction house, to whom queries can be addressed. It is, of course, up to you to decide whose opinion you will accept, bearing in mind that sometimes advice is worth what it costs (usually nothing).

If you are uncertain about any aspect of an auction, be sure to read the exposition published in the preface material to the catalogue. If you have any questions, be sure to ask and get the answers.

When it is sale time, you have to be alert, since the auctioneers often go at a rapid pace. There is not a lot of time in which to dwell on whether or not you want to go another notch up in the bidding. There again, having set a limit and standing by it is important—preventing one from going out of control.

Another advantage of auction buying is the educational value: Often the tremendous variety at these sales allows the collector and collector/dealer the chance to see a great deal of material and to quickly learn about values, about different types of guns, about what collectors want, and countless other things one should know.

The sale also presents an opportunity to meet a number of people in the gun business: fellow collectors, fellow dealers, journalists, photographers, and more.

Although it is possible for good clients to get some time from most auction houses in which to pay for purchases, most will charge a penalty, storage charges, and interest for objects not paid for within the prescribed time period.

It is illegal in many states and municipalities for "shills" to run up prices at auctions, or for the consigners themselves to arrange to have prices artificially run up. Also illegal is the often-discussed practice of an auctioneer taking a price off a chandelier, or "off the wall." However, for auction houses that have reserve figures on lots, the auctioneer has the right to bid on behalf of the owner until that protective figure is reached.

A ring of collaborators, in which persons agree not to bid on certain items or to allow an agreed-upon bidder to buy something without competition, is also illegal.

ANTIQUE SHOPS

Although antiques dealers often have broad general knowledge, many know just enough to price their material. And sometimes not enough to realize when they are really trying to get too much—and you are simply not willing to pay more than a fair figure. Thinking back over the years, the author can recollect only a few instances in which the countless hours he has spent in antiques shops paid off in finding a good gun. In most instances he enjoyed the visits, and may have found some other object of antiquity to purchase, thus at least getting his reward from that aspect of the visit.

Often the antiques dealer already has a client in mind, who will see any and all guns that come into the store or gallery. But if you do call on antiques shops, be sure to have a business card, or a want list, or some other means of leaving an impression.

Popular antique-arms specialist and New York gallery owner Martin Lane (at right), with his friend Nick Fallana. They are holding the Colt Texas Paterson revolver donated by entertainer Johnny Cash to the Metropolitan Museum of Art for the 1985 benefit auction at Christie's, New York. The guitar was part of the sale lot, and was signed by Johnny—who also made an unusual appearance as a guest auctioneer, assisted by Brian Cole, one of America's foremost auctioneers (later appointed director of Butterfield's galleries in Los Angeles).

YARD OR GARAGE SALES

Such informal sales are highly unlikely to be productive. But it is still a good idea to have that business card or other giveaway that could eventually turn up a treasure from new contacts. I have never found a firearms-related object in a yard or garage sale. On the other hand, there are a few collectors and dealers who have. Gerald Fox, one of the old-time collectors, bought a rare and original Walker Colt revolver brought to him by a mother whose lucky son found the gun in a garbage can on his way home from school. Imagine finding a Walker model, one of the great prizes of arms collecting, in an ash can!

ADVERTISING IN TRADE PUBLICATIONS AND ELSEWHERE

Judging from the number of dealers and collector/dealers who run advertisements in trade magazines and other likely venues, there must be something to the exposure and the costs. Such advertising might often seem more like the "institutional" kind, for image and prestige purposes. But in the early days of collecting the effort often paid off. With the diminishing number of guns coming out of private homes and other non-gun-collector sources, a respectful person with a dedicated interest in firearms might actually be lucky with those sources—despite the costs involved.

Try a display ad in a publication like *The Gun Report* or *Man at Arms,* or even the more expensive *Outdoor Life,* and see what happens. But be certain to weigh the advantages and the disadvantages. William M. Locke, for decades the acknowledged dean of arms collectors, occasionally ran small display advertisements. But it was his network of contacts and friends, which he had developed since he was in his twenties, that led to many of the guns he was able to locate. Further, actively attending gun shows and, in those days, an occasional auction, as well as an unending correspondence and telephone follow-ups, were all good reasons for his dominant role in arms collecting for over forty years.

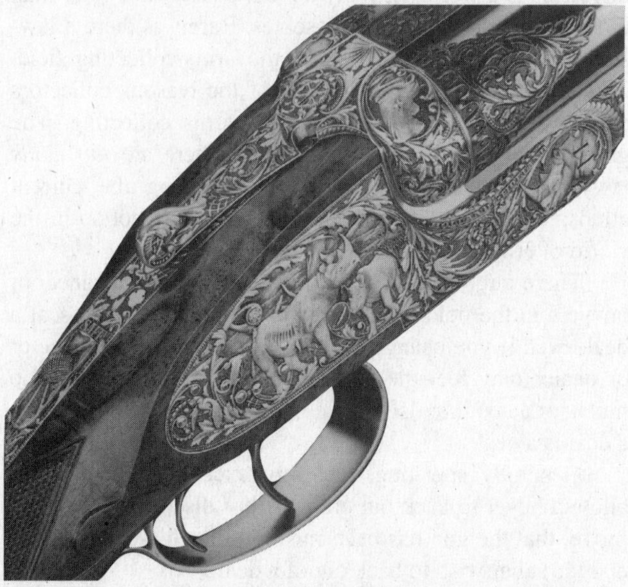

The Holland & Holland SCI 2000 Donation Double Barrel Rifle, a Royal Model relief engraved by Philippe Grifnee with decorative scrolls and floral motifs, and African rhinoceros motifs, symbolic of Safari Club International's vital role in bringing African rhino populations back from threatened extinction. Realized $280,000 at the featured Grand Banquet auction at the 2000 SCI convention, Reno.

Running an advertisement, however, requires responsibility. If people respond to your ads, and you don't in turn respond to them, they will soon become discouraged. The author virtually never advertises, although, in a way, each of his books is like a business card. That follow-up is crucial, and is simply a part of being efficient and professional, and successful.

FIREARMS INDUSTRY AND COLLECTOR/DEALER SHOWS

For the gun enthusiast, whether collector, shooter, or any other person keen on the considerable variety of firearms-related hobbies and vocations, there are three major trade and collector shows, often held in Las Vegas, which are comparable to "the greatest shows on earth." Conveniently, these three shows generally take place within a week's time of each other, in late January and early February.

First is the SHOT Show, a true extravaganza, with over 25,000 persons in attendance, representing virtually all the companies and individuals who make up the contemporary firearms, ammunition, and accessory industries.

The second of these events is the annual meeting and show of Safari Club International, complete with U.S. senators and congressmen, and (in 2000) former President George Bush, General Schwartzkopf, and former Vice President Dan Quayle. There were several hundred exhibitors, among them professional hunters from around the world, and gunmakers like Beretta, Connecticut Shotgun Mfg. Co., J. Purdey & Sons, Holland & Holland, Ltd, J. Rigby & Co., Ltd, Westley Richards, and Sturm, Ruger & Co.; sporting apparel firms the likes of Hunting World, Inc., and Euro Chasse; great taxidermists like the legendary Michael Boyce; numerous talented wildlife artists, including Guy Coheleach; and thousands of dedicated hunter-conservationists.

Finally, oriented more for the collector of antique, vintage, and contemporary firearms—and therefore most important for readers of this book—is Wallace Beinfeld's Antique Arms Show, held for approximately thirty-five years at the Hotel Sahara. Beginning in the summer of 1997, this three-times-a-year event is held at the spacious convention center of the Hotel Riviera. Featuring most of the top dealers, many leading collectors, and a throng of visiting collectors and the public, this show is truly "world-class."

For decades one of the premier shows, the National Rifle Association Annual Meetings takes place usually in late April or early May, and is held at various large cities around the country. Further, the 1996 annual meeting was joined by a separate show aimed at recognition of the importance of arms collecting to the future of gun ownership in America: the NRA Gun Collectors Show and Conference, first held at Opryland, Nashville, Tennessee, in mid-September. The 2000 show is scheduled for July 28–30, in Kansas City, Missouri (see NRA chapter, page 59, for further information).

These quite extraordinary events reflect the tremendous numbers of persons who share a devotion and a dedication to firearms.

WRITING ARTICLES AND BOOKS, I.E., ESTABLISHING EXPERT CREDENTIALS

Although he never had the above-noted goal in mind, the author's writings, and his dedication to the world of firearms, have inevitably led to an avalanche of phone calls, e-mail, snail-mail (regular mail via post office), media notices of interest, and word-of-mouth leads. Further, on publication of each book, the author's appearance in promotions at gun shows, on radio and TV interviews, and at press parties in New York City and elsewhere, all precipitate even more leads and inquiries.

The results have been satisfying and rewarding, though they have meant sixteen- and eighteen-hour days along the way, working at that backbreaking pace virtually nonstop for decades.

However, no one in the field of arms collecting is not pleased to be busy. This is like being paid for pursuing one's hobby, a dream job to virtually everyone who makes a living in the arms-collecting arena.

TRAVELING AND FIREARMS

For up-to-date information on what travelers need to know about firearms, the NRA-ILA publishes a brochure entitled *Guide to the Interstate Transportation of Firearms*.* To quote from this publication:

> Federal law prohibits the carrying of any firearm, concealed or unconcealed, on or about the person or in carry-on baggage while aboard an aircraft. Unloaded firearms not accessible to the passenger while aboard the aircraft are permitted when:
>
> 1. The passenger has notified the airline when checking the baggage that the firearm is in the baggage and that it is unloaded.
>
> 2. The baggage in which the firearm is carried is locked, and only the passenger checking the baggage retains a key.
>
> 3. The baggage is carried in an area, other than the flight crew compartment, that is inaccessible to passengers. . . .

The brochure states further, regarding other carriers:

> Any passenger who owns or legally possesses a firearm being transported aboard any common or contract carrier for movement with the passenger in interstate or foreign commerce must deliver the unloaded firearm into the custody of the pilot, captain, conductor, or operator of such common or contract carrier for the duration of the trip. Check with each carrier before your trip to avoid problems.
>
> Bus companies usually refuse to transport firearms. Trains usually allow the transportation of encased long guns, if they are dissassembled or the bolt is removed.

The brochure also explains the ins and outs of transporting firearms interstate in your automobile, something particularly important to dealers, collector/dealers, and collectors when traveling to and from gun shows.

THE ETIQUETTE AND TECHNIQUE OF BUYING GUNS

A lot of what follows is simply common sense, but it reflects the particular mores of the arms-collecting fraternity. This is a world virtually devoid of lawyers, other than those who are collectors themselves. Rarely is there a lawsuit brought against anyone in the arms-collecting field. This gentlemanly conduct is one of the reasons collectors derive such joy and pleasure from arms collecting. The greed of some lawyers (we all agree there are *too many* lawyers) has been instrumental in creating the current atmosphere of litigation madness. But this is not so in the world of arms collecting.

There are several reasons for the insignificance of lawyers in the field. First, a handshake is enough to seal a deal, even if you change your mind. Sometimes a collector or dealer may feel the next day that perhaps he paid too much, or acted impulsively, in making a purchase. Too bad; a deal is a deal.

Generally speaking, the only exceptions that would allow a buyer to back out are if he has discovered, and can prove, that the gun has been misrepresented—or if both he and the seller wish to back out of a deal.

In making an offer on a gun, the buyer has made, in effect, a verbal commitment to purchase. Should the seller agree to those points, you have a deal.

In these days of long-winded contracts on such purchases as real estate, cars, or other expensive merchandise, it may be a surprise to the novice to learn that a deal on a costly firearm could be a simple exchange of payment, or

*Available from the NRA-ILA Grassroots, 11250 Waples Mill Road, Fairfax, VA 22030-9400; (800) 392-8683.

trade, with a simple bill of sale. The author has sold firearms for over $500,000, for which he received a check and the buyer received a one-page bill of sale. Generally, however, a valuable antique of that distinction will also be accompanied by papers and documents, a pedigree, and possibly even copies of photographs, articles, and books relevant to the item's history and other merits.

Dealers normally give a three-day inspection privilege for merchandise that has been sold through the mail, by fax, over the phone, or over the Internet.

If the buyer feels he should have an expert look at the piece, he should bloody well be sure that the "expert" really is qualified. Nothing is more annoying to a dealer who sells a piece in good faith than to find that the collector wants to return the item because "someone" feels the item has been refinished, or is otherwise not as represented. The author more than once has had to assure collectors that a Paterson Colt does indeed have its original finish—although few can tell for sure, since these arms are often misleading: high polishes brought about high-gloss blues, but sometimes the factory workmen leaned hard on the polishing wheel, thereby overpolishing, and sometimes leaving the genuine markings weak.

Another common failing is for collectors to question the finish on mint Colts from the Hartford period. The author remembers his amusement when one well-meaning writer remarked how disappointed he was in the quality of the Samuel Colt Collection at the Wadsworth Atheneum: "Too bad most of the guns were refinished." Fact is, nearly all the Colts at the Atheneum are in perfect, unfired condition, including the world's finest Paterson Colt revolver. The exceptions are two revolvers (a Navy with a reblued barrel and a Belt Model Paterson refinished overall, undoubtedly by the Colt factory in the 19th century).

PRICES QUOTED

Bear in mind that at gun shows, and even in dealers' lists, the buyer is permitted to try to haggle, up to a point. Some dealers will not back off a dime. At gun shows, the sticker price is often considered the price at which negotiations begin. The author likes to state simply, "What's your best price on this piece?" But other techniques include: "How about a clergyman's discount?" and "I'm interested in this piece, at a price of $XXX." Another means is simply to offer some items in trade. Once you offer a trade or a specified price, you are committed to follow through if the seller agrees to your offer.

It is not unusual for the quoted or list price of a piece to be as much as 10 to 15 percent above what the seller will actually take. One collector, known for his sense of humor, says that he takes the quoted price, divides that by four, and then offers half of that.

Although the arms-collecting field truly does not have a ticker-tape type source of values for collectors firearms, used guns are another matter. These are easier to figure, since most are still in production, and therefore readily available through publications like *Gun List, Shotgun News,* and *Gun Journal.* Further, many are in gun shops and sporting-goods stores around the country. And manufacturers publish catalogues and lists, which help to provide guidance.

Antique and obsolete firearms for the collector are, however, another matter entirely. Some of these pieces are so rare that many collectors will never see an example in their lifetime. At the same time, the buyer has to be able to judge which of these are going to appreciate, and which are, perhaps, extremely rare, but not necessarily wanted by most collectors.

Thus it is easier for a Colt or Winchester collector, because there are more collectors keen on owning these pieces, and therefore more willing to spend top dollar. The market is stronger for them, because more people want to own examples. And there is more reference material that can provide guidance to the keen buyer. *Flayderman's Guide to Historical American Arms and Their Values* is an important source, specific to a great many variations, some of which do not appear in this price guide, since this volume also includes a great many modern arms, and European ones as well.

A collector should not be flip in trying to buy something he wants, making an outrageously low offer. On the other hand, he can get a feel for how determined the seller is to realize a particular price—and might well enjoy the sales pitch the dealer or dealer/collector will present. After a while the buyer can recognize B.S. as opposed to solid expertise, experience, and sincerity.

MAKING AN OFFER

The fact that most gun shows are only two-day affairs does not allow a lot of time for one to make a decision. Further, in that arena, there are a great many experienced and knowledgeable individuals who are capable of making a decision quickly. You may well find some great piece, a "sleeper" that no one else has spotted. You have to act fast, or that item is gone. When the author was doing about thirty gun shows a year, he would prowl about as the show opened, looking for treasures. He saw others doing the same, some of them quite aggressively, to the point that they might help the seller unwrap his wares! You may not have the opportunity to make a phone call (though that's much easier now, with cellular phones), and someone else may be looking over your shoulder ready to pounce.

Asking a dealer or other seller to hold something at a gun show is unfair unless your decision will come quickly. Sometimes the shows settle down after the first couple of hours, and if you have tied up a piece and then decide not to take it, that could damage the item, killing its sale to others.

KILLING A GUN

A collector or dealer has "killed" a gun when he has "bad-mouthed" it with comments detrimental to the future sale of that piece. Killing can happen through some irresponsible person who claims the gun is refinished or otherwise altered, or that it has been faked or is otherwise not as represented. A few dealers and collectors have the reputation for "bad-mouthing" or "poison-gassing" guns. Dealing with irresponsible assaults on the integrity of firearms is part of the education of the serious arms collector. The big-mouth who "bad-mouths" a good gun is likely also to be the kind of boor who will do the same to the reputation of someone who often does not deserve that kind of treatment.

The author has written approximately 1,000 letters of documentation on collectors firearms. Many of these are on perfectly authentic pieces that did not have the advantage of "factory" letters. Or the letters were needed because some supposed expert had claimed the gun had serious defects.

FACTORY LETTERS

Colt's Manufacturing Co., Smith & Wesson, the Marlin Firearms Co., and Ruger are four major firms that maintain records, which can be accessed by collectors, sometimes on a fee basis, sometimes for free. The records of Winchester were transferred to the Buffalo Bill Historical Center, Cody, Wyoming, and are available for a fee.

Factory letters tell you only what the original ledger books state about a firearm. These are not to be construed, necessarily, as "letters of authenticity." Sometimes a gun has been faked and sold with a letter stating the features present on the original gun. An example is a fake Buntline Special Colt revolver that was accompanied by a letter stating the features of an original revolver bearing the same serial number.

A factory letter is important to have with a gun—but it's not always absolutely crucial. The author has written many a letter on a perfectly authentic Single Action Army or percussion Colt for which the factory clerk somehow failed to note certain important facts; usually that omitted detail was the simple word *engraved*. Or perhaps the fact-that the grips were relief carved, or that the revolver was gold inlaid, was not noted.

Fortunately, as noted in the section on fakes, doing a truly creative job in faking an antique firearm is not easily accomplished. With experience and education, and seeing lots of original specimens, the collector will soon pick up the ability to spot most miscreants. Factory letters are, in most instances, entirely accurate, and will prove to be useful.

PAYMENT

Until a collector has established a reputation, he may encounter some difficulty in getting sellers to accept checks. Occasionally a bad-check expert will do a tap dance on a gun show, but that is extremely rare. Although there are risks in carrying around cash for acquisitions, there are some who find that the best means of closing a deal quickly. Writing a check for cash and cashing it at your bank before leaving for a show can eliminate the possible problems of dealing with sellers who won't take a check or credit cards. Increasingly sellers are accepting credit cards, and traveler's checks are another alternative.

Many dealers also offer variations of a "lay-away" plan, allowing purchase of a piece over a period of months. Usually the object remains in the possession of the seller until fully paid for.

Trading is also a viable means of closing a deal. Trade and cash immediately, trades and cash over time, or variations on the theme are all acceptable. The most creative trader of all was Johnie Bassett, who could make a down payment of $1,000 on a $40,000 sale, then give any number of postdated checks, and trade sculpture and paintings, furniture, silver, porcelains, and even guns! Johnie spoke and carried on like a good old boy, but he once confided to the author that he felt no one could out-trade him—and nobody ever did. Because of his skills, and his nerve, he owned many of the finest Colts and Winchesters in existence during his lifetime of collecting.

A final note: Collectors who become friendly with a particular dealer can often call on that dealer's connections and expertise to close a deal. Make no mistake about it, no great collector was able to put together his collection without relying in some way on the expertise and experience of a top dealer.

How to Sell Guns

Commerce in the domain of collectors firearms is a combination of selling through gun stores, through gun shows, through auction houses, through friends and acquaintances, through mail order, and, lately, through the Internet.

DIRECTLY TO COLLECTORS AND TO DEALERS

When Norm Flayderman speaks of the marketing of collectors firearms, he likes to use the term "the last frontier." Most of those in the business are self-employed; most of them are free to travel and find that they do so perhaps all too often. One never knows for sure where he or she might end up in a particular week, or month, or year. It is possible to schedule shows that are worth attending. But learning of a collection that you can buy, or take on consignment, or whatever your *modus operandi* is, may suddenly change your plans completely. In fact, while completing the manuscript for this book, the author was interrupted on three occasions by gun collections that suddenly became available, by an urgent appraisal involved in a contentious divorce case, and by the opportunity to get a rare Colt revolver he had first seen in 1962(!), still in the hands of the same owner.

A typical year for the author: besides commitments for writing articles and books, his duties include researching and writing letters of documentation for collectors and dealers specific to important guns, assisting a museum in identifying or selling a piece or a collection, identifying guns for the public, assisting Christie's with evaluations and identifications and sometimes specifically with items for auction (the author has been associated with that august firm since 1981), writing to old-time collector/dealer contacts to locate fresh guns, searching through over thirty-five years of correspondence for leads, and even occasionally dealing with the media when their interest is piqued by some timely event (such as the promotion attendant to a new collectors firearms book, or perhaps an item being sold in a public auction).

Thus, although the writer tries to plan an entire year of activity, he (like all his colleagues in the field) has to remain flexible—a distinct advantage of being self-employed. On the other hand, it has often been observed that making a living in this business is a matter of feast or famine. And with the increasing competition at finding good guns to sell, the famine part often overtakes the feast.

In order to plan out a year, my own method of operation is to try to have a new book appear each fall, which will allow for worthwhile action at a show—since many visitors to those events are desirous of keeping their libraries up to date. And while attending the shows, the opportunities are good for finding guns for collector clients—and for including some pieces on my sales table that might appeal to other collectors and dealers.

Particularly when planning to visit a European show, your schedule and plans need to be set up months in advance, since one way to get the word out that you will be at a particular event is to contact a foreign magazine—for me, luckily, my German publisher, Motorbuch Verlag—to see whether room is available for a special promotion in its booth.

One of the old-time gun dealers, now retired, used to be proud of his ability to come to a gun show with a few hundred dollars in his pocket, to buy or get some pieces "on the arm" (on consignment), and work the show so effectively that by the time Sunday afternoon rolled around, he had made a few thousand dollars! He was consistently good at this, and was able to do so because he knew guns, what they were worth, and what customers wanted. Also, it was helpful that people at the shows knew him, and expected him to come up with good material.

But what about the novice, who has to start from scratch? This is not an easy world to break into, and the novice finds out rather quickly the quality of his or her buying, trading, and selling skills.

OVEREXPOSING A GOOD GUN

The seller who may have a fine gun should be aware that if he does not go about selling it in an intelligent manner, he may very well overexpose it, and find that the best client for the piece doesn't want to buy it, sometimes at any price.

Here's what happened in a famous case from the 1980s, when a new collector located a rare and beautiful Single Action Army Colt from the mid-1870s. The revolver was richly engraved and in extraordinary condition. Not wanting to keep the piece for himself, he shopped it around trying to squeeze out the last dime by working one collector and dealer against the other. Finally, everyone who might have been interested would no longer tolerate the way the seller was marketing the gun. Further, the market took an unexpected dive, since the top collectors who might have been interested either died, changed interests, or were fed up with the squeeze tactics of the owner. Instead of being able to realize a fair price, the collector had no buyers, and eventu-

R.L. Wilson

Castle View
103-4 Ferry Road, Route 148
Hadlyme, Connecticut 06439
Tel: (860) 526-9297
Fax: (860) 526-9514
www.wilsonbooks.com
WilsonBook@aol.com

Historical Consultant
Colt's Manufacturing Co., Hartford
and to
'The Art of American Arms'
and
'Buffalo Bill's Wild West'
Museum Loan Exhibitions
'Son of a Gun' - BBC-TV
'Colt Firearms Legends' - SONY
'The Guns That Tamed the West' - A & E
'The Story of the Gun' - A & E
'Tales of the Gun' – The History Channel
'The Gun Industry in America' - BBC-TV/Open University
'Annie Oakley' - Riva Productions
Chairman, Antique Arms Committee
U.S. Society of Arms and Armour/America Remembers
Fine Colts The Dr. Joseph A. Murphy Collection

Samuel Colt Presents
The Arms Collection of Colonel Colt
L.D. Nimschke Firearms Engraver
The Evolution of the Colt
The Rampant Colt
Colt Commemorative Firearms
Theodore Roosevelt Outdoorsman
The Book of Colt Firearms
The Book of Winchester Engraving
Antique Arms Annual
Colt Pistols (with R.E. Hable)
Paterson Colt Pistol Variations (with P.R. Phillips)
The Colt Heritage
The "Russian" Colts
Colt Engraving
Rare and Historic Firearms (Christie's)
Winchester 1 of 1000
Colt's Dates of Manufacture
The Deringer in America, 2 Volumes (with L.D. Eberhart)
Colt An American Legend
Rare Firearms - A Benefit Auction (Christie's)
Winchester An American Legend
The Peacemakers
Steel Canvas
Ruger & His Guns
The Colt Engraving Book
The Official Price Guide to Gun Collecting
Buffalo Bill's Wild West (with Greg Martin)
The World of Beretta (2000)

THE L.D. NIMSCHKE
COLT THIRD MODEL DRAGOON REVOLVER
1 of 50
As Featured in
The Metropolitan Museum of Art-Christie's Benefit Auction
for the Museum's Department of Arms and Armor
October 8th 1985
Original Design by Alvin A. White
for The Heritage Guild
Revolvers Purchased In-the-White
from the Colt Factory
and Built by American Master Engravers
for The Heritage Guild, 1985-1986
Serial Number 24949
Signed on the Left Side of the Barrel Lug: A.W.

The Colt-L.D. Nimschke Third Model Dragoon 1 of 50 special series of revolvers was made in 1985 and 1986, with the original design by Alvin A. White, and the production exclusively for The Heritage Guild.

Enclosed is a copy of the advertising brochure issued in 1985, as well as a copy of relevant material from the catalogue of The Metropolitan Museum of Art, Department of Arms and Armor Benefit Auction, held by Christie's October 8th 1985. The original brochure advertised the revolver at $3,790. The revolver donated to The Metropolitan Museum auction brought $4,180.

These revolvers were supplied by the Colt factory, "in the white", at the very end of the company's production of blackpowder revolvers, in 1985. The author was involved in the manufacture of the special Heritage Guild series, and will be featuring the issue in the forthcoming book, **THE MODERN COLT BLACKPOWDER REVOLVER**, a joint project with co-author Thomas A. Conroy. The revolvers are also prominently pictured in **FINE COLTS The Dr. Joseph A. Murphy Collection**, and are featured in **THE COLT ENGRAVING BOOK**, in the chapters on Alvin A. White.

This important limited series of cased, deluxe, carved ivory-gripped Colt revolvers is worthy of the finest private or museum arms collection. Serial number 24949 is a superb example, signed on the left side of the barrel lug, **A.W.**

ally sold the revolver for about 40 percent less than the best offer he had received before the sudden changes! Over-exposure and greed had "killed" what otherwise would have been a good sale.

Bearing that in mind, anyone who wishes to dispose of a privately owned firearm, and wants to sell to or otherwise work through a dealer, would be well advised to consider any of the professionals in Appendix 4, all of whom make their living in the business; the majority are from the U.S.A., with a few from outside the country.*

CONSIGNMENTS

Sometimes an object's purchase would require such a sum that many in the business might not be able to come up with the necessary cash. Or sometimes a collector or other owner recognizes the sale might realize more by consignment of the item to a broker, dealer, or another collector who would be willing to work for a lesser profit. Most consigners will take on the sale of an item at a commission of anywhere from 10 to 20 percent. For the agreed-upon figure, the dealer or broker is normally expected to assume all the time and effort, and costs, of marketing the piece.

Consignments call for a clear understanding between parties, and, in many instances, the seller should make clear to the consigner that the object might sell in a few days or weeks, or it might require up to as much as six months, and maybe even more. Some crucial and rare pieces demand a very careful orchestration. The following is a checklist for any consignment transaction.

- Draw up a consignment document, spelling out all terms.
- Write a document or letter on the item(s), to facilitate presenting same for sale. This could well be along the lines of the documenting sample letter illustrated here.
- Think through the best way to market the item: gun shows, a personal call to the potential buyer, putting the piece on the Internet, advertising in a magazine, and so forth.
- Actually acting on the above might mean awaiting a particular gun show, the proper timing to see the scoped-out buyer, perhaps arranging for a friend to advise the potential buyer of this new item (recommending it as just right for his or her collection), and so forth.
- As in selling any item, think out carefully just the way to present it. At many gun shows, the best pieces are

*This list concentrates on professionals in the field, many of them known to the author. Should any dealer's name be omitted, kindly contact the writer for inclusion in future editions.

kept under the seller's table, being held until that right moment to show it off ("timing is everything"). Sometimes that moment is not even during the show, but perhaps with some ceremony in the privacy of a hotel or motel room.

- Once a deal is made, the seller needs to be careful that he pays off the consigner as quickly as the funds have cleared. One must not fall into the trap of delaying payment, and later finding that the client's money vanished into some other use.

Many dealers do not want to take on consignments, preferring to own objects outright. But today it is not unusual for an owner to want a greater involvement in the sale process, hoping also to receive a better price for his material.

ADVANTAGES OF SELLING AN ITEM OR A COLLECTION THROUGH AN AUCTION HOUSE

There are several advantages of selling through an auction house.

- Wide exposure for the object(s), permitting more potential buyers to be aware of its availability, and therefore, hopefully, more competition in the bidding.
- Reasonable costs, varying from 10 to 15 percent (on average), plus possible costs for photography, insurance, shipping, and other expenses. Generally there is a 10 percent premium paid by the buyer, which goes entirely to the auction house.
- Expert assistance for proper cataloguing, scheduling of the sale, advertising and promotion, and related details. An endorsement by qualified experts can be crucial in gaining the confidence of bidders.
- A qualified auction house will provide expert descriptions and produce a handsome catalogue that will encourage bidders.

If the collection or object is valuable enough, it is possible with some auction companies for the seller to obtain an advance against estimated realized prices. This amount could be as much as 50 percent of value, and possibly more. Some houses will even buy your collection outright, although this practice is not the usual *modus operandi* of auctioneers.

Some auction-house staff can even provide guidance on tax liability and other questions. And giving estimates of prices objects should realize is free of charge. On the other hand, if an appraisal is needed, or certain other services are not part of the auction *per se*, the house would normally charge a per diem fee.

Finally, when someone has put together an impressive collection, he or she might very well like to have the material covered in a book. Collections like those of Richard C. Marohn, M.D., Carl Press, Robert Howard, Charles L. Bricker, Karl Moldenhauer, Keith Neal, George Repaire, and many others have been immortalized by the handsome catalogues of their collections. The importance of this is evident by reference to the bibliography accompanying this *Price Guide*—in which several private-collection auction catalogues are noted.

A note on scheduling: tying dates between gun shows or in conjunction with special events (like the annual NRA Gun Collectors Show and Conference), and avoiding holidays and potential bad weather, are among several factors to be considered. Further, it is important to avoid offering too much of the same type of material at any one time. Some collections, like the historic Press sales held by Butterfield's, work better when spread out over a period of years.

DISADVANTAGES OF AUCTION-HOUSE SALE

Between the date of consignment and the date of actual sale there might be five to six months. Unless you are satisfied with possible partial advance payments, or can wait the approximate half year, other avenues for sale should be pursued.

- A public auction leaves no opportunity for trading an item, which some collectors prefer from time to time, as opposed to an outright sale.
- There may be some family or other professional or personal embarrassment attached to selling items at auction—a public venue open to considerable scrutiny.
- The protection price (the "reserve"), which establishes the lowest sum at which a consigner will sell an object, may be misjudged, and could be too high. As a consequence, the item might not sell. The best advice here is simply this: Do not set the protective figure so high that it will discourage bidders. The buyer does not mind bidding against another legitimate bidder, but he does not want to bid against the owner, or the owner's set restrictive figure.

  One can determine the reserve figure simply by looking at the estimates. This protective figure can never be higher than the upper end of the estimate range.

  Some sales do not reach their hoped-for figures, and it is worth contacting the auction house after a sale, in the event an item you want to buy went unsold. That might prove to be the most judicious time to make your purchase. However, it is risky to take the chance that something you want might remain unsold. If it does sell, and you still want it, try to keep track of who the purchaser was, and see if something might be arranged following the sale. If any object fails to sell, particularly if the object is an important one, it will be tainted, and might not be salable on the market again for several

BILL OF SALE FOR COLLECTOR FIREARM

(Please type or print)

RECEIVED OF ...., residing at ....

...., the sum of .... dollars ($........................) and

.... in trade in full payment of the following described firearm:

Maker's Name ....

Maker's Address ....

Country and Date of Manufacture ....

Model .... Serial Number(s) ....

Condition (See other side for NRA Condition Standards) ....

Ignition System ....

Barrel(s) .... Barrel(s) Length ....

Caliber(s) or Gauge(s) ....

Over-all Length .... Weight ....

Accessories Included ....

Markings, Engravings and Inscriptions (Describe) ....

Stock or Grips (Describe) ....

Repairs, Alterations and Replacements (Describe) ....

The term "Firearm" used in this Bill of Sale is employed in the general sense and not in reference to any legal definition which might appear in published statutes.

(over)

Historical Claims (Authenticity and Origin of Arm and/or Inscriptions, etc.) ....

Name and Address of Previous Owner ....

I certify that the information in this Bill of Sale is true and complete, and that I have the right to sell and give possession of the firearm described.

SIGNED AND SEALED this .... day of ...., 19........

(Name of Seller)

Received the firearm described in the foregoing Bill of Sale:

(Signature of Seller)

(Street Address of Seller)

(City & State of Seller)

IMPORTANT INFORMATION FOR COLLECTOR FIREARMS BUYERS

This form should be filled in and signed by the seller of the firearm, and carefully read by the buyer before accepting the firearm and paying for it.

There are many spurious firearms in circulation and some are passed along in good faith as genuine, while others are misrepresented by the seller.

There is no simple way in which a collector can 'protect' himself against buying a spurious gun. But the following rules, if heeded, will reduce the risk to a minimum.

(1) Deal with a reputable dealer or individual.
(2) If you are not sure about a gun's authenticity, have it checked by a recognized authority.
(3) Above all demand a bill of sale that is signed by the seller and includes the name and address of the seller and a full description of the gun, as represented.

If the seller will not put down in writing, above his signature, what he represents the gun to be, then don't buy the gun.

NRA CONDITION STANDARDS FOR ANTIQUE FIREARMS

FACTORY NEW—all original parts; 100% original finish; in perfect condition in every respect, inside and out.

EXCELLENT—all original parts; over 80% original finish; sharp lettering, numerals and design on metal and wood; unmarred wood; fine bore.

FINE—all original parts; over 30% original finish; sharp lettering, numerals and design on metal and wood; minor marks in wood; good bore.

VERY GOOD—all original parts; none to 30% original finish; original metal surfaces smooth with all edges sharp; clear lettering, numerals and design on metal; wood slightly scratched or bruised; bore disregarded for collectors firearms.

GOOD—some minor replacement parts; metal smoothly rusted or lightly pitted in places, cleaned or reblued; principal lettering, numerals and design on metal legible; wood refinished, scratched, bruised or minor cracks repaired; in good working order.

FAIR—some major parts replaced; minor replacement parts may be required; metal rusted, may be lightly pitted all over, vigorously cleaned or reblued; rounded edges of metal and wood; principal lettering, numerals and design on metal partly obliterated; wood scratched, bruised, cracked or repaired where broken; in fair working order or can be easily repaired and placed in working order.

POOR—major and minor parts replaced; major replacement parts required and extensive restoration needed; metal deeply pitted; principal lettering, numerals and design obliterated; wood badly scratched, bruised, cracked or broken; mechanically inoperative; generally undesirable as a collectors firearm.

Form designed by the National Rifle Association of America.

This form may be reproduced in its entirety.

years. Therefore, if one is offering items for sale by auction, do all that is possible, and legal, to make sure it will not remain unsold on sale day.

- Selling your collection might well spell the end of your collecting activity and presence: Seeing that you have disposed of your treasures, old contacts might figure you are now entirely out of the arms field. If this is not the case, then make sure they understand that fact clearly. Normally, an auction of a person's collection represents the end of his days in the field.
- Tax complications: It is possible that a private sale might have offered a means of marketing the item(s) without the public exposure an auction presents. However, one must be careful to remain within the law. For example, an object or collection sold privately could be paid for over a period of time, which could be of benefit from a tax standpoint. Such arrangements are much easier done privately than with an auction house—although evidently some houses are much more flexible than others.

Also bear in mind that you will need to prepare for the tax liability from a bulk sale; this includes figuring capital gains on objects that might well have cost relatively little when purchased years before.

The author with Beretta, Gardone, sales director Christian Verhuyck (right) and the president of the Tiro a Segno Club of Brescia, in a composition of shooting medals, banners, flags, and trophies for The World of Beretta *book.*

The Gun-Show Arena

The gun-show circuit has become, for some, a way of life. If one wanted to do so, he or she could be at a gun show virtually every weekend of the year. Texas alone probably has over 250 gun shows in a single year, and California perhaps even more! There are some regional shows that are not even published in such periodicals as *The Gun Report, Gun List,* or *Shotgun News*. For example, the author belongs to the Antique Arms Collectors Association of Connecticut; there are only fifteen active members, about a half dozen nonactive, and an even smaller number honorary; we meet monthly (except for June, July, and August), in the homes of members, and have an annual shoot and picnic. Each host member is expected to give a brief talk about a gun in his collection, or some other relevant subject, and members sometimes bring guns to the meeting to share with others; guests are also welcome. Although the club is small, the group has provided some of the most fun this writer has had in his entire career in collecting.

In the late 1960s and early 1970s, the author attended as many as thirty gun shows per year. In those days the NRA's annual meetings and shows were crucial for any collector, and top dealers like Herb Glass and Jack Malloy put on impressive displays, saving some of their best guns for unveiling at the event. Collectors groups would put on lavish exhibits, and the exclusive American Society of Arms Collectors even timed one of their semi-annual meetings to coincide with that of the NRA. However, things change, and although the NRA show is still an important event to attend, sales on the showroom floor are not permitted (except by the NRA itself), and therefore no collectors' arms dealers exhibit at all. However, the tradition of gun-collector associations displaying continues, and that remains one of the event's highlights.

Although auctions have taken away some of the luster of gun shows in recent years, these meets still have their distinct merits. Most shows are at least two-day weekends, and sometimes are of three days' duration; a few are even four days long. The shows allow for dealers and collectors and others to have the opportunity to see, and generally handle, an array of firearms, accouterments, books and other literature, and memorabilia of an often substantial mix. Although some few shows are quite restricted in what is exhibited, most are generalized. Thus, the Beinfeld Las Vegas events have antique arms and armor, but also have high-grade modern sporting arms, and for the winter show, might have contingents from the S&W, Remington, Marlin, and other collector organizations holding special meetings. For some collectors and dealers, the winter Las Vegas show can be the most important event of the year.

The shows also offer an opportunity for the enthusiast who is not an exhibitor to meet the experts, although often one is so busy that there is very little free time. At a recent show the author spent the first day entirely on his feet, not sitting down once, and never left his table to look around the show at all. Too often an exhibitor who is doing the show on his own will not find the time to leave his table to see what others have brought to the event. However, when one has a reputation as an authority, generally things are brought for that person to see anyway.

Above all, gun shows are important for anyone who wishes to remain "current" in his or her field. Since attending his first gun show as a twelve-year-old in Minnesota—that of the Minnesota Weapons Collectors Association, at the Stagecoach Museum, Shakopee—the author has attended anywhere from half a dozen shows a year up to as many as thirty. The number of collectors and dealers one meets, the amount of information absorbed, the array of guns and other material handled and seen, and the experience garnered have an incalculable impact on any gun enthusiast. The legendary antique-arms collector William M. Locke used to have a selection of show badges in his suitcase, so that he was ready at any time for all of the events he regularly attended. Show exhibits he used to set up from his own collection were absolutely mind-boggling: gold-inlaid guns, shoulder-stocked Colts, derringers, U.S. martial pistols, historical arms—and more. It was worthwhile going to shows just to see Bill Locke and his almost always present wife, Elsa, and their fascinating arsenal.

A PARTIAL LISTING OF SHOWS

To investigate the world of gun shows, check magazines like *Gun List, Shotgun News, Man at Arms, Gun Journal,* and *The Gun Report* that publish timely information far enough in advance to allow for careful scheduling by would-be attendees. For some events you will *not* get a table without planning well beforehand. At this writing the major gun shows include the following:

- Any show put on by Wallace Beinfeld, including the winter, summer, and fall Las Vegas events at the Riviera Hotel.

Famous quick-draw artist, exhibition shooter, and showman Joe Bowman with Robert Duvall, on the set of Lonesome Dove. *Without replica firearms, Westerns would have worn out the inventory of companies like Stembridge, supplying firearms to films and TV.*

- The annual NRA Gun Collectors Show, in July, held in Kansas City, Missouri.
- The Maryland Arms Collectors Show, generally held the second weekend in March, near Baltimore.
- The Texas Gun Collectors Show (a closed event, for members only), usually held in early May and early November; sometimes in Dallas, sometimes in San Antonio.
- The Houston Gun Collectors Show, held at the Astrohall, three times a year.
- The Great Western Arms Show, for years the biggest gun show in the world, by far—formerly held at the California State Fairgrounds, Pomona, the first weekend in May and the first weekend in November, with a Christmas show the third weekend in December; now seeking new site, and suing for old one.
- National Gun Day, at Louisville, Kentucky, in June, organized by Ron Dickson.
- The Georgia Arms Collectors show, held near Atlanta.
- The Tulsa, Oklahoma, shows put on by Wanenmacher Productions, held approximately a half dozen times a year.
- The CADA shows, put on by the Collectors Arms Dealers Association, and held in places like Florida, Colorado, and Illinois.
- The Winchester Club of America annual show, held in Cody, Wyoming, in late June.
- The Winchester Arms Collectors Association annual show, held the weekend before or the weekend after the above meet.
- The Colorado Gun Collectors Association Show, held in Denver at the Merchandise Mart, generally early in May.
- The Empire State Arms Collectors, held near Rochester, New York.
- The New York State Arms Collectors Syracuse Gun Show.
- The Ohio Gun Collectors Association, generally held near Cleveland and Canton.
- The Dallas Arms Collectors Show, held in Dallas a few times yearly.
- The Weapons Collectors Society of Montana, in Missoula, generally late May or early June.
- Jackson Hole Gun Show, Wyoming, generally held early in July.
- The Pottstown Gun Shows of the Pennsylvania Antique Gun Collectors Association.
- The Minnesota Weapons Collectors Association at the Civic Center Arena, St. Paul.

Who might one meet at a gun show? Besides dealers and collectors, persons often attend the shows because they have a family heirloom, or a gun or gun-related object that they've inherited, found in the attic, or whatever. In other words, the shows also present the opportunity to buy something that might be a rather exciting "find." Some exhibitors have a sign making it quite clear that they are looking for things to buy. The author used to wear a belt that had written on the back serial numbers of as-yet-unfound rare Colts, such as revolvers known to have been shipped to W. B. "Bat" Masterson, W. F. Cody, and others. Although I never found one of these guns by that means, I did occasionally find rarities that I knew of previously through research in the Colt factory ledgers: e.g., presentations from Colonel Colt and from the company. Knowing that certain pieces were documented gave me an edge, since one needs to exercise caution, in the event some clever faker has had an inscription engraved on what is otherwise a legitimate firearm.

The novice should be aware that if he expects to buy at a show, he needs to be alert and knowledgeable. At some shows fakes will be offered for sale. Although certain shows (generally the so-called "closed" ones, open to members and guests only) police what is on view, most do not. It is therefore the responsibility of the attendee to be careful, and not be taken in by something "bad." The novice should look to a friend, generally an experienced collector or dealer, who can offer guidance. The learning curve can be fairly accelerated, depending on how much time the novice can spend at shows or other opportunities. Every collector has to go through that phase of his development, and gun shows offer this opportunity better than any other venue.

HERB GLASS—MASTER OF THE GUN SHOW

The art of selling guns at gun shows is one that has been fully mastered by some of the top dealers. How one of the masters has done it for some fifty years will reveal some of the secrets of the trade.

Herb Glass began dealing in collectors firearms after his military service in World War II. By the early 1950s, he was one of the top antique-arms dealers in the world. With the retirement of James E. Serven, Glass became number one, and remained so until the 1980s.

I had the privilege of attending a great many gun shows with Glass, and seeing him in action was the equivalent of receiving a Ph.D. in marketing. First, Herb was always appropriately attired for the occasion, some shows being more formal than others. At an NRA Annual Meeting and Show he was bedecked in sports jacket and tie, but at a Texas Gun Collectors Show, he was more likely to be in Western attire, wearing his expensive Lucchese boots or jodhpurs.

He always made certain that his name tag was placed high enough on his person so the uninformed could easily read his name. Table locations were always critical, and he scoped those out, making every effort to be well placed.

From right, legendary dealer Herb Glass Sr., renowned collector Richard P. Mellon, and (representing the new generation of dealer/collectors) Herb Glass Jr., at the 15th Annual Mid-Winter Antique Arms Show in Las Vegas, February 1977. Note the array of Colt revolvers, among them two Walkers, two Dragoons, and a Belt Model No. 2 Paterson. Photo by John Battaglia, who has chronicled more gun shows than any other photographer in the history of collecting.

Carefully orchestrating displays of merchandise at shows, he also tailored the material so that guns, knives, etc., were saved for particular shows.

For the NRA and/or Las Vegas events, he might even have a special display cabinet built to feature some treasure, such as rare Colts like the Sultan of Turkey Dragoon or the E. K. Root Dragoon. For the Theodore Roosevelt Single Action Army Colt, Glass commissioned the writer to do a handsomely illustrated, detailed four-page brochure, and to build a special exhibition cabinet. The revolver and accouterments soon rested in the collection of one of his top customers and, some years later, ended up in the Autry Museum of Western Heritage.

Herb was fastidious about his table covers, about where he placed his briefcase, about the number and placement of chairs (for himself, any associate, guests, and customers). He had a handsome name plate displayed on his table, and used exhibition aids, like glass or wooden rods through trigger guards, to prop up certain pieces for emphasis. Documenting letters were a crucial part of his *modus operandi,* and over the years the author did at least 400 of these just for Herb Glass. Some of these were prepared in leather-bound books, with backup material, the covers embossed in gold leaf with such fancy titles as:

FROM COL. SAMUEL COLT
TO E. K. ROOT
THE FINEST COLT DRAGOON
PRESENTATION CASED SET
IN EXISTENCE
SERIAL No. 16461

Herb Glass could spot a prospective buyer from across a room, and had a way of giving that person his complete attention while working on a deal. He swept away any possible distractions and, if necessary, would arrange to meet the client privately, over drinks or dinner. The writer was present at some social and business events where Herb was entertaining members of the Mellon and Ford families, and everyone had a truly wonderful time.

Getting back to the gun shows: Herb was always ready to accommodate his clients with shipping arrangements or even personal delivery. Often, after he sold something important, he would arrange to exhibit the piece for the rest of the show, making delivery afterward. Wives and girlfriends were always encouraged to be present at the shows, and Glass's charm in dealing with them was certainly a part of his immense success.

Being punctual and staying at the show for the duration was also crucial. He never arrived late, was always businesslike, and did not encourage hangers-on to sponge up time with idle chatter.

Although he did not like to devote time to the politics of gun collecting, he always made his points of view known to show organizers. One reason the Las Vegas shows became so successful was his own input, advice, and encouragement to Wallace Beinfeld. Before Wally, Herb had worked closely with Harry Mann, the originator of the Hotel Sahara show concept.

Occasionally Herb would allow me a corner of his table to market a new book title. He advised on the making of signs (make them big enough to be read from a distance, make them brief and to the point, and be sure to have a front-cover dust-jacket image on the sign; then be sure to have a big enough stack of books so that you were ready for the hoped-for onslaught). The first such event for me was the NRA Show of 1962, in which I was marketing *Samuel Colt Presents,* just published the previous fall by the Wadsworth Atheneum. Herb even arranged for this shy young author to meet such luminaries as Roy Weatherby, Elmer Keith, Warren Page, and Bob Brownell—in each case encouraging their assistance in the promotion and sale of the book. When I returned to the Atheneum, all the books that had been taken to the Washington, DC, event had been sold!

Herb also made it clear that there were certain supplies that had to be available for each show; thus the checklist published below. And finally, he pointed out the importance of making a gun show a buying event, as much as it was a selling and trading event. Some sound advice from that venue: There are always too many temptations to buy, while selling is equally crucial; one has to balance the urge to possess with the hard business reality of marketing and selling, and not let the buying get ahead of the selling, thus interfering with that crucial element in any business: cash flow.

SCHEDULING AND PREPARATION

The author has a checklist that is run through at least three weeks before a show date. This serves as a reminder of anything that needs to be done in advance, such as having a sign or two made up, or getting special-rate airplane tickets, hotel reservations, and so forth. As an idea of what's involved in preparation, see the following:

- Arrange for table space well in advance (at some shows, a year in advance is appropriate, and necessary)
- Pre-advertise (in show program or magazine, or in an arms publication, indicating that you will be exhibiting at such and such a show)
- Table sign
- Name plate (often supplied by show organizer)
- Pre-ticketing at hotels and airlines (discounting possible with many airlines; accumulated miles will also allow free tickets for later trips)
- Ship display materials (screwdrivers, gun sacks for purchases, oil, tool kit, display stands for guns, price tags or stickers, business cards, packing tape, credit-card machine and forms, etc.); ship guns in advance whenever possible
- Be sure to have table covers, not only for the table top, but for covering display and sale material, etc., when the show is closed
- Credit cards, cash, checks, and the usual needs for traveling
- Hire temporary help if needed; some shows will arrange for this, or can advise how to do so
- Pocket magnifying glass (some prefer the kind with a small light for better illumination)

Some subtleties that a lot of gun-show attendees have never figured out include the following:

- Check the show schedule so you are aware of set-up time; some shows are scheduled to begin on a Friday, but allow for set-up beginning at noon or in the afternoon or evening the day before. It is at set-up time that much of the good material comes out. Many who attend shows do not go to sell, but are there to buy.
- Usually seniority is crucial in getting a good position at shows—the best location usually being near the main entrance. For either buying or selling, your table locale is important. At the foremost gun collector shows in the world—those of Wallace Beinfeld at Las Vegas—one might have to wait for someone to retire, or even die, to move up to a prime spot, or even to get any show tables. The author was able to garner one of the best spots in that premier event because he heard of the unfortunate passing of a leading dealer, and called Wally Beinfeld before even he was aware of the death.
- Wear your name badge high on your chest, so it can be read easily; if the one supplied by the show is not legible, make one that is (some shows do not supply a badge; in that case, bring your own).
- If the floor is concrete, bring a small carpet for comfort.
- For further comfort, you might even wish to bring your own chair(s); those supplied at most shows are not particularly comfortable.
- Bring bottled water along, and snacks if you wish.
- Try to have another person with you, to allow yourself the opportunity to walk around the show while your table is attended.
- Bring a portable telephone.
- Be sure to ship in advance any supplies you cannot bring to the show; this is particularly important if you are traveling by air. Save the cardboard shipping boxes, since you may need to ship something back.
- Be alert to other show attendees, in case you need to send something on to the next show. Some exhibitors actually share the services of a truck, which brings merchandise and equipment to the show and takes it back to their home or shop again.

Enjoying Your Treasures

Enjoying your treasures, and keeping good records, are crucial to any collector or dealer. Not only are there practical considerations—estate planning, profit (and loss) and taxes, and reminders for when the memory starts to go—but maintaining good files is part of the fun, almost like writing your own book! Not a few collectors, and all dealers, will end up having owned such an array of firearms that it is not only good organization to have written up this "collection," but good business as well.

In the 1960s, when doing quite a bit of research and cataloguing work for dealer Herb Glass, the author devised catalogue formats for 3 × 5 and 4 × 6 file cards, as well as for 8½ × 11 file forms. Some of these we printed up professionally, with data on the front that could be xeroxed and sent to an author and researcher, while the back had the private history of cost and value, and other data that the owner might not want to share in a public way.

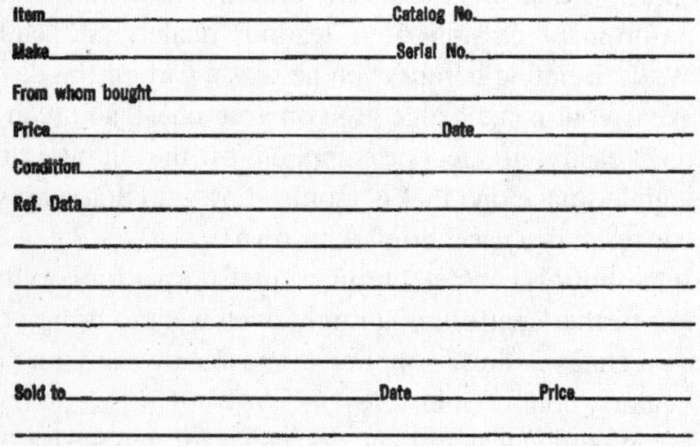
Item ____________ Catalog No. ____________
Make ____________ Serial No. ____________
From whom bought ____________
Price ____________ Date ____________
Condition ____________
Ref. Data ____________
Sold to ____________ Date ____________ Price ____________

Time passes by so quickly, especially as one advances in years, that these cards and forms became a ready and useful reference for each and every collector for whom the forms were developed. In my own instance, like the proverbial shoemaker's children having no shoes, my file records are spotty—I'm just too busy to sit down and complete the forms.

However, for virtually every important arm I've owned, some time was devoted to writing up a documenting letter. Initially under the guidance of the pioneering brilliance of Herb Glass, I developed my own letterhead and a format for such letters, which has its own characteristics. A sample letter appears on page 28. Note the following: The letter is not addressed to a particular person, so it can travel with the gun from owner to owner. The heading is designed to capture the essence of the firearm, while the body of the text logically presents the item's history and merits. If there is a relevant quotation from a book, that is presented as well—generally in the first part of the letter. Such headings as markings, a history of the original owner(s), pedigree, and a conclusion are standard features. The letters are generally kept as short as possible, but sometimes run to forty or fifty pages.

The author has actually done "books" on a collection by doing letters on each gun and then binding the results in leather. This was done for the renowned Larry Sheerin Collection, when he decided the market had peaked, had the letters prepared, and then used the letters in the sale of the collection. The leather-bound book was nearly an inch thick, and two copies were "published"—one for Larry Sheerin and the other for myself.

Over thirty-five years after first doing these letters, I have a reference collection of over 1,000, done not only on fine Colts and Winchesters, but on a variety of other makes of American arms and not a few distinguished European pieces as well. I am now trying to enter them all into my computer, although regrettably the majority were done in my B.C. period (before computer).

Printed on a copperplate-engraved letterhead and high-quality second sheets, the letters are then placed in plastilene holders, and are retained by collectors, and sometimes displayed with guns (on exhibit, or offered for sale) to the public.

Some of these letters have been mounted in leather-bound books, used in an appraisal format on some of the world's most important firearms, adapted into articles in a variety of magazines, and so forth. The author has recently entered into an agreement with the Colt company for providing authenticating letters of this nature. Contact Kathleen Hoyt, Colt Historian, for further details.

Researching each piece, and preparing the letters, has become such a pleasure that today I go virtually everywhere with a Macintosh laptop computer and can capture the essence of a gun on the spot, even sometimes doing this at night during gun shows, thus allowing the owner to keep his gun, and I have the chance to finish the letter in the privacy of my home office. The fee for these letters usually begins at $500, and I will do a letter only on a gun that warrants the time and effort, for both myself and the client.

PHOTOGRAPHY

Photographing your guns can be an extension of your hobby. Photography can be fun too—but the author has found that for him, at least, the picture-taking should be left to the professionals. When beginning my career at the Corcoran Gallery of Art and the Wadsworth Atheneum, I experimented with Nikons and Olympuses, all the while working with professionals like Eliot Elisofon of *Life* magazine and E. Irving Blomstrann (the Atheneum's photographer, who mainly concentrated on decorative art and paintings).

It soon became obvious that if I was to have first-class pictures for research and publication, the photography should be left to the professionals. Taking gun pictures is not easy; in fact, it is much more difficult than photographing virtually any other collectible: difficult angles, a combination of materials, varied finishes, challenging contrasts between such finishes as bluing, case-hardening, silver-plating, ivory, or pearl—all in one picture.

The author has worked with more than 100 photographers over the years, and has examined literally over 200,000 photographs, taken by hundreds and hundreds of photographers, most of them amateurs, but quite a few by professionals. One out of 100 of these pictures is good enough to reproduce, and acceptable for publication. The point is that gun photography is extremely difficult, and there are far fewer photographers capable of taking first-rate gun pictures than there are who can take high-quality photographs of people, or cars, or paintings, or silver, or any number of other subjects.

Having stated all of the above, for those who wish to attempt taking their own gun pictures, consider the fact that new photographic technology has led to the wonders of digital pictures, and developments in flash-assisted pictures have helped to eliminate the problems of lighting. The tips that follow from one of the best firearms photographers in the world, David Wesbrook, will help those who want to pursue their own picture-taking. A list of several of the best photographers is presented in the acknowledgments on page x, each of them freelance and capable of pictures good enough for the most demanding of publishers.

Considered by many as at the top of his art and craft, David Wesbrook studied under Frederick Sommer (a fine-arts photographer in the same league as Ansel Adams, and an innovator of the fine-arts photography movement of the 1950s). Dave has worked for some of today's most discriminating clients in the art and arms fields.

The writer used Wesbrook photographs exclusively for the dust jacket of *The Colt Engraving Book,* and sees in his pictures an artist who not only has mastered the difficult art of lighting, but understands firearms, and therefore is a master at selecting the proper angle for the best results. The material below, taken from the author's discussion with Wesbrook, is intended to guide the amateur and the professional in tackling the challenging task of taking fine-quality firearms photographs. Reviewing this material can also be helpful in the reader's decision as to whether he or she wants to take the pictures, or leave the work to a professional.

"The ideal firearms photograph shows superb detail throughout, including the shadow and highlight areas, is distortion-free with perfect focus, and is taken from the same viewpoint or aspect from which the gun would normally be viewed.

"To achieve this requires, first, a thorough knowledge and understanding of what you are photographing and how it should appear on film. Look, a gun is a piece of functional sculpture, often quite stunning in its own right. As with other forms of sculpture, there are certain angles that show and complement the line, form, and flow of shape to their best advantage. In my over twenty years at the bench as a custom gunmaker/stockmaker, first with muzzle-loaders and later with modern stocks, I've formed some definite opinions on which angles look best for the different period stylings and types of firearms being photographed. In addition, I have been privileged to study, handle, and photograph work from contemporary master gunmakers such as Monte Mandarino, Stephen Alexander, and John Bivins, as well as historic masters like Boutet and the Mantons, and exquisite 19th-century Colts and Winchesters. This knowledge of line and form is what I believe separates my work from the other firearm photographers."

VIDEOTAPING YOUR GUNS

Still another means of documenting your firearms is the use of videotape. Video equipment is available to everyone, and requires very little skill to use. As long as commentary accompanies the footage, the record presented is clear and useful. As many copies as needed can be made of the material.

Professional videos can be made for inventory and cataloguing purposes, but a written listing should accompany any tapes. Clearly this technology is not commonly used, but its potential has been realized by such auction houses as Butterfield's, Little John's, and other firms. These companies employ video aids in promoting objects for sale, and Butterfield's cooperated with a San Francisco firm in creating a video production on presentation and engraved Colt percussion firearms.

Whether videotape or computer printouts, still photographs or handwritten notes, documentation of your guns can be vital. For insurance purposes, loss claims, eventual publication, or just plain nostalgia, keeping a record of your guns can give you some of the most valuable and rewarding time you will spend with your inventory or collection.

DISPLAYS AT HOME, OFFICE, OR GUN SHOWS

For a period of approximately twenty years (from the 1960s into the 1980s), displays at gun shows were popular, so much so that cash awards were presented, as well as trophies or other prizes that were truly worth all the time, effort, and cost of competition. The best of such shows were the Las Vegas events of Wallace Beinfeld, the Baltimore Gun Collectors, and a number of other state organizations.

However, for a variety of reasons, the number of shows that continue this tradition, and the number of collectors and dealers willing to go to the trouble, have diminished. The reasons are obvious: the increased value of the objects themselves, restrictions on traveling with some types of guns, concern over damage to the objects, and—not the least—the time, energy, and money that a fine display costs the collector or dealer.

Shows that have continued the tradition are specialty collector clubs like the Colt Collectors Association, the Smith & Wesson Collectors Association, the Winchester Club of America and the Winchester Collectors Association, the Ruger Collectors Association, the Remington Society of America, the Bowie Knife Association, the American Society of Arms Collectors, and the Colorado Arms Collectors Association. Most important, the National Rifle Association continues to encourage displays, awards the finest trophies for merit, and presents ten beautiful and highly prized sterling silver medals annually for the finest guns at the annual meetings, as well as ten medals for the finest miniatures. Further, at the newly inaugurated (as of 1996) annual NRA Gun Collectors Show and Conference, special awards are also given.

Judging of these displays is voluntary, and usually the panel is composed of three experts. I have judged many such events, and like nearly all judges, I dread the responsibility. Competition can get rather fierce, and some exhibitors simply do not understand that there was a good reason they did not win the grand prize. Although from time to time politics may have had a role in a decision, this is quite rare. The judges take their responsibility quite seriously, and know that these competitions are part of the culture of arms collecting. No one wants to discourage any collector from going to the tremendous effort required to do a successful display.

The late Dr. Richard Marohn, expert and keen collector in the realm of the Colt Lightning revolver, put on some of the finest displays ever seen at any gun show. His exhibits were thoroughly researched, finely and artistically presented, and captivating for the viewer, including the general public. Think about any historical or art museum you have visited, and try to remember the displays that were of the greatest interest and provided the most pleasure. Dick Marohn's exhibits could very easily have been moved from the gun show (usually Wallace Beinfeld's Las Vegas extravaganza) and set up in most any fine museum—all that would have been necessary was to put the display behind glass.

Today, with the wizardry available through computer technology, and perhaps through the assistance of a consultant (who might be the collector's wife or girlfriend or secretary), some assistance by a talented photographer, and a knowledge of display techniques, a collector can put something together that would not only be captivating in his home gun room or library, but would be a winner at an NRA event, at Las Vegas or Denver, or at the Texas Gun Collectors Association's semi-annual shows.

Once the author worked with collector Jerry Berger of Kansas City in preparing a display on the engraving of percussion Colt firearms. This exhibit won the grand prize at a Las Vegas show, and had such a beautifully designed format (by one of Jerry's employees in his Topsy's Popcorn company) that the writer to this day has part of the presentation on display in his office complex in Hadlyme. Some of the illustrations were used in *The Colt Engraving Book* and elsewhere.

Some collectors have even had a guest book as part of the display, allowing viewers to share their comments. Sometimes a brochure was printed up to give to the public. For the late R. Q. Sutherland, the author wrote an 84-page monograph, *The Evolution of the Colt,* which was sold in conjunction with an elaborate display that won the collector the grand prize at the spring 1967 Las Vegas Sahara Antique Arms Show. To date, that monograph has been the ultimate accompaniment to a gun-show exhibition in the writer's memory!

Due to widespread distrust of journalists, most gun shows do not permit the presence of the media. Photography is generally not allowed at these events, including videotaping. However, there are times when shows or auctions present the opportunity of interfacing with the press. When that happens, the author suggests that the collector or dealer consider carefully whether he should try to become a spokesperson for guns. Sometimes our friends inadvertently turn out to be our worst enemies. People who crusade against guns (and not a few of these impact negatively the world of collectors' guns) have made their crusade into a business. Often uninformed people from the press are used to create programming or interviews that are undeservedly harsh on the world of collecting.

Some collectors and dealers are just not cut out for mainstream media interviews. They should take a long, hard look at their abilities, and make sure their interview doesn't backfire. On the other hand, experts like Greg Martin are perfectly suited for press interviews, and present an excellent image for the world of arms collecting.

Factors and Fine Points of Collecting

Most collectors not only develop their own special sphere of interest, but devise their own means of chasing after arms that appeal to them. As a general rule of thumb, in order to avoid frustration and financial disaster, the collector should set his sights on objects within a specific budget. The collector needs to establish standards of condition, originality, historical merit, and other specifics, and the lengths to which he or she will go in pursuit of goals.

What follows are the areas demanding special attention.

CONDITION, CONDITION, CONDITION

The pursuit of mint unfired guns can be quite costly, particularly if one's interest is the blue chips of gun collecting: Colts and Winchesters. Not that much less costly are Sharps rifles in perfect condition, or the best in Remington, Smith & Wessons, derringers, Marlins, fine English sporting rifles and shotguns, and so forth. In some instances, like the Colt Walker and Dragoon revolvers, there may be no mint examples available to the collector, or so few that the value is substantial.

On the other hand, the obtaining of mint examples of U.S. military metallic cartridge arms is a more realizable goal. M1 Carbines, M1 Garand rifles, Colt Model 1911 Automatic pistols, and such arms as Colt New Service .45 caliber revolvers, still are available in pristine condition. But then one must consider the laws governing such usable guns in the collectors' state and locality of residence.

Mint condition also requires careful storage of arms, and making sure that unwelcome hands do not handle the objects, leaving rust marks or working the mechanisms (causing scratches and marks). Proper care of these rarities means the use of proper oils, storage in a controlled environment, and preventing damage of any kind. Keeping the pieces for long periods in a bank vault, for example, might actually be detrimental to their finish.

HISTORY

The collector keen on history usually is not a stickler for fine condition. He understands that when Indians were pounding on some settler's door, the latter was hardly concerned about conserving for some future collector the condition of the gun he was about to shoot in self-defense! Historical guns are the ones that "speak" the most to the collector. The writer was once with Monte Hale and Gene Autry and their wives when the Autry Museum was considering purchase of some rare Theodore Roosevelt firearms and related artifacts from TR's ranching days in the Dakotas. Monte remarked about how thrilled he was with holding TR's Single Action Army and Winchester, and that "these wonderful guns are speaking to us!" He was right—and many a time one is transfixed when thinking of the many stories these fabulous rarities could tell, "if only they could talk." The author has actually had the thrill of firing TR's Single Action Army no. 92248 (now in the Autry Museum), Bat Masterson's Single Action Army no. 112737, Jesse James' S&W Schofield no. 366, and TR's double-barreled Holland & Holland elephant rifle no. 19109. He still has the cartridge casings from firing these remarkable guns, and considers those experiences among the highlights of his arms-collecting career.

ROMANCE

The craze for TV and movie Westerns in the 1950s and 1960s almost certainly influenced two generations of arms collectors, this writer among them. The author's old friend and Hollywood shooting coach Arvo Ojala met many a star, some of whom were enamored of guns. Among that group were Steve McQueen, Frank Sinatra, Sammy Davis Jr., Jerry Lewis, and Dean Martin. A prized picture in the author's collection is one showing Arvo with Marilyn Monroe, signed "Larry, my friend wish you could have been here."

Movies starring actors the likes of Steve McQueen, Arnold Schwarzenegger, Charles Bronson, Clint Eastwood, Sylvester Stallone, Steven Seagal, and Wesley Snipes have been instrumental in encouraging a cult of collectors who are more interested in modern military arms. The author believes that more than 75 percent of arms collectors are primarily keen on 20th-century firearms. Films like *Shane, Dirty Harry, The Getaway,* and *The Wild Bunch* have all influenced directions taken by gun collectors. One of the writers of some of these films, and the director of *The Wind and the Lion, Red Dawn,* and other action thrillers, is John Milius, not only a keen arms collector, but a member of the board of directors of the National Rifle Association!

MECHANICS

Many times the author has been visiting with an arms collector and finds that his home includes a machine shop.

Recently a former top executive with Allied Signal, Tony Lamb, showed me his quite respectable home workshop, and told me of having bought a somewhat rusty S&W Schofield revolver, which he cleaned with stainless-steel wool and found that under the surface rust was quite a bit of original blue finish! The artist Maxfield Parrish was both a master machinist and a dedicated collector of 19th-century U.S. martial firearms. The former chief financial officer of the Timken corporation has shown me his collection of guns and Wells Fargo items, and he too had a fine collection of machine tools.

Rare was the collectors firearm that this author and his brother Jack didn't take apart, immediately after purchase. I can still remember taking down our first antique gun purchase, serial no. 7 Manhattan .31 caliber pocket model revolver, and giving it a total cleaning (too much, in retrospect). The revolver had an engraved frame, no doubt by L. D. Nimschke, and walnut grips. But something was wrong with the mainspring, and some truly amateur home gunsmithing made it work again.

During the author's internship at the Tower of London, Norris Kennard, the Deputy Master of the Armouries, was renowned for spending part of his day in the workshops, taking apart some of the collection's rare guns. This he did with the able assistance of the master gunsmiths, since some of the pieces were complex and not easy to reassemble.

And it was the mechanics of firearms that intrigued young Samuel Colt. According to *Armsmear,* the first Colt book (1866):

> Among the traditions of his boyhood, one is given by a neighbor . . . showing at how early an age his attention was directed toward the arm with which his name was to be so intimately connected, all the world over. When about seven years of age, he one day was for some time missing, and when at last discovered, he was sitting under a tree in the field, with a pistol taken entirely to pieces, the different parts carefully arranged around him, and which he was beginning to reconstruct. He soon, to his great delight, accomplished this feat.

When the wheelock was invented, the locks were actually built by lockmakers. And manufacture of best-quality firearms commonly called upon the skills of lockmakers, stockmakers, and barrel makers. The mechanics of firearms are so fascinating that a great many collectors seek variations, most of which are identifiable based on mechanical features: squareback triggerguards, V-main springs, oval cylinder stop slots, and horizontal or vertical loading lever latches are part of the lexicon, for example, of Colt percussion firearms.

A word of caution is in order, however. Care should be taken in stripping down any gun, and for good reason: A mistake with a screwdriver can scratch a "mint" gun, botch screw heads, and otherwise damage a treasured piece. Further, grips and stocks that have never been removed may chip or lose their "seal" from metal parts, and sometimes should never be removed. Trying to punch out a barrel wedge may actually break off the wedge screw (they should always be loosened or removed before you try to tap out a wedge, particularly when all parts are tight-fitting).

Trying to remove the barrel from a fine-condition Kentucky or Plains rifle might well lead to wedges driving out keyplates, or damage to stocks. Removing some locks may chip out surrounding wood, and pulling barrel tangs might do the same.

Even working the actions on some firearms might lead to disaster: snapping hammers, breaking weakened springs, causing drag marks from the cylinder stop on cylinder surfaces, and so forth. Better to work the action or strip down a gun that has already seen a lot of takedown in its life.

ART AND CRAFTSMANSHIP

Although there are machinists and gunmakers today who can equal the skills of the old masters, the fact remains that one must truly marvel at the sheer artistry and craftsmanship exhibited by the gunmakers of past centuries. These remarkably talented craftsmen were expected to ply their craft at high standard. They could count on enthusiastic patronage from the wealthy, from governments, and later from such clients as ranchers and cowboys, Wells Fargo and other express agents, the military (both official and unofficial), hunters, sportsmen, professional marksmen and -women, and any number of others. Many of these products were not only skillfully made but quite beautiful, often elegant.

There are compelling reasons why major international museums of art exhibit fine firearms. Anyone who appreciates art, in all its forms, cannot help but be impressed by the remarkable work of the skilled gunmakers, as displayed at such institutions as The Metropolitan Museum of Art, the Art Institute of Chicago, the Buffalo Bill Historical Center, and the Autry Museum of Western Heritage.

Commemorative, Replica, and Special-Issue Firearms, and More

The tradition of special-production firearms for collectors in the modern sense was begun by Robert E. P. Cherry, of Cherry's Sporting Goods, founded in 1929. Bob Cherry, in order to celebrate the anniversary of the city of Geneseo, Illinois, ordered one hundred .22 caliber Fourth Model Colt derringer pistols with special markings from the factory (1960), and that issue began a whole new category of collectible firearms. Today his son Kevin carries on the family tradition, and is now issuing special commemorative arms, some quite elaborately engraved, under the Cherrys' trademark.

At this writing, literally hundreds of different issues have been produced since that 1960 beginning, mainly Colts and Winchesters, but the number also includes Brownings, Smith & Wessons, Marlins, Remingtons, Rugers, Lugers, and many, many more. Although the practice of issuing commemorative firearms peaked when Winchester made approximately 120,000 Buffalo Bill Model 1894s, there remains an active group of collectors keen on purchasing these modern tributes to a variety of themes. As detailed in the author's own *Colt Commemorative Firearms* books, the commemoratives generally salute a town, city, state, territorial, or national anniversary, or historical events, historical forts, historical trails, a battle or other historic event, a famous person, or a company, organization, or corporation.

This sphere of collecting offers the opportunity to purchase pieces that are in perfect, brand-new, mint condition. The guns are often quite handsomely built, sometimes richly engraved, and popular for display purposes—rarely being shot or the actions worked in any way.

When the author was employed at the Colt factory in Hartford, Connecticut, in 1964 and 1965, he was responsible for much of the design of the Colonel Samuel Colt Sesquicentennial Single Action Army revolver and the Bat Masterson Single Action Army "Lawman" commemorative .45 and .22 revolvers. Every effort was made to be as authentic as possible with these issues, and for a number of years the Colt company maintained an advisory committee made up of authorities qualified to assist in creating responsible and logical commemorative issues. The Winchester company also relied to some extent on expert advice. One of the most respected advisors for these committees was Robert E. P. Cherry himself; another was antique-arms dealer Herb Glass.

In the 1950s and 1960s, replica firearms became a valued addition to the arms market, spurred by Civil War and frontier reenactments and by the upward-spiraling value of genuine antiques. Among the leaders in this new market were Val Forgett, founder and president, Navy Arms Co., and *Guns* magazine editor William B. Edwards. Created at about the same time was the U.S. Historical Society, which quickly became the leading issuing body of best-quality special-issue firearms. The Society's first issue was the George Washington silver-mounted pistols, replicating the pair in the West Point Museum of the U.S. military academy. Later issues included such rarities as the Burr-Hamilton Wogdon flintlock dueling pistols (in cooperation with the Chase Manhattan Bank, owner of the originals), Thomas Jefferson's screwbarrel flintlock pistols (from Monticello), Carbine Williams' deluxe Single Action Army, a miniature series of Colt percussion and cartridge revolvers, and a book-cased pair of derringer percussion pistols authorized by descendants of Henry Deringer. Early in the 1990s the Society underwent a name change, to the United States Society of Arms and Armour, a.k.a. America Remembers, under the leadership of Paul Warden, president. Recent issues have included the Ruger & His Guns Tribute Vaquero revolvers, the miniature Wyatt Earp Buntline Special, and the special-issue Winchester Model 1873 rifle honoring Buffalo Bill Cody and his "pards."

Another organization that has issued several commemorative firearms is the American Historical Foundation. Among their special issues, dating back to the 1970s, are the General Patton Single Action Army, the Vietnam Tribute M14 rifle, the World War II Colt .45 M1911A1, and the Beretta Golden Centurion .40 Caliber Model 96D pistol. The founder and president of the Foundation is Robert Buerlein.

Still another firm issuing special limited editions is Colt Blackpowder, authorized maker of Colt percussion firearms, under exclusive license from Colt's Manufacturing Co. The owners of Colt Blackpowder are Louis and Anthony Imperata, and their factory complex is in Brooklyn, New York—returning a gunmaking tradition that dates back to Colonial times in that noble city.

Guns Disappearing Off the Market

A fact of life is that fine guns are disappearing off the market. Considering the magic realm of Colt firearms, with the deaths of P. R. Phillips, George A. Strichman, and other top collectors, and the vacuuming up of great guns by collectors like Robert E. Petersen and similar multi-millionaires, very few fine pieces remain among the public. Donations to museums like the Metropolitan, which received some fine Colts from Jerry D. Berger and the late John E. Parsons, as well as the Sultan of Turkey Dragoon from George and Butonne Repaire, have taken these objects out of the marketplace forever. Phil Phillips's legendary Colt collection was donated in perpetuity to the Woolaroc Museum, Raymond Wielgus donated several of his exquisite engraved and gold-inlaid arms to the Art Institute of Chicago, and collector Ed Bitters' martial pieces went to the National Museum of American History. Furthermore, the Smith & Wesson factory donated most of its extraordinary archives and arms collection to the Springfield

From the private collection of William O. Sweet, one of the most successful of American arms collectors. Many of his best pieces are now in museums. His eclectic interests ranged from Colts and Winchesters to Indian weapons to Kentucky Rifles, Mountain Man rifles, and Bowie knives. Most of his purchases came from Herb Glass.

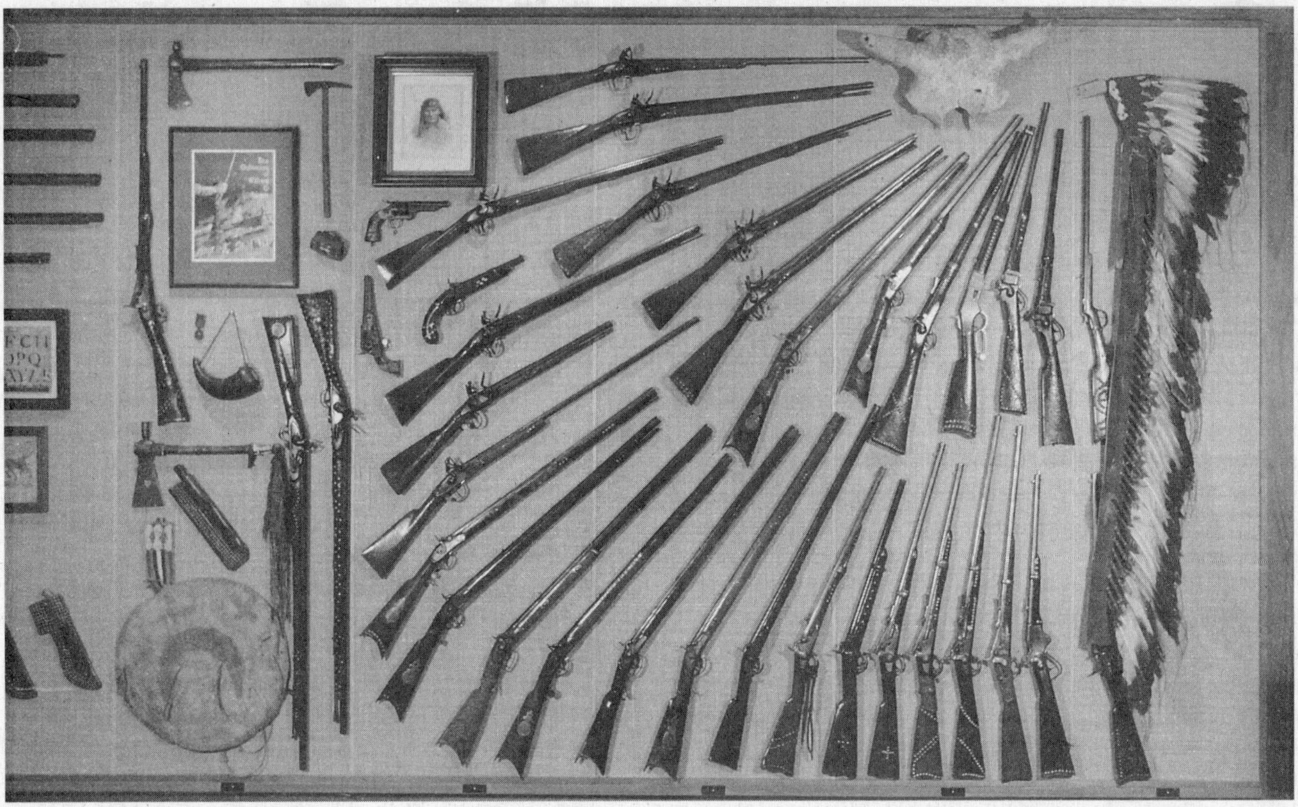

Museum, and over 3,000 guns of various types have been donated by members to the National Firearms Museum (a branch institution of the N.R.A.).

One astute collector asked me to estimate how many super Colts and super Winchesters from the 19th century had survived to date. My answer was quite a shocker, considering estimates of how many collectors are competing actively for the very best: My belief is that about 300 exceptional engraved Colt guns are known, and about that same number in Winchester lever-actions. No one will ever own these, and one can rest assured that new collectors are coming into the field on a regular basis. Sometimes the high demand within certain arenas of collecting can be truly discouraging.

From the dust jacket illustration of Fine Colts: The Dr. Joseph A. Murphy Collection, *the author with Dr. Murphy, holding historic Colt Walker and Dragon revolvers. A keen collector and student, Dr. Murphy is one whose collecting instincts and acumen have removed a significant share of fine guns from the market.*

Government-required Recordkeeping and Some BATF Rulings and Regulations

The antique-arms collector has virtually no legal problem with his arms, although muzzle-loading guns are considered illegal in certain jurisdictions, once they have been loaded and primed. On the other hand, collectors of metallic-cartridge firearms need to be aware that in some cities, such as New York, firearms that predate the federal cut-off date of 1898 may be subject to local law if they can accept cartridges that are readily available in present commerce: Thus, a Model 1873 Single Action Army and a Model 1873 Winchester, chambered for .45 Colt or .44-40 cartridges, are restricted—being considered the same as a modern gun taking the same ammunition.

Fortunately the Bureau of Alcohol, Tobacco, and Firearms issues copies of ordinances and regulations free of charge; they are regularly mailed to federal firearms license holders and to any of the public who request them. Since the number of gun laws is substantial—estimated at more than 20,000—it is a good idea for collectors interested in guns that might be subject to these regulations to be certain they have copies of these publications. Write to the BATF national headquarters at Bureau of Alcohol, Tobacco, and Firearms, Washington DC 20226.

For state and local laws, queries should be made of the state or local police (or both). All state police have a division devoted to firearms regulations. Eternal vigilance being the price of liberty, collectors should be aware of developments in some jurisdictions. The capricious New York City Council, after promising owners of so-called "assault rifles" that their firearms would never be confiscated, passed an ordinance requiring all registered assault rifles to be turned in to the authorities without compensation! Politicians are always trying to get votes, and no doubt somebody got reelected with that unproductive and truly outrageous ploy.

Nassau County, New York, tried to force owners of percussion revolvers to register their guns, just like metallic cartridge handguns, claiming that since a thug had held up a gas station with a Ruger Old Model Army, these guns should be restricted. No matter that once a gun like that is loaded, it is already covered by the same ordinance as a metallic-cartridge handgun. The author was the lead witness in a suit brought against Nassau County on this matter, before Supreme Court Justice Steven B. Derounian. The suit was filed by the Long Island Antique Gun Collectors Association Inc., the Nassau County Fish and Game Association, and others (1978). Of course, we won the case hands down.

For collectors interested in full automatic weapons, the author recommends subscribing to one of the finest magazines published on firearms: *Machine Gun News*. The address and relevant information appears in the bibliography (page 425), along with such generally better-known publications as *American Rifleman*, *American Hunter*, *Guns*, *Guns & Ammo*, *The Gun Report*, and *Man at Arms*. Collecting full automatic arms requires a particular diligence in record-keeping; certain states, like California, do not permit ownership by private citizens. The author is fortunate in living in Connecticut, which has a quite reasonable law on these arms, and he has under federal and state permits a Colt-made Thompson Submachine Gun (formerly property of the New Orleans Police Department), a Colt M16A2 Carbine with suppresser, and a Sterling 9mm submachine gun (presented to the author by the Colt company, and the only non-Colt firearm ever presented by the company). None other than famed actress Sharon Stone has been quoted in *Vanity Fair* magazine on the thrill she received when firing a Colt AR-15, accompanied by her gun-enthusiast father.

SOME BATF DEFINITIONS AND RULINGS

The BATF definition of an antique firearm is as follows*:

Under section 921(a)(16) of the Gun Control Act, the term *antique firearm* means:

> (A) Any firearm (including any firearm with a matchlock, flintlock, percussion cap, or similar type of ignition system) manufactured in or before 1898; and
>
> (B) Any replica of any firearm described in subparagraph (A) if such replica—
>
> (i) is not designed or redesigned for using rimfire or conventional centerfire fixed ammunition, or
>
> (ii) uses rimfire or conventional centerfire fixed ammunition which is no longer manufactured

*These quotations are from the BATF *Federal Firearms Regulations Reference Guide*, formerly known as *Your Guide to Federal Firearms Regulations*. The booklet is identified by federal government publication code ATF P 5300.4 (01-00), totaling 168 pages, in an 8½ × 11 format.

in the United States and which is not readily available in the ordinary channels of commercial trade.

Under section 5845(g) of the National Firearms Act, *antique firearm* means:

> . . . Any firearm not designed or redesigned for using rim fire or conventional center fire ignition with fixed ammunition and manufactured in or before 1898 (including any matchlock, flintlock, percussion cap, or similar type of ignition system or replica thereof, whether actually manufactured before or after 1898) and also any firearm using fixed ammunition manufactured in or before 1898, for which ammunition is no longer manufactured in the United States and is not readily available in the ordinary channels of commercial trade.

To illustrate the distinction between the two definitions of antique firearm under the GCA and NFA, a rifle manufactured in or before 1898 would not come under the provisions of the GCA, even though it uses conventional ammunition. However, if the rifle has a barrel of less than sixteen inches in length *and* uses conventional fixed ammunition that is available in the ordinary channels of commercial trade, it would still be a *firearm* subject to the provisions of the NFA.

An antique firearm as defined in *both* the GCA and NFA is exempt from all of the provisions and restrictions contained in both laws. Consequently, such an antique firearm may be bought, sold, transported, shipped, etc., without regard to the requirements of these laws.

Under the Arms Export Control Act, certain "antique firearms" are not subject to the import controls. These "antique firearms" are substantially the same as those exempted under the GCA, except that replicas of firearms manufactured after 1898 are exempt from the Arms Export Control Act only if they have a matchlock, flintlock, percussion cap, or similar type of ignition system. No all-inclusive list of antique firearms is published by BATF.

CURIOS AND RELICS

Quoting from the *Federal Firearms Regulations Reference Guide*, the BATF definition of this category of collectors firearm is as follows:

> As set out in the regulations (27 CFR 178.11), curios or relics include firearms which have special value to collectors because they possess some qualities not ordinarily associated with firearms intended for sporting use or as offensive or defensive weapons.
>
> Please note that ammunition is no longer classified as curios or relics since the Congress in 1986 removed the interstate controls over ammunition under the GCA.
>
> To be recognized as curios or relics, firearms must:
>
> 1. Have been manufactured at least 50 years prior to the current date, but not including replicas thereof; or
>
> 2. Be certified by the curator of a municipal, State or Federal museum which exhibits firearms to be curios or relics of museum interest; or
>
> 3. Derive a substantial part of their monetary value from the fact that they are novel, rare, or bizarre, or from the fact of their association with some historical figure, period, or event.
>
> Collectors wishing to obtain a determination whether a particular firearm qualifies for classification as a curio or relic in accordance with 27 CFR 178.26 should submit a written request for a ruling. The letter should include:
>
> (1) A complete physical description of the item.
>
> (2) Reasons the collector believes the item merits the classification.
>
> (3) Data concerning the history of the item, including production figures, if available, and market value.
>
> In some cases, actual submission of the firearm may be required prior to a determination being made. Requests should be sent to the Bureau of ATF, Firearms Technology Branch, Washington, DC 20226.
>
> ATF's classifications of curios or relics are published in ATF P 5300.12, Firearms Curios or Relics List. Curios or relics are listed in the publication under the following headings:
>
> Section I. Ammunition Classified as Curios or Relics. . . .
>
> Section II. Firearms Classified as Curios or Relics under the GCA. . . .
>
> Section III. NFA Firearms Removed From the NFA as Collectors' Items and Classified as Curios or Relics Under the GCA. . . .
>
> Section IV. NFA Firearms Classified as Curios or Relics Under the GCA. . . .

SOME OTHER DEFINITIONS

In addition to the BATF classifications of Antique and Curios and Relics, the reader should be aware of the following definitions:

Modern: Firearms manufactured post-1898, with the exception of replicas of antiques. There are special regulations dealing with Class III arms, as noted below. Various sources list serial number details that will assist in determination of the 1898 cut-off date. The author's own works are helpful with Colts; for a detailed reference on a wide variety of makes, see recent editions of Steven Fjestad's *Blue Book of Gun Values,* which is the most complete published source.

Class III Firearms: Machine guns, silencers, short-barrel shotguns (less than 18-inch barrel length), short-barrel rifles (less than 16-inch barrel length), modern-made smoothbore handguns, and firearms of modern manufacture having a rifled bore diameter in excess of .50 caliber.

Author with son Stephen, at the Winchester Club of America show, Cody, Wyoming.

An unforgettable moment for the author, presenting a copy of Colt: An American Legend *to screen legend Jimmy Stewart, with Colt's vice president of marketing Robert Morrison, at the Golden Boot Awards, Sportsman's Lodge, near Los Angeles, 1986.*

National Rifle Association of America

The first thing any serious enthusiast of firearms and the shooting sports should do to show his or her dedication to the vast arena of firearms-related pursuits is to *join the National Rifle Association of America.* With its size and comprehensive organization, and with the potency of Charlton Heston active in the fray, the NRA offers the best united front against those who do not understand guns, and do not understand hunting. The address and contact information for this unique and unsurpassed-in-significance organization is as follows:

11250 Waples Hill Road
Fairfax VA 22030
(703) 267-1000
fax: (703) 267-3913 (specifically for the Gun Collecting Program and the National Firearms Museum)
NRA-ILA Grassroots (800) 392-8683
e-mail: nra-contact@nra.org
website for NRA: http://www.nra.org

At present the award-winning NRA website averages about 2,500 visits a day! The NRA-ILA homepage on the Internet World Wide Web provides the following services, as noted in a recent release from the NRA:

> . . . allows you to search and retrieve the latest press releases, legislative alerts, state firearm law brochures, speeches by NRA officials, graphics files, fact sheets, and information on NRA programs from the Eddie Eagle Gun Safety Program . . . to Law Enforcement Training to competitive shooting events nationwide [as well as information on the NRA Museum and Gun Collector Programs].

A vital service of the NRA is the publications division, which provides members with the choice of subscription to *The American Rifleman, The American Hunter,* or *America's First Freedom* magazines, as a service of membership.

Annual NRA membership, as of 2000, is $35, the cost to become a Life Member is $750. For other membership categories and general information contact via the Internet: nra-services@nra.org.

THE NRA FOUNDATION AND NRA FOUNDATION ENDOWMENT

A nonprofit, tax-exempt organization that deserves the full support of gun enthusiasts nationwide is The NRA Foundation. The Foundation supports activities of the NRA and other organizations that foster the firearms rights of responsible American citizens. To quote from the author's guest editorial in the winter 1999 issue of the Foundation's own magazine, *Traditions,* honoring the Foundation's tenth anniversary:

From left to right, *photographed in the Beretta booth at the 1999 SHOT Show, Craig Sandler, Executive Director of NRA Operations, Ugo Gussalli Beretta, H. Wayne Sheets, Executive Director, NRA Foundation Endowment, and the author. Under discussion is the National Firearms Museum's 2001 display celebrating the 475th Anniversary of Beretta.*

> Rapidly becoming a favorite 501(c) (3) tax-exempt charity with a unique role in public education on hunting and shooting sports as well as other gun-related activities, The NRA Foundation has raised and disbursed over $21 million in one decade. And, having established an endowment of more than $5 million, the Foundation is preparing for the future by setting aside funds yielding annual returns for equally worthy grants. . . .

The mission statement of the NRA Foundation appears in the inside front cover of the *Traditions* magazine, as well as on a number of Foundation publications. To quote:

> Established in 1990, The NRA Foundation, Inc . . . raises tax-deductible contributions in support of a wide range of firearms-related public interest activities of the National Rifle Association of America and other organizations that defend and foster the Second Amendment rights of all law-abiding Americans. These activities are designed to promote firearms and hunting safety, to enhance marksmanship skills of those participating in the shooting sports, and to educate the general public about firearms in their historic, technological and artistic context. Funds granted by The NRA Foundation benefit a variety of constituencies throughout the United States including children, youth, women, individuals with physical disabilities, gun collectors, law enforcement officers, hunters and competitive shooters.

As of this writing, the author's own Educational Endowment within the Foundation totals over $30,000; and in 1999 1,000 *The Colt Heritage* posters were donated to to the National Firearms Museum shop, for sale as a means of further funding the author's Endowment. Use of the proceeds, administered by The NRA Foundation, is to the furtherance of education about firearms, particularly through the hobby of arms collecting.

The NRA Foundation Executive Director is Steven C. Anderson, and Director of the NRA Endowment is H. Wayne Sheets. They and their staffs can be reached at the same address as the NRA, and the direct line phone and fax numbers are: (703) 267-1121 and (fax) (703) 267-3834.

THE ILA

Still another organization affiliated with the National Rifle Association is the Institute of Legislative Action. Executive Director of the ILA/Administration is James Baker, often seen on television and in print. Although some elements of the press try to claim that the NRA and ILA have been losing their influence with the public and legislators, those views are open to interpretation. On the whole the ILA is highly effective, and without its hard work, and that of the NRA *per se,* the gun-haters and the hunting-haters might well have already wiped out private gun ownership and the sport of hunting, and in the process generations of immense good works in wildlife and habitat conservation.

To contact the ILA: call (703) 267-1140; fax (703) 267-3973. See also the NRA website, reachable via www.nra.org or simply by the search term nra.

BILL CLINTON NRA'S BEST RECRUITER AND GUN SALESMAN

An irony of the relentless attacks on the NRA and on gun-owners is that Bill Clinton has been instrumental in increasing NRA membership and contributions, and has caused a notable increase in gun sales throughout the United States. In his desperate attempts to leave some kind of legacy to his presidency, Clinton has misread the gun issue and the so-called polls. As a consequence, his headline-grabbing attacks on firearms have awakened a sleeping giant: the estimated 80,000,000 gun-owners in America, who see a gradual erosion of their right under the Constitution to own firearms.

Clinton's belief that "gun control" will be a deciding issue in the 2000 elections will backfire, since the true one-issue voters are pro-gun, while the gun issue is only one of many issues to consider with the majority of voters. Thus, his extreme positions will contribute to Congress remaining dominated by the Republican Party, to be joined by a Republican in the White House.

THE NRA AND ARMS COLLECTING

Programs directed at assisting and encouraging arms collecting include development of the National Firearms Museum, the NRA Gun Collectors Committee, and the NRA Gun Collectors Division, all of which are involved with promoting gun shows, encouraging proper ethics in arms collecting, and supporting the annual NRA Gun Collectors Show and Conference.

Earlier in *The Official Price Guide* is an illustration of the NRA Gun Collectors Code of Ethics and Bill of Sale, which has proven a useful reference guide for numerous collectors, and is indicative of the high standards in collecting promoted by the NRA.

Among the NRA staff actively working toward fostering public understanding of arms collecting, and working with collectors to promote the hobby, are Thomas W. (Whit) Fentem, Director, National Firearms Museum, Doug Wicklund, Curator, and Philip Schreier, Manager NRA Gun Collector Program. Overseeing Museum and Gun Collecting Division operations is Craig D. Sandler, Executive Director, NRA General Operations. A nine-member NRA Gun Collectors Committee is also involved in the NRA gun collector programs.

According to "News & Notes from NRA's Gun Collector Programs Department," the NRA's programs for gun collectors continued to evolve and expand in 1999–2000. Unfortunately, due to the Columbine school tragedy, the 1999 NRA Annual Meetings did not include exhibitors.

At the 129th Annual Meetings and Exhibits, May 19–21, 2000, Charlotte, North Carolina, the Museum and Gun Collecting Program staff and Gun Collectors Committee organized the best array of displays in NRA history.

Guest speaker for the Sunday morning Gun Collectors' awards presentation was George C. Neumann, expert and author, whose topic was "Battle Arms of Washington's Army." For readers who have never attended an NRA Annual Meeting, the gun collector displays are always a highlight of the exhibits.

A lecture series at the National Firearms Museum began in 1999, in conjunction with the Virginia Gun Collectors Association. On a quarterly basis, speakers discuss subjects of interest to collectors and firearms devotees. First of the speakers was Douglas Wicklund, Curator of the National Firearms Museum, who spoke of the role of sniper in the War Between the States. Later speakers included Harry Hunter of the National Museum of American History, on the arms collection in that institution (a division of the Smithsonian Institution), and Philip Schreier, who addressed the group on the Walker Colts of Samuel Hamilton Walker.

Among the displays that have been presented in The William B. Ruger Gallery is "The Evolution of the Allen Pepperbox," with examples from the Roger Muckherheide Collection. Dr. Joseph A. Murphy lent his pair of Walker's Walker Colt revolvers, as well as his President Franklin Pierce Colt First Model Dragoon and Model 1851 Navy presentation revolvers for exhibit, following publication of the author's *Fine Colts: The Dr. Joseph A. Murphy Collection*. The National Firearms Museum also has a Traveling Exhibit Program, which was instituted in 1990. Yet another gun collector program is that of Affiliated Club Outstanding Display Awards.

The exhibition "Ruger & His Guns" opened May 1, 2000, running through the end of the year. Based on the author's book of the same title, approximately seventy firearms from the private and corporate collection of William B. Ruger Sr., and Sturm, Ruger & Co., were handsomely displayed, augmented by visuals of paintings from the Ruger Collection, as well as blow-ups of collage illustrations from the book. The author presented a talk as part of the programs associated with the exhibition. Appropriately, the display was held in The William B. Ruger Gallery, which had been funded two years previously by Mr. Ruger. He had no idea that at some point a special display would be presented honoring his unique achievements in the worlds of firearms (including their design and collecting), manufacturing, and marketing.

An innovation launched at the 1998 Annual Show and Meetings was The National Treasures Award, the highest honor in contemporary gun collecting, donated to the NRA by Michael Zomber. Only three of these solid Gold Medals may be given in any year. The design is basically the same as the coveted Silver Medal, no more than ten of which are presented annually, for the best guns of the show.

The fifth annual NRA Gun Collectors Show & Conference was held in Kansas City, Missouri, in conjunction with the Missouri Valley Arms Collectors, July 28–30, 2000. Featured were a firearms auction to benefit the National Firearms Museum and the awarding of the E. Andrew Mowbray Trophy and seven other awards sponsored by the NRA, to honor best exhibits. Information on the annual event is available at NRA headquarters: (703) 267-1604.

In October 1999, the NRA Gun Collectors Department held its twelfth annual National Gun Collectors Leadership Seminar, at Grapevine (near Dallas), Texas. The seminar continues the tradition of meetings that disseminate information among the leadership of the affiliated gun collector organizations, of which there are presently 120. A charity auction raised more than $5,000 for National Firearms Museum programs. The Dallas Arms Collectors Association hosted the Seminar.

As a further fundraiser, Cherry's Fine Guns re-created shooting replicates of two of the Museum's masterpiece firearms: the San Juan Hill "Rough Rider" Colt Single Action Army revolver and a Trapdoor Springfield Officers Model rifle. A substantial donation from each firearm sold was presented to the National Firearms Museum.

"News & Notes From NRA's Gun Collector Programs Department" provides information to the gun collector affiliate community. For some time now, Phil Schreier and the NRA Gun Collectors Department have been producing a regular column in *Man at Arms* magazine, entitled "The NRA Page." *Man at Arms* is the official "NRA Journal for the American Arms Collector." For free mailings of "News & Notes," contact Philip Schreier, 11250 Waples Mill Road, Fairfax VA 22030 (703) 267-1601, 1604, or 1620.

The National Firearms Museum now has its own dedicated page on the Internet. The Web page domain is www/nra.org, and the e-mail address is nfmstaff@nra.org. Among other material, the website provides a photo tour of the museum and an illustrated guide to merchandise sold in the museum shop.

Commemoratives

BY KEVIN P. CHERRY

In an as yet unpublished article written for *The American Rifleman,* Larry Wilson considered the impact of commemorative firearms on the collecting world. The gist of this story is that these arms, besides offering the opportunity to collect beautiful pieces in perfect condition with strong investment potential, are an important magnet to attract many new enthusiasts to gun collecting. And in the R. L. Wilson book, *Colt Commemorative Firearms,* published by my father in 1974, James E. Serven noted:

> I have been a student of Colt firearms for many years and find nothing very unusual in the zeal of a collector who seeks factory-made Colt commemorative firearms with varied markings, different finishes, and interesting historical associations; that process has been going on among collectors for years. One veteran Oklahoma collector has twenty-one different variations of the rare Colt folding-trigger pistols made at Paterson. One could have perhaps fifty or more Colt cap-lock Navy model pistols with variations in markings, structural design, and other features.
>
> Collecting the early Colt models today, however, is not a field for one on a tight budget; many models are almost impossible to find. Where, then, do the increasing numbers of arms collectors turn? While certainly not an inexpensive pursuit, commemorative arms do open a field where there is generally a reasonable current availability of collectible items. . . .
>
> While some of the purists in Colt collecting remain critical of the commemorative pieces, it seems fair to assume that the field is wide enough to accommodate all shades of thought, and I am confident that this book will help to bring about a better understanding and a greater rapport among all who collect arms which bear the name of Colt.

These remarks also easily transfer to the subject of Winchester, Smith & Wesson, Remington, Marlin, and other marques.

Commemorative firearms on the following list fulfill these criteria:

1. The series has a stated production limit.
2. Each series has its own serial number range.
3. The production has an endorsement by the manufacturer.
4. Distribution is generally through normal channels.

The majority of these arms are classified by the BATF as curios and relics.

Among the exceptions to the above criteria are special-issue guns, such as those pieces made for "The Friends of the NRA" banquet auctions or raffles, for Ducks Unlimited dinner fund-raisers, for fish and game clubs, and so forth. These are not guns bearing endorsements by the manufacturers, nor are they distributed in the normal manner of bona fide commemorative issues.

The 1985 edition of Larry Wilson's *Colt: An American Legend* contains a list of commemorative models (pages 388–89), and a separate list of Special Editions: Hand Engraved or Etched (pages 390–91). Comparison of the two, and consideration of the above-noted criteria, make clear the commemorative nature of the former and the non-commemorative nature of the latter.

I am proud of the role my father played in establishing this major specialty in the world of arms collecting.

The course of action taken by the Colt and Winchester (U.S. Repeating Arms) firms, which adversely affected the commemorative market, should be considered here. Mistakes were made by these two major companies, which proved to be temporary setbacks. Both companies made too many models and too many examples of these models, and the issues were generally overpriced. From the early 1980s until the end of that decade, the market was idle.

But beginning about 1989, the market had absorbed the excess commemoratives, and with increased pricings of standard production, the commemorative issues regained their appeal. Prices have been returning, and the larger-caliber Colt and Winchester lever-action carbines and rifles have proven particularly attractive.

Prices in the listing that follows apply to mint guns, with their original accessories, casings, and packaging. Commemoratives that have seen use, including being shot, generally have a value equal to the same model of standard production.

Books on commemorative firearms are listed in the bibliography, in Appendix 1. Additionally, commemorative Colts and Winchesters are featured in Larry Wilson's *Colt: An American Legend* and *Winchester: An American Legend,* each of which is the official history of these prime firms in the commemorative market.

All in all, for a significant block of firearms enthusiasts, commemoratives are an important segment of the collector market, and are definitely here to stay.

Year	Description	Production	Original Retail	Current Retail
1961	Colt Genseso, Illinois, 125th Anniversary Derringer	104	$27.50	$650.00
1961	Colt Sheriff's Model, Blue & Case Hardened	478	129.95	1995.00
1961	Colt Sheriff's Model, Nickel	25	139.95	5000.00
1961	Colt 125th Anniversary Model SAA	7390	150.00	1195.00
1961	Colt Kansas Statehood Scout	6197	75.00	425.00
1961	Colt Pony Express Centennial Scout	1007	80.00	450.00
1961	Colt Civil War Centennial Pistol	24114	32.50	175.00
1961	Marlin 90th Anniversary 39A Rifle & Carbine	1000	100.00	995.00
1962	Colt Rock Island Arsenal Centennial Pistol	550	38.50	250.00
1962	Colt Columbus, Ohio Sesquicentennial Scout	200	100.00	550.00
1962	Colt Fort Findlay, Ohio Sesquicentennial Scout	110	89.50	650.00
1962	Colt Fort Findlay, Ohio Cased Pair, 22LR/22Mag	20	185.00	2500.00
1962	Colt New Mexico Golden Anniversary Scout	1000	79.95	425.00
1962	Colt Fort McPherson, Nebraska Centennial Derringer	300	28.95	395.00
1962	Colt West Virginia Statehood Centennial Scout	3451	75.00	425.00
1963	Colt West Virginia Statehood, Centennial SAA .45	600	150.00	1195.00
1963	Colt Arizona Territory Centennial Scout	5355	75.00	425.00
1963	Colt Arizona Territory Centennial SAA .45	1264	150.00	1195.00
1963	Colt Carolina Charter Tercentenary Scout	550	75.00	425.00
1963	Colt Carolina Charter Tercentenary .22/.45 Combo	250	240.00	1595.00
1963	Colt H. Cook "1 of 100" .22/.45 Combo	100	275.00	1795.00
1963	Colt Fort Stephenson, Ohio Sesq. Scout	200	75.00	550.00
1963	Colt Battle of Gettysburg Centennial Scout	1019	89.95	425.00
1963	Colt Idaho Territory Centennial Scout	902	75.00	425.00
1963	Colt Gen. John Hunt Morgan, Indiana Raid Scout	100	74.50	650.00
1964	Colt Cherry's 35th Anniversary .22/.45 Combo	100	275.00	1695.00
1964	Colt Nevada Statehood Centennial Scout	3981	75.00	425.00

Year	Description	Production	Original Retail	Current Retail
1964	Colt Nevada Statehood Centennial SAA .45	1684	$150.00	$1195.00
1964	Colt Nevada Statehood Centennial .22/.45 Combo	189	240.00	1595.00
1964	Colt Nevada State, Combo w/Extra Engraved Cylinders	577	350.00	1695.00
1964	Colt Nevada "Battle Born" Scout	981	85.00	425.00
1964	Colt Nevada "Battle Born" SAA .45	80	175.00	1395.00
1964	Colt Nevada "Battle Born" SAA .22/.45 Combo	20	265.00	2595.00
1964	Colt Montana Territorial Centennial Scout	2296	75.00	425.00
1964	Colt Montana Territorial Centennial SAA .45	850	150.00	1195.00
1964	Colt Wyoming Diamond Jubilee Scout	2356	75.00	425.00
1964	Winchester Wyoming Diamond Jubilee Mdl. 94 Carbine	1500	99.95	1295.00
1964	Remington Montana Territorial Centennial 600 Rifle	1005	124.95	495.00
1964	Colt General Hood Centennial Scout	1502	75.00	425.00
1964	Colt New Jersey Tercentenary Scout	1000	75.00	425.00
1964	Colt New Jersey Tercentenary SAA .45	249	150.00	1195.00
1964	Colt St. Louis Bicentennial Scout	801	75.00	425.00
1964	Colt St. Louis Bicentennial SAA .45	199	150.00	1195.00
1964	Colt St. Louis Bicentennial .22/.45 Combo	250	240.00	1595.00
1964	Ithaca St. Louis Bicentennial Model 49 .22 Rifle	200	34.95	195.00
1964	Colt California Gold Rush Scout	500	79.50	450.00
1964	Colt Pony Express Presentation SAA .45	1004	250.00	1395.00
1964	Colt Chamizal Treaty Scout	450	85.00	450.00
1964	Colt Chamizal Treaty SAA .45	50	170.00	1295.00
1964	Colt Chamizal Treaty .22/.45 Combo	50	280.00	1995.00
1964	Colt Col. Sam Colt Sesquicentennial Presentation SAA .45	4750	225.00	1195.00
1964	Colt Col. Sam Colt Sesquicentennial Deluxe Presentation SAA .45	200	500.00	2500.00
1964	Colt Col. Sam Colt Sesquicentennial Special Dlx. Presentation SAA .45	50	1000.00	4000.00
1964	Colt Wyatt Earp Buntline SAA .45	150	250.00	2500.00

Year	Description	Production	Original Retail	Current Retail
1965	Colt Oregon Trail Scout	1995	$75.00	$425.00
1965	Colt Joaquin Murietta .22/.45 Combo	100	350.00	1695.00
1965	Colt Forty-Niner Miner Scout	500	85.00	425.00
1965	Colt Old Fort Des Moines, Reconstruction Scout	700	89.95	450.00
1965	Colt Old Fort Des Moines, Reconstruction SAA .45	100	169.95	1195.00
1965	Colt Old Fort Des Moines, Reconstruction .22/.45 Combo	100	289.95	1695.00
1965	Colt Appomattox Centennial Scout	1001	75.00	425.00
1965	Colt Appomattox Centennial SAA .45	250	150.00	1195.00
1965	Colt Appomattox Centennial .22/.45 Combo	250	240.00	1595.00
1965	Colt General Meade Campaign Scout	1197	75.00	425.00
1965	Colt Saint Augustine Quadricentennial Scout	500	85.00	450.00
1965	Colt Kansas Cowtown Series, Wichita Scout	500	85.00	425.00
1966	Colt Kansas Cowtown Series, Dodge City Scout	500	85.00	425.00
1966	Colt Colorado Gold Rush Scout	1350	85.00	450.00
1966	Colt Oklahoma Territory Scout	1343	85.00	425.00
1966	Colt Dakota Territory Scout	1000	85.00	425.00
1966	Winchester Centennial '66 Rifle	102309	125.00	450.00
1966	Winchester Centennial '66 Carbine	102309	125.00	425.00
1966	Colt General Meade SAA .45	197	165.00	1195.00
1966	Colt Abercrombie & Fitch "Trailblazer" New York	200	275.00	1095.00
1966	Colt Kansas Cowtown Series, Abilene Scout	500	95.00	425.00
1966	Colt Indiana Sesquicentennial Scout	1745	85.00	425.00
1966	Winchester Nebraska Centennial 94 Rifle	2500	125.00	1195.00
1966	Colt Pony Express SAA .45 "4-Square"		1400.00	5995.00
1966	Colt California Gold Rush SAA .45	130	175.00	1395.00
1966	Colt Abercrombie & Fitch "Trailblazer" Chicago	100	275.00	1095.00
1966	Colt Abercrombie & Fitch "Trailblazer" San Francisco	100	275.00	1095.00
1967	Remington Canadian Centennial 742 Rifle	1000	199.95	395.00
1967	Ruger Canadian Centennial 10/22 Rifle	2000	99.95	325.00
1967	Ruger Canadian Centennial, Matched #3 Set	1900	319.00	650.00
1967	Ruger Canadian Centennial, Matched #2 Set	70	$450.00	$850.00
1967	Ruger Canadian Centennial, Matched #1 Special Deluxe Set	30	600.00	1050.00
1967	Colt Lawman Series, Bat Masterson Scout	3000	90.00	450.00
1967	Colt Lawman Series, Bat Masterson SAA .45	500	180.00	1500.00
1967	Colt Alamo Scout	4239	85.00	425.00
1967	Colt Alamo SAA .45	750	165.00	1195.00
1967	Colt Alamo .22/.45 Combo	250	265.00	1595.00
1967	Colt Kansas Cowtown Series, Coffeyville Scout	500	95.00	425.00
1967	Winchester Canadian '67 Centennial Rifle	90301	125.00	450.00
1967	Winchester Canadian '67 Centennial Carbine	90301	125.00	425.00
1967	Winchester Alaskan Purchase Centennial Carbine	1500	125.00	1495.00
1967	Colt Kansas Trail Series, Chisholm Trail Scout	500	100.00	425.00
1967	Colt WWI Series, Chateau Thierry .45 Auto	7400	200.00	695.00
1967	Colt WWI Series, Chateau Thierry Deluxe .45 Auto	75	500.00	1350.00
1967	Colt WWI Series, Chateau Thierry Special Deluxe .45 Auto	25	1000.00	2750.00
1967	H&R "Abilene Anniversary" .22 Revolver	300	83.50	150.00
1968	Colt Nebraska Centennial Scout	6999	100.00	425.00
1968	Colt Kansas Trail Series, Pawnee Trail Scout	500	110.00	425.00
1968	Winchester Illinois Sesquicentennial, 94 Carbine	37648	110.00	395.00
1968	Winchester Buffalo Bill Rifle "1 of 300"	300	1000.00	2650.00
1968	Winchester Buffalo Bill Rifle	112923	129.95	450.00
1968	Winchester Buffalo Bill Carbine	112923	129.95	425.00
1968	Colt WWI Series, Belleau Wood .45 Auto	7400	200.00	695.00
1968	Colt WWI Series, Belleau Wood Deluxe .45 Auto	75	500.00	1350.00
1968	Colt WWI Series, Belleau Wood Special Deluxe .45 Auto	25	1000.00	2750.00
1968	Colt Lawman Series, Pat Garrett Scout	2966	110.00	450.00
1968	Colt Lawman Series, Pat Garrett SAA .45	500	220.00	1295.00
1969	Colt General Nathan Bedford Forest Scout	2996	110.00	425.00
1969	Colt Kansas Trail Series, Santa Fe Trail Scout	500	120.00	425.00

Year	Description	Production	Original Retail	Current Retail
1969	Colt WWI Series, Battle of 2nd Marne, .45 Auto	7400	$220.00	$695.00
1969	Colt WWI Series, Battle of 2nd Marne, Deluxe .45 Auto	75	500.00	1350.00
1969	Colt WWI Series, Battle of 2nd Marne, Special Deluxe .45 Auto	25	1000.00	2750.00
1969	Colt Alabama Sesquicentennial Scout	2998	110.00	425.00
1969	Colt Alabama Sesquicentennial SAA .45	1	N/A	15000.00
1969	Winchester Golden Spike Carbine	69996	119.95	395.00
1969	Winchester Theodore Roosevelt Carbine	52386	134.95	425.00
1969	Winchester Theodore Roosevelt Rifle	52386	134.95	450.00
1969	Colt Golden Spike Scout	10965	135.00	450.00
1969	Colt Kansas Trail Series, Shawnee Trail Scout	500	120.00	425.00
1969	Colt WWI Series, Meuse-Argonne .45 Auto	7400	220.00	695.00
1969	Colt WWI Series, Meuse-Argonne Deluxe .45 Auto	75	550.00	1350.00
1969	Colt WWI Series, Meuse-Argonne Special Deluxe .45 Auto	25	1000.00	2750.00
1969	Colt Arkansas Territory Sesquicentennial Scout	3487	110.00	425.00
1969	Colt Lawman Series, Wild Bill Hickok SAA	500	220.00	1295.00
1969	Colt Lawman Series, Wild Bill Hickok Scout	2984	116.00	450.00
1969	Colt California Bicentennial Scout	4997	135.00	425.00
1970	Colt Kansas Fort Series, Fort Larned Scout	500	120.00	425.00
1970	Colt WWII Series, European Theater	9767	250.00	695.00
1970	Colt WWII Series, Pacific Theater	9886	250.00	695.00
1970	Winchester Northwest Territories	2500	149.95	850.00
1970	Winchester Northwest Territories, Deluxe	500	249.95	1100.00
1970	Winchester Northwest Territories, Donation	10	N/A	N/A
1970	Winchester Cowboy Commemorative Carbine	27549	125.00	450.00
1970	Winchester Cowboy Commemorative Carbine "1 of 300"	300	1000.00	2650.00
1970	Winchester Lone Star Carbine	38385	140.00	425.00
1970	Winchester Lone Star Rifle	38385	140.00	450.00
1970	Colt Texas Ranger SAA .45	1000	650.00	2250.00

Year	Description	Production	Original Retail	Current Retail
1970	Colt Texas Ranger SAA .45, Grade II	N/A	$2250.00	$5000.00
1970	Colt Texas Ranger SAA .45, Grade III	N/A	2950.00	5500.00
1970	Savage 75th Anniversary Model 99 Rifle	9999	195.00	495.00
1970	Colt Kansas Fort Series, Fort Hayes Scout	500	130.00	425.00
1970	Colt Maine Sesquicentennial Scout	2987	120.00	425.00
1970	Colt Missouri Sesquicentennial Scout	2975	125.00	425.00
1970	Colt Missouri Sesquicentennial SAA .45	888	220.00	1095.00
1970	Colt Kansas Fort Series, Fort Riley	500	130.00	425.00
1970	Colt Lawman Series, Wyatt Earp Scout	2968	125.00	495.00
1970	Colt Lawman Series, Wyatt Earp SAA .45	500	395.00	2500.00
1971	Winchester NRA Centennial Musket	23400	149.95	425.00
1971	Winchester NRA Centennial Rifle	21000	149.95	425.00
1971	Winchester Yellow Boy	4903	149.95	1150.00
1971	Winchester R.C.M.P.	9500	189.95	795.00
1971	Winchester R.C.M.P. Members Issue	4850	189.95	795.00
1971	Winchester R.C.M.P. Presentation	10	N/A	9995.00
1971	Winchester MPX	32	78.00	7995.00
1971	Colt NRA Centennial SAA .45	3475	250.00	1195.00
1971	Colt NRA Centennial SAA .357	3475	250.00	895.00
1971	Colt NRA Centennial Gold Cup .45	2478	250.00	950.00
1971	Colt 1851 Navy, U.S. Grant	4140	250.00	595.00
1971	Colt 1851 Navy, Robert E. Lee	4645	250.00	595.00
1971	Colt 1851 Navy, Lee-Grant Set	250	500.00	1350.00
1971	Colt Kansas Fort Series, Fort Scott Scout	500	130.00	425.00
1971	H&R Officer's Model .45–70	10000	250.00	495.00
1971	Marlin Zane Grey .30–30 Carbine	N/A	150.00	350.00
1971	Stevens Favorite '71 .22 Single Shot	1000	75.00	275.00
1971	Marlin 336–39A Engraved Cased Pair	1000	750.00	995.00
1972	H&R Little Big Horn, .45–70	N/A	220.00	495.00
1972	Colt Florida Sesquicentennial Scout	1996	125.00	425.00
1972	Colt Arizona Ranger Scout	3000	135.00	425.00
1972	High Standard Olympic .22 Auto	N/A	550.00	1500.00

Year	Description	Production	Original Retail	Current Retail
1973	H&R 1873 Springfield	N/A	$250.00	$495.00
1973	Smith & Wesson Texas Ranger w/Knife	10000	250.00	595.00
1973	Smith & Wesson Texas Ranger	N/A	195.00	495.00
1973	H&R Custer Memorial; Officer's Model	25	3000.00	3995.00
1973	H&R Custer Memorial, Enlisted Man's Model	243	2000.00	1995.00
1974	High Standard Griswold & Gunnison	500	175.00	250.00
1974	High Standard Presidential Derringer	N/A	150.00	250.00
1974	High Standard Leech & Rigdon	500	175.00	250.00
1974	Winchester Texas Ranger Carbine	4850	129.95	695.00
1974	Winchester Texas Ranger Presentation	150	1000.00	2650.00
1974	Winchester Apache	8600	149.95	795.00
1974	Winchester Klondike Gold Rush	10200	229.95	795.00
1974	Winchester Klondike Dawson City	25	N/A	8500.00
1974	Winchester Comanche	11511	229.95	795.00
1975	Colt Peacemaker Centennial .45	1500	300.00	1395.00
1975	Colt Peacemaker Centennial .44–40	1500	300.00	1395.00
1975	Colt Peacemaker Centennial Pair	500	625.00	2895.00
1975	High Standard Schneider & Glassick	1000	325.00	325.00
1976	Ruger Colorado Centennial Single Six	N/A	250.00	325.00
1976	Colt U.S. Bicentennial Set	1776	1695.00	1995.00
1976	Winchester U.S. Bicentennial Carbine	19999	325.00	595.00
1976	Browning Bicentennial '78 .45/70 Rifle	1000	150.00	1850.00
1976	Winchester Sioux	12000	279.95	795.00
1976	Winchester Little Big Horn	11000	229.95	795.00
1977	Colt 2nd Amendment .22	3020	194.95	425.00
1977	Winchester Wells Fargo	19999	350.00	495.00
1977	S&W 125th Anniversary Model 125	10000	350.00	495.00
1977	Winchester Cheyenne .44/40	11225	300.00	795.00
1977	Winchester Cheyenne .22	5000	319.95	695.00
1977	Colt U.S. Calvary 200th Anniversary Set	2974	995.00	1250.00
1977	Winchester "Limited Edition I"	1500	1500.00	1395.00
1977	Winchester Cherokee .30–30	9000	384.95	795.00
1977	Winchester Cherokee .22	3950	348.95	695.00
1977	Winchester Legendary Lawman	19999	375.00	495.00
1978	Browning Centennial Superposed Rifle-Shotgun	500	$7000.00	$5000.00
1978	Browning Centennial M92 .44 Magnum	6000	219.95	495.00
1978	Browning Centennial Hi-Power 9mm	3500	495.00	650.00
1978	Jonathan Browning Mountain Rifle	1000	650.00	650.00
1978	Winchester Antlered Game Carbine	19999	375.00	495.00
1978	Colt Statehood 3rd Model Dragoon	52	12500.00	6995.00
1979	Winchester Legendary Frontiersman Rifle	19999	425.00	495.00
1979	Winchester Bat Masterson	8000	650.00	795.00
1979	Winchester "Limited Edition II"	1500	1750.00	1395.00
1979	Colt Ned Buntline Single Action Army .45	2973	895.00	895.00
1980	Colt Heritage-Walker .44 Percussion	1850	1475.00	950.00
1980	Winchester Matched Set of 1000	1000	3000.00	2250.00
1980	Winchester Alberta Diamond Jubilee	2700	650.00	795.00
1980	Winchester Alberta Diamond Jubilee Deluxe	300	1900.00	1495.00
1980	Winchester Saskatchewan Diamond Jubilee	2700	695.00	795.00
1980	Winchester Saskatchewan Diamond Jubilee Deluxe	300	1695.00	1495.00
1980	Winchester Calgary Stampede	1000	2200.00	1250.00
1980	Winchester Canadian Pacific	2700	800.00	550.00
1980	Winchester Canadian Pacific, Employee Edition	2000	800.00	550.00
1980	Winchester Canadian Pacific, Presentation	300	2200.00	1100.00
1980	Winchester "Oliver Winchester"	19999	519.60	695.00
1981	Colt "John M. Browning" .45 Automatic	2986	1099.95	895.00
1981	Winchester John Wayne	50000	600.00	895.00
1981	Winchester Canadian John Wayne	999	600.00	1095.00
1981	Winchester "Duke"	1000	2250.00	2950.00
1981	Browning "American Waterfowl" Superposed	500	7000.00	3995.00
1981	Winchester U.S. Border Patrol, Members	800	950.00	595.00
1981	Winchester U.S. Border Patrol	1000	950.00	595.00
1981	Winchester John Wayne "1 of 300" Set	300	8500.00	6500.00
1981	Winchester Great Western Artists I	999	2500.00	1195.00

Year	Description	Production	Original Retail	Current Retail
1981	Winchester Great Western Artists II	999	$2500.00	$1195.00
1982	Colt John Wayne, Standard	3100	2995.00	1995.00
1982	Colt John Wayne, Deluxe	500	10000.00	7500.00
1982	Colt John Wayne, Presentation	100	20000.00	12000.00
1982	Winchester Annie Oakley .22	6000	699.00	695.00
1982	Winchester Oklahoma Diamond Jubilee	1000	2200.00	1395.00
1982	Winchester Bald Eagle, Silver	2800	895.00	595.00
1982	Winchester Bald Eagle, Gold	200	2950.00	3000.00
1983	Winchester Chief Crazy Horse	19999	600.00	595.00
1983	Colt Buffalo Bill Wild West Show Centennial SAA .45	283	1349.95	1395.00
1984	Winchester Colt	3250	3995.00	2250.00
1984	Colt "USA Edition" SAA .44–40	100	4995.00	3500.00
1984	Colt Kit Carson .22 New Frontier	951	549.95	425.00
1984	Colt Theodore Roosevelt .44/40	500	1695.00	1695.00
1984	Winchester Boy Scout 75th Anniversary 9422	15000	495.00	595.00
1984	Winchester Eagle Scout 75th Anniversary 9422	1000	1710.00	3000.00
1984	Browning A-5 "Classic" Semi-Auto Shotgun	5000	1260.00	995.00
1984	Browning Hi-Power "Classic" 9mm	5000	1000.00	850.00
1984	Browning Hi-Power "Gold Classic" 9mm	500	2000.00	1800.00
1985	Colt Texas Sesquicentennial SAA .45, Standard	1000	1836.00	1295.00
1985	Colt Texas Sesquicentennial SAA .45, Premier	75	7995.00	5000.00
1985	Winchester Texas Sesquicentennial Carbine	15000	695.00	695.00
1985	Winchester Texas Sesquicentennial, Rifle & Bowie Knife	1500	2995.00	2400.00
1985	Winchester Texas Sesquicentennial, Rifle, Carbine, & Bowie Knife Set	150	7995.00	6250.00
1986	Colt 150th Anniversary SAA .45	1000	$1595.00	$1595.00
1986	Winchester 120th Anniversary .44/40	1000	995.00	895.00
1986	Browning A-5 "Gold Classic" Shotgun	500	6500.00	3500.00
1986	Browning Superposed "Classic"	2500	2000.00	1750.00
1986	Browning Superposed "Gold Classic" Shotgun	350	6000.00	4750.00
1987	Winchester U.S. Constitution 200th Anniversary .44/40	17	12000.00	13000.00
1990	Winchester Wyoming Centennial .30–30	500	895.00	1095.00
1991	Winchester 125th Anniversary .30–30	61	4995.00	5500.00
1992	Winchester Arapaho .30–30	500	895.00	1095.00
1992	Winchester Ontario Conservation .30–30	400	1195.00	1195.00
1992	Winchester Kentucky Bicentennial .30–30	500	995.00	1095.00
1993	Winchester Nez Perce .30–30	600	950.00	1095.00
1994	Uberti Nimschke 1866 Rifle, .44/40	150	1495.00	1795.00
1994	Marlin "Century Limited" 94 Rifle, .44/40	2500	1087.90	925.00
1994	Pedersoli Creedmoor Rifle, .45/70	250	1495.00	1795.00
1995	Winchester Florida Sesquicentennial Carbine, 30/30	500	1195.00	1195.00
1995	Marlin 1895 125th Anniversary	350	1195.00	1195.00
1996	Winchester "Wild Bill Hickok" Model 94 .30/30	350	1195.00	1195.00
1996	Pedersoli Sharps Creedmoor .45/70	300	1995.00	1995.00
1997	Uberti Gustave Young Model 1866	300	1895.00	1895.00

Note: The author is grateful to Kevin Cherry for his detailed text on this increasingly complex subject. For further information, Mr. Cherry can be contacted c/o Cherry's, 3402-A Wendover Avenue, Greensboro NC 27407; telephone (336) 854-4182. Web site: http://www.cherrys.com.

U. S. Smooth Bore Pistols Designed to Fire Shotgun Shells

BY ERIC M. LARSON

As rare American cultural artifacts, certain smooth bore pistols originally manufactured in the United States in or before 1934 occupy a unique niche in U.S. firearms history and genealogy. They are highly prized by collectors, yet still inappropriately regulated strictly as machine guns by the Bureau of Alcohol, Tobacco and Firearms (ATF).

These guns were made when no federal laws (and relatively few state laws) affected firearms design. While it is rare, the most commonly encountered example is the 12¼"-barrel H&R Handy-Gun, designed to fire the 2½" .410 shotgun shell. It is one of several smooth bore pistols that competed with Marble's Game Getter Gun, a .22/.44 or .410 combination firearm with a folding shoulder stock that was first manufactured in 1908. A few smooth bore pistols (such as the 20-gauge Ithaca Auto & Burglar Gun) were marketed as defensive weapons, but most were relatively low-powered small-game guns.

Smooth bore pistols like the H&R Handy-Gun are currently regulated by the National Firearms Act (NFA) of 1934. The NFA is designed to control firearms thought to be mainly used by criminals by requiring registration of the firearms, and using prohibitive taxes to reduce their manufacture, distribution, and ownership. It is a harsh federal law to discourage illegally manufacturing, selling, or possessing hand grenades, machine guns, and similar weapons, and the cutting down of conventional shotguns or rifles (regardless of their caliber) to make concealable firearms.

Curiously, as passed in 1934, the NFA specifically excluded "a pistol or revolver," and still does today. As originally enacted, the NFA defined a "firearm" as:

> A shotgun or rifle having a barrel of less than eighteen inches in length, or any other weapon, except a pistol or revolver, from which a shot is discharged by an explosive if such weapon is capable of being concealed on the person, or a machine gun, and includes a muffler or silencer for any firearm whether or not such firearm is included within the foregoing definition.

But several original versions of the bill that eventually was enacted as the NFA included "a pistol, revolver . . . or any other firearm capable of being concealed on the person" within the definition of an NFA "firearm." Under the NFA as originally proposed, pistols and revolvers would have been regulated as strictly as machine guns.

After debate, the bill was amended to remove pistols and revolvers, but not other concealable firearms. Thus, small firearms not readily classifiable as traditional pistols or revolvers (such as cane-guns, knife-pistols, and so forth) had to be registered. But Congress did not define the terms "pistol," "revolver," "rifle," "shotgun," or "any other weapon" under the original NFA in 1934. Consequently, ATF applied the NFA using administrative regulations.

When the original NFA became effective on July 26, 1934, *all* items defined as "firearms" had to be registered, and there was a $200 tax on each transfer of ownership. The $200 rate, set to equal the cost (in 1934) of a new .45 caliber Thompson Submachine gun, was designed to be prohibitive.

Why were smooth bore pistols, which were clearly designed as handguns, deemed not to be pistols? In 1926, the Bureau of Internal Revenue determined that the H&R Handy-Gun was "not a pistol or revolver within the meaning . . . and is not, therefore, subject to tax" under the Internal Revenue Act of 1926. The 1926 Act had exempted rifles, shotguns, and ammunition from a 10 percent firearms excise tax enacted in 1918, but, because of anti-handgun politics, retained it for pistols and revolvers (the .410 Stevens Off-Hand Shot Gun, another smooth bore pistol, also was exempted).

The 1926 ruling resulted from an agitation by the H&R and Stevens manufacturers, who argued that these firearms were useful to trappers, farmers, hunters, lumberjacks, and others who worked outdoors, being relatively compact and less bulky than a firearm intended to be fired from the shoulder.

A circa 1928 H&R advertisement states: "The 'Handy-Gun' is classified by the U.S. Government as a shotgun." Other documentation of the H&R Handy-Gun's classification as a "shotgun" has not been located. Interestingly, H&R catalogues from that era state that under the laws of some states, any firearm with a barrel less than 12 inches in length was defined as a pistol; consequently, the 12¼-inch barrel caused the H&R Handy-Gun to avoid being regulated in those states as a pistol.

ATF determined that "since the manufacturer had argued successfully his point in 1926 that the H&R Handy-Gun was not a pistol, it was very easy for the Bureau in 1934 to point out . . . that the weapon could not be excepted from the definition of a firearm as defined in . . . the National Firearms Act . . . as being a pistol." "Therefore," ATF concluded, "it was easy" to place the H&R Handy-Gun within the term "firearm" as being "any other weapon" capable of being concealed on the person. ATF used this interpretation to classify all smooth bore pistols as "any other weapon" under two different rulings, each dated August 6, 1934. Ruling S.T. 772 applies to "a so-called shotgun with a pistol grip, which fires a shot shell," and Ruling S.T. 779 to a firearm that is "a single shot, single trigger, and single hammer gun with a pistol grip, and is chambered for shot loads." The test, S.T. 779 states, "is not the length of the barrel, but whether the weapon is capable of being concealed upon the person."

Because the $200 transfer tax vastly exceeded their value as firearms, no smooth bore pistol that was manufactured in 1934 was ever regularly, commercially manufactured again. Recognizing that some of these firearms have "legitimate uses," Congress reduced the $200 tax to $1 in 1938 for Marble's Game Getter Gun. The Congress declared: "The weapon to which the legislation refers may be utilized either as a shotgun or as a rifle and has legitimate uses." ATF administratively removed the 18-inch barrel variation from the NFA in 1939 because, "after reconsideration," it was not deemed concealable on the person.

In 1945, the Congress extended the $1 tax reduction to a single-shot smooth bore pistol with a barrel at least 12 inches in length. This reduction applied to the .410 and 28 gauge H&R Handy-Gun, .410 Stevens, and .410 Crescent Certified Shotgun, among others. Again Congress spoke definitively, and determined that these firearms "are particularly useful on farms and elsewhere for extermination of vermin and predatory animals, and in hunting and trapping activities where quick firing at close range is essential." The prohibitively high manufacturer, dealer, and transfer taxes, Congress found, work "an injustice both against those who need such low-powered, so-called small-game guns, and against those who make and deal in them."

In 1960, Congress changed the transfer tax to $5 for all NFA firearms classified as "any other weapon" (which included all smooth bore pistols), recognizing that they were mainly of interest to collectors and not likely to be used as weapons.

Under the Gun Control Act of 1968, Congress provided that ATF could administratively remove any firearm (except a machine gun or destructive device, such as a land mine or hand grenade) from the NFA if it determined that the firearm is primarily a collector's item and is not likely to be used as a weapon. Since 1968, it appears that ATF may have removed 50,000 to 100,000, or more, firearms from the NFA as collectors' items; and that the vast majority of these firearms were shoulder-stocked pistols of the Mauser and Luger variety. Fewer than 10,000 smooth bore pistols manufactured in or before 1934 are estimated to have survived until year 2000, out of an original production of less than 100,000 (see table). While Marble's Game Getter Gun is not a smooth bore pistol, it is included in the table because of its historical relevance.

Modern rifled-barrel pistols that are designed to fire

Estimated Total Production of Smooth Bore Pistols and Marble's Game Getter Gun Originally Commercially Manufactured in the United States in or Before 1934 by Years of Production, and the Estimated Number That Have Survived Until Year 2000, Still Under Purview of the National Firearms Act of 1934, as Amended

Name or type of firearm and years of manufacture	*Estimated original production*	*Estimated number that have survived until 2000*
Smooth bore Pistols		
.410 bore H&R Handy-Gun (1921–1934)	48,600	4,860
28 gauge H&R Handy-Gun (1921–1934)	5,400	540
.410 Crescent Certified Shotgun (1932–1934)	4,000	400
.410 Stevens "Auto Shot" and "Off Hand" pistol (1923–1934)	25,000	2,500
20 gauge Defiance Anti-Bandit Gun (1926–1927)	300	30
20 gauge Ithaca Auto & Burglar Gun, Model A (1922–1926)	2,500	250
20 gauge Ithaca Auto & Burglar Gun, Model B (1925–1934)	2,000	200
All other smooth bore pistols (circa 1867–1934)*	3,000	300
SUBTOTAL	90,800	9,080
Marble's Game Getter Gun		
.22/.44 smooth bore, Model 1908 (1908–1914)	10,000	1,000
.22/.410 smooth bore Model 1921 (1921–1942)	10,000	1,000
TOTAL	110,800	11,080

*These include the 20-gauge Remington Combination Pistol-Shotgun, .410 Victor Ejector Pistol, 20-gauge Knickerbocker Pistol, .410 or 20-gauge New Empire Auto & Burglar Gun, Marble's Game Getter .22/.44 Pistol, and others that are uncataloged and unknown at this time because of their extreme rarity (only a few, if any, may still exist). These do not include smooth bore pistols removed from the National Firearms Act of 1934, as amended, by the Bureau of Alcohol, Tobacco and Firearms (ATF) as collectors' items under the Gun Control Act of 1968.

shotgun shells are *not* subject to the NFA, that is, no federal registration with ATF or tax payment is required. The reason is that the Congress specifically exempted any pistol with a *rifled* barrel from the NFA in 1968. The pistols discussed in this research were originally manufactured with *smooth bore* barrels.

All of the smooth bore pistols and other firearms listed below are *Class III* firearms unless specifically noted. If they are not currently registered with ATF, their sale, transfer, or possession is illegal. Moreover, it is also illegal for any person to borrow or otherwise possess any NFA firearm that is registered to another person, even if the registered owner is present.

Because smooth bore pistols are not frequently bought or sold, establishing reliable values can be difficult. The values listed here are approximate, and may vary significantly according to local supply and demand. If ATF removed these rare firearms from NFA controls, as it has for 50,000 to 100,000 or more short-barreled Winchester and Marlin "trapper carbines" and various Luger, Mauser, and other shoulder-stocked pistols and other rare firearms, their values would probably increase substantially.

V.G. *Exc.*

CALIFORNIA ARMS CO.

San Jose, California, distributed circa 1926 to 1930, but manufactured by The American Machine Company in 1926–27; 2½" shotgun or tear-gas shells only; total production was probably fewer than 300. Model A has 12½" barrels and a checkered forearm; Model B has 12¼" barrels and a smooth forearm; Model C has 12" barrels and a smooth forearm.

Defiance Anti-Bandit Gun, 20 gauge, 12¼" or 12½" double barrels,
Class III, Curio .... RARE

CRESCENT FIRE ARMS CO.

Norwich, Connecticut: Knickerbocker Pistol, circa 1900s; total production unknown, nickel-plated barrels, receiver is case-hardened, right side marked AMERICAN GUN CO./NEW YORK U S A, left side marked KNICKERBOCKER, fitted with checkered pistol grip resembling that of the Model 1 and Model 2 smooth bore H&R Handy-Gun; Victor Ejector, circa 1928–30, total production unknown, left side of receiver marked Victor Ejector/ Crescent Fire Arms Co./Norwich, Conn. U.S.A., .410 on top left of receiver near breech, blued barrel marked GENUINE ARMORY STEEL, 2½" shells only; and New Empire, circa 1932, blued barrels, left side of case-colored receiver marked Crescent Fire Arms Co./Norwich, Conn. U.S.A., right side marked New Empire, probably fewer than 50 manufactured, four known specimens bear serial numbers S–1, S–13, S–18 and S–19; referred to as "Crescent Auto & Burglar Gun" in a 1932 advertisement in *Hunter Trapper Trader*.

Knickerbocker Pistol, 20 gauge, 14" double barrels,
Class III, Curio .... RARE

Victor Ejector Pistol, .410 bore, 12" single barrel,
Class III, Curio .... RARE

V.G. *Exc.*

New Empire, .410 bore or 20 gauge, 12¼" double barrels,
Class III, Curio $750 $1,100

CRESCENT-DAVIS ARMS CORP.

Norwich, Connecticut, circa 1930–32; production was probably fewer than 4,000; receiver may be blued, tiger-stripe or color case-hardened, left side marked Crescent Certified Shotgun/Crescent-Davis Arms Corp./Norwich, Conn. U.S.A.

Crescent Certified Shotgun, .410 bore, 12¼" single barrel,
Class III, Curio 650 800

Add $200 to $500 for original cardboard box.

HARRINGTON & RICHARDSON ARMS CO.

Worcester, Massachusetts, 1921–34; total production about 54,000; 8" or 12¼" .410 or 28-gauge single barrel; more than 50 variations exist; values below assume choked .410 or unchoked 28-gauge with 12¼" barrel, case-hardened receiver marked H.&R. HANDY-GUN, spur grip and plain trigger guard; early models have blued receivers and/or unchoked barrels, late models have case-hardened receivers, choked barrels and hook or no hook on triggerguard. Other values may be estimated according to scarcity in serial number table, which is a work in progress. Private-branded or trade-branded (e.g., marked ESSEX GUN WORKS or HIBBARD MODEL W. H.) variations exist; all have nickel-plated receivers and blued barrels.

Variation	*Estimated year(s) of manufacture*	*Observed serial number ranges .410 bore*	*28 gauge*
MODEL 1			
Type I	1921–22	167 to 4981	5 to 4527
Type II	1922–23	5052 to 6588	5554 to 6274
Type III	1923–24	unknown to 6817	6973 to 7067
MODEL 2			
Type I	1924–25	8276 to 14660	10539 to 29731
Type II	1925–27	15159 to 38761	none observed
Type III	1927–30	39060 to 47528	44228 to 44247
MODEL 3			
Type I	1931	47642 to 48218	unknown to 48566
Type II	1932–33	48819 to 51655	none observed
Type III	1933–34	51920 to 53691	none observed

H&R Handy-Gun, .410 bore, 12¼" choked single barrel,
Class III, Curio 350 500

H&R Handy-Gun, 28 gauge, 12¼" unchoked single barrel,
Class III, Curio 500 800

Rare variations command premiums: 8" barrel, 25% to 50%; 18" barrel, (Model 3, Type III only) 200% to 400%; unchoked .410, 20% to 50%; 28 gauge or Model 3 (only) with factory-equipped original detachable shoulder stock, 150% or more; holster, $75–$200; serial matching box, $150–$400; early boxes are extremely rare.

ITHACA GUN CO.

Ithaca, New York, 1922–34; Model A (spur on grip), 2 1/2" shells only, about 2,500 manufactured, 1922–26; Model B (no spur), 2" shells, about 2,000 manufactured; variations exist; values below assume 20-gauge, 10" double barrels.

	V.G.	Exc.
Auto & Burglar Gun, Model A, *Class III, Curio*	$1,110	$1,500
Auto & Burglar Gun, Model B, *Class III, Curio*	700	1,000

Only 11 special order or nonstandard (.410 bore, 28 gauge, and 16 gauge, with barrels from 10" to 26" in length) Auto & Burglar Guns have been documented. All are extremely rare, and command premiums of 100% or more; professional authentication is highly recommended. Original holsters (marked AUTO AND BURGLAR GUN/MADE BY/ITHACA GUN CO./ITHACA, N.Y.) are rare and worth $300–$500.

J. STEVENS ARMS CO.

Chicopee Falls, Massachusetts, Off-Hand from 1923–29, exact total production unknown, but probably about 23,000; Auto-Shot from 1929–34, about 2,000 manufactured.

	V.G.	Exc.
Off-Hand Shot Gun No. 35, .410 bore, 8" or 12 1/4" single barrel, *Class III, Curio*	300	500
Auto-Shot No. 35, .410 bore, 8" or 12 1/4" single barrel, *Class III, Curio*	350	600

MARBLE ARMS & MFG. CO.

Gladstone, Michigan, successor in 1911 to Marble Safety Axe Co. First model from 1908–14, second model from 1921–42 (total production was about 10,000 for each model). The 18" barrel variations are removed from the NFA only if an original shoulder stock is attached. In 1961, ATF ruled that if the shoulder stock is removed from any Game Getter, regardless of its barrel length, it becomes "a firearm made from a shotgun" requiring registration as a short-barreled shotgun with a $200 transfer tax rate.

	V.G.	Exc.
Marble's Game Getter Gun, Model 1908		
12" or 15" barrels, with shoulder stock attached, *Class III, Curio*	900	1,500
18" barrels, with shoulder stock attached, *Curio, Removed from NFA*	$1,000	$1,800
Marble's Game Getter Gun, Model 1921		
12" or 15" barrels, with shoulder stock attached, *Class III, Curio*	750	950
18" barrels, with shoulder stock attached, *Curio, Removed from NFA*	1,000	1,200

Boxed guns with accessories, nonstandard calibers (.25–20, .32–20, etc.) command premiums of 50% to 200% or more; add $75–$150 for original shoulder holster. Model 1908 new-in-box Game Getters command substantial prices, ranging from $2,000 up. In 1999, a new Model 1908 wooden box alone sold at auction for $2,700. In both the Model 1908 and Model 1921, 18" barrels are scarce.

	V.G.	Exc.
Marble's Game Getter Pistol, Model 1908 9" barrels, .22/.44 smooth bore, *Class III, Curio*		RARE

In approximately 1913, Marble manufactured an extremely small number of pistols with barrels ranging from 9" to 18" as experimental and special-order guns, using the Model 1908 receiver. These firearms are currently defined as "any other weapon" and must be registered; the transfer tax is $5. These firearms may be reliably identified by the lack of an inlet in the receiver to attach a shoulder stock. One known specimen bears serial number 3837.

REMINGTON ARMS CO.

Ilion, New York, c. 1867–75; 20 gauge, singleshot with rolling block action; may be used as a pistol or shotgun; usually encountered with a detachable shoulder stock and classified as a "short-barreled shotgun" by ATF ($200 transfer tax) in that configuration. Whether it qualifies for the $5 transfer tax if unaccompanied by a shoulder stock is unclear. It cannot be classified as a *Curio* because it is an *Antique* firearm manufactured before 1899; it is also a *Class III* NFA firearm because it fires fixed (cartridge) ammunition that is currently available in ordinary commerce.

	V.G.	Exc.
Remington Combination Pistol-Shotgun, 11" single barrel, *Class III*		RARE

Note: The author wishes to thank Mr. Larson for his contribution of the text in this section. For more information on smooth bore pistols, Mr. Larson may be contacted at P.O. Box 5497, Takoma Park MD 20913; telephone (301) 270-3450; e-mail: larsone@erols.com

Using This Price Guide

Given the difficulty of establishing precise values, the enclosed figures provide a general indication of value. That is to say, until the object is bought or sold, the price indicated is an estimate. However, this estimate is based on the facts that the appraiser is active in the field, has professional standards to maintain, and keeps up-to-date with changes in his field. Since we list three figures, one can determine intermediates relatively easily by noting the condition range priced. However, the most exact appraisal will come when the object is actually sold.

Factors that are not detailed in the present guide are the precise impact of such variables as engraving, any particular or unusual history (like a famous owner), out-of-the-ordinary condition, and what may be the spirited response of a client who might go overboard for a particular variation or for other sometimes hard-to-understand motivations.

Another arms-collecting legend from a distinguished family of antiquarians, Norm Flayderman holds a giant shoulder-stocked English double-action revolver. Norm's specialty of arms and militaria is highlighted by his renowned Flayderman's Guide, *a run of well over 100 highly detailed sales catalogues, and a career including big-game hunting, bird shooting, and travels worldwide.*

For assistance in determining more precise figures, the author recommends consulting other price guides, particularly *Flayderman's Guide to Antique American Firearms and Their Values* and Steven Fjestad's *Blue Book of Gun Values*. And if necessary, one can also contact any of the listed dealers and auction houses for a specific appraisal, at a pre-quoted fee. An informal appraised valuation is the usual practice of auction houses, but formal ones (for insurance, estate purposes, etc.) are generally done on a fee basis.

Of course, some arms will change hands at a less-than-appraised figure: Dealers buying are not about to pay full retail. (Although some dealers pride themselves on "paying more than guns are worth." That was, in fact, the motto of Herb Glass: "Glass pays more than guns are worth!") Also, some dealers have collector clients who, in order to obtain the best, realize that as difficult as it is to get fine guns today, they had best pay a premium and hope time will catch up to that value, or they might miss some great items.

GENERAL GUIDELINES TO DETERMINING VALUE

In considering antique firearms, when in condition of excellent to new or "mint," a range of from 50 percent to 200 percent, sometimes more and sometimes less, can be added to the given figure, determined by scarcity, demand, history, maker, and possibly other factors. To estimate value for arms in good condition, approximately 25 to 35 percent could be deducted from the very good listing. For poor condition, the deduction might be 50 percent, and possibly more. Poor-condition guns are often termed "wall hangers" in the collecting field. An exception can be "dug-up" firearms, such as a Dragoon or Walker Colt, or even a Paterson, in which the item might have a surprising worth in spite of the badly rusted condition. An intriguing dug-up Belt Model Paterson Colt is a featured display item at the Woolaroc Museum, Bartlesville, Oklahoma, and was featured in the book *Paterson Colt Pistol Variations* as the only known example of a particular variation of the Belt Model series!

For modern firearms values, for good condition, deduct approximately 25 to 35 percent from the very good listing. For fair condition, deduct approximately 40 to 60 percent. For poor, the range may well be 60 to 80 percent. Firearms in perfect or factory-new condition could have a value ranging from 30 to 70 percent above excellent, and possibly more, again determined by factors of demand, scarcity, history, maker, and so forth.

Engraved Firearms

Estimating values in this area is often particularly difficult. Not a few flintlock and early percussion arms, and even some cartridge antique arms, as well as some modern, had engraving as a standard production feature. In that case, the figures presented herewith need no adjustments. But for specially engraved or otherwise non-production embellishments, consideration must be given to added values for the decorations. The following guidelines are general; expert counsel should be consulted to be more precise.

Engraving that is lacking in quality (rough or ragged scrolls, primitive and inaccurate game or other scenes, overall crudity) could add somewhere around 25 percent for moderate amounts of decoration; if about medium, approximately 40 to 80 percent; if maximum decoration, 100 to 200 percent.

When the quality is evidently fine and factory original, the price increase range may be from 50 to 200 percent, and sometimes more, for moderate amounts; add 200 to 300 percent for medium; and perhaps as much as 300 percent, or more, for maximum coverage.

For engraving added at a later date, and not of the period, the value may actually be less. As a specific example, the Henry Rifle has been decorated by 20th-century craftsmen to the extent that perhaps half of the antique Henrys have non-original decoration! No matter how fancy this 20th-century work may be, it is detrimental to the actual value of the item.

The ultimate decoration is gold inlaying, usually accompanied by rather fine and rich engraving. The presence of such desirable decor could well increase the value of a piece 400 to 500 percent, and quite likely even more. Here, particularly, the services of a specialist are in order.

Generally less desirable (sometimes by far) than gold inlaying is gold damascening, in which the gold was added by cross-hatching the metal (generally steel) and hammering the gold into position, and sometimes engraving the precious metal once attached. These patterns can range from relatively plain on up to profuse, as seen on rare examples of Colt Model 1851 Navy revolvers, usually decorated in India. The increase in value may be as little as 25 to 50 percent, and could be as much as 200 percent, and perhaps more. Condition is especially important with such arms, since they may be rather unsightly if gold is missing and the patina is poor.

Deluxe Stock Work

The collector needs to determine whether or not the stock embellishments are standard production fare, or special. As with engraving, generalizing here is difficult: consulting an expert is generally wise. Quality of craftsmanship is also a crucial determining factor.

For relief carving, such as scrollwork, leaves, wildlife motifs, and so forth, add approximately 25 percent for minimal amounts, 25 to 50 percent for moderate, and 50 to 200 percent for profuse carvings.

For inlaying, most desirable is silver and gold wire, or plaques, sometimes with wildlife or other motifs. These too are hard to determine, but as a general rule may add 35 percent for minimal inlays, 35 to 60 percent for moderate, and 60 percent on up for profuse or particularly distinguished motifs.

As with other special decorations, checkering can add to value. Crude work can be detrimental, although one should be aware of the difference between "crude" and "folk art," as in the case of Kentucky Rifles. As a general rule, checkering (unless a standard feature) can add 10 percent on up to about 30 percent.

Ivory or mother-of-pearl grips may add 15 percent to 50 percent in value, and if carved, the amount might increase by as much as 100 percent, perhaps even more. However, quality again will be crucially important. In some cases exotic wood, such as ebony, will spiral value upward. Again, consult an expert!

Specially Marked Firearms

Consideration needs to be given to firearms with unusual markings, such as Wells Fargo & Co. or other express, mining, or other special inscriptions, police or law enforcement legends, a variety of historical inscriptions, presentation dedications, and so forth. As with engraved arms, it is impossible to generalize accurately, and sometimes the marking accounts for most of the value. As with engraving, consult a professional for specifics. In these cases condition will not be that much greater a factor in value, and often pieces are only good to very good—after all, the wear and tear shows the piece actually was used.

Express agency markings add 25 to 50 percent, perhaps more.

Police and other law enforcement markings add 25 to 50 percent, again, perhaps more.

Military markings add 25 to 75 percent; some countries, like Great Britain or Germany, will be more desirable than others.

Inscriptions or other markings of organizations or firms with romantic and adventurous associations, particularly British colonial sites, like India or Africa, could add 25 to 75 percent, and sometimes more.

Presentation inscriptions are a special category, and will often depend on the historical significance reflected in the inscription. The range here can be substantial, from an added 25 percent on up. Condition, again, may not be a critical factor, since use by the original owner can be part of the value.

Factory Mistakes in Markings

While by no means commanding astronomical prices, factory errors are intriguing to many collectors. These are not, however, comparable to upside-down airplanes on postage stamps! The increase in value may well be from 25 percent up to 100 percent, and perhaps more in very rare instances.

Special Features

When factories have modified production arms in special ways, there may be a premium for these features. The most obvious example is the Colt Buntline Special, in which the original models numbered not more than about thirty! These prizes are particularly in demand, especially since some specimens had barrels cut down (claimed for the piece traditionally ascribed as given to Bat Masterson) or were reportedly lost (the gun some say belonged to Wyatt Earp was supposedly lost by him in Alaska, dropped overboard from a river vessel).

Special barrel lengths might add from 20 to 40 percent, and possibly more. Special sights add 10 to 20 percent; special finishes, 10 to 30 percent (particularly attractive, gold or silver plating, but also extreme rarities like copper plating). Select woods, such as in Winchester, Marlin, Remington, Sharps, and Colt longarms, add from 15 to 35 percent.

With J. S. White (center), a renowned early dealer in antique firearms, and the author's brother Jack (left), at White's Highland Park, Illinois, home and sales room; c. 1953. Hard-earned newspaper route money financed the Wilson brothers' gun collection: with a total of about seventy-five Colts, Winchesters, Remingtons, S & Ws, derringers, Sharps, Civil War carbines, and other arms by the time Jack was eighteen, and the author sixteen (c. 1955).

A

	Fair	V. Good	Excellent

A & R SALES

South El Monte, Calif. Current.

HANDGUN, SELF-LOADING

	Fair	V. Good	Excellent
Government, .45 ACP, Lightweight, Patterned After Colt Govt. Model, *Modern*	$150	$200	$350

RIFLE, SELF-LOADING

	Fair	V. Good	Excellent
Mark IV Sporter, .308 Win., Clip Fed, Version of M-14, Adjustable Sights, *Modern*	155	225	400

ABBEY, GEORGE T.

Chicago, Ill., 1858–1875.

RIFLE, PERCUSSION

	Fair	V. Good	Excellent
.44, Double Barrel, Over-Under, Brass Furniture, *Antique*	350	700	1350
.44, Octagon Barrel, Brass Furniture, *Antique*	225	400	750

ABBEY, J.F. & CO.

Chicago, Ill., 1858–1875. Also made by Abbey & Foster.

RIFLE, PERCUSSION

	Fair	V. Good	Excellent
Various Calibers, *Antique*	150	300	600

SHOTGUN, PERCUSSION

	Fair	V. Good	Excellent
Various Gauges, *Antique*	200	350	650

ABILENNE

See Mossberg.

ACHA

Domingo Acha y Cia., Ermua, Spain, 1927–1937.

HANDGUN, SELF-LOADING

	Fair	V. Good	Excellent
Ruby M1916, 7.65mm, Clip Fed, *Curio*	100	150	200

ACME

Made by Hopkins & Allen, sold by Merwin & Hulbert, c. 1880.

HANDGUN, REVOLVER

	Fair	V. Good	Excellent
.22 Short R.F., 7 Shot, Spur Trigger, Solid Frame, Single Action, *Antique*	$100	$150	$225
.32 Short R.F., 5 Shot, Spur Trigger, Solid Frame, Single Action, *Antique*	100	150	250

ACME ARMS

Sold by J. Stevens Arms Co. and Cornwall Hardware Co., c. 1880.

HANDGUN, REVOLVER

	Fair	V. Good	Excellent
.22 Short R.F., 7 Shot, Spur Trigger, Solid Frame, Single Action, *Antique*	150	200	300
.32 Short R.F., 5 Shot, Spur Trigger, Solid Frame, Single Action, *Antique*	175	225	300

SHOTGUN, DOUBLE BARREL, SIDE-BY-SIDE

	Fair	V. Good	Excellent
12 Gauge, Damascus Barrel, *Antique*	125	175	300

ACME HAMMERLESS

Made by Hopkins & Allen for Hulbert Bros., 1893.

HANDGUN, REVOLVER

	Fair	V. Good	Excellent
.32 S & W, 5 Shot, Top Break, Hammerless, Double Action, 2½" Barrel, *Antique*	75	125	200
.38 S & W, 5 Shot, Top Break, Hammerless, Double Action, 3" Barrel, *Antique*	75	125	200

ACRA

Tradename used by Reinhard Fajen of Warsaw, Mo., c. 1970.

RIFLE, BOLT ACTION

	Fair	V. Good	Excellent
M18, Various Calibers, Santa Barbara Barreled Action, Mannlicher Checkered Stock, *Modern*	100	200	300
RA, Various Calibers, Santa Barbara Barreled Action, Checkered Stock, *Modern*	100	150	250
S24, Various Calibers, Santa Barbara Barreled Action, Fancy Checkering, *Modern*	100	200	250

ACTION
Modesto Santos; Eibar, Spain.

HANDGUN, SELF-LOADING

	Fair	V. Good	Excellent
#2, 7.65mm, Clip Fed, *Curio*	$50	$125	$250
Model 1920, .25 ACP, Clip Fed, *Curio*	35	75	150

ADAMS
Made by Deane, Adams, & Deane, London, England. British revolvers, particularly the percussion, but also early cartridge, are part of the warp and woof of the British Empire—on which "the sun never set." One of the most colorful periods in world history, the exquisite quality and beauty of these fine British arms symbolize the Empire, in a different way than fine British double rifles (especially those made for big game shooting in Africa and India), or best quality British shotguns (usually termed "game guns"). British (particularly English) gunmakers produced arms of such quality and distinction that even today, they are often considered the standard by which fine arms are measured. Many of these arms bore hand engraving as a customary feature of their craftsmanship. British percussion and early cartridge revolvers remain an area of collecting in which a lot of quality, history, mechanics and romance can be purchased, for a reasonable cost. Watch for these guns to move upward in price, at an increasing rate. Even Lt. Col. George Armstrong Custer had a keen affection for British revolvers, and had two bulldog types in his hands as he fell at the Little Big Horn. Some Confederate troops, particularly the cavalry, and several officers, also respected and used British revolvers.

HANDGUN, PERCUSSION

	Fair	V. Good	Excellent
12.4mm Beaumont-Adams, Revolver, Double Action, 7½" Barrel, *Antique*	500	1500	2250
12.4mm Beaumont-Adams, Revolver, Double Action, 7½" Barrel, *Antique*	500	1500	2250
12.4mm M1851, Revolver, Double Action, 7½" Barrel, *Antique*	400	1200	2000
12.4mm M1851, Revolver, Double Action, 7½" Barrel, Cased with Accessories, *Antique*	1000	2200	3250
8.1mm Pocket, Revolver, Double Action, 4½" Barrel, *Antique*	500	1000	2250
8.1mm, Revolver, Double Action, 4½" Barrel, Cased with Accessories, *Antique*	500	1500	2750

ADAMS, JOSEPH
Birmingham, England, 1767–1813.

RIFLE, FLINTLOCK

	Fair	V. Good	Excellent
.65 Officers Model Brown Bess, Musket, Military, *Antique*	500	1750	2750

ADAMY GEBRUDER
Suhl, Germany, 1921–1939.

SHOTGUN, DOUBLE BARREL, OVER-UNDER

	Fair	V. Good	Excellent
12 and 16 Ga., Automatic Ejector, Double Trigger, Engraved, Cased, *Curio*	$500	$1000	$1750

ADIRONDACK ARMS CO.
Plattsburg, N.Y., 1870–1874. Purchased by Winchester 1874.

RIFLE, LEVER ACTION

	Fair	V. Good	Excellent
Robinson 1875 Patent, First Model, Various Rimfires, Octagon Barrel, Open Rear Sight, *Antique*	850	1750	3000
Robinson Patent, Second Model, Various Calibers, Octagon Barrel, *Antique*	850	1750	3000

ADLER
Engelbrecht & Wolff; Zella St. Blasii, Germany, 1905–1906.

HANDGUN, SELF-LOADING

	Fair	V. Good	Excellent
7.25 Adler, Clip Fed, *Curio*	900	2250	3500

AERTS, JAN
Maastricht, Holland, c. 1650.

HANDGUN, FLINTLOCK

	Fair	V. Good	Excellent
Ornate Pair, Very Long Ebony Full Stock, Silver Inlay, High Quality, *Antique*			Rare

AETNA
Made by Harrington & Richardson, c. 1870–1890.

HANDGUN, REVOLVER

	Fair	V. Good	Excellent
.22 Short R.F., 7 Shot, Spur Trigger, Solid Frame, Single Action, *Antique*	100	200	300
Aetna 2½, .32 Short R.F., 5 Shot, Spur Trigger, Solid Frame, Single Action, *Antique*	125	225	325
Aetna 2, .32 Short R.F., 5 Shot, Spur Trigger, Solid Frame, Single Action, *Antique*	125	225	325

AETNA ARMS CO.
New York City, c. 1880.

HANDGUN, REVOLVER

	Fair	V. Good	Excellent
.22 Short R.F., 7 Shot, Spur Trigger, Tip-Up Barrel, *Antique*	100	225	375
.32 Short R.F., 5 Shot, Spur Trigger, Tip-Up Barrel, *Antique*	125	250	400

AFFERBACH, WILLIAM
Philadelphia, Pa., 1860–1866.

HANDGUN, PERCUSSION

	Fair	V. Good	Excellent
.41 Derringer, Full Stock, *Antique*	$300	$800	$1250

AGAWAM ARMS
Agawam, Mass., c. 1970.

RIFLE, SINGLESHOT

	Fair	V. Good	Excellent
Model M-68, .22 L.R.R.F., Lever Action, Open Sights, *Modern*	20	35	65
Model M-68M, .22 W.M.R., Lever Action, Open Sights, *Modern*	25	45	75

AJAX ARMY
Maker Unknown, sold by E. C. Meacham Co., c. 1880.

HANDGUN, REVOLVER

	Fair	V. Good	Excellent
.44 R.F., 5 Shot, 7" Barrel, Spur Trigger, Solid Frame, Single Action, *Antique*	150	350	600

AKRILL, E.
Probably St. Etienne, France, c. 1810.

RIFLE, FLINTLOCK

	Fair	V. Good	Excellent
.69, Smooth bore, Octagon Barrel, Damascus Barrel, Breech Loader, Plain, *Antique*	400	1000	2500

ALAMO
Tradename used by Stoeger Arms, c. 1958.

HANDGUN, REVOLVER

	Fair	V. Good	Excellent
Alamo, .22 L.R.R.F., Double Action, Ribbed Barrel, *Modern*	40	75	125

ALASKA
Made by Hood Firearms, sold by E. C. Meacham Co., 1873–1882.

HANDGUN, REVOLVER

	Fair	V. Good	Excellent
.22 Short R.F., 7 Shot, Spur Trigger, Solid Frame, Single Action, *Antique*	50	125	175

ALASKAN
Skinner's Sportsman's Supply, Juneau, Alaska, c. 1970.

RIFLE, BOLT ACTION

	Fair	V. Good	Excellent
Carbine, Various Calibers, Checkered Stock, Sling Swivels, *Modern*	100	225	300
Magnum, Various Calibers, Checkered Stock, Recoil Pad, Sling Swivels, *Modern*	125	275	350
Standard, Various Calibers, Checkered Stock, Sling Swivels, *Modern*	$100	$225	$325

ALBRECHT, ANDREW
Lancaster, Pa., 1779–1782. See Kentucky Rifles and Pistols.

ALBRIGHT, HENRY
Lancaster, Pa., 1740–1745. See Kentucky Rifles and Pistols.

ALDENDERFER, M.
Lancaster, Pa., 1763–1784. See Kentucky Rifles and Pistols.

ALERT
Made by Hood Firearms Co., c. 1874.

HANDGUN, REVOLVER

	Fair	V. Good	Excellent
.22 Short R.F., 7 Shot, Spur Trigger, Solid Frame, Single Action, *Antique*	75	150	200

ALEXIA
Made by Hopkins & Allen, c. 1880.

HANDGUN, REVOLVER

	Fair	V. Good	Excellent
.22 Short R.F., 7 Shot, Spur Trigger, Solid Frame, Single Action, *Antique*	75	125	175
.32 Short R.F., 5 Shot, Spur Trigger, Solid Frame, Single Action, *Antique*	75	125	175
.38 Short R.F., 5 Shot, Spur Trigger, Solid Frame, Single Action, *Antique*	75	150	200
.41 Short R.F., 5 Shot, Spur Trigger, Solid Frame, Single Action, *Antique*	75	175	250

ALEXIS
Made by Hood Firearms Co., sold by Turner & Ross Co., Boston, Mass.

HANDGUN, REVOLVER

	Fair	V. Good	Excellent
.22 Short R.F., 7 Shot, Spur Trigger, Solid Frame, Single Action, *Antique*	65	100	175

ALFA
Adolf Frank, Hamburg, Germany, c. 1900.

HANDGUN, MANUAL REPEATER

	Fair	V. Good	Excellent
"Reform" Type, .230 C.F., Four-barreled Repeater, Engraved, *Curio*	125	225	400

HANDGUN, SELF-LOADING

	Fair	V. Good	Excellent
Pocket, 6.35mm, Clip Fed, Blue, *Curio*	50	100	150

	Fair	V. Good	Excellent
RIFLE, PERCUSSION			
Back-lock, Various Calibers, Carved, Inlaid Stock, Imitation Damascus Barrel, *Antique*	$75	$125	$250
Back-lock, Various Calibers, Imitation Damascus Barrel, *Antique*	50	100	175
SHOTGUN, PERCUSSION			
Double Barrel, Various Gauges, Back-lock, Double Triggers, Damascus Barrels, *Antique*	50	125	225
Double Barrel, Various Gauges, Back-lock, Double Triggers, Damascus Barrels, Carved Stock, Engraved, *Antique*	75	200	300
SHOTGUN, DOUBLE BARREL, SIDE-BY-SIDE			
Greener Boxlock, Various Gauges, Checkered Stock, Double Triggers, *Curio*	75	200	300
Greener Boxlock, Various Gauges, Checkered Stock, Double Triggers, Engraved, *Curio*	100	200	350
SHOTGUN, SINGLESHOT			
410 add 50%; 28 gauge, 30%; 20 gauge, 15%			
Nuss Underlever, Various Gauges, Tip-Down Barrel, No Forestock, *Curio*	25	50	75
Roux Underlever, Various Gauges, Tip-Down Barrel, No Forestock, *Curio*	25	50	75
Sidebutton, Various Gauges, Tip-Down Barrel, No Forestock, *Curio*	25	50	75

ALFA

Armero Especialistas Reunidas, Eibar, Spain, c. 1920.

	Fair	V. Good	Excellent
HANDGUN, REVOLVER			
Colt Police Positive Type, .38, Double Action, Blue, *Curio*	50	100	150
S. & W. #2 Type, *Curio*	65	125	175
S. & W. M & P Type, .38, Double Action, 6 Shot, Blue, *Curio*	50	100	150

ALKARTASUNA

Spain. Made by Alkartasuna Fabrica De Armas, 1910–1922.

	Fair	V. Good	Excellent
HANDGUN, SELF-LOADING			
Alkar 1924, 6.35mm, Cartridge Counter, Grips, Clip Fed, *Curio*	100	225	350
Pocket, 7.65mm, Clip Fed, Long Grip, *Curio*	65	125	200
Pocket, 7.65mm, Clip Fed, Short Grip, *Curio*	65	125	200
Vest Pocket, 6.35mm, Clip Fed, *Modern*	50	95	175
Vest Pocket, 6.35mm, Clip Fed, Cartridge Counter, *Modern*	50	125	200

ALL RIGHT FIREARMS CO.

Lawrence, Mass., c. 1876.

	Fair	V. Good	Excellent
HANDGUN, REVOLVER			
Little All Right Palm Pistol, .22 Short R.F., Squeeze Trigger, 5 Shot, *Antique*	$300	$600	$1000

ALLEGHENY WORKS

Allegheny, Pa., 1836–1875. See Kentucky Rifles and Pistols.

ALLEN

Made by Hopkins & Allen, c. 1880.

	Fair	V. Good	Excellent
HANDGUN, REVOLVER			
.22 Short R.F., 7 Shot, Spur Trigger, Solid Frame, Single Action, *Antique*	50	125	200

ALLEN

Tradename used by McKeown's Guns of Pekin, Ill., c. 1970.

	Fair	V. Good	Excellent
SHOTGUN, DOUBLE BARREL, OVER-UNDER			
MCK 68, 12 Ga., Vent Rib, Double Triggers, Plain, *Modern*	75	175	275
Olympic 68, 12 Ga., Vent Rib, Single Selective Trigger, Automatic Ejectors, Checkered Stock, Engraved, *Modern*	100	250	425
S201 Deluxe, Various Gauges, Vent Rib, Single Trigger, Automatic Ejectors, Checkered Stock, Engraved, *Modern*	125	300	450
S201, Various Gauges, Vent Rib, Double Triggers, Checkered Stock, Light Engraving, *Modern*	100	225	375

ALLEN & THURBER

Grafton, Mass., 1837–1842; Norwich, Conn., 1842–1847. One of the most distinguished names in 19th-century American gunmaking, the products of Ethan Allen, and the several other firms with the Allen connection, continue slowly but surely to develop a dedicated following, but have yet to reach their deserved potential as collectors' items. At least for awhile, Ethan Allen rivaled Samuel Colt as a prominent gunmaker, creating a variety of guns, of solid design and quality, with production based on the American system of manufacture. Allen's history is complex, and the number of companies that included his name is profuse: E. Allen (Grafton, 1831–37) Allen & Thurber (Grafton, 1837–42; Norwich, 1842–47; Worcester, Massachusetts, 1847–54) Allen Thurber & Co. (Worcester, 1854–56) Allen & Wheelock (Worcester, 1856–65) E. Allen & Company (Worcester, 1865–71). First of Allen's firearms was a cane gun (1836); next was an underhammer pocket rifle; followed by a tube hammer pocket pistol; next was the pepperbox, the product that, more than any other, made his reputation. In time brother-in-law Charles Thurber joined as the company expanded to meet increasing demands for pepperboxes and single-shot pistols, sporting and target rifles and shotguns, and even whaling guns. In 1871 Allen died, and the company carried on as Forehand & Wadsworth. The intriguing generic name, and the

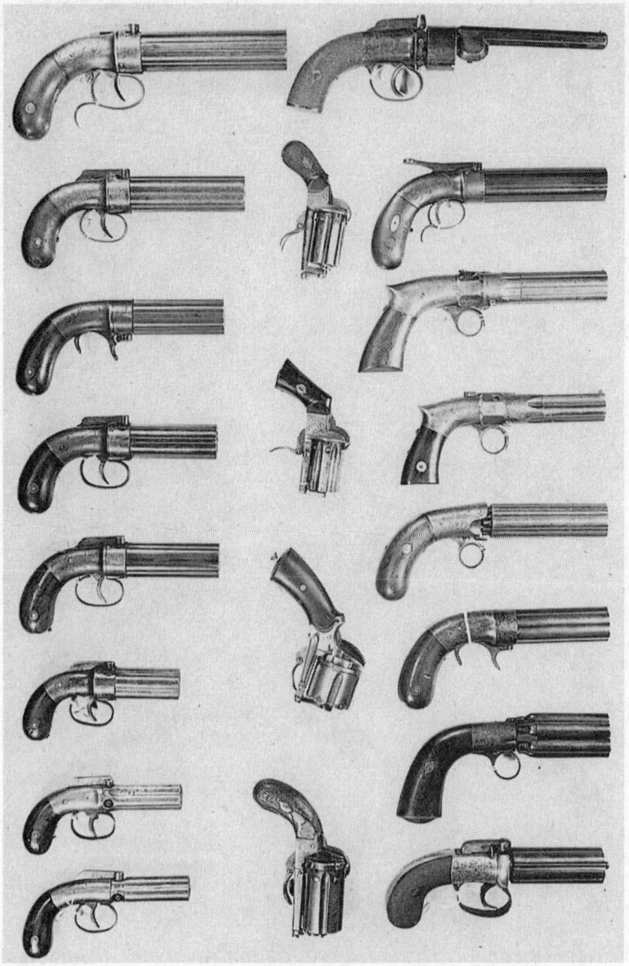

Pepperbox pistols, from top left, *Allen & Thurber Dragoon, .34 caliber, 6-shot; Allen & Wheelock 6-shot; Bacon & Co., Norwich, Ct., 6-shot underhammer; Manhattan 6-shot; Allen & Thurber, 6-shot; Manhattan 5-shot; Allen's patent, 4-shot, without nipple shield; Manhattan 3-barrel. From top* right, *English transition "Pepperbox revolver" marked A. Maloch Stirling, double-action bar hammer, by Stocking & Co., 6-shot, .28 caliber, with long thumb cocking piece and single action; Robbins & Lawrence, larger size, 4½" barrel, .30 caliber, with ringed trigger; another Robbins & Lawrence, 5-shot, .28 caliber; Blunt & Syms; Bacon & Co., underhammer; French 6-shot with individually damascened barrels and ring trigger, ebony grips; English pistol, 6-shot, with frame and grip strap of silver, and flared nipple shield. From top* center, *two French Apache pinfires; an Apache in centerfire; and another pinfire Apache.*

multi-shot nature, with a rather forbidding six charges pointed at one's adversary, meant that the pepperbox was destined to become symbolic of adventure in the Old West. The field of pepperbox arms is worthy of a solid historical treatment, and at present only rather introductory texts exist. Allen pepperboxes were the first American double-action revolving production firearms; their mechanisms were covered by two patents. First of these was that of November 11, 1837, covering the double-action system of cocking and firing by squeezing the trigger. The second patent was issued April 16, 1845, covering a design in which the revolver was cocked and fired by the trigger manually. The latter patent also simplified the mechanism of the 1837 patent. Determining the difference between an Allen pepperbox made with the 1837 patent features, or those of 1845, is the way to identify these guns: the former was built with a straight-style mainspring of one piece, within a clip at the grip frame's base. To adjust the spring's tension a screw was located on the lower front of the gripstrap. Post-1845 era guns feature a U-shaped mainspring, in which the adjustment screw appears in the center of the gripstrap at the front. The Allen and companies pepperbox line breaks down into categories based initially on the site of manufacture: Grafton, Norwich, Worcester. Further subdivision is based on size: pocket (Grafton only), medium or standard, and the rather hefty dragoon. Further classification is based on features determined by the firm's master patents, whether in 1837 (Grafton and Norwich) or 1845 (Norwich and Worcester). The pocket pepperbox calibers were .28, the medium or standard were .31, and the dragoon was .36. Since pepperboxes were manufactured in batch groupings, serial numbers were not sequential; numbers are therefore low, and of a few digits only. Still another classification by collectors is based on grip profiles: the quick drop (sharp, near right angle to frame; on Grafton and Norwich pistols of early date), slow drop (sharp angle to frame, slightly more curved than quick drop), dog leg grip, semi-dog leg grip (long shape; accompanied by German silver grip escutcheons), and late-rounded grip (majority of Worcester pistols). A standard feature was the open, relatively primitive scroll style on frames, accompanied customarily with etched scrollwork on the nipple shields (pioneer example of acid-etched embellishments on American firearms). Inscribed or cased dragoon pepperboxes are quite rare, and will command a premium. Many of the arms of Ethan Allen and the Allen companies—in addition to pepperboxes—still have a way to go to reach their deserved potential on the marketplace.

	Fair	*V. Good*	*Excellent*
HANDGUN, PERCUSSION			
.28 (Grafton) Pepperbox, 6 Shot, 3" Barrel, *Antique*	$900	$1750	$2000
.28 (Norwich) Pepperbox, 6 Shot, Bar Hammer, 3" Barrel, *Antique*	300	600	800
.28 (Norwich) Pepperbox, 6 Shot, Hammerless, 3" Barrel, *Antique*	500	1250	1750
.28, Singleshot, Bar Hammer, Various Barrel Lengths, Half-Octagon Barrel, *Antique*	300	600	980
.31 (Grafton) Pepperbox, 6 Shot, 3" Barrel, *Antique*	500	1000	1500
.31 (Norwich) Pepperbox, 6 Shot, Bar Hammer, 3" Barrel, *Antique*	150	295	650
.31 (Norwich) Pepperbox, 6 Shot, Hammerless, 3" Barrel, *Antique*	300	600	900
.31, "In-Line" Singleshot, Center Hammer, Various Barrel Lengths, Half-Octagon Barrel, *Antique*	250	450	800
.31, Singleshot, Tube Hammer, Various Barrel Lengths, Half-Octagon Barrel, *Antique*	500	1000	1500
.31, Singleshot, Under Hammer, Various Barrel Lengths, Half-Octagon Barrel, *Antique*	400	750	950

	Fair	V. Good	Excellent
.31, Singleshot, Under Hammer, Various Barrel Lengths, Saw-Handle Grip, Half-Octagon Barrel, *Antique*	$400	$800	$1200
.34, Singleshot, Side Hammer, Various Barrel Lengths, Half-Octagon Barrel, *Antique*	300	600	900
.36 (Grafton) Pepperbox, 6" Barrel, *Antique*	1000	1250	1750
.36 (Norwich) Pepperbox, 6 Shot, Bar Hammer, 6" Barrel, *Antique*	700	850	1250
.36 (Norwich) Pepperbox, 6 Shot, Ring Trigger, 6" Barrel, *Antique*	1000	1250	1500
.36, Singleshot, Bar Hammer, Various Barrel Lengths, Half-Octagon Barrel, *Antique*	550	600	900
.36, Singleshot, Center Hammer, Various Barrel Lengths, Half-Octagon Barrel, *Antique*	100	150	300
.41, Singleshot, Side Hammer, Various Barrel Lengths, Half-Octagon Barrel, *Antique*	550	625	900

ALLEN & THURBER

Worcester, Mass., 1855–1856.

COMBINATION WEAPON, PERCUSSION

Over-Under, Various Calibers, Rifle and Shotgun Barrels, *Antique*	1250	1750	2250

HANDGUN, PERCUSSION

.28, Pepperbox, Bar Hammer, Various Barrel Lengths, 5 Shot, *Antique*	300	450	600
.31, Pepperbox, Bar Hammer, 5 Shot, Various Barrel Lengths, *Antique*	350	400	550
.31, Pepperbox, Ring Hammerless, 6 Shot, *Antique*	750	1000	1500
.31, Pepperbox, Thumb Hammer, 5 Shot, Various Barrel Lengths, *Antique*	750	850	1250
.34, Pepperbox, Bar Hammer, Various Barrel Lengths, 4 Shot, *Antique*	125	250	550
.36, Target Pistol, 12" Octagon Barrel, Adjustable Sights, Detachable Shoulder Stock, *Antique*	1250	2500	3500

RIFLE, PERCUSSION

.43, Singleshot, Sporting Rifle, *Antique*	200	475	725

ALLEN & WHEELOCK

Worcester, Mass., 1856–1865. Mechanically the Allen & Wheelock revolvers are fascinating since the intriguing design called for the cylinders to move back, and then move forward, in order to overlap the barrel breech with the front end of the cylinder. This allowed for a seal that prevented the easily observable (and somewhat intimidating) flash of fire escaping between cylinder and barrel on firing. In the process, the Allen & Wheelock revolvers were also more energy efficient, since the majority of the force of propulsion went out of the front of the barrel, behind the projectile. The seal of the charge on the Allen & Wheelock revolvers also helped significantly to avoid chain fires, in which the flame from a firing chamber would reflect back into adjacent chambers, and set

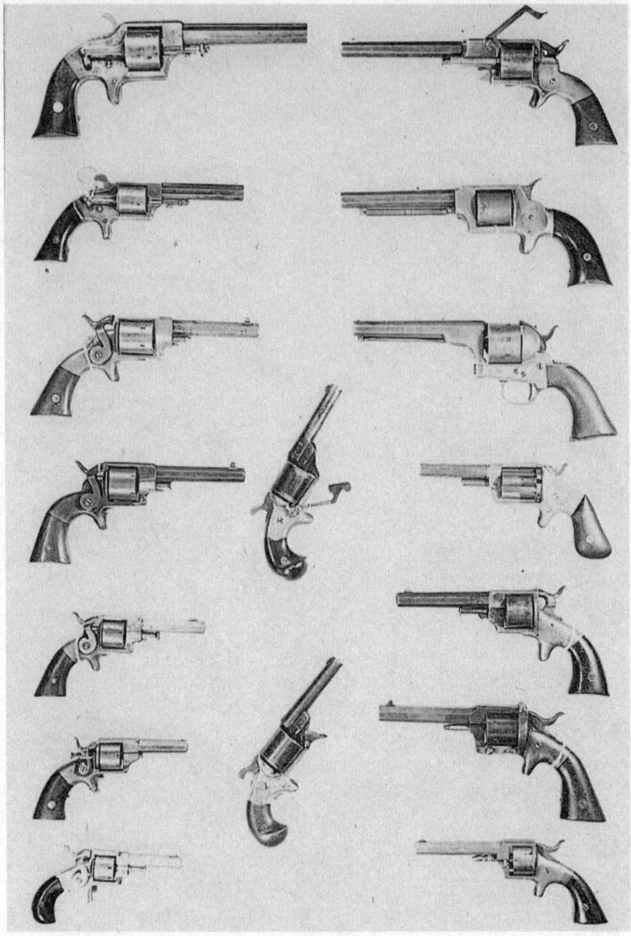

Variety of early cartridge single-action revolvers, from top left, *Plant front-loading revolver, marketed by Merwin & Bray; Eagle Arms Co. front-loading revolver, for cup-primer cartridges in .30 caliber; and two sizes of Allen & Wheelock .32 caliber sidehammer revolvers; an E. Allen & Co. .22 7-shot revolver; an Allen & Wheelock .22 7-shot revolver (both of latter have cylinder pins entering from rear); and a Forehand & Wadsworth baby-size sidehammer revolver in .22 caliber. From top* right, *an Allen & Wheelock .32 sidehammer revolver with scarce integral ejector housing on frame; J.P. Lower 6-shot revolver with 5" barrel; Moore "Seven Shooter" in .32 caliber with engraved bronze frame; Slocum sleeved cylinder revolver, .32 caliber, made by Brooklyn Arms Co.; Prescott single action in .32 caliber; Pond in .32 caliber; Pond in .22 caliber, 7-shot, with bronze frame. At lower,* center, *Moore tit-fire revolver, by National Arms Co., with hooked ejector on right side of frame; and another Moore, unusual revolver loaded from front of cylinder.*

off neighboring charges inadvertently. Having experienced chain firing, the frightening consequences, much less the loss of precious fired charges, was something to seriously consider. Still another revolving arm that had the feature of the cylinder overlapping a projection from the barrel breech was the Collier flintlock and percussion revolver.

	Fair	V. Good	Excellent
HANDGUN, PERCUSSION			
.25, Pepperbox, 4" Barrel, 5 Shot, *Antique*	$300	$475	$650
.28, Revolver, Side Hammer, Octagon Barrel, 3" Barrel, 5 Shot, *Antique*	300	500	700
.31, Revolver, Bar Hammer, Octagon Barrel, $2^1/_4$" Barrel, 5 Shot, *Antique*	125	300	450
.31, Revolver, Side Hammer, Octagon Barrel, 3" Barrel, 5 Shot, *Antique*	125	300	450
.34, Revolver, Bar Hammer, Octagon Barrel, 4" Barrel, 5 Shot, *Antique*	125	300	400
.34, Revolver, Bar Hammer, Octagon Barrel, 4" Barrel, 5 Shot, *Antique*	125	225	400
.36, Pepperbox, 6" Barrel, 6 Shot, *Antique*	400	700	1000
.36, Revolver, Center Hammer, Octagon Barrel, 5" Barrel, 6 Shot, Spur Trigger, *Antique*	225	450	800
.36, Revolver, Center Hammer, Octagon Barrel, $7^1/_2$" Barrel, 6 Shot, *Antique*	400	800	1200
.36, Revolver, Side Hammer, Octagon Barrel, 6" Barrel, 6 Shot, *Antique*	400	900	1750
.44, Revolver, Center Hammer, Half-Octagon Barrel, $7^1/_2$" Barrel, 6 Shot, *Antique*	600	1500	2500
HANDGUN, REVOLVER			
.22 Short R.F., 7 Shot, Side Hammer, Solid Frame, *Antique*	65	150	275
.25 L.F., 7 Shot, Side Hammer, Solid Frame, *Antique*	300	500	750
.32 L.F., 6 Shot, Side Hammer, Solid Frame, *Antique*	500	675	800
.32 Short R.F., 6 Shot, Side Hammer, Solid Frame, *Antique*	200	300	500
.36 L.F., 6 Shot, Side Hammer, Solid Frame, *Antique*	750	1000	1250
.38 Short R.F., 6 Shot, Side Hammer, Solid Frame, *Antique*	800	1250	1650
.44 L.F., 6 Shot, Side Hammer, Solid Frame, *Antique*	1250	1750	2250
.44 Short R.F., 6 Shot, Side Hammer, Solid Frame, *Antique*	1500	2000	2500
HANDGUN, SINGLESHOT			
.22 Short R.F., Derringer, Spur Trigger, *Antique*	250	325	425
.22 Short R.F., Large Frame, Spur Trigger, *Antique*	75	150	250
.32 Short R.F., Derringer, Spur Trigger, *Antique*	200	300	400
.32 Short R.F., Large Frame, Spur Trigger, *Antique*	$200	$275	$400
.41 Short R.F., Derringer, Spur Trigger, *Antique*	500	850	1000
RIFLE, PERCUSSION			
.36 Allen Patent, Carbine, Drop Breech Loader, *Antique*	500	750	950

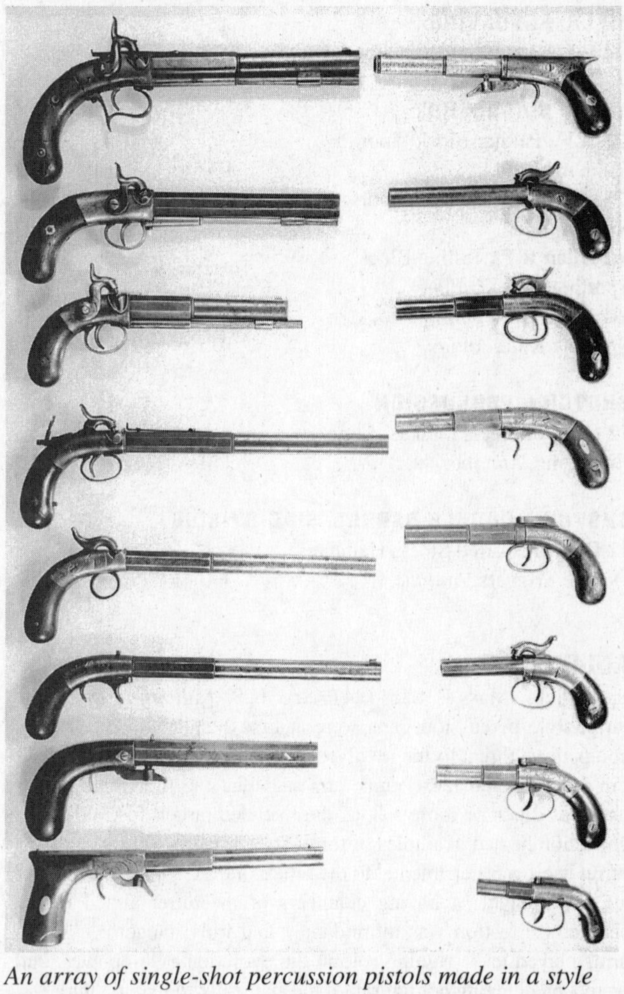

An array of single-shot percussion pistols made in a style commonly associated with New England makers, many of these arms suitable for concealing in the user's boot; from the top left, *Pocket Rifle by Allen & Thurber, Pocket Rifle by Blunt & Syms, another of the type attributed to Allen, large Pocket Rifle by Allen & Wheelock, ring trigger Pocket Rifle a scarce variation; Pocket Rifle of underhammer style attributed to Bacon & Co.; bootleg pistol with 7" barrel unsigned;* bottom *pistol signed by E. Allen, Grafton Mass. From the top* right, *a saw handle marked Cast Steel and Pocket Rifle, double-barrel pistol by Allen & Wheelock with two spur hammers and one trigger, Pocket Rifle by Marston & Co., underhammer pistol by Bacon, a Pocket Rifle by Allen & Wheelock, a double-barrel pistol by Allen & Wheelock, a bar hammer type Pocket Rifle by Allen & Wheelock, and still another Pocket Rifle marked Allen's Patent.*

	Fair	V. Good	Excellent
.36 Allen Patent, Drop Breech Loader, Sporting Rifle, *Antique*	$350	$650	$850
.38 Sidehammer, Plains Rifle, Iron Mounted, Walnut Stock, *Antique*	800	1250	1500
.44 Center Hammer, Octagon Barrel, Iron Frame, *Antique*	500	750	1000
.44 Revolver, Carbine, 6 Shot, *Antique*	3000	7500	12500

RIFLE, REVOLVING

	Fair	V. Good	Excellent
.44 L.F., Walnut Stock, 6 Shot, *Antique*	3000	7500	12500

RIFLE, SINGLESHOT

	Fair	V. Good	Excellent
.22 R.F., Falling Block, Sporting Rifle, *Antique*	100	300	500
.38 R.F., Falling Block, Sporting Rifle, *Antique*	100	285	400
.62 Allen R.F., Falling Block, Sporting Rifle, *Antique*	100	275	450
.64 Allen R.F., Falling Block, Sporting Rifle, *Antique*	100	275	450

SHOTGUN, PERCUSSION

	Fair	V. Good	Excellent
12 Ga. Double, Hammers, Light Engraving, *Antique*	350	525	750

SHOTGUN, DOUBLE BARREL, SIDE-BY-SIDE

	Fair	V. Good	Excellent
12 Ga., Checkered Stock, Hammers, Double Triggers, *Antique*	300	525	750

ALLEN, C. B.

Springfield, Mass., 1836–1841. See U.S. Military, Elgin. The turret-style percussion guns were at first thought to pose a truly competitive threat to the revolvers of Samuel Colt. However, Colt himself ridiculed these guns, and said that the firer thereof was under as much or more risk as the intended target. In Colt's own collection he had examples of turret-style firearms. The size of the turret itself was detrimental to the future of these guns. But most of all, the thought of having chambers of the turret aimed in the shooter's direction was intimidating, and truly dangerous. These arms played an intriguing role in the evolution of firepower, and were a challenging configuration mechanically to manufacture.

HANDGUN, PERCUSSION

	Fair	V. Good	Excellent
.36 Cochran Turret, 7 Shot, 4¾" Barrel, *Antique*	4000	7500	12500
.40 Cochran Turret, 7 Shot, 5" Barrel, *Antique*	6000	10000	13500

RIFLE, PERCUSSION

	Fair	V. Good	Excellent
.40 Cochran Turret, 7 Shot, Octagon Barrel, *Antique*	3000	5500	8000
.40 Cochran Turret, 9 Shot, Octagon Barrel, *Antique*	3250	5800	8000

ALLEN, ETHAN

Grafton, Mass., 1835–1837, E. Allen & Co. Worcester, Mass. 1865–1871. Became Forehand & Wadsworth.

HANDGUN, PERCUSSION

	Fair	V. Good	Excellent
.31, Pepperbox, 6 Shot, 3" Barrel, *Antique*	$400	$650	$850
.36, Pepperbox, 6 Shot, 5" Barrel, *Antique*	600	1000	1400
First Model Pocket "Rifle" Various Calibers, Various Barrel Lengths, Under Hammer, Singleshot, Saw Handle Grip, *Antique*	450	650	950
Second Model Pocket "Rifle" .31, Singleshot, Under Hammer, Half-Octagon Barrel, *Antique*	450	750	950

HANDGUN, REVOLVER

	Fair	V. Good	Excellent
.22 Short R.F., 7 Shot, Side Hammer, Sheath Trigger, *Antique*	150	300	450
.32 Short R.F., 6 Shot, Side Hammer, Sheath Trigger, *Antique*	150	275	425

HANDGUN, SINGLESHOT

	Fair	V. Good	Excellent
Derringer, .32 Short R.F., Side-Swing Barrel, Half-Octagon Barrel, *Antique*	150	300	450
Derringer, .32 Short R.F., Side-Swing Barrel, Octagon Barrel, *Antique*	125	250	400
Derringer, .41 Short R.F., Side-Swing Barrel, Round Barrel, *Antique*	500	800	1100
Derringer, .41 Short R.F., Side-Swing Barrel, Half-Octagon Barrel, *Antique*	400	750	1100
Derringer, .41 Short R.F., Side-Swing Barrel, Octagon Barrel, *Antique*	450	850	1250

RIFLE, SINGLESHOT

	Fair	V. Good	Excellent
Sidehammer Muzzleloader, .38 Caliber, Sporting Rifle, *Antique*	650	1000	1350

ALLEN, SILAS

Shrewsbury, Mass., 1796–1843. See Kentucky Rifles and Pistols.

ALLIES

Berasaluze Areitio-Arutena y Cia., Eibar, Spain, c. 1920.

HANDGUN, SELF-LOADING

	Fair	V. Good	Excellent
Model 1924, .25 ACP, Clip Fed, *Curio*	35	75	175
Pocket, .32 ACP, Clip Fed, *Curio*	35	75	175
Vest Pocket, .25 ACP, Clip Fed, *Curio*	35	75	150
Vest Pocket, .32 ACP, Clip Fed, Short Grip, *Curio*	35	75	150

ALPINE INDUSTRIES

Los Angeles, Calif., 1962–1965.

RIFLE, SELF-LOADING

	Fair	V. Good	Excellent
M-1 Carbine, .30 Carbine, Clip Fed, Military Style, *Modern*	75	150	250

ALSOP, C. R.

Middleton, Conn., 1858–1866 The author had the pleasure of acquiring an Alsop .36 caliber pocket revolver, with ivory grips, which had belonged to C.R. Alsop himself. The item, acquired from a member of the Alsop family, had only traveled about thirty miles from its original place of manufacture in over 140 years. Alsop was attempting to capitalize on the expiration of Samuel Colt's master patent on the revolver, as were Manhattan, Remington, and a number of other makers. Alsop's attempt at competing with Colt received some encouragement due to the Civil War, but in the shakeout in the arms business following the war, it was impossible for his firm to survive. These arms should increase in value as more collectors become enamored of the Civil War era, and find that the escalating prices in Colts force them to other makes, not as blue chip, but nevertheless attractive, including for their design, quality and relative scarcity.

HANDGUN, PERCUSSION

	Fair	*V. Good*	*Excellent*
.36 Navy, 5 Shot, Octagon Barrel, Spur Trigger, Top Hammer, Safety, *Antique*	$750	$1500	$3000
.36 Navy, 5 Shot, Octagon Barrel, Spur Trigger, Top Hammer, No Safety, *Antique*	1000	1500	2750
.36 Pocket, 5 Shot, Octagon Barrel, Spur Trigger, *Antique*	285	575	1500

AMERICA

Made by Bliss & Goodyear, c. 1878.

HANDGUN, REVOLVER

	Fair	*V. Good*	*Excellent*
.22 Short R.F., 7 Shot, Spur Trigger, Solid Frame, Single Action, *Antique*	65	125	250

AMERICA

Made by Norwich Falls Pistol Co., c. 1880.

HANDGUN, REVOLVER

	Fair	*V. Good*	*Excellent*
.32 Long R.F., Double Action, Solid Frame, *Antique*	50	100	150

AMERICAN ARMS & AMMUNITION CO.

Miami, Florida, c. 1979. Successors to North Armament Corp. (Norarmco).

HANDGUN, SELF-LOADING

	Fair	*V. Good*	*Excellent*
TP-70, .22 L.R.R.F., Double Action, Stainless, Clip Fed, *Modern*	85	175	275
TP-70, .25 ACP, Double Action, Stainless, Clip Fed, *Modern*	75	150	250

AMERICAN ARMS CO.

Boston, Mass., 1861–1897, Milwaukee, Wisc. 1897–1901. Purchased by Marlin 1901.

HANDGUN, DOUBLE BARREL, OVER-UNDER

	Fair	*V. Good*	*Excellent*
Wheeler Pat, .22 Short R.F., 32 Short R.F., Brass Frame, Spur Trigger, *Antique*	$250	$425	$650
Wheeler Pat, .32 Short R.F., Brass Frame, Spur Trigger, *Antique*	300	450	650
Wheeler Pat, .41 Short R.F., Brass Frame, Spur Trigger, *Antique*	400	600	850

HANDGUN, REVOLVER

	Fair	*V. Good*	*Excellent*
.32 S & W, 5 Shot, Double Action, Top Break, *Antique*	75	125	175
.32 S & W, 5 Shot, Double Action, Top Break, Hammerless, *Antique*	125	175	225
.32 S & W, 5 Shot, Single Action, Top Break, Spur Trigger, *Antique*	100	150	200

SHOTGUN, DOUBLE BARREL, SIDE-BY-SIDE

	Fair	*V. Good*	*Excellent*
12 Ga., Semi-Hammerless, Checkered Stock, *Antique*	150	400	600
Whitmore Patent, 10 Ga., 2⅞", Hammerless, Checkered Stock, *Antique*	150	400	625
Whitmore Patent, 12 Ga., Hammerless, Checkered Stock, *Antique*	150	450	675

SHOTGUN, SINGLESHOT

	Fair	*V. Good*	*Excellent*
12 Ga., Semi-Hammerless, Checkered Stock, *Antique*	50	100	175

AMERICAN ARMS INTERNATIONAL

Salt Lake City, Utah. Current.

RIFLE, SELF-LOADING

	Fair	*V. Good*	*Excellent*
American 180, .22 L.R.R.F., 177 Round Drum Magazine, Peep Sights, *Modern*	300	500	700

Extra Magazine, Add 50-75
Laser-Lok, Sight System, Add $350-$450

AMERICAN BARLOCK WONDER

Made by Crescent for Sears-Roebuck & Co. See Crescent Fire Arms Co., Shotgun, Double Barrel, Side-by-Side; Shotgun, Single Shot.

AMERICAN BOY

Made by Bliss & Goodyear for Townley Hdw. Co.

HANDGUN, REVOLVER

	Fair	*V. Good*	*Excellent*
.32 Short R.F., Single Action, Solid Frame, Spur Trigger, 7 Shot, *Antique*	75	125	250

AMERICAN BULLDOG

Made by Johnson, Bye & Co., Worcester, Mass., 1882–1900.

HANDGUN, REVOLVER

	Fair	V. Good	Excellent
.22 Short R.F., 7 Shot, Spur Trigger, Solid Frame, Single Action, *Antique*	$50	$100	$175
.32 S & W, 5 Shot, Spur Trigger, Solid Frame, Single Action, *Curio*	50	100	150
.32 S & W, 5 Shot, Spur Trigger, Solid Frame, Single Action, *Curio*	50	100	150
.32 Short R.F., 5 Shot, Spur Trigger, Solid Frame, Single Action, *Antique*	50	100	175
.38 Short R.F., 5 Shot, Spur Trigger, Solid Frame, Single Action, *Antique*	50	100	175
.41 Short C.F., 5 Shot, Spur Trigger, Solid Frame, Single Action, *Antique*	50	100	200

AMERICAN CHAMPION

SHOTGUN, SINGLESHOT

	Fair	V. Good	Excellent
M1899, 12 Gauge, Plain, *Modern* .	50	75	100

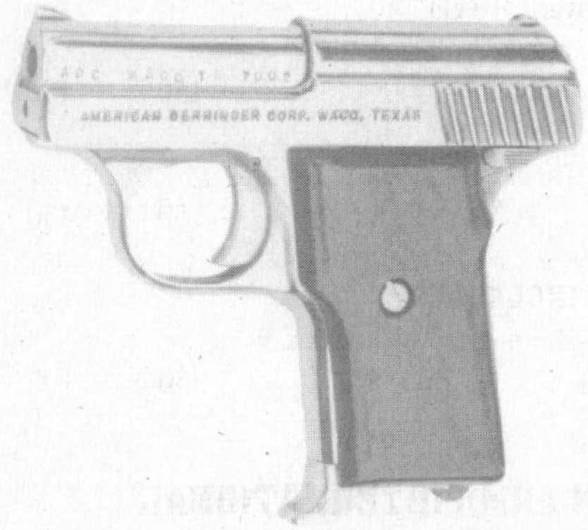

American Derringer ADSS, .25 Auto

AMERICAN DERRINGER CORP.

Waco, Texas, 1979 to date.

HANDGUN, DOUBLE BARREL, OVER-UNDER

	Fair	V. Good	Excellent
Model AD, .32 S & W Long, Remington Style Derringer, Stainless Steel, Spur Trigger, Hammer, *Modern*	100	150	175
Model AD, .357 Mag., Remington Style Derringer, Stainless Steel, Spur Trigger, Hammer, *Modern* ...	100	150	175
Model AD, .38 Spec., Remington Style Derringer, Stainless Steel, Spur Trigger, Hammer, *Modern* ...	100	150	175
Model AD, .41 Mag., Remington Style Derringer, Stainless Steel, Spur Trigger, Hammer, *Modern* ...	100	175	275
Model AD, .44 Mag., Remington Style Derringer, Stainless Steel, Spur Trigger, Hammer, *Modern* ...	100	200	275
Model AD, .45 ACP., Remington Style Derringer, Stainless Steel, Spur Trigger, Hammer, *Modern* ...	100	150	200
Model AD, .45 Win Mag., Remington Style Derringer, Stainless Steel, Spur Trigger, Hammer, *Modern*	$125	$225	$350
Model ADL, Various Calibers, Remington Style Derringer, Stainless Steel, Lightweight, Spur Trigger, Hammer, *Modern*	100	125	150

HANDGUN, SELF-LOADING

	Fair	V. Good	Excellent
Model ADBS, .25 ACP, Clip Fed, Blue, *Modern*	25	50	100
Model ADM, .250 Mag., Clip Fed, Stainless Steel, *Modern*	35	75	150
Model ADMB, .250 Mag., Clip Fed, Blue, *Modern*	25	50	100
Model ADSS, .25 ACP, Clip Fed, Stainless Steel, *Modern*	25	50	100

HANDGUN, SINGLESHOT

	Fair	V. Good	Excellent
Model ADS, Various Calibers, Remington Style Derringer, Stainless Steel, Spur Trigger, Hammer, *Modern*	75	125	200

AMERICAN EAGLE

Made by Hopkins & Allen, 1870–1898.

HANDGUN, REVOLVER

	Fair	V. Good	Excellent
.22 Short R.F., 7 Shot, Spur Trigger, Solid Frame, Single Action, *Antique*	75	125	200
.32 Short R.F., 5 Shot, Spur Trigger, Solid Frame, Single Action, *Antique*	75	150	225

AMERICAN FIREARMS CO.

San Antonio, Texas, 1966–1974.

HANDGUN, SELF-LOADING

	Fair	V. Good	Excellent
.22 L.R.R.F., Clip Fed, Stainless Steel, *Modern*	75	125	175
.25 ACP, Clip Fed, Blue, *Modern* .	100	125	175
.25 ACP, Clip Fed, Stainless Steel, *Modern*	125	150	200
.380 ACP, Clip Fed, Stainless Steel, *Modern*	175	300	450

AMERICAN GUN CO.

Made by Crescent Fire Arms Co. Sold By H. & D. Folsom Co. See Crescent Fire Arms Co. for shotguns.

HANDGUN, REVOLVER

	Fair	V. Good	Excellent
.32 S & W, 5 Shot, Double Action, Top Break, *Curio*	100	150	175

AMERICAN STANDARD TOOL CO.

Newark, N.J., 1865–1870, successor to Manhattan Firearms Co.

HANDGUN, PERCUSSION

	Fair	V. Good	Excellent
Hero, .34, Screw Barrel, Center Hammer, Spur Trigger, *Antique* ...	$75	$125	$200

HANDGUN, REVOLVER

	Fair	V. Good	Excellent
.22 Short R.F., 7 Shot, Spur Trigger, Tip-Up, *Antique*	125	250	400

AMERICUS

Made by Hopkins & Allen, 1870–1900.

HANDGUN, REVOLVER

	Fair	V. Good	Excellent
.22 Short R.F., 7 Shot, Spur Trigger, Solid Frame, Single Action, *Antique*	50	100	150
.32 Short R.F., 5 Shot, Spur Trigger, Solid Frame, Single Action, *Antique*	50	100	175

AMSDEN, B.W.

Saratoga Springs, N.Y., 1852.

COMBINATION WEAPON, PERCUSSION

	Fair	V. Good	Excellent
.40-16 Ga., Double Barrel, Rifled, *Antique*	350	650	950

RIFLE, PERCUSSION

	Fair	V. Good	Excellent
.40, Octagon Barrel, Set Trigger, Rifled, *Antique*	200	400	600

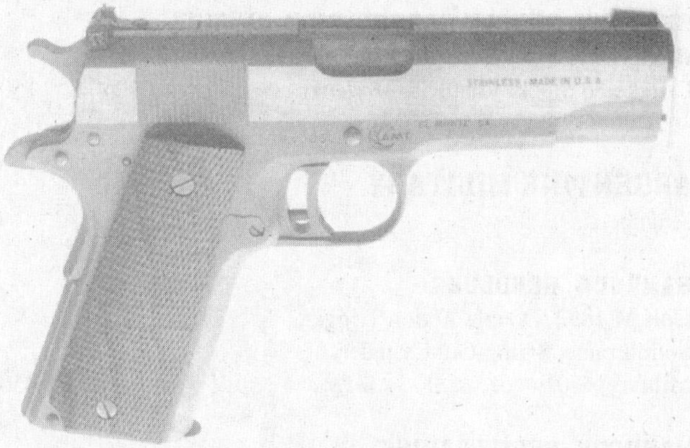

AMT Skipper

A M T

Arcadia Machine & Tool, since 1976 in Arcadia, Calif. See Auto Mag.

HANDGUN, SELF-LOADING

	Fair	V. Good	Excellent
Back Up, .22 L.R.R.F., Stainless Steel, Clip Fed, *Modern*	150	225	300
Back Up, .380 ACP, AMT, Stainless Steel, Clip Fed, *Modern*	150	225	300
Back Up, .380 ACP, OMC, Stainless Steel, Clip Fed, *Modern*	125	150	175
Back Up, .380 ACP, TDE, Stainless Steel, Clip Fed, *Modern*	$100	$175	$250
Combat Skipper, .45 ACP, Stainless Steel, Clip Fed, Fixed Sights, *Modern*	200	300	400
Government, .45 ACP, Stainless Steel, Clip Fed, Fixed Sights, *Modern* ...	200	300	400
Hardballer, .45 ACP, Stainless Steel, Clip Fed, Adjustable Sights, *Modern*	200	325	425
Lightning, .22 L.R., Stainless Steel, 5" Bull Barrel, Adjustable Sights, As Above, Fixed Sights, As Above, 6½" Bull Barrel, Adjustable Sights, As Above, Fixed Sights	150	225	250
Lightning, .22 L.R., Stainless Steel, 6½" Tapered Barrel, Adjustable Sights, As Above, Fixed Sights ...	150	225	250
Longslide, .45 ACP, Stainless Steel, Clip Fed, Adjustable Sights, *Modern*	250	400	500
Skipper, .45 ACP, Stainless Steel, Clip Fed, Adjustable Sights, *Modern*	200	350	450

ANDRUS & OSBORNE

Canton, Conn., 1847–1850, moved to Southbridge, Mass., 1850–1851.

HANDGUN, PERCUSSION

	Fair	V. Good	Excellent
.36 Underhammer, Boot Pistol, Half-Octagon Barrel, *Antique*	200	300	400

ANGSTADT, A. & J.

Berks County, Pa., 1792–1808. See Kentucky Rifles and U.S. Military.

ANGSTADT, PETER

Lancaster County, Pa., 1770–1777. See Kentucky Rifles and Pistols.

ANGUSH, JAMES

Lancaster, Pa., 1771. See Kentucky Rifles and Pistols.

ANNELY, L.

London, England, 1650–1700.

HANDGUN, FLINTLOCK

	Fair	V. Good	Excellent
.62, Holster Pistol, Brass Mounting, *Antique*	225	700	950

ANSCHUTZ

Zella Mehlis, Germany, 1922–1938, 1945 to date in Ulm, West Germany. Also see Savage Arms Co. for rifle listings.

HANDGUN, REVOLVER

	Fair	V. Good	Excellent
J.G.A., 7mm C.F., Folding Trigger, Pocket Revolver, *Curio*	65	125	200

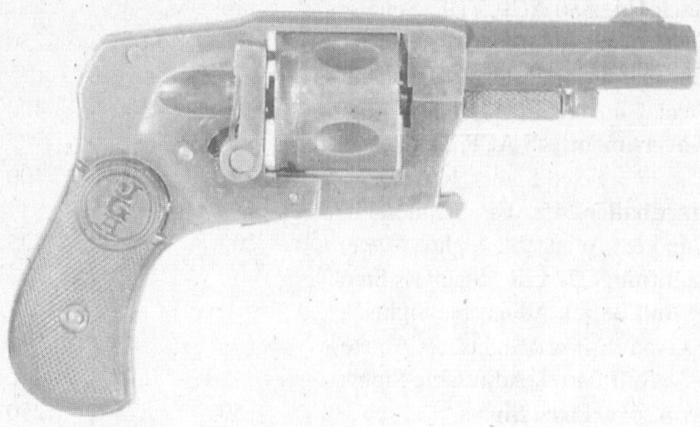

Anschutz J. G. Revolver

ANSCHUTZ, E.
Philadelphia, Pa., c. 1860.

	Fair	V. Good	Excellent
RIFLE, PERCUSSION			
.36 Schutzen Rifle, Octagon Barrel, Target, *Antique*	$625	$1500	$2200

ANSCHUTZ, UDO
Zella Mehlis, Germany, 1927–1939.

HANDGUN, SINGLESHOT			
Record-Match M1933, .22 L.R.R.F., Free Pistol, Martini Action, Fancy Stocks, Target Sights, *Curio*	250	450	700
Record-Match M210, .22 L.R.R.F., Free Pistol, Martini Action, Fancy Stocks, Target Sights, Light Engraving, *Curio*	300	750	900

ANSTADT, JACOB
Kutztown, Pa., 1815–1817. See Kentucky Rifles and Pistols.

APACHE
Fab. de Armas Garantazadas, Spain, c. 1920.

HANDGUN, REVOLVER			
Colt Police Positive Type, .38 Double Action, 6 Shots, *Curio*	35	75	125

APACHE
Made by Ojanguren y Vidosa; Eibar, Spain.

HANDGUN, SELF-LOADING			
.25 ACP, Clip Fed, *Modern*	75	150	200

APAOLOZO HERMANOS
Zumorraga, Spain, c. 1925.

	Fair	V. Good	Excellent
HANDGUN, REVOLVER			
Colt Police Positive Type, .38 Spec., Double Action, *Curio*	$35	$75	$125

APEX RIFLE CO.
Sun Valley, Calif., c. 1952.

RIFLE, BOLT ACTION			
Apex Eight, Various Calibers, 8 Lbs., Monte Kennedy Stock, Standard Grade, No Sights, *Modern*	100	200	350
Bantam Light Sporter, Various Calibers, 7 Lbs., Monte Kennedy Stock, Standard Grade, No Sights, *Modern*	125	250	400
Bench Rester, Various Calibers, Monte Kennedy Laminated Stock with Rails, Bull Barrel, Canjar Trigger, *Modern*	125	250	475
Reliable Nine, Various Calibers, 9 Lbs., Monte Kennedy Stock, Standard Grade, No Sights, *Modern*	100	200	350
Varmint & Target, Various Calibers, Monte Kennedy Target Stock, Heavy Barrel, No Sights, *Modern*	125	250	425

ARAMBERRI
Spain.

SHOTGUN, DOUBLE BARREL, SIDE-BY-SIDE			
Boxlock, 12 Gauge, Single Trigger, Checkered Stock, Vent Rib, *Modern*	75	125	150

ARGENTINE MILITARY
Aramberri.

HANDGUN, REVOLVER			
Colt M 1892, Double Action Trigger, Solid Frame, Swing-Out Cylinder, Military, *Curio*	125	300	450
HANDGUN, SELF-LOADING			
Ballester-Molina, .45 ACP, Clip Fed, *Curio*	200	350	500
Ballester-Rigaud, .45 ACP, Clip Fed, *Curio*	200	400	500
Modelo 1916 (Colt 1911), 11.25mm, Clip Fed, *Curio*	200	500	650
Modelo 1927 (Colt 1911A1), .45 ACP, Clip Fed, *Curio*	200	500	700
Steyr M1905, 7.63 Mannlicher, *Curio*	125	275	325
RIFLE, BOLT ACTION			
M 1891, 7.65 Argentine, Carbine, Open Rear Sight, Full Stocked Military, *Curio*	100	200	300

	Fair	V. Good	Excellent
M 1891, 7.65 Argentine, Rifle, Full Stocked Military, *Curio*	$100	$200	$350
M 1909, 7.65 Argentine, Carbine, Open Rear Sight, Full-Stocked Military, *Modern*	100	225	300
M 1909, 7.65 Argentine, Rifle, Full Stocked Military, *Curio*	100	225	300

RIFLE, SINGLESHOT

M 1879, .43 Mauser, Rolling Block, *Antique*	100	250	350

ARISTOCRAT

Made by Hopkins & Allen for Suplee Biddle Hardware, 1870–1900.

HANDGUN, REVOLVER

.22 Short R.F., 7 Shot, Spur Trigger, Solid Frame, Single Action, *Antique*	50	75	150
.32 Short R.F., 5 Shot, Spur Trigger, Solid Frame, Single Action, *Antique*	50	75	175

ARISTOCRAT

Made by Stevens Arms.

SHOTGUN, DOUBLE BARREL, SIDE-BY-SIDE

M 315, Various Gauges, Hammerless, Steel Barrel, *Modern*	50	100	150

ARIZAGA, GASPAR

Eibar, Spain.

HANDGUN, SELF-LOADING

.32 ACP, Clip Fed, *Modern*	50	100	150

ARMALITE

Costa Mesa, Calif. The author had the pleasure of being on a partridge shoot in Spain with the inventor of some of the Armalite products, the creator of the basis for the AR-15 and M16 series and a number of other .223-based firearms, Gene Stoner. It was a pleasure listening to this giant in contemporary firearms design and entrepreneurship sharing his extraordinary experiences. Some of those achievements and adventures were included in Edward Ezell's excellent work, *The Black Rifle.* The fascinating high-tech nature of the Armalite arms, and other .223-based firearms, are popular with a significant number of arms collectors. Following the market for this type of arm has proven that sometimes the type draws extremely well in sales figures.

RIFLE, SELF-LOADING

AR-180.223 Rem., Clip Fed, Folding Stock, *Modern*	400	750	950
AR-7 Explorer, .22 L.R.R.F., Clip Fed, *Modern*	50	75	100
AR-7 Explorer Custom, .22 L.R.R.F., Checkered Stock, Clip Fed, *Modern*	50	100	150

SHOTGUN, SELF-LOADING

	Fair	V. Good	Excellent
AR-17, 12 Ga. Lightweight, *Modern*	$200	$300	$400

ARMI JAGER

Turin, Italy. Imported by E.M.F.

HANDGUN, REVOLVER

Dakota Sheriff, Various Calibers, Single Action, Western Style, 3 1/2" Barrel, *Modern*	75	125	200
Dakota Target, Various Calibers, Single Action, Western Style, Adjustable Sights, Various Barrel Lengths, *Modern*	100	150	200
Dakota, .22 L.R.R.F. and .22 W.M.R., Single Action, Western Style, Various Barrel Lengths, *Modern*	75	125	175
Dakota, .22 L.R.R.F., Single Action, Western Style, Various Barrel Lengths, *Modern*	50	100	150
Dakota, Various Calibers, Single Action, Western Style, Various Barrel Lengths, *Modern*	75	125	175
Dakota, Various Calibers, Single Action, Western Style, Buntline Barrel Lengths, *Modern*	75	125	175
Dakota, Various Calibers, Single Action, Western Style, Engraved Barrel Lengths, *Modern*	125	225	325

RIFLE, SELF-LOADING

AP-74, .22 L.R.R.F., Military Stock, Wood Stock, *Modern*	50	75	100
AP-74, .32 ACP, Military Style, Wood Stock, *Modern*	50	75	125
AP-74 Commando, .22 L.R.R.F., Military Style, Wood Stock, *Modern*	50	75	125
AP-74 Standard, .22 L.R.R.F., Military Style, Plastic Stock, *Modern*	25	50	100
AP-74 Standard, .32 ACP, Military Style, Plastic Stock, *Modern*	50	75	125

ARMINEX LTD.

Scottsdale, Ariz., since 1982–1985.

HANDGUN, SELF-LOADING

Trifire, .45 A.C.P., 9 mm Luger, or .38 Super, Blue or Nickel, Clip Fed, Hammer, Adjustable Sights, *Modern*	200	350	500
Trifire Presentation, .45 A.C.P., 9 mm Luger, or .38 Super, Cased, Blue or Nickel, Clip Fed, Hammer, Adjustable Sights, *Modern*	300	400	550

Arminex Trifire Standard

Arminex Trifire Target

ARMINIUS

Friedrich Pickert, Zella-Mehlis, Germany, 1922–1939.

HANDGUN, REVOLVER

	Fair	V. Good	Excellent
Model 1, .22 L.R.R.F., Hammerless, *Curio*	$100	$200	$350
Model 2, .22 L.R.R.F., Hammer, *Curio*	100	250	300
Model 3, .25 ACP, Hammerless, Folding Trigger, *Curio*	75	125	200
Model 4, 5.5 Velo Dog, Hammerless, Folding Trigger, *Curio*	50	75	150
Model 5/1, 7.5mm Swiss, Hammer, *Curio*	50	100	175
Model 5/2, 7.62 Nagant, Hammer, *Curio*	50	100	175
Model 7, .320 Revolver, Hammer, *Curio*	50	75	125
Model 8, .320 Revolver, Hammerless, Folding Trigger, *Curio*	100	125	150
Model 9, .32 ACP, Hammer, *Curio*	75	125	175
Model 10, .32 ACP, Hammerless, Folding Trigger, *Curio*	50	100	150
Model 13, .380 Revolver, Hammer, *Curio*	50	100	150
Model 14, .380 Revolver, Hammerless, *Curio*	50	100	150

HANDGUN, SINGLESHOT

	Fair	V. Good	Excellent
TP 1, .22 L.R.R.F., Target Pistol, Hammer, *Modern*	$100	$200	$250
TP 2, .22 L.R.R.F., Hammerless, Set Triggers, *Modern*	100	225	275

ARMINIUS

Herman Weihrauch Sportwaffenfabrik, Mellrichstadt/Bayern, West Germany, before 1968; for current models, see F.I.E.

HANDGUN, REVOLVER

	Fair	V. Good	Excellent
HW-3, .22 L.R.R.F., *Modern*	25	50	75
HW-3, .32 S & W Long, *Modern*	25	50	75
HW-5, .22 L.R.R.F., *Modern*	25	50	75
HW-5, .32 S & W Long, *Modern*	25	50	75
HW-7, .22 L.R.R.F., *Modern*	25	50	75
HW-9, .22 L.R.R.F., Adjustable Sights, *Modern*	25	50	75

ARMSPORT

Importers discontinued 1993, Miami, Fla.

HANDGUN, FLINTLOCK

	Fair	V. Good	Excellent
Kentucky, .45, Reproduction	25	50	85

HANDGUN, PERCUSSION

	Fair	V. Good	Excellent
1847 Colt Walker, .44, Reproduction, *Antique*	75	125	250
1851 Colt Navy, .36, Brass Frame, Reproduction	50	75	100
1851 Colt Navy, .36, Steel Frame, Reproduction	50	100	125
1851 Colt Navy, .44, Brass Frame, Reproduction	50	75	100
1851 Colt Navy, .44, Steel Frame, Reproduction	50	100	125
1860 Colt Army, .44, Brass Frame, Reproduction	50	75	100
1860 Colt Army, .44, Steel Frame, Reproduction	50	100	125
Corsair, .44, Double Barrel, Reproduction	25	50	75
Kentucky, .45 or .50, Reproduction	25	50	75
New Hartford Police, .36, Reproduction	25	50	100
New Remington Army, .44, Blue, Brass Trigger Guard, Reproduction	50	75	100
New Remington Army, .44, Stainless Steel, Brass Trigger Guard, Reproduction	50	75	125
Patriot, .45, Target Sights, Set Triggers, Reproduction	50	75	100
Spiller & Burr, .36, Solid Frame, Brass Frame, Reproduction	50	75	100
Whitney, .36, Solid Frame, Brass Trigger Guard, Reproduction	50	75	100

RIFLE, BOLT ACTION

	Fair	V. Good	Excellent
Tikka, Various Calibers, Open Sights, Checkered Stock, Clip Fed, *Modern*	$250	$350	$600

RIFLE, LEVER ACTION

	Fair	V. Good	Excellent
Premier 1873 Winchester, Various Calibers, Carbine, Engraved, Reproduction, *Modern*	200	500	750
Premier 1873 Winchester, Various Calibers, Rifle, Engraved, Reproduction, *Modern*	250	600	900

RIFLE, FLINTLOCK

	Fair	V. Good	Excellent
Deluxe Hawkin, .50, Reproduction	75	125	175
Deluxe Kentucky, .45, Reproduction	100	150	200
Hawkin, .45, Reproduction	75	125	175
Kentucky, .45, Reproduction	100	125	150

RIFLE, PERCUSSION

	Fair	V. Good	Excellent
Deluxe Hawkin, Various Calibers, Reproduction	125	150	175
Deluxe Kentucky, .45, Reproduction	100	150	200
Hawkin, Various Calibers, Reproduction	100	125	150
Kentucky, .45 or .50, Reproduction	50	100	150

COMBINATION WEAPON, OVER-UNDER

	Fair	V. Good	Excellent
Tikka Turkey Gun, 12 Ga. and .222 Rem., Vent Rib, Sling Swivels, Muzzle Break, Checkered Stock, *Modern*	200	400	550

RIFLE, DOUBLE BARREL, SIDE-BY-SIDE

	Fair	V. Good	Excellent
Emperor, Various Calibers, Holland and Holland Type Sidelock, Engraved, Checkered Stock, Extra Barrels, Cased, *Modern*	5000	9500	15000
Emperor Deluxe, Various Calibers, Holland and Holland Sidelock, Fancy Engraving, Checkered Stock, Extra Barrels, *Modern*	6000	11500	17500

RIFLE, DOUBLE BARREL, OVER-UNDER

	Fair	V. Good	Excellent
Emperor, Various Calibers, Checkered Stock, Engraved, Extra Barrels, Cased, *Modern*	4000	7000	10000
Express, Various Calibers, Checkered Stock, Engraved, *Modern*	2000	3000	4000

SHOTGUN, PERCUSSION

	Fair	V. Good	Excellent
Hook Breech, Double Barrel, Side-by-Side, 10 and 12 Gauges, Reproduction	100	175	250

SHOTGUN, DOUBLE BARREL, OVER-UNDER

	Fair	V. Good	Excellent
Model 2500, 12 and 20 Ga., Checkered Stock, Adjustable Choke, Single Selective Trigger, *Modern*	250	450	650
Premier, 12 Ga., Skeet Grade, Checkered Stock, Engraved, *Modern*	600	900	1200

SHOTGUN, DOUBLE BARREL, SIDE-BY-SIDE

	Fair	V. Good	Excellent
Express, 12 and 20 Gauges, Holland and Holland Type Sidelock, Engraved, Checkered Stock, *Modern*	$1500	$2500	$3000
Goose Gun, 10 Ga. $3^1/_2$" Mag., Checkered Stock, *Modern*	275	375	475
Side-by-Side, 12 and 20 Gauges, Checkered Stock, *Modern*	225	325	425
Western Double, 12 Ga. Mag. 3", Outside Hammers Double Trigger, *Modern*	200	300	400

SHOTGUN, SINGLESHOT

	Fair	V. Good	Excellent
Monotrap, 12 Ga., Checkered Stock, *Modern*	500	750	1000
Monotrap, 12 Ga., Two Barrel Set, Checkered Stock, *Modern*	700	900	1200

ARMSTRONG, JOHN

Gettysburg, Pa., 1813–1817. Also See Kentucky Rifles and Pistols. Having owned some truly handsome, and sometimes quite striking, John Armstrong pieces, the author regards these fine guns as among the most artistic and appealing of American firearms, and at the front rank of Kentucky Rifles. This quality and style of rifle belongs in any American museum of art that purports to document and celebrate native achievements in decorative arts. One of America's indigenous art forms, a Kentucky Rifle by an artisan like John Armstrong is a true icon of American creativity and ingenuity. Armstrong excelled at gunmaking pure and simple, but his rifles also represented elegance, a mastery of the use of steel, silver and brass, beauty of design, and a lovely hand at rococo relief carving. An example of Armstrong's work should be displayed in the collection of American decorative arts at the White House—and surely that will happen. Watch for the Kentucky Rifle to become one of the darlings of the American antiques world, and continue to escalate in demand, and in price.

ARRIOLA HERMANOS

Eibar, Spain, c. 1930.

HANDGUN, REVOLVER

	Fair	V. Good	Excellent
Colt Police Positive Copy, .38 Spec., Double Action, *Curio*	25	50	100

ARRIZABALAGA, HILOS DE CALIXTO

Eibar, Spain, c. 1915.

HANDGUN, SELF-LOADING

	Fair	V. Good	Excellent
Ruby Type, .32 ACP, Clip Fed, Blue, *Curio*	75	125	150

ASCASO, FRANCISCO

Tarassa, Spain, c. 1937.

HANDGUN, SELF-LOADING

	Fair	V. Good	Excellent
Astra 400 Copy, 9mm, Clip Fed, Military Type, *Curio*	300	500	700

ASHEVILLE ARMORY

Asheville, N.C., 1861–1864.

RIFLE, PERCUSSION

	Fair	V. Good	Excellent
.58 Enfield Type, Rifled, Brass Furniture, Military, *Antique*	$2500	$5000	$7500

ASTRA

Founded in 1908 as Unceta y Esperanza in Eibar, Spain. In 1913 moved to Guernica, Spain, and the name was reversed to Esperanza y Unceta; name changed again in 1926 to Unceta y Cia.; named changed again in 1953 to Astra-Unceta y Cia.

HANDGUN, REVOLVER

	Fair	V. Good	Excellent
250, .22 L.R.R.F., Double Action, Small Frame, *Modern*	50	100	150
250, .22 W.M.R., Double Action, Small Frame, *Modern*	50	100	150
250, .32 S & W Long, Double Action, Small Frame, *Modern*	50	100	150
250, .38 Special, Double Action, Small Frame, *Modern*	75	125	175
357 Magnum, .357 Magnum, Double Action, Adjustable Sights, *Modern*	125	200	275
357 Magnum, .357 Magnum, Double Action, Adjustable Sights, Stainless Steel, *Modern*	200	250	300
44 Magnum, .44 Magnum, Double Action, Adjustable Sights, *Modern*	250	300	350

Astra .44 Magnum

	Fair	V. Good	Excellent
960, .38 Special, Double Action, Adjustable Sights, *Modern*	50	100	175
Cadix, .22 L.R.R.F., Double Action, Adjustable Sights, *Modern*	35	75	150
Cadix, .22 W.M.R., Double Action, Adjustable Sights, *Modern*	50	100	150
Cadix, .32 S & W Long, Double Action, Adjustable Sights, *Modern*	50	100	150
Cadix, .38 Special, Double Action, Adjustable Sights, *Modern*	125	150	175
Inox, .38 Special, Stainless Steel, Double Action, Small Frame, *Modern*	100	150	200
Match, .38 Special, Double Action, Adjustable Sights, *Modern*	$50	$100	$175
Model 41, .41 Magnum, Blue, *Modern*	225	250	275
Model 45, .45 Colt, Blue, *Modern*	250	300	350

HANDGUN, SELF-LOADING

Chrome Plating, Add $25.00-$45.00

Light Engraving, Add $60.00-$110.00

	Fair	V. Good	Excellent
A-50, Various Calibers, Blue, Single Action, *Modern*	75	150	225
A-80, Various Calibers, Double Action, Blue, Large Magazine, *Modern*	225	300	375
A-80, Various Calibers, Double Action, Chrome, Large Magazine, *Modern*	200	300	400
Constable, Various Calibers, Blue, *Modern*	200	250	300

Astra Constable

	Fair	V. Good	Excellent
Constable Pocket, Various Calibers, Blue, *Modern*	200	250	300
Constable Sport, Various Calibers, Blue, *Modern*	200	250	300
Constable Target, .22 L.R.R.F., Blue, *Modern*	250	300	350
Model 100, .32 ACP, *Curio*	175	225	275
Model 100 Special, .32 ACP, 9 Shot, *Curio*	200	250	300
Model 1000, .23 ACP, 12 Shot, *Modern*	300	400	500
Model 1911, .32 ACP, *Curio*	75	125	150
Model 1915, .32 ACP, *Curio*	75	125	150
Model 1916, .32 ACP, *Curio*	75	125	150
Model 1924, .25 ACP, *Curio*	50	100	125
Model 200 Firecat, .25 ACP, Early Model, Concave Indicator Cut, *Modern*	50	125	150
Model 200 Firecat, .25 ACP, Late Model, Long Clip, *Modern*	75	125	175
Model 200 Firecat, .25 ACP, Late Model, Rear Indicator, *Modern*	50	100	150

Astra M1911 .32

Astra Model 200 with Long Clip

	Fair	V. Good	Excellent
Model 2000 Camper or Cub, Conversion Kit Only	$50	$75	$100
Model 2000 Camper, .22 Short R.F., *Modern*	100	200	250
Model 2000 Cub, .22 Short R.F., *Modern*	100	150	200
Model 2000 Cub, .25 ACP, *Modern*	125	150	175
Model 300, .32 ACP, Clip Fed, *Modern*	100	200	300
Model 300, .32 ACP, Nazi-Proofed, Clip Fed, *Curio*	275	375	475
Model 300, .380 ACP, Clip Fed, *Modern*	125	225	325
Model 300, .380 ACP, Nazi-Proofed, Clip Fed, *Curio*	300	400	500

Astra Cub

	Fair	V. Good	Excellent
Model 3000 (Late), .380 ACP, Clip Fed, *Modern*	$150	$200	$250
Model 400, .32 ACP, *Modern*	200	300	400
Model 400, 9mm Bayard Long, *Modern*	225	300	375
Model 400, 9mm Bayard Long, Nazi-Proofed, Clip Fed, *Curio*	300	600	750
Model 4000 Falcon, .22 L.R.R.F., Clip Fed, *Modern*	300	400	500
Model 4000 Falcon, .32 ACP, Clip Fed, *Modern*	200	250	300
Model 4000 Falcon, .380 ACP, Clip Fed, *Modern*	200	250	300
Model 4000 Falcon, Conversion Kit Only	50	75	100
Model 5000 Sport (Constable), .22 L.R.R.F., Target Pistol, Clip Fed, *Modern*	200	250	300
Model 600, .32 ACP, Clip Fed, *Modern*	100	200	300
Model 600, 9mm Luger, Clip Fed, *Modern*	100	200	300
Model 600, 9mm Luger, Nazi-Proofed, Clip Fed, *Curio*	200	400	600
Model 700 Special, .32 ACP, 12 Shots, Clip Fed, *Modern*	200	500	600
Model 700, .32 ACP, Clip Fed, *Curio*	200	450	500
Model 7000, .22 L.R.R.F., Clip Fed, *Modern*	75	125	175
Model 800 Condor, .380 ACP, Clip Fed, *Modern*	700	850	1000
Model 900, 7.63 Mauser, Holster Stock, *Modern*	400	1000	1500
Model TS-22, .22 L.R.R.F., Target Pistol, Single Action, Clip Fed, *Modern*	125	225	325

RIFLE, SELF-LOADING

	Fair	V. Good	Excellent
Model 1000, .32 ACP, Clip Fed, *Modern*	200	325	450
Model 3000 (Early), .32 ACP, *Modern*	75	125	175

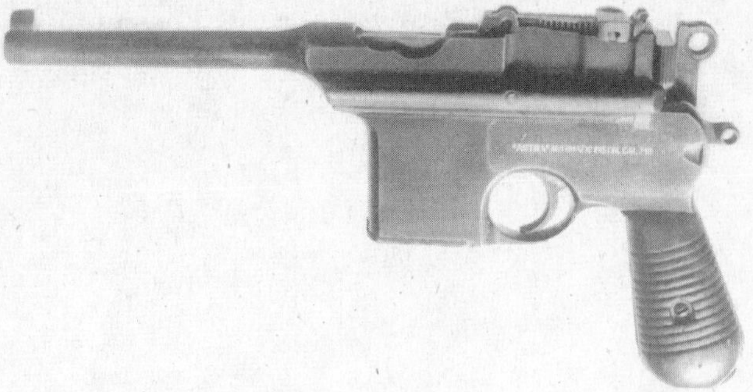

Astra Model 900

Astra TS-22

	Fair	V. Good	Excellent
Model 3000 (Late), .22 L.R.R.F., *Modern*	$50	$100	$150
Model 3000 (Late), .32 ACP, *Modern*	50	100	175
Model 800 Condor, 9mm Luger, *Curio*	250	450	650
Model 902, 7.63 Mauser, *Modern*	300	700	1000

SHOTGUN, DOUBLE BARREL, OVER-UNDER

Model 650, 12 Gauge, Checkered Stock, Double Triggers, Vent Rib, *Modern*	125	200	275
Model 650E, 12 Gauge, Checkered Stock, Double Triggers, Vent Rib, Selective Ejectors, *Modern*	150	250	375
Model 750 Skeet, 12 Gauge, Checkered Stock, Single Trigger, Vent Rib, Selective Ejectors, *Modern*	200	350	500
Model 750 Trap, 12 Gauge, Checkered Stock, Single Trigger, Vent Rib, Selective Ejectors, *Modern*	200	350	500
Model 750, 12 Gauge, Checkered Stock, Double Trigger, Vent Rib, *Modern*	100	150	300
Model 750E, 12 Gauge, Checkered Stock, Single Trigger, Vent Rib, Selective Ejectors, *Modern*	150	350	525
Model ID-13, 12 Gauge, Checkered Stock, Single Trigger, Selective Ejectors, Vent Rib, *Modern*	175	325	475

SHOTGUN, DOUBLE BARREL, SIDE-BY-SIDE

	Fair	V. Good	Excellent
Model 805, Various Gauges, Checkered Stock, Double Triggers, *Modern*	$75	$125	$200
Model 811, 10 Gauge Magnum, Checkered Stock, Double Triggers, *Modern*	115	195	275

SHOTGUN, SINGLESHOT

Cyclops, Various Gauges, Checkered Stock, *Modern*	50	75	100

ATIS

Ponte S. Marco, Italy.

SHOTGUN, SELF-LOADING

12 Ga., Lightweight, Vent Rib, *Modern*	75	150	225
12 Ga., Lightweight, Vent Rib, Left-Hand, *Modern*	75	150	225

ATKIN, HENRY E. & CO.

London, England, 1874–1900. This distinguished gunmaker has a history tied to that of J. Purdey & Sons. Atkin's own mechanical innovations influenced the work of Purdey, and the reader should consult the Hon. Richard Beaumont's landmark work on J. Purdey & Sons, to appreciate that connection.

SHOTGUN, DOUBLE BARREL, SIDE-BY-SIDE

Raleigh, 12 Gauge, Sidelock, Double Triggers, Checkered Stock, Engraved, Automatic Ejectors, "Purdey" Barrels, *Curio*	4000	7000	10000

ATLAS

Domingo Acha y Cia., Ermua, Spain, c. 1920.

HANDGUN, SELF-LOADING

Vest Pocket, .25 ACP, Clip Fed, *Curio*	75	100	125

ATLAS ARMS

Chicago, Ill., from about 1962 to 1972.

HANDGUN, DOUBLE BARREL, OVER-UNDER

Derringer, .22 L.R.R.F., Remington Style, *Modern*	50	75	100
Derringer, .38 Spec., Remington Style, *Modern*	50	100	125

SHOTGUN, DOUBLE BARREL, OVER-UNDER

Grand Prix, 12 or 20 Gauge, Merkel Type Sidelock, Single Selective Trigger, Fancy Engraving, Automatic Ejectors, *Modern*	300	600	800
Model 65, Various Gauges, Boxlock, Double Trigger, Vent Rib, *Modern*	100	200	300

	Fair	V. Good	Excellent
Model 65-ST, Various Gauges, Boxlock, Single Trigger, Vent Rib, *Modern*	$125	$250	$400
Model 87, Various Gauges, Merkel Type Sidelock, Single Trigger, Vent Rib, Engraved, *Modern*	250	350	450
Model 150, Various Gauges, Boxlock, Single Trigger, Vent Rib, *Modern*	125	250	400
Model 150, Various Gauges, Boxlock, Single Trigger, Vent Rib, Automatic Ejectors, *Modern*	175	300	425
Model 160, Various Gauges, Boxlock, Single Trigger, Vent Rib, Automatic Ejectors, *Modern*	250	350	450
Model 180, Various Gauges, Boxlock, Single Trigger, Vent Rib, Automatic Ejectors, Light Engraving, *Modern*	250	375	500
Model 750, Various Gauges, Merkel Type Sidelock, Single Trigger, Vent Rib, Engraved, *Modern*	250	350	450
Model 750, Various Gauges, Merkel Type Sidelock, Single Trigger, Vent Rib, Engraved, Automatic Ejectors, *Modern*	200	375	550

SHOTGUN, DOUBLE BARREL, SIDE-BY-SIDE

	Fair	V. Good	Excellent
Model 145, Various Gauges, Boxlock, Vent Rib, Engraved, Hammerless, Checkered Stock, *Modern*	175	300	425
Model 200, Various Gauges, Boxlock, Double Triggers, Hammerless, Checkered Stock, *Modern*	87	175	275
Model 204, Various Gauges, Boxlock, Single Trigger, Hammerless, Checkered Stock, *Modern*	175	225	275
Model 206, Various Gauges, Boxlock, Single Trigger, Automatic Ejector, Hammerless, Checkered Stock, *Modern*	200	275	350
Model 208, Various Gauges, Boxlock, Double Triggers, Vent Rib, Recoil Pad, *Modern*	175	250	325
Model 500, Various Gauges, Boxlock, Double Triggers, Vent Rib, Recoil Pad, *Modern*	175	250	325

SHOTGUN, SINGLESHOT

	Fair	V. Good	Excellent
Insuperable 101, Various Gauges, Vent Rib, Engraved, Checkered Stock, *Modern*	50	75	100
Trap Gun, 12 Gauge, Automatic Ejector, Engraved, Checkered Stock, *Modern*	300	425	525

AUBREY

Made by Meriden Arms Co., sold by Sears, Roebuck, 1900–1930.

HANDGUN, REVOLVER

	Fair	V. Good	Excellent
.32 S & W, 5 Shot, Double Action, Top Break, *Modern*	$55	$75	$95
.38 S & W, 5 Shot, Double Action, Top Break, *Modern*	55	75	95

AUDAX

Trade name of Manufacture d'Armes Des Pyrenees, Hendaye, France, marketed by La Cartoucherie Francaise, Paris, 1931–1939.

HANDGUN, SELF-LOADING

	Fair	V. Good	Excellent
.25 ACP, Clip Fed, Magazine Disconnect, Grip Safety, *Curio*	55	75	95
.32 ACP, Clip Fed, Magazine Disconnect, Blue, *Curio*	55	75	95

AUSTRALIAN MILITARY

RIFLE, BOLT ACTION

	Fair	V. Good	Excellent
Mk. III, .303 British, Clip Fed, WW I Issue, *Curio*	100	150	225
Mk. III, .303 British, Clip Fed, WW II Issue, *Curio*	100	150	200

RIFLE, SINGLESHOT

	Fair	V. Good	Excellent
Martini, .310 Greener, Small Action, *Curio*	150	200	250

AUSTRIAN MILITARY

HANDGUN, PERCUSSION

	Fair	V. Good	Excellent
.54 Dragoon, with Shoulder Stock, Singleshot, *Antique*	225	450	750

HANDGUN, REVOLVER

	Fair	V. Good	Excellent
M1898 Rast & Gasser, 8mm Rast & Gasser, *Curio*	150	250	400

HANDGUN, SELF-LOADING

	Fair	V. Good	Excellent
M1907 Roth Steyr, 8mm Roth-Steyr, *Curio*	300	400	500
M1908 Steyr, 8mm Roth-Steyr, *Curio*	300	350	400
M1911 Steyr Hahn, 9mm Steyr, *Curio*	275	325	375
M1912 Steyr Hahn, 9mm Steyr, *Curio*	200	250	300
Mannlicher 1901, 7.63 Mannlicher, *Curio*	1500	2000	2750
Mannlicher 1905, 7.63 Mannlicher, *Curio*	250	350	500

HANDGUN, SINGLESHOT

	Fair	V. Good	Excellent
Werder Lightning, 11mm, *Antique*	400	650	800

HANDGUN, TUBELOCK

	Fair	V. Good	Excellent
.69 Dragoon, with Shoulder Stock, Singleshot, *Antique*	250	350	450

	Fair	V. Good	Excellent
RIFLE, BOLT ACTION			
M1883 Schulhof, 11.15 × 58R Werndl, 8 Shot, *Antique*	$200	$375	$575
M1885 Steyr, 11.15 × 58R Werndl, Straight-Pull, *Antique*	200	375	450
M1886 Steyr, 11.15 × 58R Werndl, Straight-Pull Bolt, *Antique*	150	200	300
M1888, 8 × 50R Mannlicher, *Antique*	125	150	175
M1888/90, 8 × 50R Mannlicher, *Antique*	125	150	175
M1890, 8 × 50R Mannlicher, Carbine, *Antique*	125	150	175
M1895, 8 × 50R Mannlicher, *Curio*	100	150	175
M1895, 8 × 50R Mannlicher, Carbine, *Modern*	100	150	250
M1895 Stutzen, 8 × 50R Mannlicher, *Curio*	100	125	250

AUTO MAG

Started at Pasadena, Calif., in 1968, and moved to North Hollywood, Calif., when purchased by TDE in 1971. Marketed by TDE, Jurras Associates, and High Standard. See A M T. Without question these arms are in demand partly because of their popularity in Hollywood shoot-em-ups. This is a handful of gun to shoot, but will knock bowling pins down one after another, and has a strong following among sport and recreation shooters.

	Fair	V. Good	Excellent
HANDGUN, SELF-LOADING			
Alaskan Model, .44 AMP, Clip Fed, Stainless Steel, Hammer, Adjustable Sights, Cased, *Modern*	1000	1600	2250
First Model (Pasadena), .44 AMP, Clip Fed, Stainless Steel, Hammer, Adjustable Sights, Cased, *Modern*	1250	1750	2200
High Standard, .44 AMP, Clip Fed, Stainless Steel, Hammer, Adjustable Sights, Cased, *Modern*	1200	1500	1800
Jurras Custom Model 200, .44 AMP, Clip Fed, Stainless Steel, Hammer, Adjustable Sights, Cased, *Modern*	1750	2350	2500
Model 160, .357 AMP, Clip Fed, Stainless Steel, Hammer, Adjustable Sights, Cased, *Modern*	1200	1700	1800
Model 170, .41 JMP, Clip Fed, Stainless Steel, Hammer, Adjustable Sights, Cased, *Modern*	$1000	$1400	$1850
Model 180, .44 AMP, Clip Fed, Stainless Steel, Hammer, Adjustable Sights, Cased, *Modern*	1250	1750	2150
Model 260, .357 AMP, Clip Fed, Stainless Steel, Hammer, Adjustable Sights, Cased, *Modern*	950	1250	1500
Model 280, .44 AMP, Clip Fed, Stainless Steel, Hammer, Adjustable Sights, Cased, *Modern*	800	1100	1500

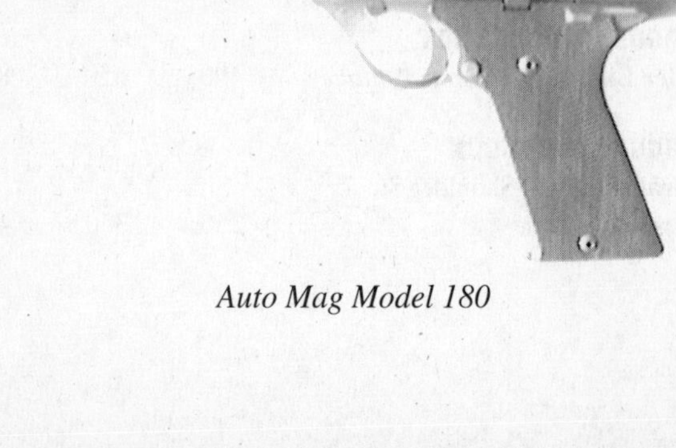

Auto Mag Model 180

AUTOMATIC

Made by Hopkins & Allen, c. 1900.

	Fair	V. Good	Excellent
HANDGUN, REVOLVER			
.32 S & W, 5 Shot, Top Break, Hammerless, Double Action, *Curio*	65	125	200
.38 S & W, 5 Shot, Top Break, Hammerless, Double Action, *Curio*	65	125	200

AUTOMATIC HAMMERLESS

Made by Iver Johnson, c. 1900.

	Fair	V. Good	Excellent
HANDGUN, REVOLVER			
.22 L.R.R.F., 7 Shot, Double Action, Top Break, Hammerless, *Curio*	50	100	150
.32 S & W, 5 Shot, Top Break, Hammerless, Double Action, *Curio*	35	75	125
.38 S & W, 5 Shot, Top Break, Hammerless, Double Action, *Curio*	35	75	125

AUTOMATIC PISTOL

Spain.

	Fair	V. Good	Excellent
HANDGUN, SELF-LOADING			
Pocket, .32 ACP, Clip Fed, *Modern*	25	50	75

AUTOMATIC POLICE

See Forehand & Wadsworth.

AUTO-ORDNANCE CORP

Presently West Hurley, New York; formerly Bridgeport, Connecticut. See also Thompson and Numrich Arms Co. A native of Kentucky, John Taliaferro Thompson graduated from the U.S. Military Academy, West Point, in 1882. Beginning in 1890 he served in the Ordnance Department of the U.S. Army. After the Spanish-American War Thompson's services became paramount in the modernization of U.S. service small arms and ammunition. He developed a position of distinction as a designer and military arms expert, and was a key figure in the evolution of the Model 1911 Colt Automatic Pistol and the .45 ACP cartridge, and in their adoption by U.S. forces. Following retirement from the Army, Thompson joined the Remington Arms Co. (1914) as chief consulting engineer. Thompson formed the Auto-Ordnance Corporation in 1916, with the financial backing of venture capital businessman and entrepreneur Thomas Fortune Ryan. Ryan was later described by an associate as "the most adroit, suave, and noiseless man American finance has ever known." In the process of designing a practical automatic rifle, Thompson's tests and research concluded that a hand-held gun in the .45 ACP cartridge would be superior to all competition. His new gun became the Thompson Submachine Gun, in .45 ACP caliber—one of the world's first. Initially termed by its inventor as a "trench broom" the Thompson, or Tommy Gun, quickly became popular. But in 1917 plans by Thompson for the new firearm were interrupted by his return to active miltary service during the U.S. involvement in World War I. Wartime experience convinced the inventor, more than he ever realized, that his design had a bright future. In December 1918, returning to a civilian career, Thompson retired with the rank of Brigadier General. Friendly with Colt's president W.C. Skinner, Thompson soon saw his submachine gun entered into production by Colt's Pt. F.A. Mfg. Co. The Auto-Ordnance advertisement of 1921 noted: "The ideal weapon for the protection of large estates, ranches, plantations, etc." Purchases were made by police departments and other law enforcement agencies (Texas Rangers included), mining companies and steel makers, a number of foreign governments, and the U.S. government and selected armed services. Automaker Henry Ford acquired a few examples, a reflection of his fascination with firearms; also he wanted to be ready to deal with the potential problem of strikes at Ford Motor Company. Regrettably, particularly to the inventor and manufacturer, the Tommy Gun got its reputation in the hands of Prohibition-era gangsters. Bonnie and Clyde, John Dillinger, Machine Gun Kelly, Baby Face Nelson, Ma Barker and her sons, and Pretty Boy Floyd contributed to the renown of the "chopper," "Chicago piano," "typewriter" or "Tommygun." The most infamous of all incidents, in which two Thompsons played key roles, was the Valentine's Day Massacre of February 14, 1929. Thompson sales shot back up during World War II, with the new majority owner of Auto-Ordnance, Wall Street businessman Russell Maguire. Great Britain, France, and the U.S. Army ordered a large number of guns: over 1,750,000 were built, plus the equivalent of another quarter million in the form of spare parts. These were made in Utica, New York (on contract by Savage Arms) and Bridgeport, Connecticut (by Auto-Ordnance). Among the employees of the firm in Bridgeport was the young inventor and designer William B. Ruger, then a fledgling, but brilliant, gun designer. With its popularity in film and TV programs, the Thompson became one of the world's best-known firearms. The gun became as much a symbol of the Roaring '20s era as did jazz, flappers, speakeasies, and bathtub gin. The Tommy Gun's role in America has earned it a monumental status on all fronts: as a cultural icon and historically, socially, criminally, militarily, and cinematically.

	Fair	*V. Good*	*Excellent*
AUTOMATIC WEAPON, SUBMACHINE GUN			
M1 (not Colt made)	$1000	$3500	$5000
M1A (not Colt made)	750	2500	4000
Model 1921, Submachine Gun (Colt-made)	3000	7500	10000
Model 1927, Submachine Gun (Colt-made)	5000	10000	15000
Model 1928, Submachine Gun (Colt-made)	2000	5000	7500

	Fair	*V. Good*	*Excellent*
HANDGUN, SELF-LOADING			
1991 A1 Various Calibers, Based on the Colt Pistol, *Modern*	$200	$300	$400
ZG-51 "Pit Bull,", Compact Model of the 1911 A1, 3.5" Barrel, *Modern*	250	350	400
CARBINE SELF-LOADING (THOMPSON REPLICAS)			
1927 A1 "Submachine Gun," .45 ACP, 16" Barrel, *Modern*	250	450	600
1927 A1 Deluxe "Submachine Gun," .45 ACP, Finned Barrel, Adjustable Sights, Pistol-Grip Forearm, *Modern*	300	600	800
1927 A1C "Submachine Gun," .45 ACP, Aluminum Alloy Receiver, *Modern*	250	525	600
1927 A3 "Submachine Gun," .22 LR, 16" Barrel, Aluminum Alloy Receiver, *Modern*	200	300	450
1927 A5 "Submachine Gun/Pistol," .45 ACP, Compact Variation, 13" Finned Barrel, Aluminum Alloy Receiver, No Shoulder Stock, *Modern*	250	525	600

AUTO-POINTER

Made by Yamamoto Mfg. Co., Imported by Sloans.

SHOTGUN, SELF-LOADING			
12 and 20 Gauges, Tube Feed, Checkered Stock, *Modern*	100	200	300

AUTOSTAND

Made for ManuFrance by Mre. d'Armes des Pyrenees.

HANDGUN, SINGLESHOT			
E-1 (Unique), .22 L.R.R.F., Target Pistol, Adjustable Sights, *Curio*	25	50	75

AVENGER

HANDGUN, REVOLVER			
.32 Long R.F., 5 Shot, Single Action, Spur Triggers, *Antique*	50	75	125

AVION

Azpiri y Cia., Eibar, Spain, c. 1915.

HANDGUN, SELF-LOADING			
Vest Pocket, .25 ACP, Clip Fed, *Curio*	50	75	125

AYA

Aguirre y Aranzabal, Spain. Now Imported by Ventura.

SHOTGUN, DOUBLE BARREL, OVER-UNDER			
Model 37 Super, Various Gauges, Single Selective Trigger, Automatic Ejectors, Fancy Engraving, Sidelock, *Modern*	1000	1750	2500

SHOTGUN, DOUBLE BARREL, SIDE-BY-SIDE

	Fair	V. Good	Excellent
Bolero, Various Gauges, Single Trigger, Checkered Stock, *Modern*	$300	$325	$350
Matador, Various Gauges, Single Selective Trigger, Checkered Stock, Selective Ejector, *Modern*	275	325	375
Matador II, Various Gauges, Single Selective Trigger, Checkered Stock, Selective Ejector, Vent Rib, *Modern*	275	350	425
Model 1, Various Gauges, Automatic Ejectors, Sidelock, Fancy Checkering, Engraved, Lightweight, *Modern*	1000	1500	2000
28 ga and 410 ga add 25%			
Model 117, 12 Gauge, Sidelock, Single Selective Trigger, Engraved, Checkered Stock, *Modern*	450	650	725
Model 2, Various Gauges, Automatic Ejector, Sidelock, Engraved, Checkered Stock, Double Trigger, *Modern*	650	950	1250
28 ga and 410 ga add 20%			
Model 53E, 12 and 20 Gauges, Sidelock, Single Selective Trigger, Fancy Checkering, Fancy Engraving, *Modern*	1000	1500	1950
Model 56, 12 and 20 Gauges, Sidelock, Raised Matted Rib, Fancy Checkering, Fancy Engraving, *Modern*	1750	2500	3000
Model 76, 12 and 20 Gauges, Automatic Ejectors, Single Selective Trigger, Engraved, Checkered Stock, *Modern*	185	375	650
Model 76, .410 Gauge, Double Triggers, Engraved, Checkered Stock, *Modern*	$200	$375	$550
Model 400, Various Gauges, Single Trigger, Checkered Stock, *Modern*	165	325	575
Model 400E, Various Gauges, Single Selective Trigger, Checkered Stock, Selective Ejector, *Modern*	250	375	450
Model XXV/SL, 12 Ga., Sidelock, Automatic Ejector, Engraved Checkered Stock, *Modern*	900	1250	1600

AZANZA Y ARRIZABALAGA

Eibar, Spain, c. 1916.

HANDGUN, SELF-LOADING

	Fair	V. Good	Excellent
M1916, .32 ACP, Clip Fed, Long Grip, *Curio*	50	100	150

AZUL

Eulegio Aristegui, Eibar, Spain, c. 1930.

HANDGUN, SELF-LOADING

	Fair	V. Good	Excellent
Azul, .25 ACP, Clip Fed, Hammerless, *Curio*	50	75	125
Azul, .32 ACP, Clip Fed, Hammer, *Curio*	50	100	150
Azul, .32 ACP, Clip Fed, Hammerless, *Curio*	50	75	125
Azul, 7.63mm Mauser, Copy of Broomhandle Mauser, *Curio*	275	550	950

B

	Fair	V. Good	Excellent

BABCOCK
c. 1880.

HANDGUN, REVOLVER

.32 Short R.F., 5 Shot, Spur Trigger, Solid Frame, Single Action, *Antique*	$50	$75	$150

BABY BULLDOG

HANDGUN, REVOLVER

.22 L.R.R.F., Double Action, Hammerless, Folding Trigger, *Modern*	50	75	150
.32 Short R.F., Double Action, Hammerless, Folding Trigger, *Modern*	50	75	125

BABY RUSSIAN
Made by American Arms Co., c. 1890.

HANDGUN, REVOLVER

.38 S & W, 5 Shot, Single Action, Spur Trigger, Top Break, *Curio* ...	75	125	225

BACKHOUSE, RICHARD
Easton, Pa., 1774–1781. See Kentucky Rifles.

BACKUP
See TDE and AMT.

BACON ARMS CO.
Norwich, Conn., 1858–1891. Also known as Bacon & Co. and Bacon Mfg. Co. The role of James Bacon in the development of Manhattan Fire Arms Co. is part of the reason that his firearms are increasingly in demand. Civil War identification and association with the Old West will increasingly impact Bacon values. It is possible to purchase these arms at a reasonable cost now, but as Colts continue to head out-of-sight, the Bacon, in its revolver configuration, is a Colt look-alike that has its own genuine and worthwhile appeal. Also made handguns marked with trade names as follows, q.v.: Big Bonanza, Bonanza, Conqueror, Daisy, Express, Fitch & Waldo, Gem, Governor, C. W. Hopkins, Little Giant.

HANDGUN, PERCUSSION

.34, Boot Gun, Underhammer, Half-Octagon Barrel, *Antique*	100	200	350

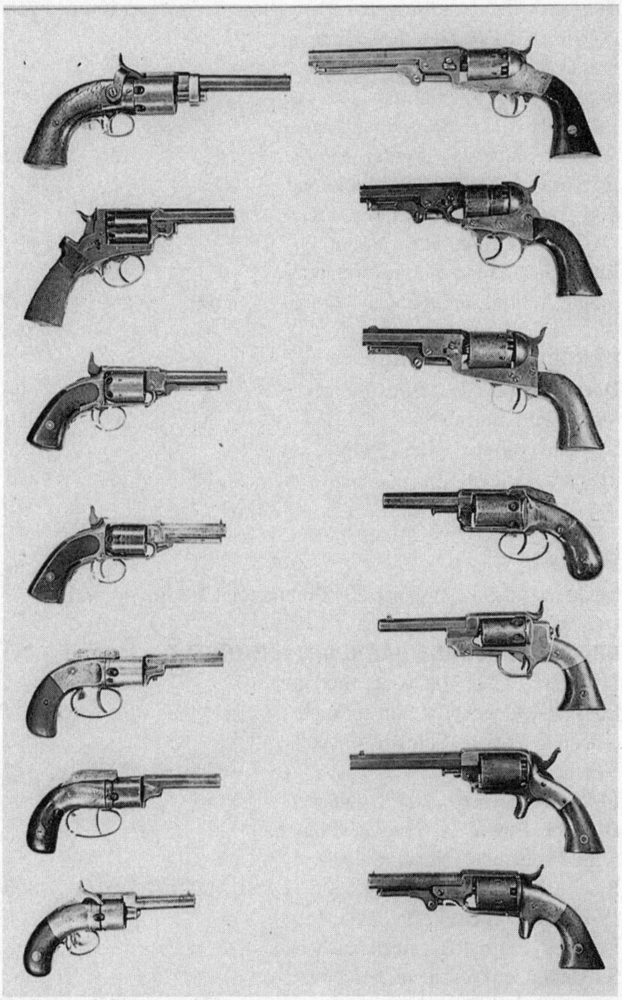

From top left, Massachusetts Arms Co. Wesson & Leavitt Patent .31, 6-shot Belt Model revolver; a double-action Massachusetts Arms Co. Pocket revolver marked made for Adams Revolving Arms Co. N.Y., .31 caliber, 5-shot; two variations of Warner single-action .28 Pocket revolvers, and Ells Patent .28 caliber revolvers; another variation of Warner Pocket revolver with etched ring-groove cylinder and offset hammer, .28 caliber. From top right, Manhattan Pocket Model .31 with 6" barrel and 12 locking grooves on cylinder; Cooper double-action .36 caliber 5-shot revolver; Manhattan Belt Model in .36 caliber, 4" barrel; Allen & Wheelock .31 caliber Pepperbox revolver of transition type with bar hammer and bag grips, double action; Allen & Wheelock .31 caliber Pocket Model, sidehammer, 5-shot; Allen sheath trigger Police Model in .36 caliber; and unmarked Pocket Model with .31 caliber 5-shot cylinder, attributed to Bacon Arms Co.

	Fair	V. Good	Excellent
6 Shot, Fluted Barrel, Pepperbox, Underhammer, Pocket Pistol, *Antique*	$350	$600	$900

HANDGUN, REVOLVER

	Fair	V. Good	Excellent
.22 Short R.F., 7 Shot, Spur Trigger, Solid Frame, Single Action, *Antique*	75	150	250
.32 Short R.F, 6 Shot, Solid Frame, Single Action with Trigger Guard, *Antique*	75	150	300
.32 Short R.F., 5 Shot, Spur Trigger, Solid Frame, Single Action, *Antique*	75	150	300
.32 Short R.F., 6 Shot, Solid Frame, Spur Trigger, Single Action, *Antique*	85	175	300
"Navy," .38 Long R.F., 6 Shot, $7\frac{1}{2}$" Barrel, Solid Frame, Spur Trigger, Single Action, *Antique*	100	200	425

HANDGUN, SINGLESHOT

	Fair	V. Good	Excellent
Derringer, .32 R.F., Spur Trigger, Side-Swing Barrel, *Antique*	85	200	350
SS Percussion, .31 Cal., Ring Trigger, *Antique*	85	200	275

BAIKAL

Made in U.S.S.R., imported by Commercial Trading Imports.

SHOTGUN, DOUBLE BARREL, OVER-UNDER

	Fair	V. Good	Excellent
IJ-27E1C, 12 or 20 Gauge, Boxlock, Engraved, Checkered Stock, Single Selective Trigger, Selective Ejectors, Vent Rib, *Modern*	115	225	375
IJ-27E1C Silver, 12 or 20 Gauge, Boxlock, Engraved, Checkered Stock, Single Selective Trigger, Selective Ejectors, Vent Rib, *Modern*	100	200	300
IJ-27E1C Super, 12 or 20 Gauge, Boxlock, Engraved, Checkered Stock, Single Selective Trigger, Selective Ejectors, Vent Rib, *Modern*	175	350	550
MC-109, 12 Gauge, Sidelock, Engraved, Checkered Stock, Single Selective Trigger, Selective Ejectors, Vent Rib, *Modern*	1750	2500	3250
MC-5-105, 20 Gauge, Boxlock, Engraved, Checkered Stock, Double Triggers, Solid Rib, Cased, *Modern*	400	875	1200
MC-6-105, 12 Gauge, Boxlock, Engraved, Checkered Stock, Double Triggers, Solid Rib, Cased, *Modern*	475	950	1500
MC-7-105, 12 or 20 Gauge, Boxlock, Engraved, Checkered Stock, Single Triggers, Selective Ejectors, Solid Rib, Cased, *Modern*	1000	1700	2400
MC-8-105, 12 Gauge, Trap or Skeet, Boxlock, Engraved, Checkered Stock, Single Trigger, Solid Rib, Cased, *Modern*	900	1400	2000
TOZ-34E, 12 or 28 Gauge, Boxlock, Engraved, Checkered Stock, Double Triggers, Vent Rib, *Modern*	$200	$325	$500

SHOTGUN, DOUBLE BARREL, SIDE-BY-SIDE

	Fair	V. Good	Excellent
IJ-58MAE, 12 or 20 Gauge, Boxlock, Engraved, Checkered Stock, Double Triggers, *Modern*	50	100	200
MC-110, 12 or 20 Gauge, Boxlock, Engraved, Checkered Stock, Double Triggers, Solid Rib, Cased, *Modern*	1000	1500	2000
MC-111, 12 Gauge, Sidelock, Engraved, Checkered Stock, Single Selective Trigger, Selective Ejectors, Cased, *Modern*	1750	2500	3250

SHOTGUN, SINGLESHOT

	Fair	V. Good	Excellent
IJ-18E, 12 or 20 Gauge, Checkered Stock, *Modern*	25	50	75

BAKER GUN & FORGING CO.

Batavia, N.Y., 1886–1919.

RIFLE, SELF-LOADING

	Fair	V. Good	Excellent
Batavia, .22 Short, Clip Fed, *Curio*	100	200	300

SHOTGUN, DOUBLE BARREL, SIDE-BY-SIDE

Single Trigger, Add $90.00–165.00
Deduct 50% for Damascus Barrels
Automatic Ejectors, Add $110.00–225.00

	Fair	V. Good	Excellent
Batavia Leader, Various Gauges, Sidelock, Double Trigger, Checkered Stock, *Curio*	200	400	550
Batavia Special, Various Gauges, Sidelock, Double Trigger, Checkered Stock, Automatic Ejectors, *Curio*	200	300	400
Black Beauty, Various Gauges, Sidelock, Double Trigger, Checkered Stock, *Curio*	225	450	675
Black Beauty Special, Various Gauges, Sidelock, Double Trigger, Checkered Stock, Automatic Ejectors, *Curio*	300	700	900
Deluxe ($1,000 Grade), Various Gauges, Sidelock, Fancy Wood, Fancy Engraving, Fancy Checkering, Automatic Ejector, *Curio*	1750	3500	5000
Deluxe ($300 Grade), Various Gauges, Sidelock, Fancy Wood, Fancy Engraving, Fancy Checkering, Automatic Ejectors, *Curio*	1500	2950	3750
Expert, Various Gauges, Sidelock, Fancy Wood, Fancy Engraving, Fancy Checkering, Automatic Ejectors, *Curio*	900	1850	2500
Grade A, Various Gauges, Sidelock, Hammerless, Engraved, Damascus Barrel, *Curio*	100	200	350
Grade B, Various Gauges, Sidelock, Hammerless, Engraved, Damascus Barrels, *Curio*	100	200	300

	Fair	V. Good	Excellent
Grade C Batavia, Various Gauges, Boxlock, Hammerless, Engraved, Damascus Barrels, *Curio*	$100	$175	$300
Grade H Deluxe, Various Gauges, Sidelock, Fancy Engraving, *Curio*	900	2500	3500
Grade L Pigeon, Various Gauges, Sidelock, Fancy Engraving, *Curio*	700	1550	2150
Grade N Krupp Trap, 12 Ga., Sidelock, Engraved, *Curio*	500	950	1400
Grade R, Various Gauges, Sidelock, Light Engraving, *Curio*	500	1000	1500
Grade S, Various Gauges, Sidelock, Light Engraving, *Curio*	300	800	1100
Model 1896, 10 and 12 Gauges, Hammers, *Curio*	125	225	400
Model 1897, Various Gauges, Hammers, *Curio*	125	225	400
New Baker Model, 10 and 12 Gauges, Hammers, *Curio*	125	250	400
Paragon, Various Gauges, Sidelock, Double Trigger, Engraved, Fancy Checkering, *Curio*	700	1100	1450
Paragon, Various Gauges, Sidelock, Double Trigger, Engraved, Fancy Checkering, Automatic Ejectors, *Curio*	900	1500	2000
Paragon Special, *Curio*	1000	1750	2350

SHOTGUN, SINGLESHOT

	Fair	V. Good	Excellent
Elite, 12 Ga., Vent Rib, Fancy Engraving, *Curio*	350	775	1250
Sterling, 12 Ga., Vent Rib, Light Engraving, *Curio*	325	550	775
Superba 12 Ga., Trap Grade, Fancy Wood, Fancy Engraving, Fancy Checkering, Automatic Ejectors, *Antique*	1125	1950	2775

BAKER GUN CO.

Made in Belgium for H & D Folsom Arms Co.

SHOTGUN, DOUBLE BARREL, SIDE-BY-SIDE

	Fair	V. Good	Excellent
Various Gauges, Hammerless, Damascus Barrel, *Antique*	50	100	175
Various Gauges, Hammerless, Steel Barrel, *Antique*	75	125	200
Various Gauges, Outside Hammers, Damascus Barrel, *Antique*	50	75	175
Various Gauges, Outside Hammers, Steel Barrel, *Antique*	75	150	200

SHOTGUN, SINGLESHOT

	Fair	V. Good	Excellent
Various Gauges, Hammer, Steel Barrel, *Antique*	25	50	75

BAKER, EZEKIEL

London, England, 1784–1825.

HANDGUN, PERCUSSION

	Fair	V. Good	Excellent
.58, Holster Pistol, Round Barrel, Light Ornamentation, *Antique*	$300	$550	$800

BAKER, JOHN

Providence, Pa., 1768–1775. See Kentucky Rifles.

BAKER, W. H. & CO.

Marathon, N.Y., 1870, Syracuse, N.Y. 1878–1886.

COMBINATION WEAPON, DRILLING

	Fair	V. Good	Excellent
Hammer Drilling, Various Gauges, Damascus Barrels. Front Trigger Break, *Antique*	225	450	725

RIFLE, PERCUSSION

	Fair	V. Good	Excellent
.60, Brass Furniture, Scope Mounted, Target, Octagon Barrel, *Antique*	1250	2000	2750

SHOTGUN, DOUBLE BARREL, SIDE-BY-SIDE

	Fair	V. Good	Excellent
Hammer Double, 10 and 12 Gauges, Damascus Barrels, Front Trigger Break, *Antique*	175	275	375

BALL & WILLIAMS

Worcester, Mass., 1861–1866.

RIFLE, SINGLESHOT

	Fair	V. Good	Excellent
Ballard, .44 Long R.F., Milliary, Carbine, Falling Block, *Antique*	300	600	1200
Ballard, .46 Long R.F., Kentucky Rifle, Falling Block, *Antique*	550	750	925
Ballard, Various Rimfires, Falling Block, Sporting Rifle, *Antique*	300	425	550
Ballard, Various Rimfires, Military, Falling Block, *Antique*	335	675	1200
Merwin & Bray, .54 Ballard R.F., Military, Carbine, Falling Block, *Antique*	315	625	1200
Merwin & Bray, Various Rimfires, Falling Block, Sporting Rifle, *Antique*	350	525	750

BALLARD & CO.

Worcester, Mass., 1861–1971. Also see U.S. Military.

RIFLE, SINGLESHOT

	Fair	V. Good	Excellent
#2 (Marlin), Various Calibers, Falling Block, Sporting Rifle, *Antique*	700	1000	1350
#3 Gallery (Marlin), Various Calibers, Falling Block, Target Rifle, *Antique*	50	400	1200
#3 Gallery (Marlin), Various Rimfires, Falling Block, Target Rifle, *Antique*	650	950	1350
#3-F Gallery (Marlin), .22 Long R.F., Falling Block, Target Rifle, Fancy Wood, *Antique*	700	1000	1300

	Fair	V. Good	Excellent
#4 Perfection (Marlin), Various Calibers, Falling Block, Target Rifle, Target Sights, Set Triggers, Octagon Barrel, *Antique*	$1000	$1500	$2000

Three variations of Ballard single-shot sporting rifles. Note barrel bands of center rifle, indicating military styling. Top, *rifle with Ball & Williams markings.* Center, *an early military model with Brown Mfg. Co. markings.* Bottom, *a Hunters rifle.*

BALLARD RIFLE

Made by Ball & Williams, 1861–1866; Merrimack Arms & Mfg. Co., 1866–1869, Brown Mfg. Co., 1869–1873; J. M. Marlin from 1875. Although definitely an "also-ran" in the pantheon of 19th-century American long-gun makers, the Ballard stands as one of the most important and successful of U.S. singleshots, and was a well-made and designed competitior in that market. Civil War, Wild West, and target match identifications will contribute to the steady rise in and demand by collectors in these arms. James J. Grant's series on singleshot rifles are vital to the collector who wishes to pursue the Ballards, which fit into this highly popular area of the fine and historic in firearms.

RIFLE, SINGLESHOT

	Fair	V. Good	Excellent
#1½ Hunter (Marlin), .40-65 Ballard Everlasting, Falling Block, Sporting Rifle, Open Rear Sight, *Antique*	300	1000	1650
#1 Hunter (Marlin), .44 Long R F/C F, Falling Block, Sporting Rifle, Recoil Pad, *Antique*	300	900	1500
#2 (Marlin), .44-40 WCF, Falling Block, Sporting Rifle, Open Rear Sight, *Antique*	400	1000	1650
#2 (Marlin), Various Calibers, Falling Block, Sporting Rifle, Recoil Pad, Early Model, *Antique*	400	1000	1650
#3½ (Marlin), .40-65 Ballard Everlasting, Falling Block, Target Rifle, Target Sights, Octagon Barrel, *Antique*	500	1500	2350
#3 Gallery (Marlin), .22 Short R.F., Falling Block, Target Rifle, Early Model, *Antique*	$200	$800	$1250
#4½ (Marlin), .40-65 Ballard Everlasting, Falling Block, Mid-Range Target Rifle, Checkered Stock, *Antique*	500	1500	2300
#4½ (Marlin), .45-70 Government, Falling Block, Sporting Rifle, *Antique*	500	1500	2500
#4½ (Marlin), Various Calibers, Falling Block, Mid-Range Target Rifle, Target Sights, Fancy Wood, *Antique*	1250	2500	4000
#4½ (Marlin), Various Calibers, Falling Block, Sporting Rifle, *Antique*	500	1000	1500
#4 Perfection (Marlin), Various Calibers, Falling Block, Target Rifle, Target Sights, Set Trigger, Early Model, *Antique*	600	1500	2500
#5 Pacific (Marlin), .45-70 Government, Falling Block, Target Rifle, Open Rear Sight, Set Trigger, Octagon Barrel, *Antique*	700	2000	3000
#5 Pacific (Marlin), Various Calibers, Falling Block, Target Rifle, Open Rear Sight, Set Trigger, Octagon Barrel, *Antique*	600	1750	2350
#6½ (Marlin), .40-65 Ballard Everlasting, Falling Block, Off-Hand Target Rifle, Target Sights, Set Trigger, *Antique*	600	2700	3750
#6½ (Marlin), Various Calibers, Falling Block, Mid-Range Target Rifle, *Antique*	900	2700	3750
#6 Pacific (Marlin), Various Calibers, Falling Block, Schutzen Rifle, Target Sights, Fancy Wood, Set Triggers, *Antique*	1200	3500	5000
#7 A (Marlin), .44-100 Ballard Everlasting, Falling Block, Long Range Target Rifle, Target Sights, Set Trigger, *Antique*	1100	3000	4500
#7 A-1 (Marlin), .44-100 Ballard Everlasting, Falling Block, Long Range Target Rifle, Target Sights, Set Trigger, Fancy Wood, *Antique*	1200	3500	5000
#7 A-1 (Marlin), .44-75 Ballard Everlasting, Falling Block, Creedmore Long Range, Target Sights, Fancy Wood, Set Trigger, *Antique*	1250	3500	5000
#7 A-1 Extra Deluxe, .44-100 Ballard Everlasting, Falling Block, Long Range Target Rifle, Target Sights, Set Trigger, Fancy Wood, *Antique*	1250	4000	6500
#8 (Marlin), .44-75 Ballard Everlasting, Falling Block, Creedmore Long Range, Target Sights, Pistol-Grip Stock, Set Trigger, *Antique*	1200	3000	4500

	Fair	V. Good	Excellent
#9 (Marlin), .44-75 Ballard Everlasting, Falling Block, Creedmore Long Range, Target Sights, Set Trigger, *Antique*	$1000	$2000	$2500
(Ball & Williams), .54 Ballard R.F., Military, Carbine, Falling Block, *Antique*	300	750	1250
(Ball & Williams), .44 Long R.F., Military, Carbine, Falling Block, *Antique*	200	500	1250
(Ball & Williams), .46 Long R.F., Kentucky Rifle, Falling Block, *Antique*	400	850	1350
(Ball & Williams), Various Rimfires, Falling Block, Sporting Rifle, *Antique*	200	475	800
(Ball & Williams), Various Rimfires, Military, Falling Block, *Antique*	300	750	1200
1½ Hunter (Marlin), .45-70 Government, Falling Block, Sporting Rifle, Open Rear Sight, Set Trigger, *Antique*	500	1000	2000
1¾ Far West (Marlin), .40-65 Ballard Everlasting, Falling Block, Sporting Rifle, Open Rear Sight, Set Trigger, *Antique*	400	800	1750
1¾ Far West (Marlin), .45-70 Government, Falling Block, Sporting Rifle, Open Rear Sight, Set Trigger, *Antique*	500	1000	1750
5½ Montana (Marlin), .45-100 Sharps, Falling Block, Sporting Rifle, Octagon Barrel, *Antique*	750	3000	4500
Brown Mfg. Co., .44 Long R.F., Falling Block, Mid-Range Target Rifle, *Antique*	300	800	1250
Hunter, .44 Long R F/C F, Falling Block, Sporting Rifle, Recoil Pad, *Antique*	300	800	1250
Merrimack Arms, .44 Long R.F., Falling Block, Carbine, *Antique*	300	800	1250
Merrimack Arms, .46 Long R.F., Falling Block, Military, *Antique*	300	800	1250
Merrimack Arms, .56-52 Spencer R.F., Falling Block, Military, *Antique*	300	800	1250
Merrimack Arms, Various Rimfires, Falling Block, Sporting Rifle, *Antique*	300	800	1250
Merwin & Bray, Various Rimfires, Falling Block, Sporting Rifle, *Antique*	285	575	1100

BANG-UP

Made by Hopkins & Allen, c. 1880.

HANDGUN, REVOLVER

	Fair	V. Good	Excellent
.22 Short R.F., 7 Shot, Spur Trigger, Solid Frame, Single Action, *Antique*	50	100	150

BARKER, F.A.

Fayetteville, N.C., 1860–1864. See Confederate Military.

BARKER, T.

Made by Crescent; also made in Belgium. See Crescent Fire Arms Co., Shotgun, Double Barrel, Side-By-Side; Shotgun, Singleshot.

BARLOW, J.

Moscow, Ind., 1836–1840. See Kentucky Rifles.

BARNETT & SON

London, England, 1750–1832.

RIFLE, FLINTLOCK

	Fair	V. Good	Excellent
.75, 3rd. Model Brown Bess, Musket, Military, *Antique*	$650	$1250	$1850

BARNETT, J. & SONS

London, England, 1835–1875.

RIFLE, PERCUSSION

	Fair	V. Good	Excellent
.577, C.W. Enfield, Rifled, Musket, Military, *Antique*	300	700	1000

BARRETT, J.

Wythesville, Va., 1857–1865. See Confederate Military.

BAUER FIREARMS (FRASER ARMS CO.)

Fraser, Mich.

HANDGUN, SELF-LOADING

	Fair	V. Good	Excellent
25-Bicentennial, .25 ACP, Clip Fed, Pocket Pistol, Stainless Steel, Hammerless, Engraved, *Modern*	75	150	225
25-SS, .25 ACP, Clip Fed, Pocket Pistol, Stainless Steel, Hammerless, *Modern*	65	125	200

COMBINATION WEAPON, OVER-UNDER

	Fair	V. Good	Excellent
Rabbit, .22/.410, Metal Frame, Survival Gun, *Modern*	75	100	125

BAUER, GEORGE

Lancaster, Pa., 1770–1781. See Kentucky Rifles.

BAY STATE ARMS CO.

Uxbridge & Worcester, Mass., 1873–1874.

RIFLE, SINGLESHOT

	Fair	V. Good	Excellent
.32 Long R.F., Dropping Block, *Antique*	100	200	300
Various Calibers, Target Rifle, *Antique*	300	700	1000

SHOTGUN, SINGLESHOT

	Fair	V. Good	Excellent
Davenport Patent, 12 Ga., *Antique*	$125	$200	$275

BAYARD

Belgium. Made by Anciens Etablissments Pieper, c. 1900. Also see Bergmann and Danish Military.

HANDGUN, REVOLVER

	Fair	V. Good	Excellent
S & W Style, .32 S&W Long, Double Action, *Curio*	50	75	125
S & W Style, .38 S&W, Double Action, *Curio*	50	75	125

HANDGUN, SELF-LOADING

	Fair	V. Good	Excellent
Bergmann/Bayard 1910, 9mm Bayard, Clip Fed, Blue, Commercial, *Curio*	500	1000	1500
Bergmann/Bayard 1910, 9mm Bayard, Clip Fed, Blue, Commercial, with Holster/Stock, *Curio*	1000	1500	2000
Model 1908 (1910) Pocket, .32 ACP, Blue, Clip Fed, *Curio*	100	275	350
Model 1908 (1910) Pocket, .32 ACP, Blue, Clip Fed, German Military, *Curio*	200	300	400
Model 1908 (1910) Pocket, .32 ACP, Nickel, Clip Fed, *Curio*	75	125	200

Bayard Model 1908 (1910) .32 ACP

	Fair	V. Good	Excellent
Model 1908 (1911) Pocket, .380 ACP, Blue, Clip Fed, *Curio*	75	125	250
Model 1908 (1911) Pocket, .380 ACP, Nickel, Clip Fed, *Curio*	75	125	250
Model 1908 (1912) Pocket, .25 ACP, Blue, Clip Fed, *Curio*	100	250	300
Model 1908 (1912) Pocket, .25 ACP, Nickel, Clip Fed, *Curio*	100	250	300
Model 1923 Pocket, Early, .25 ACP, Blue, Clip Fed, With Magazine Safety, *Curio*	100	200	275
Model 1923 Pocket, Early, .32 ACP, Blue, Clip Fed, With Magazine Safety, *Curio*	100	200	275
Model 1923 Pocket, Early, .380 ACP, Blue, Clip Fed, With Magazine Safety, *Curio*	125	250	350
Model 1923 Pocket, Standard, .25 ACP, Blue, Clip Fed, No Magazine Safety, *Curio*	$100	$200	$250
Model 1923 Pocket, Standard, .32 ACP, Blue, Clip Fed, No Magazine Safety, *Curio*	100	250	300
Model 1923 Pocket, Standard, .380 ACP, Blue, Clip Fed, No Magazine Safety, *Curio*	125	275	350
Model 1930 Pocket, .25 ACP, Blue, Clip Fed, *Curio*	125	200	275

Bayard Model 1930

	Fair	V. Good	Excellent
Model 1930 Pocket, .32 ACP, Blue, Clip Fed, *Curio*	125	200	275
Model 1930 Pocket, .380 ACP, Blue, Clip Fed, *Curio*	225	300	375

RIFLE, SINGLESHOT

	Fair	V. Good	Excellent
Boy's Rifle, .22 L.R.R.F., Plain, Takedown, *Curio*	25	50	75
Half-Auto Carbine, .22 Short, Checkered Stock, *Curio*	25	50	75
Half-Auto Carbine, .22 Short, Plain, *Curio*	25	50	75

SHOTGUN, DOUBLE BARREL, SIDE-BY-SIDE

	Fair	V. Good	Excellent
Hammer, 12 Gauge, Double Triggers, Fancy Engraving, Boxlock, Steel Barrels, *Curio*	75	125	225

Hammer, *12 Gauge, Double Triggers,*

Beeman Agner M80

	Fair	V. Good	Excellent
Light Engraving, Boxlock, Damascus Barrels, *Curio*	$50	$75	$150
Hammer, 12 Gauge, Double Triggers, Light Engraving, Boxlock, Steel Barrels, *Curio*	50	75	150
Hammerless, 12 Gauge, Double Triggers, Light Engraving, Boxlock, Steel Barrels, *Curio*	75	125	200

BECK, GIDEON

Lancaster, Pa., 1780–1788. See Kentucky Rifles and Pistols.

BECK, ISAAC

Miffinberg, Pa., 1830–1840.

RIFLE, PERCUSSION

	Fair	V. Good	Excellent
.47, Octagon Barrel, Brass Furniture, *Antique*	400	1200	1500

BECK, JOHN

Lancaster, Pa., 1772–1777. See Kentucky Rifles and Pistols.

BEEMAN PRECISION FIREARMS

San Raphael, Calif., Importers.

HANDGUN, PERCUSSION

	Fair	V. Good	Excellent
Hege-Siber, English, .33, Checkered Stock, Light Engraving, Cased, Reproduction, *Antique*	250	500	750
Hege-Siber, French, .33, Checkered Stock, Engraved, Gold Inlays, Cased, Reproduction, *Antique*	375	750	1250
PB Aristocrat, .36 or .44, Single Set Trigger, Fluted Stock, Reproduction, *Antique*	100	175	250

HANDGUN, SELF-LOADING

	Fair	V. Good	Excellent
Agner M80, .22 L.R.R.F., Clip Fed, Stainless Steel, Adjustable Target Grips, Adjustable Trigger, *Modern*	600	925	1200
FAS Model 601, .22 Short R.F., Clip Fed, Target Grip, Rapid Fire, Target Pistol, *Modern*	400	650	1000

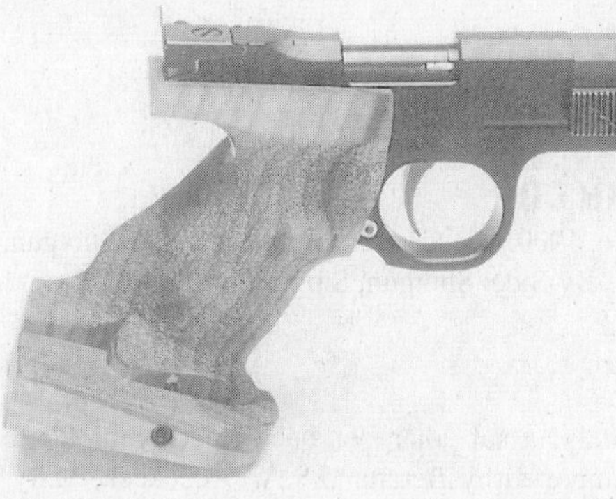

Beeman FAS Model 601

	Fair	V. Good	Excellent
FAS Model 602, .22 L.R.R.F., Clip Fed, Target Grip, Match Pistol, *Modern*	$500	$800	$1250
FAS Model 603, .32 S&W Wadcutter, Clip Fed, Target Grips, Match Pistol, *Modern*	550	800	1250
Unique Model 69, .22 L.R.R.F., Clip Fed, Adjustable Target Grips, Match Pistol, *Modern*	400	700	1000
Unique Model 823-U, .22 Short R.F., Clip Fed, Adjustable Target Grips, Rapid Fire Match Pistol, *Modern*	400	700	1000

RIFLE, BOLT ACTION

	Fair	V. Good	Excellent
Feinwerkbau 2000 Match, .22 L.R.R.F., Singleshot, Adjustable Trigger, Adjustable Target Stock, *Modern*	400	750	1100

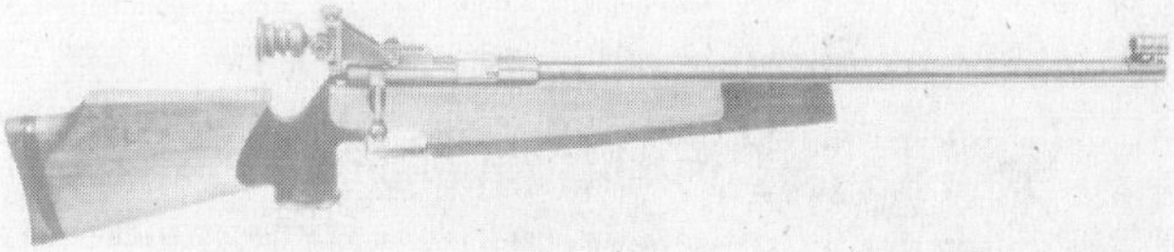

Beeman Feinwerkbau 2000 Match

	Fair	V. Good	Excellent
Feinwerkbau 2000 Mini, .22 L.R.R.F., Singleshot, Adjustable Trigger, Adjustable Target Stock, *Modern*	400	700	800
Feinwerkbau 2000 Running Target, .22 L.R.R.F., Singleshot, Adjustable Trigger, Adjustable Target Stock, *Modern*	450	750	900
Feinwerkbau 2000 Universal, .22 L.R.R.F., Singleshot, Adjustable Trigger, Adjustable Target Stock, *Modern*	750	750	900
Feinwerkbau Free Rifle, .22 L.R.R.F., Singleshot, Adjustable Electric Trigger, Adjustable Target Stock, Counterweights, Hook Buttplate, *Modern*	500	1000	1250
Krico Model 302, .22 L.R.R.F., Clip Fed, Checkered Stock, Open Sights, *Modern*	200	400	500
Krico Model 304, .22 L.R.R.F., Clip Fed, Checkered Stock, Mannlicher Stock, Set Triggers, Open Sights, *Modern*	200	450	600
Krico Model 340, .22 L.R.R.F., Metallic Silhouette Match Rifle, Clip Fed, Checkered Stock, Target Stock, *Modern*	250	625	800
Krico Model 340, .22 L.R.R.F., Mini-Sniper Match Rifle, Clip Fed, Checkered Stock, Target Stock, *Modern*	250	650	800
Krico Model 400, .22 Hornet, Clip Fed, Checkered Stock, Open Sights, *Modern*	300	650	850

	Fair	V. Good	Excellent
Krico Model 420, .22 Hornet, Clip Fed, Checkered Stock, Set Triggers, Mannlicher Stock, Open Sights, Sling Swivels, *Modern*	$250	$650	$900
Krico Model 600, Various Calibers, Clip Fed, Checkered Stock, Open Sights, Sling Swivels, Recoil Pads, *Modern*	300	800	1000
Krico Model 620, Various Calibers, Clip Fed, Checkered Stock, Set Triggers, Mannlicher Stock, Open Sights, Sling Swivels, *Modern*	300	775	1000
Krico Model 640, Various Calibers, Deluxe Varmint Rifle, Clip Fed, Checkered Stock, Target Stock, *Modern*	250	625	900
Krico Model 650, Various Calibers, Sniper/Match Rifle, Clip Fed, Checkered Stock, Target Stock, *Modern*	400	850	1100

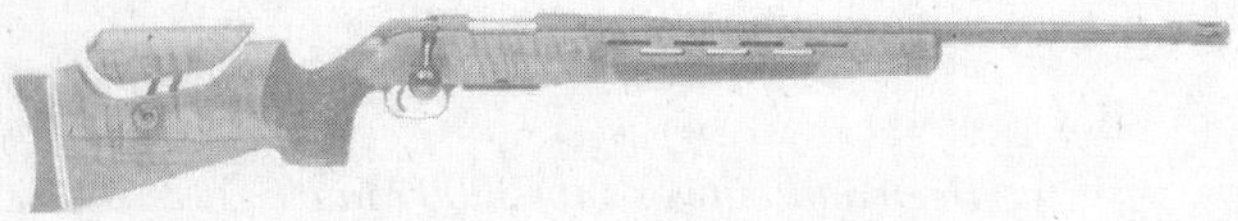

Beeman Krico Model 650

	Fair	V. Good	Excellent
Krico Model 700, Various Calibers, Clip Fed, Checkered Stock, Open Sights, Sling Swivels, Recoil Pad, *Modern*	300	850	1100
Krico Model 720, Various Calibers, Clip Fed, Checkered Stock, Set Triggers, Mannlicher Stock, Open Sights, Sling Swivels, *Modern*	300	800	1000
Weihrauch HW60, .22 L.R.R.F., Singleshot Target Rifle, Target Sights, Target Stock, Heavy Barrel, *Modern*	250	525	650

SHOTGUN, DOUBLE BARREL, OVER-UNDER

	Fair	V. Good	Excellent
Fabarm Gamma, 12 Gauge, Field Model, Single Selective Trigger, Checkered Stock, Vent Rib, *Modern*	300	700	850
Fabarm Gamma, 12 Gauge, Skeet Model, Single Selective Trigger, Checkered Stock, Vent Rib, *Modern*	350	775	900
Fabarm Gamma, 12 Gauge, Trap/Skeet Combo, 2 Barrels, Single Selective Trigger, Checkered Stock, Vent Rib, *Modern*	350	800	1000

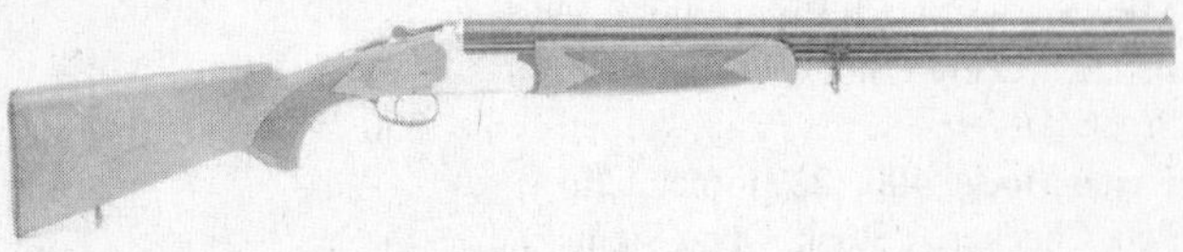

Beeman Fabarm Gamma

BEERSTECHER, FREDERICK

Lewisburg, Pa., 1849–1860.

HANDGUN, PERCUSSION

	Fair	V. Good	Excellent
.40, Double Shot, Superimposed Loading, Derringer Style, *Antique*	$2500	$4500	$6500

BEHOLLA

Made by Becker & Hollander, Suhl, Germany c. 1910. Also made under this patent were the Stenda, Leonhardt, and Menta.

HANDGUN, SELF-LOADING

	Fair	V. Good	Excellent
.32 ACP, Clip Fed, Commercial, Blue, Hard Rubber Grips, *Curio*	200	250	300
.32 ACP, Clip Fed, Commercial, Blue, Wood Grips, *Curio*	150	200	250
.32 ACP, Clip Fed, Military, Blue, Hard Rubber Grips, *Curio*	150	200	250
.32 ACP, Clip Fed, Military, Blue, Wood Grips, *Curio*	150	200	250

BELGIAN MILITARY

Also see Browning, Fabrique Nationale.

RIFLE, BOLT ACTION

	Fair	V. Good	Excellent
M 1889 Mauser, Carbine, Military, *Curio*	250	325	350
M 1889 Mauser, Military, *Curio*	275	300	325
M 1924, Various Calibers, Military, *Curio*	200	225	300
M 1930, Various Calibers, Military, *Curio*	200	225	300
M 1934/30, Various Calibers, Military, *Curio*	175	200	250
M 1935 Mauser, Military, *Curio*	250	275	350
M 1936 Mauser, Military, *Curio*	125	150	200
M 1950, .30-06 Springfield, Military, *Curio*	225	250	300

RIFLE, SELF-LOADING

	Fair	V. Good	Excellent
M 1949, .30-06 Springfield, Military, *Curio*	150	300	450
M 1949, Various Calibers, Military, *Curio*	125	250	375

BELL, JOHN

Carlisle, Pa., c. 1800. See Kentucky Rifles and Pistols.

BELLMORE GUN CO.

Made by Crescent, c. 1900. See Crescent Fire Arms Co., Shotgun, Double Barrel, Side-By-Side; Shotgun, Singleshot.

BENELLI

Made in Urbino, Italy; a subsidiary of Fabbrica d'Armi Pietro Beretta SpA, and imported by Beretta U.S.A., Accokeek, Maryland. Self-loading and pump shotguns, as well as target pistols.

	Fair	V. Good	Excellent
HANDGUN, SELF-LOADING			
B 76, 9mm Luger, Clip Fed, Blue, *Modern*	$200	$375	$550
RIFLE, SELF-LOADING			
Model 940, .30-06 Springfield, Clip Fed, Open Sights, Recoil Pad, Sling Swivels, *Modern*	325	400	550
SHOTGUN, SELF-LOADING			
Model 123V Deluxe, 12 Gauge, Engraved Model, Checkered Stock, Vent Rib, *Modern*	150	350	500
Model 123V, 12 Gauge, Standard Model, Checkered Stock, Vent Rib, *Modern*	150	325	500
Model SL 121MI, 12 Gauge, Police, Open Sights, Checkered Stock, Recoil Pad, *Modern*	150	300	500
Model SL 121V, 12 Gauge, Slug Gun, Open Sights, Checkered Stock, Recoil Pad, *Modern*	150	300	500
Model SL 201, 20 Gauge, Checkered Stock, Plain Barrel, *Modern*	150	275	450
Special Skeet, 12 Gauge, White Receiver, Checkered Stock, Vent Rib, *Modern*	250	400	525
Special Trap, 12 Gauge, White Receiver, Checkered Stock, Vent Rib, *Modern*	250	375	525

BENFER, AMOS

Beaverstown, Pa., c. 1810. See Kentucky Rifles and Pistols.

BERETTA

Beretta, Pietro, Gardone, Val Trompia, Italy; est. by 1526. Beretta U.S.A. Corporation formed in 1977. The author has written a fresh book on Beretta, entitled *The World of Beretta: An International Legend.* With a history dating back nearly 500 years, the firm is recognized as the oldest industrial operation in the world—and considering the significance of gunmakers and gunmaking in the evolution of manufacturing, it is fitting that a gunmaker is the world's oldest manufacturer. Truly the Gucci, Armani, or Ferrari of firearms, the company has remained in the hands of the same family for fourteen generations; it is currently under the leadership of Ugo Gussalli Beretta and his sons (the fifteenth generation) Pietro and Franco. Beretta is known to have been an active and successful business as early as 1526, as documented in a transaction between the firm and the City of Venice, for the production of gun barrels. Later the Berettas developed state-of-the-art production and marketing skills, particularly in the 19th and 20th centuries, and today it boasts landmark galleries in New York City and Dallas, Texas, and a satellite factory in Accokeek, Maryland, in addition to its truly impressive world headquarters in Gardone, Val Trompia, Italy. Beretta's other subsidiaries include Franchi and Benelli (q.v.). The company's museum, available by appointment, is the finest of its type of any contemporary gunmaker. Despite the size of the company, Beretta's master gunmakers are also capable of producing some of the world's most beautiful, accurate, and mechanically brilliant firearms. The fact that it is a Beretta handgun, the M9 (a variation of the Model 92), which is the standard sidearm of the U.S. government, speaks volumes for the firm's designing, manufacturing, and marketing abilities.

	Fair	V. Good	Excellent
Hammer Model Side-by-Side Double Barrel Shotguns			
Stella Model	$400	$800	$1350
Vittoria Model	500	1000	1600
Piccione Model (Pigeon)	600	1250	2100
Hammerless Boxlock Side-by-Side Double Barrel			
The Stella Model	400	800	1350
The P.B. Model, Models 9, 10, 11, 1009, 1010, 1011, 311 premium for finely engraved pieces	500	900	1650
The Pigeon Model 7 and 10 and the 1011, 311, 311E premium for finely engraved pieces	700	1200	1850
Model 1050 Hammerless Sidelock, type 1930–31, with Holland & Holland sidelocks	500	900	1600
Model 409PB, 410, 410E, 411E, Boxlock Action; 20 Gauge Only. Hand Engraved. Select Walnut Stock; Straight or Pistol-Grip; Premium for Higher Grades			
409PB, 28 ga	850	1200	1750
20 gauge	400	750	1100
16 gauge	400	600	900
12 gauge	400	600	900
410, 10 ga	600	850	1350
410E, 28 gauge	1600	3000	4600
20 gauge	800	1200	2100
12 gauge	600	900	1500
411E, 28 ga	1600	3000	4750
20 gauge	1000	1500	3000
12 gauge	800	1200	2250
Model 450 E, 450 EL, 450 EELL, 12 gauge only. Premier grade walnut stocks; snap-fastening forearm. Straight or semi-pistol grip stocks; premium for higher grades			
450 E	3000	4500	6500
450 EL	4500	6000	9500
450 EELL	4500	6000	10000
Model 425, 426, 426 E, Successor to Model 409PB; 12 gauge, engraved, select walnut stocks; premium for higher grades.	800	1200	1650
Add $125 for Model 426 and 426E			
Model 424, Same as Model 425, but "with a positive double bolt only and plain border scroll" engraving; 20, 16, and 12 gauges.	800	1200	1650
Model 427 E, various gauges; sidelock; premium for higher grades	1200	1600	2150

	Fair	V. Good	Excellent
Model 451, 451 E, 451 EL, 451 EELL, 12 gauge, basically a hand-built gun, "alongside the normal standard production," the company will make guns with barrels in various lengths and chokes; premium for higher grades.			
451	$2500	$5000	$7500
451 E	7000	9250	16000
451 EL	10000	15000	20000
451 EELL	15000	20000	25000
625	500	700	1000
625 Onyx	900	1200	1750
626 Onyx Magnum	900	1200	1750
627 EL Field	1800	2400	3000
627 EL Sport	1800	2400	3000
627 EELL	2800	3500	4750
452	15000	22500	28500
Add $5400 for extra set of barrels			
452 EELL	20000	31000	38500
470 Silver Hawk, 470 EL, 470 EELL; current boxlock, side-by-side, 20 and 12 gauge; premium for higher grades			
470 Silver Hawk	2000	2600	3500
470 EL	3800	4500	5500
470 EELL	6500	9500	12500

OVER-AND-UNDERS

	Fair	V. Good	Excellent
SO series, including SO1, SO2, SO3, SO4, SO5, SO6, SO9, most models in 12 gauge only, and listings as follows in that gauge unless indicated otherwise; some models also built in 16, 20, 28, 410 gauges, highest grades of over-and-unders in the line, from the Premium Grade line. Premium paid for engraving, and particularly for special engravings by exceptional artisans, usually even more so when signed. Added value also for scarce gauges, especially 28 and 410.			
SO1, 12 gauge	2000	2750	5000
SO2, 12 gauge	2000	2500	4000
SO3, 12 gauge	3000	3800	5500
SO3EL, 12 gauge	3000	4500	7000
SO3EELL, 12 gauge	5000	7500	10000
SO4, 12 gauge	3250	4500	6500
SO5, 12 gauge	8000	12000	16500
Trap add $4000 for Trap Combo Set			
SO5EELL, 12 gauge	6000	10000	14000
SO5 Deluxe (CCH)	7000	11000	15000
SO6 Competition, 12 gauge	15000	17500	23500
SO6EELL	22500	29500	39500
SO6EESS	22500	27000	38500
SO9, 12 gauge	22500	27000	38500
Available in .410, 28, 20, and 12 gauge			
SO9EELL	38000	50000	75000
Vandalia, 12 gauge single barrel trap gun; designed from SO series	$8000	$10000	$15000
ASE (1947–1964) 12 ga	1000	1500	2000
20 gauge	2500	3200	4000
ASE, ASEL and ASE Deluxe, boxlocks of high grade, 12, 20 gauge, from the Premium Grade line.			
ASE, 12 gauge	3000	5500	7500
ASE Gold	5000	8000	10000
ASE 90 Deluxe	8000	15500	20500
ASE L, 20 gauge	2500	3500	4500
12 gauge	1500	2500	3000
ASE EELL, 20 ga	4000	6000	8500
12gauge	1500	2500	3500
S 55 B, S 56 E, S 57 E, S 57 EL, 12, 20 gauge, an early upper grade of boxlock			
S 55 B	300	500	750
S 56 E	350	500	750
S57E SST	500	750	1000
S57 EL	700	1500	2500
58 Skeet	400	650	900
58 Trap	400	650	900
S 680, 12 gauge only, **S 680 Trap, S 680 Skeet, S 680 Sporting (Clays)**			
680	800	1000	1350
680 Skeet	750	925	1250
680 Trap	800	1000	1350
682 Continental Course	1000	1500	2500
682 Gold Sport	1000	1500	2500
682 Super Sport	1000	1500	2500
682 Gold Trap (Gold X)	1200	1900	2400
682 Mono Top Combo (Gold X)	1800	2500	3200
682 Gold Trap Adj. Stock	1800	2700	3200
682 Mono	900	1250	1600
682 Gold Live Bird	1000	1500	2250
682 Un-Single	1000	1500	2250
682 Gold X Super Trap	1000	1500	2250
682 Gold Super Trap (Top Combo, Gold X)	1500	2000	3300
682 Top Mono Super Trap	1100	1600	2350
685	350	575	800
686 Onyx, 12 and 20 ga	600	750	1250
686 Onyx Ultralight	800	1200	1500
686 Ultralight Deluxe	1000	1400	1800
686 Essential	400	700	1000
686 Silver Pigeon/Perdiz 28, 20, and 12 ga	700	900	1300
686 Silver Pigeon Combo in 28 and 20 ga	1000	1400	2000
686 International	700	900	1200
686 Sport Special Sporting	800	1200	1600
687 Silver Pigeon	1000	1400	1800
687 Silver Pigeon II	1000	1400	1800
687 Ducks Unlimited	1000	1450	1950
687 Tercentennial	1250	1950	2500
Silver Essential, 12 gauge	500	650	950
687 EELL Diamond Pigeon Trap	2800	3500	4200
687 EELL Diamond Trap Top Mono	2400	3400	4500

	Fair	V. Good	Excellent
687 EELL X Top Mono Trap Combo	$2850	$4000	$5100
S686 Onyx, 20 and 12 gauge, marking in script on receiver.	700	1000	1350
Whitewing, variation of the S686 Essential	600	850	1200
Silver Pigeon, 28, 20, and 12 gauge,	700	900	1350
Silver Pigeon 20/28 Gauge Combo Set	1000	1400	2000
S687 Silver Pigeon,	800	1350	1800
S687 Silver Pigeon II	800	1250	1750
Ultralight, 12 gauge	700	1100	1600
Ultralight Deluxe, Giubileo (Jubilee), in .410, 28, 20, and 12 gauges	5000	8000	12500
687E	500	700	1000
S687L, .410, 28, 20, and 12 gauges	1200	1500	2000
687 Engraved Course	1350	1700	2200
S687 EELL Diamond Pigeon	2000	3500	4500
S687 Diamond Pigeon 20/28 Combo Set	2500	4500	5500
S687 EL Gold Pigeon	2200	3000	4000
S687 EL Gold Pigeon 20/28 Combo Set	2700	4000	5000
Tricentennial Model 1000 Replica Percussion Over-and-Under Muzzleloader, 12 gauge, 300 only, 30" barrels, with engraving, black-powder only	900	2300	3000
Model 687 Gold and Black Tercentennial 12 gauge, 28", gold inlaid and blued, 300 only	1000	1700	3000
Model S687 Commemorative Tercentennial, 12 gauge, engraved with game scenes and scrollwork, gray finished, 200 only	1000	1850	3250
Monocanna Ripieghevole (Folding Single-Shot) Shotgun, 1922 patent, the folding shotgun first appeared in the catalog of 1925. Over 500,000 made, primarily in 16, 20, 24, and 28 gauges; joined in ensuing years by 32, 36, .410, and 9mm rimfire, and by larger variation in 12, 10, and 8.			
Models listed as 12, 13, 012, 013, 13 bis, 013 bis, 1012, 1013, 1013 bis, 312, 313, 313 bis, 312 bis, 412, 413, 413 bis, 412 bis, 1930, 930, and 414	100	200	300
premium for engraved examples, with special finish and stocks			

SELF-LOADING SHOTGUNS (GAS OPERATED).

Note: Were also military and law enforcement versions of some of the following models, some will bring premium.

	Fair	V. Good	Excellent
Model 60 and Model 60 Deluxe, 12 gauge only	500	800	1200
Model 61, Model 60 Lusso, improved version of Model 60, 12 gauge only	800	1200	2000
Model 300, aluminum alloy receiver, 12 gauge	300	400	500
300 Deluxe (Lusso)	$700	$1100	$2000
A 300 20 and 12 gauge	300	400	500
A 300 De Luxe, finely engraved frame, gold-plated trigger; silver shield on stock	700	1100	2000
A 300 Magnum	300	400	500
A 300 Super Lusso, Slug Barrel for A 300	500	700	1100
A 300 in 20 ga	400	500	600
A 300 in 12 gauge	350	450	550
A 300 De Luxe in 12–20 gauge	700	1100	2000
A 300 Extra De Luxe in 12 only	900	1400	2400
A 300 Magnum in 12 only	300	400	500
A 300 Slug in 12 gauge only	350	450	550
300 Trap	300	350	450
300/301 Skeet	350	450	550
300/301 Magnum	350	450	550
Model A-301, 12 and 20 gauge	350	450	550
A-301 De Luxe	700	1100	2000
A-301 Super De Luxe	850	1250	2250
Models A-300/A-301 and derivatives: 12 gauge	300	400	500
A-301 Magnum	350	450	600
301 Slug 12 and 20 ga	400	450	600
Model A302, with universal receiver, cut-off to magazine, and floating sight ribs, and Mobilchoke	300	400	600
302 Super Lusso	1250	1750	2250
A303, 12 and 20 gauge	400	500	750
A303 Slug - 12 and 20 gauge	350	450	650
A303 Engraved	500	700	1000
A303 Deluxe	600	800	1200
A303 Youth	350	450	650
303 Upland	400	500	650
303 Waterfowl	350	450	650
303 Sporting	450	550	750
303 Skeet	425	525	700
303 Super Skeet	550	700	1000
303 Trap	425	500	750
303 Super Trap	575	700	1000
Blowback operated self-loading shotguns, 12 gauge			
1200F	300	400	500
1200 Riot	300	400	500
1201 Field Magnum	300	400	550
1201 FP Riot	325	425	675
1201 FP	325	425	675
Gas Operated			
A 304 series, a derivation of the A 390 series, 12 and 20 gauge	400	600	850
A 390, 12 gauge, variations of **Silver Mallard; Gold Mallard, Silver Mallard Matte; Silver Mallard Slug**			
A 390 Silver Mallard	400	500	650
AL390, unique self-regulating gas valve, 20 and 12 gauge			
AL390 Silver Mallard, 20 and 12 gauge	400	500	700
AL390 Field Deluxe, Gold Mallard	400	550	850
AL390 Silver Mallard Synthetic	400	500	700

	Fair	V. Good	Excellent
AL390 Silver Mallard Camo	$400	$550	$750
AL390 Silver Mallard Slug	400	550	750
AL390 Silver Mallard Youth	400	500	750
AL390 Sporting Silver Mallard	450	550	750
AL390 Sport Sporting Collection	450	550	750
AL390 Gold Sporting	550	650	1000
AL390 Sport Sporting Youth	450	525	750
AL390 Diamond Sport	1750	2250	2750
AL390 Sport Skeet	425	500	725
AL390 Sport Super Skeet	500	700	1000
AL390 Sport Trap	500	700	850
AL 390 Sport Super Trap	500	700	1000
390 Lioness	1200	1500	2500
390 470 Anniversary	1200	1500	2500
RS 151	200	300	500
RS 200	225	350	550
RS 202	250	375	575
AL390 Camo, AL390 Silver Mallard Slug			
AL390 Lioness, 12 and 20 gauge, named after the city of Brescia, the "Lioness of Italy." Limited edition of 1,526 in each gauge	1250	1750	3000
AL391 Urika, model added in 1999, 20 and 12 gauge	400	700	1000
Urika Gold, Urika Gold, Urika Sporting	400	750	1000
A304 Lark and Pintail, A304 Silver Lark, A304 Silver Lark Slug, A304 Gold Lark-Black, A304 Gold Lark-White			
Silver Lark	250	350	450
Gold Lark	325	400	500
Ruby Lark	375	500	700
AL 1, 12 and 20 ga	300	350	500
AL 2	250	300	500
AL 2 Skeet	300	350	500
AL 2 Trap	300	350	500
AL 2 Magnum	325	375	500
AL 3 Field, Magnum, Skeet and Trap	275	350	500
AL 3 Deluxe Trap	500	650	800
412 (12, 20, 28 and .410 ga)	125	150	200
Pintail ES 100 (Victoria)	400	675	825
Pintail ES 100 Rifled Slug	500	700	985
Pintail Slug (Victoria)	300	400	600
Pump Action Shotguns			
RS 151, 12 gauge	250	350	500
RS 200, 12 gauge	250	350	500
RS 200 Lusso, engraved, with select walnut stocks	400	950	1200
RS 200 P, variation for law enforcement, 12 gauge only	250	350	500
RS 202, 12 gauge, **RS 202 P,** 12 gauge, **RS 202 MI,** 12 gauge	300	450	550

MILITARY RIFLES

BOLT-ACTION RIFLES

	Fair	V. Good	Excellent
Model 1891 Carcano Rifle, 6.5mm	200	300	500
Model 1891 Carcano Carbine, 6.5mm	250	350	550
Model 1891 TS Carcano Carbine, 6.5mm	$275	$375	$575
Model 1891 Carcano Carbine/24, 6.5mm	275	375	575
Model 1938 Carcano Rifle, 7.35mm	250	350	550
Model 1938 Carcano Carbine, 7.35mm	275	375	575
Model 1938 TS Carcano Carbine, 7.35mm	275	375	575
Model 1938 Carcano Rifle, 6.5mm	250	350	550
Model 1938 Carcano Carbine, 6.5mm	275	375	575
Model 1938 TS Carcano Carbine, 6.5mm	275	375	575
Model 1941 Carcano Rifle, 6.5mm	250	350	550
Model 1938 "I," 6.5mm × 50 (Arisaka)	350	550	950
Model 70/87/916 Wetterly, Alterations of the Model 1870 and Model 1870/87 Wetterly Rifles, to 6.5mm caliber	275	375	575

SELF-LOADING

	Fair	V. Good	Excellent
Model 31 6.5mm Rifle	300	500	750
Model 37 7.35mm Rifle	300	500	750
U.S. Garand Self-loading Rifle, Made Under License by Beretta, .30M1	800	1200	1800
M1LS, lightened and shortened M1, the feed and ammunition remaining the same	900	1400	2200
BM59, 7.62NATO (.308), Note: if full automatic capacity, requires Federal license	800	1200	1800
Mark I, BM 59R, developed from BM 59; including device reducing rate of full-auto fire.	800	1350	2000
BM 59D, vertical pistol grip, bipod; rate reducer (for improved control on full automatic fire)	800	1450	2200
BM 59GL, with grenade launcher system	800	1450	2200
BM 60CB, with controlled-burst mechanism	800	1450	2200
Mark Ital, same as Mark I, but with Beretta grenade launch system with tri-compensator and bayonet lug, winter trigger, bipod, and hinged buttplate	900	1500	2350
Mark Ital TA, special variation for Alpine troops; derived from Mark III, below	900	1500	2200
Mark Ital Para, special shortened variation for paratroops; derived from Mark III, below	900	1500	2200
Mark II same as Mark I, but with vertical pistol grip, winter trigger, bipod, hinged buttplate; weight of approximately one pound greater than Mark I	900	1500	2200

	Fair	V. Good	Excellent
Mark III, Same as Mark I, but with vertical pistol grip, bipod, folding steel stock which accommodated grenade launch system	$900	$1500	$2350
Mark Ital-A, as Mark III, but with detachable grenade launcher with tri-compensator and bayonet lug	900	1500	2200
BM59SL, self-loading version	800	1200	1600
70 Sport variation of the military AR70 rifle for civilian sale	600	1100	1500

SERVICE PISTOLS

	Fair	V. Good	Excellent
Model 1915 Pistol (9mm Glisenti)	250	500	750
Model 1915 and Model 1917 Pistol (7.65mm)	250	500	750
Model 1922 Pistol, Patent 1915–1919 (7.65mm)	200	450	700
Model 1923 Pistol, Patent 1915–1919 (9mm Glisenti)	225	500	850
Model 1931/1932 Pistols, Patent 1915–1919 (7.65mm)	250	550	950
Model 1934 Pistol, Patent 1915–1919 (7.65mm) Marketing in the United States under the tradename Cougar; succeeded by the 70 Series pistols, in .380 caliber, under the same trade name	150	250	450
Model 1932 and 1934 Pistol, Patent 1915–1919 (9mm short)	250	500	750
Model 1935 Pistol (7.65mm) **a.k.a. Model 935, 935, 935 bis, 935 D.D., 1935, 1935 bis**	125	250	500
Premium for engraved pistols			

Beretta Model 1935.32 ACP

	Fair	V. Good	Excellent
Model 951 (9mm Parabellum) In the late 1960s, advertised as Model 104, 9mm Parabellum; few only made in .32ACP (7.65mm Browning) and bring premium	125	250	550
Premium for Israeli and Brigadier models			
Helwan, An Egyptian-made copy of the Model 951; despite Arabic markings on the slide, the pistol is an accurate, authorized-by-Beretta copy of Model 951	225	400	600
951 Berhama (a.k.a. Modello 51 Berhama), target variation of Model 951 for Egyptian armed forces	$250	$450	$750
951 Target, Derived by Beretta from the Egyptian Modello 951 Berhama	275	475	675
952 (.30 Luger, 7.65 Parabellum) target version of the Model 951, brought out in 1971	250	450	650
952 Special, .30 Luger (7.65mm Parabellum) caliber; target variation of Model 952	250	450	650
951A and 951R, Automatic and burst-control, selective-fire variations of Model 951 (requires Federal license to own)	450	750	1250
951A, longer barrel, elongated frame, and the slide and hammer of increased bulk and weight; fold-down handgrip. Higher-capacity magazines of 10, 15, or 20 rounds	300	500	850
951R, fixed handgrip mounted on front of frame; higher capacity magazines of 10 or 15 rounds.	350	650	1000
951, with Alloy Frame, built for testing by Italian police. Slides heavier and of stronger construction	400	700	1200

MEDIUM FRAME PISTOLS

	Fair	V. Good	Excellent
Model 948 (.22 long rifle), 948 was the .22LR (5.6mm) version of Model 950, on frame of the 7.65mm pistol. For the U.S. market, imported under the trade names "Plinker" and "Featherweight."	65	125	250
Model 948 A.A., Model 948 bis	100	225	500
Model 70 Medium Frame Pistol (5.6mm, 7.65mm, 9mm short), Successor to Model 1935, and remaining in the line through the 1980s, Variations were available in .22LR (5.6), .32 ACP (7.65mm), and .380 ACP (9mm short) calibers. Model 70 series succeeded by Model 81 Series (specifically Models 84BB, 85BB, and 86), in 1985 catalog	100	225	500
70 C.L., same as Model 70, but chrome-plated	100	175	300
70 C.I., same as Model 70, but engraved, chrome-plated (first listed in 1967 price list)	100	175	300
70 Bis, same as Model 70, but engraved, chrome-plated	175	300	575
70 A.L., same as Model 70, but silver-plated	100	175	300
70 A.I., same as Model 70, but engraved, silver-plated; with spare magazine in case	175	300	575
70 D.I., same as Model 70, but engraved, gold-plated; mother-of-pearl grips; spare magazine, deluxe case	225	450	1000

	Fair	V. Good	Excellent
70 Ergal, first advertised in 1967, alloy frame. In 1971, advertised as 1 lb., 2 oz. (520gr)	$100	$175	$300
100, first listed in the 1971 catalog: "Directly derived from the [Model 74, *q.v.*], in larger calibre [.32ACP (7.65mm)] . . . faithfully repeats all its characteristics, including the adjustable rear sight blade, except for the weight, which is 530gr (1 lb., 3 oz.)"	125	200	350
From the 1980 catalog, revised listings:			
70 in 7.65 mm, larger trident logo at top of grips; larger spur on front of magazine at bottom	125	200	350
70S in 9mm short, left grip panel with thumb rest; larger spur on front of magazine at bottom; P. BERETTA and MADE IN ITALY marking surrounding push button magazine release at bottom of left grip panel	125	200	350
70S in .22LR, left grip panel with thumb rest; larger spur on front of magazine at bottom	125	200	350
Model 71 Medium Frame Pistol, "Same pistol as model 70, specially redesigned for .22LR rim fire shells. Light alloy body . . ." Model 71 series succeeded by Model 81 Series (specifically the Models 87 and the Model 89 Target), in 1985 catalog, although Model 71 listed therein as well.			
Caliber: .22LR.	125	200	350
Major Production Variations: initial listings of Models 71, 72, 73, and 74 from catalog of c. 1962.			
71 A.L., same as Model 71, but silver-plated	125	200	350
71 A.I., same as Model 71, but engraved, silver-plated, and with spare magazine and case	200	500	950
72, same as Model 71, with 5.906" (150mm) barrel; with short barrel 3.51" (90mm) as spare; no front sight on slide, rather on each barrel	150	225	300
73, same as Model 71, with front and rear sight fixed on barrel; enlarged grips for 10-round magazine	150	225	300
74, same as Model 73 except for frame in aluminum alloy	150	225	300
75, same pistol, in .22LR caliber, as Model 71, with 5.906" barrel, suitable for target training, 8-Round magazine; lacking adjustable rear sight as on Model 74	150	250	350
71 in .22LR, available also with (150mm) barrel; walnut grips on request	150	250	350

	Fair	V. Good	Excellent
Model 81 Double-Action Medium Frame Pistol, .32ACP (7.65 mm Browning) version of the Model 84.			
81 B Deluxe, limited number series, hand-engraved	$200	$450	$750
82 B, Model 81 B, but in 32ACP (7.65mm)	150	250	350
87 BB, identical to Model 85 BB (*q.v.*), but in .22LR caliber	175	300	550
Model 84 Double-Action Medium Frame Pistol, derivation of Model 81 Series of double and single-action pistols, first listed in the 1980 catalog.			
Model 84 B, .380ACP (9mm short)	200	300	600
84 B Deluxe, limited number series, hand-engraved	275	500	1000
85 B, same as 84 B, but in .380 (9mm short)	200	300	600
84 BB,	250	400	800
85 BB, as above, but 21.8 oz weight	250	400	800
86, same as Model 84 BB, but 4.33" barrel	250	400	600
86 BB	250	400	600
87 BB, in .22LR, with heft and feel of .380 models	250	400	600
87BB Long Barrel, .22LR, 6" barrel	250	400	600
84 F, advanced 84 BB features, plus combat-style frame	250	400	600
85 F, like 85 BB, but with combat-style frame, grooved triggerguard (for two-hand support)	275	425	650
83 F, same as 85 F, but with 4" barrel, 7-round single-column magazine	275	425	650
Browning BDA .380, produced by Beretta for Fabrique Nationale, using Beretta frame and magazine	200	400	600
The Cheetah Series, .380ACP (9mm short)	200	300	600
84 Cheetah Nickel, as above, but nickel-plated finish	200	400	600
85 Cheetah, same as 84 Cheetah, but slimmer profile	200	400	600
85 Cheetah Nickel, as above, but nickel plated	200	400	600
83 Cheetah, same as 85 Cheetah, but with 4" barrel, 7-round single-column magazine	225	425	650
86 Cheetah, tip-up barrel design (successor to Model 84 BB); same as Model 84 BB, but 4.4" barrel; 7.3" overall length	250	400	750
87 Cheetah, in .22LR, with heft and feel of .380 models	225	425	650
87 Cheetah Long Barrel, .22LR, 6" barrel	225	425	650
Model 90 Double-Action Medium Frame Pistol, Medium frame Model 90, the first Beretta automatic pistol with a double-action trigger system, .32 ACP (7.65mm Browning)	100	200	300

POCKET HANDGUNS	Fair	V. Good	Excellent
Pocket Pistols, 6.35mm (.25ACP)			
Model 1920 Pocket Pistol, Patent 1919, .25ACP (6.35mm Browning)	$125	$250	$400
Model 1926 Pocket Pistol, Patent 1919 (6.35mm), .25ACP (6.35mm Browning)	125	250	375
Model 18, standard model	125	250	375
Model 19, engraved, fine bluing	200	500	850
Model 20, lavishly engraved, nickel-plated (not listed after 1926 catalog)	450	850	1300
Model 21, deluxe engraved, finest workmanship, richly gold-plated	650	1000	1950
Model 1926–31 Pocket Pistol, Patent 1919 (6.35mm), .25ACP (6.35mm Browning)	125	250	350
Model 1934 Pocket Pistol, Patent 1919 (6.35mm), .25ACP (6.35 mm Browning)	125	250	350
Model 318 Pocket Pistol (6.35mm), .25ACP(6.35mm Browning),	125	250	325
318, 319, 320, 321 (as above)			
Model 418 Pocket Pistol (6.35), .25ACP (6.35mm Browning)	125	250	325
418, as above; final listing in catalog of c. 1959	125	250	325
419, engraved and finely blued	200	450	850
420, richly engraved and nickel-plated (toward end of production, listed as chrome-plated)	450	850	1300
420 bis, same as model 420, but with tortoise-shell grips	550	950	1400
421, deluxe engraved, finest workmanship, richly gold-plated; tortoise-shell grips noted in 1956 catalog	650	1000	1950
Pocket Pistols, 5.6mm Rimfire &/or 6.35mm Centerfire **Model 950 Pocket Pistol,** Marketed in the United States as the Minx (in .22 short) and the Jetfire (in .25ACP)	70	125	175
6.35mm (.25ACP) initially, then the .22 short (5.6mm) as the 950 C.C., added c. 1956	70	125	175
950 cc	70	125	175
950 cc Special,	100	150	200
New Model 950, from 1958 catalog; .25ACP (6.35)	100	150	200
950 A.A., 1958 catalog; elegantly engraved, silver-plated, tortoise-shell grips,	650	1000	1950
950 A.L., same as 950 B both in 6.35 and .22 short, but silver-plated and special finish	150	200	300
950 A.I., same as 950 B (see below) both in 6.35mm and .22 short	150	200	300
950 D.I., same as 950 A.I., but gold-plated, with tortoise-shell grips	225	300	400
Model 950 B Pocket Pistol (6.35mm, 5.6mm), .25ACP (6.35mm); variation also in .22 short	70	125	200

	Fair	V. Good	Excellent
950 A.A., deluxe embellished	$175	$225	$400
950 A.L., same as 950 B both in 6.35 and .22 short, but silver-plated and special finish	100	200	350
950 A.I., same as 950 B both in 6.35 and .22 short, but engraved, silver-plated, and mother-of-pearl-style grips; special finish; deluxe case	225	500	800
950 D.I., same as 950 A.I., but gold-plated	250	550	900
950 C.L.,	100	200	300
950 C.C., .22 short	100	200	300
950 C.C. Special, in .22 short with longer barrel. Right side of slide marked: MADE IN BRAZIL.	100	200	300
Model 950 BS Pocket Pistol (5.6mm and 6.35mm), U.S. tradenames for Model 950 BS; continued those from earlier period: Minx for the .22 short and Jetfire for the .25ACP, .25ACP (6.35mm) and .22 short (5.6mm)	100	200	300
950 BS Nickel, nickel-plated version	100	200	300
950 BS EL, blued, with gold inlays and partial gold-plating	225	500	700
.22 Minx Pocket Pistol, .22 short or LR	100	200	300
***.25 Jetfire Pocket Pistol,** .25ACP	100	200	300
***Model 950 Jetfire Pocket Pistol,** .25ACP (6.35mm)	100	200	300
Major Production Variations:			
950 Jetfire, as above, matte black finish	100	200	300
950 Jetfire Nickel, nickel-plated finish	100	200	300
950 Jetfire EL, blued, with gold inlays, partial gold-plating	225	500	700
Model 20 Pocket Pistol, .25ACP (6.35mm)	100	200	300
Model 21 Pocket Pistol, a restyled version of the Model 20, in .22LR	100	200	300
Model 21A Pocket Pistol, Replacement pistol to the Model 20 and Model 21, .22LR and .25ACP	100	200	300
21A Nickel, as above, but nickel-plated with blued hammer, trigger, and magazine	100	200	300
21A Engraved, deluxe version of Model 21A, with gold accented slide, gold-plated trigger, hammer, magazine release button, magazine, and selected other small parts	225	500	850
***Model 21 Bobcat Pocket Pistol,** .22LR and .25ACP	100	200	300
21 Bobcat Nickel, nickel-plated	100	200	300
21 Bobcat EL, engraved, with gold inlaid slide; smooth walnut grips, gold-plated hammer, trigger, barrel lock and grip screws	225	425	750

SMALL FRAME PISTOLS

	Fair	V. Good	Excellent
Note: 1996 catalog listed the 3022 Tomcat, a .22 long rifle variation of the Tomcat. However, pistol did not become a standard product in the line.			
***3032 Tomcat,** .32ACP	$100	$200	$350
Model 949 Target Pistol, aka the 949 Olimpionica, .22 short	85	175	275
Model 949 L.R. Target Pistol, as above, but chambered for .22LR cartridges	85	175	275
Model 949 Corto Competition Target Pistol, .22 short	85	185	275
Model 949 C.C. Competition Target Pistol, As above, but chambered for .22LR	85	185	275
Olimpionica Competition Target Pistol, .22 short or LR	85	185	275
Olympic Competition Target Pistol, .22 short or LR. Model 949 pistol continues in catalog of 1964, joined by the "new Beretta Olympic Mod 80 .22 Short," pistol (*q.v.*)	100	200	325
Model 76 Competition Target Pistol, Model was derived from Model 70–71 series, .22LR	200	350	550
Model 102 or the New Sable,	175	300	450
Model 80 Olimpionica Competition Target Pistol, .22 short	200	350	500
Model 89 Standard Competition Target Pistol, .22LR	250	400	650
***Model 89 Gold Standard Competition Pistol,** .22LR	275	450	700
Sable, Model 102 Competition Target Pistol, .22LR	275	450	700

THE 8000 SERIES COUGAR GROUP

Not to be confused with .380 caliber Cougars brought out in the United States through importers J. L. Galef & Son, the 8000 Series pistols a classification of large caliber pistols, designed from the bottom up

	Fair	V. Good	Excellent
Cougar, Medium or Compact Frame Pistol, 9mmx19 (Model 8000), .40 S & W (Model 8040), and (as of 1998) .45ACP (Model 8045)	300	400	600
Premium for .45 caliber			
8000/8040 Mini-Cougar Series, 1" shorter in grip, approximately two ounces lighter, 8-shot magazine (.40 S & W) and 10 (9mm)	300	400	600

Model 92 and Its Variations

FS Models, Double/single action, with external ambidextrous manual safety, decocking lever, trigger bar disconnect, rotating firing pin striker.

D Models, Double action only, no safety lever (slick slide).

G Models, Double/single action, with external ambidextrous decocking lever, rotating firing pin striker. Trigger bar disconnect.

	Fair	V. Good	Excellent
Model 92 Series, 9mm Parabellum= 9mm x19=9mm. NATO, later joined by 9mm x 21 IMI and .40 S & W. 15 shots, staggered; built of metal stampings; variations with capacities of 17, 13, 11, 10, and 8. **Barrel Length:** 4.92" (125mm), 1st series	$275	$500	$800
Model 92S, Modified from the Model 92, with the manual safety mounted on the rear of the slide, rather than on the rear section of the frame; second series	250	400	600
Model 92S-1, Group of test pistols built by Beretta for early U.S. Air Force trials, in seeking a new U.S. service handgun; c. 1979–80	1250	1750	3000
92SB, firing pin lock safety device, restyled safety levers on slide, grips with full checkering	315	400	600
Model 92FS (98FS, 96), Successor to the Model 92SB. Pistol is the same as the Model 98FS in caliber 9mm x 21 IMI, and the Model 96 in .40 S & W. Lightweight aluminum alloy frame machined with combat triggerguard, innovative triple safety mechanism. Ambidextrous manual safety	300	400	600
Model 92F, Civilian version of the M9 pistol	300	400	550
Model 92FSS, Stainless steel version of the Model 92FS	400	500	600
92FS and 96EL Models, Special high polish, blued slides; with gold ***P. Beretta*** signature on slide	400	550	700
92FS and 98FS Deluxe Models, Hand-engraved slide and receiver, richly blued; select figured walnut stocks	2200	3750	5000
*Model 96G, Model 92 in .40 S & W caliber	350	450	600

DOUBLE ACTION ONLY

	Fair	V. Good	Excellent
Model 92D, Introduced in 1992, identical to the 92DS, without manual safety (lever also eliminated)	225	325	450
Model 96D, Same as the Model 92D, but chambered for .40 S & W caliber	225	325	450
Model 92DS, Same as the Model 92D, but fitted with manual safety lever on the slide	225	325	450
Model 96DS, Same as the Model 96D, in .40 S & W caliber, and fitted with manual safety lever on the slide	225	300	450
Model 98, Model 92SB pistols chambered for 7.65mm Parabellum, for Italian citizens, to whom 9mm Parabellum (military calibers) were prohibited	250	325	500

	Fair	V. Good	Excellent
Model 92FS Inox, 9mmm Parabellum version of the 92FS in stainless steel; frame of anodized aluminum alloy .	$400	$500	$700
Model 98FS Inox, 9mmx21 IMI caliber variation of the stainless Model 92FSS	425	525	700
Model 96 Inox, .40 S & W caliber variation of the stainless Model 92FSS	425	525	700
Deluxe Models of the Model 98FS, 98FS Inox, and Model 96 Inox Series Pistols, Blued variations, hand engraved; walnut grips without checkering, with gold escutcheon on left-grip panel. Includes pistols finished in silver and gold-plating	2200	3750	5000
Model 98SB Compact, Variation of the Model 98, with stepped-down frame, shortened slide and barrel, reduced capacity magazine	300	400	500
Model 98SB Compact Type M, . .	325	425	525
Model 92SB-C (SB Compact; First Series), Based on the Model 92SB, but with reduced sized features, shortened slide and barrel length, lessened height	325	425	525
Model 92SB Compact (Second Series), Developed from the Model 92SB-C, and quickly recognizable with the flaring profile to the lower front of the gripstrap and contrasting angle to the backstrap	300	425	525
Model 96 Compact, Matched in size to the Model 92F Compact; introduced 1992; 9-shot .40 S & W caliber version of the Model 92FC	400	500	600
Model 92FS Compact, Made from 92FS, with reduced dimensions, yet keeping large magazine capacity (13 rounds); all safety and technical features of 92FS	400	500	600
Model 92FS, Type M Compact, Continued height and length dimensions of the Model 92 Compact pistols, Second Series; frame 1¼" thick, 8-shot magazine	400	500	600
Model 99, 7.65 caliber, blued finish, rounded triggerguard	400	500	600
Model 92SBCM, 9mm blued, with rounded triggerguard; discontinued as import item to United States, 1991	450	550	700
Model 92FCM, Bruniton, matte black, finish, chrome-plating to barrel, squared front to triggerguard, slide retention feature	450	550	700
Centurion, variation of the 92FS and 96, On Model 92FS frame, combined withe the shorter slide and barrel of the compact series, 9mm or .40 S & W, originally made with 11 (.40 S & W) and 15 (9mm) magazines; after 1996 U.S. federal law, restricted to 10-shot magazine	$225	$325	$500

TARGET VARIATIONS OF THE MODEL 92

	Fair	V. Good	Excellent
Model 92, Model 96, and Model 98 Combat Competition Pistols, 9mmx19, 9mmx21 IMI and .40 S & W (see table), 15-shot magazine for 9mm variants; 11 for .40 S & W (note restrictions may apply to magazine capacity), 5.9" barrel (15mm) or optional short version of 4.9" (125mm)	400	700	1000
Model 92, Model 96, and Model 98 Stock Competition Pistols, based on Brigadier design; identical to Combat Competition Models noted above	400	700	1000
Model 98FS Target Pistol, 5.9" (150mm barrel), with aluminum counterweight sleeve	450	750	1100
Also available in .40 S & W caliber **(Model 96 Target)**			
Also available in .40 S & W caliber **(Model 96 Conversion Kit)**	450	750	1100
Model 92, Model 96, and Model 98 Combat Short Pistol, built with 4.9" (125mm) barrel; optional Combo version with 5.9" (150mm) barrel assembly included, and recoil spring guide	450	750	1100
Model 92FS Combat, Modified for improved performance in combat-style pistol competition. Single Action only	450	750	1100
Model 98FS Combat, As above, developed from the 98FS	450	750	1100

.22 RIMFIRE AND OTHER SMALL CALIBER RIFLES

	Fair	V. Good	Excellent
Wetterly Rifles, Patented alteration of the bolt action Wetterly Model 1870 and the Model 1870–87 Wetterly-Vitali into hunting calibers, .22 long rifle, 16, 20, 24, 28, and 32.	150	250	350
.22 Flobert Gallery Rifles, Flobert Warnant rifle, in 6mm and 9mm calibers, a single shot with a breech mechanism which pivoted backwards, while a security system pivoted up and forward	100	150	250

AIR RIFLES

	Fair	V. Good	Excellent
Guglielmo (William) Tell air rifle, in 4½mm caliber; cocked by bending the gun in half	100	150	250

THE CARABINA OLIMPIONICA "BERETTA" AND SUBSEQUENT RIFLES IN THE SERIES

	Fair	V. Good	Excellent
.22 rimfire rifles are sometimes identified as Flobert type, Magazines held 4 or 8 cartridges. The barrel length was 520mm. Olimpionica appeared again, in 1947–48 (83), and in 1949 (84). Olimpia and Unione Italiana Tiro a Segno.	$125	$225	$350
Carabina "Beretta" Sport, Sporting model, with simpler, open sights. The operating mechanism was the same as the more advanced Olimpionica. Barrel length of 500mm; weight at 2.8kg.	125	225	350
The Sport, Super Sport, and Olimpia .22 Rifles			
Olimpia 23.6" barrel	125	225	350
Super Sport	150	275	400
As above, but with cheekpiece stock and more advanced overall design			
Olimpia (Mod. Unione)	175	300	425
Super Olimpia, for 1967, a sophisticated bolt action single-shot match rifle for international shooting	225	350	450
Model Sport, "light sporting rifle," .22 long rifle. 20.5" barrel	125	225	350
Model Super Sport .22 long rifle, 23.6" barrel	150	275	400
Model Olympia (Union Model), .22 long rifle. 23.6" barrel	150	250	350
Model W XXII, built for the Weatherby Company, of Southgate, California. Self-loading only, .22 long rifle, 24" barrel	100	175	300
Model W XXII De Luxe, 24" barrel	1000	175	300
Super Sport X, .22 long rifle rimfire, 5 and 10 round magazines, 23.6" barrel	150	275	400
Olimpia X .22 long rifle rimfire, 5 and 10 round magazines, 23.6" barrel	150	275	400
Model 90 Single Shot, 9mm and .22 long rifle, and .22 short cartridges, breech mechanism was a pivoting block	75	150	225
9mm barrel length 68mm	75	150	225
.22 short, .22 long rifle	75	150	225
Sako Bolt Action Rifle, in three action lengths, 500 Series, Short Action, .222 Rem. and .223 Rem., 5 round magazines. 24" barrels	300	400	500
Variations:			
500 Custom 222 Rem., .223 Rem., .243 Win., .270 Win., .30–06 Spr., .308 Win.			
500 Custom	400	500	700
500 S	400	525	700
500 DL	800	1250	1450
500 DLS	1000	1250	1500
500 EELL	1000	1400	1650
501	300	450	600
501 Deluxe, As above, but with better grade of stock, with pistol grip cap and forend cap	$700	$1250	$1500
501 Series, Medium Action, .243 Win. and .308 Win., 5 round magazines. 23" barrels	300	450	600
501 S	350	525	650
501 DLS	900	1300	1600
501 EELL	900	1400	1700
501 EELL S	1000	1500	1800
502 Series, Long Action, .300 Win. Mag., .30–06, .270 Win. 7mm Rem. Mag. and .375 H & H Mag. 4 rounds (.300, 7mm, .375); 5 rounds (.270 and .30–06), 24" barrels	500	750	1000
Standard Models, Close-grained European walnut stock, with Schnabel forend, hand checkered, full pistol grip, rubber recoil pad	400	550	750
502 S	400	550	750
Note; DL Models: Select European walnut stock with cheekpiece, contrasting grip cap and forend tip, hand checkered, full pistol grip, rubber recoil pad.			
502 DL	850	1250	1550
502 DLS	900	1250	1600
Note: EELL Models: Highly figured European walnut stock with cheek piece, deep diamond hand-cut checkered; contrasting pistol grip cap and forend tip, fully engraved receiver and magazine floorplate, with game head and gold inlay and P. Beretta signature.			
502 EELL	1000	1350	1700
502 EELL S	1100	1400	1800

MATO BOLT-ACTION SPORTING RIFLE

	Fair	V. Good	Excellent
.270 Win., .280 Rem., .30–06 Springfield, 7mm Rem. Mag., .300 Win. Mag., 338 Win. Mag., .375 Holland & Holland Mag. 4-shot magazines for .270, .280, and .30–06; 3 for remaining calibers; 23.6" barrel length	950	1200	1500
Mato Deluxe	800	2200	2600
Add $400 for .375 H & H			

EXPRESS DOUBLE BARREL RIFLES

	Fair	V. Good	Excellent
SS0 Over-and-Under Express Rifles, .375 Holland & Holland Mag., .458 Win. Mag. 25.5" barrels, with solid rib	8500	12000	16500
SS06 and SS06 EELL Over-and-Under Express Rifles, SS05	10000	14000	17500
SS06, .375 Holland & Holland Mag., .458 Win. Mag.; 9.3x74R, added 1992. (25.5")	18000	25000	35000
Add $5900 extra set of barrels			

	Fair	V. Good	Excellent
SS06 EELL Gold (1992 catalog), sling swivels on SS06 EEL; European-style silhouette cheekpiece; rubber recoil pad; blued, receiver hand-engraved with game scenes, or color case-hardened with gold inlaid animals. In custom-fitted case	$20000	$27000	$38000
S689 Express Over-and-Under Sporting Rifle, .30–06 Springfield, 9.3x74R. 23" barrels	2750	3350	3950
Add $2200 for extra 20 gauge interchangeable barrel			
S689EELL, available with deluxe engraving and gold inlaying, gold stock plaque; mounts for quick detachable scope, 20 gauge interchangeable barrel on request.	8000	14000	22000
Add $3500.			
S689 Sable Express Over-and-Under Sporting Rifles, Gold and Diamond Sable in .30–06 and 9.3x74R only. Silver Sable also in .444 Marlin. 60 cm (23") and 62 cm (24") with solid rib barrels.			
EELL Diamond Sable, gold inlaid games heads on case-hardened receiver with full side plates. With leather custom-fitted case	6000	9000	12000
Gold Sable, light scroll engraving, color case-hardened receiver; 20 gauge interchangeable barrel available on request	2850	4500	5500
Silver Sable, open barrel construction (no center or top rib), specially styled receiver	2500	3000	3500
455 EELL Side-by-Side Express Rifle, 455 375 H & H Mag., .416 Rigby, .458 Win. Mag. .470 Nitro Express, and .500 Nitro Express. 23" and 25" barrels, with solid rib, and raised rib at breech.	25000	36000	47000
455 EELL, as above, but with custom-made engraving, signed by artisan; highly detailed Bulino-style game-scene engraving and/or intricate scroll work. Select walnut briar stock and forend. Elegant leather case, with accessories	40000	52000	62000

BERETTA, GIOVANNI

Brescia, Italy, c. 1700.

HANDGUN, SNAPHAUNCE

	Fair	V. Good	Excellent
Belt Pistol, Engraved, Carved, Light Ornamentation, *Antique*	1200	3000	4250

BERGMANN

Gaggenau, Germany, 1892–1944: Company renamed Bergmann Erben 1931. Also see Bayard.

HANDGUN, SELF-LOADING

	Fair	V. Good	Excellent
Bergmann Mars, 9mmB, Clip Fed, *Curio*	$1200	$3250	$3750
Bergmann/Bayard, Model 1908, 9mmB, Clip Fed, *Curio*	600	1500	1750
Bergmann/Bayard, Model 1910, 9mmB, Clip Fed, *Curio*	400	1200	1500
Bergmann/Bayard, Model 1910/21, 9mmB, Clip Fed, *Curio*	800	1600	1850
Erben Model I, .25 ACP, Clip Fed, *Modern*	100	275	325
Erben Model II, .25 ACP, Clip Fed, *Modern*	125	300	350
Erben Special, .32 ACP, Clip Fed, *Modern*	125	325	375
Model 1894, 5mm, Blow Back, Clip Fed, *Antique*	2000	5000	6500
Model 1894, 8mm, Blow Back, Clip Fed, *Antique*	2000	3500	4250
Model 1896 #2, 5mm, Small Frame, Clip Fed, *Curio*	900	2200	2700
Model 1896 #3, 6.5mm, Clip Fed, *Curio*	800	2000	2500
Model 1896 #4, 8mm, Military, Clip Fed, *Curio*	900	2100	2600
Model 1897 #5, 7.8mm, Clip Fed, *Curio*	900	2200	2700
Model 1899 #6, 8mm, Clip Fed, *Curio*	800	1750	2000
Model 2, .25 ACP, Clip Fed, *Modern*	100	250	350
Model 2A, .25 ACP, Einhand, Clip Fed, *Modern*	150	300	400
Model 3, .25 ACP, Long Grip, Clip Fed, *Modern*	125	250	300
Model 3A, .25 ACP, Einhand, Long Grip, Clip Fed, *Modern*	75	250	350

RIFLE, SELF-LOADING

	Fair	V. Good	Excellent
Model 1897, Karabiner, 7.8mm, Long Barrel, Detachable Stock, *Modern*	2000	4400	5500

BERLIN, ABRAHAM

Caston, Pa., 1773–1786. See Kentucky Rifles and Pistols.

BERNARDELLI

Vincenzo Bernardelli, Gardone, Val Trompia, Italy.

HANDGUN, REVOLVER

	Fair	V. Good	Excellent
Standard, .22 L.R.R.F., or .32 S & W Long, Double Action, Blue, *Modern*	100	200	275
Target, .22 L.R.R.F., Double Action, Blue, Target Sights, *Modern*	100	200	275
Target, .22 L.R.R.F., Double Action, Engraved, Chrome Plated, Target Sights, *Modern*	125	350	425

HANDGUN, SELF-LOADING

	Fair	V. Good	Excellent
M1956, 9mm Luger, Clip Fed, *Curio*	$400	$975	$1250
Model 100, .22 L.R.R.F., Clip Fed, Blue, Target Pistol, *Modern*	100	250	300
Model 60, .22 L.R.R.F., Clip Fed, Blue, *Modern*	75	125	175
Model 60, .22 L.R.R.F., Clip Fed, Blue, 8" Barrel, Detachable Front Sight, Adjustable Sights, *Modern*	125	275	350
Model 60, .32 ACP, Clip Fed, Blue, *Modern*	75	150	200
Model 60, .380 ACP, Clip Fed, Blue, Modern	75	150	200
Model 80, .22 L.R.R.F., Clip Fed, Blue, *Modern*	75	125	175
Model 80, .22 L.R.R.F., Clip Fed, Blue, 6" Barrel, *Modern*	75	125	200
Model 80, .32 ACP, Clip Fed, Blue, *Modern*	75	125	175
Model 80, .380 ACP, Clip Fed, Blue, *Modern*	75	125	200
Model V P, .22 L.R.R.F., Clip Fed, Blue, *Modern*	75	150	200
Model V P, .25 ACP, Clip Fed, Blue, *Modern*	50	100	175
Standard, .22 L.R.R.F., Clip Fed, Blue, *Modern*	50	100	175
Standard, .22 L.R.R.F., Clip Fed, Blue, 6" Barrel, Detachable Front Sight, *Modern*	75	150	225
Standard, .22 L.R.R.F., Clip Fed, Blue, 10" Barrel, Detachable Front Sight, *Modern*	100	225	350
Standard, .22 L.R.R.F., Clip Fed, Blue, 8" Barrel, Detachable Front Sight, *Modern*	75	150	275
Standard, .32 ACP, Clip Fed, Blue, *Modern*	75	150	200
Standard, .32 ACP, Clip Fed, Blue, 10" Barrel, Detachable Front Sight, *Modern*	150	350	425
Standard, .32 ACP, Clip Fed, Blue, 6" Barrel, Detachable Front Sight, *Modern*	100	225	300
Standard, .32 ACP, Clip Fed, Blue, 8" Barrel, Detachable Front Sight, *Modern*	125	325	400
Standard, .380 ACP, Clip Fed, Blue, *Modern*	$75	$150	$250
Standard, 9mm Luger, Clip Fed, Blue, *Modern*	100	325	450

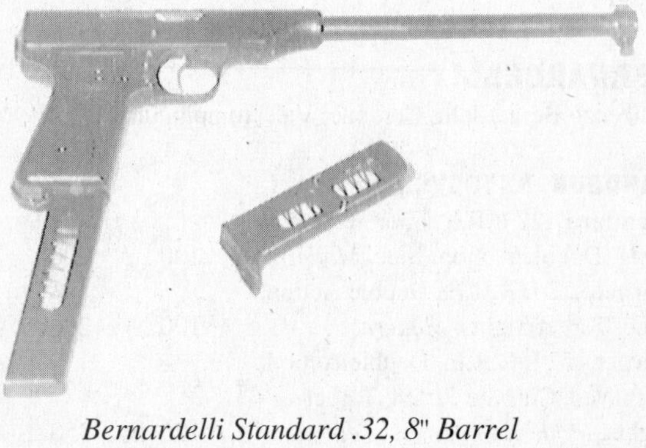

Bernardelli Standard .32, 8" Barrel

RIFLE, DOUBLE BARREL, OVER-UNDER

	Fair	V. Good	Excellent
Various Calibers, Checkered Stock, Engraved, *Modern*	400	975	1200

SHOTGUN, DOUBLE BARREL, SIDE-BY-SIDE

	Fair	V. Good	Excellent
Brescia, 12 and 20 Gauges, Checkered Stock, Hammer, *Modern*	500	1200	1650
Elio, 12 Ga., Checkered Stock, Light Engraving, Lightweight Selective Ejector, *Modern*	300	775	950
Game Cock Premier, 12 and 20 Gauges, Checkered Stock, Single Trigger, Selective Ejector, *Modern*	300	700	850
Game Cock, *Modern*	225	575	675
Holland Deluxe, Various Gauges, Sidelock, Fancy Engraving, Fancy Checkering, Automatic Ejector, *Modern*	2000	3850	4500
Holland Presentation, Various Gauges, Sidelock, Fancy Engraving, Fancy Checkering, Automatic Ejector, *Modern*	2200	5500	6500
Holland, Various Gauges, Sidelock, Engraved, Checkered Stock, Automatic Ejector, *Modern*	1500	3350	4250
Italia, 12 and 20 Gauges, Checkered Stock, Hammer, Light Engraving, *Modern*	300	725	875
Roma #3, Various Gauges, Engraved, Checkered Stock, Automatic Ejector, *Modern*	350	750	825
Roma #4, Various Gauges, Fancy Engraving, Fancy Checkering, Automatic Ejector, *Modern*	250	650	875
Roma #6, Various Gauges, Fancy Engraving, Fancy Checkering, Automatic Ejector, *Modern*	350	825	950
St. Uberto F.S., 12 and 16 Gauges, Checkered Stock, Double Trigger, Automatic Ejector, *Modern*	300	750	875
Wesley Richards, Various Gauges, Checkered Stock, Light Engraving, Double Trigger, *Modern*	700	1650	2250
Wesley Richards, Various Gauges, Fancy Checkering, Fancy Engraving, Single Trigger, Selective Ejector, Vent Rib, *Modern*	900	3000	3750

BERNARDON-MARTIN

St. Etienne, France, 1906–1912.

HANDGUN, SELF-LOADING

	Fair	V. Good	Excellent
Automatique Francais, .32 ACP, Clip Fed, *Curio*	100	225	300

BERSA
Baraldo S.A.C.I. Argentina.

	Fair	V. Good	Excellent
HANDGUN, SELF-LOADING			
Model 62, .22 L.R.R.F., Clip Fed, Blue, *Modern*	$75	$100	$150
Model 622, .22 L.R.R.F., Clip Fed, Blue, *Modern*	50	100	150
Model 644, .22 L.R.R.F., Clip Fed, Blue, *Modern*	50	100	150
Model 97, .380 ACP, Clip Fed, Blue, *Modern*	75	125	175

BERTUZZI
Gardone, Val Trompia, Italy; Imported by Ventura.

	Fair	V. Good	Excellent
SHOTGUN, DOUBLE BARREL, OVER-UNDER			
Zeus, 12 Ga., Sidelock, Automatic Ejector, Single Selective Trigger, Fancy Checkering, Fancy Engraving, *Modern*	2500	6500	8500
Zeus Extra Lusso, 12 Ga., Sidelock, Automatic Ejector, Single Selective Trigger, Fancy Checkering, Fancy Engraving, *Modern*	3000	8500	12500

BICYCLE
Bicycle by Harrington & Richardson, c. 1895.

	Fair	V. Good	Excellent
HANDGUN, REVOLVER			
.22 L.R.R.F., Top Break, Double Action, *Curio*	50	100	150
.32 S & W, 5 Shot, Double Action, Top Break, *Curio*	50	75	125

BICYCLE
France.

	Fair	V. Good	Excellent
HANDGUN, SINGLESHOT			
.22 L.R.R.F., Auto Styling, *Modern*	100	275	350

BIG BONANZA
Made by Bacon Arms Co., c. 1880.

	Fair	V. Good	Excellent
HANDGUN, REVOLVER			
.22 Short R.F., 7 Shot, Spur Trigger, Solid Frame, Single Action, *Antique*	75	125	175

BIG HORN ARMS CO.
Watertown, S.D.

	Fair	V. Good	Excellent
HANDGUN, SINGLESHOT			
Target Pistol, .22 Short, Plastic Stock, Vent Rib, *Modern*	50	100	150

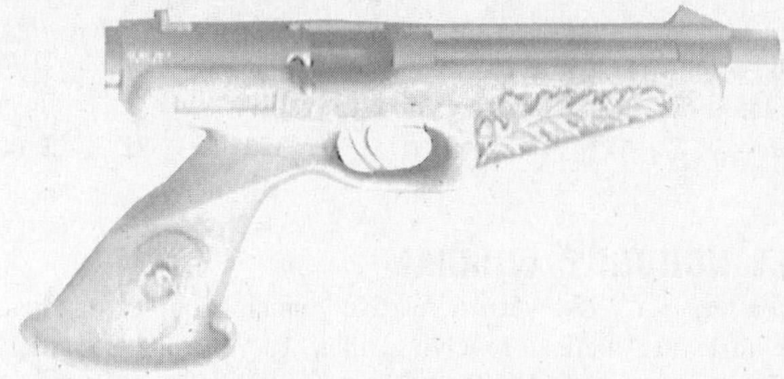

Big Horn .22 Pistol

Early arms collector Dr. Howard Andrews, of Philadelphia, holding a favorite Billinghurst-style rifle. The good doctor's collection was sold by James E. Serven a few years after World War II. The author purchased the Serven papers in the early 1980s, and several illustrations in the Price Guide *are from negatives in that archive. It would have been nearly impossible to put together the arms needed for such illustrations today, except at considerable expense. Due to the high value of many fine guns, most collectors are able only to concentrate on specific themes. To assemble such a variety of arms would require coordinating the assembling of thousands of pieces, from over one hundred different private collections. Such a task would be extremely expensive and logistically supremely challenging. Some photographs show tags used on items by Serven in doing his cataloging.*

	Fair	V. Good	Excellent
SHOTGUN, SINGLESHOT			
12 Ga. Short, Plastic Stock, *Modern*	$50	$75	$100

BILLINGHURST, WILLIAM

Rochester, N.Y., 1843–80. A relatively small group of devotees specializes in American revolving rifles. The tremendous variety in these arms, coupled with their intriguing mechanisms, are a challenge to even the most advanced of arms collectors. Overshadowed largely by Colt revolving longarms, the competitor arms have not yet got in stride in terms of collector value. Billinghurst was one of the best makers, even having assistants who left to make their own revolving longarms. Some Billinghurst revolving rifles have a California connection, and they are deserving of a premium of at least 20 percent. The type also includes the relatively scarce transition ignition system variation, dating between the flintlock and the percussion known as the pill lock.

	Fair	V. Good	Excellent
HANDGUN, PERCUSSION			
Buggy Pistol, Various Calibers, Detachable Stock, Heavy Barrel, *Antique*	700	2000	3000
RIFLE, PERCUSSION			
.36, Revolver, 7 Shot, Octagon Barrel, *Antique*	1250	2500	3500
.40, Revolver, 7 Shot, Octagon Barrel, *Antique*	1250	3000	4000
RIFLE, PILL LOCK			
.40, 7 Shot, Octagon Barrel, *Antique*	1250	2750	3500
.40, Carbine, 7 Shot, Octagon Barrel, *Antique*	1250	2750	3500

BISBEE, D. H.

Norway, Me., 1835–1860.

	Fair	V. Good	Excellent
RIFLE, PERCUSSION			
.44, Octagon Barrel, Silver Inlay, *Antique*	500	1750	2250

BISON

Imported from Germany by Jana International, c. 1971.

	Fair	V. Good	Excellent
HANDGUN, REVOLVER			
.22 L.R.R.F., Adjustable Sights, Western Style, Single Action, *Modern*	25	50	75
.22 LR/.22 WMR Combo, Adjustable Sights, Western Style, Single Action, *Modern*	25	50	75

BITTERLICH, FRANK J.

Nashville, Tenn., from about 1855 until about 1867.

	Fair	V. Good	Excellent
HANDGUN, PERCUSSION			
Derringer, .40, Plain, *Antique*	$600	$1200	$1500

BITTNER, GUSTAV

Vejprty, Bohemia, Austria-Hungary, c. 1893.

	Fair	V. Good	Excellent
HANDGUN, MANUAL REPEATER			
Model 1893, 7.7mm Bittner, Box Magazine, Checkered Stocks, *Antique*	1000	2500	3000

BLAKE, ANN

London, England, c. 1812.

	Fair	V. Good	Excellent
HANDGUN, FLINTLOCK			
Holster Pistol, .62, Walnut Stock, *Antique*	200	575	725

BLANCH, JOHN A.

London, England, 1809–1835.

	Fair	V. Good	Excellent
HANDGUN, PERCUSSION			
.68 Pair, Double Barrel, Side by Side, Officer's Belt Pistol, Engraved, Silver Inlay, Steel Furniture, Cased with Accessories, *Antique*	1500	4000	5000
Pair, Pocket Pistol, Converted from Flintlock, High Quality, Cased with Accessories, *Antique*	1000	3000	4000

BLAND, T & SONS

London & Birmingham, England, from 1876.

	Fair	V. Good	Excellent
SHOTGUN, DOUBLE BARREL, SIDE-BY-SIDE			
12 Ga., Boxlock, *Adjustable Choke*, Color Case Hardened Frame, Engraved, *Antique*	800	2000	2500

BLANGLE, JOSEPH

Gratz, Styria, Austria, c. 1670.

	Fair	V. Good	Excellent
RIFLE, WHEELLOCK			
Brass Furniture, Engraved, Silver Inlay, Light Ornamentation, Full-Stocked, *Antique*	2000	6000	7500

BLEIBERG

London, England, c. 1690.

	Fair	V. Good	Excellent
HANDGUN, FLINTLOCK			
Holster Pistol, Engraved, Silver Inlay, High Quality, *Antique*	2500	6000	7500

BLICKENSDOERFER & SCHILLING

St. Louis, Mo., 1871–1875.

RIFLE, PERCUSSION

	Fair	V. Good	Excellent
.48, Octagon Barrel, Fancy Wood, Brass Furniture, *Antique*	$400	$1200	$1500

BLISS & GOODYEAR

Connecticut, also made guns under trade names America, American Boy, and Challenge.

BLOODHOUND

Made by Hopkins & Allen, c. 1880.

HANDGUN, REVOLVER

.22 Short R.F., 7 Shot, Spur Trigger, Solid Frame, Single Action, *Antique*	75	150	250

BLUE JACKET

Made by Hopkins & Allen, c. 1880.

HANDGUN, REVOLVER

Model 1, .22 Short R.F., 7 Shot, Spur Trigger, Solid Frame, Single Action, *Antique*	75	150	250
Model 2, .32 Short R.F., 5 Shot, Spur Trigger, Solid Frame, Single Action, *Antique*	75	125	200

BLUE WHISTLER

Made by Hopkins & Allen, c. 1880.

HANDGUN, REVOLVER

.32 Short R.F., *Antique*	75	100	200

BLUMENFELD

Memphis, Tenn., c. 1970.

SHOTGUN, DOUBLE BARREL, SIDE-BY-SIDE

Arizaga, 20 Gauge, Double Triggers, Checkered Stock, *Modern*	75	125	200

SHOTGUN, SELF-LOADING

Volunteer Pointer, 12 Gauge, Checkered Stock, *Modern*	75	125	225

BLUNT, ORISON, & SYMS

N.Y.C., 1837–1865. An important gunmaker and dealer of its time, the firm of Blunt & Syms was significant for several reasons, not the least of which was its capability to manufacture prototype firearms for budding inventors–among them Samuel Colt. The prototype Walker model revolver, preserved in the Colt Collection of Firearms, Raymond Baldwin Museum of Connecticut History, was built for Colt by Blunt & Syms, and is so documented in the transcript of the Colt vs. Massachussetts Arms Co. trial of 1851. Blunt & Syms also made a working example of the Artemus Wheeler patent flintlock revolving longarm, which has survived in excellent condition, and is considered likely to have been built as an exhibit in that same trial.

HANDGUN, PERCUSSION

	Fair	V. Good	Excellent
Belt Pepperbox, Various Calibers, Ring Trigger, *Antique*	$150	$375	$450
Boot Pistol, Various Calibers, Bar Hammer, *Antique*	125	325	375
Boot Pistol, Various Calibers, Ring Trigger, *Antique*	150	375	425
Boot Pistol, Various Calibers, Side Hammer, *Antique*	150	350	400
Boot Pistol, Various Calibers, Side Hammer, Ramrod, *Antique*	150	350	400
Boot Pistol, Various Calibers, Underhammer, *Antique*	125	325	375
Dragoon Pepperbox, Various Calibers, Ring Trigger, *Antique*	150	600	850
Pocket Pepperbox, Various Calibers, Ring Trigger, *Antique*	150	400	450

RIFLE, PERCUSSION

.37, Octagon Barrel, Brass Furniture, *Antique*	200	525	625

BOITO

Brazil.

HANDGUN, SINGLESHOT

.44 C.F., Break-Open, Hammer, Blue, *Modern*	50	75	100

SHOTGUN, DOUBLE BARREL, OVER-UNDER

O/U, 12 or 20 Gauge, Checkered Stock, *Modern*	75	125	175

SHOTGUN, DOUBLE BARREL, SIDE-BY-SIDE

S/S, 12 or 20 Gauge, Checkered Stock, *Modern*	50	100	150

SHOTGUN, SINGLESHOT

SS, 12 or 20 Gauge, Checkered Stock, *Modern*	25	50	75

BONANZA

Made by Bacon Arms Co.

HANDGUN, REVOLVER

Model 1½, .22 Short R.F., 7 Shot, Spur Trigger, Solid Frame, Single Action, *Antique*	75	150	200

BOND, EDWARD

London, England, 1800–1830.

	Fair	V. Good	Excellent
HANDGUN, FLINTLOCK			
.68, Pair Officers' Type, Holster Pistol, Brass Furniture, Plain, *Antique*	$1000	$2500	$4000

BOND, WM.
London, England, 1798–1812.

HANDGUN, FLINTLOCK			
Pair, Folding Bayonet, Belt Pistol, Box Lock, Cannon Barrel, Brass Frame and Barrel, Cased with Accessories, *Antique*	1500	4500	6500

BONEHILL, C.G.
Birmingham, England, c. 1880.

SHOTGUN, DOUBLE BARREL,SIDE X SIDE			
.450 N.E. 3¼", Under-Lever, Recoil Pad, Plain, *Modern*	800	2000	3000

BONIWITZ, JAMES
Lebanon, Pa., c. 1775. See Kentucky Rifles.

BOOWLES, R.
London, England, c. 1690.

HANDGUN, FLINTLOCK			
Holster Pistol, Engraved, Iron Mounts, Medium Quality, *Antique*	500	1000	1500

BORCHARDT
Made by Ludwig Lowe, Berlin, Germany, 1893–1897. In 1897 acquired by D.W.M., superseded by the Luger in 1900. Lowe was an American gun designer who spent quite a few years in Europe, and the Borchardt self-loading pistol is truly a brilliant piece of engineering, as well as an example of gunmaking ingenuity of the application of machine tools. A student of modern art would find the Borchardt very sculptural, and a quite beautiful engraved and gold inlaid example by Raymond Wielgus is part of the Art Institute of Chicago's firearms collection.

HANDGUN, SELF-LOADING			
DWM, 7.65mm, Borchardt, 8 Shot Magazine, Blue, with 6½" Barrel and Walnut Grips, Cased with Accessories, *Curio*	6000	12500	17500
Lowe, 7.65mm, Borchardt, 8 Shot Magazine, Blue, with 6½" Barrel and Walnut Grips, Cased with Accessories, Deduct 40% without Case and Accessories	7000	15000	20000

BOSS & CO. LTD.
London, England 1832 to Date.

	Fair	V. Good	Excellent
SHOTGUN, DOUBLE BARREL, OVER-UNDER			
12 Ga., Single Selective Trigger, Straight Grip, Vent Rib, Trap Grade, Cased, *Curio*	$5000	$15000	$27500
16 Ga., Double Trigger, Plain, *Curio*	5000	15000	25000
20 Ga., Single Selective Trigger, Vent Rib, High Quality, *Curio*	6000	20000	32500
SHOTGUN, DOUBLE BARREL, SIDE-BY-SIDE			
12 Ga., Vent Rib, Fancy Wood, Fancy Checkering, Fancy Engraving, *Curio*	4000	10000	15000
Pair, 12 Ga., Straight Grip, Plain, Cased, *Curio*	9000	22500	30000

BOSTON BULLDOG
Made by Iver Johnson, sold by J. P. Lovell & Sons, Boston, Mass.

HANDGUN, REVOLVER			
.22 Short R.F., 7 Shot, Double Action, Solid Frame, *Curio*	50	100	150
.32 S & W, 5 Shot, Double Action, Solid Frame, *Curio*	50	100	150
.32 Short R.F., 5 Shot, Double Action, Solid Frame, *Curio*	50	100	150
.38 S & W, 5 Shot, Double Action, Solid Frame, *Curio*	50	100	150
.38 Short R.F., 5 Shot, Double Action, Solid Frame, *Curio*	50	100	150

BOSWORTH
Lancaster Pa., 1760–1775. See Kentucky Rifles.

BOUTET, NICHOLAS NOEL
Workshops at Versailles, under appointment from the Emperor Napoleon. As gunmaker to the Emperor, Boutet was one of the greatest of all artist in arms, and actually bore the title Director Artiste. His artistry spanned the years from the pre–French Revolution (1785) through the Revolution, Directory, Consulate, Empire, Restoration, and Paris periods. The total aesthetic philosophy of Boutet's attention to exquisite form and detail utilizing the finest materials available while reflecting the influences of rococo and neoclassicism figure in an appreciation of these magnificent firearms. Several of Boutet's design drawings have survived, adding to the fascination with this great gunmaker and artist. Boutet arms represent the decorative arts at their finest level of development in a functional artifact, and other than in specialized studies, the field is largely unknown and studied outside of curators and collectors. Many of the renowned Boutet pieces are in institutions such as the Army Museum (Paris), the Royal Armouries Museum, The Hermitage Museum, the Wallace Collection, The Victoria and Albert Museum, and The Metropolitan Museum of Art that contain extraordinary examples of the finest of Boutet's work. A few private collections also contain exceptional specimens. In addition to the grand presentation and ultra-fine

pieces, firearms of the Imperial Guard of Napoleon figure prominently in the pantheon of Boutet firearms. There are four grades of quality which have been established for Boutet arms. These are as follows: Plain, with no ornamentation on stocks or checkering; blued or browned barrels; minimal engraving. Medium, with stocks checkered; engraving more elaborate; blued barrels. High, with choice select woods; checkering more refined with bordering; carving on stocks; elaborate engraving in combination with silver wire inlays or minimal engraved silver plaques; tooled barrels; blued or browned; edges engraved; mounts deluxe, engraved or sculptured steel. Deluxe, with inlaid gold or silver engraved plaques; mounts cast silver or gold. High presentation provenance with fish-scale checkering on stocks; combination of choice woods. The author is grateful to Professor Dean Taylor for his assistance in preparing the Boutet section and values.

MUSKET

	Fair	*V. Good*	*Excellent*
Civilian Blunderbuss, Full-stocked; high quality; bayonet sometimes present; engraved mounts; "Entse Boutet/manufre A Versailles."	$7500	$20000	$32500
Flint Musket (Velites De La Guarde An XII. 1803), Three brass barrel bands; "Manufre A Versailles"	2500	6000	9000
Flint Musket Fusil D'Infanterie De La Guarde, Three brass bands; "Manufre A Versailles" (Consular) Note: Marked: "Mre Imple De Versailles" for Imperial Guard.	2500	6000	8000
Flint Musketoon, (Chasseur A Cheval/Consular and Imperial Guard); Two brass bands; half-stocked; "Manufre A Versailles."	2500	6000	10000
Flint Musketoon, (Consular and Imperial Guard Grenadier A Cheval); Three brass bands; full-stocked; "Manufre A Versailles."	2500	7000	12500
Flintlock Mousqueton Imperial Guard (Arm of Honour), Two silver barrel bands; round barrel rifled; all mounts silver with presentation plaque in stock; inscribed "Mre. Imple De Versailles"	7500	15000	25000
Flintlock Mousqueton Imperial Guard (Chasseurs), Two brass barrel bands; round barrel rifled; "Manufre Imple De Versailles."	2500	8000	12000
Flintlock Musket (De Gardes Du Corp); Guards of the King, 2nd type; special pan (Bassinet Laiton A Tambour)	3000	10000	13500
Flintlock Musket (Des Ecoles Militaires), Military School Cadets; Special pan, of rotary pattern.	1250	3500	5000
Flintlock Musket (Fusil), Model 1777 (Infantry)	900	2500	3500
Flintlock Musket Model ANIX (Dragoon)	900	2500	3500
Flintlock Musket of Reward (De Recompense), Honor Presentation. Silver mounts and commemorative plaque in butt.	$4000	$10000	$15000
Flintlock Musketoon of Reward, (as above)	4000	10000	17500
High Grade Flintlock Blunderbuss Pistol, Blued Barrel; engraved iron mounts.	4000	12000	20000
High Grade Officer's Musket, Iron Mounts; spurred hammer; three barrel mounts; "Manufre A Versailles."	2500	7000	10000
Military Blunderbuss (Mamelukes), Half-stocked; brass mounts; swan hammer; octagonal; round barrel; "Entse Boutet. Mre Imple De Versailles." (overlapped into Empire).	5000	15000	20000
Musket of the Consular Dragoons, Open pan; three brass bands; middle one large.	1500	3000	4000
Musket of the Infantry (Consular Guard), Open pan; three brass barrel bands.	1000	2500	3000
Musket of the Infantry (Guard Imperial), Open pan; three brass barrel bands.	4000	8000	12000
Officer's Blunderbuss Flintlock, High to deluxe quality; full-stocked; iron engraved mounts; swan hammer.	4000	10000	15000
Officer's Blunderbuss Flintlock, Half-stocked; brass mounts; iron barrel; "Manfre De Versailles."	3000	8000	10000
Pill Lock High Grade Pistol, "Boutet A Versailles"; sculptured iron mounts; half-stocked; c. 1825.	4000	10000	15000

HANDGUN, PERCUSSION

	Fair	*V. Good*	*Excellent*
Half-Stocked High Grade Percussion Pistol, Gold carving on hammer; fish scale checkering; barrel "Boutet A Versailles"; circa 1818, *Antique*	5000	12000	17500
Percussion Back Action Lock Officer's Pistol, Medium to high quality; "Boutet A Paris"; silver mounts; ebony stock; c. 1828, *Antique*	3000	7000	8500

HANDGUN, POCKET PISTOL

	Fair	*V. Good*	*Excellent*
Flintlock Double Barrel Pocket Pistol, High grade checkering and carving; frizzen spring integral with barrel; "Boutet Directeur Artiste"; "Manufre De Versaille, *Antique*	9000	20000	25000
Flintlock Over-and-Under Deluxe Grade Presentation Pistol, c. 1814; gold engraved plaques; gold work breech and barrels. Note: cased with all accessories: $250,000 Excellent, *Antique*	20000	60000	80000

	Fair	V. Good	Excellent
Flintlock Pocket Pistol, Converted 1820s; high butt spurs; carving at barrel tang. "Boutet/Arqre Ordre Du Roi, Versailles"; c. 1788, *Antique*	$4000	$10000	$15000
Pocket/Muff Flintlock Pistol, Medium to high quality; checkering and minimal carving; short smooth bores; no spring on frizzen (built-in barrel), *Antique*	2500	5000	9000
Pocket/Muff Flintlock Pistol, Plain to medium quality; short smooth bores; spring on frizzen; no checkering, *Antique*	1500	5500	8000

HANDGUN, MULTI-BARREL

	Fair	V. Good	Excellent
Flintlock Four Barrel Pistol with Tap Action Lock, Plain quality; "Boutet A Versailles."	2000	7000	9000

TARGET PISTOLS

	Fair	V. Good	Excellent
Officer's Flintlock Target Pistol, Full stocked; medium quality; set triggers as in Austrian Yaeger rifles; high quality lock "Manuf. A Versailles"; multi-groove rifling; barrel marked "Manufacture D'Armes De Versailles," *Antique*	3000	8000	10000

RIFLE, FLINTLOCK

	Fair	V. Good	Excellent
Carbine (Cavalry Model); Model 1793 (short), Model 1793 (short), swan hammer, one brass barrel band; octagonal rifled barrel; full-stocked, *Antique*	4000	10000	12500
Carbine (Civilian) High Grade, Plain wood; iron mounts; "Manufre Versailles"; octagonal rifled barrel.	4000	10000	12500
Carbine (Infantry Model), Model 1793 (long); swan hammer; two brass barrel bands; octagonal rifled barrel; full-stocked.	3000	7500	10000
Carbine (Infantry); Model AN XII (1803–1804), Reinforced hammer; two barrel bands; octagonal rifled barrel; full-stocked.	4000	10000	12500
Deluxe Grade Flintlock Rifle, Full-stocked; engraved silver inlaid plaques; silver-mounted ebony sculpture behind triggerguard; octagonal gold ornamented barrel, *Antique*	7000	30000	50000
Flintlock Carbines, Plain to medium quality; octagonal rifled barrels; full stocked, *Antique*	3000	10000	15000
Flintlock Deluxe Carbines, Octagonal rifled barrels; medium to high quality, *Antique*	4000	20000	30000
Flintlock Rifle, "Manufacture Royale A Versailles" Silver mounts (c. 1815); plain stock, well carved behind triggerguard; engraved animals on lockplate; spurred hammer, *Antique*	$6000	$30000	$50000
Takedown Carriage Carbine, Engraved "Equipage De, S.A.R. Monseigneur Le Duc de Berri" and "Manufre Royale A Versailles"; spurred hammer; c. 1815.	5000	15000	18500

RIFLE, DOUBLE BARREL, OVER-UNDER

	Fair	V. Good	Excellent
Cased Double Barrel, Over-and-Under Rifle, High deluxe grade with horn flasks and full accessories; "Manufacture Imperiale D'Armes De Versailles."	50000	200000	275000

PISTOLS, FLINTLOCK

	Fair	V. Good	Excellent
Cavalry Flintlock Pistol; Model AN XIII, Half-stocked; brass mounts; "Manufre Imp. Versailles."	2000	6000	7500
Cavalry Trooper's Model AN IX (1800–1801), Full-stocked; brass mounts; "Mre Nle. A. Versailles."	2500	6000	7500
Civilian Flintlock Belt Pistol, With Spring Bayonet; Queen Anne style lock; "Boutet A Versailles	3000	7000	9000
Consular Guard Flintlock Dragoon Pistol, Full-stocked; plain brass butt; smoothbore., *Antique*	3000	8000	11000
Deluxe Grade Muff Flintlock Pistols, (1804–14)	6000	20000	30000
Flintlock Holster Pistol, Bright chiseled iron mounts; "Boutet A Versailles"; High butt spurs; wood carved at barrel tang; c. 1789.	3000	8000	11000
Flintlock Long Horse Pistol in Oriental, Far Eastern manner, Deluxe grade; silver and gold plaques; silver wire inlays; round smooth bore; barrel profuse gold ornamentation, *Antique*	7500	20000	25000
Flintlock Muff Pistol, Cannon barrel, plain grade; c. 1819, *Antique*	2000	6000	8000
Flintlock Naval Presentation Pistol (AN X), 1801, Deluxe quality; silver butt naval themes; extensive silver plaques and wire inlay work; "Boutet Directeur Artiste" and "Boutet A Versailles." Note: cased with full accesories and provenance: 200,000.	7500	40000	60000
Flintlock Pistol (Military-Gardes Du Corps Du Roi), 2nd Model (1816); Blued plain barrel; three fleurs-de-lis on, *Antique*	3000	7500	10000
Flintlock Pistol (Military: "National Guard"), c. 1816. Plain brass butt; "Mre Royale De Versailles," *Antique*	5000	12000	15000

	Fair	V. Good	Excellent
Flintlock Pistol (Model 1763–1766), Brass mounts; round barrel smooth bore; full stocked; "Manufre Royale De Versailles," *Antique*	$3500	$10000	$12500
Grade Deluxe Flint Dueling Pistols, Chased silver mounts; gold-engraved inlaid plaques, roller on frizzen. Gold work on octagonal barrel. Note: cased with full accessories; Excellent: 300,000.	7500	25000	30000
Half-Stocked High Grade Flintlock Pistol, Gold carving on hammer; fish scale checkering; barrel "Boutet A Versailles"; circa 1818, *Antique*	7500	25000	30000
High Grade Flintlock Blunderbuss Pistol, Blued barrel; engraved iron mounts.	4000	17000	22000
High-grade flint dueling pistols, Double cased with flint seconds pistols. Full accessories; half-stocked; "Manufre A Versailles/Boutet Directeur Artiste."	60000	200000	275000
Holster Pistol, Bright chiseled iron mounts; "Boutet A Versailles"; high butt spurs; wood carved at barrel tang; c. 1789, *Antique*	3500	8000	11000
Mameluke Guard Flintlock (Flagbearer), Full-stocked; round barrel; smoothbore; brass mounts.	5000	15000	20000
Mameluke Guard Flintlock Belt Pistol, Half-stocked; brass mounts; "Ent. se Boutet," "Manuf. De Versailles," *Antique*	3500	15000	18500
Mameluke Guard Flintlock Horse Pistol, Full-stocked; brass mounts; rifled bore, *Antique*	4500	16000	19000
Mameluke Guard Flintlock Officer's Pistol, Half-stocked; iron mounts; rifled bore, *Antique*	6000	18000	22000
Medium to High Grade Half-Stocked Flintlock Pistol, "Boutet Directeur Artiste, Manufacture A Versailles"; checkered stock; ebony butt inlay.	5500	18000	22000
Medium to High Grade Muff Flintlock Pistols, (1804–14), *Antique*	4000	12000	15000
Officer's Flintlock Belt Pistol, Iron mounted; plain quality; "Mre De Versailles," *Antique*	2000	5000	7000
Officer's Flintlock Pistol, Iron mounted; plain quality; triggerguard extension (a battle axe); "Manufre De Versailles."	3000	7000	9000
Officer's Flintlock Pistol, Octagonal barrel, marked "Manufre Royale"; lockplate "Manufre A Versailles"; engraved iron mounts; multi-groove rifling, *Antique*	2500	7000	9000
Officer's Flintlock Pistol, Plain quality, "Boutet A Versailles"; c. 1785, *Antique*	$2500	$6000	$8000
Officer's Flintlock Pistol (Admiral's), Butt cap in silver (head of Neptune and Anchor); full silver	9000	25000	30000
Officer's Flintlock Pistol (Cheveau Leger), Light Horse Cavalry of the King; "Mfre Royale De Versailles" reinforced hammer; Fleur De Lis front of triggerguard, brass mounts, *Antique*	4000	12000	15000
Officer's Flintlock Pistol (Eagle Bearer Model 1809), Butt cap in silver (crown, "N", crossed oak, laurel branches); half-stocked; round barrel; rifled, iron mounts.	9000	25000	30000
Officer's Flintlock Pistol (Empress Dragoons), Butt cap in silver (crown, "N" and crossed oak; laurel branches); round blued barrel; smooth bore; iron mounts.	4000	12000	15000
Officer's Flintlock Pistol (Fortress Staff Officers Model), Iron mounts and plain iron butt cap; overall proportions as in Medusa pistol.	2500	7000	10000
Officer's Flintlock Pistol (Gendarmerie De La Maison Du Roi), King's Special Police; full-stocked; octagonal barrel; "Gendarmerie Du Roi" and "Manufre Royale De Versailles," *Antique*	4000	12000	15000
Officer's Flintlock Pistol (General Staff Officers Model), Plain silver butt cap; iron mounts.	3000	12000	15000
Officer's Flintlock Pistol (General's), Butt cap in silver (head of Medusa); octagon rifled bore; plain iron mounts; regulation issue. With deluxe silver mounts and cased: Excellent: $60,000	6000	15000	20000
Officer's Flintlock Pistol (Hussards), Butt cap in silver (head of Jupiter with lightning bolts); plain iron mounts; octagonal round barrel; half-stocked	6000	20000	30000
Officer's Flintlock Pistol (Infantry Officer), Butt cap in silver, crown, "N," crossed oak, laurel branches; longer barrel than eagle bearer. Marked "Boutet A Versailles"; iron mounts; round rifled barrel; half-stocked.	6000	20000	30000
Officer's Flintlock Pistol (Infantry Officer), Iron plain buttcap; half stocked; marked "Boutet A Versailles" or "Manuf. Imple De Versailles."; mounts or iron; round barrel; rifled.	4000	12000	15000

	Fair	V. Good	Excellent
Officer's Flintlock Pistol (Line Officer), Same as Infantry Officer only with hammer and iron butt cap.	$4000	$12000	$16000
Officer's Flintlock Pistol (Marshal's), Butt cap in silver (head of Jupiter or Zeus with lightning bolts); plain iron mounts; octagon blued rifles bore; regulation issue.	7000	20000	25000
Officer's Flintlock Pistol (Model IX); 1800–1801, Custom High Grade; silver-fluted butt; silver mounts; slender proportions; checkered; "Mre Nle Versailles."	4000	12000	15000
Officer's Pistol ("General" Level), Full-stocked; round barrel, rifled; silver butt cap (axe and sword motif).	7500	20000	25000
Officer's Pistol of Reward, Full stocked; medium to high quality; multi-groove rifling; "Entreprise Boutet" and "Boutet Directeur Artiste," *Antique*	4000	9000	12000
Officer's Pistol of Reward (Pistolet de Recompence), Full-stocked; multi-groove rifling; iron mounts; medium to high quality; "Boutet et Fils A Versailles."	5000	15000	20000
Officer's Pistol of Reward, Flintlock Model, Full stocked; medium to high quality; multi-groove rifling; "Enterprise Boutet" and "Boutet Directeur Artiste," *Antique*	4000	9000	12000
Officer's Presentation Deluxe Cased Flintlock Sets, With accessories, full-stocked, much wood carving; sculptured hammers; "Boutet A Versailles," *Antique*	30000	120000	180000
Pistols of Reward, Single piece; flintlock; full-stocked and "high" quality (double price for a cased pair), *Antique*	8000	25000	30000

PISTOL, PERCUSSION (ORIGINAL)

	Fair	V. Good	Excellent
Half-stocked High Grade Percussion Pistol, Gold carving on hammer; fish scale checkering; barrel "Boutet A Versailles"; c. 1818.	6000	17000	20000

SHOTGUN, FLINTLOCK

	Fair	V. Good	Excellent
Civilian Double Barrel Flintlock Fowler, Sculptured silver mounts; "Boutet Arq. Du Monsieur A. Versailles"; gold ornamentation on barrels; c. 1785.	8000	25000	30000
Flintlock Fowlers, Medium to high quality grades; "Manufre Royale A Versailles"	6000	17000	20000

BOY'S CHOICE

Made by Hood Firearms Co., c. 1875.

HANDGUN, REVOLVER

	Fair	V. Good	Excellent
.22 Short R.F., 7 Shot, Spur Trigger, Solid Frame, Single Action, *Antique*	$50	$125	$175

BOYINGTON, JOHN

S. Coventry, Conn., 1841–1847.

RIFLE, PERCUSSION

	Fair	V. Good	Excellent
.50, Octagon Barrel, Brass Furniture, *Antique*	400	775	1000

BREDA

Brescia, Italy, Diana Import Co., Current.

SHOTGUN, DOUBLE BARREL, OVER-UNDER

	Fair	V. Good	Excellent
.410 Ga., Light Engraving, Checkered Stock, *Modern*	250	425	500

SHOTGUN, SELF-LOADING

	Fair	V. Good	Excellent
"Magnum," 12 Ga., Mag. 3", Checkered Stock, Vent Rib, Lightweight, *Modern*	150	400	500
Grade 1, 12 Ga., Checkered Stock, Vent Rib, Lightweight, Engraved, *Modern*	150	425	500
Grade 2, 12 Ga., Fancy Checkering, Vent Rib, Lightweight, Fancy Engraving, *Modern*	200	575	650
Grade 3, 12 Ga., Fancy Checkering, Vent Rib, Lightweight, Fancy Engraving, *Modern*	300	750	900
Standard, 12 Ga., Checkered Stock, Plain Barrel, Lightweight, *Modern*	125	300	375
Standard, 12 Ga., Checkered Stock, Vent Rib, Lightweight, *Modern*	100	250	325

BRETTON

St. Etienne, France.

SHOTGUN, DOUBLE BARREL, OVER-UNDER

	Fair	V. Good	Excellent
Deluxe, 12 Gauge, Engraved, Dural Frame, Double Triggers, Barrels Can Be Unscrewed, *Modern*	225	600	750
Standard, 12 gauge, Dural Frame, Double Triggers, Barrels Can Be Unscrewed, *Modern*	200	500	625

B.R.F.

Successor to Pretoria Arms Factory, South Africa, 1950s.

SHOTGUN, SELF-LOADING

	Fair	V. Good	Excellent
"Junior," .25 ACP, Clip Fed, Blue, *Modern*	75	225	300

	Fair	V. Good	Excellent
"Junior," .25 ACP, Clip Fed, Blue, Low Slide, *Modern*	$75	$175	$225
"Junior," .25 ACP, Clip Fed, Blue, PAF Logo on Slide, *Modern*	75	200	300
"Junior," .25 ACP, Clip Fed, Blue, Raised Sight Rib, *Modern*	100	225	275
"Junior," .25 ACP, Clip Fed, Blue, Rough Ground Slide, *Modern*	75	175	200
"Junior," .25 ACP, Clip Fed, Factory Chrome Plated, *Modern*	100	325	400
"Junior", for Cocking Indicator, Add $75-$125			

BRIGGS, WILLIAM

Norristown, Pa., 1848–1875.

SHOTGUN, PERCUSSION

	Fair	V. Good	Excellent
12 Ga., Underhammer, *Antique*	100	275	350

BRITARMS

Aylesbury, England.

HANDGUN, SELF-LOADING

	Fair	V. Good	Excellent
M2000 Mk.II, .22 L.R.R.F., Clip Fed, Target Pistol, *Modern*	300	650	775

BRITISH BULLDOG

Made by Forehand & Wadsworth.

HANDGUN, REVOLVER

	Fair	V. Good	Excellent
.32 S & W, 5 Shot, Double Action, Solid Frame, *Modern*	50	75	150
.38 S & W, 5 Shot, Double Action, Solid Frame, *Modern*	50	75	150
.44 S & W, 5 Shot, Double Action, Solid Frame, *Modern*	50	100	200

BRITISH MILITARY

This section has been completely revised from the First Edition by Ian Skennerton, Editor, Arms & Militaria Press, publishers of books and monographs, and of *International Arms & Militaria Collector*, P.O. Box 80, Labrador 4215 Australia.

MUSKET, FLINTLOCK

	Fair	V. Good	Excellent
.66 Paget carbine, 16" Barrel, Smooth bore, Brass Furniture	1200	1500	1800
.70 Baker, Rifle, Musket Bore, Brass Furniture With Patchbox	1500	1750	2000
.75 Long Land Patt., 46" Barrel, Smooth bore, Brass Furniture, Bannister Rail Stock, Swan Neck Cock on Lock, Wooden Rammer, *Antique*	2500	5000	7500
.75 Short Land Patt., 42" Barrel, Smooth bore, Brass Furniture	1750	3500	5500
.75 India Pattern, 39" Barrel, Smooth bore, Brass Furniture	1000	1750	2750
.625 Baker, Rifle, Carbine Bore, Brass Furniture and Patchbox	$1850	$2500	$3000

MUSKET, PERCUSSION

	Fair	V. Good	Excellent
.75 P1839, 39" Barrel, Smooth bore, Converted Lock, Brass Furniture, Round Barrel Securing Pins	1000	1250	1750
.75 P1842, 39" Barrel, Smooth bore, V-notch Backsight, Brass Furniture, Flat Barrel Securing Pins	1100	1400	1900
.577 P1853, Enfield Rifle, 3-Band, 39" Barrel, Brass Furniture, Steel Rammer	1200	1500	2000
.577 P1853, Enfield Artillery Carbine, P53, P58 or P61 Model, 24" Barrel, 2-Band, Sword Bar on Barrel, Brass furniture	1200	1500	2000
.577 P1856, Short Sergeants Rifle, Enfield, 2-Band, 33" Barrel, Iron Furniture	1200	1500	2000
.577 P1858, Short Naval Rifle, Enfield, 2-Band, 33" Barrel, Brass Furniture	1400	1750	2250
.577 Lancaster, Rifle, Sappers & Miners, 31.6" Barrel, Brass Furniture Although Colonial Issues Often Had Iron Furniture	1500	1800	2300
.577 P1856, Cavalry Carbine, 21" Barrel, Captive Rammer, Ladder Backsight, Brass Furniture	1500	1800	2300
.653 P1840 Constabulary, Carbine, 26" Barrel, Smooth bore, No Backsight, Brass Furniture	1100	1350	1650
.653 P1844 Yeomanry, Carbine, 20" Barrel, Smooth bore, Saddle Ring, V-notch Backsight, Brass Furniture	1200	1400	1800
.653 Dbl.-barrel "Cape," Carbine, Colonial Service, Saddle Ring, Brass Furniture, Smooth bore or Rifled, Back Action Locks	1500	2000	2500
.702 P1851 Minie, Rifle, 39" Barrel, Brass Furniture	1200	1500	1800
.704 Brunswick, Rifle, Brass Furniture and Patchbox	1200	1500	1800
.758 Altered P1840 Sea Service, 30" Barrel, Smooth bore or Rifled, Brass Furniture, Some Converted Others New Mfg.	1200	1500	1800

PISTOL, FLINTLOCK

	Fair	V. Good	Excellent
.58, New Land, M1796 Tower, Belt Hook, Brass Furniture, *Antique*	1200	1950	2750
.67, George III Tower, Cavalry Pistol, Brass Furniture, Swivel Rammer, *Antique*	800	1450	2400
.80, Modified M1796 Spooner, Holster Pistol, Plain Brass Furniture, *Antique*	900	1600	2750

PISTOL, PERCUSSION

	Fair	V. Good	Excellent
.57 Sea Service, Smooth bore, 6" Barrel, Usually With Belt Hook, *Antique*	450	600	750

	Fair	V. Good	Excellent
753 Cavalry, Pistol, Musket Bore, 9" Barrel, Swivel Rammer	$550	$650	$800
.577 Cavalry, Pistol, 8" Barrel, Pattern 1861, Rifled, Swivel Rammer	550	650	800
.577 Cavalry, Pistol, 10" Barrel, Pattern 1856, for Lancers, Rifled, Swivel Rammer	550	650	800
.577 Cavalry, Pistol, 10" Barrel, Pattern 1856, Lancers Pattern, Detachable Butt	550	650	800

PISTOL, REVOLVER

	Fair	V. Good	Excellent
.476 Mk I, Enfield, 5⅞" Barrel, Top Break, .450 Boxer, Henry Rifling, *Antique*	500	650	800
.476 Mk II, Enfield, 5⅞" Barrel, Top Break, .450 Boxer, Henry Rifling, *Antique*	500	650	800
.450 Webley RIC (Royal Irish Constabulary), Revolver, Police and Official Issue, *Antique*	250	350	450
.455 Webley Mk I, Revolver, Top Break, Round Butt, Military, *Antique*	300	400	550
.455 Webley Mk I*, Revolver, Top Break, Round Butt, Military, *Antique*	300	400	550
.455 Webley MK I**, Revolver, Top Break, Round Butt, Military, *Antique*	300	400	550
.455 Webley MK II, Revolver, Top Break, Round Butt, Military, *Antique*	300	400	550
.455 Webley MK II*, Revolver, Top Break, Round Butt, Military, *Antique*	300	400	550
.455 Webley MK II**, Revolver, Top Break, Round Butt, Military, *Antique*	300	400	550
.455 Webley Mk III, Revolver, Top Break, Round Butt, Military, *Antique*	350	450	600
.455 Webley Mk IV, Revolver, Top Break, Round Butt, Military, *Curio*	350	450	600
.455 Webley Mk V, Revolver, Top Break, Round Butt, Military, *Curio*	350	450	600
.455 Webley Mk VI, Revolver, Top Break, Square Butt, Military, *Curio*	400	450	650

PISTOL, SELF-LOADING

	Fair	V. Good	Excellent
M1911A1 Colt, .455 Webley Auto, Clip Fed, 7-rd	1250	1500	1800
.455 Webley Mk I, Clip Fed, 7-rd, RAN Issue	850	1000	1250
.455 Webley Mk I No.2, Clip Fed, 7-rd RAF Issue, Cut for Shoulder Stock	4000	5000	6000

RIFLE, SINGLESHOT

	Fair	V. Good	Excellent
.577 Snider-Enfield, 3-Band, Military	400	525	650
.577 Snider-Enfield, 2-Band Short Rifle, Military	400	475	600
.577 Snider-Enfield, Artillery Carbine, Military	375	475	575
.577 Snider-Enfield, Cavalry Carbine, Military	350	450	550
.450 Martini-Henry, Mk I, II and III Rifle, Military	400	450	500
.450 Martini-Henry, Mk IV Long Lever, Military	$350	$400	$450
.450 Martini-Henry, Carbine, Artillery or Cavalry	400	450	500
.303 Martini-Metford, Rifle, Colonial Service	500	700	900
.303 Martini-Metford, Carbine, Mk I or II, Artillery or Cavalry	475	550	650
.303 Martini-Metford, Carbine Cavalry, Mk III	425	475	550
.303 Martini-Enfield, Rifle, Mk I or Mk II	350	425	500
.303 Martini-Enfield, Carbine, Mk I, II or III, Artillery or Cavalry	300	375	450
.310 Cadet Martini, Westley Richards Mfg, Vic. Gov't	325	350	375
.310 Cadet Martini, BSA or Greener Mfg, Australian Gov't	300	325	350

RIFLE, BOLT ACTION, MLM

	Fair	V. Good	Excellent
.303 Lee-Metford Mk I, Safety Catch on Body, Lewes Sights, 8-rd Straight-Line Mag (Longer), 30.2" Barrel, Hand Groove Forewood	750	950	1250
.303 Lee-Metford Mk I*, No Safety, Barleycorn Sights, 8-rd Straight-Line Magazine (Longer), 30.2" Barrel, Hand-Grooved Forewood	600	750	900
.303 Lee-Metford Mk II, No Safety, Barleycorn Sights, 10-rd Staggered-Line Magazine, 30.2" Barrel, Deeley Bolthead	800	1000	1200
.303 Lee-Metford Mk II*, Safety Catch on Bolt Cocking Piece, Otherwise Similar to MLM Mk II Rifle	850	1050	1250
.303 Lee-Metford Carbine, Safety Catch on Bolt Cocking Piece, 20.75" Barrel, Recessed Sling Bar in Butt, Short 6-rd Magazine	650	750	850

RIFLE, BOLT ACTION, MLE

	Fair	V. Good	Excellent
.303 Lee-Enfield Mk I & II*, Safety Catch on Bolt Cocking Piece, 30.2" Barrel, Same as the Mk II* MLM except for Enfield Rifling	450	575	700
.303 Lee-Enfield Carbine, Similar to MLM Carbine, except Enfield Rifling and Absence of Sling Bar in the Butt	550	650	750
.303 R.I.C. Lee-Enfield Carbine, 20. 75" Barrel With Provision for Fixing the Patt. 1888 Sword Bayonet	450	550	650
.303 Lee-Enfield Charger Loader (CLLE) Conversion, SMLE-Type Charger Guide Fitted, Improved Sighting for Later Ammunition	475	600	725

	Fair	V. Good	Excellent
RIFLE, BOLT ACTION, SMLE			
.303 SMLE Mk I, I* and Cond. Mk II Series, 25.2" Barrel, Sliding Charger Guide, Top of Bolthead, Mag Cut-Off, Long Range Dial Sights	$450	$550	$650
.303 SMLE Mk III and Cond. Mk IV, Similar to Mk I Series Except Simplified Leaf Backsight and Protector, Bridge Charger Guide, Etc.	350	425	500
.303 No. 1 Mk III* (SMLE Mk III*), Same as Mk III But No Mag Cut-Off, Long Range Dial Sights, Backsight Windage Adjustment, Etc. Also Made by Lithgow, Australia and Ishapore, India	150	225	300
.303 No. 1 Mk III* Sectionised Model, Full Length	750	950	1200
.303 SMLE and No. 4 Sectionised Actions, Short Barrel	350	450	550
.22RF Short Rifle Variants, 25.2" Barrels, Minor Differences	200	300	400
.22RF Long Rifle Variants, 30.2" Barrels, Minor Differences	250	350	450
.22RF No. 2 Mk IV*, Also Mfg/Cond. at Lithgow & Ishapore	200	275	350
.303 SMLE Mk V, Troop Trials Model, Enfield 1922–24, Folding Aperture Backsight, Approximately 20,000 Made	400	500	600
.303 No. 1 Mk VI, Trials Rifles, 1929–30, Enfield, 1,025 Made	600	750	900
.303 No. 1 Mk III* Sniper, Telescopic Sights, Factory Conversions	950	1250	1600
.303 No. 1 EY Grenade Launcher, Wire-Bound Reinforcing	300	350	400
.276 Patt. 1913, Enfield Trials Rifle, 1,251 Manufactured in 1912–13	1000	1400	1800
.303 Patt. 1914 (No. 3 Mk I*), U.S. Contract Production by the Winchester (W), Remington (RE), and Eddystone (E) Factories	250	300	350
.303 No. 3 Mk I* (F), Fitted With Fine-Range Adjustment on the Folding Leaf Backsight, Only on Winchester Models	300	350	400
.303 No. 3 Mk I* (T), Cond. by P.P. Co. Using Winchester Mfg. Rifles and Patt. 1918 Scope; 2,001 Units Were Set Up In 1918	1250	1500	1750
.303 No. 3 Mk I* (T)A, Cond. by Alex Martin, Glasgow, in WW2, 421 Winchester Mk I* (F) Rifles With WW1 Aldis and P.P. Co. Scopes	1000	1250	1500
.303 SMLE, Shortened and Lightened, Trials, Lithgow	1500	2000	2300
.303 No. 4 Mk I, Trials, Mfg. Enfield 1931–33, Approximately 2,500 Produced, Many Later Upgraded to WW2 Production Style	500	650	800
.303 No. 4 Mk 1, Manufactured in U.K. Only, by R.O.F. Fazakerley, R.O.F. Maltby and B.S.A. Shirley	$200	$250	$300
.303 No. 4 Mk 1 and I*, Manufactured in U.S.A. by Stevens Savage & by Long Branch SAL in Canada	220	280	350
.303 No. 4 Canadian Lightweight, Trials Model, Few Made	1500	2000	2500
.303 No. 4 Mk 2, Mk 1/2 and 1/3 Conversions, U.K. Mfg. Only for the Mk 2 Model, and Conversion of Earlier Mk I and I* to 1/2 and 1/3	250	300	350
.303 No. 4 Mk I (T) Sniper, w/No. 32 Scope, Cond. by Holland & Holland in U.K. and Long Branch in Canada. Issued in Chest	1500	1750	2000
.303 No. 5 Mk I, Jungle Carbine, UK Production Only	300	350	400
.303 No. 6 Mk I and Mk I/I, Jungle Carbine Trials, Lithgow	2500	2750	3000
.410 Musket, Rifle Factory Ishapore Conversion to Single Loader	150	200	250
.22RF No. 5, Trials, 103 Rifles Assembled by BSA in 1944	1200	1650	2100
.22RF No. 7 Trainer, Cond. by Long Branch (Single Loader) and by BSA (Magazine Feed), Cond. on the No. 4 Action	350	450	550
.22RF No. 8 Trainer, Cond. by BSA and Fazakerley on No. 4 Action	350	450	550
.22RF No. 9 Trainer, Cond. for the Royal Navy by Parker Hale, Using the No. 4 Action, Single Loader Only	350	450	550
7.62mm 2A, Ishapore SMLE, 12-rd Clip	200	250	300
7.62mm L39A1 Target, Cond. Enfield, Single Loader	800	900	1000
7.62mm L42A1 Sniper, Cond. Enfield, 10-rd Clip	1000	1250	1500
.303 L59A1 Drill Purpose, For Cadet Training	250	300	350
HANDGUN, FLINTLOCK			
.58, New Land M1796 Tower, Long Tapered Round Barrel, Belt Hook, Brass Furniture, *Antique*	850	2000	2750
.67, George III Tower, Cavalry Pistol, Military, Tapered Round Barrel, Brass Furniture, *Antique*	800	1500	2500
.80, Modified M1796 Spooner, Holster Pistol, Plain Brass Furniture, *Antique*	900	1900	3000
HANDGUN, REVOLVER			
#2 Mk I R.A.F., .38 S & W, Military, Top Break, *Curio*	150	300	350
#2 Mk I, .38 S & W, Military, Top Break, *Curio*	150	300	350
S & W M38/200, .38 S & W, Solid Frame, Swing-Out Cylinder, Double Action, Military, *Curio*	100	175	275

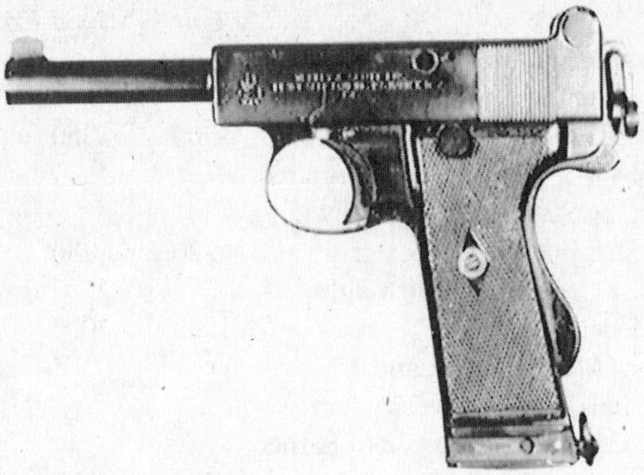

British Military Webley MK 1 No. 2.455

BRNO

Ceska Zbrojovka, Brno, Czechoslovakia, since 1922. Widely recognized and respected within the universe of arms manufacturing, BRNO has developed, over the years, some highly reliable and straight-shooting designs, deserving of distinction worldwide. The professional hunter Ian Manning of Zambia, South Africa, and Botswana, swore by this piece, and said it rivaled any bolt action sporting rifle he had ever used.

	Fair	V. Good	Excellent
RIFLE, BOLT ACTION			
21 H, Various Calibers, Sporting Rifle, Express Sights, Cheekpiece Checkered Stock, Set Trigger, *Modern*	$300	$675	$750
22 F, Various Calibers, Sporting Rifle, Express Sights, Mannlicher Checkered Stock, Set Trigger, *Modern*	275	650	825
Model I, .22 L.R.R.F., Sporting Rifle, Express Sights, 5 Shot Clip, Checkered Stock, Set Trigger, *Modern*	150	350	400
Model II, .22 L.R.R.F., Sporting Rifle, Express Sights, 5 Shot Clip, Fancy Wood, Set Trigger, *Modern*	100	275	375
Z-B Mauser, .22 Hornet, Sporting Rifle, Express Sights, 5 Shot Clip, Checkered Stock, Set Trigger, *Modern*	250	650	900
ZKB 680 Fox, .22 Rem., Clip Fed, Checkered Stock, Sling Swivels, *Modern*	200	350	475
ZKM 452, .22 L.R.R.F., Clip Fed, Checkered Stock, Tangent Sights, *Modern*	50	100	150
RIFLE, SELF-LOADING			
ZKM 581, .22 L.R.R.F., Clip Fed, Checkered Stock, Tangent Sights, *Modern*	100	300	375
RIFLE, DOUBLE BARREL, OVER-UNDER			
Super Express, Various Calibers, Fancy Checkering, Sidelock, Engraved, Double Triggers, *Modern*	1000	2500	3500
Super Express Grade III, Various Calibers, Fancy Checkering, Sidelock, Fancy Engraving, Double Triggers, *Modern*	$1500	$3500	$4000
Super Express Grade IV, Various Calibers, Fancy Checkering, Sidelock, Fancy Engraving, Double Triggers, *Modern*	2050	4000	5000
SHOTGUN, DOUBLE BARREL, OVER-UNDER			
Super, 12 Gauge, Fancy Checkering Sidelock, Plain, Ejectors, Double Triggers, *Modern*	235	600	725
Super Grade I, 12 Gauge, Fancy Checkering, Sidelock, Fancy Engraving, Ejectors, Double Triggers, *Modern*	500	1500	2000
Super Grade IV, 12 Gauge, Fancy Checkering, Sidelock, Engraved, Ejectors, Double Triggers, *Modern*	375	900	1200
ZH 303 Field, 12 Gauge, Boxlock, Checkered Stock, *Modern*	150	400	500
SHOTGUN, DOUBLE BARREL, SIDE-BY-SIDE			
ZP 47, 12 Gauge, Sidelock, Double Triggers, Extractors, Checkered Stock, *Modern*	100	275	350
ZP 49, 12 Gauge, Sidelock, Double Triggers, Ejectors, Checkered Stock, *Modern*	200	450	525

BROCKWAY, NORMAN S.

West Brookfield, Mass., 1861–1867, Bellows Falls, Vt., 1867–1900.

RIFLE, PERCUSSION			
Various Calibers, Target Rifles, *Antique*	800	3000	3500

BRONCO

Echave y Arizmendi, Eibar, Spain, 1911–1974.

HANDGUN, SELF-LOADING			
1918 Vest Pocket, .32 ACP, Clip Fed, *Curio*	50	100	150
Vest Pocket, .25 ACP, Clip Fed, *Modern*	50	100	150
Vest Pocket, .25 ACP, Clip Fed, Light Engraving, *Modern*	50	125	200

BRONCO

Imported by Garcia, c. 1970.

COMBINATION WEAPON, OVER-UNDER			
.22/.410, Skeleton Stock, *Modern*	50	75	100
RIFLE, SINGLESHOT			
Skeleton Stock, *Modern*	25	50	75

	Fair	V. Good	Excellent
SHOTGUN, SINGLESHOT			
.410 Ga., Skeleton Stock, *Modern*	$50	$100	$150

BROOKLYN ARMS

Brooklyn, N.Y., 1863–1867. Not generally known in the firearms collecting field, or often thought of, the City of Brooklyn played a vital role in the history of American gunmaking. Revolvers like the Slocum are extremely well made, and were among several makes of revolving arms developed to try to take advantage of the expiration of Colonel Colt's master revolver patent, and the demand for arms developing during the Civil War. Brooklyn-made arms are a worthy subject for collecting.

	Fair	V. Good	Excellent
HANDGUN, REVOLVER			
Slocum Patent, .32 R.F., 5 Shot Cylinder with Sliding Chambers, Spur Trigger, Single Action, Engraved, *Antique*	150	400	500

BROWN MFG. CO.

Newburyport, Mass., 1869–73. Also see Ballard Rifle.

	Fair	V. Good	Excellent
HANDGUN, SINGLESHOT			
Southerner Derringer, .41 R.F., Side-Swing Barrel, Spur Trigger, Brass Frame, *Antique*	150	350	450
RIFLE, BOLT ACTION			
1853 Long Enfield, .58 U.S. Musket, Converted from Percussion, Brass Furniture, *Antique*	200	600	800
U.S. M1861 Musket, .58 U.S. Musket, Converted from Percussion, Brass Furniture, *Antique*	300	800	1000

BROWN PRECISION CO.

San Jose, Calif., since 1975.

	Fair	V. Good	Excellent
RIFLE, BOLT ACTION			
Sporter, Various Calibers, Fiberglass Stock, Rem. 700 Action, Sling Swivels, *Modern*	300	750	900

BROWN, JOHN & SONS

Fremont, N.J., 1840–1871.

	Fair	V. Good	Excellent
RIFLE, PERCUSSION			
.50, Target Rifle, Scope Mounted, Set Trigger, *Antique*	825	4000	5000
Various Calibers, Sporting Rifle, *Antique*	600	3000	4000

BROWNING

Established 1870 in St. Louis, Mo., 1880 to Date, Ogden/Morgan, Utah. (See Fabrique Nationale.) Primary Manufacturer Fabrique National in Herstal and Liege, Belgium. Also see Commemoratives. The unique role of John M. Browning in the history of firearms presents an extraordinary chapter that has never fully been documented. The author has visited the Browning/FN complex in Herstal, Belgium, as well as the Browning Museum in Ogden, Utah. Both are a must for any dedicated arms collector, whether or not one is keen on Brownings per se. This company has not lost its touch in the manufacture of high-quality firearms. Browning firearms are among the finest mass-produced products ever made, and continue to attract hundreds of thousands of clients on a worldwide basis. As more books appear, and more collectors realize there is a small but determined army of Browning collectors and devotees, prices will exceed their present steady rise. Playing a further role in promoting Browning arms as collectibles is the Browning Collectors Association.

	Fair	V. Good	Excellent
HANDGUN, SELF-LOADING			
Baby Standard, .25 ACP, Clip Fed, *Modern*	$100	$225	$325
Baby, .25 ACP, Clip Fed, Lightweight, Nickel Plated, *Modern*	150	300	375
Baby, .25 ACP, Clip Fed, Renaissance, Nickel Plated, Engraved, *Modern*	250	600	800
BDA 38 Super, .38 Super, Clip Fed, Double Action, Fixed Sights, *Modern*	250	475	600
BDA 380, .380 ACP, Clip Fed, Double Action, Fixed Sights, *Modern*	150	300	400
BDA 380, .380 ACP, Clip Fed, Double Action, Fixed Sights, Nickel, *Modern*	150	300	375
BDA 45, .45 ACP, Clip Fed, Double Action, 7 Shot, *Modern*	200	325	400
BDA 9, 9mm Luger, Clip Fed, Double Action, 9 Shot, *Modern*	150	300	400
Challenger II, .22 L.R.R.F., Clip Fed, Adjustable Sights, *Modern*	100	175	225
Challenger III, .22 L.R.R.F., Clip Fed, Adjustable Sights, *Modern*	100	150	200

Browning Challenger III

	Fair	V. Good	Excellent
Challenger, .22 L.R.R.F., Clip Fed, Checkered Wood Grips, Adjustable Sights, *Modern*	125	250	300
Challenger, .22 L.R.R.F., Clip Fed, Gold Line, Checkered Wood Grips, Gold Inlays, Engraved, *Modern*	425	1200	1500

	Fair	V. Good	Excellent
Challenger, .22 L.R.R.F., Clip Fed, Renaissance, Checkered Wood Grips, Fancy Engraving, Nickel Plated, *Modern*	$325	$1000	$1250
Classic Hi Power Pistol, 9mm, Engraved with Lynx and Bald Eagle, *Modern*	500	1200	1500
Gold Classic Hi Power Pistol, 9mm, Engraved with Lynx and Bald Eagle, *Modern*	500	1500	1850

Browning—Gold Classic Hi Power Pistol

	Fair	V. Good	Excellent
Hi Power "FM" Argentine, 9mm, Clip Fed, Made under License, Military, *Modern*	200	425	500
Hi Power Estonian, 9mm, Clip Fed, Military, *Curio*	400	1000	1250
Hi Power Inglis #1 Mk I*, 9mm, Tangent Stocks, Slotted for Shoulder Stock, Military, *Curio*	350	650	800
Hi Power Inglis #1 Mk I*, 9mm, Tangent Stocks, with Shoulder Stock, Military, *Curio*	400	825	1050
Hi Power Inglis #1 Mk I, 9mm, Tangent Stocks, Slotted for Shoulder Stock, Military, *Curio*	350	650	800
Hi Power Inglis #2 Mk I*, 9mm, Fixed Sights, Slotted for Shoulder Stock, Military, *Curio*	350	650	750
Hi Power Inglis #2 Mk I, 9mm, Fixed Sights, Military, *Curio*	350	650	750
Hi Power Louis XVI, Fancy Engraving, Nickel Plated, Adjustable Sights, Cased, *Modern*	400	875	1050
Hi Power Louis XVI, Fancy Engraving, Nickel Plated, Fixed Sights, Cased, *Modern*	400	850	1000
Hi Power Renaissance, 9mm, Clip Fed, Nickel Plated, Engraved, *Modern*	400	850	1000
Hi Power Renaissance, 9mm, Clip Fed, Nickel Plated, Engraved, Adjustable Sights, *Modern*	400	850	1100
Hi Power Renaissance, 9mm, Clip Fed, with Ring Hammer, Nickel Plated, Engraved, *Modern*	500	900	1250
Hi Power Standard, 9mm, Clip Fed, with Ring Hammer, *Modern*	$200	$400	$450
Hi Power Standard, 9mm, Clip Fed, with Spur Hammer, *Modern*	200	375	400
Hi Power Standard, 9mm, Clip Fed, with Spur Hammer, Adjustable Sights, *Modern*	200	375	450
Hi Power Standard, 9mm, Clip Fed, with Spur Hammer, with Tangent Sights, *Modern*	250	575	650
Hi Power Standard, 9mm, Clip Fed, with Spur Tangent Sights, Slotted for Shoulder Stock, *Modern*	350	850	1000
Hi Power Standard, 9mm, Nickel Plating, Add 5%			
Hi Power, 9mm, Clip Fed, Military, *Curio*	200	375	450
Hi Power, 9mm, Clip Fed, Military, Tangent Sights, *Curio*	250	650	800

Browning Hi Power 9mm Military

	Fair	V. Good	Excellent
Hi Power, 9mm, Clip Fed, Military, Tangent Sights, with Detachable Shoulder Stock, *Curio*	225	575	800
Hi Power, 9mm, Clip Fed, Nazi-Marked Military, *Curio*	250	500	600
Hi Power, 9mm, Clip Fed, Nazi-Marked Military, Tangent Sights, *Curio*	350	850	1000
Hi Power, 9mm, Clip Fed, Nazi-Marked Military, Tangent Sights, *Curio*	350	850	1000
Hi Power, 9mm, Clip Fed, Nazi-Marked Military, Tangent Sights, with Detachable Shoulder Stock, *Curio*	1000	1500	1750
Hi Power, 9mm, Clip Fed, Pre-War Military, Tangent Sights, *Curio*	500	850	1000
Hi Power, 9mm, Clip Fed, Pre-War Military, Tangent Sights, with Detachable Shoulder Stock, *Curio*	700	1250	1500

	Fair	V. Good	Excellent
Medalist Goldline, .22 L.R.R.F., Clip Fed, Checkered Wood Target Grips, Wood Forestock, Gold Inlays, Engraved, *Modern*	$500	$1200	$1500
Medalist International Early Model, .22 L.R.R.F., Clip Fed, Checkered Wood Target Grips, Target Sights, *Modern*	300	600	750
Medalist International Second Model, .22 L.R.R.F., Clip Fed, Checkered Wood Target Grips, Gold Inlays, Engraved, Target Sights, *Modern*	300	550	600
Medalist Renaissance, .22 L.R.R.F., Clip Fed, Checkered Wood Target Grips, Fancy Engraving, Target Sights, *Modern*	500	1200	1500
Medalist, .22 L.R.R.F., Clip Fed, Checkered Wood Target Grips, Wood Forestock, Target Sights, *Modern*	300	575	750
Model 1900, .32 ACP, Clip Fed, *Curio*	100	200	275
Model 1900, .32 ACP, Clip Fed, Military, *Curio*	125	275	325
Model 1900, .32 ACP, Clip Fed, Early Type, No Lanyard Ring, *Curio*	150	325	425
Model 1903, 9mm Browning Long, Clip Fed, *Curio*	200	350	450

Browning M1903 9mm

Model 1903, 9mm Browning Long, Clip Fed, Cut for Shoulder Stock, Military, *Curio*	400	750	900
Model 1903, 9mm Browning Long, Clip Fed, Cut for Shoulder Stock, with Holster Stock, Military, *Curio*			
Model 1903, 9mm Browning Long, Clip Fed, Light Engraving, *Curio*	250	500	650
Model 1903, 9mm Browning Long, Clip Fed, Military, *Curio*	200	450	500
Model 1903, 9mm Browning Long, Swedish Contract, Clip Fed, *Curio*	150	250	275
Model 1905, First Variation, .25 ACP, Clip Fed, Grip Safety, Nickel, *Modern*	125	250	325
Model 1905, First Variation, .25 ACP, Clip Fed, Grip Safety, *Modern*	125	225	275

	Fair	V. Good	Excellent
Model 1905, Second Variation, .25 ACP, Clip Fed, Grip Safety, Nickel, *Modern*	$100	$200	$250
Model 1910, .32 ACP, Clip Fed, *Curio*	100	225	300
Model 1910, .32 ACP, Clip Fed, Military, Curio	150	325	400
Model 1910, .32 ACP, Clip Fed, German Police, *Modern*	150	275	325
Model 1910, .32 ACP, Clip Fed, Japanese Military, *Curio*	150	300	400
Model 1910, .32 ACP, Clip Fed, Peruvian Military, *Curio*	150	275	325
Model 1910, .32 ACP, Clip Fed, Syrian Police, *Curio*	150	300	350
Model 1910, .380 ACP, Clip Fed, *Curio*	150	300	350
Model 1922, .32 ACP, Clip Fed, *Curio*	100	200	250
Model 1922, .32 ACP, Clip Fed, Nazi-Marked Military, *Curio*	100	250	300
Model 1922, .32 and .380 ACP, Clip Fed, *Curio*	75	175	225
Model 1922, .32 and .380 ACP, Clip Fed, Renaissance, Nickel Plated, Engraved, *Curio*	400	750	850
Model 1922, .380 ACP, Clip Fed, *Curio*	100	225	275
Model 1922, .380 ACP, Clip Fed, Dutch Military, *Curio*	125	250	300

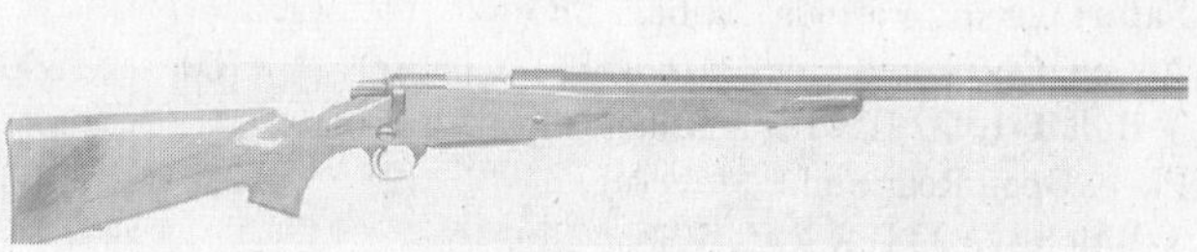

Browning BBR

Model 1922, .380 ACP, Clip Fed, Nazi-Marked, Military, *Curio*	150	300	400
Model 1922, .380 ACP, Clip Fed, Turkish Military, *Curio*	100	225	300
Model 1922, .380 ACP, Clip Fed, Waffenampt Proofed, *Curio*	150	300	350
Model 1922, .380 ACP, Clip Fed, Yugoslavian Military, *Curio*	$100	$200	$300
Nomad, .22 L.R.R.F., Clip Fed, Plastic Grips, Adjustable Sights, *Modern*	100	250	300
Renaissance Set, Baby .389 Hi Power, Nickel Plated, Engraved, *Modern*	1500	3000	3500

RIFLE, BOLT ACTION

Model BBR, Various Calibers, Checkered Stock, *Modern*	200	350	400
Exhibition Olympian Grade, Various Calibers, Gold Inlays, Fancy Wood, Fancy Checkering, Engraved, *Modern*	4000	8500	9500
Medallion Grade, .458 Win. Mag., Long Action, Fancy Wood, Fancy Checkering, Engraved, Open Rear Sight, *Modern*	500	1250	1500

	Fair	V. Good	Excellent
Medallion Grade, Various Calibers, Long Action, Magnum, Fancy Wood, Fancy Checkering, Engraved, *Modern*	$600	$1400	$1600
Medallion Grade, Various Calibers, Short Action, Fancy Wood, Fancy Checkering, Engraved, *Modern* ...	500	1150	1400
Olympian Grade, .458 Win. Mag., Long Action, Fancy Wood, Fancy Checkering, Engraved, *Modern* ...	1500	3000	3500
Olympian Grade, Various Calibers, Long Action, Fancy Wood, Fancy Checkering, Fancy Engraving, *Modern*	1200	2500	3000
Olympian Grade, Various Calibers, Long Action, Magnum, Fancy Wood, Fancy Checkering, Fancy Engraving, *Modern*	1500	2750	3250
Olympian Grade, Various Calibers, Medium Action, Fancy Wood, Fancy Checkering, Fancy Engraving, *Modern*	1200	2500	3000
Olympian Grade, Various Calibers, Short Action, Fancy Wood, Fancy Checkering, Engraved, *Modern* ...	1000	2250	2750
Safari Grade, Various Calibers, Long Action, Checkered Stock, *Modern* .	350	725	850
Safari Grade, Various Calibers, Long Action, Magnum, Checkered Stock, *Modern*	400	800	1000
Safari Grade, Various Calibers, Medium Action, Checkered Stock, *Modern*	350	700	825
Safari Grade, Various Calibers, Short Action, Checkered Stock, *Modern* .	300	700	800
T-Bolt T-1, .22 L.R.R.F., 5 Shot Clip, Plain, Open Rear Sight, *Modern* ...	125	250	300
T-Bolt T-1, .22 L.R.R.F., 5 Shot Clip, Plain, Open Rear Sight, Left-Hand, *Modern*	125	225	275
T-Bolt T-2, .22 L.R.R.F., 5 Shot Clip, Checkered Stock, Fancy Wood, Open Rear Sight, *Modern*	150	325	400

RIFLE, LEVER ACTION

	Fair	V. Good	Excellent
BL-22 Grade 1, .22 L.R.R.F., Tube Feed, Checkered Stock, *Modern*	100	200	250
BL-22 Grade 2, .22 L.R.R.F., Tube Feed, Checkered Stock, Light Engraving, *Modern*	125	225	275
BL-22, Belgian Manufacture, Add 15%-25%			
Model 81 BLR, Various Calibers, Center-Fire, Plain, Clip Fed, Checkered Stock, *Modern*	150	300	350
Model 92 Centennial, Tube Feed, Open Sights, *Modern*	200	325	375
Model 92, .357 Mag., Tube Feed, Open Sights, *Modern*	150	275	325
Model 92, .44 Mag., Tube Feed, Open Sights, *Modern*	150	300	350

Browning B-92

RIFLE, PERCUSSION

	Fair	V. Good	Excellent
J. Browning Mountain Rifle, Various Calibers, Singleshot, Octagon Barrel, Open Rear Sight, Single Set Trigger, Brass Finish, Reproduction, *Antique*	$175	$450	$600
Mountain Rifle, Various Calibers, Singleshot, Octagon Barrel, Open Rear Sight, Single Set Trigger, Browned Finish, Reproduction, *Antique*	125	300	400

RIFLE, SELF-LOADING

	Fair	V. Good	Excellent
Auto-Rifle Grade I, .22 L.R.R.F., Tube Feed, Takedown, Open Rear Sight, Checkered Stock, *Modern* ..	150	300	375
Auto-Rifle Grade I, .22 Short, Tube Feed, Takedown, Open Rear Sight, Checkered Stock, *Modern*	200	350	450

Browning Auto-Rifle Grade I

	Fair	V. Good	Excellent
If Not Belgian Made, deduct. 40–50%.			
Auto-Rifle Grade II, .22 L.R.R.F., Tube Feed, Takedown, Open Rear Sight, Satin Chrome Receiver, Engraved, *Modern*	500	1000	1250
Auto-Rifle Grade III, .22 L.R.R.F., Takedown, Satin Chrome Receiver, Fancy Wood, Fancy Checkering, Fancy Engraving, Cased, *Modern* .	800	1850	2250

Browning BAR 22

	Fair	V. Good	Excellent
Auto-Rifle, Belgian Mfg., Add 20%-30%			
BAR Grade 1, Various Calibers, Center-Fire, Checkered Stock, Plain, *Modern*	200	400	500
BAR Grade 2, Various Calibers, Center-Fire, Checkered Stock, Light Engraving, *Modern*	250	500	575

	Fair	V. Good	Excellent
BAR Grade 3, Various Calibers, Center-Fire, Fancy Wood, Fancy Checkering, Engraved, *Modern*	$300	$650	$800
BAR Grade 4, Various Calibers, Center-Fire, Fancy Wood, Fancy Checkering, Fancy Engraving, *Modern*	565	1125	1500
BAR Grade 5, Various Calibers, Center-Fire, Fancy Wood, Fancy Checkering, Fancy Engraving, Gold Inlays, *Modern*	600	2000	2500

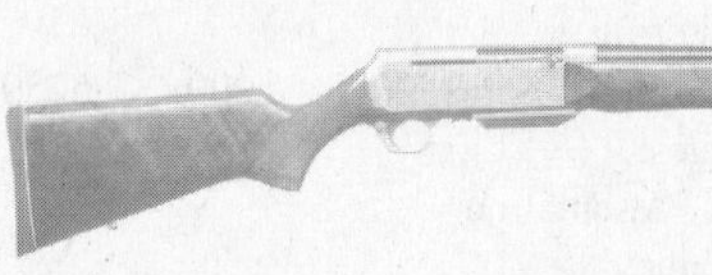

Browning BAR

	Fair	V. Good	Excellent
BAR, Various Calibers, Center-Fire, Belgian Mfg., Add 15%-25%			
BAR, Various Calibers, Center-Fire, Magnum Calibers, Add 10%			
BAR-22 Grade I, .22 L.R.R.F., Checkered Stock, *Modern*	100	200	225
BAR-22 Grade II, .22 L.R.R.F., Checkered Stock, *Modern*	150	275	325
Classic Light, 12 Gauge, Engraved with Mallard Ducks, Labrador Retriever, and Portrait of John M. Browning, *Modern*	500	900	1100
Gold Classic Light, 12 Gauge, Engraved with Mallard Ducks, Labrador Retriever, and Portrait of John M. Browning, *Modern*	1000	2000	2500

RIFLE, SINGLESHOT

	Fair	V. Good	Excellent
Model 78, .30-06, 1 of 50 Bicentennial Rifle, .30-06 Caliber, Commemorative, *Curio*	500	2000	2500
Model 78, Various Calibers, Various Barrel Styles, Checkered Stock, *Modern*	1500	5000	6000

RIFLE, DOUBLE BARREL, OVER-UNDER

	Fair	V. Good	Excellent
Express Rifle, .30/06 or .270 Win., Engraved, Fancy Wood, Fancy Checkering, Cased, *Modern*	1200	2000	2500

RIFLE, SLIDE ACTION

	Fair	V. Good	Excellent
BPR, .22 L.R.R.F., Grade I, Checkered Stock, *Modern*	100	150	200
BPR, .22 Mag., Grade I, Checkered Stock, *Modern*	125	175	225
BPR, .22 Mag., Grade II, Checkered Stock, Engraved, *Modern*	325	350	375

SHOTGUN, DOUBLE BARREL, OVER-UNDER

	Fair	V. Good	Excellent
Citori Grade I, 12 Ga., Skeet Grade, Vent Rib, Checkered Stock, *Modern*	$400	$750	$850
Citori Grade I, 12 Ga., Trap Grade, Vent Rib, Checkered Stock, *Modern*	400	850	1000
Citori Grade II, Trap and Skeet Models, Add 10%			
Citori Grade II, Various Gauges, Hunting Model, Engraved, Checkered Stock, Single Selective Trigger, *Modern*	400	800	950
Citori Grade V, Trap and Skeet Models, Add 10%			
Citori Grade V, Various Gauges, Fancy Engraving, Checkered Stock, Single Selective Trigger, *Modern*	600	1250	1400
Citori, 12 and 20 Gauges, Standard Grade, Vent Rib, Checkered Stock, *Modern*	300	725	850
Citori, 12 Ga., Early Model, Vent Rib, Checkered Stock, *Modern*	350	700	750

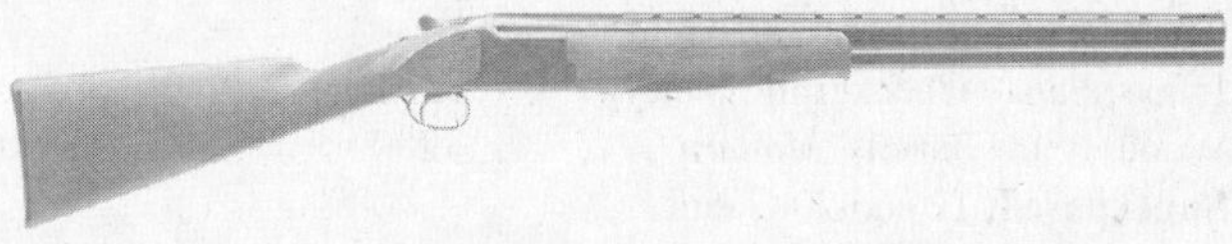

Browning Citori Superlight

	Fair	V. Good	Excellent
Citori, 12 Gauge, Magnum, Vent Rib, Checkered Stock, *Modern*	400	850	1000
Classic, 20 Gauge, 26" Barrel, Engraved with Bird Dogs, Pheasant, and Quail, *Modern*	700	1500	1750
Gold Classic, 20 Gauge, 26" Barrel, Engraved with Bird Dogs, Pheasant, and Quail, *Modern*	2000	4500	5000
Grand Liege, 12 Ga., Engraved, Single Trigger, Checkered Stock, *Modern*	350	700	800
Liege, 12 Ga., Engraved, Single Trigger, Checkered Stock, Modern	300	525	600
ST-100, 12 Ga., Trap Special, Engraved, Checkered Stock, *Modern*	700	1750	2000

Browning Gold Classic Light

	Fair	V. Good	Excellent
Superposed Bicentennial, Fancy Engraving, Gold Inlays, Fancy Wood, Fancy Checkering, Cased, Commemorative, *Modern*	$3000	$7500	$9000
Superposed, 12 and 20 Gauges, Lightning Hunting Model, Presentation Grade 4, Fancy Engraving, with Sideplates, Gold Inlays, Fancy Checkering, Fancy Wood, Extra Barrels, *Modern*	2500	5750	7000
Superposed, 12 and 20 Gauges, Lightning Hunting Model, Presentation Grade 4, Fancy Engraving, with Sideplates, Fancy Checkering, Fancy Wood, Extra Barrels, *Modern*	2500	5250	6000
Superposed, 12 and 20 Gauges, Lightning Hunting Model, Presentation Grade 2, Fancy Engraving, Fancy Checkering, Fancy Wood, Extra Barrels, *Modern*	1500	3500	3750
Superposed, 12 and 20 Gauges, Lightning Hunting Model, Presentation Grade 2, Fancy Engraving, Gold Inlays, Fancy Checkering, Fancy Wood, Extra Barrels, *Modern*	1200	3000	3750
Superposed, 12 and 20 Gauges, Lightning Hunting Model, Presentation Grade 1, Engraved, Gold Inlays, Fancy Checkering, Fancy Wood, *Modern*	1000	2250	2500
Superposed, 12 and 20 Gauges, Lightning Hunting Model, Presentation Grade 1, Engraved, Fancy Checkering, Fancy Wood, *Modern*	900	2000	2250
Superposed, 12 and 20 Gauges, Lightning Skeet Model, Presentation Grade 4, Fancy Engraving, with Sideplates, Gold Inlays, Fancy Checkering, Fancy Wood, *Modern*	2500	5500	6750
Superposed, 12 and 20 Gauges, Lightning Skeet Model, Presentation Grade 4, Fancy Engraving, with Sideplates, Fancy Checkering, Fancy Wood, Extra Barrels, *Modern*	2500	5500	6750
Superposed, 12 and 20 Gauges, Lightning Skeet Model, Presentation Grade 3, Fancy Engraving, Gold Inlays, Fancy Checkering, Fancy Wood, *Modern*	2000	4750	6000
Superposed, 12 and 20 Gauges, Lightning Skeet Model, Presentation Grade 2, Fancy Engraving, Gold Inlays, Fancy Checkering, Fancy Wood, *Modern*	1500	3000	3500
Superposed, 12 and 20 Gauges, Lightning Skeet Model, Presentation Grade 1, Engraved, Gold Inlays	800	2000	2750
Superposed, 12 and 20 Gauges, Lightning Skeet Model, Presentation Grade 1, Engraved, Fancy Checkering, Fancy Wood, *Modern*	$700	$1900	$2500
Superposed, 12 and 20 Gauges, Super-Light Hunting Model, Presentation Grade 4, Extra Barrels, Fancy Engraving, with Sideplates, Gold Inlays, Fancy Checkering, Fancy Wood, *Modern*	2500	5750	6750
Superposed, 12 and 20 Gauges, Super-Light Hunting Model, Presentation Grade 4, Fancy Engraving, with Sideplates, Fancy Checkering, Fancy Wood, Extra Barrels, *Modern*	2500	5000	6250
Superposed, 12 and 20 Gauges, Super-Light Hunting Model, Presentation Grade 2, Fancy Engraving, Fancy Checkering, Fancy Wood, Extra Barrels, *Modern*	1500	3000	4000
Superposed, 12 and 20 Gauges, Super-Light Hunting Model, Presentation Grade 2, Fancy Engraving, Gold Inlays, Fancy Checkering, Fancy Wood, Extra Barrels, *Modern*	1250	3000	3750
Superposed, 12 and 20 Gauges, Super-Light Hunting Model, Presentation Grade 1, Engraved, Gold Inlays, Fancy Checkering, Fancy Wood, *Modern*	1000	2250	2750
Superposed, 12 and 20 Gauges, Super-Light Hunting Model, Presentation Grade 1, Engraved, Fancy Checkering, Fancy Wood, *Modern*	900	2000	2500
Superposed, 12 Ga., Broadway Trap Model, Presentation Grade 4, Fancy Engraving, with Sideplates, Gold Inlays, Fancy Checkering, Fancy Wood, *Modern*	2500	5500	6500
Superposed, 12 Ga., Broadway Trap Model, Presentation Grade 4, Fancy Engraving, with Sideplates, Fancy Checkering, Fancy Wood, *Modern*	2500	5000	6000
Superposed, 12 Ga., Broadway Trap Model, Presentation Grade 3, Fancy Engraving, Gold Inlays, Fancy Checkering, Fancy Wood, *Modern*	2000	4000	5250
Superposed, 12 Ga., Broadway Trap Model, Presentation Grade 2, Fancy Engraving, Fancy Checkering, Fancy Wood, *Modern*	1500	3500	4000
Superposed, 12 Ga., Broadway Trap Model, Presentation Grade 2, Fancy Engraving, Gold Inlays, Fancy Checkering, Fancy Wood, *Modern*	1200	3000	3500
Superposed, 12 Ga., Broadway Trap Model, Presentation Grade 1, Engraved, Gold Inlays, Fancy Checkering, Fancy Wood, *Modern*	900	2250	3000

	Fair	V. Good	Excellent
Superposed, 12 Ga., Broadway Trap Model, Presentation Grade 1, Engraved, Fancy Checkering, Fancy Wood, *Modern*	$800	$2000	$2750
Superposed, 12 Ga., Lightning Trap Model, Presentation Grade 4, Fancy Engraving, with Sideplates, Gold Inlays, Fancy Checkering, Fancy Wood, *Modern*	2500	5000	6000
Superposed, 12 Ga., Lightning Trap Model, Presentation Grade 4, Fancy Engraving, with Sideplates, Fancy Checkering, Fancy Wood, *Modern*	2250	4500	5500
Superposed, 12 Ga., Lightning Trap Model, Presentation Grade 3, Fancy Engraving, Gold Inlays, Fancy Checkering, Fancy Wood, *Modern*	2000	4000	4500
Superposed, 12 Ga., Lightning Trap Model, Presentation Grade 2, Fancy Engraving, Fancy Checkering, Fancy Wood, *Modern*	1200	3000	3750
Superposed, 12 Ga., Lightning Trap Model, Presentation Grade 2, Fancy Engraving, Gold Inlays, Fancy Checkering, Fancy Wood, *Modern*	1000	2500	3250
Superposed, 12 Ga., Lightning Trap Model, Presentation Grade 1, Engraved, Gold Inlays, Fancy Checkering, Fancy Wood, *Modern*	800	2200	2750
Superposed, 12 Ga., Lightning Trap Model, Presentation Grade 1, Engraved, Fancy Checkering, Fancy Wood, *Modern*	700	2000	2500
Superposed, 28 Ga. or .410 Ga., Lightning Hunting Model, Presentation Grade 4, Fancy Engraving, with Sideplates, Gold Inlays, Fancy Checkering, Fancy Wood, *Modern*	2200	4500	5500
Superposed, 28 Ga. or .410 Ga., Lightning Hunting Model, Presentation Grade 4, Fancy Engraving, with Sideplates, Gold Inlays, Fancy Checkering, Fancy Wood, *Modern*	2200	4500	5500
Superposed, 28 Ga. or .410 Ga., Lightning Hunting Model, Presentation Grade 4, Fancy Engraving, with Sideplates, Fancy Checkering, Fancy Wood, *Modern*	2000	4000	5000
Superposed, 28 Ga. or .410 Ga., Lightning Hunting Model, Presentation Grade 3, Fancy Engraving, Gold Inlays, Fancy Checkering, Fancy Wood, *Modern*	1500	3500	4500
Superposed, 28 Ga. or .410 Ga., Lightning Hunting Model, Presentation Grade 2, Fancy Engraving, Fancy Checkering, Fancy Wood, Modern	1500	3000	3500

	Fair	V. Good	Excellent
Superposed, 28 Ga. or .410 Ga., Lightning Hunting Model, Presentation Grade 2, Fancy Engraving, Gold Inlays, Fancy Checkering, Fancy Wood, *Modern*	$1500	$3200	$4000
Superposed, 28 Ga. or .410 Ga., Lightning Hunting Model, Presentation Grade 1, Engraved, Gold Inlays, Fancy Checkering, Fancy Wood, *Modern*	1000	2500	3000
Superposed, 28 Ga. or .410 Ga., Lightning Hunting Model, Presentation Grade 1, Engraved, Fancy Checkering, Fancy Wood, *Modern*	900	2000	2500
Superposed, 28 Ga. or .410 Ga., Lightning Skeet Model, Presentation Grade 4, Fancy Engraving, with Sideplates, Gold Inlays, Fancy Checkering, Fancy Wood, *Modern*	2200	4500	5500
Superposed, 28 Ga. or .410 Ga., Lightning Skeet Model, Presentation Grade 4, Fancy Engraving, with Sideplates, Gold Inlays, Fancy Checkering, Fancy Wood, *Modern*	2200	4500	5250
Superposed, 28 Ga. or .410 Ga., Lightning Skeet Model, Presentation Grade 4, Fancy Engraving, with Sideplates, Fancy Checkering, Fancy Wood, *Modern*	1700	4200	5000
Superposed, 28 Ga. or .410 Ga., Lightning Skeet Model, Presentation Grade 3, Fancy Engraving, Gold Inlays, Fancy Checkering, Fancy Wood, *Modern*	1500	3700	4500
Superposed, 28 Ga. or .410 Ga., Lightning Skeet Model, Presentation Grade 2, Fancy Engraving, Fancy Checkering, Fancy Wood, *Modern*	1000	3000	3500
Superposed, 28 Ga. or .410 Ga., Lightning Skeet Model, Presentation Grade 2, Fancy Engraving, Gold Inlays, Fancy Checkering, Fancy Wood, *Modern*	1200	3200	4000
Superposed, 28 Ga. or .410 Ga., Lightning Skeet Model, Presentation Grade 1, Engraved, Gold Inlays, Fancy Checkering, Fancy Wood, *Modern*	1000	2500	3250
Superposed, 28 Ga. or .410 Ga., Lightning Skeet Model, Presentation Grade 1, Engraved, Fancy Checkering, Fancy Wood, *Modern*	900	2000	2750

Superposed, For .410 or 28 Gauge, Add 15%-25%

Superposed, For 20 Gauge, Add 10%-15%

Superposed, Pre-1977, Lightning Skeet, Add 5%-10%

Superposed, Pre-1977, 4-Barrel, Skeet Set, Add 275%-300%

	Fair	V. Good	Excellent
Superposed, Pre-1977, Broadway Trap Model, Add 8%-13%			
Superposed, Pre-1977, Extra Barrel, Add 35%-40%			
Superposed, Pre-1977, Lightning Trap Model, Add 5%-10%			
Superposed, Pre-1977, Super-Light Lightning, Add 15%-20%			
Superposed, Pre-1977, Vent Rib, Pre-War, Add 10%-15%			
Superposed, Pre-War, Raised Solid Rib, Add $60.00-$90.00			
Superposed, Various Gauges, Pre-1977, Diana Grade Hunting Model, Satin Nickel-Plated Frame, Fancy Engraving, Fancy Checkering, Fancy Wood, *Modern*	$1500	$3500	$4500
Superposed, Various Gauges, Pre-1977, Exhibition Grade, Fancy Engraving, Fancy Checkering, Fancy Wood, Gold Inlays, *Modern*	4000	8000	10000
Superposed, Various Gauges, Pre-1977, Grade 1, Engraved, Checkered Stock, Vent Rib, Single Selective Trigger, *Modern*	700	1700	2000
Superposed, Various Gauges, Pre-1977, Midas Grade Hunting Model, Fancy Engraving, Fancy Checkering, Fancy Wood, Gold Inlays, *Modern*	2500	5000	6000
Superposed, Various Gauges, Pre-1977, Pigeon Grade Hunting Model, Satin Nickel-Plated Frame, Fancy Engraving, Fancy Checkering, Fancy Wood, *Modern*	1000	2000	3000
Superposed, Various Gauges, Pre-1977, Pointer Grade, Fancy Engraving, Fancy Checkering, Single Selective Trigger, *Modern*	1200	2700	3500
Superposed, Various Gauges, Pre-1977, Super Exhibition Grade, Fancy Wood, Fancy Checkering, Fancy Engraving, Gold Inlays, *Modern*	5000	10000	18000
Superposed, Various Gauges, Presentation Grade 1, Extra Sets of Barrels, Add for each: $725.00-$1100.00			
Superposed, Various Gauges, Presentation Grade 2, Extra Sets of Barrels, Add for each: $825.00-$1250.00			
Superposed, Various Gauges, Presentation Grade 3, Extra Sets of Barrels, Add for each: $900.00-$1500.00			
Superposed, Various Gauges, Presentation Grade 4, Extra Sets of Barrels, Add for each: $1200.00-$1700.00			

SHOTGUN, DOUBLE BARREL, SIDE-BY-SIDE

	Fair	V. Good	Excellent
B-SS, 12 and 20 Gauges, Checkered Stock, Field Grade, *Modern*	200	400	500
B-SS, 12 and 20 Gauges, Checkered Stock, Grade II, Engraved, *Modern*	$300	$800	$975
B-SS, 12 and 20 Gauges, Checkered Stock, Sporter Grade, *Modern*	250	500	600

SHOTGUN, SELF-LOADING

	Fair	V. Good	Excellent
Auto-5, Various Gauges, Vent Rib, Add $50.00-$75.00			
Auto-5, 12 and 20 Gauges, Magnum, Checkered Stock, Light Engraving, Plain Barrel, *Modern*	200	350	450
Auto-5, 12 and 20 Gauges, Skeet Grade, Checkered Stock, Light Engraving, Vent Rib, *Modern*	200	350	550
Auto-5, 12 Ga., Trap Grade, Vent Rib, Checkered Stock, *Modern*	200	400	475
Auto-5, 16 Ga., $2\frac{9}{16}$", Pre-WW2, Checkered Stock, Light Engraving, Plain Barrel, *Modern*	100	200	275
Auto-5, 16 Gauge, Sweet Sixteen, Lightweight, Checkered Stock, Light Engraving, Plain Barrel, *Modern*	150	300	400
Auto-5, For Belgian Make Add 15%-25%			
Auto-5, Various Gauges, Buck Special, Checkered Stock, Light Engraving, Plain Barrel, *Modern*	200	400	525
Auto-5, Various Gauges, Grade 2, Pre-WW2, Plain Barrel, Fancy Engraving, *Modern*	425	850	1200
Auto-5, Various Gauges, Grade 2, Pre-WW2, Plain Barrel Fancy Engraving, Gold Inlays, *Modern*	900	2000	2500
Auto-5, Various Gauges, Grade IV, Plain Barrel, Fancy Engraving, *Modern*	1200	2500	3000
Auto-5, Various Gauges, Lightweight, Checkered Stock, Light Engraving, Plain Barrel, *Modern*	200	450	525
Auto-5, Various Gauges, Raised Solid Rib, Add $50.00-$75.00			
B-80, 12 Gauge, Lightweight, Checkered Stock, Vent Rib, *Modern*	150	300	375

Browning B-80

	Fair	V. Good	Excellent
Double-Auto, 12 and 20 Gauges, Checkered Stock, Engraved, Plain Barrel, *Modern*	150	300	400
Double-Auto, 12 Ga., Trap Model, Add 10%-15%			
Double-Auto, 12 Gauge, Checkered Stock, Engraved, Vent Rib, Barrel, *Modern*	200	400	500

	Fair	V. Good	Excellent
Double-Auto, Skeet Model, Add 10%-15%			
Double-Auto, Vent Rib, Add $50.00-$75.00			
Model 2000 Montreal Olympic, 12 Ga., Trap Grade, Vent Rib, Engraved, Gold Inlays, Commemorative, Tube Feed, Checkered Stock, *Modern*	$400	$900	$2100
Model 2000, 12 and 20 Gauges, Buck Special, Open Rear Sight, Tube Feed, Checkered Stock, *Modern*	175	250	325
Model 2000, 12 and 20 Gauges, Skeet Grade, Vent Rib, Tube Feed, Checkered Stock, *Modern*	200	275	350
Model 2000, 12 and 20 Gauges, Vent Rib, Tube Feed, Checkered Stock, *Modern*	175	250	325
Model 2000, 12 Ga., Trap Grade, Vent Rib, Tube Feed, Checkered Stock, *Modern*	175	275	325

SHOTGUN, SINGLESHOT

	Fair	V. Good	Excellent
BT-99, 12 Ga., Pigeon Grade, Checkered Stock, Engraved, Vent Rib, *Modern*	400	850	1000
BT-99, 12 Ga., Trap Grade, Vent Rib, Checkered Stock, Engraved, *Modern*	300	650	750
BT-99, 12 Ga., Trap Grade, Vent Rib, with extra Single Trap Barrel, Checkered Stock, Engraved, *Modern*	300	675	850

SHOTGUN, SLIDE ACTION

	Fair	V. Good	Excellent
BPS, 12 Ga., Buck Special, Rifle Sights, *Modern*	125	300	375
BPS, 12 Ga., Checkered Stock, Vent Rib, *Modern*	125	300	375
BPS, 12 Ga., Invector Trap, Checkered Stock, Vent Rib, *Modern*	100	275	300

BRUTUS

Made by Hood Firearms Co., c. 1875-76.

HANDGUN, REVOLVER

	Fair	V. Good	Excellent
.22 Short R.F., 7 Shot, Spur Trigger, Solid Frame, Single Action, *Antique*	50	100	175

BSA

Birmingham Small Arms, Ltd., Birmingham, England, from 1885.

RIFLE, BOLT ACTION

	Fair	V. Good	Excellent
Imperial, Various Calibers, Sporting Rifle, Muzzle Brake, Checkered Stock, Open Rear Sight, *Modern*	85	200	275
Imperial, Various Calibers, Sporting Rifle, Muzzle Brake, Checkered Stock, Open Rear Sight, Lightweight, Modern	100	200	275
Majestic Deluxe, .458 Win. Mag., Sporting Rifle, Muzzle Brake, Lightweight, Checkered Stock, Open Rear Sight, *Modern*	$125	$225	$325
Majestic Deluxe, Various Calibers, Sporting Rifle, Checkered, Stock, Open Rear Sight, *Modern*	100	200	275
Majestic Deluxe, Various Calibers, Sporting Rifle, Muzzle Brake, Lightweight, Checkered Stock, Open Rear Sight, *Modern*	100	200	275
Model CF-2, Various Calibers, Sporting Rifle, Checkered Stock, Open Rear Sights, *Modern*	115	275	375
Model CF-2, Various Calibers, Sporting Rifle, Checkered Stock, Double Set Triggers, Open Rear Sights, *Modern*	150	300	400
Monarch Deluxe, Various Calibers, Sporting Rifle, Checkered Stock Open Rear Sight, *Modern*	100	200	300
Monarch Deluxe, Various Claibers, Varmint, Heavy Barrel, Checkered Stock, Open Rear Sight, *Modern*	150	225	300

RIFLE, SINGLESHOT

	Fair	V. Good	Excellent
#12 Martini, *Modern*	100	200	300
#12/15 Martini, .22 L.R.R.F., Target, Target Sights, Target Stock, *Modern*	125	250	350
#12/15 Martini, .22 L.R.R.F., Target, Target Sights, Target Stock, Heavy Barrel, *Modern*	125	300	375
#13 Martini, .22 Hornet, Sporting Rifle, Checkered Stock, *Modern*	150	300	375
#13 Martini, .22 L.R.R.F., Target, Target Sights, Checkered Stock, *Modern*	125	200	275
#15 Martini, .22 L.R.R.F., Target, Target Sights, Target Stock, *Modern*	175	350	450
Centurian Martini, .22 L.R.R.F., Target, Target Sights, Target Stock, Target Barrel, *Modern*	125	300	375
International Martini, .22 L.R.R.F., Target, Target Sights, Heavy Barrel, Target Stock, *Modern*	125	325	400
International MK 2 Martini, .22 L.R.R.F., Target, Target Sights, Target Stock, *Modern*	150	325	400
International MK 2 Martini, .22 L.R.R.F., Target, Target Sights, Target Stock, Heavy Barrel, *Modern*	125	300	375
International MK 3 Martini, .22 L.R.R.F., Target, Target Sights, Target Stock, Heavy Barrel, Modern	150	325	400
Mark V, .22 L.R.R.F., Heavy Barrel, Target Rifle, Target Sights, Target Stock, *Modern*	200	400	475

	Fair	V. Good	Excellent
Martini I S U, .22 L.R.R.F., Target Rifle, Target Sights, Target Stock, *Modern*	$175	$400	$475

RIFLE, SLIDE ACTION

	Fair	V. Good	Excellent
.22 L.R.R.F., Clip Fed, Takedown, *Modern*	50	125	150
.22 L.R.R.F., Tube Feed, Takedown, *Modern*	50	125	150

BUCHEL, ERNST FRIEDRICH

Zella Mehlis, Germany, 1919–1926.

HANDGUN, SINGLESHOT

	Fair	V. Good	Excellent
Luna, .22 L.R.R.F., Rotary Breech, Free Pistol, Set Triggers, Light Engraving, *Curio*	300	650	800
Model W.B., .22 L.R.R.F., Roux Action, Target Pistol, Hammerless, Tip-Down Barrel, *Curio*	225	400	500
Practice, .22 Short R.F., Warnant Action, Hammer, Target Pistol, *Curio*	150	225	300
Tell I, .22 L.R.R.F., Rotary Breech, Free Pistol, Set Triggers, Light Engraving, *Curio*	300	700	850
Tell II, .22 L.R.R.F., Rotary Breech, Free Pistol, Set Triggers, Light Engraving, *Curio*	300	700	850

BUDDY ARMS

Fort Worth, Tex., during the early 1960s.

HANDGUN, DOUBLE BARREL, OVER-UNDER

	Fair	V. Good	Excellent
Double Deuce, .22 L.R.R.F., Remington Derringer Copy, *Modern*	25	50	100

BUDISCHOWSKY

Made by Norton Armament (Norarmco), Mt. Clemens, Mich., 1973–1977.

Budischowsky TP-70

HANDGUN, SELF-LOADING

	Fair	V. Good	Excellent
TP-70, .22 L.R.R.F., Clip Fed, Double Action, Pocket Pistol, Stainless Steel, Steel Hammer, *Modern*	$200	$350	$425
TP-70, .25 ACP, Clip Fed, Double Action, Pocket Pistol, Stainless Steel, Hammer, Presentation, Custom Serial Number, *Curio*	400	800	950
TP-70, .25 ACP, Clip Fed, Double Action, Pocket Pistol, Stainless Steel, Hammer, Modern	175	250	325

BUFALO

Gabilondo y Cia., Elgobar, Spain.

HANDGUN, SELF-LOADING

	Fair	V. Good	Excellent
Model 1920, .25 ACP, Clip Fed, *Modern*	50	100	150
Pocket, .32 ACP, Clip Fed, *Modern*	50	100	150

BUFFALO ARMS

Tonawanda, N.Y.

HANDGUN, DOUBLE BARREL, OVER-UNDER

	Fair	V. Good	Excellent
Model 1, .357 Mag., Hammer, Blue or Nickel, *Modern*	50	75	100

BUFFALO BILL

Sold by Homer Fisher Co.

HANDGUN, REVOLVER

	Fair	V. Good	Excellent
.22 Short R.F., 7 Shot, Spur Trigger, Solid Frame, Single Action, *Antique*	50	100	150

BUFFALO STAND

Tradename used by ManuFrance.

HANDGUN, SINGLESHOT

	Fair	V. Good	Excellent
Bolt Action, .22 L.R.R.F., Target Pistol, *Modern*	25	50	100

BUHAG

Buchsenmacher-Handwerkgenossenschaft M.B.H. of Suhl, East Germany.

HANDGUN, SELF-LOADING

	Fair	V. Good	Excellent
Olympia, .22 Short R.F., Clip Fed, Target Pistol, *Modern*	200	375	550

BULL DOZER

Made by Norwich Pistol Co., sold by J. McBride & Co., c. 1875–1883.

	Fair	V. Good	Excellent
HANDGUN, REVOLVER			
.22 Short R.F., 7 Shot, Spur Trigger, Solid Frame, Single Action, *Antique*	$50	$100	$175
.38 Short R.F, 5 Shot, Spur Trigger, Solid Frame, Single Action, *Antique*	50	100	200
.41 Short R.F., 5 Shot, Spur Trigger, Solid Frame, Single Action, *Antique*	75	200	250
.44 Short R.F., 5 Shot, Spur Trigger, Solid Frame, Single Action, *Antique*	100	250	325

BULLARD REPEATING ARMS CO.

Springfield, Mass., 1987–1989. Designed and built by an S & W alumnus, the Bullard rifle was perceived as a viable competitor to the lever-action Winchester. The rifle was even popular with such dignitaries as Theodore Roosevelt, who posed with one and some thieves he had captured while out West in the Dakotas. That rifle, with a distinctive engraved plaque on the right side of the butt-stock, has yet to be discovered. One of Gustave Young's master-works as an arms engraver was a Bullard rifle, exquisitely engraved and evidently used as a promotional and display piece. Of further importance, Bullard rifles represent some of the finest American gunmaking of the second half of the 19th century, although they simply do not have the aesthetic appeal of a Winchester or a Marlin lever-action.

RIFLE, LEVER ACTION

Various Calibers, Light Engraving, Add $55.00-$160.00
Various Calibers, Medium Engraving, Add $220.00-$435.00
Various Calibers, Octagon Barrel, Add $75.00-$110.00
Various Calibers, Ornate Engraving, Add $775.00-$1150.00
Various Calibers, Target Sights, Add $125.00-$185.00
Various Calibers, Fancy Checkering, Add $75.00-$110.00
Various Calibers, for Express Sights, Add $110.00-$160.00
Various Calibers, for Fancy Wood, Add $30.00-$50.00
Various Calibers, for Lyman Sights, Add $45.00-$75.00
Various Calibers, for Standard Checkering, Add $35.00-$50.00
Various Calibers, Full Nickel Plating, Add $55.00-$80.00
Various Calibers, Half-Octagon Barrel, Add $35.00-$65.00

	Fair	V. Good	Excellent
Carbine, Various Calibers, Open Rear Sight, Carbine, *Antique*	2500	4500	5500
Military, Musket, with Bayonet, Open Rear Sight, *Antique*	2500	5000	6000
Various Calibers, Large Frame, Tube Feed, Round Barrel, Plain, Open Rear Sight, Sporting Rifle, *Antique*	1000	2500	3250
Various Calibers, Small Frame, Tube Feed, Round Barrel, Plain, Open Rear Sights, Sporting Rifle, *Antique*	$1000	$2000	$2750
RIFLE, SINGLESHOT			
Military, Full-Stocked, with Bayonet, Open Rear Sight, *Antique*	3000	6500	7500
Military, Full-Stocked, with Bayonet, Open Rear Sight, Carbine, *Antique*	5000	8000	10000
Various Calibers, Schuetzen Target Rifle, Octagon Barrel, Target Sights, Swiss Buttplate, Checkered Stock, *Antique*	1200	3500	4500
Various Calibers, Target Gallery/Hunting, Lightweight, Open Rear Sights, *Antique*	900	2000	2500
Various Rimfires, Target Gallery/Hunting, .22 Caliber, Open Rear Sights, *Antique*	600	1200	1750
Various Rimfires, Target Rifle, Octagon Barrel, Target Sights, Swiss Buttplate, Checkered Stock, *Antique*	1200	3000	4000

BULLDOG

Made by Forehand & Wadsworth.

	Fair	V. Good	Excellent
HANDGUN, REVOLVER			
.32 S & W, 7 Shot, Double Action, Solid Frame, *Curio*	50	75	100
.38 S & W, 6 Shot, Double Action, Solid Frame, *Curio*	50	75	100
.44 S & W, 5 Shot, Double Action, Solid Frame, *Curio*	35	75	125

BULLS EYE

c. 1875.

	Fair	V. Good	Excellent
HANDGUN, REVOLVER			
.22 Short R.F., 7 Shot, Spur Trigger, Solid Frame, Single Action, *Antique*	50	100	150

BULWARK

Beistegui Hermanos, Eibar, Spain.

	Fair	V. Good	Excellent
HANDGUN, SELF-LOADING			
.25 ACP, External Hammer, Clip Fed, Blue, *Curio*	125	225	325
.25 ACP, Hammerless, Clip Fed, Blue, Curio	50	100	150
.32 ACP, External Hammer, Clip Fed, Blue, *Curio*	75	175	300
.32 ACP, Hammerless, Clip Fed, Blue, *Curio*	50	100	150

BUMFORD

London, England, 1730–1760.

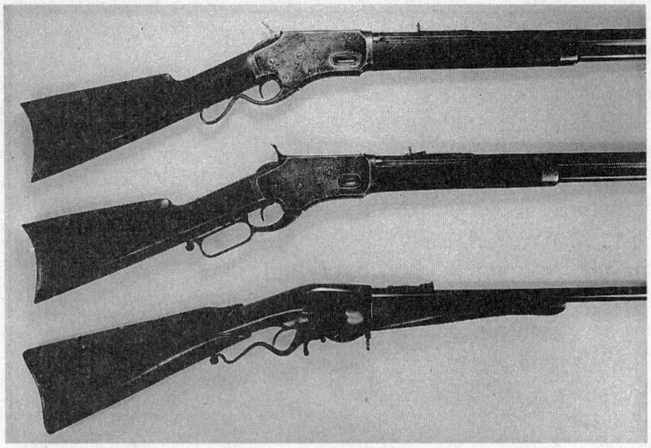

From the top, *Burgess–G. W. Morse patent .45–70 Canadian Mounted Police Model, with long forend secured by two barrel bands;* center, *Remington-Keene bolt-action Sporting Rifle in .45–70; and Bullard .45 caliber lever-action Sporting Rifle.*

	Fair	V. Good	Excellent
HANDGUN, FLINTLOCK			
.38, Pocket Pistol, Boxlock, Queen Anne Style, Screw Barrel, Silver Inlay, *Antique*	$325	$600	$775

BURGESS, ANDREW

Oswego, N.Y., 1874–1887. A prolific inventor of great ingenuity and talent, Burgess was also an adept marketer. Once, with a new collapsible and quick takedown shotgun, Burgess gave a demonstration before Theodore Roosevelt in his own office (TR was then commissioner, New York Police Department). That masterfully orchestrated and dramatic showing, which proved to Roosevelt the cleverness of Burgess's design, is a classic story of firearms audacity and entrepreneurship! An entire book has been written, by researcher and collector Sam Maxwell, on the Burgess patents and the inventor's widespread influence in the firearms field.

	Fair	V. Good	Excellent
RIFLE, LEVER ACTION			
Model 1876, .45-70 Government, Tube Feed, Octagon Barrel, *Antique*	$500	$2000	$2500
RIFLE, SLIDE ACTION			
Various Calibers, Folding Gun, with Case, *Antique*	425	1200	1500
SHOTGUN, SLIDE ACTION			
12 Ga., Folding Gun, with Case, *Antique*	300	800	1000
12 Ga., Takedown, Solid Rib, Light Engraving, *Antique*	250	600	750

BUSHMASTER

Gwinn Arms Co., Winston-Salem, N.C.

HANDGUN, SELF-LOADING			
Bushmaster, .223 Rem., Clip Fed, *Modern*	175	250	325
RIFLE, SELF-LOADING			
.223 Rem., Clip Fed, Folding Stock, *Modern*	200	275	350
.223 Rem., Clip Fed, Wood Stock, *Modern*	200	250	300

C

C.A.C.

Made by A.I.G. Corp., North Haven, Conn. Distributed by Mossberg.

HANDGUN, SELF-LOADING

	Fair	V. Good	Excellent
Combat, .45 ACP, Clip Fed, Stainless Steel, *Modern*	$200	$375	$500

CADET

Sold by Maltby-Curtis Co.

HANDGUN, REVOLVER

	Fair	V. Good	Excellent
.22 Long R.F., 7 Shot, Single Action, Solid Frame, Spur Trigger, *Antique*	50	100	150

CALDERWOOD, WILLIAM

Phila., Pa., 1808–1816. See Kentucky Rifles and Pistols and U.S. Military.

CANADIAN MILITARY

Canadian Military.

HANDGUN, SELF-LOADING

	Fair	V. Good	Excellent
Hi Power Inglis #1 Mk I, 9mm, Tangent Sights, Slotted for Shoulder Stock, Military, *Curio* with stock	400	600	750
Hi Power Inglis #1 Mk I*, 9mm, Tangent Sights, Slotted for Shoulder Stock, Military, *Curio* with stock	400	600	750
Hi Power Inglis #2 Mk I, 9mm, Fixed Sights, Military, *Curio* with stock	200	400	600
Hi Power Inglis #2 Mk I*, 9mm, Tangent Sights, Slotted for Shoulder Stock, Military, *Curio* with stock	300	600	750

RIFLE, BOLT ACTION

	Fair	V. Good	Excellent
1907 MK 2 Ross, .303 British, Full-Stocked, Military, *Curio*	150	250	350
1910 MK 3 Ross, .303 British, Full-Stocked, Military, *Curio*	150	275	350
SMLE #4 Mk.1*, .303 British, Clip Fed, *Curio*	75	150	225

CAPT. JACK

Made by Hopkins & Allen, 1871–1875.

HANDGUN, REVOLVER

	Fair	V. Good	Excellent
.22 Short R.F., 7 Shot, Spur Trigger, Solid Frame, Single Action, *Antique*	$50	$125	$150

CAROLINE ARMS

Made by Crescent Firearms Co., 1892–1900. See Crescent Fire Arms Co., Shotgun, Double Barrel, Side-By-Side; Shotgun, Single Shot.

SHOTGUN, SINGLESHOT

	Fair	V. Good	Excellent
Various Gauges, Hammer, Steel Barrel, *Modern*	25	50	75

CARPENTER, JOHN

Lancaster, Pa., 1771–1790. See Kentucky Rifles.

CARROLL, LAWRENCE

Philadelphia, Pa., 1786–1790. See Kentucky Rifles.

CARTRIDGE FIREARMS

Cartridge Firearms.

COMBINATION WEAPON, DRILLING

For whatever reason, drillings have never proven a popular collectors' item in the United States. The author has seen many of these over the years, most wanting in condition, and most of odd calibers by American standards. Although Theodore Roosevelt himself, one of the world's most experienced hunters, had at least one drilling in his sporting arsenal, the type never caught on in the United States. Hardly any were manufactured by American gunmakers. The combination of a rifle with a double barrel shotgun made the weapon generally too heavy. Further, when Americans go hunting we are either going after something which would require a rifle or a shotgun—but not both. Therefore, one would buy rifles of various calibers for certain types of game, and shotguns of different gauges and chokes for bird shooting—but not buy a gun which could take birdshot in two barrels and rifle bullets in the third. The author has shot in Europe, where many of the hunters used drillings. Even then he preferred to have a rifle and a shotgun handy, and rarely did he miss the chance to fire at something because he had the wrong gun in hand. The drilling is, therefore, mainly of interest to the Europeans, and has yet to capture the collecting imagination of Americans.

	Fair	V. Good	Excellent
German, Various Calibers, Light Engraving, *Modern*	$300	$600	$850

HANDGUN, REVOLVER

	Fair	V. Good	Excellent
.22 Short, Small Pocket Pistol, Double Action, *Modern*	25	50	75
.22 Short, Small Pocket Pistol, Folding Trigger, *Modern*	50	100	150
.25 ACP, Small Pocket Pistol, Double Action, *Modern*	25	50	75
.25 ACP, Small Pocket Pistol, Folding Trigger, *Modern*	25	50	100
11mm Pinfire, Lefaucheux Military Style, *Antique*	100	200	250
11mm Pinfire, Lefaucheux Military Style, Engraved, *Antique*	125	250	300
7.62mm Nagent, Nagent Style Gas Seal, Solid Frame, Double Action, *Modern*	50	100	150
7mm Pinfire, Pocket Pistol, Folding Trigger, Engraved, *Antique*	50	100	150
Belgian Proofs, Various Calibers, Top Break, Double Action, Medium Quality, *Modern*	25	50	75
Belgian Proofs, Various Calibers, Top Break, Double Action, Engraved, Medium Quality, *Modern*	50	75	125
Belgian Proofs, Various Calibers, Top Break, Double Action, Folding Trigger, Medium Quality, *Modern*	50	75	125
Chinese Copy of Colt Police Positive, .38 Special, Double Action, Solid Frame, Swing-Out Cylinder, Low Quality, *Modern*	25	50	75
Chinese Copy of Police Positive, 9mm Luger, Double Action, Solid Frame, Swing-Out Cylinder, Low Quality, *Modern*	25	50	75
Chinese Copy of S&W M-10, .38 Special, Double Action, Solid Frame, Swing-Out Cylinder, Low Quality, *Modern*	25	50	75
Copy of Colt SAA, Various Calibers, Western Style, Single Action, Low Quality, *Modern*	25	50	100
Copy of Colt SAA, Various Calibers, Western Style, Single Action, Medium Quality, *Modern*	75	150	200
Copy of S&W Russian Model, Various Calibers, Break, Single Action, Low Quality, *Antique*	50	100	150
Copy of S&W Russian Model, Various Calibers, Top Break, Single Action, Medium Quality, *Antique*	75	150	250
Copy of S&W Russian Model, Various Calibers, Top Break, Single Action, High Quality, *Antique*	125	350	500
Spanish Copy of S&W M-10, .38 Special, Double Action, Solid Frame, Swing-Out Cylinder, Low Quality, *Modern*	$25	$50	$75
Spanish Copy of S&W M-10, .32-20 WCF, Double Action, Solid Frame, Swing-Out Cylinder, Low Quality, *Modern*	25	50	75
Spanish Copy of S&W M-10, .38 Special, Double Action, Solid Frame, Swing-Out Cylinder, Low Quality, *Modern*	25	50	75
Various Centerfire Calibers, Bulldog Style, Double Action, Solid Frame, *Modern*	25	50	75
Various Centerfire Calibers, European Military Style, Double Action, Solid Frame, *Modern*	50	100	150
Various Centerfire Calibers, Folding Trigger, Open Top Frame, *Modern*	50	75	100
Various Centerfire Calibers, Gasser Style, Solid Frame, Double Action, *Modern*	50	125	150
Various Centerfire Calibers, Small Pocket Pistol, Hammerless, Folding Trigger, with Safety, *Modern*	50	75	100
Various Centerfire Calibers, Warnant Style, Top Break, Double Action, *Modern*	50	125	150

HANDGUN, SELF-LOADING

	Fair	V. Good	Excellent
Chinese Broomhandle, 7.63 Mauser, Low Quality, *Modern*	100	250	350
Chinese Copy of FN 1900, Various Calibers, Clip Fed, Low Quality, *Modern*	50	75	100
Chinese Pocket Pistols, Various Calibers, Clip Fed, Low Quality, *Modern*	50	75	100
Copy of Colt M1911, .45 ACP, Clip Fed, Military, High Quality, *Modern*	100	250	300
Spanish Pocket Pistols, .25 ACP, Clip Fed, Low Quality, *Modern*	50	75	100
Spanish Pocket Pistols, .32 ACP, Clip Fed, Low Quality, *Modern*	50	100	125
Spanish Pocket Pistols, .32 ACP, Clip Fed, Low Quality, Ruby Style, *Modern*	50	100	125

HANDGUN, SINGLESHOT

	Fair	V. Good	Excellent
Flobert Style, Various Configurations, *Modern*	25	75	125
.22 R.F, Fancy Target Pistol, Hammerless, Set Triggers, *Modern*	150	300	425
.22 Short, Fancy German Target Pistol, Tip-Up Barrel, Engraved, Set Triggers, *Modern*	200	400	500
.22 Short, Target Pistol, Tip-Up Barrel, Plain, *Modern*	50	75	125

RIFLE, BOLT ACTION

	Fair	V. Good	Excellent
Various Centerfire Calibers, Commercial Sporting Rifle, Low Quality, *Modern*	$50	$75	$125
Various Rimfire Calibers, Singleshot, Checkered Stock, European, *Modern*	25	75	100
Arabian Copies, Various Calibers, Military, Reproduction, Low Quality, *Modern*	25	50	75

RIFLE, SINGLESHOT

	Fair	V. Good	Excellent
Various Calibers, Flobert Style, Checkered Stock, *Modern*	50	75	100
Various Calibers, Warnant Style, Checkered Stock, *Modern*	50	100	125
Belgian Proofs, .22 Long R.F., Tip-Up, Octagon Barrel, Medium Quality, *Antique*	50	100	125

SHOTGUN, DOUBLE BARREL, SIDE-BY-SIDE

	Fair	V. Good	Excellent
Belgian Proofs, Various Gauges, Damascus Barrel, Low Quality, Outside Hammers, *Modern*	50	100	125
English Proofs, Various Gauges, Damascus Barrel, Low Quality, Outside Hammers, Modern	50	150	200
No Proofs, Various Gauges, Damascus Barrel, Low Quality, Outside Hammers, *Modern*	50	100	125
Various Gauges, American, Hammerless, Damascus Barrel, *Modern*	50	125	150
Various Gauges, American, Hammerless, Steel Barrel, *Modern*	50	125	175
Various Gauges, American, Outside Hammers, Damascus Barrel, *Modern*	50	125	150
Various Gauges, American, Outside Hammers, Steel Barrel, *Modern*	50	125	175

SHOTGUN, SINGLESHOT

	Fair	V. Good	Excellent
"Zulu," 12 Ga., Converted from Perc. Musket, Trap Door Action, *Antique*	50	100	125
Various Gauges, American, Hammer, Steel Barrel, *Modern*	50	75	100
Various Gauges, Warnant Style, Checkered Stock, *Modern*	50	75	100

CEBRA

Arizmendi, Zulaika y Cia., Eibar, Spain.

HANDGUN, SELF-LOADING

	Fair	V. Good	Excellent
Pocket, .25 ACP, Clip Fed, *Curio*	50	100	125

CELTA

Tomas de Urizar y Cia., Eibar, Spain, c. 1935.

HANDGUN, SELF-LOADING

	Fair	V. Good	Excellent
Pocket, .25 ACP, Clip Fed, *Curio*	50	100	125

CENTENNIAL

Made by Deringer Rifle & Pistol Works 1876.

HANDGUN, REVOLVER

	Fair	V. Good	Excellent
.22 Short R.F., 7 Shot, Spur Trigger, Tip-Up, *Antique*	$100	$250	$375
.32 Short R.F., 5 Shot, Spur Trigger, Solid Frame, Single Action, *Antique*	75	150	225
.38 Short R.F., 5 Shot, Spur Trigger, Solid Frame, Single Action, *Antique*	75	150	225
Centennial '76, .38 Long R.F., 5 Shot, Single Action, Spur Trigger, Tip-Up, *Antique*	100	250	375
Model 2, .32 R.F., 5 Shot, Single Action, Spur Trigger, Tip-Up, *Antique*	100	250	375

CENTRAL

Made by Stevens Arms.

SHOTGUN, DOUBLE BARREL, SIDE-BY-SIDE

	Fair	V. Good	Excellent
Model 215, 12 and 16 Gauges, Outside Hammers, Steel Barrel, *Modern*	50	150	200
Model 311, Various Gauges, Hammerless, Steel Barrel, *Modern*	50	150	200
Model 315, Various Gauges, Hammerless, Steel Barrel, *Modern*	50	150	200

SHOTGUN, SINGLESHOT

	Fair	V. Good	Excellent
Model 94, Various Gauges, Takedown, Automatic Ejector, Plain Hammer, *Modern*	25	50	75

CENTRAL ARMS CO.

Made by Crescent for Shapleigh Hardware Co., c. 1900. See Crescent Fire Arms Co., Shotgun, Double Barrel, Side-by-Side; Shotgun, Single Shot.

CHALLENGE

Made by Bliss & Goodyear, c. 1878.

HANDGUN, REVOLVER

	Fair	V. Good	Excellent
.32 Short R.F., 5 Shot, Spur Trigger, Solid Frame, Single Action, *Antique*	75	150	200

CHAMPION

c. 1870.

HANDGUN, REVOLVER

	Fair	V. Good	Excellent
.22 Short R.F., *Antique*	75	150	200

CHAMPLIN FIREARMS

Enid, Oklahoma. The author was privileged to have visited this fine and important firm of riflemakers and dealers. The expertise present is impressive, under the direction of George Caswell, veteran of many hunts in Africa and shooter of virtually every double rifle type and cartridge known to humanity. Probably America's leading expert on double rifles, this company deals in more of those guns than perhaps any other firm in the world. You can also fly in with your double rifles and have the experts help select the proper loads for truly accurate shooting and best performance. Not a few of these arms over the years have lost the accompanying data on the proper bullets and powders; and quite a few have lost the original ammunition sold with the rifles. Further, after about 25 to 30 years a centerfire rifle cartridge may well no longer work properly. Answers to questions on subjects of that nature are a specialty of Champlin Firearms. The firm's custom-made sporting rifles and shotguns are also of a high quality; those too can be tested with Champlin's expertise available, to guarantee a faultless hunt. The company publishes a catalogue and also handles selected reference books and videos.

	Fair	V. Good	Excellent
RIFLE, BOLT ACTION			
Basic Rifle, with Quarter Rib, Express Sights, Add $185.00-$270.00			
Basic Rifle, Fancy Checkering, Add $30.00-$45.00			
Basic Rifle, Fancy Wood, Add $55.00-$90.00			
Basic Rifle, Various Calibers, Adjustable Trigger, Round or Octagon Tapered Barrel, Checkered Stock, *Modern*	$1500	$3000	$4500
SHOTGUN, DOUBLE BARREL, OVER-UNDER			
12 Ga., Extra Barrels, Add $175.00-$250.00			
Model 100, 12 Ga., Field Grade, Checkered Stock, Vent Rib, Single Selective Trigger, Engraved, *Modern*	250	600	900
Model 100, 12 Ga., Skeet Grade, Checkered Stock, Vent Rib, Single Selective Trigger, Engraved, *Modern*	250	650	1000
Model 100, 12 Ga., Trap Grade, Checkered Stock, Vent Rib, Single Selective Trigger, Engraved, *Modern*	300	700	1000
Model 500, 12 Ga., Field Grade, Checkered Stock, Vent Rib, Single Selective Trigger, Engraved, *Modern*	425	900	1350
Model 500, 12 Ga., Skeet Grade, Checkered Stock, Vent Rib, Single Selective Trigger, Engraved, *Modern*	450	1000	1450
Model 500, 12 Ga., Trap Grade, Checkered Stock, Vent Rib, Single Selective Trigger, Engraved, *Modern*	450	975	1450
SHOTGUN, SINGLESHOT			
Model SB 100, 12 Ga., Trap Grade, Checkered Stock, Vent Rib, Single Selective Trigger, Engraved, *Modern*	250	600	900
Model SB 500, 12 Ga., Trap Grade, Checkered Stock, Vent Rib, Single Selective Trigger, Engraved, *Modern*	$400	$900	$1350

CHAPUIS

St. Bonnet-le-Chateau, France.

	Fair	V. Good	Excellent
SHOTGUN, DOUBLE BARREL, SIDE-BY-SIDE			
Progress RBV, R20, 12 or 20 Gauge, Automatic Ejectors, Sideplates, Double Triggers, Checkered Stock, *Modern*	500	900	1400
Progress RG, 12 or 20 Gauge, Automatic Ejectors, Double Triggers, Checkered Stock, *Modern*	800	1800	2200
Progress Slug, 12 or 20 Gauge, Automatic Ejectors, Slug Barrel, Double Triggers, Checkered Stock, *Modern*	800	1800	2300

CHARLES DALY

Trade name on guns made in Suhl, Germany, prior to WWII, and by Miroku and Breda after WWII. The quality of Daly guns kept their firm's name brand recognition, and value, at a high level. These arms continue in demand primarily as shooters, rather than as collectors' items. The products of this firm reflect an enlightened management, and Daly was one of the first to capitalize on the talented gunmaking industry evolved in Japan after World War II. Among firms of distinction who sold Daly guns were Abercrombie & Fitch, whose reputation as a knowledgeable source of high-grade arms continued into the 1980s.

	Fair	V. Good	Excellent
COMBINATION WEAPON, DRILLING			
Diamond, Various Calibers, Fancy Engraving, Fancy Checkering, *Modern*	3000	6000	8000
Regent Diamond, Various Calibers, Fancy Engraving, Fancy Checkering, Fancy Wood, *Modern*	2000	4500	6000
Superior, Various Calibers, Engraved, *Modern*	700	1200	2000
RIFLE, BOLT ACTION			
.22 Hornet, 5 Shot Clip, Checkered Stock, *Modern*	300	600	800
SHOTGUN, DOUBLE BARREL, OVER-UNDER			
For 28 Ga., Add 25%-40%			
12 Ga., For Wide Vent Rib, Add $25.00-$45.00			
Various Gauges, Field Grade, Light Engraving, Single Selective Trigger, Automatic Ejector, Post-War, *Modern*	175	300	700
Commander 100, Various Gauges, Automatic Ejector, Checkered Stock, Single Trigger, *Modern*	200	400	700

	Fair	V. Good	Excellent
Commander 100, Various Gauges, Automatic Ejector, Checkered Stock, Double Trigger, *Modern*	$150	$375	$500
Commander 200, Various Gauges, Automatic Ejector, Checkered Stock, Engraved, Single Trigger, *Modern*	300	600	800
Commander 200, Various Gauges, Double Trigger, *Modern*	250	500	750
Diamond, 12 Ga., Trap Grade, Selective Ejector, Single Selective Trigger, Post-War, *Modern*	300	600	850
Diamond, 12 or 20 Gauges, Field Grade, Trap Grade, Selective Ejector, Single Selective Trigger, Post-War, *Modern*	250	500	750
Diamond, 12 or 20 Gauges, Skeet Grade, Trap Grade, Selective Ejector, Single Selective Trigger, Post-War, *Modern*	300	600	850
Diamond, Various Gauges, Double Trigger, Automatic Ejector, Fancy Engraving, Fancy Checkering, *Modern* Pre-War	1000	3000	5000
Empire, Various Gauges, Double Trigger, Automatic Ejector, Checkered Stock, Engraved, *Modern* Pre-War	700	2000	3000
Superior, 12 Ga., Trap Grade, Automatic Ejector, Single Selective Trigger, Post-War, *Modern*	200	400	600
Superior, Various Gauges, Field Grade, Trap Grade, Automatic Ejector, Single Selective Trigger, Post-War, *Modern*	200	350	500
Superior, Various Gauges, Skeet Grade, Trap Grade, Automatic Ejector, Single Selective Trigger, Post-War, *Modern*	200	400	600
Venture, 12 Ga., Trap Grade, Single Trigger, Monte Carlo Stock, Post-War, *Modern*	125	250	375
Venture, 12 or 20 Gauges, Field Grade, Single Trigger, Trap Grade, Post-War, *Modern*	125	250	375
Venture, 12 or 20 Gauges, Skeet Grade, Single Trigger, Trap Grade, Post-War, *Modern*	175	300	450
SHOTGUN, DOUBLE BARREL, SIDE-BY-SIDE			
Diamond, Various Gauges, Double Trigger, Fancy Engraving, Fancy Checkering, Fancy Wood, Automatic Ejector, *Modern* Pre-War	2000	3500	5000
Empire, Various Gauges, Double Trigger, Engraved, Checkered Stock, Automatic Ejector, *Modern* Pre-War	900	2000	3000
Empire, Various Gauges, Vent Rib, Single Trigger, Checkered Stock, Engraved, Post-War, *Modern* Pre-War	150	250	350

	Fair	V. Good	Excellent
Regent Diamond, Various Gauges, Double Trigger, Fancy Engraving, Fancy Checkering, Fancy Wood, Automatic Ejector, *Modern* Pre-War	$1500	$3000	$4000
Superior, Various Gauges, Double Trigger, Light Engraving, Checkered Stock, *Modern* Pre-War	425	900	1400
SHOTGUN, SELF-LOADING			
Novamatic, 12 Ga., Mag. 3", Takedown, Vent Rib, Checkered Stock, Magnum, *Modern*	150	275	350
Novamatic, 12 Ga., Takedown, Trap Grade, Vent Rib, Checkered Stock, Monte Carlo Stock, *Modern*	150	275	375
Novamatic, 12 or 20 Gauges, Takedown, Plain Barrel, Checkered Stock, Lightweight, *Modern*	125	225	325
Novamatic, 12 or 20 Gauges, Takedown, Plain Barrel, Checkered Stock, Lightweight, Interchangeable Choke Tubes, *Modern*	125	300	400
Novamatic, 12 or 20 Gauges, Takedown, Vent Rib, Checkered Stock, Lightweight, *Modern*	150	225	350
Novamatic, 12 or 20 Gauges, Takedown, Vent Rib, Checkered Stock, Lightweight, Interchangable Choke Tubes, *Modern*	125	225	300
Novamatic, 20 Ga., Takedown, Checkered Stock, Magnum, Lightweight, *Modern*	200	250	350
Novamatic Super Light, 12 and 20 Gauges, Takedown, Plain Barrel, Checkered Stock, *Modern*	125	200	300
Novamatic Super Light, 12 and 20 Gauges, Takedown, Plain Barrel, Checkered Stock, Interchangeable Choke Tubes, *Modern*	100	175	350
Novamatic Super Light, 12 and 20 Gauges, Takedown, Vent Rib, Checkered Stock, *Modern*	75	150	325
SHOTGUN, SINGLESHOT			
Empire, 12 Ga., Trap Grade, Fancy Engraving, Fancy Wood, Automatic Ejector, *Modern*	2150	3450	5000
Sextuple Empire, 12 Ga., Trap Grade, Fancy Checkering, Fancy Engraving, Fancy Wood, Automatic Ejector, *Modern*	2000	3675	5500
Sextuple Regent Diamond, 12 Ga., Trap Grade, Fancy Checkering, Fancy Engraving, Fancy Wood, Automatic Ejector, *Modern*	2575	4625	7000
Superior, 12 Ga., Trap Grade, Monte Carlo Stock, Selective Ejector, Engraved, Post-War, *Modern*	175	275	400

CHAROLA Y ANITUA

Garate, Anitua y Cia., Eibar, Spain, c. 1898.

HANDGUN, SELF-LOADING

	Fair	*V. Good*	*Excellent*
Charola, 5mm Clement, Locked Breech, Box Magazine, Belgian Made, *Curio*	$300	$800	$1000
Charola, 5mm Clement, Locked Breech, Box Magazine, Spanish Made, *Curio*	250	600	800

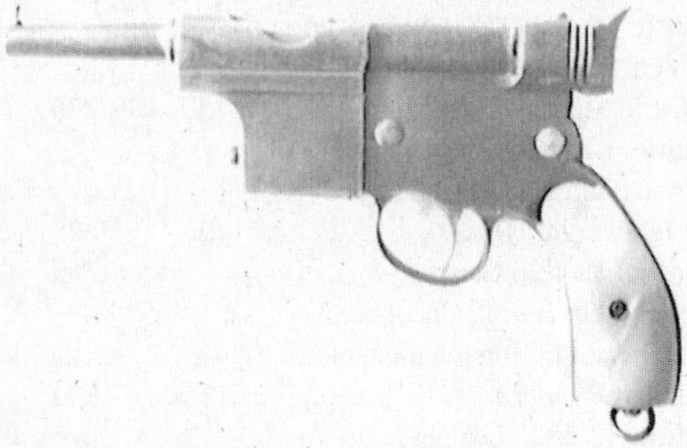

Charola y Anitua, Spanish

CHARTER ARMS

Stratford, Conn., since 1965. The brainchild of engineer and gun designer Doug McLanahan, aided in time by business head Dave Ecker, Charter Arms developed a solid line of handguns, beginning with the Undercover. When misguided thinking at the Colt company led to their reducing production and marketing of snub-nosed, self-defense revolvers (like the Cobra and Detective Special), Doug McLanahan, an employee of Sturm, Ruger & Co—recognizing Ruger's own hesitation to produce snub-nose revolvers—stepped into a ready market. McLanahan used to vacation on Mississippi paddle-wheelers as a means of relaxing and increasing his output of designs and innovative products. In the late 1960s the author was involved in helping Charter Arms to develop an engraving line, even to the point of the company's advertising deluxe examples, in different grades. One deluxe example, engraved and with gold inlay and executed for Dave Ecker, was featured on the cover of *Shooting Times* magazine. Brochures were also printed up in promoting the new concept. Production was extremely limited, however, and these arms will bring a premium of five to seven times the value of the standard unembellished models.

HANDGUN, REVOLVER

	Fair	*V. Good*	*Excellent*
Milestone Limited Edition, .44 Special, Bulldog, Engraved, Silver Plated, Cased with Accessories, *Modern*	400	800	1250
Bulldog Tracker, .357 Magnum, Double Action, Blue, Adjustable Sights, *Modern*	125	200	300
Bulldog, .44 Special, Double Action, Blue, *Modern*	125	175	250

Charter Arms Bulldog Tracker.357 Magnum, 6" Barrel

	Fair	*V. Good*	*Excellent*
Bulldog, .44 Special, Double Action, Nickel Plated, *Modern*	$125	$200	$300
Bulldog, .44 Special, Double Action, Stainless, *Modern*	125	225	300
Off-Duty, .38 SPL, 5 Shot, 2" Barrel, Stainless, *Modern*	125	225	300
Off-Duty, .38 SPL, 5 Shot, 2" Barrel, Steel Frame, *Modern*	100	150	225
Pathfinder, .22 L.R.R.F., Adjustable Sights, Bulldog Grips, Double Action, *Modern*	100	175	250
Pathfinder, .22 L.R.R.F., Adjustable Sights, Bulldog Grips, Double Action, Stainless Steel, *Modern*	125	225	300
Pathfinder, .22 L.R.R.F., Adjustable Sights, Square-Butt, Double Action, *Modern*	75	125	250
Pathfinder, .22 WMR, Adjustable Sights, Double Action, Bulldog Grips, *Modern*	75	125	250
Pathfinder, .22 WMR, Adjustable Sights, Double Action, Square-Butt, *Modern*	75	125	250
Police Bulldog, .32 H&R Magnum, 4" Bull Barrel, Checkered Grips, Blue, *Modern*	100	175	250
Police Bulldog, .38 Special, 1" Bull Barrel, Stainless, *Modern*	100	250	300

Charter Arms Police Bulldog

	Fair	V. Good	Excellent
Police Bulldog, .38 Special, 4" Tapered Barrel, Square Grips, Stainless, *Modern*	$100	$175	$300
Police Bulldog, .38 Special, Double Action, Blue, Adjustable Sights, *Modern*	100	175	250
Police Bulldog Tracker, .357 Magnum, 2½" Barrel, Blue, *Modern*	100	200	300
Police Bulldog Tracker, .357 Magnum, 4" Barrel, Bulldog Grips, Blue, *Modern*	100	200	300
Police Undercover, .32 H&R Magnum, 2" Barrel, Checkered Panel Grips, Blue, *Modern*	100	175	275
Police Undercover, .38 Special, 2" Barrel, Blue, Pocket Hammer, *Modern*	100	175	275
Police Undercover, Law Enforcement Version, .38 Special, Five Shot, Neoprene Grips, *Modern*	125	250	325
Target Bulldog, .357 Magnum, Double Action, Blue, Adjustable Sights, *Modern*	125	250	325
Target Bulldog, .44 Special, Double Action, Blue, Adjustable Sights, Modern	175	250	325
Undercover, .38 Special, Double Action, Blue, Bulldog Grips, *Modern*	100	150	250
Undercover, .38 Special, Double Action, Blue, *Modern*	100	150	250
Undercover, .38 Special, Double Action, Nickel Plated, *Modern*	100	150	250
Undercover, .38 Special, Double Action, Stainless Steel, *Modern*	100	175	275
Undercoverette, .32 S & W Long, Double Action, Blue, Bulldog Grips, *Modern*	100	150	250

HANDGUN, SELF-LOADING

	Fair	V. Good	Excellent
Explorer II, .22 L.R.R.F., Clip Fed, Takedown, *Modern*	50	75	125

Charter Arms M40 Double Action Pistol

	Fair	V. Good	Excellent
Explorer SII, .22 L.R.R.F., Clip Fed, Takedown, 6" and 10" Optional Barrels, *Modern*	$75	$100	$175
Model 40, .22 L.R., 8 Shot Mag, Checkered Walnut Gripstock, Stainless, *Modern*	125	200	300

Charter Arms M79K, .380 Caliber

	Fair	V. Good	Excellent
Model 79K, .380 Autoloader, 7 Shot Mag, Checkered Gripstock, Stainless, *Modern*	150	250	350
Model 79K32, .32 Caliber Autoloader, 7 Shot Mag, Stainless, *Modern*	150	250	350

RIFLE, SELF-LOADING

	Fair	V. Good	Excellent
AR-7 Explorer, .22 L.R.R.F., Clip Fed, Takedown, *Modern*	50	100	175

CHASE, WILLIAM

Pandora, Ohio, 1854–1860.

COMBINATION WEAPON, PERCUSSION

	Fair	V. Good	Excellent
Various Calibers, Double Barrel, *Antique*	300	800	1250

CHEROKEE ARMS CO.

Made by Crescent, C. M. McClung & Co., Tennessee, c. 1900. See Crescent Fire Arms Co., Shotgun, Double Barrel, Side-by-Side; Shotgun, Singleshot.

CHERRINGTON, THOMAS P.

Cattawissa, Pa., 1847–1858.

RIFLE, PILL LOCK

	Fair	V. Good	Excellent
.40, Revolver, Octagon Barrel, *Antique*	1000	2000	3000

CHESAPEAKE GUN CO.

Made by Crescent, c. 1900.

SHOTGUN, DOUBLE BARREL, SIDE-BY-SIDE

	Fair	V. Good	Excellent
Various Gauges, Hammerless, Damascus Barrel, *Modern*	$50	$125	$250
Various Gauges, Hammerless, Steel Barrel, *Modern*	50	100	200
Various Gauges, Outside Hammers, Damascus Barrel, *Modern*	50	125	200
Various Gauges, Outside Hammers, Steel Barrel, *Modern*	50	100	200

28 ga. and 410 ga. add 25%

SHOTGUN, SINGLESHOT

	Fair	V. Good	Excellent
Various Gauges, Hammer, Steel Barrel, *Modern*	25	50	100

CHICAGO ARMS CO.

Sold by Fred Bifflar Co. Made by Meriden Firearms Co., 1870–1890.

HANDGUN, REVOLVER

	Fair	V. Good	Excellent
.32 S & W, 5 Shot, Double Action, Top Break, *Antique*	50	100	150
.38 S & W, 5 Shot, Double Action, Top Break, *Antique*	50	100	150
.38 S & W, Top Break, Hammerless, Double Action, Grip Safety, *Antique*	50	100	150

CHICAGO FIRE ARMS CO.

Chicago, Ill., 1883–1894. One of the most intriguing of oddities in the history of American firearms, these bizarre little handguns were sometimes built with deluxe grip panels, like mother-of-pearl, and were supremely well made. Loading was achieved by unscrewing one of the side panels and then inserting the cartridges from the center of a radiating chamber. It is not uncommon to find these arms in excellent condition, since it appears that not too many were ever fired. The mechanisms were quite simple, but the type had fierce competition, and sales proved disappointing. Examples found in the original pasteboard box will bring a premium of at least an additional 25 percent.

HANDGUN, PALM PISTOL

	Fair	V. Good	Excellent
.32 Extra Short R.F., Blued, *Antique*	500	1200	1750
.32 Extra Short R.F., Nickel, *Antique*	400	1000	1450

Chicago Fire Arms Palm Pistol

CHICHESTER

Made by Hopkins & Allen, c. 1880.

HANDGUN, REVOLVER

	Fair	V. Good	Excellent
.38 Short R.F., 5 Shot, Spur Trigger, Solid Frame, Single Action, *Antique*	$50	$125	$175

CHIEFTAIN

Made by Norwich Pistol Co., c. 1880.

HANDGUN, REVOLVER

	Fair	V. Good	Excellent
.32 Short R.F., 5 Shot, Spur Trigger, Solid Frame, Single Action, *Antique*	50	125	175

CHILEAN MILITARY

RIFLE, BOLT ACTION

	Fair	V. Good	Excellent
M1895 Carbine, 7mm Mauser, Military, *Curio*	150	275	325
M1895 Rifle, 7mm Mauser, Military, *Curio*	150	225	300
M1895 Short Rifle, 7mm Mauser, Military, *Curio*	150	250	300

CHINESE MILITARY

HANDGUN, SELF-LOADING

	Fair	V. Good	Excellent
Makarov, 9mm Mak., Clip Fed, *Modern*	300	650	850
Tokarev, 7.62mm Tokarev, Clip Fed, *Modern*	150	300	400

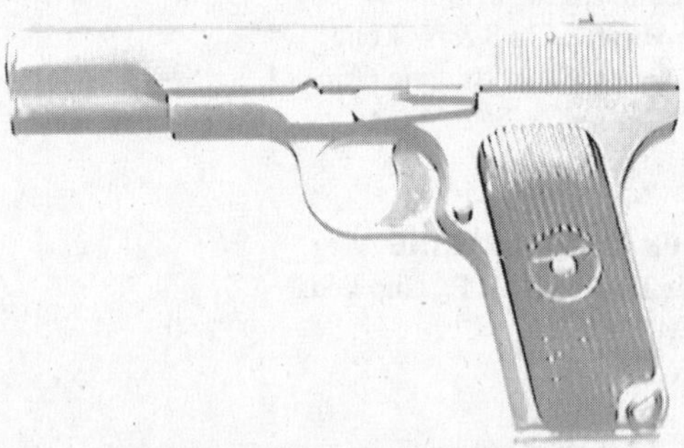

Chinese Military Tokarev

	Fair	V. Good	Excellent
Walther PPK Type, .32 A.C.P., Double Action, Blue, Clip Fed, Military, *Modern*	300	650	800

RIFLE, BOLT ACTION

	Fair	V. Good	Excellent
Type 53 (Nagent), 7.62 × 54R Russian, *Modern*	35	100	150

	Fair	V. Good	Excellent
RIFLE, SELF-LOADING			
SKS, 7.62 × 39 Russian, Folding Bayonet, Military, *Modern*	$75	$125	$150

CHINESE NATIONALIST MILITARY

HANDGUN, SELF-LOADING			
Hi Power, 9mm Luger, Clip Fed, Military, Tangent Sights, *Curio*	200	400	600
Hi Power, 9mm Luger, Clip Fed, Military, Tangent Sights, with Detachable Shoulder Stock, *Curio*	300	600	850
RIFLE, BOLT ACTION			
Kar 98k Type 79, 8mm Mauser, *Modern*	150	275	350
M1871 Mauser, .43 Mauser, Carbine, *Antique*	175	325	400
M1888, Hanyang, 8mm Mauser, 5 Shot, *Curio*	150	250	325
M98 Mukden, 8mm Mauser, *Modern*	200	350	425

CHIPMUNK

Medford, Ore., since 1982.

RIFLE, BOLT ACTION			
.22 L.R.R.F., Singleshot, Manual Cocking, *Modern*	50	100	175

CHURCHILL, E. J. LTD

London, England, 1892 to date. This capable London gunmaker, no relation to the Prime Minister, enjoys a justly deserved reputation as a respected member of the trade specializing in best quality firearms. Among the firm's clients was the royal family, including the Prince of Wales, later King Edward VIII and known still later (after abdication) as the Duke of Windsor. For several years Churchill belonged to Sam Cummings, the first American member of the London Gunmaker's Guild. Cummings is more generally known as the founder and former chairman of Interarms, an international small arms and armaments company headquartered in Monaco, until his death in 1998.

	Fair	V. Good	Excellent
RIFLE, BOLT ACTION			
One of 1,000, Various Calibers, Checkered Stock, Recoil Pad, Express Sights, Cartridge Trap, *Modern*	300	600	850
One of 1,000, Various Calibers, Fancy Checkering, Engraved Expressed Sights, Cartridge Trap, Cased with Accessories, *Modern*	900	1850	2750
SHOTGUN, DOUBLE BARREL, OVER-UNDER			
Premier Quality, for Raised Vent Rib, Add $350.00-$520.00			
Premier Quality, for Single Selective Trigger, Add $400.00-$535.00			
Premier Quality, Various Gauges (for 28 ga. and 410 ga. add 25%), Hammerless Sidelock, Fancy Checkering, Automatic Ejectors, Engraved, *Modern*	$5000	$12000	$17500
SHOTGUN, DOUBLE BARREL, SIDE-BY-SIDE			
Field Model, Various Gauges, Hammerless Sidelock, Fancy Checkering, Automatic Ejectors, Engraved, *Modern*	3500	6000	8000
Hercules Model XXV, Various Gauges, Hammerless Sidelock, Engraved, Fancy Checkering, Fancy Wood, Cased, *Modern*	3500	6000	8000
Imperial Model XXV, Various Gauges, Hammerless Sidelock, Fancy Checkering, Automatic Ejectors, Engraved, *Modern*	4000	7500	10000
Premier Quality, Various Gauges, Hammerless Sidelock, Fancy Checkering, Automatic Ejectors, Engraved, *Modern*	6000	10000	13000
Regal Model XXV, Various Gauges, Hammerless Sidelock, Fancy Checkering, Automatic Ejectors, Engraved, *Modern*	2000	3750	5250
Utility Model, Various Gauges, Boxlock, Double Triggers, Color Case with Hardened Frame, Engraved, *Modern*	2000	3500	5000
For Single Selective Trigger, Add $375.00-$535.00 (28 and 410 ga. add 20–25%)			

CHYLEWSKI, WITOLD

Austria, 1910–1918. Pistols made by S.I.G.

HANDGUN, SELF-LOADING			
Einhand, .25 A.C.P., Clip Fed, Blue, No Locking Screw, *Curio*	300	500	700
Einhand, .25 A.C.P., Clip Fed, Blue, with Locking Screw, *Curio*	300	500	700

Chylewski .25 with Locking Screw

CLARK, F. H.

Memphis, Tenn., c. 1860.

HANDGUN, PERCUSSION

	Fair	V. Good	Excellent
Derringer, .41, German Silver Mountings, *Antique*	$400	$800	$1250

CLARKSON, J.

London, England, 1680–1740.

HANDGUN, FLINTLOCK

	Fair	V. Good	Excellent
.32, Pocket Pistol, Queen Anne Style, Box Lock, Screw Barrel, Silver Furniture, *Antique*	250	600	1000

CLASSIC ARMS

Palmer, Mass.

HANDGUN, PERCUSSION

	Fair	V. Good	Excellent
.36 Duckfoot, 3 Shot, Brass Frame, Reproduction, *Antique*	15	25	50
.36 Ethan Allen, Pepperbox, 4 Shot, Brass Frame, Reproduction, *Antique*	15	25	50
.36 Snake-Eyes, Double Barrel, Side-by-Side, Brass Frame, Reproduction, *Antique*	15	25	50
.36 Twister, 2 Shot, Brass Frame, Reproduction, *Antique*	15	25	50
.44 Ace, Rifled, Brass Frame, Reproduction, *Antique*	15	25	50

CLEMENT, CHARLES

Liège, Belgium, 1886–1914.

HANDGUN, SELF-LOADING

	Fair	V. Good	Excellent
M1903, 5.5mm Clement, Clip Fed, Blue, *Curio*	100	200	300

Clement M1903 5mm

	Fair	V. Good	Excellent
M1907, .25 ACP, Clip Fed, Blue, *Curio*	125	250	325
M1907, .32 ACP, Clip Fed, Blue, *Curio*	125	275	375
M1908, .25 ACP, Clip Fed, Blue, *Curio*	$200	$325	$400
M1910, .25 ACP, Clip Fed, Blue, *Curio*	125	225	350
M1910, .32 ACP, Clip Fed, Blue, *Curio*	125	275	400
M1912 Fulgor, .32 ACP, Clip Fed, Blue, *Curio*	200	450	650

RIFLE, SELF-LOADING

	Fair	V. Good	Excellent
Clement-Neumann, .401 Win., Clip Fed, Checkered Stock, Matted Rib, *Curio*	250	450	650

SHOTGUN, DOUBLE BARREL, SIDE-BY-SIDE

	Fair	V. Good	Excellent
Various Gauges, Hammerless, Damascus Barrel, *Curio*	65	125	200
Various Gauges, Hammerless, Steel Barrel, *Curio*	75	150	225
Various Gauges, Outside Hammers, Damascus Barrel, *Curio*	65	125	200

CLEMENT, J. B.

Belgium.

SHOTGUN, DOUBLE BARREL, SIDE-BY-SIDE

	Fair	V. Good	Excellent
Various Gauges, Hammerless, Steel Barrel, *Modern*	75	150	225
Various Gauges, Outside Hammers, Steel Barrel, *Modern*	100	150	200

CLERKE

Santa Monica, Calif.

HANDGUN, REVOLVER

	Fair	V. Good	Excellent
32-200, .32 S & W, Nickel Plated, *Modern*	15	25	50
CF200, .22 L.R.R.F., Nickel Plated, *Modern*	15	25	50

RIFLE, SINGLESHOT

	Fair	V. Good	Excellent
Hi-Wall, Various Calibers, Fancy Wood, *Modern*	150	200	250
Hi-Wall Deluxe, Various Calibers, Octagon Barrel, Fancy Wood, *Modern*	150	250	300
Hi-Wall Deluxe, Various Calibers, Octagon Barrel, Set Trigger, Fancy Wood, *Modern*	150	275	325

CLIMAS

Made by Stevens Arms.

SHOTGUN, SINGLESHOT

	Fair	V. Good	Excellent
Model 90, Various Gauges, Takedown, Automatic Ejector, Plain Hammer, *Modern*	25	50	75

CLIPPER

Maker unknown, c. 1880.

HANDGUN, REVOLVER

	Fair	V. Good	Excellent
.22 Short R.F., 7 Shot, Spur Trigger, Solid Frame, Single Action, *Antique*	$50	$100	$150

CODY MANUFACTURING CO.

Chicopee, Mass., 1957–1959.

HANDGUN, REVOLVER

	Fair	V. Good	Excellent
Thunderbird, .22 R.F., 6 Shot, Double Action, Aluminum with Steel Liners, *Modern*	50	100	125

COGSWELL & HARRISON

London, England, 1770 to date; Branch in Paris, 1924–1938. Cogswell & Harrison was another respected member of the London gun trade. Due to increased competition and operating costs, and gradually worsening U.K. gun laws, Cogswell finally closed its doors in the early 1990s.

HANDGUN, REVOLVER

	Fair	V. Good	Excellent
S & W Victory, .38 Special, Double Action, Swing-Out Cylinder, Refinished and Customized, Rebored from .38 S & W and may be unsafe with .38 Spec., *Modern*	75	150	250

RIFLE, BOLT ACTION

	Fair	V. Good	Excellent
BSA-Lee Speed, .303 British, Sporting Rifle, Express Sights, Engraved, Checkered Stock, Commercial, *Modern*	275	600	800

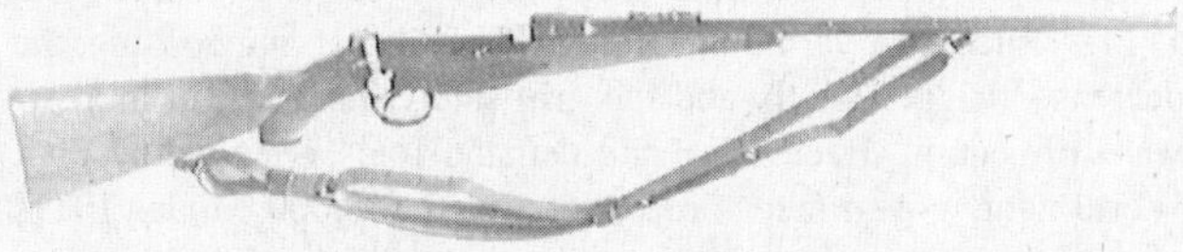

Cogswell & Harrison Lee Speed

SHOTGUN, DOUBLE BARREL, SIDE-BY-SIDE

	Fair	V. Good	Excellent
Avant Tout (Konor), Various Gauges, Box Lock, Automatic Ejector, Fancy Checkering, Fancy Engraving, Double Trigger, *Modern*	1000	2025	2450
Avant Tout (Konor), Various Gauges, Box Lock, Automatic Ejector, Fancy Checkering, Fancy Engraving, Single Trigger, *Modern*	1000	2350	2750
Avant Tout (Konor), Various Gauges, Box Lock, Automatic Ejector, Fancy Checkering, Fancy Engraving, Single Selective Trigger, *Modern*	1000	2500	3000
Avant Tout (Rex), Various Gauges, Box Lock, Automatic Ejector, Checkered Stock, Light Engraving, Double Trigger, *Modern*	$700	$1450	$1750
Avant Tout (Rex), Various Gauges, Box Lock, Automatic Ejector, Checkered Stock, Light Engraving, Single Trigger, *Modern*	500	1000	1350
Avant Tout (Rex), *Modern*	900	1500	1850
Avant Tout (Sandhurst), Various Gauges, Box Lock, Automatic Ejector, Fancy Checkering, Engraved, Double Trigger, *Modern*	1000	1875	2500
Avant Tout (Sandhurst), Various Gauges, Box Lock, Automatic Ejector, Fancy Checkering, Engraved, Single Trigger, *Modern*	900	2000	2750
Avant Tout (Sandhurst), Various Gauges, Box Lock, Automatic Ejector, Fancy Checkering, Engraved, Single Selective Trigger, *Modern*	1200	2250	3250
Huntic, Various Gauges, Sidelock, Automatic Ejector, Checkered Stock, Double Trigger, *Modern*	1200	2500	3250
Huntic, Various Gauges, Sidelock, Automatic Ejector, Checkered Stock, Single Trigger, *Modern*	1200	2750	3750
Huntic, Various Gauges, Sidelock, Automatic Ejector, Checkered Stock, Single Selective Trigger, *Modern*	1300	2750	3750
Markor, Various Gauges, Box Lock, Automatic Ejector, Checkered Stock, Double Trigger, *Modern*	500	1000	1650
Markor, Various Gauges, Box Lock, Checkered Stock, Double Trigger, *Modern*	300	800	1200
Primic, Various Gauges, Sidelock, Automatic Ejector, Fancy Engraving, Fancy Checkering, Double Trigger, *Modern*	1200	3000	3750
Primic, Various Gauges, Sidelock, Automatic Ejector, Fancy Engraving, Fancy Checkering, Single Trigger, *Modern*	1500	3500	4500
Primic, Various Gauges, Sidelock, Automatic Ejector, Fancy Engraving, Fancy Checkering, Single Selective Trigger, *Modern*	1500	3000	4275
Victor, Various Gauges, Sidelock, Automatic Ejector, Engraved, Checkered Stock, Double Trigger, *Modern*	2000	4000	5250
Victor, Various Gauges, Sidelock, Automatic Ejector, Engraved, Checkered Stock, Single Trigger, *Modern*	2200	4500	5875
Victor, Various Gauges, Sidelock, Automatic Ejector, Engraved, Checkered Stock, Single Selective Trigger, *Modern*	2500	5000	6750

COLON

Antonio Azpiri y Cia. Eibar, Spain 1914–1918.

HANDGUN, SELF-LOADING

	Fair	V. Good	Excellent
Pocket, .25 ACP, Clip Fed, *Curio*	$75	$100	$125

COLON

Made by Orbea Hermanos Eibar, Spain, c. 1925.

HANDGUN, REVOLVER

	Fair	V. Good	Excellent
Colt Police Positive Copy, .32/20 Double Action, Blue, *Curio*	75	100	125

COLONIAL

Fabrique d'Armes de Guerre de Grand Precision, Eibar, Spain.

HANDGUN, SELF-LOADING

	Fair	V. Good	Excellent
.25 ACP, Clip Fed, Blue, *Modern*	35	75	125
.32 ACP, Clip Fed, Blue, *Modern*	50	100	150

COLT

Paterson, N.J., 1836–1841. Whitneyville, Conn., 1847–1848. Hartford, Conn., 1848 to Date; London, England, 1853–1857. Also see U.S. Military. Also see Commemorative Section. Founded by Samuel Colt in 1836, the company that bears his name is the original manufacturer of the world's first successful revolving firearms. One of America's oldest gunmakers, and possessor of one of history's most respected brand names, Colt is to firearms as Kodak is to the camera, Ford to the automobile, and Rolex to the wristwatch. Most famous—and most attractive—of all Colt revolvers is the Single Action Army—known popularly as the Peacemaker, Thumb-Buster, Hogleg, Equalizer and Plowhandle. Popular Colt factory designations are the Bisley (a distinct variation) and the Frontier Six-Shooter (both noted in barrel markings on specific examples). Collectors have added their own array of appellations: U.S. Martial, Buntline, Long-Flute, Rimfire, and Sheriff's or Storekeeper's model. U.S. Ordnance tests of the predecessor arm, the Model 1872 Open Top .44, had not proved successful. But within a matter of months Colt followed up with the Single Action Army. The new design featured solid-frame construction, .45 caliber, $7\frac{1}{2}$" barrel, with blued and case-hardened finish, and grips of oil-stained one-piece walnut. The new revolver combined the most practical attributes of the Open Top .44, sharing a similar interior mechanism and frame size as the 1851 Navy and 1860 Army cap and ball predecessor models. Samuel Colt's design expertise was therefore carried over into the Single Action, a model introduced 10 years after the Colonel's death. Unlike the majority of cap and ball Colt revolvers, the barrel was a screw-in type. The ejector mechanism, for the breech-loading metallic cartridges, was mounted alongside the barrel. In 1873 the U.S. Ordnance adopted the new revolver for service. The Ordnance Department's favorable reception was followed up by contracts from the government totaling 37,063, from 1873 to 1891. The revolvers accepted by Ordnance are clearly marked with the U.S. stamped on the left side of the frame, inspector initials on the grips (often with date markings denoting year of acceptance), and minute inspector initial stampings on various other parts. Collectors pursue variations based on calibers, barrel lengths, markings, technical features (like machine cuts), low and otherwise special serial numbers, engraving, finishes, grips, and such an exotic rarity as the long-barreled Buntline Special. Manufacture was from 1873 to 1940, and from 1956 to date. Researching shipping ledgers of the Colt plant (a service of Colt's Historical Department) allows for tracing most of the prewar and all of the postwar production. Unfortunately, factory records are missing on the majority of the first 30,000 revolvers shipped, which were primarily government purchases. With its enormous appeal and striking beauty, more enthusiasts and collectors specialize in the Single Action Army than any other Colt revolver. Historically and artistically this is the ne plus ultra of all Colt firearms. The model's popularity is reflected in the total production from its introduction until modern times, including prewar, postwar, commemorative, Bisleys, Flattop Targets, the Buntlines, and special order guns from the Colt Custom Shop in excess of 650,000. Initially advertised as "The Most Powerful Automatic Pistol Made," the Model 1911 is the most famous of all handgun designs by John Browning, and is a bona fide firearms masterpiece. This classic pistol stands to this day as one of Colt's and Browning's major contributions to the long and complex history of firearms development. The first .45ACP pistol, however, was not the Model 1911. Its predecessor model was the 1905, of which only 6100 were manufactured. The U.S. government ordered 200 of these, followed by another 201, in a variant known as the Model 1907. The latter were for tests by the Springfield Armory. As exemplified in a fascinating series of development types, including the rare 1909 and 1910, Colt engineers and John Browning created the Model 1911. The resultant pistol is a classic in simplicity, design, performance, and manufacturability. From the basic Model 1911 eventually evolved a veritable industry of clones, in a variety of calibers, intended for sport hunting, target shooting, combat pistol shooting, self-defense, law enforcement and special issue "commemorative" collecting. The Colt-made Model 1911 and its successors are the record holder as the largest quantity ever made of any Colt handgun: over four million, and still going strong. The technical features which differentiate the Model 1911 from the Model 1911A1 successor variation are the arched mainspring housing, the decreased trigger width, and the grip safety increased in its rearward projection. Because of the demand for service in the First World War, government orders totaling 2,550,000 Model 1911s were placed. Only a relatively small number of pistols were delivered. American service involvement in the war was limited to the years 1917–18. Tooling up time by contracted companies proved lengthy, and among those who had been awarded contracts were the Winchester Repeating Arms Co., Lanston Monotype Machine Co., National Cash Register Co., Burroughs Adding Machine Co., Savage Arms Co., A.J. Savage Munitions Co., Caron Brothers Mfg. Co., and Dominion Rifle Plant—North American Arms Co., Ltd. The Springfield Armory, also under contract for licensed manufacture, performed best by far; the historic institution produced a total of 25,767, from 1914–18. Manufacture was from 1911 to late 1923; then succeeded by the M1911A1; approximately 130,000 civilian and 700,000 military Model 1911s were produced. The civilian range is relatively simple; the military rather complex, with individual ranges of the Colt factory, from 1911 (1 on up to approximately 700,000 range in 1924); the Remington-UMC, 1918–19 (1-21676), and specific range by

Springfield Armory (began 1914, with 72751; and completed, with gaps, in 1918 with the high serial 133186). Since adoption of the Model 1911A1, production soared, with an estimated number of that variation and its successors in excess of 3,000,000. Note: the assistance of Martin J. Lane (Martin Lane Historical Americana Gallery) in review of the Colt section is gratefully appreciated. Note: For more detailed information concerning rarity, see *The Book of Colt Firearms.*

Fair V. Good Excellent

PATERSON HANDGUNS

.28 caliber Baby Paterson No. 1 revolver, approximately 500 manufactured; serial number from 1 on up; various barrel lengths; octagonal barrel; no loading lever. *Antique* $7000 $18500 $32500

.31 caliber Belt Model No. 2 Paterson, straight grip, without loading lever; approximately 850 manufactured (including No. 3 with flared grip), serial number from 1 on up; various barrel lengths; octagonal barrel. Antique 9500 23500 45000

.31 caliber Belt Model No. 3 Paterson, flared grip, without loading lever; approximately 850 manufactured (including No. 2 Model with straight grip); serial number from 1 on up; various barrel lengths; octagonal barrel. Added premium if cased set with extra cylinder and accessories. *Antique* 10000 28500 47500

.31 caliber Belt Model No. 3 Paterson, flared grip and loading lever; relatively limited number from approximately 850 manufactured (including No. 2 Model with straight grip); various barrel lengths; octagonal barrel. Added premium if cased set with extra cylinder and accessories. *Antique* 12500 36500 52500

.36 caliber Holster Model or Texas Paterson, flared grip, without loading lever; approximately 1,000 manufactured; serial number from 1 on up; various barrel lengths, but $7\frac{1}{2}$" and 9" standard; octagonal barrel. Added premium if cased set with extra cylinder and accessories. *Antique* 17500 46500 75000

.36 caliber Holster Model or Texas Paterson, flared grip and loading lever; relatively limited production from approximately 1,000 manufactured; various barrel lengths, but $7\frac{1}{2}$" and 9" standard; octagonal barrel. Added premium if cased set with extra cylinder and accessories; different contents when loading lever present. *Antique* $20000 $52500 $80000

Fair V. Good Excellent

.28 caliber No. 1 Improved or Ehlers Model, round back cylinder and loading lever. Barrel address does not include "Mfg. Co." in marking. Added premium if cased set with accessories. Limited production of 500 (including .31 caliber Ehlers Model); serial number from 1 on up; octagonal barrel. *Antique* 10500 26500 47500

.31 caliber No. 2 Improved or Ehlers Model, round back cylinder and loading lever. Barrel address does not include "Mfg. Co." in marking. Added premium if cased set with accessories. Limited production of 500 (including .28 caliber Ehlers Model); serial number from 1 on up; octagonal barrel. Antique 10500 28500 55000

PATERSON LONGARMS

No. 1 Ring Lever Revolving Rifle, topstrap over cylinder; 200 only manufactured, in .34, .36, .38, .40 and .44 caliber (8 or 10 shots); serial number from 1 on up; octagonal barrel. *Antique* 6500 16000 42500

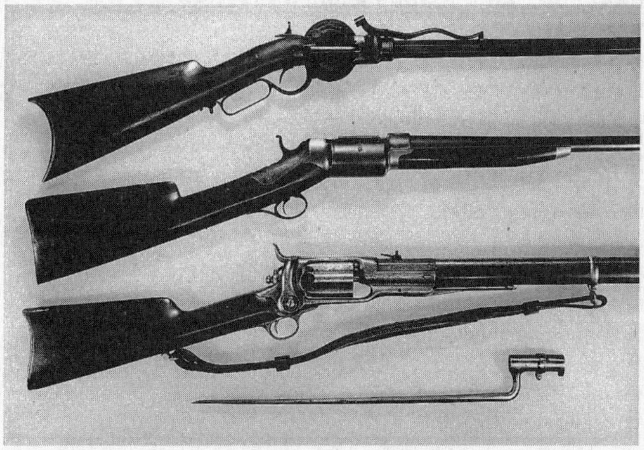

Three American Revolving rifles of the second half of the 19th century: from the top, a P. W. Porter 9-shot pill-lock in .50 caliber (dated 1851); a 4-shot Roper in 12-gauge; and a Model 1855 Colt Sidehammer Rifled Musket with angular bayonet accessory, 5-shot, .56 caliber.

	Fair	V. Good	Excellent
No. 2 Ring Lever Revolving Rifle, without topstrap over cylinder; 500 manufactured, in .44 caliber (8 or 10 shots); serial number from 1 on up; octagonal barrel. *Antique*	$5500	$14500	$37500
Model 1839 Revolving Carbine, .525 smooth bore caliber; approximately 950 produced; serial number from 1 on up; 6 shots; round barrel with faceted breech. *Antique*	5500	18500	40000
Variation with smooth cylinders (no roll engraved scene), formerly known as Albert Foster Jr. Carbines; sold by Colt in early Hartford period; often found in excellent condition. *Antique*	5000	14000	32500
Model 1839 Revolving Shotgun, .62 caliber; approximately 225 produced; serial number from 1 on up; 6 shots; round barrel, faceted breech. *Antique*	4000	12500	27500

THE WALKER COLT, MADE IN WHITNEYVILLE, CONNECTICUT, IN THE WHITNEY ARMORY.

	Fair	V. Good	Excellent
Walker Colt Revolver, .44 caliber, 6 shots, 9" part round/part octagonal barrel; with military markings of Cos. A, B, C, D from 1 to approximately 220, and E Co. from 1 to 120. *Antique*	20000	57500	100000
Walker Colt revolver, .44 caliber, 6 shots, 9" part round/part octagonal barrel; with civilian serial range of 1001 up to 1100. *Antique*	20000	57500	100000

HANDGUNS AND LONGARMS OF HARTFORD MANUFACTURE

	Fair	V. Good	Excellent
Whitneyville-Hartford Transition Dragoon revolver, .44 caliber, 6 shots, $7^1/_2$" half round/half octagonal barrel; serial range approximately 1101 through 1340. One of the most rare of all Colt revolvers. Variations primarily of Walker style grip profiling into frame at rear or of straight-backed frame at juncture with front of grip. *Antique*	15000	42500	80000
First Model Dragoon Revolver, .44 caliber, 6 shots, $7^1/_2$" half round/half octagonal barrel; round cylinder stop grooves on cylinder; squareback triggerguard; serial range approximately 1341 through 8000; total production approximately 7,000. *Antique*	4000	20000	47500

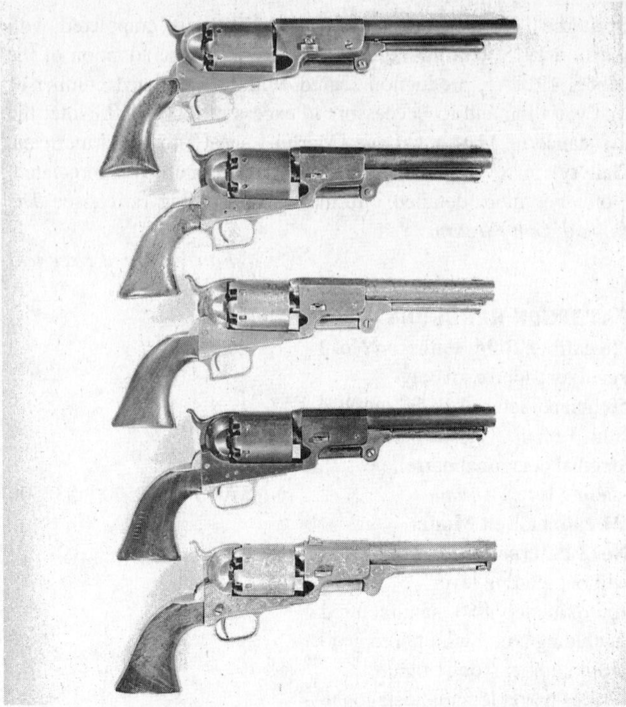

Colt .44 caliber percussion revolvers, from top, *the Walker Model, First Model Dragoon, Second Model, Third Model with vertical loading lever latch, and Third Model cut for attachable shoulder stock and with horizontal lever latch (and deluxe engraved by Nimschke).*

	Fair	V. Good	Excellent
Fluck pre-First Model Dragoon Revolver, .44 caliber, 6 shots, $7^1/_2$" half round/half octagonal barrel; serial range approximately 2216 through 2215; round stop grooves on cylinder; believed made to replace Walker Models which failed in service. Small serial numbers, some reworked Walker parts; with Ordnance stamps. *Antique*	$4500	$22500	$52500
Second Model Dragoon revolver, .44 caliber, 6 shots, $7^1/_2$" half round/half octagonal barrel, squared cylinder stop slots, squareback triggerguard; serial range approximately 8000 through 10700; approximately 2,700 made. Premium for Massachusetts or C.L. Dragoon specimens. *Antique*	4000	17500	37500
Third Model Dragoon Revolver, .44 caliber, 6 shots, $7^1/_2$" half round/half octagonal barrel, squared cylinder stop slots, roundback triggerguard; serial range approximately 10500 through 19500. Premium paid for variation with attachable shoulder stock, revolvers with steel gripstraps, and 8" barrel specimens. *Antique*	3000	14500	30000

	Fair	*V. Good*	*Excellent*
Shoulder Stock, First Model, two projections engaging two slots on backstrap. *Antique*	$2750	$4750	$8500
Shoulder Stock, Second Model, one projection into backstrap; clamp on butt. *Antique*	1750	3750	8000
Shoulder Stock, Third Model, hooks into cutouts on recoil shield, and clamp on butt. *Antique*	1500	2800	6500
Hartford-English Dragoon Revolver, .44 caliber, 6 shots, 7 1/2" half round/half octagonal barrel, squared cylinder stop slots, roundback triggerguard, serial range from 1 to 700, most have New York barrel address markings. Premium paid for early examples, some of which have hand-engraved frame and barrel address markings, and some of which have squareback triggerguards. Antique	2750	12000	24000
Model 1848 Baby Dragoon Pocket Model Revolver, .31 caliber, 5 shots; 3", 4", 5" and 6" octagonal barrel lengths; squareback triggerguards; early production without loading levers. Some of later production built with levers; some levers added later by private gunsmiths. Serial range 1 through approximately 14000 (overlap with Model 1849 Pocket Model); made c. 1848 to 1850. *Antique*	1750	4750	13500
Model 1849 Pocket Model Revolver, .31 caliber, 5 or 6 shots, 3", 4", 5" and 6" octagonal barrel lengths; with loading levers. Serial range approximately 12000 (overlap with Baby Dragoon) to approximately 340000; made c. 1850 to 1873. Numerous variations; premium paid for some of these, such as revolver with steel gripstraps, full nickel-plating, and 3" barrel version with loading lever. *Antique*	700	900	2450
Model 1849 Pocket Model Revolver, Wells Fargo variation, generally 3" or 4" barrels, without loading levers; .31 caliber. 5 or 6 shots. *Antique*	900	3000	8500
Model 1849 Pocket Revolver, London manufacture, 4", 5" and 6" barrel lengths; 5 shots; generally with Col. Colt London barrel address markings. Approximately 11,000 produced, in own serial range from 1 on up. *Antique*	450	850	2350

	Fair	*V. Good*	*Excellent*
Model 1851 Navy or Belt Revolver, .36 caliber, 7 1/2" barrel, 6 shots; total made approximately 215,000, in own serial range from 1 on up. Numerous variations bring premiums, including specimens with barrels exceeding 7 1/2" or shorter than 7 1/2", cutaways, specially marked examples, full nickel-plating.			
Model 1851 early production, First Model, squareback triggerguard, wedge over screw in barrel; serial range approximately 1 to 1250. Antique	$3750	$13500	$22500
Model 1851 early production, Second Model, squareback triggerguard, screw over wedge in barrel; serial range approximately 1250 to 4,200. *Antique*	1750	4000	16500
Model 1851 standard production, so-called Third Model, small round triggerguard; serial range approximately 4200 to 85000. *Antique*	900	2750	8500
As above, with U.S. markings and Ordnance inspector stampings; steel gripstraps. *Antique*	1000	3250	10000
Model 1851 standard production, Fourth Model, large round triggerguard; serial range approximately 85000 to 215000. *Antique*	750	2650	8500
As above, with U.S. markings and Ordnance inspector stampings; steel gripstraps. *Antique*	2250	4650	13500
Third and Fourth Model Navy Specimen, cut for attachable shoulder stocks. *Antique*	1500	3250	12500
Shoulder stock, First Model, two projections engaging two slots on backstrap. *Antique*	1500	3750	7500
Shoulder stock, Second Model, one projection into backstrap; clamp on butt. *Antique*	1200	3250	6500
Shoulder Stock, Third Model, hooks into cutouts on recoil shield, and clamp on butt. *Antique*	950	2500	4500
London Model 1851 Revolver, .36 caliber, 7 1/2" octagonal barrel, with blued or silver-plated steel gripstraps. Manufactured in London, c. 1853–57; total of approximately 42,000. Not to be confused with examples made in Hartford with London barrel addresses and proof stampings. Premium paid for variations, such as early examples with special barrel markings, squareback triggerguards. *Antique*	800	2350	6750

	Fair	V. Good	Excellent
Model 1855 Sidehammer Revolver, .28 caliber (Model 3A in .31 caliber), 5 shots; 3½" octagonal barrels (3 7/16" for Model 1A), blued. Manufactured c. 1855–1861; total of 28,000. Variations 1 and 1A, 2, and 3A. Premium for 1, 1A and 3A due to rarity. *Antique* . . .	$500	$1350	$3750
Model 1855 Sidehammer Revolver, .31 caliber (Models 4, 5 and 5A, 6 and 6A, and 7 and 7A); 5 shots; 3½" and 4½" barrels (3½" for Model 4; octagonal for Model 4; balance of variations round), blued. Manufactured c. 1860–1870; total of 14,000. Premium for Model 4, Model 6 and 6A, and Model 7 and 7A (screw in cylinder variation). *Antique*	400	1000	4000
Model 1855 Sidehammer Revolving Longarms, various calibers and barrel lengths. Two basic frame types, one having 5 shots generally and the other 6 shots. Several variations:			
Sporting Rifles, total of approximately 3,500, in .36, .40, .44, .50, and .56 calibers. Premium paid for rare calibers and unusual barrel lengths. *Antique*	1000	3250	9250
Military Rifles, sling swivels and barrel bands; total of approximately 9,310 made, in calibers .44 and .56 (with 25 or less only in .64 caliber). Premium for rare caliber and unusual barrel lengths; and when bayonet present. *Antique* .	2350	4500	17500
Carbines, total of approximately 4,435 made, in calibers .36, .40, .44, .50, and .56 (.36, .40 and .50 rare). Premium for rare caliber and unusual barrel lengths. *Antique*	1250	4000	12500
Shotguns, in 10 gauge (.75 caliber) and 20 gauge (.60 caliber); approximately 1,100 made, in own serial number range. Premium for unusual barrel lengths. *Antique*	1000	2750	7000
Model 1861 Single Shot Rifled Musket; .58 caliber; standard with 40" barrel; finished bright. Colt markings on lockplate and date 1861, 1862, 1863 or 1864. Not serial numbered. *Antique*	500	1350	3000
Single Shot Target Rifle, only a handful produced. .52 caliber (approx.); 28½" barrel (will vary); not serial numbered. Premium if false muzzle present. *Antique*	1250	3500	9250

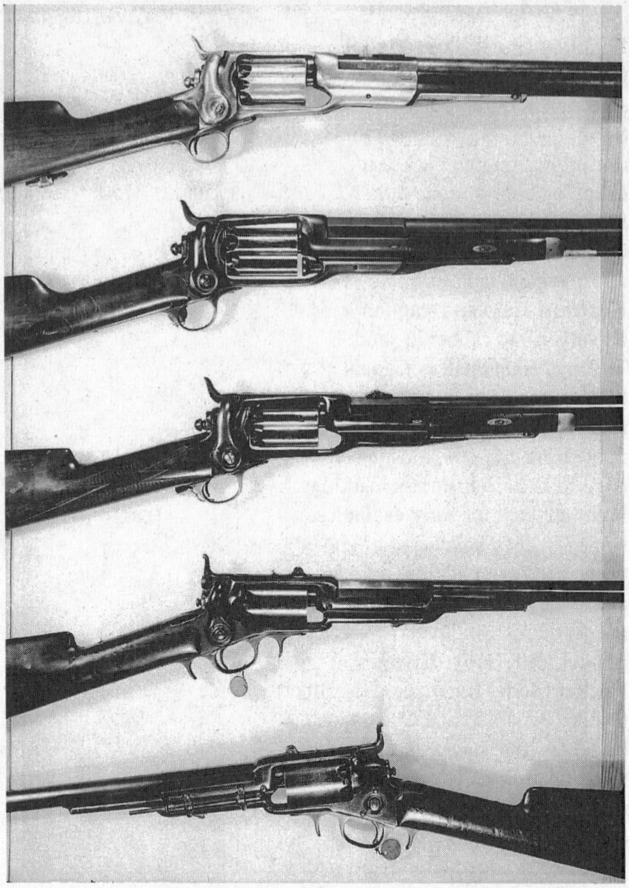

Colt Model 1855 longarms, from the top, *Rifled Musket, Shotgun, Sporting Rifle, and the First Model Sporting Rifle (lacking fore end, and fitted with automatic oiler for charges in cylinder).*

	Fair	V. Good	Excellent
Model 1860 Army Revolver, .44 caliber, 6 shot rebated cylinder; total production 200,500. Standard model with 8" round barrel with creeping style ramrod, cylinder engraved with naval engagement roll scene; Army-size grips of walnut. *Antique*	$950	$3250	$9500
Military variation of the above, 4-screw frame, cut for shoulder stock; premium if inspector markings on grips and various metal parts. *Antique*	900	4500	11500
7½" barrel, fluted cylinder, rare early production with Army size grips; Navy size grips bring premium. *Antique*	1000	4750	13500
8" barrel, fluted cylinder, scarce early production. *Antique*	950	4250	12500
Model 1860 Army Revolver, London barrel address. *Antique*	950	4250	12500

	Fair	V. Good	Excellent
Model 1860 attachable shoulder stock, First Model, two projections engaging two slots on backstrap. *Antique*	$1150	$2750	$7000
Model 1860 attachable shoulder stock, Second Model, one projection into backstrap; clamp on butt. *Antique*	1000	2250	6000
Model 1860 attachable shoulder stock, Third Model, hooks into cutouts on recoil shield, and clamp on butt. *Antique*	900	1850	5000
Model 1861 Navy Revolver, .36 caliber, 6 shots, $7^1/_2$" barrel. 38,843 made (some converted to metallic cartridge). *Antique*	750	2250	7000
Model 1861 Navy Revolver, rare early variation with half-fluted cylinder. *Antique*	2750	17500	30000
Model 1861 Navy Revolver, U.S. martial markings. *Antique*	1000	3250	15000
Model 1861 Navy Revolver, London barrel address markings. *Antique*	1200	2750	10000
Model 1862 Police Revolver, .36 caliber, 5 shot half fluted, rebated cylinders, $4^1/_2$", $5^1/_2$" and $6^1/_2$" round barrels. Approximately 47,000 made (40 percent were the 1862 Pocket Navy; some built as metallic cartridge conversions). Early specimens bring premium and have Hartford barrel address and low serial numbers. Premium for steel-grip revolvers and London barrel address markings. *Antique*	500	1250	3500
Trapper's Model, $3^1/_2$" barrel variation, without attachable loading lever; about 50 produced. *Antique*	1250	3750	12500
Model 1862 Pocket Pistol of Navy Caliber Revolver; .36 caliber, 5 shots, $4^1/_2$", $5^1/_2$" and $6^1/_2$" octagonal barrels; stagecoach holdup roll scene on rebated cylinder. Premium paid for London barrel address variation. *Antique*	500	1250	4000

CONVERSIONS AND EARLY SINGLE ACTION REVOLVERS

(Conversions of revolvers from percussion models. Total by factory estimated at approximately 46,000, built primarily c. 1869–c. 1878.)

	Fair	V. Good	Excellent
Thuer conversions: all handguns with 6 shot cylinders; any conversions of this type done on any models other than those listed below are rare and will bring premium; estimated total of all types 5,000			
Model 1849 Pocket Revolver, *Antique*	$1950	$4000	$10000
Model 1851 Navy Revolver, *Antique*	1650	4500	11500
Model 1860 Army Revolver, *Antique*	1900	4750	11000
Model 1861 Navy Revolver. *Antique*	3250	4250	11000
Model 1862 Police Revolver. *Antique*	1650	4250	11000
Model 1860 Army Revolver, Richards Conversion, .44 Colt c.f.; 6 shots; 8" barrels; approximately 9,000 made, most in range from 1 on up. *Antique*	550	2250	6000
Model 1860 Army Revolver, Richards-Mason Conversion, .44 Colt c.f.; 6 shots; 7 $^1/_2$" and 8" barrels; approximately 2,100 made, within high range of Richards Conversions. *Antique*	700	2500	9000
Model 1851 Navy Conversions, .38 r.f. and .38 c.f. calibers; 6 shots; $7^1/_2$" barrels; approximately 3,800 made. Premium for U.S. Navy markings. *Antique*	700	1900	4950
Model 1861 Navy Conversions, .38 r.f. and .38 c.f. calibers; 6 shots; $7^1/_2$" barrels; approximately 2,200 made). Premium for .38 r.f. and for U.S. Navy marked revolvers. *Antique*	700	2200	5500
Model 1862 Police and Pocket Navy conversions, .38 r.f. and .38 c.f. calibers; 5 shots; $3^1/_2$", $4^1/_2$", $5^1/_2$" and $6^1/_2$" barrel lengths. Total of approximately 24,000 in various configurations.			
$4^1/_2$" Octagonal Barrel Model, .38 rimfire (built from Pocket Navy). *Antique*	450	1250	2750
Round Barrel Pocket Navy with Ejector, .38 r.f. and c.f. *Antique*	400	1250	2850
Model 1862 Police/Pocket Navy with Ejector, .38 r.f. and c.f. *Antique*	400	1250	2750
Round (Cartridge) Barrel Model with Ejector, .38 r.f. and c.f. *Antique*	400	1000	2750
$3^1/_2$" Round (Cartridge) Barrel Model, .38 r.f. and c.f. *Antique*	300	900	2000

	Fair	V. Good	Excellent
Model 1871–72 Open Top Frontier .44 Single Action Revolver, .44 rimfire; 6 shot cylinder with naval engagement roll scene; 7 1/2" round barrels (8" barrels bring premium); total of approximately 7,000 in own serial range from 1 on up. *Antique*	$1100	$5000	$11500
Single Action Army Revolver, first generation, built from 1873 until c. 1940; in a total of approximately 30 calibers (.32-20, .38-40, .44-40 and .45 Colt the most common); and several barrel lengths from 2" up to 16" (4 3/4", 5 1/2" and 7 1/2" most common); serial numbered from 1 on up to 357859 (310386 with standard frame; 917 flattop target models; 44,350 Bisley models, and 976 Bisley flattop target models)			
Standard production model, 4 3/4", 5 1/2" and 7 1/2" barrel lengths, in common calibers, with walnut or hard rubber grips. Early production bring premium. *Antique*	1650	3250	8250
Early production revolvers, with so-called "pinched frame" feature; serial range 1 to approximately 165. *Antique*	8500	25000	65000
U.S. Martial, with U.S. frame stamping and inspector markings; .45 caliber, 7 1/2" barrel. *Antique*	3200	8000	15500
U.S. Martial variation, "Artillery Model," 5 1/2", rebuilt revolvers sent back to Colt factory; are refinished and with mixed serial numbers. *Antique*	2250	4500	7000
Rimfire, own serial range from 1 to approximately 1800; premium for .22 caliber; most were made in .44 caliber and with 7 1/2" barrels. *Antique*	3750	12500	25000
Colt Frontier Six-Shooter, with etched barrel marking of that legend on left side; .44-40 caliber; serial range 21000 to 65000. *Antique*	3250	7000	12500
Sheriff's Model, Storekeeper variation, without ejector rod or rod housing; customary barrel length 3" or 4". *Antique*	4250	11500	19500
Long-Flute Cylinder variation, found in serial range 330001 to 331480; cylinders from double action revolver production. *Antique*	2750	5250	8500

	Fair	V. Good	Excellent
Single Action Army Flattop Target Model Revolver, various calibers from .22 rimfire up to .476 Eley; various barrel lengths. Premiums for unusual barrel lengths and calibers. *Antique*	$2750	$5500	$9500
Bisley Model Single Action Army Revolver, various calibers from .32 Colt up to .455 Eley; various barrel lengths. Premiums for unusual barrel lengths and calibers, and for Sheriff's Model. *Antique*	1600	3250	5000
Bisley Flattop Target Model Revolver, various calibers from .32 Colt rimfire up to .455 Eley; various barrel lengths. Premiums for unusual barrel lengths and calibers. *Antique*	2250	4500	8500
Post–World War II Single Action Army Revolver, from 1956 to date; serial range began at 0001SA, when reached total of approximately 100000 the company placed SA in front of the serial number, e.g., SA00001. Calibers .38 Special, .357 Magnum, .44 Special, and .45 Colt; 4 3/4", 5 1/2", and 7 1/2" barrels. Premium for Sheriff's Models, unusual barrel lengths, and special calibers. *Modern*	500	1000	1850
New Frontier Single Action Army Revolver, 1961 into 1970s. .357 Magnum, .44 Special and .45 Colt calibers, 4 3/4", 5 1/2" and 7 1/2" barrels. *Modern*	350	700	950
Frontier Scout Revolvers, .22 rimfire and .22 magnum rimfire; 6 shots, 4 3/4" and 9 1/2" barrels standard. Serial numbers began with 1000Q; suffix changed to F, 1958. *Modern*	150	200	300

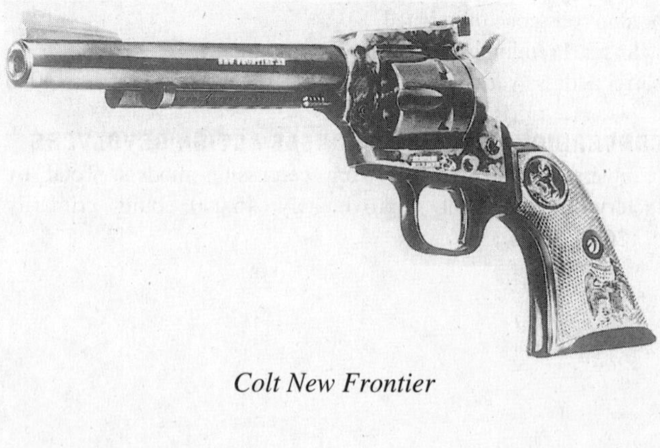

Colt New Frontier

	Fair	*V. Good*	*Excellent*
K Series Frontier Scout Revolver, as above; production began with P suffix, beginning with 999P, 1962; then changed to K, beginning with 1K, 1960. *Modern*	$125	$175	$250

DERRINGERS AND POCKET REVOLVERS

	Fair	*V. Good*	*Excellent*
First Model Derringer pistol, .41 short rimfire; $2^{1}/_{2}$" barrel; all metal construction; total made 6,500, from 1 on up; 1870–90. *Antique*	400	1350	3250
Second Model Derringer pistol, .41 short rimfire (approx. 200 in c.f.); $2^{1}/_{2}$" barrel; with checkered walnut grips; total made 9,000, from 1 on up; 1870–90. *Antique*	350	1300	2750
Third Model (Thuer) Derringer pistol, .41 short rimfire (limited number in .41 c.f.); $2^{1}/_{2}$" barrel; total production approximately 45,000, from 1 on up; c. 1875 through early 20th century. *Antique*	300	500	1000
Fourth Model Derringer, .22 rimfire; $2^{1}/_{2}$" barrel; D and N suffix to serial numbers; total made of approximately 112,000, from 1959–63. *Modern*	150	400	700
Lord and Lady Derringer, .22 short rimfire; $2^{1}/_{2}$" barrel; from 1001 on up, with DER suffix; approximately 12,000 cased pairs of Lord and 3,000 cased pairs of Lady Model made in 1970, with some production thereafter; valued as cased pairs. *Modern*	250	800	1250
Cloverleaf House Model Revolver, .41 short and long rimfire; 4 shots (Cloverleaf), 5 shots (House Pistol); $1^{1}/_{2}$" and 3" barrels; House Pistol with $2^{5}/_{8}$" barrel only; approximately 10,000 made, from 1 on up. Premium for $1^{1}/_{2}$" barrel.			
Cloverleaf House Model, 4-shot cylinder. *Antique*	350	650	1500
House Model, 5-shot cylinder. *Antique*	300	600	1350
Open Top Pocket Model Revolver, .22 short and long rimfire, 7 shots; $2^{3}/_{4}$" and $2^{7}/_{8}$" barrels; approximately 114,200 made, from 1 on up. Premium for early model with integral ejector. *Antique*	150	325	750
New Line .22 Revolver, .22 short and long rimfire; 7 shots; $2^{1}/_{4}$" barrel; approximately 55,343 made, from 1 on up. Premium for first model (1 through 16000 serial range); c. 1873–77. *Antique*	125	275	650
New Line .30 Caliber Revolver, .30 short and long rimfire; 5 shots; $1^{3}/_{4}$" and $2^{1}/_{4}$" barrels; approximately 11,000 made, from 1 on up; c. 1874–76. *Antique*	$175	$375	$1250
New Line .32 Caliber Revolver, .32 short and long rimfire, 32 short and long centerfire; 5 shots; $2^{1}/_{4}$" and 4" barrels; approximately 22,000 made, from 1 on up; c. 1873–84. *Antique*	150	350	1000
New Line .38 Caliber Revolver, .38 short and long rimfire, .38 short and long centerfire; $2^{1}/_{4}$" and 4" barrels; approximately 5,500 made, serial numbered with .41 New Lines, from 1 on up; c. 1874–80. *Antique*	150	350	1000
New Line .41 Caliber Revolver, .41 short and long rimfire, .41 short and long centerfire; $2^{1}/_{4}$" and 4" barrels; approximately 7,000 made, serial numbered with .38 New Line, from 1 on up; c. 1874–79. *Antique*	175	500	1350
New House Model Revolver, .38 and .41 short and long centerfire (premium for .32 short and long centerfire); 5 shots; $2^{1}/_{4}$" barrel; approximately 4,000 made, numbered with New Line .32, .38 and .41 pistols and Police Model pistols; c. 1880–86. *Antique*	150	500	1650
New Police Model Revolver, .32, .38 and .41 short and long centerfire; 5 shots; $2^{1}/_{4}$" (without ejector) and $4^{1}/_{2}$", 5" and 6" barrels (with ejector); approximately 3,500 to 4,000 made (.32 and .41 rare), numbered with .32 New Line and .38 and .41 House pistols; c. 1882–86. Known as Cop & Thug Model, due to depiction on composition hard rubber grips of policeman and thug. *Antique*	250	1000	4000

DOUBLE ACTION REVOLVERS

	Fair	*V. Good*	*Excellent*
Model 1877 Lightning Revolver, .38 Colt, .41 Colt (rare in .32 Colt, about 200 made, brings premium); 6 shots; $2^{1}/_{2}$", $3^{1}/_{2}$" (without ejector), $4^{1}/_{2}$", 6" barrels standard, various lengths from $1^{1}/_{2}$" to 10"; 166,849 made; c. 1877–09.			
Standard model, without ejector; premium for checkered rosewood grips, early serial numbers. *Antique*	225	425	1000

	Fair	V. Good	Excellent
Standard model, ejector; premium for checkered rosewood grips, early serial numbers. *Antique*	$225	$400	$1000
Specimens with London barrel address markings and British proof stampings. *Antique*	275	500	1200
Model 1878 Frontier Revolver, .22 rimfire, .32-20, .38-40, .38 Colt, .44 Russian, .44 German Government, .44 S & W, .44-40, .45 Colt, and .450, .455 and .476 Eley; 6 shots; 2 1/2" to 12" barrels (standard 3" and 4" without ejector and 4 3/4", 5 1/2" and 7 1/2" with ejector); 51,210 made; c. 1878–1905.			
Standard model, without ejector. *Antique*	325	600	1100
Standard model, ejector. *Antique*	400	700	1350
Specimens with London barrel address markings and British proof stampings. *Antique*	400	700	1300
Alaskan or Philippine variation, with oversize triggerguard; U.S. inspector markings; .45 caliber; lanyard swivel on butt; 4,600 made (range 43401–48097). *Antique*	450	750	1750

DOUBLE ACTION SWINGOUT CYLINDER MODELS

	Fair	V. Good	Excellent
Model 1889 Navy Revolver, .38 Colt, .38 S & W (scarce), and .41 Colt calibers; 6 shots; 3", 4 1/2" and 6" barrels; 31,000 made, from 1 on up; c. 1889–94. *Antique*	250	850	1950
Model 1889 Navy Revolver, U.S. Navy contract. *Antique*	375	1000	2250
Models 1892, 1894, 1895, 1896, 1901 and 1903 New Army and Navy Revolvers, .38 Colt, .38 S & W, .41 Colt and .32-20; 6 shots; barrel lengths from 2" to 6"; 291,000 made, from 1 on up; c. 1892–1907 (succeeded by Army Special). *Antique and modern*	150	300	700
As above, U.S. Navy purchases. *Antique*	250	500	1250
As above, U.S. Army purchases. *Antique and modern*	225	400	1000
Army Special Revolver, .32-20, .38 Colt, .38 S & W Special, .41 Colt; 6 shots; barrel lengths from 4" to 6"; 240,000 made, from 291000 to 540000 (overlaps with Official Police Model); c. 1908–28. *Modern*	200	350	1000
Model 1905 Marine Corps Revolver, .38 Colt, .38 S & W Special; 6 shots; 6" barrel; 926 made; from 10001 on up; c. 1905–09. *Modern*	700	1350	2750
Official Police Revolver, .32-20, .38 Colt, .38 Colt Special, .38-44 S & W; 6 shots; 4", 5" and 6" barrels; more than 400,000 made, range continued from Army Special (with overlap) at 513216 to approximately 9828163 (some numbers not used); plus a series of .22 revolvers numbered in own range (30,000 made; 1930 to 1967); c. 1927 to early 1970s. Succeeded by J series revolvers, which began 1969. Premium for military and police marked specimens. *Modern*	$175	$275	$500
Commando Revolver, .38 Special; 6 shots; 2", 4" and 6" barrels (4" standard); 50,617 made; from 1 on up; c. 1942–45; parkerized finish. *Modern*	125	225	450
Marshal Revolver, .38 Special; 6 shots; 2" and 4" barrels; 2,500 made, in range from 833352-M, from Official Police range; c. 1954–56. *Modern*	175	275	600
Officers Model Revolver, **Officers Model Target**, **Officers Model Special** and **Officers Model Match**, various calibers, from .32 Colt Police Positive to .38 Special, with several chamberings; 4" and 6" barrels most common, but range of from 4" to 7 1/2" lengths; 15,000 made, beginning at 229881 in Army Special and continuing in Official Police ranges); c. 1904–49; and resumed with serial changes in 1950, 1953 and 1970; complex sequence of models and serial sequences. Premium for earlier revolvers, pre–World War II, with better quality finish. *Modern*	200	325	700
New Service and Shooting Master Revolvers, New Service in production from 1898 through 1944; total 356,000 made, from 1 on up; calibers .38 Colt on up to .476 Eley; 6 shots; 2" up to 7 1/2" barrels. Earlier production brings premium.			
Standard Model. *Modern*	225	400	900
Shooting Master (flattop target) Model. *Modern*	275	450	1050
Model 1909 U.S. Army and U.S. Navy variation, .45 caliber, 5 1/2", serial range 30000 to 50000. *Modern*	325	550	1100
Model 1909 U.S. Marine Corps, USMC marked; varnished and checkered walnut grips. *Modern*	325	600	1200

	Fair	V. Good	Excellent
Model 1917 U.S. Army, serial range 150000 to 310000; .45 and .45 ACP; 5 1/2". *Modern*	$225	$450	$950
Camp Perry Single Shot Pistol, .22 long rifle; 8" and 10" barrels; 2,488 made; from 1 on up; c. 1920–41. *Modern*	525	800	1350
New Pocket Model Revolver, .32 Colt, .32 S & W; 6 shot; 2 1/2" to 6" barrels; 30,000 made, from 1 on up; c. 1893–1905; Pocket Positive continued serial number from 30000. *Modern*	175	275	600
Pocket Positive Model Revolver, several variants of .32 centerfire cartridge; 2" to 6" barrels; 6 shot; 130,000 made, from 30000 up to 159000; c. 1905–43. *Modern*	175	350	650
New Police .32 and New Police Target Model Revolvers, .32 Colt, .32 S & W, .32 Colt New Police; 6 shot; 2 1/2", 4", and 6" barrels; 49,500 made, from 1 on up; c. 1896–1907. Majority of production New Police; premium for Police Target (was in 6" barrel only). *Modern*	200	350	700

Colt Police Positive, Late

	Fair	V. Good	Excellent
Police Positive .32 and Police Positive Target Model Revolvers, various .32 caliber cartridges; 6 shot; 2 1/2", 4", 5" and 6" barrels; 199,000 made, from 49500 on up to 238623; c. 1907–43. Majority of production Police Positive; premium for Police Positive Target (was in 6" barrel only and totalled only 3351 made). *Modern*	200	350	650
Pequano Model Police Positive Revolver, .32 Police Positive; 2", 2 1/2", 4", 5" and 6" barrels; few thousand only made; c. 1933–1941, in serial range 226000 to 237000. *Modern*	$225	$325	$750
Police Positive .22 Target Revolver, Models G and C, .22 rimfire and various .32 c.f. calibers; 6" barrel; four series of serial numbers used; most of production in range from 1 on up to approximately 45741; c. 1910–41. *Modern*	225	375	750
Police Positive .38 Model Revolver, .38 Colt Police Positive (New Police) and .38 S & W calibers; 6 shot; 2", 4", 5" and 6" barrels; 200,000 made, from 1 to 177000, then 329000 on (latter shared with Bankers Special and .32 Police Positive on .38 frame); c. 1905–43. *Modern*	225	375	800
Bankers' Special Revolver, .22 long rifle, .38 Colt Police Positive (New Police) and .38 S & W; 6 shot; 2" barrel; more than 35,000 made, in Police Positive .38 range from 177000 through 185000 and 329000 through 406725; c. 1928–43. *Modern*	225	425	850
Police Positive Special Revolver, .32-20, .32 New Police, .38 Colt, .38 Special, .38 New Police, .38 S & W Special, .38-44 S & W Special and .38 smoothbore (rare); 6 shot; 2", 4", 4 1/2", 5" and 6" barrels; over 650,000 made, from 1 on up; c. 1908 into the 1970s; note variations in serial numbers, including with letter prefixes beginning 1969 (A10000 to A59999). Premium for pre–World War II revolvers, which show better quality of manufacture. Late model has special barrel design, with shrouded ejector rod. *Modern*	225	450	900
Detective Special Revolver, various .32 and .38 calibers; 6 shot; 2" and 3" (latter for .38 only) barrels; over 350,000 made; serial numbered with Police Positive Special from 331000; A prefix numbers began 1969; c. 1927 into the 1970s. *Modern*	225	450	900
Border Patrol Revolver, .38 Special; 6 shot; 4" heavy bull barrel; 400 made, in range of 610000 through 620000; c. 1952. *Modern*	375	550	1100

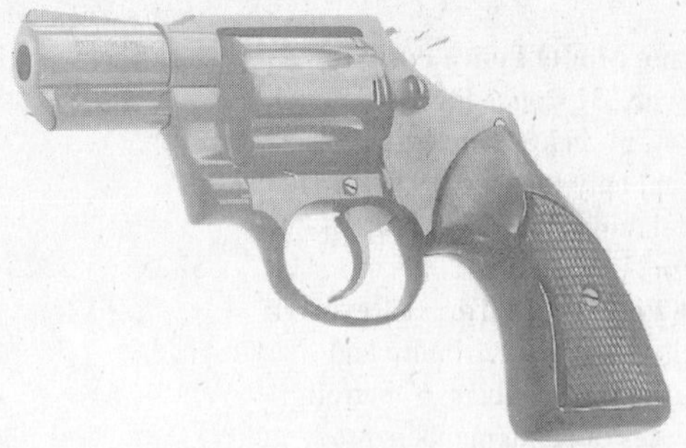

Colt Detective Special

	Fair	V. Good	Excellent
Diamondback Revolver, .22 long rifle, .38 Special; 6 shot; 2½" and 4" barrel; Python styling with distinctive weighted and ventilated rib barrel; more than 50,000 made, c. 1966 into the 1970s; from D1001 on up. *Modern*	$225	$400	$800
Cobra Revolver, .22 long rifle, .32 Colt New Police; .38 Colt New Police, .38 Special; 6 shot; 2", 3" 4" and 5" barrels; aluminum alloy frame; over 240,000 made, from 1LW on up (numbered with Agent, Courier, and Aircrewman models); from 1950 into the 1970s; A prefix serial numbers begun in 1969. *Modern*	225	375	800
Aircrewman Revolver, .38 Special; 6 shot; 2" barrel; aluminum alloy barrel and cylinder; 1,189 made; majority destroyed due to safety problem with ammunition; numbered in Cobra and Courier serial range with LW suffix; most in 2901LW to 7775LW serial group; Air Force buttstrap numbers, from 1 to 1189; made 1951. *Modern*	325	700	900
Courier Revolver, .22 long rifle, .32 S & W long and short and .32 New Police; 6 shot; 3" barrel; aluminum alloy frame; approximately 3,000 made; in serial range of Cobra and Agent revolvers; c. 1953–56. *Modern*	225	450	800
Agent Revolver, .38 Special; 6 shot; 2" barrel; aluminum alloy frame with diminutive grip; over 50,000 made; c. 1962 into 1970s; in serial range of Cobra Model. *Modern*	225	400	750

	Fair	V. Good	Excellent
Trooper Revolver, .22 long rifle, .38 Special, .357 Magnum; 4" and 6" barrels; production began 1954, from 1 on up; serial range with .357 Model through 1961; shared with Officer's Model Match from 1953 into 1970s; J series began 1969 with J1001. *Modern*	$175	$275	$550
.357 Magnum Revolver, .38 Special and .357 Magnum; 6 shot; 4" and 6" barrels; from 1953 to 1961, from 1 on up; rare early production of 259 in 1953; number shared with Trooper Model; discontinued in 28000 range, 1961. *Modern*	175	275	500
Python Revolver, .357 Magnum; 6 shots; 2½", 4" and 6" barrels; from 1955 to date, from 1 on up; prefix E begun in 1969 with five digit number. Over 200,000 made to date. Python Hunter variation will bring premium, as will earlier specimens. *Modern*	275	375	550

Colt Python .357 Magnum

MK III Series, Trooper, Metropolitan, Lawman, Official Police and Officers Model Match, production began with J-serial prefix in 1969; revolvers often called the J-series; .38 Special and .357 Magnum calibers, with some models in .22 Long Rifle. Premium for nickel plating.

	Fair	V. Good	Excellent
Lawman MK III, .357 Magnum, various barrel lengths, 6 shots. *Modern*	125	275	550
Lawman MK V, .357 Magnum, various barrel lengths, 6 shots. *Modern*	125	275	550

Colt Lawman MK V

	Fair	V. Good	Excellent
Metropolitan MK III, .38 Special, 4" barrel, 6 shots. *Modern*	$150	$250	$500
Official Police MK III, .38 Special, 6 shot. *Modern*	150	250	500

SELF-LOADING PISTOLS

	Fair	V. Good	Excellent
Model 1900 Automatic, .38 rimless, smokeless; 7-shot magazine; 6" barrel; 3,500 made, from 1 on up; c. 1900–03; serial range continued by Sporting Model 1902 pistols. Premium for rear sight functioning as hammer safety. *Modern*	2250	4500	7000
Navy contract of above pistols, USN numbers as well as commercial serial numbers; rare. *Modern*	2250	4950	8500
Army contract of above pistols, first series, 75 only; J.T.T. inspector marking; scarce. *Modern*	3250	8000	18500
Army contract of above pistols, second series; 200 only; R.A.C. inspector marking; scarce. *Modern*	3750	4750	16000
Model 1902 Sporting Automatic, .38 rimless, smokeless; 7-shot magazine; 6" barrel; 7,500 made, from approximately 3500 up to 10999 and from 30000 to 30190; c. 1903–08; premium for location of serrations on front of slide. *Modern*	550	1250	2250
Model 1902 Military Automatic, .38 rimless, smokeless; 8-shot magazine; 6" barrel; 18,000 made, from 15001 back to 11000; then from 30200 to 47266 (numbered with Model 1903 Pocket Automatic c. 1918–29); c. 1902–29; premium for location of serrations on front of slide. *Modern*	550	1250	2500
Model 1902 Military Automatic with U.S. Army markings (R.A.C. and J.T.T. inspectors); serial range 15001 to 15200. *Modern*	2250	5500	9000

	Fair	V. Good	Excellent
Model 1903 Pocket (Hammer) Automatic, .38 rimless, smokeless; 7-shot magazine; 4½" barrel; 26,000 made, from 16001 to 47226 (shared numbers from 30200 on up with Model 1902 Military Pistol); c. 1903–29. *Modern*	$225	$750	$1000
Model 1903 Hammerless .32 Pocket Automatic, .32 ACP; 8-shot magazine; 4" and 3¾" barrel; 572,215 made; from 1 on up; c. 1903–45.			
1st Model, serial range 1 to 71999. *Modern*	225	450	800
2nd Model, range 72000 to 105050. *Modern*	175	375	750
3rd Model, range 105051 to 468096. *Modern*	150	350	600
4th Model (commercial), range 468097 to 554000. *Modern*	175	350	650
4th Model (military), U.S. PROPERTY marking on frame; range 554001 to 572214. *Modern*	325	850	1500
Model 1908 .38 Hammerless Pocket Automatic, .380 ACP; 7-shot magazine; 3¾" barrel; 138,009 made; from 1 on up; c. 1908–45.			
1st Model, range 1 to 6251. *Modern*	225	550	700
2nd Model, range 6252 to 92893. *Modern*	175	450	600
3rd Model (Commercial), range 92894 to 133649. *Modern*	150	325	500
3rd Model (Military), range 133650 to 138009; marked U.S. PROPERTY on frame. *Modern*	550	1300	1750
Model 1908 .25 Hammerless Automatic, .25ACP; 6-shot magazine; 2" barrel; 409,061 made, from 1 on up; c. 1908–41.			
Early model, up through approximately serial 20000. *Modern*	175	450	600
Standard model, post 20000 serial range, with 1910 or 1910 and 1917 patent dates on slide. *Modern*	150	350	450
Military variation, U.S. PROPERTY marking on frame; limited production of less than 1,000. *Modern*	550	1850	3500
Junior Colt .25/22 Automatic and **Colt Automatic Caliber .25**, .22 short and .25ACP; 6-shot magazines; 2¼" barrel; over 75,000 made; serial range began with 1CC, shared between both models. *Modern*	175	275	400

	Fair	V. Good	Excellent
Model 1905 .45 Automatic, .45 rimless, smokeless; 7-shot magazine; 5" barrel; 6,100 made, from 1 on up. Premium for early production with 1897 and 1902 patent markings on slide.			
Standard model. *Modern*	$850	$2250	$3000
U.S. Government Contract, 1907, numbered 1 to 200; K.M. inspector marking. *Modern*	4250	9500	13500
Shoulder stock variation, with stock designed to also act as holster. *Modern*	4250	10500	16500
Model 1909 Prototype/ Experimental Automatic, .45ACP; 7-shot magazine; 5" barrel; approximately 23 made, from 1 on up; c. 1909. *Curio*	7750	16500	22500
Model 1911 Automatic, Commercial serial series (with C prefix from C1 through C240227 and C suffix from 240228C through 1970 at 336169C); 7-shot magazine; 5" barrel.			
Early specimens, with 1897, 1902, 1905, 1911 patent dates on slide; C1 to approximately C4500. *Modern*	850	1750	2500
Standard production, range C4500 to C130000; straight mainspring housing. *Modern*	450	1200	1500
.455 British Contract, own serial range W10001 to W21000; c. 1915–16. *Modern*	550	1100	1350
Russian Contract, marked ANGLO ZAKAZIVAT in cyrilic; about 14,500 made, within serial range C50000 to C85000. *Modern*	1050	3650	4750
Military Serial Series, complex numbering. Early production, range from 1 to 629500; straight mainspring housing; premium for low numbers. *Modern*	450	1100	1750
As above, but with U.S.N. markings. *Modern*	1100	2800	3750
Model 1911A1, serial range 700001 to 2380013; RS inspector stamp; arched mainspring housing. Premium for blued over Parkerized finish. *Modern*	375	800	1100
Ithaca Gun Co. variation, ITHACA GUN CO. on slide. *Modern*	400	900	1100
North American Arms Co. variation, approximately 100 only made. *Modern*	4250	9500	13500
Remington Rand, Inc. variation, several ranges of numbers; approximately 900,000 made. *Modern*	350	700	1100

	Fair	V. Good	Excellent
Remington-UMC variation, serial range 1 to 21676, with Colt and Remington-UMC slide marks. *Modern*,	$425	$1000	$1300
Singer Mfg. Co. variation, range S800001 to S800500; 500 only made. *Modern*	3500	9000	11500
Springfield Armory variation, range 72751 to 133186; 25,767 made. *Modern*	700	1650	2200
Union Switch & Signal Co. variation, range 1041405 to 1096404; approximately 40,000 made. *Modern*	400	800	1000
First Model National Match .45 Automatic, .45ACP, 7-shot magazine; 5" barrel; approximately 10,000 made; serial within commercial series pistols, with C prefix; c. 1933–41. *Modern*	900	2250	2950
Ace .22 Automatic, .22 long rifle; 10-shot magazine; 4³/₄" barrel; approximately 11,000 made; from 1 on up; c. 1931–41. *Modern*	650	1750	2250
Service Model Ace Automatic Pistol, .22 long rifle; 10-shot magazine; 5" barrel; approximately 13,500 made, with SM prefix to serial numbers; c. 1937–45. *Modern*	750	1700	2500
.22-.45 Conversion Unit, .22 long rifle; 10-shot magazine; 5" barrel; more than 5,000 made; c. 1938–1970s. *Modern*	175	275	400
.45-.22 Conversion Unit, .45 ACP; 7-shot magazine; serial range U1 to U112; made 1938–1940. *Modern*	375	900	1300
.38 AMU Automatic (Kit), .38 AMU caliber; 9-shot magazine; 5" barrel; from Model 1911 and 1911A1 serial ranges; some from Super .38 serial range; limited production, from c. 1958. *Modern*	625	1850	2250
.38 Special Kit, made for dealer Gil Hebard; c. 1964 to early 1970s; .38 Special and .45ACP; variation from .38 AMU; approximately 500 .38 Special Kits (suffix H) and over 1,200 .45ACP (suffix O). *Modern*	650	1850	2250
Super .38 Automatic, .38 rimless, smokeless (.38ACP) and .38 Super; 9-shot magazine; 5" barrel; in excess of 200,000 made, from 1 on up; production into 1970s; CS prefix begun 1969. *Modern*	750	1700	2750

	Fair	V. Good	Excellent
Super Match .38 Automatic, scarce variation of the Super 38; from c. 1935 to 1941, serial numbered in Super 38 sequence; production estimated at 3,000 to 5,000. *Modern*	$950	$2750	$3750
Gold Cup National Match Automatic, .45 mid range, .45ACP, .38 Special mid range or wad-cutter; 5-shot magazines; 5" barrels; more than 40,000 made in .45, more than 10,000 in .38; .45 range 10NM on up, in 1970 new series began with 70N prefix; .38 range 100NMR to 7000NMR; .38 National Match with MS suffix, in 1961, 101 through 855MS only (premium for this scarce variation). *Modern*	425	750	1000
Gold Cup MK III, 9mm Luger, .38 Special, .45ACP. *Modern*	375	750	1000
Mark IV/80 Gold Cup National Match, .45ACP. *Modern*	450	750	1000
Springfield Armory National Match, from 1955 through 1965; total of approximately 16,000 made; made from service pistols. *Modern*	400	750	1000
Government Model Mark IV, .38 Super, .45ACP. *Modern*	425	800	1000
Government Model Mark IV/ Series 80, various calibers including 9mm Luger and .45ACP. *Modern*	325	650	800
Officer's Model ACP MK IV/80, .45ACP; 6-shot magazine. *Modern*	350	700	800
Commander Model Automatic, 9mm Luger, .38 Super, .45ACP; 9-shot (38 and 9mm) and 7-shot magazines; 4¼" barrels; in excess of 100,000; serial markings with 00 prefix through 65; LW suffix through 1968; CLW prefix from 1969; aluminum alloy frame. *Modern*	325	600	750
Combat Commander variation, with steel frame. *Modern*	400	600	750
Mark IV/80 Combat Commander, 9mm Luger, .45ACP. *Modern*	375	600	750
Government Model Mark IV/80, .380; 7-shot magazine. *Modern*	225	450	700
Government Model Mark IV/ 80 Combat, .380; 7-shot magazine; light weight. *Modern*	225	450	600
Woodsman Automatic Target Pistol, .22 long rifle; 10-shot magazine; 4½" and 6½" barrels; total made through 1932, approximately 84,000; from 1 on up; from 1915. Sport and Target Models made from 1943. Original Woodsman series obsolete after serial range 157000 (1943). *Modern*	$275	$500	$850
Pre-Woodsman Add. 25%			
4½" barrel add. 25%			
Spl. sights Add. 10%			
Woodsman Target and Sport Model, .22 long rifle; 10-shot magazine; 4½" and 6½"; (later 6"; Target Model) barrels; 35,000 Sport and 38,000 Target pistols from 1932 through 1943, serial numbers from 1-S on up, to 241811-S; approximately 90,000 Sport and 90,000 Target pistols from 1947 through 1970. Postwar pistols identified by S suffix; new series begun 1969, 001001-S on up. *Modern*	300	550	850
4½" Barrel add. 25%			
S suffix subtract 25%			
First Model Match Target Woodsman, .22 long rifle; 10-shot magazine; 6½" heavy target barrel; from 1938 to 1942, 15,100 made; serials with MT prefix, from MT-1 on up. *Modern*	750	1600	1850
Second and Third Model Match Target Woodsman, .22 long rifle; 10-shot magazine; 4½" and 6½" barrels; from 1948 into 1970s more than 100,000 made; S-suffix in range begun 1947, shared with postwar Sport and Target Model pistols. *Modern*	225	650	800
4½" barrel add 20%			
Challenger and Huntsman Models, .22 long rifle; 10-shot magazine; 4½" and 6" barrels; total of Challenger (1950–55) at 77,143, numbering began with 1-C; total of Huntsman (c. 1955 into 1970s) more than 70,000, numbering continued C suffix series, with 90001-C. *Modern*	225	375	600
4½" barrel add 10%			
Woodsman Targetsman Model, .22 long rifle; 10-shot magazine; 6" barrel; made from 1959, with serial range 129300-C; total made into early 1970s in excess of 40,000. *Modern*	225	475	650

Fair V. Good Excellent

CARTRIDGE LONGARMS

Berdan Military Rifle and Carbine, .42 caliber bottle necked c.f.; single shot; 32½" (rifle) and 14¼" (carbine) barrel lengths; approximately 30,000 made, from 1 on up; c. 1866–70.

Russian marked military rifles, approximately 30,000 made. *Antique* $275 $900 $1350

Russian marked carbines, approximately not more than 25 made. *Antique* 2650 5500 7500

Carbines marked with Colt and Hartford, Connecticut address, not more than 25 made. *Antique* 3250 6000 8500

Military rifles marked with Colt, Hartford, not more than 100. *Antique* 2250 3750 4660

Custom-made Target Rifles on the Berdan action, not more than 30 (three models, 1st, 2nd and 3rd type), *Antique* 3750 7750 10000

Colt-Laidley Military Rifle, single shot rolling block breechloading rifle; .45 c.f. and .50 c.f., 25 of each caliber; c. 1867. *Antique* 2250 4250 5500

Colt-Franklin Military Rifle, .45-70 caliber; 9-shot gravity feed magazine; 32½" barrel; bolt action; approximately 50 made; c. 1887–88. *Antique* 3250 6750 8500

Model 1878 Double Barrel Hammer Shotgun, 10 and 12 gauge; 28", 30" and 32" standard barrel lengths (known lengths from 18" to 34"); 22,683 made, from 1 on up; c. 1878–89.

Standard model, with moderate embellishments and checkered stocks. *Antique* 750 1600 2250

Better-grade guns, panel scene engraving; higher grade stockwork and checkering. *Antique* 925 2950 3500

Model 1878 Double Barrel Sporting Rifle, .45-70, .45-85 Express, .45-90 and .45-100 calibers; approximately 40 made, serial numbers from 1 on up, and nos. 293 and 397 from Model 1878 shotgun range; c. 1879–85 (appear to be special order only). *Antique* 7500 17500 25000

Fair V. Good Excellent

Model 1883 Double Barrel Shotgun, 8, 10 and 12 gauge; standard barrel lengths 28", 30" and 32" (known lengths from 18" to 36"); approximately 7366 made, from 1 on up, with gap from 3056-4057; c. 1883–95.
8 ga. add 25%
34" and 36" barrels add 10%

Standard model, moderate embellishments and checkered stocks. *Antique* $650 $1750 $2250

Better-grade guns, panel scene engraving; higher grade stockwork and checkering. *Antique* 1000 2850 5500

Colt-Burgess Lever Action Rifle, .44-40 caliber; 25½" (rifle) and 20" (carbine) barrels; 6403 made, from 1 on up; c. 1883–85. *Antique* . 1200 3200 6500

LIGHTNING SLIDE ACTION MAGAZINE RIFLES

Medium Frame Model, .32-20, .38-40, and .44-40 calibers; 20" (carbine) and 26" (rifle) barrels, with some variations; shortest from 8" to longest of 34"; 89,777 made, from 1884–1902.
Spl. barrel length add. 20%

Standard rifle, 1883 patent dates on barrel; lacks cover on top of breech. *Antique* 550 1250 2250

Standard rifle, with 1883, '85, '86 and '87 patent date markings; and sliding cover on top of breech. *Antique* 450 1150 1650

Carbine, .44-40. *Antique* 750 2000 3000

Baby Carbine, 5¼ lbs. weight, with special lightweight barrel. *Antique* 950 2250 4000

Military Rifle or Carbine, .44-40; with bayonet lug and sling swivel. *Antique* 1100 2750 4500

San Francisco Police Department Rifles, .44-40; markings of SFP 1 to SFP 401, on lower tang; blued finish. *Antique* 525 2000 2500

Small Frame Model, .22 short and long rifle; 24" barrel length standard lengths known from 9½" to 26"; total 89,912 made, serials from 1 on up; c. 1887/1904. *Antique* 425 850 1250

Large Frame or Express Model, .38-56, .40-60, .45-60, .45-65, .45-85 and .50-95 Express; 22" (carbine) and 28" (rifle) barrels; variations from 22" to 36" standard length for .50-95 Express; total 6,496 made, from 1 on up; c. 1887–94.
50 cal. add 15%
Spl. barrel length add 10%

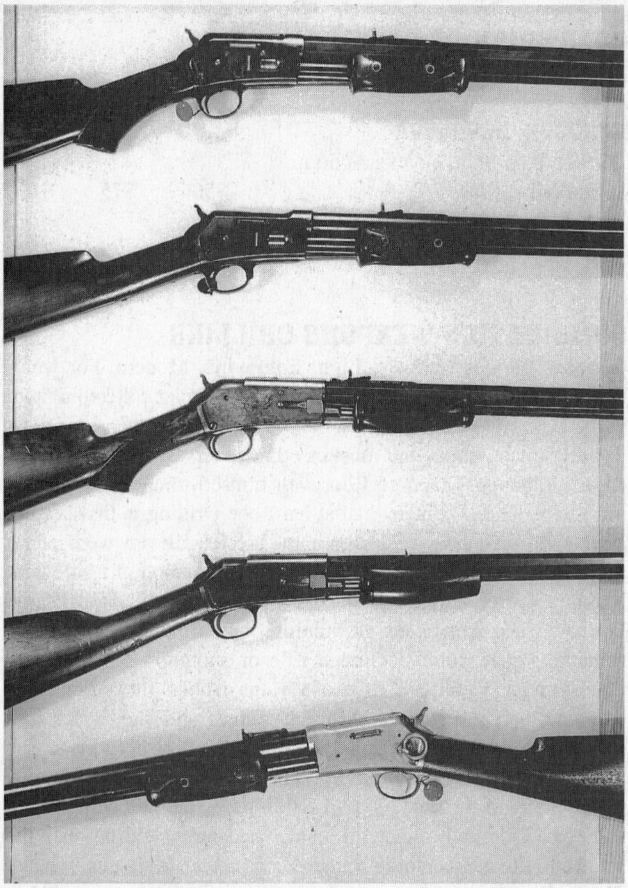

Medium and small frame Colt Lightning slide action rifles; from the top, *deluxe medium frame with semi-pistol grip stock; standard model with plain stocks; two .22 rimfire rifles (small frame) in deluxe and standard stock versions; and a medium frame Saddle Ring carbine.*

	Fair	*V. Good*	*Excellent*
Standard Rifle, round or octagonal barrel. *Antique*	$2000	$5250	$7500
Carbine, weight 9 lbs. *Antique*	2200	5750	8500
Baby Carbine, lightweight barrel; weight 8 lbs. *Antique*	2500	6750	9500
Colt '57" Bolt Action Sporting Rifle, .30-06 and .243 calibers, with FN Mauser actions; serial nos. from 1 on up; approximately 5,000 made, in 1957. *Modern*	300	550	750
Coltsman Bolt Action Rifle, Standard, Deluxe and Custom grades, .30-06, .300 Magnum, .243, and .308 calibers, with Sako and FN actions; approximately 10,000 made (including the Standard and Custom rifles of 1963–65); 1958–62. *Modern*	350	600	800

	Fair	*V. Good*	*Excellent*
Coltsman Bolt Action Rifle, Standard and Custom grades, .223, .243, .308, .264, and .30-06 calibers; with Sako actions; approximately 10,000 made (including Standard, Deluxe and Custom grades made 1958–62); 1963–65; premium for Custom grade. *Modern*	$350	$600	$850
Colt Sauer Bolt Action Sporting Rifle, Grand African, .458 Magnum; box magazine. *Modern*	500	700	1000
Colt Sauer Bolt Action Sporting Rifle, Grand Alaskan, .375 H & H Magnum; box magazine. *Modern*	400	900	1750
Colteer 1-22 Bolt Action Rifle, .22 short, long, long rifle and .22 magnum; single shot; 20" and 22" barrels; made without serial numbers; approximately 25,000 made, c. 1957–66. *Modern*	75	150	250
Colteer, Stagecoach and Courier .22 Autoloader Rifles, .22 long rifle; over 85,000 made in total of the three models; c. 1964–early 1970s. Colteer; 15 shots, with 19 3/8" barrel; over 50,000 made. *Modern*	100	250	350
Stagecoach, 13 shots; with 16 1/2" barrel; over 25,000 made, from 1965. *Modern*	150	250	400
Courier, made from 1970. *Modern*	100	250	350

AR-15 Self-loading Sporter Rifle, .223 (5.56mm) caliber; 21" barrel with flash supressor; serial numbers from SP0001 on up; c. 1964 to present; over 100,000 made.

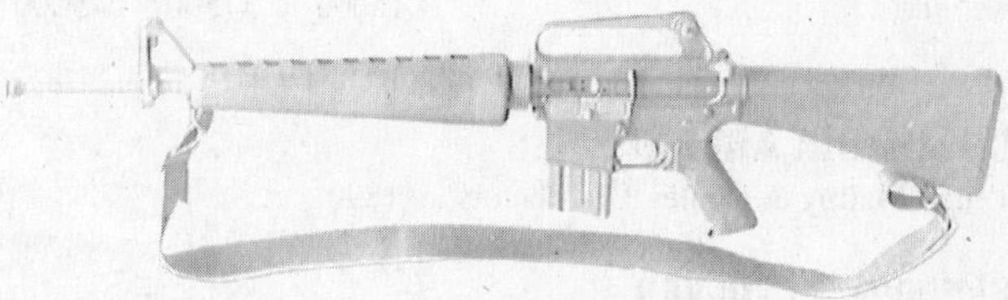

Colt AR- 15

Early model with bayonet lug add 10%

	Fair	*V. Good*	*Excellent*
Standard Self-loading Rifle configuration, early model with smooth composition stocks. *Modern*	750	1750	2500
Later version, with ribbed forend; standard barrel length. *Modern*	750	1250	2000
Carbine Variation, with ribbed forend. *Modern*	750	1350	2500

	Fair	V. Good	Excellent
Pump Shotgun, 12, 16 and 20 gauges; 3-shot tubular magazine; 26" and 28" barrels; various chokes; total of approximately 2,000; serial numbers from supplier's range, vary from as low as 15000 to as high as 105000 (most within range 60000 to 62600, or higher; c. 1961–65. *Modern*	$100	$250	$450
Self-loading Shotgun, 12 and 20 gauges; 4-shot tubular magazine; 26", 28", 30" and 32" barrels; 5,293 made, numbered in unusual ranges, with C0 prefix; c. 1962–66. *Modern*	150	250	450
Double Barrel Shotgun, 12, 12 magnum and 16 gauges; 26", 28" and 30" barrels; 25 to 50 made, in range 47000 to 469000; c. 1961–62. *Modern*	250	450	950
Colt-Sharps Single Shot Falling Block Sporting Rifle, .17, .22-250 Remington, .243 Winchester, .25.06 Remington, 7mm Remington Magnum, .30-06 Springfield, .375 H & H Magnum; 25", 26" and 28" barrels; approximately 500 made, from 1 on up (CS prefix to numbers); c. 1970 into early 1970s. *Modern*	750	1250	1950
Gatling Gun, crank-operated mechanical repeating firearm, with box and Accles feed magazines; made in a variety of calibers from .30 to 1". See Gatling Gun Co. for historical information. Values vary somewhat, based on popularity of calibers, markings, presence of original carriage, mounts, and accessories, and condition. Approximate value range. *Antique*	15000	37500	75000

COLUMBIA ARMORY

Tenn., Maltby & Henley Distributors, c. 1890.

HANDGUN, REVOLVER

	Fair	V. Good	Excellent
New Safety, .22 L.R.R.F., 7 Shot, Double Action, Solid Frame, Grip Safety, *Modern*	75	100	125
New Safety, .32 S & W, 5 Shot, Double Action, Solid Frame, Grip Safety, *Modern*	75	100	125
New Safety, .38 S & W, 5 Shot, Double Action, Solid Frame, Grip Safety, *Modern*	100	125	150

COLUMBIAN

Made by Foehl & Weeks, Philadelphia, Pa., c. 1890.

HANDGUN, REVOLVER

	Fair	V. Good	Excellent
.32 S & W, 5 Shot, Double Action, Solid Frame, *Curio*	$50	$75	$100
.38 S & W, 5 Shot, Double Action, Solid Frame, *Curio*	50	75	100

COMBINATION WEAPONS DRILLING

German, Various Calibers, Light Engraving, Modern. For whatever reason, Drillings have never proven a popular collectors' item in the U.S. The author has seen many of these over the years, most wanting in condition, and most of odd calibers by American standards. Although Theodore Roosevelt himself, one of the world's most experienced hunters, had at least one Drilling in his sporting arsenal, the type never caught on in the U.S. Hardly any were manufactured by American gunmakers. The combination of a rifle with a double-barrel shotgun made the weapon generally too heavy. Further, when Americans go hunting, they are either going after something that would require a rifle or shotgun—but not both. Therefore one would buy rifles of various calibers for certain types of game, and shotguns of different gauges and chokes for bird shooting—and not buy a gun that could take birdshot in two barrels and rifle bullets in the third. The author has shot in Europe, where many of the hunters used Drillings. Even then he preferred to have a rifle and a shotgun handy, and rarely did he miss the chance to fire at something because he had the wrong gun in hand. The Drilling is, therefore, mainly of interest to Europeans, and has yet to capture the collecting imagination of Americans.

COMET

HANDGUN, REVOLVER

	Fair	V. Good	Excellent
.32 Long R.F., 7 Shot, Single Action, Spur Trigger, Solid Frame, *Antique*	35	75	150

COMINAZZO OR COMINAZZI

Family of Armorers in Brescia, Italy, from c. 1593 to c. 1875. Barrels by this distinguished dynasty of Brescian gunmakers were instrumental in earning a deserved worldwide reputation for quality, continued today by such august gunmakers as Beretta, Rizzini, and Fabbri. The author visited the palazzo of Brescian industrialist Luigi Marzolli in 1960, and was proudly shown glass display cases filled with Brescian steel-mounted wheellock, miquelet, and flintlock pistols, many of them with barrels marked Cominazzo or Cominazzi. Marzolli was so proud of his collection that on his death a number of the pieces, including miscellaneous arms and armor (primarily Italian) became a special display of the city of Brescia, where they were installed in the Castle overlooking the city. These barrels were respected for accuracy, sturdiness, reliability, and beauty. Some of the most exquisite Brescian, steel-mounted firearms are featured in the Arms and Armor galleries of the Metropolitan Museum of Art, as well as certain of the European and British museums featuring arms and armor.

	Fair	V. Good	Excellent
HANDGUN, FLINTLOCK			
.54, Mid-1600s, Belt Pistol, Brass Furniture, Ornate, *Antique*	$2000	$4150	$6000
HANDGUN, WHEEL LOCK			
Ebony Full Stock, Ivory Pom, Holster Pistol, German Style, Military, Engraved, *Antique*	2000	5000	7500

COMMANDER

	Fair	V. Good	Excellent
HANDGUN, REVOLVER			
.32 Long R.F., 7 Shot, Single Action, Spur Trigger, Solid Frame, *Antique*	50	100	150

COMMANDO ARMS

Made by Volunteer Enterprises in Knoxville, Tenn., since 1969. Company name changed to Commando Arms in 1978.

	Fair	V. Good	Excellent
RIFLE, SELF-LOADING			
Commando MK III, .45 ACP, Clip Fed, Horizontal Fore end, with Compensator, Carbine, *Modern* ...	100	225	275
Commando MK III, .45 ACP, Clip Fed, Vertical Fore end, with Compensator, Carbine, *Modern* ...	100	250	325
Commando MK 9, 9mm Luger, Clip Fed, Horizontal Fore end, with Compensator, Carbine, *Modern* ...	100	225	300
Commando MK 9, 9mm Luger, Clip Fed, Vertical Fore end, with Compensator, Carbine, *Modern* ...	100	250	325
Commando MK 45, .45 ACP, Clip Fed, Horizontal Fore end, with Compensator, Carbine, *Modern* ...	100	225	300
Commando MK 45, .45 ACP, Clip Fed, Vertical Fore end, with Compensator, Carbine, *Modern* ...	100	250	325

COMMERCIAL

See Smith, Otis A.

COMPEER

Made by Crescent for Van Camp Hardware, c. 1900. See Crescent Fire Arms Co., Shotgun, Double Barrel, Side-by-Side; Shotgun, Singleshot.

CONE, D.D.

Washington, D.C., c. 1865.

	Fair	V. Good	Excellent
HANDGUN, REVOLVER			
.22 Long R.F., 7 Shot, Single Action, Spur Trigger, Solid Frame, *Antique*	75	125	200
.32 Long R.F., 6 Shot, Single Action, Spur Trigger, Solid Frame, *Antique*	$75	$150	$225

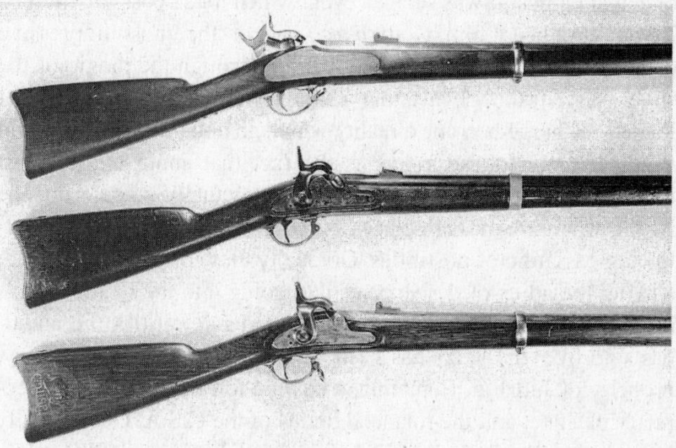

From top, *a Lindsay two-shot single-barrel Musket in .58 caliber; a Confederate rifled Musket of the Model 1861 style, .58 caliber, with brass trim, the lock marked* Fayetteville, *with an eagle and C.S.A., 1862; and a .58 caliber U.S. rifled Musket by Providence Tool Co., dated 1864.*

CONFEDERATE MILITARY

One of the most dramatic and important sagas of the Confederate States of America was her desperate struggle at supplying adequate ordnance. The Union's adeptness at creating and manufacturing firearms and ammunition was a major reason for its victory. The Confederacy was able to capture large quantities of firearms and ammunition, as well as heavy ordnance, but keeping these arms in repair and supplying backup in terms of ammunition, percussion caps, and accessories was a struggle. The Civil War collecting craze really gathered steam during the centennial years—1961–65. Collecting was particularly challenging then and remains so for those whose interests center on C.S.A. arms. During the centennial years an inordinate amount of faking took place since the use of a simple stamp, like C.S.A., was enough to place an otherwise common piece into the world of scarcity. The collector in the area of Confederate arms must, therefore, apply great caution and truly become an expert—or have the availability of competent expertise. A trip to the Confederate Museum and the White House of the Confederacy in Richmond will not only help in the learning process but provide more than enough inspiration for the enjoyment of one of the most fascinating of all areas in the arms collecting world. To actually see such vital artifacts as firearms carried by heroic military figures the likes of Robert E. Lee, John Singleton Mosby, J. E. B. Stuart, and Albert Sydney Johnston is no less than thrilling. Viewing the beautifully filmed Ken Burns documentary, *The Civil War,* adds greatly to an understanding of the enormity and passion of the conflict itself. Further, visiting such historical places as Civil War battlefield sites (particularly Gettysburg), the Harpers Ferry Armory National Historic Site, and the McLean House (the Appomattox Court House Historic Site, where Lee surrendered to Grant) will add to an understanding of this complex, far-reaching, and traumatic period in American history. Some of the museum and battlefield sites can help in an appreciation of Confederate weaponry by permitting an opportunity to view original examples. Further, demonstrations are now often held at these sites, with uniformed participants firing guns and often cannon. And in some cases, reenactments are held of actual battles. It was such an event which made possible the Ted Turner–produced film *Gettysburg,* one of the most impressive dramatizations ever done of any battle. Through the magic of the silver screen the devastating cannon fire and the tragedy of Pickett's Charge become a reality which no book or painting could ever capture. Not surprising is the fact that some of the most remarkable of C.S.A. arms and artifacts actually come from the North, where many such pieces were taken as trophies of war following cessation of hostilities. Gradually these original rarities are leaving the attics of descendants and going into the hands of collectors and museums. Among the Confederate rarities the author has sold over the years has been an inscribed Model 1851 Navy, property of Judah P. Benjamin, a key aid to President Davis, Secretary of State, and the financial brains of the C.S.A. Occasionally he has researched a Colt Model 1860 Army having a Southern history: Samuel Colt kept shipping arms into the South until the beginning of hostilities in April 1861. These scarce and highly desirable firearms bring a premium, and shipping records actually give such Southern destinations as Richmond, Virginia. Colt was sympathetic to the South and had a number of friends who became officers of the C.S.A. or served in other official capacities. Among those to whom he had presented firearms were Johnston, Governor Moore of Alabama, and Jefferson Davis himself. However, by far the bulk of Civil War material that he has seen and handled over the years has been Union-oriented, a reflection of the rarity of C.S.A. arms and artifacts.

HANDGUN, PERCUSSION

	Fair	V. Good	Excellent
.36 Columbus, Revolver, Brass Trigger Guard, 6 Shot, *Antique*			Rare
.36 Dance Box, Revolver, Iron Frame, 6 Shot, *Antique*			Rare
.36 Griswold & Gunnison, Revolver, Brass Frame, 6 Shot, Serial No. is the Only Marking, *Antique*			Rare
.36 Leech & Co., Revolver, Brass Grip Frame, 6 Shot, *Antique*			Rare
.36 Leech & Rigdon, Revolver, Brass Grip Frame, 6 Shot, *Antique*			Rare
.36 Rigdon & Ansley, Revolver, Brass Grip Frame, 6 Shot, *Antique*			Rare
.36 Shawk & McLanahan, Revolver, Brass Frame, 6 Shot, *Antique*			Rare
.36 Spiller & Burr, Revolver, Brass Frame, 6 Shot, *Antique*			Rare
.36 T.W. Cofer, Revolver, Brass Frame, 6 Shot, *Antique*			Rare
.44 Dance Bros., Revolver, Brass Grip Frame, 6 Shot, *Antique*			Rare
.44 Tucker & Sherrod, Revolver, Copy of Colt Dragoon, serial number is the only marking, *Antique*			Rare
.54 J. and F. Garrett, Singleshot, Brass Barrel, Converted from Flintlock, *Antique*	$1000	$3000	$4250
.54 Palmetto, Singleshot, Brass Furniture, *Antique*			Rare
.58 Fayetteville, Singleshot, Rifled, *Antique*			Rare
.58 Fayetteville, Singleshot, Rifled, with Shoulder Stock, *Antique*			Rare

RIFLE, PERCUSSION

	Fair	V. Good	Excellent
.52, "P," Tallahassee, Breech Loader, Carbine, *Antique*			Rare
.52, Tarpley, Breech Loader, Carbine, Brass Breech, *Antique*			Rare

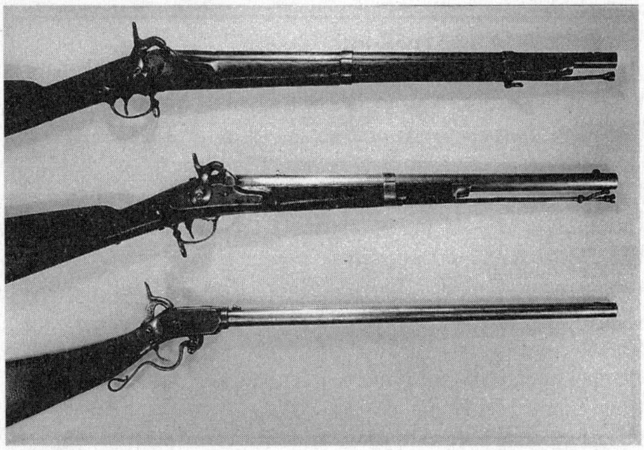

From the top, Confederate percussion carbine marked Richmond Va. 1864, *.58 caliber; with a Model 1854–type Confederate carbine marked* C.S.A. *and* P; *and a Confederate carbine, looking very much like a Maynard, but with brass frame; .52 caliber.*

	Fair	V. Good	Excellent
.54, L.G. Sturdivant, Brass Furniture, Rifled, Serial No. is the Only Marking, *Antique*			Rare
.54, Wytheville-Hall, Muzzle Loader, Rifled, Brass Frame, *Antique*			Rare
.57, Tyler, Texas Enfield, Brass Furniture, *Antique*			Rare
.58, Cook & Brother, Artillery Carbine, Brass Furniture, Military, *Antique*			Rare
.58, Cook & Brother, Infantry Type, Brass Furniture, Military, *Antique*			Rare
.58, Cook & Brother, Musketoon, Brass Furniture, Military, *Antique*			Rare
.58, D.C., Hodgkins & Co., Iron Mounts, Rifled, Carbine, *Antique*			Rare
.58, Dickson, Nelson & Co., Military, Carbine, *Antique*			Rare
.58, Dickson, Nelson & Co., Military, Rifle, *Antique*			Rare

	Fair	V. Good	Excellent
.58, Fayetteville, Brass Furniture, 2 Bands, Rifled, *Antique*			Rare
.58, Georgia, Brass Furniture, Rifled, *Antique*			Rare
.58, H.C. Lamb & Co., Brass Furniture, 2 Bands, Rifled, *Antique*			Rare
.58, Palmetto, "Mississippi" Rifle, *Antique*			Rare
.58, Richmond, Carbine, *Antique*			Rare
.58, Richmond, Musket, Rifled, *Antique*			Rare
.58, Tallahassee, Carbine, Brass Furniture, 2 Bands, *Antique*			Rare
.58, Whitney, U.S. Contract 1861, Rifle, Musket, *Antique*			Rare
.62, Richmond Navy, Musketoon, Smoothbore, *Antique*			Rare
.69, Prussian Musket, Brass Furniture, Military, *Antique*			Rare
.69, Whitney, Model 1861, Rifled, Brass Furniture, *Antique*			Rare

RIFLE, SINGLESHOT

.50, Morse, Musket, Breech Loader, *Antique*			Rare
.58, S.C. Robinson, Model 1861, Brass Furniture, Breech Loader, Carbine, Imitation Sharps, *Antique*			Rare
.71, Morse, Carbine, Breech Loader, *Antique*			Rare

CONN. ARMS & MFG. CO.

Naubuc, Conn., 1863–1869. The Hammond Bulldog was a well-built, relatively hard-hitting handgun, with but one drawback: it was a singleshot only, and therefore was no competition in terms of firepower with arms like the Colt 1860 Army or the mammoth Colt Dragoons. A legitimate Civil War handgun, though none was issued to troops; a foot soldier might well have one as a backup piece. The mechanism was simple, and the design is reflected by the Bulldog name. This arm is one that will often turn up in excellent condition, suggesting that relatively few were ever put to service use. If found in the original pasteboard box, add a premium of 25 percent.

HANDGUN, SINGLESHOT

	Fair	V. Good	Excellent
Hammond Patent Bull-Dozer, .44 R.F., Pivoting Breechblock, Hammer, Spur Trigger, *Antique*	$125	$225	$350
Hammond Patent Bulldog, .44 R.F., Pivoting Breechblock, Hammer, Spur Trigger, *Antique*	100	200	325
Hammond Patent Bulldog, .44 R.F., Pivoting Breechblock, Hammer, Spur Trigger, Very Long Barrel, *Antique*	150	300	450

CONN. ARMS CO.

Norfolk, Conn. 1862–1869.

HANDGUN, REVOLVER

	Fair	V. Good	Excellent
Wood's Patent, .28 T.F., Tip-Up Barrel, 6 Shot, Spur Trigger, *Antique*	$75	$175	$325

CONNECTICUT SHOTGUN MFG. CO.,

New Britain, Connecticut. See also A. H. Fox Gun Co. Founded by Tony Galazan, accomplished dealer and expert in best-quality sporting arms, Connecticut Shotgun Mfg. Co. specializes in producing the highest grade of over-and-under and side-by-side shotguns, with the top of their line a Fabbri look-alike, also influenced by Boss & Co. styling. Priced competitively, the design and workmanship is on a par with any sporting gun in the world today, and a visit to the workshop reminds one of Old World European standards of excellence. Without taking a nickel of aid or a moment of time from the State of Connecticut, Galazan has created a Mecca for the connoisseur of fine guns, in a state that was known for years as a trasher of industrial companies, through high taxes and truly idiotic politics.

A.H. FOX SHOTGUN PRICES* & EXTRAS FITTED TO NEW GUNS - AUGUST 1999

Gauges Available: 16, 20, 28 & .410	CE Grade	XE Grade	DE Grade	FE Grade	Exhibition
Standard Gun Prices	$ 11,000	$12,500	$15,000	$20,000	$30,000
Add for 28 & .410 Gauge Guns	1,500	1,500	1,500	$1,500	—
Selective Single Trigger	1,200	1,200	1,200	$1,200	—
Beavertail Forend	650	650	—	—	—
Krupp Steel Barrels	200	200	200	200	—
Turkish Circassian Walnut Upgrades:					
Two Star	300	—	—	—	—
Three Star	600	400	—	—	—
Four Star	1,100	900	600	—	—
Exhibition	2,200	2,000	1,700	1,500	—
Butt: Checkered	250	250	—	—	—
Skeleton	650	650	650	650	—
Heel & Toe Plates	650	650	650	650	—
Leather Covered Pad	350	350	—	—	—
Extra Set of Barrels & Forend:					
Multi Gauge Set	5,600	6,100	6,600	7,500	8,200
Same Gauge Set	4,500	4,800	5,300	6,000	6,500
Custom Initials:					
Engraved on Trigger Guard	200	200	200	—	—
Gold Inlay on Trigger Guard	250	250	250	—	—
Gold Stock Shield or Oval	350	350	350	—	—
Signature Gold Inlay on Trigger Guard	500	500	500	—	—
Gold Inlay on Barrels "*Made for* [your name]"	500	500	500	—	—
Best Traditional Trunk Case with Accessories	850	850	850	—	—

*Does not include state or local sales tax, if applicable.

Call us for a quote on custom engraving, gold inlay work or if you wish to order a Monte Carlo Stock or Cheek Piece

To order an A. H. Fox gun, complete the Order Blank, including the gauge of gun ordered, and send it to us along with a fifty percent deposit. We will confirm the receipt of your deposit, the configuration of your gun, its anticipated delivery date and price. You will be notified three weeks prior to completion of your gun, which will be shipped when we receive your final payment.

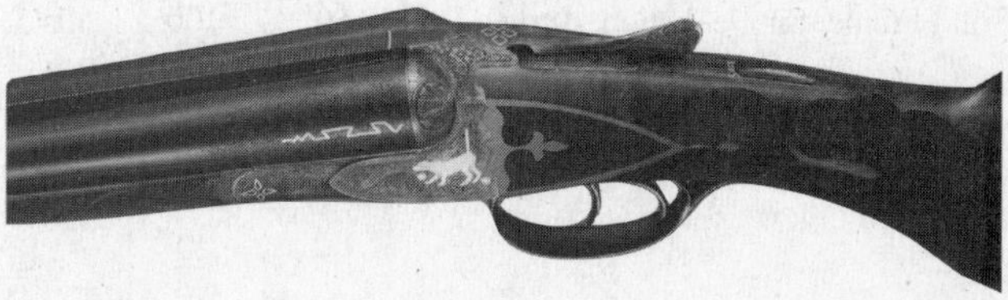

The A. Galazan Over and Under Full Sidelock Double Barrel Shotgun. Shipments were initiated in the fall of 1994, with the first guns limited to 20 and 28 gauge guns, each built to customer specifications. Design characteristics of the A. Galazan features a gun "with the lowest possible profile, best mechanical design, and a distinctly English looking forend." Delivery is with English blued barrels and case-hardened colors or a polished action, forend metal and triggerguard, with traditional bluing on the balance of metal parts. Competition or sporting models were later added, in 12, 16, 20, 28, or .410 gauges. Guns are custom-made, with standard details such as traditional rose and scroll hand engraving, walnut stocks of best quality Turkish circassian walnut, single nonselective trigger, nonautomatic safety, choice of stock and butt style, barrel length, engraving or gold inlaid signature or initials, and gun weight. Among optional features are best quality oak and leather trunk cases with accessories, extra sets of barrels, and custom engraving. Specially built leather casings are also being developed exclusively for Galazan.

Manufacture of the guns is entirely in the United States, at the Galazan shop in New Britain, Connecticut. Receiver, forend metal, sidelock plates, and all other metal parts are machined in house, from solid forgings. All the polishing, fitting, and finishing of the A. Galazan is done manually, by master gunsmiths. More than 1,000 man hours are required to complete a single gun. While the A. Galazan is made in the United States, a number of these guns are engraved in Italy, by some of the world's finest artisans. Distinguished engravers from other countries are also available with special arrangements. Base price for the A. Galazan gun is $38,000.

CONQUERER

Made by Bacon Arms Co., c. 1880.

HANDGUN, REVOLVER

	Fair	V. Good	Excellent
.22 Short R.F., 7 Shot, Spur Trigger, Solid Frame, Single Action, *Antique*	$50	$100	$175
.32 Short R.F., 5 Shot, Spur Trigger, Solid Frame, Single Action, *Antique*	50	100	175

CONSTABLE, RICHARD

Philadelphia, Pa., 1817–1851.

HANDGUN, PERCUSSION

	Fair	V. Good	Excellent
Dueling Pistols, Cased Pair, with Accessories, *Antique*	$1200	$3000	$6500

RIFLE, PERCUSSION

	Fair	V. Good	Excellent
.44, Octagon Barrel, Brass Furniture, *Antique*	700	1500	1900

CONTENTO

See Ventura Imports.

CONTINENTAL

Made by Hood Firearms Co., successors to Continental Arms Co.; Sold by Marshall Wells Co., Duluth, Minn., c. 1870.

HANDGUN, REVOLVER

	Fair	V. Good	Excellent
.22 Short R.F., 7 Shot, Spur Trigger, Solid Frame, Single Action, *Antique*	50	100	175
.32 Short R.F., 5 Shot, Spur Trigger, Solid Frame, Single Action, *Antique*	50	100	175

CONTINENTAL

Made by Jules Bertrand, Liège, Belgium, c. 1910.

HANDGUN, SELF-LOADING

	Fair	V. Good	Excellent
Pocket, .25 ACP, Clip Fed, *Curio*	100	175	250

CONTINENTAL

Made by Stevens Arms.

RIFLE, BOLT ACTION

	Fair	V. Good	Excellent
Model 52, .22 L.R.R.F., Singleshot, Takedown, *Modern*	25	50	75

SHOTGUN, DOUBLE BARREL, SIDE-BY-SIDE

	Fair	V. Good	Excellent
Model 215, 12 and 16 Gauges, Outside Hammers, Steel Barrel, *Modern*	50	100	175
Model 311, Various Gauges, Hammerless, Steel Barrel, *Modern*	65	125	200
Model 315, Various Gauges, Hammerless, Steel Barrel, *Modern*	75	125	175

SHOTGUN, SINGLESHOT

	Fair	V. Good	Excellent
Model 90, Various Gauges, Takedown, Automatic Ejector, Plain Hammer, *Modern*	25	50	75

CONTINENTAL

Rheinische Waffen u. Munitionsfabrik. Cologne, Germany.

	Fair	V. Good	Excellent
HANDGUN, SELF-LOADING			
.25 ACP, Clip Fed, Blue, *Curio*	$75	$150	$225
.32 ACP, Clip Fed, Webley Copy, Blue, *Curio*	125	200	275

CONTINENTAL ARMS CO.

Norwich, Conn., 1866–1867.

HANDGUN, PEPPERBOX			
Continental 1, .22 R.F., 7 Shot, Spur Trigger, Solid Frame, *Antique*	200	450	600
Continental 2, .32 R.F., 5 Shot, Spur Trigger, Solid Frame, *Antique*	250	525	650

CONTINENTAL ARMS CO.,

New York City. Founded by the brothers Joe and Ted Tonkin, and located at a site on exclusive Fifth Avenue, Continental Arms ordered double rifles and fine side-by-side and over-and-under shotguns for a discriminating clientele—among them Prince Abdul Reza of Iran, President Dwight D. Eisenhower, and the first violinist of the Berlin Philharmonic Orchestra. The author met both Joe and Ted, and made a habit of visiting their walnut-paneled showroom while on trips to New York City. Ted died trying to fight back a robber in a theft in their fourth-floor emporium, while Joe's gun failed to fire. Joe carried on for years, finally retiring early in the 1990s when he was into his 80s. Both Ted and Joe were charming gentlemen of the old school, with Ted the arms expert and buyer and Joe the businessman. You never knew who you would encounter in the store, and the author was interviewed there for the BBC-TV by English broadcaster, critic, and columnist Bernard Levin. The piece was for a television program based on Levin's book *A Walk Down Fifth Avenue.* Considering the antigun bias of the British press, the segment in the book was quite flattering, to some extent the result of the author having brought along a rather stunning Colt Third Model Dragoon revolver decorated by Tiffany & Co., described by Levin as "absolutely beautiful."

COONAN ARMS, INC.

St. Paul, Minn., since 1982.

HANDGUN, SELF-LOADING			
Comp. 1, .357 Magnum, Standard Production Model, Stainless Steel, Clip Fed, Adjustable Sights, *Modern*	300	900	1050
Model A, .357 Magnum, Single Action, Stainless, *Modern*	250	550	700
Model B, .357 Magnum, Pre-Production Model, Serial Numbers under 1000, Stainless Steel, Clip Fed, Adjustable Sights, *Modern*	175	550	700

COOPER FIREARMS MFG. CO.

Philadelphia, Pa., 1851–1869. This cleverly produced Colt look-alike was basically a double-action copy of the Colt Model 1849 Pocket. Philadelphia was a gunmaking center of no little skill and ingenuity. Among prominent gunmakers, the city also boasted, for a while at least, the Sharps company, and had prominent dealers the likes of J. C. Grubb & Co., E. K. Tryon, and Krider. Cooper not only made a fair quantity of Navy and Pocket handguns, the company manufactured a handful of exquisitely embellished and cased pairs. Two such sets were richly engraved, plated in silver, with ivory grips; fitted in velvet-lined, contour-fitted cases of carefully crafted woods.

	Fair	V. Good	Excellent
HANDGUN, PERCUSSION			
Navy, .31, 5 Shots, Double Action, *Antique*	$300	$800	$1250
Pocket, .31, 5 or 6 Shots, Double Action, *Antique*	250	800	1250

C.O.P.

M & N Distributers, Torrance, Calif.

HANDGUN, REPEATER			
Model Mini, .22 L.R.R.F., Four Barrels, Aluminum Frame, Hammerless, Double Action, *Modern*			
Model Mini, .22 W.M.R., Four Barrels, Stainless Steel, Hammerless, Double Action, *Modern*	200	350	400
Model SS-1, .357 Mag., Four Barrels, Stainless Steel, Hammerless, Double Action, *Modern*	125	250	300
HANDGUN, SELF-LOADING			
TP-70 AAI, .22 L.R.R.F., Double Action, Clip Fed, Stainless Steel, Hammer, *Modern*	75	125	175
TP-70 AAI, .25 A.C.P., Double Action, Clip Fed, Stainless Steel, Hammer, Modern	75	125	175

COPELAND, F.

Made by Frank Copeland, Worcester, Mass., 1868–1874.

HANDGUN, REVOLVER			
.22 Short R.F., 7 Shot, Spur Trigger, Solid Frame, Single Action, *Antique*	100	200	250
.32 Short R.F., 5 Shot, Spur Trigger, Solid Frame, Single Action, *Antique*	100	175	225

COQ

Spain, c. 1900.

HANDGUN, SELF-LOADING			
K-25, .25 ACP, Clip Fed, *Modern*	50	75	125

CORNFORTH

London, England, 1725–1760.

HANDGUN, FLINTLOCK

	Fair	V. Good	Excellent
Pair, Belt Pistol, Brass Barrel, Brass Furniture, Plain, *Antique*	$1400	$3500	$5000

COSENS, JAMES

Gunmaker in Ordinary to Charles II, England, late 1600s.

HANDGUN, FLINTLOCK

	Fair	V. Good	Excellent
Pair, Holster Pistol, Silver Furniture, Engraved Silver Inlay, High Quality, *Antique*	4500	11000	18500

COSMI

Made for Abercrombie & Fitch, c. 1960.

SHOTGUN, SELF-LOADING

	Fair	V. Good	Excellent
12 or 20 Gauge, Top Break, Engraved, Checkered Stock, Vent Rib, *Modern*	1200	3000	4000

COSMOPOLITAN ARMS CO.

Hamilton, Ohio, 1860–1865. Also see U.S. Military.

RIFLE, PERCUSSION

	Fair	V. Good	Excellent
.45, Sporting Rifle, *Antique*	600	1200	1500
.50, Carbine, *Antique*	500	1000	1350

COWELS & SMITH

Chicopee Falls, Mass., 1863–1876. Became Cowels & Son in 1871.

HANDGUN, SINGLESHOT

	Fair	V. Good	Excellent
.22 R.F., Side-Swing Barrel, Hammer, Spur Trigger, *Antique*	75	150	225
.30 R.F., Side-Swing Barrel, Hammer, Spur Trigger, *Antique*	75	150	250

COWLES & SON

Cowles & Smith, 1866–1871, Cowles & Son, 1871–1876, in Chicopee Falls, Mass.

HANDGUN, SINGLESHOT

	Fair	V. Good	Excellent
.22 Short R.F., Brass Frame, Side Swing Barrel, *Antique*	100	185	300

CRAFT PRODUCTS

HANDGUN, SELF-LOADING

	Fair	V. Good	Excellent
.25 ACP, Clip Fed, *Modern*	50	75	125

CREEDMORE

Made by Hopkins & Allen, c. 1870.

HANDGUN, REVOLVER

	Fair	V. Good	Excellent
#1, .22 Short R.F., 7 Shot, Spur Trigger, Solid Frame, Single Action, *Antique*	$75	$125	$175

CRESCENT

Made by Norwich Falls Pistol Co., c. 1880.

HANDGUN, REVOLVER

	Fair	V. Good	Excellent
.32 Short R.F, 5 Shot, Spur Trigger, Solid Frame, Single Action, *Antique*	75	125	175

CRESCENT FIRE ARMS CO.

Norwich, Conn., 1892; purchased by H & D Folsom in 1893, and absorbed by Stevens Arms & Tool 1926. Also manufactured single and double barrel shotguns marked with the following tradenames: American Barlock Wonder, American Gun Co., T. Barker, Bellmore Gun Co., Carolina Arms Co., Elgin Arms Co., Empire Arms Co., Enders Oakleaf, Essex, Faultless Goose Gun, F. F. Forbes, Harrison Arms Co., Hartford Arms Co., Hermitage Arms Co., Howard Arms, Interstate Arms Co., Lee Special, Metropolitan, Mississippi Valley Arms Co., Mohawk, National Arms Co., New Rival, New York Arms Co., Not-Nac Mfg. Co., Oxford Arms Co., Peerless, Perfection, Piedmont, Pioneer, Quail, Queen City, Rev-O-Noc, Charles Richter, Rickard Arms, Rummel, Southern, Sportsman, Springfield Arms, Square Deal, State Arms Co., Sterling Arms Co., Sullivan Arms Co., Tiger, U.S. Arms Co., Victor, Victor Special, Virginia Arms Co., Winfield Arms Co., Winoca Arms Co., Wolverine Arms Co., Worthington Arms Co.

SHOTGUN, DOUBLE BARREL, SIDE-BY-SIDE

	Fair	V. Good	Excellent
Various Gauges, Hammerless, Damascus Barrel, *Modern*	50	200	300
Various Gauges, Hammerless, Steel Barrel, Modern	100	225	325
Various Gauges, Outside Hammers, Damascus Barrel, *Modern*	75	175	250
Various Gauges, Outside Hammers, Steel Barrel, *Modern*	100	200	300

SHOTGUN, SINGLESHOT

	Fair	V. Good	Excellent
Various Gauges, Hammer, Steel Barrel, *Modern*	50	75	125

CRIOLLA

Hispano Argentine Automoviles, Buenos Aires, Argentina, c. 1935.

HANDGUN, SELF-LOADING

	Fair	V. Good	Excellent
La Criolla, .22 L.R.R.F., Colt M1911, Ace Copy, Clip Fed, Blue, *Modern*	200	400	500

	Fair	V. Good	Excellent

CROWN JEWEL

Made by Norwich Falls Pistol Co., c. 1880.

HANDGUN, REVOLVER

	Fair	V. Good	Excellent
.32 Short R.F., 5 Shot, Spur Trigger, Solid Frame, Single Action, *Antique*	$75	$125	$200

CRUCELEGUI

Spain, Imported by Mandall Shooting Supplies, Scottsdale, Ariz.

SHOTGUN, DOUBLE BARREL, SIDE-BY-SIDE

	Fair	V. Good	Excellent
Model 150, 12 or 20 Gauges, Outside Hammers, Double Trigger, *Modern*	75	150	200

CRUSO

Made by Stevens Arms.

RIFLE, BOLT ACTION

	Fair	V. Good	Excellent
Model 53, .22 L.R.R.F., Singleshot, Takedown, *Modern*	25	50	75

SHOTGUN, SINGLESHOT

	Fair	V. Good	Excellent
Model 90, Various Gauges, Takedown, Automatic Ejector, Plain Hammer, *Modern*	25	50	75

CUMBERLAND ARMS CO.

Made by Crescent for Hibbard-Spencer Bartlett Co., c. 1900. See Crescent Fire Arms Co., Shotgun, Double Barrel, Side-by-Side; Shotgun, Single Shot.

C.V.A.

(Connecticut Valley Arms), Haddam, Conn; later relocated to Norcross, Ga. The author visited the early factory of Connecticut Valley Arms in Haddam, Connecticut, in the 1970s. The enterprise had been launched by David Silk, formerly with the export department of the Remington Arms Co., and later export manager for Colt. While with these firms he learned of the capabilities of Spanish gunmakers in Eibar for turning out replica arms at reasonable prices. The result was Silk's creation of Connecticut Valley Arms, later C.V.A. Eventually selling the company, it was later moved to Norcross, Georgia.

HANDGUN, FLINTLOCK

	Fair	V. Good	Excellent
.45 Kentucky, Brass Furniture, Reproduction	$25	$50	$100

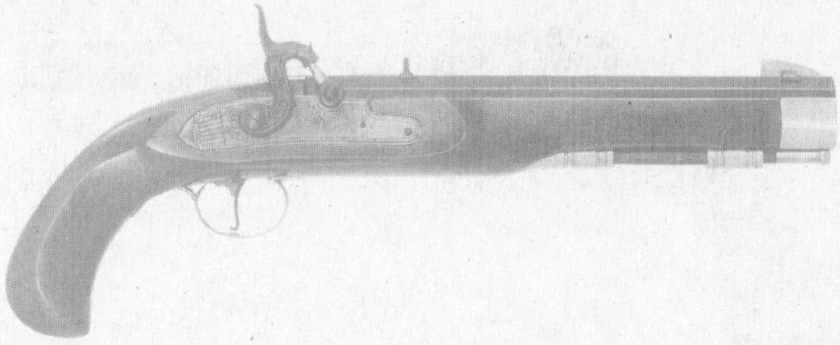

CVA Kentucky Pistol

	Fair	V. Good	Excellent
.50 Hawken, Brass Furniture, Reproduction	35	75	150

HANDGUN, PERCUSSION

	Fair	V. Good	Excellent
.45 Kentucky, Brass Furniture, Reproduction	25	50	100
.45 or .50 Mountain Pistol, Brass Furniture, Reproduction	25	50	125

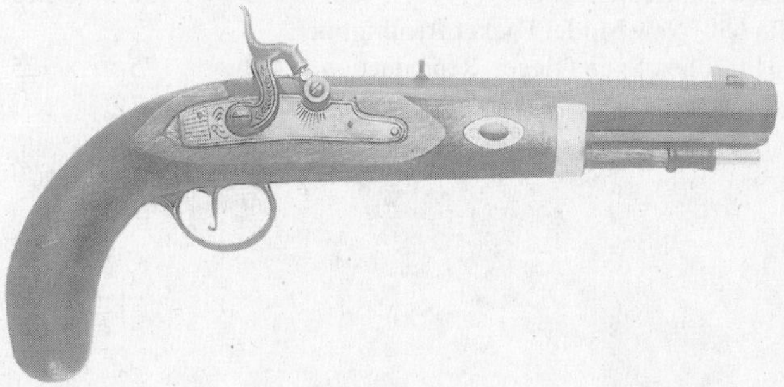

CVA Mountain Pistol

	Fair	V. Good	Excellent
.45 Philadelphia Derringer, Reproduction	15	25	100
.45 Tower Pistol, Brass Furniture, Reproduction	15	25	100
.50 Hawken, Brass Furniture, Set Triggers, Reproduction	25	50	125
.45 Colonial Pistol, Brass Furniture, Reproduction	15	25	75
PP258, Pioneer, .32 Caliber, Octagonal Barrel, Reproduction	50	85	125
PP640, Prospector, .44 Caliber, Singleshot, Reproduction	50	75	125

HANDGUN, REVOLVER

	Fair	V. Good	Excellent
RV 630, 1858 Remington Army, .44 Caliber, One Piece Frame, Reproduction	$75	$150	$200

CVA Prospector Pistol

	Fair	V. Good	Excellent
RV 632, 1858 Remington Army, .44 Caliber, Brass Frame, Reproduction	50	125	175
RV600, 1851 Colt Navy, .36 Caliber, Six Shot, Brass Frame, Reproduction	50	75	150
RV610, 1860 Colt Army, .44 Caliber, Six Shot, Reproduction	100	150	225
RV650, New Model Pocket Remington, .31 Caliber, Spur Trigger, Reproduction	50	75	125

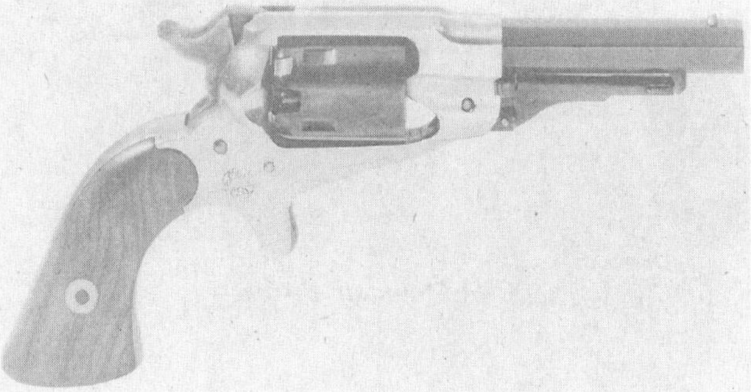

CVA New Pocket Remington

	Fair	V. Good	Excellent
RVF620, 1861 Colt Navy, .44 Caliber, Steel Frame, Reproduction	50	125	200
RVF622, 1861 Colt Navy, .44 Caliber, Steel Frame, Reproduction	35	75	150

RIFLE, FLINTLOCK

	Fair	V. Good	Excellent
.45 Kentucky Rifle, Brass Furniture, Reproduction	50	100	175
.45 or .50 Mountain Rifle, German Silver Furniture, Reproduction	50	125	225
.50 Frontier Rifle, Brass Furniture, Reproduction	50	100	175
.50 or .54 Hawken Rifle, Brass Furniture, Reproduction	$75	$125	$200
FR503, Squirrel Rifle, .32 Caliber, Double Set Triggers, Reproduction	100	200	275
FR504, Pennsylvania Long Rifle, .50 Caliber, Brass Butt Plate, Reproduction	125	300	400

RIFLE, PERCUSSION

	Fair	V. Good	Excellent
.45 Kentucky Rifle, Brass Furniture, Reproduction	35	85	150
.45 or .50 Frontier Rifle, Brass Furniture, Reproduction	50	100	175
.45, .50, .54, or.58 Mountain Rifle, German Silver Furniture, Reproduction	75	125	200
.50 .54 Hawken Rifle, Brass Furniture, Reproduction	75	125	200
.58 Zouave, Brass Furniture, Reproduction	50	100	175
PR403, Squirrel Rifle, .32 Caliber, Right Handed Model, Reproduction	125	175	250
PR404, Pennsylvania Long Rifle, .50 Caliber, Brass Butt Plate, Reproduction	100	300	400

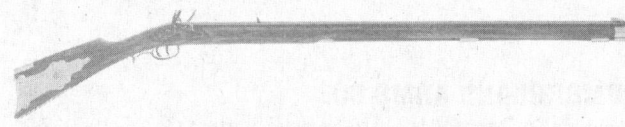

CVA Pennsylvania Long Rifle

	Fair	V. Good	Excellent
PR407, Big Bore Mountain Rifle, .54 Caliber, Undecorated Stock, Beavertail Cheekpiece, Reproduction	150	300	325
PR456, Squirrel Rifle, .32 Caliber, Left Handed Model, Reproduction	125	175	250

SHOTGUN, DOUBLE BARREL, SIDE-BY-SIDE

	Fair	V. Good	Excellent
PS409, .12 Gauge, Percussion, Muzzleloading, Reproduction	100	225	300

SHOTGUN, SINGLE BARREL

	Fair	V. Good	Excellent
FB557, Blunderbuss, .69 Caliber, Flintlock, Brass Trigger, Reproduction	100	225	300

CZ

Czechoslovakia from 1918 to date. This listing includes both Ceska Zbrojovka Brno and Ceskslovenska Zbrojovka. Also see Brno.

HANDGUN, REVOLVER

	Fair	V. Good	Excellent
Grand, .357 Mag., Double Action, Swing-Out Cylinder, *Modern*	75	125	175
Grand, .38 Spec., Double Action, Swing-Out Cylinder, *Modern*	75	125	175

	Fair	V. Good	Excellent
ZKR 551, .38 Spec., Single Action, Swing-Out Cylinder, Target Pistol, *Modern*	$100	$175	$250

HANDGUN, SELF-LOADING

	Fair	V. Good	Excellent
"Vest Pocket" CZ 1945, .25 ACP, Clip Fed, *Modern*	75	150	200
CZ 1924 Navy, .380 ACP, Clip Fed, Nazi-Proofed, *Curio*	400	800	1200

CZ VZ 38

	Fair	V. Good	Excellent
CZ 1938, .380 ACP, Clip Fed, Double Action, Curio	125	250	325
CZ 1938, .380 ACP, Clip Fed, Double Action, Nazi-Proofed, *Curio*	400	800	1000
CZ 1938, .380 ACP, Clip Fed, Double Action, with Safety, *Curio*	350	750	1000
CZ 70, .32 ACP, Clip Fed, Blue, Double Action, *Modern*	75	150	200
CZ 75, 9mm P. Clip Fed, Double Action, Blue, *Modern*	125	300	375
CZ NB 50 Police, .32 ACP, Clip Fed, Double Action, *Curio*	75	275	375
CZ1922, .380 ACP, Clip Fed, *Curio*	125	300	400
CZ1922, .380 ACP, Clip Fed, *Curio*	100	250	350
CZ1924, .380 ACP, 10 Shot, Long Grip, Clip Fed, *Curio*	200	550	700
CZ1924, .380 ACP, Clip Fed, *Curio*	150	300	375
CZ1924, .380 ACP, Clip Fed, *Curio*	100	250	350
CZ1936, .25 ACP, Clip Fed, *Curio*	100	225	275
CZ27 Communist, .32 ACP, Clip Fed, *Curio*	100	150	200

CZ VZ 27

	Fair	V. Good	Excellent
CZ27 Early Luftwaffe, .32 ACP, Clip Fed, Nazi-Proofed, *Curio*	$200	$350	$450
CZ27 Late Luftwaffe, .32 ACP, Clip Fed, Nazi-Proofed, *Curio*	175	300	400
CZ27 Navy, .32 ACP, Clip Fed, Nazi-Proofed, Curio	200	400	550
CZ27 Police, .32 ACP, Clip Fed, Nazi-Proofed, *Curio*	175	350	500
CZ27 Postwar, .32 ACP, Clip Fed, Commercial, Curio	100	175	250
CZ27 Pre-War, .32 ACP, Clip Fed, Commercial, *Curio*	150	300	425
CZ50, .32 ACP, Clip Fed, Double Action, Military, *Modern*	75	125	200
CZ52, 7.62mm Tokarev, Clip Fed, Single Action, *Curio*	65	100	175
Duo, .25 ACP, Clip Fed, *Modern*	75	125	200
Fox, .25 ACP, Clip Fed, *Curio*	100	275	350
Niva, .25 ACP, Clip Fed, *Curio*	100	275	350
PAV, .22 ACP, Clip Fed, *Modern*	50	75	125

HANDGUN, SINGLESHOT

	Fair	V. Good	Excellent
Drulov 75, .22 L.R.R.F., Top Break, Target Pistol, Target Sights, *Modern*	100	200	275
Model P, .22 L.R.R.F., Top Break, Target Pistol, *Modern*	100	175	275
Model P, 6mm Flobert, Top Break, Target Pistol, *Modern*	75	150	250

RIFLE, BOLT ACTION

	Fair	V. Good	Excellent
ZKK 600, Various Calibers, Checkered Stock, Express Sights, *Modern*	200	400	550
ZKK 602, Various Magnum Calibers, Checkered Stock, Express Sights, *Modern*	200	500	650

SHOTGUN, DOUBLE BARREL, OVER-UNDER

	Fair	V. Good	Excellent
Model 581, 12 Gauge, Checkered Stock with Cheekpiece, *Modern*	225	450	600

CZAR

Made by Hood Firearms Co., c. 1876.

HANDGUN, REVOLVER

	Fair	V. Good	Excellent
.22 Short R.F., 7 Shot, Spur Trigger, Solid Frame, Single Action, *Antique*	50	100	200

CZAR

Made by Hopkins & Allen, c. 1880.

HANDGUN, REVOLVER

	Fair	V. Good	Excellent
.22 Short R.F., 7 Shot, Spur Trigger, Solid Frame, Single Action, *Antique*	50	100	175
.32 Short R.F., 5 Shot, Spur Trigger, Solid Frame, Single Action, *Antique*	75	125	200

CZECHOSLOVAKIAN MILITARY

Also see German Military, CZ.

RIFLE, BOLT ACTION

	Fair	V. Good	Excellent
GEW 33 /40, 8mm Mauser, Military, Nazi-Proofed, Carbine, *Curio*	$150	$300	$450
Gewehr 24 T, 8mm Mauser, Military, Nazi-Proofed, *Curio*	$75	$150	$250
VZ 24, 8mm Mauser, Military, *Curio*	65	125	200
VZ 33, 8mm Mauser, Military, Carbine, *Curio*	75	125	175

D

DAISY
Made by Baçon Arms Co., c. 1880.

HANDGUN, REVOLVER

	Fair	V. Good	Excellent
.22 Short R.F., 7 Shot, Spur Trigger, Solid Frame, Single Action, *Antique*	$50	$75	$250

DAKIN GUN CO.
San Francisco, Ca., c. 1960.

SHOTGUN, DOUBLE BARREL, OVER-UNDER

	Fair	V. Good	Excellent
Model 170, Various Gauges, Light Engraving, Checkered Stock, Double Triggers, Vent Rib, *Modern*	200	450	550

SHOTGUN, DOUBLE BARREL, SIDE-BY-SIDE

	Fair	V. Good	Excellent
Model 100, 12 or 20 Gauges, Boxlock, Light Engraving, Double Triggers, *Modern*	150	300	400
Model 147, Various Magnum Gauges, Boxlock, Light Engraving, Double Triggers, Vent Rib, *Modern*	150	350	425
Model 215, 12 or 20 Gauges, Sidelock, Fancy Engraving, Fancy Wood, Ejectors, Single Selective Trigger, Vent Rib, *Modern*	400	800	1000

DALBY, DAVID
Lincolnshire, England, c. 1835.

HANDGUN, FLINTLOCK

	Fair	V. Good	Excellent
.50, Pocket Pistol, Box Lock, Screw Barrel, Folding Trigger, Silver Inlay, *Antique*	150	350	500

DALY ARMS CO.
New York City, c. 1890.

HANDGUN, REVOLVER

	Fair	V. Good	Excellent
.22 Long R.F., 6 Shot, Double Action, Ring Trigger, Solid Frame, *Antique*	100	200	300
Peacemaker, .32 Short R.F., 5 Shot, Spur Trigger, Solid Frame, Single Action, *Antique*	50	150	200

DANIELS, HENRY & CHARLES
Chester, Conn., 1835–1850.

RIFLE, PERCUSSION

	Fair	V. Good	Excellent
Turret Rifle, .40, Underhammer, 8 Shot, Manual Repeater, Octagon Barrel, *Antique*	$3500	$6500	$8000

DANISH MILITARY

HANDGUN, REVOLVER

	Fair	V. Good	Excellent
9.1mm Ronge 1891, Military, Top Break, Hammer-Like Latch, *Antique*	200	400	500

HANDGUN, SELF-LOADING

	Fair	V. Good	Excellent
M1910, 9mm B, Made by Pieper, Clip Fed, *Curio*	200	500	700
M1910/21, 9mm B, Converted from M1910, Clip Fed, *Curio*	200	400	500
M1910/21, 9mm B, Made by Danish Army Arsenal, Clip Fed, *Curio*	225	500	600
S.L.G. SG/8 9mm Luger, Clip Fed, Military, *Curio*	500	1000	1350

RIFLE, BOLT ACTION

	Fair	V. Good	Excellent
M1889 Krag, 8 × 54 Krag-Jorgensen, Carbine, *Antique*	200	400	500
M98 Mauser, 6.5 × 57, Haerens Vabenarsenal, *Curio*	150	250	350

RIFLE, SINGLESHOT

	Fair	V. Good	Excellent
M1867, Remington Rolling Block, Full Stock, *Antique*	200	400	500

Danton.25

DANTON

Made by Gabilondo y Cia., Elgoibar, Spain, 1925–1933.

HANDGUN, SELF-LOADING

	Fair	V. Good	Excellent
Pocket, .25 ACP, Clip Fed, *Curio*	$50	$100	$150
Pocket, .25 ACP, Grip Safety, Clip Fed, *Curio*	75	125	175
Pocket, .32 ACP, Clip Fed, *Curio*	50	100	175
Pocket, .32 ACP, Grip Safety, Clip Fed, *Curio*	75	125	175

DARDICK

Hamden, Conn., 1954–1962. Certainly one of the ugliest of all firearms, the Dardick system depended partly on the use of a special capsule which contained the cartridge. The capsule, with the round included, was known as a tround because of its triangular cross-section. The author remembers as a boy watching the *Today* show on television and seeing Dardick himself demonstrating his new creation. These were the days before the assassination of President John F. Kennedy, an event that made firearms an unwelcome subject to the media.

HANDGUN, REVOLVER

	Fair	V. Good	Excellent
Series 1100, .38 Dardick Tround, Double Action, Clip Fed, 3" Barrel, 11 Shot, *Modern*	200	400	500
Series 1500, .22, Double Action, Clip Fed, 2" and 11" Barrels, *Modern*	200	400	500
Series 1500, .30, Double Action, Clip Fed, $4^3/_4$" Barrel, *Modern*	300	750	800
Series 1500, .38 Dardick Tround, Double Action, Clip Fed, 6" Barrel, 15 Shot, *Modern*	250	450	650

For Carbine Conversion Unit .22, Add $25.00–$395.00

For Carbine Conversion Unit .38, Add $215.00–$325.00

DARNE

St. Etienne, France.

SHOTGUN, DOUBLE BARREL, SIDE-BY-SIDE

	Fair	V. Good	Excellent
Bird Hunter, Various Gauges, Sliding Breech, Ejectors, Double Triggers, Checkered Stock, *Modern*	400	800	1000
Hors Serie #1, Various Gauges, Sliding Breech, Ejectors, Fancy Engraving, Checkered Stock, *Modern*	1500	3200	4500
Magnum, 12 or 20 Gauges 3", Sliding Breech, Ejectors, Double Triggers, Checkered Stock, *Modern*	1000	2250	3250
Pheasant Hunter, Various Gauges, Sliding Breech, Ejectors, Light Engraving, Checkered Stock, *Modern*	1000	2000	2750
Quail Hunter, Various Gauges, Sliding Breech, Ejectors, Engraved, Checkered Stock, *Modern*	$1200	$2750	$3750

DAVENPORT, W. H.

Providence, R.I., 1880–1883, Norwich, Conn. 1890–1900.

SHOTGUN, DOUBLE BARREL, SIDE-BY-SIDE

	Fair	V. Good	Excellent
8 Ga., *Modern*	100	250	300

SHOTGUN, SINGLESHOT

	Fair	V. Good	Excellent
Various Gauges, Hammer, Steel Barrel, *Modern*	75	150	200

DAVIDSON

Spain Mfg. by Fabrica de Armas, imported by Davidson Firearms Co., Greensboro, N.C.

SHOTGUN, DOUBLE BARREL, SIDE-BY-SIDE

	Fair	V. Good	Excellent
73 Stagecoach, 12 or 20 Gauges, Magnum, Checkered Stock, *Modern*	100	225	275
Model 63B, 12 and 20 Gauges, Magnum, Engraved, Nickel Plated, Checkered Stock, *Modern*	100	175	250
Model 63B, Various Gauges, Engraved, Nickel Plated, Checkered Stock, *Modern*	75	125	200
Model 673B, 10 Ga. $3^1/_2$", Magnum, Engraved, Nickel Plated, Checkered Stock, *Modern*	100	200	275
Model 69 SL, 12 and 20 Gauges, Sidelock, Light Engraving, Checkered Stock, *Modern*	125	325	400

DAVIS INDUSTRIES

Current manufacturer in Chino, Calif.

HANDGUN, DOUBLE BARREL, OVER-UNDER

	Fair	V. Good	Excellent
Model D-22, *Modern*	25	50	75
Model D-22, .22 L.R.R.F., Remington Derringer Style, Black, Teflon, *Modern*	25	50	75
Model D-22, .25 ACP, Remington Derringer Style, Black Teflon, *Modern*	25	50	75
Model D-22, .25 ACP, Remington Derringer Style, Chrome, *Modern*	25	50	75

DAVIS, N. R. & CO.

Freetown Mass., 1853–1917. Merged with Warner Co. of Norwich, Conn., and became Davis-Warner Arms Co. It was not active between 1920 and 1922, but in 1930 started again as Crescent-Davis Arms Co., Norwich. This included Crescent Fire Arms Co. They relocated in Springfield, Mass., 1931–1932, and were taken over in 1932 by Stevens Arms.

	Fair	V. Good	Excellent
RIFLE, PERCUSSION			
.45, Octagon Barrel, *Antique*	$200	$400	$700
SHOTGUN, PERCUSSION			
#1 Various Gauges, Double Barrel, Side by Side, Damascus Barrel, Outside Hammers, *Antique*	100	325	500
#3 Various Gauges, Double Barrel, Side by Side, Damascus Barrel, Outside Hammers, *Antique*	100	275	450
SHOTGUN, DOUBLE BARREL, SIDE-BY-SIDE			
Various Gauges, Hammerless, Damascus Barrel, *Modern*	50	100	200
Various Gauges, Hammerless, Steel Barrel, *Modern*	50	125	250
Various Gauges, Outside Hammers, Damascus Barrel, *Modern*	50	100	200
Various Gauges, Outside Hammers, Steel Barrel, *Modern*	50	100	200
SHOTGUN, SINGLE BARREL			
Various Gauges, Hammer, Steel Barrel, *Modern*	25	50	100

DAY ARMS CO.

San Antonio, Tex.

HANDGUN, SELF-LOADING			
Conversion Unit Only, .22 L.R.R.F., For Colt M1911, Clip Fed	100	125	150

DEAD SHOT

L. W. Pond Co.

HANDGUN, REVOLVER			
.22 Long R.F., 6 Shot, Single Action, Solid Frame, Spur Trigger, *Antique*	175	225	275

DEANE, ADAMS & DEANE

See Adams.

Debatir .25

DEBATIR

	Fair	V. Good	Excellent
HANDGUN, SELF-LOADING			
.25 ACP, Clip Fed, *Curio*	$75	$150	$225
.32 ACP, Clip Fed, *Curio*	100	175	250

DEBERIERE, HENRY

Phila., Pa., 1769–1774. See Kentucky Rifles and Pistols.

DECKER, WILHELM

Zella St. Blasii, Germany, c. 1913.

HANDGUN, REVOLVER			
Decker, .25 ACP, Hammerless, 6 Shot, *Curio*	300	650	750
Mueller Special, .25 ACP, Hammerless, 6 Shot, *Curio*	300	675	775

DEFENDER

Made by Iver-Johnson, sold by J. P. Lovell Arms, 1875–1895.

HANDGUN, REVOLVER			
#89, .22 Short R.F., 7 Shot, Spur Trigger, Solid Frame, Single Action, *Antique*	50	100	150
#89, .32 Short R.F., 5 Shot, Spur Trigger, Solid Frame, Single Action, *Antique*	75	125	175
.22 Short R.F., 7 Shot, Spur Trigger, Solid Frame, Single Action, *Antique*	50	100	175
.32 Short R.F., 5 Shot, Spur Trigger, Solid Frame, Single Action, *Antique*	75	125	175

DEFENDER

N. Shore & Co., Chicago, Ill., c. 1922.

HANDGUN, KNIFE PISTOL			
#215, .22 R.F., 3" Overall Length, 1 Blade	50	100	175

DEFIANCE

Made by Norwich Falls Pistol Co., c. 1880.

HANDGUN, REVOLVER			
.22 Short R.F., 7 Shot, Spur Trigger, Solid Frame, Single Action, *Antique*	50	100	175

DEHUFF, ABRAHAM

Lancaster, Pa., c. 1779. See Kentucky Rifles and Pistols.

	Fair	V. Good	Excellent

DEK-DU

Tomas de Urizar y Cia., Eibar, Spain, c. 1910.

HANDGUN, REVOLVER

	Fair	V. Good	Excellent
Velo Dog, .25 ACP, 12 Shots, Folding Trigger, *Curio*	$75	$125	$175
Velo Dog, 5.5mm Velo Dog, 12 Shots, Folding Trigger, *Curio*	50	100	150

DELPHIAN

Made by Stevens Arms.

SHOTGUN, SINGLESHOT

	Fair	V. Good	Excellent
Model 90, Various Gauges, Takedown, Automatic Ejector, Plain Hammer, *Modern*	25	50	75

DELU

Fab. d'Armes Delu & Co.

HANDGUN, SELF-LOADING

	Fair	V. Good	Excellent
.25 ACP, Clip Fed, *Curio*	75	150	175

DEMRO

Manchester, Conn.

HANDGUN, SELF-LOADING

	Fair	V. Good	Excellent
T.A.C. XF-7 Wasp, .45 ACP or 9mm Luger, Clip Fed, *Modern*	150	300	350

RIFLE, SELF-LOADING

	Fair	V. Good	Excellent
T.A.C. Model 1 Carbine, .45 ACP or 9mm Luger, Clip Fed, Fixed Stock, *Modern*	100	225	350
T.A.C. XF-7 Wasp Carbine, .45 ACP or 9mm Luger, Clip Fed, Folding Stock, *Modern*	150	350	400

DERINGER RIFLE AND PISTOL WORKS

Philadelphia, Pa., 1870–1880.

HANDGUN, REVOLVER

	Fair	V. Good	Excellent
Centennial '76, .38 Long R.F., 5 Shot, Single Action, Spur Trigger, Tip-up, *Antique*	150	350	500
Model 1, .22 Short R.F., 7 Shot, Spur Trigger, Tip-up, *Antique*	125	300	400
Model 2, .22 Short R.F., 7 Shot, Spur Trigger, Tip-up, *Antique*	75	200	300
Model 2, .32 Long R.F., 5 Shot, Single Action, Spur Trigger, Tip-up, *Antique*	100	200	300

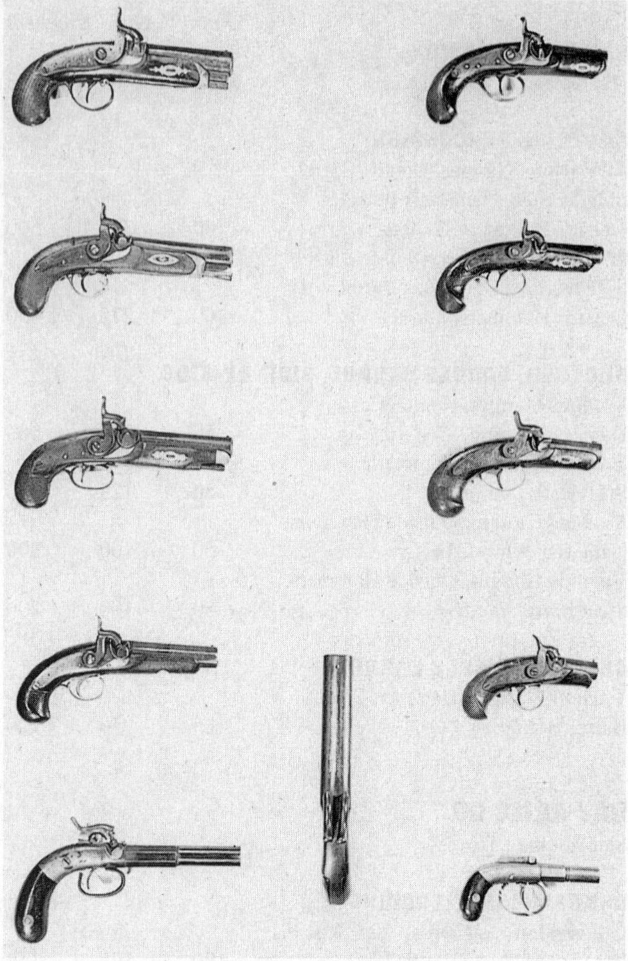

Selection of Derringer pocket pistols, of varying sizes; from top left, *first two marked Deringer but likely of Belgian manufacture; third possibly of Belgian make but early H. Deringer styling; fourth scarce Southern derringer by F. Glassick & Co., Memphis, Tennessee; so-called Pocket Rifle by Marston & Co. At* center, *double-barrel pistol by Allen & Wheelock. From top* right, *New York derringer marked Gillespie; derringer-type possible Belgian-make; by H. Deringer and with agent marking Man'd. for F.H. Clark & Co., Memphis, Tenn.; Derringer-type with inscription K.B. to J.C. but no maker's name (likely Belgian make); and Pocket Rifle marked B & S-New York, made by Blunt & Syms.*

DERINGER, HENRY, JR.

Philadelphia, Pa., 1806–1868. Also see U.S. Military. The inventor, designer, and gunmaker Henry Deringer Jr., testified on his own behalf in the celebrated trademark trial of *Henry Deringer* v. *Adolphus J. Plate,* a suit brought against dealer A. J. Plate, for his role in the manufacture of spurious pistols (by Slotter & Co.) that were marked with the Deringer trademark. The stamp, marked on the breech of the barrel and the lockplate, precisely duplicated the original. In fact, this was likely a stamp made for Deringer himself: DERINGER PHILA—The percussion ignition system was only coming into use in the 1830s, and Deringer was among the first to employ it. The use of the percussion system was instrumental in making practical, concealable firearms, like the Deringer pistol, as they were also in the evolution of practical revolvers, like the Colt. Deringer's role in manfacturing military and naval arms under government contract was crucial in his awareness and knowledge of developments in firearms technology. Among the most famous names in firearms history, Henry Deringer developed his pocket pistols beginning around 1826, proceeding through an evolution to a design which had been firmly established by the mid-19th century. By the time of his death, in 1868, over 15,000 pairs had been manufactured. The type became so recognizable that "Deringer's pistols" achieved worldwide renown to become "the derringer pistol"—a specific type and style of pocket protector recognized wherever men knew about guns. Competitors quickly seized upon the popularity of the derringer. Within a short time, a flood of counterfeit arms hit the market, a problem which plagued the inventor until his death, at the age of eighty-two. It is due to this dilemma that much more is known about Deringer and his rivals than about many other American gunmakers: Deringer sued the most blatant counterfeiter, and won. The civil suit he initiated was successfully prosecuted by his estate, and remains today as a landmark in trademark infringement law. This was the first case to award the amount of profit by the defendant as the damages to the plaintiff—in Deringer's case this was $1,700. Deringer also made military arms, as well as a variety of civilian types: holster and belt pistols, a box-lock martial model (for the U.S. Navy), and even long arms—especially military rifles of the 1814 and 1817 patterns. His Kentucky rifles were often exquisite, with rich tiger-stripe maple stocks and handsome inlays. An elegant Deringer Kentucky rifle was used in an infamous duel between Congressman Cilley of Maine, and a Mr. Graves (1838); they fought at a range of 80 yards; Cilley was killed on the third round of the engagement. The last of the Deringer production were .22 and .32 rimfire, single action pocket revolvers of which approximately 6,900 were made in .22 caliber (1873–79), and 4,000 in .32 (1874–79). But the percussion pocket pistol remains Henry Deringer's greatest legacy. These were carried by ladies and gentlemen, soldiers, gold miners, riverboat gamblers, and a broad array of other humanity, occasionally as a final arbiter in a dispute. Among the first pairs was that made for U.S. Army officer and Ordnance official Colonel George Talcott, dating from the 1830s. Among other well-known owners were pioneer Minnesota governor Alexander Ramsey (a gift from one of Deringer's sons, Calhoun) and the soon-to-be internationally celebrated William F. Cody. The most infamous of all Deringers is the pistol used by John Wilkes Booth in the assassination of President Abraham Lincoln, April 14, 1865. Ironically, Lincoln's opponent in the Presidential campaign of 1860, Senator Stephen A. Douglas, carried a pair of Deringers, and it has been speculated that Lincoln himself may well have owned a pair. Manufacture of the percussion Deringer was from the 1830s to 1868. Production of the metallic cartridge Deringer revolvers was under supervision of I. Jones Clark, from c. 1870 to 1880.

HANDGUN, PERCUSSION

	Fair	*V. Good*	*Excellent*
Dueller, .41, Back Lock, German Silver Mounts, *Antique*	$1000	$2750	$4000
Medium Pocket, .41, Back Lock, German Silver Mounts, *Antique*	600	1500	2250
Pocket, .41, Back Lock, German Silver Mounts, *Antique*	375	1250	2000

DERINGER, HENRY, SR.

Richmond, Va., & Philadelphia, Pa., 1768–1814. See Kentucky Rifles and Pistols; U.S. Military.

DERR, JOHN

Lancaster, Pa., 1810–1844. See Kentucky Rifles and Pistols.

DESPATCH

Made by Hopkins & Allen, c. 1875.

HANDGUN, REVOLVER

	Fair	*V. Good*	*Excellent*
.22 Short R.F., 7 Shot, Spur Trigger, Solid Frame, Single Action, *Antique*	$75	$125	$175

DESTROYER

Made in Spain by Isidro Gaztanaga, 1914–1933, reorganized as Gaztanaga, Trocoala y Ibarzabal, 1933–1936.

HANDGUN, SELF-LOADING

	Fair	*V. Good*	*Excellent*
Destroyer, .25 ACP, Clip Fed, *Curio*	75	125	175

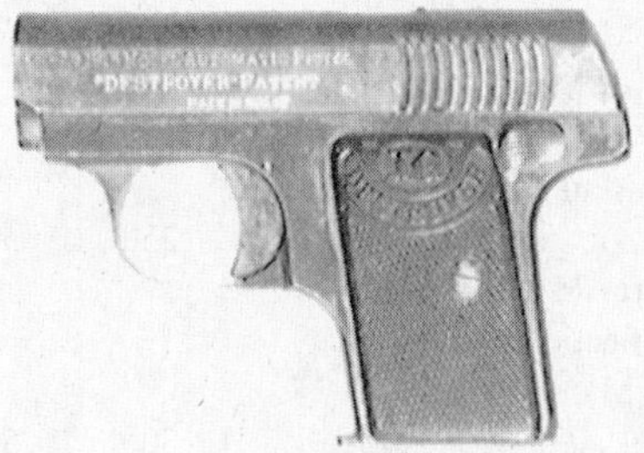

Destroyer .25

	Fair	*V. Good*	*Excellent*
Destroyer, .32 ACP, Clip Fed, Long Grip, *Curio*	75	150	200
Model 1913, .25 ACP, Clip Fed, *Modern*	75	125	175
Model 1919, .32 ACP, Clip Fed, *Modern*	75	125	175
Super Destroyer, .32 ACP, Clip Fed, *Modern*	100	175	225

DESTRUCTOR

Iraola Salaverria, Eibar, Spain.

HANDGUN, SELF-LOADING

	Fair	*V. Good*	*Excellent*
.25 ACP, Clip Fed, *Modern*	50	100	150
.32 ACP, Clip Fed, *Modern*	75	125	175

DETONICS

Seattle, Washington. This cleverly designed series of pistols features the scaled down Government Model .45, designed for concealment. Although recoil is substantial, the .45 ACP cartridge is so powerful that the mini-arm proved instantly popular, and received an enormous amount of publicity. Eventually the Colt company introduced its own scaled-down pistol, the Officer's Model ACP; that too became extremely popular. The Detonics is only one of several knock-offs of the orginal Colt/Browning Government Model .45.

HANDGUN, SELF-LOADING

	Fair	*V. Good*	*Excellent*
Mark I, .45 ACP, Combat Modifications, Clip Fed, Pocket Pistol, Matt Blue, *Modern*	$200	$450	$600
Mark II, 9mm P., Combat Modifications, Clip Fed, Pocket Pistol, Matt Blue, *Modern*	200	375	450
Mark III, .38 Super, Combat Modifications, Clip Fed, Pocket Pistol, Matt Blue, *Modern*	200	400	500
Combat Master, .45 ACP, Combat Modifications, Clip Fed, Pocket Pistol, Matt Blue, *Modern*	300	675	775
Combat Master, .45 ACP, Combat Modifications, Clip Fed, Pocket Pistol, Matt Blue, Adjustable Sights, *Modern*	300	650	775
Combat Master Mk. V, .38 Super, Combat Modifications, Clip Fed, Pocket Pistol, Matt Stainless, *Modern*	300	600	750
Combat Master Mk. V, .45 ACP, Combat Modifications, Clip Fed, Pocket Pistol, Matt Stainless, *Modern*	250	500	650
Combat Master Mk. V, 9mm P., Combat Modifications, Clip Fed, Pocket Pistol, Matt Stainless, *Modern*	300	500	650
Combat Master Mk. VI, .45 ACP, Combat Modifications, Clip Fed, Pocket Pistol, Polished Stainless, Adjustable Sights, *Modern*	350	600	750
Combat Master Mk. VI, .451 Mag., Combat Modifications, Clip Fed, Pocket Pistol, Polished Stainless, Adjustable Sights, *Modern*	400	700	850
Combat Master Mk. VI, 9mm P., Combat Modifications, Clip Fed, Pocket Pistol, Polished Stainless, Adjustable Sights, *Modern*	350	750	875

Detonics Mark VI

	Fair	*V. Good*	*Excellent*
Combat Master Mk. VII, .38 Super, Combat Modifications, Clip Fed, Pocket Pistol, Matt Stainless, No Sights, Lightweight, *Modern* ..	$400	$700	$850
Combat Master Mk. VII, .45 ACP, Combat Modifications, Clip Fed, Pocket Pistol, Matt Stainless, No Sights, Lightweight, *Modern* ..	400	700	800
Combat Master Mk. VII, .451 Mag., Combat Modifications, Clip Fed, Pocket Pistol, Matt Stainless, No Sights, Lightweight, *Modern*	400	800	1000
Combat Master Mk. VII, 9mm P., Combat Modifications, Clip Fed, Pocket Pistol, Matt Stainless, No Sights, Lightweight, *Modern* ..	400	850	1000
MC2 Military Combat, .38 Super, Clip Fed, Pocket Pistol, Matt Stainless, *Modern*	300	600	700
MC2 Military Combat, .45 ACP, Clip Fed, Pocket Pistol, Matt Stainless, *Modern*	250	575	650
MC2 Military Combat, 9mm P., Clip Fed, Pocket Pistol, Matt Stainless, *Modern*	300	600	700
Scoremaster, .45 ACP, I.P.S.C. Target Pistol, Target Sights, Stainless Steel, *Modern*	300	750	950
Scoremaster, .451 Mag., I.P.S.C. Target Pistol, Target Sights, Stainless Steel, *Modern*	500	1000	1250

DIAMOND

Made by Stevens Arms.

SHOTGUN, SINGLESHOT

Model 89 Dreadnaught, Various Gauges, Hammer, *Modern*	50	75	100
Model 90, Various Gauges, Takedown, Automatic Ejector, Plain Hammer, *Modern*	25	50	75
Model 95, 12 and 16 Gauge, Takedown, *Modern*	25	50	75

DIANE

Erquiaga, Muguruzu, y Cia., Eibar, Spain, c. 1923.

HANDGUN, SELF-LOADING

.25 ACP, Clip Fed, Blue, *Curio* ...	75	150	200

DIANE

Made by Wilkinson Arms, Covina, Calif.

HANDGUN, SELF-LOADING

Standard Model, .25 ACP, Clip Fed, *Modern*	75	100	125

DICKINSON, J. & L.

Also E. L. & J. Dickinson, Springfield, Mass., 1863–1880.

HANDGUN, SINGLESHOT

	Fair	V. Good	Excellent
.22 R.F., Brass Frame, Pivoting Barrel, Rack Ejector, *Antique*	$200	$350	$400
.32 R.F., Brass Frame, Pivoting Barrel, Rack Ejector, *Antique*	100	250	300

DICKSON

Made in Italy for American Import Co. until 1968.

HANDGUN, SINGLESHOT

Detective, .25 ACP, Clip Fed, *Modern*	75	100	125

DICTATOR

Made by Hopkins & Allen, c. 1880.

HANDGUN, REVOLVER

.22 Short R.F., 7 Shot, Spur Trigger, Solid Frame, Single Action, *Antique*	75	125	175
.32 Short R.F., 5 Shot, Spur Trigger, Solid Frame, Single Action, *Antique*	75	125	175
#2, .32 Short R.F., 5 Shot, Spur Trigger, Solid Frame, Single Action, *Antique*	100	150	200

DIXIE GUN WORKS

Union City, Tenn. The author remembers a trip to Tennessee as a boy to visit relatives living in Memphis, when the unending pleas of brother Jack and self led to a detour in order to visit the operations of Turner Kirkland's Dixie Gun Works at Union City. The trip was in 1953 and Kirkland had already developed his own empire. We were amazed at the vast quantities of replacement parts, replica guns, antique arms, and even collectors' cars.Years later, when *Sports Afield* magazine compiled a list of the most important firearms personalities in that publication's 100 years of existence, Turner's name was among them. Today the Dixie Gun Works annual catalogue is massive. The firm exhibits at the NRA Show and at IWA, as well as the SHOT Show, and has developed a book line, continues to deal in antique arms, and remains at the forefront of replica and muzzle-loading firearms interests.

HANDGUN, FLINTLOCK

Tower, .67, Brass Furniture, Reproduction	50	100	175

HANDGUN, PERCUSSION

	Fair	V. Good	Excellent
Army, .44 Revolver, Buntline, Reproduction	50	100	175
Navy, .36 Revolver, Buntline, Brass Frame, Engraved, Reproduction	75	150	225
Navy, .36 Revolver, Buntline, Brass Frame, Reproduction	100	150	225
Spiller & Burr, .36 Revolver, Buntline, Brass Frame, Reproduction	$50	$100	$175
Wyatt Earp, .44 Revolver, Buntline, Brass Frame, Reproduction	50	100	150
Wyatt Earp, .44 Revolver, Buntline, Brass Frame, with Shoulder Stock, Reproduction	75	150	200

RIFLE, LEVER ACTION

Win. 73 (Italian), .44-40 WCF, Tube Feed, Octagon Barrel, Carbine, *Modern*	200	350	500
Win. 73 (Italian), .44-40 WCF, Tube Feed, Octagon Barrel, Color Cased Hardened Frame, Engraved, *Modern*	250	400	550

RIFLE, FLINTLOCK

1st. Model Brown Bess, .75, Military, Reproduction	125	250	400
2nd. Model Brown Bess, .74, Military, Reproduction	150	300	450
Coach Guard, .95, Blunderbuss, Brass Furniture, Reproduction	50	100	200
Day Rifle, .45, Double Barrel, Over-Under, Swivel Breech, Brass Furniture, Reproduction	75	125	175
Deluxe Pennsylvania, .45, Kentucky Rifle, Full-Stocked, Brass Furniture, Light Engraving, Reproduction	150	300	400
Deluxe Pennsylvania, .45, Kentucky Rifle, Full-Stocked, Brass Furniture, Reproduction	125	250	400
Kentuckian, .45, Kentucky Rifle, Full-Stocked, Brass Furniture, Reproduction	50	100	175
Kentuckian, .45, Kentucky Rifle, Full-Stocked, Brass Furniture, Reproduction, Carbine	75	150	250
Musket, .67, Smoothbore, Reproduction, Carbine	50	100	150
Squirrel Rifle, .45, Kentucky Rifle, Full-Stocked, Brass Furniture, Reproduction	125	250	325
York County, .45, Kentucky Rifle, Full-Stocked, Brass Furniture, Reproduction	75	150	200

RIFLE, PERCUSSION

Day Rifle, .45, Double Barrel, Over-Under, Swivel Breech, Brass Furniture, Reproduction	100	225	300
Deluxe Pennsylvania, .45, Kentucky Rifle, Full-Stocked, Brass Furniture, Reproduction	100	275	350
Deluxe Pennsylvania, .45, Kentucky Rifle, Full-Stocked, Brass Furniture, Light Engraving, Reproduction	100	275	375

	Fair	V. Good	Excellent
Dixie Hawkin, .45, Half-Stocked, Octagon Barrel, Set Trigger, Brass Furniture, Reproduction	$75	$150	$225
Dixie Hawkin, .50, Half-Stocked, Octagon Barrel, Set Trigger, Brass Furniture, Reproduction	75	150	225
Enfield Two-Band, .577, Musketoon, Military, Reproduction	50	125	225
Kentuckian, .45, Kentucky Rifle, Full-Stocked, Brass Furniture, Reproduction	75	125	200
Kentuckian, .45, Kentucky Rifle, Full-Stocked, Brass Furniture, Reproduction, Carbine	100	200	275
Musket, .66, Smoothbore, Reproduction	75	125	200
Plainsman, .45, Half-Stocked, Octagon Barrel, Reproduction	100	200	275
Plainsman, .50, Half-Stocked, Octagon Barrel, Reproduction	75	150	300
Squirrel Rifle, .45, Kentucky Rifle, Full-Stocked, Brass Furniture, Reproduction	125	300	400
Target, .45, Half-Stocked, Octagon Barrel, Reproduction	50	95	150
York County, .45, Kentucky Rifle, Full-Stocked, Brass Furniture, Reproduction	75	135	185
Zouave M 1863, .58, Military, Reproduction	100	175	250

SHOTGUN, PERCUSSION

	Fair	V. Good	Excellent
12 Gauge, Double Barrel, Side-by-Side, Double Trigger, Reproduction	75	100	200
28 Gauge, Single Barrel, Reproduction	75	100	200

SHOTGUN, FLINTLOCK

	Fair	V. Good	Excellent
Fowling Piece, 14 Gauge, Single Barrel, Reproduction	100	150	225

DOBSON T.

London, England, c. 1780.

HANDGUN, FLINTLOCK

	Fair	V. Good	Excellent
.64, Presentation, Holster Pistol, Gold Inlays, Engraved, Half- Octagon Barrel, High Quality, *Antique*	1250	3000	4500

DOMINO

Made in Italy, imported by Mandell Shooting Sports. Also see Beeman.

Precision Firearms

HANDGUN, SELF-LOADING

	Fair	V. Good	Excellent
Model O.P. 601, .22 Short, Target Pistol, Adjustable Sights, Target Grips, *Modern*	500	900	1250
Model O.P. 602, .22 L.R., Target Pistol, Adjustable Sights, Target Grips, *Modern*	$500	$1000	$1250

DREADNOUGHT

Made by Hopkins & Allen, c. 1880.

HANDGUN, REVOLVER

	Fair	V. Good	Excellent
.22 Short R.F., 7 Shot, Spur Trigger, Solid Frame, Single Action, *Antique*	50	100	150
.32 Short R.F., 5 Shot, Spur Trigger, Solid Frame, Single Action, *Antique*	75	125	175

DREYSE

Dreyse Rheinische Metallwaren Machinenfabrik, Sommerda, Germany, since 1889. In 1936 merged and became Rheinmetall-Borsig, Dusseldorf, Germany.

HANDGUN, SELF-LOADING

	Fair	V. Good	Excellent
M1907, .32 ACP, Clip Fed, *Curio*	75	125	175
M1907, .32 ACP, Clip Fed, Early Model, *Curio*	75	150	200
M1910, 9mm Luger, Clip Fed, *Curio*	1000	2500	3000
Rheinmetall, .32 ACP, Clip Fed, *Curio*	100	225	275

Dreyse Model 1907 Late

	Fair	V. Good	Excellent
Vest Pocket, .25 ACP, Clip Fed, *Curio*	75	150	200
Vest Pocket, .25 ACP, Clip Fed, Early, *Curio*	100	175	225

RIFLE, SELF-LOADING

	Fair	V. Good	Excellent
Carbine, .32 ACP, Clip Fed, Checkered Stock, *Curio*	200	375	450

DRIPPARD, F.

Lancaster, Pa., 1767–1773. See Kentucky Rifles and Pistols.

DRISCOLL, J. B.

Springfield, Mass., c. 1870.

HANDGUN, SINGLESHOT

	Fair	V. Good	Excellent
.22 R.F., Brass Frame, Spur Trigger, *Antique*	150	300	450

DUBIEL ARMS CO.

Sherman, Tex., since 1975.

RIFLE, BOLT ACTION

	Fair	V. Good	Excellent
Custom Rifle, Various Calibers, Various Styles, Fancy Wood, *Modern*	$700	$1500	$2250

DUMARESD, B.

Marseille, France, probably c. 1730.

HANDGUN, FLINTLOCK

	Fair	V. Good	Excellent
Holster Pistol, Engraved, Horn Inlays, Ornate, Silver Furniture, *Antique*	800	1650	2250

DUMOULIN & DELEYE

Liège, Belgium. Makers of best quality double rifles and bolt action sporting rifles, this firm manufactured a magnificent double barrel rifle for the author in 1972. The rifle was similar to the style of Holland & Holland and was made up partly for hunting use, and partly as a sample of engraving for the author's A. A. White Engravers, Inc. This exquisite rifle has taken Cape Buffalo, leopard, lion and elephant, and remains one of the author's most prized possessions. Engraving was by K. C. Hunt, A. A. White, Rene Delcour, Philippe Grifnee, Denise Thirion, and Hans Obiltschnig. Although gunmaker Dumoulin (son of the gunmaker running Dumoulin Freres et. Cie.) referred to the rifle as a "jungle" (due to the combination of six engravers on one piece), it nevertheless must rank among the finest rifles ever built by that firm.

DUMOULIN FRERES ET CIE

Milmort, Belgium, since 1849.

RIFLE, BOLT ACTION

	Fair	V. Good	Excellent
African Pro, Various Calibers, Fancy Checkering, Fancy Engraving, Fancy Wood, *Modern*	2000	4000	5000
Safari Sportsman, Various Calibers, Fancy Checkering, Engraved, Fancy Wood, *Modern*	1500	3000	4000
Safari, Various Calibers, Fancy Checkering, Engraved, *Modern*	1000	2000	3250

RIFLE, DOUBLE BARREL, SIDE-BY-SIDE

	Fair	V. Good	Excellent
Europa, Various Calibers, Fancy Checkering, Engraved, Fancy Wood, *Modern*	$3000	$5000	$6000

DUO FRANTISEK DUSEK

Opocno, Czechoslovakia, 1926–1948. Ceska Zbrojovka from 1948 to date.

HANDGUN, SELF-LOADING

	Fair	V. Good	Excellent
Duo, .25 ACP, Clip Fed, *Modern*	100	200	250

DUTCH MILITARY

HANDGUN, REVOLVER

	Fair	V. Good	Excellent
Model 1871 Hemberg, 9.4mm, Military, *Antique*	150	300	350

RIFLE, BOLT ACTION

	Fair	V. Good	Excellent
Beaumont-Vitale M1871/88, Military, *Antique*	75	150	225
Model 95, 6.5mm Mannlicher, Carbine, Full Stock, *Curio*	75	100	150
Model 95, 6.5mm Mannlicher, Full Stock, *Curio*	75	125	150

RIFLE, FLINTLOCK

	Fair	V. Good	Excellent
.70, Officer's Type, Musket, Brass Furniture, *Antique*	500	1250	1500

DUTTON, JOHN S.

Jaffrey, N.H., 1855–1870.

RIFLE, PERCUSSION

	Fair	V. Good	Excellent
.36, Target Rifle, Swiss Buttplate, Octagon Barrel, Target Sights, *Antique*	450	1200	1600

DWM

Deutsche Waffen und Munitionsfabrik, Berlin, Germany, 1896–1945. Also see Luger and Borchardt.

HANDGUN, SELF-LOADING

	Fair	V. Good	Excellent
Pocket, .32 ACP, Clip Fed, *Curio*	100	250	350

E

E.A.

Echave y Arizmendi, Eibar, Spain, 1911–1975. Also see Echasa and MAB.

HANDGUN, SELF-LOADING

	Fair	V. Good	Excellent
1916 Model, .25 ACP, Clip Fed, *Curio*	$65	$100	$150

E.A.

Eulogio Arostegui, Eibar, Spain, c. 1930.

HANDGUN, SELF-LOADING

.25 ACP, Clip Fed, Blue, Dog Logo on Grips, *Modern*	50	100	125

EAGLE

Made by Iver Johnson, c. 1879–1886.

HANDGUN, REVOLVER

.22 Short F.F., 7 Shot, Spur Trigger, Solid Frame, Single Action, *Antique*	50	100	150
.32 Short R.F., 5 Shot, Spur Trigger, Solid Frame, Single Action, *Antique*	50	100	150
.38 Short R.F., 5 Shot, Spur Trigger, Solid Frame, Single Action, *Antique*	75	200	300
.44 Short R.F., 5 Shot, Spur Trigger, Solid Frame, Single Action, *Antique*	125	300	400

EAGLE ARMS CO.

New York City, c. 1865. Marketed by Plant's Manufacturing Company, New Haven, Conn.

HANDGUN, REVOLVER

.30 Cup Primed Cartridge, 6 Shot, Single Action, Spur Trigger, Solid Frame, *Antique*	200	400	550
.30 Cup Primed Cartridge, 6 Shot, Single Action, Spur Trigger, Tip-up, *Antique*	250	525	700
.42 Cup Primed Cartridge, 6 Shot, Single Action, Spur Trigger, Iron Frame, *Antique*	450	850	1000
.42 Cup Primed Cartridge, 6 Shot, Single Action, Spur Trigger, Tip-up, *Antique*	450	950	1250

EARLHOOD

Made by E. L. Dickinson Co., Springfield, Mass., 1870–1880.

HANDGUN, REVOLVER

	Fair	V. Good	Excellent
.32 Short R.F., 5 Shot, Spur Trigger, Solid Frame, Single Action, *Antique*	$50	$125	$175

EARLY, AMOS

Dauphin Co., Pa. See Kentucky Rifles.

EARLY, JACOB

Dauphin Co., Pa. See Kentucky Rifles.

EARTHQUAKE

See Earlhood.

EASTERN

Made by Stevens Arms.

SHOTGUN, DOUBLE BARREL, SIDE-BY-SIDE

Model 311, Various Gauges, Hammerless, Steel Barrel, *Modern*	100	175	250

SHOTGUN, SINGLESHOT

Model 94, Various Gauges, Takedown, Automatic Ejector, Plain Hammer, *Modern*	25	50	75

EASTERN ARMS CO.

Made by Meriden Firearms and sold by Sears, Roebuck.

HANDGUN, REVOLVER

.32 S & W, 5 Shot, Double Action, Top Break, *Modern*	50	75	100
.38 S & W, 5 Shot, Double Action, Top Break, *Modern*	75	100	125

EASTFIELD

See Smith & Wesson.

ECHABERRIA, ARTURA

Spain, c. 1790.

	Fair	V. Good	Excellent
HANDGUN, MIQUELET-LOCK			
Pair, Holster Pistol, Plain, Brass Furniture, *Antique*	$1500	$4000	$5500

ECHASA

Tradename used in the 1950s by Echave, Arizmendi y Cia., Eibar, Spain.

	Fair	V. Good	Excellent
HANDGUN, SELF-LOADING			
Model GZ MAB, .22 L.R.R.F., Clip Fed, Hammer, *Modern*	50	100	150

Echasa GZ-MAB

	Fair	V. Good	Excellent
Model GZ MAB, .25 ACP, Clip Fed, Hammer, *Modern*	75	125	150
Model GZ MAB, .32 ACP, Clip Fed, Hammer, *Modern*	75	125	175

ECLIPSE

Made by Johnson, Bye & Co., c. 1875.

	Fair	V. Good	Excellent
HANDGUN, SINGLESHOT			
.25 Short R.F., Derringer, Spur Trigger, *Antique*	50	100	125

EDGESON

Lincolnshire, England, 1810–1830.

	Fair	V. Good	Excellent
HANDGUN, FLINTLOCK			
.45, Pair, Box Lock, Screw Barrel, Pocket Pistol, Folding Trigger, Plain, *Antique*	500	1200	1750

EDMONDS, J.

See Kentucky Rifles.

EGG, CHARLES

London, England, c. 1850.

	Fair	V. Good	Excellent
HANDGUN, PERCUSSION			
Pepperbox, .36, 6 Shot, 3½" Barrels, *Antique*	$165	$325	$600

EGG, DURS

London, England, 1770–1840. Also see British Military.

	Fair	V. Good	Excellent
HANDGUN, FLINTLOCK			
.50, Dueling Type, Holster Pistol, Octagon Barrel, Steel Furniture, Light Ornamentation, *Antique*	750	2000	2750
HANDGUN, PERCUSSION			
6 Shot, Pepperbox, Fluted Barrel, Pocket Pistol, Engraved, *Antique*	1000	1500	2250

EGYPTIAN MILITARY

	Fair	V. Good	Excellent
HANDGUN, SELF-LOADING			
Tokagypt M-58, 9mm Luger, Clip Fed, *Curio*	150	300	400
RIFLE, SELF-LOADING			
Hakim, .22 L.R.R.F., Training Rifle, Military, *Modern*	125	250	300
Hakim, 8mm Mauser, Military, *Modern*	100	175	275

84 GUN CO.

Eighty-Four, Pa., c. 1973.

	Fair	V. Good	Excellent
RIFLE, BOLT ACTION			
Classic Rifle, Various Calibers, Checkered Stock, Grade 1, *Modern*	125	250	300
Classic Rifle, Various Calibers, Checkered Stock, Grade 2, *Modern*	150	300	400
Classic Rifle, Various Calibers, Checkered Stock, Grade 3, *Modern*	200	400	500
Classic Rifle, Various Calibers, Checkered Stock, Grade 4, *Modern*	300	600	800
Lobo Rifle, Various Calibers, Checkered Stock, Grade 1, *Modern*	200	350	450
Lobo Rifle, Various Calibers, Checkered Stock, Grade 2, *Modern*	200	400	500
Lobo Rifle, Various Calibers, Checkered Stock, Grade 3, *Modern*	300	600	800
Lobo Rifle, Various Calibers, Checkered Stock, Grade 4, *Modern*	350	800	1200
Pennsy Rifle, Various Calibers, Checkered Stock, Grade 1, *Modern*	200	350	450
Pennsy Rifle, Various Calibers, Checkered Stock, Grade 2, *Modern*	250	450	550
Pennsy Rifle, Various Calibers, Checkered Stock, Grade 3, *Modern*	300	600	800
Pennsy Rifle, Various Calibers, Checkered Stock, Grade 4, *Modern*	350	900	1100

	Fair	V. Good	Excellent
Pennsy Rifle, Various Calibers, Checkered Stock, Standard Grade, *Modern*	$150	$250	$325

EL FAISAN

SHOTGUN, DOUBLE BARREL, SIDE-BY-SIDE

	Fair	V. Good	Excellent
El Faisan, .410 Gauge, Folding Gun, Double Trigger, Outside Hammers, *Modern*	50	75	100

EL TIGRE

RIFLE, LEVER ACTION

	Fair	V. Good	Excellent
Copy of Winchester M1892, 44-40 WCF, Tube Feed, *Modern*	200	400	600

ELECTOR

Made by Hopkins & Allen, c. 1880.

HANDGUN, REVOLVER

	Fair	V. Good	Excellent
.22 Short R.F., 7 Shot, Spur Trigger, Solid Frame, Single Action, *Antique*	50	100	150
.32 Short R.F., 5 Shot, Spur Trigger, Solid Frame, Single Action, *Antique*	75	125	175

ELECTRIC

Made by Forehand & Wadsworth, 1871–1880.

HANDGUN, REVOLVER

	Fair	V. Good	Excellent
.32 Short R.F., 5 Shot, Spur Trigger, Solid Frame, Single Action, *Antique*	75	125	175

ELGIN ARMS CO.

Made by Crescent for Fred Bifflar & Co., Chicago, Ill. See Crescent Fire Arms Co., Shotgun, Double Barrel, Side-by-Side; Shotgun, Single Shot.

ELGIN CUTLASS PISTOLS

Springfield, Mass. Made by C. B. Allen, and Merrill, Mossman & Blair. Blades made by Ames Sword Co., c. 1835. One of the more unusual oddities and among the most sought-after of rarities in arms collecting, the most desirable of Elgin Cutlass pistols were those made for U.S. Navy service on the Wilkes South Seas Expedition of 1838–42; some of these arms also made their way to the American West. Touted as the "Elgin patent Bowie knives with pistol attached will shoot and cut at the same time," the unusual pistol was protected by a patent of 1837. The naval design was made in a total of about 150, by C. B. Allen, Springfield, Massachusetts; and examples are known to have been sold in St. Louis in December 1838. The stylings by Merrill, Mossman & Blair and by Mossman & Blair, made in nearby Amherst, Massachusetts, had barrels of approximately three to six inches, and were chambered for .34 to .54 calibers.

HANDGUN, PERCUSSION

	Fair	V. Good	Excellent
Allen Small Frame, 35-41 Cal., 4"- 5" Octagonal Barrel and $7\frac{1}{2}$" - 10" Blade, *Antique*	$3000	$5000	$7000
M.M.&B. Medium Frame, .31-36 Cal., 4" Round Barrel and $8\frac{3}{4}$" - $9\frac{1}{2}$" Blade, *Antique*	2500	4500	5750
U.S. Navy Model (Allen), 54 Cal., 5" Octagonal Barrel and 11" Blade, *Antique*	6000	12500	17500

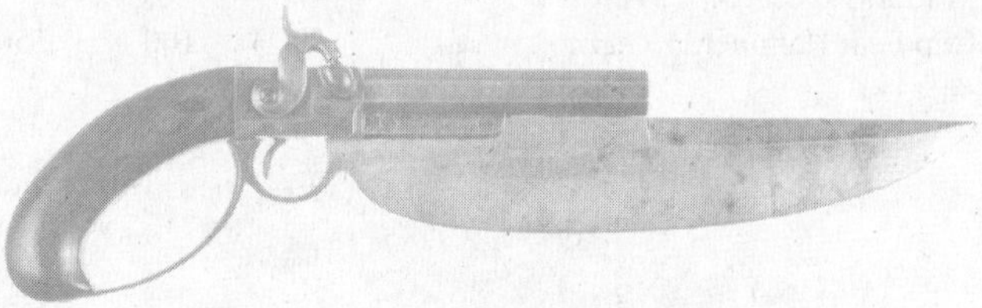

Elgin Cutlass Pistol, .54 Caliber

ELLIS, REUBEN

Albany, N.Y., 1808–1829.

RIFLE, FLINTLOCK

	Fair	V. Good	Excellent
Ellis-Jennings, .69, Sliding Lock for Multiple Loadings, 4 shot, *Antique*	7000	16000	22500
Ellis-Jennings, .69, Sliding Lock for Multiple Loadings, 10 shot, *Antique*	10000	26000	32500

E.M.F.

(Early and Modern Firearms Co., Inc.) Studio City, Calif.

HANDGUN, REVOLVER

	Fair	V. Good	Excellent
California Dragoon, .44 Magnum, Single Action, Western Style, Engraved, *Modern*	125	225	300
Dakota, Various Calibers, Single Action, Western Style, *Modern*	125	175	275
Dakota, Various Calibers, Single Action, Western Style, Engraved, *Modern*	125	250	350
Dakota, Various Calibers, Single Action, Western Style, Nickel Plated, *Modern*	125	200	300
Dakota, Various Calibers, Single Action, Western Style, Nickel Plated, Engraved, *Modern*	125	275	375
Dakota Buntline, Various Calibers, 12" Barrel, Single Action, Western Style, *Modern*	100	200	300
Dakota Buckhorn, Various Calibers, $16\frac{1}{4}$" Barrel, Single Action, Western Style, *Modern*	125	200	300
Dakota Buckhorn, Various Calibers, $16\frac{1}{4}$" Barrel, Single Action, Western Style, with Shoulder Stock, *Modern*	100	200	325
Dakota Sheriff, Various Calibers, Single Action, Western Style, *Modern*	125	225	300

	Fair	V. Good	Excellent
Super Dakota, Various Calibers, Single Action, Western Style, Magnum, *Modern*	$100	$225	$325
Outlaw 1875, Various Calibers, Single Action, Remington Style, Engraved, *Modern*	100	175	275
Outlaw 1875, Various Calibers, Single Action, Remington Style, Engraved, *Modern*	125	225	350
Thermodynamics, .357 Magnum, Solid Frame, Swing-out Cylinder, Vent Rib, Stainless Steel, *Modern*	75	150	250

HANDGUN, SINGLESHOT

	Fair	V. Good	Excellent
Baron, .22 Short R.F., Derringer, Gold Frame, Blue Barrel, Wood Grips, *Modern*	25	50	75
Baron, Count, Etc., Derringer, if Cased Add $10.00-$15.00			
Baroness, .22 Short R.F., Derringer, Gold Plated, Pearl Grips, *Modern*	25	50	75
Count, .22 Short R.F., Derringer, Blue, Wood Grips, *Modern*	15	25	50
Rolling Block, .357 Magnum, Remington Copy, *Modern*	50	100	150

RIFLE, LEVER ACTION

	Fair	V. Good	Excellent
1866 Yellowboy Carbine, Various Calibers, Brass Frame, Winchester Copy, *Modern*	200	375	475
1866 Yellowboy Carbine, Various Calibers, Brass Frame, Winchester Copy, Engraved, *Modern*	200	450	625
1873 Carbine, Various Calibers, Winchester Copy, *Modern*	200	375	475
1873 Rifle, Various Calibers, Winchester Copy, *Modern*	350	500	650
1873 Rifle, Various Calibers, Winchester Copy, Engraved, *Modern*	200	350	575

EM-GE

Gerstenberger & Eberwein, Gussenstadt, Germany.

HANDGUN, REVOLVER

	Fair	V. Good	Excellent
Model 220 KS, .22 L.R.R.F., Double Action, *Modern*	25	50	75
Model 223, .22 W.M.R., Double Action, *Modern*	25	50	75
Target Model 200, .22 L.R.R.F., Double Action, Target Sights, Vent Rib, *Modern*	50	75	100

EMPIRE

Made by Jacob Rupertus, 1858–1888.

HANDGUN, REVOLVER

	Fair	V. Good	Excellent
.22 Short R.F., 7 Shot, Spur Trigger, Solid Frame, Single Action, *Antique*	50	125	175
.38 Short R.F., 5 Shot, Spur Trigger, Solid Frame, Single Action, *Antique*	$100	$200	$300
.41 Short R.F., 5 Shot, Spur Trigger, Solid Frame, Single Action, *Antique*	125	225	300

EMPIRE ARMS

Made by Meriden and distributed by H. & D. Folsom.

HANDGUN, REVOLVER

	Fair	V. Good	Excellent
.32 S & W, 5 Shot, Double Action, Top Break, *Modern*	50	100	125
.38 S & W, 5 Shot, Double Action, Top Break, *Modern*	50	100	125

EMPIRE ARMS CO.

Made by Crescent for Sears, Roebuck & Co., c. 1900. See Crescent Fire Arms Co., Shotgun, Double Barrel, Side-by-Side; Shotgun, Singleshot.

EMPIRE STATE

Made by Meriden Firearms, and distributed by H & D Folsom.

HANDGUN, REVOLVER

	Fair	V. Good	Excellent
.32 S & W, 5 Shot, Double Action, Top Break, *Modern*	50	75	100
.38 S & W, 5 Shot, Double Action, Top Break, *Modern*	50	75	100

EMPRESS

Made by Jacob Rupertus, 1858–1888.

HANDGUN, REVOLVER

	Fair	V. Good	Excellent
.32 Short R.F., 5 Shot, Spur Trigger, Solid Frame, Single Action, *Antique*	100	175	225

ENCORE

Made by Johnson-Bye, also by Hopkins & Allen, 1847–1887.

HANDGUN, REVOLVER

	Fair	V. Good	Excellent
.22 Short R.F., 7 Shot, Spur Trigger, Solid Frame, Single Action, *Antique*	50	100	150
.32 Short R.F., 5 Shot, Spur Trigger, Solid Frame, Single Action, *Antique*	75	125	175
.38 R.F., 5 Shot, Spur Trigger, Solid Frame, Single Action, *Antique*	100	150	200

ENDERS OAKLEAF

Made by Crescent for Shapleigh Hardware Co., St. Louis, Mo. See Crescent Fire Arms Co., Shotgun, Double Barrel, Side-by-Side; Shotgun, Singleshot.

ENTERPRISE

Made by Enterprise Gun Works, Pittsburgh, Pa., c. 1875.

	Fair	V. Good	Excellent
HANDGUN, REVOLVER			
#1, .22 Short R.F., 7 Shot, Spur Trigger, Solid Frame, Single Action, *Antique*	$75	$125	$175
#2, .32 Short R.F., 5 Shot, Spur Trigger, Solid Frame, Single Action, *Antique*	100	150	225
#3, .38 Short R.F., 5 Shot, Spur Trigger, Solid Frame, Single Action, *Antique*	125	175	250
#4, .41 Short R.F., 5 Shot, Spur Trigger, Solid Frame, Single Action, *Antique*	150	300	375

ERBI

	Fair	V. Good	Excellent
SHOTGUN, DOUBLE BARREL, SIDE-BY-SIDE			
Deluxe Ejector Grade, 12 and 20 Gauge, Raised Matted Rib, Double Trigger, Checkered Stock, Beavertail Fore End, Automatic Ejector, *Modern*	100	175	350
Field Grade, 12 and 20 Gauge, Raised Matted Rib, Double Trigger, Checkered Stock, *Modern*	100	150	275

ERIKA

Francios Pfannl, Krems, Austria, 1913–1926.

	Fair	V. Good	Excellent
HANDGUN, SELF-LOADING			
4.25mm, Clip Fed, Blue, *Curio*	250	450	650

ERMA

Erfurter Maschinen u. Werkzeugfabrik, Erfurt, Germany, prior to WWII, and after the war became Erma-Werke, Munich-Dachau, West Germany. Imported by Excam, Miami, Fla.

	Fair	V. Good	Excellent
HANDGUN, REVOLVER			
Model 440, .38 Spec., Double Action, Swing-Out Cylinder, Stainless, *Modern*	75	150	200
Model 442, .22 L.R.R.F., Double Action, Swing-Out Cylinder, Blue, *Modern*	75	125	175
Model 443, .22 W.M.R., Double Action, Swing-Out Cylinder, Blue, *Modern*	75	125	175
HANDGUN, SELF-LOADING			
EP-22, .22 L.R.R.F., Clip Fed, *Modern*	75	150	200
EP-25, .25 ACP, Clip Fed, *Modern*	100	175	225
ET-22 Luger, .22 L.R.R.F., Clip Fed, *Modern*	125	200	275
ET-22 Luger, .22 L.R.R.F., Clip Fed, with Conversion Kit, Cased with Accessories, *Modern*	$200	$350	$450
FB-1, .25 ACP, Clip Fed, *Modern*	50	75	125
KGP-68 (Baby), .32 ACP, Clip Fed, *Modern*	125	250	325
KGP-68 (Baby), .380 ACP, Clip Fed, *Modern*	150	275	325
KGP-69, .22 L.R.R.F., Clip Fed, *Modern*	125	250	325
LA-22 PO 8, .22 L.R.R.F., Clip Fed, *Modern*	125	200	275
New Model Target, .22 L.R.R.F., Clip Fed, *Modern*	125	250	300
Old Model Target, .22 L.R.R.F., Clip Fed, *Modern*	125	225	250
RX-22, .22 L.R.R.F., Double Action, Clip Fed, *Modern*	100	175	225
RIFLE, BOLT ACTION			
EG-61, .22 L.R.R.F., Singleshot, Open Sights, *Modern*	50	75	100
M1957 KK, .22 L.R.R.F., Military Style Training Rifle, *Modern*	50	75	100
M98 Conversation Unit, .22 L.R.R.F., Clip Fed, Cased, *Modern*	125	250	300
Master Target, .22 L.R.R.F., Checkered Stock, Peep Sights, *Modern*	75	125	175
RIFLE, LEVER ACTION			
EG-71, .22 L.R.R.F., Tube Feed, *Modern*	50	100	150
EG-712, .22 L.R.R.F., Tube Feed, *Modern*	75	125	175
EG-712 L, .22 L.R.R.F., Tube Feed, Octagon Barrel, Nickel Silver Receiver, *Modern*	125	200	275
EG-73, .22 W.M.R., Tube Feed, *Modern*	100	150	200
RIFLE, SELF-LOADING			
EGM-1, .22 L.R.R.F., Clip Fed, *Modern*	100	125	150
EM-1, .22 L.R.R.F., Clip Fed, *Modern*	100	125	150
ESG22, .22 L.R.R.F., Clip Fed, *Modern*	100	125	150
ESG22, .22 W.M.R., Clip Fed, *Modern*	100	175	250

ESSEX

Made by Crescent for Belknap Hardware Co., Louisville, Ky. See Crescent Fire Arms Co., Shotgun, Double Barrel, Side-by-Side; Shotgun, Single Shot.

ESSEX

Made by Stevens Arms.

	Fair	V. Good	Excellent

RIFLE, BOLT ACTION

Model 50, .22 L.R.R.F., Singleshot, Takedown, *Modern*	$15	$25	$50
Model 53, .22 L.R.R.F., Singleshot, Takedown, *Modern*	15	25	50
Model 56 Buckhorn, .22 L.R.R.F., 5 Shot Clip, Open Rear Sights, *Modern*	15	25	50

SHOTGUN, DOUBLE BARREL, SIDE-BY-SIDE

Model 515, Various Gauges, Hammerless, *Modern*	50	100	200

ESSEX

Makers of pistol frames in Island Pond, Vt.

HANDGUN, SELF-LOADING

Colt M1911 Copy, .45 ACP, Parts Gun, *Modern*	125	200	300

ESTEVA, PEDRO

Spain, c. 1740.

HANDGUN, FLINTLOCK

Pair, Belt Pistol, Silver Inlay, Silver Furniture, Engraved, Half-Octagon Barrel, *Antique*	3000	7500	10000

EVANS RIFLE MFG. CO.

Mechanics Falls, Maine, 1868–1880. Not known particularly for its grace and beauty, nevertheless the Evans lever-action repeating magazine rifle was one of the most intriguing of designs from the second half of the 19th century. With a spiral magazine design, a total of 28 or 34 cartridges could be inserted in the rifle loading port (located in the butt), allowing the shooter a substantial supply of ammunition—far more than conventional Winchesters. Despite the mechanical innovations, the Evans production had the distinct disadvantage of exceptional weight, and poor, butt-heavy balance. Among celebrity owners of Evans rifles were W. F. "Buffalo Bill" Cody and Mexican President and keen arms collector Porfirio Diaz. At present Cody's Evans, a gift from the factory, is on display at the Cody Firearms Museum, and perhaps the most exquisitely engraved specimen known is at the Royal Military College Museum, Kingston, Ontario. The L. D. Nimschke engraving record illustrates some handsome designs developed by L.D.N. and engraved on a few specimens.

RIFLE, LEVER ACTION

New Model, .44 C.F., Tube Feed, Dust Cover, Carbine, *Antique*	375	900	1350
New Model, .44 C.F., Tube Feed, Dust Cover, Military Musket, *Antique*	500	1200	1600
New Model, .44 C.F., Tube Feed, Dust Cover, Sporting Rifle, *Antique*	325	800	1100
Old Model, .44 C.F., Upper Buttstock Only, Tube Feed, Sporting Rifle, *Antique*	500	1000	1250

Two Spencer lever-action breechloading carbines, the top an early .52 rimfire example, and the center an example in .50 caliber, the Model 1865, by Burnside Rifle Co., sometimes known as "The Indian Model." At bottom, an Evans lever-action carbine in .44 caliber, made at Mechanics Falls, Maine; capacity of 26 cartridges.

	Fair	V. Good	Excellent

EVANS, STEPHEN

Valley Forge, Pa., 1742–1797. See Kentucky Rifles and U.S. Military.

EVANS, WILLIAMS

London, England, 1883–1900.

SHOTGUN, DOUBLE BARREL, SIDE-BY-SIDE

Pair, 12 Gauge, Double Trigger, Plain, Cased, *Modern*	$2500	$5000	$9500
Pair, 12 Gauge, Double Trigger, Straight Grip, Cased, *Modern*	3000	6000	10000

EXCAM

Importers, Hialeah, Fla. Also see Erma and Tanarmi.

HANDGUN, DOUBLE BARREL, OVER-UNDER

TA-38, .38 Special, 2 Shot, Derringer, *Modern*	50	75	100

HANDGUN, REVOLVER

Buffalo Scout TA-22, .22 L.R.R.F., Western Style, Single Action, Brass Backstrap, *Modern*	50	75	100
Buffalo Scout TA-22, .22 LR/.22 WMR Combo, Western Style, Single Action, Brass Backstrap, *Modern*	75	125	150
Buffalo Scout TA-22, .22 LR/.22 WMR Combo, Western Style, Single Action, Brass Backstrap, Target Sights, *Modern*	50	125	150
Buffalo Scout TA-76, .22 L.R.R.F., Western Style, Single Action, *Modern*	50	100	125

	Fair	V. Good	Excellent
Buffalo Scout TA-76, .22 LR/.22 WMR Combo, Western Style, Single Action, *Modern*	$75	$125	$150
Warrior, .22 L.R.R.F., Double Action, Blue, Vent Rib, *Modern*	50	75	100
Warrior, .22 LR/.22 WMR Combo, Double Action, Blue, Vent Rib, *Modern*	75	100	125
Warrior, .357 Magnum, Double Action, Blue, Vent Rib, Target Sights, *Modern*	75	125	150
Warrior, .38 Spec., Double Action, Blue, Vent Rib, Target Sights, *Modern*	75	100	125

HANDGUN, SELF-LOADING

	Fair	V. Good	Excellent
GT-22, .22 L.R.R.F., Clip Fed, *Modern*	50	125	150
GT-26, .25 ACP, Clip Fed, Steel Frame, *Modern*	50	100	125
GT-27, .25 ACP, Clip Fed, *Modern*	50	100	125
GT-27, .25 ACP, Clip Fed, Steel Frame, *Modern*	50	100	125
GT-32, .32 ACP, Clip Fed, *Modern*	50	100	125
GT-32, .32 ACP, Clip Fed, 12 Shot, *Modern*	50	100	125
GT-380, .25 ACP, Clip Fed, Engraved, *Modern*	50	100	125
GT-380, .380 ACP, Clip Fed, *Modern*	50	100	125
GT-380, .380 ACP, Clip Fed, 11 Short, *Modern*	$100	$150	$170
RX-22, .22 L.R.R.F., Clip Fed, *Modern*	50	100	125

EXCELSIOR

Made by Norwich Pistol Co., c. 1880.

HANDGUN, REVOLVER

	Fair	V. Good	Excellent
.32 Short R.F., 5 Shot, Spur Trigger, Solid Frame, Single Action, *Antique*	75	125	175

EXCELSIOR

Made in Italy.

SHOTGUN, DOUBLE BARREL, SIDE-BY-SIDE

	Fair	V. Good	Excellent
Super 88, 12 Ga. Mag 3", Boxlock, Checkered Stock, *Modern*	150	275	350

EXPRESS

Made by Bacon Arms Co., c. 1880.

HANDGUN, REVOLVER

	Fair	V. Good	Excellent
.22 Short R.F., 7 Shot, Spur Trigger, Solid Frame, Single Action, *Antique*	75	125	175

F

F.I.E.

Firearms Import & Export Corp., Miami, Fla.

	Fair	V. Good	Excellent
HANDGUN, DOUBLE BARREL, OVER-UNDER			
D 38, .38 Special, Derringer, *Modern*	$35	$50	$100
D 86, .38 Special, Derringer, *Modern*	55	75	100
HANDGUN, FLINTLOCK			
Kentucky, .44, Belt Pistol, Engraved, Reproduction	15	25	50
Kentucky, .44, Belt Pistol, Reproduction	15	25	50
Tower, .69	15	25	40
HANDGUN, PERCUSSION			
Baby Dragoon, .31, Revolver, Engraved, Reproduction	15	50	75
Baby Dragoon, .31, Revolver, Reproduction	15	50	75
Kentucky, .44, Belt Pistol, Engraved, Reproduction	15	50	75
Kentucky, .44, Belt Pistol, Reproduction	15	50	75
Navy, .36, Revolver, Engraved, Reproduction	15	50	75
Navy, .36, Revolver, Reproduction.	15	40	60
Navy, .44, Revolver, Engraved, Reproduction	15	50	75
Navy, .44, Revolver, Reproduction	15	40	60
Remington, .36, Revolver, Engraved, Reproduction	15	50	75
Remington, .36, Revolver, Reproduction	15	40	60
Remington, .44, Revolver, Engraved, Reproduction	15	50	75
Remington, .44, Revolver, Reproduction	15	40	60
HANDGUN, REVOLVER			
Arminius, .22 L.R.R.F., Double Action, Swing-out Cylinder, Fixed Sights, Chrome, *Modern*	25	50	75
Arminius, .22 L.R.R.F., Double Action, Swing-out Cylinder, Adjustable Sights, Blue, *Modern*	25	60	80
Arminius, .22 L.R.R.F., Double Action, Swing-out Cylinder, Adjustable Sights, Chrome, *Modern*	50	75	100
Arminius, .22 L.R.R.F., Double Action, Swing-out Cylinder, Adjustable Sights, Blue, Target, *Modern*	$50	$75	$100
Arminius, .22 L.R.R.F., Double Action, Swing-out Cylinder, Adjustable Sights, Chrome, Target, *Modern*	50	75	100
Arminius, .22 LR/.22 WMR Combo, Double Action, Swing-out Cylinder, Fixed Sights, Chrome, *Modern*	50	100	125
Arminius, .22 LR/.22 WMR Combo, Double Action, Swing-out Cylinder, Adjustable Sights, Chrome, *Modern*	50	100	125
Arminius, .22 LR/.22 WMR Combo, Double Action, Swing-out Cylinder, Adjustable Sights, Blue, *Modern*	50	100	125
Arminius, .22 LR/.22 WMR Combo, Double Action, Swing-out Cylinder, Adjustable Sights, Blue, Target, *Modern*	50	100	125
Arminius, .32 S & W, Double Action, Swing-out Cylinder, Adjustable Sights, Blue, Target, *Modern*	50	75	100
Arminius, .32 S & W, Double Action, Swing-out Cylinder, Adjustable Sights, Chrome, Target, *Modern*	50	100	125
Arminius, .357 Magnum, Double Action, Swing-out Cylinder, Adjustable Sights, Chrome, Target, *Modern*	50	100	125
Arminius, .357 Magnum, Double Action, Swing-out Cylinder, Adjustable Sights, Blue, Target, *Modern*	75	125	150
Arminius, .38 Special, Double Action, Swing-out Cylinder, Adjustable Sights, Blue, Target, *Modern*	50	100	125
Arminius, .38 Special, Double Action, Swing-out Cylinder, Adjustable Sights, Chrome, Target, *Modern*	50	100	125
Arminius, .38 Special, Double Action, Swing-out Cylinder, Blue, *Modern*	25	50	75
Arminius, .38 Special, Double Action, Swing-out Cylinder, Chrome, *Modern*	25	50	75
Buffalo Scout, .22LR/.22 WMR Combo, Single Action, Western Style, *Modern*	50	75	100
Buffalo, .22 L.R.R.F., Single Action, Western Style, ., *Modern*	15	40	60
Guardian, .22 L.R.R.F., Double Action, Swing-out Cylinder, *Modern*	15	40	60
Guardian, .22 L.R.R.F., Double Action, Swing-out Cylinder, Chrome, *Modern*	15	40	60

	Fair	V. Good	Excellent
Guardian, .32 S & W, Double Action, Swing-out Cylinder, *Modern*	$15	$40	$60
Guardian, .32 S & W, Double Action, Swing-out Cylinder, Chrome, *Modern*	15	40	60
Hombre, .357 Magnum, Single Action, Western Style, Steel Frame, *Modern*	75	150	200
Hombre, .44 Mag, Single Action, Western Style, Steel Frame, *Modern*	100	175	225
Hombre, .45 L.C., Single Action, Western Style, Steel Frame, *Modern*	100	175	225
Legend, .22 L.R.R.F., Single Action, Western Style, Steel Frame, *Modern*	25	75	100
Legend, .22LR/.22 WMR Combo, Single Action, Western Style, Steel Frame, *Modern*	50	100	125
Texas Ranger, .22LR/.22 WMR Combo, Single Action, Western Style, Steel Frame, *Modern*	50	100	125

HANDGUN, SELF-LOADING

	Fair	V. Good	Excellent
Best, .25 ACP, Hammer, Steel Frame, Blue, *Modern*	50	75	100
Guardian, .25 ACP, Hammer, Blue, *Modern*	25	50	75
Guardian, .25 ACP, Hammer, Chrome, *Modern*	25	50	75
Guardian, .25 ACP, Hammer, Gold Plated, *Modern*	25	50	75
Interdynamics KG-9, 9mm Luger, Clip Fed, *Modern*	150	325	375
Interdynamics Mini-99, 9mm Luger, Clip Fed, *Modern*	125	200	250
Super Titan II, .32 ACP, Hammer, Steel Frame, Blue, 13 Shot, *Modern*	50	75	100
Super Titan II, .380 ACP, Hammer, Steel Frame, Blue, 12 Shot, *Modern*	75	150	175
Titan, .25 ACP, Hammer, Blue, *Modern*	25	40	60
Titan, .25 ACP, Hammer, Chrome, *Modern*	25	40	60
Titan, .32 ACP, Hammer, Steel Frame, Blue, *Modern*	50	75	100
Titan, .32 ACP, Hammer, Steel Frame, Chrome, *Modern*	50	75	100
Titan, .32 ACP, Hammer, Steel Frame, Engraved, Blue, *Modern*	50	75	100
Titan, .32 ACP, Hammer, Steel Frame, Engraved, Chrome, *Modern*	50	75	100
Titan, .380 ACP, Hammer, Steel Frame, Blue, *Modern*	50	100	125
Titan, .380 ACP, Hammer, Steel Frame, Chrome, *Modern*	50	100	125
Titan, .380 ACP, Hammer, Steel Frame, Engraved, Blue, *Modern*	75	150	175
Titan, .380 ACP, Hammer, Steel Frame, Engraved, Chrome, *Modern*	100	175	200
TZ-75, 9mm. Luger, Clip Fed, Double Action, Hammer, Adjustable Sights, Wood Grips, *Modern*	$125	$225	$275

RIFLE, FLINTLOCK

	Fair	V. Good	Excellent
Kentucky, .45, Engraved, Reproduction	50	100	125
Kentucky, .45, Reproduction	40	80	100

RIFLE, PERCUSSION

	Fair	V. Good	Excellent
Berdan, .45, Reproduction	50	100	125
Kentucky, .45, Engraved, Reproduction, *Antique*	50	100	125
Kentucky, .45, Reproduction, *Antique*	40	80	100
Zoave, .58, Reproduction, *Antique*	50	100	125

COMBINATION WEAPON, OVER-UNDER

	Fair	V. Good	Excellent
Combo, 30/30-20 Ga., *Modern*	50	100	125

SHOTGUN, DOUBLE BARREL, OVER-UNDER

	Fair	V. Good	Excellent
OU, 12 and 20 Ga., Field Grade, Vent Rib, *Modern*	100	200	225
OU 12 T, 12 Ga., Trap Grade, Vent Rib, *Modern*	125	200	225
OU-S, 12 and 20 Ga., Skeet Grade, Vent Rib, *Modern*	125	225	250

SHOTGUN, DOUBLE BARREL, SIDE-BY-SIDE

	Fair	V. Good	Excellent
Brute, Various Gauges, Short Barrels, Short Stock, *Modern*	50	100	150
DB, Various Gauges, Hammerless, *Modern*	50	75	125
DB Riot, Various Gauges, Hammerless, *Modern*	50	75	125

SHOTGUN, SINGLESHOT

	Fair	V. Good	Excellent
S.O.B., 12 and 20 Gauges, Short Barrel, Short Stock, *Modern*	25	40	60
SB 12 16 20.410, Various Gauges, Hammer, *Modern*	25	40	60
SB 40, 12 Ga., Hammer, Button Break, *Modern*	25	40	60
SB 41, 20 Ga., Hammer, Button Break, *Modern*	25	40	60
SB 42, .410 Ga., Hammer, Button Break, *Modern*	25	40	60
SB Youth, Various Gauges, Hammer, *Modern*	25	40	60

FABRIQUE D'ARMES DE GUERRE

Spain, c. 1900.

HANDGUN, SELF-LOADING

	Fair	V. Good	Excellent
Paramount, .25 ACP, Clip Fed, *Modern*	75	150	200

FABRIQUE D'ARMES DE GUERRE DE GRAND

HANDGUN, SELF-LOADING

	Fair	V. Good	Excellent
Bulwak, .25 ACP, Clip Fed, *Modern*	$75	$125	$150
Colonial, .25 ACP, Clip Fed, *Modern*	75	150	175
Colonial, .32 ACP, Clip Fed, *Modern*	75	175	200
Helvece, .25 ACP, Clip Fed, *Modern*	75	125	150
Jupiter, .32 ACP, Clip Fed, *Modern*	75	125	150
Libia, .32 ACP, Clip Fed, *Modern*	75	150	175
Looking Glass, .32 ACP, Clip Fed, *Modern*	75	150	175
Looking Glass, .32 ACP, Clip Fed, Grip Safety, *Modern*	75	175	200
Trust, .25 ACP, Clip Fed, *Modern*	75	125	150

FABRIQUE NATIONALE

Herstal, Belgium, from 1889. Also see Browning and Belgian Military. One of Europe's most historic gunmakers, FN was given a boost in its product line by the willingness of John M. Browning to license the firm to manufacture shotguns, handguns and other arms of his invention. In 1967 the author was on a firearms tour of Europe, and through his friend, arms engraver Rene Delcour, was given a tour of the FN workshops. The enormity of the firm was truly impressive and the engraving studio alone then employed over 125 artisans in the FN section, and about 50 in the Browning Arms Co. studio. There was some consternation at the time, since management had entered into arrangements of having production of some products done in Japan. Employees in Herstal saw the demise of their national operations, due to the less expensive, but high quality Japanese work. Some workmen from Belgium were actually chastised for going to Japan to teach the new machinists. Alas, the concerns of the Belgian workers were well founded. Today FN is much smaller than in those days—the bulk of the engraving is now executed by a consortium of craftsmen; that substantial studio no longer exists. John Browning became a national hero in Belgium, and was responsible for the employment of literally thousands of workmen over the years. It was, in fact, in Belgium, in 1926, while working at the FN factory on a new project, where the brilliant inventor and designer died.

RIFLE, BOLT ACTION

	Fair	V. Good	Excellent
Mauser 98 Military Style, 30/06, Military Finish, Military Stock, Commercial, *Modern*	100	200	300
Mauser 98 Military Style, Various Military Calibers, Military Finish, Military Stock, Commercial, *Modern*	75	150	225
Mauser Deluxe Presentation, Various Calibers, Sporting Rifle, Fancy Wood, Engraved, *Modern*	500	850	1250
Mauser Deluxe, Various Calibers, Sporting Rifle, Checkered Stock, Engraved, *Modern*	300	525	750
Mauser Supreme, Various Calibers, Sporting Rifle, Checkered Stock, *Modern*	$300	$500	$750
Mauser Supreme, Various Calibers, Sporting Rifle, Checkered Stock, Magnum, *Modern*	300	575	750
Model 1925 Deluxe, .22 L.R.R.F., Singleshot, Checkered Stock, *Modern*	50	75	100
Model 1925, .22 L.R.R.F., Singleshot, *Modern*	25	50	75

RIFLE, SELF-LOADING

	Fair	V. Good	Excellent
FN FAL, .308 Win., Clip Fed, Commercial, *Modern*	400	750	1000
FN LAR Competition, .308 Win., Clip Fed, Commercial, Flash Hider, *Modern*	700	1400	1750
FN LAR Heavy Barrel, .308 Win., Clip Fed, Commercial, Synthetic Stock, Bipod, *Modern*	800	1650	2000
FN LAR Heavy Barrel, .308 Win., Clip Fed, Commercial, Wood Stock, Bipod, *Modern*	800	1750	2100
FN LAR Paratrooper, .308 Win., Clip Fed, Commercial, Folding Stock, *Modern*	500	800	1000
FNC Competition, .223 Rem., Clip Fed, Commercial, Flash Hider, *Modern*	500	850	1100
FNC Paratrooper, .223 Rem., Clip Fed, Commercial, Folding Stock, *Modern*	600	1000	1250
M-49 Egyptian, 8mm Mauser, Clip Fed, Military, *Modern*	100	150	225
Model 1949, 30/06, Clip Fed, Military, *Modern*	150	350	450
Model 1949, 7mm or 9mm Mauser, Clip Fed, Military, *Modern*	150	275	400

SHOTGUN, BOLT ACTION

	Fair	V. Good	Excellent
9mm Shotshell, *Modern*	75	125	150

FALCON FIREARMS

Northridge, Calif.

HANDGUN, SELF-LOADING

	Fair	V. Good	Excellent
Portsider, .45 ACP, Clip Fed, Stainless Steel, *Modern*	250	400	500

FAMARS

Gardone, Val Trompia, Italy. The joint creation of Mario Abbiatico and Remo Salvinelli, Famars rapidly built an international reputation as one of Europe's finest gunmakers. When the author first visited the firm's factory, in the early 1970s, it was a relatively small operation, along a quiet street in Gardone, Val Trompia. In the 1980s the company built an impressive, modern structure along the main highway through Gardone. This new building has more than ample space, with the most modern equipment in a comfortable production complex, with a handsome showroom and offices.

Fair V. Good Excellent

Abbiatico's books on fine guns were instantly popular, and alerted the world to the extraordinary work carried on in Val Trompia, not only by Famars, but by such companies as Fabbri, Rizzini, Piotti, and of course Beretta. Many would argue that considering price and quality, performance and reliability, the Italian best quality shotgun is as good as, if not better than, any made anywhere in the world today.

SHOTGUN, DOUBLE BARREL, SIDE-BY-SIDE

	Fair	V. Good	Excellent
Hammer Gun, Various Gauges, Automatic Ejector, Fancy Wood, Fancy Engraving, Double Trigger, *Modern*	$3500	$7000	$12500
Sidelock Gun, Various Gauges, Automatic Ejector, Double Trigger, Fancy Engraving, Fancy Wood, *Modern*	4500	10000	11500

Add 10% for 28 and 410 ga.

FARNOT, FRANK

Lancaster, Pa., 1779–1783. See Kentucky Rifles and Pistols.

FARNOT, FREDERICK

Lancaster, Pa., 1779–1782. See Kentucky Rifles and Pistols.

FARROW ARMS CO.

Holyoke, Mass. Established by William Farrow, 1878–1885. Became Farrow Arms Co. about 1885 and moved to Mason, Tenn., in 1904, then to Washington, D.C., in 1904 and remained in business until 1917.

RIFLE, SINGLESHOT

	Fair	V. Good	Excellent
#1, .30 Long R.F., Target Rifle, Octagon Barrel, Target Sights, Fancy Wood, *Antique*	1500	4000	6000
#2, .30 Long R.F., Target Rifle, Octagon Barrel, Target Sights, *Antique*	1000	3000	5000

FAST

Echave, Arizmendi y Cia, Eibar, Spain.

HANDGUN, SELF-LOADING

	Fair	V. Good	Excellent
Model 221, .22 L.R.R.F., Clip Fed, Blue, *Modern*	45	95	125
Model 221, .22 L.R.R.F., Clip Fed, Chrome, *Modern*	50	100	125
Model 631, .25 ACP, Clip Fed, Blue, *Modern*	50	100	125
Model 631, .25 ACP, Clip Fed, Chrome, *Modern*	50	100	125
Model 761, .32 ACP, Clip Fed, Blue, *Modern*	50	100	125
Model 761, .32 ACP, Clip Fed, Chrome, *Modern*	50	100	125
Model 901, .380 ACP, Clip Fed, Blue, *Modern*	50	125	150
Model 901, .380 ACP, Clip Fed, Chrome, *Modern*	$75	$150	$175

FAULTLESS GOOSE GUN

Made by Crescent for John M. Smythe Hdw. Co., Chicago, Ill. See Crescent Fire Arms Co., Shotgun, Double Barrel, Side-by-Side; Shotgun, Singleshot.

FAVORITE

Made by Johnson-Bye Co., c. 1874–1884.

HANDGUN, REVOLVER

	Fair	V. Good	Excellent
#1, .22 Short R.F., 7 Shot, Spur Trigger, Solid Frame, Single Action, *Antique*	75	125	150
#2, .32 Short R.F., 5 Shot, Spur Trigger, Solid Frame, Single Action, *Antique*	75	125	150
#3, .38 Short R.F., 5 Shot, Spur Trigger, Solid Frame, Single Action, *Antique*	100	150	200
#4, .41 Short R.F., 5 Shot, Spur Trigger, Solid Frame, Single Action, *Antique*	125	200	250

FAVORITE NAVY

Made by Johnson-Bye Co., c. 1874–1884.

HANDGUN, REVOLVER

	Fair	V. Good	Excellent
.44 Short R.F., 5 Shot, Spur Trigger, Solid Frame, Single Action, *Antique*	150	300	375

FAY, HENRY C.

Lancaster, Mass., c. 1837.

RIFLE, PERCUSSION

	Fair	V. Good	Excellent
.58, Military, *Antique*	1500	2750	3750

FECHT, G. VAN DER

Berlin, Germany, c. 1733.

RIFLE, FLINTLOCK

	Fair	V. Good	Excellent
Yaeger, Half-Octagon Barrel, Brass Furniture, Engraved, Carved, *Antique*	2000	4500	6000

FEDERAL ARMS

Made by Meriden Firearms, sold by Sears-Roebuck.

HANDGUN, REVOLVER

	Fair	V. Good	Excellent
.32 S & W, 5 Shot, Double Action, Top Break, *Modern*	50	75	100
.38 S & W, 5 Shot, Double Action, Top Break, *Modern*	50	75	100

FEMARU

Made by Femaru Fegyver es Gepgyar (Fegyvergyar) Pre-War; Post-War Made by Femaru es Szerszamgepgyar, N.V., Budapest, Hungary. Also see Frommer, Hungarian Military.

HANDGUN, SELF-LOADING

	Fair	V. Good	Excellent
M 29, .380 ACP, Clip Fed, Military, *Curio*	$125	$175	$275
M 37, .32 ACP, Clip Fed, Nazi-Proofed, *Modern*	150	250	325
M 37, .380 ACP, Clip Fed, Military, *Modern*	125	200	275
M 37, .380 ACP, Clip Fed, Nazi-Proofed, *Modern*	175	300	400

FENNO

Lancaster Pa., 1790–1800. See Kentucky Rifles and Pistols.

FERLACH

Genossenschaft der Buchsenmachermeister, Ferlach, Austria. One of the world's great gun centers, like Val Trompia in Italy, Ferlach is in a remote part of Austria, and is only reachable by car. The author visited this small city in 1972, and was quite overwhelmed by the quality of workmanship, and the number of dedicated craftsmen and gunmakers. A visit to the gunmaking school demonstrated that the future of fine gunmaking in Ferlach was assured. In the intervening years, a magnificent book was published on German and Austrian gun engravers, and the style of Ferlach guns has undergone a significant transformation. Fine makers like Peter Hofer, Wilfried Glanzning, Ludwig Borovnik and Schiering have built some of the most exquisite arms of all time. The style and ingenuity of the work of some makers reveals not only mechanical wizardry, but the artistic influence of British and Italian gunmakers. As a result, not all Ferlach arms have that old strongly Germanic look. One of the most appealing aspects of contemporary gunmaking is that the creations of the best of these craftsmen rival the work of the finest gunmakers in history. In the exalted realm of the world's greatest gunmakers, the Ferlach masters play a significant role.

RIFLE, DOUBLE BARREL, SIDE-BY-SIDE

	Fair	V. Good	Excellent
Standard Grade, Various Calibers, Boxlock, Engraved, Checkered Stock, Fancy Wood, *Modern*	1500	3000	4000
Standard Grade, Various Calibers, Sidelock, Engraved, Checkered Stock, Fancy Wood, *Modern*	2000	4500	6500

FERREE, JACOB

Lancaster, Pa., 1774–1784. See Kentucky Rifles and U.S. Military.

FESIG, CONRAD

Reading, Pa., 1779–1790. See Kentucky Rifles and Pistols.

FIALA

Made for Fiala Arms & Equipment Co. by Blakslee Forging Co., New Haven, Conn.

HANDGUN, MANUAL REPEATER

	Fair	V. Good	Excellent
.22 L.R.R.F., Clip Fed, Target Pistol, *Curio*	$200	$400	$450
.22 L.R.R.F., Clip Fed, Target Pistol, with Shoulder Stock, 20" Barrel, 3" Barrel, Cased, *Curio*	500	900	1150

FIEHL & WEEKS FIRE ARMS MFG. CO.

Philadelphia, Pa., c. 1895.

HANDGUN, REVOLVER

	Fair	V. Good	Excellent
.32 S & W, 5 Shot, Top Break, Hammerless, Double Action, *Modern*	50	75	100

FIEL

Erquiaga, Muguruzu y Cia., Eibar, Spain, c. 1920.

HANDGUN, SELF-LOADING

	Fair	V. Good	Excellent
Fiel #1, .25 ACP, Clip Fed, Eibar Style, *Curio*	50	100	125
Fiel #1, .32 ACP, Clip Fed, Eibar Style, *Curio*	50	100	125
Fiel #2, .25 ACP, Clip Fed, Breech Bolt, *Curio*	50	100	125

FIGTHORN, ANDREW

Reading, Pa., 1779–1790. See Kentucky Rifles.

FINNISH LION

Made by Valmet, Jyvaskyla, Finland.

RIFLE, BOLT ACTION

	Fair	V. Good	Excellent
Champion, .22 L.R.R.F., Singleshot, Free Rifle, Thumbhole Stock, Target Sights, Heavy Barrel, *Modern*	225	450	550
Match, .22 L.R.R.F., Singleshot, Target Rifle, Thumbhole Stock, Target Sights, *Modern*	200	350	500
Standard, .22 L.R.R.F., Singleshot, Target Rifle, Target Stock, Target Sights, U.I.T. Rifle, *Modern*	175	250	400

FIREARMS CO. LTD.

Made in England for Mandall Shooting Supplies.

RIFLE, BOLT ACTION

	Fair	V. Good	Excellent
Alpine Custom, Various Calibers, Checkered Stock, Recoil Pad, Open Rear Sight, *Modern*	200	275	350

	Fair	V. Good	Excellent
Alpine Standard, Various Calibers, Checkered Stock, Recoil Pad, Open Rear Sight, *Modern*	$150	$250	$350

FIREARMS INTERNATIONAL

Washington, D.C.

HANDGUN, REVOLVER

	Fair	V. Good	Excellent
Regent, .22 L.R.R.F., 7 Shot, Various Barrel Lengths, Blue, *Modern*	50	75	100
Regent, .22 L.R.R.F., 8 Shot, Various Barrel Lengths, Blue, *Modern*	50	75	100

HANDGUN, SELF-LOADING

	Fair	V. Good	Excellent
Combo, .22 L.R.R.F., Unique Model L Pistol with Conversion Kit for Stocked Rifle, *Modern*	75	125	150
Model D, .380 ACP., Clip Fed, Adjustable Sights, Blue, *Modern*	75	125	175
Model D, .380 ACP., Clip Fed, Adjustable Sights, Chrome, *Modern*	100	150	175
Model D, .380 ACP., Clip Fed, Adjustable Sights, Matt Blue, *Modern*	75	125	175

SHOTGUN, DOUBLE BARREL, SIDE-BY-SIDE

	Fair	V. Good	Excellent
Model 400, Various Gauges, Single Trigger, Checkered Stock, *Modern*	125	175	275
Model 400E, Various Gauges, Single Selective Trigger, Checkered Stock, Selective Ejector, Vent Rib, *Modern*	150	225	325
Model 400E, Various Gauges, Single Selective Trigger, Selective Ejector, *Modern*	125	200	300

FIREARMS SPECIALTIES

Owosso, Mich., c. 1972.

HANDGUN, REVOLVER

	Fair	V. Good	Excellent
.45/70 Custom Revolver, Brass Frame, Single Action, Western Style, *Modern*	400	700	1000

FIREARMS, CUSTOM-MADE

This category covers some of the myriad special firearms that are built to an individual's specifications by a competent gunsmith, and not by the original factory. Most firearms in this class will appeal only to a person who happens to want the same special features, and because of this many of these guns will sell for less than the cost of the conversion. The collector or investor in this area of firearms should bear in mind that something built to his own specifications may or may not appreciate significantly in value. Most crucial in determining long-term value are such factors as the reputation and quality of the gunmaker, the make and the action, the caliber, barrel length, type wood, quality of the wood grain and finish, and amount of personalization evident in the decoration or inscriptions. Unless the client is famous or renowned for one reason or another, the monogram or name on a piece might be detrimental to future salability, although in some instances the monogram or name could be removed and replaced by that of the new owner or by some other decoration or inscription.

HANDGUN, PERCUSSION

	Fair	V. Good	Excellent
Target Revolver, Various Calibers, Tuned, Target Sights, Reproduction	$100	$200	$300

HANDGUN, REVOLVER

	Fair	V. Good	Excellent
"F.B.L." Conversion, .38 Special, Cut Trigger Guard, Spurless Hammer, Short Barrel, *Modern*	100	250	325
P.P.C. Conversion, .38 Special, Heavy Barrel, Rib with Target Sights, Target Trigger, Target Grips, *Modern*			
Recoil Compensation Devices or Ports, Add $25.00-$45.00			

HANDGUN, SELF-LOADING

	Fair	V. Good	Excellent
M1911A1, Combat Conversion, Extended Trigger Guard, Ambidextrous Safety, Special Slide Release, Ported, Combat Sights, *Modern*	200	400	600
M1911A1, Double Action Conversion, Add $95.00-$175.00			
M1911A1, I.P.S.C. Conversion, Extended Trigger Guard, Ambidextrous Safety, Special Slide Release, Ported, Target Sights, Extended Grip Safety, *Modern*	200	400	600

HANDGUN, SINGLESHOT

	Fair	V. Good	Excellent
Silhouette Pistol, Various Calibers, Bolt Action, Thumbhole Stock, Target Sights, Target Trigger, *Modern*	150	300	500

RIFLE, BOLT ACTION

	Fair	V. Good	Excellent
Sporting Rifle, Various Calibers, Checkered Stock, Recoil Pad, Simple Military Conversion, *Modern*	75	150	250
Sporting Rifle, Various Calibers, Fancy Stock, High Quality Commercial Parts, Fancy Checkering, Stock Inlays, *Modern*	100	200	275
Sporting Rifle, Various Calibers, Fancy Stock, High Quality Commercial Parts, Fancy Checkering, Stock Inlays, Engraved, *Modern*	150	350	475
Sporting Rifle, Various Calibers, Fancy Stock, High Quality Commercial Parts, Fancy Checkering, Stock Inlays, Engraved, Gold Inlays, *Modern*	250	550	700
Sporting Rifle, Various Calibers, Fancy Wood, Recoil Pad, Fancy Military Conversion, *Modern*	100	200	275

	Fair	V. Good	Excellent
Sporting Rifle, Various Calibers, Mauser 1871 Action, Checkered Stock, *Antique*	$75	$125	$225
Sporting Rifle, Various Calibers, Plain Stock, Commercial Parts, *Modern*	100	200	300

RIFLE, SINGLESHOT

Target Rifle, Centerfire Calibers, Fancy, Target Sights, Built on Various Moving Block Actions, *Modern*	125	200	300
Target Rifle, Centerfire Calibers, Plain, Target Sights, Built on Various Bolt Actions, *Modern*	100	225	350
Target Rifle, Centerfire Calibers, Plain, Target Sights, Built on Various Moving Block Actions, *Modern*	100	175	300
Target Rifle, Rimfire Calibers, Plain, Target Sights, Built on Various Moving Block Actions, *Modern*	75	150	250

FIREBIRD

Made by Femaru for German exporter for U.S. Sales.

HANDGUN, SELF-LOADING

Tokagypt Type, 9mm Luger, Clip Fed, Blue, *Modern*	200	400	500

FITCH & WALDO

New York City, c. 1862–67. Made by Bacon Mfg. Co., Norwich, Conn.

HANDGUN, REVOLVER

Pocket Model, .31, 5 Shot, *Antique*	200	500	750

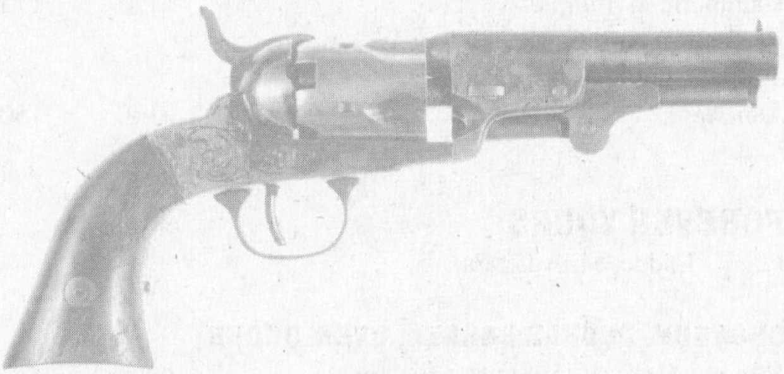

Fitch & Waldo Pocket Revolver, .31 Caliber

FLINTLOCK

Establishing values in this area is worthy of a book unto itself. Variables in the reputation of makers, national and regional styles, quality of workmanship, calibers, dates of manufacture, technical features of mechanisms and mounts, and many other features present a challenge to the appraiser. The figures presented herewith are approximate only. As an example, the author was privileged to have found a flintlock pistol by the renowned French maker Piraube at a bar near New Haven, Connecticut. Piraube was one of the most respected gunmakers of his day and was honored with apartments in the Louvre, where his shop could manufacture arms under appointment to the king. The barrel of this truly exceptional pistol was gold damascened with an inscription indicating Piraube's address at the Louvre, and testifying to his status as gunmaker to Louis XIV. Furthermore, the pistol bore the coat of arms of the Swedish King, to whom a garniture of guns by Piraube had been presented by Louis XIV. For some time the owner of the bar was reluctant to sell this pistol. He knew the gun was valuable, but had been frustrated in his attempts to determine its true worth. Finally, he had exhausted the patience of several collector/dealers and dealers, all of whom had been knocking on the bar owner's door. Norm Flayderman bought the pistol, and it was soon sold to the author, acting on behalf of client and friend, John B. Solley III. Despite the fact that the Piraube had been restocked in the 18th century, the workmanship was so magnificent that the pistol is a featured piece in the magnificent collections of the Metropolitan Museum of Art. The Piraube is a classic example of the difficulty of determining value for some arms, even though this pistol is an extreme case, in value far more exalted than most flintlocks that the reader is likely to encounter.

HANDGUN, FLINTLOCK

	Fair	V. Good	Excellent
.28, English, Pocket Pistol, Queen Anne Style, Box Lock, Screw Barrel, Plain, *Antique*	$225	$475	$650
.40, Herdsman Pistol, Long Tapered Round Barrel, Silver Furniture, *Antique*	200	300	400
.45, French, Mid-1700s, Screw Barrel, Long Cannon Barrel, Silver Furniture	700	1500	1850
.60, Continental, Early 1700s, Holster Pistol, Half-Octagon Bar Engraved, High Quality	1000	2500	3000
.60, Oval Bore, Box Lock, Pocket Pistol, Steel Furniture	400	750	1150
.62, Crantham English, Holster Pistol, Brass Furniture, Plain	250	650	850
.63, Spanish, Mid-1600s, Holster Pistol, Silver Inlay, Engraved	2000	4000	4500
.65, Arabian, Holster Pistol, Flared, Round Barrel, Low Quality	75	150	250
.68, Tower, Continental, Plain	200	350	450
English Lock, mid-1600s, Military, Holster Pistol, Iron Mounts, Plain	1700	3000	3750
English, Early 1700s, Pocket Pistol, Box Lock, Double Barrel, Screw Barrel, Low Quality	200	400	500
English, Early 1700s, Pocket Pistol, Queen Anne Style, Box Lock, Screw Barrel, All Metal	400	800	1000
English, Mid-1600s, Button Trigger, Brass Barrel, Octagon Fish-tail Butt	1500	2500	3250
French Officer's Type, c. 1650, Steel Furniture, Rifled	1500	2700	3250
French Sedan Mid-1600s, Long Screw Barrel, Rifled, Plain	1500	2500	3250

	Fair	V. Good	Excellent
RIFLE, FLINTLOCK			
.64, Continental, Carbine, Musket, Brass Furniture	$300	$600	$750
.72, Continental, 1650, Musket, Brass Furniture, Plain	500	1000	1350
SHOTGUN, FLINTLOCK			
.65, American Hudson Valley	800	1600	2250

FOLGER, WILLIAM H.

Barnsville, Ohio, 1830–1854. Also see Kentucky Rifles.

FOLK'S GUN WORKS

Bryan, Ohio, 1860–1891.

	Fair	V. Good	Excellent
RIFLE, SINGLESHOT			
.32 L.R.R.F., Side Lever, Octagon Barrel, *Antique*	200	325	400

FONDERSMITH, JOHN

Strasburg, Pa., 1749–1801. See Kentucky Rifles, U.S. Military.

FORBES, F. F.

Made by Crescent, c. 1900. See Crescent Fire Arms Co., Shotgun, Double Barrel, Side-by-side; Shotgun, Singleshot.

FOREHAND & WADSWORTH

Worchester, Mass. Successors and sons-in-law to Ethan Allen, 1871–1902. In 1872 the name was changed to Forehand & Wadsworth, in 1890 to Forehand Arms. Co.

	Fair	V. Good	Excellent
HANDGUN, REVOLVER			
.22 Short R.F. Side Hammer, 7 Shot, Single Action, Solid Frame, *Antique*	75	175	250
.41 Short R.F. Center Hammer, Single Action, Spur Trigger, Solid Frame, *Antique*	100	250	400
American Bulldog, .32 S & W, 6 Shot, Double Action, Solid Frame, *Antique*	50	100	150
British Bulldog, .38 S & W, 6 Shot, Double Action, Solid Frame, Antique	100	225	300
British Bulldog, .44 S & W, 6 Shot, Double Action, Solid Frame, *Antique*	125	300	375
New Army, .44 Russian, 6 Shot, Single Action, Solid Frame, *Antique*	800	2500	3250
Old Army, .44 Russian, 6 Shot, Single Action, Solid Frame, 7½" Barrel, *Antique*	800	2500	3250
Swamp Angel, .41 Short R.F., 5 Shot, Single Action, Solid Frame, Spur Trigger, *Antique*	$100	$225	$375
Terror, .32 Short R.F., 5 Shot, Single Action, Solid Frame, Spur Trigger, *Antique*	75	125	225
HANDGUN, SINGLESHOT DERRINGER			
.22 Short R.F., Spur Trigger, Side-swing Barrel, *Antique*	100	300	375
.41 Short R.F., Spur Trigger, Side-swing Barrel, *Antique*	300	600	850

FOREHAND ARMS CO.

	Fair	V. Good	Excellent
HANDGUN, REVOLVER			
.32 S & W, 5 Shot, Double Action, Solid Frame, 2" Barrel, *Antique*	50	75	125

Forehand Arms Co., .32 S&W

	Fair	V. Good	Excellent
.38 S & W, 5 Shot, Double Action, Solid Frame, 2" Barrel, *Antique*	50	75	175
Perfection Automatic, .32 S & W, 5 Shot, Double Action, Top Break, Hammerless, *Antique*	75	125	175
Perfection Automatic, .32 S & W, 5 Shot, Double Action, Top Break, *Antique*	75	100	150

FOREVER YOURS

Flaig's Lodge, Millvale, Pa.

	Fair	V. Good	Excellent
SHOTGUN, DOUBLE BARREL, OVER-UNDER			
Various Gauges, Automatic Ejector, Checkered Stock, Vent Rib, Double Trigger, *Modern*	300	550	750
Various Gauges, Automatic Ejector, Checkered Stock, Vent Rib, Single Trigger, *Modern*	250	550	800

FOULKES, ADAM

Easton & Allentown, Pa., 1773–1794. See Kentucky Rifles and U.S. Military.

FOUR ACE CO.

Brownsville, Texas.

HANDGUN, SINGLESHOT

	Fair	V. Good	Excellent
Four Ace, Derringer, Presentation Case Add $10.00-$15.00			
Four Ace Model 200, .22 Short R.F., Derringer, 4 Shot, Spur Trigger, *Modern*	$25	$50	$75
Four Ace Model 200, .22 Short R.F., Derringer, 4 Shot, Spur Trigger, Nickel Plated, Gold Plated, *Modern*	25	50	75
Four Ace Model 202, .22 L.R.R.F., Derringer, 4 Shot, Spur Trigger, Nickel Plated, Gold Plated, *Modern*	25	50	75
Four Ace Model 202, .22 L.R.R.F., Derringer, 4 Shot, Spur Trigger, *Modern*	25	50	75
Four Ace Model 204, .22 L.R.R.F., Derringer, 4 Shot, Spur Trigger, Stainless Steel, *Modern*	25	50	75
Little Ace Model 300, .22 Short R.F., Derringer, Side-swing Barrel, Spur Trigger, *Modern*	25	50	75

FOX

Foxco Products, Inc. Manchester, Conn. Also see Demro, T.A.C.

RIFLE, SELF-LOADING

	Fair	V. Good	Excellent
Model #1, 9mm Luger or .45 ACP, Carbine, Clip Fed, *Modern*	85	175	275

FOX, A. H. GUN CO.

Philadelphia, Pa. Formerly Philadelphia Arms Co., from 1903. A subsidiary of Savage Arms Co., 1930–1942. Also see Savage Arms Co., and Connecticut Shotgun Mfg. Co. Though famous today for his fine shotguns, Ansley H. Fox (1875–1948) was also a prolific designer and inventor and an entrepreneurial businessman, who excelled in automobiles, munitions, machine guns, real estate, and fishing reels. Fox lived in times which saw extraordinary advancements in science and technology, two devastating world wars, and rapid changes in virtually every sphere of human interest. Of all his achievements, the most distinguished were in the field of firearms, and the Fox was promoted as "The Finest Gun in the World." At the age of eighteen, Fox applied to the U.S. Patent Office for protection on a break-open open side-by-side shotgun, with concealed hammers, which were cocked by the opening action of the barrels. The innovative design revealed a simplicity and functionalism reflecting true mechanical brilliance—there were no less than 19 patentable features, as issued July 3, 1894 (No. 522,464). Soon thereafter, the youthful inventor submitted still another design, an improvement on the original, with twelve more specific features! Fox was on his way. Beginning his arms-making enterprise under the name of the National Arms Company, in Baltimore, in 1897, the firm went through several evolutionary steps, and what eventually emerged, in 1904, was the A. H. Fox Gun Co. of Philadelphia. Importantly, the firearms industry was experiencing the dramatic change from black to smokeless powders, an improvement which also meant added stress to materials, and the resultant likelihood of breakdowns—particularly so with shotguns fired repeatedly, as in competitive shotgun shooting. The inventor himself was destined to become one of America's leading live pigeon shooters, but his gunmaking and designing interests were a distraction. Accordingly, he was described in an 1896 *American Field* article as "something of a shot, but, having devoted more of his time to developing his mechanical ideas than to shooting, does not rank as an expert. No doubt in time this will be rectified." From 1900 through 1902 Fox was a sales representative and professional shotgun shooter, an employee of the Winchester Repeating Arms Co. With innovations in gun designs, augmented by a national reputation as an experienced and highly competitive shotgunner, Fox (termed by some the "boy inventor") quickly made a name for himself and his guns. In fact, it appears that Fox's tournament shooting was done with guns of his own designs. In 1909 the company was the first gunmaker to exhibit at the Grand American Handicap Tournament, the World Series of trapshooting. The same year, a special 12-gauge side-by-side gun was built for President Theodore Roosevelt to take on his celebrated safari to Africa. TR wrote Fox that it was "the most beautiful gun I have ever seen. I am extremely proud that I am to have such a beautiful bit of American workmanship with me." Still another satisfied Fox gun owner was the legendary Ty Cobb, one of the greatest stars in the annals of baseball. Fox guns were awarded the Gold Medal at the Panama-Pacific International Exposition, in San Francisco (1915), for the best double shotguns and single trigger mechanism. The company capitalized on awards and quotations from satisfied shooters. Contemporary Fox guns, made by the Connecticut Shotgun Manufacturing Co., rival and sometimes surpass the artistry of the original A. H. Fox firm. The author has toured the new firm's factory in New Britain, Connecticut, and was amazed at the quality of workmanship, and at the collection of talent, many of them artisans from European gunmaking centers. Tony Galazan, founder of the company, has made Connecticut again a center of manufacture of some of the world's finest and most innovative shotguns.

SHOTGUN, DOUBLE BARREL, SIDE-BY-SIDE

	Fair	V. Good	Excellent
Various Gauges, Beavertail Forend Add 10%-15%			
Various Gauges, For Vent Rib Add $295.00-$495.00			
Various Gauges, Single Selective Trigger Add $295.00-$495.00			
Various Grades, for 20 Ga. Add 50%-75%			
A Grade, Various Gauges, Box Lock, Light Engraving, Checkered Stock, *Modern*	$600	$1200	$1650
AE Grade, Various Gauges, Box Lock, Light Engraving, Checkered Stock, Automatic Ejector, *Modern*	700	1500	1850
BE Grade, Various Gauges, Box Lock, Engraved, Checkered Stock, Automatic Ejector, *Modern*	1000	2000	2500
CE Grade, Various Gauges, Box Lock, Engraved, Fancy Checkering, Automatic Ejector, *Modern*	2000	4500	5500

	Fair	V. Good	Excellent
DE Grade, Various Gauges, Box Lock, Fancy Engraving, Fancy Checkering, Fancy Wood, Automatic Ejector, *Modern*	$3000	$7000	$10000
FE Grade, Various Gauges, Box Lock, Fancy Engraving, Fancy Checkering, Fancy Wood, Automatic Ejector, *Modern*	5000	10000	13500
HE Grade, 12 and 20 Gauge, Box Lock, Light Engraving, Checkered Stock, Automatic Ejector, *Modern*	1200	2200	2750
SP Grade, Various Gauges, Box Lock, Checkered Stock, *Modern*	400	800	1200
SP Grade, Various Gauges, Box Lock, Checkered Stock, Automatic Ejector, *Modern*	450	900	1350
SP Grade, Various Gauges, Box Lock, Skeet Grade, Automatic Ejector, Checkered Stock, *Modern*	500	950	1350
SP Grade, Various Gauges, Box Lock, Skeet Grade, Checkered Stock, *Modern*	400	750	1150
Sterlingworth, Various Gauges, Box Lock, Checkered Stock, Hammerless, *Modern*	400	800	1150
Sterlingworth, Various Gauges, Box Lock, Checkered Stock, Hammerless, Automatic Ejector, *Modern*	500	1000	1350
Sterlingworth, Various Gauges, Box Lock, Skeet Grade, Checkered Stock, *Modern*	400	900	1250
Sterlingworth, Various Gauges, Box Lock, Skeet Grade, Checkered Stock, Automatic Ejector, *Modern*	550	1100	1400
Sterlingworth Deluxe, Various Gauges, Box Lock, Checkered Stock, Hammerless, Recoil Pad, *Modern*	500	1000	1350
Sterlingworth Deluxe, Various Gauges, Box Lock, Checkered Stock, Hammerless, Recoil Pad, Automatic Ejector, *Modern*	600	1250	1600
XE Grade, Various Gauges, Box Lock, Fancy Engraving, Fancy Checkering, Fancy Wood, Automatic Ejector, *Modern*	2750	5500	10000

SHOTGUN, SINGLESHOT

	Fair	V. Good	Excellent
JE Grade, 12 Gauge, Trap Grade, Vent Rib, Automatic Ejector, Engraved, Fancy Checkering, *Modern*	700	1500	2000
KE Grade, 12 Gauge, Trap Grade, Vent Rib, Automatic Ejector, Engraved, Fancy Checkering, *Modern*	1500	2500	3250
LE Grade, 12 Gauge, Trap Grade, Vent Rib, Automatic Ejector, Fancy Engraving, Fancy Checkering, *Modern*	1700	3500	4750
ME Grade, 12 Gauge, Trap Grade, Vent Rib, Automatic Ejector, Fancy Engraving, Fancy Checkering, *Modern*	$2500	$6500	$8500

FRANCAIS

France. Made by Manufacture d'Armes Automatiques Francaise.

HANDGUN, SELF-LOADING

	Fair	V. Good	Excellent
Prima, .25 ACP, Clip Fed, *Modern*	50	100	125

FRANCHI

Brescia, Italy. In the 1990s Franchi became a subsidiary of Fabbrica d'Armi Pietro Beretta, SpA; imported by Beretta U.S.A., Accokeek, Maryland. In addition to its own production, Franchi built guns to the specifications of other companies, among these Colt of Hartford.

RIFLE, SELF-LOADING

	Fair	V. Good	Excellent
Centennial, .22 L.R.R.F., Checkered Stock, Tube Feed, Takedown, *Modern*	125	275	350
Centennial Deluxe, .22 L.R.R.F., Checkered Stock, Tube Feed, Takedown, Light Engraving, *Modern*	150	325	425
Centennial Gallery, .22 Short R.F., Checkered Stock, Tube Feed, Takedown, *Modern*	125	250	350

SHOTGUN, DOUBLE BARREL, OVER-UNDER

	Fair	V. Good	Excellent
Alcione, 12 Ga., Field Grade, Automatic Ejectors, Single Selective Trigger, Vent Rib, *Modern*	200	400	800
Alcione, 12, Vent Rib, Single Selective Trigger, Automatic Ejector, Engraved, *Modern*	200	450	850
Alcione, 12, Vent Rib, Single Selective Trigger, Automatic Ejector, Engraved, *Modern*	400	875	1000
Aristocrat, 12 Ga., Imperial Grade, Automatic Ejectors, Single Selection Trigger, Vent Rib, *Modern*	800	1800	2200
Aristocrat, 12 Ga., Monte Carlo Grade, Automatic Ejectors, Single Selective Trigger, Vent Rib, *Modern*	1000	2500	3250
Barrage Skeet, 12 Ga., Vent Rib, Single Selective Trigger, Automatic Ejector, Recoil Pad, *Modern*	500	900	1250
Barrage Trap, 12 Ga., Vent Rib, Single Selective Trigger, Automatic Ejector, Recoil Pad, *Modern*	500	900	1200
Dragon Skeet, 12 Ga., Vent Rib, Single Selective Trigger, Automatic Ejector, Recoil Pad, *Modern*	400	800	1000
Dragon Trap, 12 Ga., Vent Rib, Single Selective Trigger, Automatic Ejector, Recoil Pad, *Modern*	400	800	1000

	Fair	V. Good	Excellent
Falconet Buckskin, 12 and 20 Ga., Vent Rib, Single Selective Trigger, Automatic Ejector, *Modern*	$300	$475	$650
Falconet Ebony, 12 and 20 Ga., Vent Rib, Single Selective Trigger, Automatic Ejector, *Modern*	250	425	600
Falconet Peregrine 400, 12 and 20 Ga., Vent Rib, Single Selective Trigger, Automatic Ejector, *Modern*	300	575	750
Falconet Peregrine 451, 12 and 20 Ga., Vent Rib, Single Selective Trigger, Automatic Ejector, *Modern*	250	500	700
Falconet Pigeon, 12 Ga., Vent Rib, Single Selective Trigger, Automatic Ejector, Fancy Engraving, Fancy Checkering, *Modern*	600	1000	1300
Falconet Silver, 12 Ga., Vent Rib, Single Selective Trigger, Automatic Ejector, *Modern*	300	550	700
Falconet Super, 12 Ga., Vent Rib, Single Selective Trigger, Automatic Ejector, *Modern*	350	650	800
Falconet Super Deluxe, 12 Ga., Vent Rib, Single Selective Trigger, Automatic Ejector, *Modern*	400	750	1000
Model 2003, 12 Ga., Trap Grade, Vent Rib, Single Selective Trigger, Automatic Ejector, *Modern*	500	1075	1350
Model 2005/2, 12 Ga., Trap Grade, Vent Rib, Single Selective Trigger, Automatic Ejector, Extra Shotgun Barrel, *Modern*	1000	2000	2350
Model 2005/3, 12 Ga., Trap Grade, Vent Rib, Single Selective Trigger, Automatic Ejector, Extra Shotgun Barrel, Custom Choke, *Modern*	1000	2250	2650
Model 255, 12 Ga., Vent Rib, Single Selective Trigger, Automatic Ejector, *Modern*	250	500	600

SHOTGUN, DOUBLE BARREL, SIDE-BY-SIDE

	Fair	V. Good	Excellent
Airone, 12 Ga., Box Lock, Hammerless, Checkered Stock, Automatic Ejector, *Modern*	450	800	1100
Astore, 12 Ga., Box Lock, Hammerless, Checkered Stock, *Modern*	350	700	900
Astore 5, 12 Ga., Box Lock, Hammerless, Checkered Stock, Light Engraving, *Modern*	700	1500	1850
Condor, Various Gauges, Sidelock, Engraved, Checkered Stock, Automatic Ejector, *Modern*	2500	5000	7500
Imperial, Various Gauges, Sidelock, Engraved, Checkered Stock, Automatic Ejector, *Modern*	4500	8500	12500
Imperial Monte Carlo #11, Various Gauges, Sidelock, Fancy Engraving, Fancy Checkering, Automatic Ejector, *Modern*	6000	18500	35000
Imperial Monte Carlo #5, Various Gauges, Sidelock, Fancy Engraving, Fancy Checkering, Automatic Ejector, *Modern*	$5000	$13500	$27500
Imperial Monte Carlo Extra, Various Gauges, Sidelock, Fancy Engraving, Fancy Checkering, Automatic Ejector, *Modern*	7000	8500	40000
Imperiales, Various Gauges, Sidelock, Engraved, Checkered Stock, Automatic Ejector, *Modern*	4500	8500	15000

SHOTGUN, SELF-LOADING

	Fair	V. Good	Excellent
Dynamic (Heavy), 12 Ga., Checkered Stock, Slug, Open Rear Sight, *Modern*	150	275	400
Dynamic (Heavy), 12 Ga., Plain Barrel, *Modern*	150	250	375
Dynamic (Heavy), 12 Ga., Skeet Grade, Vent Rib, Checkered Stock, *Modern*	150	275	425
Dynamic (Heavy), 12 Ga., Vent Rib, *Modern*	150	300	400
Eldorado, 12 and 20 Ga., Vent Rib, Engraved, Fancy Checkering, Lightweight, *Modern*	150	350	500
Hunter, 12 and 20 Ga., Vent Rib, Engraved, Checkered Stock, Lightweight, *Modern*	200	400	600
Model 500, 12 Ga., Vent Rib, Checkered Stock, *Modern*	150	250	450
Model 500, 12 Ga., Vent Rib, Checkered Stock, Engraved, *Modern*	200	350	550
Slug Gun, 12 and 20 Ga., Open Rear Sights, Sling Swivels, *Modern*	200	350	550
SPAS 12, 12 gauge, Combat Shotgun, Folding Stock, Rifle Sights, Lightweight, *Modern*	250	400	600
Standard, 12 and 20 Ga., Plain Barrel, Lightweight, Checkered Stock, *Modern*	200	325	500
Standard, 12 and 20 Ga., Solid Rib, Lightweight, Checkered Stock, *Modern*	200	350	500
Standard, 12 and 20 Ga., Vent Rib, Lightweight, Checkered Stock, *Modern*	200	375	500
Standard Magnum, 12 and 20 Gauges, Vent Rib, Lightweight, Checkered Stock, *Modern*	150	250	400
Superange (Heavy), 12 and 20 Gauges, Magnum, Plain Barrel, Checkered Stock, *Modern*	150	250	400
Superange (Heavy), 12 and 20 Gauges, Magnum, Vent Rib, Checkered Stock, *Modern*	200	375	500
Wildfowler (Heavy), 12 and 20 Gauges, Magnum, Vent Rib, Checkered Stock, Engraved, *Modern*	200	375	500

SHOTGUN, SINGLESHOT

	Fair	V. Good	Excellent
Model 2004, 12 Ga., Trap Grade, Vent Rib, Automatic Ejector, *Modern*	$500	$900	$1100
Model 3000/2, 12 Ga., Trap Grade, Vent Rib, Automatic Ejector, with Choke Tubes, *Modern*	1000	2000	2850

FRANCI, PIERO INZI

Brescia, Italy, c. 1640.

HANDGUN, WHEEL LOCK

	Fair	V. Good	Excellent
Octagon-Barrel, Dagger, Handle Butt, *Antique*	2000	4000	6000

FRANCOTTE, AUGUST

Liège, Belgium, 1844 to date, also London, England, 1877–1893. One of the most memorable moments in the author's career in the arms field was visiting Francotte while the last of the family was still at the helm. Monsieur Francotte, a direct descendant of the founder, gave the writer a tour of the old facility, and signed some original photographs taken of specially built display guns exhibited by the firm at world's fairs and expositions. This gracious old gentleman, then in his 70s, took justifiable pride in the creations of his family, but his sadness at having no heirs who could carry on the business was clearly evident. Francotte was then much like the J. Purdey & Sons of continental Europe, still making superior sporting arms for a discriminating clientele—many of these clients decendants of clients of Francotte from earlier generations. The new owners have done an admirable job of maintaining the quality and reputation of the firm although the factory site is now primarily a showroom, with much of the work sub-contracted to highly competent artisans from Liège and surrounding locales.

HANDGUN, REVOLVER

	Fair	V. Good	Excellent
Bulldog, Various Calibers, Double Action, Solid Frame, *Curio*	50	100	200
Military Style, Various Calibers, Double Action, *Antique*	50	100	200

HANDGUN, SELF-LOADING

	Fair	V. Good	Excellent
Vest Pocket, .25 ACP, Clip Fed, *Curio*	100	200	250

Also * Pre-WWII Bonus, add 20%
28 and 410 ga, add 40%

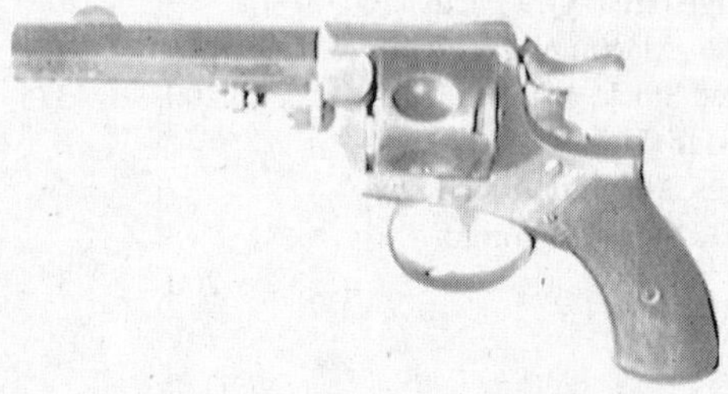

Francotte Bulldog Revolver

HANDGUN, SINGLESHOT

	Fair	V. Good	Excellent
Target Pistol, .22 L.R.R.F., Toggle Breech, *Modern*	$200	$400	$500

RIFLE, DOUBLE BARREL, SIDE-BY-SIDE

	Fair	V. Good	Excellent
Luxury Double, .458 Win., Sidelock, Hammerless, Double Triggers, Fancy Engraving, *Curio*	9000	17500	25000
*Pre-War II Double Rifles S x S and u/u in Various Small and Large cal. add 10%	4000	8000	17500

SHOTGUN, DOUBLE BARREL, SIDE-BY-SIDE

	Fair	V. Good	Excellent
A & F #14, Various Gauges, Box Lock, Automatic Ejector, Checkered Stock, Engraved, Hammerless, *Curio*	900	1750	2250
*Pre-War II Bonus add 20%			
28 + 410 ga add 40%			
A & F #20, Various Gauges, Box Lock, Automatic Ejector, Checkered Stock, Engraved, Hammerless, *Curio*	1100	2750	3500
A & F #25, Various Gauges, Box Lock, Automatic Ejector, Checkered Stock, Engraved, Hammerless, *Curio*	1500	3200	3750
A & F #30, Various Gauges, Box Lock, Automatic Ejector, Checkered Stock, Engraved, Hammerless, *Curio*	2000	3800	4750
A & F #45, Various Gauges, Box Lock, Automatic Ejector, Checkered Stock, Engraved, Hammerless, *Curio*	1600	3500	4250
A & F Jubilee, Various Gauges, Box Lock, Automatic Ejector, Checkered Stock, Light Engraving, Hammerless, *Curio*	600	1250	1750
A & F Knockabout, Various Gauges, Box Lock, Automatic Ejector, Checkered Stock, Hammerless, *Curio*	500	1000	1350
Francotte Original, Various Gauges, Box Lock, Automatic Ejector, Checkered Stock, Hammerless, Engraved, *Curio*	900	2000	3250
Francotte Special, Various Gauges, Box Lock, Automatic Ejector, Checkered Stock, Hammerless, Light Engraving, *Curio*	750	1500	2500
Model 10/18E/628, Various Gauges, Box Lock, Automatic Ejector, Checkered Stock, Hammerless, Light Engraving, *Curio*	1500	3000	4000
Model 10594, Various Gauges, Box Lock, Automatic Ejector, Checkered Stock, Hammerless, Engraved, *Curio*	1500	2500	3500
Model 11/18E, Various Gauges, Box Lock, Automatic Ejector, Checkered Stock, Hammerless, Engraved, *Curio*	1500	2500	3250
Model 120.HE/328, Various Gauges, Sidelock, Automatic Ejector, Checkered Stock, Hammerless, Fancy Engraving, *Curio*	3500	7000	10000

	Fair	V. Good	Excellent
Model 4996, Various Gauges, Box Lock, Automatic Ejector, Checkered Stock, Hammerless, Light Engraving, *Curio*	$750	$1500	$2750
Model 6886, Various Gauges, Box Lock, Automatic Ejector, Checkered Stock, Hammerless, *Curio*	750	1500	2750
Model 6930, Various Gauges, Box Lock, Automatic Ejector, Checkered Stock, Hammerless, Light Engraving, *Curio*	750	1500	2750
Model 6982, Various Gauges, Box Lock, Automatic Ejector, Checkered Stock, Hammerless, Engraved, *Curio*	1200	2500	3750
Model 8455, Various Gauges, Box Lock, Automatic Ejector, Checkered Stock, Hammerless, *Curio*	1000	2500	3750
Model 8457, Various Gauges, Box Lock, Automatic Ejector, Checkered Stock, Hammerless, Engraved, *Curio*	1000	2500	3750
Model 9/40.SE, Various Gauges, Box Lock, Automatic Ejector, Checkered Stock, Hammerless, Fancy Engraving, *Curio*	3500	7000	10000
Model 9/40E/38321, Various Gauges, Box Lock, Automatic Ejector, Checkered Stock, Hammerless, Engraved, *Curio*	1500	3000	5000
Model SOB.E/11082, Various Gauges, Box Lock, Automatic Ejector, Checkered Stock, Hammerless, Engraved, *Curio*	2500	5000	7000

FRANKLIN, C. W.

Belgium, c. 1900.

SHOTGUN, DOUBLE BARREL, SIDE-BY-SIDE

Various Gauges, Hammerless, Damascus Barrel, *Modern*	50	125	225
Various Gauges, Hammerless, Steel Barrel, *Modern*	75	150	250
Various Gauges, Outside Hammers, Damascus Barrel, *Modern*	50	125	225
Various Gauges, Outside Hammers, Steel Barrel, *Modern*	75	125	225

SHOTGUN, SINGLESHOT

Various Gauges, Hammer, Steel Barrel, *Modern*	25	50	75

FRANKONIA

Frankonia Jagd, arms dealers and manufacturers in West Germany. Publishers of one of the most beautiful and comprehensive arms-related catalogues in the world, Frankonia remains in the family of the founders. The author has had the pleasure of meeting the patriarch of the family, and one of his sons, at the IWA show in Nuremberg. Among manufacturers represented by Frankonia are a wide array of European and American gunmakers, not the least of which, Sturm, Ruger & Co., has been a featured Frankonia brand for many years. The company's significance in today's sporting Germany is broad-based, having several stores located throughout the country, catering to a dedicated and enthusiastic clientele.

	Fair	V. Good	Excellent

RIFLE, BOLT ACTION

Favorit, Various Calibers, Set Triggers, Checkered Stock, *Modern*	$100	$275	$350
Favorit Deluxe, Various Calibers, Set Triggers, Checkered Stock, *Modern*	200	350	500
Favorit Leichtmodell, Various Calibers, Lightweight, Set Triggers, Checkered Stock, *Modern*	200	400	525
Safari, Various Calibers, Target Trigger, Checkered Stock, *Modern*	250	425	550
Stutzen, Various Calibers, Carbine, Set Triggers, Full Stock, *Modern*	250	400	500

RIFLE, SINGLESHOT

Heeren Rifle, Various Calibers, Fancy Engraving, Fancy Wood, Octagon Barrel, *Modern*	1200	2500	4000
Heeren Rifle, Various Calibers, Fancy Engraving, Fancy Wood, Round Barrel, *Modern*	1000	2000	2750

FRASER

Formerly Bauer Firearms, Fraser, Mich.

HANDGUN, SELF-LOADING

.25 ACP, Stainless Steel, Clip Fed, Hammerless, Browning Baby Style, *Modern*	75	100	125

FRASER, D. & J.

Edinburgh, Scotland, 1870–1900.

RIFLE, DOUBLE BARREL, SIDE-BY-SIDE

.360 N.E. #2, Automatic Ejector, Express Sights, Engraved, Extra Set of Barrels, Cased with Accessories, *Modern*	4500	8500	12500

FRAZIER, CLARK K.

Rawson, Ohio.

RIFLE, PERCUSSION

Matchmate Offhand, Various Calibers, Under-Hammer, Thumbhole Stock, Heavy Barrel, Reproduction, *Antique*	250	450	650

FRAZIER, JAY

Tyler, Wash., c. 1974.

RIFLE, SINGLESHOT

	Fair	V. Good	Excellent
Creedmore Rifle, Various Calibers, Single Set Trigger, Vernier Sights, Skeleton Buttplate, Pistol Grip Stock, *Modern*	$300	$600	$900
Schuetzen Rifle, Various Calibers, Single Set Trigger, Vernier Sights, Helm Buttplate, Palm Rest, False Muzzle, *Modern*	300	600	900

FREEDOM ARMS

Freedom, Wyo.

HANDGUN, REVOLVER

	Fair	V. Good	Excellent
FA-BG, "Minute Man,".22 L.R.R.F., Spur Trigger, 3" Barrel, Single Action, *Modern*	75	175	275
FA-S, "Bostonian,".22 L.R.R.F., Spur Trigger, 3" Barrel, Single Action, *Modern*	75	175	300
FA-S, "Ironsides,".22 W.M.R., Matte Finish, Spur Trigger, 1" Barrel, Single Action, *Modern*	75	175	300
FA-S, "Patriot,".22 L.R.R.F., Matte Finish, Spur Trigger, 1" Barrel, Single Action, *Modern*	75	125	250
FA-S, .22 L.R.R.F., Stainless Steel, Matte Finish, Spur Trigger, 1 3/4" Barrel, Single Action, Buckel/Rev. Combo, *Modern*	100	200	300

For High Gloss Finish, Add $5.00-$10.00

See also line of modern single action revolvers in the firm's detailed catalogues.

FRENCH MILITARY

For the American collector, French military arms are extremely important, primarily those of the period from the American Revolution through the Civil War era. French styling, calibers, and materials heavily influenced the design not only of American military arms, but of weapons like swords and cutlasses. The first U.S. martial handgun, the North & Cheney singleshot flintlock pistol, was copied from the French Model 1777 Charleville. Many other similarities can be pointed out by comparing French models with those adopted by the American Ordnance. Napoleonic arms are a popular pursuit with some very successful Americans, among them the designer Bill Blass and jewelry manufacturer Christopher Ross, both of New York City. The late Calvin Bullock, owner of a Wall Street investment banking firm, was also a keen Napoleonic collector; his impressive holdings were sold by Sotheby's several years after World War II. Visitors to Paris are missing one of the most impressive of museums should they not spend at least a day at the Musée de l'Armée at the site of the Invalides and of Napoleon's tomb. There one can marvel at the world's most magnificent collection of French military arms, accouterments, and uniforms.

HANDGUN, FLINTLOCK

	Fair	V. Good	Excellent
.69 AN XIII, Officer's Pistol, Made in France, *Antique*	$375	$800	$1200
.69 AN XIII, Officer's Pistol, Made in Occupied Country, *Antique*	375	800	1100

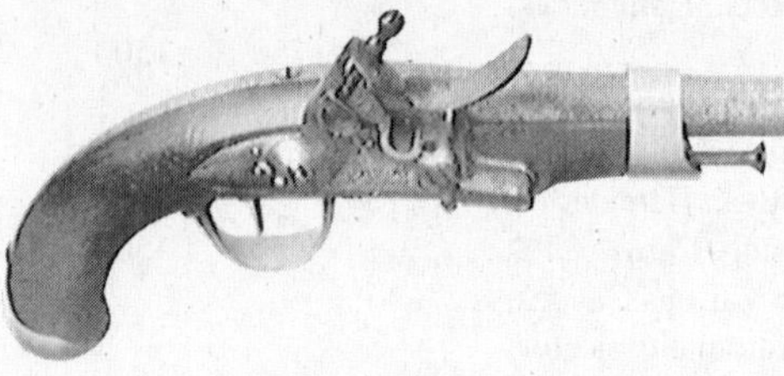

French Military AN XIII

	Fair	V. Good	Excellent
.69 Charleville 1777, Cavalry Pistol, Brass Furniture, Belt Hook, *Antique*	500	1200	1650

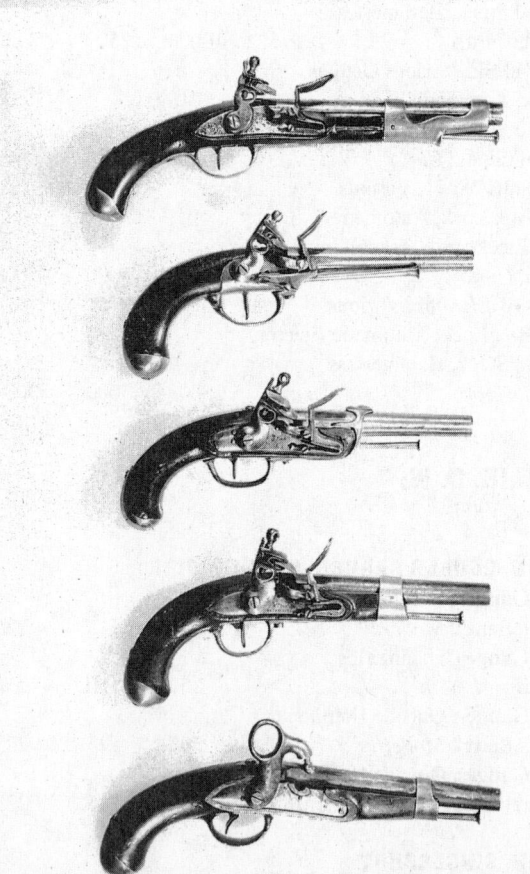

French military flintlock pistols; from top, *Model 1763, dated 1793; Model 1777, St. Etienne markings, this the type on which North & Cheney U.S. martial pistol based; Model 1799 known as "Depareille" model; Model AN 13 (1804), with lock marking* Mre Imple de Versailles; *converted flintlock Model 1815, with odd ring-type hammer.*

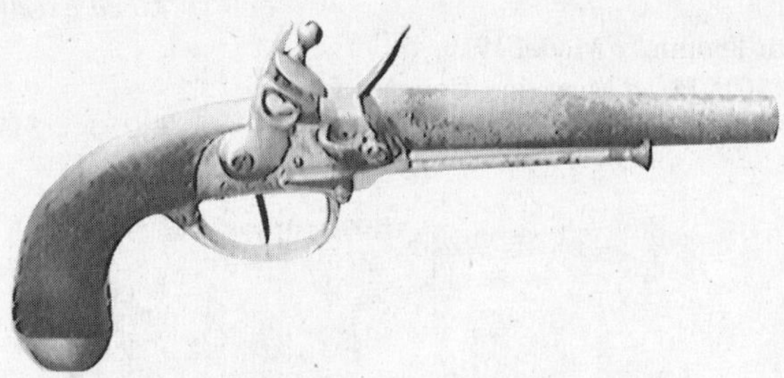
French Military M1777 Charleville

	Fair	V. Good	Excellent
.69 Charleville 1810, Cavalry Pistol, Brass Furniture, Plain, *Antique*	$400	$800	$1350
.69 Charleville 1810, Cavalry Pistol, Brass Furniture, Converted from Flintlock, Plain, *Antique*	200	400	750
.69 Model 1763, Belt Pistol, Military, *Antique*	500	1000	1600

HANDGUN, REVOLVER

Model 1873, 11mm French Ordnance, Double Action, Solid Frame, *Antique*	100	200	350
Model 1873 Officer's, 11mm French Ordnance, Double Action, Solid Frame, *Antique*	100	225	350

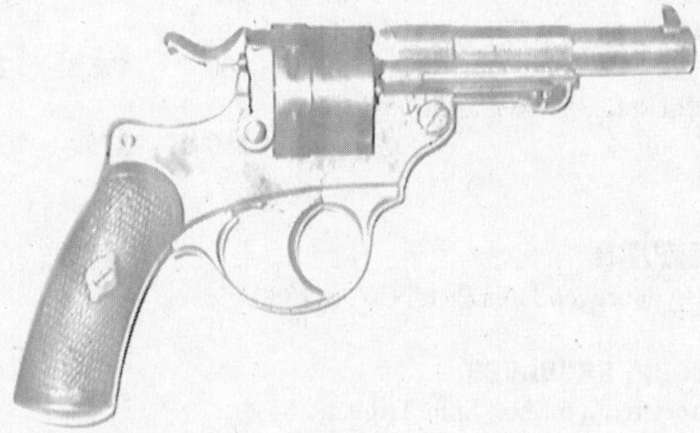
French Military M1873 Revolver

Model 1892, 8mm Lebel Revolver, Double Action, Solid Frame, *Curio*	100	200	250
Model 1915, 8mm Lebel Revolver, Double Action, Solid Frame, Spanish Contract, *Curio*	100	200	250

HANDGUN, SELF-LOADING

M.A.B. Model C, 7.65mm, Clip Fed, *Curio*	100	225	250
M.A.B. Model C, 7.65mm, Clip Fed, Nazi Proofed, *Curio*	150	325	350
M.A.B. Model D, 7.65mm, Clip Fed, *Curio*	100	200	225
M.A.B. Model D, 7.65mm, Clip Fed, Nazi Proofed, *Curio*	125	250	300
Model 1935-A, 7.65 MAS, Clip Fed, Black Paint, *Curio*	75	125	150

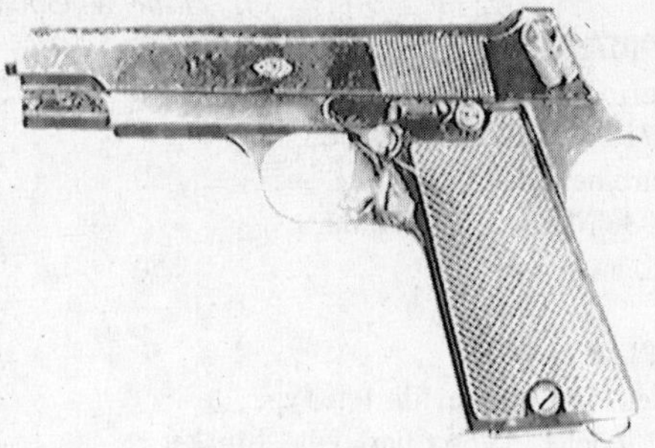
French Military M1935A

	Fair	V. Good	Excellent
Model 1935-A, 7.65 MAS, Clip Fed, Blued, *Curio*	$75	$150	$175
Model 1935-A, 7.65 MAS, Clip Fed, Nazi Proofed, *Curio*	100	225	250
Model 1935-A, 7.65 MAS, M.A.C., Clip Fed, *Curio*	100	250	300
Model 1935-S, 7.65 MAS, M.A.C. M-1, Clip Fed, *Curio*	150	325	350
Model 1935-S, 7.65 MAS, M.A.C., Clip Fed, Nazi Proofed, *Curio*	150	400	450
Model 1935-S, 7.65 MAS, SACM, Clip Fed, *Curio*	100	200	225
Model 1935-S, 7.65 MAS, SAGEM M-1, Clip Fed, Nazi Proofed, *Curio*	100	250	300
Model 1950, 9mm Luger, M.A.S., Clip Fed, *Modern*	150	350	475

French Military M1950

RIFLE, BOLT ACTION

6.5 X 53.5 Daudetau, Carbine, *Curio*	40	80	100
Model 1874, 11 × 59R Gras, *Antique*	100	200	250
Model 1874, 11 × 59R Gras, Carbine, *Antique*	100	200	300
Model 1886/93 Lebel, 8 × 50R Lebel, *Curio*	50	75	100

French Military Daudetau Rifle

	Fair	V. Good	Excellent
Model 1907/15 Remington, 8 × 50R Lebel, *Curio*	$75	$125	$175
Model 1916 St. Etienne, 8 × 50R Lebel, Carbine, *Curio*	50	125	200
Model 1936 MAS, 7.5 × 54 MAS, with Bayonet, *Curio*	50	75	150

RIFLE, FLINTLOCK

	Fair	V. Good	Excellent
.69, Model 1763 Charleville 1st. Type, Musket, Model 1763/66 Charleville, Musket, *Antique*	800	2000	2750

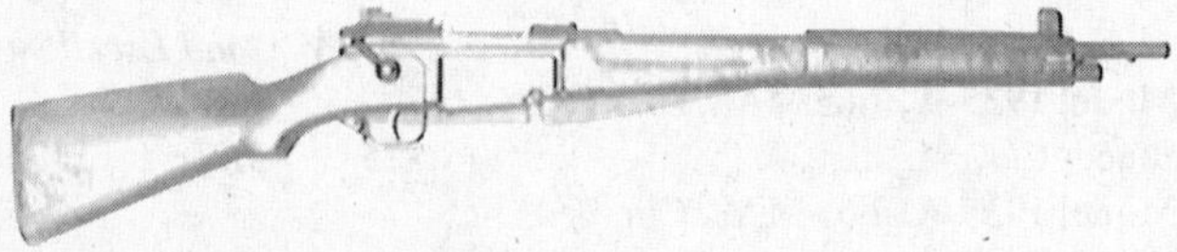

French Military Model 1935 MAS Rifle

RIFLE, PERCUSSION

	Fair	V. Good	Excellent
Model 1840, Short Rifle, *Antique*	400	800	1100

FROMMER

Made by Femaru-Fegyver-Es Gepgyar R.T. (Fegyvergyar), Budapest, Hungary. Also see Femaru.

HANDGUN, SELF-LOADING

	Fair	V. Good	Excellent
Baby Pocket, .32 ACP, Clip Fed, *Curio*	75	150	200
Baby Pocket, .380 ACP, Clip Fed, *Curio*	100	175	225
Liliput, .22 L.R.R.F., Clip Fed, *Curio*			Rare
Liliput, .25 ACP, Clip Fed, *Curio*	150	300	350

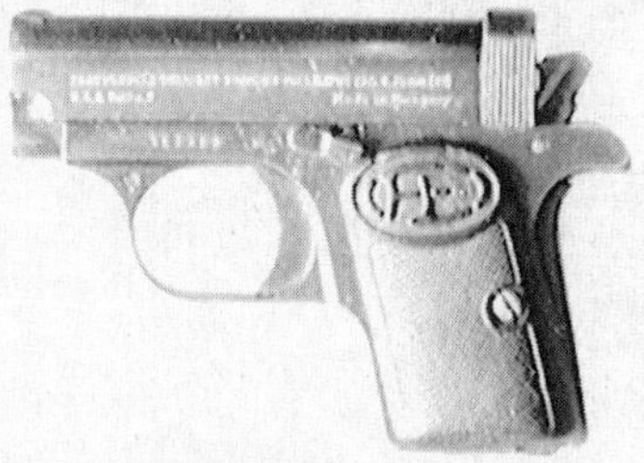

Frommer Liliput

	Fair	V. Good	Excellent
Roth-Frommer Model 1901, 8mm Roth Sauer, Fixed Magazine, Commercial, *Curio*	700	1500	1850
Roth-Frommer Model 1901, 8mm Roth Sauer, Fixed Magazine, Military Test, *Curio*	900	2000	2350
Roth-Frommer Model 1906, 7.65mm Roth Sauer, Clip Fed, Commercial, *Curio*	600	1250	1750
Roth-Frommer Model 1906, 7.65mm Roth Sauer, Fixed Magazine, Commercial, *Curio*	500	1100	1450
Roth-Frommer Model 1910, .32 ACP, Fixed Magazine, Commercial, *Curio*	$500	$1250	$1750

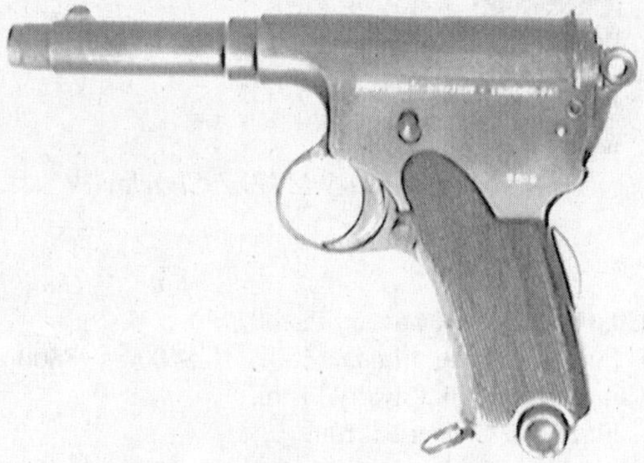

Frommer Roth-Frommer 1910

	Fair	V. Good	Excellent
Roth-Frommer Model 1910, .32 ACP, Fixed Magazine, Police, *Curio*	600	1500	1850
Stop Pocket, .32 ACP, Commercial, Clip Fed, *Curio*	100	200	300
Stop Pocket, .32 ACP, M-19 Military, Clip Fed, *Curio*	100	175	250
Stop Pocket, .32 ACP, Police, Clip Fed, *Curio*	125	225	300
Stop Pocket, .32 ACP, WW-1 Military, Clip Fed, *Curio*	100	175	250
Stop Pocket, .380 ACP, Military, Clip Fed, *Curio*	150	275	350

FRONTIER

Made by Norwich Falls Pistol Co., c. 1880.

HANDGUN, REVOLVER

	Fair	V. Good	Excellent
.32 Short R.F., 5 Shot, Spur Trigger, Solid Frame, Single Action, *Antique*	50	100	175

FRYBERG, ANDREW

Hopkintown, Mass., c. 1905.

	Fair	V. Good	Excellent
.32 S & W, 5 Shot, Top Break, Double Action, Modern	75	100	125
.32 S & W, 5 Shot, Top Break, Hammerless, Double Action, *Modern*	75	100	125
.38 S & W, 5 Shot, Top Break, Double Action, *Modern*	75	100	125
.38 S & W, 5 Shot, Top Break, Hammerless, Double Action, *Modern*	75	100	125

FTL

Covina, Calif.

HANDGUN, SELF-LOADING

	Fair	V. Good	Excellent
.22 L.R.R.F., Clip Fed, Chrome Plated, *Modern*	50	100	150

G

	Fair	V. Good	Excellent

GALAND, CHARLES FRANCOIS

From 1865 until about 1910 with plants in London, England, Paris, France, and Liège, Belgium.

HANDGUN, REVOLVER

	Fair	V. Good	Excellent
Galand, Various Calibers, Double Action, Underlever Extraction, *Curio*	$125	$350	$500
Galand-Perrin, Various Calibers, Double Action, Underlever Extraction, *Curio*	125	350	500
Galand-Sommerville, 7-12mm, Double Action, Underlevel Extraction, *Curio*	125	350	500
Galand-Sommerville, 7-12mm, Double Action, Underlever Extraction, *Curio*	150	350	500
Le Novo, .25 ACP, Double Action, Folding Trigger, *Curio*	100	175	250

SHOTGUN, PERCUSSION

	Fair	V. Good	Excellent
Various Gauges, Checkered Stock, Double Barrel, Plain, *Antique*	100	200	350

SHOTGUN, DOUBLE BARREL, SIDE-BY-SIDE

	Fair	V. Good	Excellent
Various Gauges, Checkered Stock, Plain, Hammers, *Curio*	75	125	250

GALEF

Importers in New York City.

HANDGUN, REVOLVER

	Fair	V. Good	Excellent
Stallion, 22LR/.22 WMR Combo, Western Style, Single Action, *Modern*	50	75	125

HANDGUN, SELF-LOADING

	Fair	V. Good	Excellent
Brigadier, 9mm Luger, Beretta, Clip Fed, *Modern*	100	250	350
Cougar, .380 ACP, Beretta, Clip Fed, *Modern*	100	200	275
Jaguar, .22 L.R.R.F., Beretta, Clip Fed, *Modern*	75	150	225
Puma, .32 ACP, Beretta, Clip Fed, *Modern*	75	150	225
Sable, .22 L.R.R.F., Beretta, Clip Fed, Adjustable Sights, *Modern*	75	150	225

RIFLE, BOLT ACTION

	Fair	V. Good	Excellent
BSA Monarch, Various Calibers, Checkered Stock Magnum Action, *Modern*	$125	$225	$300
BSA Monarch, Various Calibers, Checkered Stock, *Modern*	100	200	300
BSA Monarch Varmint, Various Calibers, Checkered Stock, Heavy Barrel, *Modern*	125	250	350

SHOTGUN, DOUBLE BARREL, OVER-UNDER

	Fair	V. Good	Excellent
Golden Snipe, 12 and 20 Gauges, Beretta, Single Selective Trigger, Automatic Ejector, Engraved, Fancy Checkering, *Modern*	200	425	600
Golden Snipe, 12 and 20 Gauges, Beretta, Single Trigger, Automatic Ejector, Engraved, Fancy Checkering, *Modern*	150	350	500
Golden Snipe, 12 and 20 Gauges, Skeet Grade, Single Trigger, Automatic Ejector, Engraved, Checkered Stock, *Modern*	200	450	600
Golden Snipe, 12 Ga., Trap Grade, Single Trigger, Automatic Ejector, Engraved, Checkered Stock, *Modern*	200	450	600
Golden Snipe Deluxe, 12 and 20 Gauges, Beretta, Single Selective Trigger, Automatic Ejector, Fancy Engraving, Fancy Checkering, *Modern*	200	475	600
Silver Snipe, 12 and 20 Gauges, Beretta, Single Selective Trigger, Checkered Stock, Light Engraving, *Modern*	150	325	450
Silver Snipe, 12 and 20 Gauges, Beretta, Single Trigger, Checkered Stock, *Modern*	150	300	400
Silver Snipe, 12 and 20 Gauges, Skeet Grade, Single Trigger, Vent Rib, Engraved, Checkered Stock, *Modern*	200	375	475
Silver Snipe, 12 Ga., Trap Grade, Single Trigger, Vent Rib, Engraved, Checkered Stock, *Modern*	175	375	475
Zoli Golden Snipe, 12 and 20 Gauges, Vent Rib, Single Trigger, Adjustable Choke, Engraved, Checkered Stock, *Modern*	175	400	500

	Fair	V. Good	Excellent
Zoli Silver Snipe, 12 and 20 Gauges, Vent Rib, Single Trigger, Engraved, Checkered Stock, *Modern*	$150	$350	$450

SHOTGUN, DOUBLE BARREL, SIDE-BY-SIDE

	Fair	V. Good	Excellent
M213CH, 10 Ga. 3½", Double Trigger, Checkered Stock, Light Engraving, Recoil Pad, *Modern*	100	250	400
M213CH, Various Gauges, Double Trigger, Checkered Stock, Light Engraving, Recoil Pad, *Modern*	75	125	250
Silver Hawk, 10 Ga. 3½", Beretta, Double Trigger, Magnum, *Modern*	200	450	600
Silver Hawk, 12 and 20 Gauges, Double Trigger, Engraved, Checkered Stock, *Modern*	150	325	450
Silver Hawk, 12 Ga. Mag. 3", Beretta, Double Trigger, Magnum, *Modern*	150	325	450
Silver Hawk, 12 Ga. Mag. 3", Beretta, Single Trigger, Magnum, *Modern*	175	375	500
Silver Hawk, Various Gauges, Beretta, Double Trigger, Lightweight, *Modern*	150	275	400
Silver Hawk, Various Gauges, Beretta, Double Trigger, Lightweight, *Modern*	150	350	500
Zabala 213, 10 Ga. 3½", Double Trigger, *Modern*	75	150	300
Zabala 213, 12 and 20 Gauges, Double Trigger, *Modern*	75	125	225
Zabala 213, 12 and 20 Gauges, Double Trigger, Vent Rib, *Modern*	75	125	225
Zabala Police, 12 and 20 Gauges, Double Trigger, *Modern*	75	125	225

SHOTGUN, SELF-LOADING

	Fair	V. Good	Excellent
Gold Lark, 12 Ga., Beretta, Vent Rib, Light Engraving, Checkered Stock, *Modern*	100	200	325
Ruby Lark, 12 Ga., Beretta, Vent Rib, Fancy Engraving, Fancy Checkering, *Modern*	150	300	450
Silver Gyrfalcon, 12 Ga., Beretta, Checkered Stock, *Modern*	50	100	300
Silver Lark, 12 Ga., Beretta, Checkered Stock, *Modern*	75	125	300

SHOTGUN, SINGLESHOT

	Fair	V. Good	Excellent
Companion, Various Gauges, Folding Gun, Checkered Stock, *Modern*	25	50	75
Companion, Various Gauges, Folding Gun, Checkered Stock, Vent Rib, *Modern*	25	50	75
Monte Carlo, 12 Ga., Trap Grade, Vent Rib, Engraved, Checkered Stock, *Modern*	100	225	400

SHOTGUN, SLIDE ACTION

	Fair	V. Good	Excellent
Gold Pigeon, 12 Ga., Beretta, Vent Rib, Fancy Engraving, Fancy Checkering, *Modern*	150	300	400
Ruby Pigeon, 12 Ga., Beretta, Vent Rib, Fancy Engraving, Fancy Checkering, *Modern*	$200	$400	$700
Silver Pigeon, 12 Ga., Beretta, Light Engraving, Checkered Stock, *Modern*	175	325	650

GALESI

Industria Armi Galesi, Brescia, Italy, since 1910.

HANDGUN, SELF-LOADING

	Fair	V. Good	Excellent
Galesi, 6.35mm, Clip Fed, *Curio*	75	200	300
Model 30, 6.35mm, Clip Fed, *Curio*	75	200	300
Model 30, 7.65mm, Clip Fed, *Curio*	75	200	300
Model 9, .22 L.R.R.F., Clip Fed, *Curio*	50	100	175

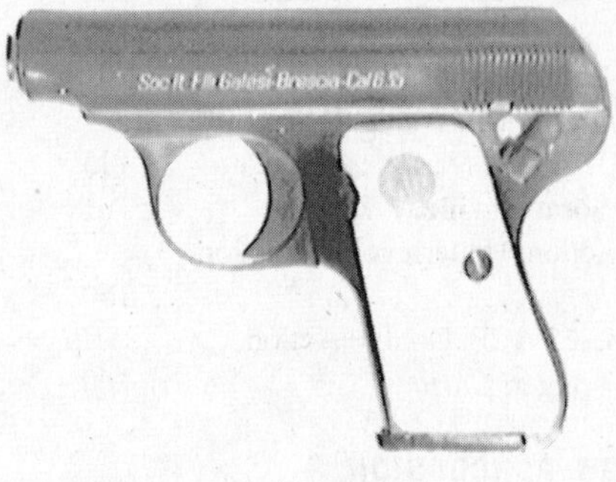

Galesi Model 9 Pistol

	Fair	V. Good	Excellent
Model 9, .32 ACP, Clip Fed, *Curio*	50	100	200
Model 9, .380 ACP, Clip Fed, *Curio*	75	150	225

GALLATIN, ALBERT

See Kentucky Rifles and Pistols.

GALLUS

Retoloza Hermanos, Eibar, Spain, c. 1920.

HANDGUN, SELF-LOADING

	Fair	V. Good	Excellent
.25 ACP, Clip Fed, Blue, *Curio*	50	100	175

GAMBA

Renato Gamba, Brescia, Italy.

RIFLE, SINGLESHOT

	Fair	V. Good	Excellent
Mustang, Various Calibers, Holland Type Sidelock Action, Set Triggers, Checkered Stock, Engraved, Zeiss Scope, *Modern*	3000	7500	12000

	Fair	V. Good	Excellent
RIFLE, DOUBLE BARREL, OVER-UNDER			
Safari, Various Calibers, Boxlock, Checkered Stock, Engraved, Double Triggers, *Modern*	$1500	$3000	$5500
SHOTGUN, DOUBLE BARREL, SIDE-BY-SIDE			
London, 12 or 20 Ga., Sidelock, Checkered Stock, Engraved, *Modern*	3000	6500	10000
Oxford, 12 or 20 Ga., Boxlock, Checkered Stock, Engraved, *Modern*	1100	2500	4500

GANDER, PETER

Lancaster, Pa., 1779–1782. See Kentucky Rifles.

GARATE, ANITUA

Eibar, Spain, c. 1915.

	Fair	V. Good	Excellent
HANDGUN, REVOLVER			
Pistol O.P. #Mk.I, .455 Webley, British Military, *Curio*	75	150	250
HANDGUN, SELF-LOADING			
.32 ACP, Clip Fed, Long Grip, *Curio*	75	125	175

GARBI

Amas Garbi, Eibar, Spain.

	Fair	V. Good	Excellent
SHOTGUN, DOUBLE BARREL, SIDE-BY-SIDE			
Model 51-A, Various Gauges, Boxlock, Checkered Stock, Engraved, *Modern*	200	400	650
Model 60-A, Various Gauges, Sidelock, Checkered Stock, Engraved, *Modern*	225	550	750
Model 60-B, Various Gauges, Sidelock, Checkered Stock, Engraved, Automatic Ejectors, *Modern*	600	1250	1750

GARRISON

Made by Hopkins & Allen, c. 1880–1890.

	Fair	V. Good	Excellent
HANDGUN, REVOLVER			
.22 Short R.F., 7 Shot, Spur Trigger, Solid Frame, Single Action, *Antique*	75	125	175

GARRUCHA

Made by Amadeo Rossi, São Leopoldo, Brazil.

	Fair	V. Good	Excellent
HANDGUN, DOUBLE BARREL, SIDE-BY-SIDE			
.22 L.R.R.F., Double Triggers, Outside Hammers, *Modern*	25	50	75

GASSER

Leopold Gasser, Vienna, Austria.

	Fair	V. Good	Excellent
HANDGUN, REVOLVER			
Montenegrin Gasser, 10.7mm Montenegrin, Double Action, Break Top, Ring Extractor, *Antique*	$175	$375	$500
Rast & Gasser, 8mm R&G, Double Action, Solid Frame, *Curio*	100	200	300

GASTINNE RENETTE

Paris, France, since 1812. Like his Uncle Napoleon Bonaparte, Napoleon III was a keen arms devotee and collector, and was also renowned for his skills as a bird shooter. Napoleon III was a patron of such distinguished gunmakers as Gastinne Renette and Galvain, and was presented some fine American-made guns by various makers. The author has had the pleasure of owning, if only briefly, an extraordinary cased fowling piece and a cased pair of exquisite percussion pistols made for Napoleon III by Gastinne Renette. While visiting Paris in the late 1980s, the author was invited to fire a Colt Python at the Gastinne Renette private shooting gallery, a vestige from the original company used in the 19th century to practice target shooting and dueling! The gallery is located below street level of the store, and has much of the original decorative interior intact. Gastinne Renette today is one of the most elegant showrooms of any arms dealer in the world, and remains at a Paris address used by the firm since the 19th century. The sport of game shooting is alive and well in France, ably assisted and encouraged by the remarkable and historic firm of Gastinne Renette.

	Fair	V. Good	Excellent
RIFLE, DOUBLE BARREL, SIDE-BY-SIDE			
Chapuis Standard, Various Calibers, Boxlock Action, Engraved, Checkered Stock, Double Trigger, Open Sights, *Modern*	1000	2000	3250
Chapuis de Luxe, Various Calibers, Boxlock Action with Sideplates, Fancy Engraving, Checkered Stock, Double Trigger Open Sights, *Modern*	1500	2500	3750
Chapuis President, Various Calibers, Boxlock Action with Sideplates, Engraved, Gold Inlays, Checkered Stock, Double Trigger, Open Sights, *Modern*	1700	2800	4250
Chapuis, For Claw Mounts Add $150.00-$250.00			
Chapuis, With 20 Gauge Barrels Add $550.00-$850.00			
SHOTGUN, DOUBLE BARREL, OVER-UNDER			
Bretton Baby Luxe, Lightweight, Double Trigger, Checkered Stock, Engraved, Chrome Frame, *Modern*	200	400	650
Bretton Baby Standard, Lightweight, Double Trigger, Checkered Stock, *Modern*	150	350	600
Bretton Baby-Elite, Lightweight, Double Trigger, Checkered Stock, *Modern*	150	375	650

SHOTGUN, DOUBLE BARREL, SIDE-BY-SIDE

	Fair	*V. Good*	*Excellent*
Model 105, 12 or 20 Gauge, Boxlock Action, Engraved, Fancy Wood, Checkered Stock, Double Trigger, *Modern*	$600	$1250	$1650
Model 202, 12 or 20 Gauge, Boxlock Action with Sideplates, Fancy Engraving, Fancy Wood, Checkered Stock, Double Trigger, *Modern*	1700	3500	4750
Model 353, 12 or 20 Gauge, Sidelock Action, Fancy Engraving, Fancy Wood, Checkered Stock, Double Trigger, *Modern*	3000	6000	9000
Model 98, 12 or 20 Gauge, Boxlock Action, Engraved, Fancy Wood, Checkered Stock, Double Trigger, *Modern*	1100	2000	2750

GATLING ARMS & AMMUNITION CO

Birmingham, England, c. 1890.

HANDGUN, REVOLVER

Dimancea, .38 &.45 Caliber, Hammerless, Twist Opening, Double Action, *Antique*	400	800	1100

GATLING GUN COMPANY

Hartford, Connecticut; production est. 1866, in conjunction with the Colt's Patent Fire Arms Mfg. Co., Inc. Inventor of the first successful crank-operated repeating gun, Dr. Richard Gatling (1818–1903) created the machine while he was residing in Indianapolis, Indiana, a successful doctor of medicine. A prolific inventor who also patented a bicycle, a flush toilet, torpedo boats, a cultivator, a cleaning system, a casting system, and a cast steel gun, the Gatling Gun was designed for defense of buildings, bridges, and causeways. Gatling demonstrated his first working model in 1862, with six revolving barrels, each with its own bolt. Cocking and firing were by a cam action, via a gear-drive mechanism. The original design fired paper cartridges, ignited by percussion caps. Rimfire ammunition soon succeeded the percussion and the Gatling was adopted by the U.S. Army in 1866, with the first example chambered for the newly adopted .50 caliber government cartridge. With adequate protection for his designs from the U.S. Patent Office, Gatling approached the Colt's Patent Fire Arms Mfg. Co., known to be receptive to creative inventors, to contract their production of his revolutionary design. Accordingly, all the Gatling Guns made in America, from the Model 1866 onward, were built by Colt's. The company marking appears on the breeches either in hand-engraved inscriptions, or embossed on cast bronze plaques. Until Gatling Guns became obsolete and the company was dissolved in 1912, most of the officers of the Colt company were one and the same as those of the Gatling Gun Co. The inventor himself served as Gatling Gun Co. president until 1897, when he was succeeded by Colt's president, John H. Hall. In the same year, the Gatling Gun Co. was absorbed by Colt's. Evolutionary design changes led from the first guns, the Models of 1862, to the Models 1865, 1866, 1871–73, '74, '75, '76, '77, '79, '81, '83, '85, '86, '87, '89, '91, '92, '93, '93 Electric, the Police Gatling (Model 1893 Bulldog), '95, 1900, '03, and the Models 1903–06. Gatlings earned worldwide popularity, primarily in the armed services of many European countries, as well as in South America, and even in Africa and China. Gatlings were chambered for nearly every major military cartridge in use during their period of manufacture: from the smallest of these, the .30, on up to the largest, the 1". The name "gat" was derived from an abbreviation of the Gatling Gun, as a generic term for firearms. By the end of the gun's production, examples had even been adapted for operating under electric power, with a cyclic rate of 3,000 rounds per minute. Colt's had entered into agreements with the inventor John M. Browning for manufacture of a gas-operated, belt-feed machine gun, in 1895. Those arrangements assured the company's dominance in machine guns until well into the Twentieth Century. See Colt for value listings.

Fair V. Good Excellent

GAULOIS

Tradename used by Mrs. Francaise de Armes et Cycles de St. Etienne, France, 1897–1910.

HANDGUN, MANUAL REPEATER

Palm Pistol, 8mm, Engraved, *Curio*	$250	$750	$1500

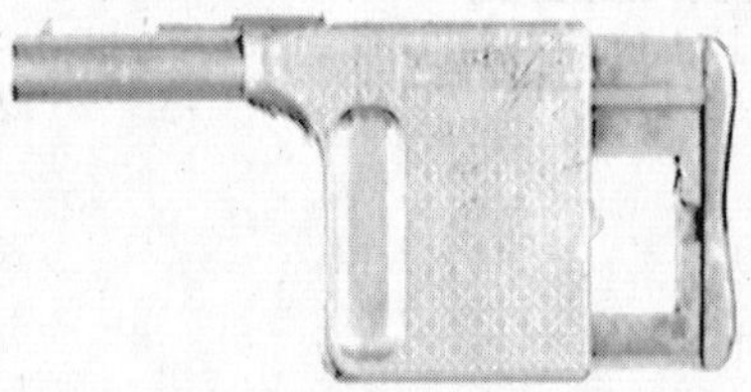

Gaulois Palm Pistol

GAUTEC, PETER

Lancaster, Pa., c. 1780 Kentucky Rifles and Pistols.

GAVAGE

Fab. d'Armes de Guerre de Haute Precision Armand Gavage, Liege, Belgium, c. 1940.

HANDGUN, SELF-LOADING

7.65mm, Clip Fed, Blue, *Curio*	75	200	350

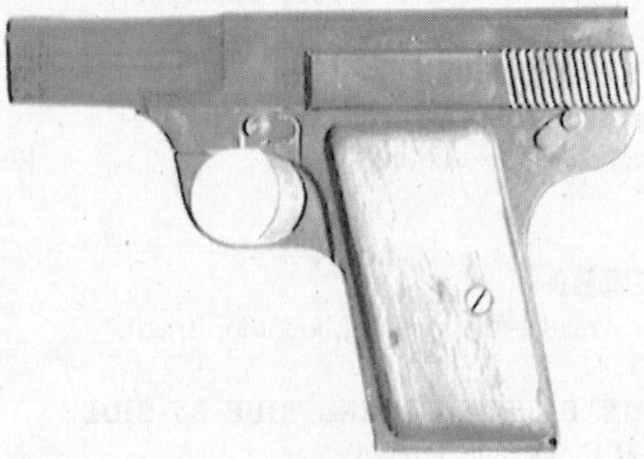

Gavage .32 Pistol

	Fair	V. Good	Excellent
7.65mm, Clip Fed, Blue, Nazi-Proofed, *Curio*	$200	$400	$550

GECADO

Suhl, Germany, by G. C. Dornheim.

HANDGUN, SELF-LOADING

	Fair	V. Good	Excellent
Model 11, .25 ACP, Clip Fed, *Modern*	75	100	150

GECO

Tradename used by Gustav Genschow, Hamburg, Germany.

HANDGUN, REVOLVER

	Fair	V. Good	Excellent
Bulldog, .32 ACP, Double Action, *Modern*	50	100	150
Velo Dog, .25 ACP, Double Action, *Modern*	50	100	150

SHOTGUN, DOUBLE BARREL, SIDE-BY-SIDE

	Fair	V. Good	Excellent
12 Gauge, Checkered Stock, Double Triggers, Plain, *Modern*	75	125	175

GEM

Made by Bacon Arms Co., c. 1880.

HANDGUN, REVOLVER

	Fair	V. Good	Excellent
.22 Short R.F., 7 Shot, Spur Trigger, Solid Frame, Single Action, *Antique*	100	175	225

GEM

Made by J. Stevens Arms & Tool, Chicopee Falls, Mass.

HANDGUN, SINGLESHOT

	Fair	V. Good	Excellent
.22 or .30 R.F., Side-Swing Barrel, Spur Trigger, *Antique*	75	125	200

GERMAN MILITARY

Also see: Walther, Mauser, Luger. For centuries Germany was a militaristic country. German military firearms have a distinctive businesslike style, but also exhibit the Germanic qualities of practicality and serviceability. Although there is a tremendous interest in World War II Nazi arms and memorabilia, some gun shows are reluctant to permit the display and sale of these artifacts. Ironically, not a few of the collectors interested in such material are Jewish, despite the horrendous treatment of Jews by Hitler and his minions. Interest in Nazi material should by no means be considered a reflection of political bent in favor of Nazi philosophies. The relics of that period often reveal solid craftsmanship, interesting designs, and engineering orginality. One of the specialists in Nazi and Imperial German collectibles, for many years, has been the Mohawk Arms firm in Utica, New York. Catalogues the company has produced have been substantial and are at times like a textbook of that field of interest.

HANDGUN, FLINTLOCK

	Fair	V. Good	Excellent
Model 1830, .63, Military, *Antique*	$450	$800	$1200

HANDGUN, PERCUSSION

	Fair	V. Good	Excellent
Model 1860, .63, Military, *Antique*	250	550	750

HANDGUN, REVOLVER

	Fair	V. Good	Excellent
Model 1879 Troopers Model, 11mm German Service, Solid Frame, Single Action, Safety, 7" Barrel, 6 Shot, *Antique*	175	400	650

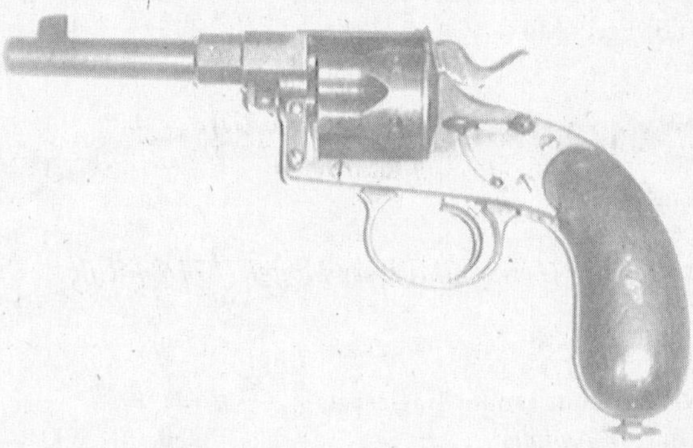

German Military Model 1879 Revolver

	Fair	V. Good	Excellent
Model 1883 Officer's Model, 11mm German Service, Solid Frame, Single Action, Safety, 5" Barrel, 6 Shot, *Antique*	150	350	550

RIFLE, BOLT ACTION

	Fair	V. Good	Excellent
GEW 88 Commission, 8 × 57 JRS, Clip Fed, *Antique*	35	75	125
GEW 98 (Average), 8mm Mauser Military, *Curio*	100	175	250
GEW 98 Sniper, 8mm Mauser, Scope Mounted, Military, *Curio*	300	750	1100
K98K Sniper, 8mm Mauser, Scope Mounted, Military, *Curio*	300	700	1100
KAR 98 (Average), 8mm Mauser Military, Carbine, *Curio*	100	200	300
KAR 98A (Average), 8mm Mauser Military, Carbine, *Curio*	100	200	300
M-95, 8mm Mauser, Steyr-Mannlicher, German Military, Nazi- Proofed, *Curio*	75	150	225
M-95, 8mm Mauser, Steyr-Mannlicher, German Military, Carbine Nazi-Proofed, *Curio*	75	150	225
Model 1871 Mauser, .43 Mauser, Carbine, Singleshot, Military, *Antique*	200	500	800

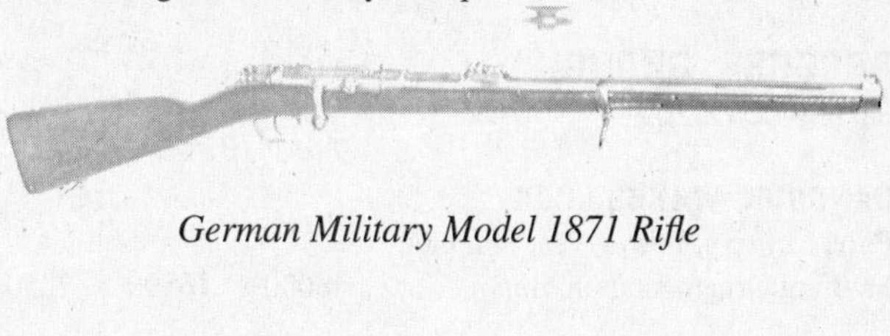

German Military Model 1871 Rifle

	Fair	V. Good	Excellent
Model 1871 Mauser, .43 Mauser, Singleshot, Military, *Antique*	$150	$300	$500
Model 1936 Falke KK, .22 L.R.R.F., Training Rifle, Military, *Curio*	35	75	225
Model 29/40, 8mm Mauser, Nazi-Proofed, Military, *Curio*	50	100	225
Model 3 3/40, 8mm Mauser, Nazi-Proofed, Military, *Curio*	65	125	250
Model 45 Mauser, .22 L.R.R.F., Training Rifle, Military, *Curio*	75	150	275
Model 71/84 Mauser, .43 Mauser, Tube Feed, Military, *Antique*	175	325	550

German Military Model 1871/84 Rifle

	Fair	V. Good	Excellent
Needle Gun, 11mm, Singleshot, Military, *Antique*	250	600	950
VK-98, 8mm Mauser, Nazi-Proofed, Military, *Curio*	75	175	300
VZ-24 BRNO, 8mm Mauser, Nazi-Proofed, Military, *Curio*	65	125	250

RIFLE, PERCUSSION

	Fair	V. Good	Excellent
M1839, .69, Musket, Brass Furniture, Military, *Antique*	200	450	750
M1842, .75, Musket, Brass Furniture, Military, *Antique*	150	400	700

RIFLE, SELF-LOADING

	Fair	V. Good	Excellent
G43, 8mm Mauser, Clip Fed, 10 Shot, Military, *Curio*	125	275	450
GEW 41, 8mm Mauser, 10 Shot, Military, *Curio*	250	425	600
GEW 41(W), 8mm Mauser, 10 Shot, Military, *Curio*	175	375	600
KAR 43 Sniper, 8mm Mauser, Scope Mounted, Clip Fed, 10 Shot, Military, *Curio*	325	700	1350
VG 2, 8mm Mauser, Clip Fed, 10 Shot, Military, *Curio*	150	300	600

RIFLE, SINGLESHOT

	Fair	V. Good	Excellent
Model 1869 Werder, 11.5mm, Bavarian, *Antique*	350	700	950

GESSCER, GEORG

Saxony, 1591–1611.

HANDGUN, WHEEL LOCK

	Fair	V. Good	Excellent
Pair, Military, Inlays, Pear Pommel, Medium Ornamentation, *Antique*	8000	16500	22500

GEVARM

Gevelot, St. Etienne, France.

RIFLE, SELF-LOADING

	Fair	V. Good	Excellent
Model A3, .22 L.R.R.F., Target Sights, Clip Fed, *Modern*	$50	$100	$150
Model A6, .22 L.R.R.F., Open Sights, Clip Fed, *Modern*	75	100	125
Model A7, .22 L.R.R.F., Target Sights, Clip Fed, *Modern*	50	100	150

GIBRALTER

Made by Stevens Arms.

SHOTGUN, SINGLESHOT

	Fair	V. Good	Excellent
Model 116, Various Gauges, Hammer, Automatic Ejector, Raised Matted Rib, *Modern*	25	50	75

GILL, THOMAS

London, England, 1770–1812.

HANDGUN, FLINTLOCK

	Fair	V. Good	Excellent
.68, Pocket Pistol, Octagon Barrel, Plain, High Quality, *Antique*	400	800	1150

GLASER WAFFEN

Zurich, Switzerland.

HANDGUN, SINGLESHOT

	Fair	V. Good	Excellent
Target Pistol, .22 L.R.R.F., Toggle Breech, Francotte, *Modern*	150	350	450

RIFLE, BOLT ACTION

	Fair	V. Good	Excellent
Custom Rifle, Various Calibers, Fancy Wood, *Modern*	500	1150	1750

RIFLE, SINGLESHOT

	Fair	V. Good	Excellent
Heeren Rifle, Various Calibers, Engraved, Fancy Wood, *Modern*	900	2000	2750

GLASSBRENNER, DAVID

Lancaster, Pa., c. 1800. See Kentucky Rifles.

GLAZIER, JOHN

Belleville, Ind., c. 1820. See Kentucky Rifles.

GLENFIELD

See Marlin.

GLENN, ROBERT
Edinburgh, Scotland, c. 1860. Made fine copies of Highland Pistols.

HANDGUN, SNAPHAUNCE

	Fair	V. Good	Excellent
Replica Highland, All Brass, Engraved, Ovoid Pommel, *Antique*	$1100	$2750	$3150

GLISENTI
Soc. Siderugica Glisenti, Turin, Italy, c. 1889–1930.

HANDGUN, REVOLVER

	Fair	V. Good	Excellent
M1889, 10.4mm Glisenti, Double Action, Folding Trigger, Military, *Curio*	75	125	175
M1889, 10.4mm Glisenti, Double Action, Trigger Guard, Military, *Curio*	75	125	175

HANDGUN, SELF-LOADING

	Fair	V. Good	Excellent
Brixia, 9mm Glisenti, Clip Fed, Hard Rubber Grips, *Curio*	200	375	450
M1906, 7.63 Mauser, Clip Fed, Military, *Curio*	200	475	600
M1910 Army, 9mm Glisenti, Clip Fed, Wood Grips, *Curio*	200	500	650
M1910 Navy, 9mm Glisenti, Clip Fed, Hard Rubber Grips, *Curio*	250	575	725

GOFF, DANIEL
London, England, 1779–1810.

HANDGUN, FLINTLOCK

	Fair	V. Good	Excellent
Dueling Pistols, .50, Cased pair, with Accessories, *Antique*	1000	2750	5000

GOLCHER, JAMES
Philadelphia, Pa., 1820–1833. Locks with Golcher markings are often seen on arms made by other gunmakers, which sometimes is the source of confusion in trying to identify the maker of a particular firearm. The name on the barrel generally is indicative, in this period, of the gunmaker's identity; the name on the lock often merely identifies the maker of the lock only.

GOLCHER, JOHN
Easton, Pa., c. 1775.

GOLCHER, JOSEPH
Philadelphia, Pa., c. 1800.

GOLDEN EAGLE
Nikko Arms Co. Ltd, Tochigi, Japan.

RIFLE, BOLT ACTION

	Fair	V. Good	Excellent
Model 7000, Various African Calibers, Grade 1, Checkered Stock, *Modern*	$225	$475	$650
Model 7000, Various African Calibers, Grade 2, Checkered Stock, *Modern*	300	625	850
Model 7000, Various Calibers, Grade 1, Checkered Stock, *Modern*	200	425	600
Model 7000, Various Calibers, Grade 2, Checkered Stock, *Modern*	250	575	750

SHOTGUN, DOUBLE BARREL, OVER-UNDER

	Fair	V. Good	Excellent
Model 5000 Grandee, 12 and 20 Gauges, Field Grade 3, Vent Rib, Checkered Stock, Fancy Engraving, Gold Overlay, *Modern*	900	2250	3000
Model 5000 Grandee, 12 and 20 Gauges, Skeet Grade 3, Vent Rib, Checkered Stock, Fancy Engraving, Gold Overlay, *Modern*	900	2000	2750
Model 5000 Grandee, 12 and 20 Gauges, Trap Grade 3, Vent Rib, Checkered Stock, Fancy Engraving, Gold Overlay, *Modern*	900	2000	2750
Model 5000, 12 and 20 Gauges, Field Grade 2, Vent Rib, Checkered Stock, Light Engraving, Gold Overlay, *Modern*	500	1000	1500
Model 5000, 12 and 20 Gauges, Field Grade, Vent Rib, Checkered Stock, Light Engraving, Gold Overlay, *Modern*	350	725	1000
Model 5000, 12 and 20 Gauges, Skeet Grade 2, Vent Rib, Checkered Stock, Light Engraving, Gold Overlay, *Modern*	425	950	1250
Model 5000, 12 and 20 Gauges, Skeet Grade, Vent Rib, Checkered Stock, Light Engraving, Gold Overlay, *Modern*	350	800	1000
Model 5000, 12 and 20 Gauges, Trap Grade 2, Vent Rib, Checkered Stock, Light Engraving, Gold Overlay, *Modern*	400	950	1250
Model 5000, 12 and 20 Gauges, Trap Grade, Vent Rib, Checkered Stock, Light Engraving, Gold Overlay, *Modern*	400	875	1100

GONTER, PETER
Lancaster, Pa., 1770–1778. See Kentucky Rifles.

GOOSE GUN
Made by Stevens Arms.

	Fair	V. Good	Excellent
SHOTGUN, SINGLESHOT			
Model 89 Dreadnaught, Various Gauges, Hammer, *Modern*	$25	$50	$75

GOVERNOR
Made by Bacon Arms Co.

	Fair	V. Good	Excellent
HANDGUN, REVOLVER			
.22 Short R.F., 7 Shot, Spur Trigger, Solid Frame, Single Action, *Antique*	75	125	200

GOVERNOR
Various makers, c. 1880.

	Fair	V. Good	Excellent
HANDGUN, REVOLVER			
.32 S & W, 5 Shot, Double Action, Top Break, *Modern*	50	75	125
.38 S & W, 5 Shot, Double Action, Top Break, *Modern*	50	75	125

GRAEFF, WM.
Reading, Pa., 1751–1784. See Kentucky Rifles.

GRANT HAMMOND
New Haven, Conn., 1915–1917.

	Fair	V. Good	Excellent
HANDGUN, SELF-LOADING			
U.S. Test, .45 ACP, Clip Fed, Hammer, *Curio*	4000	8000	12500

GRANT, W. L.
Manufactured by Wm. Uhlinger, Phil., Penn.

	Fair	V. Good	Excellent
HANDGUN, REVOLVER			
.22 Long R.F., 6 Shot, Single Action, Solid Frame, Spur Trigger, *Antique*	100	200	350
.22 Short R.F., 6 Shot, Single Action, Solid Frame, Spur Trigger, *Antique*	100	200	375

GRAVE, JOHN
Lancaster, Pa., 1769–1773. See Kentucky Rifles.

GREAT WESTERN ARMS CO.
Venice, Calif. Moved to North Hollywood, Calif. in 1959. Last address Los Angeles, Calif., 1953–1961. See also Hy Hunter. The Great Western firm was the operation of Hy Hunter, a flamboyant arms dealer and entrepreneur with a great many Hollywood connections. As a boy the author remembers seeing advertisements of Hy Hunter, and articles and pictures of him with such show business types as Mel Tormé, Audie Murphy, and several of the TV and movie Western stars. Although relatively short-lived, Hunter and his company had a strong impact on the popularity of single action style firearms, on guns as collectibles, and on the use of the single action for sport and target shooting and in the rapidly growing hobby of quick-draw.

	Fair	V. Good	Excellent
HANDGUN, DOUBLE BARREL, OVER-UNDER			
Double Derringer, .38 Spec., Remington Copy, *Modern*	$75	$150	$200
HANDGUN, REVOLVER			
Buntline, Various Calibers, Single Action, Western Style, *Modern*	300	650	850
Deputy, .22 L.R.R.F., Single Action, Western Style, *Modern*	100	200	300
Frontier, .22 L.R.R.F., Target Model, Single Action, Western Style, *Modern*	150	300	450
Frontier, Various Calibers, Single Action, Western Style, *Modern*	300	500	650

GREAT WESTERN GUN WORKS
Pittsburgh, Pa., 1860 to about 1923. Catalogs by the Great Western Gun Works have proven a valuable source in researching various arms built and sold in the period of this firm's years of operation. Well illustrated, and covering a breadth of guns, these catalogs are among the most comprehensive and informative of arms-related publications from the 19th and early 20th century.

	Fair	V. Good	Excellent
HANDGUN, REVOLVER			
.22 Short R.F., 7 Shot, Spur Trigger, Solid Frame, Single Action, *Antique*	75	125	175
RIFLE, PERCUSSION			
No. 5, Various Calibers, Various Barrel Lengths, Plains Rifle, Octagon Barrel, Brass Fittings, *Antique*	250	575	750

GREEK MILITARY

	Fair	V. Good	Excellent
RIFLE, BOLT ACTION			
M 1903 Mannlicher Schoenauer, 6.5mm M.S., Military, *Curio*	100	225	300
M 1903 Mannlicher Schoenauer, 8mm Mauser, Military, *Curio*	125	225	300
M 1930 F N Short Rifle, 8mm Mauser, Military, *Curio*	125	250	325

GREENER, W. W.
Established in 1829 in Northumberland, England, as W. Greener, moved to Birmingham, England, in 1844; name changed to W. W. Greener in 1860, and to W. W. Greener & Son in 1879. William Greener was author of one of the most widely read arms books of all time: *The Gun, or a Treatise on the Various Descriptions of Small Fire-Arms,* published in London, 1835, and in numerous editions thereafter. This book is a must for any enthusiast of collectors firearms. The text includes a history of firearms, with illustrations based on Greener's own experience, as well as expositions on a variety of matters involving gun design, performance and ammunition. Later editions are of particular interest due to develop-

ments in firearms technology, a science in which Greener was well informed. When the Greener firm closed its doors, Val Forgett was the successful purchaser of the remaining stock and numerous records and files.

	Fair	V. Good	Excellent
SHOTGUN, DOUBLE BARREL, SIDE-BY-SIDE			
Various Gauges, Single Non-Selective Trigger Add $280.00-$400.00			
Various Gauges, Single Selective Trigger Add $385.00-$475.00			
Crown DH-55, Various Gauges, Box Lock, Automatic Ejector, Checkered Stock, Fancy Engraving, *Modern*	$1600	$3000	$3500
Empire, 12 Ga., Mag. 3", Box Lock, Hammerless, Light Engraving, Checkered Stock, *Modern*	600	1250	1650
Empire, 12 Ga., Mag. 3", Box Lock, Hammerless, Light Engraving, Checkered Stock, Automatic Ejector, *Modern*	700	1500	2150
Empire Deluxe, 12 Ga., Mag. 3", Box Lock, Hammerless, Engraved, Checkered Stock, *Modern*	600	1400	2000
Empire Deluxe, 12 Ga., Mag. 3", Box Lock, Hammerless, Engraved, Checkered Stock, Automatic Ejector, *Modern*	700	1550	2250
Farkiller F35, 10 Ga. 3½", Box Lock, Hammerless, Engraved, Checkered Stock, *Modern*	1100	2500	3250
Farkiller F35, 10 Ga. 3½", Box Lock, Hammerless, Engraved, Checkered Stock, Automatic Ejector, *Modern*	1500	3250	4750
Farkiller F35, 12 Ga., Mag. 3", Box Lock, Hammerless, Engraved, Checkered Stock, *Modern*	1100	2250	3250
Farkiller F35, 12 Ga., Mag. 3", Box Lock, Hammerless, Engraved, Checkered Stock, Automatic Ejector, *Modern*	1600	3000	4000
Farkiller F35, 8 Ga., Box Lock, Hammerless, Engraved, Checkered Stock, *Modern*	1100	2500	3250
Farkiller F35, 8 Ga., Box Lock, Hammerless, Engraved, Checkered Stock, Automatic Ejector, *Modern*	1600	3250	4250
Jubilee DH-35, Various Gauges, Box Lock, Automatic Ejector, Checkered Stock, Engraved, *Modern*	900	2000	3000
Royal DH-75, Various Gauges, Box Lock, Automatic Ejector, Checkered Stock, Fancy Engraving, *Modern*	1700	3700	4750
Sovereign DH-40, Various Gauges, Box Lock, Automatic Ejector, Checkered Stock, Engraved, *Modern*	900	2150	3250
SHOTGUN, SINGLESHOT			
G.P. Martini, 12 Ga., Checkered Stock, Takedown, *Modern*	175	300	425

GREGORY

Mt. Vernon, Ohio, 1837–1842. See Kentucky Rifles.

GREIFELT & CO

Suhl, Germany, from 1885.

	Fair	V. Good	Excellent
COMBINATION WEAPON, DRILLING			
Various Calibers, Engraved, Checkered Stock, *Curio*	$1200	$3000	$3750
Various Calibers, Fancy Wood, Fancy Checkering, Engraved, *Curio*	1700	4000	5000
RIFLE, BOLT ACTION			
Sport, .22 Hornet, Checkered Stock, Express Sights, *Curio*	450	850	1350
COMBINATION WEAPON, OVER-UNDER			
Various Calibers, Solid Rib, Engraved, Checkered Stock, *Curio*	2700	5000	7000
Various Calibers, Solid Rib, Engraved, Checkered Stock, Automatic Ejector, *Curio*	3000	5800	7500
SHOTGUN, DOUBLE BARREL, OVER-UNDER			
Various Gauges, For Vent Rib Add $300.00-$400.00			
Various Gauges, Single Trigger, Add $350.00-$450.00			
#1, .410 & 28 Ga., Automatic Ejector, Fancy Engraving, Checkered Stock, Fancy Wood, Solid Rib, *Modern*	1300	3000	4250
#1, Various Gauges, Automatic Ejector, Fancy Engraving, Checkered Stock, Fancy Wood, Solid Rib, *Modern*	1300	2750	3750
#3, .410 & 28 Ga., Automatic Ejector, Engraved, Checkered Solid Rib, *Modern*	1000	2500	3500
#3, Various Gauges, Automatic Ejector, Engraved, Checkered Stock, Solid Rib, *Modern*	800	1750	2750
Model 143E, Various Gauges, Automatic Ejector, Engraved, Checkered Stock, Solid Rib, Double Trigger, *Modern*	900	2000	3000
Model 143E, Various Gauges, Automatic Ejector, Engraved, Checkered Stock, Vent Rib, Single Selective Trigger, *Modern*	900	2250	3250
SHOTGUN, DOUBLE BARREL, SIDE-BY-SIDE			
Model 103, 12 and 16 Gauge, Box Lock, Double Trigger, Checkered Stock, Light Engraving, *Modern*	700	1500	2000

	Fair	V. Good	Excellent
Model 103E, 12 and 16 Gauge, Box Lock, Double Trigger, Checkered Stock, Light Engraving, Automatic Ejector, *Modern*	$700	$1600	$2000
Model 22, 12 and 16 Gauge, Box Lock, Double Trigger, Checkered Stock, Engraved, *Modern*	700	1500	1950
Model 22E, 12 and 16 Gauge, Box Lock, Double Trigger, Checkered Stock, Engraved, Automatic Ejector, *Modern*	700	1750	2250

GREYHAWK ARMS CORP.

South El Monte, Calif., c. 1975.

RIFLE, SINGLESHOT

	Fair	V. Good	Excellent
Model 74, Various Calibers, Rolling Block, Octagon Barrel, Open Rear Sight, Reproduction, *Modern*	75	100	150

GRIFFIN & HOWE

N.Y.C., 1923–1976, subsidiary of Abercrombie & Fitch, 1930–1976, privately held company after 1976. Maker of custom rifles. Showrooms and shop opened in Bernardsville, N.J., 1987. Rifles by Griffin & Howe rank among the finest custom-made arms in the history of American gunmaking—and among the finest bolt action rifles made anywhere. Built on a variety of actions—though Mausers have been the primary type—G & H rifles have their own designated serial range, and a classic quality and style. The present showroom is at 36 West 44th Street, New York City, and a New Jersey showroom and workshops are in Bernardsville. Griffin himself was a cabinet maker, who had a keen appreciation of fine guns. His preference in stock styling was the traditional English, and that's what he set out to make. Other gunsmithing firms then rebuilding Springfield bolt action rifles, in the World War I period, included Fred Adolph of New York state, Louis Wundhammer of Los Angeles, and R. F. Sedgely of Philadelphia. Riflemen Townsend Whelen and E. C. Crossman wrote about the new sporter Springfields, which had a positive affect on the demand. Colonel Whelen was instrumental in putting Griffin together with master metal worker James V. Howe, then foreman of Frankford Arsenal's machine shop. At a May 1923 meeting which included Griffin, Howe, Whelen, James M. Holsworth and James L. Gerry, Griffin & Howe was established, with a shop and showroom set up at 234 East 39th Street, New York City. Howe, in a matter of months, left to join a competitor, Hoffman Arms Co., of Cleveland, Ohio, and would later write a classic work on gun and stock making, metalwork and engraving: *The Modern Gunsmith.* Griffin, then the only active employee, continued toiling for another five years, uncertain if the business would prove a success. Despite the stock market crash of 1929, Griffin & Howe remained active, aided by a significant order from the Springfield Armory, to build stocks for international match rifles. By c. 1930 approximately 840 G & H rifles had been made. From March to October 1930 the company was known as Griffin & Hobbs, Inc., at which time G & H serial numbers started with 1000. The company name reverted back to Griffin & Howe soon after the firm became a subsidiary of Abercrombie & Fitch, in September of 1930. Springfield Conversions to sporting rifles continued to be the main output, but Mauser actions became increasingly popular. During World War II the company devoted its time and talents to defense work, including triggers for anti-aircraft guns, as well as parts for airplane factories, sidemounts for Garand M1 rifles (23,000 of them by war's end), and special mounts for telescopic sights for the British Enfield bolt action rifle (only 50 prototypes were delivered due to the abrupt end of war). After World War II Griffin & Howe returned to the manufacture of big game sporting rifles. However, by 1975 Abercrombie & Fitch was in liquidation, and employee Bill Ward was able to buy G & H. From 1960 through 1987 the workshop and later showrooms were located in downtown New York. Ward's share in the company was subsequently sold and the company is presently under the management of Joe Prather, one of the owners. By 1998 Griffin & Howe had built over 300 custom sporting rifles. Business lines the firm has developed over the years include sale of new and second-owner shotguns, clothing and accessories, a full-time shooting program for shotgunners, booking hunting and shooting trips, and continuing the traditional gunsmithing and repairs. Among celebrity clients of G & H: Gary Cooper, Jack O'Connor, Clark Gable, Ernest Hemingway, Robert Ruark, Dwight D. Eisenhower, William B. Ruger, William E. Simon, and Henry Kravis.

GROOM, RICHARD

London, England, c. 1855.

HANDGUN, FLINTLOCK

	Fair	V. Good	Excellent
.68, East India Company, Calvary Pistol, Military, Tapered Round Barrel, Brass Furniture, *Antique*	$800	$1800	$2250

GROSS ARMS CO.

Tiffin, Ohio, 1862–1865.

HANDGUN, POCKET REVOLVER

	Fair	V. Good	Excellent
.25 Short R.F., 7 Shot, Spur Trigger, Tip-Up, *Antique*	100	200	300
.30 Short R.F., 7 Shot, Spur Trigger, Tip-Up, *Antique*	100	200	300

GRUENEL

Gruenig & Elmiger, Malters, Switzerland.

RIFLE, BOLT ACTION

	Fair	V. Good	Excellent
Match 300m, Various Calibers, Offhand Target Rifle, Target Sights, Ventilated Forestock, Palm Rest, Hook Buttplate, *Modern*	600	1000	1500
Model K 31, .308 Win., U.I.T. Target Rifle, Target Sights, Ventilated Forestock, *Modern*	350	750	1000
U.L.T. Standard, .308 Win., Target Rifle, Target Sights, Ventilated Forestock, *Modern*	350	700	1000

GUARDIAN

Made by Bacon Arms Co., c. 1880.

HANDGUN, REVOLVER

	Fair	V. Good	Excellent
.22 Short R.F., 7 Shot, Spur Trigger, Solid Frame, Single Action, *Antique*	$75	$125	$200
.32 Short R.F., 5 Shot, Spur Trigger, Solid Frame, Single Action, *Antique*	75	150	250

GUMPH, CHRISTOPHER

Lancaster, Pa., 1779–1803. See Kentucky Rifles and Pistols.

GUSTAF, CARL

See Husqvarna Vapenfabrik Akitiebolag.

GUSTLOFF WERKE

Suhl, Germany.

HANDGUN, SELF-LOADING

	Fair	V. Good	Excellent
.32 ACP, Clip Fed, Hammer, Single Action, *Modern*	$600	$1200	$1500
.380 ACP, Clip Fed, Hammer, Single Action, *Modern*	1200	2500	3250

RIFLE, BOLT ACTION

	Fair	V. Good	Excellent
Mauser M98, 8mm Mauser, Military, *Curio*	75	175	275
Model KKW, .22 L.R.R.F., Pre-WW2, Singleshot, Tangent Sights, Military Style Stock, *Modern*	150	350	500

SHOTGUN, DOUBLE BARREL, SIDE-BY-SIDE

	Fair	V. Good	Excellent
16 Ga., Engraved, Color Case Hardened Frame, *Modern*	150	400	500

GYROJET

See M.B. Associates.

H

	Fair	V. Good	Excellent

H & D
Henrion & Dassy, Liege, Belgium, c. 1900.

HANDGUN, SELF-LOADING

	Fair	V. Good	Excellent
H & D Patent, .25 ACP, Clip Fed, *Curio*	$75	$150	$225

HACKET, EDWIN AND GEORGE
London, England, c. 1870.

SHOTGUN, DOUBLE BARREL, SIDE-BY-SIDE

	Fair	V. Good	Excellent
10 Ga. $2^7/_8$", Damascus Barrel, Plain, *Antique*	100	200	350

HADDEN, JAMES
Philadelphia, Pa., c. 1769. See Kentucky Rifles and Pistols.

HAEFFER, JOHN
Lancaster, Pa., c. 1800. See Kentucky Rifles and Pistols.

HAENEL, C. G.
C. G. Haenel Waffen und Fahrradfabrik, Suhl, Germany 1840–1945.

HANDGUN, SELF-LOADING

	Fair	V. Good	Excellent
Schmiesser Model 1, .25 ACP, Clip Fed, *Curio*	125	225	300

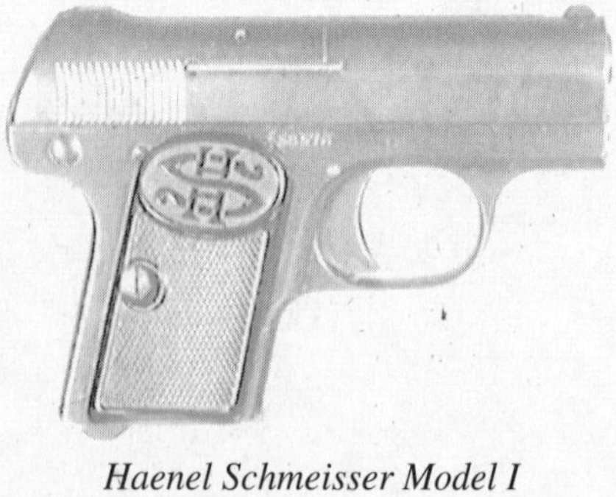

Haenel Schmeisser Model I

	Fair	V. Good	Excellent
Schmeisser Model 2, .25 ACP, Clip Fed, *Curio*	125	250	350

RIFLE, BOLT ACTION

	Fair	V. Good	Excellent
Model 88, Various Calibers, Sporting Rifle, Half-Octagon Barrel, Open Rear Sights, *Curio*	$150	$300	$600
Model 88 Sporter, Various Calibers, 5 Shot Clip, Half-Octagon Barrel, Open Rear Sights, *Curio*	150	350	450

HAFDASA
Hispano Argentina Fab. de Automoviles, Buenos Aires, Argentina, c. 1935.

HANDGUN, SELF-LOADING

	Fair	V. Good	Excellent
.22 L.R.R.F., Blowback, *Curio*	150	375	475

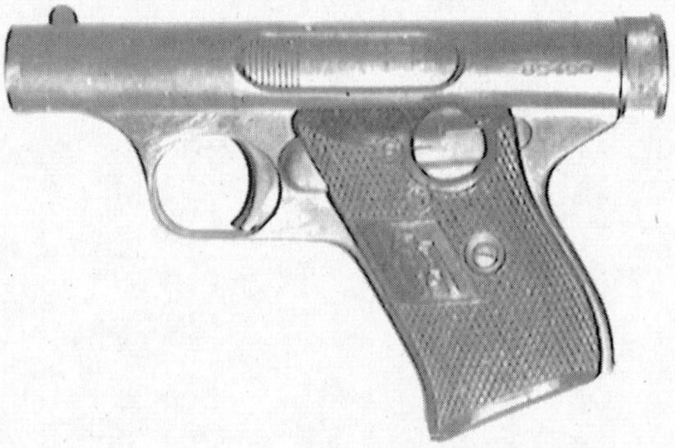

Hafdasa

HALF-BREED
Made by Hopkins & Allen, c. 1880.

HANDGUN, REVOLVER

	Fair	V. Good	Excellent
.32 Short R.F., 5 Shot, Spur Trigger, Solid Frame, Single Action, *Antique*	75	125	175

HAMMERLI
Lenzburg, Switzerland. One of the world leaders in highly accurate target guns, the Hammerli name is synonymous with Olympic level target shooting.

HANDGUN, REVOLVER

	Fair	V. Good	Excellent
Dakota, Various Calibers, Single Action, Western Style, *Modern*	100	250	325
Virginian, Various Calibers, Single Action, Western Style, *Modern*	100	225	325

HANDGUN, SELF-LOADING

	Fair	V. Good	Excellent
Model 200 Walther Olympia, .22 L.R.R.F., Target Pistol, *Modern*	$325	$600	$850
Model 200 Walther Olympia, .22 L.R.R.F., Target Pistol, Muzzle Brake, *Modern*	325	650	900
Model 201 Walther Olympia, .22 L.R.R.F., Target Pistol, Adjustable Grips, *Modern*	300	600	900
Model 202 Walther Olympia, .22 L.R.R.F., Target Pistol, Adjustable Grips, *Modern*	350	700	1000
Model 203 Walther Olympia, .22 L.R.R.F., Target Pistol, Adjustable Grips, *Modern*	350	650	950
Model 203 Walther Olympia, .22 L.R.R.F., Target Pistol, Adjustable Grips, Muzzle Brake, *Modern*	350	725	1000
Model 204 Walther Olympia, .22 L.R.R.F., Target Pistol, *Modern*	325	700	1000
Model 205 Walther Olympia, .22 L.R.R.F., Target Pistol, Fancy Wood, *Modern*	350	775	1000
Model 205 Walther Olympia, .22 L.R.R.F., Target Pistol, Fancy Wood, Muzzle Brake, *Modern*	400	900	1250
Model 206, .22 L.R.R.F., Target Pistol, *Modern*	300	650	1000
Model 207, .22 L.R.R.F., Target Pistol, Adjustable Grips, *Modern*	300	650	1000
Model 208 Deluxe, .22 L.R.R.F., Target Pistol, Clip Fed, Adjustable Grips, *Modern*	1600	3000	4000
Model 208, .22 L.R.R.F., Target Pistol, Clip Fed, Adjustable Grips, *Modern*	700	1500	2000
Model 209, .22 Short R.F., Target Pistol, 5 Shot Clip, Muzzle Brake, *Modern*	325	700	1000
Model 210, .22 L.R.R.F., Target Pistol, Adjustable Grips, *Modern*	400	800	1100
Model 211, .22 L.R.R.F., Target Pistol, Clip Fed, *Modern*	700	1500	2000
Model 212, .22 L.R.R.F., Target Pistol, Clip Fed, *Modern*	700	1500	2000
Model 215, .22 L.R.R.F., Target Pistol, Clip Fed, *Modern*	400	850	1100
Model 230, .22 Short R.F., Target Pistol, 5 Shot Clip, *Modern*	300	575	800
Model 232, .22 Short R.F., Target Pistol, 5 Shot Clip, Adjustable Grips, *Modern*	300	625	900
Model 232, .22 Short R.F., Target Pistol, 5 Shot Clip, Adjustable Grips, Left-Hand, *Modern*	275	600	900
280, .22 L.R.R.F., Target Pistol, Clip Fed, Conversion Unit Only, *Modern*	250	525	750
280, .22 Short, Clip Fed, Target Pistol, Cased with Accessories, *Modern*	800	1500	1950
280, .32 Wadcutter, Clip Fed, Target Pistol, Cased with Accessories, *Modern*	$800	$1750	$2350

HANDGUN, SINGLESHOT

	Fair	V. Good	Excellent
Match Pistol, .22 L.R.R.F., Target Pistol, Round Barrel, *Modern*	300	500	700
Model 100, .22 L.R.R.F., Target Pistol, *Modern*	350	750	900
Model 100 Deluxe, .22 L.R.R.F., Target Pistol, *Modern*	425	800	1000
Model 101, .22 L.R.R.F., Target Pistol, *Modern*	350	775	1000
Model 102, .22 L.R.R.F., Target Pistol, *Modern*	400	800	1000
Model 102 Deluxe, .22 L.R.R.F., Target Pistol, *Modern*	400	825	1100
Model 103, .22 L.R.R.F., Target Pistol, Carved, *Modern*	400	850	1150
Model 103, .22 L.R.R.F., Target Pistol, Carved, Inlays, *Modern*	425	1000	1350
Model 104, .22 L.R.R.F., Target Pistol, Round Barrel, *Modern*	300	750	900
Model 105, .22 L.R.R.F., Target Pistol, Octagon Barrel, *Modern*	400	875	1100
Model 107, .22 L.R.R.F., Target Pistol, Octagon Barrel, *Modern*	400	850	1100
Model 107 Deluxe, .22 L.R.R.F., Target Pistol, Octagon Barrel, Engraved, *Modern*	525	1150	1450
Model 120 H.B., .22 L.R.R.F., Target Pistol, Heavy Barrel, Left-Hand, Adjustable Grips, *Modern*	225	550	750
Model 120-1, .22 L.R.R.F., Target Pistol, Heavy Barrel, *Modern*	200	400	650
Model 120-1, .22 L.R.R.F., Target Pistol, Heavy Barrel, Adjustable Grips, *Modern*	200	400	650
Model 150, .22 L.R.R.F., Target Pistol, *Modern*	700	1500	2000
Model 152 Electronic, .22 L.R.R.F., Target Pistol, *Modern*	800	1750	2250

RIFLE, BOLT ACTION

	Fair	V. Good	Excellent
Model 45, .22 L.R.R.F., Singleshot, Thumbhole Stock, Target Sights, with Accessories, *Modern*	250	500	800
Model 54, .22 L.R.R.F., Singleshot, Thumbhole Stock, Target Sights, with Accessories, *Modern*	250	525	850
Model 503, .22 L.R.R.F., Singleshot, Thumbhole Stock, Target Sights, with Accessories, *Modern*	250	500	800
Model 506, .22 L.R.R.F., Singleshot, Thumbhole Stock, Target Sights, with Accessories, *Modern*	250	550	850
Olympia 300 Meter, Various Calibers, Singleshot, Thumbhole Stock, Target Sights, with Accessories, *Modern*	300	675	900
Sporting Rifle, Various Calibers, Set Triggers, Fancy Wood, Checkered Stock, Open Sights, *Modern*	250	525	850

	Fair	V. Good	Excellent
Tanner, Various Calibers, Singleshot, Thumbhole Stock, Target Sights, with Accessories, *Modern*	$300	$750	$1000

HAMPTON, JOHN

Dauphin County, Pa. See Kentucky Rifles and Pistols.

HARD PAN

Made by Hood Firearms Co., c. 1875.

HANDGUN, REVOLVER

.22 Short R.F., 7 Shot, Spur Trigger, Solid Frame, Single Action, *Antique*	50	100	175
.32 Short R.F., 5 Shot, Spur Trigger, Solid Frame, Single Action, *Antique*	75	125	200

HARPERS FERRY ARMS CO.

RIFLE, FLINTLOCK

.72 Lafayette, Musket, Reproduction	150	250	325

RIFLE, PERCUSSION

.51 Maynard, Carbine, Breech Loader, Reproduction	100	150	300
.58, 1861 Springfield, Rifled, Musket, Reproduction	100	150	300

HARRINGTON & RICHARDSON ARMS CO.

Wesson & Harrington, 1874–1986. Also see the Commemoratives chapter. The Harrington & Richardson company traces its heritage back to such firms as Frank Wesson and Wesson and Harrington, and was founded in 1871. From the outset the Worcester, Massachusetts, company dedicated its manufacturing acumen to producing a line of firearms which were of good quality and utility, reasonably priced. Some collectors would term the handgun products of H & R as "Saturday Night Specials." However, a review of the extraordinary display cabinet of Harrington & Richardson revolvers, at the firm's stand in the Philadelphia Centennial Exhibition of 1876, exhibits some of the finest examples of pocket-sized revolvers ever made in 19th-century America. These early revolvers were models of Frank Wesson and Gilbert Harrington production, and were intended to show off H & R's product line in the finest possible light. Quality of fit, finish, engraving, and grips rivaled even that of the more experienced and more famous Colt Patent Fire Arms Mfg. Co. and the Remington Arms Co.

HANDGUN, REVOLVER

Abilene Anniversary, .22 L.R.R.F., Commemorative, *Curio*	75	150	200
American, Various Calibers, Double Action, Solid Frame, *Modern*	25	50	75
Auto Ejecting, Various Calibers, Top Break, Hammer, Double Action, *Modern*	75	100	150
Bobby, Various Calibers, 6 Shot, Top Break, Double Action, *Modern*	35	75	100

Harrington & Richardson Auto Ejecting

	Fair	V. Good	Excellent
Bulldog, Various Calibers, Double Action, Solid Frame, *Modern*	$50	$75	$100
Defender, .38 S & W, Top Break, 6 Shot, Double Action, Adjustable Sights, *Modern*	75	100	150
Expert, .22 L.R.R.F., Top Break, 9 Shot, Double Action, Wood Grips, *Modern*	75	125	175
Expert, .22 W.R.F., Top Break, 9 Shot, Double Action, Wood Grips, *Modern*	75	125	175
Hammerless, Various Calibers, Double Action, Solid Frame, *Modern*	50	75	100
Hunter (Early), .22 L.R.R.F., 7 Shot, Solid Frame, Wood Grips, Double Action, *Modern*	50	75	100
Hunter (Late), .22 L.R.R.F., 9 Shot, Solid Frame, Wood Grips, Double Action, *Modern*	50	75	100
Model 4, Various Calibers, Double Action, Solid Frame, *Modern*	50	75	100
Model 40, Various Calibers, Top Break, Hammerless, Double Action, *Modern*	75	100	150
Model 5, .32 S & W Double Action, 5 Shot, Solid Frame, *Modern*	50	75	100
Model 6, .22 L.R.R.F., Double Action, 7 Shot, Solid Frame, *Modern*	50	75	100
Model 603, .22 W.M.R., 9 Shot, Solid Frame, Double Action, Swing-Out Cylinder, Adjustable Sights, *Modern*	50	100	150
Model 604, .22 W.M.R., 9 Shot, Solid Frame, Double Action, Swing-Out Cylinder, Adjustable Sights, *Modern*	75	125	175
Model 622, .22 L.R.R.F., Solid Frame, 6 Shot, Double Action, *Modern*	25	50	75
Model 632, .32 S & W Long, Solid Frame, 6 Shot, Double Action, *Modern*	50	75	100
Model 633, .32 S & W Long, Solid Frame, 6 Shot, Chrome, Double Action, *Modern*	25	50	75
Model 649, .22LR/.22 W.M.R. Combo, Western Style, 9 Shot, Double Action, Adjustable Sights, *Modern*	75	100	150

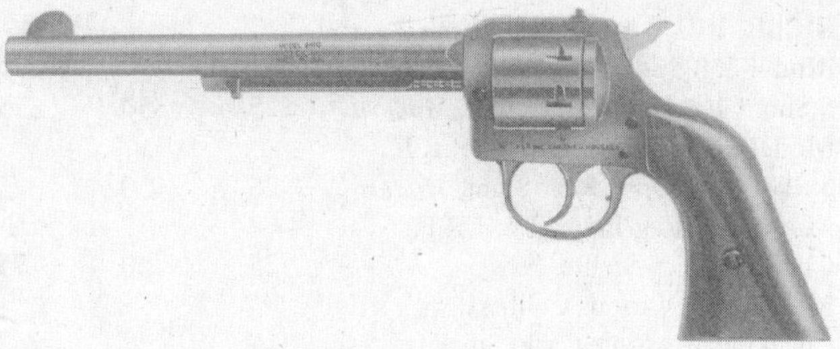

Harrington & Richardson M649, .22 Caliber

	Fair	V. Good	Excellent
Model 650, .22LR/.22 W.M.R. Combo, Western Style, 9 Shot, Double Action, Adjustable Sights, *Modern*	$75	$125	$175
Model 666, .22LR/.22 W.M.R. Combo, Solid Frame, 9 Shot, Double Action, *Modern*	75	125	175
Model 676, .22LR/.22 W.M.R. Combo, Western Style, 9 Shot, Double Action, Adjustable Sights, *Modern*	75	125	175
Model 676-12", .22LR/.22 W.M.R. Combo, Western Style, 9 Shot, Double Action, Adjustable Sights, *Modern*	75	125	175
Model 686, .22LR/.22 W.M.R. Combo, Western Style, 9 Shot, Double Action, Adjustable Sights, *Modern*	75	125	175
Model 732, .32 S & W Long, Solid Frame, 6 Shot, Double Action, Swing-Out Cylinder, *Modern*	50	100	150
Model 733, .32 S & W Long, Solid Frame, 6 Shot, Double Action, Swing-Out Cylinder, *Modern*	75	100	150
Model 766, .22 L.R.R.F., Top Break, 7 Shot, Double Action, Wood Grips, *Modern*	50	100	150
Model 766, .22 W.M.F., Top Break, 7 Shot, Double Action, Wood Grips, *Modern*	50	100	150
Model 826, .22 W.M.R., 6 Shot, Double Action, Adjustable Sights, Swing-Out Cylinder, *Modern*	50	100	150
Model 829, .22 L.R.R.F., 9 Shot, Double Action, Adjustable Sights, Swing-Out Cylinder, *Modern*	50	100	150
Model 832, .32 S & W, 6 Shot, Double Action, Adjustable Sights, Swing-Out Cylinder, *Modern*	50	100	150
Model 900, .22 L.R.R.F., Solid Frame, 9 Shot, Double Action, *Modern*	50	75	100
Model 901, .22 L.R.R.F., Solid Frame, 9 Shot, Double Action, *Modern*	50	75	100
Model 922 (Early), .22 L.R.R.F., 9 Shot, Solid Frame, Wood Grips, Octagon Barrel, Double Action, *Modern*	50	75	100
Model 922 (Early), .22 L.R.R.F., 9 Shot, Solid Frame, Double Action, *Modern*	50	75	100

	Fair	V. Good	Excellent
Model 922 (Late), .22 L.R.R.F., 9 Shot, Solid Frame, Swing-Out Cylinder, Double Action, *Modern*	$50	$100	$150
Model 925, .22 L.R.R.F., 9 Shot, Solid Frame, Double Action, Swing-Out Cylinder, *Modern*	50	100	150
Model 925, .38 S & W, Solid Frame, 5 Shot, Adjustable Sights, *Modern*	50	100	150
Model 926, .22 L.R.R.F., 5 Shot, Solid Frame, Adjustable Sights, *Modern*	75	110	150
Model 926, .38 S & W, Solid Frame, 5 Shot, Adjustable Sights, *Modern*	50	100	150
Model 929, .22 L.R.R.F., 9 Shot, Solid Frame, Double Action, Swing-Out Cylinder, *Modern*	25	75	125

Harrington & Richardson M929, .22 Caliber

	Fair	V. Good	Excellent
Model 930, .22 L.R.R.F., 9 Shot, Solid Frame, Double Action, Swing-Out Cylinder, Adjustable Sights, *Modern*	50	100	150
Model 939, .22 L.R.R.F., 9 Shot, Solid Frame, Double Action, Swing-Out Cylinder, Adjustable Sights, *Modern*	50	100	150
Model 940, .22 L.R.R.F., 9 Shot, Solid Frame, Double Action, Swing-Out Cylinder, *Modern*	25	75	125
Model 949, .22 L.R.R.F., 9 Shot, Western Style, Double Action, Adjustable Sights, *Modern*	50	100	150
Model 950, .22 L.R.R.F., 9 Shot, Western Style, Double Action, Adjustable Sights, *Modern*	50	100	150
Model 976, .22 Checkered Grip, Case Hardened Frame, *Modern*	25	75	125
Model 999 (Early), .22 L.R.R.F., 9 Shot, Top Break, Double Action, Adjustable Sights, *Modern*	75	125	175
Model 999 (Early), .22 W.R.F., Top Break, 9 Shot, Double Action, Adjustable Sights, *Modern*	75	125	175
Model 999 (Engraved), .22 L.R.R.F., Top Break, 9 Shot, Double Action, Adjustable Sights, *Modern*	100	250	400

	Fair	V. Good	Excellent
New Defender, .22 L.R.R.F., Top Break, 9 Shot, Double Action, Wood Grips, Adjustable Sights, *Modern*	$75	$150	$200
Special, .22 L.R.R.F., Top Break, 9 Shot, Double Action, Wood Grips, *Modern*	50	100	150
Special, .22 W.R.F., Top Break, 9 Shot, Double Action, Wood Grips, *Modern*	75	125	175
Sportsman No. 199, .22 L.R.R.F., Single Action, 9 Shot, Top Break Adjustable Sights, *Modern*	50	75	125
Target (Early), .22 L.R.R.F., Top Break, 9 Shot, Double Action, Wood Grips, *Modern*	75	125	175
Target (Early), .22 W.R.F., Top Break, 9 Shot, Double Action, Wood Grips, *Modern*	75	125	175
Target (Hi Speed), .22 L.R.R.F., Top Break, 9 Shot, Double Action, Wood Grips, *Modern*	75	125	175
Target (Hi Speed), .22 W.R.F., Top Break, 9 Shot, Double Action, Wood Grips, *Modern*	75	125	175
Trapper, .22 L.R.R.F., 7 Shot, Solid Frame, Wood Grips, Double Action, *Modern*	50	100	150
Vest Pocket, Various Calibers, Double Action, Solid Frame, Spurless Hammer, *Modern*	25	50	75
Young America, Various Calibers, Double Action, Solid Frame, *Modern*	25	50	75

HANDGUN, SELF-LOADING

	Fair	V. Good	Excellent
Self-Loading, .25 ACP, Clip Fed, *Modern*	100	275	350
Self-Loading, .32 ACP, Clip Fed, *Modern*	125	225	300

Harrington & Richardson .32 Pistol

HANDGUN, SINGLESHOT

	Fair	V. Good	Excellent
U.S.R.A. Target, .22 L.R.R.F., Top Break, Adjustable Sights, Wood Grips, *Modern*	200	400	650
For 6" or 7" Barrel add 25%			

RIFLE, BOLT ACTION

	Fair	V. Good	Excellent
Model 250 Sportster, .22 L.R.R.F., 5 Shot Clip, Open Rear Sight, *Modern*	$25	$50	$75
Model 251 Sportster, .22 L.R.R.F., 5 Shot Clip, Open Rear Sight, *Modern*	25	50	75
Model 265 Reg'lar, .22 L.R.R.F., Clip Fed, Peep Sights, *Modern*	25	50	75
Model 300, Various Calibers, Cheekpiece, Monte Carlo Stock, Checkered Stock, *Modern*	150	300	350
Model 301, Various Calibers, Checkered Stock, Mannlicher, *Modern*	150	350	400
Model 317, Various Calibers, Checkered Stock, Monte Carlo Stock, *Modern*	150	275	325
Model 317P, .223 Rem., Fancy Checkering, Monte Carlo Stock, Fancy Wood, *Modern*	200	450	500
Model 330, Various Calibers, Checkered Stock, Monte Carlo Stock, *Modern*	150	225	275
Model 333, Various Calibers, Monte Carlo Stock, *Modern*	150	225	275
Model 340, Various Calibers, Monte Carlo Stock, Recoil Pad, *Modern*	150	250	300
Model 365 ACE, .22 L.R.R.F., Singleshot, Peep Sights, *Modern*	25	50	75
Model 370, Various Calibers, Target Stock, Heavy Barrel, *Modern*	150	300	350
Model 450 Medalist, .22 L.R.R.F., 5 Shot Clip, No Sights, Target Stock, *Modern*	75	125	150
Model 451 Medalist, .22 L.R.R.F., 5 Shot Clip, Lyman Sights, Target Stock, *Modern*	75	125	175
Model 465 Targeteer, .22 L.R.R.F., Clip Fed, Peep Sights, *Modern*	50	75	100
Model 465 Targeteer Jr., .22 L.R.R.F., Clip Fed, Peep Sights, *Modern*	50	75	100
Model 5200 Match, .22 L.R.R.F., Target Rifle, Single Shot, Heavy Barrel, No Sights, *Modern*	125	225	275
Model 5200 Sporter, .22 L.R.R.F., Targert Rifle, Clip Fed, Target Sights, Checkered Stock, *Modern*	125	225	275
Model 750 Pioneer, .22 L.R.R.F., Singleshot, Open Rear Sight, *Modern*	25	50	75
Model 751 Pioneer, .22 L.R.R.F., Singleshot, Open Rear Sight, Mannlicher, *Modern*	25	50	75
Model 765 Pioneer, .22 L.R.R.F., Singleshot, Open Rear Sight, *Modern*	25	50	75
Model 852 Fieldsman, .22 L.R.R.F., Tube Feed, Open Rear Sight, *Modern*	25	50	75
Model 865 Plainsman, .22 L.R.R.F., 5 Shot Clip, Open Rear Sights, *Modern*	25	50	75
Model 866 Plainsman, .22 L.R.R.F., 5 Shot Clip, Open Rear Sight, Mannlicher, *Modern*	25	50	75

RIFLE, PERCUSSION

	Fair	V. Good	Excellent
Huntsman .45, Top Break, Side Lever, Rifled, Reproduction, *Antique*	$50	$75	$100
Huntsman .50, Top Break, Side Lever, Rifled, Reproduction, *Antique*	50	75	100
Model 175, .45 or .58 Caliber, Springfield Style, Open Sights, Reproduction, *Antique*	75	125	175
Model 175 Deluxe, .45 or .58 Caliber, Springfield Style, Open Sights, Checkered Stock, Reproduction, *Antique*	125	225	275

RIFLE, SELF-LOADING

	Fair	V. Good	Excellent
Model 150 Leatherneck, .22 L.R.R.F., 5 Shot Clip, Open Rear Sight, *Modern*	50	75	100
Model 151 Leatherneck, .22 L.R.R.F., 5 Shot Clip, Peep Sights, *Modern*	50	75	100
Model 165 Leatherneck, .22 L.R.R.F., Clip Fed, Heavy Barrel, Peep Sights, *Modern*	75	100	125
Model 308, Various Calibers, Checkered Stock, Monte Carlo Stock, *Modern*	150	275	325
Model 360, Various Calibers, Checkered Stock, Monte Carlo Stock, *Modern*	125	250	300
Model 361, Various Calibers, Checkered Stock, Monte Carlo Stock, *Modern*	150	275	325
Model 60 Reising, .45 ACP, Clip Fed, Carbine, Open Rear Sight, *Modern*	150	350	400
Model 65 General, .22 L.R.R.F., Clip Fed, Heavy Barrel, Peep Sights, *Modern*	100	200	250
Model 700, .22 W.M.R., Monte Carlo Stock, 5 Shot Clip, *Modern*	75	125	150
Model 700 Deluxe, .22 W.M.R., Monte Carlo Stock, 5 Shot Clip, *Modern*	125	200	225
Model 800 Lynx, .22 L.R.R.F., Clip Fed, Open Rear Sight, *Modern*	50	75	100

RIFLE, SINGLESHOT

	Fair	V. Good	Excellent
1871 Springfield Deluxe, .45-70 Government, Trap Door Action, Carbine, Light Engraving, *Modern*	125	350	400
1871 Springfield Officers', .45-70 Government, Commemorative, Trap Door Action, *Curio*	150	300	400
1871 Springfield Standard, .45-70 Government, Trap Door Action, Carbine, *Modern*	100	250	300
1873 Springfield Officers', .45-70 Government, Trap Door Action, Light Engraving, Peep Sights, *Modern*	150	300	400
1873 Springfield Standard, .45-70 Government, Trap Door Action, Commemorative, *Modern*	100	200	300
Custer Memorial Enlisted Model, .45-70 Government, Commemorative, Trap Door Action, Carbine, Fancy Engraving, Fancy Wood, *Curio*	500	1000	1200
Custer Memorial Officers' Model, .45-70 Government, Commemorative, Trap Door Action, Carbine, Fancy Engraving, Fancy Wood, *Curio*	$1100	$2200	$2750
Little Big Horn Springfield Standard, .45-70 Government, Commemorative, Trap Door Action, Carbine, *Curio*	150	300	450
Model 157, Various Calibers, Top Break, Side Lever, Automatic Ejector, Open Rear Sights, Mannlicher, *Modern*	25	50	75
Model 158 Topper, Various Calibers, Top Break, Side Lever, Automatic Ejector, Open Rear Sight, *Modern*	25	50	75
Model 158 Topper, Various Calibers, Top Break, Side Lever, Automatic Ejector, Open Rear Sight, Extra Set of Rifle Barrels, *Modern*	50	75	100
Model 158 Topper, Various Calibers, Top Break, Side Lever, Automatic Ejector, Open Rear Sight, Extra Shotgun Barrel, *Modern*	50	75	100
Model 163, Various Calibers, Top Break, Side Lever, Automatic Ejector, Open Rear Sight, *Modern*	25	50	75
Model 172 Springfield, .45-70 Government, Trap Door Action, Carbine, Engraved, Silver Plated, Tang Sights, Checkered Sights, *Modern*	150	350	550
Model 755 Sahara, .22 L.R.R.F., Singleshot, Open Rear Sight, Mannlicher, *Modern*	25	50	75
Model 760 Sahara, .22 L.R.R.F., Singleshot, Open Rear Sight, *Modern*	25	50	75
Shikari, .44 Magnum, Top Break, Side Lever, Automatic Ejector, *Modern*	25	50	75
Shikari, .45-70 Government, Top Break, Side Lever, Automatic Ejector, *Modern*	50	75	100

RIFLE, SLIDE ACTION

	Fair	V. Good	Excellent
Model 422, .22 L.R.R.F., Tube Feed, Open Rear Sight, *Modern*	50	100	125

SHOTGUN, BOLT ACTION

	Fair	V. Good	Excellent
Model 348 Gamemaster, 12 and 16 Gauges, Tube Feed, Takedown, *Modern*	25	50	75
Model 349 Deluxe, 12 and 16 Gauges, Tube Feed, Takedown, Adjustable Choke, *Modern*	25	50	75
Model 351 Huntsman, 12 and 16 Gauges, Tube Feed, Takedown, Monte Carlo Stock, Adjustable Choke, *Modern*	25	50	75

SHOTGUN, PERCUSSION

	Fair	V. Good	Excellent
Huntsman 12 Ga., Top Break, Side Lever, Reproduction, *Antique*	$50	$75	$100

SHOTGUN, DOUBLE BARREL, OVER-UNDER

	Fair	V. Good	Excellent
Model 1212, 12 Ga., Field Grade, Vent Rib, Single Selective Trigger, *Modern*	150	325	450
Model 1212 Waterfowl, Ga. Mag. 3", Field Grade, Vent Rib, Single Selective Trigger, *Modern*	150	350	450

SHOTGUN, DOUBLE BARREL, SIDE-BY-SIDE

	Fair	V. Good	Excellent
Model 404, Various Gauges, Hammerless, *Modern*	75	150	200
Model 404C, Various Gauges, Hammerless, Checkered Stock, *Modern*	75	125	175

SHOTGUN, SELF-LOADING

	Fair	V. Good	Excellent
Model 403, .410 Ga., Takedown, *Modern*	75	150	250

SHOTGUN, SINGLESHOT

	Fair	V. Good	Excellent
Folding Gun, Various Gauges, Top Break, Hammer, Automatic Ejector, *Modern*	25	50	75
Model #1 Harrich, 12 Ga., Vent Rib, Engraved, Fancy Checkering, *Modern*	600	1250	1550
Model 148, Various Gauges, Top Break, Side Lever, Automatic Ejector, *Modern*	25	50	75
Model 158, Various Gauges, Top Break, Side Lever, Automatic Ejector, *Modern*	25	50	75
Model 159, Various Gauges, Top Break, Side Lever, Automatic Ejector, *Modern*	25	50	75
Model 162 Buck, 12 Ga., Top Break, Side Lever, Automatic Ejector, Peep Sights, *Modern*	25	50	75
Model 176, 10 Ga. 3½", Top Break, Side Lever, Automatic Ejector, *Modern*	25	50	75
Model 188 Deluxe, Various Gauges, Top Break, Side Lever, Automatic Ejector, *Modern*	15	25	50
Model 198 Deluxe, Various Gauges, Top Break, Side Lever, Automatic Ejector, *Modern*	15	25	50
Model 3, Various Gauges, Top Break, Hammerless, Automatic Ejector, *Modern*	25	50	75
Model 459 Youth, Various Gauges, Top Break, Side Lever, Automatic Ejector, *Modern*	25	50	75
Model 48, Various Gauges, Top Break, Hammer, Automatic Ejector, *Modern*	25	50	75
Model 480 Youth, Various Gauges, Top Break, Side Lever, Automatic Ejector, *Modern*	$25	$50	$75
Model 488 Deluxe, Various Gauges, Top Break, Hammer, Automatic Ejector, *Modern*	25	50	75
Model 490 Youth, Various Gauges, Top Break, Side Lever, Automatic Ejector, *Modern*	25	50	75
Model 5, Various Gauges, Top Break, Lightweight, Automatic Ejector, *Modern*	50	75	100
Model 6, Various Gauges, Top Break, Heavyweight, Automatic Ejector, *Modern*	50	75	100
Model 7, Various Gauges, Top Break, Automatic Ejector, *Modern*	25	50	75
Model 8 Standard, Various Gauges, Top Break, Automatic Ejector, *Modern*	25	50	75
Model 9, Various Gauges, Top Break, Automatic Ejector, *Modern*	25	50	75
Model 98, Various Gauges, Top Break, Side Lever, Automatic Ejector, *Modern*	25	50	75

SHOTGUN, SLIDE ACTION

	Fair	V. Good	Excellent
Model 400, Various Gauges, Solid Frame, *Modern*	75	150	200
Model 400, Various Gauges, Solid Frame, Vent Rib, *Modern*	75	150	200
Model 401, Various Gauges, Solid Frame, Adjustable Choke, *Modern*	75	150	200
Model 402, .410 Ga., Solid Frame, *Modern*	75	150	200
Model 440, Various Gauges, Solid Frame, *Modern*	75	150	200

HARRIS, HENRY

Payton, Pa., 1779–1783. See Kentucky Rifles.

HARRISON ARMS CO.

Made in Belgium for Sickles & Preston, Davenport, Iowa. See Crescent Fire Arms Co., Shotgun, Double Barrel, Side-by-Side; Shotgun, Singleshot.

HARTFORD ARMS & EQUIPMENT CO.

Hartford, Conn., 1929–1932. Acquired by High Standard Arms Co. in 1932.

HANDGUN, MANUAL REPEATER

	Fair	V. Good	Excellent
.22 L.R.R.F., Singleshot Target, Clip Fed, Target Pistol, *Curio*	200	400	600

HANDGUN, SELF-LOADING

	Fair	V. Good	Excellent
1st Model, .22 L.R.R.F., Clip Fed, Target Pistol, *Curio*	150	300	450
2nd Model, .22 L.R.R.F., Target Pistol, *Curio*	150	300	450

HARTFORD ARMS CO.

Made by Crescent for Simmons Hardware Co., St. Louis, Mo. See Crescent Fire Arms Co., Shotgun, Double Barrel, Side-by-Side; Shotgun, Singleshot.

HARTFORD ARMS CO.

Made by Norwich Falls Pistol Co., c. 1880.

HANDGUN, REVOLVER

	Fair	V. Good	Excellent
.32 Short R.F., 5 Shot, Spur Trigger, Solid Frame, Single Action, *Antique*	$75	$125	$200

HARVARD

Made by Crescent, c. 1900. See Crescent Fire Arms Co., Shotgun, Double Barrel, Side-by-Side; Shotgun, Singleshot.

HAUCK, WILBUR

West Arlington, Vt., c. 1950.

RIFLE, SINGLESHOT

	Fair	V. Good	Excellent
Target Rifle, Various Calibers, Target Sights, Target Stock, Adjustable Trigger, *Modern*	200	450	600

HAWES FIREARMS

Van Nuys, Calif. Manufactured by J. P. Sauer und Sohn, Eckernforde, Germany.

HANDGUN, REVOLVER

	Fair	V. Good	Excellent
Chief City Marshall, .45 Colt, Western Style, Single Action, Brass Grip Frame, Adjustable Sights, *Modern*	75	125	250
Chief Marshall, .357 Magnum, Western Style, Single Action, Brass Grip Frame, Adjustable Sights, *Modern*	75	125	250
Chief Marshall, .44 Magnum, Western Style, Single Action, Brass Grip Frame, Adjustable Sights, *Modern*	75	125	250
Denver Marshall, .22 L.R.R.F., Western Style, Single Action, Brass Grip Frame, Adjustable Sights, *Modern*	50	75	125
Denver Marshall, .22 L.R.R.F./ .22 W.M.R. Combo, Western Style, Single Action, Adjustable Sights, *Modern*	75	125	175
Montana Marshall, .22 L.R.R.F., Western Style, Single Action, Brass Grip Frame, *Modern*	50	75	125
Montana Marshall, .22 L.R.R.F./ .22 W.M.R. Combo, Western Style, Single Action, Brass Grip Frame, *Modern*	75	125	175
Montana Marshall, .357 Magnum/ 9mm Combo, Western Style, Single Action, Brass Grip Frame, *Modern*	$100	$200	$300
Montana Marshall, .44 Magnum, Western Style, Single Action, Brass Grip Frame, *Modern*	75	150	200
Montana Marshall, .44 Magnum/ .44-40 Combo, Western Style, Single Action, Brass Grip Frame, *Modern*	100	200	275
Montana Marshall, .45 Colt, Western Style, Single Action, Brass Grip Frame, *Modern*	75	150	250
Montana Marshall, .45 Colt/.45 ACP Combo, Western Style, Single Action, Brass Grip Frame, *Modern*	100	200	300
Silver City Marshall, .22 L.R.R.F., Western Style, Single Action, Brass Grip Frame, *Modern*	50	75	125
Silver City Marshall, .22 L.R.R.F./ .22 W.M.R., Western Style, Single Action, Brass Grip Frame, *Modern*	75	125	175
Silver City Marshall, .357 Magnum/ 9mm Combo, Western Style, Single Action, Brass Grip Frame, *Modern*	100	200	250
Silver City Marshall, .44 Magnum, Western Style, Single Action, Brass Grip Frame, *Modern*	100	150	250
Silver City Marshall, .44 Magnum/ .44-40 Combo, Western Style, Single Action, Brass Grip Frame, *Modern*	100	200	275
Silver City Marshall, .45 Colt, Western Style, Single Action, Brass Grip Frame, *Modern*	75	150	225
Silver City Marshall, .45 Colt/.45 ACP Combo, Western Style, Single Action, Brass Grip Frame, *Modern*	100	200	300
Texas Marshall, .22 L.R.R.F., Western Style, Single Action, Nickel Plated, *Modern*	50	75	100
Texas Marshall, .22 L.R.R.F./ 22 W.M.R., Combo, Western Style, Single Action, Nickel Plated, *Modern*	75	125	150
Texas Marshall, .357 Magnum, Western Style, Single Action, Nickel Plated, *Modern*	75	125	200
Texas Marshall, .357 Magnum/ 9mm Combo, Western Style, Single Action, Nickel Plated, *Modern*	100	200	275
Texas Marshall, .44 Magnum, Western Style, Single Action, Nickel Plated, *Modern*	75	150	225
Texas Marshall, .44 Magnum/ .44-40 Combo, Western Style, Single Action, Nickel Plated, *Modern*	100	200	300
Texas Marshall, .45 Colt, Western Style, Single Action, Nickel Plated, *Modern*	75	150	250

	Fair	V. Good	Excellent
Texas Marshall, .45 Colt/.45 ACP Combo, Western Style, Single Action, Nickel Plated, *Modern*	$100	$200	$300

HANDGUN, SELF-LOADING

.25 ACP, Clip Fed, *Modern*	75	100	175

HANDGUN, SINGLESHOT

Stevens Favorite Copy, .22 L.R.R.F., Tip-Up, Plastic Grips, *Modern*	50	75	125
Stevens Favorite Copy, .22 L.R.R.F., Tip-Up, Plastic Grips, Target Sights, *Modern*	50	75	125
Stevens Favorite Copy, .22 L.R.R.F., Tip-Up, Rosewood Grips, *Modern*	75	100	150

HAWKEN, J. & S.

Jacob and Samuel Hawken, St. Louis, Mo., 1822–1862. John Gemmer purchased the business and continued it until 1890. Jacob Hawken came to St. Louis, Missouri from Maryland, having once been employed by the Harpers Ferry Armory. Hawken and James Lakenen, of Virginia, were in St. Louis as early as 1819, evidently in business as partners. Gunmakers in St. Louis had distinct advantages over those back East, since having the opportunity to speak directly with clients off the frontier allowed for convenient access to the market, and the benefit of their expertise on design and performance. Samuel Hawken joined his older brother in St. Louis, in 1822, setting up a business a few blocks distant. On the death of Lakenen, the brothers established the J & S Hawken shop. Guns so marked are within the years c. 1825 to 1850. Of rugged proportions and substantial calibers, Hawken rifles could stand up to the demands of tough frontier service. Furthermore, these handsomely styled arms were renowned for their accuracy. The Hawken soon became the standard by which all so-called "Rocky Mountain" rifles were judged. Customary mounts on the Hawkens were of iron, proving stronger than brass. The supreme Hawken rifle, made from the late 1830s into the 1840s, customarily had a barrel of about 38" length, heavy in weight, and of about .50 to .53 caliber. The stock was of maple, of half length in the forend, with an oval contoured cheekpiece. Average weight was a substantial 11 pounds. Hawkens were considered accurate up to and somewhat beyond 200 yards. Considering the tremendous interest in the great American West, Hawken rifles, made in limited numbers, and suffering from a high attrition rate, are among the most prized of frontier weaponry—a sure thing to increase in value and demand over the years. And with these arms, condition is not particularly important, since each dent, scratch, mar and scar likely represents some unknown adventure in the hands of some of the most fearsome men who courageously trod the frontier.

RIFLE, PERCUSSION

Gemmer Plains Rifle, Various Calibers, Hawken Style, *Antique* ..	2000	5000	8500
Hawken Plains Rifle, Various Calibers, Hawken Style, *Antique* ..	7500	15000	27500

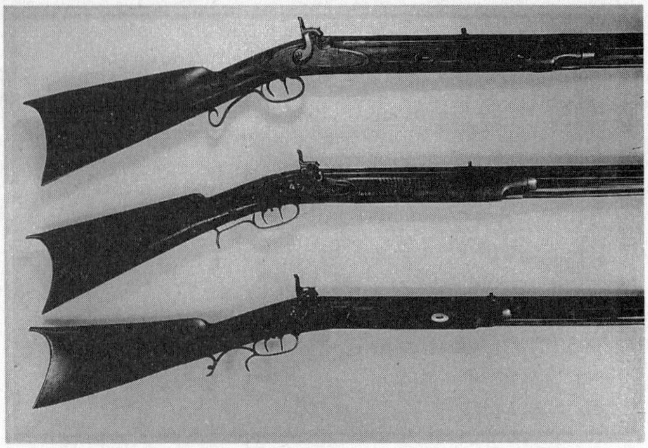

From top, *an S. Hawken percussion Plains rifle, made in .54 caliber, with iron mounts and without patchbox; a Leman, Lancaster, Plains rifle in .42 caliber and with artifically striped maple halfstock; and an A. Wurfflein, Philadelphia Plains rifle with back-action lock and in .50 caliber.*

HAWKINS, HENRY

Schenectady, N.Y., 1769–1775. See Kentucky Rifles.

H.D.H.

Mre. d'Armes HDH, Liege, Belgium, c. 1910.

HANDGUN, REVOLVER

	Fair	V. Good	Excellent
10 Shot, Various Calibers, Double Action, *Curio*	$200	$400	$600
20 Shot, Various Calibers, Over-Under Barrels, Two Row Cylinder, Double Action, *Curio*	250	600	800
Constabulary Type, Various Calibers, Double Action, *Curio*	75	125	150
Ordnance Type, Various Calibers, Double Action, *Curio*	75	150	225
"Velo-Dog," Various Calibers, Folding Trigger, Double Action, Hammerless, *Curio*	50	175	250

HECKERT, PHILIP

York, Pa., 1769–1779. See Kentucky Rifles and Pistols.

HECKLER & KOCH

Oberndorf/Neckar, Germany. Recognized and respected for their quality, design, and engineering, H & K arms are rated amongst the finest performing sporting, target, self-defense, and military arms made today.

HANDGUN, SELF-LOADING

HK, Various Calibers, Clip Fed, Conversion Kit Only, *Each*	50	150	350

	Fair	V. Good	Excellent
HK, Various Calibers, Clip Fed, Double Action, with Conversion Kits All 4 Calibers, *Modern*	$250	$500	$750
HK P-7(PSP), 9mm Luger, Squeeze Cocking, *Modern*	250	575	800
HK P-9S, .45 ACP, Clip Fed, Double Action, *Modern*	175	325	550

Heckler & Koch P-9S Sport Competition

	Fair	V. Good	Excellent
HK P-9S, .45 ACP, Target Model, Clip Fed, Double Action, *Modern*	150	350	550
HK P-9S, .45 ACP, with Extra 8" Barrel, Clip Fed, Double Action, *Modern*	200	400	750
HK-4, .22 L.R.R.F., Clip Fed, Double Action, *Modern*	200	400	750
HK-4, .25 ACP, Clip Fed, Double Action, *Modern*	150	275	550
HK-4, .32 ACP, Clip Fed, Double Action, *Modern*	150	225	500
HK-4, .32 ACP, Clip Fed, Double Action, French Made, *Modern*	125	250	500
HK-4, .32 ACP, Clip Fed, Double Action, German Police, *Modern*	150	300	550
HK-4, .380 ACP, Clip Fed, Double Action, *Modern*	150	375	575
P-9S, 9mm Luger, Clip Fed, Double Action 5 1/2" Barrel, Target Sights, *Modern*	150	350	525
P-9S Combat, 9mm Luger, Clip Fed, Double Action 4" Barrel, *Modern*	200	425	650
P-9S Combat, 9mm Luger, Clip Fed, Double Action 4" Barrel with .30 Luger Conversion Kit, *Modern*	300	625	950
P-9S Competition Kit, 9mm Luger, Clip Fed, Double Action, Extra Barrel, Target Sights, Target Grips, *Modern*	300	650	950
VP-70Z, 9mm Luger, Clip Fed, Double Action, 18 Shot Clip, *Modern*	150	300	500

RIFLE, SELF-LOADING

	Fair	V. Good	Excellent
HK 770, .308 Win., Sporting Rifle, Checkered Stock, Monte Carlo Stock, *Modern*	250	550	800
HK 91 A-2 Package, .308 Win., Clip Fed, Sporting Version of Military Rifle, with Compensator, Polygonal Rifling, *Modern*	$700	$1500	$2250
HK 91 A-2, .308 Win., Clip Fed, Sporting Version of Military Rifle, with Compensator, *Modern*	600	1000	1500
HK 91 A-2, .308 Win., Clip Fed, Sporting Version of Military Rifle, Folding Stock with Compensator, Polygonal Rifling, *Modern*	600	1250	1750
HK 91 A-3, .308 Win., Clip Fed, Sporting Version of Military Rifle, Folding Stock with Compensator, *Modern*	600	1250	1750
HK 91, .22 L.R.R.F., Clip Fed, Conversion Kit Only	300	600	1100
HK 91/93, For Scope Mount Add $75.00-$120.00			
HK 91/93, Light Bipod, Add $40.00-$60.00			
HK 93 A-2, .223 Rem., Clip Fed, Sporting Version of Military Rifle, with Compensator, *Modern*	500	1000	1500
HK 93 A-3, .223 Rem., Clip Fed, Sporting Version of Military Rifle, Folding Stock with Compensator, *Modern*	550	1250	1650

Heckler & Koch HK 93 A-3

	Fair	V. Good	Excellent
HK 94 A-2, 9mm Luger, Clip Fed, Carbine, Standard Stock, *Modern*	750	1750	2500

Heckler & Koch HK 94 A-2

	Fair	V. Good	Excellent
HK 94 A-3, 9mm Luger, Clip Fed, Carbine, Folding Stock, *Modern*	800	1850	2500
Model 270, .22 L.R.R.F., Clip Fed, Checkered Stock, Open Rear Sight, *Modern*	150	300	550
Model 300, .22 WMR, Clip Fed, Checkered Stock, Open Rear Sight, *Modern*	200	425	650

	Fair	V. Good	Excellent
Model 630, .223 Rem., Clip Fed, Checkered Stock, Open Rear Sight, *Modern*	$250	$500	$800
Model 940, .30/06, Clip Fed, Checkered Stock, Open Rear Sight, *Modern*	250	550	850
Model SL 6, .223 Rem., Clip Fed, Military Style Carbine, Open Rear Sight, *Modern*	200	450	750
Model SL 7, .308 Win., Clip Fed, Military Style Carbine, Open Rear Sight, *Modern*	175	425	700

Heckler & Koch SL 7

HEGE

Tradename of Hebsacker Gesellschaft and Hege GmbH, established in 1959 in Schwabisch Halle, West Germany. Now in Uberlingen/Bodensee, West Germany. Also see Beeman Precision Firearms. Founder and president Frederick Hebsacker, a talented master gunsmith, is also a master marketer and consummate entrepreneur in the domain of muzzle loading and replica firearms. His highly detailed catalog and stock of arms and accessories rank among the finest in the world. Among the exquisite products in the Hege catalog are finely made muzzle loaders, built to Hebsacker's own specifications, and based on such original arms as Manton flintlock dueling pistols and a complete line of muzzle loading revolvers. Some of the more refined of these arms are partially built by such best-quality gunmakers as Uberti, and then perfected still further in the Hege workshops.

HANDGUN, PERCUSSION

Silber Pistol, .33 Caliber, British Style, Engraved, Cased, Reproduction, *Antique*	150	375	600
Silber Pistol, .33 Caliber, French Style, Engraved, Gold Inlays, Cased, Reproduction, *Antique*	300	600	900

HANDGUN, SELF-LOADING

AP-63, .32 ACP, Clip Fed, Double Action, *Modern*	150	275	425
AP-66, .32 ACP, Clip Fed, Double Action, *Modern*	150	225	400
AP-66, .380 ACP, Clip Fed, Double Action, *Modern*	100	250	425

COMBINATION WEAPON, OVER-UNDER

President, Various Calibers, Box Lock, Solid Rib, Double Trigger, Checkered Stock, *Modern*	300	675	900

Hege AP-66.32

RIFLE, MATCHLOCK

	Fair	V. Good	Excellent
Zeughaus Musket, .63 Caliber, Heavy Swiss Style, Plain, Reproduction, *Antique*	$100	$250	$400

HEINZELMANN, C.E.

Plochigen, Germany, 1921–1928.

HANDGUN, SELF-LOADING

Heim, .25 ACP, Clip Fed, Blue, *Curio*	100	200	400

HELFRICHT

Alfred Krauser Waffenfabrik, Zella Mehlis, Germany, 1921–1929.

HANDGUN, SELF-LOADING

Model 1, .25 ACP, Clip Fed, *Curio*	200	425	600
Model 2, .25 ACP, Clip Fed, *Curio*	200	400	600
Model 3, .25 ACP, Clip Fed, *Curio*	200	400	600
Model 4, .25 ACP, Clip Fed, *Curio*	150	350	550

HELVICE

Fab. d'Armes de Guerre de Grand Precision, Eibar, Spain.

HANDGUN, SELF-LOADING

.25 ACP, Clip Fed, *Modern*	50	125	150

HENNCH, PETER

Lancaster, Pa., 1770–1774. See Kentucky Rifles.

HENRY GUN CO.

Belgium, c. 1900.

SHOTGUN, DOUBLE BARREL, SIDE-BY-SIDE

Various Gauges, Hammerless, Damascus Barrel, *Modern*	75	150	250
Various Gauges, Hammerless, Steel Barrel, *Modern*	75	175	300
Various Gauges, Outside Hammers, Damascus Barrel, *Modern*	75	150	300

	Fair	V. Good	Excellent
Various Gauges, Outside Hammers, Steel Barrel, *Modern*	$125	$250	$450

SHOTGUN, SINGLESHOT

Various Gauges, Hammer, Steel Barrel, *Modern*	50	75	100

HENRY, ALEXANDER

Edinburgh, Scotland, 1869–1895. One of the most respected of British gunmakers, Alexander Henry's influence continues to this day, as reflected in such contemporary arms as the Ruger No. 1 Sporting rifle, which features a "Henry-style forend." A number of Henry sporting rifles are in the private arms collection of William B. Ruger, some of which appear in the author's *Ruger & His Guns.* The design and quality of Alexander Henry rifles reflects the masterful skills of British Empire gunmakers. Collecting in this area of interest tends to be expensive, although specimens are available showing a fair amount of use, and thus at more reasonable prices.

RIFLE, DOUBLE BARREL, SIDE-BY-SIDE

.500/450 BPE, Damascus Barrel, Engraved, Fancy Checkering, Ornate, Cased with Accessories, Hammerless, *Antique*	2500	5000	8500

HERCULES

Made by Stevens Arms.

SHOTGUN, DOUBLE BARREL, SIDE-BY-SIDE

M 315, Various Gauges, Hammerless, Steel Barrel, *Modern*	75	150	200
Model 215, 12 and 16 Gauges, Outside Hammers, Steel Barrel, *Modern*	75	150	200
Model 311, Various Gauges, Hammerless, Steel Barrel, *Modern*	75	175	225
Model 3151, Various Gauges, Hammerless, Recoil Pad, Front & Rear Bead Sights, *Modern*	75	175	300
Model 5151, Various Gauges, Hammerless, Steel Barrel, *Modern*	75	175	300

SHOTGUN, SINGLESHOT

Model 94, Various Gauges, Takedown, Automatic Ejector, Plain Hammer, *Modern*	25	50	100

HERMETIC

Tradename used by Bernadon-Martin, St. Etienne, France, c. 1912.

HANDGUN, SELF-LOADING

B.M., .32 ACP, Clip Fed, *Curio*	100	275	375

HERMITAGE

Made by Stevens Arms.

SHOTGUN, SINGLESHOT

	Fair	V. Good	Excellent
Model 90, Various Gauges, Takedown, Automatic Ejector, Plain Hammer, *Modern*	$25	$50	$75

HERMITAGE ARMS CO.

Made by Crescent for Grey & Dudley Hdw. Co., Nashville, Tenn. See Crescent Fire Arms Co., Shotgun, Double Barrel, Side-by-Side; Shotgun, Singleshot.

HERO

Made by Manhattan/American Standard.

HANDGUN, SINGLESHOT PISTOL

.34 Caliber, American Standard, Spur Trigger, Solid Frame, Single Action, *Antique*	100	200	300
.34 Caliber, Manhattan, Spur Trigger, Solid Frame, Single Action, *Antique*	100	225	325

HEROLD

Tradename of Franz Jager & Co., Suhl, Germany, 1923–1939.

RIFLE, BOLT ACTION

Herold Repetierbuchse, .22 Hornet, Set Triggers, Checkered Stock, *Modern*	400	750	1000

HERTERS

Distributor & Importer in Waseca, Minn.

HANDGUN, REVOLVER

Guide, .22 L.R.R.F., Swing-Out Cylinder, Double Action, *Modern*	50	75	100
Power-Mag, .357 Magnum, Western Style, Single Action, *Modern*	75	100	125
Power-Mag, .401 Herter Mag., Western Style, Single Action, *Modern*	75	100	125
Power-Mag, .44 Magnum, Western Style, Single Action, *Modern*	75	125	150
Western, .22 L.R.R.F., Single Action, Western Style, *Modern*	25	50	75

RIFLE, BOLT ACTION

Model J-9 Hunter, Various Calibers, Plain, Monte Carlo Stock, *Modern*	75	150	250
Model J-9 Presentation, Various Calibers, Checkered Stock, Monte Carlo Stock, Sling Swivels, *Modern*	75	175	250
Model J-9 Supreme, Various Calibers, Checkered Stock, Monte Carlo Stock, Sling Swivels, *Modern*	100	200	300
Model U-9 Hunter, Various Calibers, Plain, Monte Carlo Stock, *Modern*	75	125	200

	Fair	V. Good	Excellent
Model U-9 Presentation, Various Calibers, Checkered Stock, Monte Carlo Stock, Sling Swivels, *Modern*	$75	$150	$250
Model U-9 Supreme, Various Calibers, Checkered Stock, Sling Swivels, Monte Carlo Stock, *Modern*	75	175	275

SHOTGUN, SELF-LOADING

	Fair	V. Good	Excellent
Model SL-18, 12 Ga. 3", Checkered Stock, *Modern*	100	225	300

SHOTGUN, SINGLESHOT

	Fair	V. Good	Excellent
Model 151, Various Gauges, Hammer, *Modern*	25	75	125

HESS, JACOB

Stark Co., Ohio, 1842–1860. See Kentucky Rifles.

HESS, SAMUEL

Lancaster, Pa., c. 1771. See Kentucky Rifles.

HEYM

Franz W. Heym, 1934–1945 in Suhl, Germany, now in Munnerstadt, Germany.

COMBINATION WEAPON, DRILLING

	Fair	V. Good	Excellent
Model 33, Various Calibers, Hammerless, Double Triggers, Engraved, Checkered Stock, Express Sights, *Curio*	2000	4500	6000
Model 37, Various Calibers, Hammerless, Sidelock, Double Rifle Barrels, Engraved, Checkered Stock, *Curio*	2500	5000	7500
Model 37, Various Calibers, Hammerless, Sidelock, Engraved, Checkered Stock, *Curio*	2500	4500	7000
Model 37 Deluxe, Various Calibers, Hammerless, Sidelock, Double Rifle Barrels, Engraved, Checkered Stock, *Curio*	3000	6000	9000

RIFLE, BOLT ACTION

	Fair	V. Good	Excellent
Model SR-20, Various Calibers, Fancy Wood, Double Set Triggers, *Curio*	500	1000	1500
Model SR-20 Hunter, Various Calibers, Fancy Wood, Double Set Triggers, *Curio*	350	950	1250

COMBINATION WEAPON, OVER-UNDER

	Fair	V. Good	Excellent
Model 22S, Various Calibers, Single Set Trigger, Checkered Stock, Light Engraving, *Curio*	900	2000	2750
Model 55BF (77BF), Various Calibers, Boxlock, Double Triggers, Checkered Stock, Engraved, *Curio*	1500	2500	3250
Model 55BFSS (77BFSS), Various Calibers, Sidelock, Double Triggers, Checkered Stock, *Curio*	$1500	$3500	$4500

RIFLE, SINGLESHOT

	Fair	V. Good	Excellent
Model HR-30, Various Calibers, Fancy Wood, Engraved, Single Set Trigger, Ruger Action, Round Barrel, *Curio*	700	1500	2250
Model HR-38, Various Calibers, Fancy Wood, Engraved, Single Set Trigger, Ruger Action, Octagon Barrel, *Curio*	800	1700	2350

RIFLE, DOUBLE BARREL, OVER-UNDER

	Fair	V. Good	Excellent
Model 88-B, Various Calibers, Boxlock, Engraved, Checkered Stock, *Curio*	2000	5000	9000
Model 88-B Safari, Various Calibers, Sidelock, Engraved, Checkered Stock, *Curio*	2200	6000	12000

SHOTGUN, DOUBLE BARREL, OVER-UNDER

	Fair	V. Good	Excellent
Model 55F (77F), Various Gauges, Boxlock, Engraved, Checkered Stock, Double Triggers, *Curio*	1500	3750	4750
Model 55FSS (77FSS), Various Gauges, Sidelock, Engraved, Checkered Stock, Double Triggers, *Curio*	1700	4000	5000

HIGGINS, J. C.

Tradename used by Sears-Roebuck, 1946–1962.

HANDGUN, REVOLVER

	Fair	V. Good	Excellent
Model 88, .22 L.R.R.F., *Modern*	25	50	75
Model 88 Fisherman, .22 L.R.R.F., *Modern*	25	50	75
Ranger, .22 L.R.R.F., *Modern*	25	50	75

HANDGUN, SELF-LOADING

	Fair	V. Good	Excellent
Model 80, .22 L.R.R.F., Clip Fed, Hammerless, *Modern*	50	75	100
Model 85, .22 L.R.R.F., Clip Fed, Hammer, *Modern*	75	100	125

RIFLE, BOLT ACTION

	Fair	V. Good	Excellent
Model 228, .22 L.R.R.F., Clip Fed, *Modern*	15	25	50
Model 229, .22 L.R.R.F., Tube Feed, *Modern*	15	25	50
Model 245, .22 L.R.R.F., Singleshot, *Modern*	15	25	50
Model 51, Various Calibers, Checkered Stock, *Modern*	100	175	225
Model 51 Special, Various Calibers, Checkered Stock, Light Engraving, *Modern*	125	225	275

	Fair	V. Good	Excellent
RIFLE, LEVER ACTION			
.22 WMR, *Modern*	$25	$50	$75
Model 45, Various Calibers, Tube Feed, Carbine, *Modern*	25	50	75
RIFLE, SELF-LOADING			
Model 25, .22 L.R.R.F., Clip Fed, *Modern*	15	25	50
Model 31, .22 L.R.R.F., Tube Feed, *Modern*	25	50	75
RIFLE, SLIDE ACTION			
Model 33, .22 L.R.R.F., Tube Feed, *Modern*	25	50	75
SHOTGUN, BOLT ACTION			
Model 10, Various Gauges, Tube Feed, 5 Shot, *Modern*	25	50	75
Model 11, Various Gauges, Tube Feed, 3 Shot, *Modern*	50	50	50
SHOTGUN, DOUBLE BARREL, SIDE-BY-SIDE			
Various Calibers, Plain, Takedown, Hammerless, *Modern*	75	150	200
SHOTGUN, SELF-LOADING			
Model 66, 12 Ga., Plain Barrel, *Modern*	75	125	200
Model 66, 12 Ga., Plain Barrel, Adjustable Choke, *Modern*	75	150	200
Model 66, 12 Ga., Vent Rib, Adjustable Choke, *Modern*	75	150	200
Model 66 Deluxe, 12 Ga., *Modern*	75	150	200
SHOTGUN, SINGLESHOT			
Various Calibers, Takedown, Adjustable Choke, Plain, Hammer, *Modern*	25	50	75
SHOTGUN, SLIDE ACTION			
Model 20 Deluxe, 12 Ga., *Modern*	75	125	175
Model 20 Deluxe, 12 Ga., Vent Rib, Adjustable Choke, *Modern*	75	125	175
Model 20 Special, 12 Ga., Vent Rib, Adjustable Choke, *Modern*	75	150	225
Model 20 Standard, 12 Ga., *Modern*	50	100	175

HIGH STANDARD

High Standard Mfg. Co., 1926 to the present, first in New Haven, Conn., then as High Standard Sporting Firearms in Hamden, Conn., now as High Standard, Inc. in East Hartford, Conn.; reorganized and factory now in Dallas, Texas, with office in Hartford. The product lines of the High Standard company commenced with .22 rimfire self-loading pistols, and developed into one of the finest lines in the history of target and sport handguns of that caliber. In the post–World War II years, attempts were made to fill out the product line, eventually contributing to the company's temporary demise. One of the most capable engineers and designers to work for High Standard was Harry Sefried II, whose years of creative engineering at Winchester (assisting "Carbine" Williams) and at Sturm, Ruger, & Co. (under William B. Ruger) established him as one of the 20th century's most talented arms innovators. The High Standard Sentinel series of revolvers was one of Sefried's creations, achieving over the million mark in sales. After difficulties with the East Hartford operation, the company was reorganized, and presently has a production facility in Dallas, Texas, and office in Hartford, Connecticut.

	Fair	V. Good	Excellent
HANDGUN, DOUBLE BARREL, OVER-UNDER			
Derringer, .22 L.R.R.F., Double Action, Top Break, Electroless, Nickel Plated, Hammerless, Walnut Grips, Cased, *Modern*	$75	$150	$225
Derringer, .22 L.R.R.F., Double Action, Top Break, Nickel Plated, Hammerless, Cased, *Modern*	75	150	225
Derringer, .22 WMR, Double Action, 2 Shot, *Modern*	75	150	225
Derringer, .22 WMR, Double Action, Top Break, Electroless, Nickel Plated, Hammerless, Walnut Grips, Cased, *Modern*	75	175	250
Derringer, .22 WMR, Double Action, Top Break, Nickel Plated, Hammerless, Cased, *Modern*	75	175	250
Derringer, 22 L.R.R.F., Double Action, 2 Shot, *Modern*	75	125	225
Gold Derringer, .22 WMR, Double Action, 2 Shot, *Modern*	125	250	425
Silver Derringer, .22 WMR, Double Action, Top Break, Hammerless, Cased, *Modern*	100	200	325
HANDGUN, PERCUSSION			
.36, Griswald & Gunnison, Revolver, Commemorative, Cased, Reproduction, *Antique*	100	200	300
.36 Leech & Rigdon, Revolver, Commemorative, Cased, Reproduction, *Antique*	100	200	300
.36 Schneider & Glassick, Revolver, Commemorative, Cased, Reproduction, *Antique*	100	250	350
HANDGUN, REVOLVER			
For Nickel Plating, Add $7.50-$12.50			
Crusader, Deluxe Pair, .44 Mag. & .45 Colt, Commemorative, Double Action, Swing-Out Cylinder, Gold Inlays, Engraved, *Modern*	500	1000	1750
Double-Nine, .22 L.R.R.F., Double Action, Western Style, *Modern*	75	125	175
Double-Nine, .22 LR/.22 WMR Combo, Double Action, Western Style, Alloy Frame, *Modern*	75	150	225
Double-Nine, .22 LR/.22 WMR Combo, Double Action, Western Style, *Modern*	75	150	225

	Fair	V. Good	Excellent
Double-Nine Deluxe, .22 LR/.22 WMR Combo, Double Action, Western Style, Adjustable Sights, *Modern*	$100	$200	$300
Durango, .22 L.R.R.F., Double Action, Western Style, *Modern*	50	100	150
High Sierra, .22 LR/.22 WMR Combo, Double Action, Western Style, Octagon Barrel, *Modern*	75	125	175
High Sierra Deluxe, .22 LR/.22 WMR Combo, Double Action, Western Style, Octagon Barrel, Adjustable Sights, *Modern*	75	150	225
Kit Gun, .22 L.R.R.F., Double Action, 9 Shot, Swing-Out Cylinder, Adjustable Sights, *Modern*	75	125	200
Longhorn, .22 LR/.22 WMR Combo, Double Action, Adjustable Sights, Western Style, *Modern*	100	150	225
Longhorn, .22 LR/.22 WMR Combo, Double Action, Western Style, Alloy Frame, *Modern*	75	100	175
Longhorn, .22 LR/.22 WMR Combo, Double Action, Western Style, *Modern*	75	125	200

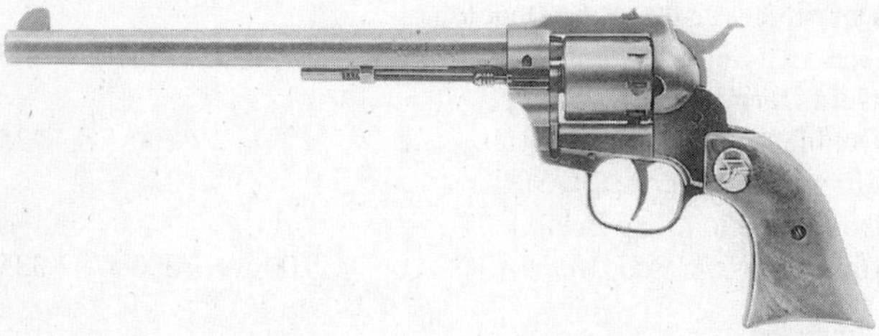

High Standard Longhorn

	Fair	V. Good	Excellent
Natchez, .22 LR/.22 WMR Combo, Double Action, Western Style, Birdshead Grip, Allow Frame, *Modern*	50	75	125
Posse, .22 LR/.22 WMR Combo, Double Action, Western Style, Brass Gripframe, *Modern*	75	100	150
Sentinel, .22 L.R.R.F., Double Action, Swing-Out Cylinder, *Modern*	50	100	150
Sentinel Deluxe, .22 L.R.R.F., Double Action, Swing-Out Cylinder, *Modern*	75	150	200
Sentinel Imperial, .22 L.R.R.F., Double Action, Swing-Out Cylinder, *Modern*	75	150	200
Sentinel Mk I, .22 L.R.R.F., Double Action, Swing-Out Cylinder, *Modern*	75	125	200
Sentinel Mk I, .22 L.R.R.F., Double Action, Swing-Out Cylinder, Adjustable Sights, *Modern*	$75	$150	$200
Sentinel Mk II, .357 Magnum, Double Action, Swing-Out Cylinder, *Modern*	75	100	150
Sentinel Mk III, .357 Magnum, Double Action, Swing-Out Cylinder, Adjustable Sights, *Modern*	50	100	175
Sentinel Mk IV, .22 L.R.R.F., Double Action, Swing-Out Cylinder, Adjustable Sights, *Modern*	75	125	200

High Standard Sentinel

	Fair	V. Good	Excellent
Sentinel Mk IV, .22 WMR, Double Action, Swing-Out Cylinder, Adjustable Sights, *Modern*	50	100	225
Sentinel Mk IV, .22 WMR, Double Action, Swing-Out Cylinder, *Modern*	75	100	225
Sentinel Snub, .22 L.R.R.F., Double Action, Swing-Out Cylinder, *Modern*	50	75	175

HANDGUN, SELF-LOADING

	Fair	V. Good	Excellent
"Benner Olympic," .22 L.R.R.F., Supermatic, Military, Engraved, *Curio*	300	650	1000
10-X Custom, .22 L.R.R.F., Heavy Barrel, Military Grip, Target Sights, *Modern*	700	1500	1950
Citation (Early), .22 L.R.R.F., Supermatic, Clip Fed, Hammerless, Tapered Barrel, *Modern*	150	350	500
Citation (Early), .22 L.R.R.F., Supermatic, Clip Fed, Hammerless, Heavy Barrel, *Modern*	150	375	550
Citation (Late), .22 L.R.R.F., Supermatic, Clip Fed, Hammerless, Frame-Mounted Rear Sight, Heavy Barrel, *Modern*	175	375	475
Citation (Late), .22 L.R.R.F., Supermatic, Military, Hammerless, Frame-Mounted Rear Sight, Fluted Barrel, *Modern*	175	350	450

	Fair	V. Good	Excellent
Citation (Late), .22 L.R.R.F., Supermatic, Military, Hammerless, Frame-Mounted Rear Sight, Heavy Barrel, *Modern*	$175	$375	$600
Duramatic, .22 L.R.R.F., Clip Fed, Hammerless, *Modern*	75	150	225
Field King, .22 L.R.R.F., Clip Fed, Hammerless, Heavy Barrel, *Modern*	100	200	275
Flight King, .22 Short R.F., Clip Fed, Hammerless, *Modern*	100	200	275
Flight King, .22 Short R.F., Clip Fed, Hammerless, Extra Barrel, *Modern*	125	225	300
Flight King, .22 Short R.F., Clip Fed, Hammerless, Lightweight, *Modern*	100	200	275
Flight King, .22 Short R.F., Clip Fed, Hammerless, Lightweight, Extra Barrel, *Modern*	125	225	300
For Nickel Plating, Add $20.00-$35.00			
Model A, .22 L.R.R.F., Clip Fed, Hammerless, *Curio*	175	400	550
Model B, .22 L.R.R.F., Clip Fed, Hammerless, *Curio*	175	350	500
Model B, .22 L.R.R.F., Navy, Clip Fed, Hammerless, *Curio*	200	475	625
Model C, .22 Short R.F., Clip Fed, Hammerless, *Curio*	200	450	600
Model D, .22 L.R.R.F., Clip Fed, Hammerless, Heavy Barrel, *Curio*	225	450	600
Model E, .22 L.R.R.F., Clip Fed, Hammerless, Heavy Barrel, Target Grips, *Curio*	300	650	900
Model G-380, .380 ACP, Clip Fed, Hammer, Takedown, *Curio*	200	425	600
Model G-B, .22 L.R.R.F., Clip Fed, Hammerless, Takedown, *Curio*	200	400	550
Model G-B, .22 L.R.R.F., Clip Fed, Hammerless, Takedown, Extra Barrel, *Curio*	200	450	600
Model G-D, .22 L.R.R.F., Clip Fed, Hammerless, Takedown, *Curio*	225	500	700
Model G-D, .22 L.R.R.F., Clip Fed, Hammerless, Takedown, Extra Barrel, *Curio*	250	550	750
Model G-E, .22 L.R.R.F., Clip Fed, Hammerless, Takedown, Extra Barrel, *Curio*	400	800	1000
Model G-E, .22 L.R.R.F., Clip Fed, Hammerless, Takedown, *Curio*	350	750	1000
Model G-O, .22 Short, Clip Fed, Hammerless, Takedown, Extra Barrel, *Curio*	450	900	1150
Model G-O, .22 Short, Clip Fed, Hammerless, Takedown, *Curio*	400	850	1000
Model H-A, .22 L.R.R.F., Clip Fed, Hammer, *Curio*	250	550	700
Model H-B, .22 L.R.R.F., Clip Fed, Hammer, *Curio*	175	375	550

	Fair	V. Good	Excellent
Model H-D Military, .22 L.R.R.F., Clip Fed, Hammer, Heavy Barrel, Thumb Safety, *Curio*	$125	$250	$375
Model H-D, .22 L.R.R.F., Clip Fed, Hammer, Heavy Barrel, *Curio*	150	300	450
Model H-E, .22 L.R.R.F., Clip Fed, Hammer, Heavy Barrel, Target Grips, *Curio*	600	1250	1650
Model SB, .22 L.R.R.F., Clip Fed, Hammerless, Smoothbore, Class 3	200	400	550
Olympic I.S.U., .22 Short R.F., Clip Fed, Hammerless, Military, Frame-Mounted Rear Sights, *Modern*	225	500	700
Olympic I.S.U., .22 Short R.F., Clip Fed, Hammerless, Frame-Mounted Rear Sights, *Modern*	250	525	700
Olympic I.S.U., .22 Short R.F., Supermatic, Clip Fed, Hammerless, Military, *Modern*	250	550	750
Olympic I.S.U., .22 Short R.F., Supermatic, Clip Fed, Hammerless, *Modern*	250	525	750
Olympic, .22 Short R.F., Clip Fed, Hammerless, *Modern*	250	475	600
Olympic, .22 Short R.F., Clip Fed, Hammerless, Extra Barrel, *Modern*	250	575	775
Plinker, .22 L.R.R.F., Clip Fed, Hammer, *Modern*	75	150	250
Sharpshooter (Late), .22 L.R.R.F., Military Grip, Clip Fed, Hammerless, *Modern*	150	375	500
Sharpshooter, .22 L.R.R.F., Clip Fed, Hammerless, *Modern*	150	350	500

High Standard Sharpshooter

	Fair	V. Good	Excellent
Sport King (Late), .22 L.R.R.F., Military Grip, Clip Fed, Hammerless, *Modern*	125	225	350
Sport King, .22 L.R.R.F., Clip Fed, Hammerless, *Modern*	100	250	375
Sport King, .22 L.R.R.F., Clip Fed, Hammerless, Extra Barrel, *Modern*	125	250	375
Sport King, .22 L.R.R.F., Clip Fed, Hammerless, Lightweight, *Modern*	125	250	375

	Fair	V. Good	Excellent
Sport King, .22 L.R.R.F., Clip Fed, Hammerless, Lightweight, Extra Barrel, *Modern*	$150	$300	$425
Supermatic, .22 L.R.R.F., Clip Fed, Hammerless, *Modern*	200	450	625
Supermatic, .22 L.R.R.F., Clip Fed, Hammerless, Extra Barrel, *Modern*	200	450	625
Survival Pack, .22 L.R.R.F., Sharpshooter (Late), Electroless Nickel Plated, Cased with Accessories, *Modern*	125	250	400
Tournament, .22 L.R.R.F., Supermatic, Clip Fed, Hammerless, *Modern*	175	375	500
Tournament, .22 L.R.R.F., Supermatic, Clip Fed, Hammerless, Military, *Modern*	175	350	500
Trophy (Early), .22 L.R.R.F., Supermatic, Clip Fed, Hammerless, *Modern*	200	475	650
Trophy (Late), .22 L.R.R.F., Supermatic, Military, Hammerless, Frame-Mounted Rear Sight, Fluted Barrel, *Modern*	200	400	600
Trophy (Late), .22 L.R.R.F., Supermatic, Military, Hammerless, Frame-Mounted Rear Sight, Heavy Barrel, *Modern*	225	500	750
Victor, .22 L.R.R.F., Heavy Barrel, Military Grip, Solid Rib, Target Sights, *Modern*	225	450	650
Victor, .22 L.R.R.F., Heavy Barrel, Military Grip, Vent Rib, Target Sights, *Modern*	250	500	750

RIFLE, BOLT ACTION

	Fair	V. Good	Excellent
Hi Power Deluxe, Various Calibers, Monte Carlo Stock, Checkered Stock, *Modern*	100	200	350
High Power, Various Calibers, Field Grade, *Modern*	75	175	325

RIFLE, SELF-LOADING

	Fair	V. Good	Excellent
Sport King, .22 L.R.R.F., Field Grade, Carbine, Tube Feed, *Modern*	50	75	125
Sport King, .22 L.R.R.F., Field Grade, Tube Feed, *Modern*	50	75	125
Sport King Deluxe, .22 L.R.R.F., Tube Feed, Monte Carlo Stock, Checkered Stock, *Modern*	50	100	175
Sport King Special, .22 L.R.R.F., Tube Feed, Monte Carlo Stock, *Modern*	50	75	125

RIFLE, SLIDE ACTION

	Fair	V. Good	Excellent
.22 L.R.R.F., Flight-King, Tube Feed, Monte Carlo Stock, *Modern*	50	75	125

SHOTGUN, DOUBLE BARREL, OVER-UNDER

	Fair	V. Good	Excellent
Shadow Indy, 12 Ga., Single Selective Trigger, Selective Ejectors, Checkered Stock, Engraved, *Modern*	$200	$400	$600
Shadow Seven, 12 Ga., Single Selective Trigger, Selective Ejectors, Checkered Stock, Light Engraving, *Modern*	150	300	450

SHOTGUN, SELF-LOADING

	Fair	V. Good	Excellent
12 Ga., Supermatic, Field Grade, *Modern*	75	150	200
20 Ga. Mag., Supermatic, Field Grade, *Modern*	75	150	200
20 Ga. Mag., Supermatic, Skeet Grade, Vent Rib, *Modern*	75	150	300
Deer Gun, 12 Ga., Supermatic, Open Rear Sight, Recoil Pad, *Modern*	100	175	300
Deluxe, 20 Ga. Mag., Supermatic, Recoil Pad, *Modern*	100	175	300
Deluxe, 20 Ga. Mag., Supermatic, Recoil Pad, Vent Rib, *Modern*	100	175	300
Deluxe, Recoil Pad, *Modern*	75	150	275
Deluxe, Recoil Pad, Vent Rib, *Modern*	100	175	300
Duck Gun, 12 Ga. Mag., 3", Supermatic, Recoil Pad, Field Grade, *Modern*	100	175	300
Duck Gun, 12 Ga. Mag., 3", Supermatic, Vent Rib, Recoil Pad, *Modern*	100	175	300
Model 10B, 12 Ga., Riot Gun, *Modern*	200	400	550
Skeet Grade, Vent Rib, Recoil Pad, *Modern*	200	350	500
Special, 12 Ga., Field Grade, Adjustable Choke, *Modern*	100	175	300
Special, 20 Ga. Mag., Supermatic, Field Grade, Adjustable Choke, *Modern*	100	175	300
Trap Grade, Vent Rib, Recoil Pad, *Modern*	150	300	450
Trophy, 20 Ga. Mag., Supermatic, Recoil Pad, Vent Rib, Adjustable Choke, *Modern*	100	200	300
Trophy, Recoil Pad, Vent Rib, Adjustable Choke, *Modern*	100	175	275

SHOTGUN, SLIDE ACTION

	Fair	V. Good	Excellent
.410 Ga. 3", Flight-King, Field Grade, *Modern*	75	125	225
.410 Ga. 3", Flight-King, Skeet Grade, *Modern*	75	150	250
12 and 20 Gauges, Flight-King, Field Grade, *Modern*	75	125	225
12 Ga., Flight-King, Trap Grade, Vent Rib, Recoil Pad, *Modern*	100	200	300

	Fair	V. Good	Excellent
12 Ga., Flight-King, Skeet Grade, Vent Rib, Recoil Pad, *Modern*	$100	$200	$300
28 Ga., Flight-King, Field Grade, *Modern*	75	150	250
28 Ga., Flight-King, Skeet Grade, Vent Rib, *Modern*	100	200	300
Brush Gun, 12 Ga., Flight-King, Open Rear Sight, *Modern*	75	125	225
Deluxe, .28 Ga., Flight-King, Vent Rib, *Modern*	100	200	300
Deluxe, .410 Ga. 3", Flight-King, Vent Rib, *Modern*	100	200	300
Deluxe, 12 and 20 Gauges, Flight-King, Recoil Pad, Vent Rib, *Modern*	75	150	250
Deluxe, 12 and 20 Gauges, Flight-King, Recoil Pad, *Modern*	75	125	225
Deluxe Brush Gun, 12 Ga., Flight-King, Peep Sights, Sling Swivels, *Modern*	75	175	275
Riot, 12 Ga., Flight-King, Open Rear Sight, *Modern*	75	150	250
Riot, 12 Ga., Flight-King, Plain Barrel, *Modern*	75	150	250
Special, 12 and 20 Gauges, Flight-King, Field Grade, Adjustable Choke, *Modern*	75	150	250
Trophy, 12 and 20 Gauges, Flight-King, Recoil Pad, Vent Rib, Adjustable Choke, *Modern*	75	150	250

HIJO

Tradename used by Sloan's of N.Y.C.

HANDGUN, SELF-LOADING

Hijo, .25 ACP, Clip Fed, *Modern*	50	75	100
Hijo Military, .22 L.R.R.F., Clip Fed, *Modern*	75	100	125

HILL, S. W.

See Kentucky Rifles and Pistols.

HILLEGAS, J.

Pottsville, Pa. 1810–1830. See Kentucky Rifles.

HILLIARD, D. H. & GEORGE C.

D. H. Hilliard, Cornish, New Hampshire, 1842–1877 taken over by George C. Hilliard and operated 1877–1880.

HANDGUN, PERCUSSION

.34, Underhammer Target Pistol, *Antique*	300	700	850

HINO-KOMORO

Kumaso Hino and Tomisiro Komoro, Tokyo, Japan, c. 1910.

HANDGUN, SELF-LOADING

	Fair	V. Good	Excellent
Blow-Forward, 7.65mm, Clip Fed, *Curio*	$1600	$3000	$3250

HOCKLEY, JAMES

Chester County, Pa., 1769–1771. See Kentucky Rifles.

HOLDEN, CYRUS B.

Worchester, Mass., c. 1861–1880.

RIFLE, SINGLESHOT

Model 1862, .44 Henry, Octagon Barrel, *Antique*	325	650	775
Tip-Up, .22 R.F., Nickel Plated Frame, Blued Barrel, *Antique*	225	500	600

HOLLAND & HOLLAND

London, England, since 1835; showrooms later opened in New York and Paris. One of the world's most respected gunmakers, Holland & Holland remained in the hands of the family until well into the 20th century. In the early 1990s, after a period of years as a stock-ownership company, the firm was bought 100 percent by Chanel. President of Chanel Alain Wertheimer is a devoted firearms enthusiast, a keen shot, and a highly talented entrepreneur. Under his patronage Holland & Holland has entirely modernized its London factory, created some of the finest showrooms for any product in London, Paris, and New York City, and is spearheading a revival in the British arms trade. Add premium for guns embellished by renowned engravers.

RIFLE, BOLT ACTION

Best Quality, Various Calibers, Express Sights, Checkered Stock, *Modern*	2750	5000	12500
Best Quality, Various Calibers, Express Sights, Fancy Checkering, Engraved, *Modern*	3150	5000	17500

RIFLE, DOUBLE BARREL, SIDE-BY-SIDE

#2, Various Calibers, Sidelock, Checkered Stock, Engraved, Hammerless, Non Ejector *Modern*	4500	9500	20000
Deluxe, Various Calibers, Sidelock, Automatic Ejector, Fancy Engraving, Fancy Checkering, Double Trigger, Ejector *Modern*	9000	22500	35000
Royal, Various Calibers, Sidelock, ejector Automatic Ejector, Fancy Engraving, Fancy Checkering, Double Trigger, *Modern*	10000	27500	55000
In 470, 500 and 500/465	17500	45000	75000

SHOTGUN, DOUBLE BARREL, OVER-UNDER

Deluxe Royal, 12 Ga., Sidelock, Automatic Ejector, Fancy Engraving, Fancy Checkering, Double Triggers, *Modern*	12000	27000	40000

	Fair	V. Good	Excellent
Deluxe Royal, 12 Ga., Sidelock, Automatic Ejector, Fancy Engraving, Fancy Checkering, Single Trigger, *Modern*	$15000	$30000	$45000
Royal Model (Late), 12 Ga., Sidelock, Automatic Ejector, Fancy Engraving, Fancy Checkering, Double Triggers, *Modern*	15000	30000	45000
Royal Model (Late), 12 Ga., Sidelock, Automatic Ejector, Fancy Engraving, Fancy Checkering, Single Trigger, *Modern*	15000	30000	45000
Royal Model (Old), 12 Ga., Sidelock, Automatic Ejector, Fancy Engraving, Fancy Checkering, Double Triggers, *Modern*	8000	17500	25000
Royal Model (Old), 12 Ga., Sidelock, Automatic Ejector, Fancy Engraving, Fancy Checkering, Single Trigger, *Modern*	9000	20000	27500

SHOTGUN, DOUBLE BARREL, SIDE-BY-SIDE

	Fair	V. Good	Excellent
Badminton, Various Gauges, Sidelock, Automatic Ejector, Fancy Engraving, Fancy Checkering, Double Triggers, *Modern*	3500	7500	9500
Badminton, Various Gauges, Sidelock, Automatic Ejector, Fancy Engraving, Fancy Checkering, Single Trigger, *Modern*	4000	8000	10000
Centenary Royal, 12 Ga. 2", Sidelock, Automatic Ejector, Fancy Engraving, Fancy Checkering, Double Triggers, *Modern*	5750	12500	17500
Deluxe, Various Gauges, Sidelock, Automatic Ejector, Fancy Engraving, Fancy Checkering, Double Triggers, *Modern*	5750	12500	17500
Deluxe, Various Gauges, Sidelock, Automatic Ejector, Fancy Engraving, Fancy Checkering, Single Trigger, *Modern*	6500	15000	19500
Dominion, 12 Ga. 2", Sidelock, Automatic Ejector, Engraved, Checkered Stock, Double Triggers, *Modern*	2750	5000	6500
Dominion, Various Gauges, Sidelock, Automatic Ejector, Engraved, Checkered Stock, Double Triggers, *Modern*	1900	4000	5500
Northwood, Various Gauges, Boxlock, Automatic Ejector, Checkered Stock, Engraved, *Modern*	2000	4500	6000
Riviera, Various Gauges, Extra Shotgun Barrel, Automatic Ejector, Fancy Engraving, Fancy Checkering, Double Triggers, *Modern*	4000	8000	12500
Royal, Various Gauges, Sidelock, Automatic Ejector, Fancy Engraving, Fancy Checkering, Double Triggers, *Modern*	$3750	$10000	$14500
Royal, Various Gauges, Sidelock, Automatic Ejector, Fancy Engraving, Fancy Checkering, Single Trigger, *Modern*	5500	12000	17500
Royal Ejector Grade, 12 Ga. Mag. 3", Single Selective Trigger, Vent Rib, Pistol-Grip Stock, Cased with Accessories, *Modern*	5000	10000	14500
28 ga. and 410 ga. add 25%			

SHOTGUN, SINGLESHOT

	Fair	V. Good	Excellent
Standard Super Trap, 12 Ga., Boxlock, Automatic Ejector, Vent Rib, Fancy Engraving, Checkered Stock, *Modern*	1800	3500	5000
Deluxe Super Trap, 12 Ga., Boxlock, Automatic Ejector, Vent Rib, Fancy Engraving, Checkered Stock, *Modern*	2000	5500	8500
Exhibition Super Trap, 12 Ga., Boxlock, Automatic Ejector, Vent Rib, Fancy Engraving, Checkered Stock, *Modern*	3500	7500	10000

HOLLIS, CHAS. & SONS

London, England.

SHOTGUN, DOUBLE BARREL, SIDE-BY-SIDE

	Fair	V. Good	Excellent
12 Ga., Hammerless, Engraved, Fancy Checkering, Fancy Wood, *Modern*	1200	2500	3250

HOLLIS, RICHARD

London, England, 1800–1850.

HANDGUN, FLINTLOCK

	Fair	V. Good	Excellent
.68, Holster Pistol, Round Barrel, Brass Furniture, Plain, *Antique*	250	550	950

SHOTGUN, PERCUSSION

	Fair	V. Good	Excellent
12 Ga., Double Barrels, Double Triggers, Hook Breech, Light Engraving, Checkered Stock, *Antique*	300	650	1000

HOLMES, BILL

Fayetteville, Ark.

SHOTGUN, SINGLESHOT

	Fair	V. Good	Excellent
Supertrap, 12 Ga., Various Action Types, Checkered Stock, *Modern*	800	1650	2250

HOOD FIREARMS CO.

Norwich, Conn., c. 1875. Also made handguns with selected trade name markings, as follows: Alaska, Alert, Alexis, Boy's Choice, Continental, Czar, Hard Pan, International, Liberty, Little John, Marquis of Lorne, Rob Roy, Robin Hood, Scout, Tramps Terror, Turner & Ross, Union Jack, Victoria, Wide Awake.

HANDGUN, REVOLVER

	Fair	V. Good	Excellent
.32 Short R.F., 5 Shot, Spur Trigger, Solid Frame, Single Action, *Antique*	$75	$125	$200

HOPKINS & ALLEN

Norwich, Conn., 1868–1914, taken over by Marlin-Rockwell in 1914. Also see Bacon Arms Co. and Merwin Hulbert & Co. The following trade names also made by Hopkins & Allen, q.v.: Acme Hammerless, Alexia, Allen, American Eagle, American Gun Co., Aristocrat, Automatic, Bang-Up, Bloodhound, Blue Jacket, Blue Whistler, Capt. Jack, Chicnester, Creedmore, Czar, Despatch, Dictator, Elector, Encore, Garrison, Half-Breed, Imperial Arms, Mountain Eagle, Paragon, Parole, Ranger, Tower's Police Safety, Universal, You Bet. Although considered by some collectors as second-grade guns, Hopkins & Allen's production spread throughout the U.S. and proved to see active service in the American West. One of their most historic production was a pocket revolver, finely engraved on one of the ivory grip panels; A. Lincoln.

HANDGUN, PERCUSSION REVOLVER

	Fair	V. Good	Excellent
Dictator, .36 Caliber, 5 Shot, Octagon Barrel, *Antique*	150	375	500

HANDGUN, REVOLVER

	Fair	V. Good	Excellent
Model 1876 Army, .44-40 WCF, Solid Frame, Single Action, 6 Shot, Finger-Rest Trigger Guard, *Antique*	250	550	750
Safety Police, .22 L.R.R.F., Top Break, Double Action, Various Barrel Lengths, *Curio*	75	150	300
Safety Police, .32 S & W, Top Break, Double Action, Various Barrel Lengths, *Curio*	75	125	275
Safety Police, .38 S & W, Top Break, Double Action, Various Barrel Lengths, *Curio*	75	125	275
XL .30 Long, .30 Long R.F., Solid Frame, Spur Trigger, Single Action, 5 Shot, *Antique*	75	150	300
XL 1 Double Action, .22 Short R.F., Solid Frame, Folding Hammer, *Curio*	50	100	250
XL 3 Double Action, .32 S & W, Solid Frame, Folding Hammer, *Curio*	50	75	125
XL Bulldog, .32 S & W, Solid Frame, Folding Hammer, *Curio*	50	100	150
XL Bulldog, .32 Short R.F., Solid Frame, Folding Hammer, *Curio*	50	75	125
XL Bulldog, .38 S & W, Solid Frame, Folding Hammer, *Curio*	50	75	125
XL CR .22 Short R.F., Solid Frame, Spur Trigger, Single Action, 7 Shot, *Antique*	$125	$150	$200
XL Double Action, .32 S & W, Solid Frame, Folding Hammer, *Curio*	50	75	100
XL Double Action, .38 S & W, Solid Frame, Folding Hammer, *Curio*	50	75	100
XL Navy, .38 Short R.F., Solid Frame, Single Action, 6 Shot, *Antique*	250	500	700
XL No. 1, .22 Short R.F., Solid Frame, Spur Trigger, Single Action, 7 Shot, *Antique*	100	150	200
XL No. 2, .30 Short R.F., Solid Frame, Spur Trigger, Single Action, 5 Shot, *Antique*	100	175	225
XL No. 3, .32 Short R.F., Solid Frame, Spur Trigger, Single Action, 5 Shot, Safety Cylinder, *Antique*	100	175	225
XL No. 4, .38 Short R.F., Solid Frame, Spur Trigger, Single Action, 5 Shot, *Antique*	100	175	225
XL No. 5, .38 S & W, Solid Frame, Spur Trigger, Single Action, 5 Shot, *Antique*	150	350	450
XL No. 5, .38 Short R.F., Solid Frame, Spur Trigger, Single Action, 5 Shot, Safety Cylinder, Engraved, *Antique*	150	300	450
XL No. 6, .41 Short R.F., Solid Frame, Spur Trigger, Single Action, 5 Shot, *Antique*	100	175	300
XL No. 7, .41 Short R.F., Solid Frame, Spur Trigger, Single Action, 5 Shot, Swing-Out Cylinder, *Antique*	100	225	350
XL No. 8 Army, .44 R.F., Solid Frame, Single Action, 6 Shot, *Antique*	400	800	1250
XL Police, .38 Short R.F., Solid Frame, Single Action, 6 Shot, *Antique*	200	400	650

HANDGUN, SINGLESHOT

	Fair	V. Good	Excellent
New Model Target, .22 L.R.R.F., Top Break, 10" Barrel, Adjustable Sights, Target Grips	150	300	500
Single Shot Derringer, .22 Short R.F., $1^{3}/_{4}$" Barrel Pivots Downward for Loading, Folding Trigger, Single Action, *Antique*	400	900	1350
XL Derringer, .41 Short R.F., Spur Trigger, Single Action, *Antique*	225	475	700

RIFLE, BOLT ACTION

	Fair	V. Good	Excellent
American Military, .22 L.R.R.F., Singleshot, Takedown, Open Rear Sight, Round Barrel, *Curio*	100	200	350

RIFLE, FLINTLOCK

	Fair	V. Good	Excellent
"Kentucky," .31, Octagon Barrel, Full-Stocked, Brass Furniture, Reproduction (Numrich), *Antique*	100	175	325

	Fair	V. Good	Excellent
"Kentucky," .36, Octagon Barrel, Full-Stocked, Brass Furniture, Reproduction (Numrich), *Antique*	$100	$175	$275
"Kentucky," .45, Octagon Barrel, Full-Stocked, Brass Furniture, Reproduction (Numrich), *Antique*	100	175	275
"Minute Brush," .50, Octagon Barrel, Full-Stocked, Carbine Reproduction (Numrich), *Antique*	100	175	275
"Minuteman Brush," .45, Octagon Barrel, Full-Stocked, Carbine Reproduction (Numrich), *Antique*	100	175	275
"Minuteman," .31, Octagon Barrel, Full-Stocked, Brass Furniture, Reproduction (Numrich), *Antique*	100	175	275
"Minuteman," .36, Octagon Barrel, Full-Stocked, Brass Furniture, Reproduction (Numrich), *Antique*	75	150	250
"Minuteman," .45, Octagon Barrel, Full-Stocked, Brass Furniture, Reproduction (Numrich), *Antique*	100	175	275
"Minuteman," .50, Octagon Barrel, Full-Stocked, Brass Furniture, Reproduction (Numrich), *Antique*	100	175	275
"Pennsylvania," .31, Octagon Barrel, Half-Stocked, Brass Furniture, Reproduction (Numrich), *Antique*	100	150	250
"Pennsylvania," .36, Octagon Barrel, Half-Stocked, Brass Furniture, Reproduction (Numrich), *Antique*	75	150	250
"Pennsylvania," .45, Octagon Barrel, Half-Stocked, Brass Furniture, Reproduction (Numrich), *Antique*	100	175	275
"Pennsylvania," .50, Octagon Barrel, Half-Stocked, Brass Furniture, Reproduction (Numrich), *Antique*	75	150	250

RIFLE, PERCUSSION

	Fair	V. Good	Excellent
"Buggy Deluxe," .36, Under-Hammer, Octagon Barrel, Carbine, Reproduction (Numrich), *Antique*	50	75	125
"Buggy Deluxe," .45, Under-Hammer, Octagon Barrel, Carbine, Reproduction (Numrich), *Antique*	50	100	150
"Deer Stalker," .58, Under-Hammer, Octagon Barrel, Reproduction (Numrich), *Antique*	50	75	150
"Heritage," .36, Under-Hammer, Octagon Barrel, Brass Furniture, Reproduction (Numrich), *Antique*	50	100	175

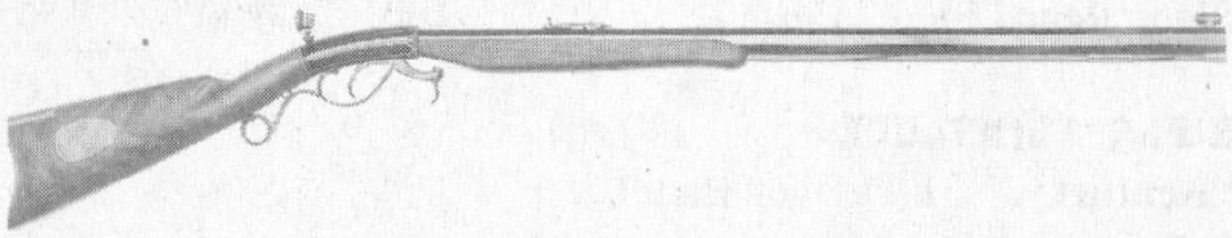

Hopkins & Allen Heritage Rifle

	Fair	V. Good	Excellent
"Heritage," .45, Under-Hammer, Octagon Barrel, Brass Furniture, Reproduction (Numrich), *Antique*	$50	$100	$200
"Kentucky," .31, Full-Stocked, Octagon Barrel, Brass Furniture, Reproduction (Numrich), *Antique*	75	150	250
"Kentucky," .36, Full-Stocked, Octagon Barrel, Brass Furniture, Reproduction (Numrich), *Antique*	75	150	250
"Kentucky," .45, Full-Stocked, Octagon Barrel, Brass Furniture, Reproduction (Numrich), *Antique*	75	150	250
"Minuteman Brush," .45, Full-Stocked, Octagon Barrel, Carbine, Reproduction (Numrich), *Antique*	75	150	250
"Minuteman Brush," .50, Full-Stocked, Octagon Barrel, Carbine, Reproduction (Numrich), *Antique*	75	175	275
"Minuteman," .31, Full-Stocked, Octagon Barrel, Brass Furniture, Reproduction (Numrich), *Antique*	75	150	275
"Minuteman," .36, Full-Stocked, Octagon Barrel, Brass Furniture, Reproduction (Numrich), *Antique*	75	150	275
"Minuteman," .45, Full-Stocked, Octagon Barrel, Brass Furniture, Reproduction (Numrich), *Antique*	75	150	275
"Minuteman," .50, Full-Stocked, Octagon Barrel, Brass Furniture, Reproduction (Numrich), *Antique*	75	125	225
"Offhand Deluxe," .36 Under-Hammer, Octagon Barrel, Reproduction (Numrich), *Antique*	50	75	125
"Offhand Deluxe," .45 Under-Hammer, Octagon Barrel, Reproduction (Numrich), *Antique*	50	75	125
"Offhand Deluxe," .45 Under-Hammer, Octagon Barrel, Reproduction (Numrich), *Antique*	50	75	125
"Pennsylvania," .31, Half-Stocked, Octagon Barrel, Brass Furniture, Reproduction (Numrich), *Antique*	75	125	200
"Pennsylvania," .36, Half-Stocked, Octagon Barrel, Brass Furniture, Reproduction (Numrich), *Antique*	75	150	250
"Pennsylvania," .45, Half-Stocked, Octagon Barrel, Brass Furniture, Reproduction (Numrich), *Antique*	75	150	250
"Pennsylvania," .50, Half-Stocked, Octagon Barrel, Brass Furniture, Reproduction (Numrich), *Antique*	75	150	250
"Target," .45, Under-Hammer, Octagon Barrel, Reproduction (Numrich), *Antique*	50	75	125
.45, Double Barrel, Over-Under, Swivel Breech, Brass Furniture, Reproduction (Numrich), *Antique*	50	100	200

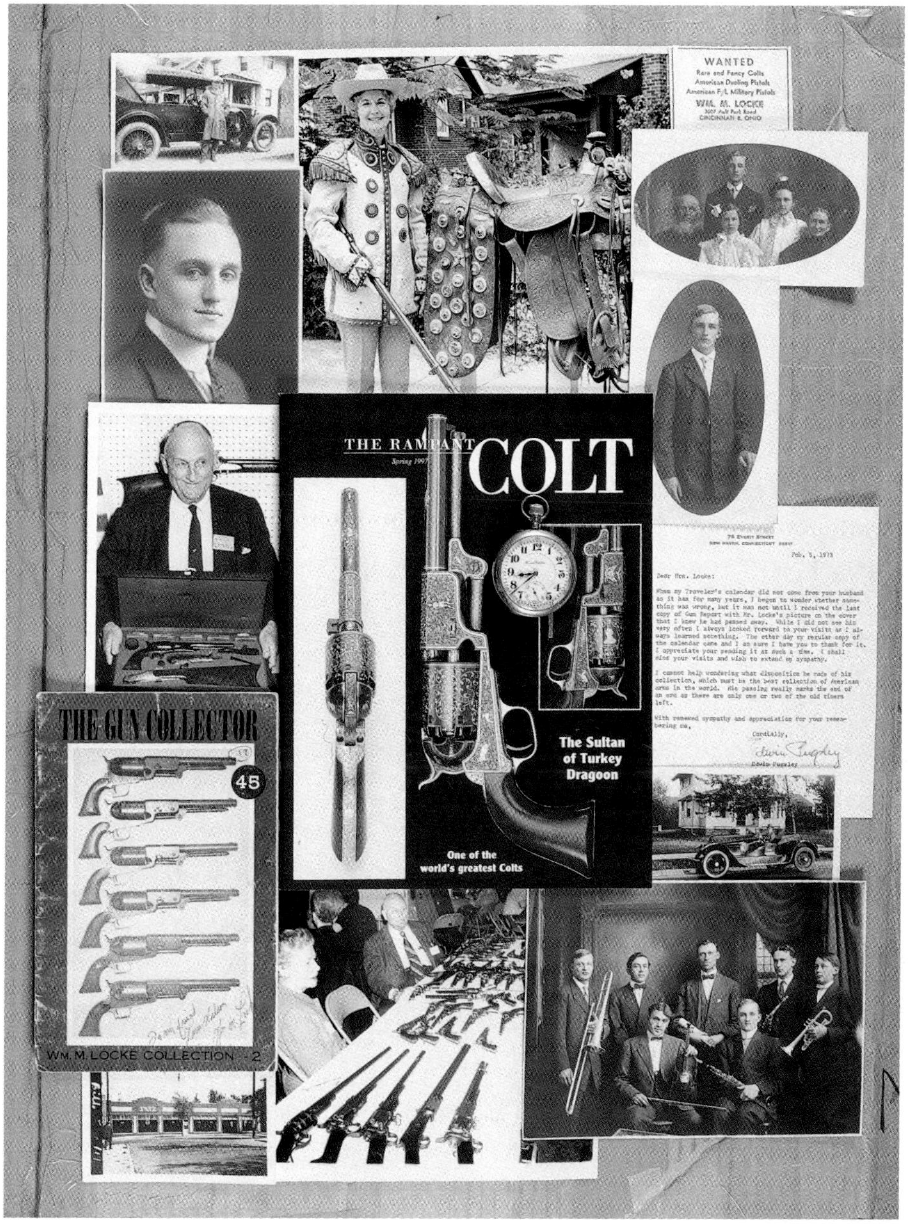

Tribute to the foremost collector of American arms, William M. Locke. At top right, *the simple advertisement that he placed in several publications over the years, seeking guns for the collection.* Top right, *family picture with parents, and his two sisters.* Upper left, *young Bill Locke at age sixteen, taken in 1912. He had been born William Matthew Locke, in Mt. Ayr, Iowa, May 22, 1894. The orchestra photograph was taken in 1913; he played the clarinet. Automobile photographs reflect his dealership in Stutz cars. At* lower left, *the agency in Omaha, 1919. Image seated in Stutz Bearcat dates from 1920, in front of house in Omaha. Standing in front of Stutz touring car, taken 1924. The pocket watch was Locke's from c. 1913–15.*

At left, *at the National Rifle Association meeting of 1961, in St. Louis, Missouri, holding one of his favorite sets, the Colt Model 1860 Army number 183226.* Bottom center, *at an Ohio Gun Collectors Association meeting, 1971, with a table full of fine Colts and other make firearms. Mrs. Elsa Locke at* left, *a frequent companion at shows, and traveling cross-country seeking fine guns.*

Top left, *the Doc Carver Silver Dollar Saddle (now collection Buffalo Bill Historical Center, Cody), and the Diamond Dick Show Jacket, worn by Margaret Trent, June 1966.* The Rampant Colt *pictures the most important firearm in the Locke Collection, the Sultan of Turkey Third Model Dragoon, no. 12407.*

The Gun Collector *was one of two issues, which featured Colt, and some other makes of arms from the collection. The other issue was no. 39. See also* Antique Arms Annual *1971, which featured the collection on pages 144–151, with a memoir by Locke himself. Note letter at* right center, *from Edwin Pugsley, for many years an executive of Winchester and himself a gun-collecting legend, paying tribute to Locke. With the passing a few years later of Mr. Pugsley, the end of an era had indeed been reached.*

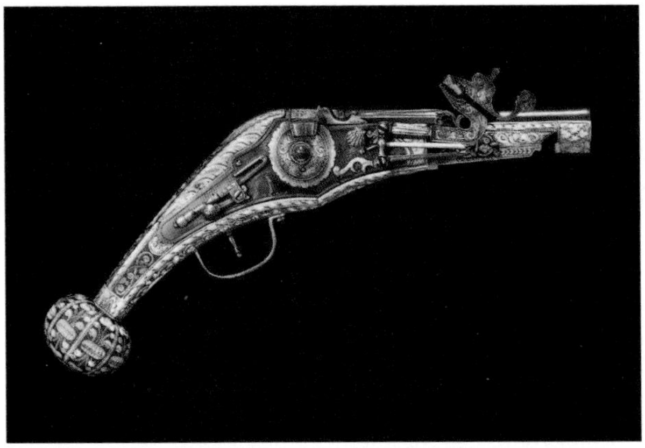

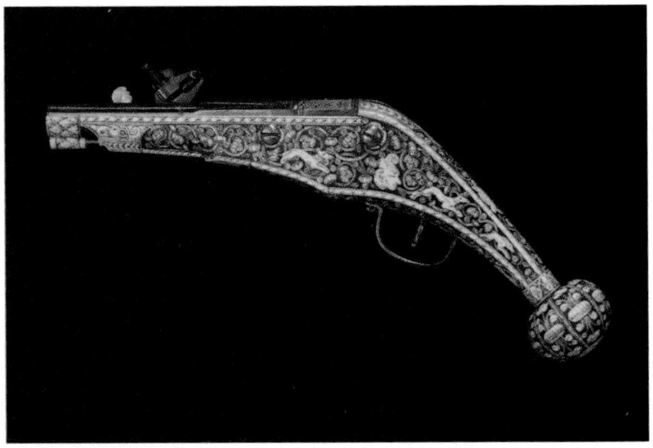

From Christie's, London: exceptional 120-bore wheelock puffer-style pistol, made for a boy, dated 1586, probably Saxon. The finest example to appear on the market of a child's wheelock pistol; only two other examples sold in modern times. Realized $82,000 (£49,900) at the sale of December 16, 1999 (lot 344).

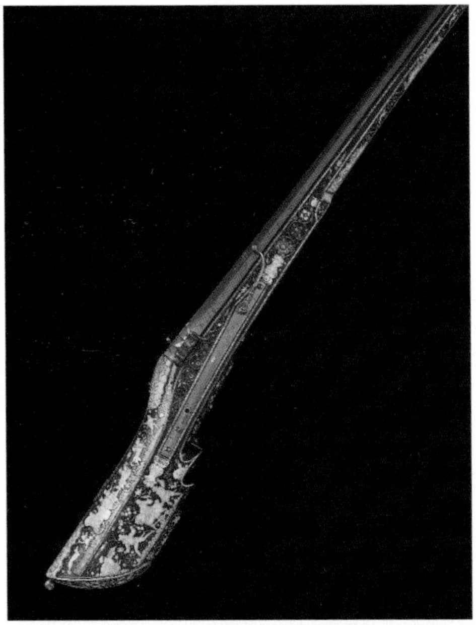

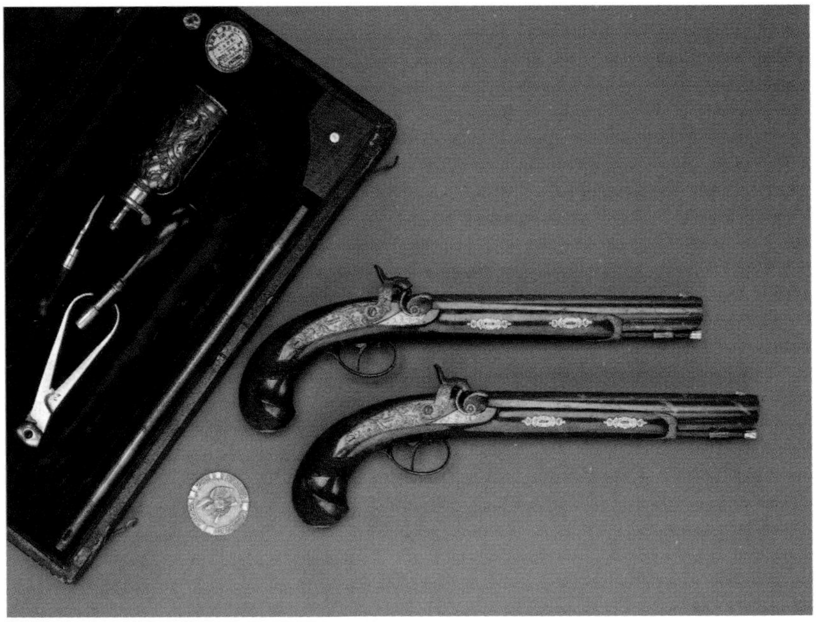

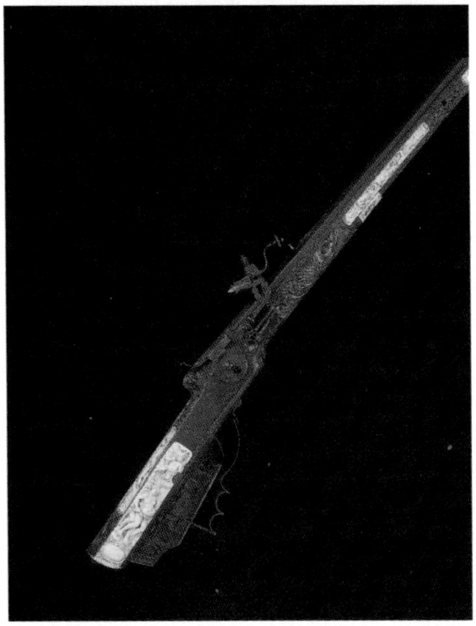

Above: *Sold by Little John's Auction Service, Inc., at November 9, 1999, sale, the finest known pair of Henry Deringer dueling pistols, the 14¾-inch barrels marked MAND FOR/A. MILLSPAUGH,/WASHINGTON, LA. Formerly in the William M. Locke and R. B. Berryman collections. Sold for $275,000.*

Left, top: *From the Barons Nathaniel and Albert Von Rothschild arms and armor sale, July 15, 1999: lot 83, a 16-bore German snap matchlock competition target rifle, Nuremberg, late 16th century, the barrel marking indicating Peter Danner as maker. Scenes inlaid on stock taken from prints by Nuremberg artist Virgil Solis (1514–62). Approximately twenty similar guns known; primarily in museums. Rifle reached a figure of $93,000 (£56,500).*

Left, bottom: *Another Von Rothschild sale gun, lot 84, a 54-bore German wheelock sporting rifle, stocked by Johann Michael Maucher, one of the most distinguished South German stockmakers and carvers of the 17th century. Schwabisch-Gmund, c. 1670. Gun made for display, rather than actual use. Sold for $174,000 (£106,000).*

Silver-mounted flintlock rifle at left *by J. B. Bartlett Bros., Binghampton, New York, for E. G. Roberts, and presented to Rezin Bowie, brother of knife-fighting legend Jim Bowie. Colt Single Actions at* center left *and* right *engraved by John McGraw in the late 1930s and 1940s (courtesy Little John's Auction Service). Bohlin silver-mounted holster rig from the Montie Montana collection; with Will & Finck ivory-handled, silver-mounted San Francisco knife and half-horse/half-alligator Bowie by Woodhead & Hartley, Sheffield (courtesy Butterfield's). Auction catalogs and promotions represent some of the major sales of 1999 and 2000. Miniatures by Aldo Uberti & Co. (sold in 2000 to Fabbrica d'Armi Pietro Beretta SpA), plus gambling memorabilia, sword and dagger objects, daguerreotype case and Bowie knife portrait, from Peter Buxtun Collection. Wrangler Award from National Cowboy Hall of Fame, for* Buffalo Bill's Wild West *book, from Greg Martin Collection. Snapshots taken at Butterfield's preview party at the Pebble Beach (California) home of Dennis and Karen Levett, during the Concourse d'Elegance, August 1999. Robert M. Lee and Anne Brockinton, with Sergio Pinanfarina and wife, at the Concourse.* Fine Colts *cover near snapshots of collector Dr. Joseph A. Murphy, with daughter Kate. Rolex watches from author's and Greg Martin collections.* (COURTESY OF DOUGLAS SANDBERG)

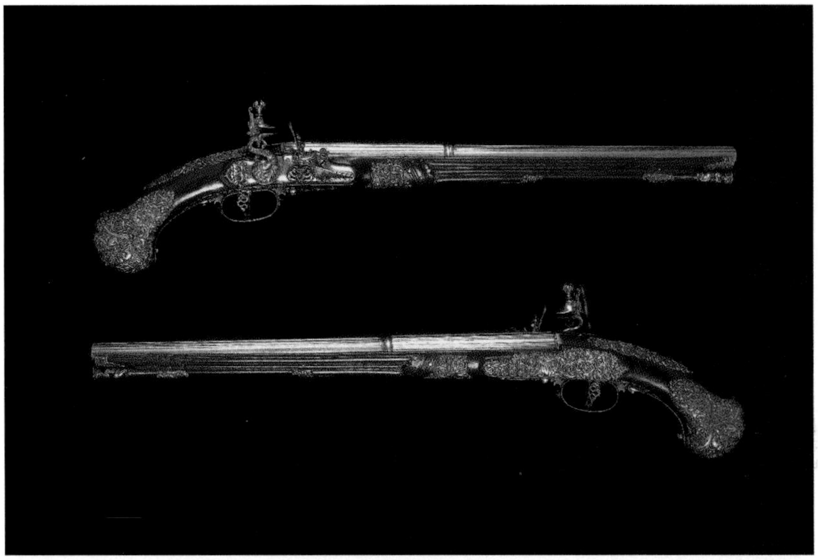

Left: *From Christie's, London: Yet another masterpiece from the Von Rothschild sale, lot 91, a pair of 40-bore Brescian flintlock holster pistols, by Pietro Manani, c. 1660–70. Approximately thirty-eight examples known of the work of Manani, recognized by Nolfo diCarpegna as "one of the most active craftsmen of his time." Barrels marked* LAZARO LAZARINO COMINAZZO. *Realized $120,000 (£73,000).*

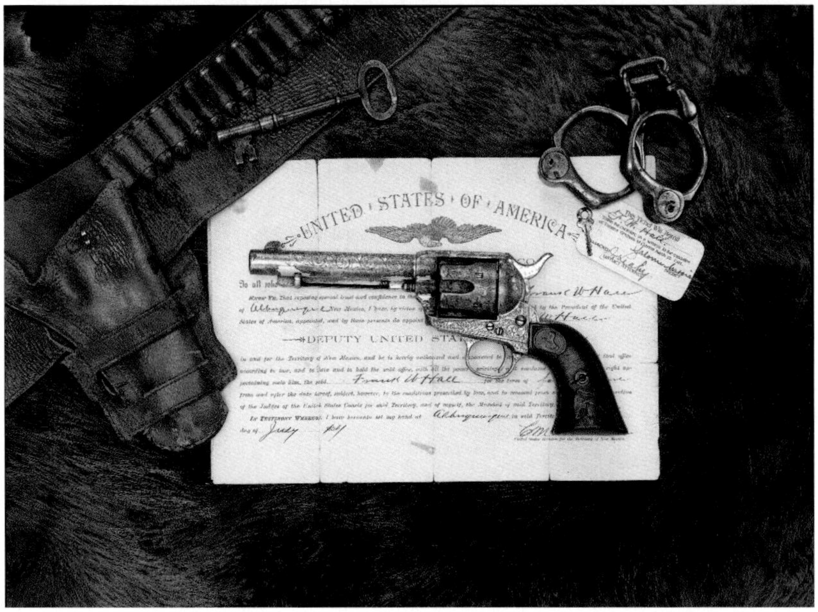

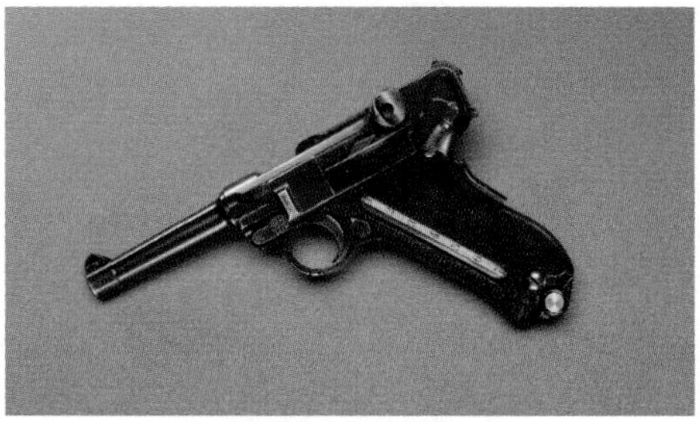

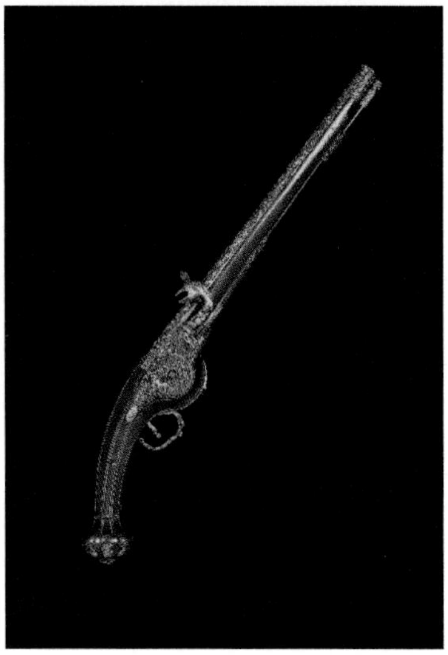

Above: *From the Little John's Auction event of November 8, 1999, the R. B. Berryman Collection: the Blackjack Ketchum Single Action Army Colt, number 128145, factory engraved in the Helfricht shop, with holster, and numerous accompanying documents and memorabilia. Reached a price of $231,000*

Right, top: *From Little John's Auction Services, Important Firearms Auction sale of November 9, 1999: Baby Paterson cased set from the William M. Locke Collection, serial number 404; finest example known of this model. Lot 770, realized $253,000.*

Right, center: *Model 1902 American Eagle "cartridge counter" Luger, 9mm; serial number 22449. One of the most desirable, and rare, of all Luger pistols. Lot 795, realized $29,700.*

Right, bottom: *Also from the Von Rothschild sale, lot 93, a 38-bore French wheelock holster pistol, signed* Agrisole, *c. 1620. Sold for $254,000 (£155,500), a world record auction price for a single European antique firearm.*

Framed at left *and* right *with side-by-side shotguns by the late Mario Beschi (20-gauge, single trigger) and Bottega dell'Artigiano (12-gauge, double trigger) respectively, and at* top *by Model 94 Winchester from series built by Pachmayr; the publications are an array of auction and dealer catalogs, gunmaker publications, and the Metropolitan Museum of Art's helmet display, opened early in 2000. Two important new books on fine guns and engraving are* Les Plus Belles Gravures d'armes de Chasse, *by Claude Gaier, and* Legendary Sporting Guns *by Eric Joly. Not pictured is* British Gun Engraving *by Douglas Tate (see "The Season in Review: 1999–2000"). Simeon North flintlock dueling pistol at* top left, *from North family estate. Outstanding contemporary work from Ferlach gunmaker Peter Hofer, pictured* lower right *and* top right; *work was admired in his spectacular display at Safari Club International convention, Reno, 2000. On cover of* The Shooting Field, *magnificent double rifle by Holland & Holland, termed the SCI 2000, fetched $280,000 price at SCI auction. Dixie's annual catalog with tribute of each issue to celebrity gun enthusiast; the 2000 edition—all 720 pages of it—was dedicated to Harry Carey, Jr. At* bottom right, *author with gun enthusiast David E. Davis, Jr., dean of automotive journalists, on publication of his* Thus Spake David E., *at the Concourse d'Italiano, Carmel, California. At* bottom, *antique-style cartridge boxes by Cheyenne Cartridge Boxes, handsomely designed for use by Single Action Shooting Society competitors.*

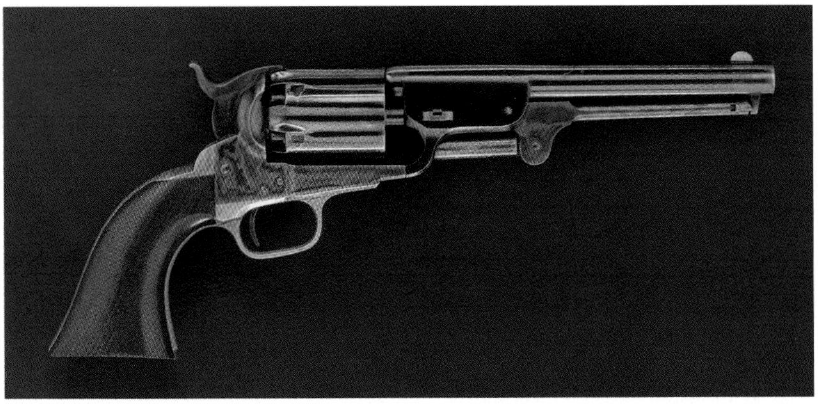

Three rarities from Butterfield's Millennium Sale of November 15–16, 1999: Experimental Colt Third Model Dragoon revolver, serial number 4, .44 caliber. Lot 5006, reached $442,500.

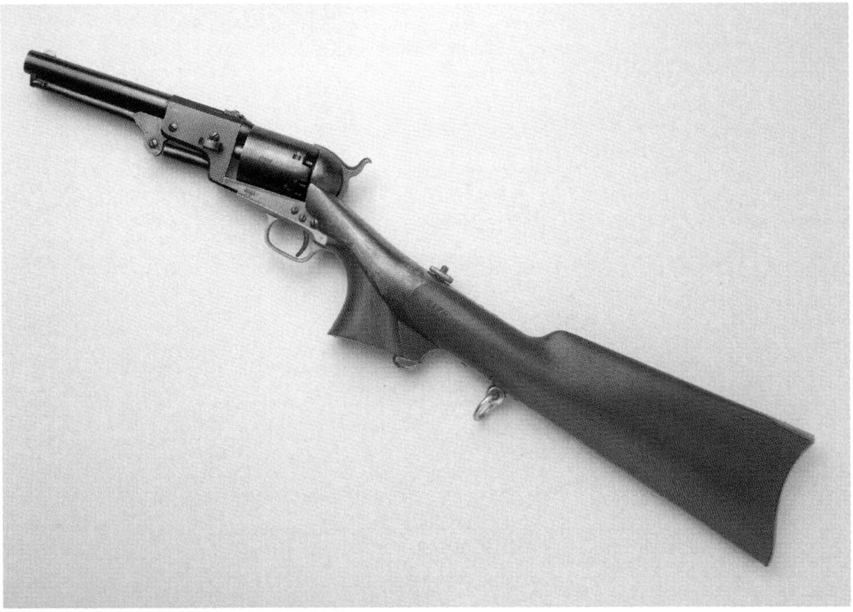

Colt Third Model Dragoon with matching shoulder stock, serial number 17022, from the Hegeman and U.S. Cartridge Co. collections. Lot 5001, reached $167,500.

Unique German experimental system Luger self-loading military rifle; 26-inch barrel. Lot 6011, realized $112,500.

Opposite: *A sampling of dealer and auction house catalogs, with snapshots and brochures from gunmakers, gun advocacy groups, the NRA Whittington Center, and institutions with arms like the Higgins Armory Museum, Autry Museum of Western Heritage, the King Ranch Museum, and the Detroit Institute of Arts. Rare Ruger medallion at* lower left, *given to employees at Christmas 1999 in celebration of 50th anniversary. Single Action Shooting Society book and brochure, in recognition of fast-growing shooting sport. Galazan/Connecticut Shotgun Manufacturing Co. catalog and big-game cartridge block symbolic of extraordinary achievements of New Britain–based dealer and gunmaker of international distinction. CD* 100 Guns *from the J. M. Davis Arms & Historical Museum ("The Largest Gun Collection in the World"), Claremore, Oklahoma.*

Collectable Arms International Incorporated
Griffin & Howe
More than YOU MIGHT HAVE THOUGHT WE WERE!
BARRETT-SMYTHE
HOLLAND & HOLLAND
NRA WHITTINGTON CENTER BUILDER
Buffalo Bill's WILD WEST
Heroic!
HAPPY TRAILS
NAVY ARMS COMPANY
BONHAMS
KNIGHTSBRIDGE
The Benn Hunter Collection of Antique & Modern Firearms
Smith & Wesson
Model 3 Schofield
The NRA Whittington Center
NRA WHITTINGTON CENTER
Guided Hunts
Entering A New Millennium
IMAX
ALAMO
THE PRICE OF FREEDOM
Galazan
BUTTERFIELDS
DAVID CONDON
100 GUNS
KING RANCH
MUSEUM
WITHERELL'S
Join SASS
THE SINGLE ACTION SHOOTING SOCIETY
BEYOND THE WILD BUNCH
The Applegate Collection
J.C. DEVINE INC.
RUGER
DANGEROUS GAME
CARTRIDGES for SPORTING RIFLES
champlin firearms inc.
1999 NSSF PROMOTIONAL MATERIALS CATALOG
NSSF
Collector Arms Dealers Association
CADA
SPECIAL INSURANCE PROGRAM
REX STARK
IMPORTANT FIXED PRICE CATALOG
Petersen
BISMUTH
Asprey & Garrard
Firearms Engravers Guild of America
"Artisans in Metal"
Beretta
U.S.A.

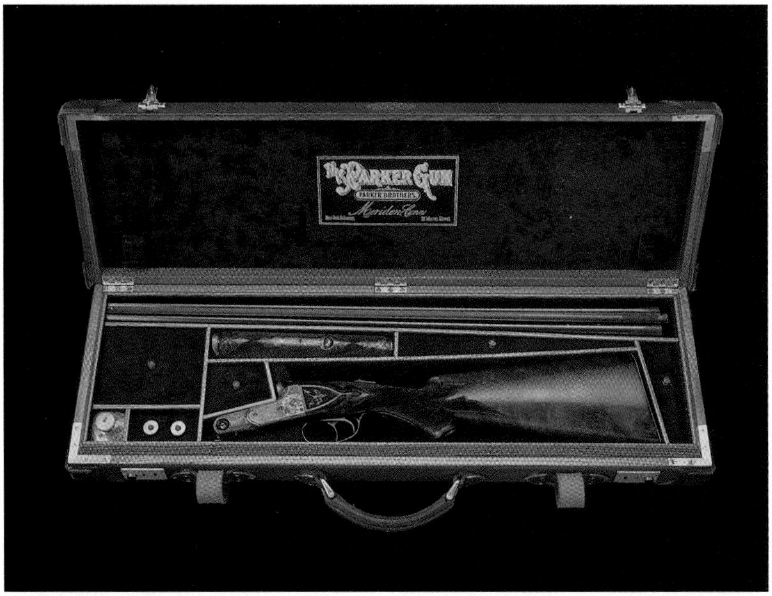

From Butterfield's May 24–25, 1999, sale, Parker A-1 Special 28-gauge double barrel exhibition shotgun, serial 191049; 26-inch barrels, believed to be "The Little Persuader." Lot 2413, realized $101,500. One of four known examples.

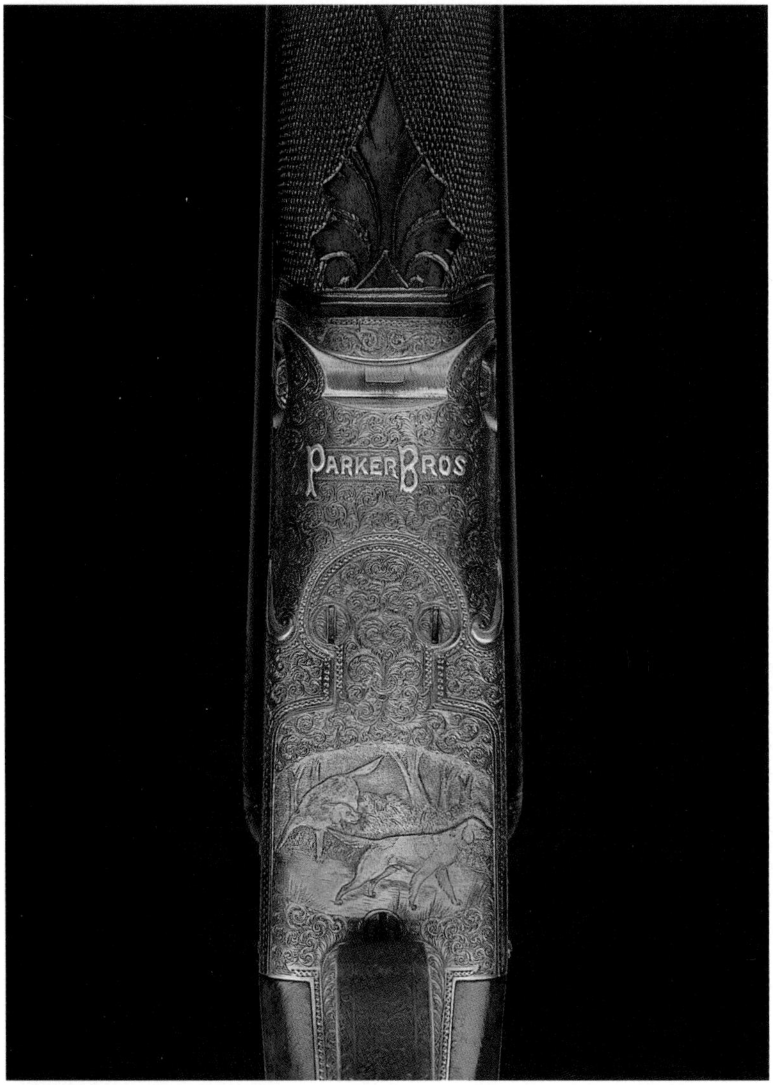

Another Parker shotgun from the May 24–25 sale, .410 gauge BHE double barrel shotgun, serial 221960; 28-inch barrels. Lot 2418, realized $101,500. One of two known examples.

The author with Tony Galazan, founder and owner of Connecticut Shotgun Manufacturing Company, and H. Wayne Sheets, Director, the NRA Foundation Endowment. Taken at the Safari Club International show, January 2000, Reno. Tony and Wayne hold display samples of the celebrated CSM over-and-unders, while the author is holding a Fox exhibition grade. See "Introduction: The Season in Review" for further information on this amazing American company.

The author with Craig Sandler, executive director of Operations, NRA. Formerly in law enforcement, and a keen shooter and gun enthusiast, Sandler is directly involved on a full-time, flat-out basis in fighting to defend the right of responsible U.S. citizens to possess, collect, and use firearms.

	Fair	V. Good	Excellent
RIFLE, SINGLESHOT			
Model 1881 (XL), Various Calibers, Falling Block, Takedown, Lever Action, Round Barrel, Open Rear Sight, *Antique*	$150	$375	$500
Model 1881 Junior, .22 L.R.R.F., Falling Block, Takedown, Lever Action, Round Barrel, Open Rear Sight, *Antique*	150	350	525
No. 1922 New Model Junior, .22 L.R.R.F., Falling Block, Takedown, Lever Action, Octagon Barrel, Open Rear Sight, *Curio*	100	200	300
No. 1925 New Model Junior, .25 Short R.F., Falling Block, Takedown, Lever Action, Octagon Barrel, Open Rear Sight, *Curio*	125	250	350
No. 1932 New Model Junior, .32 Long R.F., Falling Block, Takedown, Lever Action, Octagon Barrel, Open Rear Sight, *Curio*	125	225	325
No. 1938 New Model Junior, .38 S & W, Falling Block, Takedown, Lever Action, Octagon Barrel, Open Rear Sight, *Curio*	125	250	350
No. 2922 New Model Junior, .22 L.R.R.F., Falling Block, Takedown, Lever Action, Octagon Barrel, Checkered Stock, Open Rear Sight, *Curio*	100	225	325
No. 2925 New Model Junior, .25 Short R.F., Falling Block, Takedown, Lever Action, Octagon Barrel, Checkered Stock, Open Rear Sight, *Curio*	125	250	350
No. 2932 New Model Junior, .32 Long R.F., Falling Block, Takedown, Lever Action, Octagon Barrel, Checkered Stock, Open Rear Sight, *Curio*	125	250	350
No. 2938 New Model Junior, .38 S & W, Falling Block, Takedown, Lever Action, Octagon Barrel, Checkered Stock, Open Rear Sight, *Curio*	125	275	350
No. 3922 Schüetzen Target, .22 L.R.R.F., Falling Block, Takedown, Lever Action, Octagon Barrel, Checkered Stock, Swiss Buttplate, *Antique*	400	800	1200
No. 3925 Schüetzen Target, .25-20 WCF, Falling Block, Takedown, Lever Action, Octagon Barrel, Checkered Stock, Swiss Buttplate, *Antique*	550	1000	1650
No. 722, .22 L.R.R.F., Rolling Block, Takedown, Round Barrel, Open Rear Sight, *Curio*	50	100	175
No. 822, .22 L.R.R.F., Rolling Block, Takedown, Lever Action, Round Barrel, Open Rear Sight, *Curio*	75	125	175
No. 832, .32 Short R.F., Rolling Block, Takedown, Lever Action, Round Barrel, Open Rear Sight, Curio	$75	$150	$225
No. 922 New Model Junior, 22 L.R.R.F., Falling Block, Takedown, Lever Action, Round Barrel, Open Rear Sight, *Curio*	75	150	225
No. 925 New Model Junior, .25 Short R.F., Falling Block, Takedown, Lever Action, Round Barrel, Open Rear Sight, *Curio*	75	150	225
No. 932 New Model Junior, .32 Long R.F., Falling Block, Takedown, Lever Action, Round Barrel, Open Rear Sight, *Curio*	75	125	200
No. 938 New Model Junior, .38 S & W, Falling Block, Takedown, Lever Action, Round Barrel, Open Rear Sight, *Curio*	100	225	300
SHOTGUN, DOUBLE BARREL, SIDE-BY-SIDE			
No. 100, 12 and 16 Ga., Double Trigger, Outside Hammers, Checkered Stock, Steel Barrel, *Curio*	100	200	400
No. 110, 12 and 16 Ga., Double Trigger, Hammerless, Checkered Stock, Steel Barrel, *Curio*	100	175	250
SHOTGUN, SINGLESHOT			
New Model, Various Gauges, Hammer, Top Break, Damascus Barrel, Checkered Stock, *Curio*	50	75	100
New Model, Various Gauges, Hammer, Top Break, Steel Barrel, *Curio*	50	75	100
New Model, Various Gauges, Hammer, Top Break, Steel Barrel, Automatic Ejector, Checkered Stock, *Curio*	50	75	100

HOPKINS, C. W.

Made by Bacon Mfg. Co., Norwich, Conn.

	Fair	V. Good	Excellent
HANDGUN, REVOLVER			
.32 Short R.F., Single Action, Solid Frame, Swing-Out Cylinder, *Antique*	125	350	550
.38 Caliber (Navy), Single Action, Solid Frame, Swing-Out Cylinder, *Antique*	250	575	800

HOROLT, LORENZ

Nuremberg, Germany, c. 1600.

	Fair	V. Good	Excellent
HANDGUN, WHEEL LOCK			
Long Barreled, Holster Pistol, Hexagonal Ball Pommel, Light Ornamentation, *Antique*	3500	7500	10000

HOUILLER, BLANCHAR

Paris, France, c. 1845.

HANDGUN, PERCUSSION

	Fair	V. Good	Excellent
Pepperbox, .48, 6 Shot, *Antique*	$175	$375	$600

HOWARD ARMS

Made by Crescent for Fred Bifflar & Co. See Crescent Fire Arms Co., Shotgun, Double Barrel, Side-by-Side; Shotgun, Singleshot.

HOWARD ARMS

Made by Meriden Firearms Co.

HANDGUN, REVOLVER

	Fair	V. Good	Excellent
.32 S & W, 5 Shot, Double Action, Top Break, *Modern*	50	75	100
.38 S & W, 5 Shot, Double Action, Top Break, *Modern*	50	75	100

HOWARD BROTHERS

Detroit, Mich., c. 1868.

RIFLE, SINGLESHOT

	Fair	V. Good	Excellent
.44 Henry R.F., Round Barrel, *Antique*	150	375	600

HUMBERGER, PETER JR.

Ohio, 1791–1852. See Kentucky Rifles.

HUMBERGER, PETER SR.

Pa., 1774–1791, then Ohio, 1791–1811. See Kentucky Rifles.

HUMMER

Belgium, for Lee Hdw., Kansas.

SHOTGUN, DOUBLE BARREL, SIDE-BY-SIDE

	Fair	V. Good	Excellent
Various Gauges, Hammerless, Steel Barrel, *Modern*	100	175	225
Various Gauges, Outside Hammers, Damascus Barrel, *Modern*	75	150	200
Various Gauges, Outside Hammers, Steel Barrel, *Modern*	75	150	200

SHOTGUN, SINGLESHOT

	Fair	V. Good	Excellent
Various Gauges, Hammer, Steel Barrel, *Modern*	25	50	75

HUNGARIAN MILITARY

HANDGUN, SELF-LOADING

	Fair	V. Good	Excellent
29M Femaru, 7.65mm, Clip Fed, Blue, Miltary, *Curio*	150	350	450
37M Femaru, 7.65mm, Clip Fed, Blue, Miltary, *Curio*	$125	$250	$350
Frommer, Stop Pocket, .380 ACP, Clip Fed, Blue, Military, *Curio*	100	225	325

RIFLE, BOLT ACTION

	Fair	V. Good	Excellent
1935M, 8mm, Mannlicher, Military, *Curio*	100	225	325
1943M, 8mm Mauser, Mannlicher, Military, *Curio*	150	325	425

Hungarian Military 37M Femaru

HUNTER ARMS

See L. C. Smith.

HUNTING WORLD

New York City. A dedicated sportsman and gun enthusiast, Hunting World's founder and president Bob Lee began collecting custom-made rifles while still a youth, carrying on correspondence with prominent riflemen the likes of Jack O'Connor and Elmer Keith. Lee's knowledge of fine guns of all periods is prodigious, and his hunting experiences around the world have established him as one of the 20th century's premier sportsmen and firearms authorities. It was only natural, therefore, that he would venture into the world of gunmaking, with his own line of best-quality game guns. The relatively limited production was based on the Holland & Holland system, style and quality, even to the detail of having K. C. Hunt design and embellish the prototype gun. That sample piece served as the standard pattern for the remaining production, done in Spain by gunmakers at a high level of quality and performance. These game guns are no longer in production.

SHOTGUN, DOUBLE BARREL, SIDE-BY-SIDE

	Fair	V. Good	Excellent
Royal Deluxe Game Gun, 12 or 20 Gauges, Sidelock, Fancy Wood, Engraved, *Modern*	1700	3500	4500

HUSQVARNA VAPENFABRIK AKITIEBOLAG

HANDGUN, REVOLVER

	Fair	V. Good	Excellent
Model 1887 Swedish Nagent, 7.5mm, Double Action, Blue, Military, *Antique*	150	400	500

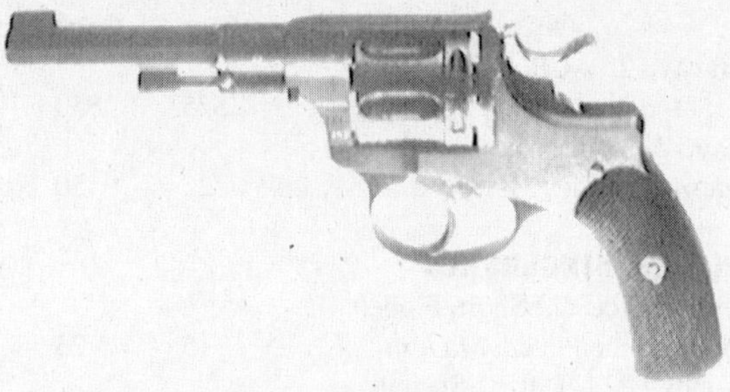

Husqvarna M1887 Revolver

	Fair	V. Good	Excellent
HANDGUN, SELF-LOADING			
Model 40 "Lahti," 9mm Browning Long, Clip Fed, Swedish Military, *Curio*	$150	$300	$400
Model L-35 "Lahti," 9mm Browning Long, Clip Fed, Finnish Military, *Curio*	400	800	1100
RIFLE, BOLT ACTION			
1000 Super Grade, Various Calibers, Sporting Rifle, Checkered Stock, Monte Carlo Stock, *Curio*	150	300	400
1100 Deluxe, Various Calibers, Sporting Rifle, Checkered Stock, *Curio*	150	300	400
1622, .22 L.R.R.F., Clip Fed, Sling Swivels, *Curio*	50	100	150
1951, Various Calibers, Sporting Rifle, Checkered Stock, *Curio*	150	300	425
3000 Crown Grade, Various Calibers, Sporting Rifle, Checkered Stock, Monte Carlo Stock, *Curio*	175	350	450
3100 Crown Grade, Various Calibers, Sporting Rifle, Checkered Stock, *Curio*	175	325	425
4000, Various Calibers, Sporting Rifle, Checkered Stock, Lightweight, Monte Carlo Stock, *Curio*	175	350	450
4100, Various Calibers, Sporting Rifle, Checkered Stock, Lightweight, *Curio*	175	325	425
456, Various Calibers, Sporting Rifle, Checkered Stock, Lightweight, Full-Stocked, *Curio*	175	375	500
6000 Imperial, Various Calibers, Sporting Rifle, Checkered Stock, Fancy Wood, Express Sights, *Curio*	200	425	650
8000 Imperial Grade, Various Calibers, Sporting Rifle, Checkered Stock, Engraved, Monte Carlo Stock, Fancy Wood, *Curio*	200	425	650
9000 Crown Grade, Various Calibers, Sporting Rifle, Checkered Stock, Monte Carlo Stock, *Curio*	150	325	450
Gustav CG-T, Various Calibers, Singleshot, Target Stock, Heavy Barrel, *Curio*	125	250	350
Gustav Grade II, Various Calibers, Sporting Rifle, Checkered Stock, *Curio*	$175	$375	$500
Gustav Grade II, Various Calibers, Sporting Rifle, Checkered Stock, Left-Hand, *Curio*	200	400	600
Gustav Grade II, Various Calibers, Sporting Rifle, Checkered Stock, Magnum Action, *Curio*	175	375	500
Gustav Grade III, Various Calibers, Sporting Rifle, Checkered Stock, Magnum Action, Left-Hand, *Curio*	200	400	600
Gustav Grade III, Various Calibers, Sporting Rifle, Checkered Stock, Magnum Action, Light Engraving, Left-Hand, *Curio*	200	400	600
Gustav Grade III, Various Calibers, Sporting Rifle, Checkered Stock, Magnum Action, Light Engraving, *Curio*	200	450	650
Gustav Grade III, Various Calibers, Sporting Rifle, Checkered Stock, Light Engraving, *Curio*	200	450	650
Gustav Grade III, Various Calibers, Sporting Rifle, Checkered Stock, Light Engraving, Left-Hand, *Curio*	200	425	625
Gustav Grade V, Various Calibers, Sporting Rifle, Checkered Stock, Engraved, *Curio*	300	600	800
Gustav Grade V, Various Calibers, Sporting Rifle, Checkered Stock, Engraved, Left-Hand, *Curio*	275	575	800
Gustav Grade V, Various Calibers, Sporting Rifle, Checkered Stock, Engraved, Magnum Action, *Curio*	300	600	800
Gustav Grade V, Various Calibers, Sporting Rifle, Checkered Stock, Engraved, Magnum Action, Left-Hand, *Curio*	300	625	825
Gustav Swede, Various Calibers, Sporting Rifle, Checkered Stock, *Curio*	150	300	450
Gustav Swede Deluxe, Various Calibers, Sporting Rifle, Checkered Stock, Light Engraving, *Curio*	150	300	450
Gustav V-T, Various Calibers, Varmint, Target Stock, Heavy Barrel, *Curio*	200	400	525
Hi Power, Various Calibers, Sporting Rifle, Checkered Stock, *Curio*	150	300	400
P 3000 Presentation, Various Calibers, Sporting Rifle, Checkered Stock, Engraved, Fancy Wood, *Curio*	300	625	825

HUTZ, BENJAMIN

Lancaster, Pa., c. 1802. See Kentucky Rifles.

HVA

See Husqvarna.

HY HUNTER

Burbank, Calif. See also Great Western Arms Co.

HANDGUN, DOUBLE BARREL, OVER-UNDER

	Fair	V. Good	Excellent
Automatic Derringer, .22 L.R.R.F., Blue, *Modern*	$15	$25	$50

HANDGUN, REVOLVER

	Fair	V. Good	Excellent
Chicago Cub, .22 Short, 6 Shot, Folding Trigger, *Modern*	15	25	50
Detective, .22 L.R.R.F., Double Action, 6 Shot, *Modern*	25	50	75
Detective, .22 W.M.R., Double Action, 6 Shot, *Modern*	25	50	75
Frontier Six Shooter, .22 L.R.R.F., Single Action, Western Style, *Modern*	25	50	75
Frontier Six Shooter, .22 LR/.22 WRF Combo, Single Action, Western Style, *Modern*	25	50	75
Frontier Six Shooter, .357 Mag., Single Action, Western Style, *Modern*	50	125	150
Frontier Six Shooter, .44 Mag., Single Action, Western Style, *Modern*	75	150	175
Frontier Six Shooter, .45 Colt, Single Action, Western Style, *Modern*	50	125	150

HANDGUN, SELF-LOADING

	Fair	V. Good	Excellent
Maxim, .25 ACP, Clip Fed, *Modern*	25	50	75
Militar, .22 L.R.R.F., Double Action, Hammer, Clip Fed, Blue, *Modern*	25	50	100
Militar, .32 ACP, Double Action, Hammer, Clip Fed, Blue, *Modern*	50	75	100
Militar, .380 ACP, Double Action, Hammer, Clip Fed, Blue, *Modern*	50	100	125
Panzer, .22 L.R.R.F., Clip Fed, Blue, *Modern*	25	50	75
Stingray, .25 ACP, Clip Fed, Blue, *Modern*	$25	$50	$75
Stuka, .22 Long, Clip Fed, Blue, *Modern*	25	50	75

HANDGUN, SINGLESHOT

	Fair	V. Good	Excellent
Accurate Ace, .22 Short, Flobert Type, Chrome Plated, *Modern*	15	25	50
Favorite, .22 L.R.R.F., Stevens Copy, *Modern*	25	50	75
Favorite, .22 W.M.R., Stevens Copy, *Modern*	25	50	75
Gold Rush Derringer, .22 L.R.R.F., Spur Trigger, *Modern*	15	25	50
Target, .22 L.R.R.F., Bolt Action, *Modern*	15	25	50
Target, .22 W.M.R., Bolt Action, *Modern*	15	25	50

HY SCORE ARMS

Brooklyn, N.Y.

HANDGUN, REVOLVER

	Fair	V. Good	Excellent
.22 L.R.R.F., Double Action, *Modern*	15	25	50

HYPER

Jenks, Okla. Discontinued 1984.

RIFLE, SINGLESHOT

	Fair	V. Good	Excellent
Hyper-Single Rifle, Various Calibers, Fancy Wood, No Sights, Falling Block, Fancy Checkering, *Modern*	800	1750	2250
Hyper-Single Rifle, Various Calibers, Fancy Wood, No Sights, Falling Block, Fancy Checkering, Stainless Steel Barrel, *Modern*	900	2000	2500

I

I G
Grey, of Dundee, c. 1630.

HANDGUN, SNAPHAUNCE

	Fair	V. Good	Excellent
Belt Pistol, Engraved, Ovoid Pommel, All Metal, *Antique*	$9000	$20000	$27500

I P
Germany, 1580–1600.

RIFLE, WHEELOCK

	Fair	V. Good	Excellent
.60, German Style, Brass Furniture, Light Ornamentation, Horn Inlays, Set Trigger, *Antique*	1900	4000	6000

IAB SHOTGUNS
Brescia, Italy. Imported by Puccinelli Co., San Anselmo, Calif.

SHOTGUN, DOUBLE BARREL, OVER-UNDER

	Fair	V. Good	Excellent
C-300 Super Combo, 12 Ga., Vent Rib, Single Selective Trigger, Checkered Stock, with 2 Extra Single Barrels, *Modern*	1100	2250	2750
C-3000 Combo, 12 Ga., Vent Rib, Single Selective Trigger, Checkered Stock, with 2 Extra Single Barrels, *Modern*	900	1750	2000

SHOTGUN, SINGLESHOT

	Fair	V. Good	Excellent
S-300, 12 Ga., Vent Rib, Checkered Stock, Trap Grade, *Modern*	450	1000	1250

IMPERIAL ARMS
Made by Hopkins & Allen, c. 1880.

HANDGUN, REVOLVER

	Fair	V. Good	Excellent
.32 Short R.F., 5 Shot, Spur Trigger, Solid Frame, Single Action, *Antique*	50	125	150
.38 Short R.F., 5 Shot, Spur Trigger, Solid Frame, Single Action, *Antique*	75	150	175

IMPERIAL REVOLVER
c. 1880.

HANDGUN, REVOLVER

	Fair	V. Good	Excellent
.22 Short R.F., 7 Shot, Spur Trigger, Solid Frame, Single Action, *Antique*	$50	$125	$150
.32 Short R.F., 5 Shot, Spur Trigger, Solid Frame, Single Action, *Antique*	75	150	175

I.N.A.
Industria Nacional de Armas, São Paulo, Brazil.

HANDGUN, REVOLVER

	Fair	V. Good	Excellent
Tiger, .22 L.R.R.F., Single Action, Western Style, *Modern*	25	50	75
Tiger, .32 S&W Long, Single Action, Western Style, *Modern*	25	50	75

INDIA MILITARY
RIFLE, BOLT ACTION

	Fair	V. Good	Excellent
No. 1 Mk.III, S.M.L.E., .303 British, Clip Fed, Ishapore, *Curio*	75	150	175

INDIAN ARMS
Detroit, Mich., c. 1976. Discontinued.

HANDGUN, SELF-LOADING

	Fair	V. Good	Excellent
.380 ACP, Clip Fed, Stainless Steel, Vent Rib, Double Action, *Modern*	125	300	400

INDIAN SALES
Cheyenne, Wyo.

HANDGUN, REVOLVER

	Fair	V. Good	Excellent
HS-21, .22 L.R.R.F., Double Action, Blue, *Modern*	15	25	50

HANDGUN, SELF-LOADING

	Fair	V. Good	Excellent
Model 4, .25 ACP, Clip Fed, Blue, *Modern*	25	50	75

INGRAM
Invented by Gordon Ingram. Made by Police Ordnance Co., Los Angeles, Calif., and Military Armament Corp., Georgia. Discontinued 1982.

	Fair	V. Good	Excellent
SELF-LOADING WEAPON			
MAC 10, .45, ACP or 9mm, Clip Fed, Folding Stock, Open-Bolt, *Modern*	$200	$400	$600
MAC 10A1, 9mm Luger or .45 ACP, Clip Fed, Folding Stock, Closed Bolt, *Modern*	200	400	700
MAC 11, .380 ACP, Clip Fed, Folding Stock, Smaller Version of MAC 10, *Modern*	250	500	750

INGRAM, CHARLES

Glasgow, Scotland, c. 1860.

SHOTGUN, DOUBLE BARREL, SIDE-BY-SIDE			
Extra Set of Rifle Barrels, High Quality, Cased with Accessories, Engraved, Checkered Stock, *Antique*	3000	6500	7500

INHOFF, BENEDICT

Berks County, Pa., 1781–1783. See Kentucky Rifles.

INTERARMS

Alexandria, Virginia. Founded by Samuel Cummings, the company also maintains facilities in the U.K., Europe, and the Far East. On the 40th anniversary, Richard S. Winter, Executive Vice President based in Alexandria, Virginia, wrote the following history, at the same time a tribute to the company founder: "The history of Interarms is colorful. To some it engages a degree of mystique. Founded in 1953, it gained physical permanency in 1957 with the establishment of offices and warehouses along the Potomac River in historic Alexandria, Virginia. Its beginning was stimulated by the introduction of completely new marketing concepts which were reflective of market interest. Many continue to reflect on an unprecedented decade of unequaled firearm values. Incoming shipments of Mausers, Enfields, Springfields, Garands, M-1 Carbines, Colts, Lugers, Walthers, Webleys, Smith & Wessons, Lahtis and all of the variations thereof, plus hundreds of other military/civilian models were virtual treasure hunts destined to please the hunter, plinker, targeteer, collector, history buff, and, above all, those in search of sound firearms at affordable prices. This era carried with it a boom to gunsmiths, hobbyists, accessory manufacturers, plus untold numbers of others directly or indirectly associated with our traditional enjoyment of firearms. These were also prized by large, time-honored chains, such as Sears and Montgomery Ward—yes, the list also included giant cosmopolitan retailers, such as Gimbels and Macy's. An added dimension was generated in satisfying a refreshing new surge in firearm interest. During this period, a few domestic manufacturers sought to curb an imagined threat to their industry through a petition filed with the Office of Civil and Defense Mobilization. This was successfully resisted by Interarms with the stalwart support of a few high brigades of firearms dealers. Ultimately, domestic manufacturers were also beneficiaries as manifested by the upswing in firearm sales during the years thereafter. Many who had purchased those reliable military obsoletes decided to trade upward for commercial counterparts with a bit more sophistication and cosmetic allure. Millions of military surplus bargains introduced thousands of shooters into the world of firearms due to an irresistible introductory investment. Some of these fine relics can still be found on dealer shelves or at gun shows at prices which have multiplied. Starting with Walther and Mauser, we moved our attention to Star, Astra, Rossi, Zastava, Howa, Norinco, and many others. This signaled a corporate reorganization, which emphasized a restructuring of our Marketing Division. It called for an upgraded commercial approach, including the organizing of professional salesmen to make our products known to essentially every major distributor. This was concurrent with keeping in close contact with as many dealers as possible and upon whom we are dependent. Our specialized national sales organization is today second to none. Sales of new commercial products soon caught and surpassed previous sales revenue. Thanks to dealer and consumer responsiveness, this upward curve has continued without interruption." Soon after the death of Cummings in 1998, Interarms was sold to Karl Walther GmbH.

INTERCHANGEABLE

Belgium, Tradename Schoverlin-Daley & Gales, c. 1880.

	Fair	V. Good	Excellent
SHOTGUN, DOUBLE BARREL, SIDE-BY-SIDE			
Various Gauges, Outside Hammers, Damascus Barrel, *Curio*	$100	$200	$350

INTERDYNAMIC

Miami, Fla., c. 1979. Sold by F.I.E.

HANDGUN, SELF-LOADING			
KG-99, 9mm Luger, Clip Fed, SMG Styling, *Modern*	225	475	600

INTERNATIONAL

Made by Hood Firearms, c. 1875.

HANDGUN, REVOLVER			
.22 Short R.F., 7 Shot, Spur Trigger, Solid Frame, Single Action, *Antique*	75	125	175
.32 Short R.F., 5 Shot, Spur Trigger, Solid Frame, Single Action, *Antique*	75	125	175

INTERNATIONAL DISTRIBUTORS

Miami, Fla.

RIFLE, BOLT ACTION			
Mauser Type, Various Calibers, Checkered Stock, Sling Swivels, Recoil Pad, *Modern*	75	150	250

INTERSTATE ARMS CO.

Made by Crescent for Townley Metal & Hdw., Kansas City, Mo. See Crescent Fire Arms Co., Shotgun, Double Barrel, Side-by-Side; Shotgun, Singleshot.

ISRAELI MILITARY

This list includes both military arms and the commercial arms made by Israeli Military Industries (I.M.I.). Also see Magnum Research, Inc. (M.R.I.).

HANDGUN, REVOLVER

	Fair	V. Good	Excellent
S & W Model 10 Copy, 9mm Luger, Solid Frame, Swing-Out Cylinder, Double Action, Military, *Modern*	$250	$500	$625

RIFLE, SELF-LOADING

	Fair	V. Good	Excellent
Galil, .223 Rem., Clip Fed, Assault Rifle, Folding Stock, *Modern*	400	800	1000
Galil, .308 Win., Clip Fed, Assault Rifle, Folding Stock, *Modern*	425	900	1100
UZI, 9mm Luger, Clip Fed, Folding Stock, Commercial, *Modern*	400	850	1090

ITALGUNS INTERNATIONAL

Cusago, Italy.

HANDGUN, REVOLVER

	Fair	V. Good	Excellent
Western Style, Various Calibers, Single Action, *Modern*	50	125	175
Western Style, Various Calibers, Single Action, Automatic Hammer Safety, *Modern*	50	125	175

COMBINATION WEAPON, OVER-UNDER

	Fair	V. Good	Excellent
Various Calibers, Checkered Stock, Double Triggers, *Modern*	100	275	350

SHOTGUN, DOUBLE BARREL, OVER-UNDER

	Fair	V. Good	Excellent
Model 125, 12 Gauge, Checkered Stock, Vent Rib, Double Triggers, *Modern*	100	200	275
Model 150, 12 or 20 Gauges, Checkered Stock, Vent Rib, Single Trigger, *Modern*	100	225	300

ITALIAN MILITARY

Also See Beretta. Anyone who has visited Val Trompia, about a 90-minute drive northeast of Milan, comes away with a realization that Italian gunmakers are capable of designs and manufacture in the firearms genre rivaling, or surpassing, the work of any gunmakers anywhere in the world. The Beretta Museum, in Gardone, best exemplifies these exemplary craftsmen and mechanics. The collection of military arms on display there is of particular interest because it not only demonstrates Italian proficiency, but exhibits substantial numbers of military arms made in other nations, including the United States. The adoption by U.S. armed forces of the Beretta M9 self-loading 9mm pistols is proof in itself of the extraordinary capability of Italian gunmakers in the military small arms arena.

HANDGUN, REVOLVER

	Fair	V. Good	Excellent
Service Revolver, 10.4mm, Double Action, 6 Shot, Folding Trigger, *Curio*	$50	$100	$250

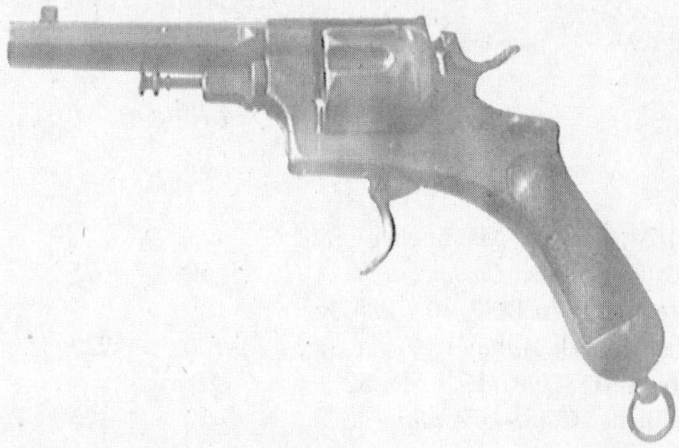

Italian Military Service Revolver Folding Trigger

	Fair	V. Good	Excellent
Service Revolver, 10.4mm, Double Action, 6 Shot, Trigger Guard, *Curio*	50	100	125

HANDGUN, SELF-LOADING

	Fair	V. Good	Excellent
Brixia, 9mm Glisenti, Clip Fed, *Curio*	150	375	600
M1910 Glisenti Army, 9mm, Clip Fed, *Curio*	150	400	650

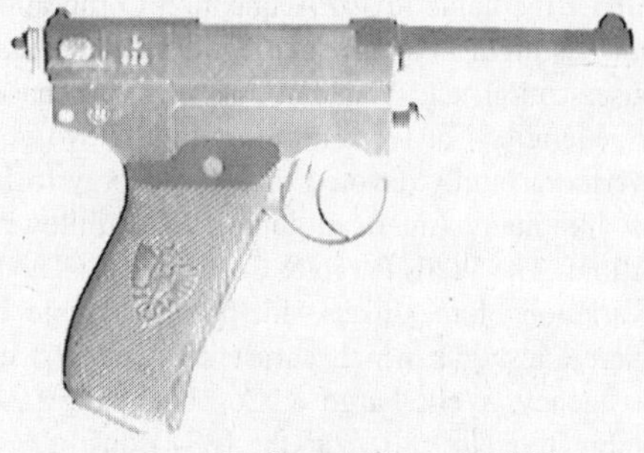

Italian Military M910

	Fair	V. Good	Excellent
M1934 Beretta, .380 ACP, Clip Fed, *Curio*	150	275	375

RIFLE, BOLT ACTION

	Fair	V. Good	Excellent
M1891, 6.5 × 52 Mannlicher-Carcano, *Curio*	50	75	100
M38, 7.35mm, Terni, Military, *Curio*	50	75	100
M91 T.S., 6.5 × 52 Mannlicher-Carcano, Carbine, Folding Bayonet, *Curio*	50	75	100
M91 T.S. (Late), 6.5 × 52 Mannlicher-Carcano, Carbine, Folding Bayonet, *Curio*	50	75	100

	Fair	V. Good	Excellent
M91/24, 6.5 × 52 Mannlicher-Carcano, *Curio*	$50	$75	$100

Italian Military M91/24 Rifle

M91/24, 6.5 × 52 Mannlicher-Carcano, Carbine, *Curio*	50	75	125
Vetterli M1870/1887, 10.4 × 47R Italian Vetterli, *Antique*	100	225	375
Vetterli M1870/87/15, 6.5 × 52 Mannlicher-Carcano, *Antique*	50	125	175

ITHACA GUN CO.

Ithaca, N.Y., 1883–1986. Absorbed Lefever Arms Co., Syracuse Arms Co., Union Firearms Co., and Wilkes Barre Gun Co. Also see the commemorative section. The founders of Ithaca were William H. Baker, John VanNatta, Dwight McIntyre, and Leroy Smith, latter and associate George Livermore becoming sole owners and operators by 1894. Smith and Baker, a prolific gun designer, both took out patents for shotgun designs, and the growing concern, along a raceway from Fall Creek, had additions to the initial structure in 1890, 1904, and 1917. It is ironic that although Ithaca's Cornell University is a world-renowned educational institution, the city is often better known as the site of the Ithaca Gun Co. In 1986 Ithaca closed for a short period, reopening early in 1987, under the name Ithaca Acquisition Corporation. In Ithaca's long and distinguished past, gun companies the likes of Lefever, Syracuse, Union, and Wilkes-Barre were purchased or absorbed. Four generations of the Smith family and two generations of the Livermore family devoted time and energy to Ithaca Gun, which has, like many American gunmakers, a following of near cult proportions. The Wells Fargo & Co. Shotguns: The Flues Model was a variation of the Ithaca side-by-side double barrel hammer and hammerless gun which attracted the interest of the historic express agency, Wells Fargo & Co., beginning c. 1909. The company's directive No. 280, from the 1884 Book of Instructions, stated: "Guards and Messengers will be furnished with suitable firearms, if needed, by requisition on the Stationery and Supply Department, San Francisco." Directive No. 1056, from the 1902 Book of Instructions, further stated: "Messengers on all important routes are required to travel armed for defense, in case of attack." Ithaca's Flues Model joined the line in 1908, the year the first ten were built by employee Emil Flues. As detailed in company catalogues, the gun boasted a new three-piece lock, developed by Flues, "the noted inventor." Wells Fargo & Co. had its own arsenal, for issue to its agents and messengers, in dealing with the threat of hold-up men. Revolvers were usually by Colt or Smith & Wesson, rifles by Winchester, and shotguns by such makers as L. C. Smith, Remington, and Ithaca. From 1907 to 1917, approximately 749 shotguns were sold to Wells Fargo & Co. by the Ithaca Gun Co. From 1908 through 1925, approximately 223,000 shotguns of the Flues model were built (4,700 of them single barrel trap guns.) Among shooters of these guns, the two most famous were Annie Oakley and John Philip Sousa, whose "Stars and Stripes Forever" is a time-honored favorite of marching bands. Wells Fargo & Co. Markings: On lock plate and frame water table: W.F. & Co. EX., accompanied by property number. On barrel rib: Wells Fargo & Co. followed by property number. Ithaca records do not record all of the Wells Fargo & Co. numbers. Most of those numbers known are in the mid and late 400, late 500 and early 600 range. Variations: Grade X Hammer Models, frames heavily constructed, all barrels of A quality, guns in configuration of: 12 gauge, 26" fluid steel barrels; 10 gauge, 24" twisted steel barrels; 12 gauge, 24" fluid steel barrels. Dates of Orders: Between February of 1909 and 1917: steel barrels; 1911 through 1917, serial ranges 211000, 219000, 223000, 228000, 230000, 233000, 241000, 251000, 253000, 255000, 256000, 262000, 263000, 265000, 275000, 279000, 281000, 282000, 12 gauge, 24" fluid steel barrels. On cessation of express operations in 1918, the records of the Wells Fargo & Co. Express went to American Railway Express Co., later the Railway Express Agency. These records have been of virtually no assistance to collectors over the years. Because of imaginative faking not a few bogus markings of Wells Fargo & Co. stamps have been placed on guns never property of the firm. The exercise of caution is important to any enthusiast keen on possessing a genuine Wells Fargo shotgun. Thus, the records of the Ithaca Gun Co. are of immeasurable value in assessing express guns of their manufacture. The company's deluxe shotgun production revived with the introduction of the finely made side-by-side shotgun in 1998; contact Ithaca Classic Doubles, The Old Station, No. 5 Railroad Street, Victor, NY 14564.

	Fair	V. Good	Excellent
RIFLE, BOLT ACTION			
LSA 55, Various Calibers, Monte Carlo Stock, Cheekpiece, Heavy Barrel, *Modern*	$150	$350	$450
LSA 55, Various Calibers, Monte Carlo Stock, Open Rear Sight, *Modern*	150	325	400
LSA 55 Deluxe, Various Calibers, Monte Carlo Stock, Cheekpiece, No Sights, Scope Mounts, *Modern*	150	350	450
LSA 65 Deluxe, Various Calibers, Monte Carlo Stock, Cheekpiece, No Sights, Scope Mounts, *Modern*	150	325	425
LSA 65, Various Calibers, Monte Carlo Stock, Open Rear Sight, *Modern*	150	300	400
RIFLE, LEVER ACTION			
Model 49, .22 L.R.R.F., Singleshot, *Modern*	50	75	100
Model 49, .22 WMR, Singleshot, *Modern*	50	75	100
Model 49 Deluxe, .22 L.R.R.F., Singleshot, Fancy Wood, *Modern*	75	100	125
Model 49 Presentation, .22 L.R.R.F., Singleshot, Engraved, Fancy Checkering, *Modern*	75	125	150
Model 49 R, .22 L.R.R.F., Tube Feed, *Modern*	50	75	100
Model 49 St. Louis, .22 L.R.R.F., Bicentennial, Fancy Wood, Singleshot, *Curio*	35	75	150

	Fair	V. Good	Excellent
Model 49 Youth, .22 L.R.R.F., Singleshot, *Modern*	$25	$50	$75
Model 72, .22 L.R.R.F., Tube Feed, *Modern*	50	100	125
Model 72, .22 WMR, Tube Feed, *Modern*	75	125	150
Model 72 Deluxe, .22 L.R.R.F., Tube Feed, Octagon Barrel, *Modern*	75	125	175

COMBINATION WEAPON, OVER-UNDER

	Fair	V. Good	Excellent
LSA 55 Turkey Gun, 12 Ga./.222, Open Rear Sight, Monte Carlo Stock, *Modern*	250	500	625

RIFLE, SELF-LOADING

	Fair	V. Good	Excellent
X-15 Lightning, .22 L.R.R.F., Clip Fed, *Modern*	50	100	150
X5-C Light Lightning, .22 L.R.R.F., Clip Fed, *Modern*	50	75	100
X5-T Lightning, .22 L.R.R.F., Tube Feed, *Modern*	50	75	100

SHOTGUN, DOUBLE BARREL, OVER-UNDER

	Fair	V. Good	Excellent
Model 500, 12 and 20 Gauges, Field Grade, Selective Ejector, Vent Rib, *Modern*	150	350	450
Model 500, 12 Ga. Mag. 3", Field Grade, Selective Ejector, Vent Rib, *Modern*	150	375	475
Model 600 Combo Set, Various Gauges, Skeet Grade, Selective Ejector, Vent Rib, Cased, *Modern*	300	600	850
Model 600, 12 and 20 Gauges, Field Grade, Selective Ejector, Vent Rib, *Modern*	200	400	500
Model 600, 12 and 20 Gauges, Skeet Grade, Selective Ejector, Vent Rib, *Modern*	200	475	600
Model 600, 12 Ga., Trap Grade, Selective Ejector, Vent Rib, *Modern*	200	400	550
Model 600, 12 Ga., Trap Grade, Selective Ejector, Vent Rib, Monte Carlo Stock, *Modern*	200	400	550
Model 600, 28 and.410 Gauges, Skeet Grade, Selective Ejector, Vent Rib, *Modern*	250	575	750
Model 680 English, 12 and 20 Gauges, Field Grade, Selective Ejector, Vent Rib, Modern	225	450	600
Model 700 Combo Set, Various Gauges, Skeet Grade, Selective Ejector, Vent Rib, Cased, *Modern*	400	900	1300
Model 700, 12 and 20 Gauges, Skeet Grade, Selective Ejector, Vent Rib, *Modern*	300	600	800
Model 700, 12 Ga., Trap Grade, Selective Ejector, Vent Rib, *Modern*	300	600	800
Model 700, 12 Ga., Trap Grade, Selective Ejector, Vent Rib, Monte Carlo Stock, *Modern*	$300	$600	$900
Parazzi MT-6, 12 Ga., Skeet Grade, Automatic Ejector, Vent Rib, Cased, *Modern*	1500	3250	4000
Parazzi MT-6, 12 Ga., Trap Grade, Automatic Ejector, Vent Rib, Cased, *Modern*	1500	3000	3750
Perazzi Competition 1, 12 Ga., Skeet Grade, Automatic Ejector, Vent Rib, Single Trigger, Cased, *Modern*	1500	3000	3750
Perazzi Competition 1, 12 Ga., Trap Grade, Automatic Ejector, Vent Rib, Single Trigger, Cased, *Modern*	800	1750	2350
Perazzi Light Game Model, 12 Ga., Automatic Ejector, Vent Rib, Single Trigger, *Modern*	800	1600	2200
Perazzi Mirage Special 4-Barrel Set, Various Gauges, Skeet Grade, Automatic Ejector, Vent Rib, Cased, *Modern*	4000	8000	12500
Perazzi Mirage Special, 12 Ga., Trap Grade, Automatic Ejector, Vent Rib, Cased, *Modern*	2000	4500	7500
Perazzi MX-7 Combo, 12 Ga., Trap Grade, Automatic Ejector, Vent Rib, Cased, *Modern*	2000	4000	7000

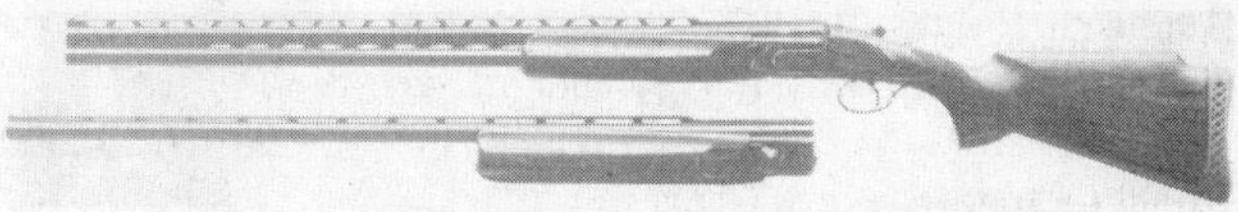

Ithaca Perazzi Combination

SHOTGUN, DOUBLE BARREL, SIDE-BY-SIDE

Early Model, Serial Numbers under 425,000, Deduct 50%

Outside Hammers, Deduct Another 20%-30%

	Fair	V. Good	Excellent
#2 Grade, 10 Ga. Magnum, Hammerless, Beavertail Forend, Double Trigger, *Modern*	700	1500	2200
#2 Grade, 12 Ga., Hammerless, Beavertail Forend, Double Trigger, Checkered Stock, *Modern*	500	1050	1350
#3 Grade, 10 Ga. Magnum, Hammerless, Beavertail Forend, Double Trigger, *Modern*	900	2000	2750
#3 Grade, 12 Ga., Hammerless, Double Trigger, Engraved, Checkered Stock, *Modern*	600	1125	1450
#3 Grade, 16 Ga., Hammerless, Beavertail Forend, Engraved, Checkered Stock, Double Trigger, *Modern*	500	1050	1350
#3 Grade, 20 Ga., Hammerless, Double Trigger, Engraved, Checkered Stock, *Modern*	700	1500	1850

	Fair	V. Good	Excellent
#4 E Grade, 12 Ga., Hammerless, Automatic Ejector, Vent Rib, Beavertail Forend, *Modern*	$1200	$2750	$3350
#4 E Grade, 16 Ga., Hammerless, Automatic Ejector, Vent Rib, Fancy Checkering, Engraving, *Modern*	1500	3250	4000
#4 E Grade, 20 Ga., Hammerless, Automatic Ejector, Beavertail Forend, Fancy Checkering, Engraving, *Modern*	1600	3500	4250
#5 E Grade, 10 Ga. Mag., Hammerless, Automatic Ejector, Vent Rib, Beavertail Forend, *Modern*	1200	3000	4250
#5 E Grade, 12 Ga., Hammerless, Automatic Ejector, Vent Rib, Fancy Checkering, Engraving, *Modern*	1400	3250	4000
#5 E Grade, 16 Ga., Hammerless, Automatic Ejector, Beavertail Forend, Fancy Checkering, Fancy Engraving, *Modern*	1500	3250	4000
#5 E Grade, 20 Ga., Hammerless, Automatic Ejector, Fancy Checkering, Fancy Engraving, Double Trigger, *Modern*	1500	4000	4750
#7 E Grade, Various Gauges, Hammerless, Automatic Ejector, Vent Rib, Beavertail Forend, *Modern*	2000	5000	7000
$1000 Grade, 12 Ga., Hammerless, Automatic Ejector, Single Selective Trigger, Vent Rib, Beavertail Forend, *Curio*	4000	9000	12500
$1000 Grade, 16 and 20 Gauges, Hammerless, *Curio*	4000	10000	13500
$2000 Grade, 12 Ga., Hammerless, Automatic Ejector, Single Selective Trigger, Ornate, *Modern*	3500	8500	12500
$2000 Grade, 16 Ga., Hammerless, Automatic Ejector, Single Selective Trigger, Vent Rib, Ornate, *Modern*	4000	11000	15000
$2000 Grade, 20 Ga., Hammerless, Automatic Ejector, Single Selective Trigger, Beavertail Forend, Ornate, *Modern*	5000	12000	17500
Field Grade, Hammerless, 10 Ga. Magnum, Beavertail Forend, *Modern*	700	1750	2250
Field Grade, Hammerless, 10 Ga. Magnum, Double Trigger, *Modern*	600	1500	2000
Field Grade, Various Gauges, Hammerless, Beavertail Forend, Double Trigger, *Modern*	300	700	1150
Field Grade, Various Gauges, Hammerless, Double Trigger, Checkered Stock, *Modern*	250	550	800

20 ga. add 25%
28 ga. add 40%
410 ga. add 50%

SHOTGUN, LEVER ACTION

	Fair	V. Good	Excellent
Model 66, Various Gauges, Singleshot, *Modern*	$50	$75	$100
Model 66, Various Gauges, Singleshot, Ventilated Rib, *Modern*	75	100	125
Model 66 Youth, Various Gauges, Singleshot, *Modern*	25	50	75

SHOTGUN, PISTOL

	Fair	V. Good	Excellent
Auto Burglar, Various Gauges, Double Barrel, Side by Side, Short Shotgun, *Curio*	300	650	900

SHOTGUN, SELF-LOADING

	Fair	V. Good	Excellent
5KB 300 Standard, 12 and 20 Gauges, *Modern*	100	200	300
5KB 300 Standard, 12 and 20 Gauges, Vent Rib, *Modern*	100	225	325
5KB 300 XL Standard, 12 and 20 Gauges, *Modern*	125	275	325
5KB 300 XL Standard, 12 and 20 Gauges, Vent Rib, *Modern*	150	300	400
5KB 900 XL Deluxe, 12 and 20 Gauges, Vent Rib, *Modern*	125	275	375
5KB 900 XL MR Deluxe, 12 and 20 Gauges, Vent Rib, *Modern*	125	275	375
5KB 900 XL Slug, 12 and 20 Gauges, Open Rear Sight, *Modern*	125	275	375
5KB 900 XL, 12 and 20 Gauges, Skeet Grade, *Modern*	150	325	425
5KB 900 XL, 12 Ga., Trap Grade, *Modern*	150	325	425
5KB 900 XL, 12 Ga., Trap Grade, Monte Carlo Stock, *Modern*	150	350	450
Mag 10 Deluxe, 10 Ga. 3½", Takedown, Vent Rib, Fancy Wood, Checkered Stock, *Modern*	250	500	850
Mag 10 Standard, 10 Ga. 3½", Takedown, Recoil Pad, Checkered Stock, Sling Swivels, *Modern*	225	475	800
Mag 10 Standard, 10 Ga. 3½", Takedown, Vent Rib, Recoil Pad, Checkered Stock, Sling Swivels, *Modern*	300	600	900
Mag 10 Supreme, 10 Ga. 3½", Takedown, Vent Rib, Fancy Wood, Engraved, Checkered Stock, *Modern*	300	600	950
Model 51 Presentation, 12 and 20 Gauges, Skeet Grade, Takedown, Checkered Stock, Fancy Wood, Recoil Pad, *Modern*	325	750	1000
Model 51 Standard, 12 and 20 Gauges, Takedown, Checkered Stock, *Modern*	125	225	325
Model 51 Standard, 12 and 20 Gauges, Takedown, Vent Rib, Checkered Stock, *Modern*	150	300	425

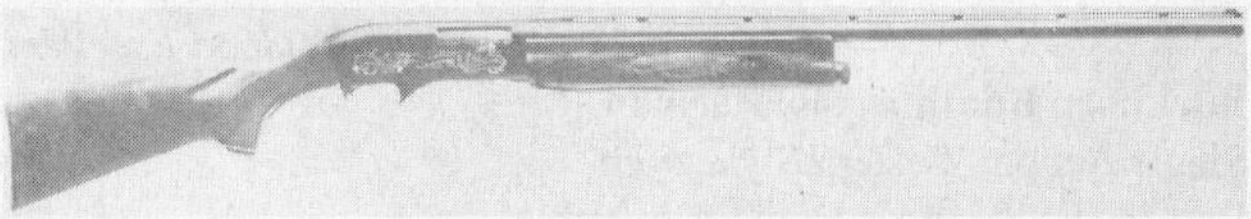

Ithaca Model 51

	Fair	V. Good	Excellent
Model 51 Turkey Gun, 12 Ga., Trap Grade, Takedown, Checkered Stock, Fancy Wood, Recoil Pad, *Modern*	$150	$300	$500
Model 51A Deerslayer, 12 Ga., Takedown, Open Rear Sight, Sling Swivels, *Modern*	125	275	375
Model 51A Waterfowler, 12 Ga., Trap Grade, Monte Carlo Stock, Fancy Wood, Recoil Pad, *Modern*	150	325	425
Model 51A, Magnum 12 Ga., Takedown, Vent Rib, Recoil Pad, *Modern*	150	325	425

SHOTGUN, SINGLESHOT

	Fair	V. Good	Excellent
$5000 Grade, 12 Ga., Trap Grade, Automatic Ejector, Ornate, *Modern*	3000	7500	9500
4 E Grade, 12 Ga., Trap Grade, Automatic Ejector, Engraved, Fancy Checkering, *Modern*	450	1000	1400
5 E Grade, 12 Ga., Trap Grade, Automatic Ejector, Fancy Engraving, Fancy Checkering, *Modern*	900	2000	2700
7 E Grade, 12 Ga., Trap Grade, Automatic Ejector, Fancy Engraving, Fancy Checkering, *Modern*	1700	4000	6000
Century 12 Ga., Trap Grade, Automatic Ejector, Engraved, Checkered Stock, *Modern*	200	425	575
Century II, 12 Ga., Trap Grade, Automatic Ejector, Engraved, Checkered Stock, *Modern*	225	475	575
Perazzi Competition, 12 Ga., Trap Grade, Automatic Ejector, Vent Rib, Cased, *Modern*	400	950	1450
Victory Grade, 12 Ga., Automatic Ejector, Checkered Stock, Vent Rib, Trap Grade, *Modern*	300	600	900

SHOTGUN, SLIDE ACTION

Model 37, Extra Vent Rib Barrel, Add $60.00-$85.00

Model 37, for Extra Barrel, Add $50.00-$75.00

	Fair	V. Good	Excellent
Model 37 Deerslayer, Various Gauges, Takedown, Checkered Stock, Recoil Pad, Open Rear Sight, *Modern*	125	275	375
Model 37 Deerslayer, Various Gauges, Takedown, Fancy Wood, Checkered Stock, Recoil Pad, Open Rear Sight, *Modern*	125	250	350
Model 37 DSPS, 12 Ga., Takedown, Checkered Stock, 5 Shot, Open Rear Sight, *Modern*	$100	$200	$300
Model 37 DSPS, 12 Ga., Takedown, Checkered Stock, 8 Shot, Open Rear Sight, *Modern*	100	225	325
Model 37 English Ultralite, 12 or 20 Gauge, Takedown, Checkered Stock, Recoil Pad, *Modern*	125	250	350
Model 37 Field Grade, Various Gauges, Takedown, Plain, *Modern*	75	150	350
Model 37 Presentation, Various Gauges, Takedown, Skeet Grade, Fancy Wood, Checkered Stock, *Modern*	450	1000	1400
Model 37 Riotgun, 12 Ga., Takedown, Parkerized, 5 Shot, *Modern*	150	225	325
Model 37 Standard, Various Gauges, Takedown, Checkered Stock, *Modern*	100	200	300
Model 37 Trenchgun, 12 Ga., Takedown, Parkerized, 5 Shot, *Modern*	150	300	400
Model 37, 12 Ga., Takedown, Bicentennial, Engraved, Fancy Wood, Checkered Stock, *Modern*	150	325	425
Model 37-$1000 Grade, Various Gauges, Takedown, Fancy Wood, Fancy Checkering, Fancy Engraving, Gold Inlays, *Modern*	1700	4000	6000
Model 37-$5000 Grade, Various Gauges, Takedown, Fancy Wood, Fancy Checkering, Fancy Engraving, Gold Inlays, *Modern*	1500	3500	6000
Model 37-D, Various Gauges, Takedown, Checkered Stock, Beavertail Forend, *Modern*	100	225	325
Model 37-DV, Various Gauges, Takedown, Checkered Stock, Recoil Pad, *Modern*	100	225	325
Model 37-R Deluxe, Various Gauges, Takedown, Solid Rib, Fancy Wood, Checkered Stock, *Modern*	100	225	325
Model 37-R, Various Gauges, Takedown, Solid Rib, Checkered Stock, *Modern*	100	200	300
Model 37-R, Various Gauges, Takedown, Solid Rib, Plain, *Modern*	75	150	250
Model 37-S, Various Gauges, Takedown, Skeet Grade, Checkered Stock, Fancy Wood, *Modern*	150	325	425
Model 37-T, Various Gauges, Takedown, Trap Grade, Checkered Stock, Fancy Wood, *Modern*	150	325	425
Model 37-V Standard, Various Gauges, Takedown, Checkered Stock, Vent Rib, *Modern*	100	225	325
Model 37T Target, Various Gauges, Takedown, Trap Grade, Fancy Wood, Checkered Stock, *Modern*	150	350	450

IVER JOHNSON

Started as Johnson & Bye, 1871, in Worcester, Mass. In 1883 became Iver Johnson's Arms & Cycle Works. 1891–1982 at Fitchburg, Mass., relocated to Jacksonville, Ark. in 1982. Acquired by American Military Arms in 1987. All operations ceased in 1993. The following trade names also marked on selected handguns by this firm, q.v.: Automatic Hammerless, Boston Bulldog, Defender, Eagle. Although not one of the major gunmakers in terms of reputation, beauty or rarity, Iver Johnson produced a vast quantity of firearms, for a broad-based clientele, at reasonable prices. The latter years of Iver Johnson were under the ownership and direction of Louis Imperata, prominent New York arms dealer and gunmaker. Owners of John Jovino, Inc., Louis Imperata, later joined by his son Anthony, have been a major force in U.S. gunmaking. For years Jovino was the leading Colt jobber, and for much of the 1970s the Imperatas were involved, through Iver Johnson, in the production of Colt Blackpowder revolvers, the parts having been supplied from Gardone, Val Trompia, Italy, primarily by the Uberti Co. and Armi San Marco. Though no longer operating as Iver Johnson, the Imperatas are the licensed manufacturers of the Colt Blackpowder production of the 1990s.

HANDGUN, PERCUSSION

	Fair	*V. Good*	*Excellent*
.36 1861 Navy, Revolver, Reproduction, *Antique*	$25	$50	$75
.36 New Model Navy, Revolver, Reproduction, *Antique*	25	50	75
.36 Pocket Model, Revolver, Reproduction, *Antique*	25	50	75
.36 Remington Army, Revolver, Reproduction, *Antique*	25	50	75
.44 1860 Army, Revolver, Reproduction, *Antique*	25	50	75
.44 Confederate Army, Revolver, Reproduction, *Antique*	25	50	75
.44 Remington Army, Revolver, Reproduction, *Antique*	50	75	100
.44 Remington Target, Revolver, Reproduction, *Antique*	50	75	100
Prince, .30, Singleshot, Spur Trigger, Various Barrel Lengths, Screw Barrel, *Antique*	150	300	400
Uncle Sam 1871, .30, Singleshot, Spur Trigger, Various Barrel Lengths, *Antique*	125	250	350

HANDGUN, REVOLVER

	Fair	*V. Good*	*Excellent*
.22 Supershot, .22 L.R.R.F., 7 Shot, Blue, Wood Grips, Top Break, Double Action, *Modern*	50	75	100
Armsworth M855, .22 L.R.R.F., 8 Shot, Single Action, Top Break, Adjustable Sights, Wood Grips, *Modern*	50	100	150
Buckhorn Buntline, .357 Magnum, Single Action, Western Style, with Detachable Shoulder Stock, Adjustable Sights, 18" Barrel, *Modern*	125	275	375
Buckhorn Buntline, .44 Magnum, Single Action, Western Style, with Detachable Shoulder Stock, Adjustable Sights, 18" Barrel, *Modern*	$150	$300	$400
Buckhorn Buntline, .45 Colt, Single Action, Western Style, with Detachable Shoulder Stock, Adjustable Sights, 18" Barrel, *Modern*	150	275	375
Buckhorn, .357 Magnum, Single Action, Western Style, Color Case Hardened Frame, Adjustable Sights, 12" Barrel, *Modern*	100	175	375
Buckhorn, .357 Magnum, Single Action, Western Style, Color Case Hardened Frame, Adjustable Sights, Various Barrel Lengths, *Modern*	75	125	325
Buckhorn, .44 Magnum, Single Action, Western Style, Color Case Hardened Frame, Adjustable Sights, Various Barrel Lengths, *Modern*	100	175	375
Buckhorn, .45 Colt, Single Action, Western Style, Color Case Hardened Frame, Adjustable Sights, Various Barrel Lengths, *Modern*	75	150	350
Buckhorn, .45 Colt, Single Action, Western Style, Color Case Hardened Frame, Adjustable Sights, 12" Barrel, *Modern*	100	175	275
Cadet, .22 WMR, 8 Shot, Solid Frame, Double Action, Plastic Stock, Blue, *Modern*	25	50	75
Cadet, .32 S & W Long, 5 Shot, Solid Frame, Double Action, Plastic Stock, Nickel Plated, *Modern*	25	50	75
Cadet, .32 S & W, 5 Shot, Solid Frame, Double Action, Plastic Stock, Blue, *Modern*	25	50	75
Cadet, .38 Special, 5 Shot, Solid Frame, Double Action, Plastic Stock, Blue, *Modern*	25	50	75
Cadet, .38 Special, 5 Shot, Solid Frame, Double Action, Plastic Stock, Nickel Plated, *Modern*	25	50	75
Cattleman, .357 Magnum, Single Action, Western Style, Color Case Hardened Frame, Various Barrel Lengths, *Modern*	100	150	250
Cattleman, .447 Magnum, Single Action, Western Style, Color Case Hardened Frame, Various Barrel Lengths, *Modern*	100	175	275
Cattleman, .45 Colt, Single Action, Western Style, Color Case Hardened Frame, Various Barrel Lengths, *Modern*	75	125	225
Champion Target, .22 L.R.R.F., 8 Shot, Single Action, Top Break, Adjustable Sights, Wood Grips, *Modern*	50	100	200

	Fair	V. Good	Excellent
Model 1900 Target, .22 L.R.R.F., 7 Shot, Blue, Wood Grips, Solid Frame, Double Action, *Modern*	$65	$125	$250
Model 1900, .22 L.R.R.F., 7 Shot, Blue, Double Action, Solid Frame, *Modern*	50	75	125
Model 1900, .22 L.R.R.F., 7 Shot, Nickel Plated, Double Action, Solid Frame, *Modern*	50	75	125
Model 1900, .32 S & W Long, 6 Shot, Blue, Double Action, Solid Frame, *Modern*	50	75	125
Model 1900, .32 S & W Long, 6 Shot, Nickel Plated, Double Action, Solid Frame, *Modern*	50	75	125
Model 1900, .32 Short R.F., 6 Shot, Blue, Double Action, Solid Frame, *Modern*	50	75	125
Model 1900, .32 Short R.F., 6 Shot, Nickel Plated, Double Action, Solid Frame, *Modern*	50	100	175
Model 1900, .38 S & W, 5 Shot, Blue, Double Action, Solid Frame, *Modern*	50	100	175
Model 1900, .38 S & W, 5 Shot, Nickel Plated, Double Action, Solid Frame, *Modern*	50	100	175
Model 50A Sidewinder, .22 L.R.R.F., 8 Shot, Solid Frame, Double Action, Plastic Stock, Western Style, *Modern*	25	50	75
Model 50A Sidewinder, .22 L.R.R.F., 8 Shot, Solid Frame, Double Action, Wood Grips, Western Style, *Modern*	25	50	75
Model 55, .22 L.R.R.F., 8 Shot, Solid Frame, Double Action, Wood Grips, Blue, *Modern*	25	50	75
Model 55-S Cadet, .32 S & W, 5 Shot, Solid Frame, Double Action, Plastic Stock, Blue, *Modern*	25	50	75
Model 55-S Cadet, .38 S & W, 5 Shot, Solid Frame, Double Action, Plastic Stock, Blue, *Modern*	25	50	75
Model 55-SA Cadet, .22 L.R.R.F., 8 Shot, Solid Frame, Double Action, Plastic, Blue, *Modern*	25	50	75
Model 55-SA Cadet, .32 S & W, 5 Shot, Solid Frame, Double Action, Plastic Stock, Blue, *Modern*	25	50	75
Model 55-SA Cadet, .38 S & W, 5 Shot, Solid Frame, Double Action, Plastic Stock, Blue, *Modern*	25	50	75
Model 55A, .22 L.R.R.F., 8 Shot, Solid Frame, Double Action, Wood Grips, Blue, *Modern*	50	75	100
Model 55A, .22 L.R.R.F., 8 Shot, Solid Frame, Double Action, Wood Grips, Blue, *Modern*	50	75	100
Model 55A, .22 L.R.R.F., 8 Shot, Solid Frame, Double Action, Plastic Stock, Blue, *Modern*	$50	$75	$100
Model 55S, .22 L.R.R.F., 8 Shot, Solid Frame, Double Action, Plastic Stock, Blue, *Modern*	25	50	75
Model 57 Target, .22 L.R.R.F., 8 Shot, Solid Frame, Double Action, Plastic Stock, Adjustable Sights, *Modern*	50	75	100
Model 57 Target, .22 L.R.R.F., 8 Shot, Solid Frame, Double Action, Wood Grips, Adjustable Sights, *Modern*	50	75	100
Model 57-A Target, .22 L.R.R.F., 8 Shot, Solid Frame, Double Action, Plastic Stock, Adjustable Sights, *Modern*	50	75	100
Model 57-A Target, .22 L.R.R.F., 8 Shot, Solid Frame, Double Action, Wood Grips, Adjustable Sights, *Modern*	50	75	100
Model 66 Trailsman, .22 L.R.R.F., 8 Shot, Top Break, Double Action, Wood Grips, Adjustable Sights, *Modern*	50	75	100
Model 67 Viking, .22 L.R.R.F., 8 Shot, Top Break, Double Action, Plastic Stock, Adjustable Sights, *Modern*	50	75	100
Model 67S Viking, .32 S & W, 5 Shot, Top Break, Double Action, Plastic Stock, Adjustable Sights, *Modern*	50	75	100
Model 67S Viking, .38 S & W, 5 Shot, Top Break, Double Action, Plastic Stock, Adjustable Sights, *Modern*	25	50	75

Iver Johnson Trailsman

	Fair	V. Good	Excellent
Model 76S Viking, .22 L.R.R.F., 8 Shot, Top Break, Double Action, Plastic Stock, Adjustable Sights, *Modern*	50	75	100
Petite, .22 Short Nickel Plated, Folding Trigger, 5 Shot, "Baby" Style, *Antique*	100	200	250

	Fair	V. Good	Excellent
Safety, .22 L.R.R.F., 7 Shot, Top Break, Double Action, Hammer, Blue, *Modern*	$50	$100	$175
Safety, .22 L.R.R.F., 7 Shot, Top Break, Double Action, Hammer, Nickel Plated, *Modern*	50	125	175
Safety, .22 L.R.R.F., 7 Shot, Top Break, Double Action, Hammerless, Blue, *Modern*	50	125	175
Safety, .22 L.R.R.F., 7 Shot, Top Break, Double Action, Hammerless, Nickel Plated, *Modern*	50	125	175
Safety, .32 S & W Long, 6 Shot, Top Break, Double Action, Hammer, Blue, *Modern*	50	100	175
Safety, .32 S & W Long, 6 Shot, Top Break, Double Action, Hammer, Nickel Plated, *Modern*	50	100	175
Safety, .32 S & W Long, 6 Shot, Top Break, Double Action, Hammerless, Blue, *Modern*	50	100	175
Safety, .32 S & W, 5 Shot, Top Break, Double Action, Hammer, Nickel Plated, *Modern*	50	125	175
Safety, .32 S & W, 5 Shot, Top Break, Double Action, Hammer, Blue, *Modern*	50	100	175
Safety, .32 S & W, 5 Shot, Top Break, Double Action, Hammerless, Blue, *Modern*	50	125	175
Safety, .32 S & W, 5 Shot, Top Break, Double Action, Hammerless, Nickel Plated, *Modern*	50	125	175
Safety, .38 S & W, 5 Shot, Top Break, Double Action, Hammerless, Nickel Plated, *Modern*	50	125	175
Sealed 8 Protector, .22 L.R.R.F., 8 Shot, Blue, Wood Grips, Top Break, Double Action, *Modern*	50	125	175
Sealed 8 Supershot, .22 L.R.R.F., Adjustable Sights, Blue, Wood Grips, Top Break, Double Action, *Modern*	50	125	175
Sealed 8 Target, .22 L.R.R.F., 8 Shot, Blue, Wood Grips, Solid Frame, Double Action, *Modern*	50	100	175
Sidewinder, .22LR/.22 WMR Combo, Western Style, 4" Barrel, Adjustable Sights, *Modern*	25	85	150
Sidewinder, .22LR/.22 WMR Combo, Western Style, 6" Barrel, Adjustable Sights, *Modern*	25	85	150
Supershot 9, .22 L.R.R.F., 9 Shot, Adjustable Sights, Blue, Wood Grips, Top Break, *Modern*	50	115	150
Supershot M 844, .22 L.R.R.F., 8 Shot, Double Action, Top Break, Adjustable Sights, Wood Grips, *Modern*	25	100	125
Swing Out Model 1879, .38 S & W, 5 Shot, Swing Right, Forward Hinge, Solid Frame, *Antique*	100	275	350

	Fair	V. Good	Excellent
Swing Out, .22 L.R.R.F., Swing-Out Cylinder, 4" Barrel, Double Action, Wood Grips, Blue, *Modern*	$25	$75	$100
Swing Out, .22 L.R.R.F., Swing-Out Cylinder, 4" Barrel, Double Action, Adjustable Sights, Blue, *Modern*	50	125	150
Swing Out, .22 L.R.R.F., Swing-Out Cylinder, 6" Barrel, Double Action, Adjustable Sights, Blue, *Modern*	50	100	125
Swing Out, .22 L.R.R.F., Swing-Out Cylinder, Various Barrel Lengths, Double Action, Wood Grips, Blue, *Modern*	25	75	100
Swing Out, .22 WMR, Swing-Out Cylinder, 4" Barrel, Double Action, Wood Grips, Blue, *Modern*	25	75	100
Swing Out, .22 WMR, Swing-Out Cylinder, 4" Barrel, Double Action, Adjustable Sights, Blue, *Modern*	50	125	150
Swing Out, .22 WMR, Swing-Out Cylinder, 6" Barrel, Double Action, Adjustable Sights, Blue, *Modern*	25	100	125
Swing Out, .22 WMR, Swing-Out Cylinder, Various Barrel, Lengths, Double Action, Wood Grips, Blue, *Modern*	50	75	100
Swing Out, .32 S & W Long, Swing-Out Cylinder, 4" Barrel, Double Action, Wood Grips, Blue, *Modern*	75	100	125
Swing Out, .32 S & W Long, Swing-Out Cylinder, 4" Barrel, Double Action, Adjustable Sights, Blue, *Modern*	75	125	150
Swing Out, .32 S & W Long, Swing-Out Cylinder, 6" Barrel, Double Action, Adjustable Sights, Blue, *Modern*	50	100	125
Swing Out, .32 S & W Long, Swing-Out Cylinder, Various Barrel Lengths, Double Action, Wood Grips, Blue, *Modern*	50	75	100
Swing Out, .32 S & W Long, Swing-Out Cylinder, Various Barrel Lengths, Double Action, Wood Grips, Nickel Plated, *Modern*	50	100	125
Swing Out, .38 Special, Swing-Out Cylinder, 4" Barrel, Double Action, Wood Grips, Blue, *Modern*	50	100	125
Swing Out, .38 Special, Swing-Out Cylinder, 4" Barrel, Double Action, Adjustable Sights, Blue, *Modern*	50	125	150
Swing Out, .38 Special, Swing-Out Cylinder, 6" Barrel, Double Action, Adjustable Sights, Blue, *Modern*	50	125	150
Swing Out, .38 Special, Swing-Out Cylinder, Various Barrel Lengths, Double Action, Wood Grips, Blue, *Modern*	50	100	125

	Fair	V. Good	Excellent
Swing Out, .38 Special, Swing-Out Cylinder, Various Barrel Lengths, Double Action, Wood Grips, Nickel Plated, *Modern*	$50	$100	$125
Target 9, .22 L.R.R.F., 9 Shot, Blue, Solid Frame, Wood Grips, Double Action, *Modern*	50	100	125
Trailblazer, .22LR/.22 WMR Combo, Single Action, Western Style, Color Case Hardened Frame, Adjustable Sights, *Modern*	50	125	150
Trigger-Cocking, .22 L.R.R.F., 8 Shot, Single Action, Top Break, Adjustable Sights, Wood Grips, *Modern*	50	125	150

HANDGUN, SELF-LOADING

	Fair	V. Good	Excellent
Model TP-22, .22 L.R.R.F., Double Action, Hammer, Clip Fed, Blue, *Modern*	100	175	225
Model TP-25, .25 ACP, Double Action, Hammer, Clip Fed, Blue, *Modern*	100	150	200
Pony, .380 ACP, Hammer, Clip Fed, Blue, *Modern*	100	200	300
Pony, .380 ACP, Hammer, Clip Fed, Nickel Plated, *Modern*	100	175	275
Pony, .380 ACP, Hammer, Clip Fed, Stainless, *Modern*	100	225	300
PP30 Enforcer, .30 M1 Carbine, Clip Fed, Blue, *Modern*	100	200	300

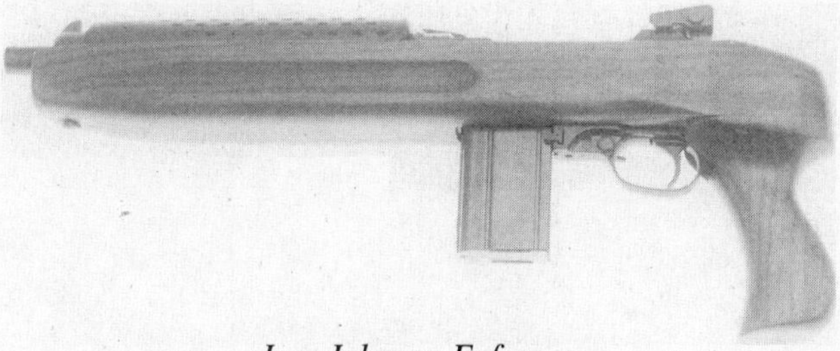

Iver Johnson Enforcer

	Fair	V. Good	Excellent
PP30S Enforcer, .30 M1 Carbine, Clip Fed, Stainless, *Modern*	100	225	325
Trailsman, .22 L.R.R.F., Clip Fed, Blue, *Modern*	75	125	250

HANDGUN, SINGLESHOT

	Fair	V. Good	Excellent
Eclipse 1872, .22 R.F., Spur Trigger, Side-Swing Barrel, Hammer, *Antique*	100	250	325

RIFLE, BOLT ACTION

	Fair	V. Good	Excellent
Model 2X, .22 L.R.R.F., Singleshot, Takedown, *Modern*	25	50	75
Model X, .22 L.R.R.F., Singleshot, Takedown, *Modern*	25	50	75

RIFLE, SELF-LOADING

	Fair	V. Good	Excellent
PM30G, .30 Carbine, Clip Fed, Military Style, Carbine, *Modern*	$75	$175	$300

Iver Johnson PM30G

	Fair	V. Good	Excellent
PM30P, .30 Carbine, Clip Fed, Telescoping Stock, Carbine, *Modern*	75	200	300
PM30PS Paratrooper, .30 M1 Carbine, Clip Fed, Stainless, *Modern*	100	250	375
PM5.7 Spitfire, 5.7 Spitfire, Clip Fed, Military Style, *Modern*	75	150	225
SC30F, .30 Carbine, Clip Fed, Folding Stock, Carbine, *Modern*	100	175	275
SC30F, .30 Carbine, Clip Fed, Paratrooper, Carbine, Stainless, *Modern*	100	200	300
SC30S, .30 Carbine, Clip Fed, Plastic Stock, Carbine, Stainless, *Modern*	75	150	350

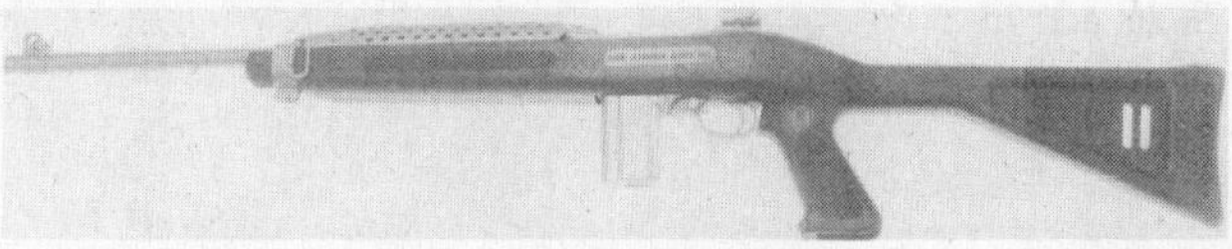

Iver Johnson SC30SS

	Fair	V. Good	Excellent
SC5.7S, 5.7 Spitfire, Clip Fed, Carbine, *Modern*	75	150	250
SC5.7S, 5.7 Spitfire, Clip Fed, Folding Stock, Carbine, *Modern*	75	150	250
SC5.7S, 5.7 Spitfire, Clip Fed, Plastic Stock, *Modern*	50	125	225
SC5.7S, 5.7 Spitfire, Clip Fed, Plastic Stock, Stainless, *Modern*	75	175	275

SHOTGUN, DOUBLE BARREL, OVER-UNDER

	Fair	V. Good	Excellent
Silver Shadow, 12 Gauge, Double Trigger, Checkered Stock, *Modern*	100	250	250
Silver Shadow, 12 Gauge, Double Trigger, Checkered Stock, Light Engraving, Vent Rib, *Modern*	125	300	400
Silver Shadow, 12 Gauge, Single Trigger, Checkered Stock, *Modern*	150	350	450
Silver Shadow, 12 Gauge, Single Trigger, Checkered Stock, Light Engraving, Vent Rib, *Modern*	150	375	475

SHOTGUN, DOUBLE BARREL, SIDE-BY-SIDE

	Fair	V. Good	Excellent
Hercules, Various Gauges, Double Trigger, Automatic Ejector, Hammerless, Checkered Stock, *Modern*	175	400	550

	Fair	V. Good	Excellent
Hercules, Various Gauges, Double Trigger, Checkered Stock, Hammerless, *Modern*	$175	$375	$475
Hercules, Various Gauges, Single Trigger, Automatic Ejector, Hammerless, Checkered Stock, *Modern*	175	450	600
Hercules, Various Gauges, Single Trigger, Hammerless, Checkered Stock, *Modern*	175	425	575
Knox-All, Various Gauges, Double Trigger, Hammer, Checkered Stock, *Modern*	150	300	450
Skeeter, Various Gauges, Double Trigger, Hammerless, *Modern*	300	700	950
Skeeter, Various Gauges, Skeet Grade, Single Selective Trigger, Hammerless, *Modern*	350	800	1000
Skeeter, Various Gauges, Skeet Grade, Single Selective Trigger, Automatic Ejector, Hammerless, *Modern*	500	1000	1350
Skeeter, Various Gauges, Skeet Grade, Single Trigger, Hammerless, *Modern*	350	800	1050
Super, *Modern*	300	700	850
Super, 12 Gauge, Trap Grade, Double Trigger, Hammerless, *Modern*	275	600	750

20 ga. add 10%
28 ga. add 25–30%
410 ga. add 40–50%

	Fair	V. Good	Excellent
Super, 12 Gauge, Trap Grade, Single Trigger, Hammerless, Modern	$325	$700	$900

SHOTGUN, SINGLESHOT

	Fair	V. Good	Excellent
Champion, Various Gauges, Automatic Ejector, *Modern*	25	50	75
Mat Rib Grade, Various Gauges, Raised Matted Rib, Automatic Ejector, Checkered Stock, *Modern*	50	75	100
Side Snap, 12 Gauge, Damascus Barrel, Hammer, *Antique*	25	50	75
Side Snap, 12 Gauge, Steel Barrel, Hammer, *Antique*	50	75	100
Top Snap, 12 Gauge, Steel Barrel, Hammer, *Antique*	50	75	100
Trap Grade, 12 Gauge, Vent Rib, Checkered Stock, *Modern*	100	300	450

IZARRA

Made by Bonifacio Echeverra, Eibar, Spain, c. 1918.

HANDGUN, SELF-LOADING

	Fair	V. Good	Excellent
.32 ACP, Clip Fed, Long Grip, *Curio*	100	150	225

J

J & R
Burbank, Calif.

	Fair	V. Good	Excellent
RIFLE, SELF-LOADING			
Model 68, 9mm Luger, Clip Fed, Flash Hider, Takedown, *Modern*	$100	$150	$225

JACKRABBIT
Continental Arms Corp., New York City, c. 1960.

	Fair	V. Good	Excellent
RIFLE, SINGLESHOT			
Handy Gun, .44 Magnum, Detachable Shoulder Stock, *Modern*	50	75	100
SHOTGUN, SINGLESHOT			
Handy Gun, .410, Detachable Shoulder Stock, *Modern*	25	50	75

JACKSON ARMS CO.
Made by Crescent for C. M. McClung & Co., Knoxville, Tenn. See Crescent Fire Arms Co., Shotgun, Double Barrel, Side-by-Side; Shotgun, Single Shot.

JACKSON HOLE RIFLE CO.
Jackson Hole, Wyo., c. 1970.

	Fair	V. Good	Excellent
RIFLE, BOLT ACTION			
Custom, Various Calibers, with 3 Interchangeable Barrels, Fancy Checkering, Fancy Wood, *Modern*	400	850	1000
Presentation, Various Calibers, with 3 Interchangeable Barrels, Fancy Checkering, Fancy Wood, Engraved, *Modern*	450	1000	1350
Sportsman, Various Calibers, with 3 Interchangable Barrels, Checkered Stock, *Modern*	350	750	950

JAGA
Frantisek Dusek, Opocno, Czechoslovakia, c. 1930.

	Fair	V. Good	Excellent
HANDGUN, SELF-LOADING			
.25 ACP, Clip Fed, Blue, *Curio*	75	125	150

JAGER
Germany, 1960–1975.

	Fair	V. Good	Excellent
HANDGUN, REVOLVER			
Jager, .22LR/.22 WMR Combo, Single Action, Western Style, Adjustable Sights, *Modern*	$50	$100	$125
Jager, .22LR/.22 WMR Combo, Single Action, Western Style, *Modern*	50	75	100
Jager Centerfire, Various Calibers, Single Action, Western Style, Adjustable Sights, *Modern*	75	125	150
Jager Centerfire, Various Calibers, Single Action, Western Style, *Modern*	50	100	125

JAGER
Suhl, Germany.

	Fair	V. Good	Excellent
HANDGUN, SELF-LOADING			
.32 ACP, Clip Fed, Commercial, *Curio*	100	200	300
.32 ACP, Clip Fed, Military, *Curio*	100	200	325

JAGER, F. & CO.
See Herold.

JANSSEN FRERES
Liege, Belgium, c. 1925.

	Fair	V. Good	Excellent
SHOTGUN, DOUBLE BARREL, SIDE-BY-SIDE			
Various Gauges, Hammerless, Steel Barrel, *Curio*	100	175	250

JAPANESE MILITARY
Although prior to the 1950s and 1960s few would consider Japanese military arms of any quality, a number of surplus and captured rifles came to America as trophies of war. Some Japanese military arms were altered by amateur (and a few professional) gunsmiths into sporting arms. The Nambu military pistols developed a fairly enthusiastic following, and the Baby Nambu became one of the genre's most popular and valued handguns. No less a figure than William B. Ruger was inspired to manufacture a prototype Baby Nambu in .22 caliber. This exquisite and diminutive self-loading pistol was test-fired by a member of Sturm, Ruger's board of directors—without a single malfunction. The pistol was built based on Ruger's design drawings and might well have become another Ruger success story, but at the time there was government pressure against manufacture of pocket repeating arms, a

factor in Ruger's decision to withdraw the model from consideration for a production run. The result: one of the most rare of all Ruger firearms.

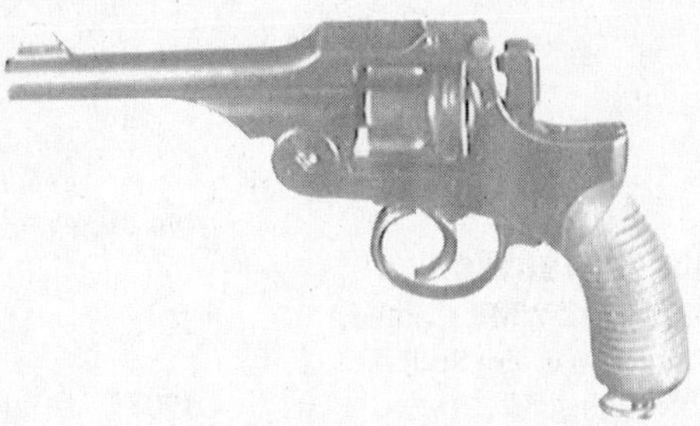

Japanese Military Type 26 Revolver

Japanese Military Type 14 Pistol

	Fair	*V. Good*	*Excellent*
HANDGUN, REVOLVER			
Model 26, 9mm, Military, *Curio*	$125	$250	$350
HANDGUN, SELF-LOADING			
Baby Nambu, 7mm Nambu, "TGE," Clip Fed, Military, *Curio*	1000	2000	3000
Baby Nambu, 7mm Nambu, Clip Fed, Military, *Curio*	1100	2000	2750
Type 14 Nambu, 8mm Nambu, Clip Fed, Large Trigger Guard, Military, *Curio*	150	350	450
Type 14 Nambu, 8mm Nambu, Clip Fed, Small Trigger Guard, Military, *Curio*	200	425	525
Type 1902 "Grandpa," 8mm Nambu, Tokyo Arsenal, Clip Fed, Military, Curio	1200	3000	3750
Type 1904 "Papa," 8mm Nambu, TGE Commercial, Clip Fed, *Curio*	700	1500	1950
Type 1904 "Papa," 8mm Nambu, TGE Navy, Clip Fed, Military, *Curio*	600	1250	1750
Type 1904 "Papa," 8mm Nambu, Thailand, Clip Fed, Military, *Curio*	450	1000	1400
Type 1904 "Papa," 8mm Nambu, Tokyo Arsenal, Clip Fed, Military, *Curio*	450	1000	1400
Type 94, 8mm Nambu, Clip Fed, Military, *Curio*	$125	$225	$325
RIFLE, BOLT ACTION			
Japanese "Siamese Mauser," 8 × 52R Cal., Made by Japan for the Government of Siam in the Early 1920s. A Modified 98 Mauser, Bolt Action, 30-Inch Barrel, *Curio*	50	100	150
Model 38 (1905), 6.5 × 50 Arisaka, Military, *Curio*	50	125	175
Model 38 (1905), 6.5 × 50 Arisaka, Military, Carbine, *Curio*	75	150	275
Model 44 (1911), 6.5 × 50 Arisaka, Military, Carbine, *Curio*	100	225	375
Model 99 (1939), 7.7 × 58 Arisaka, Military, Open Rear Sight, *Curio*	75	125	200
Type 30 (1897), 6.5 Aisaka, Bolt Action, 31-Inch Barrel, Often Referred to as the "Hook Safety Rifle," *Curio*	75	150	225
Type 38 Carbine, 6.5 Cal., Arisaka, 19-Inch Barrel, Modified for Paratroop Use by the addition of a Hinge to the Wrist of the Stock for Folding, Somewhat Rare, *Curio*	75	300	500
Type 38, 6.5 × 50 Arisaka, Late Model, Military, *Curio*	75	125	225
Type 44, 6.5 × 50 Arisaka, Folding Bayonet, Military, *Curio*	100	225	325
Type 97 Sniper Rifle, Arisaka, 31-Inch Barrel, Specially Selected for Extreme Accuracy and Then Fitted with Telescopic Sight, *Curio*	150	325	550
Type 99 Type 2 Take Down Rifle, 7.7 Cal., Arisaka, 25-Inch Barrel, A Standard Type 99 Rifle Modified to Break in Half for Compact Paratroop Use, Very Rare, *Curio*	125	275	450
Type 99, 7.7 Cal., Arisaka, 31-Inch Barrel, Five Shot Mauser Type Magazine, Bolt Action, Long Barrel Infantry Model, Becoming Scarce, *Curio*	75	125	175
Type 99, 7.7 × 58 Arisaka, Aircraft Sights Dust Cover, Military, *Curio*	100	225	300

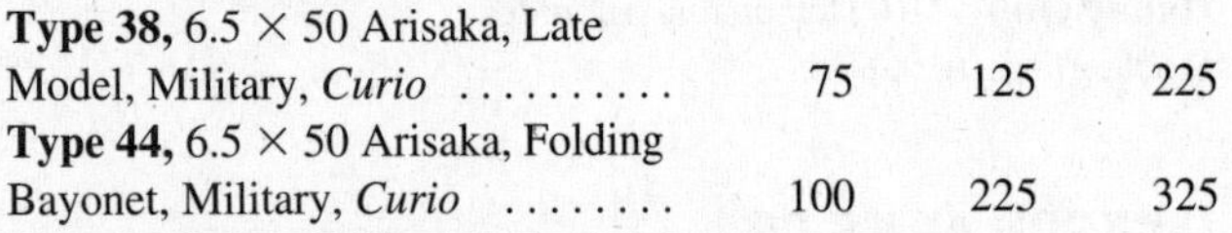

Japanese Military Type 99 Rifle

JENNINGS FIREARMS, INC.

Carson City, Nev.

HANDGUN, SELF-LOADING			
Model J-22, .22 L.R.R.F., Clip Fed, Black Teflon Plate, *Modern*	25	50	75

	Fair	V. Good	Excellent
Model J-22, .22 L.R.R.F., Clip Fed, Satin Nickel Plate, *Modern*	$25	$50	$75

JEWEL

Made by Hood Firearms Co., c. 1876.

HANDGUN, REVOLVER

#1, .22 Short R.F., 7 Shot, Spur Trigger, Solid Frame, Single Action, *Antique*	75	150	200

J.G.L.

Jos. G. Landmann, Holstein, Germany, c. 1968.

RIFLE, SELF-LOADING

JGL-68 Model 1, .22 L.R.R.F., Clip Fed, Carbine Style, *Modern*	25	50	75
JGL-68 Model 2, .22 L.R.R.F., Clip Fed, Vertical Grip & Foregrip, *Modern*	25	50	75
JGL-68 Model 3, .22 L.R.R.F., Clip Fed, Vertical Grip, *Modern*	25	50	75

JIEFFCO

Mre. Liegoise d'Armes a Feu Robar et Cie, Liège, Belgium, c. 1912–1914.

HANDGUN, SELF-LOADING

.25 ACP, Clip Fed, Blue, *Curio*	75	150	200
.32 ACP, Clip Fed, Blue, *Curio*	75	150	200

JIEFFCO

Tradename used by Davis-Warner on pistols made by Robar et Cie., c. 1920.

HANDGUN, SELF-LOADING

New Model Melior, .25 ACP, Clip Fed, *Curio*	75	150	200

JO-JO-AR

Hijos de Arrizabalaga, Eibar, Spain, c. 1920.

HANDGUN, SELF-LOADING

.380 ACP, Tip-up, Clip Fed, Hammer, Spur Trigger, Military, *Curio*	100	200	300
9mm Bergmann, Tip-up, Clip Fed, Hammer, Spur Trigger, Military, *Curio*	75	150	250

JOFFRE

Spain, c. 1900.

	Fair	V. Good	Excellent
HANDGUN, SELF-LOADING			
M1916, .32 ACP, Clip Fed, *Modern*	$50	$100	$150

JOHNSON & BYE CO.

Worcester, Mass. The following trade names also marked on selected guns made by this firm, q.v.: American Bulldog, Eclipse, Encore, Favorite, Favorite Navy, Lion, Tycoon.

JOHNSON AUTOMATICS

Providence, R.I. Also see U.S. Military.

RIFLE, BOLT ACTION

Diamond Cherry Featherweight, Various Calibers, Engraved, Carved Cherry Stock, Muzzle Brake, *Modern*	450	1000	1350
Honey Featherweight, Various Calibers, Engraved, Carved Stock, Muzzle Brake, Gold and Silver Inlays, *Modern*	700	1500	1850
Laminar Sporter, Various Calibers, Laminated Stock, *Modern*	275	650	950

RIFLE, SELF-LOADING

Model 1941, .30-06 Springfield, Miliatry, *Curio*	600	1500	2250
Model 1941, 7mm Mauser, Military, *Curio*	400	1000	1350

JONES, CHARLES

Lancaster, Pa., 1780. See Kentucky Rifles.

JONES, J.N. & CO.

London, England, c. 1760.

HANDGUN, FLINTLOCK

.60, George III, Navy Pistol, Brass Barrel, Brass Furniture, Military, *Antique*	550	1250	1650

HANDGUN, PERCUSSION

.58, Holster Pistol, Converted from Flintlock, Brass Furniture, Plain, *Antique*	500	1100	1500

JUPITER

Fabrique d'Armes de Guerre de Grand Precision, Eibar, Spain.

HANDGUN, SELF-LOADING

.32 ACP, Clip Fed, Blue, *Curio*	50	125	150

K

KABA SPEZIAL

Made by August Menz, Suhl, Germany, for Karl Bauer & Co., Berlin, Germany, c. 1925.

HANDGUN, SELF-LOADING

	Fair	V. Good	Excellent
Liliput, .25 ACP, Clip Fed, Blue, *Modern*	$100	$225	$300
Liliput, .32 ACP, Clip Fed, Blue, *Modern*	100	250	325

KABA SPEZIAL

Made by Francisco Arizmendi, Eibar, Spain.

HANDGUN, SELF-LOADING

	Fair	V. Good	Excellent
.25 ACP, Clip Fed, Blue, *Modern*	75	150	200

KART

HANDGUN, SELF-LOADING

	Fair	V. Good	Excellent
For Colt Government Target, .22 L.R.R.F., Conversion Unit Only	75	150	200
Target, .22 L.R.R.F., Clip Fed, M1911 Frame, 6" Barrel, *Modern*	250	575	750

KASSNAR IMPORTS

Harrisburg, Pa.

RIFLE, BOLT ACTION

	Fair	V. Good	Excellent
Model M-14S, .22 L.R.R.F., Clip Fed, Checkered Stock, *Modern*	25	50	100
Model M-15S, .22 WMR, Clip Fed, Checkered Stock, *Modern*	25	50	100
Model M-1400, .22 L.R.R.F., Clip Fed, Checkered Stock, *Modern*	25	50	100
Model M-1500, .22 WMR, Clip Fed, Checkered Stock, *Modern*	50	75	125
Parker Hale Midland, Various Calibers, Checkered Stock, Open Sights, *Modern*	100	200	250
Parker Hale Super, Various Calibers, Checkered Stock, Open Sights, Monte Carlo Stock, *Modern*	100	250	325
Parker Hale Varmint, Various Calibers, Checkered Stock, Open Sights, Varmint Stock, *Modern*	125	275	325

RIFLE, SELF-LOADING

	Fair	V. Good	Excellent
Model M-16, .22 L.R.R.F., Clip Fed, Military Style, *Modern*	40	75	125
Model M-20S, .22 L.R.R.F., *Modern*	$40	$75	$125

SHOTGUN, DOUBLE BARREL, OVER-UNDER

	Fair	V. Good	Excellent
Fias SK-1, 12 and 20 Gauges, Double Trigger, Checkered Stock, *Modern*	150	300	400
Fias SK-3, 12 and 20 Gauges, Single Selective Trigger, Checkered Stock, *Modern*	150	325	425
Fias SK-4, 12 and 20 Gauges, Single Selective Trigger, Checkered Stock, Automatic Ejector, *Modern*	150	375	500
Fias SK-4D, 12 and 20 Gauges, Single Selective Trigger, Fancy Checkering, Fancy Wood, Engraved, Automatic Ejector, *Modern*	175	400	550
Fias SK-4T, 12 Ga., Trap Grade, Single Selective Trigger, Automatic Ejector, Checkered Stock, Wide Vent Rib, *Modern*	200	425	500

SHOTGUN, DOUBLE BARREL, SIDE-BY-SIDE

	Fair	V. Good	Excellent
Zabala, Various Gauges, Checkered Stock, Double Triggers, *Modern*	75	200	300

SHOTGUN, SINGLESHOT

	Fair	V. Good	Excellent
Taiyojuki, Various Gauges, Top Break, Plain, *Modern*	25	35	65

KEFFER, JACOB

Lancaster, Pa., c. 1802. See Kentucky Rifles and Pistols.

KEIM, JOHN

Reading, Pa., 1820–1839. See Kentucky Rifles and Pistols.

KENTUCKY RIFLES AND PISTOLS

Often alone in the wilderness and totally self-reliant, the American frontiersman from the mid-18th to the second quarter of the 19th century depended for survival on his wits and courage, his skill in the wilderness, and his most important possession: his Kentucky Rifle. No possession held greater importance or meaning that these flintlock firearms, often termed the first original American art form. The Kentucky was the necessary instrument for providing meat for the table, for protection against Indian attack, or militarily against other adversaries (French, British, or Spanish), and was a source of aesthetic pleasure due to its intrinsic beauty. These arms reminded man in the wilderness of the civilization he had left behind, in hunting, exploring, and settling virgin territory. To quote from the author's *Steel Canvas*:

> A fine Kentucky is a masterwork created with primitive tools on the frontier. Although it has roots in its European predecessor arms, the Kentucky rifle is distinctly and uniquely American. The greatest Kentucky riflemakers were masters of many skills and crafts; silversmiths, lockmakers, barrelmakers, polishers, finishers, ironmongers, furniture makers, brass makers, jewelers, engravers, and designers. And the Kentucky is the one artifact from pioneer America that required these combined skills in a single craftsmen.

Termed by some the "Pennsylvania Rifle," since many of these arms were built there, Kentucky Rifles expressed in wood and metal the attitude of strength and independence that fostered a young nation. For the most part Kentuckys are custom guns, and, aside from general similarities, virtually all are different, even those by the same maker. To add to the problem of price generalization, gunsmiths purchased parts from various makers and there may be three different names on a single gun, or no name at all. The main considerations in determining value are: 1. period of manufacture; 2. identity of maker; 3. type of ignition; 4. quality of workmanship; 5. decoration; 6. originality; and 7. condition. The literature on Kentucky Rifles and Pistols continues to grow, and this area of collecting has tremendous potential, even though some arms have already reached six-figure prices, and at present the Kentucky is generally undervalued.

	Fair	*V. Good*	*Excellent*
RIFLE, FLINTLOCK			
High Quality, Fancy Decoration, *Antique*	$5000	$12000	$16500
Moderate Quality, Medium Decoration, *Antique*	3000	8000	11000
Moderate Quality, Plain, *Antique*	1250	4000	6000
Over-Under, Swivel-Breech, High Quality, *Antique*	9000	20000	27500
Over-Under, Swivel-Breech, Medium Quality, *Antique*	8000	17500	22500
Over-Under, Swivel-Breech, Plain, *Antique*	4000	8500	12500
Deduct 30%-40%, if Converted from Percussion			
RIFLE, PERCUSSION			
Add 20%, if Converted from Flintlock Percussion			
High Quality, Fancy Decoration, *Antique*	4000	8500	11500
Moderate Quality, Medium Decoration, *Antique*	2000	4000	6000
Moderate Quality, Plain, *Antique*	900	2000	3000
Over-Under, High Quality, Swivel Breech, *Antique*	6000	10000	13500
Over-Under, Medium Quality, Swivel Breech, *Antique*	3500	7500	9500
Over-Under, Medium Quality, Swivel Breech, Plain, *Antique*	2000	4000	6000

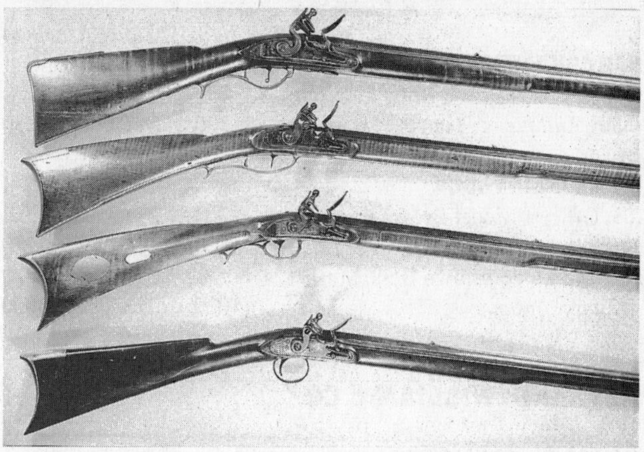

From the top, flintlock Kentucky type rifles with Ketland lock but otherwise unmarked, next with barrel marked S. Miller *and lock marked* Ross, *next marked* J. J. Henry-Boulton *on lock; and bottom with lock marked* A. W. Spies.

	Fair	*V. Good*	*Excellent*
PISTOLS, FLINTLOCK			
High Quality, Fancy Decoration, *Antique*	$4000	$8000	$12500
Moderate Quality, Medium Decoration, *Antique*	3000	6500	8500
PISTOL, PERCUSSION (ORIGINAL)			
High Quality, Fancy Decoration, *Antique*	1600	3000	4000
Moderate Quality, Medium Decoration, *Antique*	800	1750	2250
PISTOLS, PERCUSSION (CONVERTED FLINTLOCK)			
High Quality, Fancy Decoration, *Antique*	2000	4000	5500
Moderate Quality, Medium Decoration, *Antique*	1500	3000	4000

KETLAND & CO

Birmingham & London, England, 1760–1831. Also see Kentucky Rifles. The Ketland marking, a name not infrequently found marked on locks, is often mistakenly thought to be the manufacturer of a variety of arms. Generally speaking, Ketland supplied the lock only, while the identity of the maker needs to be determined either by identification through the barrel marking, or by interpreting the style.

HANDGUN, FLINTLOCK			
.58, Holster Pistol, Plain, Tapered Round Barrel, Brass Furniture, *Antique*	500	1200	1750
.62, Belt Pistol, Brass Barrel, Brass Furniture, Light Ornamentation, *Antique*	700	1700	2250

KETLAND, T.

Birmingham, England, 1750–1829.

	Fair	V. Good	Excellent
HANDGUN, FLINTLOCK			
.69, Pair, Belt Pistol, Brass Furniture, Plain, *Antique*	$1200	$2700	$3250
RIFLE, FLINTLOCK			
.65, Officers Model Brown Bess, Musket, Military, *Antique*	1500	3000	3750
.73, 2nd Model Brown Bess, Musket, Military, *Antique*	1000	2250	3000

KETLAND, WILLIAM & CO.

	Fair	V. Good	Excellent
HANDGUN, FLINTLOCK			
.63, Holster Pistol, Round Barrel, Plain, *Antique*	600	1350	1750

KETTNER, ED

Suhl, Thuringia, Germany, 1922–1939.

	Fair	V. Good	Excellent
COMBINATION WEAPON, DRILLING			
12 X 12 X 10.75 X 65R Collath, Engraved, Checkered Stock, Sling Swivels, *Curio*	900	2200	2750

KIMBALL, J. M. ARMS CO.

Detroit, Mich., c. 1955–1958.

	Fair	V. Good	Excellent
HANDGUN, SELF-LOADING			
Combat Model, .30 Carbine, 3" Barrel, Clip Fed, Blue, Short Barrel, *Modern*	400	800	1000
Target Model, .30 Carbine, 5" Barrel, Clip Fed, Blue, Adjustable Sights, *Modern*	400	800	1000
Standard Model, .22 Hornet, Clip Fed, Blue, *Modern*	600	1200	1500

KIMBER

Clackamas, Ore., 1980–1991.

	Fair	V. Good	Excellent
RIFLE, BOLT ACTION			
Model 82 Match, .22 L.R.R.F., Checkered Stock, Clip Fed, No Sights, *Modern*	600	1250	1750
Model 82 Varmint, .22 W.M.R., Checkered Stock, Clip Fed, No Sights, *Modern*	300	600	1000
Model 82C Classic, .22 L.R.R.F., Checkered Stock, Clip Fed, No Sights, Monte Carlo Stock, *Modern*	400	800	1200
Model 82C Super America, .22 L.R.R.F., Checkered Stock, Clip Fed, No Sights, Monte Carlo Stock, *Modern*	400	850	1250

KIMEL INDUSTRIES

Mathews, N.C.

	Fair	V. Good	Excellent
HANDGUN, DOUBLE BARREL, OVER-UNDER			
Twist, .22 Short R.F., Swivel Breech, Derringer, Spur Trigger, *Modern*	$25	$50	$75

KING NITRO

Made by Stevens Arms.

	Fair	V. Good	Excellent
RIFLE, BOLT ACTION			
Model 53, .22 L.R.R.F., Singleshot, Takedown, *Modern*	50	100	150
SHOTGUN, DOUBLE BARREL, SIDE-BY-SIDE			
M 315 Various Gauges, Hammerless, Steel Barrel, *Modern*	75	125	175

KINGLAND 10-STAR

Made by Crescent for Geller, Wards, & Hasner, St. Louis, Mo. See Kingland Special.

KINGLAND SPECIAL

Made by Crescent for Geller, Wards & Hasner, St. Louis, Mo. See Crescent Fire Arms Co., Shotgun, Double Barrel, Side-by-Side; Shotgun, Singleshot.

KIRIKKALE

Makina ve Kimya Endustrisi Kurumu Kirrikale, Ankara, Turkey.

	Fair	V. Good	Excellent
HANDGUN, SELF-LOADING			
MKE, 7.65mm & 9mmk, Clip Fed, Double Action, *Modern*	150	325	450

KITTEMAUG

c. 1880.

	Fair	V. Good	Excellent
HANDGUN, REVOLVER			
.32 Short R.F., 5 Shot, Spur Trigger, Solid Frame, Single Action, *Antique*	75	150	225

KLEINGUENTHER'S

Seguin, Texas.

	Fair	V. Good	Excellent
HANDGUN, REVOLVER			
Reck R-18, .357 Magnum, Adjustable Sights, Western Style, Single Action, *Modern*	50	100	150
RIFLE, BOLT ACTION			
K-10, .22 L.R.R.F., Single Shot, Tangent Sights, *Modern*	25	50	75

	Fair	V. Good	Excellent
K-12, .22 L.R.R.F., Clip Fed, Checkered Stock, *Modern*	$25	$50	$75
K-13, .22 W.M.R., Clip Fed, Checkered Stock, *Modern*	50	100	150
K-14 Insta-fire, Various Calibers, Checkered Stock, No Sights, Recoil Pad, *Modern*	300	700	900
K-15, .22 L.R.R.F., Clip Fed, Checkered Stock, *Modern*	50	100	150
K-15 Insta-fire, Various Calibers, Checkered Stock, No Sights, Recoil Pad, *Modern*	400	800	1100
V2130, Various Calibers, Checkered Stock, Recoil Pad, *Modern*	100	200	275

RIFLE, DOUBLE BARREL, OVER-UNDER

Model 222, .22 W.M.R., Plain, *Modern*	75	125	175

SHOTGUN, DOUBLE BARREL, OVER-UNDER

Condor, 12 Gauge, Single Selective Trigger, Automatic Ejector, Vent Rib, *Modern*	150	375	500
Condor, 12 Gauge, Skeet Grade, Single Selective Trigger, Automatic Ejector, Wide Vent Rib, *Modern*	200	400	500

SHOTGUN, DOUBLE BARREL, SIDE-BY-SIDE

Brescia, 12 Gauge, Hammerless, Light Engraving, Double Trigger, *Modern*	100	200	300

SHOTGUN, SELF-LOADING

12 Ga., Checkered Stock, Vent Rib, Engraved, Left Hand, *Modern*	100	200	300
12 Ga., Checkered Stock, Vent Rib, Engraved, Right Hand, *Modern*	100	175	275

KLETT, SIMON

Leipzig, c. 1620.

RIFLE, WHEEL LOCK

.54, Rifled, Octagon Barrel, Brass Furniture, Medium Ornamentation, Engraved, High Quality, *Antique*	4500	10000	13500

KNICKERBOCKER

Made by Crescent H & D Folsom, c. 1900. See Crescent Fire Arms Co., Shotgun, Double Barrel, Side-by-Side.

KNICKERBOCKER

Made by Stevens Arms.

SHOTGUN, DOUBLE BARREL, SIDE-BY-SIDE

Model 311, Various Gauges, Hammerless, Steel Barrel, *Modern*	75	150	200

KNOCKABOUT

Made by Stevens Arms.

SHOTGUN, DOUBLE BARREL, SIDE-BY-SIDE

	Fair	V. Good	Excellent
Model 311, Various Gauges, Hammerless, Steel Barrel, *Modern*	$75	$150	$200

KNOXALL

Made by Crescent, c. 1900.

SHOTGUN, DOUBLE BARREL, SIDE-BY-SIDE

Various Gauges, Hammerless, Steel Barrel, *Modern*	75	150	200
Various Gauges, Outside Hammers, Steel Barrel, *Modern*	75	150	200

KODIAK MFG. CO.

North Haven, Conn., c. 1965. Despite the prodigious knowledge and experience with fine sporting arms of George Rowbottom, a principal in the company, the Mfg. Co. was relatively short-lived.

RIFLE, BOLT ACTION

Model 98 Brush Carbine, Various Calibers, Checkered Stock, *Modern*	75	150	225
Model 99 Deluxe Brush Carbine, Various Calibers, Checkered Stock, *Modern*	75	150	225
Model 100 Deluxe Rifle, Various Calibers, Checkered Stock, *Modern*	75	175	300
Model 100M Deluxe Rifle, Various Magnum Calibers, Checkered Stock, *Modern*	100	225	325
Model 101 Ultra, Various Calibers, Monte Carlo Stock, *Modern*	75	175	300
Model 101M Ultra, Various Magnum Calibers, Monte Carlo Stock, *Modern*	125	250	375
Model 102 Ultra Varmint, Various Calibers, Heavy Barrel, *Modern*	100	200	300

RIFLE, SELF-LOADING

Model 260 Autoloader, .22 L.R.R.F., Tube Feed, Open Sights, 22" Barrel, *Modern*	100	200	300
Model 260 Autoloader Carbine, .22 L.R.R.F., Tube Feed, Open Sights, 20" Barrel, *Modern*	100	225	325
Model 260 Magnum, .22 W.M.R., Tube Feed, Open Sights, 22" Barrel, *Modern*	125	250	350
Model 260 Magnum Carbine, .22 W.M.R., Tube Feed, Open Sights, 20" Barrel, *Modern*	100	225	325

KOHOUT & SPOL

Kdyne, Czechoslovakia, 1928–1945.

HANDGUN, SELF-LOADING

	Fair	V. Good	Excellent
Mars, 6.35mm, Clip Fed, *Curio*	$75	$175	$250
Mars, 7.65mm, Clip Fed, *Curio*	100	200	275

KOMMER, THEODOR

Zella Mehlis, Germany, c. 1920.

HANDGUN, SELF-LOADING

	Fair	V. Good	Excellent
Model I, 6.35mm, Clip Fed, *Curio*	125	275	375

Kommer Model I

	Fair	V. Good	Excellent
Model II, 6.35mm, Clip Fed, *Curio*	125	250	350
Model III, 6.35mm, Clip Fed, *Curio*	100	225	325
Model IV, 7.65mm, Clip Fed, *Curio*	150	300	400

KORTH

Wilhelm Korth Waffenfabrik, Ratzburg, West Germany. One of the world's finest revolving handguns, the Korth has a well-deserved reputation for excellence in engineering, and for quality of manufacture. These arms also rank as one of the most expensive out-of-the-box revolvers produced today.

HANDGUN, REVOLVER

	Fair	V. Good	Excellent
Target, Various Calibers, 6 Shot, *Modern*	700	1750	2250

KRAFT, JACOB

Lancaster, Pa., 1771–1782. See Kentucky Rifles and Pistols.

KRICO

Stuttgart, West Germany. Also see Beeman's.

RIFLE, BOLT ACTION

	Fair	V. Good	Excellent
.22 Rem. Carbine, Checkered Stock, Double Set Triggers, *Modern*	250	575	675
.22 Rem. Rifle, Checkered Stock, Double Set Triggers, *Modern*	250	550	650
Model 302, .22 L.R.R.F., Clip Fed, Checkered Stock, Open Sights, *Modern*	300	625	725
Model 304, .22 L.R.R.F., Clip Fed, Checkered Stock, Mannlicher Stock, Set Triggers, Open Sights, *Modern*	$300	$625	$725
Model 311, .22 L.R.R.F., Checkered Stock, Double Set Trigger, *Modern*	150	300	400
Model 340, .22 L.R.R.F., Metallic Silhouette Match Rifle, Clip Fed, Checkered Stock, Target Stock, *Modern*	300	600	700
Model 340, .22 L.R.R.F., Mini-Sniper Match Rifle, Clip Fed, Checkered Stock, Target Stock, *Modern*	300	650	750
Model 351, .22 WMR, Checkered Stock, Double Set Triggers, *Modern*	250	500	600
Model 354, .22 WMR, Checkered Stock, Double Set Triggers, *Modern*	300	600	700
Model 400, .22 Hornet, Clip Fed, Checkered Stock, Open Sights, *Modern*	300	625	725
Model 420, .22 Hornet, Clip Fed, Checkered Stock, Set Triggers, Mannlicher Stock, Open Sights, Sling Swivels, *Modern*	400	800	900
Model 600, Various Calibers, Clip Fed, Checkered Stock, Open Sights, Sling Swivels, Recoil Pad, *Modern*	400	800	1100
Model 600 Export, Various Calibers, Checkered Stock, Double Set Triggers, *Modern*	200	400	500
Model 600 Luxus, Various Calibers, Checkered Stock, Double Set Triggers, *Modern*	225	475	575
Model 620, Various Calibers, Clip Fed, Checkered Stock, Set Triggers, Mannlicher Stock, Open Sights, Sling Swivels, *Modern*	425	900	1250
Model 620 Luxus, Various Calibers, Checkered Stock, Double Set Triggers, *Modern*	250	550	650
Model 640, Various Calibers, Deluxe Varmint Rifle, Clip Fed, Checkered Stock, Target Stock, *Modern*	500	1025	1250
Model 650, Various Calibers, Sniper/Match Rifle, Clip Fed, Checkered Stock, Target Stock, *Modern*	450	950	1300
Model 700, Various Calibers, Clip Fed, Checkered Stock, Open Sights, Sling Swivels, Recoil Pad, *Modern*	325	750	1000
Model 700 Export, Various Calibers, Checkered Stock, Double Set Triggers, *Modern*	250	550	750
Model 700 Luxus, Various Calibers, Checkered Stock, Double Set Triggers, *Modern*	300	600	800

	Fair	V. Good	Excellent
Model 720, Various Calibers, Clip Fed, Checkered Stock, Set Triggers, Mannlicher Stock, Open Sights, Sling Swivels, *Modern*	$450	$950	$1150
Model 720 Luxus, Various Calibers, Checkered Stock, Double Set Triggers, *Modern*	350	775	950
Model DJV, .22 Various Calibers, Checkered Target Stock, Double Set Triggers, *Modern*	250	500	600
Special Varmint, .222 Rem., Checkered Stock, Heavy Barrel, Double Set Triggers, *Modern*	250	550	650

KRIEGHOFF GUN CO.

Suhl, Germany, 1886–1945, and from 1945 to date in Ulm, West Germany. Also see shotguns of Ulm. For many years these highly respected sporting guns have been imported by Hal Du Pont, of the Du Pont chemical family. With their Germanic styling, solid construction, and high-quality Krieghoffs are not inexpensive, but they have had a strong following for decades. The vast majority, however, are sold not to collectors, but to active shooters.

COMBINATION WEAPON, DRILLING

	Fair	V. Good	Excellent
Neptun, Various Calibers, Hammerless, Engraved, Fancy Checkering, Sidelock, *Modern*	3500	8000	11500
Neptun Dural, Various Calibers, Hammerless, Engraved, Fancy Checkering, Sidelock, *Modern*	3500	8000	11500
Neptun Primus, Various Calibers, Hammerless, Fancy Checkering, Fancy Engraving, Sidelock, *Modern*	6000	12000	16500

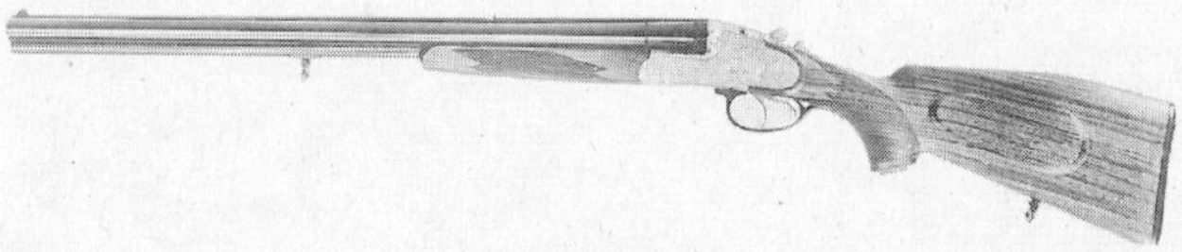

Krieghoff Neptun

	Fair	V. Good	Excellent
Neptun Primus Dural, Various Calibers, Hammerless, Fancy Checkering, Fancy Engraving, Sidelock, Lightweight, *Modern*	6000	12500	17500
Trumpf, Various Calibers, Hammerless, Engraved, Fancy Checkering, *Modern*	3000	6000	8500

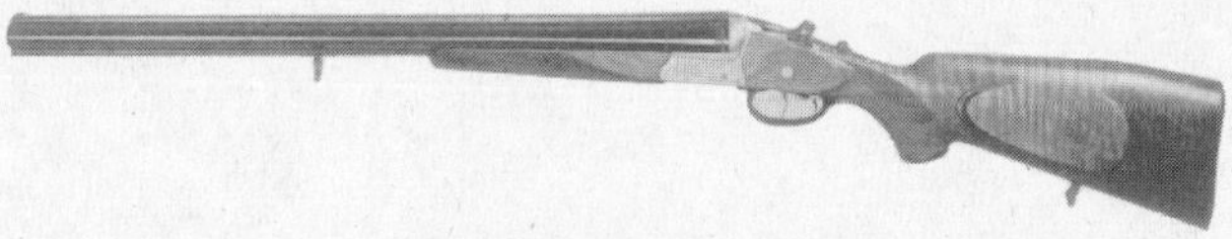

Krieghoff Trumpf

	Fair	V. Good	Excellent
Trumpf Dural, Various Calibers, Hammerless, Engraved, Fancy Checkering, Lightweight, *Modern*	$3000	$6200	$7500

RIFLE, DOUBLE BARREL, OVER-UNDER

	Fair	V. Good	Excellent
Teck, Various Calibers, Hammerless, Engraved, Fancy Checkering, *Modern*	2500	5500	7000
Teck Dural, Various Calibers, Hammerless, Engraved, Fancy Checkering, Lightweight, *Modern*	2500	6000	8000
Ulm, Various Calibers, Hammerless, Engraved, Fancy Checkering, Sidelock, *Modern*	3000	7500	9000
Ulm Dural, Various Calibers, Hammerless, Engraved, Fancy Checkering, Sidelock, *Modern*	3700	8000	10000
Ulm Primus, Various Calibers, Hammerless, Engraved, Fancy Checkering, Sidelock, *Modern*	3500	8000	11500

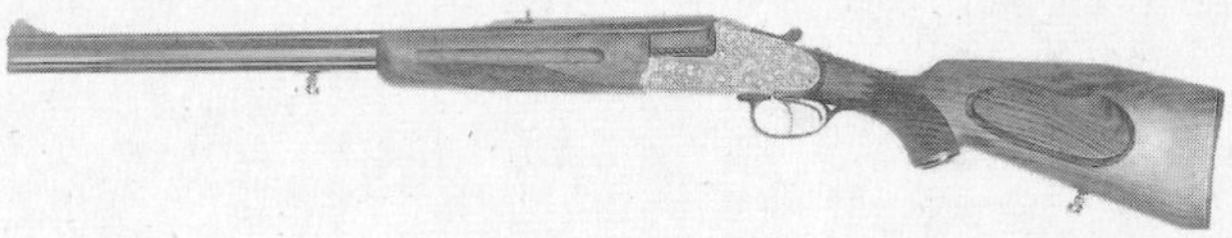

Krieghoff Ulm

	Fair	V. Good	Excellent
Ulm Primus Dural, Various Calibers, Hammerless, Engraved, Fancy Checkering, Sidelock, Lightweight, *Modern*	3500	8500	11000

SHOTGUN, DOUBLE BARREL, OVER-UNDER

	Fair	V. Good	Excellent
Crown, 12 Gauge, Trap Grade, *Modern*	8000	16000	19500
Exhibition, 12 Gauge, Trap Grade, *Modern*	9000	25000	32500
Extra Barrel, Add $800.00–$1,000.00			
Monte Carlo, 12 Gauge, Trap Grade, *Modern*	5000	11000	14500
Munchen, Various Gauges, Skeet Grade, *Modern*	2500	5000	7500
San Remo, 12 Gauge, Trap Grade, *Modern*	2700	6000	8500
Standard, 12 Gauge, Field Grade, *Modern*	1400	3500	5000
Standard, 12 Gauge, Trap Grade, *Modern*	2000	4500	5500

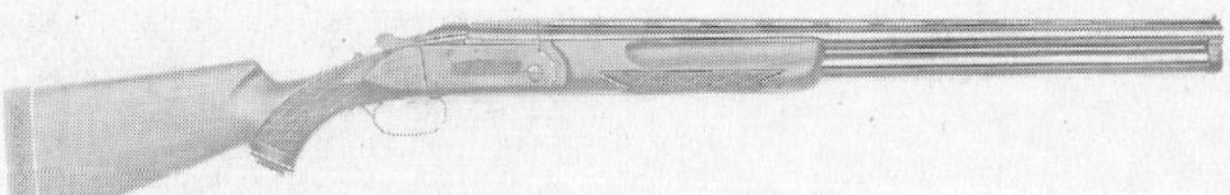

Krieghoff Standard

	Fair	V. Good	Excellent
Standard, Various Gauges, Skeet Grade, *Modern*	$1600	$3500	$4750
Super Crown, 12 Gauge, Trap Grade, *Modern*	7000	15000	20000

KROYDEN

Tradename used by Savage Arms Corp.

RIFLE, SELF-LOADING

.22 L.R.R.F., Tube Feed, Plain Stock, *Modern*	25	50	75

KRUSCHITZ

Vienna, Austria.

RIFLE, BOLT ACTION

Mauser 98, .30/06, Checkered Stock, Double Set Triggers, *Modern*	100	250	350

Kynoch Schlund Revolver

KYNOCH GUN FACTORY

Birmingham, England. Late 1880s.

HANDGUN, REVOLVER

	Fair	V. Good	Excellent
Schlund, .32, .38, &.45 Calibers, Concealed Hammer, Top Break, Double Trigger, Cocking, *Antique*	$400	$850	$1150

L

	Fair	V. Good	Excellent

LA SALLE

Tradename used by Manufrance.

SHOTGUN, SELF-LOADING

	Fair	V. Good	Excellent
Custom, 12 Ga., Checkered Stock, *Modern*	$100	$250	$350

SHOTGUN, SLIDE ACTION

	Fair	V. Good	Excellent
12 Gauge, Checkered Stock, Fancy Wood, *Modern*	100	250	300
12 Gauge, Field Grade, Plain, *Modern*	100	225	300
20 Gauge, Field Grade, Plain, *Modern*	75	150	225

LAHTI

Developed and made by Valtion Kivaarithedas, Jyvaskyla, Finland. Also made by Husqvarna in Sweden.

HANDGUN, SELF-LOADING

	Fair	V. Good	Excellent
L-35 Finnish, 9mm Luger, Clip Fed, Military, *Curio*	300	750	1100
M 40 Swedish, 9mm Luger, Clip Fed, Military, *Modern*	150	275	400

LAKESIDE

Made by Crescent for Montgomery Ward & Co., c. 1900. See Crescent Fire Arms Co., Shotgun, Double Barrel, Side-by-Side; Shotgun, Singleshot.

LAMES

Chiavari, Italy.

SHOTGUN, DOUBLE BARREL, OVER-UNDER

	Fair	V. Good	Excellent
California, 12 Gauge, Trap Grade, Automatic Ejector, Single Selective Trigger, Vent Rib, Checkered Stock, *Modern*	300	675	925
Field Grade, 12 Gauge, Automatic Ejector, Single Selective Trigger, Vent Rib, Checkered Stock, *Modern*	150	350	450
Skeet Grade, 12 Gauge, Automatic Ejector, Single Selective Trigger, Vent Rib, Checkered Stock, *Modern*	200	500	625
Trap Grade, 12 Gauge, Automatic Ejector, Single Selective Trigger, Vent Rib, Monte Carlo Stock, *Modern*	$200	$400	$600

LANBER

Lanber Armas, S.A., Zaldibar, Spain.

SHOTGUN, DOUBLE BARREL, OVER-UNDER

	Fair	V. Good	Excellent
Model 844 ST, 12 Gauge, Double Triggers, Checkered Stock, Light Engraving, *Modern*	100	200	300
Model 844 MST, 12 Gauge 3", Double Triggers, Checkered Stock, Light Engraving, *Modern*	100	200	300
Model 844 EST, 12 Gauge, Automatic Ejector, Double Triggers, Checkered Stock, Light Engraving, *Modern*	100	200	300
Model 844 EST CHR, 12 Gauge, Automatic Ejector, Double Triggers, Checkered Stock, Light Engraving, *Modern*	125	250	350
Model 2004 LCH, 12 Gauge, Trap Grade, Automatic Ejector, Single Trigger, Checkered Stock, Light Engraving, Lanber Choke, *Modern*	125	250	400
Model 2004 LCH, 12 Gauge, Skeet Grade, Automatic Ejector, Single Trigger, Checkered Stock, Light Engraving, Lanber Choke, *Modern*	125	250	400
Model 2004 LCH, 12 Gauge, Automatic Ejector, Single Trigger, Checkered Stock, Light Engraving, Lanber Choke, *Modern*	125	250	400

LANCASTER, CHARLES

London, England, 1889–1936.

RIFLE, BOLT ACTION

	Fair	V. Good	Excellent
Various Calibers, Sporting Rifle, Checkered Stock, *Curio*	450	1000	1400
Double Rifles Various cal.	1500	4000	5500

LANCELOT

HANDGUN, SELF-LOADING

	Fair	V. Good	Excellent
.25 ACP, Clip Fed, Blue, *Modern*	75	150	175

	Fair	V. Good	Excellent

LANE & READ
Boston, Mass., 1826–1835.

SHOTGUN, PERCUSSION

	Fair	V. Good	Excellent
28 Gauge, Double Barrel, Side-by-Side, Light Engraving, Checkered Stock, *Antique*	$200	$400	$550

LANG, JOSEPH
London, England, established in 1821.

HANDGUN, PERCUSSION

	Fair	V. Good	Excellent
Pair, Double Barrel, Over-Under, Officer's Belt Pistol, Light Engraving, Cased with Accessories, *Antique*	1800	4000	5500

SHOTGUN, SINGLESHOT

	Fair	V. Good	Excellent
12 Gauge, Plain, Trap Grade, *Modern*	600	1200	1650

LANGENHAN
Friedrich Langenhan Gewehr u. Fahrradfabrik, Zella Mehlis, Germany.

HANDGUN, SELF-LOADING

	Fair	V. Good	Excellent
Model I, 7.65mm, Clip Fed, Military, *Modern*	100	225	300

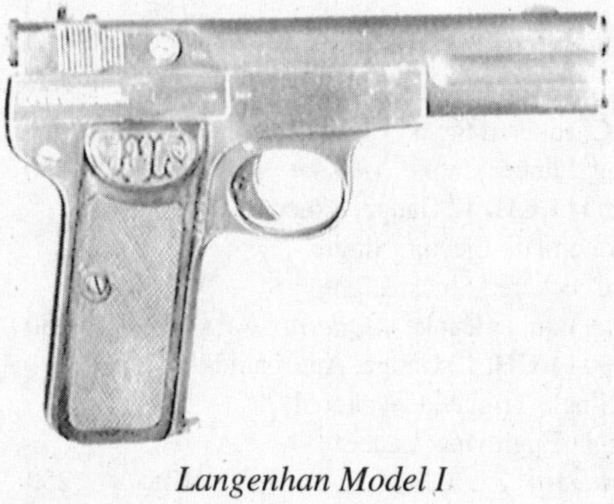

Langenhan Model I

	Fair	V. Good	Excellent
Model II, 6.35mm, Clip Fed, *Modern*	125	275	325
Model III, 6.35mm, Clip Fed, *Modern*	125	275	325

LAURONA
Spain.

SHOTGUN, DOUBLE BARREL, OVER-UNDER

	Fair	V. Good	Excellent
Model 67-G, 12 Gauge 3", Checkered Stock, Vent Rib, Double Triggers, *Modern*	75	150	225

LEADER
Possibly Hopkins & Allen, c. 1880.

HANDGUN, REVOLVER

	Fair	V. Good	Excellent
.22 Short R.F., 7 Shot, Spur Trigger, Solid Frame, Single Action, *Antique*	$75	$150	$200
.32 Short R.F., 5 Shot, Spur Trigger, Solid Frame, Single Action, *Antique*	75	150	200

LEADER GUN CO.
Made by Crescent for Charles William Stores Inc., c. 1900. See Crescent Fire Arms Co., Shotgun, Double Barrel, Side-by-Side; Shotgun, Singleshot.

LEATHER, JACOB
York, Pa., 1779–1802. See U.S. Military, Kentucky Rifles.

LE BARON

RIFLE, FLINTLOCK

	Fair	V. Good	Excellent
.69 Presentation, Silver Furniture, Fancy Wood, Fancy Checkering, Fancy Engraving, *Antique*	1900	4000	6000

LE BASQUE

HANDGUN, SELF-LOADING

	Fair	V. Good	Excellent
7.65mm, Clip Fed, Blue, *Modern*	100	150	250

LEBEAU-COURALLY
Liège, Belgium, since 1865. One of the finest gunmakers of sporting arms in the world, it was this firm that produced an exquisite double-barrel sporting rifle in .375 H & H Magnum and .458 Winchester Magnum (interchangeable barrels) for use in the film and video *In the Blood,* shot in Tanzania. The author had the pleasure of using this rifle on safari, and in between duties as a player in the production, hunted zebra with world-renowned professional hunter Robin Hurt. The rifle was later sold to a keen collector, proud owner of one of the finest double-barrel elephant, lion, and Cape buffalo rifles built in modern times. Many collectors, including this writer, regard the Lebeau-Courally as in the top-rank of European sporting rifles and shotguns.

RIFLE, DOUBLE BARREL, SIDE-BY-SIDE

	Fair	V. Good	Excellent
Ardennes, Various Calibers, Fancy Engraving, Double Triggers, Checkered Stock, Automatic Ejector, Boxlock, Fancy Wood, *Modern*	6000	12000	22500
St. Hubert, Various Calibers, Fancy Engraving, Double Triggers, Checkered Stock, Automatic Ejector, Sidelocks, Fancy Wood, *Modern*	9000	20000	37500

	Fair	V. Good	Excellent
SHOTGUN, DOUBLE BARREL, SIDE-BY-SIDE			
Grand Russe, 12 Gauge, Fancy Engraving, Double Triggers, Checkered Stock, Automatic Ejector, Boxlock, Fancy Wood, *Modern*	$3250	$8000	$15000
Sologne, 12 Gauge, Medium Engraving, Double Triggers, Checkered Stock, Automatic Ejector, Boxlock with Sideplates, Fancy Wood, *Modern*	4000	9500	17500

LEE ARMS CO.

Wilkes-Barre, Pa., c. 1870. Also see Red Jacket.

HANDGUN, REVOLVER			
.22 Short R.F., 7 Shot, Spur Trigger, Solid Frame, Single Action, *Antique*	75	150	200
.32 Short R.F., 5 Shot, Spur Trigger, Solid Frame, Single Action, *Antique*	75	150	200
.32 Short R.F., Spur Trigger, Nickel Plated, *Antique*	75	125	175

LEE SPECIAL

Made by Crescent for Lee Hardware, Salinas, Kans., c. 1900. See Crescent Fire Arms Co., Shotgun, Double Barrel, Side-by-Side; Shotgun, Singleshot.

LEFAUCHEUX

Paris, France, c. 1865. The use of revolvers by Lefaucheux in the Civil War has added to the appeal of these arms to the American collector. As pinfire cartridges became harder and harder to obtain, many of these revolvers became useless. A genuine C.S.A.-marked and/or pedigreed specimen will command a premium, sometimes several multiples of its value without such association. Another patron of Lefaucheux was the youthful Theodore Roosevelt—his first shotgun, a gift from his father, was a 12 gauge pinfire by this maker. The gun is part of the collection of the Sagamore Hill National Historic Site, Oyster Bay, New York. Of this piece TR would later recollect that it was "an excellent gun for a clumsy and often absent-minded boy."

HANDGUN, REVOLVER			
12mm Pinfire, Model 1863, Double Action, Finger Rest Trigger Guard, *Antique*	200	400	600
9mm Pinfire, Double Action, Folding Trigger, Belgian, *Antique*	100	200	350
9mm Pinfire, Double Action, Paris, *Antique*	125	250	400
SHOTGUN, DOUBLE BARREL, SIDE-BY-SIDE			
Various Pinfire Gauges, Double Triggers, Hammers, *Antique*	75	125	200

LEFEVER SONS & CO.

Syracuse, N.Y. Nichols & Lefever, 1876–1878; D. M. Lefever, 1879–1889; Lefever Arms Co., 1889–1899; Lefever, Sons & Co., 1899–1926. Purchased by Ithaca Gun Co. 1926. Lefever marked guns manufactured until 1948. Once ranked among America's premier manufacturers of fine shotguns, Lefever continues to this day as a master restorer and finisher of quality sporting shotguns and other arms in Lee Center, New York.

	Fair	V. Good	Excellent
SHOTGUN, DOUBLE BARREL, SIDE-BY-SIDE			
B, Various Gauges, Sidelock, Hammerless, Fancy Checkering, Fancy Engraving, Monte Carlo Stock, *Curio*	$2200	$5500	$7500
BE, Various Gauges, Sidelock, Hammerless, Fancy Checkering, Fancy Engraving, Monte Carlo Stock, Automatic Ejector, *Curio*	4000	8500	10500
C, Various Gauges, Sidelock, Hammerless, Fancy Checkering, Fancy Engraving, Monte Carlo Stock, *Curio*	1600	3500	5000
CE, Various Gauges, Sidelock, Hammerless, Fancy Checkering, Fancy Engraving, Monte Carlo Stock, Automatic Ejector, *Curio*	2000	4500	6500
D, Various Gauges, Sidelock, Hammerless, Fancy Checkering, Engraved, Monte Carlo Stock, *Curio*	900	2500	3500
DE, Various Gauges, Sidelock, Hammerless, Fancy Checkering, Engraved, Monte Carlo Stock, Automatic Ejector, *Curio*	900	2750	3750
DS, Various Gauges, Sidelock, Hammerless, Checkered Stock, *Curio*	400	850	1150
DSE, Various Gauges, Sidelock, Hammerless, Checkered Stock, Automatic Ejector, *Curio*	500	1250	1750
E, Various Gauges, Sidelock, Hammerless, Fancy Checkering, Engraved, *Curio*	600	1750	2250
EE, Various Gauges, Sidelock, Hammerless, Fancy Checkering, Engraved, *Curio*	900	2250	2750
F, Various Gauges, Sidelock, Hammerless, Checkered Stock, Engraved, *Curio*	450	1000	1500
FE, Various Gauges, Sidelock, Hammerless, Checkered Stock, Engraved, Automatic Ejector, *Curio*	550	1250	1750
G, Various Gauges, Sidelock, Hammerless, Checkered Stock, Light Engraving, *Curio*	550	1250	1750
GE, Various Gauges, Sidelock, Hammerless, Checkered Stock, Light Engraving, Automatic Ejector, *Curio*	700	1500	2000
H, Various Gauges, Sidelock, Hammerless, Checkered Stock, Light Engraving, *Curio*	450	1000	1500

	Fair	V. Good	Excellent
HE, Various Gauges, Sidelock, Hammerless, Checkered Stock, Light Engraving, Automatic Ejector, *Curio*	$600	$1250	$1650
Nitro Special, Various Gauges, Boxlock, Double Triggers, Checkered Stock, *Curio*	200	425	650
Nitro Special, Various Gauges, Boxlock, Single Triggers, Checkered Stock, *Curio*	250	500	725

SHOTGUN, SINGLESHOT

A Grade Skeet, 12 Gauge, Hammerless, Vent Rib, Checkered Stock, Automatic Ejector, *Curio*	450	1000	1400
Long Range, Various Gauges, Field Grade, Hammerless, Checkered Stock, *Curio*	150	300	450
Trap Grade, 12 Gauge, Hammerless, Vent Rib, Checkered Stock, Automatic Ejector, *Curio*	250	500	650

LEFEVRE, PHILIP
Beaver Valley, Pa., 1731–1756. See Kentucky Rifles.

LEFEVRE, SAMUEL
Strasbourg, Pa., 1770–1771. See Kentucky Rifles.

LE FRANCAISE
Mre. Francaise de Armes et Cycles de St. Etienne, St. Etienne, France.

HANDGUN, SELF-LOADING

Army Model, 9mm French Long, Clip Fed, *Curio*	400	800	1000
Champion, 6.35mm, Clip Fed, Long Grip, *Curio*	125	250	325
Le Francais, 7.65mm, Clip Fed, *Curio*	150	350	425
Pocket Model, 6.35mm, Clip Fed, *Curio*	100	175	275
Policeman, 6.35mm, Clip Fed, *Curio*	200	400	600
Staff Officer's, 6.35mm, Clip Fed, *Curio*	150	300	450

Le Francaise Policeman

	Fair	V. Good	Excellent

LEIGH, HENRY
Belgium, c. 1890.

SHOTGUN, DOUBLE BARREL, SIDE-BY-SIDE

Various Gauges, Outside Hammers, Damascus Barrel, *Curio*	$100	$200	$400

LEITNER, ADAM
York Co., Pa. See Kentucky Rifles and Pistols.

LE MARTINY

HANDGUN, SELF-LOADING

6.35mm, Clip Fed, Blue, *Curio*	50	100	150

LE MONOBLOC
Jules Jacquemart, Liège, Belgium, c. 1910.

HANDGUN, SELF-LOADING

6.35mm, Clip Fed, *Curio*	100	200	300

LENNARD
Lancaster, Pa., 1770–1772. See Kentucky Rifles and Pistols.

LEONHARDT
H. M. Gering & Co., Arnstadt, Germany, c. 1917.

HANDGUN, SELF-LOADING

Army, 7.65 ACP, Clip Fed, *Curio*	100	175	225
Gering, 7.65 ACP, Clip Fed, *Curio*	100	220	275

Leonhardt Gering

LE PAGE
Made by Manufacter d'Armes Le Page, Liège, Belgium.

HANDGUN, SELF-LOADING

7.65mm, Clip Fed, *Curio*	150	375	450
9mm Browning Long, Clip Fed, Adjustable Sights, *Curio*	200	450	600
9mm Browning Long, Clip Fed, Adjustable Sights, Detachable Shoulder Stock, *Curio*	400	1000	1350

Le Page

	Fair	V. Good	Excellent
9mm Short, Clip Fed, Adjustable Sights, *Curio*	$200	$400	$500

LE PAGE, JEAN

Paris, 1746–1834. French gunmaker of premier-quality dueling, target, and exhibition-grade firearms. To many, Le Page carried on with the mantle of excellence and quality which had been worn by Boutet for many years.

LEPCO

HANDGUN, SELF-LOADING

6.35mm, Clip Fed, Blue, *Modern*	50	100	150

Lepco

L.E.S.

Skokie, Ill.

HANDGUN, SELF-LOADING

P-18, 9mm Luger, Matte Stainless Steel, Clip Fed, Hammer, Double Action, *Modern*	100	225	300
P-18 Deluxe, 9mm Luger, Polished Stainless Steel, Clip Fed, Hammer, Double Action, *Modern*	125	250	350

LE SANS PARIEL

Mre. d'Armes des Pyrenees.

HANDGUN, SELF-LOADING

	Fair	V. Good	Excellent
6.35mm, Clip Fed, Blue, *Curio*	$75	$125	$175

LESCHER

Philadelphia, Pa., c. 1730. See Kentucky Rifles and Pistols.

LESCONNE, A.

France, c. 1650.

HANDGUN, FLINTLOCK

Pair, Engraved, Silver Inlay, Long Screw Barrel, Rifled, Belt Hook, *Antique*	3000	8000	12500

LE TOUTACIER

Mre. d'Armes des Pyrenees.

HANDGUN, SELF-LOADING

6.35mm, Clip Fed, Blue, *Curio*	50	125	175

LIBERTY

Made by Hood Firearms, 1880–1900.

HANDGUN, REVOLVER

.22 Short R.F., 7 Shot, Spur Trigger, Solid Frame, Single Action, *Antique*	75	150	200
.32 Short R.F., 5 Shot, Spur Trigger, Solid Frame, Single Action, *Antique*	75	150	200

LIBERTY

Montrose, Calif.

HANDGUN, REVOLVER

Mustang, .22 L.R.R.F., Single Action, Western Style, Adjustable Sights, *Modern*	25	50	75
Mustang, .22 LR/.22 WMR Combo, Single Action, Western Style, Adjustable Sights, *Modern*	25	50	75

LIBERTY

Retolaza Hermanos, Eibar, Spain, c. 1920.

HANDGUN, SELF-LOADING

M1924, 6.35mm, Clip Fed, *Curio*	50	125	175
Model 1914, 7.65mm, Clip Fed, Blue, *Curio*	75	150	200
Model 1914, 7.65mm, Clip Fed, Blue, Long Grip, *Curio*	75	150	200

Liberty M1924

Liberty Long Grip

LIBERTY CHIEF
Miroku Firearms, Kochi, Japan.

HANDGUN, REVOLVER	Fair	V. Good	Excellent
Model 6, .38 Spec., Double Action, Blue, *Modern*	$50	$125	$150

LIBIA
Made by Beistegui Hermanos, c. 1920.

HANDGUN, SELF-LOADING	Fair	V. Good	Excellent
6.35mm, Clip Fed, Blue, *Curio*	75	175	225
7.65mm, Clip Fed, Blue, *Curio*	100	200	250

LIEGEOISE D'ARMES A FEU
Robar et Cie., Liege, Belgium, c. 1920.

HANDGUN, SELF-LOADING	Fair	V. Good	Excellent
New Model Melior, 6.35mm, Clip Fed, Blue, *Curio*	75	150	200
Spanish Copy, 6.35mm, Blue, Clip Fed, *Curio*	50	100	150
Spanish Copy, 7.65mm, Blue, Clip Fed, *Curio*	50	125	175

LIGHTNING
Echave y Arizmendi, Eibar, Spain, c. 1920.

HANDGUN, SELF-LOADING	Fair	V. Good	Excellent
6.35mm, Clip Fed, Blue, *Curio*	$50	$125	$175

LIGNITZ, I. H.
Continental, c. 1650.

HANDGUN, WHEEL LOCK	Fair	V. Good	Excellent
Brass Barrel, Holster Pistol, Medium Ornamentation, *Antique*	2900	6500	9500

LIGNOSE
Successors to Theodor Bergmann, Suhl, Germany, c. 1925.

HANDGUN, SELF-LOADING	Fair	V. Good	Excellent
For Original Wood Grips, Add 10%–15%			
Model 2, 6.35mm, Clip Fed, *Curio*	100	150	225
Model 2A, 6.35mm, Clip Fed, Einhand, Steel Cocking Piece, *Curio*	100	200	275

Lignose 2A

	Fair	V. Good	Excellent
Model 3A, 6.35mm, Clip Fed, Long Grip, Einhand, Brass Cocking Piece, *Curio*	100	200	275

LILIPUT
August Menz, Suhl, Germany, c. 1920.

HANDGUN, SELF-LOADING	Fair	V. Good	Excellent
4.25mm Liliput, Clip Fed, Blue, *Curio*	200	400	500
6.35mm, Clip Fed, Blue, *Curio*	75	125	200

LION
Made by Johnson Bye & Co., c. 1870–1880. Sold by J. P. Lovell, Boston, Mass.

HANDGUN, REVOLVER	Fair	V. Good	Excellent
#1, .22 Short R.F., 7 Shot, Spur Trigger, Solid Frame, Single Action, *Antique*	75	150	200
#2, .32 Short R.F., 5 Shot, Spur Trigger, Solid Frame, Single Action, *Antique*	75	150	200

	Fair	V. Good	Excellent
#3, .38 Short R.F., 5 Shot, Spur Trigger, Solid Frame, Single Action, *Antique*	$75	$150	$200
#4, .41 Short R.F., 5 Shot, Spur Trigger, Solid Frame, Single Action, *Antique*	75	175	225

LITTLE GIANT

Made by Bacon Arms Co., c. 1880.

HANDGUN, REVOLVER

.22 Short R.F., 7 Shot, Spur Trigger, Solid Frame, Single Action, *Antique*	75	150	225

LITTLE JOHN

Made by Hood Firearms, c. 1876.

HANDGUN, REVOLVER

.22 Short R.F., 7 Shot, Spur Trigger, Solid Frame, Single Action, *Antique*	75	150	225

LITTLE JOKER

Made by John M. Marlin, New Haven, Conn., 1873–1875.

HANDGUN, REVOLVER

.22 Short R.F., 7 Shot, Spur Trigger, Solid Frame, Single Action, *Antique*	75	175	225

LITTLE PET

Made by Stevens Arms.

SHOTGUN, SINGLESHOT

Model 958, .410 Gauge, Automatic Ejector, Hammer, *Modern*	25	50	100
Model 958, 32 Gauge, Automatic Ejector, Hammer, *Modern*	25	50	100

LITTLE TOM

Alois Tomiska, Pilsen, Czechoslovakia, 1909–1918.

HANDGUN, SELF-LOADING

6.35mm, Clip Fed, Blue, Hammer, *Curio*	150	300	400
7.65mm, Clip Fed, Blue, Hammer, *Curio*	150	350	450

LITTLE TOM

Wiener Waffenfabrik, Vienna, Austria, 1918–1925.

HANDGUN, SELF-LOADING

	Fair	V. Good	Excellent
6.35mm, Clip Fed, Blue, Hammer, *Curio*	$150	$275	$325

LJUTIC INDUSTRIES, INC.

Yakima, Wash. Shooters swear by their Ljutics, considered at the highest rank of trap shooting shotguns. The author remembers when these arms first came on the market; one of the early buyers and most vociferous endorsers of the Ljutic was Herb Glass, antique arms dealer and collector, who, with his wife Vi, shot trap for years. The only shortcomings for these guns were their ugly lines, compared to rivals like the Perazzi and Beretta. But performance on the trap field was what counted—and at that the Ljutic proved without peer.

SHOTGUN, DOUBLE BARREL, OVER-UNDER

Bi-Gun Set, Various Calibers, Vent Rib, Skeet Grade, Checkered Stock, with 4 Sets of Barrels, *Modern*	4500	10000	14500
Bi-Gun, 12 Gauge, Vent Rib, Trap Grade, Checkered Stock, *Modern*	2900	6500	9000

SHOTGUN, SELF-LOADING

Bi Matic, 12 Gauge, Vent Rib, Trap Grade, Checkered Stock, *Modern*	800	1800	2750

SHOTGUN, SINGLESHOT

Dyn-A-Trap, 12 Gauge, for Custom Stock Add $170.00-$300.00			
Dyn-A-Trap, 12 Gauge, Release Trigger, Add $150.00-$250.00			
Dyn-A-Trap, 12 Gauge, Trap Grade, Checkered Stock, Vent Rib, *Modern*	800	1800	2500
Mono-Gun, 12 Gauge, for Extra Barrel Add $565.00-$750.00			
Mono-Gun, 12 Gauge, Release Trigger Add $220.00-$300.00			
Mono-Gun, 12 Gauge, Trap Grade, Checkered Stock, Olympic Rib, *Modern*	1600	3500	5000
Mono-Gun, 12 Gauge, Trap Grade, Checkered Stock, Vent Rib, *Modern*	1400	3000	4500
X-73, 12 Gauge, Trap Grade, Checkered Stock, Vent Rib, *Modern*	900	2000	3000
X-73, 12 Gauge, for Extra Barrel Add $435.00-$600.00			
X-73, 12 Gauge, Release Trigger Add $220.00-$300.00			

LLAMA

Gabilondo y Cia., Elgoibar, Spain, from 1930 to date. Imported by Stoeger Arms.

HANDGUN, REVOLVER

Chrome Plate, Add 20%–30%

	Fair	V. Good	Excellent
Commanche I, .22 L.R.R.F., Swing-Out Cylinder, Double Action, Blue, *Modern*	$100	$175	$250
Commanche II, .38 Special, Swing-Out Cylinder, Double Action, Blue, *Modern*	100	175	250
Commanche III, .357 Magnum, Swing-Out Cylinder, Double Action, Blue, *Modern*	100	200	275
Engraving, Add 25%–35%			
Gold Damascening, Add 300%-400%			
Martial, .38 Special, Swing-Out Cylinder, Double Action, Blue, *Modern*	75	150	200
Super Commanche IV, .44 Magnum, Swing-Out Cylinder, Double Action, Blue, *Modern*	100	250	300
Super Commanche V, .357 Magnum, Swing-Out Cylinder, Double Action, Blue, *Modern*	100	225	275

HANDGUN, SELF-LOADING

	Fair	V. Good	Excellent
Chrome Plate, Add 20%-30%			
Engraving, Add 25%-35%			
Gold Damascening, Add 300%-400%			
Model I, .32 ACP. Clip Fed, Blue, *Modern*	100	175	225
Model II, .380 ACP. Clip Fed, Blue, *Modern*	100	200	250
Model III, .380 ACP. Clip Fed, Blue, *Modern*	100	175	225
Model IIIA, .380 ACP. Clip Fed, Grip Safety, Blue, *Modern*	100	200	250
Model IV, 9mm Bergmann, Clip Fed, Blue, *Modern*	100	175	225
Model V, .38 ACP. Clip Fed, Blue, *Modern*	100	175	225
Model VII, .38 ACP. Clip Fed, Blue, *Modern*	100	225	300
Model VIII, .38 ACP. Grip Safety, Blue, *Modern*	125	250	325
Model IX, .45 ACP. Clip Fed, Blue, *Modern*	125	275	325
Model IXA, .45 ACP. Clip Fed, Blue, *Modern*	125	275	325
Model X, .32 ACP. Clip Fed, Blue, *Modern*	100	175	225
Model XA, .32 ACP. Clip Fed, Grip Safety, Blue, *Modern*	100	200	250
Model XI, 9mm Luger, Clip Fed, Blue, *Modern*	125	275	325
Model XV, .22 L.R.R.F., Clip Fed, Grip Safety, Blue, *Modern*	125	225	275
Omni, 9mm Luger or .45 ACP, Clip Fed, Double Action, Blue, Military, *Antique*	150	350	425

LOBINGER, JOHANN

Vienna, Austria, c. 1780.

RIFLE, FLINTLOCK

	Fair	V. Good	Excellent
Yaeger, Smooth bore, Half-Octagon Barrel, Silver Furniture, Carved, *Antique*	$1400	$3500	$4750

LONG RANGE WONDER

Tradename used by Sears, Roebuck & Co.

SHOTGUN, SINGLESHOT

	Fair	V. Good	Excellent
12 Ga., Hammer, Break-Open, *Modern*	25	50	75

LONG TOM

Made by Stevens Arms.

SHOTGUN, SINGLESHOT

	Fair	V. Good	Excellent
Model 90, Various Gauges, Takedown, Automatic Ejector, Plain, Hammer, *Curio*	25	50	100
Model 95, 12 and 16 Gauges, Hammer, Automatic Ejector, *Curio*	25	50	100

LONGINES

Cooperative Orbea, Eibar, Spain, c. 1920.

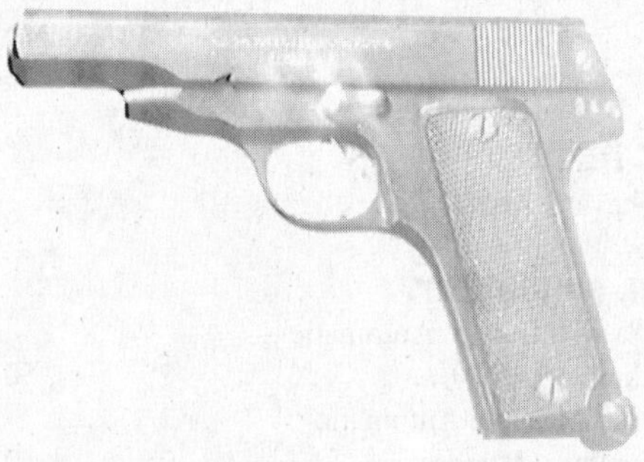

Longines

HANDGUN, SELF-LOADING

	Fair	V. Good	Excellent
7.65mm, Clip Fed, *Curio*	100	175	225

LOOKING GLASS

Domingo Acha and Acha Hermanos, Ermua, Spain, c. 1920.

HANDGUN, SELF-LOADING

	Fair	V. Good	Excellent
6.35mm, Clip Fed, Hammer, *Curio*	75	125	200
6.35mm, Clip Fed, Hammerless, *Curio*	50	100	175
7.65mm, Clip Fed, Long Grip, Hammer, *Curio*	75	150	225
7.65mm, Clip Fed, Long Grip, Hammerless, *Curio*	75	125	175

LORD, J.

Orwigsburg, Pa., 1842–55. See Kentucky Rifles.

LOWELL ARMS CO.

Lowell, Mass., 1854–68.

HANDGUN, REVOLVER

	Fair	V. Good	Excellent
.22 Short R.F., 7 Shot, Spur Trigger, Tip-up, *Antique*	$150	$300	$400
.32 Long R.F., 6 Shot, Spur Trigger, Tip-up, Single Action			
.38 Long R.F., 6 Shot, Spur Trigger, Tip-up, Single Action, *Antique*	150	350	450

RIFLE, SINGLESHOT

	Fair	V. Good	Excellent
.38 Long R.F., *Antique*	150	350	425

LOWER, J. P.

Philadelphia, Pa., c. 1875.

HANDGUN, REVOLVER

	Fair	V. Good	Excellent
.22 Long R.F., 7 Shot, Single Action, Solid Frame, Spur Trigger, *Antique*	100	225	300
.32 Long R.F., 7 Shot, Single Action, Solid Frame, Spur Trigger, *Antique*	150	325	400

LUGER

Made by various companies for commercial and military use from 1900-45. Also see Mauser and German Military. The German Luger ranks among the world's great handguns, and was one of the first successful self-loading pistols. Its ingenious mechanism allows takedown simply by removal of the toggle on the left side of the receiver, above the trigger. These beautiful and functional arms have a substantial following of dedicated collectors. Although a careful study of these arms is important to the collector, to avoid being taken in by a fake or refinished example, the rewards of Luger collecting are many. These are one of the arms field's most consistent performers in terms of steady increase in value. Variations have been well established, several books on the subject are in print, and experts like Ralph Shattuck, Fred Datig, and the Simpsons (father and son) are keen to share their expertise with new and seasoned collectors alike. Note: The author is grateful to John R. Hansen Jr., of Hansen & Co., Southport, Connecticut, for his assistance in establishing the values of the pistols listed in this section.

HANDGUN, SELF-LOADING

	Fair	V. Good	Excellent
1900 Bulgarian, .30 Luger, *Curio*	3000	7000	8000
1900 Commercial, .30 Luger, *Curio*	900	2225	2500
1900 Eagle, .30 Luger, *Curio*	900	2000	2250
1900 Swiss Commercial, .30 Luger, *Curio*	900	2250	2500
1900 Swiss Military, .30 Luger, *Curio*	900	2250	2500
1900 Swiss Military, .30 Luger, Wide Trigger, *Curio*	900	2500	3000
1902 Commercial, 9mm Luger, *Curio*	$2200	$5500	$6500
1902 Eagle, 9mm Luger, *Curio*	2400	5000	5500
1902 Prototype, .30 Luger and 9mm Luger, *Curio*			Rare
1902 Test, .30 Luger and 9mm Luger, *Curio*	3000	6000	7000
1902, .30 Luger and 9mm Luger, Carbine, Blue, Curio Add 50% For Stock	2700	6500	9000
1902, 9mm Luger, Cartridge Counter, *Curio*	6000	12500	15000
1902-3 Presentation, .30 Luger, Carbine, *Curio*	3000	10000	12000
1903 Commercial, .30 Luger, *Curio*	3000	6500	8000
1904 Navy, 9mm Luger, *Curio*	4000	10000	12500
1906 Brazilian, .30 Luger, *Curio*	550	1200	1650
1906 Bulgarian, .30 Luger, *Curio*	1500	3750	4500
1906 Bulgarian, 9mm Luger, *Curio*	1400	3000	3500
1906 Commercial, .30 Luger, *Curio*	700	1500	1750

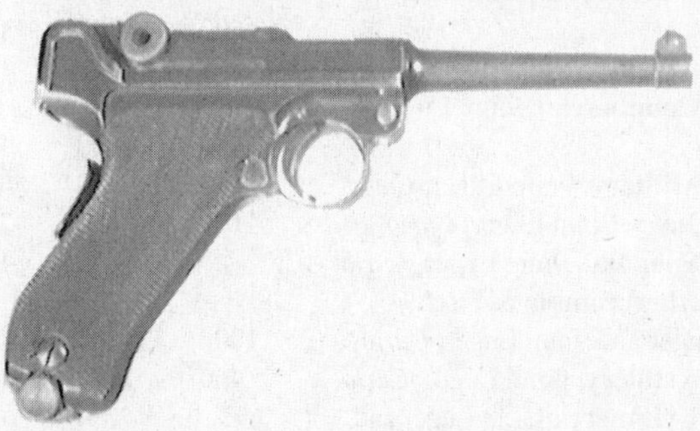

Luger 1906 Commercial

	Fair	V. Good	Excellent
1906 Commercial, 9mm Luger, *Curio*	800	1750	2100
1906 Dutch, 9mm Luger, *Curio*	700	1500	1950
1906 Eagle, .30 Luger, *Curio*	800	1500	2200
1906 Eagle, 9mm Luger, *Curio*	1100	2500	3000
1906 French, .30 Luger, *Curio*	1500	3000	3500
1906 Navy Commercial, 9mm Luger, *Curio*	1500	3000	4000
1906 Navy Military, 9mm Luger, *Curio*	1200	2500	3000

Luger 1906 Navy

	Fair	V. Good	Excellent
1906 Portuguese Army, .30 Luger, *Curio*	$600	$1250	$1500
1906 Portuguese Navy, .30 Luger, *Curio*	3000	6500	7000
1906 Portuguese Navy Crown, .30 Luger and 9mm Luger, *Curio*	3000	6500	7250
1906 Russian, 9mm Luger, *Curio*	3500	7500	9500
1906 Swiss Commercial, .30 Luger, *Curio*	900	2000	2350
1906 Swiss Military, .30 Luger, *Curio*	800	1900	2250
1906 Swiss Police, .30 Luger, *Curio*	900	2250	2500
1908 Bolivian, 9mm Luger, *Curio*	1500	3500	4000
1908 Bulgarian, 9mm Luger, *Curio*	900	2000	2500
1908 DWM Commercial, 9mm Luger, *Curio*	350	750	900
1908 Military, 9mm Luger, *Curio*	300	575	650
1908 Navy Commercial, .30 Luger, *Curio*	1500	3000	3500
1908 Navy Military, 9mm Luger, *Curio*	900	2250	2500
1913 Commercial, 9mm Luger, *Curio*	600	1400	1650
1914 Artillery, 9mm Luger, *Curio*	550	1250	1500
1914 Commercial, 9mm Luger, *Curio*	450	1000	1250
1914 Military, 9mm Luger, *Curio*	350	750	850
1914 Navy, 9mm Luger, *Curio*	1100	2450	2600
1918 Spandau, 9mm Luger, *Curio*			Rare
1920 Abercrombie & Fitch, .30 Luger and 9mm Luger, *Curio*	1900	4000	4500
1920 Artillery, 9mm Luger, *Curio*	450	1000	1300
1920 Commercial, .30 Luger and 9mm Luger, *Curio*	250	550	600
1920 Navy, 9mm Luger, *Curio*	700	1800	2000
1920 Simson, 9mm Luger, *Curio*	325	700	800
1920 Swiss Commercial, .30 Luger and 9mm Luger, *Curio*	550	1250	1500
1920 Swiss Rework, .30 Luger and 9mm Luger, *Curio*	550	1200	1550
1920-21, .30 Luger and 9mm Luger, *Curio*	250	500	650
1921 Krieghoff, .30 Luger, *Curio*	1100	2500	2800
1923 Commercial "Safe-Loaded," .30 Luger and 9mm Luger, *Curio*	450	1000	1250
1923 Commercial Krieghoff, 9mm Luger, *Curio*	550	1250	1500
1923 Commercial, .30 Luger and 9mm Luger, *Curio*	300	650	750
1923 Dutch, 9mm Luger, *Curio*	550	1200	1450
1923 Finnish Army, 9mm Luger, *Curio*	250	550	600
1923 Simson Commercial, 9mm Luger, *Curio*	800	1800	2000
1923 Simson Military, 9mm Luger, *Curio*	900	2000	2250
1923 Stoeger, .30 Luger and 9mm Luger, *Curio*	900	2250	2750

	Fair	V. Good	Excellent
1924 Bern, .30 Luger, *Curio*	$600	$1500	$2500
1924-7 Simson, 9mm Luger, Dated Chamber, *Curio*	1100	2500	3000
1929 Bern, .30 Luger and 9mm Luger, *Curio*	700	1750	2000
1930-33 Death Head, 9mm Luger, *Curio*	550	1250	1500
1933 K.I., 9mm Luger, *Curio*	400	850	1000
1933-35 Dutch, 9mm Luger, Royal Dutch Air Force, *Curio*	600	1450	1650
1933-35 Mauser Commercial, 9mm Luger, *Curio*	550	1250	1500
1934 P Commercial Krieghoff, .30 Luger and 9mm Luger, *Curio*	1100	2250	2500
1934 P Commercial, Krieghoff, 9mm Luger, *Curio*	900	2000	2250
1934 Sideframe, Krieghoff, 6" Barrel, 9mm Luger, *Curio*	1100	2500	3000
1935 Portuguese, "GNR,".30 Luger, *Curio*	800	1750	2000
1936 Persian, 9mm Luger, *Curio*	1400	3000	3500
1936-37, 9mm Luger, Krieghoff, *Curio*	800	1750	2250
1936-39, .30 Luger and 9mm Luger, 4" Barrel, *Curio*	350	750	900
1936-40 Dutch Banner, 9mm Luger, *Curio*	800	1500	1750
1936-9 S/42, 9mm Luger, *Curio*	325	750	875
1937-39 Banner Commercial, .30 Luger, 4" Barrel, *Curio*	700	1500	1750
1938, 9mm Luger, *Curio*	1200	2500	2650
1939-40 42, 9mm Luger, *Curio*	300	625	750
1940 42/44 byf, 9mm Luger, *Curio*	300	600	750
1940 Mauser Banner, .30 Luger and 9mm Luger, *Curio*	550	1250	1500
1940, 9mm Luger, Krieghoff, *Curio*	1000	2250	2500

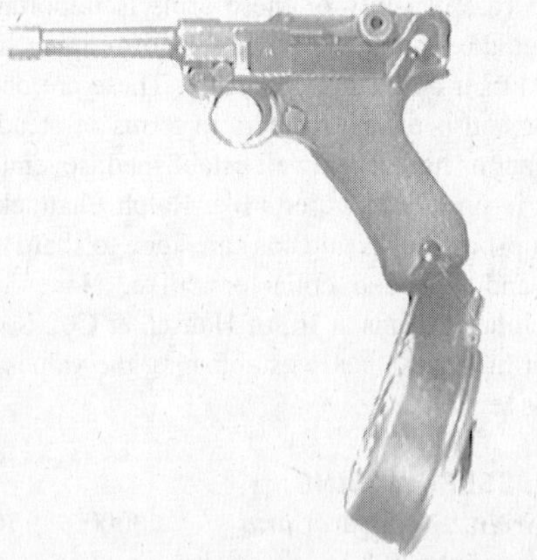

Luger 1940-42 with Snail Drum

	Fair	V. Good	Excellent
1941-42 byf, 9mm Luger, *Curio*	350	750	900
1941-44, 9mm Luger, Krieghoff, *Curio*	1000	2250	2750
1945, 9mm Luger, Krieghoff, *Curio*	2500	5000	7500

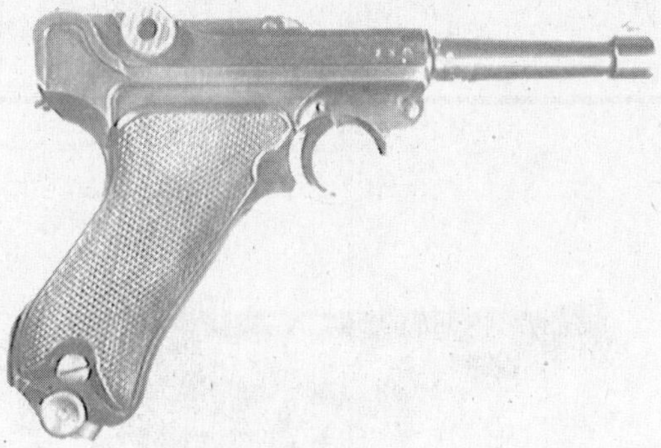

Luger 1941-42 byf

Luger VOPO

	Fair	V. Good	Excellent
36, 9mm Luger, Krieghoff, *Curio*	$1100	$2500	$3000
41 & 42 Banner, 9mm Luger, *Curio*	650	1450	1650
42/41, 9mm Luger, *Curio*	400	800	950
Artillery, Stock Only, *Curio*	150	300	350
Austrian Banner, 9mm Luger, *Curio*	700	1500	1850
Banner Commercial, .30 Luger, 4" Barrel, *Curio*	700	1500	1750
Double Date, 9mm Luger, *Curio*	250	550	700
G.L. Baby, 9mm Luger, *Curio*			Rare
G-S/42, 9mm Luger, *Curio*	300	650	800
Ideal, Holster Stock, *Curio*	450	1000	1250
K U, 9mm Luger, *Curio*	550	1200	1500
K-S/42 Navy, 9mm Luger, *Curio*	1100	2250	2800
K-S/42, 9mm Luger, *Curio*	900	2000	2500
Mauser Banner Commercial, 9mm Luger, *Curio*	600	1250	1750
Navy Stock Only	250	500	650
Post War, 9mm Luger, Krieghoff, *Curio*	700	1500	1750
S/42 Navy, 9mm Luger, *Curio*	400	850	1000
Snail Drum, Magazine, *Curio*	250	500	800
Stoeger Luger Carbine, .22 L.R.R.F., Clip Fed, Alloy Frame, *Modern*	150	375	475
Stoeger Luger, .22 L.R.R.F., Clip Fed, Alloy Frame, *Modern*	100	225	300
Stoeger Luger, .22 L.R.R.F., Clip Fed, Alloy Frame, Checkered Wood Grips, Early, *Modern*	100	250	325
Stoeger Target Luger, .22 L.R.R.F., Clip Fed, Alloy Frame, *Modern*	100	250	325
U.S. Test Eagle 1900, .30 Luger, *Curio*	1200	2500	3000
Vickers Commercial, 9mm Luger, *Curio*	1400	3000	3500
Vickers Military, 9mm Luger, *Curio*	900	2000	2500
VOPO, 9mm Luger, Clip Fed, *Modern*	600	1250	1450

LUR-PANZER

Echave y Arizmendi, Eibar, Spain.

HANDGUN, SELF-LOADING

	Fair	V. Good	Excellent
Luger Type, .22 L.R.R.F., Toggle Action, Clip Fed, *Modern*	$75	$125	$175

LYMAN GUN SIGHT CORP.

Middlefield, Conn.

HANDGUN, PERCUSSION

.36 1851 Navy, Color Case Hardened Frame, Engraved Cylinder, Reproduction	50	100	175
.36 New Model Navy, Brass Trigger Guard, Solid Frame, Reproduction	25	75	150
.44 1860 Army, Color Case Hardened Frame, Engraved Cylinder, Reproduction	50	100	175
.44 New Model Army, Brass Trigger Guard, Solid Frame, Reproduction	50	100	175

RIFLE, FLINTLOCK

Plains Rifle, Various Calibers, Brass Furniture, Set Trigger, Reproduction	100	200	275

RIFLE, PERCUSSION

Plains Rifle, Various Calibers, Brass Furniture, Set Trigger, Reproduction	75	150	225
Trade Rifle, Various Calibers, Brass Furniture, Set Trigger, Reproduction	50	125	200

RIFLE, SINGLESHOT

Centennial, 45/70 Government, Ruger #1, Commemorative, Cased with Accessories, *Modern*	600	1200	1650

M

MAADI

RIFLE, SELF-LOADING

	Fair	V. Good	Excellent
Paratrooper AKM, 7.62 × 39mm, Clip Fed, Assault Rifle, *Modern*	$350	$750	$1150
Standard AKM, 7.62 × 39mm, Clip Fed, Assault Rifle, *Modern*	350	750	1050

MAB

Mre. d'Armes Automatiques Bayonne, Bayonne, France, since 1921.

HANDGUN, SELF-LOADING

	Fair	V. Good	Excellent
Modele A, 6.35mm, Clip Fed, *Modern*	75	150	200

MAB Modele A

	Fair	V. Good	Excellent
Modele B, 6.35mm, Clip Fed, *Modern*	100	225	275
Modele C, .380 ACP, Clip Fed, *Modern*	100	225	275
Modele C, 7.65mm, Clip Fed, *Modern*	100	200	250
Modele C/D, .380 ACP, Clip Fed, *Modern*	75	175	225
Modele C/D, 7.65mm, Clip Fed, *Modern*	75	150	200
Modele D, .380 ACP, Clip Fed, *Modern*	75	175	225
Modele D, 7.65mm, Clip Fed, *Modern*	75	150	200
Modele D, 7.65mm, Clip Fed, French Military, *Curio*	100	225	275
Modele E, 6.35mm, Clip Fed, Long Grip, *Modern*	100	200	250
Modele F, .22 L.R.R.F., Clip Fed, Hammer, 3" Barrel, *Modern*	75	175	225

MAB Modele E

	Fair	V. Good	Excellent
Modele F, .22 L.R.R.F., Clip Fed, Hammer, 5" Barrel, *Modern*	$100	$200	$275
Modele GZ, 7.65mm, Clip Fed, *Modern*	75	175	225
Modele Le Chasseur, .22 L.R.R.F., Clip Fed, Hammer, Target Grips, *Modern*	100	200	250
Modele PA-15, 9mm Luger, Clip Fed, Hammer, *Modern*	150	350	425
Modele R Court, 7.65mm, Clip Fed, Hammer, *Modern*	125	275	350
Modele R Longue, 7.65 MAS, Clip Fed, Hammer, *Modern*	125	250	325
Modele R Para, 9mm Luger, Clip Fed, Hammer, *Curio*	150	350	450
Modele R, 7.65mm, Clip Fed, *Modern*	125	250	325

Nazi Navy Proofs, Add 40%-50%
Nazi Proofs, Add 20%-30%
W.A.C. Markings, Deduct 5%-10%
(Importer Winfield Arms Co., Los Angeles, Calif.)

M.A.C.

(Military Armament Corp.) See Ingram.

MACLEOD

Doune, Scotland, 1711–1750.

HANDGUN, FLINTLOCK

	Fair	V. Good	Excellent
.54, All Steel, Engraved, Ram's Horn Butt, *Antique*	1400	3000	4250

MAGNUM RESEARCH INC.

Minneapolis, Minn. Also see Israeli Military.

	Fair	V. Good	Excellent

HANDGUN, SELF-LOADING

	Fair	V. Good	Excellent
Desert Eagle, .357 Magnum, Clip Fed, Interchangeable Barrels, Gas Operated, Blue, *Modern*	$250	$600	$850

MAICHE, A.

France.

HANDGUN, FLINTLOCK

	Fair	V. Good	Excellent
.56, Brass Mountings, Holster Pistol, *Antique*	225	400	650

MALTBY-CURTIS

Agent for Norwich Pistol Co., 1875–1881.

HANDGUN, REVOLVER

	Fair	V. Good	Excellent
.22 Short R.F., 7 Shot, Spur Trigger, Solid Frame, Single Action, *Antique*	75	150	200
.32 Short R.F., 5 Shot, Spur Trigger, Solid Frame, Single Action, *Antique*	75	150	200

MALTY-HENLEY & CO.

New York City, 1878–1899. Made by Columbia Armory, Tenn.

HANDGUN, REVOLVER

	Fair	V. Good	Excellent
Spencer Safety Hammerless, .32 S & W, 5 Shot, Top Break, Hammerless, Double Action, *Curio*	100	200	300

MAMBA

Made by Relay Products in Johannesburg, South Africa, and Navy Arms in the U.S.

HANDGUN, SELF-LOADING

	Fair	V. Good	Excellent
Navy Mamba, 9mm Luger, Stainless, Double Action, *Modern*	150	300	350
Relay Mamba, 9mm Luger, Stainless, Double Action, *Modern*	200	425	500
Rhodesian Mamba, 9mm Luger, Stainless, Double Action, *Modern*	700	1500	2250

MANHATTAN FIREARMS MFG. CO.

Newark, N.J., 1849–1864. Their closeness in appearance and quality to Colt Model 1849 Pocket and Model 1851 Navy and to early Smith & Wesson .22 rimfire revolvers have contributed to the demand for Manhattan firearms. The late James U. Blanchard III commissioned the author to do a comprehensive book, *The Guns of Manhattan,* for publication in 2003. The Blanchard Foundation has over 600 Manhattans, among them the most historic known example, a cased Navy revolver presented to Ulysses S. Grant by men of his command while in Louisiana during the Civil War. Richly engraved and handsomely plated and blued, the revolver's inscription was neatly incised on the butt of the checkered ivory grips. *The Guns of Manhattan,* though featuring Manhattan firearms, will also focus on other guns made in New York City, on dealers in arms, and on New York residents like Theodore Roosevelt and Colt Board Chairman Donald E. Zilkha, both keen enthusiasts of firearms.

HANDGUN, PERCUSSION

	Fair	V. Good	Excellent
Bar Hammer, Double Action, Screw Barrel, Singleshot, *Antique*	$150	$300	$400

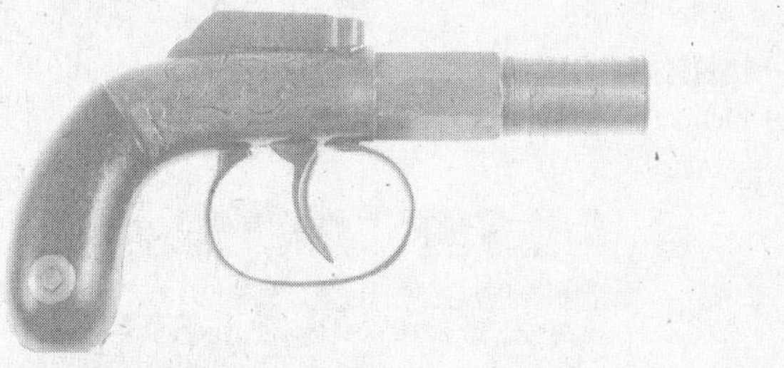

Manhattan Bar Hammer, .31 Caliber

	Fair	V. Good	Excellent
Hero, Singleshot, Derringer, *Antique*	125	250	350
Pepperbox, .28, 3 Shot, Double Action, *Antique*	300	650	900
Pepperbox, .28, 6 Shot, Double Action, *Antique*	250	550	750
Revolver, .31, Pocket Model, Single Action, *Antique*	200	400	600
Revolver, .36, Navy Model, Single Action, *Antique*	350	700	950
Revolver, Pocket, .22 Cal. Cartridge, *Antique*	175	375	525

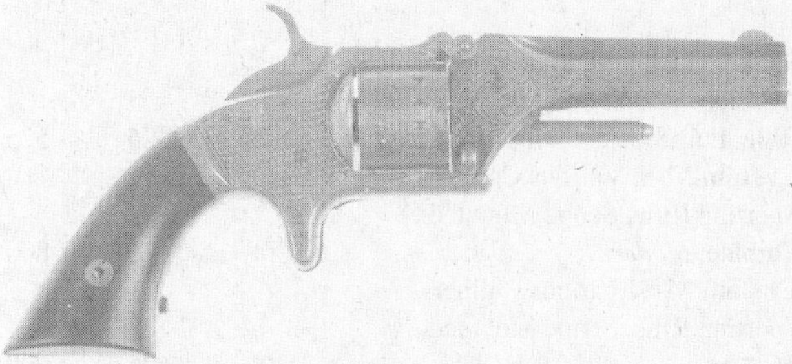

Manhattan Second Model, .22 Caliber

MANHURIN

Mre. de Machines du Haut-Rhin, Mulhouse-Bourtzwiller, France. Also see Walther.

HANDGUN, REVOLVER

	Fair	V. Good	Excellent
Model 73 Police, .357 Magnum, Double Action, Swing-Out Cylinder, *Modern*	400	900	1250
Model 73 Sport, .357 Magnum, Double Action, Swing-Out Cylinder, *Modern*	500	1000	1350

MANN

Fritz Mann Werkzeugfabrik, Suhl, Germany, 1919–1924.

HANDGUN, SELF-LOADING

	Fair	V. Good	Excellent
.25 ACP, Clip Fed, *Curio*	$150	$300	$400
Pocket, .32 ACP, Clip Fed, *Curio*	150	300	400
Pocket, .380 ACP, Clip Fed, *Curio*	150	325	425

MANN, MICHEL

Uhlenberg, Germany, c. 1630.

Mann Pocket

HANDGUN, WHEEL LOCK

	Fair	V. Good	Excellent
Miniature, All Metal, Gold Damascened, Ball Pommel, *Antique*	1600	3500	4750

MANNLICHER-SCHOENAUER

Steyr-Daimler-Puch, Steyr, Austria.

RIFLE, BOLT ACTION

	Fair	V. Good	Excellent
Alpine, Various Calibers, Sporting Rifle, Full-Stocked, *Modern*	200	425	525
Custom M-S, Various Calibers, Sporting Rifle, Scope Mounted, Carbine, *Modern*	300	650	800
Custom M-S, Various Calibers, Sporting Rifle, Scope Mounted, *Modern*	300	675	900
High Velocity, Various Calibers, Sporting Rifle, Set Trigger, *Modern*	350	750	1000
High Velocity, Various Calibers, Sporting Rifle, Takedown, Set Trigger, *Modern*	350	775	1050
M-72 LM, Various Calibers, Sporting Rifle, Full-Stocked, *Modern*	350	750	1000
M-72 S, Various Calibers, Sporting Rifle, *Modern*	350	775	1050
M-72 T, Various Calibers, Sporting Rifle, *Modern*	400	800	1150
Magnum M-S, Various Calibers, Sporting Rifle, Monte Carlo Stock, Set Trigger, *Modern*	400	825	1200
MCA, Various Calibers, Sporting Rifle, Carbine, Monte Carlo Stock, *Modern*	425	875	1250
MCA, Various Calibers, Sporting Rifle, Monte Carlo Stock, *Modern*	$425	$850	$1225
Model 1903, Various Calibers, Sporting Rifle, Carbine, Set Trigger, Full-Stocked, *Modern*	450	900	1250
Model 1905, 9 × 56 M.S., Sporting Rifle, Carbine, Set Trigger, Full-Stocked, *Modern*	450	900	1275
Model 1908, Various Calibers, Sporting Rifle, Carbine, Set Trigger, Full-Stocked, *Modern*	450	925	1300
Model 1910, 9.5 × 57 M.S., Sporting Rifle, Carbine, Set Trigger, Full-Stocked, *Modern*	450	950	1300
Model 1924, .30-06 Springfield, Sporting Rifle, Carbine, Set Trigger, Full-Stocked, *Modern*	500	1000	1350
Model 1950, 6.5 × 54 M.S., Sporting Rifle, Carbine, Set Trigger, Full-Stocked, *Modern*	400	850	1225
Model 1950, Various Calibers, Sporting Rifle, Carbine, Set Trigger, Full-Stocked, *Modern*	400	850	1225
Model 1950, Various Calibers, Sporting Rifle, Set Trigger, *Modern*	350	750	1000
Model 1952, 6.5 × 54 M.S., Sporting Rifle, Carbine, Set Trigger, Full-Stocked, *Modern*	400	900	1250
Model 1952, Various Calibers, Sporting Rifle, Carbine, Set Trigger, Full-Stocked, *Modern*	400	800	1200
Model 1952, Various Calibers, Sporting Rifle, Set Trigger, *Modern*	300	650	850
Model 1956, Various Calibers, Sporting Rifle, Carbine, Set Trigger, Full-Stocked, *Modern*	350	750	950
Model 1956, Various Calibers, Sporting Rifle, Set Trigger, *Modern*	350	725	925
Model L Varmint, Various Calibers, Checkered Stock, Set Trigger, *Modern*	225	475	625
Model M Professional, Various Calibers, Checkered Stock, Set Trigger, *Modern*	175	375	525
Model M, Various Calibers, Checkered Stock, Set Trigger, *Modern*	250	550	750
Model ML 79, Various Calibers, Checkered Stock, Set Trigger, *Modern*	350	700	950
Model S, Various Calibers, Checkered Stock, Set Trigger, *Modern*	300	625	850
Model S/T Magnum, Various Calibers, Checkered Stock, Set Trigger, *Modern*	300	650	850
Model SSG Match, .308 Win., Synthetic Target Stock, Set Triggers, Walther Peep Sights, *Modern*	250	575	750
Model SSG, .308 Win., Synthetic Target Stock, Set Triggers, *Modern*	200	450	650
Premier, Various Calibers, Sporting Rifle, Fancy Checkering, Engraved, *Modern*	250	575	750

	Fair	V. Good	Excellent
Premier, Various Calibers, Sporting Rifle, Magnum Action, Fancy Checkering, Engraved, *Modern*	$600	$1250	$1550

RIFLE, DOUBLE BARREL, SIDE-BY-SIDE

Mustang, Various Calibers, Standard, Checkered Stock, Sidelock, *Modern*	2600	5000	7500
Mustang, Various Calibers, Standard, Checkered Stock, Sidelock, Engraved, *Modern*	2700	5500	7500

RIFLE, DOUBLE BARREL, OVER-UNDER

Safari 72, .375 H & M Mag., Checkered Stock, Engraved, Double Trigger, *Modern*	1400	3000	4500
Safari 77, Various Calibers, Checkered Stock, Engraved, Double Trigger, Automatic Ejector, *Modern*	1900	4000	5000

SHOTGUN, DOUBLE BARREL, OVER-UNDER

Edinbourgh, 12 Ga., Checkered Stock, Vent Rib, *Modern*	600	1250	1650

SHOTGUN, DOUBLE BARREL, SIDE-BY-SIDE

Ambassador English, 12 and 20 Gauges, Checkered Stock, Sidelock, Automatic Ejectors, Engraved, *Modern*	3200	7000	9250
Ambassador Executive, 12 and 20 Gauges, Checkered Stock, Sidelock, Automatic Ejectors, Fancy Engraving, *Modern*	5500	12000	16500
Ambassador Extra, 12 and 20 Gauges, Checkered Stock, Sidelock, Automatic Ejectors, Engraved, *Modern*	3100	6500	8500
Ambassador Golden Black, 12 and 20 Gauges, Checkered Stock, Sidelock, Automatic Ejectors, Engraved, Gold Inlays, *Modern*	4100	8500	10500
London, 12 and 20 Gauges, Checkered Stock, Sidelock, Automatic Ejectors, Engraved, Cased, *Modern*	1100	2250	3000
Oxford Field, 12 and 20 Gauges, Checkered Stock, Automatic Ejectors, Engraved, *Modern*	450	1000	1750

MANTON J. & CO.

Belgium, c. 1900.

SHOTGUN, DOUBLE BARREL, SIDE-BY-SIDE

Various Gauges, Hammerless, Damascus Barrel, *Modern*	75	150	300
Various Gauges, Hammerless, Steel Barrel, *Modern*	75	150	300
Various Gauges, Outside Hammers, Damascus Barrel, *Modern*	75	150	300
Various Gauges, Outside Hammers, Steel Barrel, *Modern*	75	150	300

SHOTGUN, SINGLESHOT

	Fair	V. Good	Excellent
Various Gauges, Hammer, Steel Barrel, *Modern*	$25	$50	$75

MANTON, JOSEPH

London, England, 1795–1838. One of the giants in the history of gunmaking, Joe Manton's reputation was such that he was considered a legend in his own lifetime. An exhaustively detailed and superbly illustrated Manton book, by David Back and Keith Neal, has been instrumental in the strength of the market of these guns. Among Joe Manton's distinctions were his development of the elevated barrel rib, the gravitating stop (prevented accidental firing during loading) and an improved patent breech. The spirit of Manton lives on in the British gun trade: across the street from the Holland & Holland London factory is the gravesite of Manton, carved with the following inscription written by Colonel Peter Hawker:

IN MEMORY OF
MR JOSEPH MANTON, WHO DIED UNIVERSALLY REGRETTED
ON THE 29TH DAY OF JUNE 1838. AGED 66 YEARS.
THIS HUMBLE TABLET IS PLACED HERE BY HIS AFFLICTED FAMILY
MERELY TO MARK WHERE ARE DEPOSITED HIS MORTAL REMAINS
BUT AN EVERLASTING MONUMENT TO HIS UNRIVALLED GENIUS
IS ALREADY ESTABLISHED IN EVERY QUARTER OF THE GLOBE.
BY HIS CELEBRITY AS THE GREATEST ARTIST IN FIRE ARMS THAT EVER THE
WORLD PRODUCED, AS THE FOUNDER AND THE FATHER
OF THE MODERN GUN TRADE AND AS A MOST SCIENTIFIC INVENTOR
IN OTHER DEPARTMENTS NOT ONLY FOR THE BENEFIT
OF HIS FRIENDS AND THE SPORTING WORLD
BUT FOR THE GOOD OF HIS KING AND COUNTRY

HANDGUN, FLINTLOCK

Pair, Octagon Barrel, Dueling Pistols, Gold Inlays, Light Engraving, Cased with Accessories, *Antique*	3000	6500	8500

HANDGUN, PERCUSSION

.55, Pair, Dueling Pistols, Octagon Barrel, Light Ornamentation, Cased with Accessories, *Antique*	1900	4000	6000

SHOTGUN, PERCUSSION

12 Ga. Double Barrel, Side-by-Side, Damascus Barrels, Light Engraving, Gold Inlays, *Antique*	450	1250	1750

MANUFRANCE

Manufacture Francaise de Armes et Cycles de St. Etienne, St. Etienne, France. Also see Le Francaise. 1902–Date.

HANDGUN, SELF-LOADING

Model 1911 Astra-Manufacture, .32 ACP, Clip Fed, Blue, *Curio*	75	125	200

RIFLE, BOLT ACTION

Buffalo Match, .22 L.R.R.F., Target Rifle, *Modern*	75	150	225

	Fair	V. Good	Excellent
Club, .22 L.R.R.F., Singleshot, Carbine, *Modern*	$50	$75	$125
Club, .22 L.R.R.F., Singleshot, Carbine, Checkered Stock, *Modern*	50	100	175
Mauser K98 Sporter, .270 Win., Sporterized, Checkered Stock, *Modern*	50	125	200
Mauser K98 Sporter, .270 Win., Sporterized, Plain, *Modern*	50	100	175
Rival, 375 H & H Mag., Checkered Stock, *Modern*	100	250	325

RIFLE, SELF-LOADING

Reina, .22 L.R.R.F., Carbine, Clip Fed, *Modern*	45	125	175
Sniper, .22 W.M.R., Carbine, Clip Fed, *Modern*	75	150	225

SHOTGUN, DOUBLE BARREL, OVER-UNDER

Falcor Field, 12 Ga., Vent Rib, Automatic Ejector, Single Selective Trigger, Checkered Stock, *Modern*	250	575	750
Falcor Sport, 12 Ga., Vent Rib, Automatic Ejector, Single Selective Trigger, Checkered Stock, Extra Barrels, *Modern*	350	725	850
Falcor Trap, 12 Ga., Vent Rib, Automatic Ejector, Single Selective Trigger, Checkered Stock, *Modern*	300	625	875

SHOTGUN, DOUBLE BARREL, SIDE-BY-SIDE

Ideal DeLuxe, 12 Ga. 3", Fancy Engraving, Checkered Stock, Double Triggers, *Modern*	800	1750	2150
Ideal Prestige, 12 Ga. 3", Fancy Engraving, Checkered Stock, Double Triggers, *Modern*	1100	2500	3250
Robust, 12 Ga. 3", Checkered Stock, Double Triggers, *Modern*	150	350	550
Robust Luxe, 12 Ga. 3", Engraved, Automatic Ejectors, Checkered Stock, Double Triggers, *Modern*	275	600	850

SHOTGUN, SELF-LOADING

Perfex Special, *Modern*	150	325	450
Perfex, 12 Ga., Checkered Stock, *Modern*	150	300	425

SHOTGUN, SINGLESHOT

Simplex, 12 Gauge, Sling Swivels, *Modern*	75	125	150

SHOTGUN, SLIDE ACTION

Rapid, 12 or 16 Gauges, Plain, *Modern*	75	150	225

MARK X

Made in Zestavia, Yugoslavia. Imported by Interarms.

RIFLE, BOLT ACTION

	Fair	V. Good	Excellent
Alaskan, Various Calibers, Magnum, Open Rear Sights, Checkered Stock, Sling Swivels, *Modern*	$125	$250	$425
Cavalier, Various Calibers, Cheekpiece, Checkered Stock, Open Rear Sight, Sling Swivels, *Modern*	125	225	400
Mannlicher, Various Calibers, Carbine, Full-Stocked, Checkered Stock, Open Rear Sight, Sling Swivels, *Modern*	125	250	425
Marquis, Various Calibers, Carbine, Mauser Action, *Modern*	200	425	600
Standard, Various Calibers, Checkered Stock, Open Rear Sight, Sling Swivels, *Modern*	100	225	325
Viscount, Various Calibers, Plain, Open Rear Sight, Checkered Stock, Sling Swivels, *Modern*	75	175	300

MARKWELL ARMS CO.

Chicago, Ill.

HANDGUN, PERCUSSION

.41 Derringer, Singleshot, Brass Furniture, Reproduction	12	25	50
.44 C S A 1860, Revolver, 6 Shot, Brass Frame, Reproduction	25	50	75
.44 New Army, Revolver, 6 Shot, Brass Triggerguard, Reproduction	25	50	75
.45 Colonial, Singleshot, Brass Furniture, Reproduction	15	25	50
.45 Kentucky, Singleshot, Brass Furniture, Reproduction	15	25	50
.45 Loyalist, Singleshot, Brass Furniture, Set Trigger, Adjustable Sights, Reproduction	25	50	75

RIFLE, PERCUSSION

.45 Hawken, Brass Furniture, Reproduction	50	75	100
.45 Kentucky, Brass Furniture, Reproduction	25	50	75
.45 Super Kentucky, Brass Furniture, Set Trigger, Reproduction	75	100	125

MARLIN FIREARMS CO.

New Haven, Conn. J. M. Marlin, from 1870–1881. Marlin Firearms from 1881–1915. Marlin-Rockwell Corp., 1915–1926. From 1926 to date as Marlin Firearms Co., North Haven, Ct. Also see Ballard. Also see the Commemorative Section. John Mahlon Marlin was a former employee of Colt's Pt. F.A. Mfg. Co., who began his career as a gun manufacturer in 1863, with a singleshot derringer pistol. By the early 1880s his fledgling company was manufacturing lever-action rifles rivaling those of Winchester (both firms were neighbors, in New Haven, Connecticut). Marlin also built Ballard singleshot rifles and single- and double-action revolvers. First in his line of lever-action repeating rifles was the Model of 1881. Unlike O. F. Winchester, who was primarily an investor and businessman, John Marlin was an inventor and designer, and was issued several patents. The company's New Haven factory, an impressive brick building which still stands on Willow Street, was erected at the turn of the century. In 1901, on the death of John M. Marlin, the business assumed a new direction under his sons Mahlon H. and J. Howard. The sons sold the business in 1915, and Marlin became part of the Marlin-Rockwell Corporation. By the early 1920s the company, which had gone through various changes, was heavily in debt. Known by 1921 as the Marlin Firearms Corporation, the firm was sold in 1924 to Frank Kenna, Sr. The Marlin Firearms Company has remained under the sole ownership of the Kenna family ever since.

	Fair	V. Good	Excellent
HANDGUN, REVOLVER			
Model 1887, .32 and.38, Double Action, Top Break, *Antique*	$150	$300	$425
Standard 1875, .30 R.F., Tip Up, Spur Trigger, *Antique*	100	225	300
XX Standard 1873, .22 R.F., Tip Up, Spur Trigger, *Antique*	200	425	650
XX Standard 1873, .22 R.F., Tip Up, Spur Trigger, Octagon Barrel, *Antique*	150	375	500
XXX Standard 1872, .30 R.F., Tip Up, Spur Trigger, Antique	175	375	500
XXX Standard 1872, .30 R.F., Tip Up, Spur Trigger, Octagon Barrel, *Antique*	175	350	450
RIFLE, BOLT ACTION			
Glenfield M10, .22 L.R.R.F., Singleshot, *Modern*	15	25	50
Glenfield M20, .22 L.R.R.F., Clip Fed, *Modern*	25	50	75
Model 100, .22 L.R.R.F., Singleshot, Open Rear Sight, Takedown, *Modern*	15	25	50
Model 100-S, .22 L.R.R.F., Singleshot, Peep Sights, Takedown, *Modern*	50	75	100
Model 100-SB, .22 L.R.R.F., Singleshot, Smoothbore, Takedown, *Modern*	15	25	50
Model 101, .22 L.R.R.F., Singleshot, Open Rear Sight, Takedown, Beavertail Forend, *Modern*	25	50	75
Model 101-DL, .22 L.R.R.F., Singleshot, Takedown, Peep Sights, Beavertail Forend, *Modern*	25	50	75
Model 122, .22 L.R.R.F., Singleshot, Open Rear Sight, Monte Carlo Stock, *Modern*	25	50	75
Model 322 (Sako), .222 Rem., Clip Fed, Peep Sights, Checkered Stock, *Modern*	125	275	350
Model 455 (FN), Various Calibers, Peep Sights, Monte Carlo Stock, Checkered Stock, *Modern*	150	300	375
Model 65, .22 L.R.R.F., Singleshot, Open Rear Sight, *Modern*	25	50	75

	Fair	V. Good	Excellent
Model 65E, .22 L.R.R.F., Singleshot, Peep Sights, *Modern*	$25	$50	$75
Model 780, .22 L.R.R.F., Clip Fed, Open Rear Sight, *Modern*	50	75	100
Model 781, .22 L.R.R.F., Tube Feed, Open Rear Sight, *Modern*	50	75	100
Model 782, .22 WMR., Clip Fed, Open Rear Sight, *Modern*	50	75	100
Model 783, .22 WMR, Tube Feed, Open Rear Sight, *Modern*	50	100	125

Marlin 783 with 200 Scope

Model 80, .22 L.R.R.F., Clip Fed, Open Rear Sight, Takedown, *Modern*	25	50	75
Model 80 DL, .22 L.R.R.F., Clip Fed, Beavertail Forend, Takedown, Peep Sights, *Modern*	25	50	75
Model 80C, .22 L.R.R.F., Clip Fed, Beavertail Forend, Takedown, Open Rear Sight, *Modern*	25	50	75
Model 80E, .22 L.R.R.F., Clip Fed, Peep Sights, Takedown, *Modern*	25	50	75
Model 81, .22 L.R.R.F., Tube Feed, Takedown, Open Rear Sight, *Modern*	25	50	75
Model 81C, .22 L.R.R.F., Tube Feed, Takedown, Open Rear Sight, Beavertail Forend, *Modern*	25	50	75
Model 81DL, .22 L.R.R.F., Tube Feed, Takedown, Peep Sights, Beavertail Forend, *Modern*	25	50	75
Model 81E, .22 L.R.R.F., Tube Feed, Takedown, Peep Sights, *Modern*	25	50	75
Model 81G, .22 L.R.R.F., Tube Feed, Takedown, Open Rear Sight, Beavertail Forend, *Modern*	25	50	75
Model 980, .22 WMR, Clip Fed, Monte Carlo Stock, Open Rear Sight, *Modern*	50	75	125
RIFLE, LEVER ACTION			
Centennial Set 336-39 (1970), Fancy Checkering, Fancy Wood, Engraved, Brass Furniture, *Curio*	450	1000	1450
Glenfield M 30 A, .30-30 Win., Tube Feed, *Modern*	75	125	200
M1894 (Late), .357 Magnum, Tube Feed, Open Rear Sight, *Modern*	100	200	275
M1894 (Late), .41 Magnum, Tube Feed, Open Rear Sight, *Modern*	100	200	275
M1894 (Late), .44 Magnum, Tube Feed, Open Rear Sight, *Modern*	100	225	300

Marlin Cased Centennial Pair

	Fair	V. Good	Excellent
M1895 (Late), .45-70 Government, Tube Feed, Open Rear Sight, *Modern*	$125	$250	$375
Model 1881 Standard, Various Calibers, Tube Feed, Open Rear Sight, *Antique*	500	1000	1400
Model 1888, Various Calibers, Tube Feed, Open Rear Sight, *Antique*	900	2500	3250
Model 1889 Standard, Various Calibers, Tube Feed, Open Rear Sight, *Antique*	300	650	900
Model 1891, .22 L.R.R.F., Tube Feed, Open Rear Sight, *Antique*	800	2000	2750
Model 1892 Over #177382, Various Calibers, Tube Feed, *Modern*	250	800	1250
Model 1892, Various Calibers, Tube Feed, Open Rear Sight, *Antique*	300	800	1250
Model 1893 over #177304, Various Calibers, Tube Feed, Solid Frame, Octagon Barrel, *Modern*	300	800	1250
Model 1893 over #177304, Various Calibers, Tube Feed, Solid Frame, Round Barrel, *Modern*	300	700	1150
Model 1893 over #177304, Various Calibers, Tube Feed, Solid Frame, Round Barrel, Carbine, *Modern*	300	800	1250
Model 1893 over #177304, Various Calibers, Tube Feed, Takedown, Octagon Barrel, *Modern*	300	800	1250
Model 1893 over #177304, Various Calibers, Tube Feed, Takedown, Round Barrel, *Modern*	275	700	1100
Model 1893 over #177304, Various Calibers, Tube Feed, Sporting Carbine, 5 Shot, *Modern*	325	650	1050
Model 1893 over #177304, Various Calibers, Tube Feed, Sporting Carbine, Takedown, 5 Shot, *Modern*	400	800	1250
Model 1893 over #177304, Various Calibers, Tube Feed, Full-Stocked, with Bayonet, *Modern*	1500	4500	7500
Model 1893, Various Calibers, Tube Feed, Musket, with Bayonet, *Antique*	2000	5000	8000
Model 1893, Various Calibers, Tube Feed, Solid Frame, Octagon Barrel, *Antique*	500	1200	1750

	Fair	V. Good	Excellent
Model 1893, Various Calibers, Tube Feed, Solid Frame, Round Barrel, *Antique*	$400	$1000	$1350
Model 1893, Various Calibers, Tube Feed, Solid Frame, Round Barrel, Carbine, *Antique*	400	1000	1350
Model 1893, Various Calibers, Tube Feed, Sporting Carbine, 5 Shot, *Antique*	400	1000	1350
Model 1893, Various Calibers, Tube Feed, Sporting Light Weight Rifle Takedown, 5 Shot, *Antique*	550	1200	1650
Model 1893, Various Calibers, Tube Feed, Takedown, Octagon Barrel, *Antique*	700	1500	1950
Model 1893, Various Calibers, Tube Feed, Takedown, Round Barrel, *Antique*	600	1300	1600
93 in. 25/36 cal. add 15%			
93 in. 32/40 or 38/55 cal. add 10%			
93 in. 32 spl. cal. deduct 15%			
Model 1894 over #175431, Various Calibers, Tube Feed, Takedown, Octagon Barrel, *Modern*	500	1000	1350
Model 1894 over #175431, Various Calibers, Tube Feed, Takedown, Round Barrel, *Modern*	400	800	1250
Model 1894 over #175431, Various Calibers, Tube Feed, Solid Frame, Octagon Barrel, *Modern*	500	1000	1350
Model 1894 over #175431, Various Calibers, Tube Feed, Solid Frame, Round Barrel, *Modern*	400	800	1250
Model 1894, Various Calibers, Tube Feed, Solid Frame, Octagon Barrel, *Antique*	600	1200	1750
Model 1894, Various Calibers, Tube Feed, Solid Frame, Round Barrel, *Antique*	500	1000	1350
Model 1894, Various Calibers, Tube Feed, Takedown, Octagon Barrel, *Antique*	600	1200	1750
Model 1894, Various Calibers, Tube Feed, Takedown, Round Barrel, *Antique*	500	1000	1350
Model 1895 Carbine over #167531, Various Calibers, Tube Feed, Takedown, Octagon Barrel, *Modern*	2000	7000	12500
Model 1895 Carbine, Various Calibers, Tube Feed, Takedown, Octagon Barrel, *Antique*	3500	9000	13500
Model 1895 Lightweight over #167531, Various Calibers, Tube Feed, Solid Frame, Octagon Barrel, *Modern*	500	2000	3000
Model 1895 Lightweight, Various Calibers, Tube Feed, Solid Frame, *Antique*	600	2000	2500

	Fair	V. Good	Excellent
Model 1895 Standard over #167531, Various Calibers, Tube Feed, Solid Frame, Round Barrel, *Modern*	$700	$1600	$1950
Model 1895 Standard, Various Calibers, Tube Feed, Solid Frame, *Antique*	800	1800	2150
Model 1897 over #177197, .22 L.R.R.F., Tube Feed, Takedown, *Modern*	550	1200	1600
Model 1936 Carbine	200	400	600
Model 1897, .22 L.R.R.F., Tube Feed, Takedown, *Antique*	550	1200	1600
Model 336 Marauder, Various Calibers, Tube Feed, Carbine, Open Rear Sight, Straight Grip, *Modern*	150	400	650
Model 336 Zane Grey, .30-.30 Win., Tube Feed, Octagon Barrel, Open Rear Sight, *Modern*	150	300	450
Model 336, .219 Zipper, Tube Feed, Sporting Carbine, Open Rear Sight, 5 Shot, *Modern*	250	600	950
94 Musket w/Bayonet.	1500	3500	8750
94 in. 44/40 cal. add 15%			
94 in. 45/70 cal. add 15%			
Model 336, Various Calibers, Tube Feed, Sporting Carbine, Open Rear Sight, 5 Shot, *Modern*	175	225	300
Model 336A, Various Calibers, Tube Feed, Sporting Rifle, Open Rear Sight, 5 Shot, *Modern*	150	225	300

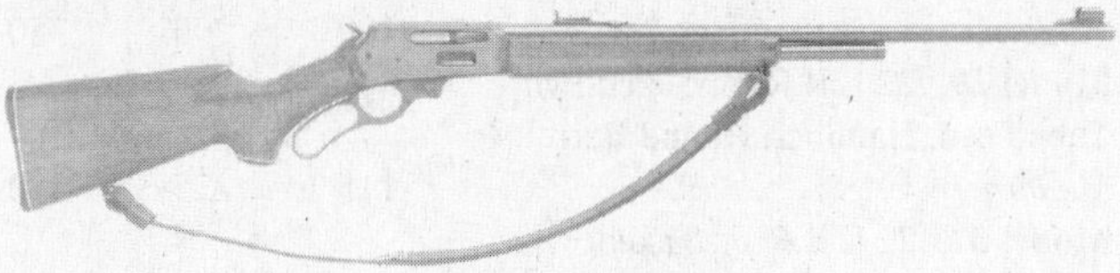

Marlin 336A

	Fair	V. Good	Excellent
Model 336A-DL, Various Calibers, Tube Feed, Sporting Rifle, Open Rear Sight, 5 Shot, Checkered Stock, *Modern*	125	175	250
Model 336C, Various Calibers, Tube Feed, Carbine, Open Rear Sight, *Modern*	125	175	250
Model 336T, .44 Magnum, Tube Feed, Carbine, Open Rear Sight, Straight Grip, *Modern*	125	175	250
Model 336T, Various Calibers, Tube Feed, Carbine, Open Rear Sight, Straight Grip, *Modern*	125	175	250
Model 36, Various Calibers, Tube Feed, Beavertail Forend, Open Rear Sight, Carbine, *Modern*	150	225	300

	Fair	V. Good	Excellent
Model 36, Various Calibers, Tube Feed, Beavertail Forend, Open Rear Sight, Sporting Carbine, 5 Shot, *Modern*	$150	$250	$325
Model 36A, Various Calibers, Tube Feed, Beavertail Forend, Open Rear Sight, 5 Shot, *Modern*	150	225	300
Model 36DL, Various Calibers, Tube Feed, Fancy Checkering, Open Rar Sight, 5 Shot, *Modern*	150	250	375
Model 39 Article II, .22 L.R.R.F., Takedown, Tube Feed, Hammer, Octagon Barrel, *Modern*	150	275	350
Model 39 Article II, .22 L.R.R.F., Takedown, Tube Feed, Hammer, Octagon Barrel, Carbine, *Modern*	150	325	400
Model 39 Century, .22 L.R.R.F., Takedown, Tube Feed, Hammer, Octagon Barrel, *Modern*	150	250	350

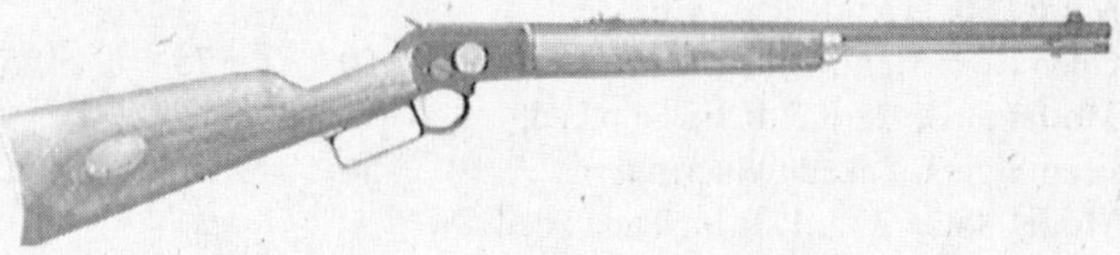

Marlin 39 Century Ltd.

	Fair	V. Good	Excellent
Model 39 M, .22 L.R.R.F., Takedown, Tube Feed, Hammer, Round Barrel, Carbine, *Modern*	150	250	325
Model 39, .22 L.R.R.F., Takedown, Hammer, Octagon Barrel, *Modern*	200	750	1150
Model 39A Mountie, .22 L.R.R.F., Takedown, Tube Feed, Hammer, Round Barrel, *Modern*	150	200	350
Model 39A, .22 L.R.R.F., Takedown, Tube Feed, Hammer, Round Barrel, *Modern*	150	200	300

Marlin 39A

	Fair	V. Good	Excellent
Model 444, .444 Marlin, Tube Feed, Monte Carlo Stock, Open Rear Sight, Straight Grip, *Modern*	150	200	275
Model 56, .22 L.R.R.F., Clip Fed, Open Rear Sight, Monte Carlo Stock, *Modern*	100	125	200
Model 57, .22 L.R.R.F., Tube Feed, Open Rear Sight, Monte Carlo Stock, *Modern*	100	125	200
Model 57M, .22 WMR., Tube Feed, Open Rear Sight, Monte Carlo Stock, *Modern*	125	150	200

	Fair	V. Good	Excellent
Model 62, Various Calibers, Clip Fed, Open Rear Sight, Monte Carlo Stock, *Modern*	$175	$200	$300

RIFLE, SELF-LOADING

	Fair	V. Good	Excellent
Glenfield M40, .22 L.R.R.F., Tube Feed, *Modern*	75	100	150
Glenfield M60, .22 L.R.R.F., Tube Feed, *Modern*	25	50	100
Model 49 DL, .22 L.R.R.F., Tube Feed, Open Rear Sight, *Modern*	50	75	125

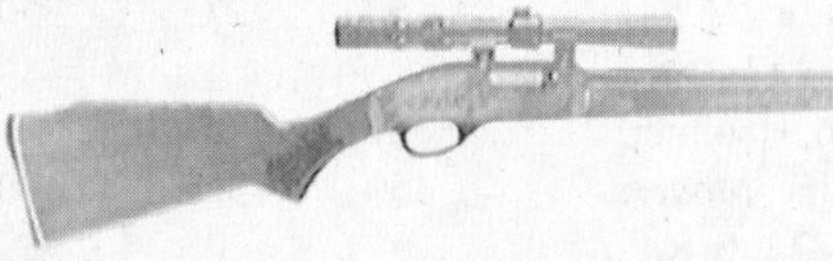

Marlin Model 49 DL

	Fair	V. Good	Excellent
Model 50, .22 L.R.R.F., Clip Fed, Open Rear Sight, Takedown, *Modern*	50	75	125
Model 50E, .22 L.R.R.F., Clip Fed, Peep Sights, Takedown, *Modern*	50	75	125
Model 88C, .22 L.R.R.F., Tube Feed, Takedown, Open Rear Sight, *Modern*	50	75	125
Model 88DL, .22 L.R.R.F., Tube Feed, Takedown, Peep Sights, *Modern*	75	100	150
Model 89C, .22 L.R.R.F., Clip Fed, Takedown, Open Rear Sight, *Modern*	50	75	125
Model 89DL, .22 L.R.R.F., Clip Fed, Takedown, Peep Sights, *Modern*	75	100	150
Model 98, .22 L.R.R.F., Tube Feed, Solid Frame, Open Rear Sight, Monte Carlo Stock, *Modern*	50	75	125
Model 989 G, .22 L.R.R.F., Clip Fed, Open Rear Sight, Monte Carlo Stock, *Modern*	25	50	100
Model 989, .22 L.R.R.F., Clip Fed, Open Rear Sight, Monte Carlo Stock, *Modern*	25	50	100

Marlin Model 989 M-2

	Fair	V. Good	Excellent
Model 99 M-1, .22 L.R.R.F., Tube Feed, Open Rear Sight, Monte Carlo Stock, *Modern*	25	50	100

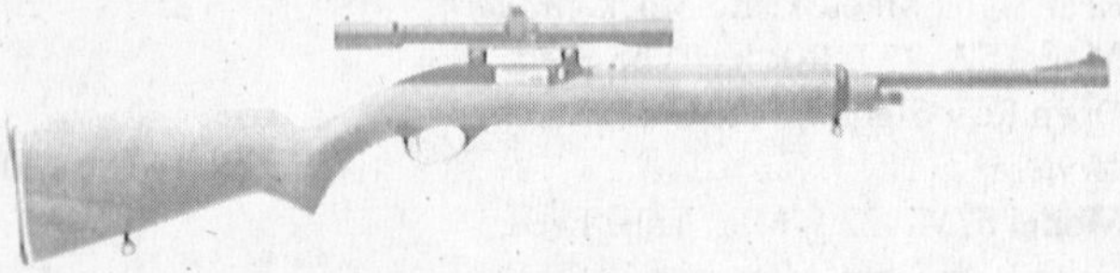

Marlin Model 99 M-1

	Fair	V. Good	Excellent
Model 99 M-2, .22 L.R.R.F., Clip Fed, Open Rear Sight, *Modern*	$25	$50	$75
Model 99, .22 L.R.R.F., Tube Feed, Open Rear Sight, *Modern*	25	50	75
Model 990, .22 L.R.R.F., Tube Feed, Open Rear Sight, Monte Carlo Stock, *Modern*	25	50	75
Model 995, .22 L.R.R.F., Clip Fed, Open Rear Sight, *Modern*	25	50	75
Model 99C, .22 L.R.R.F., Tube Feed, Open Rear Sight, Monte Carlo Stock, *Modern*	25	50	75
Model 99DL, .22 L.R.R.F., Tube Feed, Open Rear Sight, Monte Carlo Stock, *Modern*	25	50	75
Model A-1, .22 L.R.R.F., Clip Fed, Takedown, Open Rear Sight, *Modern*	25	50	75
Model A-1E, .22 L.R.R.F., Clip Fed, Takedown, Peep Sights, *Modern*	25	50	75

RIFLE, SLIDE ACTION

	Fair	V. Good	Excellent
Model 18, .22 L.R.R.F., Solid Frame, Tube Feed, Hammer, *Modern*	125	250	375
Model 20, .22 L.R.R.F., Takedown, Tube Feed, Hammer, Octagon Barrel, *Modern*	125	225	350
Model 25, .22 Short R.F., Takedown, Tube Feed, Hammer, *Modern*	125	250	400
Model 27, Various Calibers, Takedown, Tube Feed, Hammer, Octagon Barrel, *Modern*	100	200	350
Model 27-S, Various Calibers, Takedown, Tube Feed, Hammer, Round Barrel, *Modern*	100	200	350
Model 29, .22 L.R.R.F., Takedown, Tube Feed, Hammer, Round Barrel, *Modern*	115	225	350
Model 32, .22 L.R.R.F., Takedown, Tube Feed, Hammerless, Octagon Barrel, *Modern*	150	250	350
Model 38, .22 L.R.R.F., Takedown, Tube Feed, Hammerless, Octagon Barrel, *Modern*	150	250	350

SHOTGUN, BOLT ACTION

	Fair	V. Good	Excellent
Glenfield, 12 Ga. 3", Clip Fed, *Modern*	50	75	100
Model 55, 12 Ga. 3", Clip Fed, Adjustable Choke, *Modern*	75	100	125

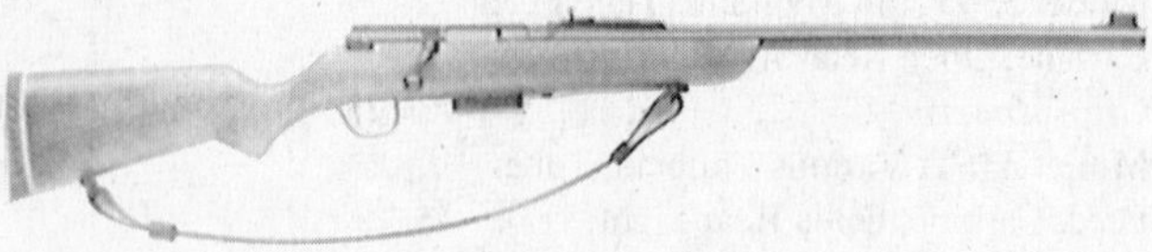

Marlin Model 55 Slug Gun

	Fair	V. Good	Excellent
Model 55, Various Gauges, Clip Fed, *Modern*	50	75	100

	Fair	V. Good	Excellent
Model 55, Various Gauges, Clip Fed, Adjustable Choke, *Modern*	$75	$100	$150
Model 55 Goose Gun, 12 Ga. 3", Clip Fed, *Modern*	75	150	200
Model 55S, 12 Ga. 3", Clip Fed, *Modern*	75	125	175
Model Super Goose, 10 Ga. 3 1/2", Clip Fed, *Modern*	100	175	225

SHOTGUN, DOUBLE BARREL, OVER-UNDER

	Fair	V. Good	Excellent
Model 90, 12 and 16 Gauges, Checkered, Double Triggers, *Modern*	150	350	425
Model 90, 12 and 16 Gauges, Checkered, Single Triggers, *Modern*	200	400	500
Model 90, 20 Gauge, Checkered Stock, Double Triggers, Modern	200	425	500
Model 90, 20 Gauge, Checkered Stock, Single Triggers, *Modern*	200	475	550
Model 90, 410 Gauge as above	300	600	750

SHOTGUN, LEVER ACTION

	Fair	V. Good	Excellent
Four-Tenner, .410 Ga., Tube Feed, *Modern*	500	1000	1350

SHOTGUN, SLIDE ACTION

	Fair	V. Good	Excellent
Glenfield Model 778, 12 Ga., Hammerless, Tube Feed, *Modern*	100	175	250
Model 120, 12 Ga. 3", Hammerless, Tube Feed, *Modern*	125	250	325
Model 16 A, 12 Ga., Hammer, Tube Feed, *Modern*	125	250	300
Model 16 B, 12 Ga., Hammer, Tube Feed, Checkered Stock, *Modern*	150	350	425
Model 16 C, 12 Ga., Hammer, Tube Feed, Checkered Stock, Fancy Wood, Light Engraving, *Modern*	200	450	750
Model 16 D, 12 Ga., Hammer, Tube Feed, Checkered Stock, Fancy Wood, Engraved, *Modern*	400	850	1150
Model 17, 12 Ga., Hammer, Tube Feed, *Modern*	200	400	500
Model 1898 A, 12 Ga., Hammer, Tube Feed, *Modern*	150	325	425
Model 1898 B, 12 Ga., Hammer, Tube Feed, Checkered Stock, *Modern*	150	375	475
Model 1898 C, 12 Ga., Hammer, Tube Feed, Checkered Stock, Fancy Wood, Light Engraving, *Modern*	250	600	850
Model 1898 D, 12 Ga., Hammer, Tube Feed, Checkered Stock, Fancy Wood, Engraved, *Modern*	700	1500	1950
Model 19 A, 12 Ga., Hammer, Tube Feed, *Modern*	150	275	325
Model 19 B, 12 Ga., Hammer, Tube Feed, Checkered Stock, *Modern*	150	350	425
Model 19 C, 12 Ga., Hammer, Tube Feed, Checkered Stock, Fancy Wood, Light Engraving, *Modern*	225	600	850
Model 19 D, 12 Ga., Hammer, Tube Feed, Checkered Stock, Fancy Wood, Engraved, *Modern*	$500	$1500	$1850
Model 21 B, 12 Ga., Hammer, Tube Feed, Checkered Stock, *Modern*	200	350	450
Model 21 C, 12 Ga., Hammer, Tube Feed, Checkered Stock, Fancy Wood, Light Engraving, *Modern*	250	500	700
Model 21 D, 12 Ga., Hammer, Tube Feed, Checkered Stock, Fancy Wood, Engraved, *Modern*	400	1500	1850
Model 21 Field, 12 Ga., Hammer, Tube Feed, *Modern*	150	250	300
Model 24 B, 12 Ga., Hammer, Tube Feed, Checkered Stock, *Modern*	200	350	425
Model 24 C, 12 Ga., Hammer, Tube Feed, Checkered Stock, Fancy Wood, Light Engraving, *Modern*	250	500	750
Model 24 D, 12 Ga., Hammer, Tube Feed, Checkered Stock, Fancy Wood, Engraved, *Modern*	600	1500	1850
Model 24 Field, 12 Ga., Hammer, Tube Feed, *Modern*	125	250	325
Model 26 Field, 12 Ga., Hammer, Tube Feed, *Modern*	175	225	300
Model 28 A, 12 Ga., Hammerless, Tube Feed, *Modern*	225	250	325
Model 28 B, 12 Ga., Hammerless, Tube Feed, Checkered Stock, *Modern*	200	350	450
Model 28 C, 12 Ga., Hammerless, Tube Feed, Checkered Stock, Fancy Wood, Light Engraving, *Modern*	200	425	550
Model 28 D, 12 Ga., Hammerless, Tube Feed, Checkered Stock, Fancy Wood, Engraved, *Modern*	400	1000	1350
Model 28 Trap, 12 Ga., Hammerless, Tube Feed, *Modern*	200	400	600
Model 30 A, 12 Ga., Hammer, Tube Feed, *Modern*	200	275	350
Model 30 B, 12 Ga., Hammer, Tube Feed, Checkered Stock, *Modern*	200	350	450
Model 30 C, 12 Ga., Hammer, Tube Feed, Checkered Stock, Fancy Wood, Light Engraving, *Modern*	200	450	750
Model 30 D, 12 Ga., Hammer, Tube Feed, Checkered Stock, Fancy Wood, Engraved, *Modern*	500	1500	1850
Model 31 B, 12 Ga., Hammerless, Tube Feed, Checkered Stock, *Modern*	200	350	450
Model 31 D, 12 Ga., Hammerless, Tube Feed, Checkered Stock, Fancy Wood, Engraved, *Modern*	400	1400	1650
Model 31 Field, 12 Ga., Hammerless, Tube Feed, *Modern*	150	250	375
Model 31C, 12 Ga., Hammerless, Tube Feed, Checkered Stock, Fancy Wood, Light Engraving, *Modern*	300	600	900
Model 44 Field, 12 Ga., Hammerless, Tube Feed, *Modern*	150	350	425

	Fair	V. Good	Excellent
Model 63 Field, 12 Ga., Hammerless, Tube Feed, *Modern*	$150	$325	$375
Premier Mark I, 12 Ga., Hammerless, Tube Feed, *Modern*	150	200	275
Premier Mark II, 12 Ga., Hammerless, Tube Feed, *Modern*	150	225	275
Premier Mark IV, 12 Ga., Hammerless, Tube Feed, Vent Rib, *Modern*	150	250	325

MAROCCINI

Frabricca Fucili da Caccia di Luciano Maroccini, Gardone, Val Trompia, Italy.

SHOTGUN, DOUBLE BARREL, OVER-UNDER

Field Master Commander, 12 Gauge Magnum, Police Style, Detachable Buttstock, Double Triggers, Boxlock, *Modern*	200	425	500
Field Master I, Various Gauges, Checkered Stock, Sling Swivels, Double Triggers, Boxlock, *Modern*	150	325	400
Field Master II, Various Gauges, Checkered Stock, Single Trigger, Boxlock, Automatic Ejectors, *Modern*	150	350	450

SHOTGUN, DOUBLE BARREL, SIDE-BY-SIDE

Mondial, 12 Gauge, Checkered Stock, Sling Swivels, Double Triggers, Boxlock, *Modern*	50	100	175

MARQUIS OF LORNE

Made by Hood Arms Co. Norwich, Conn., c. 1880.

HANDGUN, REVOLVER

.22 Short R.F., 7 Shot, Spur Trigger, Solid Frame, Single Action, *Antique*	75	150	200
.32 Short R.F., 5 Shot, Spur Trigger, Solid Frame, Single Action, *Antique*	100	175	225

MARS

Kohout & Spolecnost, Kydne, Czechoslovakia, c. 1925.

HANDGUN, SELF-LOADING

Mars, 6.35mm, Clip Fed, Blue, *Curio*	100	200	275
Mars, 7.65mm, Clip Fed, Blue, *Curio*	100	250	325

MARS

Spain, c. 1920.

HANDGUN, SELF-LOADING

Automat Pistole Mars, 6.35mm, Clip Fed, *Curio*	50	100	175

MARS AUTOMATIC PISTOL SYNDICATE

Distributors of the Gabbet Fairfax pistol made by Webley & Scott, Birmingham, England, 1902–1904.

	Fair	V. Good	Excellent
HANDGUN, SELF-LOADING			
.45 Long, Clip Fed, Blue, Hammer, *Curio*	$5500	$12000	$16500
9mm, Clip Fed, Blue, Hammer, *Curio*	3750	8000	11500

MARSHWOOD

Made by Stevens Arms.

SHOTGUN, DOUBLE BARREL, SIDE-BY-SIDE

M 315, Various Gauges, Hammerless, Steel Barrel, *Modern*	75	150	200

MARSTON, STANHOPE

New York City, c. 1850s.

HANDGUN, PERCUSSION

Swivel Breech, .31, Two Barrels, Ring Trigger, Bar Hammer, *Antique*	400	850	1150

MARSTON, WILLIAM W.

New York City, 1850–1875.

HANDGUN, PERCUSSION

Breech Loader, .35, Half Octagon Barrel, Engraved, *Antique*	800	1800	2250
Pepperbox, .31, Double Action, 6 Shot, Bar Hammer, *Antique*	250	500	750
Pocket, .31, Bar Hammer, Double Action, Screw Barrel, *Antique*	150	300	425
Singleshot, .36, Bar Hammer, Single Action, Screw Barrel, *Antique*	150	350	450

MARTE

Erquiaga, Muguruzu y Cia, Eibar, Spain, c. 1920.

HANDGUN, SELF-LOADING

.25 ACP, Clip Fed, Blue, *Curio*	75	125	175

MARTIAN

Martin a Bascaran, Eibar, Spain, 1916–1927.

HANDGUN, SELF-LOADING

6.35mm, Clip Fed, Eibar Type, *Curio*	50	100	150
6.35mm, Clip Fed, Triggerguard Takedown, *Curio*	100	200	250
7.65mm, Clip Fed, Eibar Type, *Curio*	75	125	175
7.65mm, Clip Fed, Triggerguard Takedown, *Curio*	100	225	275

Martian

MARTIAN COMMERCIAL

Martin A Bascaran, Eibar, Spain, 1919–1927.

HANDGUN, SELF-LOADING

	Fair	V. Good	Excellent
6.35, Clip Fed, Eibar Type, *Curio*	$75	$125	$175
6.35, Clip Fed, Eibar Type, *Curio*	75	150	200

MARTIN, ALEXANDER

Glasglow & Aberdeen, Scotland, 1922–1928.

RIFLE, BOLT ACTION

.303 British, Sporting Rifle, Express Sights, Engraved, Fancy Wood, Cased, *Curio*	400	950	1450

MASSACHUSETTS ARMS

Made by Stevens Arms.

SHOTGUN, DOUBLE BARREL, SIDE-BY-SIDE

Model 311, Various Gauges, Hammerless, Steel Barrel, *Modern*	75	150	200

SHOTGUN, SINGLESHOT

Model 90, Various Gauges, Takedown, Automatic Ejector, Plain, Hammer, *Modern*	25	50	75
Model 94, Various Gauges, Takedown, Automatic Ejector, Plain, Hammer, *Modern*	25	50	75

MASSACHUSETTS ARMS CO.

Chicopee Falls, Mass., 1850–1866. Also see Adams.

HANDGUN, PERCUSSION

	Fair	V. Good	Excellent
Maynard Belt Revolver, .31, 6 Shot, *Antique*	400	800	1000
Maynard Pocket Revolver, .28, 6 Shot, *Antique*	300	600	850
Wesson & Leavitt Belt Revolver, .31, 6 Shot, *Antique*	450	1000	1350
Wesson & Leavitt Dragoon Revolver, .40, 6 Shot, *Antique*	$1500	$3750	$5500

MATADOR

Made in Spain for Firearms International, Washington, D.C.

SHOTGUN, DOUBLE BARREL, SIDE-BY-SIDE

Matador II, 12 or 20 Gauges, Checkered Stock, Single Trigger, Selective Ejectors, *Modern*	100	200	300

MATCHLOCK ARMS EXAMPLES

RIFLE, MATCHLOCK

.45, India mid-1600s, 4 Shot, Revolving Cylinder, Light Ornamentation, Brass Furniture, *Antique*	2100	4500	6500
.57, Japanese Full Stock Musket, Octagon Barrel, Silver Inlay, Brass Furniture, *Antique*	800	1800	2750

MAUSER

Germany Gebruder Mauser et Cie from 1854–1890. From 1890–1994 is known as Mauser-Werke. 1894 to date Mauser-Werke Oberndorf Waff Ensysteme GmbH. Also see German Military, Luger.

HANDGUN, REVOLVER

Colt Type, .38 Spec., Double Action, 6 Shot, 2" Barrel, *Curio*	75	125	200
M 78 Zig Zag, 10.6mm, Tip-Up, *Antique*	1500	3500	5000
M 78 Zig Zag, 7.6mm, Tip-Up, *Antique*	1250	3250	4750
M 78 Zig Zag, 9mm Mauser, Tip-Up, *Antique*	1250	3250	4750
M 78 Zig Zag, Tip-Up, Fancy Engraving, *Antique*	1750	4500	6500

HANDGUN, SELF-LOADING

Chinese Shansei, .45 ACP, with Shoulder Stock, *Curio*	1900	4000	5250
HSc 1 of 5,000, .380 ACP, Blue, Post-War, Cased, *Modern*	100	200	300
HSc Army, .32 ACP., Nazi-Proofed, *Curio*	150	325	400
HSc Navy, .32 ACP., Nazi-Proofed, *Curio*	250	500	600
HSc NSDAP SA, .32 ACP., Nazi-Proofed, *Curio*	300	600	800
HSc Police, .32 ACP., Nazi-Proofed, *Curio*	150	300	400
HSc Swiss, .32 ACP., *Curio*	450	950	1350
HSc, .32 ACP, Nickel Plated, Post-War, *Modern*	150	275	350

Mauser M 78 Zig Zag

From the top right, two Borchardt semi-automatics (both Model 1892s in 7.65 Luger), a Mauser Model 1912 broomhandle military pistol, a Luger in 7.65 caliber with American eagle on receiver, and a Browning High-Power Model 1935 in 9mm. From the top left, an Austrian Mun & Waffenfabr. Summerda A.-G, V. Dreyse; a Mannlicher Model 1905 by Waffenfabrik Steyr; next a System Mannlicher Model 1905 by Waffenfabrik Steyr in 7.63 Mannlicher caliber and with 6" barrel; a Roth-Steyr Model 1908 in 8m/m Steyr; a Steyr-Hahn Model 1911, also I 9mm Steyr; and finally, bottom center, an Italian Glisenti in 9mm.

	Fair	V. Good	Excellent
HSc, .32 ACP, Post-War, Blue, *Modern*	$125	$250	$325
HSc, .32 ACP. Pre-War, Nazi-Proofed, Commercial, *Curio*	200	425	600
HSc, .32 ACP. Pre-War, Prototype, Commercial, *Curio*	150	300	425
HSc, .380 ACP, Blue, Post-War, *Modern*	125	250	350
HSc, .380 ACP, Nickel Plated, Post-War, *Modern*	150	275	375
M 1896 (Early), 7.63 Mauser, Small Ring, *Curio*	500	1100	1650
M 1896 (Italian), 7.63 Mauser, Slabside, *Curio*	500	1100	1650
M 1896 Banner, 7.63 Mauser, *Curio*	500	1000	1450
M 1896 Bolo, 7.63 Mauser, Post-War, *Curio*	400	800	1250
M 1896 French Police, 7.63 Mauser, *Curio*	400	800	1250
M 1896 Persian, 7.63 Mauser, *Curio*	450	900	1350
M 1896 Police, 7.63 Mauser, *Curio*	200	600	850
M 1896 System Mauser, 7.63 Mauser, With Conehammer, *Curio*	1000	2000	2750
M 1896 Turkish, 7.63 Mauser, Conehammer, *Curio*	500	1000	1450
M 1896 WW I, 7.63 Mauser, Military, *Curio*	200	400	750
M 1896 WW I, 9mm Luger, Military, *Curio*	500	1350	1750

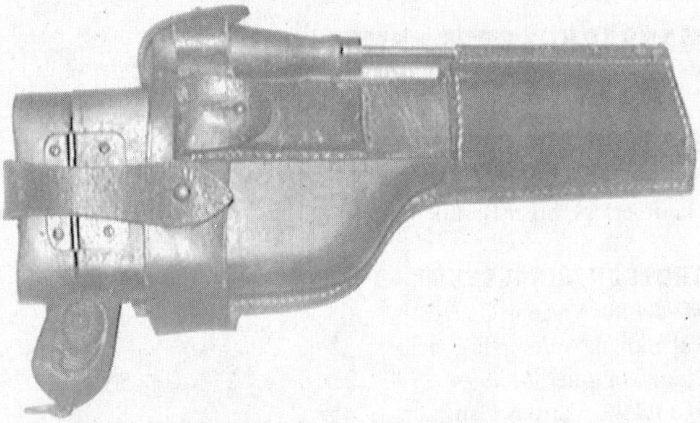

Mauser M 1896 WWI with Holster Stock

	Fair	V. Good	Excellent
M 1896, 7.63 Mauser, 10 Shot, Conehammer, *Curio*	1100	2500	3250
M 1896, 7.63 Mauser, 10 Shot, Fixed Sight Conehammer, *Curio*	1200	2750	3500
M 1896, 7.63 Mauser, Conehammer with Shoulder Stock, *Curio*	1000	2000	2650
M 1896, 7.63 Mauser, Fixed Sight Conehammer with Shoulder Stock, *Curio*	1000	2000	2750
M 1896, 7.63 Mauser, Flatside, *Curio*	500	1200	1750
M 1896, 7.63 Mauser, Pre-War, Commercial, *Curio*	200	500	750

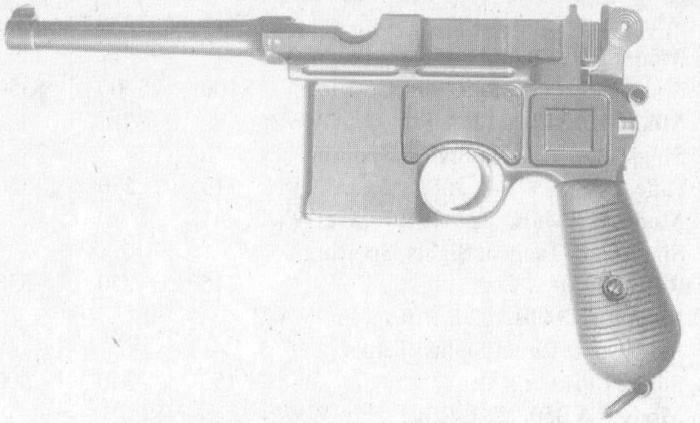

Mauser 1896 Conehammer

	Fair	V. Good	Excellent
M 1896, 7.63 Mauser, Transitional, *Curio*	$500	$1000	$1500
M 1896, Factory Engraving Add 300%			
M 1896, Original Holster Stock Add 20%-35%			
M 1896, 20-Shot Model Add 50%-80%			
M 1896, 40-Shot Model Add 100%			
M 1896, 6-Shot Model Add 75%-100%			
M 1906/08, 7.63 Mauser, Clip Fed, *Curio*	9000	25000	33500
M 1910, .25 ACP, Clip Fed, *Curio*	150	300	425

Mauser M 1910

Mauser M 1914

	Fair	V. Good	Excellent
M 1912/14, 9mm Luger, Clip Fed, *Curio*	$7000	$17500	$23500
M 1914 Army, .32 ACP, Clip Fed, *Curio*	150	275	350
M 1914 Early, .32 ACP, Clip Fed, *Curio*	125	225	300
M 1914 Humpback, .32 ACP, Long Barrel, Clip Fed, *Curio*	1100	2500	3520
M 1914 Navy, .32 ACP, Clip Fed, *Curio*	150	300	400
M 1914 Post-War, .32 ACP, Clip Fed, *Modern*	100	175	250
M 1914 War Commercial, .32 ACP, Clip Fed, *Curio*	100	200	300
M 1934 Navy, .32 ACP, Clip Fed, *Curio*	250	500	800
M 1934 Police, .32 ACP, Clip Fed, *Curio*	150	300	425
M 1934, .32 ACP, Clip Fed, *Curio*	125	250	400
New Model Carbine, 9mm Luger, 12" Barrel, Grip Safety, *Modern*	2000	4500	6500
Parabellum Bulgarian, .30 Luger, Grip Safety, Commemorative, *Modern*	450	1000	1450
Parabellum Cartridge Counter, 9mm Luger, Grip Safety, Commemorative, *Modern*	900	2000	2750
Parabellum P.O8, .30 Luger, 6" Barrel, Grip Safety, *Modern*	200	450	600
Parabellum PO 8, .30 Luger, 4" Barrel, Grip Safety, *Modern*	250	575	750
Parabellum PO 8, 9mm Luger, Various Barrel Lengths, Grip Safety, *Modern*	250	500	700
Parabellum Russian, .30 Luger, Grip Safety, Commemorative, *Modern*	450	1000	1450
Parabellum Sport, .30 or 9mm Luger, Heavy Barrel, Target Sights, *Modern*	550	1200	1550
Parabellum Swiss, 7.65mm, 6" Barrel, Grip Safety, *Modern*	200	400	600
Parabellum Swiss, 9mm Luger, 4" Barrel, Grip Safety, *Modern*	225	450	650
W T P I, 6.35mm, Clip Fed, *Modern*	100	250	425
W T P II, 6.35mm, Clip Fed, *Modern*	200	450	700

RIFLE, BOLT ACTION

	Fair	V. Good	Excellent
Model 10 Varminter, .22-250 Post-War, Heavy Barrel, Monte Carlo Stock, Checkered Stock, *Modern*	600	1400	1850
Model 2000, Various Calibers, Post-War, Monte Carlo Stock, Checkered Stock, *Modern*	150	300	400
Model 3000, Various Calibers, Post-War, Left-Hand, Magnum Action, Monte Carlo Stock, Checkered Stock, *Modern*	200	425	550

Mauser W T P

	Fair	V. Good	Excellent
Model 3000, Various Calibers, Post-War, Left-Hand, Monte Carlo Stock, Checkered Stock, *Modern*	$200	$450	$600
Model 3000, Various Calibers, Post-War, Magnum Action, Monte Carlo Stock, Checkered Stock, *Modern*	225	475	600
Model 3000, Various Calibers, Post-War, Monte Carlo Stock, *Modern*	200	400	525
Model 4000, Various Calibers, Varmint, Checkering, Flared, *Modern*	150	350	500
Model 66S, Various Calibers, Post-War, Takedown, Monte Carlo Stock, Checkered Stock, *Modern*	600	1250	1750
Model 66S Safari, Various Calibers, Post-War, Takedown, Monte Carlo Stock, Checkered Stock, Magnum, *Modern*	800	1750	2500
Model 98, Various Calibers, Sporting Rifle, Full-Stocked, Pre-WW2, Military, Commercial, *Modern*	150	325	425
Model A, Various Calibers, Sporting Rifle, Pre-WW2, Magnum Action, *Curio*	1400	3000	4250
Model A, Various Calibers, Sporting Rifle, Pre-WW2, Short Action, *Curio*	1500	3250	4500
Model A British, Various Calibers, Sporting Rifle, Express Sights, Pre-WW2, *Curio*	1400	3000	4750
Model A British, Various Calibers, Sporting Rifle, Peep Sights, Pre-WW2, Octagon Barrel, Set Trigger, *Curio*	1600	3500	5500
Model B, Various Calibers, Sporting Rifle, Pre-WW2, Octagon Barrel, Set Trigger, *Curio*	900	2000	3250
Model B, Various Calibers, Sporting Rifle, Pre-WW2, Set Trigger, Express Sights, *Curio*	900	2000	3000
Model DSM 34, .22 L.R.R.F., Pre-WW2, Singleshot, Tangent Sights, Military Style, Stock, *Curio*	150	275	400
Model EL 320, .22 L.R.R.F., Pre-WW2, Singleshot, Sporting Rifle, Adjustable Sights, *Curio*	100	225	350
Model EN 310, .22 L.R.R.F., Pre-WW2, Singleshot, Open Rear Sight, *Curio*	$100	$200	$350
Model ES 340, .22 L.R.R.F., Pre-WW2, Singleshot, Tangent Sights, Sporting Rifle, *Curio*	115	250	350
Model ES 340B, .22 L.R.R.F., Pre-WW2, Singleshot, Tangent Sights, Sporting Rifle, *Curio*	115	250	350
Model ES 340B, .22 L.R.R.F., Pre-WW2, Singleshot, Target Sights, Target Stock, *Curio*	150	350	500
Model ES 350, .22 L.R.R.F., Pre-WW2, Singleshot, Target Sights, Target Stock, *Curio*	200	400	550
Model K, Various Calibers, Sporting Rifle, Pre-WW2, Short Action, *Curio*	200	425	650
Model KKW, .22 L.R.R.F., Pre-WW2, Singleshot, Tangent Sights, Military Style Stock, *Curio*	150	350	450
Model M, Various Calibers, Express Sights, Carbine, *Modern*	250	550	725
Model M, Various Calibers, Sporting Rifle, Pre-WW2, Full-Stocked, Tangent Sights, Carbine, *Curio*	200	450	650
Model MM 410, .22 L.R.R.F., Pre-WW2, 5 Shot Clip, Tangent Sights, Sporting Rifle, *Curio*	150	300	425
Model MM 410B, .22 L.R.R.F., Pre-WW2, 5 Shot Clip, Tangent Sights, Sporting Rifle, *Curio*	175	350	500
Model MS 350B, .22 L.R.R.F., Pre-WW2, 5 Shot Clip, Target Sights, Target Stock, *Curio*	200	425	550
Model MS 420, .22 L.R.R.F., Pre-WW2, 5 Shot Clip, Tangent Sights, Sporting Rifle, *Curio*	125	275	400
Model MS 420B, .22 L.R.R.F., Pre-WW2, 5 Shot Clip, Tangent Sights, Target Stock, *Curio*	150	350	450
Model S, Various Calibers, Sporting Rifle, Pre-WW2, Full-Stocked, Set Trigger, Carbine, *Curio*	900	2000	2750
Standard, Various Calibers, Sporting Rifle, Set Trigger, Pre-WWI, *Curio*	1100	2500	3250
Various Calibers, Sporting Rifle, Pre-WWI, Military, Commercial, *Curio*	700	1500	2000
Various Calibers, Sporting Rifle, Set Trigger, Pre-WWI, Short Action, *Curio*	1100	2500	3350
Various Calibers, Sporting Rifle, Set Trigger, Pre-WWI, Carbine, Full-Stocked, *Curio*	800	1750	2750

RIFLE, SELF-LOADING

	Fair	V. Good	Excellent
M 1896, 7.63 Mauser, Carbine, *Curio*	1900	4000	5500

	Fair	V. Good	Excellent
RIFLE, DOUBLE BARREL, OVER-UNDER			
Model Aristocrat, .375 H & H Magnum, Fancy Checkering, Engraved, Open Rear Sight, Cheekpiece, Double Trigger, *Modern*	$1200	$2650	$3250
Model Aristocrat, Various Calibers, Fancy Checkering, Engraved, Open Rear Sight, Cheekpiece, Double Trigger, *Modern*	1000	1900	2450
SHOTGUN, BOLT ACTION			
16 Gauge, *Modern*	75	100	150
SHOTGUN, DOUBLE BARREL, OVER-UNDER			
Model 610, 12 Gauge, Skeet Grade, with Conversion Kit, Vent Rib, Checkered Stock, *Modern*	800	1500	1950
Model 610, 12 Gauge, Trap Grade, Vent Rib, Checkered Stock, *Modern*	350	750	1250
Model 620, 12 Gauge, Automatic Ejector, Double Trigger, Vent Rib, Fancy Wood, *Modern*	400	800	1150
Model 620, 12 Gauge, Automatic Ejector, Single Selective Trigger, Vent Rib, Fancy Wood, *Modern*	400	850	1250
Model 620, 12 Gauge, Automatic Ejector, Single Trigger, Vent Rib, Fancy Wood, *Modern*	350	700	1050
Model 71E, 12 Gauge, Field Grade, Double Trigger, Checkered Stock, *Modern*	150	325	450
Model 72E, 12 Gauge, Skeet Grade, Checkered Stock, Light Engraving, *Modern*	200	450	700
Model 72E, 12 Gauge, Trap Grade, Checkered Stock, Light Engraving, *Modern*	200	450	700
SHOTGUN, DOUBLE BARREL, SIDE-BY-SIDE			
Model 496, 12 Gauge, Trap Grade, Vent Rib, Single Trigger, Checkered Stock, Box Lock, *Modern*	225	500	700
Model 545, 12 and 20 Gauges, Single Trigger, Recoil Pad, Checkered Stock, Box Lock, *Modern*	200	450	650
Model 580, 12 Gauge, Engraved, Fancy Checkering, Fancy Wood, *Modern*	400	800	1150
SHOTGUN, SINGLESHOT			
Model 496, 12 Gauge, Trap Grade, Engraved, Checkered Stock, *Modern*	250	500	650
Model 496 Competition, 12 Gauge, Trap Grade, Engraved, Fancy Wood, Fancy Checkering, *Modern*	300	650	850

MAYER & SOEHNE

Arnsberg, W. Germany.

	Fair	V. Good	Excellent
HANDGUN, REVOLVER			
Target, .22 L.R.R.F., Break Top, 5 Shot, Target Sights, Double Action, *Modern*	$50	$100	$150

MAYESCH

Lancaster, Pa., 1760–1770. See Kentucky Rifles and Pistols.

MAYOR, FRANCOIS

Lausanne, Switzerland.

	Fair	V. Good	Excellent
HANDGUN, SELF-LOADING			
Rochat, 6.35mm, Clip Fed, *Modern*	250	500	750

MBA

San Ramon, Calif., 1965–1975.

	Fair	V. Good	Excellent
HANDGUN, POCKET PISTOL			
Gyrojet, For Nickel Plating, Add 10%-15%			
Gyrojet, For U.S. Property Stamping Add 75%-100%			
Gyrojet Mark I Model A, Clip Fed, *Modern*	250	550	750
Gyrojet Mark I Model A Exp., Clip Fed, *Modern*	400	800	1050
Gyrojet Mark I Carbine Model B Exp., Clip Fed, *Modern*	450	1000	1350
Gyrojet Mark I Carbine Model B Snub, Clip Fed, *Modern*	450	950	1250
Gyrojet Mark I Carbine Model B, Clip Fed, *Modern*	350	750	1150
Gyrojet Mark I Carbine Model C, Clip Fed, *Modern*	300	650	850
Gyrojet Mark I, Clip Fed, Presentation Cased with Accessories, *Modern*	700	1500	1950

MCCOY, ALEXANDER

Philadelphia, Pa., 1779. See Kentucky Rifles.

MCCOY, KESTER

Lancaster, Pa. See Kentucky Rifles and Pistols.

MCCULLOUGH, GEORGE

Lancaster, Pa., 1770–1773. See Kentucky Rifles.

MEIER, ADOLPHUS

St. Louis, Mo., 1845–1850.

RIFLE, PERCUSSION

	Fair	V. Good	Excellent
.58 Plains Type, Double Barrel, Side by Side, Half-Octagon Barrel, Rifled, Plain, *Antique*	$900	$2250	$3000

MELIOR

Liège, Belgium. Made by Robar et Cie. 1900–1959.

HANDGUN, SELF-LOADING

	Fair	V. Good	Excellent
New Model Pocket, .22 L.R.R.F., Clip Fed, *Modern*	75	150	175
New Model Pocket, .380 ACP, Clip Fed, *Modern*	75	150	175
New Model Pocket, 7.65mm, Clip Fed, *Modern*	50	125	150
New Model Vest Pocket, .22 Long R.F., Clip Fed, *Modern*	50	125	150
New Model Vest Pocket, 6.35mm, Clip Fed, *Modern*	75	150	175
Old Model Pocket, 7.65mm, Clip Fed, *Modern*	75	150	175
Old Model Vest Pocket, 6.35mm, Clip Fed, *Modern*	75	150	175
Target, .22 L.R.R.F., Clip Fed, Long Barrel, *Modern*	100	200	250

MENDOZA

Mexico City, Mexico.

HANDGUN, SINGLESHOT

	Fair	V. Good	Excellent
K-62, .22 L.R.R.F., *Modern*	50	100	125

RIFLE, BOLT ACTION

	Fair	V. Good	Excellent
Modelo Conejo, .22 L.R.R.F., 2 Shot, *Modern*	75	125	175

MENTA

Made by August Menz, Suhl, Germany, c. 1916.

HANDGUN, REVOLVER

	Fair	V. Good	Excellent
7.65mm, Clip Fed, Commercial, *Curio*	100	250	300
7.65mm, Clip Fed, Military, *Curio*	150	300	350

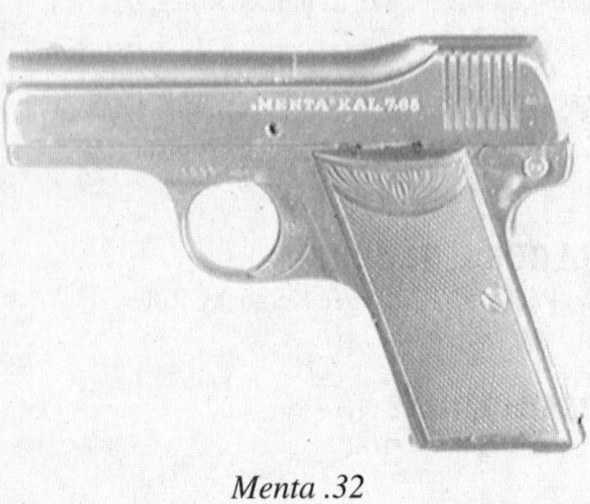

Menta .32

MENZ, AUGUST

Suhl, Germany, 1912–1937. Also see Menta.

HANDGUN, SELF-LOADING

	Fair	V. Good	Excellent
Lilliput, 6.35mm, Clip Fed, *Curio*	$150	$300	$400
Model I, 7.65mm, Clip Fed, *Curio*	100	250	325

Menz Model I

	Fair	V. Good	Excellent
Model II, 7.65mm, Clip Fed, *Curio*	125	275	350
Model III, 7.65mm, Clip Fed, Hammer, *Curio*	150	350	450
P & B Special, .380 ACP, Clip Fed, Hammer, Double Action, *Curio*	300	725	950
P & B Special, 7.65mm, Clip Fed, Hammer, Double Action, *Curio*	250	500	750

MERCURY

Made by Robar et Cie., Liège, Belgium, for Tradewinds.

RIFLE, SELF-LOADING

	Fair	V. Good	Excellent
M 622 VP, .22 L.R.R.F., Clip Fed, *Modern*	50	100	300

SHOTGUN, DOUBLE BARREL, SIDE-BY-SIDE

	Fair	V. Good	Excellent
Mercury, 10 Gauge 3", Hammerless, Magnum, Checkered Stock, Double Trigger, *Modern*	85	170	350
Mercury, 12 and 20 Gauges, Hammerless, Magnum, Checkered Stock, Double Trigger, *Modern*	80	160	325

MERIDEN FIRE ARMS CO.

Meriden, Conn., 1907–1909. Also made handguns marked with trade names as follows: Aubrey, Eastern Arms Co., Empire Arms, Empire State, Federal Arms, Howard Arms.

HANDGUN, REVOLVER

	Fair	V. Good	Excellent
.38 S & W, 5 Shot, Top Break, Hammerless, Double Action, *Modern*	50	100	175

RIFLE, SINGLESHOT

	Fair	V. Good	Excellent
Model 10, .22 L.R.R.F., *Modern*	25	50	125

	Fair	V. Good	Excellent
RIFLE, SLIDE ACTION			
Model 15, .22 L.R.R.F., Tube Feed, *Modern*	$100	$200	$300

MERKEL

Gebruder Merkel, Suhl, Germany, from 1920. After WWII, VEB Fahrzeug u. Jagdwaffenwerk Ernst Thalmann, Suhl, East Germany.

	Fair	V. Good	Excellent
COMBINATION WEAPON, DRILLING			
Model 142, Various Calibers, Pre-WW2, Double Trigger, Engraved, Checkered Stock, *Curio*	1000	2200	2750
Model 142, Various Calibers, Pre-WW2, Double Trigger, Checkered Stock, *Curio*	800	1500	2250
Model 145, Various Calibers, Pre-WW2, Double Trigger, Engraved, Checkered Stock, *Curio*	700	1500	2250
COMBINATION WEAPON, OVER-UNDER			
Model 210, Various Calibers, Pre-WW2, Engraved, Checkered Stock, *Curio*	600	1750	2500
Model 211E, Various Calibers, Engraved, Checkered Stock, Automatic Ejector, *Modern*	800	1500	2250
Model 213E, Various Calibers, Sidelock, Fancy Checkering, Fancy Engraving, Automatic Ejector, *Modern*	1200	3000	4750
Model 313E, Various Calibers, Sidelock, Fancy Checkering, Fancy Engraving, Automatic Ejector, *Modern*	1500	3500	5250
RIFLE, DOUBLE BARREL, OVER-UNDER			
Model 220E, Various Calibers, Pre-WW2, Checkered Stock, Engraved, *Curio*	2200	4000	5500
Model 221E, Various Calibers, Engraved, Checkered Stock, Automatic Ejector, *Curio*	2500	5000	6250
Model 323E, Various Calibers, Sidelock, Fancy Checkering, Fancy Engraving, Automatic Ejector, *Modern*	3000	7000	9500
SHOTGUN, DOUBLE BARREL, OVER-UNDER			
Model 100, Various Gauges, Pre-WW2, Plain Barrel, Checkered Stock, *Curio*	400	850	1250
Model 100, Various Gauges, Pre-WW2, Raised Matted Rib, Checkered Stock, *Curio*	500	1000	1350
Model 101, Various Gauges, Pre-WW2, Raised Matted Rib, Checkered Stock, Light Engraving, *Curio*	500	1050	1350
Model 101E, Various Gauges, Pre-WW2, Raised Matted Rib, Checkered Stock, Light Engraving, Automatic Ejector, *Curio*	500	1100	1450
Model 200, Various Gauges, Pre-WW2, Raised Matted Rib, Checkered Stock, Light Engraving, *Curio*	$450	$950	$1350
Model 201, Various Gauges, Pre-WW2, Raised Matted Rib, Checkered Stock, Engraved, *Curio*	550	1250	1650
Model 201E, Various Gauges, Pre-WW2, Raised Matted Rib, Checkered Stock, Engraved, Automatic Ejector, *Curio*	700	1500	1950
Model 202, Various Gauges, Pre-WW2, Raised Matted Rib, Fancy Checkering, Fancy Engraving, *Curio*	900	2000	2500
Model 202E, Various Gauges, Pre-WW2, Raised Matted Rib, Fancy Checkering, Fancy Engraving, Automatic Engraving, *Curio*	1000	2250	2750
Model 203E, Various Gauges, Sidelock, Fancy Checkering, Fancy Engraving, Automatic Ejector, *Modern*	1200	2650	3500
Model 204E, Various Gauges, Pre-WW2, Sidelock, Fancy Checkering, Fancy Engraving, Automatic Ejector, *Curio*	1900	4250	5500
Model 300, Various Gauges, Pre-WW2, Raised Matted Rib, Checkered Stock, Engraved, *Curio*	700	1750	2500
Model 300E, Various Gauges, Pre-WW2, Raised Matted Rib, Checkered Stock, Engraved, Automatic Ejector, *Curio*	800	1950	2750
Model 301, Various Gauges, Pre-WW2, Raised Matted Rib, Fancy Checkering, Engraved, *Curio*	1500	3500	4500
Model 301E, Various Gauges, Pre-WW2, Raised Matted Rib, Fancy Checkering, Engraved, Automatic Ejector, *Curio*	2100	4500	5750
Model 302, Various Gauges, Pre-WW2, Raised Matted Rib, Fancy Checkering, Fancy Engraving, Automatic Ejector, *Curio*	3250	7250	9000
Model 303E, Various Gauges, Sidelock, Single Selective Trigger, Automatic Ejector, Fancy Engraving, Fancy Checkering, *Modern*	4500	9500	13500
SHOTGUN, DOUBLE BARREL, SIDE-BY-SIDE			
Model 127, Various Gauges, Pre-WW2, Sidelock, Fancy Engraving, Fancy Checkering, Automatic Ejector, *Curio*	7000	15000	19500
Model 130, Various Gauges, Pre-WW2, Fancy Engraving, Fancy Checkering, Automatic Ejector, *Curio*	3500	8500	12500

	Fair	V. Good	Excellent
Model 147E, Various Gauges, Fancy Checkering, Fancy Engraving, *Modern*	$600	$1250	$1500
Model 147E, Various Gauges, Fancy Checkering, Fancy Engraving, Single Selective Trigger, *Modern*	700	1450	1750
Model 147S, Various Gauges, Fancy Checkering, Fancy Engraving, Sidelock, *Modern*	1500	3250	4000
Model 147S, Various Gauges, Fancy Checkering, Fancy Engraving, Sidelock, Single Selective Trigger, *Modern*	1900	4000	5000
Model 47E, Various Gauges, Checkered Stock, Engraved, *Modern*	400	850	1250
Model 47E, Various Gauges, Single Selective Trigger, Checkered Stock, Engraved, *Modern*	450	950	1350
Model 47S, Various Gauges, Sidelock, Checkered Stock, Engraved, *Modern*	1200	2500	3250
Model 47S, Various Gauges, Sidelock, Single Selective Trigger, Checkered Stock, Engraved, *Modern*	1300	2750	3500

MERRILL CO.

Formerly in Rockwell City, Iowa, now in Fullerton, Calif.

HANDGUN, SINGLESHOT

	Fair	V. Good	Excellent
Sportsman, For Extra 14" Barrel and Dies Add $125.00-$185.00			
Sportsman, For Extra Barrel Add $75.00-$110.00			
Sportsman, Wrist Attachment Add $15.00-$25.00			
Sportsman, Various Calibers, Target Pistol, Top Break, Adjustable Sights, Vent Rib, *Modern*	150	300	425

MERRIMAC ARMS & MFG. CO.

Newburyport, Mass. Absorbed by Brown Mfg. Co., Worcester, Mass., 1861–1866. Also see Ballard.

HANDGUN, SINGLESHOT

	Fair	V. Good	Excellent
Southerner, .41 Short R.F., Derringer, Iron Frame, Light Engraving, *Antique*	250	500	700

RIFLE, DOUBLE BARREL, SIDE-BY-SIDE

	Fair	V. Good	Excellent
Various Calibers, Octagon Barrel, *Antique*	450	950	1350

SHOTGUN, SINGLESHOT

	Fair	V. Good	Excellent
20 Gauge, Falling Block, *Antique*	125	250	375

MERVEILLEUX

Rouchouse, Paris, France.

HANDGUN, MANUAL REPEATER

	Fair	V. Good	Excellent
Palm Pistol, 6mm, Engraved, Nickel Plated, *Curio*	$300	$600	$900

MERWIN & BRAY

Worcester, Mass., 1864–1868. Became Merwin & Simpkins in 1868 and also Merwin-Taylor & Simpkins the same year, also within the same year became Merwin, Hulbert & Co. Also see Ballard, Merwin, Hulbert & Co.

HANDGUN, REVOLVER

	Fair	V. Good	Excellent
"Navy," .32 Short R.F., 6 Shot, Single Action, Solid Frame, Finger-Rest Trigger Guard, *Antique*	200	400	550
"Navy," .38 Short R.F., 6 Shot, Single Action, Solid Frame, Finger-Rest Trigger Guard, *Antique*	200	475	650
"Original," .28 Cup Primed Cartridge, 6 Shot, Single Action, Spur Trigger, Tip-Up, *Antique*	300	600	750
"Original," .30 Cup Primed Cartridge, 6 Shot, Single Action, Spur Trigger, Tip-Up, *Antique*	300	650	850
"Original," .42 Cup Primed Cartridge, 6 Shot, Single Action, Spur Trigger, Tip-Up, *Antique*	350	700	900
"Original," Various Cup-Primed Calibers, Extra Cylinder, Percussion, Add $95.00-$160.00			
.22 Short R.F., 7 Shot, Single Action, Solid Frame, Spur Trigger, *Antique*	75	150	250
.28 Cup Primed Cartridge, 6 Shot, Single Action, Spur Trigger, Solid Frame, *Antique*	75	150	250
.30 Cup Primed Cartridge, 6 Shot, Single Action, Spur Trigger, Solid Frame, *Antique*	125	175	300
.31 R.F., 6 Shot, Single Action, Solid Frame, Spur Trigger, *Antique*	75	125	225
.32 Short R.F., 6 Shot, Single Action, Solid Frame, Spur Trigger, *Antique*	75	125	225
.42 Cup Primed Cartridge, 6 Shot, Single Action, Spur Trigger, Solid Frame, *Antique*	100	200	300
.42 Cup Primed Cartridge, 6 Shot, Single Action, Spur Trigger, Solid Frame, 6" Barrel, *Antique*	150	375	500
Reynolds, .25 Short R.F., 5 Shot, Single Action, Spur Trigger, 3" Barrel, *Antique*	100	175	250

HANDGUN, SINGLESHOT

	Fair	V. Good	Excellent
.32 Short R.F., Side-Swing Barrel, Brass Frame, 3" Barrel, Spur Trigger, *Antique*	100	225	325

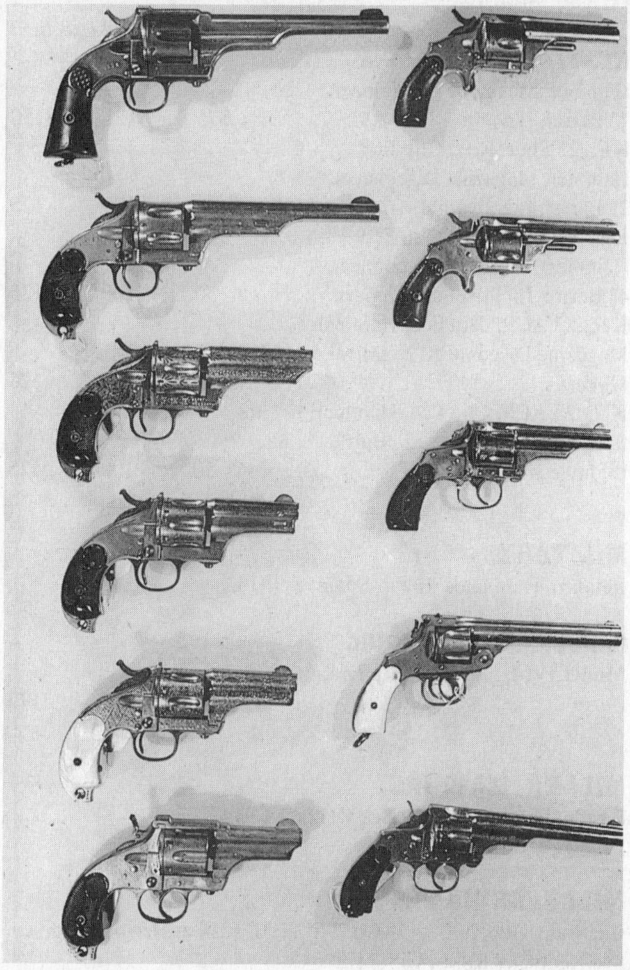

Merwin & Hulbert revolvers, large frame Army Models in column at left including scarce Pocket Army with presentation engraving; three smaller frame .38 caliber variations at top right; below Hopkins & Allen topbreak in .38 caliber, and Merwin & Hulbert .38 with 5½" barrel, both with folding hammer spurs.

MERWIN, HULBERT & CO.

Successors to Merwin & Bray, et al., in 1868, and became Hulbert Bros. in 1892. Out of business in 1896. The author was introduced to the innovative and high-quality guns of Merwin & Hulbert by Stan Nelson, the gunsmith and gun dealer at the Stagecoach Museum, Shakopee, Minnesota. The innovative mechanisms, featuring a twist of the barrel to allow for ejection and then manual reloading, were unique in the arms trade, and required highly competent gunmakers for their construction.

HANDGUN, REVOLVER

	Fair	*V. Good*	*Excellent*
Army Model, "Safety Hammer," Add $65.00–$100.00			
Army Model, .44-40 WCF, Belt Pistol, 7" Barrel, Double Action, Round Butt, 6 Shot, *Antique*	$700	$1700	$2500
Army Model, .44-40 WCF, Belt Pistol, 7" Barrel, Single Action, Square Butt, 6 Shot, *Antique*	800	2000	2750
Army Model, .44-40 WCF, Pocket Pistol, 3½" Barrel, Double Action, Round Butt, 6 Shot, *Antique*	$700	$1500	$2000
Army Model, .44-40 WCF, Pocket Pistol, 3½" Barrel, Single Action, Square Butt, 6 Shot, *Antique*	800	1500	2000
Army Model, Extra Barrel, Add $200.00–$300.00			
Pocket Model, .32 S & W, 5 Shot, Double Action, *Antique*	150	300	550
Target Model, .32 S & W, 7 Shot, Double Action, *Antique*	150	325	450

MESSERSMITH, JACOB

Lancaster, Pa., 1779–1782. See Kentucky Rifles and Pistols.

METEOR

Made by Stevens Arms.

RIFLE, BOLT ACTION

Model 52, .22 L.R.R.F., Singleshot, Takedown, *Modern*	15	25	50

METROPOLITAN

Made by Crescent for Siegel Cooper Co., New York City, c. 1900. See Crescent Fire Arms Co., Shotgun, Double Barrel, Side-by-Side; Shotgun, Singleshot.

METROPOLITAN POLICE

Made by Norwich Falls Pistol Co., Norwich, Conn., c. 1885.

HANDGUN, REVOLVER

.32 Short R.F., 5 Shot, Spur Trigger, Solid Frame, Single Action, *Antique*	75	125	175

METZGER, J.

Lancaster, Pa., c. 1728. See Kentucky Rifles.

MEUHIRTER, S.

See Kentucky Rifles.

MEXICAN MILITARY

HANDGUN, SELF-LOADING

Obregon, .45 ACP, Clip Fed, Military, *Modern*	800	1750	2250

RIFLE, BOLT ACTION

M1902 Mauser, 7mm, Military, *Curio*	150	275	325
M1936 Mauser, 7mm, Military, *Curio*	150	250	300

	Fair	V. Good	Excellent
RIFLE, SELF-LOADING			
M1908 Mondragon, 7mm, Clip Fed, S.I.G., *Curio*	$1100	$2500	$3250

MIDLAND

Imported from England by Jana International, c. 1973.

	Fair	V. Good	Excellent
RIFLE, BOLT ACTION			
Midland, Various Calibers, Checkered Stock, Open Sights, *Modern*	100	225	325

MIIDA

Tradename of Marubeni America Corp. on Japanese shotguns.

	Fair	V. Good	Excellent
SHOTGUN, DOUBLE BARREL, OVER-UNDER			
Model 612, 12 Gauge, Field Grade, Checkered Stock, Light Engraving, Single Selective Trigger, Vent Rib, *Modern*	350	700	1000
Model 2100, 12 Gauge, Skeet Grade, Checkered Stock, Engraved, Single Selective Trigger, Vent Rib, *Modern*	400	800	1100
Model 2200 S, 12 Gauge, Skeet Grade, Checkered Stock, Engraved, Single Selective Trigger, Wide Vent Rib, *Modern*	400	900	1200
Model 2200 T, 12 Gauge, Trap Grade, Checkered Stock, Engraved, Single Selective Trigger, Wide Vent Rib, *Modern*	450	1000	1400
Model 2300 S, 12 Gauge, Skeet Grade, Fancy Wood, Engraved, Single Selective Trigger, Vent Rib, *Modern*	500	1100	1450
Model 2300 T, 12 Gauge, Trap Grade, Fancy Wood, Engraved, Single Selective Trigger, Vent Rib, *Modern*	700	1400	1750
Model Grandee, 12 Gauge, Fancy Engraving, Fancy Wood, Gold Inlays, Single Selective Trigger, Vent Rib, *Modern*	800	1750	2250

MIKROS

Tradename of Manufacture d'Armes Des Pyrenees, Hendaye, France, 1934–1939, 1958 to date.

	Fair	V. Good	Excellent
HANDGUN, SELF-LOADING			
6.35mm, Clip Fed, Magazine Disconnect, *Modern*	75	150	175
7.65mm, Clip Fed, Magazine Disconnect, *Modern*	75	150	175
KE, .22 Short R.F., Clip Fed, Hammer, Magazine Disconnect, 2" Barrel, *Modern*	75	125	150
KE, .22 Short R.F., Clip Fed, Hammer, Magazine Disconnect, 4" Barrel, *Modern*	$75	$125	$150
KE, .22 Short R.F., Clip Fed, Hammer, Magazine Disconnect, 2" Barrel, Lightweight, *Modern*	50	100	125
KE, .22 Short R.F., Clip Fed, Hammer, Magazine Disconnect, 4" Barrel, Lightweight, *Modern*	50	100	125
KN, .25 ACP, Clip Fed, Hammer, Magazine Disconnect, 2" Barrel, *Modern*	50	100	125
KN, .25 ACP, Clip Fed, Hammer, Magazine Disconnect, 2" Barrel, Lightweight, *Modern*	50	100	125

MILITARY

Retolaza Hermanos, Eibar, Spain, c. 1915.

	Fair	V. Good	Excellent
HANDGUN, SELF-LOADING			
Model 1914, 7.65mm, Clip Fed, *Curio*	75	125	175

MILLER, MATHIAS

Easton, Pa., 1771–1788. See Kentucky Rifles.

MILLS, BENJAMIN

Charlottesville, N.C., 1784–1790, 1790–1814 at Harrodsburg, Ky. See Kentucky Rifles, U.S. Military.

MINNEAPOLIS FIREARMS CO.

Minneapolis, Minn., c. 1883.

	Fair	V. Good	Excellent
HANDGUN, PALM PISTOL			
The Protector, .32 Extra Short R.F., Nickel Plated, *Antique*	500	1300	1850

MIQUELET-LOCK EXAMPLES

	Fair	V. Good	Excellent
HANDGUN, MIQUELET-LOCK			
.52 Arabian, Holster Pistol, Tapered Round Barrel, Low Quality, *Antique*	150	300	450
.55, Russian Cossack Type, Tapered Round Barrel, Steel Furniture, Silver Furniture, *Antique*	350	700	950
Central Italian 1700s, Holster Pistol, Brass Furniture, Brass Overlay Stock, Medium Quality, *Antique*	900	2250	3000
Pair Cominazzo Early 1700s, Steel Inlay, Medium Quality, Holster Pistol, *Antique*	1400	3250	4250
Pair Late 1700s, Pocket Pistol, Medium Quality, Brass Furniture, Light Ornamentation, *Antique*	800	1750	2750

	Fair	V. Good	Excellent
Pair Spanish Late 1600s, Belt Hook, Brass Overlay Stock, High Quality, *Antique*			Rare
Ripoll Type Late 1600s, Blunderbuss, Brass Inlay, *Antique*	$1900	$4250	$5500
Ripoll Type Late 1600s, Blunderbuss, Silver Inlay, *Antique*	3100	7000	10000

RIFLE, MIQUELET-LOCK

	Fair	V. Good	Excellent
Mid-Eastern, Gold Inlays, Cannon Barrel, Front & Rear Bead Sights, Silver Overlay Stock, Silver Furniture, *Antique*	1600	3500	4750
Mid-Eastern 1700s, Damascus Barrel, Gold Inlays, Many Semi-Precious Gem Inlays, Silver Furniture, Ornate, *Antique*	3100	6500	9500

MIROKU

Tokyo, Japan.

HANDGUN, REVOLVER

	Fair	V. Good	Excellent
Model 6, .38 Spec., Double Action, Swing-Out Cylinder, *Modern*	75	125	150

RIFLE, LEVER ACTION

	Fair	V. Good	Excellent
.22 L.R.R.F., Tube Feed, Plain, *Modern*	100	225	275

Miroku .22 Lever Action

	Fair	V. Good	Excellent
Center Fire, Various Calibers, Checkered Stock, Clip Fed, *Modern*	100	200	250

RIFLE, SELF-LOADING

	Fair	V. Good	Excellent
.22 L.R.R.F., Takedown, Tube Feed Through Butt, *Modern*	100	175	225

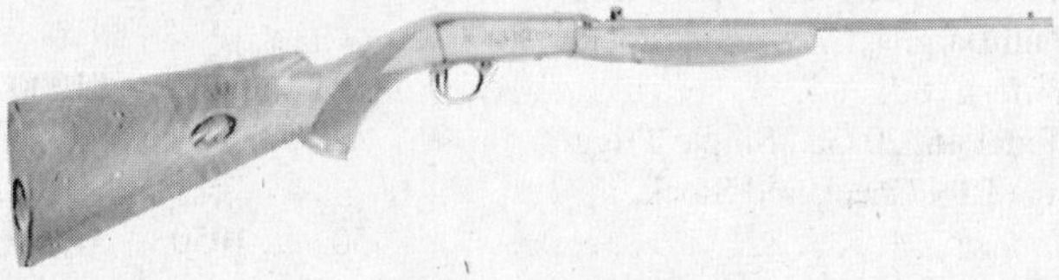

Miroku .22 Auto

RIFLE, SINGLESHOT

	Fair	V. Good	Excellent
Model 78, Various Calibers, Checkered Stock, Falling Block, *Modern*	150	325	400

SHOTGUN, DOUBLE BARREL, OVER-UNDER

	Fair	V. Good	Excellent
Model 3800, 12 Ga., Checkered Stock, Vent Rib, *Modern*	$200	$425	$600
Model H.S.W. DeLuxe, 12 Ga., Checkered Stock, Vent Rib, Engraved, *Modern*	400	800	1000

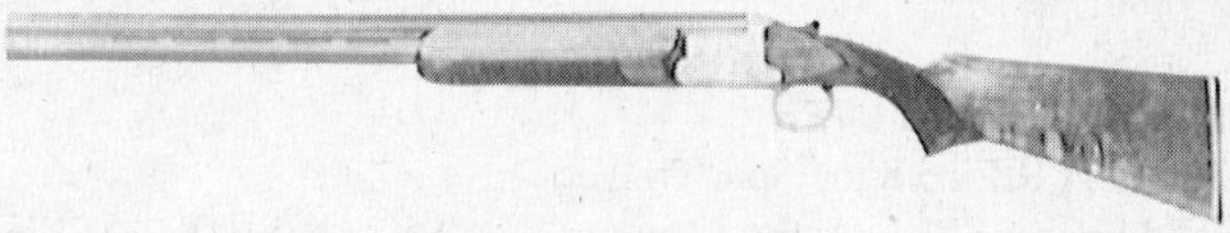

Miroku Model 3800

MISSISSIPPI VALLEY ARMS CO.

Made by Crescent for Shapleigh Hardware, St. Louis, Mo. See Crescent Fire Arms Co., Shotgun, Double Barrel, Side-by-Side; Shotgun, Singleshot.

MITCHELL ARMS

HANDGUN, DOUBLE BARREL, OVER-UNDER

	Fair	V. Good	Excellent
Derringer, .357 Magnum, Spur Trigger, *Modern*	75	125	175

HANDGUN, REVOLVER

	Fair	V. Good	Excellent
Army, Various Calibers, Single Action, Western Style, *Modern*	125	175	250

MITRAILLEUSE

Mre. de Armes et Cycles de St. Etienne, St. Etienne, France, c. 1893–1897.

HANDGUN, PALM PISTOL

	Fair	V. Good	Excellent
Mitrailleuse, 8mm, Engraved, Nickel Plated, *Antique*	300	600	900

MOHAWK

Made by Crescent for Blish, Mize & Stillman, c. 1900. See Crescent Fire Arms Co., Shotgun, Double Barrel, Side-by-Side; Shotgun, Singleshot.

MOLL, DAVID

Hellerstown, Pa., 1814–1833. See Kentucky Rifles.

MOLL, JOHN

Hellerstown, Pa., 1770–1794. See Kentucky Rifles.

MOLL, JOHN JR.

Hellerstown, Pa., 1794–1824. See Kentucky Rifles.

MOLL, JOHN III

Hellerstown, Pa., 1824–1863. See Kentucky Rifles.

MOLL, PETER

Hellerstown, Pa., 1804–1833, with Brother John Moll Jr. Made some of the finest Kentucky Rifles in Pa. See Kentucky Rifles.

MONARCH

c. 1880.

HANDGUN, REVOLVER

	Fair	V. Good	Excellent
.32 Short R.F., 5 Shot, Spur Trigger, Solid Frame, Single Action, *Antique*	$50	$100	$175

MONARCH

Made by Hopkins & Allen, c. 1880.

HANDGUN, REVOLVER

	Fair	V. Good	Excellent
#1, .22 Short R.F., 7 Shot, Spur Trigger, Solid Frame, Single Action, *Antique*	50	100	175
#2, .32 Short R.F., 5 Shot, Spur Trigger, Solid Frame, Single Action, *Antique*	75	125	200
#3, .38 Short R.F., 5 Shot, Spur Trigger, Solid Frame, Single Action, *Antique*	75	125	200
#4, .41 Short R.F., 5 Shot, Spur Trigger, Solid Frame, Single Action, *Antique*	100	250	325

MONDIAL

Gaspar Arrizaga, Eibar, Spain.

HANDGUN, SELF-LOADING

	Fair	V. Good	Excellent
Model 1, 6.35mm, Clip Fed, Grip Safety, Magazine Disconnect, *Modern*	100	200	275
Model 2, 6.35mm, Clip Fed, Blue, *Modern*	75	150	225

Mondial Model 2

MONITOR

Made by Stevens Arms.

SHOTGUN, DOUBLE BARREL, SIDE-BY-SIDE

	Fair	V. Good	Excellent
Model 311, Various Gauges, Hammerless, Steel Barrel, *Modern*	75	125	200

SHOTGUN, SINGLESHOT

	Fair	V. Good	Excellent
Model 90, Various Gauges, Takedown, Automatic Ejector, Plain, Hammer, *Modern*	$25	$50	$75

MOORE PATENT FIREARMS CO.

Brooklyn, N.Y., 1863–1883. Since the teat-fire metallic cartridge had a relatively short presence on the gun market, Moore revolvers tend to be found in excellent condition. A standard feature was the presence of engraving, and sometimes of etched decoration (the latter on the cylinders, the former on the frames). Moore derringers were held in high regard, and the company was succeeded by the National, which in turn was bought out by the Colt Company (1870), which continued the production of its own First and Second Model derringer pistols. Moore firearms, therefore, have a direct association with the Colt Company, and some Colt enthusiasts include examples in their collections.

HANDGUN, REVOLVER

	Fair	V. Good	Excellent
.32 T.F., Spur Trigger, Single Action, Brass Frame, No Extractor, *Antique*	150	300	500
Engraved	300	600	850

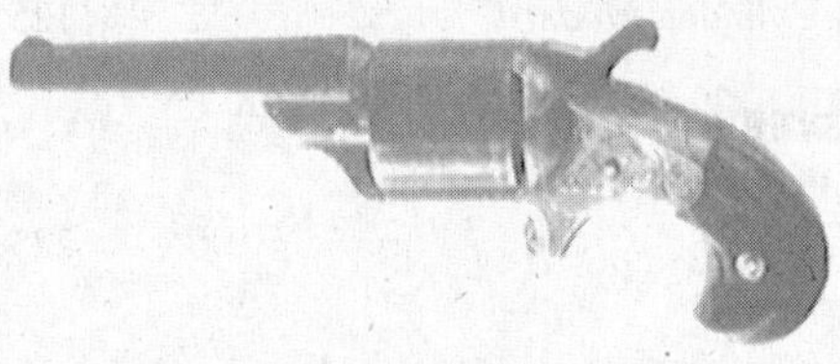

Moore .32 R.F

	Fair	V. Good	Excellent
Williamson's Patent, .32 T.F., Brass Frame, Hook Extractor, *Antique*	150	350	600

HANDGUN, SINGLESHOT

	Fair	V. Good	Excellent
.41 Short R.F., Derringer, Brass Frame, *Antique*	300	800	1150

MORRONE

Rhode Island Arms Co., Hope Valley, R.I., c. 1951.

SHOTGUN, DOUBLE BARREL, OVER-UNDER

	Fair	V. Good	Excellent
Model 46, 12 Ga., Single Trigger, Plain Barrels, Checkered Stock, *Modern*	350	750	1000
Model 46, 20 Ga., Single Trigger, Vent Rib, Checkered Stock, *Modern*	450	1050	1350

MORTIMER, H. W. & SON

London, England, 1800–1802.

HANDGUN, FLINTLOCK

	Fair	V. Good	Excellent
.45, Barrel Duckfoot, Pocket Pistol, Steel Barrel and Frame, Plain, *Antique*	1900	4000	6000

MOSSBERG, O. F. & SONS

New Haven, Conn., 1919 to date. Fitchburg & Chicopee Falls, Mass., 1892–1919 as Oscar F. Mossberg. Interest in Mossberg firearms among collectors was given a boost by publication of *Mossberg—More Gun for the Money* by Victor and Cheryl Halvin. The Halvins also were instrumental in the formation of the National Mossberg Collectors Association.

HANDGUN, MANUAL REPEATER

	Fair	V. Good	Excellent
Brownie, .22 L.R.R.F., Top Break, Double Action, Rotating Firing Pin, 4 Barrels, 4 Shot, *Modern*	$100	$160	$200

HANDGUN, REVOLVER

	Fair	V. Good	Excellent
Abilene, .357 Mag., Single Action, Western Style, Adjustable Sights, Various Barrel Lengths, *Modern*	150	275	350

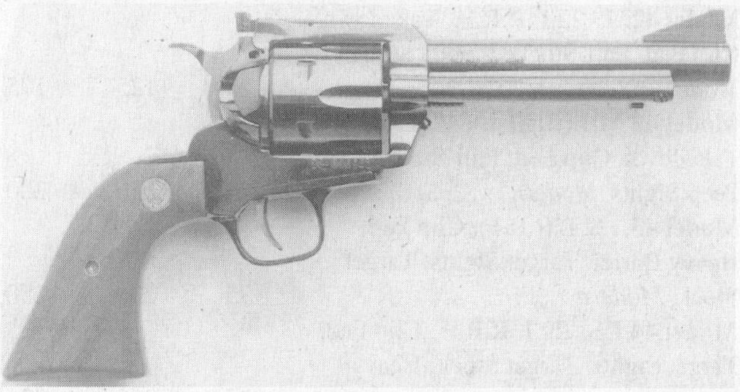

Mossberg Abilene, .357 Magnum

	Fair	V. Good	Excellent
Abilene, .44 Mag., Single Action, Western Style, Adjustable Sights, Various Barrel Lengths, *Modern*	150	300	450

Mossberg Abilene, .44 Magnum

	Fair	V. Good	Excellent
Abilene Silhouette, .357 Mag., Single Action, Western Style, Adjustable Sights, 10" Barrel, *Modern*	150	325	400

RIFLE, BOLT ACTION

	Fair	V. Good	Excellent
Model 10, .22 L.R.R.F., Singleshot, Takedown, *Modern*	50	75	100
Model 14, .22 L.R.R.F., Singleshot, Takedown, Peep Sights, *Modern*	50	75	100
Model 140B, .22 L.R.R.F., Clip Fed, Peep Sights, Monte Carlo Stock, *Modern*	$50	$100	$150
Model 140K, .22 L.R.R.F., Clip Fed, Open Rear Sights, Monte Carlo Stock, *Modern*	50	75	100
Model 142A, .22 L.R.R.F., Clip Fed, Carbine, Monte Carlo Stock, Peep Sights, *Modern*	75	125	150
Model 142A, .22 L.R.R.F., Clip Fed, Peep Sights, *Modern*	75	100	125
Model 142K, .22 L.R.R.F., Clip Fed, Carbine, Monte Carlo Stock, *Modern*	75	100	125
Model 142K, .22 L.R.R.F., Clip Fed, Open Rear Sights, *Modern*	50	75	100
Model 144, .22 L.R.R.F., Clip Fed, Heavy Barrel, Target Stock, Target Sights, *Modern*	75	150	175
Model 144LS, .22 L.R.R.F., Clip Fed, Heavy Barrel, Lyman Sights, Target Stock, *Modern*	125	175	225
Model 146B, .22 L.R.R.F., Takedown, Tube Feed, Monte Carlo Stock, Peep Sights, *Modern*	75	125	150
Model 20, .22 L.R.R.F., Singleshot, Takedown, *Modern*	50	75	100
Model 25, .22 L.R.R.F., Singleshot, Takedown, Peep Sights, *Modern*	50	75	100
Model 25A, .22 L.R.R.F., Singleshot, Takedown, Peep Sights, *Modern*	75	100	125
Model 26B, .22 L.R.R.F., Singleshot, Takedown, Peep Sights, *Modern*	50	75	100
Model 26C, .22 L.R.R.F., Singleshot, Takedown, Open Rear Sight, *Modern*	50	75	100
Model 30, .22 L.R.R.F., Singleshot, Takedown, Peep Sights, *Modern*	50	75	100
Model 320B, .22 L.R.R.F., Singleshot, Peep Sights, *Modern*	75	100	125
Model 320K, .22 L.R.R.F., Singleshot, Open Rear Sight, Monte Carlo Stock, *Modern*	50	75	100
Model 321K, .22 L.R.R.F., Singleshot, Open Rear Sight, *Modern*	50	75	100
Model 340B, .22 L.R.R.F., Clip Fed, Peep Sights, *Modern*	75	100	125
Model 340K, .22 L.R.R.F., Clip Fed, Open Rear Sight, *Modern*	50	75	100
Model 340M, .22 L.R.R.F., Clip Fed, Full-Stocked, Carbine, *Modern*	125	175	225
Model 341, .22 L.R.R.F., Clip Fed, Open Rear Sight, *Modern*	50	75	100
Model 342K, .22 L.R.R.F., Clip Fed, Open Rear Sight, *Modern*	50	75	100
Model 346B, .22 L.R.R.F., Tube Feed, Peep Sights, Monte Carlo Stock, *Modern*	75	100	125

	Fair	V. Good	Excellent
Model 346K, .22 L.R.R.F., Tube Feed, Monte Carlo Stock, Open Rear Sight, *Modern*	$75	$100	$125
Model 352K, .22 L.R.R.F., Clip Fed, Monte Carlo Stock, Open Rear Sight, Carbine, *Modern*	50	75	100
Model 430, .22 L.R.R.F., Tube Feed, Monte Carlo Stock, Checkered Stock, Open Rear Sight, *Modern*	50	75	100
Model 432, .22 L.R.R.F., Tube Feed, Western Style, Carbine, *Modern*	50	75	100
Model 50, .22 L.R.R.F., Takedown, Tube Feed, Open Rear Sight, *Modern*	75	125	150
Model 51, .22 L.R.R.F., Takedown, Tube Feed, Peep Sight, *Modern*	75	125	150
Model 51M, .22 L.R.R.F., Takedown, Tube Feed, Peep Sight, Full-Stocked, *Modern*	75	125	150

RIFLE, LEVER ACTION

	Fair	V. Good	Excellent
Model 400, .22 L.R.R.F., Tube Feed, Open Rear Sight, *Modern*	100	150	200
Model 402, .22 L.R.R.F., Tube Feed, Open Rear Sight, Monte Carlo Stock, *Modern*	100	150	200
Model 472, Various Calibers, Pistol-Grip Stock, Tube Feed, Open Rear Sight, *Modern*	75	125	200
Model 472C, Various Calibers, Straight Grip, Tube Feed, Open Rear Sight, Carbine, *Modern*	75	125	175

RIFLE, SELF-LOADING

	Fair	V. Good	Excellent
Model 151K, .22 L.R.R.F., Takedown, Tube Feed, Open Rear Sight, *Modern*	50	100	150
Model 151M, .22 L.R.R.F., Takedown, Tube Feed, Peep Sights, Full-Stocked, *Modern*	75	125	175
Model 152, .22 L.R.R.F., Clip Fed, Monte Carlo Stock, Peep Sights, Carbine, *Modern*	75	125	175
Model 152K, .22 L.R.R.F., Clip Fed, Monte Carlo Stock, Open Rear Sight, Carbine, *Modern*	50	100	150
Model 350K, .22 L.R.R.F., Clip Fed, Monte Carlo Stock, Open Rear Sight, *Modern*	25	50	75
Model 351C, .22 L.R.R.F., Tube Feed, Monte Carlo Stock, Open Rear Sight, Carbine, *Modern*	50	75	100
Model 351K, .22 L.R.R.F., Tube Feed, Monte Carlo Stock, Open Rear Sight, *Modern*	50	75	100
Model 35, .22 L.R.R.F., Singleshot, Target Stock, Target Sights, *Modern*	100	175	250
Model 35A, .22 L.R.R.F., Singleshot, Target Stock, Target Sights, *Modern*	100	200	225

	Fair	V. Good	Excellent
Model 35A-LS, .22 L.R.R.F., Singleshot, Target Stock, Lyman Sights, *Modern*	$100	$225	$275
Model 35B, .22 L.R.R.F., Singleshot, Target Sights, Heavy Barrel, Target Stock, *Modern*	100	225	300
Model 40, .22 L.R.R.F., Takedown, Tube Feed, Open Rear Sight, *Modern*	50	75	100
Model 42, .22 L.R.R.F., Takedown, Clip Fed, Open Rear Sight, *Modern*	50	75	100
Model 42A, .22 L.R.R.F., Takedown, Clip Fed, Peep Sights, *Modern*	50	75	100
Model 42B, .22 L.R.R.F., Takedown, 5 Shot Clip, Peep Sights, *Modern*	50	75	100
Model 42C, .22 L.R.R.F., Takedown, 5 Shot Clip, Open Rear Sight, *Modern*	50	75	100
Model 42M, .22 L.R.R.F., Takedown, Clip Fed, Full-Stocked, Peep Sights, *Modern*	75	125	175
Model 42 MB (British), .22 L.R.R.F., Takedown, Clip Fed, Full-Stocked, Peep Sights, *Modern*	75	150	200
Model 43, .22 L.R.R.F., Clip Fed, Heavy Barrel, Target Sights, Target Stock, *Modern*	75	200	250
Model 44 US, .22 L.R.R.F., Clip Fed, Target Sights, Target Stock, Heavy Barrel, *Modern*	125	250	325
Model 44B, .22 L.R.R.F., Target Stock, Clip Fed, Target Sights, *Modern*	100	200	275
Model 45, .22 L.R.R.F., Takedown, Tube Feed, Peep Sights, *Modern*	75	125	175
Model 45A, .22 L.R.R.F., Takedown, Tube Feed, Peep Sights, *Modern*	75	125	175
Model 46, .22 L.R.R.F., Takedown, Tube Feed, Peep Sights, *Modern*	75	125	175
Model 46-ALS, .22 L.R.R.F., Takedown, Tube Feed, Lyman Sights, *Modern*	100	175	250
Model 46B, .22 L.R.R.F., Takedown, Tube Feed, Peep Sights, *Modern*	50	100	150
Model 46M, .22 L.R.R.F., Takedown, Tube Feed, Full-Stocked, Peep Sights, *Modern*	50	100	150
Model 46M, .22 L.R.R.F., Takedown, Tube Feed, Open Rear Sight, *Modern*	75	125	175
Model 46T, .22 L.R.R.F., Takedown, Tube Feed, Heavy Barrel, Target Stock, Peep Sights, *Modern*	100	150	200
Model 83D, .410 Ga., Takedown, 3 Shot, *Modern*	75	150	200
Model 85D, .20 Ga., Takedown, 3 Shot, Adjustable Choke, *Modern*	50	75	125
Model L45A, .22 L.R.R.F., Takedown, Tube Feed, Open Rear Sight, *Modern*	75	150	200

	Fair	V. Good	Excellent
RIFLE, SINGLESHOT			
Model L, .22 L.R.R.F., Lever Action, Falling Block, Takedown, *Modern*	$150	$275	$350
RIFLE, SLIDE ACTION			
Model K, .22 L.R.R.F., Takedown, Tube Feed, Hammerless, *Modern*	100	175	225
Model M, .22 L.R.R.F., Takedown, Tube Feed, Hammerless, Octagon Barrel, *Modern*	100	175	250
SHOTGUN, BOLT ACTION			
Model 173, .410 Ga., Takedown, Singleshot, *Modern*	50	75	100
Model 173Y, .410 Ga., Clip Fed, Singleshot, *Modern*	50	75	100
Model 183D, .410 Ga., Takedown, 3 Shot, *Modern*	50	75	100
Model 183K, .410 Ga., Takedown, Adjustable Choke, Clip Fed, *Modern*	50	75	100
Model 183T, .410 Ga., Clip Fed, *Modern*	50	75	100
Model 185D, 20 Ga., Takedown, 3 Shot, *Modern*	50	75	100
Model 185K, 20 Ga., Takedown, 3 Shot, Adjustable Choke, *Modern*	50	75	100
Model 190D, 16 Ga., Takedown, Clip Fed, *Modern*	50	75	100
Model 190K, 16 Ga., Takedown, Adjustable Choke, Clip Fed, *Modern*	50	75	100
Model 195D, 12 Ga., Takedown, Clip Fed, *Modern*	50	75	100
Model 195K, 12 Ga., Takedown, Adjustable Choke, Clip Fed, *Modern*	50	75	100
Model 385K, 20 Ga., Clip Fed, Adjustable Choke, *Modern*	50	75	100
Model 385T, 12 Ga. Mag. 3", Clip Fed, Adjustable Choke, *Modern*	50	75	100
Model 390K, 16 Ga., Clip Fed, Adjustable Choke, *Modern*	50	75	100
Model 390T, 16 Ga., Clip Fed, *Modern*	50	75	100
Model 395K, 12 Ga. Mag. 3", Clip Fed, Adjustable Choke, *Modern*	50	75	100
Model 395S, 12 Ga. Mag. 3", Clip Fed, Open Rear Sight, *Modern*	50	75	100
Model 395T, 12 Ga., Clip Fed, *Modern*	50	75	100

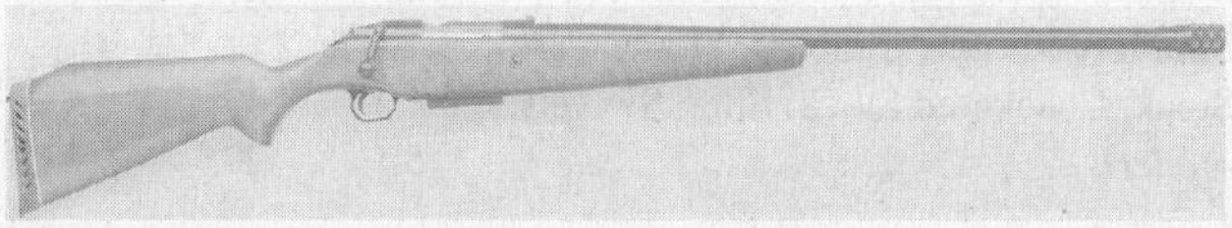

Mossberg 395K, 12 Gauge

	Fair	V. Good	Excellent
Model 73, .410 Ga., Takedown, Singleshot, *Modern*	$50	$75	$125
Model 800, Various Calibers, Open Rear Sight, Monte Carlo Stock, *Modern*	100	175	225
Model 800D, Various Calibers, Monte Carlo Stock, Checkpiece, Checkered Stock, Open Rear Sight, *Modern*	100	200	250
Model 800M, Various Calibers, Open Rear Sight, Full-Stocked, *Modern*	100	200	250
Model 800SM, Various Calibers, Scope Mounted, Monte Carlo Stock, *Modern*	100	225	275
Model 800V, Various Calibers, No Sights, Monte Carlo Stock, Heavy Barrel, *Modern*	100	200	250
Model 810, Various Calibers, Magnum Action, Open Rear Sight, Monte Carlo Stock, *Modern*	100	200	250
Model 810, Various Calibers, Open Rear Sight, Long Action, Monte Carlo Stock, *Modern*	100	200	250
Model B, .22 L.R.R.F., Singleshot, Takedown, *Modern*	25	50	75
Model L42A, .22 L.R.R.F., Takedown, Clip Fed, Peep Sights, Left-Hand, *Modern*	50	75	100
Model L43, .22 L.R.R.F., Clip Fed, Heavy Barrel, Target Sights, Target Stock, Left-Hand, *Modern*	50	125	175
Model L45A, .22 L.R.R.F., Takedown, Tube Feed, Peep Sights, *Modern*	50	100	150
Model L46A-LS, .22 L.R.R.F., Takedown, Tube Feed, Lyman Sights, Left-Hand, *Modern*	75	125	175
Model R, .22 L.R.R.F., Takedown, Tube Feed, Open Rear Sight, *Modern*	25	50	75
SHOTGUN, SLIDE ACTION			
Cruiser, 12 Ga., One-Hand Grip, Nickel Plated, *Modern*	75	150	200
Model 200D, 12 Ga., Clip Fed, Adjustable Choke, *Modern*	50	100	150
Model 200K, 12 Ga., Clip Fed, Adjustable Choke, *Modern*	50	100	150
Model 500 Super, Checkered Stock, Vent Rib, *Modern*	100	200	300
Model 500A, 12 Ga. Mag. 3", Field Grade, *Modern*	100	175	225
Model 500AA, 12 Ga. Mag. 3", Trap Grade, *Modern*	100	225	300
Model 500AHTD, Trap Grade, High Vent Rib, with Choke Tubes, *Modern*	150	350	500

	Fair	V. Good	Excellent
Model 500AK, Field Grade, Adjustable Choke, *Modern*	$100	$200	$300
Model 500AKR, Field Grade, Adjustable Choke, Vent Rib, *Modern*	100	225	300
Model 500AM, Field Grade, Magnum, *Modern*	100	175	250
Model 500AMR, Field Grade, Magnum, Vent Rib, *Modern*	100	175	250
Model 500AR, Field Grade, Vent Rib, *Modern*	100	175	250
Model 500AS, Field Grade, Open Rear Sight, *Modern*	100	200	300
Model 500ATR, Trap Grade, Vent Rib, *Modern*	100	200	300
Model 500B, 16 Ga., Field Grade, *Modern*	100	200	275
Model 500BK, 16 Ga., Adjustable Choke, *Modern*	100	175	275
Model 500BS, 16 Ga., Open Rear Sight, *Modern*	100	175	275
Model 500C, 20 Ga., Field Grade, *Modern*	100	175	275
Model 500CK, 20 Ga., Field Grade, Adjustable Choke, *Modern*	100	175	275
Model 500CKR, 20 Ga., Field Grade, Vent Rib, Adjustable Choke, *Modern*	100	175	275
Model 500CR, 20 Ga., Field Grade, Vent Rib, *Modern*	100	175	275
Model 500CS, 20 Ga., Field Grade, Open Rear Sight, *Modern*	100	200	300
Model 500E, .410 Ga., Field Grade, *Modern*	100	175	275
Model 500EK, .410 Ga., Field Grade, Adjustable Choke, *Modern*	100	200	300
Model 500EKR, .410 Ga., Field Grade, Vent Rib, Adjustable Choke, *Modern*	100	175	275
Model 500ER, .410 Ga., Field Grade, Vent Rib, *Modern*	100	175	275

MOSTER, GEO.

Lancaster, Pa., 1771–1779. See Kentucky Rifles and Pistols.

MOUNTAIN EAGLE

Made by Hopkins & Allen, c. 1880.

HANDGUN, REVOLVER

	Fair	V. Good	Excellent
.32 Short R.F., 5 Shot, Spur Trigger, Solid Frame, Single Action, *Antique*	50	100	150

M.S.

Modesto Santos, Eibar, Spain, c. 1920.

HANDGUN, SELF-LOADING

	Fair	V. Good	Excellent
Action, 7.65mm, Clip Fed, Blue, *Curio*	$75	$125	$175
Model 1920, .25 ACP, Clip Fed, Blue, *Curio*	50	100	150

MT. VERNON ARMS

Belgium, c. 1900.

SHOTGUN, DOUBLE BARREL, SIDE-BY-SIDE

	Fair	V. Good	Excellent
Various Gauges, Hammerless, Damascus Barrel, *Modern*	50	150	200
Various Gauges, Hammerless, Steel Barrel, *Modern*	50	175	225
Various Gauges, Outside Hammers, Damascus Barrel, *Curio*	50	150	200
Various Gauges, Outside Hammers, Steel Barrel, *Modern*	50	150	225

SHOTGUN, SINGLESHOT

	Fair	V. Good	Excellent
Various Gauges, Hammer, Steel Barrel, *Modern*	25	50	75

MUGICA

Jose Mugica, Eibar, Spain, tradename on Llama pistols. See Llama for equivalent models.

MUSGRAVE

South Africa.

RIFLE, BOLT ACTION

	Fair	V. Good	Excellent
Mk. III, Various Calibers, Checkered Stock, *Modern*	150	275	350
Premier NR5, Various Calibers, Checkered Stock, *Modern*	150	300	400
Valiant NR6, Various Calibers, Checkered Stock, *Modern*	150	250	325

MUSKETEER

Tradename used by Firearms International, Washington, D.C., c. 1968.

RIFLE, BOLT ACTION

	Fair	V. Good	Excellent
Carbine, Various Calibers, Monte Carlo Stock, Checkered Stock, Sling Swivels, *Modern*	150	300	400
Deluxe, Various Calibers, Monte Carlo Stock, Checkered Stock, Sling Swivels, *Modern*	150	325	425
Mannlicher, Various Calibers, Full Stock, *Modern*	150	275	375
Sporter, Various Calibers, Monte Carlo Stock, Checkered Stock, Sling Swivels, *Modern*	150	275	375

MUTTI, GEROLIMO

Brescia, c. 1680.

HANDGUN, SNAPHAUNCE

	Fair	V. Good	Excellent
Pair, Belt Pistol, Brass Mounts, Engraved, Ornate, *Antique*	$5000	$13000	$17500

MUTTI, GIESU

Brescia, c. 1790.

HANDGUN, SNAPHAUNCE

	Fair	V. Good	Excellent
Pair, Engraved, Belt Hook, Medium Ornamentation, *Antique*	$4000	$8500	$12500

N

NAPOLEON

Made by Thomas Ryan, Jr., Pistol Mfg. Co., c. 1870–1876.

HANDGUN, REVOLVER

	Fair	V. Good	Excellent
.22 Short R.F., 7 Shot, Spur Trigger, Solid Frame, Single Action, *Antique*	$75	$125	$175
.32 Short R.F., 5 Shot, Spur Trigger, Solid Frame, Single Action, *Antique*	75	150	200

NATIONAL

Made by Norwich Falls Pistol Co., c. 1880.

HANDGUN, REVOLVER

	Fair	V. Good	Excellent
.32 Short R.F., 5 Shot, Spur Trigger, Solid Frame, Single Action, *Antique*	75	150	225
.38 Short R.F., 5 Shot, Spur Trigger, Solid Frame, Single Action, *Antique*	75	150	225

HANDGUN, SINGLESHOT

	Fair	V. Good	Excellent
.41 Short R.F., Derringer, All Metal, Light Engraving, *Antique*	100	300	700

NATIONAL ARMS CO.

Made by Crescent, c. 1900. See Crescent Fire Arms Co., Shotgun, Double Barrel, Side-by-Side; Shotgun, Singleshot.

NATIONAL ORDNANCE

South El Monte, Calif.

RIFLE, BOLT ACTION

	Fair	V. Good	Excellent
1903A3, .30-06 Springfield, *Modern*	75	125	175

RIFLE, SELF-LOADING

	Fair	V. Good	Excellent
Garand, .30-06 Springfield, *Modern*	200	400	600
M-1 Carbine, .30 Carbine, Clip Fed, *Modern*	75	125	175
M-1 Carbine, .30 Carbine, Clip Fed, Folding Stock, Reweld, *Modern*	75	150	200
Tanker Garand, .308 Win., Reweld, Military, *Modern*	200	400	600

NAVY ARMS

Ridgefield, N.J., 1959–Date. Factory opened up in Martinsburg, W. Va., in early 1990s. A true pioneer in and unequivocal advocate of blackpowder shooting. Val Forgett deserves credit for much of the revival of muzzle-loaders in contemporary shooting and collecting. Just prior to the Civil War centennial, Forgett was confident that the shooting public would welcome accurately made replicas of bygone firearms. His Navy Arms Co. has been in the vanguard of this movement ever since. The extraordinary array of the company's product line can only be fully appreciated by visiting the company store, in Ridgefield, New Jersey, by carefully scrutinizing Navy Arms Co. color catalogs, or by visiting the Navy Arms and Gibbs Rifle factory site in Martinsburg, West Virginia. The Governor's Place, Williamsburg, Virginia, was outfitted with panoplies of flintlock pistols and muskets, and of swords, by Val Forgett and Navy Arms Co. The brilliant displays of these guns were instrumental in re-creating the original atmosphere and ambiance of one of colonial America's most striking public architectural landmarks.

HANDGUN, FLINTLOCK

	Fair	V. Good	Excellent
.44 "Kentucky," Belt Pistol. Brass Furniture, Brass Barrel, Reproduction	$100	$200	$325
.44 "Kentucky," Belt Pistol. Brass Furniture, Reproduction	100	200	325
.577 Scotch Black Watch, Military, Belt Pistol, all Metal, Reproduction	100	225	350
.69 M1763 Charleville, Military, Belt Pistol, Reproduction	150	375	500
.69 M1763 Charleville, Military, Belt Pistol, Reproduction	100	225	350
.69 M1777 Charleville, Military, Belt Pistol, Reproduction	100	225	350
.69 Tower, Military, Belt Pistol, Reproduction	50	100	200

A Engraving Pistol, Add $115.00-$225.00
A Engraving Rifle, Add $145.00-$300.00
B Engraving Pistol, Add $140.00-$300.00
B Engraving Rifle, Add $215.00-$450.00
C Engraving Pistol, Add $265.00-$500.00
C Engraving Rifle, Add $495.00-$1000.00
Presentation Case Only, Add $25.00-$50.00
Silver Plating, Add $95.00-$250.00
Tiffany Grips Only, Add $155.00-$350.00

HANDGUN, PERCUSSION

	Fair	V. Good	Excellent
.36 M1851 New Navy, Revolver, Brass Grip Frame, Reproduction	100	200	300
.36 M1851 New Navy, Revolver, Silver-Plated Grip Frame, Reproduction	100	200	300

	Fair	V. Good	Excellent
.36 M1853, Revolver, Pocket Pistol, 4½" Barrel, Reproduction	$100	$200	$300
.36 M1853, Revolver, Pocket Pistol, 5½" Barrel, Reproduction	100	200	300
.36 M1853, Revolver, Pocket Pistol, 6½" Barrel, Reproduction	100	200	300
.36 M1860 Reb, Revolver, Brass Frame, Reproduction	100	200	300
.36 M1860 Sheriff, Revolver, Brass Frame, Reproduction	100	200	300
.36 M1861 Navy, Revolver, Engraved Cylinder, Reproduction	100	200	300
.36 M1861 Navy, Revolver, Fluted Cylinder, Reproduction	100	200	300
.36 M1861, Revolver, Sheriff's Model, with Short Barrel, Reproduction	100	200	300
.36 M1862 Police, Revolver, 5 Shot, Brass Grip Frame, Cased with Accessories, Reproduction	100	250	350
.36 M1862 Police, Revolver, 5 Shot, Brass Grip Frame, 4½" Barrel, Reproduction	100	200	300
.36 M1862 Police, Revolver, 5 Shot, Brass Grip Frame, 5½" Barrel, Reproduction	100	200	300
.36 M1862 Police, Revolver, 5 Shot, Brass Grip Frame, 6½" Barrel, Reproduction	100	200	300
.36 M1862 Police, Revolver, Fancy Engraving, Silver Plated, Gold Plated, Reproduction	100	800	1150
.36 M1863, Revolver, Sheriff's Model, with Short Barrel, Reproduction	100	200	300
.36 Remington, Revolver, Target Pistol, Adjustable Sights, Reproduction	100	225	325
.36 Spiller & Burr, Revolver, Solid Frame, Reproduction	100	175	275
.44 "Kentucky," Belt Pistol, Brass Furniture, Brass Barrel, Reproduction	100	225	325
.44 "Kentucky," Belt Pistol, Brass Furniture, Reproduction	100	175	325
.44 First Model Dragoon, Revolver, Brass Grip Frame, Reproduction	100	225	325
.44 M1847 Walker, Revolver, Brass Grip Frame, Engraved, Gold Inlays, Reproduction	200	450	575
.44 M1847 Walker, Revolver, Brass Grip Frame, Reproduction	100	250	350
.44 M1860 Army, Revolver, Engraved Cylinder, Reproduction	75	150	250
.44 M1860 Army, Revolver, Fluted Cylinder, Reproduction	75	150	250
.44 M1860 Reb, Revolver, Shoulder Stock Only, Reproduction	25	50	100
.44 M1860 Sheriff, Revolver, Brass Frame, Reproduction	100	125	100
.44 M1860, Revolver, Sheriff's Model, with Short Barrel, Reproduction	100	175	325
.44 Remington Army, Revolver, Nickel Plated, Reproduction	$100	$225	$325
.44 Remington, Revolver, Solid Frame, Reproduction	100	150	250
.44 Remington, Revolver, Stainless Steel, Reproduction	100	225	325

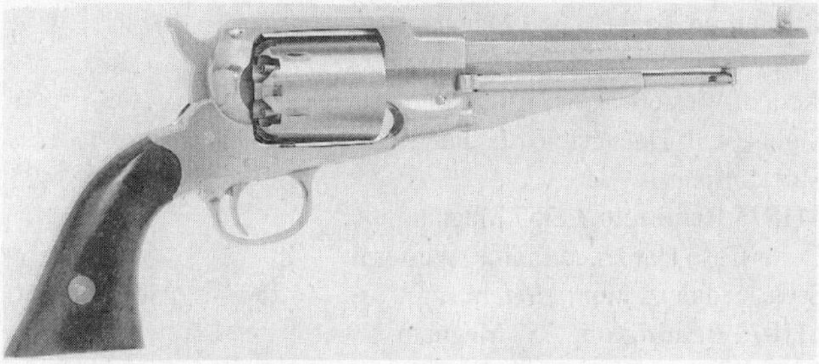

Navy Arms .44 Remington Stainless

	Fair	V. Good	Excellent
.44 Remington, Revolver, Target Pistol, Adjustable Sights, Reproduction	100	225	325
.44 Second Model, Dragoon, Revolver, Brass Grip Frame, Reproduction	150	300	450
.44 Third Model Dragoon, Revolver, Brass Grip Frame, with Detachable Shoulder Stock, Reproduction	150	350	500
.44 Third Model Dragoon, Revolver, Brass Grip Frame, Reproduction	150	325	450
.44 Third Model Dragoon, Revolver, Buntline, with Detachable Shoulder Stock, Reproduction	150	350	500
.58 M1806, Harper's Ferry, Brass Furniture, Military, Belt Pistol, Reproduction	75	150	250
.58 M1855, Harper's Ferry, Holster Pistol, Military, with Detachable Shoulder Stock, Reproduction	100	200	300

Navy Arms Harper's Ferry 1806

	Fair	V. Good	Excellent
.58 M1855, Harper's Ferry, Shoulder Stock Only	25	50	75

HANDGUN, REVOLVER

	Fair	V. Good	Excellent
Cattleman, Various Calibers, Color Case Hardened Frame, Single Action, Western Style, *Modern*	150	300	425

	Fair	V. Good	Excellent
Cattleman Buntline, .45 Colt, Color Case Hardened Frame, Single Action, Western Style, Adjustable Sights, with Detachable Shoulder Stock, *Modern*	$200	$425	$525
Cattleman Carbine, Various Calibers, Color Case Hardened Frame, Single Action, Western Style, Adjustable Sights, *Modern*	200	400	500
Cattleman Target, .357 Magnum, Color Case Hardened Frame, Single Action, Western Style, Adjustable Sights, with Detachable Shoulder Stock, *Modern*	150	325	425
M1875 Remington, .357 Magnum, Color Case Hardened Frame, Western Style, Single Action, *Modern*	125	250	350
M1875 Remington, .357 Magnum, Nickel Plated, Western Style, Single Action, *Modern*	150	300	450
M1875 Remington, .44-40 WCF, Color Case Hardened Frame, Western Style, Single Action, *Modern*	150	300	400
M1875 Remington, .44-40 WCF, Nickel Plated, Western Style, Single Action, *Modern*	150	325	425
M1875 Remington, .45 Colt, Color Case Hardened Frame, Western Style, Single Action, *Modern*	150	275	375
M1875 Remington, .45 Colt, Nickel Plated, Western Style, Single Action, *Modern*	150	300	400
M1875 Remington, .45 Colt, Stainless Steel, Western Style, Single Action, *Modern*	150	325	425

HANDGUN, SINGLESHOT

	Fair	V. Good	Excellent
Rolling Block, .22 Hornet, Half-Octagon Barrel, Color Case Hardened Frame, Adjustable Sights, *Modern*	100	250	350
Rolling Block, .22 L.R.R.F., Half-Octagon Barrel, Color Case Hardened Frame, Adjustable Sights, *Modern*	100	200	300
Rolling Block, .357 Magnum, Half-Octagon Barrel, Color Case Hardened Frame, Adjustable Sights, *Modern*	100	250	250

RIFLE, BOLT ACTION

	Fair	V. Good	Excellent
Mauser '98, .45-70 Government, Carbine, Checkered Stock, *Modern*	100	225	325
Mauser '98, .45-70 Government, Checkered Stock, *Modern*	100	225	325

RIFLE, LEVER ACTION

	Fair	V. Good	Excellent
M1873 1 of 1000, .44-40 WCF, Blue Tube, Octagon Barrel, Steel Buttplate, Engraved, *Modern*	300	675	1000
M1873-".101," .22 L.R.R.F., Color Case Hardened Frame, Tube Feed, Round Barrel, Steel Buttplate, Carbine, *Modern*	150	300	550
M1873-".101," .44-40 WCF, Color Case Hardened Frame, Tube Feed, Octagon Barrel, Steel Buttplate, *Modern*	$250	$550	$750
M1873-".101," .44-40 WCF, Color Case Hardened Frame, Tube Feed, Round Barrel, Steel Buttplate, Carbine, *Modern*	300	600	800
M1873-".101," Trapper, .22 L.R.R.F., Color Case Hardened Frame, Tube Feed, Round Barrel, Steel Buttplate, *Modern*	150	300	400
M1873-".101," Trapper, .44-40 WCF, Color Case Hardened Frame, Tube Feed, Round Barrel, Steel Buttplate, *Modern*	200	425	525
Yellowboy Trapper, .22 L.R.R.F., Brass Frame, Tube Feed, Round Barrel, Brass Buttplate, *Modern*	200	400	550
Yellowboy Trapper, .38 Special, Brass Frame, Tube Feed, Round Barrel, Brass Buttplate, *Modern*	200	425	575
Yellowboy Trapper, .44-40 WCF, Brass Frame, Tube Feed, Round Barrel, Brass Buttplate, *Modern*	325	600	800
Yellowboy, .22 L.R.R.F., Brass Frame, Tube Feed, Round Barrel, Brass Buttplate, Saddle-Ring Carbine, *Modern*	150	300	425
Yellowboy, .38 Special, Brass Frame, Tube Feed, Octagon Barrel, Brass Buttplate, *Modern*	200	400	525
Yellowboy, .38 Special, Brass Frame, Tube Feed, Round Barrel, Brass Buttplate, Saddle-Ring Carbine, *Modern*	200	400	525
Yellowboy, .44-40 WCF, Brass Frame, Tube Feed, Octagon Barrel, Brass Buttplate, *Modern*	300	600	800
Yellowboy, .44-40 WCF, Brass Frame, Tube Feed, Round Barrel, Brass Buttplate, Saddle-Ring Carbine, *Modern*	300	600	800

RIFLE, FLINTLOCK

	Fair	V. Good	Excellent
.45 "Kentucky," Carbine, Brass Furniture, Reproduction	150	300	400
.45 "Kentucky," Long Rifle, Brass Furniture, Reproduction	150	300	400
.58 M1803, Harper's Ferry, Brass Furniture, Military, Reproduction	150	325	500

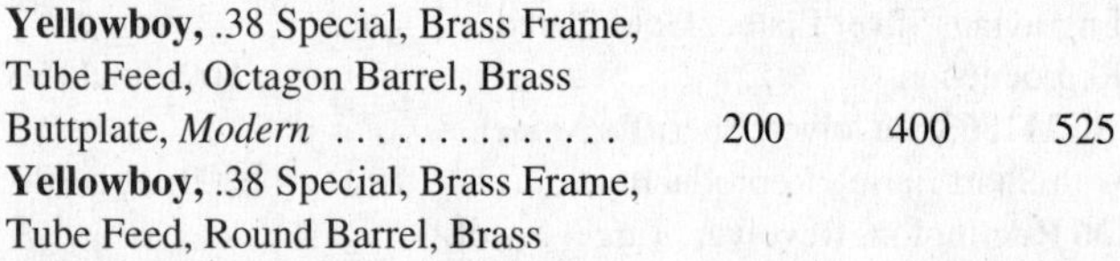

Navy Arms .58 1803 Harper's Ferry

	Fair	V. Good	Excellent
.69 M1795 Springfield, Musket, Modern Reproduction	200	400	525

	Fair	V. Good	Excellent
.69 M1809 Springfield, Musket, Modern Reproduction	$200	$400	$525
.75 Brown Bess (Jap), Musket, Modern Reproduction	200	400	525
.75 Brown Bess, Carbine, Modern Reproduction	250	500	650
.75 Brown Bess, Musket, Modern Reproduction	250	500	650

Navy Arms Brown Bess Rifle

RIFLE, PERCUSSION

	Fair	V. Good	Excellent
.44 Remington, Revolving, Carbine, Brass Furniture, Reproduction	125	200	300
.45 "Kentucky," Carbine, Brass Furniture, Reproduction	125	275	375
.45 "Kentucky," Carbine, Brass Furniture, Reproduction	125	275	400
.45 "Kentucky," Long Rifle, Brass Furniture, Reproduction	125	275	400
.45 Hawken Hurricane, Octagon Barrel, Brass Furniture, Reproduction	150	300	425
.45 Morse, Octagon Barrel, Brass Frame, Reproduction	100	200	325
.50 Hawken Hurricane, Octagon Barrel, Brass Furniture, Reproduction	150	325	450
.50 Morse, Octagon Barrel, Brass Frame, Reproduction	100	225	350
.54 Gallagher, Carbine, Military, Steel Furniture, Reproduction	150	300	450
.577 M1853 3-Band, Military, Musket, (Parker-Hale), Reproduction	150	375	500
.577 M1858 2-Band, Military, Rifled, (Parker-Hale), Reproduction	150	325	450
.577 M1861, Military, Musketoon, (Parker-Hale), Reproduction	150	325	450
.58 Buffalo Hunter, Round Barrel, Brass Furniture, Reproduction	150	300	425

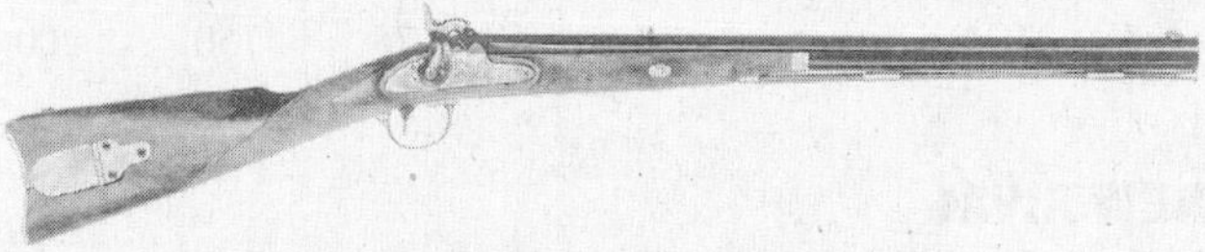

Navy Arms .58 Buffalo Hunter

	Fair	V. Good	Excellent
.58 Hawken Hunter, Octagon Barrel, Brass Furniture, Reproduction	150	325	425
.58 J.P. Murray Artillery Carbine, Brass Furniture, Military, Reproduction	$150	$300	$400
.58 M1841 Mississippi Rifle, Brass Furniture, Military, Reproduction	150	300	400
.58 M1863 Springfield, Military, Rifled, Musket, Reproduction	150	300	400

Navy Arms 1863 Springfield

	Fair	V. Good	Excellent
.58 M1864 Springfield, Military, Rifled, Musket, Reproduction	150	325	425
.58 Morse, Octagon Barrel, Brass Frame, Reproduction	150	275	375
.58 Zouave 1864, Military, Carbine, Brass Furniture, Reproduction	150	300	400
.58 Zouave, Military, Reproduction	150	300	400

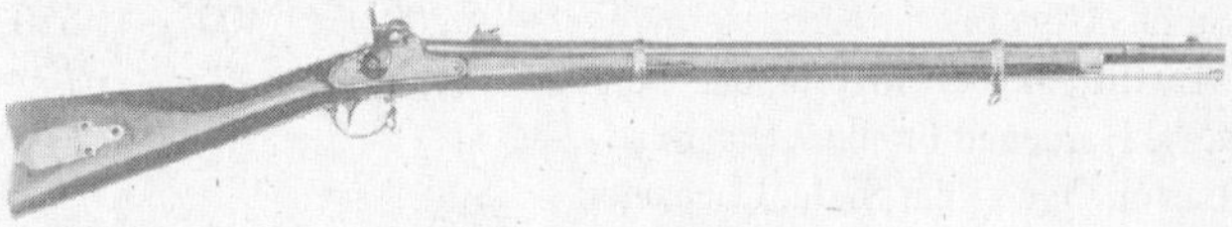

Navy Arms Zouave Rifle

RIFLE, SELF-LOADING

	Fair	V. Good	Excellent
AP-74, .22 L.R.R.F., Clip Fed, Plastic Stock, *Modern*	75	150	250
AP-74, .22 L.R.R.F., Clip Fed, Wood Stock, *Modern*	100	175	275
AP-74, .32 ACP, Clip Fed, Plastic Stock, *Modern*	100	175	275
AP-74 Commando, .22 L.R.R.F., Clip Fed, Wood Stock, *Modern*	75	150	250

RIFLE, SINGLESHOT

	Fair	V. Good	Excellent
Buffalo, .45-70 Government, Rolling Block, Color Case Hardened Frame, Octagon Barrel, Open Rear Sights, Various Barrel Lengths, *Modern*	100	200	300
Buffalo, .45-70 Government, Rolling Block, Color Case Hardened Frame, Half-Octagon Barrel, Open Rear Sights, Various Barrel Lengths, *Modern*	100	200	300
Buffalo, .50 U.S. Carbine, Rolling Block, Color Case Hardened Frame, Octagon Barrel, Open Rear Sights, Various Barrel Lengths, *Modern*	100	200	300
Buffalo, .50 U.S. Carbine, Rolling Block, Color Case Hardened Frame, Half-Octagon Barrel, Open Rear Sights, Various Barrel Lengths, *Modern*	100	175	250

	Fair	V. Good	Excellent
Creedmore, .45-70 Government, Rolling Block, Color Case Hardened Frame, Octagon Barrel, Vernier Sights, 30" Barrel, *Modern*	$150	$350	$500
Creedmore, .45-70 Government, Rolling Block, Color Case Hardened Frame, Half-Octagon Barrel, Vernier Sights, 30" Barrel, *Modern*	150	325	450
Creedmore, .50 U.S. Carbine, Rolling Block, Color Case Hardened Frame, Octagon Barrel, Vernier Sights, 30" Barrel, *Modern*	150	325	450
Creedmore, .50 U.S. Carbine, Rolling Block, Color Case Hardened Frame, Half-Octagon Barrel, Vernier Sights, 30" Barrel, *Modern*	150	325	450
Creedmore, .50-140 Sharps, Rolling Block, Color Case Hardened Frame, Octagon Barrel, Vernier Sights, 30" Barrel, *Modern*	175	375	500
Martini, .45-70 Government, Color Case Hardened Frame, Half-Octagon Barrel, Open Rear Sight, Checkered Stock, *Modern*	200	400	550
Martini, .45-70 Government, Color Case Hardened Frame, Octagon Barrel, Open Rear Sight, Checkered Stock, *Modern*	200	400	550
Rolling Block, .22 Hornet, Carbine, Color Case Hardened Frame, Adjustable Sights, *Modern*	150	300	450
Rolling Block, .22 L.R.R.F., Carbine, Color Case Hardened Frame, Adjustable Sights, *Modern*	125	250	400
Rolling Block, .357 Magnum, Carbine, Color Case Hardened Frame, Adjustable Sights, *Modern*	125	250	400

SHOTGUN, PERCUSSION

	Fair	V. Good	Excellent
Magnum Deluxe, 12 Ga., Double Barrel, Side-by-Side, Outside Hammers, Checkered Stock, Reproduction	100	200	350
Morse/Navy, 12 Ga., Singleshot, Brass Frame, Reproduction	75	150	250

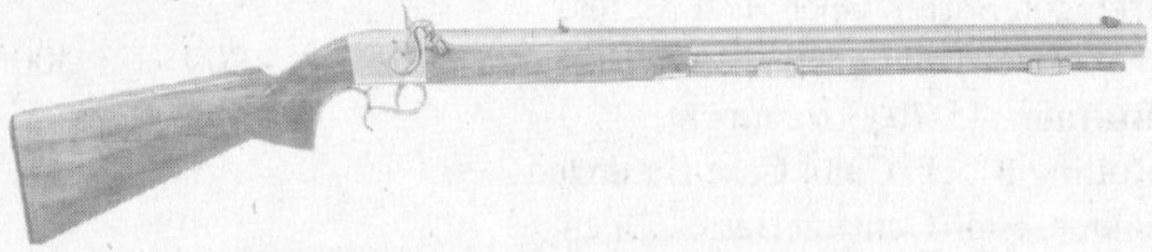

Navy Arms Morse Navy Shotgun

	Fair	V. Good	Excellent
Upland Deluxe, 12 Ga., Double Barrel, Side-by-Side, Outside Hammers, Checkered Stock, Reproduction	75	150	225
Zouave, 12 Ga., Brass Furniture, Reproduction	75	150	225

NEIHARD, PETER

Northhampton, Pa., 1785–1787. See Kentucky Rifles.

NERO

Made by Hopkins & Allen., c. 1880. Sold by C. L. Riker.

HANDGUN, REVOLVER

	Fair	V. Good	Excellent
.22 Short R.F., 7 Shot, Spur Trigger, Solid Frame, Single Action, *Antique*	$100	$200	$300
.32 Short R.F., 5 Shot, Spur Trigger, Solid Frame, Single Action, *Antique*	125	250	350

NERO

Made by J. Rupertus Arms Co., c. 1880. Sold by E. Tryon Co.

HANDGUN, REVOLVER

	Fair	V. Good	Excellent
.22 Short R.F., 7 Shot, Spur Trigger, Solid Frame, Single Action, *Antique*	125	250	325
.32 Short R.F., 5 Shot, Spur Trigger, Solid Frame, Single Action, *Antique*	150	300	375

NEW CHIEFTAIN

Made by Stevens Arms.

SHOTGUN, SINGLESHOT

	Fair	V. Good	Excellent
Model 94, Various Gauges, Takedown, Automatic Ejector, Plain, Hammer, *Modern*	25	50	75

NEW NAMBU

Shin Chuo Kogyo, Tokyo, Japan, c. 1960.

HANDGUN, REVOLVER

	Fair	V. Good	Excellent
Model 58, .38 Special, Swing-Out Cylinder, Double Action, *Modern*	75	100	175

HANDGUN, SELF-LOADING

	Fair	V. Good	Excellent
Model 57A, 9mm Luger, Clip Fed, Blue, *Modern*	100	175	225
Model 57B, .32 ACP, Clip Fed, Blue, *Modern*	75	150	200

NEW RIVAL

Made by Crescent for Van Camp Hardware & Iron Co., Indianapolis, Ind. See Crescent Fire Arms Co., Shotgun, Double Barrel, Side-by-Side; Shotgun, Singleshot.

NEW YORK ARMS CO.
Made by Crescent for Garnet Carter Co., Tenn., c. 1900. See Crescent Fire Arms Co., Shotgun, Double Barrel, Side-by-Side; Shotgun, Singleshot.

NEW YORK PISTOL CO.
New York City, c. 1870.

HANDGUN, REVOLVER

	Fair	V. Good	Excellent
.22 Short R.F., 7 Shot, Spur Trigger, Solid Frame, Single Action, *Antique*	$75	$150	$200
.32 Short R.F., 5 Shot, Spur Trigger, Solid Frame, Single Action, *Antique*	75	125	175

NEWCOMER, JOHN
Lancaster, Pa., 1770–1772. See Kentucky Rifles.

NEWHARDT, JACOB
Allentown, Pa., 1770–1777. See Kentucky Rifles.

NEWPORT
Made by Stevens Arms.

SHOTGUN, DOUBLE BARREL, SIDE-BY-SIDE

	Fair	V. Good	Excellent
Model 311, Various Gauges, Hammerless, Steel Barrel, *Modern*	75	125	175

NEWTON ARMS CO.
Buffalo, N.Y., 1914–1918, reorganized 1918–1930 as Newton Rifle Corp.

RIFLE, BOLT ACTION

	Fair	V. Good	Excellent
1st Type, Various Calibers, Sporting Rifle, Set Trigger, Checkered Stock, Open Rear Sight, *Curio*	400	850	1150
2nd Type, Various Calibers, Sporting Rifle, Set Trigger, Checkered Stock, Open Rear Sight, *Curio*	350	750	1000
Newton-Mauser, Various Calibers, Sporting Rifle, Set Trigger, Checkered Stock, Open Rear Sight, *Curio*	325	675	900

NICHOLS, JOHN
Oxford, England, 1730–1775.

HANDGUN, FLINTLOCK

	Fair	V. Good	Excellent
Holster Pistol, Engraved, Brass Furniture, High Quality, *Antique*	1300	3000	4250

NIKKO SPORTING FIREARMS
Japan. Imported by Kanematsu-Gosho U.S.A. Inc., Arlington Heights, Ill., 1958–1989. Sold in the U.S. as "Golden Eagle."

RIFLE, BOLT ACTION

	Fair	V. Good	Excellent
Model 7000, Various African Calibers, Grade 1, Checkered Stock, *Modern*	$150	$400	$625
Model 7000, Various Calibers, Grade 1, Checkered Stock, *Modern*	125	400	625

SHOTGUN, DOUBLE BARREL, OVER-UNDER

	Fair	V. Good	Excellent
Model 5000, 12 and 20 Gauge, Field Grade 2, Vent Rib, Checkered Stock, Light Engraving, Gold Overlay, *Modern*	350	775	1000
Model 5000, 12 and 20 Gauge, Field Grade, Vent Rib, Checkered Stock, Light Engraving, Gold Overlay, *Modern*	300	675	900
Model 5000, 12 and 20 Gauge, Skeet Grade 2, Vent Rib, Checkered Stock, Light Engraving, Gold Overlay, *Modern*	350	800	1000
Model 5000, 12 and 20 Gauge, Skeet Grade, Vent Rib, Checkered Stock, Light Engraving, Gold Overlay, *Modern*	325	700	950
Model 5000, 12 and 20 Gauge, Trap Grade 2, Vent Rib, Checkered Stock, Light Engraving, Gold Overlay, *Modern*	350	800	1000
Model 5000, 12 and 20 Gauge, Trap Grade, Vent Rib, Checkered Stock, Light Engraving, Gold Overlay, *Modern*	325	700	950
Model 5000 Grandee, 12 and 20 Gauge, Field Grade 3, Vent Rib, Checkered Stock, Fancy Engraving, Gold Overlay, *Modern*	700	1750	2500
Model 5000 Grandee, 12 and 20 Gauge, Skeet Grade 3, Vent Rib, Checkered Stock, Fancy Engraving, Gold Overlay, *Modern*	800	2000	2750
Model 5000 Grandee, 12 and 20 Gauge, Trap Grade 3, Vent Rib, Checkered Stock, Fancy Engraving, Gold Overlay, *Modern*	800	2000	2750

NITRO PROOF
Made by Stevens Arms.

SHOTGUN, SINGLESHOT

	Fair	V. Good	Excellent
Model 115, Various Gauges, Hammer, Automatic Ejector, *Modern*	25	50	75

NIVA
Kohout & Spolecnost, Kydne, Czechoslovakia.

HANDGUN, SELF-LOADING

	Fair	V. Good	Excellent
Niva, 6.35mm, Clip Fed, Blue, *Modern*	$50	$125	$200

NOBLE

Haydenville, Mass., 1950–1971.

RIFLE, BOLT ACTION

	Fair	V. Good	Excellent
.98 Mauser, .30-06 Springfield, Monte Carlo Stock, Open Rear Sight, *Modern*	50	100	175
Model 10, .22 L.R.R.F., Singleshot, *Modern*	15	25	50
Model 20, .22 L.R.R.F., Singleshot, *Modern*	15	25	50
Model 222, .22 L.R.R.F., Singleshot, *Modern*	25	50	75

RIFLE, LEVER ACTION

	Fair	V. Good	Excellent
Model 275, .22 L.R.R.F., Tube Feed, *Modern*	25	50	75

RIFLE, SELF-LOADING

	Fair	V. Good	Excellent
Model 285, .22 L.R.R.F., Tube Feed, *Modern*	50	75	125

RIFLE, SLIDE ACTION

	Fair	V. Good	Excellent
Model 235, .22 L.R.R.F., Wood Stock, *Modern*	50	75	125
Model 33, .22 L.R.R.F., Plastic Stock, *Modern*	25	50	75
Model 33A, .22 L.R.R.F., Wood Stock, *Modern*	50	75	125

SHOTGUN, DOUBLE BARREL, SIDE-BY-SIDE

	Fair	V. Good	Excellent
Model 420, Various Gauges, Hammerless, Checkered Stock, Recoil Pad, *Modern*	50	125	175
Model 420EK, Various Gauges, Hammerless, Checkered Stock, Recoil Pad, Fancy Wood, *Modern*	75	150	200
Model 450E, Various Gauges, Hammerless, Checkered Stock, Recoil Pad, *Modern*	100	200	300

SHOTGUN, SELF-LOADING

	Fair	V. Good	Excellent
Model 80, .410 Ga., *Modern*	75	150	275

SHOTGUN, SLIDE ACTION

	Fair	V. Good	Excellent
Model 160 Deergun, 12 and 20 Gauges, Peep Sights, *Modern*	25	100	150
Model 166L Deergun, 12 and 16 Gauges, Peep Sights, *Modern*	25	100	150
Model 166LP Deergun, 12 and 16 Gauges, Peep Sights, *Modern*	25	100	150
Model 200, 20 Ga., *Modern*	25	100	150
Model 200, 20 Ga., Adjustable Choke, *Modern*	25	100	150
Model 200, 20 Ga., Trap Grade, *Modern*	$25	$100	$175
Model 200, 20 Ga., Vent Rib, Adjustable Choke, *Modern*	25	100	175
Model 300, 12 Ga., *Modern*	25	100	175
Model 300, 12 Ga., Adjustable Choke, *Modern*	25	100	175
Model 300, 12 Ga., Trap Grade, *Modern*	50	100	175
Model 300, 12 Ga., Vent Rib, Adjustable Choke, *Modern*	50	125	200
Model 390, 12 Ga., Peep Sights, *Modern*	25	100	175
Model 40, 12 Ga., Hammerless, Solid Frame, Adjustable Choke, *Modern*	25	100	175
Model 400, .410 Ga., *Modern*	25	100	175
Model 400, .410 Ga., Adjustable Choke, *Modern*	25	100	175
Model 400, .410 Ga., Skeet Grade, *Modern*	25	100	175
Model 400, .410 Ga., Skeet Grade, Adjustable Choke, *Modern*	25	125	200
Model 50, 12 Ga., Hammerless, Solid Frame, *Modern*	25	75	125
Model 60, 12 and 16 Gauges, Hammerless, Solid Frame, Adjustable Choke, *Modern*	25	100	175
Model 60 RCLP, 12 and 16 Gauges, Hammerless, Solid Frame, Vent Rib, Adjustable Choke, Checkered Stock, *Modern*	25	100	175
Model 602, 20 Ga., *Modern*	25	100	175
Model 602CLP, 20 Ga., Adjustable Choke, *Modern*	25	100	175
Model 602RCLP, 20 Ga., Adjustable Choke, Vent Rib, *Modern*	25	100	175
Model 602RLP, 20 Ga., Vent Rib, *Modern*	25	100	175
Model 60ACP, 12 and 16 Gauges, Hammerless, Solid Frame, Adjustable Choke, Vent Rib, *Modern*	25	100	175
Model 60AF, 12 and 16 Gauges, Hammerless, Solid Frame, Vent Rib, Adjustable Choke, *Modern*	25	100	175
Model 65, 12 and 20 Gauges, Hammerless, Solid Frame, *Modern*	25	75	125
Model 662CR, 20 Ga., Vent Rib, *Modern*	25	100	150
Model 66CLP, 12 and 16 Gauges, Adjustable Choke, *Modern*	25	100	150
Model 66RCLP, 12 and 20 Gauges, Hammerless, Solid Frame, Adjustable Choke, Vent Rib, *Modern*	25	100	175
Model 66RLP, 12 and 20 Gauges, Hammerless, Solid Frame, Vent Rib, *Modern*	25	100	175
Model 66XLP, 12 and 20 Gauges, Hammerless, Solid Frame, *Modern*	25	100	175
Model 70, .410 Ga., *Modern*	25	75	125

	Fair	V. Good	Excellent
Model 70CLP, .410 Ga., Hammerless, Solid Frame, Adjustable Choke, *Modern*	$25	$100	$175
Model 70RL, .410 Ga., *Modern*	25	100	150
Model 70X, .410 Ga., *Modern*	25	75	125
Model 70XL, .410 Ga., *Modern*	25	75	125
Model 757, 20 Ga., Adjustable Choke, Lightweight, *Modern*	50	100	175

NOCK, HENRY

London & Birmingham, England, 1760–1810.

RIFLE, FLINTLOCK

	Fair	V. Good	Excellent
.65, Ellett Carbine, Musket, Military, *Antique*	700	1750	2500

SHOTGUN, PERCUSSION

	Fair	V. Good	Excellent
Fowler, Converted from Flintlock, Patent Breech, *Antique*	400	800	1350

NONPAREIL

Made by Norwich Falls Pistols Co., c. 1880.

HANDGUN, REVOLVER

	Fair	V. Good	Excellent
.32 Short R.F., 5 Shot, Spur Trigger, Solid Frame, Single Action, *Antique*	75	150	200

NORTH AMERICAN ARMS, INC.

Provo, Ut.

HANDGUN, REVOLVER

	Fair	V. Good	Excellent
.450 Magnum, Single Action, Western Style, High Polish Finish, 5 Shot, *Modern*	350	800	1250
Mini, .22 L.R.R.F., 5 Shot, Single Action, Spur Trigger, 1" Barrel, Derringer, *Modern*	50	100	175
Mini, .22 L.R.R.F., 5 Shot, Single Action, Spur Trigger, 1½" Barrel, Derringer, *Modern*	50	100	175
Mini, .22 Short, 5 Shot, Single Action, Spur Trigger, 1" Barrel, Derringer, *Modern*	50	75	150
Mini, .22 W.M.R., 5 Shot, Single Action, Spur Trigger, 1" Barrel, Derringer, *Modern*	50	125	200

NORTHWESTERNER

Made by Stevens Arms.

RIFLE, BOLT ACTION

	Fair	V. Good	Excellent
Model 52, .22 L.R.R.F., Single Action, Takedown, *Modern*	15	25	50

SHOTGUN, SINGLESHOT

	Fair	V. Good	Excellent
Model 94, Various Gauges, Takedown, Automatic Ejector, Plain, Hammer, *Modern*	$25	$50	$100

NORTON

See Budischowsky and Americam Arms & Ammunition Co.

NORWEGIAN MILITARY

HANDGUN, SELF-LOADING

	Fair	V. Good	Excellent
Mauser Model 1914, 7.65mm, Blue, Clip Fed, *Curio*	225	275	350
Model 1914, 11.25mm, Military, Clip Fed, *Curio*	325	700	950
Model 1914, 11.25mm, Military, Clip Fed, Nazi-Proofed, *Curio*	600	1250	1650

RIFLE, BOLT ACTION

	Fair	V. Good	Excellent
Model 1894 Krag, 6.5 × 55mm, Military, *Curio*	300	650	950
Model 1925 Krag Sniper, 6.5 × 55mm, Military, *Curio* with scope	350	800	1000

NORWICH PISTOL CO.

Norwich, Conn., 1875–1881. Also made handguns marked with trade names as follows: America, Bull Dozer, Chieftain, Crescent, Crown Jewel, Defiance, Exelsior, Frontier, Hartford Arms Co., Maltby-Curtis, Metropolitan Police, National, Nonpareil, Norwich Pistol Co., Patriot, Penetrator, Pinafore, Prairie King, Protection, Scott Arms Co., Spy, True Blue, U.M.C. Co., Veteran, Winfield Arms Co.

HANDGUN, REVOLVER

	Fair	V. Good	Excellent
.22 Short R.F., 7 Shot, Spur Trigger, Solid Frame, Single Action, *Antique*	100	150	200
.32 Short R.F., 5 Shot, Spur Trigger, Solid Frame, Single Action, *Antique*	75	125	175

NOT-NAC MFG. CO.

Made by Crescent for Belknap Hardware Co., Louisville, Ky. See Crescent Fire Arms Co., Shotgun, Double Barrel, Side-by-Side; Shotgun, Singleshot.

NOVA

La France Specialties, San Diego, Calif.

HANDGUN, SELF-LOADING

	Fair	V. Good	Excellent
Nova, 9mm Luger, Clip Fed, "Electrofilm" Finish, Reduced M1911 Style, *Modern*	200	400	550

NOYS, R.

Wiltshire, England, 1800–1830.

HANDGUN, FLINTLOCK

	Fair	V. Good	Excellent
Pocket Pistol, Screw Barrel, Box Lock, Steel Barrel and Frame, Plain, *Antique*	$250	$550	$950

NUMRICH ARMS CO.

West Hurley, N.Y. Also see Auto Ordnance, Thompson, Hopkins & Allen.

HANDGUN, SELF-LOADING

	Fair	V. Good	Excellent
M1911A1, .45 ACP, Clip Fed, Blue, Military Style, *Modern*	100	200	325
Model ZG-51, .45 ACP, Clip Fed, Finned Barrel, Adjustable Sights, with Compensator, (Numrich), *Modern*	100	225	350

RIFLE, SELF-LOADING

	Fair	V. Good	Excellent
Model 27A1, .45 ACP, Clip Fed, without Compensator, *Modern*	$150	$375	$550
Model 27A1, .45 ACP, Clip Fed, without Compensator, Cased with Accessories, *Modern*	225	550	750
Model 27A1 Deluxe, .45 ACP, Clip Fed, Finned Barrel, Adjustable Sights, with Compensator, *Modern*	200	450	650
Model 27A3, .22 L.R.R.F., Clip Fed, Finned Barrel, Adjustable Sights, with Compensator, *Modern*	150	300	425

NUNNEMACHER, ABRAHAM

York, Pa., 1779–1783. See Kentucky Rifles.

O

	Fair	V. Good	Excellent

OAK LEAF
Made by Stevens Arms.

SHOTGUN, SINGLESHOT

	Fair	V. Good	Excellent
Model 90, Various Gauges, Takedown, Automatic Ejector, Plain, Hammer, *Modern*	$20	$40	$65

OCCIDENTAL
Belgium, c. 1880.

SHOTGUN, DOUBLE BARREL, SIDE-BY-SIDE

	Fair	V. Good	Excellent
Various Gauges, Outside Hammers, Damascus Barrel, *Modern*	100	150	225

OLD TIMER
Made by Stevens Arms.

SHOTGUN, SINGLESHOT

	Fair	V. Good	Excellent
Model 94, Various Gauges, Takedown, Automatic Ejector, Plain, Hammer, *Modern*	20	40	65

OLYMPIC
Made by Stevens Arms.

SHOTGUN, DOUBLE BARREL, SIDE-BY-SIDE

	Fair	V. Good	Excellent
M 315, Various Gauges, Hammerless, Steel Barrel, *Modern*	75	150	200
Model 311, Various Gauges, Hammerless, Steel Barrel, *Modern*	75	150	200

SHOTGUN, SINGLESHOT

	Fair	V. Good	Excellent
Model 94, Various Gauges, Takedown, Automatic Ejector, Plain, Hammer, *Modern*	20	40	60

O.M.
Ojanguren y Marcaido, Eibar, Spain, c. 1920.

HANDGUN, REVOLVER

	Fair	V. Good	Excellent
S & W Type, Various Calibers, Double Action, Swing-Out Cylinder, Blue, *Curio*	35	75	125

OMEGA
Armero Especialistas Reunidas, Eibar, Spain, c. 1925.

HANDGUN, SELF-LOADING

	Fair	V. Good	Excellent
6.35mm, Clip Fed, *Curio*	$50	$100	$175
7.65mm, Clip Fed, Grip Safety, *Curio*	50	125	175

OMEGA
Torrance, Calif. Made by Hi-Shear Corp. 1980s.

RIFLE, BOLT ACTION

	Fair	V. Good	Excellent
Omega III, Various Calibers, No Sights, Fancy Wood, Adjustable Trigger, *Modern*	200	375	500

ORBEA HERMANOS
Orbea Hermanos and Orbea y Cia., Eibar, Spain, c. 1860–1935.

HANDGUN, REVOLVER

	Fair	V. Good	Excellent
S & W Type, .44 Russian, Double Action, Top-Break, *Antique*	35	90	145

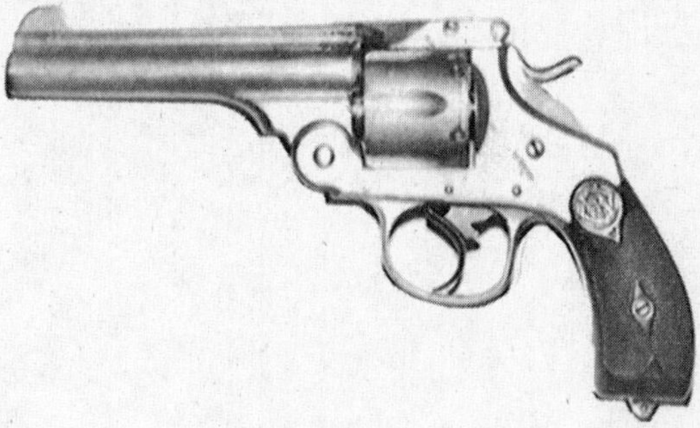

Orbea Hermanos .44

OREA
Orechowsky, Graz, Austria, c. 1930.

RIFLE, SINGLESHOT

	Fair	V. Good	Excellent
Heeren Rifle, Various Calibers, Checkered Stock, Engraved, Fancy Wood, *Modern*	500	1350	1950

ORTGIES

Germany, 1918–1921, taken over in 1921 by Deutsche-Werke, Erfurt, Germany.

HANDGUN, SELF-LOADING

	Fair	V. Good	Excellent
D Pocket, .380 ACP, Clip Fed, *Curio*	$75	$225	$325

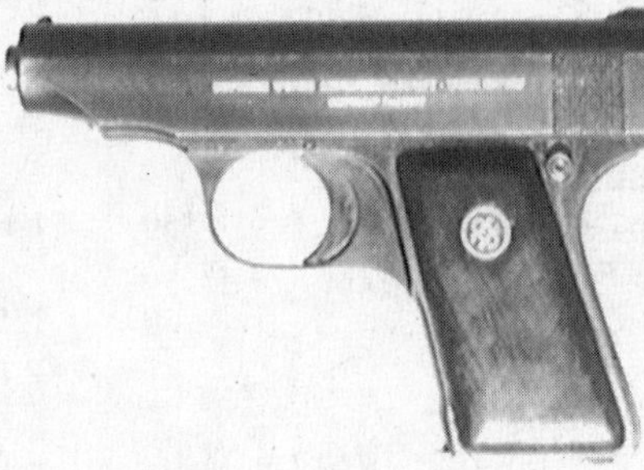

Ortgies D Pocket

	Fair	V. Good	Excellent
D Pocket, 7.65mm, Clip Fed, *Curio*	50	175	300
D Vest Pocket, 6.35mm, Clip Fed, *Curio*	60	175	300
H O Pocket, .380 ACP, Clip Fed, *Curio*	100	200	325
H O Vest Pocket, 6.35mm, Clip Fed, *Curio*	75	175	300

OSGOOD GUN WORKS

Norwich, Conn., c. 1880.

HANDGUN, REVOLVER

	Fair	V. Good	Excellent
Duplex, .22/.32 R.F., 8 Shot .22, Singleshot .32, Two Barrels, Spur Trigger, *Antique*	$300	$650	$950

OUR JAKE

HANDGUN, REVOLVER

	Fair	V. Good	Excellent
.32 R.F., Spur Trigger, Solid Frame, Hammer, *Antique*	50	125	175

OWA

Oesterreichische Werke Anstalt, Vienna, Austria, c. 1920–1925.

HANDGUN, SELF-LOADING

	Fair	V. Good	Excellent
Model 1921 Standard, 6.35mm, Clip Fed, *Curio*	100	200	300

OXFORD ARMS

Made by Stevens Arms.

SHOTGUN, DOUBLE BARREL, SIDE-BY-SIDE

	Fair	V. Good	Excellent
Model 311, Various Gauges, Hammerless, Steel Barrel, *Modern*	75	150	300

OXFORD ARMS CO.

Made by Crescent for Belknap Hdw. Co., Louisville, Ky. See Crescent Fire Arms Co., Shotgun, Double Barrel, Side-by-Side; Shotgun, Singleshot.

P

P.A.F.

Pretoria Arms Factory, Pretoria, South Africa, c. 1955.

HANDGUN, SELF-LOADING

	Fair	V. Good	Excellent
Junior, For Cocking Indicator Add 10%–15%			
Junior, 6.35mm, High Slide, Clip Fed, Blue, *Curio*	$100	$225	$300

P.A.F. Junior

	Fair	V. Good	Excellent
Junior, 6.35mm, Low Slide, Clip Fed, Blue, *Curio*	100	250	350
Junior, 6.35mm, Sight Rib, Clip Fed, Blue, *Curio*	125	275	375

PAGE, T.

Norwich, England, 1766–1776.

HANDGUN, FLINTLOCK

	Fair	V. Good	Excellent
.60, Queen Anne Style, Pocket Pistol, Screw Barrel, Box Lock, Brass Furniture, Engraved, *Antique*	600	1400	1950

PAGE-LEWIS ARMS CO.

See Stevens, J. Arms & Tool Co. for similar listings.

PALMER, THOMAS

Philadelphia, Pa., 1772–1776. See Kentucky Rifles and U.S. Military.

PALMETTO

Made by Stevens Arms.

SHOTGUN, SINGLESHOT

	Fair	V. Good	Excellent
Model 90, Various Gauges, Takedown, Automatic Ejector, Plain, Hammer, *Curio*	$20	$40	$65
Model 94, Various Gauges, Takedown, Automatic Ejector, Plain, Hammer, *Modern*	25	50	85

PANNABECKER, JEFFERSON

Lancaster, Pa., 1790–1810. See Kentucky Rifles.

PANNABECKER, JESSE

Lancaster, Pa., 1833–1860. See Kentucky Rifles.

PANTAX

Tradename used by E. Woerther, Buenos Aires, Argentina.

PANZER

G.M.F. Corp., Watertown, Ct.

HANDGUN, DOUBLE BARREL, OVER-UNDER

	Fair	V. Good	Excellent
Panzer, .22 L.R.R.F., Twist Barrel, Spur Trigger, *Modern*	25	50	75

PARAGON

Made by Stevens Arms.

SHOTGUN, DOUBLE BARREL, SIDE-BY-SIDE

	Fair	V. Good	Excellent
Model 311, Various Gauges, Hammerless, Steel Barrel, *Modern*	75	150	200

PARAGON

Possibly made by Hopkins & Allen, c. 1880.

HANDGUN, REVOLVER

	Fair	V. Good	Excellent
.32 Short R.F., 5 Shot, Spur Trigger, Solid Frame, Single Action, *Antique*	75	150	200

PARAMOUNT

Retolaza Hermanos, Eibar, Spain, c. 1920.

	Fair	V. Good	Excellent
HANDGUN, SELF-LOADING			
7.65mm, Clip Fed, *Curio*	$50	$100	$175
M 1914, 7.65mm, Clip Fed, Long Grip, *Curio*	50	125	200
Vest Pocket, 6.35mm, Clip Fed, *Curio*	50	100	175

PARKER BROTHERS

Imported from Italy by Jana International.

SHOTGUN, DOUBLE BARREL, OVER-UNDER			
California Trap Model, 12 Ga., Single Selective Trigger, Automatic Ejectors, Checkered Stock, Engraved, Double Vent Rib, *Modern*	200	475	650
Field Model, 12 Ga. 3", Single Selective Trigger, Automatic Ejectors, Checkered Stock, Engraved, Vent Rib, *Modern*	150	300	450
Field Model, 12 Ga., Single Selective Trigger, Automatic Ejectors, Checkered Stock, Engraved, Vent Rib, *Modern*	150	275	425
Monte Carlo Stock, 12 Ga., Single Selective Trigger, Automatic Ejectors, Checkered Stock, Engraved, Vent Rib, *Modern*	150	300	450
Skeet Model, 12 Ga., Single Selective Trigger, Automatic Ejectors, Checkered Stock, Engraved, Vent Rib, *Modern*	150	300	450

PARKER BROTHERS

Meriden, Conn., 1868–1934. In 1934 Parker Bros. was taken over by Remington Arms Co. Parkers occupy a key position and status among America's gunmaking legends; over 243,000 shotguns were made by that august firm from the late 1860s to 1942. The founder of the Parker enterprise was Charles (1809–1902), beginning with his patented coffee grinder. The first gun by Parker was a Model 1861 Springfield .58 caliber musket (marked Parker's Snow & Co.), built on private contract during the Civil War (total of 15,000). Still another Civil War product, the Triplett & Scott repeating carbine, was built by Parker with his partners William and George Miller, under the name Meriden Manufacturing Co. (5,000 made). From 1865 to 1867, Meriden Manufacturing also altered an unknown quantity of Model 1861 muskets, from percussion to metallic cartridge breechloaders. With his brothers, Wilbur and Dexter, Charles brought out the first double-barrel Parker shotgun in 1868. The company was known as Parker Brothers, and was established c. 1867–68. The first Parker catalog appeared in 1869, and the firm would remain in continuous operation in Meriden, until January 1934, at which time the new owners became the Remington Arms Co. However, the works were not moved to Ilion, New York, until 1938. The line was discontinued in 1942, when Remington was concentrating on wartime production. The complete line of Parker production is as follows: pre-1899—grades K, L, M, O, Q, and R; some of the following pre-date 1899, some were introduced post 1899—grades U, T, S, R, I, H, G, F, E, D, C, B, A, AA Pigeon Gun, the A1-Special, and the Invincible. Nearly 100,000 Parkers were made before 1900. Hammer models were built as late as 1920, and some appear to have been available even after that late date. The so-called "lifter" action was the first locking system on Parkers; a protrusion on the bottom of the frame was pushed upwards to break open the breech. The lifter system remained in use until about 1900. The top-lever release system was adopted well before, and became the standard after the turn of the century. The Parker marque is of such fame and of such solid design that production was revived in the post–World War II period, by both the Remington Arms Co. and by "Parker Reproductions by Winchester"—the former made in the U.S., the latter made in Japan, beginning in 1983 with the DHE grade Parker. Pre-war Parkers were advertised with such legitimate claims as "The most discriminating gun users in America shoot guns made by Parker Bros." and "Makers of guns that satisfy." Parker Bros. were instrumental in introducing several innovations to American shotgun design: among them a hammerless lock mechanism, an automatic ejector, the first 28-gauge and the first ventilated rib. Parker's single barrel trap gun became a favorite of U.S. trapshooters. The ultimate grades of Parkers were the A-1 Special and the Invincible. Only about 320 A-1 Specials were built, and only a handful of the Invincibles. One of the latter, made for Czar Nicholas II of Russia, was never shipped, due to the 1917 Revolution. Parker Bros. described the Invincible as placing "before the discriminating shooting public of the world, a gun equaled by few and excelled by none."

	Fair	V. Good	Excellent
SHOTGUN, DOUBLE BARREL, SIDE-BY-SIDE			
A-1 Special, 12 Ga., Hammerless, Double Trigger, Automatic Ejector, *Modern*	$20000	$40000	$55000
A-1 Special, 16 Ga., Hammerless, Double Trigger, Automatic Ejector, *Modern*	20000	40000	55000
A-1 Special, 20 Ga., Hammerless, Double Trigger, Automatic Ejector, *Modern*	25000	55000	80000
A-1 Special, 28 Ga., Hammerless, Double Trigger, Automatic Ejector, *Modern*	30000	65000	80000
AAHE, 12 Ga., Hammerless, Double Trigger, Automatic Ejector, *Modern*	15000	32500	40000
AAHE, 16 Ga., Hammerless, Double Trigger, Automatic Ejector, *Modern*	15000	32500	40000
AAHE, 20 Ga., Hammerless, Double Trigger, Automatic Ejector, *Modern*	17000	42500	52500
AAHE, 28 Ga., Hammerless, Double Trigger, Automatic Ejector, *Modern*	20000	52500	65000
AHE, .410 Ga., Hammerless, Double Trigger, Automatic Ejector, *Modern*	30000	57500	75000
AHE, 10 Ga., Hammerless, Double Trigger, Automatic Ejector, *Modern*	9000	22500	35000
AHE, 12 Ga., Hammerless, Double Trigger, Automatic Ejector, *Modern*	7000	17500	25000

	Fair	V. Good	Excellent
AHE, 16 Ga., Hammerless, Double Trigger, Automatic Ejector, *Modern*	$6000	$15000	$22500
AHE, 20 Ga., Hammerless, Double Trigger, Automatic Ejector, *Modern*	9000	25000	32500
AHE, 28 Ga., Hammerless, Double Trigger, Automatic Ejector, *Modern*	12000	35000	42500
Beavertail Forend, for BHE through A-1 Add 20%			
Beavertail Forend, VHE through CHE Add $300.00–$500.00			
BH, .410 Ga., Hammerless, Double Trigger, Automatic Ejector, *Modern*	12000	30000	37500
BH, 10 Ga., Hammerless, Double Trigger, Automatic Ejector, *Modern*	3000	8000	12500
BH, 12 Ga., Hammerless, Double Trigger, Automatic Ejector, *Modern*	2500	6500	8500
BH, 16 Ga., Hammerless, Double Trigger, Automatic Ejector, *Modern*	2000	6000	9000
BH, 20 Ga., Hammerless, Double Trigger, Automatic Ejector, *Modern*	4000	12000	16500
BH, 28 Ga., Hammerless, Double Trigger, Automatic Ejector, *Modern*	8000	20000	27500
CH, .410 Ga., Hammerless, Double Trigger, Automatic Ejector, *Modern*	10000	20000	27500
CH, 10 Ga., Hammerless, Double Trigger, Automatic Ejector, *Modern*	2000	6500	8500
CH, 12 Ga., Hammerless, Double Trigger, Automatic Ejector, *Modern*	1750	4750	7000
CH, 16 Ga., Hammerless, Double Trigger, Automatic Ejector, *Modern*	1750	4750	7000
CH, 20 Ga., Hammerless, Double Trigger, Automatic Ejector, *Modern*	4000	11000	15000
CH, 28 Ga., Hammerless, Double Trigger, Automatic Ejector, *Modern*	4500	13500	17500
DH, .410 Ga., Hammerless, Double Trigger, Automatic Ejector, *Modern*	9000	26500	32500
DH, 10 Ga., Hammerless, Double Trigger, Automatic Ejector, *Modern*	1500	5000	7500
DH, 12 Ga., Hammerless, Double Trigger, Automatic Ejector, *Modern*	1000	3500	5500
DH, 16 Ga., Hammerless, Double Trigger, Automatic Ejector, *Modern*	1000	3500	5250
DH, 20 Ga., Hammerless, Double Trigger, Automatic Ejector, *Modern*	$2200	$5000	$7500
DH, 28 Ga., Hammerless, Double Trigger, Automatic Ejector, *Modern*	3000	7500	12500
Early Model, Various Gauges, Outside Hammers, Damascus Barrel, Under-Lever, *Antique*	700	1750	3500
Extra Barrel, Add 30%-40%			
For Damascus Barrel, Deduct 60%-75%			
For Ejectors, Add 50% (E)			
For Upgrades, Deduct 40%-60%			
GH, .410 Ga., Hammerless, Double Trigger, Automatic Ejector, *Modern*	5000	15000	22500
GH, 10 Ga. 3½", Hammerless, Double Trigger, *Modern*	1500	3500	5000
GH, 10 Ga. 3½", Hammerless, Double Trigger, Automatic Ejector, *Modern*	2000	4000	5750
GH, 12 Ga., Hammerless, Double Trigger, *Modern*	800	1750	3250
GH, 12 Ga., Hammerless, Double Trigger, Automatic Ejector, *Modern*	1000	2500	3500
GH, 16 Ga., Hammerless, Double Trigger, *Modern*	800	1750	3000
GH, 16 Ga., Hammerless, Double Trigger, Automatic Ejector, *Modern*	1000	2500	3250
GH, 20 Ga., Hammerless, Double Trigger, *Modern*	1000	3000	4250
GH, 20 Ga., Hammerless, Double Trigger, Automatic Ejector, *Modern*	1200	3500	4750
GH, 28 Ga., Hammerless, Double Trigger, *Modern*	1200	4000	6500
GH, 28 Ga., Hammerless, Double Trigger, Automatic Ejector, *Modern*	1500	6000	9500
Invincible, 12 Ga., Hammerless, Double Trigger, Automatic Ejector, *Modern*	30000	100000	135000
Invincible, 16 Ga., Hammerless, Double Trigger, Automatic Ejector, *Modern*	30000	100000	135000
Outside Hammers with Steel Barrels, Deduct 20%-30%			
Single Selective Trigger, Add 20%			
Skeet Grade, Add 15%-25%			
Trap Grade, Add 10%-15%			
Trojan, 12 and 16 Gauges, Hammerless, Double Trigger, *Modern*	600	1200	1650
Trojan, 20 Ga., Hammerless, Double Trigger, *Modern*	800	1500	2500
Vent Rib, 20%-50%			

	Fair	V. Good	Excellent
VH, .410 Ga., Hammerless, Double Trigger, Automatic Ejector, *Modern*	$4000	$8000	$12000
VH, 12 Ga., Hammerless, Double Trigger, Automatic Ejector, *Modern*	700	1800	2500
VH, 16 Ga., Hammerless, Double Trigger, Automatic Ejector, *Modern*	700	1800	2500
VH, 20 Ga., Hammerless, Double Trigger, Automatic Ejector, *Modern*	1000	2000	2850
VH, 28 Ga., Hammerless, Double Trigger, Automatic Ejector, *Modern*	2700	6000	7500

SHOTGUN, SINGLE BARREL TRAP

	Fair	V. Good	Excellent
S.A., 12 Ga., Hammerless, Vent Rib, Automatic Ejector, *Modern*	1200	4000	5250
S.A.-1 Special, 12 Ga., Hammerless, Vent Rib, Automatic Ejector, *Modern*	6000	17000	22500
S.A.A., 12 Ga., Hammerless, Vent Rib, Automatic Ejector, *Modern*	4000	15000	20000
S.B., 12 Ga., Hammerless, Vent Rib, Automatic Ejector, *Modern*	2000	6000	9500
S.C., 12 Ga., Hammerless, Vent Rib, Automatic Ejector, *Modern*	1000	2000	3500

PARKER SAFETY HAMMERLESS

Made by Columbia Armory, Tenn., c. 1890.

HANDGUN, REVOLVER

	Fair	V. Good	Excellent
.32 S & W, 5 Shot, Top Break, Hammerless, Double Action, *Curio*	50	75	100

PARKER, WILLIAM

London, England, 1790–1840.

SHOTGUN, PERCUSSION

	Fair	V. Good	Excellent
14 Ga., Single Barrel, Smoothbore, High Quality, Cased with Accessories, *Antique*	600	1250	1600

SHOTGUN, FLINTLOCK

	Fair	V. Good	Excellent
16 Ga., Double Barrel, Side by Side, Engraved, High Quality, *Antique*	1700	3500	4500

PARKER-HALE LTD.

Birmingham, England. Purchased by Navy Arms in 1991.

HANDGUN, REVOLVER

	Fair	V. Good	Excellent
S & W Victory, .22 L.R.R.F., Conversion, Adjustable Sights, *Modern*	125	225	300

RIFLE, BOLT ACTION

	Fair	V. Good	Excellent
Model 1200, Various Calibers, Checkered Stock, Open Rear Sight, Monte Carlo Stock, *Modern*	$250	$500	$750
Model 1200M, Various Calibers, Magnum, Checkered Stock, Open Rear Sight, Monte Carlo Stock, *Modern*	250	550	750
Model 1200V, Various Calibers, Heavy Barrel, Checkered Stock, No Sights, Monte Carlo Stock, *Modern*	225	475	700

RIFLE, PERCUSSION

	Fair	V. Good	Excellent
.451, Whitworth Military Target Rifle, 3 Bands, Target Sights, Checkered Stock, Reproduction,	150	325	450
.54 Gallagher, Breech Loader, Carbine, Brass Furniture, Reproduction,	75	150	225
.58 M1853 Enfield Rifle, Rifled, Brass Funiture, Reproduction,	100	175	250
.58 M1853 Enfield, Musket, Rifled, 2 Bands, Brass Furniture, Reproduction,	100	175	250
.58 M1861 Enfield, Musketoon, Rifled, 2 Bands, Brass Furniture, Reproduction,	100	150	250

SHOTGUN, SELF-LOADING

	Fair	V. Good	Excellent
Model 640A, 12 Ga., Checkered Stock, Vent Rib, *Modern*	200	475	650
Model 640M, 10 Ga. 3", Checkered Stock, Vent Rib, *Modern*	300	600	800

PARKHILL, ANDREW

Phila., Pa., 1778–1785. See Kentucky Rifles and Pistols.

PAROLE

Made by Hopkins & Allen, c. 1880.

HANDGUN, REVOLVER

	Fair	V. Good	Excellent
.22 Short R.F., 7 Shot, Spur Trigger, Solid Frame, Single Action, *Antique*	75	150	200

PARR, J.

Liverpool, England, c. 1810.

RIFLE, FLINTLOCK

	Fair	V. Good	Excellent
.75, 3rd Model Brown Bess, Musket, Military, *Antique*	700	1400	1850

PARSONS, HIRAM

Baltimore, Md., c. 1819. See Kentucky Rifles.

PATRIOT
Made by Norwich Falls Pistol Co., c. 1880.

HANDGUN, REVOLVER

	Fair	V. Good	Excellent
.32 Short R.F., 5 Shot, Spur Trigger, Solid Frame, Single Action, *Antique*	$75	$150	$200

PECK, ABIJAH
Hartford, Conn. See U.S. Military.

PEERLESS
Made by Crescent H. & D. Folsom, c. 1900. See Crescent Fire Arms Co., Shotgun, Double Barrel, Side-by-Side; Shotgun, Singleshot.

PEERLESS
Made by Stevens.

RIFLE, BOLT ACTION

	Fair	V. Good	Excellent
Model 056 Buckhorn, .22 L.R.R.F., 5 Shot Clip, Peep Sights, *Modern*	25	50	75
Model 066 Buckhorn, .22 L.R.R.F., Tube Feed, Peep Sights, *Modern*	25	50	75
Model 53, .22 L.R.R.F., Singleshot, Takedown, *Modern*	20	40	50

PENCE, JACOB
Lancaster, Pa., 1771. See Kentucky Rifles and Pistols.

PENETRATOR
Made by Norwich Falls Pistol Co., c. 1880.

HANDGUN, REVOLVER

	Fair	V. Good	Excellent
.32 Short R.F., 5 Shot, Spur Trigger, Solid Frame, Single Action, *Modern*	75	125	200

PENNYPACKER, DANIEL
Berks County, Pa., 1773–1808. See Kentucky Rifles and Pistols.

PENNYPACKER, WM.
Berks County, Pa., 1808–1858. See Kentucky Rifles and Pistols.

PERCUSSION EXAMPLES

HANDGUN, PERCUSSION

	Fair	V. Good	Excellent
.40 English, 6 Shot, Pepperbox, Pocket Pistol, Light Engraving, German Silver Frame, Steel Barrel, *Antique*	150	400	650
.45, Pair French, Target Pistol, Octagon Barrel, Single Set Trigger, Brass Furniture, Cased with Accessories, *Antique*	$1100	$2500	$3250
.70, French Sotiau, Belt Pistol, Steel Furniture, Rifled, Octagon Barrel, *Antique*	200	450	700
Boot Pistol, Bar Hammer, Screw Barrel, *Antique*	100	200	300
Boot Pistol, Boxlock, Screw Barrel, *Antique*	100	250	325
Boot Pistol, Sidelock, Derringer Style, *Antique*	100	200	300
Pair, Dueling Pistols, Octagon Barrel, Single Set Trigger, German Silver Furniture, Medium Quality, Cased with Accessories, *Antique*	900	2000	2750

HANDGUN, REVOLVER

	Fair	V. Good	Excellent
.36, Navy Colt Type, Belgian Make, Medium Quality, *Antique*	100	200	300
.45, Adams Type, Double Action, Octagon Barrel, Plain, Cased with Accessories, *Antique*	400	850	1150

RIFLE, PERCUSSION

	Fair	V. Good	Excellent
American Indian Trade Gun, Belgian, Converted from Flintlock, Brass Furniture, *Antique*	1100	2500	3750
Benchrest, Various Calibers, Heavy Barrel, Set Triggers, Target Sights, Light Decoration, *Antique*	350	700	1000

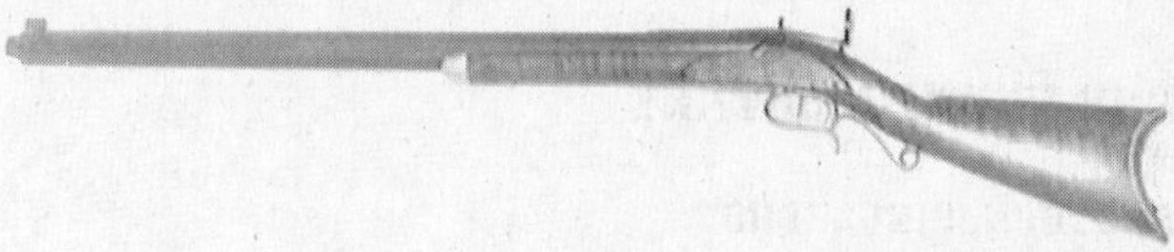

Percussion Arms, Unknown Maker Benchrest Rifle

	Fair	V. Good	Excellent
Benchrest, Various Calibers, Heavy Barrel, Set Triggers, Target Sights, Medium Decoration, *Antique*	350	800	1150
German, Schutzen Rifle, Rifled, Ivory Inlays, Gold Inlays, Ornate, *Antique*	2200	5000	7000

SHOTGUN, PERCUSSION

	Fair	V. Good	Excellent
English, 12 Ga., Double Barrel, Side by Side, Light Ornamentation, Medium Quality, *Antique*	150	400	650
English, 12 Ga., Double Barrel, Side by Side, Light Ornamentation, High Quality, Cased with Accessories, *Antique*	400	1000	1350

Fair V. Good Excellent

PERFECT
Made by Foehl & Weeks. Phila., Pa., c. 1890.

HANDGUN, REVOLVER
.38 S & W, 5 Shot, Double Action, Top Break, *Modern* $50 $75 $125

PERFECTION
Made by Crescent for H. & G. Lipscomb & Co., Nashville, Tenn. See Crescent Fire Arms Co., Shotgun, Double Barrel, Side-by-Side; Shotgun, Singleshot.

PERFECTION AUTOMATIC REVOLVER
Made by Forehand Arms Co.

HANDGUN, REVOLVER
.32 S & W, 5 Shot, Double Action, Top Break, *Antique* 50 75 125
.32 S & W, 5 Shot, Double Action, Top Break, Hammerless, *Antique* .. 50 100 150

PERLA
Frantisek Dusek, Opocno, Czechoslovakia, c. 1935.

HANDGUN, SELF-LOADING
.25 ACP, Clip Fed, Blue, *Modern* 100 175 250

PETTIBONE, DANIEL
Philadelphia, Pa., 1799–1814. See Kentucky Rifles and Pistols.

PHILIPPINE MILITARY

SHOTGUN, SINGLESHOT
WW2 Guerrilla Weapon, 12 Ga., *Modern* 50 125 200

PHOENIX
Spain, Tomas de Urizar y Cia., c. 1920.

HANDGUN, SELF-LOADING
Vest Pocket, 6.35mm, Clip Fed, *Curio* 50 125 200

PHOENIX ARMS CO.
Lowell Arms Co., Lowell, Mass., c. 1920.

HANDGUN, SELF-LOADING
Vest Pocket, .25 ACP, Clip Fed, *Curio* 200 425 550

PIC
Made in West Germany for Precise Imports Corp., Suffern, N.Y.

Phoenix Arms Co. .25

Fair V. Good Excellent

HANDGUN, REVOLVER
.22 L.R.R.F., Double Action, Blue, *Modern* $15 $50 $75

PIC .25

HANDGUN, SELF-LOADING
Vest Pocket, .22 Short R.F., Clip Fed, *Modern* 25 50 75
Vest Pocket, .25 ACP., Clip Fed, *Modern* 25 50 75

PICKFATT, HUMPHREY
London, England, 1714–1730.

HANDGUN, FLINTLOCK
Pair, Holster Pistol, Engraved, Brass Furniture, High Quality, *Antique* 3500 8000 12500
Pair, Queen Anne Style, Box Lock, Pocket Pistol, Silver Furniture, *Antique* 1100 2500 4000

PIEDMONT
Made by Crescent for Piedmont Hdw. Danville, Pa. See Crescent Fire Arms Co., Shotgun, Double Barrel, Side-by-Side; Shotgun, Singleshot.

PIEPER
Henry Pieper, Harstal, Belgium, 1859. Became Nicolas Pieper in 1898, and in 1905 became Anciens Etablissments Pieper.

	Fair	V. Good	Excellent
COMBINATION WEAPON, SIDE-BY-SIDE			
Various Calibers, Hammer, Open Rear Sight, Checkered Stock, Plain, *Curio*	$200	$375	$500
HANDGUN, SELF-LOADING			
Bayard Model 1908 Pocket, .380 ACP, Blue, Clip Fed, *Curio*	75	150	200
Bayard Model 1908 Pocket, 6.35mm, Blue, Clip Fed, *Curio*	50	125	175
Bayard Model 1923 Pocket, 6.35mm, Blue, Clip Fed, *Curio*	75	150	200
Bayard Model 1923 Pocket, 7.65mm, Blue, Clip Fed, *Curio*	100	200	250
Bayard Model 1930 Pocket, 6.35mm, Blue, Clip Fed, *Curio*	100	200	250
Model A (Army), 7.65mm, Clip Fed, 7 Shot, *Curio*	75	150	200
Model B, 7.65mm, Clip Fed, 6 Shot, *Curio*	75	125	175
Model C, 6.35mm, Clip Fed, *Curio*	75	125	175
Model C, 6.35mm, Clip Fed, Long Grip, *Curio*	75	150	200
Model D (1920), 6.35mm, Clip Fed, Tip-Up, *Curio*	75	150	200

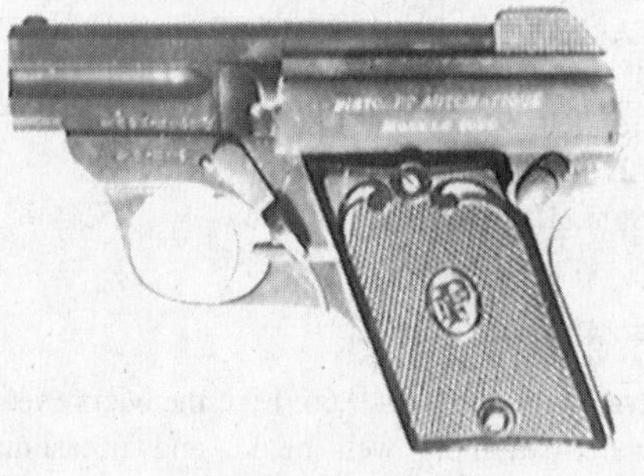

Pieper Model D

Model Legia, 6.35mm, Clip Fed, *Curio*	75	125	175
Model Legia, 6.35mm, Clip Fed, Long Grip, *Curio*	75	150	200
Model N, 7.65mm, Clip Fed, Tip-Up, 7 Shot, *Curio*	75	125	175
Model O, 7.65mm, Clip Fed, Tip-Up, 6 Shot, *Curio*	75	125	175
Model P, 6.35mm, Clip Fed, Tip-Up, *Curio*	75	150	200
RIFLE, BOLT ACTION			
Singleshot, .22 L.R.R.F., Plain, *Curio*	25	50	75
RIFLE, SELF-LOADING			
Pieper Carbine, .22 L.R.R.F., Checkered Stock, English Grip, *Curio*	50	100	150

	Fair	V. Good	Excellent
Pieper Musket, .22 L.R.R.F., Military Style Stock, *Curio*	$50	$100	$150
Pieper Musket, .22 L.R.R.F., Military Style Stock, with Bayonet, *Curio*	75	125	175
Pieper/Bayard Carbine, .22 Long, Checkered Stock, Pistol Grip, *Curio*	50	100	150
Pieper/Bayard Carbine, .22 Short, Checkered Stock, Pistol Grip, *Curio*	50	75	125
SHOTGUN, DOUBLE BARREL, SIDE-BY-SIDE			
Bayard, Various Gauges, Hammerless, Boxlock, Light Engraving, Checkered Stock, *Modern*	100	175	225
Hammer Gun, Various Gauges, Light Engraving, Steel Barrels, *Modern*	75	150	225
Hammer Gun, Various Gauges, Plain, Damascus Barrels, *Modern*	75	125	175
Hammer Gun, Various Gauges, Plain, Steel Barrels, *Modern*	75	150	200

PIEPER, ABRAHAM

Lancaster, Pa., 1801–1803. See Kentucky Rifles and Pistols.

PIEPER, HENRY

Also see Pieper.

COMBINATION WEAPON, SIDE-BY-SIDE			
Various Calibers, Double Trigger, Outside Hammers, Side Lever, *Antique*	150	375	475

PINAFORE

Made by Norwich Falls Pistol Co., c. 1880.

HANDGUN, REVOLVER			
.22 Short R.F., 7 Shot, Spur Trigger, Solid Frame, Single Action, *Antique*	75	125	200

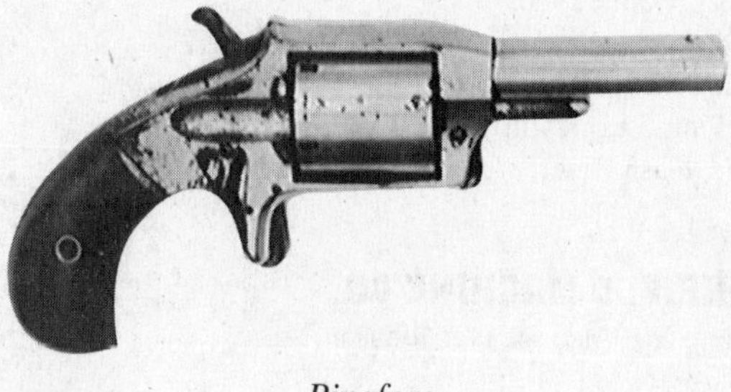

Pinafore

PINKERTON

Gaspar Arizaga, Eibar, Spain, c. 1930.

	Fair	V. Good	Excellent
HANDGUN, SELF-LOADING			
Browning Type, 6.35mm, Clip Fed, Blue, *Curio*	$75	$125	$200
Mondial Type, 6.35mm, Clip Fed, Blue, *Curio*	100	175	225

PIONEER
c. 1880.

	Fair	V. Good	Excellent
HANDGUN, REVOLVER			
.38 Short R.F., 5 Shot, Spur Trigger, Solid Frame, Single Action, *Antique*	75	150	200

PIONEER
Made by Stevens Arms.

	Fair	V. Good	Excellent
RIFLE, SELF-LOADING			
Model 87, .22 L.R.R.F., Tube Feed, Open Rear Sight, *Modern*	25	50	75

PIONEER ARMS CO.
Made by Crescent for Kruse Hardware Co. Cincinatti, Ohio. See Crescent Fire Arms Co., Shotgun, Double Barrel, Side-by-Side; Shotgun, Singleshot.

PIOTTI
Gardone, Val Trompia, Brescia, Italy. Currently imported by Ventura Imports.

	Fair	V. Good	Excellent
SHOTGUN, DOUBLE BARREL, SIDE-BY-SIDE			
Monte Carlo, 12 and 20 Gauges, Sidelock, Automatic Ejector, Single Selective Trigger, Fancy Checkering, Fancy Engraving, *Modern*	3500	7500	10000
Westlake, 12 and 20 Gauges, Sidelock, Automatic Ejector, Double Trigger, Fancy Checkering, Fancy Engraving, *Modern*	2700	6000	9000

PJK
Bradbury, Calif., 1960s.

	Fair	V. Good	Excellent
RIFLE, SELF-LOADING			
M-68, 9mm Luger, Clip Fed, Carbine, Flash Hider, *Modern*	75	150	225

PLAINFIELD MACHINE CO.
Dunellen, N.J. Also see Iver Johnson.

	Fair	V. Good	Excellent
HANDGUN, SELF-LOADING			
Super Enforcer, .30 Carbine, Clip Fed, *Modern*	100	175	250
RIFLE, SELF-LOADING			
M-1, .30 Carbine, Carbine, *Modern*	75	150	225
M-1, .30 Carbine, Carbine, Sporting Rifle, *Modern*	$75	$150	$225
M-1, 5.7mm Carbine, Carbine, *Modern*	75	125	200
M-1 Deluxe, .30 Carbine, Carbine, Sporting Rifle, Monte Carlo Stock, Checkered Stock, *Modern*	100	200	275
M-1 Paratrooper, .30 Carbine, Carbine, Folding Stock, *Modern*	100	200	275
M-1 Presentation, .30 Carbine, Carbine, Sporting Rifle, Monte Carlo Stock, Fancy Wood, *Modern*	100	200	275

PLAINFIELD ORDNANCE CO.
Middlesex, N.J.

	Fair	V. Good	Excellent
HANDGUN, SELF-LOADING			
Model 71, .22 L.R.R.F. and 25 ACP, Clip Fed, Stainless Steel, with Conversion Kit, *Modern*	100	175	250
Model 71, .22 L.R.R.F., Clip Fed, Stainless Steel, *Modern*	75	125	200
Model 71, 25 ACP, Clip Fed, Stainless Steel, *Modern*	50	100	175
Model 72, .25 ACP, Clip Fed, Lightweight, *Modern*	75	125	200
Model 72, .22 L.R.R.F. and 25 ACP, Clip Fed, Lightweight with Conversion Kit, *Modern*	100	175	250
Model 72, .22 L.R.R.F., Clip Fed, Lightweight, *Modern*	75	150	225

PLANT'S MFG. CO.
New Haven, Conn., 1860–1866. Like the Moore teat-fire revolvers, Plants were extremely well made, and occasionally are found engraved and/or inscribed and sometimes handsomely cased. Engraved examples, which demand a premium, have been observed, decorated exactly in the same style as much of the Henry Rifle engraving—undoubtedly by the same hand.

	Fair	V. Good	Excellent
HANDGUN, REVOLVER			
Army, .42 Cup Primed Cartridge, 6 Shot, Single Action, Spur Trigger, 1st Model, *Antique*	600	1250	1750
Army, .42 Cup Primed Cartridge, 6 Shot, Single Action, Spur Trigger, 2nd Model, *Antique*	450	1000	1500

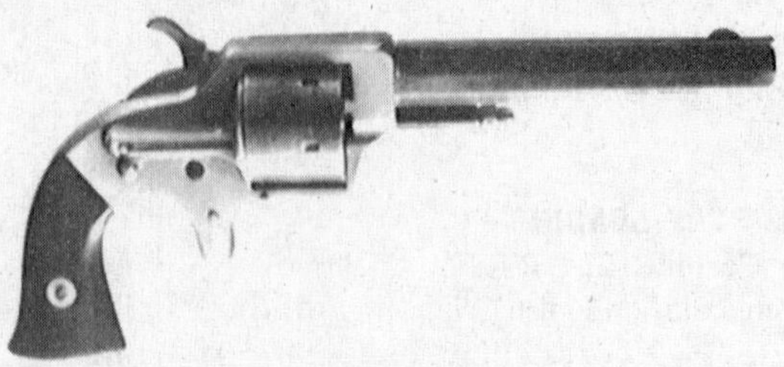

Plant's .42 C.P.

	Fair	V. Good	Excellent
Army, .42 Cup Primed Cartridge, 6 Shot, Single Action, Spur Trigger, 3rd Model, *Antique*	$500	$1200	$1650
Pocket, .30 Cup Primed Cartridge, 5 Shot, Single Action, Spur Trigger, Solid Frame, *Antique*	200	400	650

PLUS ULTRA

Gabilondo y Cia., Eibar, Spain, c. 1930.

HANDGUN, SELF-LOADING

	Fair	V. Good	Excellent
7.65mm, Extra Long Grip, Military, *Curio*	200	425	600

POND, LUCIUS W.

Worcester, Mass., c. 1863–72.

HANDGUN, REVOLVER

	Fair	V. Good	Excellent
Front Loader, .22, 7 Shot, 3½" barrel, *Antique*	250	500	700

Lucius W. Pond Seven Shot Cartridge Revolver, .22 Caliber

	Fair	V. Good	Excellent
Front Loader, .32, 7 Shot, 3½" barrel, *Antique*	200	475	600

PORTER, PATRICK W.

New York City, c. 1851–54.

HANDGUN, PERCUSSION

	Fair	V. Good	Excellent
Patent Turret Pistol, .41, 9 Shot, *Antique*	5000	10000	13500

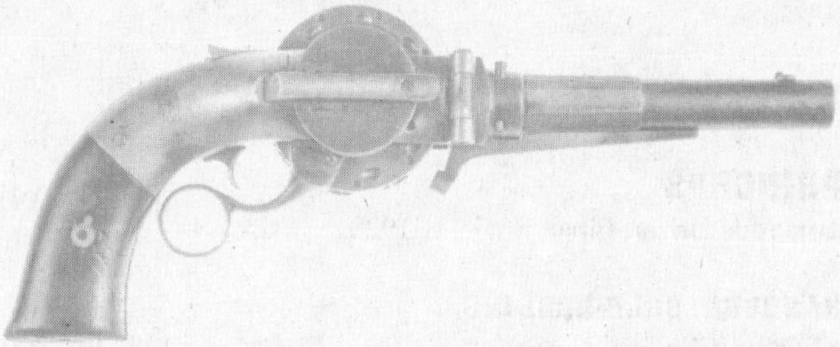

Patrick W. Porter Turret Pistol, .41 Caliber

	Fair	V. Good	Excellent
P.W. Porter Turret Rifle, 44 cal.	1000	2750	4250

PORTUGUESE MILITARY

RIFLE, BOLT ACTION

	Fair	V. Good	Excellent
Kropatchek M1886, 8mm, Tube Feed, *Antique*	$100	$200	$300
Mauser-Vergueiro, 6.5mm, Rifle, *Curio*	150	250	325

POUS, EUDAL

Spain, c. 1790.

HANDGUN, MIQUELET-LOCK

	Fair	V. Good	Excellent
Pair, Holster Pistol, Low Quality, Light Brass Furniture, *Antique*	1200	2750	3500

PRAGA

Zbrojovka Praga, Prague, Czechoslovakia, 1918–1926.

HANDGUN, SELF-LOADING

	Fair	V. Good	Excellent
Model 1921, 6.35mm, Clip Fed, Folding Trigger, *Curio*	100	200	250
Vz 21, 7.65mm, Clip Fed, *Curio*	150	275	350

Praga Praha

PRAIRIE KING

Made by Norwich Falls Pistol Co., c. 1880.

HANDGUN, REVOLVER

	Fair	V. Good	Excellent
.22 Short R.F., 7 Shot, Spur Trigger, Solid Frame, Single Action, *Antique*	75	125	175

PREMIER

Brooklyn, N.Y.

SHOTGUN, DOUBLE BARREL, SIDE-BY-SIDE

	Fair	V. Good	Excellent
Ambassador, Various Calibers, Checkered Stock, Hammerless, Double Trigger, *Modern*	150	325	400
Brush King, 12 and 20 Gauges, Checkered Stock, Hammerless, Double Trigger, *Modern*	125	225	300

	Fair	V. Good	Excellent
Continental, Various Calibers, Checkered Stock, Outside Hammers, Double Trigger, *Modern*	$100	$200	$275
Monarch, Various Calibers, Hammerless, Double Trigger, Checkered Stock, Engraved, Adjustable Choke, *Modern*	150	375	500
Presentation, Various Calibers, Adjustable Choke, Double Trigger, Fancy Engraving, Fancy Checkering, Extra Shotgun Barrel, *Modern*	400	850	1250
Regent Magnum, 10 Ga. 3½", Checkered Stock, Hammerless, Double Trigger, *Modern*	150	275	400
Regent, Various Calibers, Checkered Stock, Hammerless, Double Trigger, *Modern*	125	225	375
Regent, Various Calibers, Checkered Stock, Hammerless, Double Trigger, Extra Shotgun Barrel, *Modern*	150	300	450

PREMIER

Made by Stevens Arms.

RIFLE, BOLT ACTION

	Fair	V. Good	Excellent
Model 52, .22 L.R.R.F., Singleshot, Takedown, *Modern*	20	40	50
Model 53, .22 L.R.R.F., Singleshot, Takedown, *Modern*	25	50	75
Model 66 Buckhorn, .22 L.R.R.F., Tube Feed, Open Rear Sight, *Modern*	25	50	75

RIFLE, SLIDE ACTION

	Fair	V. Good	Excellent
Model 75, .22 L.R.R.F., Tube Feed, Hammerless, *Modern*	75	150	200

PREMIER

Made by Thomas E. Ryan, Norwich, Conn., c. 1870–1876.

HANDGUN, REVOLVER

	Fair	V. Good	Excellent
.22 Short R.F., 7 Shot, Spur Trigger, Solid Frame, Single Action, *Antique*	75	125	200
.32 Long R.F., 6 Shot, Spur Trigger, Solid Frame, Single Action, *Antique*	75	125	200

PREMIER

Tomas de Urizar y Cia, Eibar, Spain, c. 1920.

HANDGUN, SELF-LOADING

	Fair	V. Good	Excellent
6.35mm, Clip Fed, Blue, *Modern*	75	100	200

PREMIER TRAIL BLAZER

Made by Stevens Arms.

RIFLE, SLIDE ACTION

	Fair	V. Good	Excellent
Model 75, .22 L.R.R.F., Tube Feed, Hammerless, *Modern*	$75	$125	$200

PRESCOTT, E. A.

Worcester, Mass., 1860–1874.

	Fair	V. Good	Excellent
Brass Frame	100	250	350

HANDGUN, REVOLVER

	Fair	V. Good	Excellent
"Navy" .38 Short R.F., 6 Shot, Iron Frame, Single Action, Solid Frame, Finger-Rest Triggerguard, *Antique*	300	650	900
Belt .32 Short R.F., Brass Frame *Antique*	250	500	750
Pocket .22 Short R.F., 7 Shot, Brass Frame, Spur Trigger, Solid Frame, Single Action, *Antique*	200	450	750
Pocket .31 Percussion, 6 Shot, Brass Frame, Spur Trigger, Solid Frame, Single Action, *Antique*	300	600	850

PRICE, J. W.

Made by Stevens Arms.

SHOTGUN, SINGLESHOT

	Fair	V. Good	Excellent
Model 90, Various Gauges, Takedown, Automatic Ejector, Plain, Hammer, *Modern*	25	50	75

PRIMA

Mre. d'Armes des Pyrenees, Hendaye, France.

HANDGUN, SELF-LOADING

	Fair	V. Good	Excellent
6.35mm, Clip Fed, *Curio*	75	125	200

Prima

PRINCEPS

Tomas de Urizar, Eibar, Spain, c. 1920.

HANDGUN, SELF-LOADING

	Fair	V. Good	Excellent
6.35mm, Clip Fed, *Curio*	50	125	200

PRINCESS

c. 1880.

Princeps

	Fair	V. Good	Excellent
HANDGUN, REVOLVER			
.22 Short R.F., 7 Shot, Spur Trigger, Solid Frame, Single Action, *Antique*	$75	$150	$200

PROTECTION

Made by Norwich Falls Pistol Co., c. 1860.

	Fair	V. Good	Excellent
HANDGUN, REVOLVER			
Pocket .28 Percussion, 6 Shot, Spur Trigger, Solid Frame, Single Action, *Antique*	250	500	700

PROTECTOR ARMS CO.

Spain, c. 1900.

	Fair	V. Good	Excellent
HANDGUN, SELF-LOADING			
M 1918, 6.35mm, Clip Fed, *Curio*	75	125	175

PURDEY, JAMES

	Fair	V. Good	Excellent
RIFLE, PERCUSSION			
.52, Double Barrel, Side by Side, Damascus Barrel, Engraved, Fancy Wood, Gold Inlays	2750	6500	8500
RIFLE, DOUBLE BARREL, SIDE-BY-SIDE			
.500 #2 Express, Damascus Barrel, Outside Hammers, Under-Lever, Engraved, Ornate, *Antique*	1800	4000	6500

PURDEY, JAS. & SONS

London, England, 1814 to Date. Established showrooms on Madison Avenue, New York City, 1999.

	Fair	V. Good	Excellent
RIFLE, BOLT ACTION			
Sporting Rifle, Various Calibers, Fancy Wood, Checkered Stock, Express Sights, *Modern*	2200	6500	12500
RIFLE, DOUBLE BARREL, SIDE-BY-SIDE			
Various Calibers, Sidelock, Fancy Engraving, Fancy Checkering, Fancy Wood, *Modern*	17500	55000	85000
SHOTGUN, DOUBLE BARREL, OVER-UNDER			
12 Ga., Vent Rib, Single Selective Trigger, Pistol-Grip Stock, *Modern*	$12500	$37500	$65000
Purdey, Various Gauges, Sidelock, Automatic Ejector, Double Trigger, Fancy Engraving, Fancy Checkering, *Modern*	10000	37500	65000
Purdey, Various Gauges, Sidelock, Automatic Ejector, Single Trigger, Fancy Engraving, Fancy Checkering, *Modern*	10000	37500	65000
Various Gauges, Extra Barrels Only $3,000.00-$7,000.00			
Woodward, Various Gauges, Sidelock, Automatic Ejector, Double Trigger, Fancy Engraving, Fancy Checkering, *Modern*	10000	37500	65000
Woodward, Various Gauges, Sidelock, Automatic Ejector, Single Trigger, Fancy Engraving, Fancy Checkering, *Modern*	10000	37500	65000
Add 20% for 28 ga.			
Add 40% for 410 ga.			
SHOTGUN, DOUBLE BARREL, SIDE-BY-SIDE			
12 Ga., Extra Barrel, Vent Rib, Single Selective Trigger, Engraved, Cased with Accessories, *Modern*	10000	27500	45000
12 Ga., Extra Barrels, Pistol-Grip Stock, Cased with Accessories, *Modern*	10000	27500	45000
Featherweight, Various Gauges, Sidelock, Automatic Ejector, Double Trigger, Fancy Engraving, Fancy Checkering, *Modern*	10000	27500	45000
Featherweight, Various Gauges, Sidelock, Automatic Ejector, Single Trigger, Fancy Engraving, Fancy Checkering, *Modern*	10000	27500	45000
Game Gun, Various Gauges, Sidelock, Automatic Ejector, Double Trigger, Fancy Engraving, Fancy Checkering, *Modern*	10000	27500	45000
Game Gun, Various Gauges, Sidelock, Automatic Ejector, Single Trigger, Fancy Engraving, Fancy Checkering, *Modern*	10000	27500	45000
Pigeon Gun, 12 Ga., Single Selective Trigger, Vent Rib, Cased Straight Grip, *Modern*	10000	27500	45000
Pigeon Gun, Various Gauges, Sidelock, Automatic Ejector, Double Trigger, Fancy Engraving, Fancy Checkering, *Modern*	10000	22500	45000
Pigeon Gun, Various Gauges, Sidelock, Automatic Ejector, Single Trigger, Fancy Engraving, Fancy Checkering, *Modern*	10000	27500	45000

	Fair	V. Good	Excellent
Two-Inch, 12 Ga. 2", Sidelock, Automatic Ejector, Double Trigger, Fancy Engraving, Fancy Checkering, *Modern*	$7000	$15000	$27500
Two-Inch, 12 Ga. 2", Sidelock, Automatic Ejector, Single Trigger, Fancy Engraving, Fancy Checkering, *Modern*	9000	18000	27500

Various Gauges, Extra Barrels Only $2,600.00–$4,750.00
Add 20% for 28 ga.
Add 40% for 410 ga.

SHOTGUN, SINGLESHOT

	Fair	V. Good	Excellent
12 Ga., Vent Rig, Plain, Trap Grade, *Modern*	$5000	$13500	$16500

PZK

Kohout & Spolecnost, Kydne, Czechoslovakia.

HANDGUN, SELF-LOADING

	Fair	V. Good	Excellent
PZK, 6.35mm, Clip Fed, *Modern*	75	150	200

Q

QUACKENBUSH

Herkimer, N.Y., c. 1880.

	Fair	V. Good	Excellent
RIFLE, SINGLESHOT BOY'S RIFLE			
.22 R.F., Side Swing Breech, Nickel Plated, Takedown, *Curio*	$150	$300	$400

QUAIL

Made by Crescent, c. 1900. See Crescent Fire Arms Co., Shotgun, Double Barrel, Side-by-Side; Shotgun, Singleshot.

QUAIL'S FARGO

Tradename used by Dakin Gun Co. and Simmons Specialties.

	Fair	V. Good	Excellent
SHOTGUN, DOUBLE BARREL, SIDE-BY-SIDE			
12 Ga., Checkered Stock, Plain, *Modern*	$75	$150	$200

QUEEN CITY

Made by Crescent for Elmira Arms Co., c. 1900. See Crescent Fire Arms Co., Shotgun, Double Barrel, Side-by-Side; Shotgun, Singleshot.

R

RADIUM

Gabilondo y Urresti, Guernica, Spain, c. 1910.

HANDGUN, SELF-LOADING

	Fair	V. Good	Excellent
6.35mm, Fixed Magazine, Side Loading, Blue, *Curio*	$75	$150	$200

RADOM

Fabryka Broni w Radomu, Radom, Poland, c. 1930 through WWII.

HANDGUN, REVOLVER

	Fair	V. Good	Excellent
Ng 30, 7.62mm Nagant, Gas Seal, Double Action, *Curio*	150	300	375

HANDGUN, SELF-LOADING

	Fair	V. Good	Excellent
VIS 1935, 9mm Luger, Clip Fed, Military, Nazi-Production, Early, *Curio*	200	400	500

Radom, Early Nazi

	Fair	V. Good	Excellent
VIS 1935, 9mm Luger, Clip Fed, Military, Nazi-Proofed, Early Type, *Curio*	700	1500	1950
VIS 1935 Navy, 9mm Luger, Clip Fed, Military, Nazi-Production, Late, *Curio*	450	1000	1500
VIS 1935 Polish, 9mm Luger, Clip Fed, Military, *Curio*	450	1000	1500

RANDALL

Randall Firearms Mfg. Corp., Sun Valley, Calif.

HANDGUN, SELF-LOADING

	Fair	V. Good	Excellent
Compact Model, Various Calibers, Stainless Steel, M1911A1 Style, Herritt Grips, Adjustable Sights, *Modern*	$300	$600	$850
Service Model, Various Calibers, Stainless Steel, M1911A1 Style, Herritt Grips, Adjustable Sights, *Modern*	325	700	950
Target Model, Various Calibers, Stainless Steel, M1911A1 Style, Herritt Grips, Adjustable Sights with Rib, *Modern*	325	700	950

RANGER

Made by E. L. Dickinson, Springfield, Mass.

HANDGUN, REVOLVER

	Fair	V. Good	Excellent
#2, .32 Short R.F., 5 Shot, Spur Trigger, Solid Frame, Single Action, *Antique*	75	125	200

RANGER

Made by Hopkins & Allen, c. 1880.

HANDGUN, REVOLVER

	Fair	V. Good	Excellent
.22 Short R.F., 7 Shot, Spur Trigger, Solid Frame, Single Action, *Antique*	75	150	200
.32 Short R.F., 6 Shot, Spur Trigger, Solid Frame, Single Action, *Antique*	75	150	200

RANGER

Made by Stevens Arms.

RIFLE, SLIDE ACTION

	Fair	V. Good	Excellent
Model 70, .22 L.R.R.F., Solid Frame, Hammer, *Modern*	75	125	200
Model 75, .22 L.R.R.F., Tube Feed, Hammerless, *Modern*	75	150	200

SHOTGUN, DOUBLE BARREL, SIDE-BY-SIDE

	Fair	V. Good	Excellent
Model 215, 12 and 16 Gauges, Steel Barrels, Outside Hammers, *Modern*	75	125	200
Model 315, Various Gauges, Steel Barrels, Hammerless, *Modern*	75	150	200

SHOTGUN, SINGLESHOT

	Fair	V. Good	Excellent
Model 89 Dreadnaught, Various Gauges, Hammer, *Modern*	$25	$50	$75

RANGER ARMS, INC.

Gainesville, Tex., c. 1972.

RIFLE, BOLT ACTION

	Fair	V. Good	Excellent
Bench Rest/Varminter, Various Calibers, Singleshot, Target Rifle, Thumbhole Stock, Heavy Barrel, Recoil Pad, *Modern*	200	425	600
Governor Grade, Various Calibers, Sporting Rifle, Fancy Checkering, Fancy Wood, Recoil Pad, Sling Swivels, *Modern*	150	375	550
Governor Grade Magnum, Various Calibers, Sporting Rifle, Fancy Checkering, Fancy Wood, Recoil Pad, Sling Swivels, *Modern*	200	400	550
Senator Grade, Various Calibers, Sporting Rifle, Fancy Checkering, Recoil Pad, Sling Swivels, *Modern*	150	325	500
Senator Grade Magnum, Various Calibers, Sporting Rifle, Fancy Checkering, Recoil Pad, Sling Swivels, *Modern*	175	350	525
Statesman Grade, Various Calibers, Sporting Rifle, Checkered Stock, Recoil Pad, Sling Swivels, *Modern*	125	250	425
Statesman Grade Magnum, Various Calibers, Sporting Rifle, Checkered Stock, Recoil Pad, Sling Swivels, *Modern*	150	300	450

RASCH

Brunswick, Germany, 1790–1810.

RIFLE, FLINTLOCK

	Fair	V. Good	Excellent
Yaeger, Octagon Barrel, Brass Furniture, Engraved, Carved, Target Sights, *Antique*	1200	3000	4250

RATHFONG, GEORGE

Lancaster, Pa., 1774–1809. See U.S. Military, Kentucky Rifles.

RATHFONG, JACOB

Lancaster, Pa., 1810–1839. See Kentucky Rifles and Pistols.

RAVEN

Raven Arms, Industry, Calif., 1970–1991.

HANDGUN, SELF-LOADING

	Fair	V. Good	Excellent
MP-25, .25 ACP, Clip Fed, Nickel, *Modern*	15	25	50
MP-25, .25 ACP, Clip Fed, Teflon, *Modern*	$15	$25	$50
MP-25, .25 ACP, Clip Fed, Teflon, *Modern*	15	25	50
P-25, .25 ACP, Clip Fed, Blue, *Modern*	15	25	50
P-25, .25 ACP, Clip Fed, Chrome, *Modern*	15	25	50
P-25, .25 ACP, Clip Fed, Nickel, *Modern*	15	25	50

REASOR, DAVID

Lancaster, Pa., 1749–1780. See Kentucky Rifles and Pistols.

RECK

Reck Sportwaffenfabrik, Arnsberg, West Germany.

HANDGUN, REVOLVER

	Fair	V. Good	Excellent
.22 L.R.R.F., Double Action, Blue, *Modern*	15	25	50

HANDGUN, SELF-LOADING

	Fair	V. Good	Excellent
P-8, 6.35mm, Clip Fed, Blue, *Modern*	25	50	75

RED CLOUD

HANDGUN, REVOLVER

	Fair	V. Good	Excellent
.32 Long R.F., 5 Shot, Single Action, Solid Frame, Spur Trigger, *Antique*	75	150	200

RED JACKET

Made by Lee Arms, Wilkes-Barre, Pa., c. 1870.

HANDGUN, REVOLVER

	Fair	V. Good	Excellent
.22 Long R.F., 7 Shot, Single Action, Solid Frame, Spur Trigger, *Antique*	75	150	200
.32 Long R.F., 5 Shot, Single Action, Solid Frame, Spur Trigger, *Antique*	75	150	200

REED, JAMES

Lancaster, Pa., 1778–1780. See Kentucky Rifles.

REFORM

August Schueler, Suhl, Germany, 1900–1905.

HANDGUN, MANUAL REPEATER

	Fair	V. Good	Excellent
6mm R.F., 4 Barrel, Double Action, Hammer, *Curio*	250	550	750

REFORM

Spain, c. 1920.

	Fair	V. Good	Excellent
HANDGUN, SELF-LOADING			
6.35mm, Clip Fed, Blue, *Curio*	$50	$100	$150

REGENT
Gregorio Bolumburu, Eibar, Spain, c. 1925.

HANDGUN, SELF-LOADING			
6.35mm, Clip Fed, Blue, *Curio*	50	100	150

REGENT
Karl Burgsmuller, Kreiensen, Germany.

HANDGUN, REVOLVER			
.22 L.R.R.F., Double Action, Blue, *Modern*	25	50	75

REGINA
Gregorio Bolumburu, Eibar, Spain, c. 1920.

HANDGUN, SELF-LOADING			
Pocket, 7.65mm, Clip Fed, Blue, *Curio*	75	125	175
Vest Pocket, 6.35mm, Clip Fed, Blue, *Curio*	50	100	150

Regina Vest Pocket

REGNUM
Tradename used by August Menz, Suhl, Germany.

HANDGUN, MANUAL REPEATER			
6.35mm, 4 Barrels, Spur Trigger, Hammer, *Curio*	200	400	650

REID PATENT REVOLVERS
Made by W. Irving for James Reid, N.Y., 1862–1884.

HANDGUN, REVOLVER			
Model 1.22 Short R.F., 7 Shot, Spur Trigger, Solid Frame, Single Action, *Antique*	450	1000	1450
Model 2.32 Short R.F., 7 Shot, Spur Trigger, Solid Frame, Single Action, *Antique*	400	800	1150

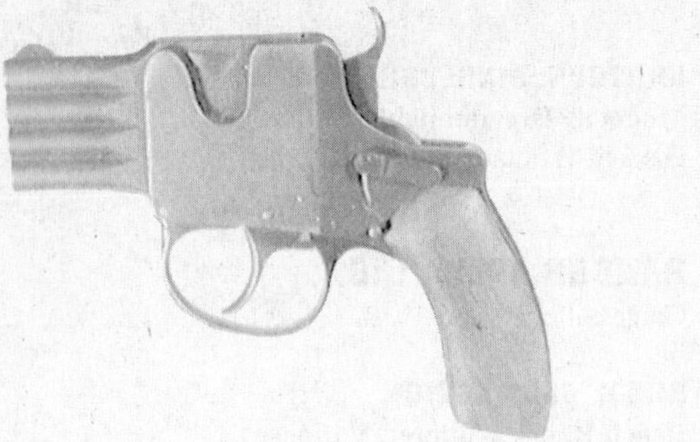

Regnum

	Fair	V. Good	Excellent
My Friend .41 Short R.F., Knuckleduster, 5 Shot, *Antique*	$1500	$3500	$4500
My Friend, .22 R.F., Knuckleduster, 7 Shot, *Antique*	350	750	1000
My Friend, .32 R.F., Knuckleduster, 7 Shot, *Antique*	400	850	1150

REIMS
Azanza y Arrizabalaga, Eibar, Spain, c. 1914.

HANDGUN, SELF-LOADING			
1914 Model, 6.35mm, Clip Fed, *Curio*	50	100	150
1914 Model, 7.65mm, Clip Fed, *Curio*	75	125	175

REINA
Mre. d'Armes des Pyrenees, Hendaye, France, c. 1930.

HANDGUN, SELF-LOADING			
7.65mm, Clip Fed, Blue, *Curio*	50	125	175

REISING
Hartford, Conn., 1916–1924.

HANDGUN, SELF-LOADING			
Target (Hartford), .22 L.R.R.F., Clip Fed, Hammer, *Curio*	250	525	750
Target (N.Y.), .22 L.R.R.F., Clip Fed, Hammer, *Curio*	300	600	800

REMINGTON ARMS CO.
Eliphalet Remington, Herkimer County, N.Y., 1816–1831. Ilion, N.Y., 1831 to Date. 1856, E. Remington & Sons; 1888, Remington Arms Co.; 1910, Remington Arms U.M.C. Co.; 1925 to Date Remington Arms Co., Ilion, N.Y. Also see the Commemorative Section. America's oldest gunmaker, Remington was founded by Connecticut-born Eliphalet Remington, in 1816, in central New York State. The site eventually came to be called Ilion; initial production was of gun barrels. An 1845 government contract was instrumental in expanding the operation for the quality manufacture of complete guns, beginning with the Jenks breechloading

rifle. As the line expanded, revolvers were added, their design—in some details—superior to the Colt, the exclusive patent for which had expired in 1857. During the Civil War, Remington was awarded substantial contracts, and the armory was expanded significantly. The founder was a skillful businessman, adept at hiring talented designers who created a solid line of firearms bearing the Remington name. The death of Eliphalet in 1861 left the business in the hands of his three sons. Philo, Eliphalet III, and Samuel Remington all carried on the family enterprise. By the end of the 1860s the company offered a more broad-based line of firearms than any other American gunmaker—primarily revolvers and rifles, derringers, rolling block breechloading pistols and rifles, a cane gun, military rifles, a percussion shotgun, and singleshot target rifles. Financial problems in the 1880s led to the purchase by the New York firm Hartley & Graham, leading jobbers of the day. The same company had established the Union Metallic Cartridge Company, Bridgeport, Connecticut, in 1867. In 1912 Remington Arms merged with Union Metallic Cartridge Company, and the name was changed to Remington-UMC. In 1935, after another reorganization, the name was changed to Remington Arms Company, Inc. From 1933 to 1993 the Du Pont Corporation owned Remington; in 1993 Du Pont's interest was bought out by the New York investment banking group of Clayton, Dubilier, Rice. Remington's fame has undergone somewhat of a revival, with a much more proactive management, and the running of the Remington stock car, on the NASCAR circuit, beginning in the 1995–96 season.

The standard general references on Remington are the newly published *The Guns of Remington Historic Firearms Spanning Two Centuries* (Madaus and Stoddard) and *Remington America's Oldest Gunmaker,* by Roy M. Marcot. Classification used herein based on the system used in the latter title. For further details, see both of these volumes.

	Fair	*V. Good*	*Excellent*
SINGLE SHOT PLAINS RIFLES WITH REMINGTON BARRELS			
Plains Rifle, Percussion, approx. .36 to .45 Caliber, Rifled Barrel	$200	$600	$950
Plains Rifle, with Over-and-Under Barrels, Percussion, approx. .36 to .45 Caliber	300	900	1200
Same, Rifle-Shotgun Combination, .36 to .45 Caliber and approx. 16 gauge	150	450	700
Side-by-Side Shotgun, Imported, Marked with Remington Name as Importer, approx. 16 gauge	100	300	500
1816–1996 COMMEMORATIVE FLINTLOCK RIFLE			
.50 Caliber Muzzleloader, 39″ Octagonal Barrel, Curly Maple Full Stock, with Brass Mountings, made for Remington by outside contractor	150	400	650
GOVERNMENT CONTRACT LONGARMS			
U.S. Navy, Jenks Breechloading Carbine, .52 Smoothbore (Later Rifled) Caliber	800	1600	2250
U.S. Model 1841 Rifle, .54 Caliber, Socket or Saber Bayonet	800	2000	2750

	Fair	*V. Good*	*Excellent*
U.S. Model 1822 Musket, Alteration to Percussion, with Rifling and Sights added, .69 Caliber	$400	$900	$1350
Merrill, Latrobe & Thomas Breechloading Carbine, Lock with Remington markings, .54–.56 Caliber	5000	12000	17500
Model 1862 Zouave Rifle, .58 Caliber	700	1600	2250
Model 1863 (Type 1) Rifled Musket .58 caliber	500	1200	1750
As above, but altered to metallic cartridge Breechloader by Remington	300	600	950
English Model P1853 Type IV Rifled-Musket, alteration to Breechloader with Trapdoor System of Remington Patent .577 Berdan Centerfire, 36¼″ Barrel	200	500	750
As above, Type III but with Second Model System of Berdan, 1867	200	500	750
REVOLVING RIFLES			
New Model Revolving Rifle, .36 Caliber, 6 Shots, 24″ to 28″ Barrels	1500	3000	4500
.44 Caliber, 6 Shots, 24″ to 28″ Barrels	1500	3200	4750
As above, but altered to metallic cartridge by Remington .38 Rimfire	800	1600	2250
.46 Rimfire	1200	2000	2750

REVOLVERS

Beals Pocket Revolvers

.31 Caliber, 5-Shots, 3″ Barrel until Third Model (then to 4″), Solid Frame, marking references Beals' patent

	Fair	*V. Good*	*Excellent*
Remington-Beals First Model (First Issue),	300	650	900
Remington-Beals First Model (Second Issue), with cylinder stops between nipples	250	600	850
Remington-Beals First Model (Third Issue), Hammer of new design, with or without cylinder stops	250	600	850
Remington-Beals First Model (Fourth Issue), without cylinder stops, marking differs from above	250	600	850
Remington-Beals First Model (Fifth Issue), Improved external revolving pawl system on left side of frame	250	600	850
Remington-Beals Second Model, Spur Trigger improvement of above	1500	4500	6000
Remington-Beals Third Model, With extended Barrel Lug, attached Loading Lever beneath Barrel, Longer Cylinder and 4″ Barrel	500	1500	2250

Note: for any of the above altered to metallic cartridge, deduct 50% in valuation, but add 50% if both percussion and cartridge cylinder present.

	Fair	V. Good	Excellent
Remington-Rider Double Action Pocket Revolver, .31 Caliber, 5 Shots, 3″ Barrel, marking references Rider's patent	$250	$600	$800
Remington-Rider Improved Double Action Pocket, as above, but with adaptations for Metallic Cartridge Cylinder, .32 Rimfire, Premium if both Percussion and Cartridge Cylinder present	250	600	800
With Cartridge Extra Cylinder	400	800	1000
New Model Pocket Revolvers, .31 Caliber, Spur Trigger, 5 Shots, 3½″ Barrel, September 14, 1858 Patent Marking			
Steel Frame	600	1200	1650
Brass Frame	200	500	750
As above, Improved New Model Pocket Conversion to Metallic Cartridge, .32 Rimfire, Premium if both Percussion and Cartridge Cylinder Present	150	350	500
New Model Police Revolver, .36 Caliber, 5 Shots, 3½″, 4½″, 5½″ and 6½″ Barrel; premium for latter	200	600	900
As above, Improved New Model Police Conversion to Metallic Cartridge	150	350	500
.38 Rimfire, premium if both Percussion and Cartridge Cylinder present	300	800	1250
New Model Police Double Action Belt Revolver, .36 Caliber, 6 Shots, 6½″ Barrel	600	1200	1650
As above, Improved New Model Police Conversion to Metallic Cartridge	300	700	1000
.38 Rimfire, premium if both Percussion and Cartridge Cylinder present	800	1600	2250
Remington-Beals Navy or Belt Revolver, .36 Caliber, 6 Shots, 7⅜″ or 7½″ Barrel	600	1200	1650
As above, with U.S. Government Inspector Markings	1000	2200	2750
Conversion to Metallic Cartridge, .38 Rimfire	300	700	1000
Model 1861 Navy or Belt Revolver, .36 Caliber, 6 Shots, 7⅜″ Barrel, Streamlined Loading Lever and Cylinder Pin System	600	1200	1650
As above, with U.S. Government Inspector Markings Conversion to Metallic Cartridge, .38 Rimfire	300	700	950
New Model Navy or Belt Revolver, .36 Caliber, 6 Shots, 7⅜″ Barrel	600	1200	1650
As above, with U.S. Government Inspector Markings	1000	2200	2750
Same as above with Anchor Marking Applied on Barrel Conversion to Metallic Cartridge	400	700	950
.38 Rimfire	400	700	950
.38 Centerfire for U.S. Navy	400	700	950
New Model Single Action Belt Revolver, .36 Caliber, 6¼″ or 6½″ Barrel	500	1000	1350

	Fair	V. Good	Excellent
Conversion to Metallic Cartridge, .38 Rimfire	$300	$550	$750
New Model Double Action Belt Revolver, .36 Caliber, 6 Shots, 6½″ Barrel, some with Rider's patent marking	500	1100	1350
Conversion to Metallic Cartridge .38 Rimfire	350	600	850
Remington-Beals Army or Holster Revolver, .44 Caliber, 6 Shots, 8″ Barrel	900	2500	3250
As above, with U.S. Government Inspector Markings Conversion to Metallic Cartridge .46 Rimfire	600	1200	1750
Model 1861 Army or Holster Revolver, .44 Caliber, 6 Shots, 8″ Barrel, Improved Cylinder Pin Removal System and Loading Lever Design	800	1750	2250
As above, with U.S. Government Inspector Markings,	1000	2000	2750
Conversion to Metallic Cartridge .46 Rimfire	600	1000	1950
New Model Army or Holster Revolver, .44 Caliber, 6 Shots, 8″ Barrel, most specimens marked NEW MODEL, larger Cutout on Barrel Lug in line with Chamber of Cylinder at Firing Position, improved Loading Lever/Cylinder in System	600	1700	2350
As above, with U.S. Government Inspector Markings, many also marked with unit identifications	800	2000	2750
Conversion to Metallic Cartridge, .46 Rimfire	600	1200	1850

CARTRIDGE SINGLE ACTION REVOLVERS

Remington-Smoot Pocket Revolver

	Fair	V. Good	Excellent
No. 1 Smoot, .30 Short Rimfire, Barrel and Frame of Single Piece, 2¾″ Barrel Early Production with Revolving Recoil Shield	500	1000	1350
Standard Model	100	250	425
No. 2 Smoot, .32 Rimfire (a few in .30 Rimfire, will Bring Premium), Straight Ejector Rod Retained by Cross Pin, 2¾″ Barrel	100	250	425
No. 3 Smoot, .38 Centerfire (also available in .38 Short Rimfire), Grip at First Bird's-head Pattern, then to Saw Handle Configuration, 3¾″ Barrel	100	250	425
No. 4 Smoot, .38 or .41 Rimfire or Centerfire, 2½″ Barrel	100	250	425
Iroquois Model, .22 Short or Long Rimfire, 7 Shots, 2¼″ Barrel	100	300	475
Model 1875 Army Revolver, .44 Centerfire, later in .44–40 and .45 Long Colt, 7½″, 5¾″ Barrels bring Premium, with Web below Barrel	1200	3000	4250

	Fair	V. Good	Excellent
Model 1888 New Model Army, Similar to above, .44–40, 5¾″ Barrel; about 500 made (possibly by Hartley & Graham, New York City); without Web below Barrel	$2000	$3750	$5000
Model 1890 New Model Army, .44–40, 5¾″ or 7½″ Barrels; without Web below	2000	5000	6500

DERRINGER PISTOLS

	Fair	V. Good	Excellent
Rider Patent Parlor Pistol, .177 Caliber (Percussion Cap and No 1 Shot), 3″ Barrel, Spur Trigger	2000	4500	5500
Vest Pocket Pistol, .22 Short Rimfire, 3¼″ Barrel	300	900	1350
Split Breech Derringer Pistol, .30 or .32 Rimfire, 3½″ Barrel	350	900	1350
Split Breech Derringer Pistol, .41 Short Rimfire, 3¾″ Barrel	300	800	1200
Remington-Elliott Single Shot Derringer, .41 Short Rimfire, 2½″ Barrel	500	1000	1350
Remington-Rider Magazine Pistol, .32 Short Rimfire, 3⅛″ Barrel	500	1000	1350
Remington-Elliott Pepperbox Zig Zag Pistol, .22 Short or Long Rimfire, 6 Shots, Ring Trigger, 3¼″ Barrel Cluster	600	1500	2150
Remington-Elliott Pepperbox Pistol, .22 Short or Long Rimfire, 5 Shots, Ring Trigger, 3″ Barrel Cluster	400	800	1250
Remington-Elliott Pepperbox Pistol, .32 Short or Long Rimfire, 4 Shots, Ring Trigger, 3¼″ Barrel Cluster	200	600	900
Over-and-Under Double Derringer .41 Rimfire, Two Shots Type I, Early Production (Model No. 1)	850	1750	2250
Type I, Transitional or Model No. 1, First Variation	850	2000	2500
Type I, Late Series or Model No. 2	400	1000	1350
Type II, or Model No. 3	400	1000	1350
Type III, or Model No. 4	400	1000	1350
Type III, Late Production, or Model No. 4	500	1100	1550

REMINGTON-RIDER ROLLING BLOCK PISTOLS

	Fair	V. Good	Excellent
U.S. Navy Model 1866 Pistol (Spur Trigger), .50–23 Rimfire, 8½″ Barrel	700	1750	2350
As above, with nickel finish, commercial model	600	1500	2000
Model 1866, with Government Inspector Markings	1000	2500	3250
U.S. Navy Model 1870 Pistol (with Triggerguard) .50–25 Rimfire or .50–25 Centerfire, 8½″ Barrel,	500	1000	1450
As above, with nickel finish, commercial model	400	900	1350
Model 1870, with Government Inspector Markings	600	1200	1750
U.S. Army Model 1871 Pistol (with Triggerguard and Spur at top of Backstrap), .50–25 Centerfire, 8″ Barrel	$500	$1000	$1750
As above, with nickel finish, commercial model	400	900	1450
Model 1871, with Government Inspector Markings	600	1150	1550
Model 1887 Target Pistol (on 1866 Navy Frame), .32 S & W Centerfire, 8½″ Barrel	700	1750	2450
Model 1891 Target Pistol (on 1866 Navy Frame), .32 S & W Centerfire, 10″ Barrel	800	2000	3000
Model 1871 Target Pistol (on 1871 Army Frame), .44 S & W Centerfire, 10″ Barrel	700	1750	2500
Model 1887 Target Pistol (on 1871 Army Frame), .22 Long Rifle, 10″ Barrel			
.25–10 Rimfire, 8″ Barrel	700	1750	2500
.44 S & W Centerfire, 10″			
Model 1891 Target Pistol (on 1871 Army Frame), .22 Short or Long Rifle, 10″ Barrel	700	1750	2500
Model 1901 Target Pistol (on 1871 Army Frame), .44 S & W Centerfire, 10″ Barrel	700	1750	2500
As above, in .22 Short or Long Rifle Caliber, 10″ Barrel	700	1750	2500

SELF-LOADING PISTOLS

	Fair	V. Good	Excellent
Pedersen Model 51 Autoloading Pistol .380ACP, 7 Round Magazine	200	500	850
.32 ACP, 8 Round Magazine	250	550	900
Colt Model 1911 Automatic Pistol, 1917–18 .45ACP, 8 Shot Magazine, REM-UMC Markings	800	1750	2350

MISCELLANEOUS PISTOLS

	Fair	V. Good	Excellent
Mark III Signal Pistols (World War I), 10-Gauge, Single Shot	50	100	175
Model XP-100 Bolt Action Single Shot Pistol (several variations, including with Box Magazine), .221 Rem. Fire Ball (variations in .22 Rimfire, .308, .223 Rem., 7mm–08, .35 Rem., .22–250 Rem., .308 Win., etc.), 10½″ Barrel (variations include with 14½″)	150	300	550
Model XP-100R, .260 Rem., .35 Rem., Blind Magazine, 14½″ Barrel, Fiberglass Stock	150	300	550

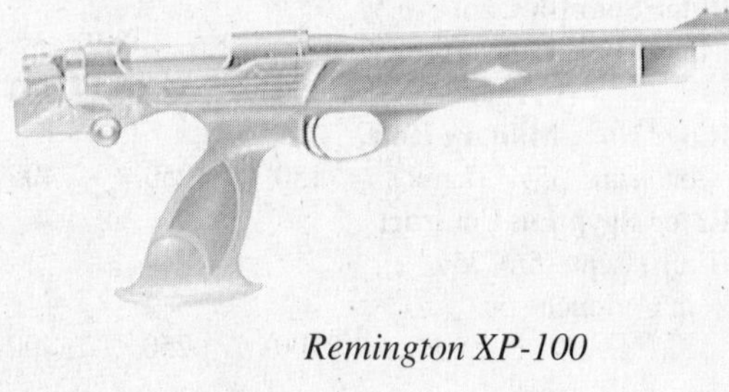

Remington XP-100

ROLLING BLOCK RIFLES, MILITARY

Note: rifles adapted for target use will bring premium.

	Fair	*V. Good*	*Excellent*
Split Breech Carbine, .56–50 Rimfire, 20″ Barrel, Geiger and Rider Patents	$700	$1200	$1750
Remington-Rider Breechloading Carbine, .56–50 Rimfire, 20″ Barrel, Rare	1000	2000	2750
Springfield Model 1863 Rifled Musket (Type II), altered to Rider System, .50–70, .58 Centerfire, 32¼″ or 39″ Barrel	700	1750	2350
U.S. Model 1861 Rifled Musket, altered to Rider System, .58 Centerfire, 32¼″ Barrel	800	2000	2650
Remington-Rider U.S. Navy Model 1867 Cadet Rifle (for U.S. Naval Academy), .50 Centerfire, 32½″ Barrel	600	1250	1750
Remington-Rider U.S. Navy Model 1870 Rifle (Type I), .50 Centerfire, 32⅝″ Barrel	600	1250	1750
Remington-Rider U.S. Navy Model 1870 Rifle (Type II) .50 Centerfire, 32⅝″ Barrel	600	1250	1750
Remington-Rider U.S. Navy Model 1871 Rifle (New York State Contract) .50–70 Centerfire, 36″ Barrel	400	900	1350
Remington-Rider Model 1871 Rifle (by Springfield Armory using Remington-Rider actions), .50–70 centerfire, 36″ Barrel	500	1000	1500
Remington-Rider Model 1871 Carbine (New York State Contract), .50–45 Centerfire, 22″ Barrel, H.B.H. Inspector Marking on Buttstock	400	900	1450
Remington-Rider Swedish Model 1868 Engineer & Artillery Musketoon (3,000 made in Ilion; balance built in Sweden on actions supplied by Remington), .50 (12mm) Rimfire, 18⅛″ Barrel	200	500	850
Remington-Rider Swedish Model 1867 Rifle (bulk built under license in Sweden, using Remington actions), 50 (12mm) Rimfire, 37⅜″ Barrel	200	500	850
Remington-Rider Swedish Model 1867 Rifle (adapted to new Caliber in Sweden, using own M1867 Rifles), 50 (12mm) Center Fire, 37⅜″ Barrel	200	500	850
Remington-Rider Spanish Model 1874 Engineer and Artillery Musketoon, .433 (11mm), 23⅛″ Barrel	200	500	850
Remington-Rider Spanish Civil Guard Rifle .433 (11mm) Centerfire, 30¼″ Barrel	150	300	550
Remington-Rider No. 1 Military Rifle, .433 (11mm) Centerfire, 35¼″ Barrel	150	250	400
Remington-Rider Egyptian Contract Rifle, .433 (11mm) Centerfire, 35⅛″ Barrel, A.D.B. in Cartouche on Buttstock	100	250	400

	Fair	*V. Good*	*Excellent*
Remington-Rider Egyptian Contract Carbine, .433 (11mm) Centerfire, 20½″ Barrel	$100	$250	$350
Remington-Rider Argentine Model 1879 Rifle, .433 (11mm) Centerfire, 36″ Round Barrel with 2¼″ Octagonal Section at Breech	125	250	400
Remington-Rider Argentine Model 1879 Carbine, .433 (11mm) Centerfire, 20½″ Round Barrel with 2¼″ Octagonal Section at Breech	125	250	400
Remington-Rider Danish Model 1867 Rifle (made at Copenhagen Arsenal under Remington license) .45 (11.7mm) Centerfire, 35½″ Barrel	125	250	400
Remington-Rider Danish Model 1867 Carbine .45 (11.7mm) Centerfire, 21″ Barrel	125	250	400
Remington-Rider Dutch Police Brevet Model 1869 Gendarmarie Carbine (built by F.U. & D. Nagant, Liege, Belgium), 11.4 mm Centerfire, 21″ Barrel, with 1½″ Octagonal Section at Breech	100	200	350
Remington Licensed Oriental Model Export Rifle (built by August Francotte, Liege), 11mm Centerfire, 27½″ Barrel	200	350	450
Remington No. 1 ½ Frame Cadet Rifle, Model No. 206, .45–70 Centerfire, 28″ Barrel	600	1250	1750
Remington New Model Small-Bore Military Rifle, Model 1896, 7mm (Mauser) Centerfire; 30″ Barrel; designed for Smokeless Powder Ammunition	100	250	400
Remington Model 1897 Military Rifle, .30–40 Centerfire, 7mm Spanish Mauser; 30⅛″ Barrel; made for Smokeless Powder	125	300	450
Remington Model 1897 Small-Bore Military Carbine, 7mm Spanish Mauser	75	200	350
Remington Model 1901 Military Rifle, Improved Model 1897; Front Sight banded to Barrel, Rear Sight improved, Rotary Extractor added	100	225	450
Remington Model 1901 Military Rifle, as above, but with Carbine Length Barrel	75	200	350
Remington Model 1902 Military Rifle, 7mm (Mauser) Centerfire, 30⅛″ Barrel; made for Smokeless Powder	100	225	400
Remington Model 1902 Military Carbine 7mm (Mauser) Centerfire, 20⅜″ Barrel; made for Smokeless Powder	75	200	350
Model 1911 Rolling Block Military Rifle, as above, but with Rem-UMC Tang Marking	125	250	400

	Fair	V. Good	Excellent
Model 1914 Lebel Military Rifle, 8mm Lebel	$100	$200	$400

ROLLING BLOCK RIFLES, CIVILIAN

	Fair	V. Good	Excellent
No. 1 Sporting Rifle (from Military Actions), .38 long, .44 Long Rimfire	600	1250	1650
In Center Fire Cartridges	700	1750	2250
No. 1 Short Range Sporting Rifle, Rimfire, Short-Range Centerfire Cartridges, Varying Barrel Lengths.	400	900	1350
No. 1 Mid Range Sporting Rifle, Centerfire Cartridges, Varying Barrel Lengths	700	1500	2150
No. 1 Long Range Creedmore Sporting Rifle, .44–90, .44–10, .44–105 Centerfire, Varying Half-round, Half Octagonal Barrel Lengths, Pistol-grip Stocks. Available in Grades A, B, C, D, and E, A being the most sophisticated	2000	5500	8000
As above, Military Variation	1000	2500	3500
No. 1 Heavy Sporting Rifle, Heavier Weight of Barrel Variation	1250	3000	4000
No. 1 Sporting Rifle, Hunter's Rifle, .38, .40, .44, and .50 Rimfire or Centerfire, Standard Features, Varying Barrel Lengths			
Rim Fire	450	900	1350
Center Fire	500	1200	1750
No. 1 Sporting Rifle, Adirondack Rifle, .45–50 Peabody Sporting Centerfire, 34″ Octagonal Barrel, Rounded Buttplate	800	1750	2250
No. 1 Sporting Rifle, Deer Rifle, .46 Long Rimfire, 24″ Round Barrel	450	900	1350
No. 1 Sporting Rifle, Buffalo Rifle, .50–70 Centerfire, 28⅛″ Octagonal Barrel	500	1200	1750
No. 1 Sporting Rifle, Black Hills Rifle, .45–60, .45–70 Centerfire, 28″ Round Barrel, Standard Features	800	1750	2250
No. 1 Short Range Target Rifle, Similar to Standard No. 1, Excepting Target Sights	1000	2750	3500
No. 1 Short Range Scheutzen Target Rifle, Similar to above, but with Scheutzen Buttplate, Special Stocks and Sights	1200	3000	3750
No. 1½ Sporting Rifle (Receiver lighter and thinner than No. 1 Series, "Economy" Model), Cartridge Range from .22 Short Rimfire to .44–40 Centerfire	450	900	1350
No. 1½ Creedmore Target Rifle, less expensive version of No. 1 Creedmore above	2000	4000	6000
No. 2 Sporting Rifle, Similar to Number 1 Series, but with smaller frame, and lighter in Weight	400	900	1350
No. 4 Rifle, Solid Frame, .22 Rimfire, .25–10 Rimfire, .32 Rimfire	150	400	650
No. 4 Rifle, Takedown Model, improved version of above, with 22½″ Barrel	$150	$400	$600
No. 4S Boy Scout Model Rifle, .22 Short Rimfire, 28″ Barrel, Leather Sling, Bayonet, Scabbard	500	1000	1450
No. 4S Military Model Rifle, Frame Marked MILITARY MODEL, as above, except in .22 Short, Long, and Long Rifle, 28″ Barrel with Shorter Front Sight Blade	500	1000	1450
No. 5 Sporting and Target Rifle, .30–30, 7mm Mauser, .30–40 Krag, .303 British (for Smokeless Ammunition)	1000	2500	3250
No. 6 Boy's Rifle, Smoothbore, .22 and .32 Rimfire, 20″ Barrel, Falling Block Action; Takedown; nearly 500,000 made	75	200	400
New Improved No. 6 Boy's Rifle, .22 Rimfire, .32 Rimfire, 24″ Barrel; Coil Springs used instead of Flat; new Safety System	75	200	400
No. 7 Target and Sporting Rifle, built on Frames of Model 1871 Army Rolling Block Pistols, .22 Short, .22 Long Rifle, .25–10 Stevens Rimfire; 24″, 26″, 28″ Barrels; Target Sights	1500	3500	4500
Coxford (Hartley & Graham) Cadet Rifle Built on Remington-Rider Model 1870 Pistol Actions, .50–25 Centerfire, 28″ Barrel	200	500	800
No. 1 Mid-Range Creedmoor Rifle, .45–70, 30″ Part Round, Part Octagonal Barrel, Walnut Stock	1250	2750	3500
No. 1 Mid-Range Sporter Rifle, .45–70, .30–30 Win., .444 Marlin, 30″ Round Barrel, Walnut Stock	800	1750	2750

REMINGTON-HEPBURN SINGLE SHOT RIFLES

	Fair	V. Good	Excellent
Remington-Hepburn No. 3 Hunting Rifle, Range of Thirteen Centerfire Calibers, from .32–20 to .45–90, available with Double-set Triggers, Extra Sights	1250	2500	3500
Remington-Hepburn No. 3 Hunters or Sporting Rifle, Range of Twenty-seven Centerfire Calibers, available with Fixed and Adjustable Front and Rear Sights	1000	2000	3000
Remington-Hepburn No. 3 Sporting Rifle, for Smokeless Powder, introduced 1903	1000	2000	3000
Remington-Hepburn No. 3 Short-Range Rifle, .38–40 Centerfire; variety of Sights available; Swiss Scheutzen Buttplates an option	900	2000	2750

	Fair	V. Good	Excellent
Remington-Hepburn No. 3 Mid-Range Rifle, range of nine Centerfire Cartridges, in .38, .40, and .45 Calibers; variety of Sights available	$1100	$2500	$3250
Remington-Hepburn No. 3 Long-Range Creedmoor Rifle, .44–77, .44–90, .44–100 Centerfire, customarily 34″ Barrels, variety of Sights, some of the Rear Types mounted on Buttstock	2000	4500	6500
Remington-Hepburn No. 3 Long-Range Military Rifle, .44–85 Centerfire, Military or Target Sights, Military Style Stock	1500	3000	4500
Remington-Hepburn No. 3 Match Rifle, Caliber Range from .25 on up to .40 Centerfire; Swiss Style Scheutzen Buttplates, Wind-gauge Spirit-level Front Sights, Vernier Rear Tang Sights	3000	9000	14500
Remington-Hepburn Walker No. 3 Scheutzen Match Rifle, .32–40 Ballard & Marlin Centerfire, other Calibers on Special Order; Scroll-contour Scheutzen under Lever, Opening the Action; Double-set Triggers, 30″ or 32″ Part Round, Part Octagonal Barrels; Elaborate Sights; Scheutzen Buttstock with Cheekpiece and Buttplate. Rare; 23 only recorded as sold	7000	22500	32500

SINGLE SHOT RIFLES, OTHER MODELS THAN ABOVE

	Fair	V. Good	Excellent
Remington-Beals, Iron Frame Model, .32 Rimfire, 27½″ Half Round, Half Octagonal Barrel	300	900	1200
Remington-Beals, Brass Frame Model, .38 Rimfire, 24″ Part Round, Part Octagonal Barrel	150	400	650
Remington No. 1 Cartridge Cane-Gun, Doghead Grip, .22 Short or Long Rimfire, 29½″ Barrel	2000	4000	6500
Remington No. 2 Cartridge Cane-Gun, Dog-head Grip, .32 Short or Long Rimfire, 26″ or 28″ Barrel	2000	4000	6500
As above, with Plain Grip, .32 Short or Long Rimfire, 30″ Barrel	900	2000	3250
As above, with Ball and Claw Handle, .32 Caliber, 27¼″ Barrel	1000	2500	3750

BOLT ACTION RIFLES

	Fair	V. Good	Excellent
Remington-Lee, Model 1879 Military Rifle, U.S. Navy Contract, .45–70, 29″ Barrel	500	1750	2500
Variation in .43 Spanish Centerfire for Foreign Market	100	300	500
(Purchased by Chinese)	200	400	650
Model 1882 Military Rifle, .45–70 and Variation in .45–70 for U.S. Army Contract	500	1500	2250
.43 Spanish Calibers	100	250	400

	Fair	V. Good	Excellent
Model 1882 Carbine, 45/70 Caliber	$600	$1750	$2350
Primarily Export Sale, 43 Spanish Caliber	125	300	450
Model 1882/85 Remington-Lee Conversion, Rifles, Carbines, alteration of the Model 1882 with improved Bolt System; in .45–70 and .43 Spanish, 45/70 Caliber	400	1200	1650
43 Spanish	100	200	325
Model 1882/85 Remington-Lee Sporting Rifle, .45–70, 30″ Half Round, Half Octagonal Barrel; Single Piece Sporting Stocks	600	1750	2500
Model 1885 Remington-Lee Military Rifle, .45–70 and .43 Spanish, 45/70 Caliber	500	1500	2250
43 Spanish	100	200	325
Model 1899 Small-Bore Remington-Lee Box Magazine Military Rifle, .30–40 Krag, 29″ Barrel	500	1500	2250
Model 1899 Small-Bore Remington-Lee Carbine, .30–40 Krag, 29″ Barrel	600	1700	2500
Model 1899 Remington-Lee Sporting Rifle, .236 Remington, .30–30, .30–40 Centerfire, 7mm Spanish Mauser, 7.65mm Belgium Mauser, .44–77, .43 Spanish, .45–70, .45–90, 24″, 26″, 28″ Barrels	600	1750	2500
Remington-Keene Bolt Action Repeating Carbine, .45–70 Centerfire, 20″ Barrel, 6 Shots	600	1500	2250
Repeating Army Rifle, .45–70 Centerfire, 32½″ Barrel, 9 Shots	1000	2500	3250
Repeating Navy Rifle, .45–70 Centerfire, 29¼″ Barrel, 9 Shots	1000	2500	3250
Repeating Frontier Rifle, .45–70 Centerfire, 24″ Barrel, 8 Shots	400	900	1250
Repeating Hunters or Sporting Rifle, .45/70 and .40–60 Centerfire, 24½″ Barrel, 9 Shots, in Grades of A, B, C, and D, the A being the most deluxe, and bringing Premium accordingly			
A	900	2250	3000
B	800	1750	2350
C	600	1250	1650
D	400	800	1200
.303 Caliber Enfield Military Rifle, 1914 Pattern, on Contract for British Government, .303 British	200	400	600
Mosin-Nagant Military Rifle, .30 Centerfire, 5 Shots	50	150	250
Remington-Enfield Model 1917 Military Rifle, .30–06	150	350	500
Model 30 (built on Model 1917 Military Action), .30–06, 24″ Barrel	200	500	700

	Fair	*V. Good*	*Excellent*
Model 30 Express and 30A Express, improved version of the above, .30–06, and .25, .30, 32, and .35 Remington; later joined by 7mm Mauser and .256 Roberts, 22″ Barrel Standard	$200	$500	$750
Model 30S Special and Variations, improved Grade of the Model 30 Express, .30–06, 7mm Mauser, .25 Remington, later joined by .257 Remington-Roberts in 24″ Barrel	200	500	750
30R Express Carbine, as above but with 20″ Barrel	250	600	850
Model 1934 (aka Model 40) Military Rifle, 7 × 57 Mauser, built on Model 1917 Enfield actions, and 30S Express Rifle actions	200	400	650
Model 1903 U.S. Military Rifle (World War II Production), .30 caliber	250	500	750
Model 1903 U.S. Military Rifle (Modified) (World War II Production), .30 Caliber	200	400	625
Model 1903A3 U.S. Military Rifle (World War II Production), .30 Caliber	200	400	600
Model 1903A4 U.S. Military Sniper's Rifle (World War II Production), .30 Caliber, with Scope	700	1200	1650
Model 721 (variations from Standard up to F Premier) (Premium for Higher Grades), .270, .30–06, .300 H & H Magnum, 24″ and 26″ Barrels Depending on Caliber	150	300	500
Model 722 (variations from Standard up to F Premier) (Premium for Higher Grades), .257 Roberts, .300 Savage, .222 Remington, .244 Remington, .308, .222 Rem. Mag., .243 Win., Short Action Version of Model 721, 24″ Barrel	150	300	500
Model 725 (variations from Standard up to F Premier), .222 Rem., .243 Win., .244 Rem., .270, .280 Rem., 30–06, 24″ Barrel, 4-shot Magazine, Monte Carlo Stock	200	400	600
Model 725 Kodiak (Larger Caliber Version of above), .375 H & H Mag., .458 Win. Mag., 26″ Barrels	750	1750	2250
Model 700 (improved version of Model 721/722) (several variations, including Law Enforcement, Sniper, Deluxe Metalwork and Stocks) (Cylindrical Receiver); current numerous Chamberings from .17 Rem. on up to .458 Win., including new 7mm Rem., Short and Long Actions to Accommodate Cartridge Sizes, varying Barrel Lengths, Walnut, Laminated, and Synthetic (including camouflage) Stocks	200	400	600
Magnum calibers Add 25%			
Model 700 Muzzleloading Rifle (several variations); current .50 and .54 Calibers, Percussion, In-line	$150	$300	$450
Model 600 Carbine (several variations) .222 Rem., .243 Rem., 6mm Rem., .308 Win., .35 Rem, 18½″ Ventilated Rib Barrel, Fixed Box Magazine, Monte Carlo Stock	150	300	450
Model 600 Magnum Carbine (several variations), .350 Rem. Mag., 6.5 Rem. Mag., 18½″ Barrel Ventilated Rib Barrel, 4-shot Box Magazine, Laminated Stock	200	400	550
Model 660 Carbine (successor to Model 600; several variations), .222 Rem., 6mm Rem., .243 Win., 308 Win., .223 Rem., 20″ Barrel, Wood Stock	150	300	450
Mohawk Carbine (cheaper version of Model 660 Carbine), .222 Rem., 6mm Rem., .243 Win., .308 Win., 18½″ Barrel, Walnut Stock	125	250	400
Model 660 Magnum Carbine (successor to Model 600 Mag. Carb., several variations), 6.5mm Rem. Mag., .350 Rem., Mag., 20″ Barrel, Laminated Stock	200	350	500
Model 788 Rifle (several variations), .222 Rem., .22–250 Rem., .243 Win., 6mm Rem., .308 Win., .30–30 Win., 7mm–08 Rem., .44 Rem. Mag., 22″ and 24″ Barrels depending on Caliber, Detachable Box Magazine, Walnut Stock	125	250	400
Model Seven Rifle (several variations); Current, .17 Rem., 222 Rem., .223 Rem., .243 Win, 7mm–08 Rem., 6mm Rem., .308 Win., 18½″ Barrel, Box Magazine with Floorplate, Walnut Stock	125	250	400
Sportsman Model 78 Rifle (based on Model 700 action), .223 Rem., .243 Win., .270 Win., .30–06, .308 Win., most with 22″ Barrel, 4-shot Box Magazine, Hardwood Stock	125	250	400

.22 RIMFIRE RIFLES, BOLT ACTION

	Fair	*V. Good*	*Excellent*
Model 33, Single Shot, .22 Short	35	75	100
As above, a Smooth bore and so marked, .22 Short Shot	100	200	300
Model 33, Type 33, Single Shot (variations include NRA Junior Target), .22 Short	100	175	275
Model 41 Targetmaster Single Shot (replacement of the Model 33 Series, in Rifled and Smooth bore), .22 Short, Long, Long Rifle, later .22 Remington Special	75	150	250
Model 411 Single Shot, .22 CB Cap Rimfire, 24″ Barrel, Plastic Stock	100	200	275
Model 510 Targetmaster (replacement for Model 33 and 41 Series) (several variations, including Smooth bore), .22 Short, Long, Long Rifle, 25″ Barrel Standard, Tubular Receiver	75	125	225

	Fair	V. Good	Excellent
Model 510X (replacement for Model 510 Targetmaster)	$75	$125	$175
Model 511 Scoremaster Repeater, .22 Short, Long, Long Rifle, 6 Shot (10-shot Magazine optional)	75	150	225
Model 511X (replacement for Model 511 Scoremaster)	75	150	225
Model 512 Sportmaster Repeater (several variations), .22 Short, Long, Long Rifle, Tubular Magazine	75	150	225
Model 513T (513TR) Matchmaster Target Rifle (several variations), .22 Short, Long, Long Rifle, 27″ Heavy Barrel, Target Sights	100	175	250
521T Junior Special Target Rifle, .22 Short, Long, Long Rifle, 25″ Barrel, 6-shot Box Magazine	50	125	200
Model 514 Single Shot (with variations), .22 Short, Long, Long Rifle, 24¾″ Barrel	40	75	125
Model 34 (variations include NRA Junior Target), .22 Short, Long, Long Rifle, Tubular Magazine	100	200	300
Model 37 Rangemaster Target (variations include 37AR, 37AS, 37AF, 37AX, 37AV, 37AM), .22 Long Rifle, 28″ Heavy Barrel, Target Sights, Competitive Level	200	400	550
Model 341 Sportmaster (improved version of Model 34) (variations include the 341PT Special, 341AT Special, 341SB Smooth bore), .22 Short, Long, Long Rifle, Heavy Target Barrel, Tubular Magazine	100	175	275
Add 25% for Smooth Bore			
Model 40X Single Shot Target Rifle (replacement for Model 37) (several variations), .22 Short, Long, Long Rifle, 24″ Barrel	200	400	550
Model 40XB Single Shot Target Rifle, .222 Rem., .222 Rem. Mag., .30–06, .300 H & H Mag., .308 Win. (7.62 NATO), 24″ Barrel	200	400	550
Model 40XB International Free Rifle (sophisticated version of above), .22 Short, Long, Long Rifle, and .308, .30–06, .222 Rem., .222 Rem. Magnum	200	400	550
Center Calibers	400	900	1150
Model 10 Single Shot Nylon Rifle, .22 Short, Long, Long Rifle, Nylon Stock	50	100	150
Model 11 Nylon Rifle, .22 Short, Long, Long Rifle, 6-shot Box Magazine (10-shot optional), Nylon Stock	50	100	150
Model 12 Nylon Rifle, .22 Short, Long, Long Rifle, Tubular Magazine, Nylon Stock	50	100	150
Models 610, 611A, 612A, 613S Single Shot (based on 500 Series Rifles, with Tubular Receiver((Scarce), .267 Rimfire, 25″ Barrel	50	125	175

	Fair	V. Good	Excellent
Model 580 Single Shot Rifle (replacement for Model 510 Series) (several variations), .22 Short, Long, Long Rifle, 24″ Barrel, Walnut Stock	$40	$75	$125
Model 581 Repeating Rifle (several variations), .22 Short, Long, Long Rifle, 24″ Barrel, 5-shot Box Magazine, Walnut Stock	50	100	150
Model 581 Repeating Rifle (Post 1986 Manufacture), as above, Plain Hardwood Stock, 24″ Barrel, Single-shot Adapter	40	75	125
Model 582 Repeating Rifle (several variations), .22 Short, Long, Long Rifle, 24″ Barrel, Tubular Magazine, Walnut Stock	40	75	125
Model 540X Single Shot Target Rifle, .22 Short, Long, Long Rifle, 26″ Barrel of Heavy Weight, Hardwood Stock with Thumb Cut Aperture	125	250	350
Model 591 Magnum Rifle, 5mm Rimfire Rem. Magnum, 4-shot Box Magazine, 24″ Barrel, Walnut Stock with Monte Carlo Comb	75	125	225
Model 592 Magnum Rifle, 5mm Rimfire Rem. Magnum, 24″ Barrel, 10-shot Tubular Magazine, Walnut Stock with Monte Carlo Comb	75	125	225
New Series Model 40-X Repeating Target Rifle (successor to Model 40-X Rangemaster Target Rifle) (variations including Bench Rest Design), .22–250 Rem., .222 Rem., .222 Rem. Mag., .223 Rem., 6mm Rem., 6mm International, 6m–47, and 7.62mm NATO Box Magazine, Wood Stock and Composition Stock Models	150	350	500
New Series Model 40-X Single Shot Target Rifle (successor to Model 40-X Rangemaster Target Rifle) (variations included a Benchrest Rifle), .22 Long Rifle, .22–250 Rem., .222 Rem., .222 Rem. Mag., .223 Rem., 6mm Rem., 6mm International, 6m–47, and 7.62mm NATO, 6.5mm × 55, 7mm Rem. Mag., .30–06, .30–338, .243 Win., 6.5mm Rem., 25–06 Rem., .300 Win. Mag., Wood Stock and Composition Stock Models	150	350	500
Model 540-XR Single Shot Rimfire Position Rifle (succeeding Model 540X Target Model), .22 Short, Long, Long Rifle, 26″ Barrels, Monte Carlo Stocks	150	300	500
Model 540-XPJR Single Shot Rimfire Position Rifle, Junior Version of above, with 1¾″ Shorter Stock	100	250	400
Model 541-S Single Shot Sporter Rifle, .22 Short, Long, Long Rifle, 24″ Barrel, 5-shot Box Magazine, Walnut Stock	200	400	550

	Fair	V. Good	Excellent
Model 541-T Custom Sporter Single Shot Rifle, .22 Short, Long, Long Rifle, 24″ Barrel, 5-shot Box Magazine, Walnut Stock	$100	$250	$350
Model 541-X Target Rifle (M13 Military designation), .22 Short, Long, Long Rifle, 27″ Heavy Barrel, 5-shot Plastic Box Magazine, Hardwood Stock	150	300	450

LEVER ACTION RIFLES

	Fair	V. Good	Excellent
Model 76 Nylon Trailrider, .22 Long Rifle, 19½″ Barrel, 14-shot Tubular Magazine	75	150	225

SINGLE BARREL SHOTGUNS

	Fair	V. Good	Excellent
No. 1 Shotgun, 20 Gauge, 30″, 32″ Barrels, Shotgun Buttplate	40	75	125
No. 2 Shotgun, 20 Gauge, 30″, 32″ Barrels, Rifle Buttplate, built using Military Rifle parts	40	75	125
Model 1893 No. 3 Single Barrel, 28, 24, 20, 16, 12, 10 Gauge, 30″, 32″, 34″ Barrels	40	75	125
28 and 24 ga. add 50%.			
No. 9 Single Barrel, or Model 1902, 28, 24, 20, 16, 12 and 10 Gauges; Button-Release Forend, Automatic Ejectors	40	75	125
28 and 24 ga. add 50%.			

OVER-AND-UNDER SHOTGUNS

	Fair	V. Good	Excellent
Model 32, with variations 32S Trap Special, 32TC Target, D Tournament, E Expert, F Premier, 32 Skeet, 32S Trap Special, 12 Gauge, Automatic Ejectors, Double Triggers (Single Selective Trigger from 1934), Open Barrel Design (no Rib between Barrels)	500	1300	2250
Model 3200 (replacement for Model 32) (variations in Field, Skeet, Trap), 12, 20, 28, .410 Gauges, several Barrel Lengths and Types, variety of Chokes	300	700	1800
Peerless Over-and-Under, 12 Gauge, 26″, 28″, or 30″ Vent Rib Barrels, Single-selective Trigger, Walnut Stock			
Model 396 Over-and-Under (current production), 12 Gauge, 28″ or 30″ Vent Rib Barrels, Walnut Stock	500	1700	2800

DOUBLE BARREL SHOTGUNS

	Fair	V. Good	Excellent
Model 1873 Remington-Whitmore Hammer-Lifter, 10 and 12 Gauge, in Three Grades	1000	2500	3250
Model 1875 Remington-Whitmore Lifter, 10 and 12 Gauge	1000	2500	3250
Model 1875 Remington-Whitmore Lifter Rifle/Shotgun Combination	1500	3500	4250
Model 1876 Lifter, variation in Hammer Profile			
Model 1878 Heavy Duck Gun, 10 Gauge, Heavy Weight and Solid Construction	$400	$900	$1250
Model 1879 Lifter Shotgun, 12 Gauge, Frame scaled down in size and weight from Model 1878, Deeley & Edge Forend Latch System	400	900	1250
Model 1882 Shotgun, 10 and 12 Gauge (two frame sizes), Standard Type Top Lever Opening and Locking System, Changed Hammer Profile, available with Auxiliary Tube for Insertion into Barrel for use as Rifle	400	900	1250
Model 1883 Shotgun, as above, but with different style Hammer	300	700	950
Model 1885 and 1887 Shotguns, 10, 12, and 16 Gauges, an improved Model 1882; Three Frame Sizes; differing Hammer Configurations	400	900	1200
Model 1889 (improved Model 1887), 10, 12 Gauge	400	900	1200
Model 1894 Hammerless, 10, 12, 16 Gauge, with or without Automatic Ejectors, Grades A, B, C, D, and E, with the latter the highest level	400	900	1200
Remington Special of the Model 1894, High-grade Gun in 12 Gauge, Barrel Length custom made to shooter's wishes. Rare	700	1250	1750
Model 1900, 12, 16 Gauge, economy version of the Model 1894	300	700	1000
Parker AHE Side-by-Side Shotguns, 20 Gauge, 28″ Vent Rib Barrels, Single-Selective Trigger, basically a custom-made gun, from Remington Custom Shop	20000	40000	55000

SINGLE BARREL TRAP GUN

	Fair	V. Good	Excellent
Model 90-T Single Barrel Trap Gun (built for Remington by Competition Arms Co.) (several variations), 12 Gauge, 32″ and 34″ Vent Rib Barrels, Walnut Stock	2250	3500	5500

SELF-LOADING SHOTGUNS

	Fair	V. Good	Excellent
Remington Autoloading, Listed in Grades from No. 1 on up through No. 6, and No. 0 Riot Grade, 12 Gauge			
Model 11 Autoloading Shotgun, listed in Grades from 11A Standard on up to 11F Premier (Premium for Higher Grades), new name for the Remington Autoloading, and Adopted by the Company in 1911, 12, later joined by 20 and 16 Gauge	100	350	450
11F Premier	1000	2000	2750
Remington Sportsman, a variation of the Model 11 (introduced 1931)	150	400	600

	Fair	V. Good	Excellent
Model 11-'48 (replacement for the Model 11) (numerous variations up to '48F Premier), 12, 16, 20 Gauge, later joined by 28 and .410	$125	$250	$400
Sportsman 58 Gas-Operated Shotgun (various Grades), 12, 16, 20 Gauge	125	250	400
Model 878 Automaster Gas-Operated Shotgun (various Grades), 12 Gauge	100	225	300
Model 1100 Gas-Operated (successor to Model 878) (several variations, including for Skeet, Trap, Sporting Clays, Field, Law Enforcement, etc.), 12, 16, 20, 28, 410, numerous Barrel Types and Lengths, variety of Stock Types	125	275	400
Sportsman 12 Model (based on 1100 Action), 12 Gauge, 28″ or 30″ Barrels, 5-shot Magazine, Wood Stock	125	275	400
Model 11-87 Premier (several variations, including Deer Gun, Synthetic Stocks, Camouflage, etc.), 12 Gauge, several Barrel Lengths, Wood Stock	125	275	400
SP (Special Purpose) 10 Magnum (with variations, including for Turkey Hunting), 10 Gauge, 26″ or 30″ Vent Rib Barrels, Walnut or Synthetic Stock, latter including Camouflage Patterns	200	350	500
Model 11-96 Euro Lightweight, 12 Gauge, 26″ or 28″ Vent Rib Barrels, Walnut Stock	200	350	500

AUTO-LOADING RIFLES

	Fair	V. Good	Excellent
Remington Autoloading Repeating Rifles, Listed in Grades from No. 1 on up to No. 6			
Model 8 Autoloading Rifle, in Grades 8A Standard, 8C Special, 8D Peerless, 8E Expert and 8F Premier, .25, .30, .32, and .35 Remington, Rimless, Centerfire Ammunition; 22″ Barrels, 5-shot Box Magazine	150	350	500
8F Premier	1500	3000	3750
Model 81, improved version of above	125	275	400
Model 81 Woodsmaster (improved versions of Model 8) (variations from Standard up through F Premier Grades) (Premium for Higher Grades), .30, .32, and .35 Remington, later .300 Savage added, 22″ Barrels, 5-shot Box Magazine	125	275	400
81F Premier	1000	2500	3250
Model 740 Woodsmaster (improved version of Model 81), .30–06, .244 Rem., .280 Rem., .308, 22″ Barrels, 4-shot Box Magazine	125	250	350
Model 742 Woodmaster (improved version of Model 740) (several variations), .243 Win., .280 Rem., .30–06, .308 Win., 6mm Rem.	150	300	400
Model Four (several variations), .243 Win., 6mm Rem., .270 Win., 7mm Express (.280) Rem., .308 Win., .30–06, later Calibers added, 22″ Barrels, Monte Carlo Stocks	$150	$350	$450
Model 7400 (several variations); current product, .243 Win., 6mm Rem., .270 Win., 7mm Express (.280) Rem., .308 Win., .30–06, later Calibers added, 22″ Barrels, Monte Carlo Stocks	150	350	425
Sportsman Model 74; current product (based on Model 7400 Action), .30–06, 22″ Barrel, 4-shot Box Magazine	150	350	425
Model 16 in Grades 16A Standard, 16C Special, 16D Peerless, and 16F Premier, .22 Rimfire, Takedown, 15 Shots, with Magazine in Butt	100	250	300
16F Premier	1000	2500	3250
Model 24 Autoloading Rifle, .22 Short Rimfire, Magazine in Stock, 19″ Barrel; later 21″ and joined by .22 Long, and variety of Grades	100	250	325
Model 241 Speedmaster (improved version of Model 24) (several variations, including Gallery Types), .22 Short, Long, and Long Rifle, 24″ Barrel, Tubular Magazine	125	250	325
Routledge-Bored Barrel variation (Smoothbore), .22 Long Rifle	400	800	1000
Model 550 Autoloading Rifle (several variations; replacement of the Model 241), .22 Short, Long, Long Rifle, 24″ Barrel, Tubular Magazine	100	200	300
Model 552 Speedmaster (several variations; replacement of Model 550), .22 Short, Long, Long Rifle, Tubular Magazine	75	175	225
Nylon 66 Rifle (several variations), .22 Long Rifle, 19$\frac{9}{10}$″ Barrel, Tubular Magazine, Nylon Stock	50	125	175
Nylon 77 Rifle (several variations), .22 Long Rifle, 5-shot Box Magazine (10-shot optional)	50	125	175
Model 522 Viper Rifle, .22 Long Rifle, Box Magazine, 20″ Barrel, Synthetic Stock and Receiver	50	125	175
Model 597 Rifle (several variations), .22 Long Rifle, Box Magazine, Laminated Wood or Synthetic Stock	50	125	175
Model 597 Magnum, as above, but Chambered for .22 Magnum, with Heavier Bolt	50	125	175

PUMP ACTION SHOTGUNS

	Fair	V. Good	Excellent
Model 1908, Listed in Grades from No. 1 on up to No. 6, along with No. 0 Riot Grade (Premium for Higher Grades), 12 Gauge	100	250	325

	Fair	*V. Good*	*Excellent*
Model 1908 Repeating Shotgun, Premium as Grades develop in quality, F Premier	$500	$1750	$2250
Model 10 Pump-Action listed in Grades from 10A Standard up to 10F Premier later joined by 10T Target with Ventilated Rib, 10TD Tournament, 10TE Expert, and 10TF Premier (Premium for Higher Grades)	125	300	450
Model 10 Trench, 12 Gauge, 23″ Barrel	200	400	500
Model 10R Trench, 12 Gauge, 20″ Barrel	200	400	500
Model 17 in Grades 17A Standard, 17B Special, 17D Tournament, 17E Expert, 17F Premier, and 17R Riot (Premium for Higher Grades), 20 Gauge, Hammerless, Takedown, 2½″ and 2″ Shells	125	350	450
Model 29 (replacement of the Model 10), in Grades from 29A Standard to 29F Premier, as well as 29T Target, 29TD Tournament, 2TE Expert, and 29TF Premier. Also in 29R Riot (Premium for Higher Grades), 12 Gauge, Hammerless, with Tubular Magazine	200	300	450
Model 31 (replacement for Model 17 and 29) made in thirty-five variations, from 31A Standard to the Highest, 31T-F Target Premier, 12 Gauge, later in 20 and 16, Side Ejection	300	450	700
New Improved Standard Weight Model 31, 12, 16, 20 Gauge	300	450	700
New Improved Lightweight Aluminum Receivers, a variety of Model 31 Guns built with Aluminum Alloy Frames, Long-Range Guns, variations of the Model 31 for Longer Range of Shooting	200	400	550
Model 870 Wingmaster (numerous variations; Premium for Higher Grades), 12, 16, 20, 28, 410, 5-shot Magazine, numerous Barrel Length options, Stock Types, Sights, etc.	100	200	300
Sportsman, 12 Gauge, 28″ and 30″ Barrel, 5-shot Magazine	100	200	350

PUMP ACTION RIFLES

	Fair	*V. Good*	*Excellent*
.22 Rimfire Calibers, Model 12 (several variations, including 12A, 12B Gallery Special, 12CS, 12C NRA Target, 12DS, 12ES, 12FS, 12D Peerless, and 12F Premier) (Premium for Higher Grades), .22 Rimfire, 14 .22 Short, 11 .22 Long, 10 .22 Long Rifle, soon thereafter changed to 15, 12, and 11, respectively; .22 Remington Special added later	100	400	500
12F Premier	1000	2500	2750
Model 121 Fieldmaster (improved version of Model 12, with several variations, including Routledge-bored Smooth bore) (Premium for Higher Grades), .22 Short, Long, Long Rifle; increased Magazine Capacity over Model 12, 24″ Barrel	$200	$400	$600
Model 572 Fieldmaster (improved version of Model 121, including a Smooth bore variation), .22 Short, Long, Long Rifle, Tubular Magazine, 23″ Barrels	100	200	300

PUMP ACTION RIFLES, CENTERFIRE CARTRIDGES

	Fair	*V. Good*	*Excellent*
Model 14 in various Grades from 14A Standard to 14F Premier, .25, .30, .32, and .35 Remington, in Grades of 14A, 14C Special, 1	200	400	600
14F Premier	1200	3500	4500
14 ½ Sporting Rifle, in 14½A Standard Grade and 14½R Carbine.	200	400	600
14½ Carbine, .38–40, .44–50, Barrel Lengths of 18½″ to 22½″	300	800	1000
Model 25 in various Grades from 25A Standard to Model 25F Premier, .25–20, .32–20, 24″ Barrel, 10-shot Tubular Magazine; Takedown	300	500	700
25R Carbine, .25–20, .32–20, 6 Shots, 18″ Barrel	400	700	1100
Model 141 Gamemaster Rifle (improved version of Model 14) (variations from 141A Standard to 141F Premier) (Premium for Higher Grades), .30, .32, and .35 Remington, 24″ Barrel	200	350	450
As above, Carbine Variation, 18½″ Barrel	300	600	800
Model 760 Gamemaster (succeeded Model 141; numerous variations; Premium for Higher Grades), .30–06, .300 Savage, .35 Remington, .270, .257 Roberts, 222 Rem, .223 Rem., .243, .244 Rem., .280 Rem., .308, 6mm Rem., 22″ Barrel, 4-shot Box Magazine	125	300	400
Model 760 Gamemaster Carbine, as above, but with 18½″ Barrel, did not include all Calibers of above	125	300	400
Model Six (improved version of Model 742/760) (several variations), .243 Win., 6mm Rem., .270 Win., .308 Win., 22″ Barrels, Synthetic Stock a later option	150	350	450
Model 7600 (Improved version of Model 742/760) (several variations), .243 Win., 6mm Rem., .270 Win., .308 Win., .280 Rem., .35 Whelen, 22″ Barrels, Synthetic Stock a later option	150	350	450
Sportsman Model 76 (based on Model 7600 Action), .30–06, 22″ Barrel, 4-shot Box Magazine, Wood Stock.	125	300	400

REPUBLIC

Spain, unknown maker.

HANDGUN, SELF-LOADING

	Fair	V. Good	Excellent
.32 ACP, Clip Fed, Long Grip, *Modern*	$75	$125	$175

RETRIEVER

Made by Thomas Ryan, Norwich, Conn., 1870–1876.

HANDGUN, REVOLVER

	Fair	V. Good	Excellent
.32 Short R.F., 5 Shot, Spur Trigger, Solid Frame, Single Action, *Antique*	75	150	200

REV-O-NOC

Made by Crescent for Hibbard-Spencer-Bartlett Co., Chicago. See Crescent Fire Arms Co., Shotgun, Double Barrel, Side-by-Side; Shotgun, Singleshot.

REVELATION

Trade name used by Western Auto.

RIFLE, BOLT ACTION

	Fair	V. Good	Excellent
Model 107, .22 WMR, Clip Fed, *Modern*	25	50	75
Model 210B, 7mm Rem. Mag., Checkered Stock, Monte Carlo Stock, *Modern*	75	150	175
Model 220A, .308 Win., Checkered Stock, Monte Carlo Stock, *Modern*	75	150	175
Model 220AD, .308 Win., Checkered Stock, Monte Carlo Stock, Fancy Wood, *Modern*	100	175	200
Model 220B, .243 Win., Checkered Stock, Monte Carlo Stock, *Modern*	75	150	175
Model 220BD, .243 Win., Checkered Stock, Monte Carlo Stock, Fancy Wood, *Modern*	75	150	200
Model 220C, .22-250, Checkered Stock, Monte Carlo Stock, *Modern*	75	150	175
Model 220CD, .22-250, Checkered Stock, Monte Carlo Stock, Fancy Wood, *Modern*	75	150	200

RIFLE, LEVER ACTION

	Fair	V. Good	Excellent
Model 117, .22 L.R.R.F., Tube Feed, *Modern*	25	50	75

RIFLE, SELF-LOADING

	Fair	V. Good	Excellent
Model 125, .22 L.R.R.F., Clip Fed, *Modern*	15	25	50

RIFLE, SINGLESHOT

	Fair	V. Good	Excellent
Model 100, .22 L.R.R.F, *Modern*	15	25	50

SHOTGUN, BOLT ACTION

	Fair	V. Good	Excellent
Model 312B, 12 Ga., Clip Fed, *Modern*	$15	$25	$50
Model 312BK, 12 Ga., Clip Fed, Adjustable Choke, *Modern*	25	50	75
Model 316B, 16 Ga., Clip Fed, *Modern*	15	25	50
Model 316BK, 16 Ga., Clip Fed, Adjustable Choke, *Modern*	15	25	50
Model 325B, 20 Ga., Clip Fed, *Modern*	15	25	50
Model 325BK, 20 Ga., Clip Fed, Adjustable Choke, *Modern*	15	25	50
Model 330, .410 Ga., Clip Fed, *Modern*	15	25	50

SHOTGUN, SLIDE ACTION

	Fair	V. Good	Excellent
Model 310, Various Gauges, Plain Barrel, Takedown, *Modern*	75	125	150
Model 310R, Various Gauges, Vent Rib, Takedown, *Modern*	75	125	150

REYNOLDS, PLANT & HOTCHKISS

Also see Plant's Mfg. Co.

HANDGUN, REVOLVER

	Fair	V. Good	Excellent
.25 Short R.F., 5 Shot, Single Action, Spur Trigger, 3" Barrel, *Antique*	75	150	225

R.G. INDUSTRIES

R.G. tradename belongs to Rohm GmbH, Sontheim/Brenz, West Germany, and after 1968 also made in Miami, Fla., for American consumption. Operations ceased in 1986.

HANDGUN, DOUBLE BARREL, OVER-UNDER

	Fair	V. Good	Excellent
RG-16, .22 WMR, 2 Shot, Derringer, *Modern*	25	50	75
RG-17, .38 Special, 2 Shot, Derringer, *Modern*	50	75	100

HANDGUN, REVOLVER

	Fair	V. Good	Excellent
Partner RG-40P, .38 Special, 6 Shot, Double Action, Swing-Out Cylinder, *Modern*	50	75	100
RG-14, .22 L.R.R.F., 6 Shot, Double Action, *Modern*	50	75	100
RG-23, .22 L.R.R.F., 6 Shot, Double Action, *Modern*	25	50	75
RG-30, .22 L.R.R.F., 6 Shot, Double Action, Swing-Out Cylinder, *Modern*	25	50	75
RG-30, .22 LR/.22 WMR Combo, 6 Shot, Double Action, Swing-Out Cylinder, *Modern*	50	75	100
RG-30, .22 WMR, 6 Shot, Double Action, Swing-Out Cylinder, *Modern*	25	50	75
RG-40, *Modern*	50	75	100

	Fair	V. Good	Excellent
RG-57, .357 Magnum, 6 Shot, Double Action, Swing-Out Cylinder, *Modern*	$50	$100	$150
RG-57, .44 Magnum, 6 Shot, Double Action, Swing-Out Cylinder, *Modern*	75	125	175
RG-63, .22 L.R.R.F., 6 Shot, Double Action, Western Style, *Modern*	15	25	50
RG-63, .22 LR/.22 WMR Combo, 6 Shot, Single Action, Western Style, *Modern*	25	50	75
RG-66T, .22 LR/.22 WMR Combo, 6 Shot, Single Action, Western Style, Adjustable Sights, *Modern*	25	50	75
RG-74, .22 L.R.R.F., 6 Shot, Double Action, Swing-Out Cylinder, *Modern*	25	50	75
RG-88, .357 Magnum, 6 Shot, Double Action, Swing-Out Cylinder, *Modern*	50	75	125

HANDGUN, SELF-LOADING

RG-25, .25 ACP, *Modern*	25	50	75
RG-26, .25 ACP, *Modern*	25	50	75

RHEINMETALL

Rheinsche Metallwaren u. Maschinenfabrik, Sommerada, Germany, 1922–1927.

HANDGUN, SELF-LOADING

7.65mm, Clip Fed, Blue, *Curio*	100	250	350

Rheinmetall

RICHARDS, JOHN

London & Birmingham, England, 1745–1810.

SHOTGUN, FLINTLOCK

Blunderbuss, Half-Octagon, Steel Barrel, Folding Bayonet, *Antique*	400	900	1250

RICHARDS, W.

Belgium, c. 1900.

RICHARDS, WESTLEY. See Westley, Richards.

SHOTGUN, DOUBLE BARREL, SIDE-BY-SIDE

	Fair	V. Good	Excellent
Various Gauges, Hammerless, Damascus Barrel, *Modern*	75	150	200
Various Gauges, Hammerless, Steel Barrel, *Modern*	$75	$150	$200
Various Gauges, Outside Hammers, Damascus Barrel, *Modern*	75	150	200
Various Gauges, Outside Hammers, Steel Barrel, *Modern*	75	150	200

SHOTGUN, SINGLESHOT

Various Gauges, Hammer, Steel Barrel, *Modern*	25	50	100

RICHARDSON INDUSTRIES

New Haven, Conn.

SHOTGUN, SINGLESHOT

Model R-5, 12 Ga., 24" Barrel, *Modern*	15	25	50

RICHLAND ARMS CO.

Importer. Bussfield, Mich.

RIFLE, PERCUSSION

Wesson Rifle, .50, Set Triggers, Target Sights, Reproduction, *Antique*	100	200	300

SHOTGUN, DOUBLE BARREL, OVER-UNDER

Model 808, 12 Ga., Single Trigger, Checkered Stock, Vent Rib, *Modern*	150	375	450
Model 810, 10 Ga. $3^{1}/_{2}$", Double Trigger, Checkered Stock, Vent Rib, *Modern*	200	450	550
Model 828, 28 Ga., Single Trigger, Checkered Stock, *Modern*	200	400	500
Model 844, 12 Ga., Single Trigger, Checkered Stock, *Modern*	125	275	375

SHOTGUN, DOUBLE BARREL, SIDE-BY-SIDE

Model 200, Various Gauges, Double Trigger, Checkered Stock, *Modern*	125	275	350
Model 202, Various Gauges, Double Trigger, Extra Shotgun Barrel, *Modern*	125	250	325
Model 707 Deluxe, 12 and 20 Gauges, Double Trigger, *Modern*	125	275	350
Model 707 Deluxe, 12 and 20 Gauges, Double Trigger, Checkered Stock, Extra Shotgun Barrel, *Modern*	150	300	400
Model 711, 10 Ga. $3^{1}/_{2}$", Double Trigger, *Modern*	125	275	375
Model 711, 12 Ga. Mag. 3", Double Trigger, *Modern*	150	300	400

RICHTER, CHARLES

Made by Crescent for New York Sporting Goods Co., c., 1900. See also Crescent Fire Arms Co., Shotgun, Double Barrel, Side-by-Side; Shotgun, Singleshot.

RICKARD ARMS

Made by Crescent for J. A. Rickard Co., Schenectady, N.Y. See Crescent Fire Arms Co., Shotgun, Double Barrel, Side-by-Side; Shotgun, Singleshot.

RIGARMI

Industria Galesi, Brescia, Italy.

HANDGUN, SELF-LOADING

	Fair	V. Good	Excellent
Militar, .22 L.R.R.F., Clip Fed, Hammer, Double Action, *Modern*	$75	$150	$200
Pocket, 7.65mm, Clip Fed, Hammer, Double Action, *Modern*	75	125	175
RG-217, .22 Long R.F., Clip Fed, *Modern*	50	75	100
RG-218, .22 L.R.R.F., Clip Fed, *Modern*	50	100	125
RG-219, 6.35mm, Clip Fed, *Modern*	50	75	100

RIGBY, JOHN & CO.

Dublin, Ireland, and London, England, from 1765–1998. Sold and relocated to 1317 Spring Street, Paso Robles, California 93446.

Founded in 1765 in Dublin, with a branch opened up in London in 1865 (the Dublin operation closed down some years thereafter), the history of J. Rigby & Co. placed it securely within the traditions of Britain's best-quality gun trade, with its specialty primarily rifles for big-game hunting, but also supplying side-by-side game guns of its own make and by Spanish manufacturers. In 1983 the firm was purchased by J. Roberts & Son. Owner and Managing Director Paul Roberts is one of the most knowledgeable contemporary shooters in the U.K., having extensive experience not only as a gunmaker and keen enthusiast of antique arms, but as a sportsman—with several African safaris, numerous bird shoots, and deer stalking adventures to his credit.

RIFLE, BOLT ACTION

	Fair	V. Good	Excellent
.275 Rigby, Sporting Rifle, Express Sights, Checkered Stock, *Modern*	3500	6500	9500
.275 Rigby, Sporting Rifle, Lightweight, Express Sights, Checkered Stock, *Modern*	4000	7000	10000
.350 Rigby, Sporting Rifle, Express Sights, Checkered Stock, *Modern*	4000	8500	12500
Big Game, .416 Rigby, Sporting Rifle, Express Sights, Checkered Stock, *Modern*	5000	12000	17500

RIFLE, DOUBLE BARREL, SIDE-BY-SIDE

	Fair	V. Good	Excellent
Best Grade, Various Calibers, Sidelock, Double Trigger, Express Sights, Fancy Engraving, Fancy Checkering, *Modern*	12000	27000	45000
Second Grade, Various Calibers, Box Lock, Double Trigger, Express Sights, Fancy Engraving, Fancy Checkering, *Modern*	3000	9000	17500
Third Grade, Various Calibers, Box Lock, Double Trigger, Express Sights, Engraved, Fancy Checkering, *Modern*	$2700	$6000	$10000

SHOTGUN, DOUBLE BARREL, SIDE-BY-SIDE

	Fair	V. Good	Excellent
Chatsworth, Various Gauges, Box Lock, Automatic Ejector, Double Trigger, Fancy Engraving, Fancy Checkering, *Modern*	1400	3000	4000
Regal, Various Gauges, Sidelock, Automatic Ejector, Double Trigger, Fancy Engraving, Fancy Checkering, *Modern*	4000	10000	14500
Sackville, Various Gauges, Box Lock, Automatic Ejector, Double Trigger, Fancy Engraving, Fancy Checkering, *Modern*	2500	4000	6500
Sandringham, Various Gauges, Sidelock, Automatic Ejector, Double Trigger, Fancy Engraving, Fancy Checkering, *Modern*	3500	7500	9500

28 ga. Add 15%
410 ga. Add 20%

RINO GALESI

Industria Galesi, Brescia, Italy.

HANDGUN, SELF-LOADING

	Fair	V. Good	Excellent
Model 9, 6.35mm, Clip Fed, Blue, *Modern*	75	100	125

RIOT

Made by Stevens Arms.

SHOTGUN, PUMP

	Fair	V. Good	Excellent
Model 520, 12 Ga., Takedown, *Modern*	75	125	150
Model 620, Various Gauges, Takedown, *Modern*	75	150	175

RIPOLI

HANDGUN, MIQUELET-LOCK

	Fair	V. Good	Excellent
Ball Butt, Brass Inlay, Light Ornamentation, *Antique*	1000	2500	3250
Pair, Fluted Barrel, Pocket Pistol, Engraved, Silver Furniture, *Antique*	3000	7000	9500

RITTER, JACOB

Philadelphia, Pa., 1775–1783. See Kentucky Rifles and Pistols.

RIVERSIDE ARMS CO.

Made by Stevens Arms & Tool Co.

	Fair	V. Good	Excellent

SHOTGUN, DOUBLE BARREL, SIDE-BY-SIDE

	Fair	V. Good	Excellent
Model 215, 12 and 16 Gauges, Outside Hammers, Steel Barrel, *Modern*	$85	$175	$250

ROB ROY

Made by Hood Firearms, Norwich, Conn., c. 1880.

HANDGUN, REVOLVER

	Fair	V. Good	Excellent
.22 Short R.F., 7 Shot, Spur Trigger, Solid Frame, Single Action, *Antique*	75	150	200

ROBBINS & LAWRENCE

Robbins, Kendall & Lawrence, Windsor, Vt., 1844–1857. Became Robbins & Lawrence about 1846. Also see Sharps, U.S. Military.

HANDGUN, PERCUSSION

	Fair	V. Good	Excellent
Pepperbox, Various Calibers, Ring Trigger, *Antique*	400	850	1150

ROBIN HOOD

Made by Hood Firearms, Norwich, Conn., c. 1875.

HANDGUN, REVOLVER

	Fair	V. Good	Excellent
.22 Short R.F., 7 Shot, Spur Trigger, Solid Frame, Single Action, *Antique*	75	125	150
.32 Short R.F., 5 Shot, Spur Trigger, Solid Frame, Single Action, *Antique*	75	150	175

ROESSER, PETER

Lancaster, Pa., 1741–1782. See Kentucky Rifles and Pistols.

ROGERS & SPENCER

Willowvale, N.Y., c. 1862.

HANDGUN, PERCUSSION

	Fair	V. Good	Excellent
.44 Army, Single Action, *Antique*	900	2000	2750

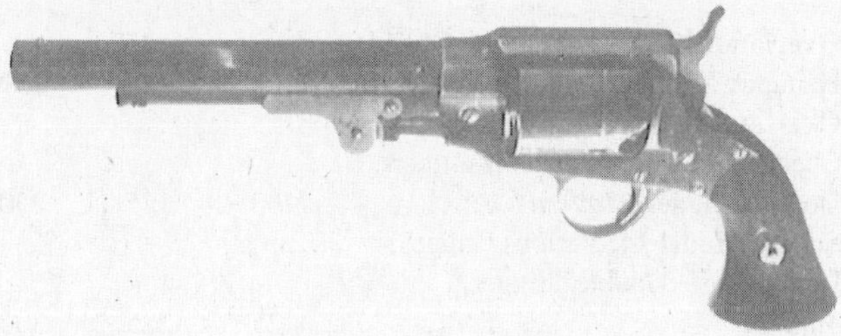

Rogers & Spencer

ROLAND

Francisco Arizmendi, Eibar, Spain, c. 1922.

HANDGUN, SELF-LOADING

	Fair	V. Good	Excellent
6.35mm, Clip Fed, Blue, *Curio*	$50	$100	$150
7.65mm, Clip Fed, Blue, *Curio*	75	125	175

ROME REVOLVER AND NOVELTY WORKS

Rome, N.Y., c. 1880.

HANDGUN, REVOLVER

	Fair	V. Good	Excellent
.32 Short R.F., 5 Shot, Spur Trigger, Solid Frame, Single Action, *Antique*	75	125	150

ROMER

Romerwerke AG, Suhl, Germany, 1924–1926.

HANDGUN, SELF-LOADING

	Fair	V. Good	Excellent
.22 L.R.R.F., Clip Fed, $2\frac{1}{2}$" and $6\frac{1}{2}$" Barrels, Blue, *Curio*	300	600	800
.22 L.R.R.F., Clip Fed, One Barrel, Blue, *Curio*	250	550	750

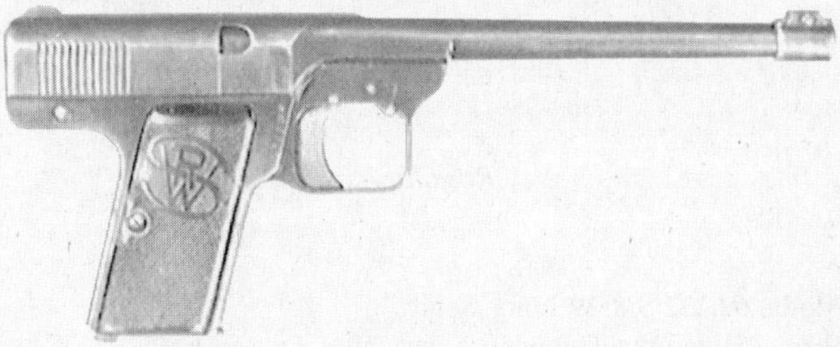

Romer

ROOP, JOHN

Allentown, Pa., c. 1775. See Kentucky Rifles.

ROSS RIFLE CO.

Quebec, Canada. Also see Canadian Military. 1896–1915.

RIFLE, BOLT ACTION

	Fair	V. Good	Excellent
Canadian Issue, .303 British, Military, *Modern*	150	300	400
Model 1903 MK I, .303 British, Sporting Rifle, Open Rear Sight, *Modern*	150	350	450
Model 1905 MK II, Various Calibers, Open Rear Sight, *Modern*	125	250	350
Model 1910 MK III, Various Calibers, Open Rear Sight, Checkered Stock, *Modern*	150	275	375

ROSSI

Amadeo Rossi S.A., Sao Leopoldo, Brazil. Also see Garrucha.

HANDGUN, REVOLVER

	Fair	V. Good	Excellent
Model 31, .38 Special, Solid Frame, Swing-Out Cylinder, 5 Shot, 4" Barrel, *Modern*	$50	$75	$100
Model 51, .22 L.R.R.F., Solid Frame, Swing-Out Cylinder, Adjustable Sights, 5 Shot, 6" Barrel, *Modern*	50	75	100
Model 68, .38 Special, Solid Frame, Swing-Out Cylinder, Adjustable Sights, 5 Shot, 3" Barrel, *Modern*	75	100	125
Model 68/2, .38 Special, Solid Frame, Swing-Out Cylinder, Adjustable Sights, 5 Shot, 2" Barrel, *Modern*	75	125	150

Rossi 68/2

	Fair	V. Good	Excellent
Model 69, .32 S & W Long, Solid Frame, Swing-Out Cylinder, Adjustable Sights, 5 Shot, 3" Barrel, *Modern*	50	75	100
Model 70, .22 Short R.F., Solid Frame, Swing-Out Cylinder, Adjustable Sights, 5 Shot, 3" Barrel, *Modern*	50	75	100
Model 88, .38 Special, Solid Frame, Swing-Out Cylinder, Adjustable Sights, Stainless Steel, 5 Shot, 3" Barrel, *Modern*	75	125	150
Model 89, The Stainless Lady, .38 Special, Stainless, 3" Barrel, *Modern*	75	150	175
Model 94, .38 Special, Medium Frame, Shrouded Ejector Rod, *Modern*	75	100	125

Rossi 94

HANDGUN, SINGLESHOT

	Fair	V. Good	Excellent
.22 Short R.F., Derringer, *Modern*	$15	$25	$50

RIFLE, SLIDE ACTION

	Fair	V. Good	Excellent
Gallery, .22 L.R.R.F., Tube Feed, Takedown, Hammer, *Modern*	50	100	125

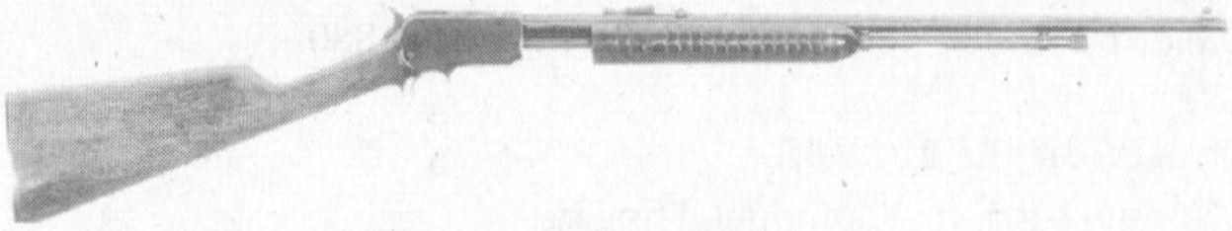

Rossi Gallery Rifle

	Fair	V. Good	Excellent
Gallery, .22 L.R.R.F., Tube Feed, Takedown, Hammer, Octagon Barrel, *Modern*	75	125	150
Saddle Ring, .357 Mag., Tube Feed, Hammer, Carbine, *Modern*	75	125	175
Saddle Ring, .357 Mag., Tube Feed, Hammer, Carbine, Nickel, *Modern*	75	150	225

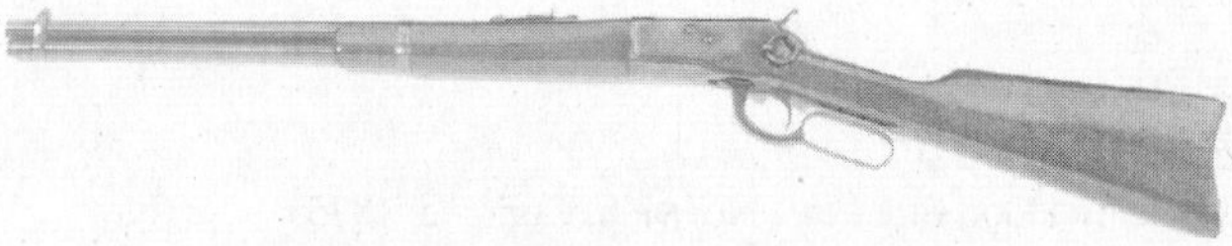

Rossi Saddle Ring Carbine Rifle

SHOTGUN, DOUBLE BARREL, SIDE-BY-SIDE

	Fair	V. Good	Excellent
12 Ga. Mag. 3", Checkered Stock, Hammerless, Double Trigger, *Modern*	125	175	225
12 Ga. Mag. 3", Hammerless, Double Trigger, *Modern*	125	175	225
Overland, 12 and 20 Gauges, Checkered Stock, Outside Hammers, Double Trigger, *Modern*	100	200	250

Rossi Overland Shotgun

	Fair	V. Good	Excellent
Overland, 12 and 20 Gauges, Outside Hammers, Double Trigger, *Modern*	100	175	250
Overland II, Various Gauges, Checkered Stock, Outside Hammers, Double Trigger, *Modern*	100	175	250
Squire Model 14, Various Gauges, Hammerless, Double Trigger, *Modern*	125	225	300

ROTTWEIL

Germany, Imported by Eastern Sports, Milford, N.H.

	Fair	V. Good	Excellent

RIFLE, DOUBLE BARREL, OVER-UNDER

	Fair	V. Good	Excellent
Standard Grade, Various Calibers, Engraved, Fancy Checkering, Open Rear Sight, *Modern*	$900	$2000	$2650

SHOTGUN, DOUBLE BARREL, OVER-UNDER

	Fair	V. Good	Excellent
American, 12 Ga., Trap Grade, Single Selective Trigger, Automatic Ejector, Vent Rib, Engraved, *Modern*	800	1800	2250
Montreal, 12 Ga., Trap Grade, Vent Rib, Single Selective Trigger, Checkered Stock, *Modern*	650	1350	1750
Olympia, 12 Ga., Skeet Grade, Single Selective Trigger, Automatic Ejector, Vent Rib, Engraved, *Modern*	700	1500	1950
Olympia, 12 Ga., Trap Grade, Single Selective Trigger, Automatic Ejector, Vent Rib, Engraved, *Modern*	700	1500	1950
Olympia 72, 12 Ga., Skeet Grade, Trap Grade, Single Selective Trigger, Checkered Stock, *Modern*	700	1450	1800
Supreme, 12 Ga., Field Grade, Single Selective Trigger, Automatic Ejector, Vent Rib, Engraved, *Modern*	700	1500	1950
Supreme, 12 Ga., Vent Rib, Single Selective Trigger, Checkered Stock, *Modern*	600	1200	1550

ROVIRO, ANTONIO

Iqualada, Spain, c. 1790.

HANDGUN, MIQUELET-LOCK

	Fair	V. Good	Excellent
Pair, Belt Pistol, Belt Hook, Engraved, Light Ornamentation, *Antique*	2200	4500	6750

ROYAL

M. Zulaika y Cia., Eibar, Spain.

HANDGUN, SELF-LOADING

	Fair	V. Good	Excellent
12 Shot, 7.65mm, Clip Fed, Long Grip, *Modern*	75	175	225
7.65mm, Clip Fed, Long Grip, *Modern*	$50	$125	$175
Mauser M1896 Type, 7.63mm, Blue, *Modern*	125	325	400
Novelty, 6.35mm, Clip Fed, Blue, *Curio*	50	100	150
Novelty, 7.65mm, Clip Fed, Blue, *Curio*	75	125	175

Royal 12 Shot

ROYAL

Possibly Hopkins & Allen, c. 1880.

HANDGUN, REVOLVER

	Fair	V. Good	Excellent
.22 Short R.F., 7 Shot, Spur Trigger, Solid Frame, Single Action, *Antique*	75	150	200
.32 Short R.F., 5 Shot, Spur Trigger, Solid Frame, Single Action, *Antique*	75	150	200

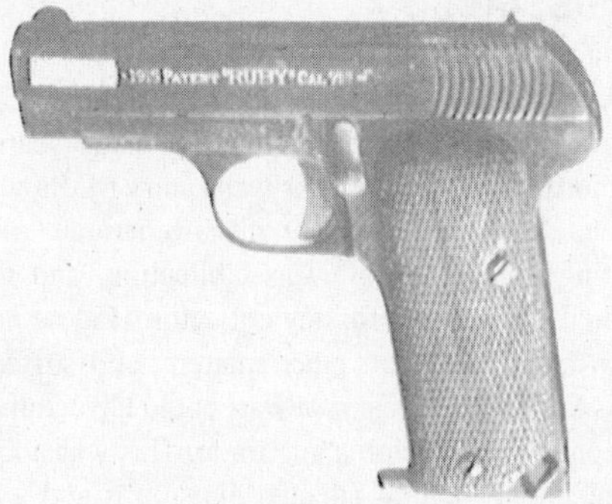

Ruby .32

RUBY

Gabilondo y Cia., Vitoria, Spain.

HANDGUN, REVOLVER

Ruby Extra, For Chrome Plating Add $35.00-$75.00

Ruby Extra, For Engraving Add $60.00-$100.00

	Fair	V. Good	Excellent
Ruby Extra Model 12, .38 Spec., Double Action, Blue, Swing-Out Cylinder, *Curio*	25	50	75
Ruby Extra Model 14, .22 L.R.R.F., Double Action, Blue, Swing-Out Cylinder, *Curio*	25	50	75
Ruby Extra Model 14, .32 S & W Long, Double Action, Blue, Swing-Out Cylinder, *Curio*	25	50	75

HANDGUN, SELF-LOADING

	Fair	V. Good	Excellent
7.35mm, Clip Fed, Blue, *Curio*	75	150	200

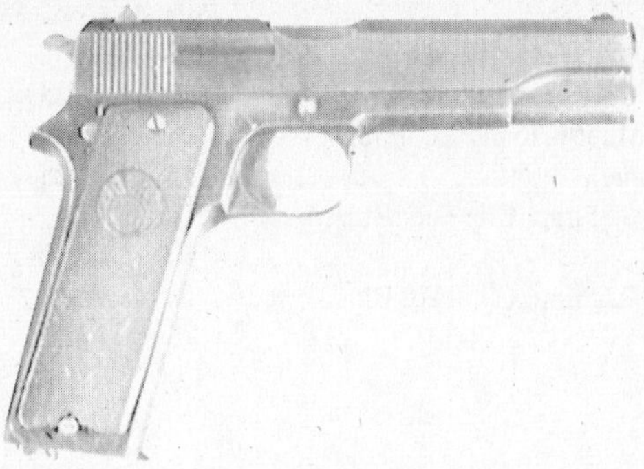

Ruby .45

Jacob Rupertus Patent Navy Six Shot, .36 Caliber

RUMMEL

Made by Crescent for A.J. Rummel Arms Co., Toledo, Ohio. See Crescent Fire Arms Co., Shotgun, Double Barrel, Side-by-Side; Shotgun, Singleshot.

RUPERTUS, JACOB

Philadelphia, Pa., 1858–1899. The gunmakers of Philadelphia included several luminaries, among them Sharps, E. K. Tryon, Henry Derringer, and Jacob Rupertus. For many years one of the leading authorities on antique arms was Henry M. Stewart, Jr., resident of Philadelphia, and truly one of the venerable "old timers" of gun collecting. Seeing the Stewart Collection, and visiting with this individual, was a treat for any collector. Had he not been preoccupied with business and other matters, and suffered from ill health in his later years, Henry Stewart could have authored a landmark book on the Philadelphia gun trade. This was a thriving arms making center with several talented gunsmiths and a few leading gun dealers—among them J. C. Grubb & Co., one of the foremost Colt jobbers, and the likely company involved in the manufacture of the unique Colt Van Syckel Dragoons—one of the most exquisite sets of Colt firearms ever made. Rupertus happened to be one of the local gunmakers represented rather substantially in the Stewart collection. Particularly in European arms, and some of the rare American pieces, the bulk of the material remains intact, at VMI, arrangements for the bequest of the collection having been made by Stewart prior to his death in 1988.

	Fair	*V. Good*	*Excellent*
HANDGUN, DOUBLE BARREL, SIDE-BY-SIDE			
.22 Short R.F., Derringer, Side-Swing Barrel, Iron Frame, Spur Trigger, *Antique*	$325	$800	$1150
HANDGUN, REVOLVER			
.22 Short R.F., 5 Shot, Spur Trigger, Solid Frame, Single Action, *Antique*	150	275	400
.22 Short R.F., Pepperbox, 8 Shot, Iron Frame, Spur Trigger, *Antique*	200	500	750
.25 Short R.F., 6 Shot, Spur Trigger, Solid Frame, Single Action, *Antique*	1400	3000	3750
.36 Patent Navy, Percussion, 6 Shot, *Antique*	2700	6000	8500
.44 Patent Army, 6 Shot, Solid Frame, Single Action, *Antique*	$2700	$6000	$8500
HANDGUN, SINGLESHOT			
.22 Short R.F., Derringer, Side-Swing Barrel, Iron Frame, Spur Trigger, *Antique*	125	250	325
.32 Short R.F., Derringer, Side-Swing Barrel, Iron Frame, Spur Trigger, *Antique*	100	200	300
.38 Short R.F., Derringer, Side-Swing Barrel, Iron Frame, Spur Trigger, *Antique*	100	225	325
.41 Short R.F., 5 Shot, Spur Trigger, Solid Frame, Single Action, *Antique*	150	350	450

RUPP, HERMAN

Pa., 1784. See Kentucky Rifles.

RUPP, JOHN

Allentown, Pa. See U.S. Military, Kentucky Rifles and Pistols.

RUPPERT, WILLIAM

Lancaster. Pa., c. 1776. See U.S. Military, Kentucky Rifles and Pistols.

RUSH, JOHN

Philadelphia, Pa., 1740–1750. See Kentucky Rifles and Pistols.

RUSSIAN MILITARY

Czarist and Communist plants include: Tula, Izshevsky, and many others. Foreign manufacturers for Czarist Russia include: SIG Neuhasen, Switzerland; St. Etienne, France; and Remington Arms Co., Winchester Repeating Arms Co., Colt's Pt. F. A. Mfg. Co., and Smith & Wesson in the United States. Foreign manufacturers for Moisin-Nagant only. Tokarev and SKS Communist Russia produced. With the collapse of the Soviet regime, tremendous changes are now taking place in Russia, as discussed in "The Year in Review" section from the first edition. Mikhail Kalashnikov, renowned inventor of the AK-47 military rifle (estimated total production to date, in excess of 35 million), has visited the United

States, once under the aegis of William B. Ruger (1992). At the NRA Show, Salt Lake City, a gala cocktail party was thrown by Sturm, Ruger & Co. at which both William B. Ruger and Mikhail Kalashnikov exchanged greetings and presents—a sure sign that the Cold War is a thing of the past. The study of Russian military arms received an impressive boost in scholarship with the publication of *Guns for the Tsar: American Technology and the Small Arms Industry in Nineteenth-Century Russia*, authored by Joseph Bradley. Although dealing with the Czarist era of the 19th and early 20th centuries, the impact of Samuel Colt, his products, and his machinery, as well as other gunmakers on Russian industry provides a fascinating area of interest. While visiting Russia in 1993 and 1995, the author was shown vast quantities of military small arms, cannon, and just about everything in between. The most comprehensive collection in this genre was at the Artillery Museum, St. Petersburg, although quite a bit of the collection was in storage and thus not available for public view. Unfortunately, in an attempt to deactivate numerous firearms, the Soviets, in their infinite wisdom, had required the museum to bore holes in the barrels and/or chambers of many cartridge firearms! Such vandalism, one would hope, is now strictly a deed of the past.

	Fair	*V. Good*	*Excellent*
HANDGUN, FREE PISTOL			
MC, .22 L.R.R.F., Clip Fed, *Modern*	$100	$200	$275
MCU, .22 Short, Clip Fed, *Modern*	100	225	325
Vostok M-TOZ-35, .22 L.R.R.F., *Modern*	250	500	650
Vostok M-TOZ-35, .22 L.R.R.F., Cased with Accessories, *Modern*	300	775	950

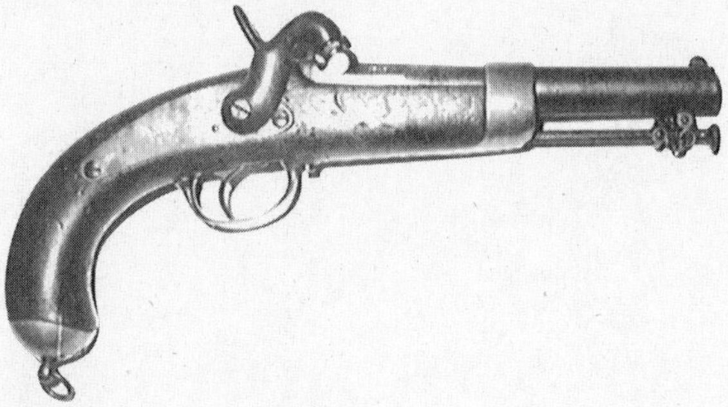

Russian Military Handgun..... Percussion	150	300	450

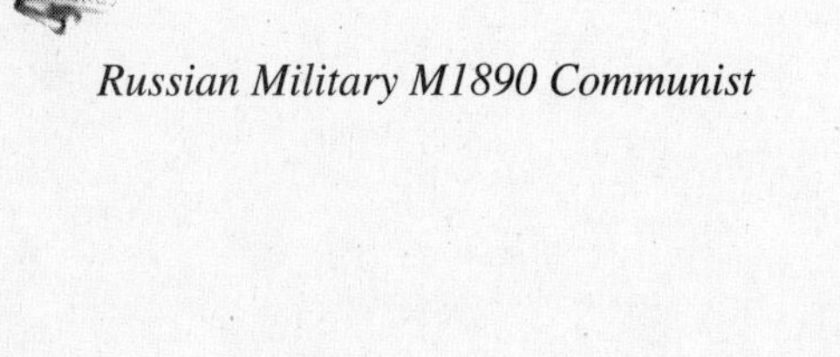

Russian Military M1890 Communist

	Fair	*V. Good*	*Excellent*
HANDGUN, REVOLVER			
M1890, 7.62mm Nagant, Gas-Seal Cylinder, Communist, *Curio*	$100	$175	$275
M1890, 7.62mm Nagant, Gas-Seal Cylinder, Imperial, *Curio*	100	200	300
M1890, 7.62mm Nagant, Gas-Seal Cylinder, Police, *Curio*	100	175	325
HANDGUN, SELF-LOADING			
Makarov, 9mm Makarov, Clip Fed, Double Action, *Modern*	300	750	1000

Russian Military Makarov

Tokarev TT-30, 7.62mm Tokarev, Clip Fed, *Modern*	100	250	350
Tokarev TT-33 Early, 7.62mm Tokarev, Clip Fed, *Modern*	100	200	300

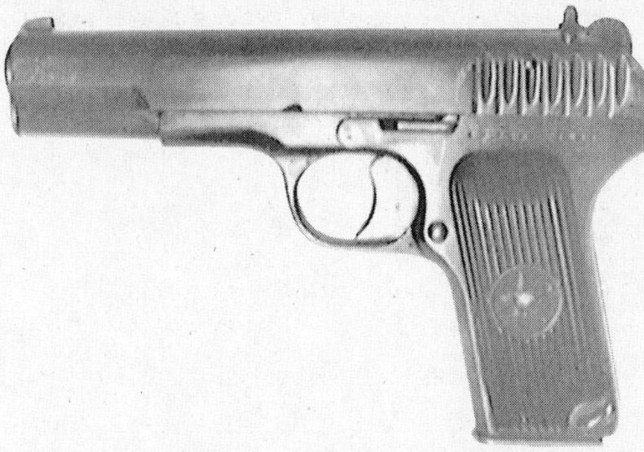

Russian Military Tokarev

RIFLE, BOLT ACTION			
1891 Moisin-Nagant, 7.62 Cal, 31-inch Barrel, Bolt Action. (The rear sight of these early rifles are graduated not in meters but in arshins. An arshin is equivalent to .78 yards. After the Revolution, Russia adopted the metric system and the sights for the Model 1891/30 and later rifles and carbines are graduated in meters.)	50	75	100

	Fair	V. Good	Excellent
1891 Remington, Same as Russian Nagent, except made in U.S.A., by Remington for export to Czarist Russia. (Few were ever delivered. Much higher quality than Russian produced models)	$75	$125	$175
1891/30 Sniper Rifle, Especially Selected for Accuracy, Bolt Handle turned down and fitted with either 4 × P.E. or 3.5 × P.U. Telescopic Sight (still in use in Russia.) Very Rare	250	575	750
1891/38 Carbine, 7.62.54 Cal., 20-inch Barrel, Hooded Front Sight, Rear Sight graduated from 100-1000 meters, no bayonet mounting	50	100	150
1938 Russian Tokarev, Self-Loading Gas Operated Rifle, Two Piece Stock, 10 Shot Magazine, Fitted with Muzzlebreak, Cleaning Rod on Right Side of Stock, First of Tokarev Series	125	275	375
1940 Tokarev Model, 24-Inch Barrel, Self-Loading Gas Operated Rifle, (Similar to Model 1938 but much more rugged, was very successful action similar to that of Belgian FN Rifle.)	100	250	350
KK M, CM 2, .22 L.R.R.F., Match Rifle, Target Sights, *Modern*	150	300	400
M1919, 7.62 × 54R Russian, Military, Carbine, *Modern*	$100	$200	$300
Russian SKS, 7.62.39M43 Cal., 20-Inch Barrel, (A Russian attempt to develop a gas operated carbine) 10 Shot Magazine, Folding Bayonet, Very Well Made	100	200	300

RWS

Rheinische-Westfalische Sperengstoff, since 1931. Now Dynamit Nobele AG, Troisdorf-Oberlar, West Germany.

RIFLE, BOLT ACTION

	Fair	V. Good	Excellent
Repeater, Various Calibers, Checkered Stock, Set Triggers, Open Sights, *Modern*	200	400	625

RYAN, THOMAS

Norwich, Conn., c. 1870.

HANDGUN, REVOLVER

	Fair	V. Good	Excellent
.22 Short R.F., 7 Shot, Spur Trigger, Solid Frame, Single Action, *Antique*	75	150	200
.32 Short R.F., 5 Shot, Spur Trigger, Solid Frame, Single Action, *Antique*	75	150	200

S

S-M CORP.

Sydney Manson, Alexandria, Va., c. 1953.

HANDGUN, SELF-LOADING

	Fair	V. Good	Excellent
Sporter, .22 L.R.R.F., Blowback, *Modern*	$50	$125	$175

SABLE

Belgium, Maker unknown.

HANDGUN, REVOLVER

	Fair	V. Good	Excellent
Baby Hammerless, .22 Short R.F., Folding Trigger, *Modern*	50	100	150

SAKO

O. Y. Sako AB, Riihmaki, Finland. Purchased in 2000 by Fabbrica d'Armi Pietro, Beretta, Gardone.

RIFLE, BOLT ACTION

	Fair	V. Good	Excellent
Deluxe (Garcia), Various Calibers, Sporting Rifle, Monte Carlo Stock, Fancy Checkering, Long Action, *Modern*	300	650	950
Deluxe (Garcia), Various Calibers, Sporting Rifle, Monte Carlo Stock, Fancy Checkering, Medium Action, *Modern*	300	650	950
Deluxe (Garcia), Various Calibers, Sporting Rifle, Monte Carlo Stock, Fancy Checkering, Short Action, *Modern*	300	650	950
Finnbear Carbine, Various Calibers, Sporting Rifle, Monte Carlo Stock, Checkered Stock, Long Action, Full-Stocked, *Modern*	300	675	1000
Finnbear, Various Calibers, Sporting Rifle, Monte Carlo Stock, Checkered Stock, Long Action, *Modern*	300	625	950
Forester Carbine, Various Calibers, Sporting Rifle, Monte Carlo Stock, Checkered Stock, Medium Action, Full-Stocked, *Modern*	300	650	950
Forester, Various Calibers, Sporting Rifle, Monte Carlo Stock, Checkered Stock, Medium Action, *Modern*	300	600	950
Forester, Various Calibers, Sporting Rifle, Monte Carlo Stock, Checkered Stock, Medium Action, Heavy Barrel, *Modern*	300	600	950
Hi-Power Mauser (FN), Various Calibers, Sporting Rifle, Monte Carlo Stock, Checkered Stock, *Modern*	$200	$475	$700
Magnum Mauser (FN), Various Calibers, Sporting Rifle, Monte Carlo Stock, Checkered Stock, *Modern*	250	575	850
Model 74 (Garcia), Various Calibers, Sporting Rifle, Monte Carlo Stock, Checkered Stock, Long Action, *Modern*	200	400	700
Model 74 (Garcia), Various Calibers, Sporting Rifle, Monte Carlo Stock, Checkered Stock, Medium Action, *Modern*	200	400	700
Model 74 (Garcia), Various Calibers, Sporting Rifle, Monte Carlo Stock, Checkered Stock, Short Action, *Modern*	200	400	700
Model 74 (Garcia), Various Calibers, Sporting Rifle, Monte Carlo Stock, Checkered Stock, Heavy Barrel, Medium Action, *Modern*	200	425	725
Model 74 (Garcia), Various Calibers, Sporting Rifle, Monte Carlo Stock, Checkered Stock, Heavy Barrel, Short Action, *Modern*	200	425	725
Model 78 (Stoeger), .22 Hornet, Sporting Rifle, Monte Carlo Stock, Checkered Stock, *Modern*	150	300	600
Model 78 (Stoeger), .22 L.R.R.F., Sporting Rifle, Monte Carlo Stock, Checkered Stock, *Modern*	125	250	500
Model 78 (Stoeger), .22 L.R.R.F., Sporting Rifle, Monte Carlo Stock, Checkered Stock, Heavy Barrel, *Modern*	200	400	650
Model 78 (Stoeger), .22 W.M.R., Sporting Rifle, Monte Carlo Stock, Checkered Stock, *Modern*	150	375	625
Vixen Carbine, Various Calibers, Sporting Rifle, Monte Carlo Stock, Checkered Stock, Short Action, Full-Stocked, *Modern*	350	750	1050
Vixen, Various Calibers, Sporting Rifle, Monte Carlo Stock, Checkered Stock, Short Action, *Modern*	300	650	900
Vixen, Various Calibers, Sporting Rifle, Monte Carlo Stock, Checkered Stock, Short Action, Heavy Barrel, *Modern*	325	700	1000

	Fair	V. Good	Excellent
RIFLE, LEVER ACTION			
Finnwolf, Various Calibers, Sporting Rifle, Monte Carlo Stock, Checkered Stock, *Modern*	$250	$525	$750

SAMPLES, BETHUEL

Urbana, Ohio. See Kentucky Rifles and Pistols.

SANDERSON

Portage, Wisc.

	Fair	V. Good	Excellent
SHOTGUN, SINGLESHOT			
M200-S 1, Various Gauges, Checkered Stock, Automatic Ejectors, Engraved, *Modern*	150	350	450
Neumann, 10 Gauge Mag., Checkered Stock, Automatic Ejectors, Engraved, *Modern*	150	350	450
Neumann, Various Gauges, Checkered Stock, Automatic Ejectors, Engraved, *Modern*	100	225	325

SANTA BARBARA

Santa Barbara of America, Inc. of Irving, Tx., on Mauser actions made in La Caruna, Spain.

	Fair	V. Good	Excellent
RIFLE, BOLT ACTION			
Sporter, Various Calibers, Custom Made, High Quality, *Modern*	75	150	225
Sporter, Various Calibers, Custom Made, Medium Quality, *Modern*	75	125	175

SARASQUETA, FELIX

Eibar, Spain, imported by Sarasquetta of N.A., Coral Gables, Fla.

	Fair	V. Good	Excellent
SHOTGUN, DOUBLE BARREL, OVER-UNDER "MERKE"			
Model 500, 12 Gauge, Checkered Stock, Boxlock, Light Engraving, Double Triggers, *Modern*	85	175	275
Model 510, 20 Gauge, Checkered Stock, Boxlock with Sideplates, Light Engraving, Double Triggers, *Modern*	75	150	225

SARASQUETE, VICTOR

Victor Sarasqueta, Eibar, Spain, from 1934.

	Fair	V. Good	Excellent
RIFLE, DOUBLE BARREL, SIDE-BY-SIDE			
Various Calibers, Sidelock, Automatic Ejector, Fancy Engraving, Fancy Checkering, *Modern*	3500	8000	9500
SHOTGUN, DOUBLE BARREL, SIDE-BY-SIDE			
#10E, Various Gauges, Sidelock, Fancy Checkering, Fancy Engraving, *Modern*	$700	$1500	$1750
#11E, Various Gauges, Sidelock, Fancy Checkering, Fancy Engraving, *Modern*	700	1600	1850
#12E, Various Gauges, Sidelock, Fancy Checkering, Fancy Engraving, *Modern*	750	1750	2000
#3, Various Gauges, Double Trigger, Checkered Stock, Light Engraving, *Modern*	250	500	700
#4, Various Gauges, Sidelock, Checkered Stock, Light Engraving, *Modern*	200	475	550
#4E, Various Gauges, Sidelock, Checkered Stock, Light Engraving, *Modern*	250	500	600
#6E, Various Gauges, Sidelock, Fancy Checkering, Engraved, *Modern*	300	650	800
#7E, Various Gauges, Sidelock, Fancy Checkering, Engraved, *Modern*	325	700	850
203, Various Gauges, Sidelock, Fancy Checkering, Fancy Engraving, *Modern*	250	525	625
203E, Various Gauges, Sidelock, Fancy Checkering, Fancy Engraving, *Modern*	300	600	700

SATA

Sabolti & Tantagiro Fabbrica o' Armi, Gardone, Val Trompia, Italy.

	Fair	V. Good	Excellent
HANDGUN, SELF-LOADING			
.22 Short, Clip Fed, Blue, *Modern*	50	125	150
6.35mm, Clip Fed, Blue, *Modern*	75	150	175

SAUER, J. P. & SOHN

1855 to date, first in Suftt, now in Eckernforde, West Germany. Also see Hawes.

	Fair	V. Good	Excellent
COMBINATION WEAPON, DRILLING			
Model 3000E, Various Calibers, Double Trigger, Engraved, Checkered Stock, *Modern*	1400	3000	3750
Model 3000E Deluxe, Various Calibers, Double Trigger, Fancy Engraving, Fancy Checkering, *Modern*	1400	3000	3750
HANDGUN, MANUAL REPEATER			
Bar Pistole, 7mm, Double Barrel, 4 Shot, Folding Trigger, *Curio*	150	325	450
HANDGUN, SELF-LOADING			
Behorden, .32 ACP, Clip Fed, *Modern*	100	200	300
Behorden, .32 ACP, Clip Fed, Lightweight, *Modern*	150	350	450

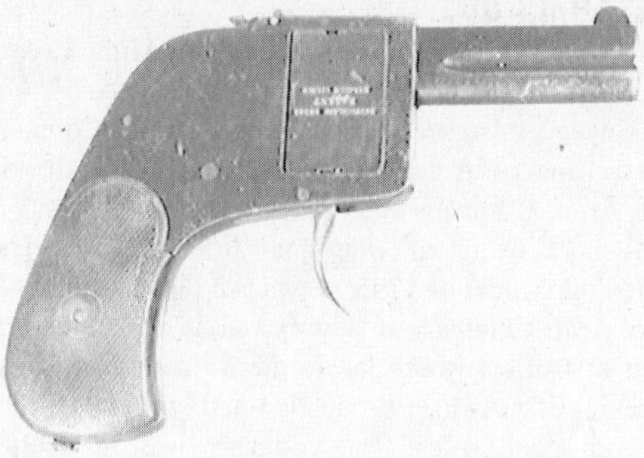

Sauer Bar Pistole

Sauer Model 38H

	Fair	V. Good	Excellent
Behorden 4mm, .32 ACP, Clip Fed, Extra Barrel, *Modern*	$300	$700	$850
Behorden Dutch Navy, .32 ACP, Clip Fed, Military, *Modern*	150	350	450
Model 1913, .25 ACP, Clip Fed, *Modern*	100	225	325
Model 38H, .380 ACP, Double Action, Clip Fed, Hammer, Nazi-Proofed, No Safety, Military, *Modern*	$125	$275	$375
Model 38H, .380 ACP, Double Action, Clip Fed, Hammer, Lightweight, *Modern*	200	475	575
Roth-Sauer, 8mm, Clip Fed, *Curio*	400	900	1200

Sauer Model 1913, .25

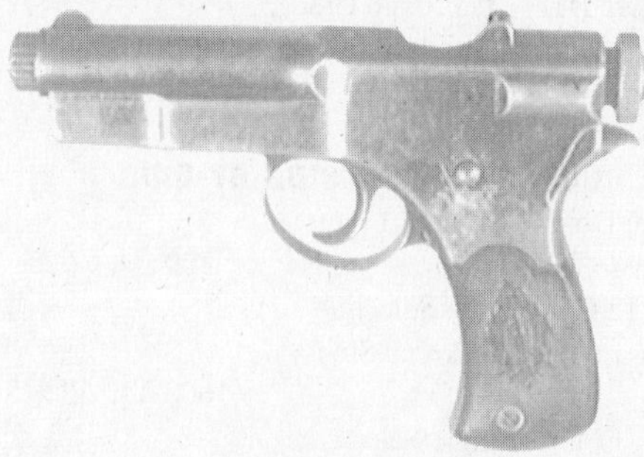

Sauer Roth-Sauer

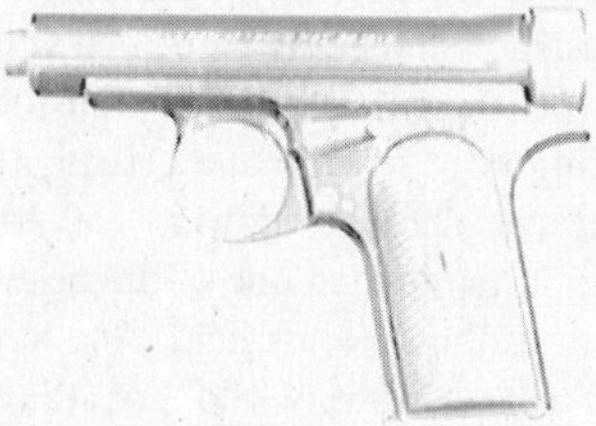

Sauer Model 1913, .32

	Fair	V. Good	Excellent
Model 1913, .32 ACP, Clip Fed, *Modern*	100	225	300
Model 28, .25 ACP, Clip Fed, *Modern*	125	250	325
Model 38H, .22 L.R., Double Action, Clip Fed, Hammer, *Curio*	700	1500	2000
Model 38H, .380 ACP, Double Action, Clip Fed, Hammer, Commercial, *Modern*	100	225	325
Model 38H, .380 ACP, Double Action, Clip Fed, Hammer, Nazi-Proofed, Military, *Modern*	100	225	325
W.T.M. 1922, .25 ACP, Clip Fed, *Modern*	150	300	400
W.T.M. 1928, .25 ACP, Clip Fed, *Modern*	125	275	350
W.T.M. 1928/2, .25 ACP, Clip Fed, *Modern*	100	225	300

RIFLE, BOLT ACTION

	Fair	V. Good	Excellent
Mauser Custom, Various Calibers, Set Trigger, Checkered Stock, Octagon Barrel, *Modern*	300	600	725

COMBINATION WEAPON, OVER-UNDER

	Fair	V. Good	Excellent
BBF, Various Calibers, Double Trigger, Set Trigger, Engraved, Checkered Stock, *Modern*	700	1700	2000
BBF Deluxe, Various Calibers, Double Trigger, Set Trigger, Fancy Engraving, Fancy Checkering, *Modern*	800	1900	2250

SHOTGUN, DOUBLE BARREL, OVER-UNDER

	Fair	V. Good	Excellent
Model 66 GR I, 12 Ga., Single Selective Trigger, Selective Ejector, Hammerless, Sidelock, Engraved, *Modern*	700	1650	1950

	Fair	V. Good	Excellent
Model 66 GR I, 12 Ga., Skeet Grade, Selective Ejector, Hammerless, Sidelock, Engraved, *Modern*	$600	$1450	$1700
Model 66 GR II, 12 Ga., Single Selective Trigger, Selective Ejector, Hammerless, Sidelock, Fancy Engraving, *Modern*	1100	2500	3000
Model 66 GR II, 12 Ga., Skeet Grade, Selective Ejector, Hammerless, Sidelock, Fancy Engraving, *Modern*	1100	2400	2750
Model 66 GR II, 12 Ga., Trap Grade, Selective Ejector, Hammerless, Sidelock, Fancy Engraving, *Modern*	1100	2350	2700
Model 66 GR III, 12 Ga., Single Selective Trigger, Selective Ejector, Hammerless, Sidelock, Fancy Engraving, *Modern*	1400	3000	3650
Model 66 GR III, 12 Ga., Skeet Grade, Selective Ejector, Hammerless, Sidelock, Fancy Engraving, *Modern*	1200	2500	3200
Model 66 GR III, 12 Ga., Trap Grade, Selective Ejector, Hammerless, Sidelock, Fancy Engraving, *Modern*	1200	2500	3200

SHOTGUN, DOUBLE BARREL, SIDE-BY-SIDE

	Fair	V. Good	Excellent
.410 Gauge, Double Trigger, Light Engraving, *Modern*	300	625	750
Artemis I, 12 Ga., Single Selective Trigger, Engraved, Checkered Stock, *Modern*	1600	3500	4750
Artemis II, 12 Ga., Single Selective Trigger, Fancy Engraving, Fancy Checkering, *Modern*	2100	4500	5750
Model Kim, Various Gauges, Double Triggers, Checkered Stock, Light Engraving, *Modern*	125	250	325
Model VIII, Various Gauges, Double Triggers, Checkered Stock, Light Engraving, *Modern*	125	250	350
Model VIII DES, Various Gauges, Single Selective Trigger, Selective Ejectors, Checkered Stock, Light Engraving, *Modern*	125	250	350
Model VIII DES-01, Various Gauges, Single Selective Trigger, Selective Ejectors, Checkered Stock, Engraved, *Modern*	150	325	400
Model VIII DES-05, Various Gauges, Single Selective Trigger, Selective Ejectors, Checkered Stock, Fancy Engraving, Sideplates, *Modern*	300	700	900
Model VIII DES-07, Various Gauges, Single Selective Trigger, Selective Ejectors, Checkered Stock, Fancy Engraving, *Modern*	200	425	575
Royal, 12 and 20 Gauges, Single Selective Trigger, Engraved, Checkered Stock, *Modern*	450	1000	1350

SAVAGE ARMS CO.

Utica, N.Y., 1893–1899, renamed Savage Arms Co., 1899. J. Stevens Arms Co. Springfield Arms Co. and A. H. Fox are all part of Savage. Also see U.S. Military. Also see Commemorative section. One of America's oldest gunmakers, the Savage Repeating Arms Company was incorporated in West Virginia in 1894, founded by inventor/designer Arthur Savage. The first Savage rifle, the Model of 1895, was made on subcontract by the Marlin Fire Arms Company of New Haven, in a quantity of 5,000. It was that first effort which led to the Model 1899, an American gunmaking icon still in production and still one of the most popular lever-action rifles. The company was re-incorporated under New York State law as the Savage Arms Company. In 1915 the firm was acquired by the Driggs-Seabury Ordnance Co., of Sharon, Pennsylvania. In 1917 the gunmaker's name was changed again, this time to Savage Arms Corporation. In 1920 Savage acquired the widely known and respected J. Stevens Arms Co., of Chicopee Falls, and operated that firm as a subsidiary until 1936, when the two were merged. Savage production facilities remained in Utica, New York until 1926 when purchasing the Page-Lewis Co., of Chicopee Falls and moving the Savage part of the plant to the Stevens facility. From 1959 production has been at Westfield, Massachusetts. From the mid-1960s the firm was renamed the Savage Arms Division of American Hardware, late the Emhart Corporation. In 1981 the division was sold, becoming Savage Industries, and from 1989, Savage Arms, Inc. Among other corporate acquisitions by Savage were the A. H. Fox Gun Co. (Philadelphia, 1930), the Davis-Warner Arms Corporation (Norwich, Connecticut, 1930), and the Crescent Fire Arms Co. (also of Norwich, 1931). The Savage line is best known for rifles and shotguns, but has also offered automatic pistols, accessories, sights, reloading tools, smokeless powder and cartridges, and more recently, indoor and outdoor range systems. In promoting the Savage automatic pistol, gunfighter-lawman-buffalo hunter W. B. "Bat" Masterson wrote complimentary articles and memoirs about the Wild West, and how the pistol would have been welcomed by the old-time shootists. Savage's emergence as a force to be reckoned with in American gunmaking coincided with the introduction of smokeless powder, a critical point of transition in the firearms field. On the cutting edge of rifle and cartridge development, the firm evolved their own .22 High Power, .250/3000, .300 and .303 calibers. For years it maintained one of the best equipped ballistic research operations in the firearms field. And having acquired gun companies the likes of Stevens and Fox, Savage had become makers of one of the world's most prestigious lines of sporting firearms. Savage was a pioneer in the use of coiled wire springs in the manufacture of sporting rifles and handguns. It was the Model 99 which established Savage's reputation, more than any other product or innovation. A long-term Savage claim has been that the 99 is the strongest lever-action rifle in the world. To demonstrate the strength and safety of the Model 99 mechanism, the inventor fired the rifle as a single shot, with thirteen parts of the mechanism removed, representing nearly one half of the breech system. He also fired the rifle without the buttstock or forearm, to demonstrate the light recoil with the .303 cartridge. In 1995 Savage celebrated the centennial of the Model 99 with the "Centennial Edition," 1,000 rifles chambered for .300 Savage, marked with serial numbers AS0001 through AS1000. The classic Model 99 had added one more landmark in its immortality. The Model 1899 Savage Rifle Sporting Rifle, Early Model, with 26" octagon or half octagon barrel, sporting sights. Carbine, 20" barrel; short forend with barrel band; carbine buttplate and sights, left side of frame with saddle ring. Saddle Gun, as above, but without saddle ring, 22" barrel, and adaptations to barrel and stock, primarily to reduce weight. Military Rifle, .303 and .30–30 calibers, 30" barrel, full length forend, two barrel bands, bayonet lug on muzzle, fitted for saber or angular bayonet. Takedown Model, round barrel, available in rifle and Featherweight versions. Featherweight Model, reduced to about six pounds, solid frame or takedown; 20" barrel, straight stock, unusual style of forearm. For modern production of A. H. Fox shotguns, see Connecticut Shotgun Mfg. Co.

From top left, Savage self-loading pistol in rare .45ACP caliber, a Savage in .380, and in .32; and a Remington .380 Pocket Model. From top right, *a Ruger .22 in Target and Standard variations (latter with 5" barrel); a Hi-Standard Model G-380, and a Reising .22 designed to compete with the Colt Woodsman. At center* a *Harrington & Richardson self-loader.*

HANDGUN, SELF-LOADING

	Fair	V. Good	Excellent
Military Model, .45 ACP. Clip Fed, Original, *Curio*	$4000	$9000	$12500
Military Model, .45 ACP. Clip Fed, Surplus, Reblue, *Curio*	3000	7000	9000
Model 1907 (1908), .32 ACP, Clip Fed, Burr Cocking Piece, (under #10,899), *Curio*	125	250	350
Model 1907 (1909), .32 ACP, Clip Fed, Burr Cocking Piece, (#'s 10900-70499), *Curio*	125	275	375
Model 1907 (1912), .32 ACP, Clip Fed, Burr Cocking Piece, (Higher # than 70500), *Curio*	$125	$250	$350
Model 1907 (1913), .380 ACP, Clip Fed, Burr Cocking Piece, *Curio*	150	325	325
Model 1907 (1914), .32 ACP, Spur Cocking Piece, *Curio*	125	250	350
Model 1907 (1914), .380 ACP, Spur Cocking Piece, *Curio*	125	250	350
Model 1907 (1918), .308 ACP, Clip Fed, Burr Cocking Piece, (After #10000B), *Curio*	150	325	375
Model 1907 (1918), .32 ACP, Clip Fed, No Cartridge Indicator, Burr Cocking Piece, *Curio*	100	225	325
Model 1907 (1918), .380 ACP, Clip Fed, Spur Cocking Piece, (After # 195000), *Curio*	100	250	350
Model 1907 Military, .32 ACP, Clip Fed, Burr Cocking Piece, *Curio*	125	275	375
Model 1907 Military, .32 ACP, Clip Fed, Burr Cocking Piece, (Portuguese Contract), *Curio*	150	375	450
Model 1907, Factory Nickel,	200	450	575
Add $50.00–$95.00			
Model 1907, Grade A Engraving (Light),	500	1000	1250
Add $100.00–$150.00			
Model 1907, Grade C Engraving (Light),	1000	2200	2650
Add $325.00–$450.00			
Model 1915, .32 ACP, Clip Fed, Hammerless, Grip Safety, *Curio*	125	250	350
Model 1915, .380 ACP, Clip Fed, Hammerless, Grip Safety, *Curio*	125	250	350
Model 1917, .32 ACP, Clip Fed, Spur Cocking Piece, Flared Grip, *Curio*	125	250	350
Model 1917, .380 ACP, Clip Fed, Spur Cocking Piece, Flared Grip, *Curio*	125	250	350
1915 and 1917 engraved as above			

HANDGUN, SINGLESHOT

	Fair	V. Good	Excellent
Model 101, .22 L.R.R.F., Western Style, Single Action, Swing-Out Cylinder, *Modern*	25	50	75

RIFLE, BOLT ACTION

	Fair	V. Good	Excellent
Model 10, .22 L.R.R.F., Target Sights, (Anschutz), *Modern*	75	150	200
Model 110, Magnum Calibers, Add $35.00			
Model 110, Various Calibers, Open Rear Sight, Checkered Stock, *Modern*	100	175	225
Model 110-B, Various Calibers, Open Rear Sight, *Modern*	100	225	300
Model 110-BL, Various Calibers, Open Rear Sight, Left-Hand, *Modern*	125	250	350

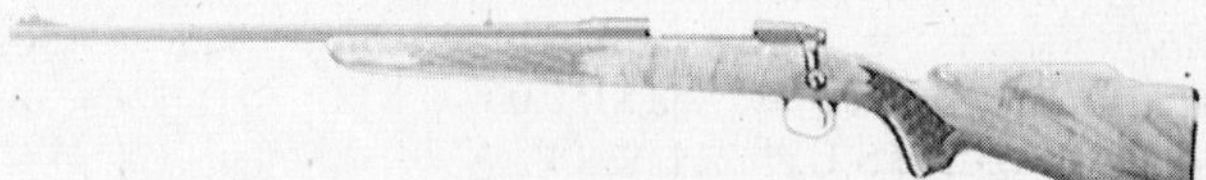

Savage 110-BL

	Fair	V. Good	Excellent
Model 110-C, Various Calibers, Clip Fed, Open Rear Sight, *Modern*	$100	$200	$300
Model 110-CL, Various Calibers, Clip Fed, Open Rear Sight, Left-Hand, *Modern*	100	225	300
Model 110-E, Various Calibers, Open Rear Sight, *Modern*	100	175	225
Model 110-EL, Various Calibers, Open Rear Sight, Left-Hand, *Modern*	100	175	250
Model 110-ES, Various Calibers, Internal Box Mag. Scope, *Modern*	125	250	325
Model 110-M, Various Calibers, Open Rear Sight, Monte Carlo Stock, Checkered Stock, Magnum Action, *Modern*	100	175	250
Model 110-MC, Various Calibers, Open Rear Sight, Monte Carlo Stock, Checkered Stock, *Modern*	75	150	200
Model 110-MCL, Various Calibers, Open Rear Sight, Monte Carlo Stock, Checkered Stock, Left-Hand, Modern	75	150	225
Model 110-ML, Various Calibers, Open Rear Sight, Monte Carlo Stock, Checkered Stock, Magnum Action, Left-Hand, *Modern*	100	175	250
Model 110-P, Various Calibers, Open Rear Sight, Fancy Wood, Monte Carlo Stock, Fancy Checkering, Sling Swivels, *Modern*	150	300	375
Model 110-PE, Various Calibers, Engraved, Fancy Checkering, Fancy Wood, Sling Swivels, *Modern*	225	550	650
Model 110-PEL, Various Calibers, Engraved, Fancy Checkering, Fancy Wood, Sling Swivels, Left-Hand, *Modern*	225	550	650
Model 110-PL, Various Calibers, Fancy Wood, Monte Carlo Stock, Fancy Checkering, Sling Swivels, Left-Hand, *Modern*	150	350	450
Model 110-S Silhouette Rifle, .308 Winchester and 7mm-08 Remington, Free Floating Barrel, Monte Carlo Stock, *Modern*	125	275	400
Model 110-V Varmint, Various Calibers, 26" Heavy Barrel, *Modern*	150	300	375
Model 111, Various Calibers, Clip Fed, Monte Carlo Stock, Checkered Stock, *Modern*	100	200	275
Model 112-V, Various Calibers, Singleshot, No Sights, *Modern*	125	250	375
Model 1407 "I.S.U.", .22 L.R.R.F., Heavy Barrel, No Sights, (Anschutz), *Modern*	200	425	500
Model 1407, Sights Only, Add $150.00			
Model 1407-L "I.S.U.," .22 L.R.R.F., Heavy Barrel, No Sights, Left-Hand, (Anschutz), *Modern*	200	450	525

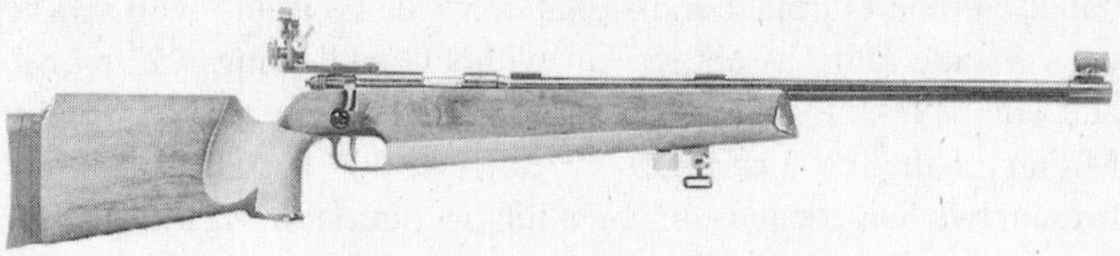

Savage Anschutz 1407

	Fair	V. Good	Excellent
Model 1408, .22 L.R.R.F., Heavy Barrel, No Sights, (Anschutz), *Modern*	$150	$350	$425
Model 1408-ED, .22 L.R.R.F., Heavy Barrel, No Sights, (Anschutz), *Modern*	200	450	525

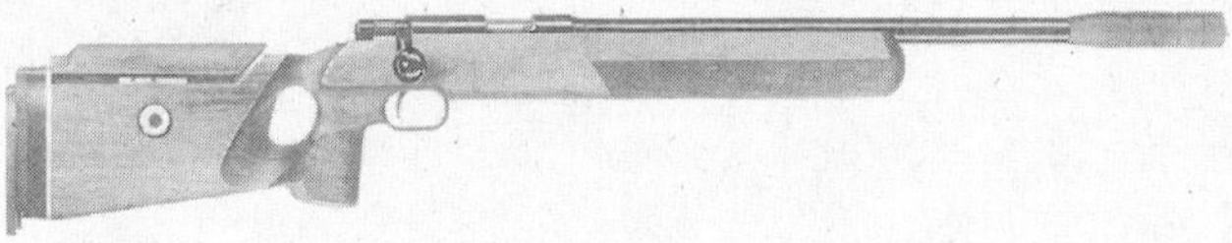

Savage Anschutz 1408-ED

Model 1408-L, .22 L.R.R.F., Heavy Barrel, No Sights, Left-Hand, (Anschutz), *Modern*	150	325	400
Model 1411 "Prone," .22 L.R.R.F., Heavy Barrel, No Sights, (Anschutz), *Modern*	200	425	525

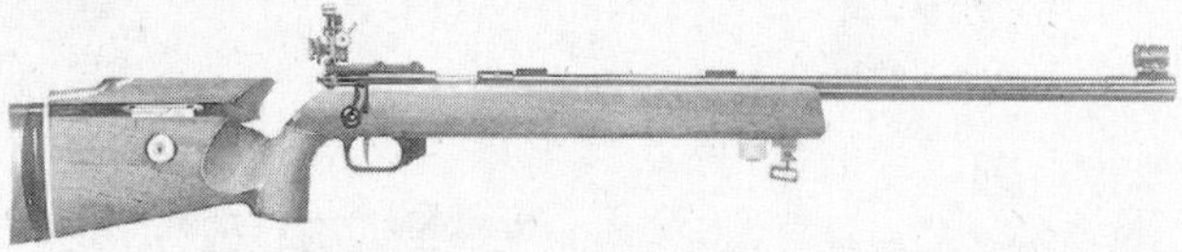

Savage Anschutz 1411

Model 1411, Sights Only, Add $125.00			
Model 1411-L "Prone," .22 L.R.R.F., Heavy Barrel, No Sights, Left-Hand, (Anschutz), *Modern*	200	425	525
Model 1413 "Match," .22 L.R.R.F., Heavy Barrel, No Sights, (Anschutz), *Modern*	300	625	725
Model 1413, .22 L.R.R.F., Sights Only, Add $125.00			
Model 1413-L "Match," .22 L.R.R.F., Heavy Barrel, No Sights, Left-Hand, (Anschutz), *Modern*	300	675	775
Model 1418, .22 L.R.R.F., Clip Fed, Mannlicher, Fancy Checkering, (Anschutz), *Modern*	150	300	400
Model 1432, .22 Hornet, Sporting Rifle, Clip Fed, Fancy Checkering, (Anschutz), *Modern*	200	425	525
Model 1433, .22 Hornet, Mannlicher, Clip Fed, Fancy Checkering, (Anschutz), *Modern*	200	450	575

	Fair	V. Good	Excellent
Model 1518, .22 WMR, Clip Fed, Mannlicher, Fancy Checkering, (Anschutz), *Modern*	$150	$300	$400
Model 1533, .222 Rem., Mannlicher, Clip Fed, Fancy Checkering, (Anschutz), *Modern*	200	450	550

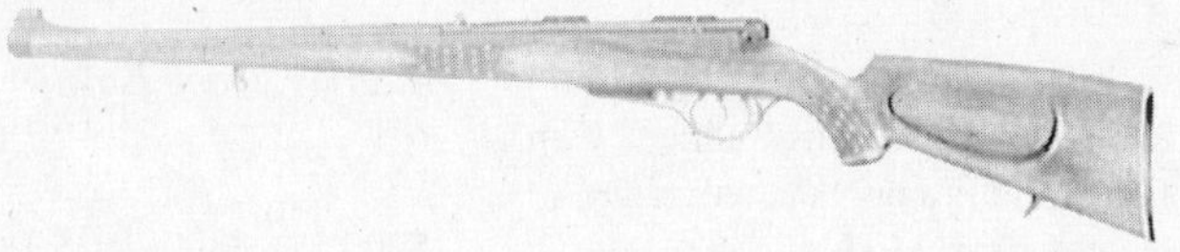

Savage Anschutz 164

	Fair	V. Good	Excellent
Model 164, .22 L.R.R.F., Sporting Rifle, Clip Fed, Checkered Stock, (Anschutz), *Modern*	100	225	300
Model 164-M, .22 WMR, Sporting Rifle, Clip Fed, Checkered Stock, (Anschutz), *Modern*	100	225	300

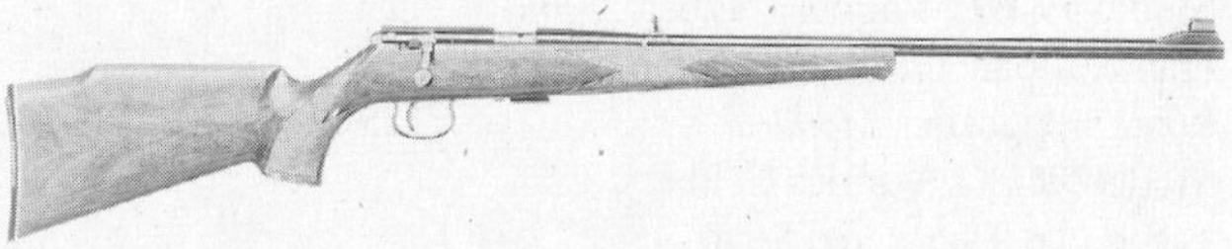

Savage Anschutz 164-M

	Fair	V. Good	Excellent
Model 19-H, .22 Hornet, 5 Shot Clip, Peep Sights, *Modern*	150	350	450
Model 19-L, .22 L.R.R.F., 5 Shot Clip, Lyman Sights, *Modern*	50	100	150
Model 19-M, .22 L.R.R.F., 5 Shot Clip, Heavy Barrel, *Modern*	50	100	150
Model 19-N.R.A., .22 L.R.R.F., 5 Shot Clip, Full-Stocked, Peep Sights, *Modern*	100	250	375
Model 19-Speed Lock, .22 L.R.R.F., 5 Shot Clip, Peep Sights, *Modern*	75	150	200
Model 1904, .22 L.R.R.F., Singleshot, Takedown, *Modern*	50	100	150
Model 1904-Special, .22 L.R.R.F., Singleshot, Takedown, Fancy Wood, *Modern*	65	125	175
Model 1905, .22 L.R.R.F., Target, Singleshot, Takedown, Swiss Buttplate, *Modern*	50	125	175
Model 1905-B, .22 L.R.R.F., *Modern*	65	100	150
Model 1905-Special, .22 L.R.R.F., Fancy Wood, *Modern*	75	150	225
Model 1911, .22 Short R.F., Target, Singleshot, Takedown, *Modern*	50	75	125
Model 20, Various Calibers, Open Rear Sight, *Modern*	100	250	325
Model 20, Various Calibers, Peep Sights, *Modern*	125	275	350

	Fair	V. Good	Excellent
Model 23A, .22 L.R.R.F., 5 Shot Clip, Open Rear Sight, *Modern*	$75	$125	$175
Model 23AA, .22 L.R.R.F., 5 Shot Clip, Open Rear Sight, Monte Carlo Stock, *Modern*	75	125	200
Model 23B, .25 WCF, 5 Shot Clip, Open Rear Sight, Monte Carlo Stock, *Modern*	75	250	325
Model 23C, .32-20 WCF, 5 Shot Clip, Open Rear Sight, Monte Carlo Stock, *Modern*	75	250	325
Model 23D, .22 Hornet, 5 Shot Clip, Open Rear Sight, Monte Carlo Stock, *Modern*	100	300	425
Model 3, .22 L.R.R.F., Singleshot, Takedown, Open Rear Sight, *Modern*	50	85	125
Model 3-S, .22 L.R.R.F., Singleshot, Takedown, Peep Sights, *Modern*	50	85	125
Model 3-ST, .22 L.R.R.F., Singleshot, Takedown, Peep Sights, Sling Swivels, *Modern*	50	85	125
Model 340, Various Calibers, Clip Fed, *Modern*	100	175	250
Model 340-C, Various Calibers, Clip Fed, Carbine, *Modern*	100	175	250
Model 340-S Deluxe, Various Calibers, Clip Fed, Peep Sights, *Modern*	125	225	300
Model 342, .22 Hornet, Clip Fed, *Modern*	100	200	275
Model 342-S, .22 Hornet, Clip Fed, Peep Sights, *Modern*	100	200	275
Model 35, .22 L.R.R.F., Clip Fed, *Modern*	50	75	100
Model 35-M, .22 W.M.R., Clip Fed, *Modern*	50	75	100
Model 36, .22 L.R.R.F., Singleshot, *Modern*	50	75	100
Model 4, .22 L.R.R.F., 5 Shot Clip, Takedown, *Modern*	50	100	125
Model 4-M, .22 WMR, 5 Shot Clip, Takedown, *Modern*	65	100	125
Model 4-S, .22 L.R.R.F., 5 Shot Clip, Takedown, Peep Sights, *Modern*	50	75	100
Model 40, Various Calibers, Open Rear Sights, *Modern*	125	275	325
Model 45 Super, Various Calibers, Peep Sights, Checkered Stock, *Modern*	150	300	375
Model 5, .22 L.R.R.F., Tube Feed, Takedown, Open Rear Sight, *Modern*	50	100	125
Model 5-S, .22 L.R.R.F., Tube Feed, Takedown, Peep Sights, *Modern*	50	100	125
Model 54, .22 L.R.R.F., Sporting Rifle, Clip Fed, Fancy Checkering, (Anschutz), *Modern*	150	350	400
Model 54-M, .22 WMR, Sporting Rifle, Clip Fed, Fancy Checkering, (Anschutz), *Modern*	175	375	425

	Fair	V. Good	Excellent
Model 63, .22 L.R.R.F., Singleshot, Open Rear Sight, *Modern*	$25	$50	$75
Model 63-K, .22 L.R.R.F., Singleshot, Open Rear Sight, *Modern*	25	50	75
Model 63-M, .22 WMR, Singleshot, Open Rear Sight, *Modern*	50	75	100
Model 64, .22 L.R.R.F., Heavy Barrel, No Sights, (Anschutz), *Modern*	100	200	275
Model 64, .22 L.R.R.F., Sights Only, Add $30.00-$55.00			
Model 64-CS, .22 L.R.R.F., Heavy Barrel, No Sights, Lightweight, (Anschutz), *Modern*	100	200	275
Model 64-CSL, .22 L.R.R.F., Heavy Barrel, No Sights, Left-Hand, Lightweight, (Anschutz), *Modern*	100	225	300
Model 64-L, .22 L.R.R.F., Heavy Barrel, No Sights, Left-Hand, (Anschutz), *Modern*	100	200	275
Model 64-S, .22 L.R.R.F., Heavy Barrel, No Sights, (Anschutz), *Modern*	100	225	275
Model 64-SL, .22 L.R.R.F., Heavy Barrel, No Sights, Left-Hand, (Anschutz), *Modern*	125	250	325
Model 65-M, .22 WMR, Clip Fed, Open Rear Sight, *Modern*	50	75	100
Model 73, .22 L.R.R.F., Singleshot, *Modern*	25	50	75
Model 73-Y Boys, .22 L.R.R.F., Singleshot, *Modern*	25	50	75
Model 89, .22 L.R.R.F., Singleshot, Open Rear Sight, *Modern*	25	50	75

RIFLE, LEVER ACTION

	Fair	V. Good	Excellent
Model 1895, .303 Savage, Hammerless, Rotary Magazine, Open Rear Sight, *Antique*	600	1300	1650
Model 1899, .30–30 Win., Hammerless, Rotary Magazine, Full-Stocked Military, *Modern*	1200	2700	3250
Model 1899, Various Calibers, Hammerless, Rotary Magazine, Open Rear Sight, *Modern*	150	350	450
Model 99, for Extra Barrel, Add $110.00-$150.00			
Model 99 E, Various Calibers, Solid Frame, Carbine, Hammerless, Rotary Magazine, *Modern*	150	500	700
Model 99-1895 Anniversary, .308 Win., Octagon Barrel, Hammerless, Rotary Magazine, *Modern*	150	325	400
Model 99-358, .358 Win., Solid Frame, Hammerless, Rotary Magazine, *Modern*	175	350	450
Model 99-A, Various Calibers, Solid Frame, Hammerless, Rotary Magazine, *Modern*	200	425	525
Model 99-B, Various Calibers, Takedown, Hammerless, Rotary Magazine, *Modern*	300	675	800

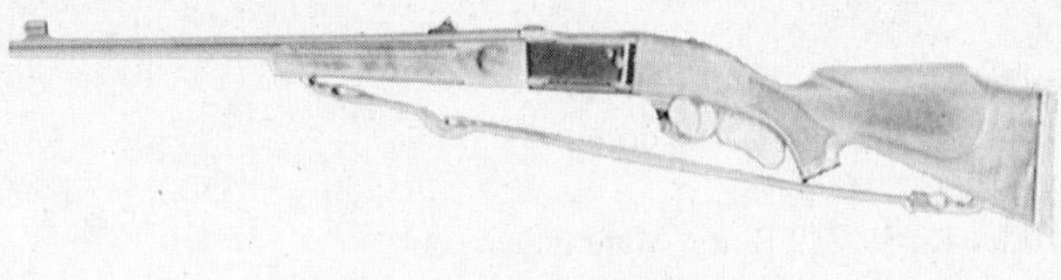

Savage Model 99-C

	Fair	V. Good	Excellent
Model 99-C, Various Calibers, Clip Fed, Solid Frame, Featherweight, Hammerless, *Modern*	$200	$400	$500
Model 99-CD, Various Calibers, Hammerless, Clip Fed, Solid Frame, Monte Carlo Stock, *Modern*	175	375	425
Model 99-D, Various Calibers, Solid Frame, Hammerless, Rotary Magazine, *Modern*	150	275	325
Model 99-DE, Various Calibers, Solid Frame, Monte Carlo Stock, Light Engraving, Hammerless, Rotary Magazine, *Modern*	250	550	675
Model 99-DL, Various Calibers, Solid Frame, Monte Carlo Stock, Hammerless, Rotary Magazine, *Modern*	125	250	300
Model 99-EG, Various Calibers, Takedown, Checkered Stock, Hammerless, Rotary Magazine, *Modern*	175	375	450
Model 99-F, Various Calibers, Featherweight, Takedown, Hammerless, Rotary Magazine, *Modern*	150	275	325
Model 99-F, Various Calibers, Solid Frame, Featherweight, Hammerless, Rotary Magazine, *Modern*	125	250	300
Model 99-G, Various Calibers, Takedown, Checkered Stock, Hammerless, Rotary Magazine, *Modern*	225	475	550
Model 99-H, Various Calibers, Carbine, Solid Frame, Hammerless, Rotary Magazine, *Modern*	200	400	500
Model 99-K, Various Calibers, Takedown, Light Engraving, Checkered Stock, Hammerless, Rotary Magazine, *Modern*	600	1200	1500
Model 99-PE, Various Calibers, Solid Frame, Monte Carlo Stock, Engraved, Hammerless, Rotary Magazine, *Modern*	600	1200	1500
Model 99-R, Various Calibers, Solid Frame, Checkered Stock, Pre-War, Hammerless, Rotary Magazine, *Modern*	200	400	500
Model 99-R, Various Calibers, Solid Frame, Checkered Stock, Hammerless, Rotary Magazine, *Modern*	125	250	300

	Fair	V. Good	Excellent
Model 99-RS, Various Calibers, Solid Frame, Peep Sights, Pre-War, Hammerless, Rotary Magazine, *Modern*	$225	$475	$550
Model 99-RS, Various Calibers, Solid Frame, Peep Sights, Hammerless, Rotary Magazine, *Modern*	150	275	350
Model 99-T, Various Calibers, Solid Frame, Featherweight, Hammerless, Rotary Magazine, *Modern*	150	275	350

38–55 cal. add 50%
32–40 cal. add 40%
25–35 cal. add 50%

COMBINATION WEAPON, OVER-UNDER

Model 24, Various Calibers, Hammer, *Modern*	75	100	150

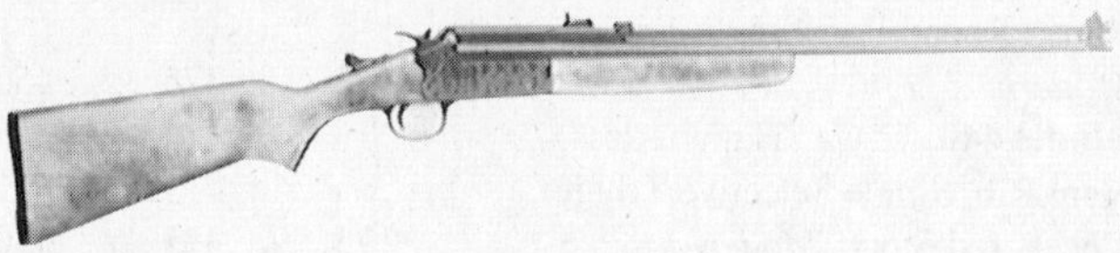

Savage Model 24

Model 24-C, .22/20 Ga., Hammer, *Modern*	75	125	150
Model 24-D, Various Calibers, Hammer, *Modern*	100	170	200
Model 24-V, Various Calibers, Checkered Stock, Hammer, *Modern*	100	225	250
Model 389, Various Calibers, Checkered Stock, Hammer, *Modern*	200	450	550

RIFLE, SELF-LOADING

Model 6, .22 L.R.R.F., Takedown, Tube Feed, Open Rear Sight, *Modern*	50	75	100
Model 6-S, .22 L.R.R.F., Takedown, Tube Feed, Peep Sights, *Modern*	75	100	125
Model 60, .22 L.R.R.F., Monte Carlo Stock, Checkered Stock, Tube Feed, *Modern*	50	75	100
Model 7, .22 L.R.R.F., 5 Shot Clip, Takedown, Open Rear Sight, *Modern*	50	75	100
Model 7-S, .22 L.R.R.F., 5 Shot Clip, Takedown, Open Rear Sight, *Modern*	75	100	125
Model 80, .22 L.R.R.F., Tube Feed, *Modern*	25	50	75
Model 88, .22 L.R.R.F., Tube Feed, *Modern*	25	50	75

	Fair	V. Good	Excellent
Model 90, .22 L.R.R.F., Carbine, Tube Feed, *Modern*	$50	$75	$100
Model 987 Stevens Rimfire, .22 Autoloader, Tubular Mag. 15 Rounds, Walnut Stock, *Modern*	75	100	125
Model 987-T Stevens Rimfire, .22 Autoloader, Tubular Mag. 15 Rounds, 4 × Scope and Mount, *Modern*	75	100	125

RIFLE, SINGLESHOT

Model 219, Various Calibers, Hammerless, Top Break, Open Rear Sight, *Modern*	75	100	125
Model 219L, Various Calibers, Hammerless, Top Break, Open Rear Sight, Side Lever, *Modern*	50	75	100
Model 221, .30–30 Win., Hammerless, Top Break, Extra Shotgun Barrel, *Modern*	50	75	100
Model 222, .30–30 Win., Hammerless, Top Break, Extra Shotgun Barrel, Modern	50	75	100
Model 223, .30–30 Win., Hammerless, Top Break, Extra Shotgun Barrel, *Modern*	50	75	100
Model 227, .30–30 Win., Hammerless, Top Break, Extra Shotgun Barrel, *Modern*	50	75	100
Model 228, .30–30 Win., Hammerless, Top Break, Extra Shotgun Barrel, *Modern*	50	75	100
Model 229, .30–30 Win., Hammerless, Top Break, Extra Shotgun Barrel, *Modern*	50	75	100
Model 71 Stevens Favorite, .22 L.R.R.F., Lever Action, Falling Block, Favorite, *Modern*	75	125	150
Model 72, .22 L.R.R.F., Lever Action, Falling Block, *Modern*	50	75	100
Model 89 Stevens Rimfire, .22 L.R.R.F., Lever Action, 18" Barrel, Sporting Sights, *Modern*	75	100	125

RIFLE, SLIDE ACTION

Model 170, Various Calibers, Open Rear Sight, *Modern*	100	150	175

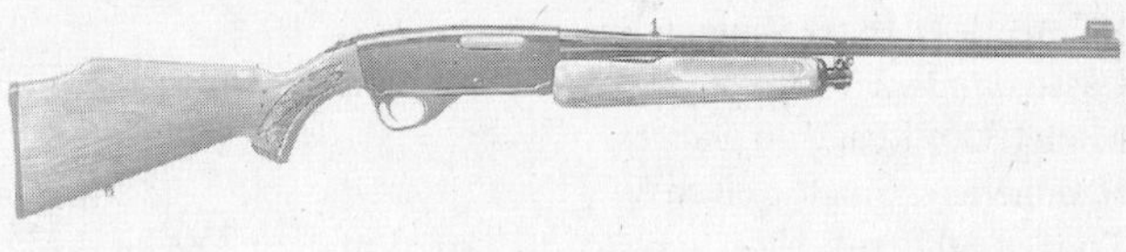

Savage 170

Model 170-C, .30–30 Win., Carbine, Open Rear Sight, *Modern*	75	125	150

	Fair	V. Good	Excellent
Model 1903, .22 L.R.R.F., Hammerless, Clip Fed, Octagon Barrel, *Modern*	$100	$175	$225
Model 1903-EF, .22 L.R.R.F., Hammerless, Clip Fed, Octagon Barrel, Fancy Wood, Engraved, *Modern*	200	450	525
Model 1903-Expert, .22 L.R.R.F., Hammerless, Clip Fed, Octagon Barrel, Checkered Stock, Light Engraving, *Modern*	100	250	300
Model 1909, .22 L.R.R.F., Half-Octagon Barrel, Takedown, Clip Fed, *Modern*	75	125	150
Model 1914, .22 L.R.R.F., Half-Octagon Barrel, Takedown, Tube Feed, *Modern*	75	175	225
Model 1914-E.F., .22 L.R.R.F., Half-Octagon Barrel, Takedown, Tube Feed, Fancy Engraving, *Modern*	525	1200	1500
Model 1914-Expert, .22 L.R.R.F., Half-Octagon Barrel, Takedown, Tube Feed, Fancy Engraving, *Modern*	500	1200	1500
Model 1914-Gold Medal, .22 L.R.R.F., Half-Octagon Barrel, Takedown, Tube Feed, Checkered Stock, Light Engraving, *Modern*	200	700	850
Model 25, .22 L.R.R.F., Tube Feed, Octagon Barrel, Open Rear Sight, Monte Carlo Stock, *Modern*	100	200	250
Model 29, .22 L.R.R.F., Tube Feed, Octagon Barrel, Open Rear Sight, Monte Carlo Stock, *Modern*	100	175	225
Model 29, .22 L.R.R.F., Tube Feed, Round Barrel, Open Rear Sight, *Modern*	75	150	175
Model 29-G, .22 Short R.F., Tube Feed, *Modern*	75	150	175

SHOTGUN, BOLT ACTION

Model 58, .410 Ga., Singleshot, *Modern*	25	50	75

SHOTGUN, DOUBLE BARREL, OVER-UNDER

Model 242, .410 Ga., Hammer, Single Trigger, *Modern*	100	200	275
Model 330, 12 and 20 Gauges, Hammerless, Extra Shotgun Barrel, Cased, *Modern*	200	425	500
Model 330, 12 and 20 Gauges, Hammerless, Single Selective Trigger, *Modern*	150	350	425
Model 333, 12 and 20 Gauges, Hammerless, Vent Rib, Single Selective Trigger, *Modern*	150	350	425
Model 333-T, 12 Ga., Hammerless, Vent Rib, Trap Grade, Single Selective Trigger, *Modern*	200	400	475

Savage Model 333

	Fair	V. Good	Excellent
Model 420, Various Gauges, Hammerless, Takedown, Double Trigger, *Modern*	$100	$250	$300
Model 420, Various Gauges, Hammerless, Takedown, Single Trigger, *Modern*	150	300	350
Model 430, Various Gauges, Hammerless, Takedown, Checkered Stock, Recoil Pad, Double Trigger, *Modern*	150	300	350
Model 430, Various Gauges, Hammerless, Takedown, Checkered Stock, Recoil Pad, Single Trigger, *Modern*	175	375	450
Model 440, 12 Ga., Hammerless, Vent Rib, Single Selective Trigger, Checkered Stock, *Modern*	175	375	450
Model 440-T, 12 Ga., Hammerless, Vent Rib, Checkered Stock, *Modern*	200	400	475
Model 444, 12 Ga., Hammerless, Vent Rib, Single Selective Trigger, Checkered Stock, Selective Ejector, *Modern*	200	425	500

RIFLE/SHOTGUN COMBINATION

Model 2400 Field Combo, .22 L.R. Top Barrel, 4 10 Bore or 20 Gauge Bottom Barrel, Walnut Stock, *Modern*	225	475	600
Model 2400-C Combo Gun Camper's Break Action, .22 L.R. Top Barrel, 20 Gauge Bottom Barrel, *Modern*	250	500	600
Model 2400-CS Camper/Survival Combo Gun, Break Action, .22 L.R. Top Barrel, 20 Gauge Bottom Barrel, Pistol Grip, Satin Nickel, *Modern*	250	550	650
Model 2400-D Combo Gun, .22 L.R., Top Barrel, 20 Gauge Bottom Barrel, Folding Rear Sight, *Modern*	250	550	650
Model 2400-V Combo Gun, Break Action, .22 Hornet, Top Barrel, 20 Gauge Bottom Barrel, Monte Carlo Stock, *Modern*	250	550	650
Model 2400-VS Camper/Survival Combo Gun, Break Action, .357 Magnum Top Barrel, 20 Gauge Bottom Barrel, Pistol Grip, Satin Nickel, *Modern*	275	575	675

SHOTGUN, DOUBLE BARREL, SIDE-BY-SIDE

Model B Fox, Various Gauges, Hammerless, Vent Rib, Double Trigger, *Modern*	100	175	225

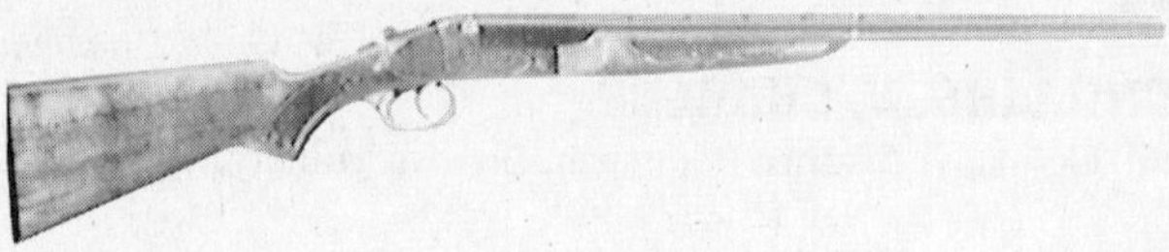

Savage Fox Model B

	Fair	V. Good	Excellent
Model B-SE Fox, Various Gauges, Hammerless, Vent Rib, Selective Ejector, Single Trigger, *Modern*	$100	$225	$300

SHOTGUN, SELF-LOADING

	Fair	V. Good	Excellent
Model 720, 12 Ga., Tube Feed, Checkered Stock, Plain Barrel, *Modern*	75	125	175
Model 720-P, 12 Ga., Checkered Stock, Adjustable Choke, *Modern*	75	125	175
Model 720-R, 12 Ga., Riot Gun, *Modern*	150	300	350
Model 721, 12 Ga., Tube Feed, Checkered Stock, Raised Matted Rib, *Modern*	75	150	200
Model 722, 12 Ga., Tube Feed, Checkered Stock, Vent Rib, *Modern*	75	200	250
Model 723, 16 Ga., Tube Feed, Checkered Stock, Plain Barrel, *Modern*	50	100	150
Model 724, 16 Ga., Tube Feed, Checkered Stock, Raised Matted Rib, *Modern*	75	125	175
Model 725, 16 Ga., Tube Feed, Checkered Stock, Vent Rib, *Modern*	75	200	250
Model 726, 12 and 16 Gauges, 3 Shot, Checkered Stock, Plain Barrel, *Modern*	75	125	150
Model 727, 12 and 16 Gauges, 3 Shot, Checkered Stock, Raised Matted Rib, *Modern*	75	125	175
Model 728, 12 and 16 Gauges, 3 Shot, Checkered Stock, Vent Rib, *Modern*	75	150	200
Model 740-C, 12 and 16 Gauges, Skeet Grade, *Modern*	100	200	250
Model 745, 12 Ga., Lightweight, *Modern*	75	150	200
Model 750, 12 Ga., *Modern*	100	175	225
Model 750-AC, 12 Ga., Adjustable Choke, *Modern*	100	175	225
Model 750-SC, 12 Ga., Adjustable Choke, *Modern*	100	175	225
Model 755, 12 and 16 Gauges, *Modern*	75	125	175
Model 755-SC, 12 and 16 Gauges, Adjustable Choke, *Modern*	75	150	200
Model 775, 12 and 16 Gauges, Lightweight, *Modern*	75	150	200
Model 775-SC, 12 and 16 Gauges, Adjustable Choke, Lightweight, *Modern*	75	150	200

SHOTGUN, SINGLESHOT

	Fair	V. Good	Excellent
Model 220, Various Gauges, Hammerless, Takedown, *Modern*	$50	$75	$100
Model 220-AC, Various Gauges, Hammerless, Takedown, Adjustable Choke, *Modern*	25	50	75
Model 220-P, Various Gauges, Hammerless, Takedown, Adjustable Choke, *Modern*	25	50	75
Model 94, Various Gauges, Hammer, Takedown, *Modern*	50	100	125
Model 94-C, Various Gauges, Hammer, Takedown, *Modern*	50	75	100

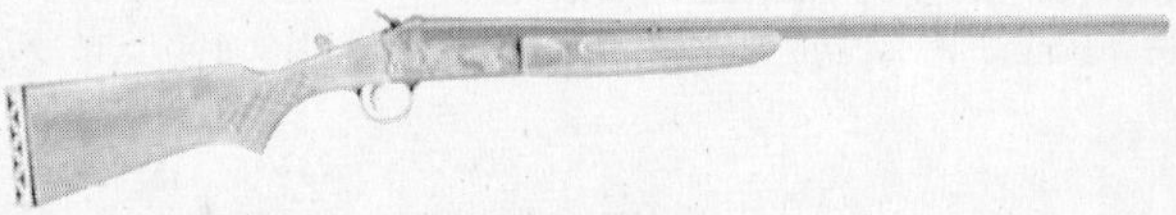

Savage Model 94-Y

	Fair	V. Good	Excellent
Model 94-Y Youth, Various Gauges, Hammer, Takedown, *Modern*	25	50	75
Model 9478, Various Gauges, Hammer, Auto Ejection, 42" to 52" Overall, *Modern*	75	100	125

SHOTGUN, SLIDE ACTION

	Fair	V. Good	Excellent
Model 21-A, 12 Ga., Hammerless, Takedown, *Modern*	75	125	150
Model 21-B, 12 Ga., Hammerless, Takedown, Raised Matted Rib, *Modern*	75	150	175
Model 21-C, 12 Ga., Hammerless, Takedown, Riot Gun, *Modern*	50	150	200
Model 21-D, 12 Ga., Hammerless, Takedown, Trap Grade, *Modern*	100	200	250
Model 21-E, 12 Ga., Hammerless, Takedown, Fancy Wood, Fancy Checkering, Vent Rib, *Modern*	125	250	300
Model 28-A, 12 Ga., Hammerless, Takedown, *Modern*	75	125	150
Model 28-B, 12 Ga., Hammerless, Takedown, Raised Matted Rib, *Modern*	75	100	175
Model 28-C, 12 Ga., Hammerless, Takedown, Riot Gun, *Modern*	50	150	200
Model 28-D, 12 Ga., Hammerless, Takedown, Trap Grade, *Modern*	100	200	250
Model 28-S, 12 Ga., Hammerless, Takedown, Fancy Checkering, *Modern*	100	200	250

Model 30, For Vent Rib, Add $15.00–$20.00

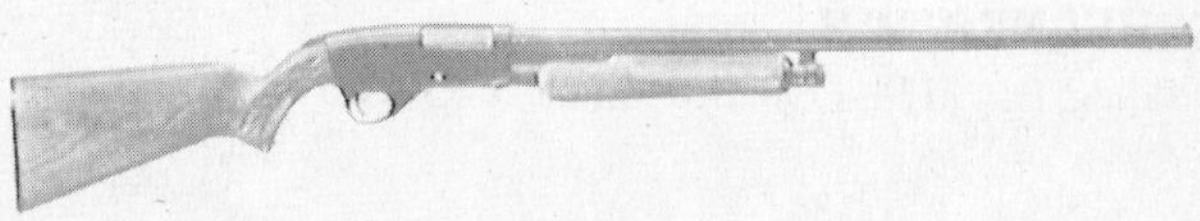

Savage Model 30

	Fair	V. Good	Excellent
Model 30, Various Gauges, Hammerless, Solid Frame, *Modern*	$75	$150	$175
Model 30-AC, Various Gauges, Hammerless, Solid Frame, Adjustable Choke, *Modern*	75	150	175
Model 30-ACL, Various Gauges, Hammerless, Solid Frame, Left-Hand, Adjustable Choke, *Modern*	75	150	175
Model 30-D, Various Gauges, Hammerless, Solid Frame, Light Engraving, Recoil Pad, *Modern*	100	200	250
Model 30-L, Various Gauges, Hammerless, Solid Frame, Left-Hand, *Modern*	75	150	175
Model 30-Slug, 12 Ga., Hammerless, Solid Frame, *Modern*	75	150	175

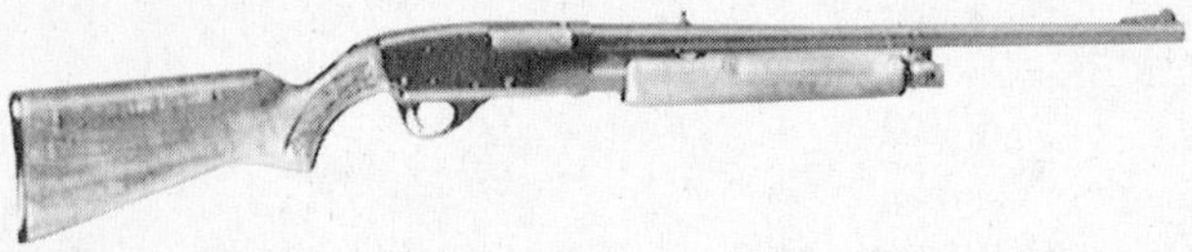

Savage Model 30-Slug

	Fair	V. Good	Excellent
Model 30-T, 12 Ga., Hammerless, Solid Frame, Monte Carlo Stock, Recoil Pad, Vent Rib, *Modern*	75	150	200
Model 67, 12 or 20 Gauge, Tubular Mag, Hammerless, Walnut Stock, *Modern*	75	150	175
Model 67-T Stevens, 12 or 20 Gauge, Three Choke Tubes, 28" Barrel, *Modern*	100	150	200
Model 67-VR Stevens, 12 Gauge, 4 Shot Tubular, Vent Ribs, *Modern*	100	175	200
Model 69-N Guard Gun, 12 Gauge, 7 Shot Tubular Mag., 18¼" Cylinder Bore, Nickel, *Modern*	100	150	200
Model 69-R Guard Gun, 12 Gauge, 5 Shot Tubular Mag., 20" Cylinder Bore, *Modern*	100	150	200
Model 69-RXL Guard Gun, 12 Gauge, 7 Shot Tubular Mag., 18¼" Cylinder Bore, *Modern*	25	150	200

SCHALL & CO.

Hartford, Conn.

HANDGUN, MANUAL REPEATER

	Fair	V. Good	Excellent
.22 L.R.R.F., Target Pistol, Clip Fed, *Curio*	150	350	425

SCHEANER, WM.

Reading, Pa., 1779–1790. See Kentucky Rifles.

SCHILLING, V. CHARLES

Suhl, Germany. Also see Bergmann, German Military.

RIFLE, BOLT ACTION

	Fair	V. Good	Excellent
Model 88 Sporter, Various Calibers, Checkered Stock, *Curio*	$150	$300	$350

SCHMIDT & HABERMANN

Suhl, Germany, 1920–1940.

COMBINATION WEAPON, OVER-UNDER

	Fair	V. Good	Excellent
Various Calibers, Pre-WW2, Engraved, Checkered Stock, *Curio*	300	650	750

SCHMIDT, ERNST

Suhl, Germany.

RIFLE, SINGLESHOT

	Fair	V. Good	Excellent
8mm Roth-Steyr, Schutzen Rifle, Engraved, Set Trigger, Takedown, Octagon Barrel, *Modern*	500	1200	1650

SCHMIDT, HERBERT

Ostheim/Rhon, Germany.

HANDGUN, REVOLVER

	Fair	V. Good	Excellent
Liberty 11, .22 L.R.R.F., Double Action, Swing-Out Cylinder, Blue, *Modern*	25	50	75
Texas Scout, .22 L.R.R.F., Western Style, Blue, *Modern*	25	50	75

SCHOUBOE

Dansk Rekylriffel Syndikat, Copenhagen, Denmark, 1902–1917.

HANDGUN, SELF-LOADING

	Fair	V. Good	Excellent
Model 1902/07, 11.35mm Sch., *Curio*	1900	4000	5500
Model 1902/10, 11.35mm Sch., *Curio*	1900	4000	5500
Model 1902/10, 11.35mm Sch., with Holster Stock, *Curio*	2500	5500	6750
Model 1903, 7.65mm, Clip Fed, Blue, *Curio*	1500	3250	4250

SCHULTZ & LARSEN

Otterup, Denmark.

HANDGUN, SINGLESHOT

	Fair	V. Good	Excellent
Free Pistol, .22 L.R.R.F., Bolt Action, Target Trigger, Target Sights, *Modern*	125	275	350

RIFLE, BOLT ACTION

	Fair	V. Good	Excellent
M54, Various Calibers, *Modern*	300	725	850

	Fair	V. Good	Excellent
Model 47, .22 L.R.R.F., Target Rifle, Thumbhole Stock, Adjustable Trigger, Singleshot, *Modern*	$250	$550	$650
Model 61, .22 L.R.R.F., Target Rifle, Thumbhole Stock, Adjustable Trigger, Singleshot, *Modern*	300	650	750
Model 62, Various Calibers, Target Rifle, Thumbhole Stock, Adjustable Trigger, Singleshot, *Modern*	400	800	950
Model 65DL, Various Calibers, Sporting Rifle, Checkered Stock, Adjustable Trigger, No Sights, Repeater, *Modern*	250	575	650
Model 68DL, .458 Win. Mag., Sporting Rifle, Checkered Stock, Adjustable Trigger, No Sights, Repeater, *Modern*	300	650	750
Model 68DL, Various Calibers, Sporting Rifle, Checkered Stock, Adjustable Trigger, No Sights, Repeater, *Modern*	275	575	650

SCHUTZEN RIFLE EXAMPLES

RIFLE, SINGLESHOT

	Fair	V. Good	Excellent
Aydt System, Various Calibers, Dropping Block, Fancy Tyrol Stock, Fancy Engraving, Target Sights, *Modern*	700	1500	2000
Aydt System, Various Calibers, Dropping Block, Plain Tyrol Stock, Light Engraving, Target Sights, *Modern*	400	1200	1500
Martini System, Various Calibers, Dropping Block, Fancy Tyrol Stock, Fancy Engraving, Target Sights, *Modern*	700	1500	2000

SCHWARZLOSE

Andreas W. Schwarlose, Berlin, Germany, 1911–1927.

HANDGUN, SELF-LOADING

	Fair	V. Good	Excellent
M 1908 Pocket, 7.65mm, Blow-Forward, Clip Fed, Grip Safety, *Curio*	200	400	475
M 1908 W.A.C. Pocket, 7.65mm, Blow-Forward, Clip Fed, Grip Safety, *Curio*	$175	$375	$450
M96 Standardt, 7.65mm Mauser, Clip Fed, Blue, *Curio*	1400	3000	3500

Schwarzlose M 1908 WAC

SCOTT ARMS CO.

Norwich Falls Pistol Co., c. 1880.

HANDGUN, REVOLVER

	Fair	V. Good	Excellent
.32 Short R.F., 5 Shot, Spur Trigger, Solid Frame, Single Action, *Antique*	75	150	175

SCOTT REVOLVER-RIFLE

Hopkins & Allen, c. 1880.

HANDGUN, REVOLVER

	Fair	V. Good	Excellent
$24\frac{1}{2}$" Brass Barrel, .38 Short R.F., 5 Shot, Spur Trigger, Solid Frame, Single Action, *Antique*	150	300	350

SCOTT, D.

Edinburgh, Scotland, 1727–1745.

HANDGUN, FLINTLOCK

	Fair	V. Good	Excellent
Queen Anne Type, .59, Screw Barrel, Holster Pistol, Marked "Edinboro," *Antique*	750	1500	1950

SCOUT

Made by Hood Firearms for Frankfurt Hardware of Milwaukee, Wisc., c. 1870.

HANDGUN, REVOLVER

	Fair	V. Good	Excellent
.32 Short R.F., 5 Shot, Spur Trigger, Solid Frame, Single Action, *Antique*	75	125	150

SCOUT

Made by Stevens.

SHOTGUN, DOUBLE BARREL, SIDE-BY-SIDE

	Fair	V. Good	Excellent
Model 311, Various Gauges, Hammerless, Steel Barrel, *Modern*	75	175	200

S.E.A.M.

Fab. d'Armes de Soc. Espanola de Armas y Municiones, Eibar, Spain.

HANDGUN, SELF-LOADING

	Fair	V. Good	Excellent
Eibar Type, 6.35mm, 11 Slide Grooves, Good Quality, Clip Fed, Blue, *Modern*	75	150	175
Eibar Type, 6.35mm, 13 Slide Grooves, Fair Quality, Clip Fed, Blue, *Modern*	50	100	125
Walther Type, 6.35mm, Clip Fed, Blue, *Modern*	100	175	225

SEARS

Sears, Roebuck & Co., Chicago, Ill. Also see Ted Williams.

RIFLE, BOLT ACTION

	Fair	V. Good	Excellent
Semi-Sporterized Mauser, 8mm Mauser, Converted Military, *Modern*	$50	$100	$125
Sporterized Mauser, 8mm Mauser, Converted Military, Recoil Pad, *Modern*	75	125	150

SHOTGUN, BOLT ACTION

	Fair	V. Good	Excellent
.410 Gauge, Clip Fed, Blue, Plain, *Modern*	25	50	75
.410 Gauge, Singleshot, Plain, *Modern*	25	40	50
12 or 20 Gauges, Clip Fed, Adjustable Choke, Blue, Plain, *Modern*	25	40	50

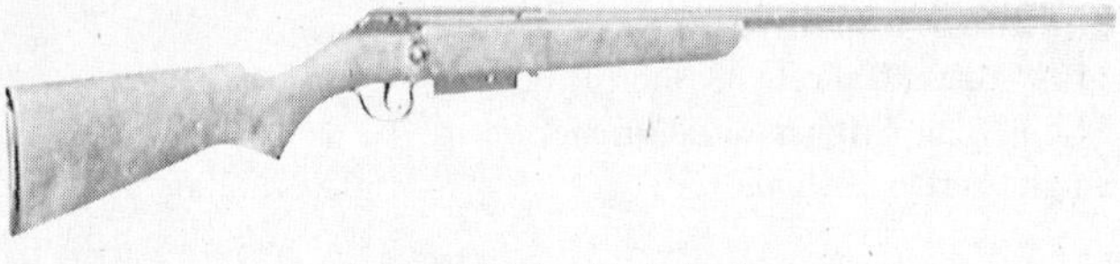

Sears 12 Ga. Bolt Action

	Fair	V. Good	Excellent
12 or 20 Gauges, Clip Fed, Blue, Plain, *Modern*	20	40	50

SHOTGUN, SINGLESHOT

	Fair	V. Good	Excellent
Various Gauges, Top Break, Plain, *Modern*	20	40	50
Youth, 20 or .410 Gauges, Plain, *Modern*	20	40	50

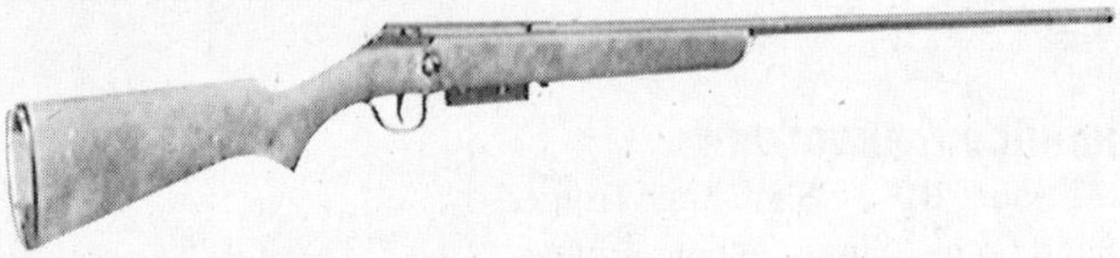

Sears Youth

SECRET SERVICE SPECIAL

Made for Fred Biffar, Chicago, by Iver Johnson and Meriden.

HANDGUN, REVOLVER

	Fair	V. Good	Excellent
.32 S & W, 5 Shot, Top Break, Hammerless, Double Action, *Modern*	25	50	75
.38 S & W, 5 Shot, Top Break, Hammerless, Double Action, *Modern*	25	50	75

SECURITY INDUSTRIES OF AMERICA

Little Ferry, N.J.

HANDGUN, REVOLVER

	Fair	V. Good	Excellent
Police Pocket, .357 Magnum, Stainless Steel, 2" Barrel, Swing-Out Cylinder, Double Action, Spurless Hammer, *Modern*	100	175	225
Security Undercover, .357 Magnum, Stainless Steel, 2" Barrel, Swing-Out Cylinder, Double Action, *Modern*	$100	$175	$225

SEDGLEY, R. F., INC.

Philadelphia, Pa., 1911–1938. Successor to Henry Kolb.

HANDGUN, REVOLVER

	Fair	V. Good	Excellent
Baby Hammerless, .22 L.R.R.F., Double Action, Folding Trigger, *Modern*	75	125	150

RIFLE, BOLT ACTION

	Fair	V. Good	Excellent
Springfield, Carbine, Various Calibers, Sporting Rifle, Lyman Sights, Checkered Stock, Full-Stocked, *Modern*	450	1150	1450
Springfield, Various Calibers, Sporting Rifle, Lyman Sights, Checkered Stock, *Modern*	400	800	1000
Springfield, Various Calibers, Sporting Rifle, Lyman Sights, Checkered Stock, Left-Hand, *Modern*	300	600	750

SELECTA

Echave y Arizmendi, Eibar, Spain.

HANDGUN, SELF-LOADING

	Fair	V. Good	Excellent
Model 1918, 6.35mm, Double Safety, Clip Fed, *Modern*	50	100	125
Model 1918, 6.35mm, Triple Safety, Clip Fed, *Modern*	50	100	125
Model 1919, 7.65mm, Double Safety, Clip Fed, *Modern*	50	100	125

Selecta Model 1919

	Fair	V. Good	Excellent
Model 1919, 7.65mm, Triple Safety, Clip Fed, *Modern*	50	100	150

SEMMERLING

Semmerling Corp., Newton, Mass. Currently manufactured by American Derringer Corp. Waco, Tex.

HANDGUN, MANUAL REPEATER

	Fair	V. Good	Excellent
LM-4, .45 ACP, Double Action, Clip Fed, *Modern*	600	1250	1500

SHAKANOOSA ARMS MFG. CO.
1862–1864. See Confederate Military.

RIFLE, PERCUSSION

	Fair	V. Good	Excellent
.58, Military (C S A), *Antique*	$5000	$10000	$13500
.58, Military, Carbine (C S A), *Antique*	4000	9000	11500

SHARPE
England, 1670–1680.

HANDGUN, FLINTLOCK

	Fair	V. Good	Excellent
Pair, Pocket Pistol, Screw Barrel, Octagon, High Quality, *Antique* ...	1400	3250	3750

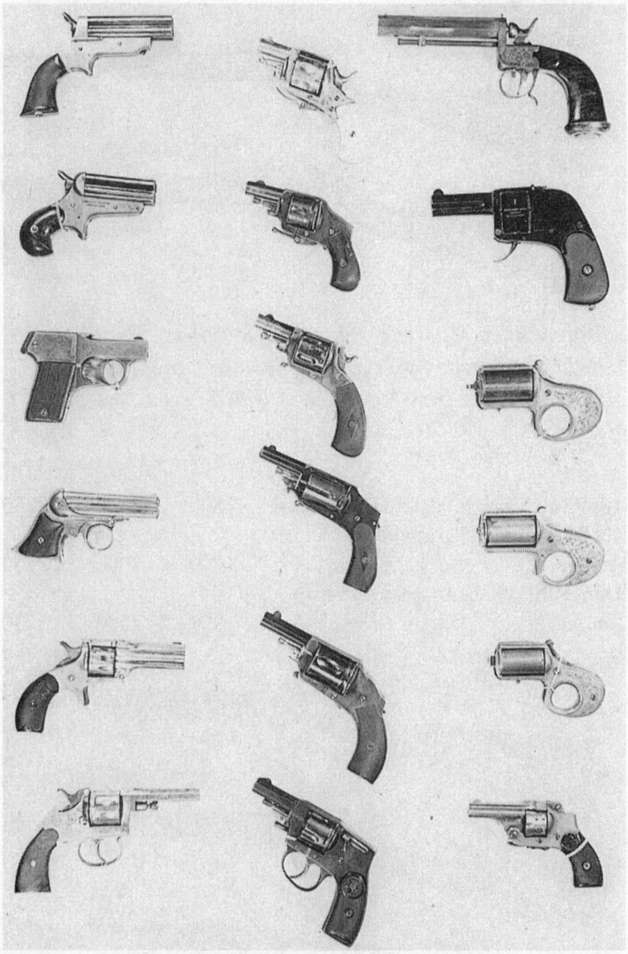

From top left, *two variations of Sharps four-barrel Pepperbox, first in .30 caliber, second in .32 with bird's head butt; Mossberg .22 Brownie 4-shot on Sharps principle; Remington 4-shot ring trigger Pepperbox; Osgood 2-barrel duplex revolver with .22/.32 super-imposed barrel; German blank or gas revolver, 10-shot; from top* right, *Belgian percussion single-shot pistol, in .22 caliber; bar pistol with flat reversible breech holding four cartridges; three variations of the Reid Knuckle Duster revolver, in .22 and .32 rimfire; and a Belgian break-open double-action Baby Hammerless revolver. From top* center, *six varieties of French Pocket metallic cartridge "suicide special" revolvers.*

SHARPS, CHRISTIAN
Mill Creek, Pa., 1848; moved to Hartford, Connecticut, in 1851 and became Sharps Rifle Mfg. Co., changing its name to Sharps Rifle Co. in 1874, continuing operations until 1881. In 1854 formed C. Sharps & Co. in Philadelphia, Pa., became Sharps & Hankins in 1862, C. Sharps & Co. again in 1866, and continued until 1880. Inventor and gun designer Christian Sharps, a native of New Jersey, was founder of the Sharps Rifle Manufacturing Company. After becoming a master machinist and gathering extensive experience in the gun trade, including at the Harpers Ferry Armory, Sharps launched his own company in Hartford, Connecticut in 1851. With Colt's Patent Fire Arms Mfg. Co. as a crosstown rival, the Sharps company concentrated on singleshot rifles with a falling block breech mechansim. However, in 1854 the inventor resigned from the firm, moving to Philadelphia. There he set up C. Sharps & Company, manufacturers of singleshot percussion pistols, followed by pepperbox-style four-barrel pistols. Sharps later joined forces with William Hankins, setting up Sharps & Hankins and adding a breech-loading carbine to the line. Sharps died in Vernon, Connecticut in 1874. The Sharps operations in Hartford, complete with a new factory built in 1853, came to be managed by Robbins & Lawrence of Windsor, Vermont. A broad line of falling block breechloading rifles made up the Sharps line, with the famed Civil War era "Beecher's Bibles" adding to the firm's notoriety. The percussion line was succeeded by metallic cartridge rifles, with similar falling block actions. Transition to the new models took place during and after the Civil War. Sales to the military and civilian trade brought substantial business to Sharps, whose buffalo rifles became part of the warp and woof of the Great American West. The "Old Reliable" trademark was stamped on the barrels of thousands of Sharps rifles, and is one of the best known of marketing slogans from nineteenth century gunmaking. The heavy-hitting, long range cartridges featured various .40, .44, .45, .50 calibers, accurate for hunting at ranges up to four and five hundred yards, and more. The true Sharps Buffalo Rifles were made in limited numbers only, with specific requirements for sights, barrel weight, and cartridges. Generally these arms were with octagonal barrels, with double set triggers, and weighed from approximately 10½ to as much as 20 pounds. Nearly coinciding with the demise of the great buffalo hunts, and in the face of stiff competition from repeating rifles, particularly the Winchester, the Sharps Rifle Company closed its doors in 1881. One of the legends of American gunmaking, the Sharps name lives on in modern firms, in the Shiloh Sharps and the Montana Armory companies, both of Big Timber, Montana. These firms, as well as Italian gunmakers, produce accurate, reliable and finely built reproductions based on the original Sharps singleshots of the nineteenth century.

HANDGUN, PERCUSSION

	Fair	V. Good	Excellent
Bryce Revolver, .25, Tip-Up, 6 Shot, Blue, Spur Trigger, Single Action, *Antique*	$800	$1750	$2350
Medium Frame Percussion Pistol, .31 & .34, *Antique*	900	2200	3250
Pistol Rifle Percussion Pistol, .31 & .38, *Antique*	1400	3000	4500
Revolver, .25, Tip-Up, 6 Shot, Blue, Spur Trigger, Single Action, *Antique*	800	1500	1950
Small Frame Percussion Pistol, .31 & .34, *Antique*	1100	2500	3500

HANDGUN, PERCUSSION REVOLVER

	Fair	V. Good	Excellent
Percussion Revolver, .25 caliber	$760	$1900	$2350

HANDGUN, MULTI-BARREL

	Fair	V. Good	Excellent
.22 R.F., Model 1A, 4 Barreled Pistol, *Antique*	150	350	450
.22 R.F., Model 1B, 4 Barreled Pistol, *Antique*	150	350	450
.22 R.F., Model 1C, 4 Barreled Pistol, *Antique*	150	300	400
.22 R.F., Model 1D, 4 Barreled Pistol, *Antique*	200	450	575
.30 R.F., Model 2C, 4 Barreled Pistol			
.30 R.F., Model 2C, 4 Barreled Pistol, *Antique*	125	350	450
.30 R.F., Model 1E, 4 Barreled Pistol, *Antique*	500	1000	1250
.30 R.F., Model 2, 4 Barreled Pistol, *Antique*	100	250	400
.30 R.F., Model 2B, 4 Barreled Pistol, *Antique*	150	350	450
.32 R.F. Bulldog, Model 4, 4 Barreled Pistol, Pin on Side of Frame, *Antique*	200	425	500
.32 R.F. Bulldog, Model 4, 4 Barreled Pistol, Screw Under Frame, *Antique*	200	400	475
.32 R.F., Model 3, 4 Barreled Pistol, *Antique*	200	400	475
.32 R.F., Model 4, 4 Barreled Pistol, Bird Head Grip, *Antique*	200	450	600
.32 R.F., Model 4, 4 Barreled Pistol, Mechanism on Hammer, *Antique*	300	750	950

HANDGUN, SINGLESHOT

	Fair	V. Good	Excellent
Medium Frame, Various Calibers, Single Action, Dropping Block, Hammer, *Antique*	900	2250	2850
Small Frame, Various Calibers, Single Action, Dropping Block, Hammer, *Antique*	900	2000	2500

Christian Sharps Patent Single Shot, .36 Caliber

RIFLE, PERCUSSION

	Fair	V. Good	Excellent
1849 Rifle, .36 & .44, *Antique*	2500	6000	12500
1850 Rifle, .36 & .44, *Antique*	2200	5000	8000
1851 Carbine, .52, Maynard Primer, *Antique*	$2500	$6000	$9000
1852 Carbine, .52, percussion Primer, *Antique*	1200	2200	3250
1853 Carbine, .52, percussion Primer, *Antique*	1000	2250	3750
1855 Carbine, .52, Maynard Primer, *Antique*	1600	3500	4750
1855 Rifle, .52, Maynard Primer, *Antique*	1600	3500	4750

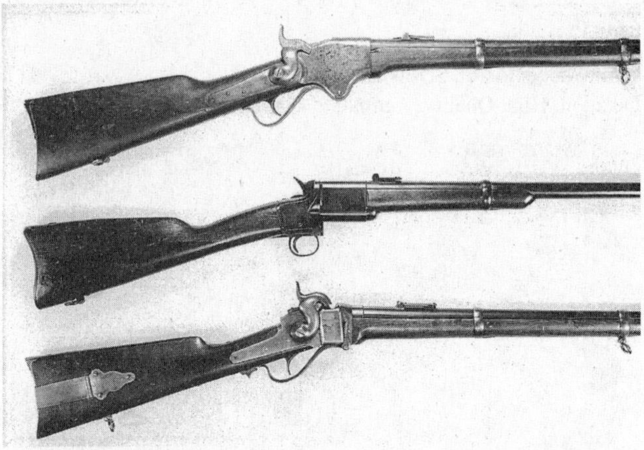

Military rifled Musket by Spencer (at top) in .52 caliber; a military-style rifle by Triplett & Scott in .56-50 Spencer rimfire; and the New Model 1863 Rifled percussion Musket by Sharps in .50-70 caliber.

	Fair	V. Good	Excellent
1859 Carbine, .52, Rim Fire, *Antique*	800	2500	3250
1863 Carbine, .52, Lawrence Cut-off, *Antique*	700	2000	2750
1863 Rifle, .52, Lawrence Cut-off, *Antique*	900	2500	3250

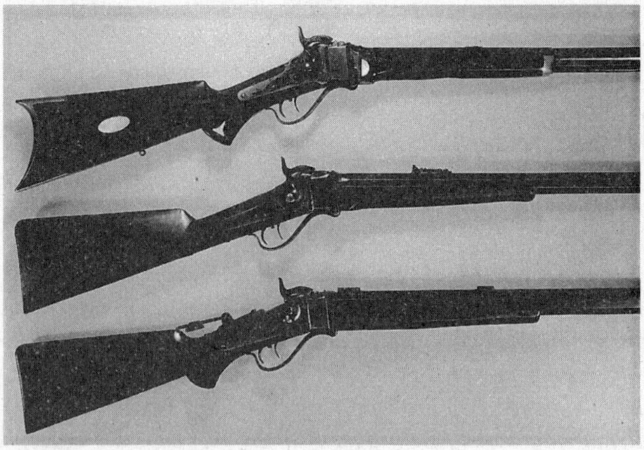

Sharps Model 1874 Sporting rifles, each with special features, including double-set triggers. The top *rifle in .40-70 caliber custom built by H. Slotterbek, Los Angeles; note silver plaque inlaid on pistol grip stock, half-octagonal barrel with cleaning rod;* center *in .45/100 caliber with Old Reliable barrel;* bottom *in .45 3 1/4" caliber with semi-pistol grip stock, tang peep sight, extra-heavy octagonal barrel, weighing 16 1/4 lbs.*

	Fair	V. Good	Excellent
RIFLE, SINGLESHOT			
1874 Hunting Rifle, Various Calibers, Open Sights, *Antique*	$1900	$4000	$5000
1874 Long Range Rifle, Various Calibers, Target Sights, *Antique*	3000	7500	9250
1874 Sporting Rifle, Various Calibers, Set Trigger, Target Sights, *Antique*	3000	3750	5000
1877 Target Rifle, .45 Caliber, *Antique*	7000	14000	18500
1878 Hunters Rifle, .40 & .45 Calibers, *Antique*	900	2200	2750
1878 Long Range Rifle, .40 & .45 Calibers, *Antique*	3000	7000	9250

SHARPSHOOTER

Hijos de Calixto Arrizabalaga, Eibar, Spain, c. 1920.

	Fair	V. Good	Excellent
HANDGUN, SELF-LOADING			
"Sharp-Shooter," .380 ACP, Clip Fed, Hammer, Hinged Barrel, Blue, *Curio*	100	125	150
"Sharp-Shooter," 6.35mm, Clip Fed, Hammer, Hinged Barrel, Blue, *Curio*	75	100	125
"Sharp-Shooter," 7.65mm, Clip Fed, Hammer, Hinged Barrel, Blue, *Curio*	75	100	125

SHATTUCK, C. S.

Hatfield, Mass., 1880–1890.

	Fair	V. Good	Excellent
HANDGUN, REVOLVER			
Lincoln/Garfield Grips, Hard Rubber, Add 20%-30%, *Antique*	100	200	275
.22 R.F., Single Action, Spur Trigger, Swing-Out Cylinder, *Antique*	100	225	300
.38 R.F., Double Action, Spur Trigger, Swing-Out Cylinder, *Antique*	150	275	325
.41 R.F., Double Action, Spur Trigger, Swing-Out Cylinder, *Antique*	200	375	425

SHAW, JOHN

London, England, c. 1688.

	Fair	V. Good	Excellent
HANDGUN, FLINTLOCK			
Holster Pistol, Engraved, Steel Mounts, High Quality, *Antique*	1900	2000	2850

SHELL, JOHN

Leslie County, Ky., 1810–1880. See Kentucky Rifles.

SHERIDEN

Racine, Wisc., 1953–1960.

	Fair	V. Good	Excellent
HANDGUN, SINGLESHOT			
Knockabout, .22 L.R.R.F., Tip-Up Barrel, Single Action, Hammer, Blue, *Modern*	75	100	125

SHILEN

Ennis, Tex.

	Fair	V. Good	Excellent
RIFLE, BOLT ACTION			
DGA Benchrest, Various Calibers, Target Rifle, *Modern*	$300	$625	$825
DGA Silhouette, Various Calibers, Target Rifle, *Modern*	225	550	650
DGA Sporter, Various Calibers, Blind Magazine, Plain Stock, *Modern*	250	550	650
DGA Varmint, Various Calibers, Heavy Barrel, *Modern*	250	550	650

SHILOH RIFLE MANUFACTURING CO.

Mfg. of Sharps Rifle Replicas, Big Timber, Mt.

	Fair	V. Good	Excellent
RIFLE, PERCUSSION			
Model 1859 New Model Cavalry Carbine, .54, Reproduction	150	325	500
Model 1862 Robinson Confederate Cavalry Carbine, .54, Reproduction	300	650	850
Model 1863 Cavalry Carbine, .54, Reproduction	250	500	700
Model 1863 New Model Military Rifle, .54, Reproduction	300	600	800
Model 1863 Sporting Rifle #2, .54, Reproduction	200	450	650
Model 1863 Sporting Rifle #3, .54, Reproduction	200	400	600
RIFLE, SINGLESHOT			
Model 1874 Business Rifle, Various Calibers, Reproduction, *Modern*	600	1200	1500
Model 1874 Hunter's Rifle, Various Calibers, Reproduction, *Modern*	600	1200	1500
Model 1874 Military Carbine, Various Calibers, Reproduction, *Modern*	250	575	750
Model 1874 Military Rifle, Various Calibers, Reproduction, *Modern*	300	650	850
Model 1874 Sporting Rifle #2, Various Calibers, Reproduction, *Modern*	600	1250	1650
Model 1874 Sporting Rifle #3, Various Calibers, Reproduction, *Modern*	600	1250	1650

SHORER, ANDREW

Northhampton, Pa., 1775–1776. See Kentucky Rifles.

SICKEL'S ARMS CO.

Belgium for Robert Sickel's & Preston Co., Davenport, Iowa.

	Fair	V. Good	Excellent
SHOTGUN, DOUBLE BARREL, SIDE-BY-SIDE			
Various Gauges, Hammerless, Damascus Barrel, *Modern*	50	100	125

	Fair	V. Good	Excellent
Various Gauges, Hammerless, Steel Barrel, *Modern*	$50	$125	$150
Various Gauges, Outside Hammers, Damascus Barrel, *Modern*	50	100	125
Various Gauges, Outside Hammers, Steel Barrel, *Modern*	50	100	135

SHOTGUN, SINGLESHOT

	Fair	V. Good	Excellent
Various Gauges, Hammer, Steel Barrel, *Modern*	50	50	75

S.I.G.

Schweizerische Industrie Gesellschaft, Neuhausen, Switzerland, since 1857.

HANDGUN, SELF-LOADING

	Fair	V. Good	Excellent
P210 Luxus, Various Calibers, Clip Fed, Fancy Engraving, Gold Inlay, High-Polish Blue Finish, Carved Wood Grips, *Modern*	1500	3000	3650
P210-1, .22 L.R.R.F., Clip Fed, Blue, High-Polish Finish, Wood Grips, *Modern*	600	1250	1500
P210-1, .22 L.R.R.F., Conversion Unit Only, *Modern*	250	500	650
P210-1, .30 Luger, Clip Fed, Blue, High-Polish Finish, Wood Grips, *Modern*	600	1350	1750
P210-1, .9mm Luger, Clip Fed, Blue, High-Polish Finish, Wood Grips, *Modern*	600	1400	1750
P210-1, Various Calibers, Clip Fed, Blue, High-Polish Finish, with 3 Caliber Conv. Units, Wood Grips, *Modern*	900	2000	2700
P210-2, .30 Luger, Clip Fed, Blue, Plastic Stock, *Modern*	450	950	1250
P210-2, .9mm Luger, Clip Fed, Blue, Plastic Stock, *Modern*	500	1000	1300
P210-5, .30 Luger, Clip Fed, Blue, Plastic Stock, Target Pistol, 6" Barrel, *Modern*	600	1200	1500
P210-5, .9mm Luger, Clip Fed, Blue, Plastic Stock, Target Pistol, 6" Barrel, *Modern*	600	1250	1500
P210-6, .30 Luger & 4mm, Clip Fed, Blue, Plastic Stock, Target Pistol, 4½" Barrel, *Modern*	$500	$1050	$1350
P210-7, .9mm Luger, Clip Fed, Blue, Plastic Stock, Target Pistol, Long Barrel, *Modern*	900	2250	2500
P 220 SIG-Sauer, Various Calibers, Clip Fed, Double Action, Blue, *Modern*	250	550	750
P 225 SIG-Sauer, .9mm Luger, Clip Fed, Double Action, Blue, *Modern*	250	525	725
P 230 SIG-Sauer, Various Calibers, Clip Fed, Double Action, *Modern*	175	350	500
P 2305L SIG-Sauer, Various Calibers, Clip Fed, Double Action, Stainless, *Modern*	200	400	500
SP 47/8 (Pre-210), 9mm Luger, Clip Fed, German Border Patrol, *Modern*	700	1750	2250
SP 47/8 (Pre-210), 9mm Luger, Clip Fed, Swiss Military, *Modern*	1100	2500	3250

S.I.G. P210-6

RIFLE, SELF-LOADING

	Fair	V. Good	Excellent
SIG AMT, .308 Win., Clip Fed, Bipod, *Modern*	700	1750	2150
SIG STG-57, 7.5 Swiss, Clip Fed, Bipod, *Modern*	1200	2500	2850

SILE

Imported by Sile Distributers, New York City.

HANDGUN, SELF-LOADING

	Fair	V. Good	Excellent
Seecamp, .25 ACP, Double Action, Clip Fed, Stainless Steel, *Modern*	100	175	200

SIMPLEX

Belgium, 1901–1906. Also see Bergmann.

HANDGUN, SELF-LOADING

	Fair	V. Good	Excellent
Simplex, 8mm Bergmann, Blue, *Curio*	600	1200	1650

SIMSON & CO.

Waffenfabrik Simson & Co., Suhl, Germany, 1910–1939. Also see Luger.

HANDGUN, SELF-LOADING

	Fair	V. Good	Excellent
M1927 Vest Pocket, .25 ACP, Clip Fed, Blue, *Curio*	225	450	550

RIFLE, BOLT ACTION

	Fair	V. Good	Excellent
Model 1933, .22 Extra Long, Singleshot, Checkered Stock, Target Sights, *Curio*	50	100	150
Precision Carbine, 9mm Shot, Singleshot, Plain, *Curio*	75	125	175
Sportrifle #7, .22 Extra Long, Singleshot, Checkered Stock, Target Sights, *Curio*	50	75	125

	Fair	V. Good	Excellent
SHOTGUN, DOUBLE BARREL, OVER-UNDER			
Trap Grade, 12 Ga., Automatic Ejectors, Checkered Stock, Engraved, Cocking Indicators, *Curio*	$700	$1500	$1850
SHOTGUN, DOUBLE BARREL, SIDE-BY-SIDE			
Astora, Various Calibers, Checkered Stock, Plain, *Curio*	150	300	400
Magnum, 12 Ga. 3", Checkered Stock, Engraved, *Curio*	350	700	800
Monte Carlo, 12 Ga., Checkered Stock, Fancy Engraving, Automatic Ejectors, Sidelock, *Curio*	700	1500	1750

SINGER

Arizmendi y Geonaga, Eibar, Spain.

	Fair	V. Good	Excellent
HANDGUN, SELF-LOADING			
6.35mm, Clip Fed, Blue, *Modern*	50	100	125
7.65mm, Clip Fed, Blue, *Modern*	75	125	150

SINGER

Frantisek Dusek, Opocno, Czechoslovakia.

	Fair	V. Good	Excellent
HANDGUN, SELF-LOADING			
Duo, 6.35mm, Clip Fed, Blue, *Modern*	50	100	125

SJOGREN

Sweden.

	Fair	V. Good	Excellent
SHOTGUN, SELF-LOADING			
12 Ga., 5 Shot, Checkered Stock, Recoil Operated, *Curio*	200	400	500

SKB

Tokyo, Japan.

	Fair	V. Good	Excellent
SHOTGUN, DOUBLE BARREL, OVER-UNDER			
Model 500, 12 and 20 Gauges, Field Grade, Selective Ejector, Vent Rib, *Modern*	225	475	550
Model 500, 12 Ga. Mag. 3", Field Grade, Selective Ejector, Vent Rib, *Modern*	250	525	600
Model 600, .410 Gauges, Skeet Grade, Selective Ejector, Vent Rib, *Modern*	250	525	600
Model 600, 12 and 20 Gauges, Field Grade, Selective Ejector, Vent Rib, *Modern*	300	625	700
Model 600, 12 and 20 Gauges, Skeet Grade, Selective Ejector, Vent Rib, *Modern*	300	625	700
Model 600, 12 Ga., Trap Grade, Selective Ejector, Vent Rib, *Modern*	300	600	700
Model 600, 12 Ga., Trap Grade, Selective Ejector, Vent Rib, Monte Carlo Stock, *Modern*	$300	$600	$700
Model 600 Combo Set, Various Gauges, Skeet Grade, Selective Ejector, Vent Rib, Cased, *Modern*	400	900	1100
Model 680 English, 12 and 20 Gauges, Field Grade, Selective Ejector, Vent Rib, *Modern*	350	700	850
Model 700, 12 and 20 Gauges, Skeet Grade, Selective Ejector, Vent Rib, *Modern*	400	825	925
Model 700, 12 Ga., Trap Grade, Selective Ejector, Vent Rib, *Modern*	400	800	1000
Model 700, 12 Ga., Trap Grade, Selective Ejector, Vent Rib, Monte Carlo Stock, *Modern*	400	800	1000
Model 700 Combo Set, Various Gauges, Skeet Grade, Selective Ejector, Vent Rib, Cased, *Modern*	700	1500	1850
SHOTGUN, SELF-LOADING			
XL 900, 12 and 20 Gauges, Skeet Grade, *Modern*	125	250	350
XL 900, 12 Ga., Trap Grade, Monte Carlo Stock, *Modern*	125	250	350
XL 900 MR, 12 and 20 Gauges, Vent Rib, *Modern*	125	225	300
XL 900 Slug, 12 and 20 Gauges, Open Rear Sight, *Modern*	125	250	350

SLOANS

Importers, New York City. Also see Charles Daly.

	Fair	V. Good	Excellent
SHOTGUN, DOUBLE BARREL, SIDE-BY-SIDE			
POS, .410 Ga., Checkered Stock, Hammerless, Double Trigger, *Modern*	75	200	250
POS, 10 Ga., $3^1/_2$", Checkered Stock, Hammerless, Double Trigger, *Modern*	75	200	250
POS, 12 and 20 Gauges, Checkered Stock, Hammerless, Double Trigger, *Modern*	75	150	200
POS Coach Gun, 12 and 20 Gauges, Checkered Stock, Outside Hammers, Double Trigger, *Modern*	75	150	200

SMITH & WESSON

Started in Norwich, Connecticut, in 1855 as Volcanic Repeating Arms Co. Reorganized at Springfield, Mass. as Smith & Wesson in 1857 (Volcanic Repeating Arms moved to New Haven, Conn. in 1856 and was purchased in 1857 by what would become Winchester Repeating Arms Co.). Smith & Wesson at Springfield, Massachusetts to date. Also see U.S. Military and the Commemorative section. One of America's oldest gunmakers, Smith & Wesson shares its early years with the predecessor firms to the Winchester Repeating Arms Co. Seventeen years older than D. B.

Wesson, Horace Smith had eighteen years of experience at the Springfield Armory, fine-tuning his expertise at factories in New Haven and Norwich, Connecticut, and at Worcester, Massachusetts. Wesson had worked with his older brothers, Edwin and Frank, themselves accomplished riflemakers, as well as with other Massachusetts gunmakers. Smith and Wesson had years of experience with Cortlandt Palmer in Norwich, building the patented magazine firearm known as the Volcanic. In 1855 the patent for that design was sold and the business relocated in New Haven, evolving eventually into the Winchester Repeating Arms Co. Smith and Wesson both served the New Haven factory as superintendents. Wesson's successor was none other than B. Tyler Henry, one of the most accomplished mechanics of his day, and the designer of both the Henry lever-action repeating rifle, and the .44 cartridge that it fired. It was the development of what became the first successful repeating handgun for metallic self-contained cartridges that reunited Smith and Wesson, only months before Samuel Colt's master revolver patent would expire, in 1857. The partners had a windfall of $18,000, from sale of the Volcanic operation. They soon had a design for a revolver, in which the cylinder was bored end to end, permitting loading of the new .22 caliber rimfire cartridge, which they termed the No. 1—the revolver also came to be known as the Model 1. An April 3, 1855, patent of inventor Rollin White had secured rights to the manufacture of a bored through cylinder. Smith and Wesson arranged for White to license their use of that feature, for a flat fee of $500 and a royalty of 25 cents per revolver. However, the agreement shrewdly specified that White himself had to defend the exclusivity of his patent, a requirement which would consume much of his royalties over the years. Within a year Smith & Wesson had established itself, and by September 1858 extra-quality plated pistols were in the line, as well as such amenities as frames plated in gold or silver, ivory grips, and hand engraving. By the 1870s and 1880s the Smith & Wesson line had expanded to one of the most complete selections of metallic cartridge handguns in the world. Mechanisms ranged from single action to double action, and, in the twentieth century, automatic pistols were introduced. Revolver calibers, for both single and double actions, ranged from the .22 short on up to the .45 S & W. A 12-gauge side-by-side shotgun, designed by D. B. Wesson, was brought out in 1868. Only about 219 were made by the Wesson Fire Arms Co. Smith & Wesson's ownership in the twentieth century has changed over the years. Bangor Punta owned the company from 1965 to 1984; present ownership is Tompkins p.l.c., of Great Britain.

	Fair	*V. Good*	*Excellent*
SHOTGUN, DOUBLE BARREL			
Shotgun, Double Barrel, Hammer, Damascus, 12 Gauge; Premium if Specially Decorated Beyond Standard	$1200	$2650	$4000
HANDGUN, REVOLVER			
.32 Double Action, .32 S & W, 1st Model, Top Break, 5 Shot, Straight-Cut Sideplate, Rocker Cylinder Stop, *Antique*	1800	3500	4250
.32 Double Action, .32 S & W, 2nd Model, Top Break, 5 Shot, Irregularly Cut Sideplate, Rocker Cylinder Stop, *Antique*	75	200	275
.32 Double Action, .32 S & W, 3rd Model, Top Break, 5 Shot, Irregularly Cut Sideplate, *Antique*	$75	$200	$250
.32 Double Action, .32 S & W, 4th Model, Round-Back Triggerguard, Top Break, 5 Shot, Irregularly Cut Sideplate, *Curio*	75	200	250
.32 Double Action, .32 S & W, 5th Model, Round-Back Triggerguard, Top Break, 5 Shot, Irregularly Cut Sideplate, Front Sight Forged on Barrel, *Curio*	75	200	250
.32 Hand Ejector 1903, .32 S & W Long, Solid Frame, Swing-Out Cylinder, 6 Shot, Double Action, *Curio*	75	200	250
.32 Hand Ejector, (Bekeart), .32 S & W Long, Solid Frame, Swing-Out Cylinder, 6 Shot, Target Sights, Double Action, *Curio*	300	800	900
.32 Hand Ejector, .32 S & W Long, 1st Model, Solid Frame, Swing-Out Cylinder, Hammer Actuated Cylinder Stop, 6 Shot, *Curio*	200	500	600
.32 Regulation Police, .32 S & W Long, Solid Frame, Swing-Out Cylinder, 6 Shot, Double Action, *Curio*	150	225	300
.32 Safety Hammerless, .32 S & W Long, 1st Model, Double Action, Top Break, 5 Shot, Push-Button Latch, *Curio*	100	250	300
.32 Safety Hammerless, .32 S & W Long, 2nd Model, Double Action, Top Break, 5 Shot, T Latch, *Curio*	100	200	275
.32 Safety Hammerless, .32 S & W, 3rd Model, Double Action, Top Break, 5 Shot, Over #170,000, *Curio*	100	200	275
.32 Single Action, .32 S & W, 10" Barrel, Add 75%-100%			
.32 Single Action, .32 S & W, 6" or 8" Barrel, Add 50%-75%			
.32 Single Action, .32 S & W, Top Break, Spur Trigger, 5 Shot, *Antique*	100	250	350
.38 D A Perfected, .38 S & W, Made With Side Latch, Hand-Ejector Action, Top Break, Double Action, *Curio*	200	450	500
.38 Double Action, .38 S & W, 1st Model, Straight-Cut Sideplate, Rocker Cylinder Stop, Double Action, Top Break, 5 Shot, *Antique*	300	700	775
.38 Double Action, .38 S & W, 2nd Model, Irregularly Cut Sideplate, Rocker Cylinder Stop, Double Action, Top Break, 5 Shot, *Antique*	100	200	250
.38 Double Action, .38 S & W, 3rd Model, Irregularly Cut Sideplate, Double Action, Top Break, 5 Shot, *Antique*	100	200	250

	Fair	*V. Good*	*Excellent*
.38 Double Action, .38 S & W, 4th Model, #'s 32701-539000, Double Action, Top Break, 5 Shot, *Curio*	$100	$200	$250
.38 Double Action, .38 S & W, 5th Model, #'s 539001-554077, Double Action, Top Break, 5 Shot, *Curio*	100	250	300
.38 Hand Ejector 1902, .38 Special, Military and Police, Solid Frame, Swing-Out Cylinder, Double Action, *Curio*	100	250	300
.38 Hand Ejector 1902, .38 Special, Military and Police, Solid Frame, Swing-Out Cylinder, Double Action, Adjustable Sights, *Curio*	200	400	500
.38 Hand Ejector 1905, .38 Special, Military and Police, Solid Frame, Swing-Out Cylinder, Double Action, *Curio*	150	300	350
.38 Hand Ejector 1905, .38 Special, Military and Police, Solid Frame, Swing-Out Cylinder, Double Action, Adjustable Sights, *Curio*	200	400	500
.38 Hand Ejector, .38 Long Colt, 1st Model, Solid Frame, Swing-Out Cylinder, No Cylinder-Pin Front-Lock, U.S. Army Model, *Curio*	400	900	1000
.38 Hand Ejector, .38 Long Colt, 1st Model, Solid Frame, Swing-Out Cylinder, No Cylinder-Pin Front-Lock, U.S. Navy Model, *Curio*	700	1400	1500
.38 Hand Ejector, .38 Special, 1st Model, Solid Frame, Swing-Out Cylinder, No Cylinder-Pin Front-Lock, Adjustable Sights, *Curio*	250	500	600
.38 Hand Ejector, .38 Special, 2nd Model, Solid Frame, Swing-Out Cylinder, *Curio*	150	250	350
.38 Hand Ejector, .38 Special, 2nd Model, Solid Frame, Swing-Out Cylinder, Adjustable Sights, *Curio*	250	500	600
.38 Safety Hammerless, .38 S & W, 1st Model-Button Latch, Release on Left Topstrap, Top Break, Double Action, *Antique*	300	700	800
.38 Safety Hammerless, .38 S & W, 2nd Model-Button Latch, Release on Top of Frame, Top Break, Double Action, *Antique*	150	250	350
2" Barrel, Add 50%			
.38 Safety Hammerless, .38 S & W, 3rd Model-Button Latch, Release on Rear Topstrap, Top Break, Double Action, *Antique*	150	250	350
2" Barrel, Add 50%			

	Fair	*V. Good*	*Excellent*
.38 Safety Hammerless, .38 S & W, 4th Model T-Shaped Latch, Top Break, Double Action, *Curio*	$150	$250	$350
2" Barrel, Add 50%			
.38 Safety Hammerless, .38 S & W, 5th Model T-Shaped Latch, Top Break, Double Action, Front Sight Forged on Barrel, Curio	150	250	300
2" Barrel, Add 50%			
.38 Single Action, .38 S & W, 1st Model, Baby Russian, Top Break, Spur Trigger, *Antique*	200	500	600
.38 Single Action, .38 S & W, 2nd Model, Top Break, Spur Trigger, Short Ejector Housing, *Antique*	150	300	350
.38 Single Action, .38 S & W, 3rd Model, Top Break, with Trigger Guard, *Curio*	400	700	800
.38 Single Action, .38 S & W, 3rd Model, Top Break, with Trigger Guard, with Extra Singleshot Barrel, *Curio*	600	1300	1500
.38 Single Action, .38 S & W, Mexican Model, Top Break, Spur Trigger, 5 Shot, *Curio*	900	2000	2500
.38 Win. Double Action, .38-40 WCF, Top Break, *Curio*	1200	2700	3000
.44 Double Action Frontier, for Target Sights, Add 30%-50%			
.44 Double Action, .44 Russian, 1st Model, Top Break, 6 Shot, *Antique*	500	1000	1200
.44 Double Action, for Target Sights, Add 20%-30%			
.44 Double Action, Wesson Favorite, 6 Shot, Lightweight, Top Break, *Antique*	1100	2700	3000
.44 Hand Ejector, .44 Special, 1st Model, Triple-Lock, Solid Frame, Swing-Out Cylinder, New Century, *Curio*	400	900	1000
.44 Hand Ejector, .44 Special, 2nd Model, Un-Shrouded Ejector Rod, Solid Frame, Swing-Out Cylinder, *Curio*	300	500	600
.44 Hand Ejector, .44 Special, 3rd Model, Shrouded Ejector Rod, Solid Frame, Swing-Out Cylinder, *Curio*	350	500	600
.44 Hand Ejector, 1st Model, for Target Sights, Add 50%			
.44 Hand Ejector, 2nd Model, for Target Sights, Add 20%-30%			
.44 Hand Ejector, 3rd Model, for Target Sights, Add 20%-30%			
.44 Hand Ejector, Calibers other than .44 Spec., Add 15%-25%			
.44 Hand Ejector, Calibers other than .44 Spec., Add 15%-25%			

	Fair	V. Good	Excellent
.44 New Model #3 Frontier, .44–40 WCF, Top Break, 6 Shot, *Antique*	$900	$2000	$2500
with Target Sights, Add 25%			
.455 MK II Hand Ejector, Solid Frame, Swing-Out Cylinder, Double Action, Military, Curio	250	500	600
22/32 Bekeart Model, .22 L.R.R.F., #'s 138220-139275, Target Pistol, Double Action, Adjustable Sights, 6" Barrel, *Curio*	300	700	1000
22/32 Kit Gun, .22 L.R.R.F., Early Model, Double Action Adjustable Sights, 4" Barrel, Pre-World War II, Curio	300	700	900
32/20 Hand Ejector 1902, .32-20 WCF, 2nd Model, Solid Frame, Swing-Out Cylinder, 6 Shot, *Curio*	200	400	500
32/20 Hand Ejector 1902, .32-20 WCF, 2nd Model, Solid Frame, Swing-Out Cylinder, 6 Shot, Adjustable Sights, *Curio*	300	600	700
32/20 Hand Ejector 1905, .32-20 WCF, Solid Frame, Swing-Out Cylinder, 6 Shot, Adjustable Sights, *Curio*	225	600	700
32/20 Hand Ejector 1905, .32-20 WCF, Solid Frame, Swing-Out Cylinder, 6 Shot, Victory Model, *Curio*	150	250	350
32/20 Hand Ejector, .32-20 WCF, 1st Model, Solid Frame, Swing-Out Cylinder, 6 Shot, No Cylinder-Pin Front-Lock, *Curio*	225	475	525
38/200 British (Model 11), .38 S & W, Military & Police, Solid Frame, Swing-Out Cylinder, Double Action, Military, *Curio*	150	300	350
First Model Schofield, .45 S & W, Top Break, Single Action, Military, *Antique*	1700	3500	4500
First Model Schofield, .45 S & W, Top Break, Single Action, Commercial, *Antique*	2200	4500	5000
First Model Schofield, .45 S & W, Wells Fargo, Top Break, Single Action, *Antique*	1500	3000	3500
Second Model Schofield, .45 S & W, Knurled Latch, Top Break, Single Action, Military, *Antique*	1600	3500	4500
Second Model Schofield, .45 S & W, Knurled Latch, Top Break, Single Action, Commercial, *Antique*	2100	4250	4750
Second Model Schofield, .45 S & W, Wells Fargo, Knurled Latch, Top Break, Single Action, *Antique*	1200	2500	3000

	Fair	V. Good	Excellent
K-22 Masterpiece, .22 L.R.R.F., 2nd Model, K-22 Hand Ejector, Speed Lock Action, Double Action, Adjustable Sights, 6" Barrel, *Modern*	$250	$500	$600
K-22 Outdoorsman, .22 L.R.R.F., 1st Model, Double Action, Adjustable Sights, 6" Barrel, *Modern*	300	600	700
K-32 Masterpiece, .32 S & W Long, 1st Model, Pre-War, 6 Shot Adjustable Sights, Target Pistol, only made 97, *Modern*	2200	4000	4500
K-32 Masterpiece, .32 S & W Long, 2nd Model, Post-War, 6 Shot, Adjustable Sights, Target Pistol, *Modern*	400	900	1200
Model "13," .357 Magnum, Double Action, Swing-Out Cylinder, *Modern*	300	500	575
Model #1, .22 Short R.F., 1st Issue, Tip-Up, Spur Trigger, 7 Shot, *Antique*	1200	3500	4500
Model #1, .22 Short R.F., 2nd Issue, Tip-Up, Spur Trigger, 7 Shot, *Antique*	150	400	500
Model #1, .22 Short R.F., 3rd Issue, Tip-Up, Spur Trigger, 7 Shot, *Antique*	100	300	400
Model #1 1/2, .32 Short R.F., 1st Issue, Tip-Up, Spur Trigger, 5 Shot, Non-Fluted Cylinder, *Antique*	150	350	450
Model #1 1/2, .32 Short R.F., 2nd Issue, Tip-Up, Spur Trigger, 5 Shot, Fluted Cylinder, *Antique*	150	350	450
Model #2 Old Army, .22 Short R.F., Tip-Up, Spur Trigger, 6 Shot, *Antique*	400	800	900
Model #3 American, .44 Henry, 1st Model, Single Action, Top Break, 6 Shot, *Antique*	3000	5500	6000
Model #3 American, .44 Henry, 2nd Model, #'s 8000-32800, Single Action, Top Break, 6 Shot, *Antique*	2500	5000	5500
Model #3 American, .44 S & W, 1st Model, Single Action, Top Break, 6 Shot, *Antique*	1600	3500	4000
Model #3 American, .44 S & W, 2nd Model, #'s 8000-32800, Single Action, Top Break, 6 Shot, *Antique*	1100	2700	3000
Model #3 Fronter, .38-40 WCF, Single Action, Top Break, 6 Shot, *Antique*	3500	6500	7000
Model #3 Fronter, .44-40 WCF, Single Action, Top Break, 6 Shot, *Antique*	1200	2700	3000
Model #3 New Model, .44 Russian, Argentine Model, Add 15%-25%			
Model #3 New Model, .44 Russian, Australian Police with Shoulder Stock, Add 50%-100%			
Model #3 New Model, .44 Russian, Japanese Navy Issue, Add 15%-25%			
Model #3 New Model, .44 Russian, Single Action, Top Break, 6 Shot, *Antique*	900	2200	2500

	Fair	V. Good	Excellent
Model #3 New Model, .44 S & W, Turkish Model, Add 15%-25%			
Model #3 New Model, Calibers, Calibers other than .44 Russian, Add 25%			
Model #3 Russian, .44 Russian, 1st Model, Single Action, Top Break, 6 Shot, Military, *Antique*	$1100	$2700	$3000
Model #3 Russian, .44 Russian, 2nd Model, Finger-Rest Triggerguard, Single Action, Top Break, 6 Shot, *Antique*	1000	2500	2750
Model #3 Russian, .44 Russian, 2nd Model, Finger-Rest Triggerguard, Single Action, Top Break, with Shoulder Stock, Antique	1750	3500	4000
Model #3 Russian, .44 Russian, 3rd Model, Front Sight Forged on Barrel, Single Action, Top Break, 6 Shot, *Antique*	1100	2500	2750
Model #3 Target, .32-44 S & W, 38-44 S & W, New Model #3, with Target Sights, Single Action, Top Break, *Curio*	900	2750	3500
Model 10, .38 Special, Double Action, Blue, Various Barrel Lengths, Swing-Out Cylinder, *Modern*	100	150	250
Model 10, .38 Special, Double Action, Swing-Out Cylinder, 4" Barrel, Heavy Barrel, Blue, *Modern*	125	175	275
Model 10, .38 Special, Double Action, Swing-Out Cylinder, 4" Barrel, Heavy Barrel, Nickel Plated, *Modern*	100	200	300
Model 10, .38 Special, Double Action, Swing-Out Cylinder, Various Barrel Lengths, Nickel Plated, *Modern*	100	200	275
Model 11 (.38/200), .38 S & W, Double Action, Swing-Out Cylinder, *Modern*	125	225	300
Model 12 (U.S.A.F. Model 13), .38 Special, Double Action, Swing-Out Cylinder, Lightweight, *Modern*	300	600	750
Model 12, .38 Special, Double Action, Swing-Out Cylinder, Various Barrel Lengths, Blue, *Modern*	125	300	400
Model 12, .38 Special, Double Action, Swing-Out Cylinder, Various Barrel Lengths, Nickel Plated, *Modern*	125	325	450
Model 14 SA, .38 Special, Single Action, Swing-Out Cylinder, 6" Barrel, Blue, Adjustable Sights, *Modern*	125	275	325
Model 14 SA, .38 Special, Single Action, Swing-Out Cylinder, 8 3/8" Barrel, Blue, Adjustable Sights, *Modern*	150	300	350
Model 14, .38 Special, Double Action, Swing-Out Cylinder, 6" Barrel, Blue, Adjustable Sights, *Modern*	125	225	275

	Fair	V. Good	Excellent
Model 14, .38 Special, Double Action, Swing-Out Cylinder, 8 3/8" Barrel, Blue, Adjustable Sights, *Modern*	$150	$250	$300
Model 15, .38 Special, Double Action, Swing-Out Cylinder, Various Barrel Lengths, Blue, Adjustable Sights, *Modern*	125	225	300
Model 15, .38 Special, Double Action, Swing-Out Cylinder, Various Barrel Lengths, Nickel Plated, Adjustable Sights, *Modern*	125	250	325

S & W Model 15

	Fair	V. Good	Excellent
Model 16, .32 S & W Long, Double Action, Swing-Out Cylinder, Adjustable Sights, Target Pistol, *Modern*	125	650	950
Model 17, .22 L.R.R.F., Double Action, Swing-Out Cylinder, 6" Barrel, Adjustable Sights, Blue, *Modern*	125	250	300
Model 17, .22 L.R.R.F., Double Action, Swing-Out Cylinder, 8 3/8" Barrel, Adjustable Sights, Blue, *Modern*	150	275	325
Model 18, .22 L.R.R.F., Double Action, Swing-Out Cylinder, 4" Barrel, Adjustable Sights, Blue, *Modern*	125	250	300
Model 19, .357 Magnum, Double Action, Swing-Out Cylinder, Various Barrel Lengths, Adjustable Sights, Blue, *Modern*	150	300	350
Model 19, .357 Magnum, Double Action, Swing-Out Cylinder, Various Barrel Lengths, Adjustable Sights, Nickel Plated, *Modern*	150	275	325
Model 1917, .45 Auto-Rim, Double Action, Swing-Out Cylinder, Brazilian Contract, + 45 ACP, *Curio*	100	200	250
Model 1917, .45 Auto-Rim, Double Action, Swing-Out Cylinder, Military, + 45 ACP, *Modern*	200	450	650
Model 20, .38 Special, Double Action, Swing-Out Cylinder, *Modern*	125	300	450
Model 21 "1950 Military," .44 Special, Double Action, Swing-Out Cylinder, Various Barrel Lengths, *Modern*	150	400	500
with Target Sights, Add 50%			

	Fair	V. Good	Excellent
Model 22 "1950. 45 Military," .45 Auto-Rim, Double Action, Swing-Out Cylinder, *Modern*	$150	$300	$400
Model 23, .38 Special, Double Action, Swing-Out Cylinder, Adjustable Sights, Target Pistol, *Modern*	300	700	800
Model 24, .44 Special, Double Action, Swing-Out Cylinder, Various Barrel Lengths, Adjustable Sights, *Modern*	225	475	525
Model 25, .45 Auto-Rim, Double Action, Swing-Out Cylinder, Target Pistol, Blue, 125th Anniversary, Cased with Accessories, + 45 ACP, *Modern*	150	300	400
Model 25, .45 Auto-Rim, Double Action, Swing-Out Cylinder, Target Pistol, Blue, *Modern*	150	300	350
with 8 3/4" Barrel, Add 25%			
Model 26,.45 Auto-Rim, Double Action, Swing-Out Cylinder, *Modern*	300	600	700
with 8 3/4" Barrel, Add 25%			
Model 27 with Registration, .357 Magnum, Double Action, Swing-Out Cylinder, Pre-World War II, Adjustable Sights, *Curio*	800	1600	1750
with 8 3/4" Barrel, Add 25%			
Model 27, .357 Magnum, Double Action, 8 3/8" Barrel, Adjustable Sights, Cased with Accessories, Nickel Plated, *Modern*	150	300	350
with 8 3/4" Barrel, Add 25%			
Model 27, .357 Magnum, Double Action, 8 3/8" Barrel, Adjustable Sights, Cased with Accessories, Blue, *Modern*	150	300	350
with 8 3/4" Barrel, Add 25%			
Model 27, .357 Magnum, Double Action, Swing-Out Cylinder, Pre-War, Adjustable Sights, *Curio*	300	750	900
with 8 3/4" Barrel, Add 25%			
Model 27, .357 Magnum, Double Action, Swing-Out Cylinder, Various Barrel Lengths, Adjustable Sights, Blue, *Modern*	150	250	300
Model 27, .357 Magnum, Double Action, Swing-Out Cylinder, Nickel Plated, *Modern*	150	250	325
Model 27, .357 Magnum, Double Action, Swing-Out Cylinder, 8 3/8" Barrel, Blue, *Modern*	150	250	350
Model 27, .357 Magnum, Double Action, Swing-Out Cylinder, 8 3/8" Barrel, Nickel Plated, *Modern*	150	250	350
Model 27, .357 Magnum, Double Action, Various Barrel Lengths, Adjustable Sights, Cased with Accessories, Nickel Plated or blue, *Modern*	150	250	300
Model 28, .357 Magnum, Double Action, Various Barrel Lengths, Adjustable Sights, Blue, Highway Patrolman, *Modern*	100	200	250

S & W Model 28

	Fair	V. Good	Excellent
Model 29, .44 Magnum, Double Action, 8 3/8" Barrel, Adjustable Sights, Swing-Out Cylinder, Blue, *Modern*	$200	$250	$350
Model 29, .44 Magnum, Double Action, 8 3/8" Barrel, Adjustable Sights, Swing-Out Cylinder, Nickel Plated, *Modern*	200	250	350
Model 29, .44 Magnum, Double Action, 8 3/8" Barrel, Adjustable Adjustable Sights, Cased with Accessories, Blue, *Modern*	225	275	375
Model 29, .44 Magnum, Double Action, 8 3/8" Barrel, Adjustable Adjustable Sights, Cased with Accessories, Nickel Plated, *Modern*	225	275	375
Model 29, .44 Magnum, Double Action, Various Barrel Lengths, Adjustable Sights, Swing-Out Cylinder, Blue, *Modern*	150	250	350
Model 29, .44 Magnum, Double Action, Various Barrel Lengths, Adjustable Sights, Swing-Out Cylinder, Nickel Plated, *Modern*	150	250	350
Model 29, .44 Magnum, Double Action, Various Barrel Lengths, Adjustable Sights, Cased with Accessories, Blue, *Modern*	175	275	375
Model 29, .44 Magnum, Double Action, Various Barrel Lengths, Adjustable Sights, Cased with Accessories, Nickel Plated, *Modern*	175	275	375
Model 30, .32 S & W Long, Double Action, Swing-Out Cylinder, *Modern*	100	200	300
Model 31, .32 S & W Long, Double Action, Swing-Out Cylinder, Various Barrel Lengths, Nickel Plated, *Modern*	100	250	350
Model 31, .32 S & W Long, Double Action, Swing-Out Cylinder, Various Barrel Lengths, Blue, *Modern*	100	200	300
Model 32, .32 S & W, Double Action, Swing-Out Cylinder, 2" Barrel, *Modern*	100	200	325
Model 33, .32 S & W, Double Action, Swing-Out Cylinder, *Modern*	100	250	350
Model 34 "Kit Gun," .22 L.R.R.F., Double Action, Swing-Out Cylinder, Various Barrel Lengths, Adjustable Sights, Blue, *Modern*	150	250	325

	Fair	V. Good	Excellent
Model 34 "Kit Gun," .22 L.R.R.F., Double Action, Swing-Out Cylinder, Various Barrel Lengths, Adjustable Sights, Nickel Plated, *Modern*	$150	$300	$350
Model 35, .22 L.R.R.F., Double Action, Swing-Out Cylinder, Target Pistol, Adjustable Sights, *Modern*	150	325	425
Model 36, .38 Special, Double Action, Swing-Out Cylinder, Various Barrel Lengths, Blue, *Modern*	100	150	250
Model 36, .38 Special, Double Action, Swing-Out Cylinder, Various Barrel Lengths, Nickel Plated, *Modern*	100	200	300

S & W Model 36

	Fair	V. Good	Excellent
Model 36, .38 Special, Double Action, Swing-Out Cylinder, 3" Barrel, Heavy Barrel, Blue, Modern	100	150	250
Model 36, .38 Special, Double Action, Swing-Out Cylinder, 3" Barrel, Heavy Barrel, Nickel Plated, *Modern*	100	200	300
Model 37, .38 Special, Double Action, Swing-Out Cylinder, Various Barrel Lengths, Lightweight, Blue, *Modern*	150	250	350
Model 37, .38 Special, Double Action, Swing-Out Cylinder, Various Barrel Lengths, Lightweight, Nickel Plated, *Modern*	150	300	400
Model 38, .38 Special, Double Action, Swing-Out Cylinder, 2" Barrel, Hammer Shroud, Blue, *Modern*	125	225	325
Model 38, .38 Special, Swing-Out Cylinder, 2" Barrel, Hammer Shroud, Nickel Plated, Double Action, *Modern*	225	275	325

S & W Model 38

	Fair	V. Good	Excellent
Model 40, .38 Special, Double Action, Swing-Out Cylinder, Hammerless, *Modern*	$200	$400	$500
Model 42, .38 Special, Double Action, Swing-Out Cylinder, Hammerless, Lightweight, *Modern*	150	275	400
Model 43, .22 L.R.R.F., Double Action, Swing-Out Cylinder, Adjustable Sights, Lightweight, *Modern*	200	300	400
Model 45 USPO, .22 L.R.R.F., Double Action, Swing-Out Cylinder, Modern	200	300	500
Model 45, .22 L.R.R.F., Double Action, Swing-Out Cylinder, Commercial, *Modern*	200	300	450
Model 48, .22 WMR, Double Action, Swing-Out Cylinder, Various Barrel Lengths, Blue, Adjustable Sights, *Modern*	150	250	400
Model 48, .22 WMR, Double Action, Swing-Out Cylinder, $8^{3}/_{8}$" Barrel, Blue, Adjustable Sights, *Modern*	150	300	425
Model 49, .38 Special, Double Action, Swing-Out Cylinder, 2" Barrel, Hammer Shroud, Nickel Plated, *Modern*	150	200	325
Model 49, .38 Special, Double Action, Swing-Out Cylinder, 2" Barrel, Hammer Shroud, Blue, *Modern*	150	200	300
Model 50, .38 Special, Double Action, Swing-Out Cylinder, Adjustable Sights, *Modern*	300	450	650
Model 51, .22 WMR, Double Action, Swing-Out Cylinder Adjustable Sights, *Modern*	200	300	400
Model 51, .22LR/.22 WMR Combo, Double Action, Swing-Out Cylinder, Adjustable Sights, *Modern*	250	325	450
Model 53, .22 Rem. Jet, Double Action, Swing-Out Cylinder Adjustable Sights, *Modern*	300	500	650
Model 53, .22 Rem. Jet, Double Action, Swing-Out Cylinder Adjustable Sights, Extra Cylinder, *Modern*	325	550	700
Model 547, 9mm Luger, Double Action, Swing-Out Cylinder, Blue, *Modern*	150	200	250
Model 56, .38 Special, Double Action, Swing-Out Cylinder 2" Barrel, Adjustable Sights, *Modern*	650	700	750
Model 57, .41 Magnum, Double Action, Swing-Out Cylinder Various Barrel Lengths, Blue, Adjustable Sights, *Modern*	200	275	350
Model 57, .41 Magnum, Double Action, Swing-Out Cylinder Various Barrel Lengths, Nickel Plated, Adjustable Sights, *Modern*	200	300	375

	Fair	V. Good	Excellent
Model 57, .41 Magnum, Double Action, Swing-Out Cylinder $8\frac{3}{8}$" Barrel, Blue, Adjustable Sights, *Modern*	$200	$300	$350
Model 57, .41 Magnum, Double Action, Swing-Out Cylinder $8\frac{3}{8}$" Barrel, Nickel Plated, Adjustable Sights, *Modern*	200	325	400
Model 57, .41 Magnum, Double Action, Swing-Out Cylinder Various Barrel Lengths, Blue, Cased with Accessories, *Modern*	150	300	400
Model 57, .41 Magnum, Double Action, Swing-Out Cylinder Various Barrel Lengths, Nickel Plated, Cased with Accessories, *Modern*	150	325	400
Model 57, .41 Magnum, Double Action, Swing-Out Cylinder $8\frac{3}{8}$" Barrel, Blue, Cased with Accessories, *Modern*	150	325	400
Model 57, .41 Magnum, Double Action, Swing-Out Cylinder $8\frac{3}{8}$" Barrel, Blue, Cased with Accessories, *Modern*	150	325	400
Model 58, .41 Magnum, Double Action, Swing-Out Cylinder 4" Barrel, Blue, *Modern*	125	250	300
Model 58, .41 Magnum, Double Action, Swing-Out Cylinder 4" Barrel, Nickel Plated, *Modern*	125	250	300
Model 581, .357 Magnum, Double Action, Swing-Out Cylinder Blue, *Modern*	100	175	200
Model 581, .357 Magnum, Double Action, Swing-Out Cylinder Nickel, *Modern*	100	175	225

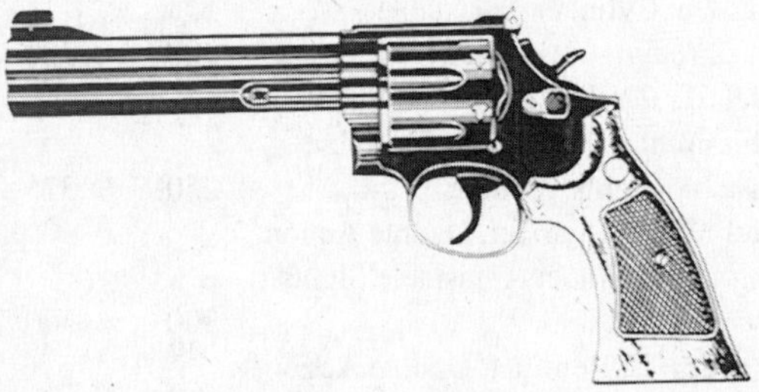

S & W Model 586

Model 586, .357 Magnum, Double Action, Swing-Out Cylinder Blue, Adjustable Sights, *Modern*	100	275	325
Model 586, .357 Magnum, Double Action, Swing-Out Cylinder Nickel, Adjustable Sights, *Modern*	250	300	350
Model 60, .38 Special, Double Action, Swing-Out Cylinder Stainless Steel, Adjustable Sights, *Modern*	250	350	450
Model 60, .38 Special, Double Action, Swing-Out Cylinder Stainless Steel, 2" Barrel, *Modern*	150	200	250

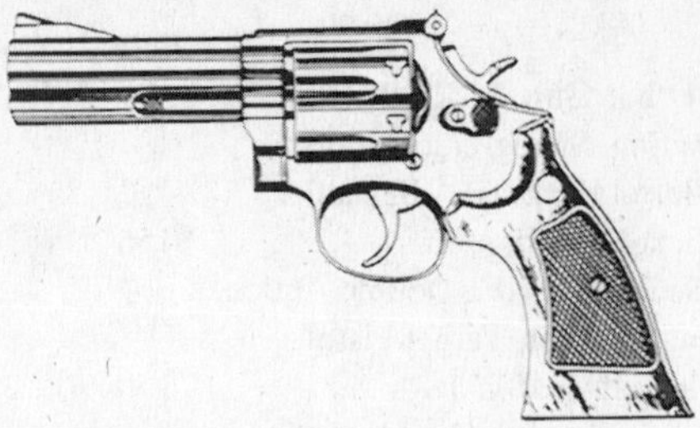

S & W Model 586 Stainless

	Fair	V. Good	Excellent
Model 60, .38 Special, Double Action, Swing-Out Cylinder High Polish Stainless Steel, 2" Barrel, Early model, *Modern*	$200	$300	$400
Model 629, .44 Magnum, Double Action, Swing-Out Cylinder Stainless Steel, Adjustable Sights, *Modern*	250	300	400
Model 629, .44 Magnum, Double Action, Swing-Out Cylinder $8\frac{3}{8}$" Barrel, Stainless Steel, Adjustable Sights, *Modern*	300	400	450
Model 63, .22 L.R.R.F., Double Action, Swing-Out Cylinder, Stainless Steel, 4" Barrel, Adjustable Sights, *Modern*	150	250	300
Model 64, .38 Special, Double Action, Swing-Out Cylinder Stainless Steel, Various Barrel Lengths, *Modern*	125	225	275
Model 649 Bodyguard, .38 Special, J Frame, 5 Shot, Stainless Steel, *Modern*	100	200	300
Model 65, .357 Magnum, Double Action, Swing-Out Cylinder Stainless Steel, 4" Barrel, Heavy Barrel, *Modern*	125	225	200
Model 650, .22 W.M.R., Double Action, Swing-Out Cylinder, Stainless Steel, *Modern*	150	200	300
Model 651, .22 W.M.R., Double Action, Swing-Out Cylinder, Stainless Steel, Adjustable Sights, *Modern*	150	200	250
Model 66, .357 Magnum, Double Action, Swing-Out Cylinder Stainless Steel, $2\frac{1}{2}$" Barrel, *Modern*	125	200	250
Model 66, .357 Magnum, Double Action, Swing-Out Cylinder Stainless Steel, Various Barrel Lengths, *Modern*	125	200	250
Model 67, .38 Special, Double Action, Swing-Out Cylinder Stainless Steel, 4" Barrel, *Modern*	125	200	250
Model 681, .357 Magnum, Double Action, Swing-Out Cylinder Stainless Steel, *Modern*	150	200	250
Model 686, .357 Magnum, Double Action, Swing-Out Cylinder Stainless Steel, Adjustable Sights, *Modern*	175	225	275

Target Models add $50 for Target Hammer, Target Trigger, and Target Stocks

	Fair	V. Good	Excellent
Model M Head Ejector, .22 Long R.F., 1st Model Ladysmith, Solid Frame, Swing-Out Cylinder, Double Action, *Curio*	$400	$900	$1200
Model M Head Ejector, .22 Long R.F., 2nd Model Ladysmith, Solid Frame, Swing-Out Cylinder, Double Action, Curio	400	800	1200
Model M Head Ejector, .22 Long R.F., 3rd Model Ladysmith, Solid Frame, Swing-Out Cylinder, Double Action, *Curio*	400	800	1200
Model M Head Ejector, .22 Long R.F., 3rd Model Ladysmith, Solid Frame, Swing-Out Cylinder, Double Action, 2$^1/_4$" & 6" Barrel, *Curio*	500	1250	2500
Victory, .38 Special Military & Police, Solid Frame, Swing-Out Cylinder, Double Action, Military, *Modern*	150	250	300

HANDGUN, SELF-LOADING

	Fair	V. Good	Excellent
.32 ACP, Blue, *Curio*	1200	2500	2750
Nickel Finish, Add 25%			
.35 S & W Automatic, Blue, *Curio*	250	525	600
Nickel Finish, Add 25%			
.35 S & W Automatic, Early Model, *Curio*	250	550	700
Nickel Finish, Add 25%			
Model 39, 9mm Luger, Double Action, Blue, *Modern*	150	275	325
Model 39, 9mm Luger, Double Action, Nickel Plated, *Curio*	150	275	350

S & W Model 39

	Fair	V. Good	Excellent
Model 39, 9mm Luger, Double Action, Steel Frame, *Curio*	400	850	950
Model 41, .22 L.R.R.F., Various Barrel Lengths, *Modern*	250	550	600
Model 41-1, .22 Short R.F., Various Barrel Lengths, *Modern*	250	525	575
Model 44, 9mm Luger, Single Action, *Modern*			
Model 46, .22 L.R.R.F., Various Barrel Lengths, *Modern*	200	425	500
Model 52A, .38 Special, Blue, *Modern*	900	2250	2500
Model 59, 9mm Luger, Double Action, Blue, *Modern*	150	325	375
Model 59, 9mm Luger, Double Action, Nickel Plated, *Modern*	$150	$325	$425
Model 61 Escort, .22 L.R.R.F., Clip Fed, Blue, *Modern*	100	225	275
Model 61 Escort, .22 L.R.R.F., Clip Fed, Nickel Plated, *Modern*	100	250	300

S & W Model 61

	Fair	V. Good	Excellent
Model 439, 9mm Luger, Double Action, Blue, *Modern*	150	300	325
Model 439, 9mm Luger, Double Action, Nickel Plated, *Modern*	150	300	350
Model 459, 9mm Luger, Double Action, Blue, *Modern*	150	325	375
Model 459, 9mm Luger, Double Action, Nickel Plated, *Modern*	150	350	400
Model 469, (12 Shot), 9mm Luger, Double Action, Blue, *Modern*	150	300	350
Model 539, 9mm Luger, Double Action, Blue, *Modern*	150	325	375
Model 539, 9mm Luger, Double Action, Nickel Plated, *Modern*	150	350	400
Model 639, 9mm Luger, Double Action, Stainless, *Modern*	150	300	350
Model 659, (12 Shot), 9mm Luger, Double Action, Stainless Steel, *Modern*	150	300	350
Model 659, 9mm Luger, Double Action, Stainless, *Modern*	150	325	375

HANDGUN, SINGLESHOT

	Fair	V. Good	Excellent
Model 1891 Set, Various Calibers, Extra Cylinder, Extra Barrel, Target Pistol, Single Action, 1st Model, *Antique*	500	1000	1200
Model 1891, .22 L.R.R.F., Target Pistol, Single Action, 1st Model, Various Barrel Lengths, *Antique*	300	700	800
Model 1891, .22 L.R.R.F., Target Pistol, Single Action, 2nd Model, No Hand or Cylinder Stop, *Curio*	300	700	800
Perfected Olympic, .22 L.R.R.F., Double Action, Top Break, Tight Bore and Chamber, Target Pistol, *Modern*	350	750	900
Perfected, .22 L.R.R.F., Double Action, Top Break, Target Pistol, *Modern*	200	600	700

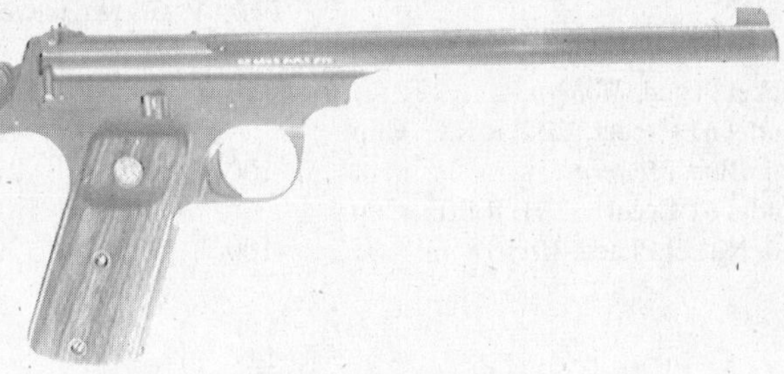

S & W Straight Line

	Fair	V. Good	Excellent
Straight Line, .22 L.R.R.F., Cased, *Curio*	$600	$1100	$1500

RIFLE, BOLT ACTION

	Fair	V. Good	Excellent
Model 1500, Various Calibers, Monte Carlo Stock, Checkered Stock, *Modern*	100	200	250
Model 1500 Deluxe, Various Calibers, Monte Carlo Stock, Checkered Stock, *Modern*	100	225	275
Model 1500 Magnum, Various Calibers, Monte Carlo Stock, Checkered Stock, *Modern*	100	200	250
Model 1500 Varmint, Various Calibers, Monte Carlo Stock, Checkered Stock, Heavy Barrel, *Modern*	100	225	275
Model 1700 Classic, Various Calibers, Monte Carlo Stock, Checkered Stock, Clip Fed, *Modern*	100	275	325
Model A, Various Calibers, Monte Carlo Stock, Checkered Stock, *Modern*	100	275	325
Model B, Various Calibers, Monte Carlo Stock, Checkered Stock, *Modern*	100	225	275
Model C, Various Calibers, Sporting Rifle, Checkered Stock, *Modern*	100	225	275
Model D, Various Calibers, Mannlicher, Checkered Stock, *Modern*	100	325	375
Model E, Various Calibers, Monte Carlo Stock, Mannlicher, *Modern*	100	325	375

RIFLE, REVOLVER

	Fair	V. Good	Excellent
Model 320, .320 S & W Rifle, Single Action, Top Break, 6 Shot, Adjustable Sights, Cased with Accessories, *Antique*	4000	8000	10000
No case but with stock	2000	5000	6500
without stock	1500	3500	4500

RIFLE, SELF-LOADING

	Fair	V. Good	Excellent
Light Rifle, MK I, 9mm Luger, Clip Fed, Carbine, *Curio*	600	1250	1500
Light Rifle, MK II, 9mm Luger, Clip Fed, Carbine, *Curio*	800	1750	2000

SHOTGUN, DOUBLE BARREL

	Fair	V. Good	Excellent
Hammer, Damascus, 12 ga., premium if specially decorated beyond standard.	$800	$1500	$3500

SHOTGUN, SELF-LOADING

	Fair	V. Good	Excellent
Model 1000 Field, 12 Ga., Vent Rib, *Modern*	125	250	300

S & W Model 1000

	Fair	V. Good	Excellent
Model 1000 Skeet, 12 Ga., Vent Rib, *Modern*	150	300	350
Model 1000 Super 12, 12 Ga., Vent Rib, *Modern*	150	375	425
Model 1000 Trap, 12 Ga., Open Sights, *Modern*	200	450	500

SHOTGUN, SLIDE ACTION

	Fair	V. Good	Excellent
Model 916 Eastfield, Various Gauges, Plain Barrel, *Modern*	75	125	150
Model 916T Eastfield, Various Gauges, Plain Barrel, *Modern*	75	150	175
Model 3000 Field, 12 Ga. 3", Vent Rib, *Modern*	100	250	275
Model 3000 Police, 12 Ga., Open Sights, *Modern*	100	225	250
Model 3000 Police, 12 Ga., Open Sights, Folding Stock, *Modern*	125	250	300
Model 3000 Slug, 12 Ga. 3", Open Sights, *Modern*	125	250	300

SMITH, ANTHONY

Northampton, Pa., 1770–1779. See Kentucky Rifles and Pistols.

SMITH, L. C. GUN CO.

Syracuse, N.Y., 1877–1890. Manufactured after 1890 by Hunter Arms, and in 1948 became a division of Marlin.

SHOTGUN, DOUBLE BARREL, SIDE-BY-SIDE

	Fair	V. Good	Excellent
Crown Grade, Various Calibers, Sidelock, Double Trigger, Automatic Ejector, Fancy Engraving, Fancy Checkering, *Curio*	2100	4750	5500
Crown Grade, Various Calibers, Sidelock, Single Selective Trigger, Automatic Ejector, Fancy Engraving, Fancy Checkering, *Curio*	2200	5000	5750
Eagle Grade, 12 Ga., Double Trigger, Checkered Stock, Vent Rib, *Curio*	1700	3500	4350
Field Grade, Various Calibers, Sidelock, Double Trigger, Checkered Stock, Light Engraving, *Curio*	250	750	1000

L.C. Smith Field Grade

	Fair	V. Good	Excellent
Field Grade, Various Calibers, Sidelock, Double Trigger, Automatic Ejector, Checkered Stock, Light Engraving, *Curio*	$450	$1000	$1350
Field Grade, Various Calibers, Sidelock, Single Trigger, Checkered Stock, Light Engraving, *Curio*	450	950	1250
Field Grade, Various Calibers, Sidelock, Single Trigger, Automatic Ejector, Checkered Stock, Light Engraving, *Curio*	550	1200	1500
Ideal Grade, Various Calibers, Sidelock, Double Trigger, Checkered Stock, Engraved, *Curio*	400	850	1150
Ideal Grade, Various Calibers, Sidelock, Double Trigger, Automatic Ejector, Checkered Stock, Engraved, *Curio*	550	1150	1450
Ideal Grade, Various Calibers, Sidelock, Single Selective Trigger, Checkered Stock, Engraved, *Curio*	450	1050	1350
Ideal Grade, Various Calibers, Sidelock, Single Selective Trigger, Automatic Ejector, Engraved, Checkered Stock, *Curio*	550	1300	1550
Monogram Grade, Various Calibers, Sidelock, Single Selective Trigger, Automatic Ejector, Engraved, Checkered Stock, *Curio*	3250	7500	9500
Skeet Grade, Various Calibers, Sidelock, Single Selective Trigger, Automatic Ejector, Engraved, Checkered Stock, *Curio*	1200	2500	3250
Skeet Grade, Various Calibers, Sidelock, Single Trigger, Automatic Ejector, Engraved, Checkered Stock, *Curio*	1200	2750	3450
Specialty Grade, Various Calibers, Sidelock, Double Trigger, Engraved, Checkered Stock, *Curio*	900	2250	3000
Specialty Grade, Various Calibers, Sidelock, Single Selective Trigger, Automatic Ejector, Engraved, Checkered Stock, *Curio*	1100	2500	3150
Trap Grade, 12 Ga., Sidelock, Single Selective Trigger, Automatic Ejector, Engraved, Checkered Stock, *Curio*	550	1250	1750

SHOTGUN, SINGLESHOT

	Fair	V. Good	Excellent
Crown Grade, 12 Ga., Trap Grade, Vent Rib, Automatic Ejector, Fancy Engraving, Fancy Checkering, *Curio*	$1200	$2500	$3250
Olympic Grade, 12 Ga., Trap Grade, Vent Rib, Automatic Ejector, Engraved, Fancy Checkering, *Curio*	600	1250	1750
Specialty Grade, 12 Ga., Trap Grade, Vent Rib, Automatic Ejector, Engraved, Fancy Checkering, *Curio*	600	1250	1750

*All L.C. Smiths—410 ga. add 50%
20 ga. add 15%

SMITH, OTIS A.

Middlefield & Rockfall, Conn., 1873–1890.

HANDGUN, REVOLVER

	Fair	V. Good	Excellent
.22 Short R.F., 7 Shot, Spur Trigger, Solid Frame, Single Action, *Antique*	100	200	275
.32 S & W, 5 Shot, Single Action, Top Break, Spur Trigger, *Antique*	100	175	250
.32 Short R.F., 5 Shot, Spur Trigger, Solid Frame, Single Action, *Antique*	100	200	275
.38 Short R.F., 5 Shot, Spur Trigger, Solid Frame, Single Action, *Antique*	100	200	275
.41 Short R.F., 5 Shot, Spur Trigger, Solid Frame, Single Action, *Antique*	200	400	650

SMITH, STOEFFEL

Pa., 1790–1800. See Kentucky Rifles and Pistols.

SMITH, THOMAS

London, England, c. 1850.

RIFLE, PERCUSSION

	Fair	V. Good	Excellent
16 Ga., Smooth bore, Octagon Barrel, Fancy Wood, Cased with Accessories, *Antique*	1100	2650	3750

SMITH, WM.

England.

HANDGUN, SELF-LOADING

	Fair	V. Good	Excellent
Pocket, 6.35mm, Clip Fed, 1906 Browning Type, *Modern*	150	375	450

SMOKER

Made by Johnson Bye & Co., 1875–1884.

	Fair	V. Good	Excellent
HANDGUN, REVOLVER			
#1, .22 Short R.F., 7 Shot, Spur Trigger, Solid Frame, Single Action, *Antique*	$75	$150	$175
#2, .32 Short R.F., 5 Shot, Spur Trigger, Solid Frame, Single Action, *Antique*	75	150	175
#3, .38 Short R.F., 5 Shot, Spur Trigger, Solid Frame, Single Action, *Antique*	75	150	175
#4, .41 Short R.F., 5 Shot, Spur Trigger, Solid Frame, Single Action, *Antique*	75	150	200

SNAPHAUNCE, EXAMPLE

	Fair	V. Good	Excellent
HANDGUN, SNAPHAUNCE			
.45 Italian Early 1700s, Holster Pistol, Half-Octagon Barrel, Engraved, Carved, High Quality, Furniture, *Antique*	900	2000	2750
Early 1800s Small, Plain, *Antique*	500	900	1350
English Late 1500s, Ovoid Pommel, Engraved, Gold, Damascened, High Quality, *Antique*	6000	15000	22500
Italian 1700s, High Quality, Belt Pistol, Light Ornamentation, *Antique*	1100	2500	3500
Italian Early 1700s, Medium Quality, Brass Furniture, Plain, *Antique*	400	800	1250
RIFLE, SNAPHAUNCE			
Arabian, .59, Ornate, Inlaid with Silver, Ivory Buttstock Inlays, *Antique*	200	450	700
Italian Mid-1600s, Half-Octagon Barrel, Carved, Engraved, Silver Inlay, Steel Furniture, Ornate, *Antique*	4000	9000	12500

SODIA, FRANZ

Ferlach, Austria.

	Fair	V. Good	Excellent
COMBINATION WEAPON, MULTI-BARREL			
Bochdrilling, Various Calibers, Fancy Wood, Fancy Checkering, Fancy Engraving, *Antique*	3000	5500	7500
Doppelbuchse, Various Calibers, Fancy Wood, Fancy Checkering, Fancy Engraving, *Antique*	1900	3750	5500
Over-Under Rifle, Various Calibers, Fancy Wood, Fancy Checkering, Fancy Engraving, *Antique*	1700	3500	5000

SOLER

Ripoll, Spain, c. 1625.

	Fair	V. Good	Excellent
HANDGUN, WHEELOCK			
Enclosed Mid-1600's, Ball Pommel, Ornate, *Antique*	4500	10000	14500

SOUTHERN ARMS CO.

Made by Crescent for H. & D. Folsom, New York City. See Crescent Fire Arms Co., Shotgun, Double Barrel, Side-by-Side, Shotgun, Singleshot.

SPAARMAN, ANDREAS

Berlin, Germany, c. 1680.

	Fair	V. Good	Excellent
RIFLE, FLINTLOCK			
.72, Jaeger, Octagon Barrel, Swamped, Rifled, Iron Mounts, Ornate, Set Trigger, *Antique*	$1800	$3500	$4750

SPANISH GUNMAKERS, FROM EIBAR

Most of the production of the Colt or FN type .25 caliber self-loading pistols, some of .32 autos, and some of double-action copies of Colt or S & W–type revolvers: Modesto Santos, Armero Especialistas Reunides, Gaspar Arizaga, Antonio Azpiri y Cia, Apaolozo Hermanos, Retolaza Hermanos, Arriola Hermanos, Orbea Hermanos Azanza y Arrizabalaga, Arrizabalaga Hilos De Calixto, Astra, Avion, Azanza y Arrizabalaga, Azul, Berasaluze Areitio-Arutena y Cia, Francisco Arizamendi, Echave y Arizmendi, Arizmendi Zulaika y Cia, Gregorio Bolumburu, Juan Esteban Bustindiu, Hijos de A Echevera, Tomas de Urizar y Cia, Antonio Azpiri y Cia, Fabbrique d'Arms de Guerre de Grand Precision (Etxezagarra & Abitua), Iraola Salaverria, Erquiaga Muguruzu y Cia, Echave y Arizmendi, Eulogio Arostegui, Anitua, Garate, Amas Garbi, Bonifacio Echeverra, Cooperative Orbea, San Martin y Cid, Martin a Bascaran, Gaspar Arrizaga, Jose Mugica, Ojanguren y Marcaido, Armero Especialistas Reunidas, Gabilondo y Cia, Gregorio Bolumburu, M. Zulaica y Cia, Felix Sarasqueta, S.E.A.M., Star, Stosel, Retolaza Hermanos, Charola y Anitua, Colon, T.A.C. (Trocaola, Aranzabal y Cia), Tomas de Urizair y Cia, Arizmendi y Geonaga, Ojanguran y Vidosa, Gaspar Arizaga, hijos de Calixto Arrizabalaga.

SPANISH MILITARY

Also see Astra, Star.

	Fair	V. Good	Excellent
HANDGUN, SELF-LOADING			
Jo-Lo-Ar, 9mm Bergmann, Clip Fed, Military, Hammer, *Curio*	250	550	700
M1913-16 Campo-Giro, 9mm Bergmann, Clip Fed, Military, *Curio*	200	425	550
RIFLE, BOLT ACTION			
Destroyer, 9mm Bayard Long, Clip Fed, Carbine, *Modern*	75	150	200
M98 La Caruna, 8mm Mauser, Military, *Curio*	75	150	200
RIFLE, SELF-LOADING			
CETME Sport, .308 Win., Clip Fed, *Modern*	600	1250	1500

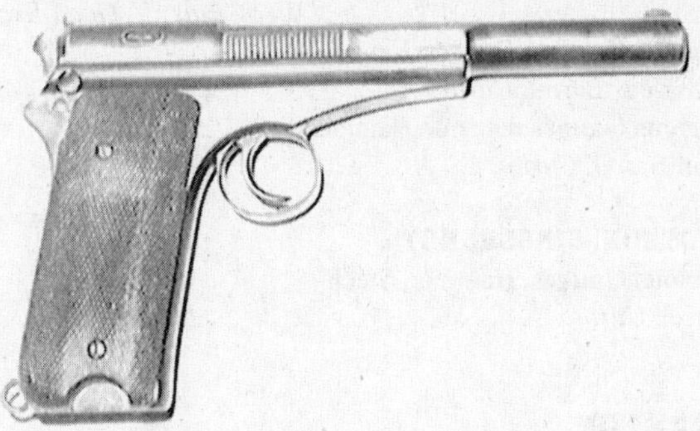

Spanish Military M1913-16

Fair V. Good Excellent

SPENCER ARMS CO.

Windsor, Conn., 1886–1888.

SHOTGUN, SLIDE ACTION

Spencer, Roper, 12 Ga., Tube Feed, *Antique* $150 $350 $475

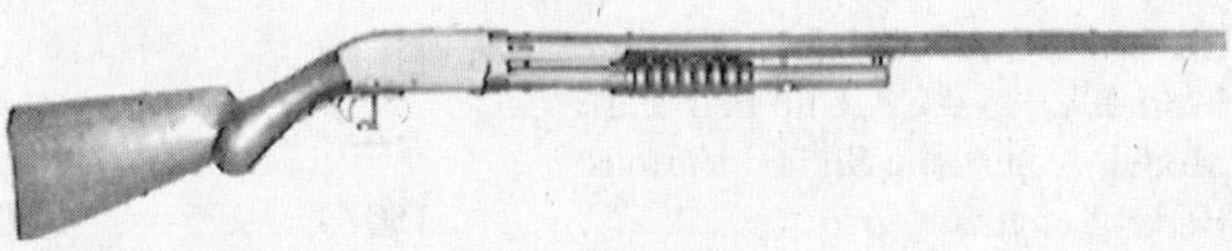

Spencer Roper

SPENCER GUN CO.

Made by Crescent for Hibbard & Spencer Bartlett, c. 1900. See Crescent Fire Arms Co., Shotgun, Double Barrel, Side-by-Side; Shotgun, Singleshot.

SPENCER SAFETY HAMMERLESS

Made by Columbia Armory, Tenn., c. 1892.

HANDGUN, REVOLVER

.38 S & W, 5 Shot, Top Break, Hammerless, Double Action, *Antique* 50 100 125

SPORTSMAN

Made by Crescent for W. Bingham Co. Cleveland, Ohio, c. 1900. See Crescent Fire Arms Co., Shotgun, Double Barrel, Side-by-Side; Shotgun, Singleshot.

SPORTSMAN

Made by Steven Arms.

SHOTGUN, DOUBLE BARREL, SIDE-BY-SIDE

M 315, Various Gauges, Hammerless, Steel Barrel, *Antique* 75 150 175

*410 ga. add 25%

Fair V. Good Excellent

SHOTGUN, SINGLESHOT

Model 90, Various Gauges, Takedown, Automatic Ejector, Plain, Hammer, *Antique* $25 $50 $75

SPRINGFIELD ARMORY

Manufactured by Springfield, Inc., Geneseo, Ill.

RIFLE, SELF-LOADING

M1A Match, .308 Win., Clip Fed, Version of M-14, *Modern* 450 1050 1250

M1A Standard, .308 Win., Clip Fed, Version of M-14, *Modern* 400 850 1000

M1A Standard, .308 Win., Clip Fed, Version of M-14, Folding Stock, *Modern* 425 950 1100

M1A Super Match, .308 Win., Clip Fed, Version of M-14, Heavy Barrel, *Modern* 550 1250 1500

SPRINGFIELD ARMS

Made by Crescent, c. 1900. See Crescent Fire Arms Co., Shotgun, Double Barrel; Shotgun, Singleshot.

SPY

Made by Norwich Falls Pistol Co., c. 1880.

HANDGUN, REVOLVER

.22 Short R.F., 7 Shot, Spur Trigger, Solid Frame, Single Action, *Antique* 75 150 175

SQUARE DEAL

Made by Crescent for Stratton-Warren Hdw. Co., Memphis, Tenn. See Crescent Fire Arms Co., Shotgun, Double Barrel, Side-by-Side; Shotgun, Singleshot.

SQUIBMAN

Made by Squires, Bingham, Makati, Philippines.

HANDGUN, REVOLVER

Model 100 D, .38 Spec., Double Action, Blue, Swing-Out Cylinder, Vent Rib, *Modern* 50 100 125

Model 100 DC, .38 Spec., Double Action, Blue, Swing-Out Cylinder, *Modern* 50 100 125

Thunder Chief, .38 Spec., Double Action, Blue, Swing-Out Cylinder, Vent Rib, Heavy Barrel, *Modern* .. 75 125 150

RIFLE, BOLT ACTION

M 14D, .22 L.R.R.F., Clip Fed, Checkered Stock, *Modern* 30 50 75

	Fair	V. Good	Excellent
M 15, .22 WMR, Clip Fed, Checkered Stock, *Modern*	$40	$60	$90

RIFLE, SELF-LOADING

	Fair	V. Good	Excellent
M-16, .22 L.R.R.F., Clip Fed, Flash Hider, *Modern*	30	60	75
M20D, .22 L.R.R.F., Clip Fed, Checkered Stock, *Modern*	30	60	75

SHOTGUN, SLIDE ACTION

	Fair	V. Good	Excellent
M 30/28, 12 Ga., Plain, *Modern*	50	75	100

ST. LOUIS ARMS CO.

Belgium for Shapleigh Hardware Co., c. 1900.

SHOTGUN, DOUBLE BARREL, SIDE-BY-SIDE

	Fair	V. Good	Excellent
Various Gauges, Hammerless, Damascus Barrel, *Modern*	75	150	175
Various Gauges, Hammerless, Steel Barrel, *Modern*	75	150	200
Various Gauges, Outside Hammers, Damascus Barrel, *Modern*	125	200	300
Various Gauges, Outside Hammers, Steel Barrel, *Modern*	125	200	300

SHOTGUN, SINGLESHOT

	Fair	V. Good	Excellent
Various Gauges, Hammer, Steel Barrel, *Modern*	25	50	75

STAGGS-BILT

Staggs Enterprises, Phoenix, Ariz., c. 1970.

COMBINATION WEAPON, OVER-UNDER

	Fair	V. Good	Excellent
20 Ga./.30–30, Top Break, Hammerless, Double Triggers, Top Break, *Modern*	75	100	125

STANDARD ARMS CO.

Wilmington, Del., 1909–1911.

RIFLE, SELF-LOADING

	Fair	V. Good	Excellent
Model G, Various Calibers, Takedown, Mag Feed, Hammerless, *Curio*	200	400	500

RIFLE, SLIDE ACTION

	Fair	V. Good	Excellent
Model M, Various Calibers, Takedown, Mag Feed, Hammerless, *Curio*	150	275	325

STANLEY

Belgium, c. 1900.

SHOTGUN, DOUBLE BARREL, SIDE-BY-SIDE

	Fair	V. Good	Excellent
Various Gauges, Hammerless, Damascus Barrel, *Curio*	75	150	175
Various Gauges, Hammerless, Steel Barrel, *Curio*	75	175	200
Various Gauges, Outside Hammers, Damascus Barrel, *Curio*	$75	$150	$175
Various Gauges, Outside Hammers, Steel Barrel, *Curio*	75	175	200

SHOTGUN, SINGLESHOT

	Fair	V. Good	Excellent
Various Gauges, Hammer, Steel Barrel, *Curio*	25	50	75

STANTON

London, England, c. 1778.

HANDGUN, FLINTLOCK

	Fair	V. Good	Excellent
.55 Officers, Belt Pistol, Screw Barrel, Box Lock, Brass, *Antique*	800	1750	2250

STAR

Made by Bonifacio Echeverria, Eibar, Spain, 1911 to date.

HANDGUN, SELF-LOADING

	Fair	V. Good	Excellent
Model A, .45 ACP, Clip Fed, Early Model, Adjustable Sights, Various Barrel Lengths, *Curio*	150	275	300

Star Model A

	Fair	V. Good	Excellent
Model A, 7.63mm, Clip Fed, *Curio*	125	250	275
Model A, 9mm Bergmann, Clip Fed, Early Model, Adjustable Sights, Various Barrel Lengths, *Curio*	100	175	225
Model A, 9mm, Clip Fed, *Curio*	125	250	275
Model A, Carbine, 7.63 Mauser, Clip Fed, Early Model, Adjustable Sights, Various Barrel Lengths, Stock Lug, *Curio*	600	1250	1500
Model A, Various Calibers, Holster Stock, Add $250.00-$500.00			
Model AS, .38 Super, Clip Fed, *Curio*	100	200	250
Model B, 9mm Luger, Clip Fed, *Curio*	100	200	250
Model B, 9mm Luger, Clip Fed, German Military Marked, *Modern*	300	650	750
Model BKM, 9mm Luger, Clip Fed, Lightweight, *Curio*	100	225	275

	Fair	V. Good	Excellent
Model BKS-Starlight, 9mm Luger, Clip Fed, Lightweight, *Curio*	$100	$225	$250
Model BM, 9mm Luger, Clip Fed, Steel Frame, *Curio*	100	200	225
Model C, 9mm Browning Long, Clip Fed, 8 Shot, *Curio*	100	175	225
Model C O, 6.35mm, Clip Fed, *Curio*	75	150	200
Model C U, 6.35mm, Clip Fed, Lightweight, *Curio*	75	125	175
Model D, .380 ACP, Clip Fed, 15 Shot Clip, *Curio*	100	175	225
Model D, .380 ACP, Clip Fed, 6 Shot, *Curio*	75	150	200
Model DK, .380 ACP, Clip Fed, Lightweight, *Curio*	125	275	300
Model E Vest Pocket, .25 ACP, Clip Fed, *Curio*	75	150	200
Model F, .22 L.R.R.F., Clip Fed, *Curio*	75	125	175
Model F R S, .22 L.R.R.F., Clip Fed, Target Pistol, Adjustable Sights, *Curio*	100	175	200
Model F T B, .22 L.R.R.F., Clip Fed, Target Pistol, *Curio*	75	150	200
Model F-Olympic, .22 Short R.F., Clip Fed, Target Pistol, *Curio*	100	200	250
Model F-Sport, .22 L.R.R.F., Clip Fed, 6" Barrel, *Curio*	75	150	200
Model FR, .22 L.R.R.F., Clip Fed, *Curio*	75	125	175
Model H, 7.65mm, Clip Fed, 7 Shot, *Curio*	75	125	175
Model HF, .22 L.R.R.F., Clip Fed, *Curio*	75	150	200
Model HK Lancer, .22 L.R.R.F., Clip Fed, Lightweight, *Curio*	75	150	175
Model HN, .380 ACP, Clip Fed, *Curio*	75	150	175
Model I, 7.65mm, Clip Fed, 9 Shot, *Curio*	100	200	225

Star Model 1 .32

	Fair	V. Good	Excellent
Model IN, .380 ACP, Clip Fed, *Curio*	100	225	275
Model M, .38 ACP, Clip Fed, *Curio*	$75	$125	$175
Model Military, 9mm, Clip Fed, *Modern*	100	225	275
Model MMS, 7.63 Mauser, Clip Fed, Stock Lug, *Curio with stock*	325	750	850
Model NZ, 6.35mm, Clip Fed, *Curio*	175	375	450
Model P, .45 ACP, Clip Fed, *Modern*	125	250	300
Model PD, .45 ACP, Clip Fed, *Modern*	125	250	300
Model S, .380 ACP, Clip Fed, *Modern*	100	175	200
Model S I, *Modern*	100	200	225
Model SM, .380 ACP, Clip Fed, *Modern*	100	200	250
Model Starfire, .380 ACP, Clip Fed, Lightweight, *Modern*	150	325	375
Model Starlet, 6.35mm, Clip Fed, Lightweight, *Modern*	100	225	250
Model Super A, .38 ACP, Clip Fed, *Modern*	100	225	250
Model Super B, 9mm Luger, Clip Fed, *Modern*	100	200	225
Model Super P, .45 ACP, Clip Fed, *Modern*	125	275	325
Model 28, 9mm Luger, Clip Fed, *Modern*	150	300	350

RIFLE, SINGLESHOT

Rolling Block, Various Calibers, Carbine, *Modern*	75	125	175

STAR GAUGE

Spain, Imported by Interarms.

SHOTGUN, DOUBLE BARREL, SIDE-BY-SIDE

12 and 20 Gauges, Checkered Stock, Adjustable Choke, Double Trigger, *Modern*	100	175	225

STARR ARMS CO.

Yonkers and Binghamton, N.Y., 1860–1868.

HANDGUN, PERCUSSION

1858 Army, .44 Revolver, 6 Shot, 6" Barrel, Double Action, *Antique*	400	1000	1250
1858 Navy, .36 Revolver, 6 Shot, 6" Barrel, Double Action, *Antique*	600	1200	1500
1863 Army, .44 Revolver, 6 Shot, 8" Barrel, Single Action, *Antique*	400	1000	1250

RIFLE, PERCUSSION

Carbine, .54, Underlever, *Antique*	500	1500	2150

RIFLE, SINGLESHOT

	Fair	V. Good	Excellent
Carbine, .52 R.F., Underlever, *Antique*	$450	$1200	$1500

STATE ARMS CO.

Made by Crescent for J. H. Lau & Co., c. 1900. See also Crescent Fire Arms Co., Shotgun, Double Barrel, Side-by-Side; Shotgun, Singleshot.

STEIGLEDER, ERNST

Suhl & Berlin, Germany, 1921–1935.

RIFLE, DOUBLE BARREL, SIDE-BY-SIDE

	Fair	V. Good	Excellent
Various Calibers, Box Lock, Engraved, Checkered Stock, Color Case Hardened Frame, *Modern*	1000	2500	3500

STENDA

Stenda Werke Waffenfabrik, Suhl, Germany, c. 1920.

HANDGUN, SELF-LOADING

	Fair	V. Good	Excellent
7.65mm, Blue, Clip Fed, *Curio*	100	175	225

STERLING ARMS CO.

Gasport and Lockport, N.Y.

HANDGUN, SELF-LOADING

	Fair	V. Good	Excellent
#283 Target 300, .22 L.R.R.F., Hammer, Adjustable Sights, Various Barrel Lengths, *Modern*	75	125	150
#284 Target 300, .22 L.R.R.F., Hammer, Adjustable Sights, Tapered Barrel, *Modern*	75	125	150
#285 Huskey, .22 L.R.R.F., Hammer, Heavy Barrel, *Modern*	50	100	125
#286 Trapper, .22 L.R.R.F., Hammer, Tapered Barrel, *Modern*	50	100	125
Model 300, .25 ACP, Blue, *Modern*	50	75	100
Model 300N, .25 ACP, Nickel Plated, *Modern*	50	75	100
Model 300S, .25 ACP, Stainless Steel, *Modern*	50	75	100
Model 302, .22 L.R.R.F., Blue, *Modern*	50	75	100
Model 302N, .22 L.R.R.F., Nickel Plated, *Modern*	50	75	100
Model 302S, .22 L.R.R.F., Stainless Steel, *Modern*	50	75	100
Model 400, .380 ACP, Blue, Clip Fed, *Modern*	100	200	225
Model 400N, .380 ACP, Nickel Plated, Clip Fed, *Modern*	100	225	250
Model 400S, .380 ACP, Stainless Steel, Clip Fed, *Modern*	125	250	275
Model 402, .22 L.R.R.F., Blue, Clip Fed, *Modern*	$75	$100	$125
Model 402, .22 L.R.R.F., Nickel Plated, Clip Fed, *Modern*	75	100	125
Model 402 MkII, .32 ACP, Blue, Clip Fed, *Modern*	75	125	150
Model 402 MkIIS, .32 ACP, Stainless Steel, Clip Fed, *Modern*	75	150	175
Model 450, .45 ACP, Clip Fed, Double Action, Adjustable Sights, Blue, *Modern*	125	275	300
Model PPL, .380 ACP, Short Barrel, Clip Fed, *Modern*	125	250	275

Sterling PPL

RIFLE, SINGLESHOT

	Fair	V. Good	Excellent
Backpacker, .22 L.R.R.F., Takedown, *Modern*	25	50	75

STERLING ARMS CORP.

Made by Crescent for H. & D. Folsom, c. 1900. See Crescent Fire Arms Co., Shotgun, Double Barrel, Side-by-Side; Shotgun, Singleshot.

STERLING REVOLVERS

c. 1880.

HANDGUN, REVOLVER

	Fair	V. Good	Excellent
.22 Short R.F., 7 Shot, Spur Trigger, Solid Frame, Single Action, *Antique*	75	150	175
.32 Short R.F., 5 Shot, Spur Trigger, Solid Frame, Single Action, *Antique*	75	150	175

STEVENS, J. ARMS & TOOL CO.

Chicopee Falls, Mass., 1864–1886. Became J. Stevens Arms & Tool Co. in 1886, absorbed Page-Lewis Arms Co., Davis-Warner Arms Co., and Crescent Firearms Co. in 1926. Became a subsidiary of Savage in 1920. Also see the Commemorative Section. Stevens received highly complimentary publicity from the use of its large frame target pistols by such famous shooters as Buffalo

Bill Cody and Annie Oakley. Following trade names marked by Stevens on various firearms: REVOLVERS, Acme Arms; SINGLE-SHOT PISTOLS, Gem; DOUBLE BARREL SHOTGUNS, Aristocrat, Central, Continental, Eastern, Essex, Hercules, King Nitro, Knickerbocker, Massachusetts Arms, Monitor, Newport, Olympic, Oxford Arms, Paragon, Ranger, Riverside Arms Co., Scout, Triumph, Wittes Hardware Co., George Worthington; SINGLE BARREL SHOTGUNS, Central, Climas, Continental, Cruso, Delphian, Diamond, Eastern, Gibralter, Goose Gun, Hercules, Hermitage, Little Pet, Massachusetts Arms, Monitor, Nitro Proof, Northwesterner, Premier; SLIDE-ACTION RIFLES, Premier, Premier trail blazer, Ranger; and PUMP-ACTION SHOTGUN, Riot.

HANDGUN, SINGLESHOT

	Fair	*V. Good*	*Excellent*
1888 #1, Various Calibers, Tip-Up, Octagon Barrel, Open Rear Sight, *Antique*	$75	$150	$200
1888 #2 "Gallery," .22 L.R.R.F., Tip-Up, Octagon Barrel, Open Rear Sight, *Antique*	75	150	200
1888 #3 "Combined Sight," Various Calibers, Tip-Up, Octagon Barrel, *Antique*	75	150	200
1888 #4 "Combined Sight," .22 L.R.R.F., Tip-Up, Octagon Barrel, *Antique*	75	150	200
1888 #5 "Expert," Various Calibers, Tip-Up, Half Octagon Barrel, *Antique*	75	150	200
1894 "New Ideal," Various Calibers, Level Action, Falling Block, Vernier Sights, *Antique*	125	275	350
Model 10, .22 L.R.R.F., Tip-Up, Target, Various Barrel Lengths, *Modern*	100	250	325
Model 23 "Sure-Shot," .22 Short R. F., Side-Swing Barrel, Hammer, *Antique*	200	400	550
Model 34 "Hunters Pet," Various Rimfires, Tip-Up, Half-Octagon Barrel, with Shoulder Stock, Vernier Sights, *Curio*	200	450	550
Model 34 "Hunters Pet," Various Rimfires, Tip-Up, Octagon Barrel, with Shoulder Stock, *Curio*	200	400	500
Model 35 Target, .22 L.R.R.F., Tip-Up, Target, Ivory Grips, Various Barrel Lengths, *Modern*	150	400	550
Model 35 Target, .22 L.R.R.F., Tip-Up, Target, Various Barrel Lengths, *Modern*	125	275	400
Model 37 "Gould," Various Calibers, Tip-Up, *Modern*	300	600	750
Model 38 "Conlin," .22 L.R.R.F., Tip-Up, *Modern*	300	700	850
Model 40 New Model Pocket Rifle, Various Calibers, Tip-Up, with Shoulder Stock, *Curio*	200	500	700
Model 41, .22 L.R.R.F., Tip-Up, Pocket Pistol, *Modern*	100	275	400

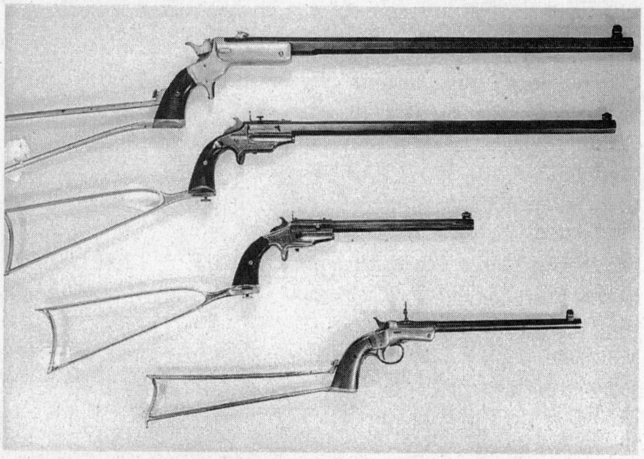

Variations of Stevens Pocket rifles, with attachable shoulder stocks. At top, The Hunter's Pet, so-called Buggy Model in .32 rimfire caliber, another in .22 rimfire (10" barrel), and bottom, *The Pocket rifle in .32 rimfire. Note differences in frame sizes, trigger types, sights, and barrels.*

	Fair	*V. Good*	*Excellent*
Model 42 Reliable Pocket Rifle, .22 L.R.R.F., Tip-Up, with Shoulder Stock, *Curio*	$250	$600	$750
Model 43 "Diamond," .22 L.R.R.F., Tip-Up, Spur Trigger, 6" Barrel, Octagon Barrel, *Modern*	100	175	250
Model 43 "Diamond," .22 L.R.R.F., Tip-Up, Spur Trigger, 10" Barrel, Octagon Barrel, *Modern*	100	200	250
Model 43 "Diamond," .22 L.R.R.F., Tip-Up, Spur Trigger, 6" Barrel, Globe Sights, *Modern*	100	200	250
Model 43 "Diamond," .22 L.R.R.F., Tip-Up, Spur Trigger, 10" Barrel, Globe Sights, *Modern*	100	225	300

RIFLE, BOLT ACTION

Model 053 Buckhorn, Various Rimfires, Singleshot, Peep Sights, *Modern*	25	50	75
Model 056 Buckhorn, .22 L.R.R.F., 5 Shot Clip, Peep Sights, *Modern*	50	75	100
Model 066 Buckhorn, .22 L.R.R.F., Tube Feed, Peep Sights, *Modern*	50	75	100
Model 083, .22 L.R.R.F., Singleshot, Peep Sights, Takedown, *Modern*	25	50	75
Model 084, .22 L.R.R.F., 5 Shot Clip, Peep Sights, Takedown, *Modern*	25	50	75
Model 086, .22 L.R.R.F., Tube Feed, Takedown, Peep Sights, *Modern*	50	75	100
Model 15, .22 L.R.R.F., Singleshot, (Springfield), *Modern*	25	50	75
Model 15Y, .22 L.R.R.F., Singleshot, *Modern*	25	50	75
Model 322, .22 Hornet, Clip Fed, Carbine, Open Rear Sight, *Modern*	100	200	250

	Fair	V. Good	Excellent
Model 322-S, .22 Hornet, Clip Fed, Carbine, Peep Sights, *Modern*	$100	$200	$250
Model 325, .30–30 Win., Clip Fed, Carbine, Open Rear Sight, *Modern*	100	175	200
Model 325-S, .30–30 Win., Clip Fed, Carbine, Peep Sights, *Modern*	100	175	200
Model 416, .22 L.R.R.F., 5 Shot Clip, Peep Sights, Target Stock, *Modern*	100	200	225
Model 419, .22 L.R.R.F., Singleshot, Peep Sights, *Modern*	50	75	100
Model 48, .22 L.R.R.F., Singleshot, Takedown, *Modern*	25	50	100
Model 49, .22 L.R.R.F., Singleshot, Takedown, *Modern*	25	50	100
Model 50, .22 L.R.R.F., Singleshot, Takedown, *Modern*	25	50	100
Model 51, .22 L.R.R.F., Singleshot, Takedown, *Modern*	25	50	100
Model 52, .22 L.R.R.F., Singleshot, Takedown, *Modern*	25	50	100
Model 53, .22 L.R.R.F., Singleshot, Takedown, *Modern*	25	50	100
Model 56 Buckhorn, .22 L.R.R.F., 5 Shot Clip, Open Rear Sight, *Modern*	25	50	75
Model 65 "Little Krag," .22 L.R.R.F., Singleshot, Takedown, *Modern*	75	200	250
Model 66 Buckhorn, .22 L.R.R.F., Tube Feed, Open Rear Sight, *Modern*	25	50	75
Model 82, .22 L.R.R.F., Singleshot, Peep Sights, (Springfield), *Modern*	25	50	75
Model 83, .22 L.R.R.F., Singleshot, Open Rear Sight, Takedown, *Modern*	15	25	50
Model 84, .22 L.R.R.F., 5 Shot Clip, Open Rear Sight, Takedown, *Modern*	25	50	75
Model 86, .22 L.R.R.F., Tube Feed, Takedown, Open Rear Sight, *Modern*	25	50	75

RIFLE, LEVER ACTION

	Fair	V. Good	Excellent
Model 425, Various Calibers, Hammer, *Curio*	200	400	500
Model 430, Various Calibers, Hammer, Checkered Stock, *Curio*	300	600	700
Model 435, Various Calibers, Hammer, Light Engraving, Fancy Checkering, *Curio*	900	2000	2500
Model 440, Various Calibers, Hammer, Fancy Checkering, Fancy Engraving, Fancy Wood, *Curio*	1900	4000	5000

COMBINATION WEAPON, OVER-UNDER

	Fair	V. Good	Excellent
Model 22-410, .22-.410 Ga., Hammer, Plastic Stock, *Modern*	50	75	100
Model 22-410, .22-.410 Ga., Hammer, Wood Stock, *Modern*	50	100	125

RIFLE, SELF-LOADING

	Fair	V. Good	Excellent
Model 057 Buckhorn, .22 L.R.R.F., 5 Shot Clip, Open Rear Sight, *Modern*	$50	$75	$100
Model 057 Buckhorn, .22 L.R.R.F., 5 Shot Clip, Peep Sights, *Modern*	50	75	100
Model 076 Buckhorn, .22 L.R.R.F., Peep Sights, Tube Feed, *Modern*	50	75	100
Model 085 Springfield, .22 L.R.R.F., 5 Shot Clip, Peep Sights, *Modern*	50	75	100
Model 76 Buckhorn, .22 L.R.R.F., Open Rear Sight, Tube Feed, *Modern*	50	75	100
Model 85 Springfield, .22 L.R.R.F., 5 Shot Clip, Open Rear Sight, *Modern*	50	75	100
Model 87, .22 L.R.R.F., Tube Feed, Open Rear Sight, *Modern*	50	75	100
Model 87-S, .22 L.R.R.F., Peep Sights, Tube Feed, *Modern*	50	75	100
Model 87K Scout, .22 L.R.R.F., Tube Feed, Open Rear Sight, Carbine, *Modern*	50	75	100

RIFLE, SINGLESHOT

	Fair	V. Good	Excellent
1888 #10 "Range," Various Calibers, Tip-Up, Half-Octagon Barrel, Fancy Wood, Vernier Sights, *Antique*	200	400	500
1888 #12 "Ladies," Various Calibers, Tip-Up, Half-Octagon Barrel, Open Rear Sight, Fancy Wood, *Antique*	300	600	700
1888 #13 "Ladies," Various Calibers, Tip-Up, Half-Octagon Barrel, Vernier Sights, *Antique*	200	400	500
1888 #14 "Ladies," Various Calibers, Tip-Up, Half-Octagon Barrel, Vernier Sights, Fancy Wood, *Antique*	300	600	700
1888 #15 "Crack Shot," Various Calibers, Tip-Up, Half-Octagon Barrel, Peep Sights, *Antique*	100	225	250
1888 #16 "Crack Shot," Various Calibers, Tip-Up, Half-Octagon Barrel, Peep Sights, Fancy Wood, *Antique*	150	300	350
1888 #22 "Ladies," Various Calibers, Tip-Up, Half-Octagon Barrel, Open Rear Sight, *Antique*	100	200	225
1888 #6 "Expert," Various Calibers, Tip-Up, Half-Octagon Barrel, Fancy Wood, *Antique*	100	200	225
1888 #7 "Premier," Various Calibers, Tip-Up, Half-Octagon Barrel, Globe Sights, *Antique*	100	175	225
1888 #8 "Premier," Various Calibers, Tip-Up, Half-Octagon Barrel, Fancy Wood, Globe Sights, *Antique*	100	225	275
1888 #9 "Range," Various Calibers, Tip-Up, Half-Octagon Barrel, Vernier Sights, *Antique*	100	175	225

	Fair	V. Good	Excellent
Model 101 Featherweight, .44-40 WCF, Lever Action, Tip-Up, Smooth bore, Takedown, Half-Octagon Barrel, *Modern*	$100	$200	$250
Model 101, with Extra 22 Barrel, .44-40 WCF, Lever Action, Tip- Up, Smooth bore, Takedown, Half-Octagon Barrel, *Modern*	100	250	300
Model 11 "Ladies," Various Rimfires, Tip-Up, Open Rear Sight, *Modern*	200	400	500
Model 12 "Marksman," Various Rimfires, Hammer, Lever Action, Tip-Up, *Modern*	75	150	175
Model 13 "Ladies," Various Rimfires, Tip-Up, Vernier Sights, *Modern*	200	400	500
Model 14 "Little Scout," .22 L.R.R.F., Hammer, Rolling Block, *Curio*	100	125	150
Model 14 1/2 "Little Scout," .22 L.R.R.F., Hammer, Rolling Block, *Modern*	75	125	150
Model 15 "Maynard Jr.," .22 L.R.R.F., Lever Action, Tip-Up, *Modern*	75	125	150
Model 15 1/2 "Maynard Jr.," .22 L.R.R.F., Lever Action, Tip-Up, *Modern*	75	125	150
Model 17, Various Rimfires, Lever Action, Takedown, Favorite, Open Rear Sight, *Modern*	75	150	175
Model 18, Various Rimfires, Lever Action, Takedown, Favorite, Vernier Sights, *Modern*	100	175	200
Model 19, Various Rimfires, Lever Action, Takedown, Favorite, Lyman Sights, *Modern*	75	150	175
Model 2, Various Rimfires, Tip-Up, Open Rear Sight, *Modern*	125	250	275
Model 20, Various Rimfires, Lever Action, Takedown, Favorite, Smoothbore, *Curio*	75	150	175
Model 26, Various Rimfires, Lever Action, Takedown, Open Rear Sight, *Curio*	75	150	175
Model 26 1/2, Various Rimfires, Lever Action, Takedown, Smoothbore, *Curio*	75	150	175
Model 27, Various Rimfires, Lever Action, Takedown, Favorite, Octagon Barrel, Open Rear Sight, *Modern*	75	175	200
Model 28, Various Rimfires, Lever Action, Takedown, Favorite, Octagon Barrel, Vernier Sights, *Modern*	100	175	200
Model 29, Various Rimfires, Lever Action, Takedown, Favorite, Octagon Barrel, Lyman Sights, *Modern*	100	175	200
Model 404, .22 L.R.R.F., Hammer, Falling Block, Target Sights, Full-Stocked, *Modern*	225	475	525
Model 414 "Armory," .22 L.R.R.F., Lever Action, Lyman Sights, *Modern*	200	400	450

	Fair	V. Good	Excellent
Model 417-0, Various Calibers, Lever Action, Walnut Hill, *Modern*	$200	$400	$450
Model 417-1, Various Calibers, Lever Action, Lyman Sights, Walnut Hill, *Modern*	250	500	600
Model 417-2, Various Calibers, Lever Action, Vernier Sights, Walnut Hill, *Modern*	250	525	625
Model 417-3, Various Calibers, Lever Action, No Sights, Walnut Hill, *Modern*	200	400	450
Model 417 1/2, Various Calibers, Lever Action, Walnut Hill, *Modern*	200	400	500
Model 418, .22 L.R.R.F., Lever Action, Takedown, Walnut Hill, *Modern*	200	400	550
Model 418 1/2, Various Rimfires, Lever Action, Takedown, Walnut Hill, *Modern*	200	450	550
Model 44 "Ideal," Various Calibers, Lever Action, Rolling Block, *Modern*	200	400	500
Model 44 1/2 "Ideal," Various Calibers, Lever Action, Falling Block, *Modern*	400	800	1000
Model 49 "Ideal," Various Calibers, Walnut Hill, Lever Action, Falling Block, Engraved, Fancy Checkering, *Modern*	800	2000	2650
Model 5, Various Rimfires, Tip-Up, Vernier Sights, *Modern*	150	250	300
Model 51 "Pope," Various Calibers, Schutzen Rifle, Lever Action, Falling Block, Engraved, Fancy Checkering, *Modern*	2000	4500	5000

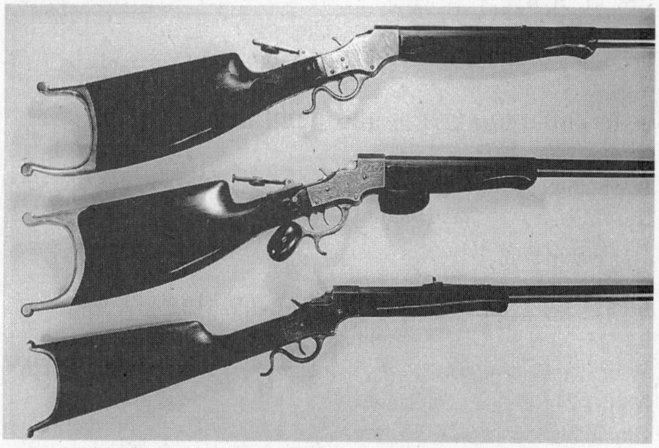

Three variations of Stevens singleshot rifles; each with Swiss butts: from the top, *deluxe off-hand model; benchrest Model 51 with scarce etched frame; and Ideal Sporting Model with No. 44 action, in .25/20 caliber.*

	Fair	V. Good	Excellent
Model 52 "Pope Jr.," Various Calibers, Schutzen Rifle, Lever Action, Falling Block, Engraved, Fancy Checkering, *Modern*	2000	4000	5500

	Fair	V. Good	Excellent
Model 54 "Pope," Various Calibers, Schutzen Rifle, Lever Action, Falling Block, Fancy Engraving, Fancy Checkering, *Modern*	$2500	$5000	$6000
Model 56 "Pope Ladies," Various Calibers, Schutzen Rifle, Lever Action, Falling Block, Fancy Checkering, *Modern*	1000	2000	2500
Model 7 "Swiss Butt," Various Rimfires, Tip-Up, Vernier Sights, *Modern*	125	350	400

RIFLE, SLIDE ACTION

	Fair	V. Good	Excellent
Model 70, .22 L.R.R.F., Hammer, Solid Frame, *Modern*	100	175	200
Model 71, .22 L.R.R.F., Hammer, Solid Frame, *Modern*	100	200	225
Model 75, .22 L.R.R.F., Tube Feed, Hammerless, *Modern*	100	200	225
Model 80, Various Rimfires, Tube Feed, Takedown, *Modern*	75	150	175

SHOTGUN, BOLT ACTION

	Fair	V. Good	Excellent
Model 237, 20 Ga., Takedown, Singleshot, (Springfield), *Modern*	20	40	50
Model 258, 20 Ga., Takedown, Clip Fed, *Modern*	25	50	75
Model 37, .410 Ga., Takedown, Singleshot, (Springfield), *Modern*	25	50	75
Model 38, .410 Ga., Takedown, Clip Fed, (Springfield), *Modern*	25	50	75
Model 39, .410 Ga., Takedown, Tube Feed, (Springfield), *Modern*	25	50	75
Model 58, .410 Ga., Takedown, Clip Fed, *Modern*	25	50	75
Model 59, .410 Ga., Takedown, Tube Feed, *Modern*	25	50	75

SHOTGUN, DOUBLE BARREL, OVER-UNDER

	Fair	V. Good	Excellent
Model 240, .410 Ga., Hammer, Plastic Stock, *Modern*	100	175	200
Model 240, .410 Ga., Hammer, Wood Stock, *Modern*	100	200	225

SHOTGUN, DOUBLE BARREL, SIDE-BY-SIDE

	Fair	V. Good	Excellent
M 315, Various Gauges, Hammerless, Steel Barrel, *Modern*	100	175	200
Model 215, 12 and 16 Gauges, Outside Hammers, Steel Barrel, *Modern*	150	225	300
Model 235, Various Gauges, Outside Hammers, Checkered Stock, Steel Barrel, *Modern*	150	250	350
Model 250, Various Gauges, Outside Hammers, Checkered Stock, Steel Barrel, *Modern*	150	250	350
Model 255, 12 and 16 Gauges, Outside Hammers, Checkered Stock, Steel Barrel, *Modern*	150	250	350
Model 260 "Twist," Various Gauges, Outside Hammers, Checkered Stock, Damascus Barrel, *Modern*	$150	$250	$350
Model 265 "Krupp," 12 and 16 Gauges, Outside Hammers, Checkered Stock, Steel Barrel, *Modern*	175	250	350
Model 270 "Nitro," Various Gauges, Outside Hammers, Checkered Stock, Damascus Barrel, *Modern*	175	250	350
Model 311 ST, Various Gauges, Hammerless, Steel Barrel, Single Trigger, *Modern*	100	200	250
Model 311, Various Gauges, Hammerless, Steel Barrel, *Modern*	100	200	250
Model 311-R Guard Gun, 12 or 20 Gauge, Double Trigger, 18½" Bore, Solid Rib, *Modern*	125	250	325
Model 3151, Various Gauges, Hammerless, Recoil Pad, Front and Rear Bead Sights, *Modern*	100	200	250
Model 330, Various Gauges, Hammerless, Checkered Stock, *Modern*	100	175	225
Model 335, 12 and 16 Gauges, Hammerless, Steel Barrel, Checkered Stock, Double Trigger, *Modern*	100	175	225
Model 345, 20 Ga., Hammerless, Checkered Stock, Steel Barrel, Double Trigger, *Modern*	100	175	225
Model 355, 12 and 16 Gauges, Hammerless, Steel Barrel, Checkered Stock, Double Trigger, *Modern*	100	175	225
Model 365 "Krupp," 12 and 16 Gauges, Hammerless, Checkered Stock, Steel Barrel, Double Trigger, *Modern*	100	175	225
Model 375 "Krupp," 12 and 16 Gauges, Hammerless, Light Engraving, Fancy Checkering, Double Trigger, Steel Barrel, *Modern*	100	200	250
Model 385 "Krupp," 12 and 16 Gauges, Hammerless, Fancy Engraving, Fancy Checkering, Double Trigger, Steel Barrel, *Modern*	100	225	275
Model 515, Various Gauges, Hammerless, *Modern*	75	150	200
Model 5151, Various Gauges, Hammerless, Steel Barrel, *Modern*	100	175	225
Model 530 ST, Various Gauges, Hammerless, Steel Barrel, Single Trigger, *Modern*	100	200	250
Model 530, Various Gauges, Hammerless, Steel Barrel, Double Trigger, *Modern*	100	175	225

	Fair	V. Good	Excellent
Model 530M, Various Gauges, Hammerless, Plastic Stock, *Modern*	$75	$150	$200

SHOTGUN, PUMP

	Fair	V. Good	Excellent
Model 520, 12 Ga., Takedown, *Modern*	75	150	175
Model 620, Various Gauges, Takedown, *Modern*	75	150	175

SHOTGUN, SELF-LOADING

	Fair	V. Good	Excellent
Model 124, 12 Ga., Plastic Stock, *Modern*	75	125	150

SHOTGUN, SINGLESHOT

	Fair	V. Good	Excellent
Various Gauges, Hammer, Automatic Ejector, *Modern*	25	50	75
Various Gauges, Hammer, Automatic Ejector, Raised Matted Rib, *Modern*	50	125	150
1888 "New Style," Various Gauges, Tip-Up, Hammer, Damascus Barrel, *Antique*	100	200	275
Model 100, Various Gauges, Ejector, Hammer, *Modern*	25	50	75
Model 102, .410 Ga., Hammer, Featherweight, *Modern*	50	125	150
Model 102, 24, 28, and 32 Gauges, Hammer, Featherweight, *Modern*	50	125	150
Model 104, .410 Ga., Hammer, Featherweight, Automatic Ejector, *Modern*	50	75	100
Model 104, 24, 28, and 32 Gauges, Hammer, Automatic Ejector, Featherweight, *Modern*	50	125	150
Model 105, 20 Ga., Hammer, *Modern*	25	50	75
Model 105, 28 Ga., Hammer, *Modern*	50	100	125
Model 106, .32 Ga., Hammer, *Modern*	75	125	150
Model 106, .410 Ga. 2½", Hammer, *Modern*	25	50	75
Model 106, .44-40 WCF., Hammer, Smoothbore, *Modern*	50	100	125
Model 107, Various Gauges, Hammer, Automatic Ejector, *Modern*	25	50	75
Model 108, .32 Ga., Hammer, Automatic Ejector, *Modern*	50	125	150
Model 108, .410 Ga. 2½", Hammer, Automatic Ejector, *Modern*	25	50	75
Model 108, .44-40 WCF., Hammer, Automatic Ejector, Smoothbore, *Modern*	50	100	125
Model 110, Various Gauges, Ejector, Checkered Stock, Hammer, *Modern*	25	50	75
Model 120, Various Gauges, Selective Ejector, Fancy Checkering, Hammer, *Modern*	50	125	150
Model 125 Ladies, .20 Ga., Automatic Ejector, Hammer, *Modern*	$25	$50	$75
Model 125 Ladies, .28 Ga., Automatic Ejector, Hammer, *Modern*	50	100	125
Model 140, Various Gauges, Selective Ejector, Hammerless, Checkered Stock, *Modern*	50	75	100
Model 160, Various Gauges, Hammer, *Modern*	25	50	75
Model 165, Various Gauges, Automatic Ejector, Hammer, *Modern*	25	50	75
Model 170, Various Gauges, Automatic Ejector, Hammer, Checkered Stock, *Modern*	25	50	75
Model 180, Various Gauges, Hammerless, Automatic Ejector, Checkered Stock, Round Barrel, *Modern*	50	75	100
Model 182, 12 Ga., Hammerless, Automatic Ejector, Light Engraving, Checkered Stock, Trap Grade, *Modern*	100	300	350
Model 185, 12 Ga., Hammerless, Automatic Ejector, Checkered Stock, Half-Octagon Barrel, *Modern*	75	125	150
Model 185, For 16 or 20 Gauge, Add 20%			
Model 185, For Damascus Barrel, Deduct 25%			
Model 190, 12 Ga., Hammerless, Automatic Ejector, Fancy Checkering, Light Engraving, Half-Octagon Barrel, *Modern*	200	300	450
Model 190, For 16 or 20 Gauge, Add 20%			
Model 190, For Damascus Barrel, Deduct 25%			
Model 195, 12 Ga., Hammerless, Automatic Ejector, Fancy Checkering, Fancy Engraving, Half-Octagon Barrel, *Modern*	200	400	650
Model 195, For 16 or 20 Gauge, Add 20%			
Model 195, For Damascus Barrel, Deduct 25%			
Model 89 Dreadnaught, Various Gauges, Hammer, *Modern*	25	50	75
Model 90, Various Gauges, Takedown, Automatic Ejector Plain, Hammer, *Modern*	25	50	75
Model 93, 12 and 16 Gauges, Hammer, *Modern*	25	50	75
Model 94, Various Gauges, Takedown, Automatic Ejector Plain, Hammer, *Modern*	25	50	75
Model 944, .410 Ga., Hammer, Automatic Ejector, (Springfield), *Modern*	25	50	75
Model 94A, Various Gauges, Hammer, Automatic Ejector, *Modern*	25	50	75

	Fair	V. Good	Excellent
Model 94C, Various Gauges, Hammer, Automatic Ejector, Modern, *Modern*	$25	$50	$75
Model 95, 12 and 16 Gauges, *Modern*	25	50	75
Model 958, .410 Ga., Automatic Ejector, Hammer, *Modern*	25	50	75
Model 958, 28 Ga., Automatic Ejector, Hammer, *Modern*	50	125	150
Model 97, 12 and 16 Gauges, Hammer, Automatic Ejector, *Modern*	25	50	75
Model 970, 12 Gauge, Hammer, Automatic Ejector, Checkered Stock, Half-Octagon Barrel, *Modern*	25	50	75

SHOTGUN, SLIDE ACTION

	Fair	V. Good	Excellent
Model 520, 12 Ga., Takedown, *Modern*	75	150	175
Model 522, 12 Ga., Trap Grade, Takedown, Raised Matted Rib, *Modern*	75	175	200
Model 620, Various Gauges, Takedown, *Modern*	100	250	275
Model 621, Various Gauges, Hammerless, Checkered Stock, Raised Matted Rib, Takedown, *Modern*	100	200	250
Model 67, Various Gauges, Hammerless, Solid Frame, (Springfield), *Modern*	75	150	175
Model 67-VR, Various Gauges, Hammerless, Solid Frame, Vent Rib, (Springfield), *Modern*	100	175	200
Model 77, 12 and 16 Gauges, Hammerless, Solid Frame, *Modern*	75	150	175
Model 77, For Vent Rib, Add $10.00-$15.00			
Model 77, Various Gauges, Hammerless, Solid Frame, *Modern*	75	150	175
Mode 77 S C, 12 and 16 Gauges, Hammerless, Solid Frame, Recoil Pad, Adjustable Choke, *Modern*	75	150	175
Model 77-AC, Various Gauges, Hammerless, Solid Frame, Adjustable Choke, *Modern*	75	125	150
Model 77-M, 12 Ga., Hammerless, Solid Frame, Adjustable Choke, *Modern*	75	125	150
Model 820, 12 Ga., Hammerless, Solid Frame, *Modern*	75	125	150

STEVENS, JAMES

SHOTGUN, PERCUSSION

	Fair	V. Good	Excellent
14 Ga., Double Barrel, Side-by-395 Side, Engraved, Light Ornamentation, *Antique*	200	450	550

STEYR

Since 1863 in Steyr, Austria, as Werndl Co.; in 1869 became Oesterreichische Waffenfabrik Gesellschaft; after WWI became Steyr Werke; in 1934 became Steyr-Daimler-Puch. Also see German Military, Austrian Military, Mannlicher-Schoenauer.

HANDGUN, SELF-LOADING

	Fair	V. Good	Excellent
Model 1901 Mannlicher, 7.63mm Mannlicher, Commercial, *Curio*	$350	$700	$950
Model 1905 Mannlicher, 7.63mm Mannlicher, Military, *Curio*	175	375	500
Model 1908, 7.65mm, Clip Fed, Tip-Up, *Modern*	100	225	275
Model 1909, 6.35mm, Clip Fed, Tip-Up, *Modern*	100	225	300
Model 1909, 7.65mm, Clip Fed, Tip-Up, *Modern*	125	250	350
Model 1911, 9mm Steyr, Commercial, *Curio*	150	350	425
Model 1912, 9mm Luger, Nazi-Proofed, Military, *Curio*	200	400	500
Model 1912, 9mm Steyr, Military, *Curio*	100	200	250
Model 1912 Roumanian, 9mm Steyr, Military, *Curio*	125	250	300
Model GB, 9mm Luger, Clip Fed, Double Action, *Modern*	200	400	500
Model SP, .32 ACP, Clip Fed, Double Action, *Modern*	250	525	600
Solohurn, .32 ACP, Clip Fed, *Modern*	100	200	300

STOCK, FRANZ

Franz Stock Maschinen u. Werkbaufabrik, Berlin, Germany, 1920–1940.

HANDGUN, SELF-LOADING

	Fair	V. Good	Excellent
6.35mm, Clip Fed, *Modern*	150	300	400
7.65mm, Clip Fed, *Modern*	125	275	400

Franz Stock .25

STOCKMAN, HANS

Dresden, Germany, 1590–1621.

HANDGUN, WHEELOCK

	Fair	V. Good	Excellent
Pair, Holster Pistol, Pear Pommel, Horn Inlays, Light Ornamentation, *Antique*	$5000	$12500	$17500

STOEGER, A. F.

Stoeger Arms Corp., New York City, now in South Hackensack, N.J. Also see Luger. Purchased in 2000 by Fabbrica d'Armi Pietro Beretta, Gardone; was a division of Sako, Finland.

COMBINATION WEAPON, DRILLING

Model 259, 3 Calibers, Side Barrel, Box Lock, Double Triggers, Checkered Stock, *Modern*	900	2000	3000
Model 297, Various Calibers, 2 Rifle Barrels, Box Lock, Double Triggers, Engraved, Checkered Stock, *Modern*	900	2000	3000
Model 300, Vierling, 4 Barrels, Box Lock, Double Triggers, Checkered Stock, *Modern*	1800	3500	4500

COMBINATION WEAPON, OVER-UNDER

Model 290, Various Calibers, Blitz System, Box Lock, Double Triggers, Engraved, Checkered Stock, *Modern*	800	1800	2250

SHOTGUN, DOUBLE BARREL, SIDE-BY-SIDE

Victor Special, 12 Ga., Checkered Stock, Double Triggers, *Modern*	100	175	275

SHOTGUN, SINGLESHOT

Model 27 Trap, 12 Ga., Engraved, Vent Rib, Checkered Stock, Recoil Pad, *Modern*	325	700	900

STOSEL

Retolaza Hermanos, Eibar, Spain.

HANDGUN, SELF-LOADING

Model 1913, 6.35mm, Clip Fed, *Modern*	75	125	175

STUART, JOHAN

Edinburgh, Scotland, 1701–1750.

HANDGUN, SNAPHAUNCE

All Steel Highland, Engraved, Scroll Butt, Ball Trigger, *Antique*	4000	8500	12500

STURM, RUGER & CO

Southport, Conn., 1946 to Date. Also see Commemorative section. The Samuel Colt of modern times and an all-American original, William B. Ruger, with his partner, Alexander McCormick Sturm, founded their company in 1949, as underdogs: They were told "it can't be done." From the $50,000 investment that launched their first pistol—the .22 Standard—the company rose to occupy a leadership role in the firearms field. Now the largest American firearms manufacturer, Sturm, Ruger & Co. has produced over 15 million pistols, revolvers, rifles, and shotguns through 1997. WIlliam B. Ruger began designing firearms at the age of 17, while growing up in Brooklyn, New York. As a youth he learned about firearms history and technology by scouring the New York Public Library and visiting shops the likes of Griffin & Howe. Ruger was fascinated not only by firearms, but by machine tools and how they could carve and shape steel. In his early 20s he unsuccessfully sought employment with various American gunmakers. But in 1939, at the request of the Ordnance Department of the U.S. Army, he worked as an engineer and designer at the Springfield Armory. During World War II Ruger designed a Light Machine Gun for the Auto-Ordnance corporation. Still another project was a sighting device for aircraft machine guns. It was at Auto-Ordnance Corporation that Ruger first learned about the advantages of investment castings, an ancient process often termed "lost wax" due to the material's role in creating the final cast part. At war's end Ruger had an advanced knowledge of design and manufacturing, and was perfectly prepared for a career in gunmaking. However, it was not until the 1949 partnership with Alexander Sturm that Ruger's experience and ideas would begin to come to fruition. With his friend Sturm supplying the start-up capital, Sturm, Ruger & Company began production with the .22 Standard, a uniquely designed self-loading pistol. Alex Sturm prepared the first advertisements, and the company's first brochure. A gifted artist and published author, Sturm also designed the company's distinctive "red eagle" logo. The .22 Standard was billed as "the first overall improvement in automatic pistol design since the Browning patent of 1905." The initial series, of which over 1,250,000 pistols were produced, was succeeded in 1982 by the Mark II Standard and target models, of which over 1,500,000 were completed by the end of 1996; production continues at an impressive pace. The .22 Standard began a continuing series of firearms products—pistols, revolvers, rifles and shotguns—which now number approximately 50 models and over 250 variations. Founder, Chairman of the Board, and Chief Executive Officer William B. Ruger continues to develop new designs. He celebrated his eighty-first birthday on June 16, 1997. Note: The assistance of John R. Hansen Jr., Executive Director, Ruger Collectors Association, in the preparation of these values is greatly appreciated. For more information on membership in this group contact the RCA at P.O. Box 240, Green Farms, Connecticut 06436. The company celebrated its 50th anniversary in 1999, which was a landmark in the history of firearms. Several new firearms were added to the line in the anniversary year, including a special issue of the .22 self-loading pistol—the MK4-50—replicating the original pistol of 1949 and available only in 1999.

HANDGUN, SELF-LOADING, RIMFIRE

	Fair	V. Good	Excellent
Standard Auto, *"Red Eagle"* ser. no. under 35000, 4¾" bbl., .22 LR, blued finish	$265	$350	$450
Mark I Target Auto, *"Red Eagle",* ser. no 15000–17000 & 25000–25300, 8⅞" bbl	300	375	475
Standard Auto, ser. no. over 35000, .22 LR, Blued finish; 4¾" & 8" bbl.	100	140	175
Marked "Hecho En Mexico"	650	850	1200
1 of 5000 stainless	275	350	400

	Fair	V. Good	Excellent
Mark I Target Auto, adjustable rear sight 5½" or 6⅞" barrel, blued finish	$140	$175	$225
5¼" bbl	280	350	450
U.S. marked	280	350	450

Ruger MK II

	Fair	V. Good	Excellent
Mark II Standard Auto, Improved features. Blued finish	110	125	200
Stainless	140	185	280
50th Anniversary	115	150	290
Mark II Target Auto, adjustable rear sight. Blued finish	130	185	310
Stainless	150	185	300
Government Model	155	195	300
U.S. marked	380	450	550
Stainless Government Model	185	220	355
Slab Side	180	235	370
Model 22/46 Auto, Zytel frame, Colt 1911 grip angle. .22 LR, 4", 4¾", 5¼" bbl & 5½" bull barrel. Stainless, fixed sights	115	145	220
Stainless, adjustable sights	150	185	265
Blued, adjustable sights	125	150	195

HANDGUN, SELF-LOADING, CENTERFIRE

	Fair	V. Good	Excellent
P85 MK II, 9mm, 15 round magazine, ambidextrous safety, 4½" bbl, aluminum frame/steel slide, cased, extra magazine. Matte black finish	200	265	335
KP85 Stainless	210	280	350
Subtract $30 if no case or extra magazine			
P89, Improved P85, 9mm or with interchangeable .30 cal. Luger barrel, Blued finish	215	270	350
Blued finish, extra .30 Luger barrel	260	315	395
KP89 Stainless	240	295	390
Stainless, extra .30 Luger barrel	280	340	435
P90, .45 ACP caliber, Matte black finish	215	290	390
KP90 Stainless	225	300	400
P91, .40 S&W caliber, Blued finish	220	295	385
KP91 Stainless	225	300	400

Ruger MK II Bull Barrel

	Fair	V. Good	Excellent
P93, 9mm, compact version, 3⁹⁄₁₀" barrel, Blued finish	$215	$265	$345
KP93 Stainless	300	350	415
P94, 9mm, ambidextrous safety or double action, Blued finish	215	265	345
KP94 Stainless	250	300	415
P95, 9mm, polymer frame, ambidextrous safety or double action, Blued finish	185	215	295
KP95 Stainless	175	225	320
P97, stainless, similar to KP94, .45 ACP caliber	210	260	370
P944, similar to P93, .40 S&W caliber, Blued finish	215	265	345
KP93 Stainless	250	300	415

HANDGUN, REVOLVER

Single Action, 1953–1973 Single Six: .22 rimfire, 4⅝", 5½", 6½" & 9½" barrel, fixed sights, black rubber or walnut grip panels, blued finish, steel ejector rod housing. There are many variations and sub variants.			
"Flatgate," ser. no. 1-6100	175	250	350
Lightweight Model, "Tri-color", ser. no. 200001–205900	200	300	450
Blue anodized aluminum frame & cylinder, ser. no. 205900/206100	350	450	550
Blue anodized aluminum frame with blue steel cylinder, ser. No. 206100–212590	200	300	450
Engraved Model, cased, 250 guns	1800	2750	3200
Contoured loading gate, ser. no. 81000–198940 4⅝" bbl.	250	350	475
5½" bbl	120	175	275
6½" bbl. (22 WRM), ser. no. 300000–342450	185	200	300
9½" bbl.	250	350	450

Add $30 for extra 22 WRM cylinder (numbered to gun), convertibles begin at ser. No. 162XXX.

	Fair	V. Good	Excellent
Same as above with redesigned grip frame profile, all finished walnut grip panels, aluminum ejector rod housing, and contoured gate. After ser. no. 196940. 4⅝" bbl.	$225	$275	$375
5½" bbl.	120	175	275
6½" bbl.	120	175	275
9½" bbl.	235	285	385
Add $30 for extra 22 WRM cylinder (numbered to gun)			
Super Single Six, same as above with flatop cylinder frame and Intregal rear sight protection, adjustable rear sight. 4⅝" bbl., 200 guns	750	1000	1400
5½" bbl.	140	200	275
6½" bbl.	140	200	275
Chrome plated, 60 guns	800	1250	2000
Add $30 for extra 22 WRM cylinder (numbered to gun)			
Blackhawk .357 mag. "Flatop," mfd. 1955–1963, approximately 42,700 made in 4⅝", 6½", and 10" barrel lengths, blued finish, black rubber or walnut grip panels, steel ejector rod housing. 4⅝" bbl.	250	375	500
6½" bbl., est. 2000 guns	350	450	700
10" bbl., est. 500 guns	750	1100	1400
Blackhawk .44 mag. "Flatop," mfd. 1956–1963, approximately 28,000 made in 6½", 7½" and 10" barrel lengths, blued finish, walnut grip panel, steel ejector rod housing. 6½" bbl.	350	495	650
7½" bbl., est 500 guns	550	700	850
10" bbl., est. 1000 guns	700	925	1200
Old Model Blackhawk, similar to Flatops with integral rear sight protection, improved grip frame profile, oiled walnut grip panels, anodized aluminum ejector rod housing, three screws on side of frame, blued finish. .357 mag. 4⅝" & 6½" bbl.	180	250	350
With extra 9mm cylinder	225	295	400
4⅝" factory brass grip frame, 385 guns	300	450	600
6½" factory brass frame, 370 guns	300	450	600
.30 carb. cal., 7½" bbl only	180	250	350
.41 mag., 4⅝" & 6½" bbl.	230	300	390
4⅝" factory brass frame, 50 guns	900	1100	1400
6½" factory brass frame, 160 guns	600	700	800
.45 LC, 4⅝" & 7½" bbl.	350	395	425
With extra .45 ACP cylinder	400	475	525
4⅝" factory brass frame, 405 guns	550	650	750
7½" factory brass frame, 190 guns	600	700	800
Super Blackhawk, .44 mag., mfd. 1959–1973. Same as Flatops with integral rear sight protection, larger steel grip frame, square back triggerguard and wide hammer spur and trigger, non-fluted cylinder, super polished and blued after ser. no. 4000. In Mahogany case, 4500 guns	$550	$750	$1000
"Long Grip Frame" in mahogany case, 300 guns	750	900	1150
In "White Cardboard Case", est. 400 guns	800	950	1200
Factory brass grip frame, 1500 guns	475	575	750
6½" bbl., 800 guns	475	575	750
Old Model Bearcat, small one piece anodized aluminum frame, similar to Remington Pocket Model, steel roll engraved cylinder, .22 caliber, mfd. 1958–1970, gold anodized aluminum triggerguard. Standard Model	200	275	350
"Alphabet", ser. prefixed with a letter	275	375	400
Blue anodized aluminum triggerguard, ser. no. 73XXX	500	650	750
Old Model Super Bearcat, steel frame, gold or blue triggerguard	200	250	350
Hawkeye single shot pistol, .256 Win. Mag. caliber, 8½" barrel, built on Super Blackhawk frame, rotating breech block, oiled walnut grip panels, 3,300 guns manufactured 1963–1964, blued finish	650	875	1200

HANDGUN, REVOLVER

Single Action, New Model, 1973–present. New Models feature a patented interlocking transfer bar system. Ruger applied this new design to its entire line of SA revolvers in 1973. The New Model is readily identifiable by two pivot pins in the side of the frame in the same location that three screws were formerly utilized in the Old Model.

	Fair	V. Good	Excellent
Single Six Convertible, fixed sight, .22 cal. with extra .22 WRM cylinder, 5½" and 6½" barrels, wood grip panels, introduced 1994. Blued finish	120	155	260
Stainless	150	185	325
Super Single Six, same as above except features intregal rear sight protection with adjustable rear sight, 4⅝", 5½", 6½", and 9½" bbl., .22 ca. With extra .22 WRM cylinder. Introduced 1973. Blued finish	120	155	260
Stainless	150	185	325
High Gloss Stainless	160	195	335
Colorado Centenial, 1975, 15,000 guns	165	200	295
.32 H&R magnum	175	275	350
.32 H&R magnum, frame is stamped SSM	260	410	425

	Fair	V. Good	Excellent
Blackhawk, adjustable rear sight, polished and blued finish, wood grip panels, introduced 1973.			
.357 mag., 4⅝" and 6½" bbl., blued finish	$145	$175	$290
With extra 9mm cylinder, blued finish	170	225	315
Stainless, 4⅝" and 6½" bbl.	175	255	410
Stainless extra 9mm cylinder, 6½" bbl. Only, 300 guns	550	650	750
Stainless High Gloss, 4⅝" and 6½" bbl.	165	250	395
.357 Maximum, 7½" and 10½" bbl., blued finish			
.30 carb. Cal., 7½" bbl. only, blued finish	145	175	290
.41 mag., 4⅝" and 6½" bbl., blued finish	145	175	290
.44 mag., 5½" bbl., blued finish	170	210	325
With extra 44/40 cylinder, blued finish	190	250	345
.45 LC, 4⅝" and 7½" bbl., blued finish	145	175	290
With extra .45ACP cylinder, blued finish, 4⅝" and 7½" bbl.	170	225	315
Stainless, 4⅝" and 7½" bbl.	175	255	410
Stainless High Gloss, 4⅝" and 7½" bbl.	165	250	395
.32-20WCF/.32 H&R mag., Buckeye Special	220	295	450
.38-40WCF/10mm auto. Buckeye Special	200	265	405
Super Blackhawk, same as Blackhawk except with wide hammer spur and trigger, longer steel grip frame with square back triggerguard, wood grip panels, .44 mag. cal. Blued finish, 4⅝", 6½", 7½", and 10½" bbl.	170	210	325
Stainless, 4⅝", 6½", 7½", and 10½" bbl.	185	225	380
Stainless High Gloss, 4⅝", 5½", and 7½" bbl.	180	220	385
Hunter, stainless 7½" bbl. only	350	400	450
Vaquero, dimensionally like Blackhawk, with rounded topstrap and sighting groove patterned after Colt SA, case colored frame, blued steel grip frame, rosewood grip panels,			
.357 mag., 4⅝" and 5½" bbl., blue/case colored	190	240	385
Stainless High Gloss, 4⅝" and 5½" bbl.	190	240	385
Bisley Vaquero, 5½" bbl. only	200	260	380
Stainless High Gloss, 5½" bbl. only	210	255	400
.44-40WCF, 4⅝", 5½" and 7½" bbl., blue/case colored	190	240	385
Stainless High Gloss, 4⅝", 5½", and 7½" bbl.	190	240	385
.44 mag., 5½" and 7½" bbl., blue/case colored	190	240	365
Stainless High Gloss, 5½" and 7½" bbl.	190	240	385
Bisley Vaquero, 4⅝" and 5½" bbl.	200	260	380
Stainless High Gloss, 4⅝" and 5½" bbl.	210	255	400
.45 LC, 4⅝", 5½", and 7½" bbl., blue/case colored	190	240	365
Stainless High Gloss, 4⅝", 5½", and 7½" bbl	190	240	365
Bisley Vaquero, 4⅝" and 5½" bbl.	200	260	380

	Fair	V. Good	Excellent
Stainless High Gloss, 4⅝" and 5½" bbl.	$210	$255	$400
Add $35 for simulated ivory grip panels			
Add $150 for engraved cylinder and simulated ivory grip panels			
Bisley Models, similar to Super Single Six and Blackhawk, features Colt Bisley style grip frame and hammer, wood grip panels, blued finish, some cylinders are not fluted and are roll marked, sights are fixed or adjustable.			
.22 LR, 6½" bbl. only	160	190	320
.32 H&R mag., 6½" bbl. only	160	190	320
.357 mag., 6½" and 7½" bbl.	160	190	320
.41 mag., 6½" and 7½" bbl.	160	190	320
.44 mag., 6½" and 7½" bbl.	160	190	320
New Model Bearcat, similar to original Bearcat, steel frame is slightly longer 4" bbl., wood grip panels, blued finish, transfer bar ignition, fixed sights.			
.22 LR cal.	125	185	280
.22LR/.22WRM cal., est. 50 guns left after recall	450	750	900

Ruger Old Army

	Fair	V. Good	Excellent
Old Army Percussion, "Black Powder Only", cap & ball, 7½" bbl., fixed or adjustable sights, .44 caliber, wood grip panels. Blued finish	135	180	335
Stainless	135	180	335
Blued finish with factory brass grip frame, est. 1500 guns	235	275	450

HANDGUN, REVOLVER, DOUBLE ACTION

	Fair	V. Good	Excellent
Speed Six, fixed sights, 2¾" and 4" bbl, spurless hammer available on request, checkered wood grip panels, mfd. 1973–1988.			
Model 207, blued finish .38 special	160	190	230
Stainless (Mod. 738)	190	220	280
Model 208, blued finish .357 mag.	180	190	230
Stainless (Mod. 737)	190	220	280
Model 209, blued finish 9mm	200	230	270
Stainless (Mod. 739)	200	230	300
Security Six, .357 magnum, adjustable sights, 2¾", 4" (heavy), and 6" bbl., checkered walnut grip panels, mfd. 1970–1985.			
Model 117, blued finish	180	195	250
Stainless (Mod. 717)	200	230	295
Add $15 for Ruger target grips			

	Fair	V. Good	Excellent
Police Service Six, fixed sights, 2¾" and 4" bbl., checkered walnut grip panels, square butt, mfd. 1976–1988.			
Model 107, blued finish, 2¾" and 4" bbl., .357 magnum	$180	$200	$250
Stainless (Mod. 707), 4" bbl.	190	210	270
Model 108, blued finish, 4" bbl., .38 special	180	200	250
Stainless (Mod. 708), 4" bbl.	190	210	270
Model 109, blued finish, 4" bbl., 9mm	185	205	275
GP-100, strengthened design, fixed or adjustable sights, rubber grip panels with wood inserts, 4", 6", and 6" heavy bbl.			
Adjustable sights, blued finish. .357 magnum	215	275	370
Stainless	235	265	390
Stainless High Gloss finish (.357 mag. only)	235	265	390
Fixed sights, blued finish, .38 special or .357 magnum	200	245	355
Stainless	220	250	375
Stainless High Gloss finish (.357 mag. only)	220	250	375
SP-101, small frame version of GP-100, fixed or adjustable sights, rubber grip panels with wood inserts, 5 and 6 round cylinders, 2½", 3$\frac{1}{16}$", and 4" bbls., Stainless only, .22, .32 H&R mag., .38 spec., 9mm, and .357 mag. calibers. Stainless or High Gloss finish	200	240	360

Ruger Redhawk

	Fair	V. Good	Excellent
Redhawk, redesigned large frame, adjustable sights, smooth wood grip panels, .357 mag., 41 mag., .44 mag., and .45 LC calibers, 5½" and 7½" bbls.			
Blued finish, .357, .41 and .44 calibers	215	295	425
Stainless, .357, .41, .44 and .45LC calibers	280	310	485
Add $40 for Ruger scope rings .357 and .41 calibers bring collector premium			
Super Redhawk, Stainless only, beefed-up frame, scope rings, .44 mag. and .454 Casuil calibers, 7½" and 9½" bbls.			
.44 magnum caliber	250	285	500
.454 Casuil caliber	375	410	625

RIFLE, LEVER ACTION

	Fair	V. Good	Excellent
Model 96 Carbine, detachable rotary magazine, hardwood stock, 18½" bbl., .22 LR, case colored lever, .22 WRM and .44 magnum calibers			
.22 LR caliber	$145	$180	$265
.22 WRM caliber	165	200	285
.44 magnum caliber	185	220	305
.44 magnum caliber with scope rings	260	295	380

RIFLES, SELF-LOADING

	Fair	V. Good	Excellent
10/22 Carbine, detachable rotary magazine, walnut, birch, laminate, black synthetic stock or deluxe checkered walnut stock, blued and stainless finish, introduced 1964. Many variations and sub-variants in this group.			
10/22 Standard Carbine	80	120	175
10/22RB Standard Carbine Stainless	100	125	200
Checkered walnut stock	100	140	195
Deluxe checkered walnut sporter stock	230	170	225
10/22T Target Model, blue finish, spiral barrel	210	225	330
10/22 T Stainless Target Model, spiral barrel	225	240	385
10/22 Fingergroove Sporter, walnut Monte Carlo stock	225	300	400
Fingergroove Sporter with checkering	450	600	800
10/22 International, walnut Mannlicher stock, 1966–1969	350	425	550
International with checkering	525	550	775
10/22 International, reintroduced 1994, birch Mannlicher stock	95	130	205
Stainless International	100	135	220
10/22 Canadian Centennial, 1967, 2000 guns	300	350	450
Ruger / Remington Canadian Centennial set, 1967, Ruger 10/22 and Remington Mod. 742 in .308 cal., 1,000 sets	350	425	700
Ruger Canadian Centennial Matched set No. 2, 1967, 70 sets	425	550	950
Ruger Can. Cent. Matched set No. 1, Deluxe, 1967, 30 sets	550	675	1150
10/22 Magnum, .22 WRM caliber, blued finish	225	280	350
.44 Standard Carbine, tubular magazine, walnut and deluxe walnut stocks, .44 magnum cal., blowback action, 1961–1985.			
Deerstalker, 1961–1962, 3,750 guns	400	550	850
Ruger .44 Standard Carbine	275	325	395
Mod. 44RS, with sling swivels and aperture rear sight	300	400	525
Mod. 44 Fingergroove Sporter	400	500	800
Mod. 44 Fingergroove Sporter with checkering	800	1000	1200
Mod. 44 International	475	600	750
Mod. 44 International with checkering	710	900	1125
Mod. 44, 25th Anniversary, 1985	300	375	500

	Fair	V. Good	Excellent
Ruger Carbine, 1998, 9mm and .40 S&W caliber	$265	$345	$485
Ruger Carbine with adjustable rear sight	290	370	490
MINI-14, gas operated, police and military styling, .223 and .222 calibers, introduced 1976.			
"Southport Model," 1,000 guns	330	425	560
MINI-14, blued finish, wood stock	265	340	450
MINI-14, Stainless, wood or black synthetic stock	280	355	485
MINI-14 Folding stock, blued finish, wood stock, disc. 1989	390	465	575
MINI-14 Folding stock, Stainless, wood stock, disc. 1989	405	480	610
MINI-14 RANCH RIFLE, blued finish scope mounts	325	380	465
MINI-14 RANCH RIFLE Stainless, scope mounts	340	395	510
MINI-14 RANCH RIFLE, Folding stock, disc. 1990	465	520	635
MINI-THIRTY, blued finish, 7.62×39 caliber	300	365	465

RIFLE, SINGLE SHOT

No. 1, falling block action, variety of calibers, forearms, barrel lengths, and sights. Blued finish. Certain calibers were made in limited quantity and command collector premium. Non-prefixed serial numbers command collector premium (approx. first 8,000 guns). Introduced 1967.

	Fair	V. Good	Excellent
No. 1-A Light Sporter, Alex Henry forearm, sights/no rings	275	415	575

Ruger #1 Sporter

	Fair	V. Good	Excellent
No. 1-B STANDARD, no sights/with rings, beavertail forearm	300	425	575
No. 1-RSI, INTERNATIONAL, Mannlicher stock, sights/no rings	275	415	590

Ruger #1 International

	Fair	V. Good	Excellent
No. 1-V VARMINT, heavy barrel, target scope blocks	275	415	575
No. 1-S MEDIUM SPORTER, medium barrel, sights/no rings	$275	$415	$575
No. 1-H TROPICAL RIFLE, heavy calibers, open sights	360	450	620

Ruger #1 Tropical

	Fair	V. Good	Excellent
No. 3 CARBINE, field version of No. 1, 1972, 1987	260	350	450

Ruger #3 Carbine

RIFLE, BOLT ACTION, ROTARY MAGAZINE

Model 77/22, detachable rotary magazine, .22LR cal., checkered walnut stock, blued finish, open sights or no sights / scope rings, introduced 1987.

	Fair	V. Good	Excellent
77/22-R, no sights w/ rings	210	265	380
77/22-RS, with sights	220	275	390
Rollmarked "77/22"	440	550	780
77/22, with green laminate stock	440	550	780
77/22-RP, all weather stainless w/synthetic stock, rings	235	265	380
77/22-RSP, all weather stainless w/synthetic stock, sights	245	275	390
77/22-VBZ VARMINT, stainless, heavy barrel, laminated stock	250	275	400
77/22-RM, .22WRM cal., blued finish, walnut stock, rings	210	265	380
77/22-RSM, .22WRM cal., blued finish, walnut stock, sights	220	275	390
77/22-RMP, .22 WRM cal., stainless, synthetic stock, rings	210	265	380
77/22-RSMP, .22WRM cal., stainless, synthetic stock, sights	220	265	390
77/22-VMBZ, .22WRM cal., stainless, heavy bbl, laminated stock	250	275	400
77/22-RH, .22 Hornet cal., blued finish, walnut stock, rings	250	275	400
77/22-RSH, .22 Hornet cal., blued finish, walnut stock, sights	260	285	410
77/22-VHZ, .22 Hornet cal., stainless, heavy bbl., laminated stock	270	290	430
77/44, .44 mag. cal., blued finish, walnut stock open sights only	245	295	485
77/44, .44 mag. cal., stainless, synthetic stock, open sights only	245	295	485

RIFLE, BOLT ACTION, BOX MAGAZINE

	Fair	V. Good	Excellent
Model 77, bolt action, variety of calibers, barrel lengths, and sights checkered walnut stock, super polished and blued finish. Certain calibers were made in limited quantities and command collector premium. Non-prefixed serial numbers and "flat bolts" command collector premium.			
77-R, round top or integral sight bases, walnut stock, no sights	$245	$325	$420
Same as above in scarce .284 cal.	295	390	465
Same as above in scarcer .350 Rem. Mag. cal.	295	425	525
77-RL, ultra light variation, no sights, disc. 1992	250	325	445
77-RLS, ultra light variation with open sights, disc. 1989	250	325	445
77-RS, open sights	265	350	460
Same as above in scarce .284 and .350 Rem. Mag. cals	330	440	575
77-PL, same as 77-R round top, except drilled and tapped for Redfield scope, no sights	245	325	420
77-ST, same as 77-PL with sights	265	350	460
77-V Varmint, heavy barrel, drilled and tapped for scope bases	245	325	430

Ruger Model 77V

	Fair	V. Good	Excellent
77-RS African, similar to 77-R, in .458 Win. Mag, cal., disc. 1991	335	400	550
77-RSC, same as African with Circassian walnut stock	400	500	675
77-RSI, International, Mannlicher stock, open sights and rings	265	325	470
Model 77 MARK II, improved M-77, bolt action, variety of calibers, barrel lengths, and sights. Super polished and blued or stainless, checkered walnut (standard) or synthetic stock, three-position safety, positive extraction, introduced 1989.			
77-R, this is standard model MARK II	245	300	410
77-RL, ultra light variation, no sights	250	310	440
77-RLS, ultra light variation with open sights	260	310	480
77-RLP Stainless, synthetic stock, w/o sights, includes rings	245	300	410
77-RS, same as 77-R with open sights	265	330	470
77-RSI, International, Mannlicher stock, open sights and rings	265	335	475
K77-RP All-Weather Stainless, synthetic stock, w/o sights	$255	$295	$415
K77-RSP All-Weather Stainless, synthetic stock, open sights	265	335	445
K77-RBZ Satin Stainless, laminate stock, rings/no sights	260	310	420
same as above with open sights and rings	270	320	430
K77-VT, Stainless, laminate stock, heavy barrel	265	335	440
77-LR, same as 77-R except left-handed	245	300	415
77K-LRBBZ Stainless, laminate stock, left-handed	255	310	420
77-RSM, heavy magnum calibers, premium wood, checkered, ebony foreand tip	750	875	1300
77-RS EXPRESS, similar to 77-RSM above, lighter calibers, premium wood, checkered, ebony forend tip	700	800	1200

SHOTGUN: OVER/UNDER

	Fair	V. Good	Excellent
Red Label, variety of gauges, barrel lengths, stocks, and chokes. Boxlock design with automatic ejectors. Polished and blued or stainless. Deluxe wood with checkering 3" chambers. Engraved models available.			
Standard Grade, early 20 ga., all blue, no screw in chokes	550	685	965
Standard Grade, early 12 ga., all blue, *500 guns*	610	755	1065
Standard Grade, 20, 28, and 12 ga. blue/stainless, screw in chokes	550	685	965
Red Label All Weather Stainless, checkered synthetic stock screw in chokes	550	685	965

Ruger Red Label

	Fair	V. Good	Excellent
Red Label Engraved, standardized patterns only Standard coverage	1000	1650	2200
⅓ coverage	1190	1840	2390
⅔ coverage (12 ga. Only)	1530	2180	2730
Red Label English Field, straight stock, 20, 28, and 12 ga.	550	685	965
Red Label Sporting Clays, 12 or 20 ga. Briley chokes, 30" barrels	550	740	1050
Red Label Sporting Clays Engraved, 12 only, ⅓ coverage	1300	1900	2500
Red Label "Woodside", 12 ga., stock extends into side plate	625	975	1425
Red Label "Woodside" Engraved, standard pattern on it	1050	1725	2200

SULLIVAN ARMS CO.

Made by Crescent for Sullivan Hardware, Anderson, S.C., c. 1900. See Crescent Fire Arms Co., Shotgun, Double Barrel, Side-by-Side; Shotgun, Singleshot.

SUPER DREADNAUGHT

Made by Stevens Arms.

SHOTGUN, SINGLESHOT

	Fair	V. Good	Excellent
Model 89 Dreadnaught, Various Gauges, Hammer, *Modern*	$25	$50	$75

SUPER RANGE GOOSE

Made by Stevens Arms.

RIFLE, SELF-LOADING

	Fair	V. Good	Excellent
Model 85 Springfield, .22 L.R.R.F., 5 Shot Clip, Open Rear Sight, *Modern*	25	50	75

SUTHERLAND, JAMES

Edinburgh, Scotland, c. 1790.

HANDGUN, FLINTLOCK

	Fair	V. Good	Excellent
.50, All Steel, Engraved, Ram's Horn Butt, *Antique*	1200	2500	3250

SUTHERLAND, RAMSEY

London and Birmingham, England, 1790–1827.

HANDGUN, FLINTLOCK

	Fair	V. Good	Excellent
.67, George III, Calvary Pistol, Military, Tapered Round Barrel, Brass Furniture, *Antique*	500	1000	1350

RIFLE, FLINTLOCK

	Fair	V. Good	Excellent
.75, 3rd Model Brown Bess, Musket, Military, *Antique*	600	1250	1650

SVENDSEN

E. Svendsen, Itasca, Ill., c. 1965.

HANDGUN, MANUAL REPEATER

	Fair	V. Good	Excellent
Four Aces, .22 Short, Four Barrels, Derringer, Spur Trigger, *Modern*	75	100	125

SWAMP ANGEL

Made by Forehand & Wadsworth, Worcester, Mass., c. 1871.

HANDGUN, REVOLVER

	Fair	V. Good	Excellent
.41 Short, 5 Shot, Spur Trigger, Solid Frame, Single Action, *Antique*	100	200	275

SWEDISH MILITARY

HANDGUN, REVOLVER

	Fair	V. Good	Excellent
M1887 Husqvarna, 7.5mm, Double Action, Blue, *Antique*	$125	$250	$300

RIFLE, BOLT ACTION

	Fair	V. Good	Excellent
M1896 Mauser, 6.5 × 55mm, Gustav, *Curio*	100	200	250

RIFLE, SINGLESHOT

	Fair	V. Good	Excellent
M1867/89 Remington, 11.7mm, Full Stock, *Antique*	150	350	425

SWEITZER, DANIEL & CO.

Lancaster, Pa., 1808–1814. See Kentucky Rifles.

SWIFT

Made by Iver Johnson, Fitchburg, Mass., 1890–1900.

HANDGUN, REVOLVER

	Fair	V. Good	Excellent
.38 S & W, 5 Shot, Double Action, Top Break, *Curio*	50	75	100
.38 S & W, 5 Shot, Top Break, Hammerless, Double Action, *Curio*	50	75	100

SWISS MILITARY

HANDGUN, REVOLVER

	Fair	V. Good	Excellent
M1872 Swiss Ordnance, 10.4mm R.F., Double Action, Blue, Military, *Antique*	400	800	1100
M1872/78 Swiss Ordnance, 10.4mm C.F., Double Action, Blue, Military, *Antique*	200	400	550
M1882 Swiss Ordnance, 7.5mm, Double Action, Blue, Military, *Antique*	75	150	225
M1882 Swiss Ordnance, 7.5mm, Double Action, Blue, Military, with Holster Stock and All Leather, *Antique*	600	1250	1750

RIFLE, BOLT ACTION

	Fair	V. Good	Excellent
Vetterli, Bern 1878, .41 Swiss R.F., Tube Feed, Military, *Antique*	100	200	300
Vetterli, Bern 1878/81, .41 Swiss R.F., Tube Feed, Military, *Antique*	100	175	300
Vetterli, Carbine, .41 Swiss R.F., Tube Feed, Military, *Antique*	400	800	1000
M1893, 7.5 × 55 Swiss, Military, *Curio*	200	400	550
M 1889/1900, 7.5 × 55 Swiss, Short Rifle, *Curio*	200	400	550
M1889, 7.5 × 55 Swiss, Military, *Modern*	100	175	250
M1911 Schmidt Rubin, 7.5 × 55 Swiss, Clip Fed, Carbine, Military, *Curio*	75	125	175

	Fair	V. Good	Excellent
M1911 Schmidt Rubin, 7.5 × 55 Swiss, Clip Fed, Military, *Curio*	$75	$100	$150

RIFLE, PERCUSSION

	Fair	V. Good	Excellent
Federal Rifle, .41 Caliber, Full Stocked, *Antique*	$350	$750	$1000

T

T.A.C.

Trocaola, Aranzabal y Cia., Eibar, Spain.

HANDGUN, REVOLVER

	Fair	V. Good	Excellent
Modelo Militar, .44 Spec., S & W Triple Lock Copy, Double Action, Blue, *Modern*	$100	$175	$225
OP No. 2 Mk I, .455 Eley, British, Double Action, Top Break, *Curio*	75	150	175
S & W Frontier Copy, .44 American, Double Action, Top Break, Blue, *Modern*	75	125	150
S & W M&P Copy, .38 Spec., Double Action, Blue, *Modern*	50	75	100

TALLARES

Tallares Armas Livianas Argentinas, Punta Alta, Argentina.

HANDGUN, SELF-LOADING

	Fair	V. Good	Excellent
T.A.L.A., .22 L.R.R.F., Clip Fed, *Modern*	75	125	150

TANARMI

Made in Italy. Imported by Excam.

HANDGUN, REVOLVER

	Fair	V. Good	Excellent
E-15, For Chrome, Add $5.00			
E-15, .22 L.R.R.F, Single Action, Western Style, *Modern*	20	40	50
E-15, .22LR/.22 WMR Combo, Single Action, Western Style, *Modern*	20	40	50
TA-22, For Chrome, Add $5.00			
TA-22, .22 L.R.R.F, Single Action, Western Style, Brass Grip Frame, *Modern*	20	40	50
TA-22, .22LR/.22 WMR Combo, Single Action, Western Style, Brass Grip Frame, *Modern*	25	50	75
TA-76, For Chrome, Add $5.00			
TA-76, .22 L.R.R.F, Single Action, Western Style, *Modern*	15	25	50
TA-76, .22LR/.22 WMR Combo, Single Action, Western Style, *Modern*	15	25	50

TANKE

HANDGUN, SELF-LOADING

	Fair	V. Good	Excellent
.25 ACP, Clip Fed, *Modern*	$50	$75	$100

TANNER

Andrae Tanner, Werkstatte fur Praszisionswaffen, Fulenbach, Switzerland.

RIFLE, BOLT ACTION

	Fair	V. Good	Excellent
300m Match, .308 Win., Offhand Target Rifle, Target Stock, Palm Rest, *Modern*	1900	3500	3850
50m Match, .22 L.R.R.F., Offhand Target Rifle, Target Stock, Palm Rest, *Modern*	1700	3250	3650
Hunting Match, Various Calibers, Checkered Monte Carlo Stock, Singleshot, *Modern*	1200	2500	2950
Standard UIT, .308 Win., Repeater, Target Rifle, Monte Carlo Target Stock, *Modern*	1900	3250	3650
Standard UIT, .308 Win., Singleshot, Target Rifle, Monte Carlo Target Stock, *Modern*	1900	3250	3650

TANQUE

Ojanguran y Vidosa, Eibar, Spain, c. 1930.

HANDGUN, SELF-LOADING

	Fair	V. Good	Excellent
6.35mm, Clip Fed, *Modern*	75	150	175

TARGA

Guiseppi Tanfoglio, Gardone, Val Trompia, Italy, imported by Excam.

HANDGUN, SELF-LOADING

	Fair	V. Good	Excellent
Chrome Plating, For All Models, Add $5.00			
GT22B, .22 L.R.R.F., Clip Fed, Blue, *Modern*	50	75	100
GT27, .25 ACP, Clip Fed, Blue, *Modern*	20	40	50
GT32C, .22 L.R.R.F., Clip Fed, Blue, *Modern*	50	75	100
GT32XBE, .32 ACP, Clip Fed, *Modern*	75	125	150
GT380B, .380 ACP, Clip Fed, Blue, *Modern*	75	100	125

	Fair	V. Good	Excellent
GT380BE, .380 ACP, Clip Fed, Engraved, Blue, *Modern*	$50	$125	$150
GT380XE, .380 ACP, Clip Fed, *Modern*	50	125	150

T.A.R.N.

Swift Rifle Co., London, England, c. 1943.

HANDGUN, SELF-LOADING

	Fair	V. Good	Excellent
Polish Air Force, 9mm Luger, Clip Fed, Blue, *Curio*	1800	3500	4350

TAURUS

Forjas Taurus S.A., Porto Alegre, Brazil.

HANDGUN, REVOLVER

	Fair	V. Good	Excellent
Model 65, .38 Special, Solid Frame, Swing-Out Cylinder, Double Action, *Modern*	100	175	225
Model 66, .38 Special, Solid Frame, Swing-Out Cylinder, Double Action, Adjustable Sights, *Modern*	100	200	250
Model 73, .32 S & W Long, Solid Frame, Swing-Out Cylinder, Double Action, Nickel Finish, *Modern*	75	150	200
Model 74, .32 S & W Long, Solid Frame, Swing-Out Cylinder, Double Action, Adjustable Sights, *Modern*	75	125	175
Model 80, .38 Special, Solid Frame, Swing-Out Cylinder, Double Action, *Modern*	75	125	175
Model 82, .38 Special, Solid Frame, Swing-Out Cylinder, Double Action, Heavy Barrel, *Modern*	75	150	175
Model 83, .38 Special, Solid Frame, Swing-Out Cylinder, Double Action, Adjustable Sights, *Modern*	75	150	175
Model 85, .38 Special, Solid Frame, Swing-Out Cylinder, Double Action, 3" Barrel, *Modern*	75	175	200
Model 86, .38 Special, Solid Frame, Swing-Out Cylinder, Double Action, Adjustable Sights, 6" Barrel, *Modern*	100	200	225
Model 94, .22 L.R.R.F., Solid Frame, Swing-Out Cylinder, Double Action, Adjustable Sights, *Modern*	75	150	175

HANDGUN, SELF-LOADING

	Fair	V. Good	Excellent
PT-92, 9mm Luger, Clip Fed, Blue, Double Action, *Modern*	150	350	400
PT-99, 9mm Luger, Clip Fed, Blue, Double Action, *Modern*	175	375	425

T.D.E.

El Monte, Calif. Also see Auto-Mag.

HANDGUN, SELF-LOADING

	Fair	V. Good	Excellent
Backup, .380 ACP, Stainless Steel, *Modern*	$100	$225	$250

TED WILLIAMS

Trade name of Sears, Roebuck, also see Sears.

RIFLE, BOLT ACTION

	Fair	V. Good	Excellent
Model 52703, .22 L.R.R.F., Singleshot, Plain, *Modern*	20	40	50
Model 52774, .22 L.R.R.F., Clip Fed, Plain, *Modern*	25	50	75
Model 53, Various Calibers, Checkered Stock, *Modern*	75	150	175

RIFLE, LEVER ACTION

	Fair	V. Good	Excellent
Model 120, .30/30 Win., Carbine, *Modern*	50	125	150

RIFLE, SELF-LOADING

	Fair	V. Good	Excellent
Model 34, .22 L.R.R.F., *Modern*	25	50	75
Model 34, .22 L.R.R.F., Carbine, *Modern*	25	50	75
Model 3T, .22 L.R.R.F., Checkered Stock, *Modern*	50	75	100
Model 52811, .22 L.R.R.F., Plain, Tube Feed, Takedown, *Modern*	25	50	75
Model 52814, .22 L.R.R.F., Checkered Stock, Clip Fed, Takedown, *Modern*	75	100	125

SHOTGUN, BOLT ACTION

	Fair	V. Good	Excellent
Model 51106, 12 or 20 Gauges, Clip Fed, Adjustable Choke, *Modern*	25	50	75
Model 51142, .410 Gauge, Clip Fed, *Modern*	25	50	75

SHOTGUN, DOUBLE BARREL, OVER-UNDER

	Fair	V. Good	Excellent
Model Laurona, 12 Ga., Checkered Stock, Light Engraving, Double Trigger, Vent Rib, *Modern*	150	325	350
Model Zoli, 12 and 20 Gauges, Checkered Stock, Light Engraving, Double Trigger, Vent Rib, *Modern*	150	275	300
Model Zoli, 12 Ga., Checkered Stock, Light Engraving, Double Trigger, Vent Rib, Automatic Ejector, *Modern*	125	275	300

SHOTGUN, DOUBLE BARREL, SIDE-BY-SIDE

	Fair	V. Good	Excellent
Model 51226, 12 and 20 Gauges, Plain, Double Trigger, *Modern*	75	125	150
Model Laurona, 12 and 20 Gauges, Checkered Stock, Light Engraving, Hammerless, *Modern*	75	150	175

	Fair	V. Good	Excellent
SHOTGUN, SELF-LOADING			
Model 300, 12 and 20 Gauges, Checkered Stock, Vent Rib, Adjustable Choke, *Modern*	$100	$175	$200
Model 300, 12 and 20 Gauges, Checkered Stock, Vent Rib, *Modern*	100	175	200
Model 300, 12 Ga., Plain, *Modern*	75	150	175
SHOTGUN, SINGLESHOT			
Model 5108, Various Gauges, Plain, *Modern*	20	40	50
SHOTGUN, SLIDE ACTION			
Model 200, 12 and 20 Gauges, Checkered Stock, Plain Barrel, *Modern*	75	125	150
Model 200, 12 and 20 Gauges, Checkered Stock, Vent Rib, Adjustable Choke, *Modern*	75	150	175
Model 200, 12 and 20 Gauges, Checkered Stock, Vent Rib, *Modern*	75	125	150
Model 200, 12 and 20 Gauges, Plain, *Modern*	50	100	125
Model 51454, .410 Ga., Plain, *Modern*	50	100	125

TEN STAR

Belgium, c. 1900.

SHOTGUN, DOUBLE BARREL, SIDE-BY-SIDE			
Various Gauges, Hammerless, Damascus Barrel, *Modern*	50	150	175
Various Gauges, Hammerless, Steel Barrel, *Modern*	75	175	200
Various Gauges, Outside Hammers, Damascus Barrel, *Modern*	50	150	175
Various Gauges, Outside Hammers, Steel Barrel, *Modern*	75	175	200
SHOTGUN, SINGLESHOT			
Various Gauges, Hammer, Steel Barrel, *Modern*	50	75	100

TERRIBLE

Hijos de Calixto Arrizabalaga, Eibar, Spain, c. 1930.

HANDGUN, SELF-LOADING			
.25 ACP, Clip Fed, Blue, *Modern*	75	125	150

TERRIER

Made by J. Rupertus, Philadelphia, Pa. Sold by Tryon Bros., c. 1880.

	Fair	V. Good	Excellent
HANDGUN, REVOLVER			
.22 Short R.F., 7 Shot, Spur Trigger, Solid Frame, Single Action, *Antique*	$100	$150	$200
.32 Short R.F., 5 Shot, Spur Trigger, Solid Frame, Single Action, *Antique*	100	150	200
.38 Short R.F., 5 Shot, Spur Trigger, Solid Frame, Single Action, *Antique*	100	150	200
.41 Short R.F., 5 Shot, Spur Trigger, Solid Frame, Single Action, *Antique*	125	300	350

TERROR

Made by Forehand & Wadsworth, c. 1870.

HANDGUN, REVOLVER			
.32 Short R.F., 5 or 6 Shot, Spur Trigger, Solid Frame, Single Action, *Antique*	75	150	175

TEUF-TEUF

Arizmendi y Goenaga, Eibar, Spain, c. 1912.

HANDGUN, SELF-LOADING			
.25 ACP, Clip Fed, Blue, *Curio*	75	125	150

TEUF-TEUF

Belgium, c. 1907.

HANDGUN, SELF-LOADING			
.25 ACP, Clip Fed, Blue, *Curio*	75	150	175

TEXAS RANGER

Made by Stevens Arms.

SHOTGUN, SINGLESHOT			
Model 95, 12 and 16 Gauges, *Modern*	20	40	50

THAMES ARMS CO

Norwich, Conn., c. 1907.

HANDGUN, REVOLVER			
.22 L.R.R.F., 7 Shot, Double Action, Top Break, *Curio*	75	150	175
.32 S & W, 5 Shot, Double Action, Top Break, *Curio*	50	100	125
.38 S & W, 5 Shot, Double Action, Top Break, *Curio*	75	125	150

THAYER, ROBERTSON & CARY

Norwich, Conn., c. 1907.

	Fair	V. Good	Excellent
HANDGUN, REVOLVER			
.32 S & W, 5 Shot, Double Action, Top Break, *Curio*	$50	$75	$100
.38 S & W, 5 Shot, Double Action, Top Break, *Curio*	50	75	100

THOMPSON

Developed by Auto-Ordnance, invented by Gen. John T. Thompson, made by various companies. Also see Numrich Arms.

HANDGUN, SELF-LOADING PISTOL/CARBINE			
Model 27A5, .45 ACP, Clip Fed, Finned Barrel, Adjustable Sights, with Compensator, (Numrich), *Modern*	200	450	550
RIFLE, SELF-LOADING			
Model 27 A 1, .45 ACP, Clip Fed, without Compensator, (Numrich), *Modern*	225	550	650
Model 27 A 1, .45 ACP, Clip Fed, without Compensator,Cased with Accessories, (Numrich), *Modern*	250	550	700
Model 27 A 1 Deluxe, .45 ACP, Clip Fed, Finned Barrel, Adjustable Sights, with Compensator, (Numrich), *Modern*	300	675	800
Model 27 A 3, .22 L.R.R.F., Clip Fed, Finned Barrel, Adjustable Sights, with Compensator, (Numrich), *Modern*	150	300	450

THOMPSON, SAMUEL

Columbus, Ohio, 1820–1822. See Kentucky Rifles.

THOMPSON/CENTER ARMS

Rochester, N.H. A relative newcomer to the family of American gunmakers, Thompson/Center was founded as a joint collaboration of inventor/designer Warren Center, and manufacturer Ken Thompson, president, K. W. Thompson Tool Co. Center had a novel firearms design, and Thompson was looking for a product to manufacture. The first Contender, the beginning of the firm's substantial line of singleshot closed breech pistols, came on the market in 1967. Since then over a million guns and over a million barrels have been made for a special dedicated clientele of handgun hunters and sihouette shooters. In 1970 the firm entered the blackpowder market by adding the Hawken singleshot muzzleloading rifle to the line, followed by the Renegade, Big Boar, Grey Hawk, Pennsylvania Hunter, White Mountain, and New Englander muzzle loaders and such innovations as the Fire Hawk and Thunder Hawk in-line ignition percussion rifles and carbines and the Scout in-line ignition rifle, carbine and pistol. With the in-line system, the percussion nipple is in a straight line with the barrel, and is struck directly from the rear by the firing pin. The design allows for fast ignition and high dependability, and the rifle resembles closely a conventional bolt-action rifle in pointability and balance. The Contender line was also expanded, by addition of a carbine design, which, like the pistols, offers the capability of interchangeable barrels. Additionally, Carbine Conversion Kits allowed adapting pistols into carbines, by changing the buttstock and forend and adding a 21" barrel. A full line of scopes and accessories rounds out the line. The New Hampshire–based firm is proud of its self-sufficiency, and is one of the few gunmakers in the world with its own investment casting foundry. The factory is equipped with state-of-the-art machinery. The company also boasts its own saw mill and kilns for walnut curing, in Perry, Kansas. Warren Center has been honored as Handgunner of the Year, a coveted trophy presented to such luminaries as William B. Ruger and Elmer Keith. The patented designs for the Contender pistol were intended to create a singleshot pistol versatile for a variety of hunting and shooting conditions and situations, with a wide choice of calibers and barrel lengths. The Contender has been made in as many as 19 centerfire pistol or rifle cartridges, and in .410 shotgun. Barrels are interchangeable in seconds: the forend is removed, the barrel pin pushed out, the new barrel installed, and the correct forend installed. The firing pin is designed with two strikers, alterable manually to rotate into position for rim or centerfire cartridges. The versatile firing pin system is designed to also serve as a safety. Still another feature is the automatic ejection system, found on selected barrels, in which the cartridge casing is totally ejected from the breech after firing. A total of over 600,000 Thompson/Center Contenders have been manufactured to date. Calibers have been: .22 L.R., .22 L.R. Match, .22 WMR, .17 Remington, .22 Hornet, .222 Remington, 7 mm T.C.U., 7-30 Waters, .30–30 Winchester, .32-20, .357 Magnum, .357 Remington Maximum, .35 Remington, .375 Winchester, 10 mm Auto, .44 Magnum, .445 Super Magnum, .45-70, .45 Colt and .410 shotgun. Barrel lengths have been: 10", 12", 14", 16", 16¼", and 21" (carbine), standard round; octagonal for .22 Long Rifle only. A disastrous fire in 1998 destroyed the company's foundry, although it was quickly rebuilt.

	Fair	V. Good	Excellent
HANDGUN, PERCUSSION			
.45 Patriot, Set Trigger, Octagon Barrel, Reproduction, *Antique*	$100	$200	$250
.45 Patriot, Set Trigger, Octagon Barrel, with Accessories, Reproduction, *Antique*	100	225	275
HANDGUN, SINGLESHOT			
Contender, Various Calibers, Adjustable Sights, *Modern*	150	325	350
Contender, Various Calibers, Adjustable Sights, Heavy Barrel, *Modern*	100	225	275
Contender, Various Calibers, Adjustable Sights, Super 14" Barrel, *Modern*	125	275	325
Contender, Various Calibers, Adjustable Sights, Vent Rib, *Modern*	150	350	375
Contender, Various Calibers, Heavy Barrel, No Sights, *Modern*	100	225	275
RIFLE, FLINTLOCK			
.45 Hawken, Set Trigger, Octagon Barrel, Reproduction, *Antique*	125	275	325

	Fair	V. Good	Excellent
.45 Hawken, Set Trigger, Octagon Barrel, with Accessories, Reproduction, *Antique*	$150	$300	$350
.50 Hawken, Set Trigger, Octagon Barrel, Reproduction, *Antique*	150	275	325
.50 Hawken, Set Trigger, Octagon Barrel, with Accessories, Reproduction, *Antique*	150	300	350
Hawken Cougar, .45 and .50 Caliber Caplock, Stainless Furniture, Reproduction, *Antique*	175	375	425

RIFLE, PERCUSSION

Cherokee, .32 or .45 Caliber, Brass Furniture, 24" Barrel, *Modern*	150	300	350

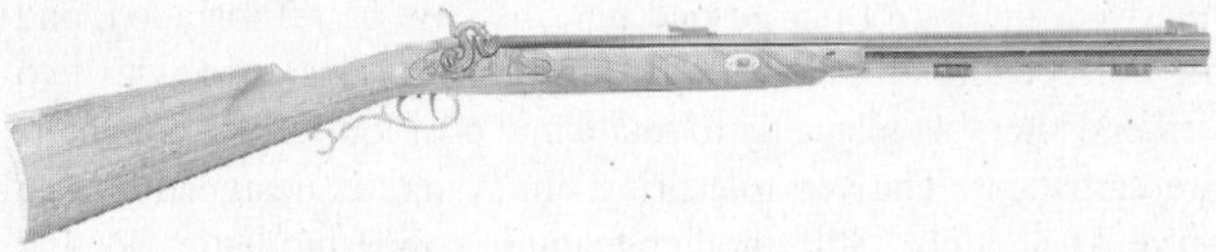

Thompson/Center Cherokee

.36 Seneca, Set Trigger, Octagon Barrel, Reproduction, *Antique*	125	250	300
.36 Seneca, Set Trigger, Octagon Barrel, with Accessories, Reproduction, *Antique*	125	275	325
.45 Hawken, Set Trigger, Octagon Barrel, Reproduction, *Antique*	125	250	300
.45 Hawken, Set Trigger, Octagon Barrel, with Accessories, Reproduction, *Antique*	125	275	325
.45 Seneca, Set Trigger, Octagon Barrel, Reproduction, *Antique*	125	250	300
.45 Seneca, Set Trigger, Octagon Barrel, with Accessories, Reproduction, *Antique*	125	275	325
.50 Hawken, Set Trigger, Octagon Barrel, Reproduction, *Antique*	125	250	300
.50 Hawken, Set Trigger, Octagon Barrel, with Accessories, Reproduction, *Antique*	125	275	325
.54 Renegade, Set Trigger, Octagon Barrel, Reproduction, *Antique*	100	225	275
.54 Renegade, Set Trigger, Octagon Barrel, with Accessories, Reproduction, *Antique*	125	250	300

RIFLE, SINGLESHOT

TCR83 Sports Rifle, Various Calibers, Interchangeable Barrels, Adjustable Double Set Triggers, *Modern*	250	500	550

THREE-BARREL GUN CO.

Moundsville, W. Va., 1906–1908, also at Wheeling, W. Va., as Royal Gun Co. and as Hollenbeck Gun Co.

	Fair	V. Good	Excellent

COMBINATION WEAPON, DRILLING

Various Calibers, Damascus barrel, *Antique*	$450	$1100	$1200

THUNDER

Martin Bascaran, Eibar, Spain, made for Alberdi, Teleria y Cia, 1912–1919.

HANDGUN, SELF-LOADING

M1919, .25 ACP, Clip Fed, *Curio*	75	100	125

TIGER

c. 1880.

HANDGUN, REVOLVER

#2, .32 Short R.F., 5 Shot, Spur Trigger, Solid Frame, Single Action, *Antique*	75	150	175

TIGER

Made by Crescent for J. H. Hill Co. Nashville, Tenn., c. 1900. See Crescent Fire Arms Co., Shotgun, Double Barrel, Side-by-Side; Shotgun, Singleshot.

TIKKA

Oy Tikkakoski AB, Tikkakoski, Finland. Purchased in 2000 by Fabbri a d'Armi Pietro Beretta, Gardone.

RIFLE, BOLT ACTION

Model 55 Deluxe, Various Calibers, Clip Fed, Checkered Stock, *Modern*	225	475	600
Model 55 Sporter, Various Calibers, Clip Fed, Checkered Stock, Heavy Barrel, *Modern*	225	475	600
Model 55 Standard, Various Calibers, Clip Fed, Checkered Stock, *Modern*	225	450	600
Model 65 Deluxe, Various Calibers, Clip Fed, Checkered Stock, *Modern*	225	475	600
Model 65 Sporter, Various Calibers, Clip Fed, Checkered Stock, Target Rifle, Heavy Barrel, *Modern*	250	550	700
Model 65 Standard, Various Calibers, Clip Fed, Checkered Stock, *Modern*	225	450	600

TINDALL & DUTTON

London, England, 1790–1820.

HANDGUN, FLINTLOCK

Pocket Pistol, Various Calibers, Boxlock, *Antique*	150	350	500

TINGLE MFG. CO.
Shelbyville, Ind.

HANDGUN, PERCUSSION

	Fair	V. Good	Excellent
Model 1960 Target, Octagon Barrel, Rifled, Reproduction, *Antique*	$75	$125	$150

RIFLE, PERCUSSION

	Fair	V. Good	Excellent
Model 1962 Target, Octagon Barrel, Brass Furniture, Rifled, Reproduction, *Antique*	100	175	200

SHOTGUN, PERCUSSION

	Fair	V. Good	Excellent
Model 1960, 10 or 12 gauges, Vent Rib, Double Barrel, Over-Under, Reproduction, *Antique*	100	200	225

TIPPING & LAWDEN
Birmingham, England, c. 1875.

HANDGUN, MANUAL REPEATER

	Fair	V. Good	Excellent
Sharps Derringer, Various Calibers, 4 Barrels, Spur Trigger, Cased with Accessories, *Antique*	300	625	800

HANDGUN, REVOLVER

	Fair	V. Good	Excellent
Thomas Patent, .450, Solid Frame, Double Action, *Antique*	250	500	675

TITAN
Guiseppi Tanfoglio, Gardone, Val Trompia, Italy. Also see F.I.E.

HANDGUN, SELF-LOADING

	Fair	V. Good	Excellent
Pocket, .25 ACP, Clip Fed, Hammer, *Modern*	25	50	75

TITAN
Retolaza Hermanos, Eibar, Spain, c. 1900.

HANDGUN, SELF-LOADING

	Fair	V. Good	Excellent
M 1913, 6.35mm, Clip Fed, *Curio*	75	100	125

TITANIC
Retoloza Hermanos, Eibar, Spain, c. 1900.

HANDGUN, SELF-LOADING

	Fair	V. Good	Excellent
M 1913, 6.35mm, Clip Fed, *Curio*	75	100	125
M 1914, 7.65mm, Clip Fed, *Curio*	75	125	150

TOMPKINS
Varsity Mfg. Co., Springfield, Mass., c. 1947.

HANDGUN, SINGLESHOT

	Fair	V. Good	Excellent
Target, .22 L.R.R.F., Full Stock, *Modern*	100	200	225

TOWER'S POLICE SAFETY
Made by Hopkins & Allen, Norwich, Conn. c. 1875.

HANDGUN, REVOLVER

	Fair	V. Good	Excellent
.38 Short R.F., 5 Shot, Spur Trigger, Solid Frame, Single Action, *Antique*	$75	$150	$175

TRADEWINDS
Tacoma, Wash. Also see HVA.

RIFLE, BOLT ACTION

	Fair	V. Good	Excellent
Husky (Early), Various Calibers, Checkered Stock, Monte Carlo Stock, *Modern*	100	225	375
Husky M-5000, Various Calibers, Checkered Stock, Clip Fed, *Modern*	125	275	325
Husqvarna Crown Grade, Various Calibers, Checkered Stock, Monte Carlo Stock, *Modern*	250	575	625
Husqvarna Imperial Custom, Various Calibers, Checkered Stock, Monte Carlo Stock, *Modern*	225	475	525
Husqvarna Imperial, Various Calibers, Checkered Stock, Monte Carlo Stock, Lightweight, *Modern*	225	500	550
Husqvarna Presentation, Various Calibers, Checkered Stock, Monte Carlo Stock, *Modern*	350	700	750
Husqvarna, Various Calibers, Checkered Stock, Monte Carlo Stock, Lightweight, *Modern*	225	525	575
Husqvarna, Various Calibers, Checkered Stock, Monte Carlo Stock, Lightweight, Full-Stocked, *Modern*	250	525	600
Model 1998, .222 Rem., No Sights, Heavy Barrel, Target Stock, *Modern*	225	475	525
Model 600K, Various Calibers, Clip Fed, No Sights, Heavy Barrel, Set Trigger, *Modern*	150	300	350
Model 600S, Various Calibers, Clip Fed, Heavy Barrel, Octagon Barrel, *Modern*	225	475	525

RIFLE, SELF-LOADING

	Fair	V. Good	Excellent
Model 260A, .22 L.R.R.F., 5 Shot Clip, Checkered Stock, *Modern*	75	150	200

SHOTGUN, DOUBLE BARREL, OVER-UNDER

	Fair	V. Good	Excellent
Gold Shadow Indy, 12 Ga., Field Grade, Engraved, Fancy Checkering, Automatic Ejector, Vent Rib, *Modern*	600	1400	1550
Gold Shadow Indy, 12 Ga., Skeet Grade, Engraved, Fancy, Checkering, Automatic Ejector, Vent Rib, *Modern*	600	1500	1750

	Fair	V. Good	Excellent
Gold Shadow Indy, 12 Ga., Trap Grade, Engraved, Fancy, Checkering, Automatic Ejector, Vent Rib, *Modern*	$650	$1450	$1600
Shadow Indy, 12 Ga., Field Grade, Automatic Ejector, Vent Rib, Checkered Stock, *Modern*	225	475	525
Shadow Indy, 12 Ga., Skeet Grade, Automatic Ejector, Vent Rib, Checkered Stock, *Modern*	250	500	550
Shadow Indy, 12 Ga., Trap Grade, Automatic Ejector, Vent Rib, Checkered Stock, *Modern*	225	525	575
Shadow-7, 12 Ga., Field Grade, Automatic Ejector, Vent Rib, *Modern*	150	325	350
Shadow-7, 12 Ga., Skeet Grade, Automatic Ejector, Vent Rib, *Modern*	150	350	375
Shadow-7, 12 Ga., Trap Grade, Automatic Ejector, Vent Rib, *Modern*	175	375	400

SHOTGUN, DOUBLE BARREL, SIDE-BY-SIDE

	Fair	V. Good	Excellent
Model G-1032, 10 Ga. 3 1/2", Checkered Stock, *Modern*	100	225	250
Model G-1228, 12 Ga. Mag. 3", Checkered Stock, *Modern*	100	250	275
Model G-2028, 20 Ga. Mag., Checkered Stock, *Modern*	125	250	275

SHOTGUN, SELF-LOADING

	Fair	V. Good	Excellent
Model D-200, 12 Ga., Field Grade, Vent Rib, Engraved, *Modern*	125	250	300
Model H-150, 12 Ga., Field Grade, *Modern*	100	200	225
Model H-170, 12 Ga., Field Grade, Vent Rib, *Modern*	100	225	275
Model T-220, 12 Ga., Trap Grade, Vent Rib, Engraved, *Modern*	125	250	300

SHOTGUN, SINGLESHOT

	Fair	V. Good	Excellent
Model M50, 10 Ga., 3 1/2" Barrel, Checkered Stock, *Modern*	75	125	175

TRAMPS TERROR

Made by Hoods Firearms Co. Norwich, Conn., c. 1870.

HANDGUN, REVOLVER

	Fair	V. Good	Excellent
.22 Short R.F., 7 Shot, Spur Trigger, Solid Frame, Single Action, *Antique*	75	150	175

TRIOMPH

Apaolozo Hermanos, Eibar, Spain.

HANDGUN, SELF-LOADING

	Fair	V. Good	Excellent
6.35mm, Clip Fed, Blue, *Modern*	50	100	125

TRIUMPH

Made by Stevens Arms.

SHOTGUN, DOUBLE BARREL, SIDE-BY-SIDE

	Fair	V. Good	Excellent
Model 311, Various Gauges, Hammerless, Steel Barrel, *Modern*	$75	$150	$175

TRUE BLUE

Made by Norwich Falls Pistols Co., c. 1880.

HANDGUN, REVOLVER

	Fair	V. Good	Excellent
.32 Short R.F., 5 Shot, Spur Trigger, Solid Frame, Single Action, *Antique*	75	125	175

TRUST

Fab. d'Armes de Guerre de Grande Precision, Eibar, Spain.

HANDGUN, SELF-LOADING

	Fair	V. Good	Excellent
6.36mm, Clip Fed, Blue, *Modern*	50	100	125
7.65mm, Clip Fed, Blue, *Modern*	75	125	150

TRUST SUPRA

Fab. d'Armes de Guerre de Grande Precision, Eibar, Spain.

HANDGUN, SELF-LOADING

	Fair	V. Good	Excellent
6.35mm, Clip Fed, Blue, *Modern*	50	100	125

TUE-TUE

C. F. Galand, Liège, Belgium, and Paris, France.

HANDGUN, REVOLVER

	Fair	V. Good	Excellent
Velo Dog, Various Calibers, Double Action, Hammerless, *Curio*	75	200	250

TURBIAUX

J. E. Turbiaux, Paris, France, c. 1885.

HANDGUN, MANUAL REPEATER

	Fair	V. Good	Excellent
Le Protector, Various Calibers, Palm Pistol, *Antique*	300	600	700

TURNER

Dublin, c. 1820.

HANDGUN, FLINTLOCK

	Fair	V. Good	Excellent
.62, *Antique*	500	1200	1650

TURNER & ROSS

Made by Hood Firearms, Norwich, Conn., c. 1875.

HANDGUN, REVOLVER

	Fair	V. Good	Excellent
.22 Short R.F., 7 Shot, Spur Trigger, Solid Frame, Single Action, *Antique*	$100	$150	$175

TWIGG

London, England, 1760–1813.

HANDGUN, FLINTLOCK

	Fair	V. Good	Excellent
.58, Pair, Belt Pistol, Flared, Octagon Barrel, Cased with Accessories, Plain, *Antique*	1500	3000	4500

TYCOON

Made by Johnson-Bye, Worcester, Mass., 1873–1887.

HANDGUN, REVOLVER

	Fair	V. Good	Excellent
#1, .22 Short R.F., 7 Shot, Spur Trigger, Solid Frame, Single Action, *Antique*	75	150	175
#2, .32 Short R.F., 5 Shot, Spur Trigger, Solid Frame, Single Action, *Antique*	75	150	200
#3, .38 Short R.F., 5 Shot, Spur Trigger, Solid Frame, Single Action, *Antique*	$75	$150	$175
#4, .41 Short R.F., 5 Shot, Spur Trigger, Solid Frame, Single Action, *Antique*	100	250	300
#5, .41 Short R.F., 5 Shot, Spur Trigger, Solid Frame, Single Action, *Antique*	100	250	325

TYROL

Made in Belgium for Tyrol Sport Arms, Englewood, Colo., c. 1963.

RIFLE, BOLT ACTION

	Fair	V. Good	Excellent
Model DC, Various Calibers, Mannlicher Style, Checkered Stock, *Modern*	150	275	350
Model DCM, Various Calibers, Mannlicher Style, Checkered Stock, Recoil Pad, *Modern*	100	225	250
Model DM, Various Calibers, Checkered Stock, *Modern*	75	150	175

U

UBERTI, ALDO & CO.

Gardone, Val Trompia, Italy (est. 1959) and Lakeville, Connecticut (est. 1987). One of the foremost makers of replica muzzle-loading and cartridge firearms, and of miniatures, Aldo Uberti established his company at about the same time Val Forgett was setting up Navy Arms Co. The two have collaborated on many projects over the years, and can be credited, along with Turner Kirkland (founder-owner, Dixie Gun Works) with the launching of the replica firearms business as a major entity within the firearms industry. The most recent project of Uberti and Navy Arms was the Schofield S & W, a complex arm to manufacture, whether in the 1870s or the 1990s. With the death of Aldo Uberti, the company continued under management by the family, ably assisted by staff. Overtures were made toward either buying the company outright, or partial family ownership with an outside investor, and in 2000 purchase was made by Fabbrica d'Armi Pietro Beretta, Gardone, Italy.

UHLINGER, W. L. & CO.

Philadelphia, Pa., c. 1880.

HANDGUN, REVOLVER

	Fair	*V. Good*	*Excellent*
.22 R.F., 7 Shot, Spur Trigger, Solid Frame, Single Action, *Antique*	$100	$225	$275
.32 Short R.F., 6 Shot, Spur Trigger, Solid Frame, Single Action, *Antique*	150	325	375

U.M.C. ARMS CO.

Probably Norwich Arms Co., c. 1880.

HANDGUN, REVOLVER

.32 Short R.F., 5 Shot, Spur Trigger, Solid Frame, Single Action, *Antique*	75	150	175

UNION

Fab. Francaise.

HANDGUN, SELF-LOADING

7.65mm, Ruby Style, Clip Fed, *Modern*	100	225	275
7.65mm, Ruby Style, with Horseshoe Magazine, *Modern*	300	650	750

UNION

France, M. Seytres.

HANDGUN, SELF-LOADING

	Fair	*V. Good*	*Excellent*
.25 ACP, Clip Fed, Long Grip, *Modern*	50	100	125
.32 ACP, Clip Fed, Long Grip, *Modern*	$75	$125	$150

UNION

Unceta y Cia., Guernica, Spain, 1924–1931.

HANDGUN, SELF-LOADING

Model I, 6.35mm, Clip Fed, *Modern*	50	100	150
Model II, 6.35mm, Clip Fed, *Modern*	75	125	150
Model III, 7.65mm, Clip Fed, *Modern*	100	150	175
Model IV, 7.65mm, Clip Fed, *Modern*	75	150	175

UNION FIREARMS CO.

Toledo, Ohio, 1903–1913.

HANDGUN, SELF-LOADING

Lefever Patent Revolver, .32 Caliber, 6 Shot, Top Break, *Curio*	800	1500	2000
Reifgraber Patent Pistol, .32 S & W, 8 Shot, *Curio*	900	2000	2500

UNION JACK

Made by Hood Firearms Norwich, Conn., c. 1880.

HANDGUN, REVOLVER

.22 Short R.F., 7 Shot, Spur Trigger, Solid Frame, Single Action, *Antique*	75	125	150
.32 Short R.F., 5 Shot, Spur Trigger, Solid Frame, Single Action, *Antique*	75	150	175

UNION REVOLVER

Maker unknown, c. 1880.

HANDGUN, REVOLVER

.22 Short R.F., 7 Shot, Spur Trigger, Solid Frame, Single Action, *Antique*	75	125	150
.32 Short R.F., 5 Shot, Spur Trigger, Solid Frame, Single Action, *Antique*	75	150	175

UNIQUE

Made by C. S. Shattuck, 1880–1915.

	Fair	V. Good	Excellent
HANDGUN, REPEATER			
Shattuck Palm Pistol, Various Calibers, 4 Shot, *Curio*	$250	$575	$1250
HANDGUN, REVOLVER			
.32 Short R.F., 5 Shot, Spur Trigger, Solid Frame, Single Action, *Antique*	75	150	200
.38 Short R.F., 5 Shot, Spur Trigger, Solid Frame, Single Action, *Antique*	75	150	200

UNIQUE

Mre. d'Armes de Pyrenees, Hendaye, France, 1923 to date.

	Fair	V. Good	Excellent
HANDGUN, SELF-LOADING			
Kreigsmodell, 7.65mm, Clip Fed, Magazine Disconnect, 9 Shot, Nazi-Proofed, Hammer, *Curio*	125	250	275
Model 10, 6.35mm, Clip Fed, Magazine Disconnect, *Modern*	75	150	200
Model 11, 6.35mm, Clip Fed, Magazine Disconnect, Safety, Cartridge Indicator, *Modern*	100	200	250
Model 12, 6.35mm, Clip Fed, Magazine Disconnect, Grip Safety, *Modern*	100	200	225
Model 13, 6.35mm, Clip Fed, Magazine Disconnect, Grip Safety, 7 Shot, *Modern*	100	200	225
Model 14, 6.35mm, Clip Fed, Magazine Disconnect, Grip Safety, 9 Shot, *Modern*	100	175	225
Model 15, 7.65mm, Clip Fed, Magazine Disconnect, 6 Shot, *Modern*	100	200	250
Model 16, 7.65mm, Clip Fed, Magazine Disconnect, 7 Shot, *Modern*	100	200	250
Model 17, 7.65mm, Clip Fed, Magazine Disconnect, 9 Shot, Nazi-Proofed, *Curio*	150	300	350
Model 17, 7.65mm, Clip Fed, Magazine Disconnect, 9 Shot, *Modern*	100	225	275
Model 18, 7.65mm, Clip Fed, Magazine Disconnect, 6 Shot, *Modern*	100	200	250
Model 19, 7.65mm, Clip Fed, Magazine Disconnect, 7 Shot, *Modern*	100	200	250
Model 20, 7.65mm, Clip Fed, Magazine Disconnect, 9 Shot, *Modern*	100	225	275
Model 21, .380 ACP, Clip Fed, Magazine Disconnect, 6 Shot, *Modern*	100	225	275
Model 51, .380 ACP, Clip Fed, Magazine Disconnect, 6 Shot, *Modern*	$100	$200	$250
Model 51, 7.65mm, Clip Fed, Magazine Disconnect, 9 Shot, *Modern*	100	200	250
Model 52, .22 L.R.R.F., Clip Fed, Hammer, Various Barrel Lengths, *Modern*	100	175	225
Model 540, 7.65mm, Clip Fed, Magazine Disconnect, 9 Shot, *Modern*	100	200	250
Model 550, *Modern*	100	200	250
Model C, 7.65mm, Clip Fed, 9 Shot, Hammer, *Modern*	100	200	250
Model D-1, .22 L.R.R.F., Clip Fed, Hammer, 3" Barrel, *Modern*	100	200	250
Model D-2, .22 L.R.R.F., Clip Fed, Hammer, Adjustable Sights, 4" Barrel, *Modern*	100	225	275
Model D-3, .22 L.R.R.F., Clip Fed, Hammer, Adjustable Sights, 8" Barrel, *Modern*	100	200	250
Model D-4, .22 L.R.R.F., Clip Fed, Hammer, Muzzle Brake, Adjustable Sights, 9½" Barrel, *Modern*	100	225	275
Model D-6, .22 L.R.R.F., Clip Fed, Hammer, Adjustable Sights, 6" Barrel, *Modern*	100	225	275
Model DES/69, .22 L.R.R.F., Clip Fed, Target Pistol, *Modern*	150	300	350
Model DES/VO 79, .22 L.R.R.F., Clip Fed, Rapid Fire Target Pistol, Gas Ports, *Modern*	300	650	750
Model DES/VO, .22 L.R.R.F., Clip Fed, Rapid Fire Target Pistol, *Modern*	250	525	600
Model E-1, .22 Short R.F., Clip Fed, Hammer, 3" Barrel, *Modern*	75	100	125
Model E-2, .22 Short R.F., Clip Fed, Hammer, Adjustable Sights, 4" Barrel, *Modern*	75	125	150
Model E-3, .22 Short R.F., Clip Fed, Hammer, Adjustable Sights, 8" Barrel, *Modern*	75	125	150
Model E-4, .22 Short R.F., Clip Fed, Hammer, Muzzle Brake, Adjustable Sights, 9½" Barrel, *Modern*	75	150	200
Model F, .380 ACP, Clip Fed, 8 Shot, Hammer, *Modern*	100	225	275
Model L (Corsair), .22 L.R.R.F., Clip Fed, Hammer, *Modern*	100	175	225
Model L (Corsair), .22 L.R.R.F., Clip Fed, Hammer, Lightweight, *Modern*	100	175	225
Model L (Corsair), .32 ACP, Clip Fed, Hammer, *Modern*	75	125	150

	Fair	V. Good	Excellent
Model L (Corsair), .32 ACP, Clip Fed, Hammer, Lightweight, *Modern*	$75	$125	$150
Model L (Corsair), .380 ACP, Clip Fed, Hammer, *Modern*	75	150	175
Model L (Corsair), .380 ACP, Clip Fed, Hammer, Lightweight, *Modern*	75	125	150
Model Mikros, .25 ACP, Clip Fed, Magazine Disconnect, 6 Shot, *Modern*	75	150	175
Model RD (Ranger), .22 L.R.R.F., Clip Fed, Hammer, *Modern*	50	75	100
Model RD (Ranger), .22 L.R.R.F., Clip Fed, Muzzle Brake, Hammer, *Modern*	50	100	125

RIFLE, BOLT ACTION

	Fair	V. Good	Excellent
Audax, .22 L.R.R.F., Checkered Stock, Open Sights, *Modern*	75	150	175
Dioptra 3121, .22 L.R.R.F., Checkered Stock, Open Sights, *Modern*	200	450	500
Dioptra 3121, .22 L.R.R.F., Checkered Stock, Target Sights, *Modern*	250	575	650
Dioptra 4131, .22 WMR., Checkered Stock, Open Sights, *Modern*	250	575	650
Model T-66, .22 L.R.R.F., Target Stock, Target Sights, Singleshot, *Modern*	175	375	425

UNITED STATES ARMS

Riverhead, N.Y., distributed by Mossberg.

HANDGUN, REVOLVER

	Fair	V. Good	Excellent
Abilene, .44 Magnum, Single Action, Western Style, Adjustable Sights, *Modern*	150	300	450
Abilene, .44 Magnum, Stainless Steel, Single Action, Western Style, Adjustable Sights, *Modern*	150	325	450
Abilene, .44 Magnum, Stainless Steel, Single Action, Western Style, 10" Barrel, Adjustable Sights, *Modern*	175	350	400
Abilene, Various Calibers, Single Action, Western Style, Adjustable Sights, *Modern*	150	300	350
Abilene, Various Calibers, Single Action, Western Style, Adjustable Sights, Stainless Steel, *Modern*	150	325	375

UNIVERSAL

Hialeah, Fla. Now owned by Iver Johnson, Inc. Currently manufactured in Jacksonville, Arkansas.

HANDGUN, SELF-LOADING

	Fair	V. Good	Excellent
Model 3000 Enforcer, .30 Carbine, Clip Fed, Blued, *Modern*	$100	$175	$200
Model 3000 Enforcer, .30 Carbine, Clip Fed, Nickel Plated, *Modern*	100	225	250
Model 3000 Enforcer, .30 Carbine, Clip Fed, Stainless, *Modern*	100	225	275

RIFLE, SELF-LOADING

	Fair	V. Good	Excellent
Model 1001, .30 Carbine, Carbine, Clip Fed, *Modern*	75	150	200
Model 1002, .30 Carbine, Carbine, Clip Fed, Bayonet Lug, *Modern*	100	200	250
Model 1003, .30 Carbine, Carbine, Clip Fed, Walnut Stock, *Modern*	75	125	175
Model 1004, .30 Carbine, Carbine, Clip Fed, Scope Mounted, *Modern*	100	200	250
Model 1010, .30 Carbine, Carbine, Clip Fed, Nickel Plated, *Modern*	100	225	275
Model 1011 Deluxe, .30 Carbine, Carbine, Clip Fed, Nickel Plated, Monte Carlo Stock, *Modern*	125	250	300
Model 1015, .30 Carbine, Carbine, Clip Fed, Gold Plated, *Modern*	125	250	300
Model 1016 Deluxe, .30 Carbine, Carbine, Clip Fed, Gold Plated, Monte Carlo Stock, *Modern*	150	300	350
Model 1025 Ferret, .256 Win. Mag., Carbine, Clip Fed, Sporting Rifle, *Modern*	100	175	225
Model 1025 Ferret, .30 Carbine, Carbine, Clip Fed, Sporting Rifle, *Modern*	100	175	225
Model 1941 Field Commander, .30 Carbine, Carbine, Clip Fed, Fancy Wood, *Modern*	100	175	225

RIFLE, SLIDE ACTION

	Fair	V. Good	Excellent
Vulcan 440, .44 Magnum, Clip Fed, Sporting Rifle, Open Rear Sight, *Modern*	75	150	200

SHOTGUN, DOUBLE BARREL, OVER-UNDER

	Fair	V. Good	Excellent
Baikal 1J-27, 12 Ga., Double Trigger, Vent Rib, Engraved, Checkered Stock, *Modern*	100	200	250
Baikal 1J-27, 12 Ga., Double Trigger, Vent Rib, Engraved, Checkered Stock, Automatic Ejector, *Modern*	100	225	275

SHOTGUN, SINGLESHOT

	Fair	V. Good	Excellent
Model 1J18, 12 Ga., Hammerless, *Modern*	25	50	75
Model 7212, 12 Ga., Trap Grade, Vent Rib, Engraved, Checkered Stock, Monte Carlo Stock, *Modern*	400	850	950

	Fair	V. Good	Excellent

UNIVERSAL

Made by Hopkins & Allen, Norwich, Conn., c. 1880.

HANDGUN, REVOLVER

.32 S & W, 5 Shot, Double Action, Solid Frame, *Curio*	$50	$75	$100

UNWIN & ROGERS

Yorkshire, England, c. 1850.

HANDGUN, PERCUSSION

Knife Pistol, with Ramrod and Mould, Cased with Accessories, *Antique*	450	1150	1750

U.S. ARMS CO.

Brooklyn, N.Y., 1874–1878.

HANDGUN, REVOLVER

.22 Short R.F., 7 Shot, Spur Trigger, Solid Frame, Single Action, *Antique*	75	125	200
.32 Short R.F., 5 Shot, Spur Trigger, Solid Frame, Single Action, *Antique*	75	150	200
.38 Short R.F., 5 Shot, Spur Trigger, Solid Frame, Single Action, *Antique*	75	150	200
.41 Short R.F., 5 Shot, Spur Trigger, Solid Frame, Single Action, *Antique*	75	150	300

U.S. Arms Co., .41

U.S. ARMS CO.

Made by Crescent for H. & D. Folsom, c. 1900. See Crescent Fire Arms Co., Shotgun, Double Barrel, Side-by-Side; Shotgun, Singleshot.

U.S. MILITARY

Establishment of the first federal armory in Springfield, Massachusetts, in 1795 was a major step forward in the evolution of American manufacturing technology. Firearms for war and peace were a necessary commodity, requiring design and engineering, standardization, and efficient production. The Armory served as a major force, indeed for decades the cutting edge, in developing the American System of Manufacture wherein Yankee ingenuity showed the world the way toward parts interchangeability and mass production. The buildings of the Springfield Armory are largely still standing, most of them converted for use by the Springfield Technical Community College. The Main Arsenal building and certain adjoining structures serve as the Springfield Armory National Historic Site, administered and staffed by the National Park Service, U.S. Department of the Interior. The Main Arsenal houses the world's largest collection of U.S. military small arms, a mecca for collectors, researchers, writers, and the public. The array of guns built at the arsenal has established the Springfield Armory as a major theme for arms collectors. The first official U.S. martial longarm was the 1795 Springfield flintlock musket, and the profusion of types and models which succeeded that landmark gun have captivated the imagination of collectors for decades.

OTHER PRODUCTION SITES FOR U.S. MILITARY FIREARMS

The Harpers Ferry Armory, in Harpers Ferry, West Virginia, began production in 1800, and the site remained in operation until largely destroyed at the beginning of the Civil War. The Armory had been a primary source of military small arms for the U.S. government, including providing flintlock rifles for the Lewis & Clark Expedition. Other significant sources were private contractors, the likes of Simeon North, I. Johnson, H. Aston, E. Remington & Sons, and a myriad of other manufacturers. The contract system, as particularly evident in the Model 1808 Flintlock production (with nineteen contractors), was particularly important to the federal government for quantities of arms in addition to what was supplied by the Springfield and Harpers Ferry armories.

PRIMARY AND SECONDARY U.S. MARTIAL ARMS

Simply stated, primary arms are those manufactured at the federal armories—Springfield and Harpers Ferry—as well as arms recognized as official U.S. service models, even if made by companies like Colt, Winchester, Remington, IBM, etc. Secondary arms are those made for issue to U.S. military and militia units on contract by various manufacturers—but never designated as official U.S. models and not made by federal armories.

THE SPRINGFIELD TRAPDOOR SERIES

Of particular popularity with collectors, the Trapdoor Springfield remained the standard U.S. military rifle for twenty years. The Trapdoor Springfield type was the first metallic cartridge breechloader to be adopted as standard issue by the Ordnance Department. Prior to commencing standard production in 1873, tens of thousands of muzzle-loading U.S. military longarms were converted under the Allin system to trapdoor breechloaders. The alteration allowed use of the new metallic cartridge ammunition which had proved its practicality during the Civil War. The First Model Allin, made in 1865, was of .58 rimfire caliber; 5,000 were built in alterations from the Model 1861 percussion musket. In 1866 another 25,000 Allin alterations were made—the Second Model Allin—in .50 centerfire caliber from the Model 1863 percussion musket. From 1868–72 51,389 Trapdoor rifles were made, also in .50 centerfire caliber. Still another major model in the evolution of the Trapdoor Springfield was the Model 1870, made in rifle and carbine versions, and an improved version of the Model 1868; production was from 1870 to 1873, with 11,533 the total manufacture. The Trapdoor Springfield was formally adopted as a .45-70 standard military service rifle in 1873. This refined and perfected model, and the predecessors noted above, may collectively be referred to as "the gun that won the West." Trapdoor Springfields served as the regulation U.S. military longarm for most of the final period of the Indian Wars, as well as in other service. Manufacture remained steady through 1893, at which time the Model 1892 Krag-Jorgensen .30 caliber bolt-action magazine rifle was adopted. Despite the acceptance of the new magazine repeaters, the Trapdoor saw service in the Spanish American War, and remained in use into the 20th century. The total production of all types of the .45–70 Trapdoor Springfield is in excess of 500,000. The Model 1873 Trapdoor remained standard in .45–70 caliber, with so many technical variations that the type is among the most sought-after of all U.S. military firearms. Carbines, rifles, and rifled muskets were the conventional types, but Cadet Rifles, Shotguns, Marksman, Long Range, and "Fencing" variations were among other variants built. For the upper ranks, the Officers Model Springfield was designed, one of the most attractive and rare of all U.S. military longarms. A striking feature common to all production is the spread eagle stamping on the lockplates, accompanied by the letters "U.S." and the name "SPRINGFIELD." Specimens were customarily blued, with oil-stained black walnut stocks. Inspector markings on the stocks are ESA (1873 to 1878), and SWP (1878 to 1893). These initials stand for Erskine S. Allin and Samuel W. Porter, Master Armourers at Springfield. In 1877 and 1878 the date stamping was also present. Buffalo Bill Cody's tried-and-true buffalo rifle, while a professional hunter for the railroad, was the Trapdoor that he affectionately called "Lucretia Borgia." Carbine versions of the Trapdoor were present in the hands of Custer's troops at the Battle of the Little Bighorn. But the most refined and sought-after variation of the Springfield Trapdoor series was the Officer's Model, made for the sporting and target use of the officer corps primarily stationed in the West. The earliest of the Trapdoor Officer's Models, like George Armstrong Custer's, was built on the Model 1868 and Model 1870 rifles in .50–70 centerfire. These arms are rare, and having been made to officer's specifications, a degree of variation will be observed. Springfield Armory records reveal totals as follows: 1873—6, 1874—7, and 1875—10. Sales of the Model 1875 Officer's Model continued until approximately 1900. Examples were on hand at the Armory until early in the 20th century, and the balance was sold to commercial firms, including the renowned emporium of military goods, Francis Bannerman Sons, of New York. Officer's Model Springfield, variation manufactured 1875–85, with a total of approximately 490, recorded in Springfield Armory records as follows: 1875—10, 1876—88, 1877—140, 1878—1, 1879—101, 1882—50, and 1885—100.

	Fair	*V. Good*	*Excellent*
HANDGUN, FLINTLOCK			
.54 M1805 (06), Singleshot, Smooth bore, Brass Mounts, Dated 1806, *Antique*	$7000	$18000	$22500
.54 M1805 (06), Singleshot, Smooth bore, Brass Mounts, Dated 1807, *Antique*	6000	10000	12500
.54 M1805 (06), Singleshot, Smooth bore, Brass Mounts, Dated 1808, Antique	6000	13000	15000
.54 M1807-8, Singleshot, Smooth bore, Brass Mounts, Various Contractors, *Antique*	3000	6500	8000
.54 M1816, Singleshot, Smooth bore, S North Army, Brass Furniture, *Antique*	700	1500	1750
.54 M1819, Singleshot, Smooth bore, S North Army, Iron Mounts, *Antique*	$700	$1500	$1750
.54 M1826, Singleshot, Smooth bore, S North Army, Iron Mounts, *Antique*	2500	5250	5500
.54 M1836, Singleshot, Smooth bore, R Johnson Army, Iron Mounts, and A. Waters, *Antique*	625	1750	2000
.64 M1808, Singleshot, Smooth bore, S North Army, Brass Furniture, *Antique*	5500	7000	8500
.69 M1799, Singleshot, North & Cheney, Brass Furniture, Brass Frame, *Antique*	12000	25000	35000
.69 M1811, Singleshot, Smooth bore, S North Army, Brass Furniture, *Antique*	2000	4500	5500
.69 M1817 (18), Singleshot, Smooth bore, Springfield, Iron Mounts, *Antique*	4000	8000	9500
HANDGUN, PERCUSSION			
.54 M1836, Singleshot, Smooth bore, U.S. Navy Conversion from Flintlock, Iron Mounts, *Antique*	$600	$1250	$1500
.54 M1842 Aston, Singleshot, Smooth bore, Brass Mounts, *Antique*	600	1000	1200
.54 M1842 Johnson, Singleshot, Smooth bore, Brass Mounts, *Antique*	600	1250	1500
.54 M1843 Deringer Army, Singleshot, Rifled, Brass Mounts, *Antique*	900	2250	2500
.54 M1843 Deringer Army, Singleshot, Smooth bore, Brass Mounts, *Antique*	600	1250	1500
.54 M1843 Deringer Navy, Singleshot, Smooth bore, Brass Mounts, *Antique*	700	1500	1750
HANDGUN, SINGLESHOT			
Liberator, .45 ACP, Military, *Curio*	300	500	600
RIFLE, BOLT ACTION			
M1871 Ward-Burton, .50 C.F., Iron Mountings, Carbine, *Antique*	900	2000	2500
M1871 Ward-Burton, .50 C.F., Iron Mountings, Rifle, *Antique*	800	1750	2000
M1882 Chaffee-Reese, 45-70, Rifle, *Antique*	900	2000	2500
M1892/6 Krag, .30-40 Krag, Rifle, *Antique*	300	700	800
M1895 Lee Straight Pull, 6mm Lee Navy, Musket, *Antique*	450	1000	1250
M1896 Krag, .30-40 Krag, Cadet, *Antique*	8000	20000	25000
M1896 Krag, .30-40 Krag, Carbine, *Antique*	500	1200	1500
M1896 Krag, .30-40 Krag, Rifle, *Antique*	400	800	900
M1898 Krag, .30-40 Krag, Carbine, *Curio*	300	700	800

	Fair	V. Good	Excellent
M1898 Krag, .30-40 Krag, Rifle, *Curio*	$150	$400	$700
M1899 Krag, .30-40 Krag, Carbine, *Curio*	400	850	1100
M1903 MKI Pedersen, . .30-06 Springfield, *Curio*	7000	15000	17500
M1903 National Match, .30-06 Springfield, Target Rifle, *Curio*	1200	2500	3000
M1903 Sniper, .30-06 Springfield, Scope Mounts, *Curio*	1400	3000	3750
M1903, .30-03 Springfield, Machined Parts, *Modern with Rod-Bayonet*	6000	15000	20000
M1903/5, .30-03 Springfield, *Curio*	3000	8000	11000
M1903/5, .30-06 Springfield, *Curio*	1100	2250	2750
M1903/7, .30-06 Springfield, Early Receivers, *Curio*	700	1750	2250
M1903/Postwar, .30-06 Springfield, *Curio*	400	800	1100
M1903/WWI, .30-06 Springfield, *Curio*	800	2000	2350
M1903A1 National Match, .30-06 Springfield, Target Rifle, *Curio*	1200	2500	3150
M1903A1, .30-06 Springfield, Parkerized, Checkered Butt, Machined Parts, *Curio*	450	1000	1350
M1917 Eddystone, .30-06 Springfield, *Curio*	300	500	600
M1917 Remington, .30-06 Springfield, *Curio*	300	525	600
M1917 Winchester, .30-06 Springfield, *Curo*	400	700	800
M1922 Trainer, .22 L.R.R.F., Target Rifle, *Curio*	1200	2500	3000
M1922M2 Trainer, .22 L.R.R.F., Target Rifle, *Curio*	500	1000	1200

RIFLE, FLINTLOCK

	Fair	V. Good	Excellent
.52, M1819 Hall Whitney, Rifled, Breech Loader, 32½" Barrel, 3 Bands, *Antique*	1500	4000	5250
.52, M1819 Hall, Rifled, Breech Loader, 32½" Barrel, 3 Bands, *Antique*	1500	4000	5250
.54, M1807 Springfield, "Indian Carbine," 27¾" Barrel, *Antique*	7500	20000	23500
.54, M1814, Rifled, 36" Barrel, *Antique*	2000	4500	5500

U.S. SPRINGFIELD TRAP/DOOR RIFLES AND CARBINES

	Fair	V. Good	Excellent
.45-70, M1873 U.S., "Trapdoor," Carbine, 22" Barrel, Single Band, *Antique*	600	1350	1750
.45-70, M1873 U.S., "Trapdoor," Rifle, 32⅝" Barrel, 2 Bands, *Antique*	450	1100	1350
.45-70, M1888 U.S., "Trapdoor," Rifle, 32⅝" Barrel, 2 Bands, Ramrod-Bayonet, *Antique*	400	1000	1300

RIFLE, PERCUSSION

	Fair	V. Good	Excellent
.57, M1841 U.S. Cadet Musket, 40" Barrel, 2 Bands, *Antique*	$4500	$9000	$12500
.57, M1851 U.S. Cadet Musket, Rifled, 40" Barrel, 2 Bands, *Antique*	600	1300	1750
.57, M1851 U.S. Cadet Musket, Smoothbore, 40" Barrel, 2 Bands, *Antique*	600	1300	1750
.58 Lindner, Breech Loader, Carbine, Rising Block, *Antique*	1250	3000	4250
.58, M1841 Contract, Rifled, 33" Barrel, 2 Bands, (Mississippi Rifle), *Antique*	900	2500	3350
.58, M1855 U.S., Carbine, Rifled, 22" Barrel, 1 Band, with Tape Priming System, *Antique*	4500	10000	13500
.58, M1855 U.S., Rifled, 40" Barrel, 3 Bands, with Tape Priming System, *Antique*	1250	4000	5000
.58, M1861 U.S., Rifled, 40" Round Barrel, 3 Bands, *Antique*	800	2000	2750
.58, M1863 U.S., Rifled, 40" Round Barrel, 3 Bands, *Antique*	800	2000	2750
.64, M1836 Hall-North, Rifled, Breech Loader, Carbine, 26⅛" Barrel, 2 Bands, *Antique*	1200	3000	3750
.69, M1842 U.S., Musket, 42" Barrel, 3 Bands, *Antique*	1100	2250	2750
.69, M1842 U.S., Rifled, Musket, 42" Barrel, 3 Bands, *Antique*	1100	2250	2750
.69, M1847 Artillery, Musketoon, 26" Barrel, 2 Bands, Steel Furniture, *Antique*	1400	3500	4250
.69, M1847 Cavalry, Musketoon, 26" Barrel, 2 Bands, Brass Furniture, *Antique*	1400	3000	3750
.69, M1847 Sappers, Musketoon, 26" Barrel, 2 Bands, Bayonet Stud on Right Side, *Antique*	1700	3500	4250
M1864 Training Rifle, Military, Wood Barrel, *Antique*	100	200	300

THE MI GARAND RIFLE

The M1 Garand was the first self-laoding rifle to be adopted as a standard service weapon. Inventor John C. Garand was born in Quebec, and moved with his family to Connecticut at the age of ten. Garand became a tool and die maker, gaining valuable experience working for Browne & Sharpe, and for the Federal Screw Corporation, from 1908 to 1914. At the beginning of World War I, Garand was in New York City employed in gauge-designing. Noting the government's testing of machine guns, Garand studied all he could on automatic weapons. He determined that his knowledge, skill, and experience with machine tools would be helpful in manufacturing self-loading firearms devoid of malfunctioning problems. Soon his independent design efforts led to employment with the National Bureau of Standards, Washington, D.C., in 1918. At the Bureau Garand devoted his efforts toward a machine gun, with the novel feature of the cartridge case primer on firing moving rearward far enough to permit unlocking and opening the bolt. Garand's abilities were soon recognized by Army Ordnance, and he was reassigned in 1919 to the Springfield Armory. The gifted inventor's mission was to develop a self-loading service rifle, quite in contrast to his machine gun work at the Bureau of Standards. Flush with valuable combat experience from World War I, an Infantry and Cavalry Board convened regularly to oversee developments of new firearms. In a test at Springfield Armory in May 1920, Garand's Model T1920—the Thompson autorifle—and three self-loading rifles—the Bang, the Hatcher, and the Berthier—were considered. The Ordnance test report recommended that further development be devoted to the Garand and Bang rifles. Guided by extensive Ordnance Department criteria, Garand and others continued to strive to create the perfect self-loading service rifle. Garand's next rifle design, the Model 1921, was favorably described by Julian S. Hatcher in *Arms and the Man*, December 15, 1921: "Its light weight, neat appearance, and simplicity of mechanism have elicited much favorable comment, but of course final judgment must be reserved until after the gun is proved by an official test." Twenty-four examples of the Model 1921 were built to allow for further testing. These rifles were specified to have barrels of 20", 21½", and 24", with 10-shot magazines. An improved Garand rifle was completed—the Model 1924—another in the quest for the ultimate self-loading service rifle. A rival designer was J. D. Pedersen, formerly of the Remington Arms Co. and described by John M. Browning himself as "the greatest living arms designer." The Pedersen rifle was of .276 caliber, while Garand's was of .30. Adoption of a new .30 caliber cartridge in 1926 (succeeding the .30 Model 1906) led Garand to abandon the principle of a primer-actuated rifle and concentrate on a gas-operated, turning bolt repeater. For the new design he experimented not only with the .30 caliber cartridge, but with the .276. A thorough test of seven rifles in 1929 led the Ordnance Board to report favorably the Pedersen Model T1 and the Garand Model T3, both in .276 caliber; the conclusion was that the Garand was superior to the Pedersen. Another twenty Garands, this time in .276 caliber, were ordered to be manufactured for field testing, as well as a single rifle to be made in .30 caliber. Although test board recommendations favored the .276 caliber, General Douglas MacArthur was in favor of .30 caliber and overruled the opinions of "the experts." Orders were given for manufacture of eighty rifles for extended test purposes, termed the U.S. Semiautomatic Rifle, Caliber .30 T1E2. While these rifles were in manufacture under the close supervision of Garand himself, the designation for the model was changed to U.S. Semiautomatic Rifle, Caliber .30, M1. By May 1934 the eighty test rifles were completed; fifty were issued to the Infantry and twenty-five to the Cavalry. When the rigorous tests were completed, the .30 M1 was recommended for adoption. The new designed was approved by the Adjutant General, January 9, 1936. All that remained was the demanding and costly task of tooling up to begin production of the rifle General George S. Patton came to respect more than any other: he termed the M1 Garand as the "greatest battle implement ever devised." Deliveries began at the Armory in September 1937. By January 1940, the production rate was up to 200 per day. Timing couldn't have been better: in 1941 America became embroiled in World War II. Manufacture began in 1936 and continued into the 1950s. A total of over 5,500,000 were produced by the Springfield Armory, Winchester, Harrington & Richardson, and International Harvester.

Variations

The M1E1 (slight variations from standard M1; limited production), M1E2 (adapted for telescopic sights; experimental)

M1E3 (experimental, with changes to bolt cam lug and operating rod's cam angle)

M1E4 (adjustments to mechanism and rapidity of operation)

M1E5 (a shortened version with folding stock and 18" barrel)

M1E6 (offset telescopic sight on sniper rifle, also permitting use of open sights)

M1E7 (later termed M1C, see below)

M1E8 (later termed M1D, see below)

M1E9 (variation of M1E4, attempt to avoid overheating problems), Model T26 (made for Pacific theater of WWII, with shortened stock and action of the M1E5)

Special Rifles, the Sniper Versions

The Models M1C and M1D, adapted for sniper use, with telescopic sight, flash suppresser, and a laced-on cheek pad. The M1Cs were built from completed rifles, while the M1Ds were specially made, since they required metal for scope mounting which was normally machined off in production.

	Fair	*V. Good*	*Excellent*
RIFLE, SELF-LOADING			
M-1 Carbine IBM, .30 Carbine, Clip Fed, *Curio*	$200	$400	$600
M-1 Carbine Inland, .30 Carbine, Clip Fed, *Curio*	200	400	600
M-1 Carbine Irwin-Pedersen, .30 Carbine, Clip Fed, *Curio*	300	700	900
M-1 Carbine Nat. Postal Meter, .30 Carbine, Clip Fed, *Curio*	300	700	900
M-1 Carbine Quality Hdw., .30 Carbine, Clip Fed, *Curio*	300	550	700
M-1 Carbine Rockola, .30 Carbine, Clip Fed, *Curio*	350	750	1000
M-1 Carbine Underwood, .30 Carbine, Clip Fed, *Curio*	200	400	600
M-1 Carbine Winchester, .30 Carbine, Clip Fed, *Curio*	400	800	1000
M-1 Garand National Match, .30-06 Springfield, Military, Target Sights, Target Trigger, Target Barrel, *Curio*	600	1200	1600
M-1 Garand Winchester, .30-06 Springfield, Pre WWII, *Curio*	500	1000	1300
M-1 Garand, .30-06 Springfield, Military, *Curio*	350	725	900
M-1A1 Carbine, .30 Carbine, Clip Fed, Folding Stock, *Modern*	400	900	1200
M1941 Johnson, .30-06 Springfield, Military, *Curio*	600	1500	1850

U.S. REVOLVER CO.

MADE BY IVER JOHNSON

.32 S & W, 5 Shot, Double Action, Solid Frame, *Modern*	50	75	100
.32 S & W, 5 Shot, Top Break, Double Action, *Modern*	50	75	100

	Fair	V. Good	Excellent
.32 S & W, 5 Shot, Top Break, Hammerless, Double Action, *Modern*	$50	$75	$100
.32 Short R.F., 5 Shot, Spur Trigger, Solid Frame, Single Action, *Antique*	125	150	175
.38 S & W, 5 Shot, Double Action, Top Break, *Modern*	50	75	100
.38 S & W, 5 Shot, Double Action, Solid Frame, *Modern*	$25	$50	$75
.38 S & W, 5 Shot, Top Break, Hammerless, Double Action, *Modern*	50	75	100

V

VALIANT
Made by Stevens Arms for Spear & Co., Pittsburgh, Pa.

RIFLE, BOLT ACTION

	Fair	V. Good	Excellent
Model 51, .22 L.R.R.F., Singleshot, Takedown, *Modern*	$20	$40	$50

VALMET
Valmet Oy, Tourula Works, Jyvaskyla, Finland.

RIFLE, SELF-LOADING

	Fair	V. Good	Excellent
M-62S, 7.62 × 39 Russian, Clip Fed, AK-47 Type, Sporting Version of Military Rifle, *Modern*	500	1000	1350
M-71S, .223 Rem., Clip Fed, AK-47 Type, Sporting Version of Military Rifle, *Modern*	300	750	1150
M78 HV, .223 Rem., Clp Fed, Bipod, *Modern*	500	1000	1350
M78 Standard, .308 Win., Clip Fed, Bipod, *Modern*	500	1000	1350

VALOR ARMS
Importers, Miami, Fla.

HANDGUN, REVOLVER

	Fair	V. Good	Excellent
.22 L.R.R.F., Double Action, Lightweight, *Modern*	20	40	50
.32 S & W, Double Action, Lightweight, *Modern*	20	40	50

VANDERFRIFT, ISSAC AND JEREMIAH
Philadelphia, Pa., 1809–1815. See Kentucky Rifles and Pistols.

VEGA
Sacramento, Calif.

HANDGUN, SELF-LOADING

	Fair	V. Good	Excellent
Vega 1911A1, .45 ACP, Stainless Steel, Clip Fed, *Modern*	150	300	400

VELO DOG
Various makers, c. 1900.

HANDGUN, REVOLVER

	Fair	V. Good	Excellent
5mm Velo Dog, Hammerless, Folding Trigger, *Curio*	$100	$200	$250
5mm Velo Dog, Hammer Folding Trigger, *Curio*	100	200	250
5mm Velo Dog, Hammerless, Trigger Guard, *Curio*	100	200	250
.25 ACP, Hammer, Folding Trigger, *Curio*	100	200	250
.25 ACP, Hammerless, Folding Trigger, *Curio*	100	200	250

VENCEDOR
San Martin y Cia., Eibar, Spain.

HANDGUN, SELF-LOADING

	Fair	V. Good	Excellent
.25 ACP, Clip Fed, Blue, *Modern*	50	100	125
.35 ACP, Clip Fed, Blue, *Modern*	50	125	150

VENTURA IMPORTS (CONTENDO)
Seal Beach, Calif. Also see Bertuzzi and Piotti.

SHOTGUN, DOUBLE BARREL, OVER-UNDER

	Fair	V. Good	Excellent
MK-1 Contento, 12 Ga., Field Grade, Automatic Ejector, Single Selective Trigger, Engraved, Checkered Stock, *Modern*	400	850	1000
MK-2 Contento, 12 Ga., Field Grade, Automatic Ejector, Single Selective Trigger, Engraved, Checkered Stock, *Modern*	500	1100	1300
MK-2 Contento, 12 Ga., Trap Grade, with Extra Single Trap Barrel, Engraved, Checkered Stock, *Modern*	650	1400	1600
MK-2 Luxe Contento, 12 Ga., Field Grade, Automatic Ejector, Single Selective Trigger, Engraved, Checkered Stock, *Modern*	500	1000	1200
MK-2 Luxe Contento, 12 Ga., Trap Grade, with Extra Single Trap Barrel, Engraved, Checkered Stock, *Modern*	700	1500	1800
MK-3 Contento, 12 Ga., Field Grade, Automatic Ejector, Single Selective Trigger, Engraved, Checkered Stock, *Modern*	600	1250	1500

	Fair	V. Good	Excellent
MK-3 Contento, 12 Ga., Trap Grade, with Extra Single Trap Barrel, Engraved, Checkered Stock, *Modern*	$900	$2000	$2650
MK-3 Luxe Contento, 12 Ga., Field Grade, Automatic Ejector, Single Selective Trigger, Engraved, Checkered Stock, *Modern*	700	1500	1800
MK-3 Luxe Contento, 12 Ga., Trap Grade, with Extra Single Trap Barrel, Engraved, Checkered Stock, *Modern*	1100	2500	3250
Nettuno Contento, 12 Ga., Field Grade, Automatic Ejector, Single Selective Trigger, Engraved, Checkered Stock, *Modern*	200	400	450

SHOTGUN, DOUBLE BARREL, SIDE-BY-SIDE

Ventura Model 51, 12 and 20 Gauges, Boxlock, Checkered Stock, *Modern*	150	350	400
Ventura Model 62 Standard, 12 and 20 Gauges, Sidelock, Checkered Stock, Engraved, *Modern*	400	800	900
Ventura Model 64 Standard, 12 and 20 Gauges, Sidelock, Checkered Stock, Engraved, *Modern*	350	775	850

VENUS

Tomas de Urizar y Cia., Eibar, Spain.

HANDGUN, SELF-LOADING

7.65mm, Clip Fed, *Modern*	50	100	150

VENUS

Venus Waffenwerk Oskar Will, Zella Mehils, Germany, c. 1912.

HANDGUN, SELF-LOADING

7.65mm, Target Pistol, Hammerless, Blue, *Curio*	250	500	700

VERNEY-CARRON

St. Etienne, France.

HANDGUN, SELF-LOADING

6.35mm, Clip Fed, Blue, *Modern*	75	150	175

SHOTGUN, DOUBLE BARREL, OVER-UNDER

Field Grade, 12 Ga., Automatic Ejectors, Checkered Stock, Engraved, *Modern*	400	800	1150

VESTA

Hijos de A. Echevera, Eibar, Spain.

HANDGUN, SELF-LOADING

Pocket, 7.65mm, Clip Fed, Long Grip, *Modern*	50	125	150

Vesta

	Fair	V. Good	Excellent
Vest Pocket, 6.35mm, Clip Fed, *Modern*	$50	$100	$125

VETERAN

Made by Norwich Falls Pistol Co., c. 1880.

HANDGUN, REVOLVER

.32 Short R.F., 5 Shot, Spur Trigger, Solid Frame, Single Action, *Antique*	75	125	175

VETO

c. 1880.

HANDGUN, REVOLVER

.32 Short R.F., 5 Shot, Spur Trigger, Solid Frame, Single Action, *Antique*	75	150	175

VICI

Belgium.

HANDGUN, SELF-LOADING

7.65mm, Clip Fed, *Modern*	50	100	125

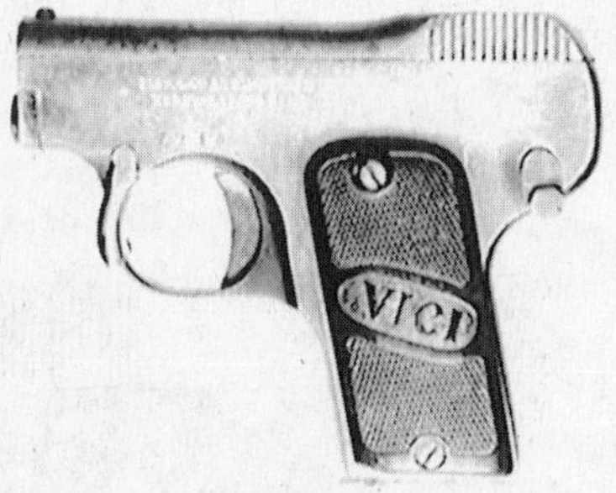

Vici

VICTOR

Francisco Arizmendi, Eibar, Spain, c. 1916.

HANDGUN, SELF-LOADING

6.35mm, Clip Fed, Blue, *Curio* ...	50	100	125

	Fair	V. Good	Excellent
7.65mm, Clip Fed, Blue, *Curio*	$50	$125	$150

VICTOR
Made by Crescent, c. 1900. See Crescent Fire Arms Co., Shotgun, Double Barrel, Side-by-Side; Shotgun, Singleshot.

VICTOR # 1
Made by Harrington & Richardson, c. 1876.

HANDGUN, REVOLVER

#1, .22 Short R.F., 7 Shot, Spur Trigger, Solid Frame, Single Action, *Antique*	75	150	200
#2, .32 Short R.F., 5 Shot, Spur Trigger, Solid Frame, Single Action, *Antique*	75	150	200
.32 S & W, 5 Shot, Single Action, Solid Frame, *Antique*	50	100	150

VICTOR SPECIAL
Made by Crescent for Hibbard-Spencer-Bartlett Co., c. 1900. See Crescent Fire Arms Co., Shotgun, Double Barrel, Side-by-Side; Shotgun, Singleshot.

VICTORIA
Made by Hood Firearms, c. 1875.

HANDGUN, REVOLVER

.32 Short R.F., 5 Shot, Spur Trigger, Solid Frame, Single Action, *Antique*	75	150	175

VICTORIA
Spain, Esperanza y Unceta, c. 1900.

HANDGUN, SELF-LOADING

6.35mm, Clip Fed, *Modern*	50	100	125
M1911, .32 ACP, Clip Fed, *Modern*	50	125	150

Victoria

	Fair	V. Good	Excellent

VICTORY
M. Zulaica y Cia., Eibar, Spain.

HANDGUN, SELF-LOADING

6.35mm, Clip Fed, *Modern*	$50	$100	$150

VILAR
Spain, 1920–1938.

HANDGUN, SELF-LOADING

Pocket, 7.65mm, Clip Fed, Long Grip, *Modern*	50	100	125

VINCITOR
M. Zulaica y Cia., Eibar, Spain.

HANDGUN, SELF-LOADING

Model 14 No. 2, 7.65mm, Clip Fed, Blue, *Curio*	50	150	175
Model 1914, 6.35mm, Clip Fed, Blue, *Curio*	50	125	150

VINDEX
Mre. d'Armes des Pyrenees, Hendaye, France.

HANDGUN, SELF-LOADING

7.65mm, Clip Fed, Blue, *Modern*	50	100	125

VIRGINIA ARMS CO.
Made by Crescent for Virginia-Caroline Co., c. 1900. See Crescent Fire Arms Co., Shotgun, Double Barrel, Side-by-Side; Shotgun, Singleshot.

VIRGINIAN
Imported and manufactured (1976–1984) by Interarms, Alexandria, Va.

HANDGUN, REVOLVER

Dragoon, Buntline, Various Calibers, Single Action, Western Style, Target Sights, Blue, *Modern*	75	200	300
Dragoon, Deputy, Various Calibers, Single Action, Western Style, Fixed Sights, Blue, *Modern*	75	175	250
Dragoon, Deputy, Various Calibers, Single Action, Western Style, Fixed Sights, Stainless Steel, *Modern*	75	175	275
Dragoon, Engraved, Various Calibers, Single Action, Western Style, Target Sights, Blue, *Modern*	100	375	500
Dragoon, Engraved, Various Calibers, Single Action, Western Style, Target Sights, Presentation Case, *Modern*	100	400	575

	Fair	V. Good	Excellent
Dragoon, Silhouette, .44 Magnum, Single Action, Western Style, Target Sights, Stainless Steel, *Modern*	$175	$225	$300
Dragoon, Standard, Various Calibers, Single Action, Western Style, Target Sights, Blue, *Modern*	100	200	250
Dragoon, Standard, Various Calibers, Single Action, Western Style, Target Sights, Stainless Steel, *Modern*	150	200	275

VITE

Echave y Arizmendi, Eibar, Spain, c. 1913.

HANDGUN, SELF-LOADING

	Fair	V. Good	Excellent
Model 1912, 6.35mm, Clip Fed, Blue, *Curio*	50	100	125
Model 1915, 7.65mm, Clip Fed, Blue, *Curio*	50	125	150

VOERE

Voere GmbH, Vohrenbach, West Germany. Owned by Mauser since 1987.

RIFLE, BOLT ACTION

	Fair	V. Good	Excellent
Model 2145, .308 Win., Match Rifle, Target Stock, *Modern*	350	700	900
Model 3145 DJV, .223 Rem., Match Rifle, Target Stock, *Modern*	250	500	600
Premier Mauser, Various Calibers, Sporting Rifle, Checkered Stock, Recoil Pad, Open Rear Sight, *Modern*	150	300	400
Shikar, Various Calibers, Sporting Rifle, Fancy Checkering, Fancy Wood, Recoil Pad, No Sights, *Modern*	$200	$450	$600
Titan-Menor, Various Calibers, Sporting Rifle, Checkered Stock, Recoil Pad, Open Rear Sight, *Modern*	150	350	500

VOERE

Voere Tiroler Jagd u. Sportwaffenfabrik, Kufstein, Austria.

RIFLE, BOLT ACTION

	Fair	V. Good	Excellent
Model 2155, Various Calibers, Sporting Rifle, Checkered Stock, Open Rear Sight, *Modern*	150	325	400
Model 2165/1, Various Calibers, Sporting Rifle, Checkered Stock, Recoil Pad, Open Rear Sight, *Modern*	200	475	600

VOLUNTEER

Made by Stevens Arms for Belknap Hardware Co., Louisville, Ky.

SHOTGUN, SINGLESHOT

	Fair	V. Good	Excellent
Model 94, Various Gauges, Takedown, Automatic Ejector, Plain, Hammer, *Modern*	25	50	75

VULCAN ARMS CO.

Made by Crescent, c. 1900. See Crescent Fire Arms Co., Shotgun, Double Barrel, Side-by-Side; Shotgun, Singleshot.

W

WAFFENFABRIK BERN

Eidgenossische Waffenfabrik, Bern, Switzerland. Also see Swiss Military.

RIFLE, BOLT ACTION

	Fair	V. Good	Excellent
Model 31, 7.5mm Swiss, Military Style, *Modern*	$250	$575	$725
Model 31 Target, 7.5mm Swiss, Military Style, Match Rifle, Target Sights, *Modern*	350	775	925

WALDMAN

Arizmendi Y Goenaga, Eibar, Spain.

HANDGUN, SELF-LOADING

	Fair	V. Good	Excellent
6.35mm, Clip Fed, *Curio*	50	100	125
7.65mm, Clip Fed, *Curio*	50	125	150

WALMAN

F. Arizmendi Y Goenaga, Eibar, Spain.

HANDGUN, SELF-LOADING

	Fair	V. Good	Excellent
.380 ACP, Clip Fed, *Curio*	75	175	225
6.35mm, Clip Fed, *Curio*	50	100	125
7.65mm, Clip Fed, *Curio*	50	125	150

WALSH FIREARMS CO.

New York City, c. 1860.

HANDGUN, PERCUSSION

	Fair	V. Good	Excellent
Navy, .36, Revolver, 12 Shot, Double-Charge Cylinder, *Antique*	1400	3500	4250
Pocket, .31, Revolver, 12 Shot, Double-Charge Cylinder, *Antique*	1000	2000	2750

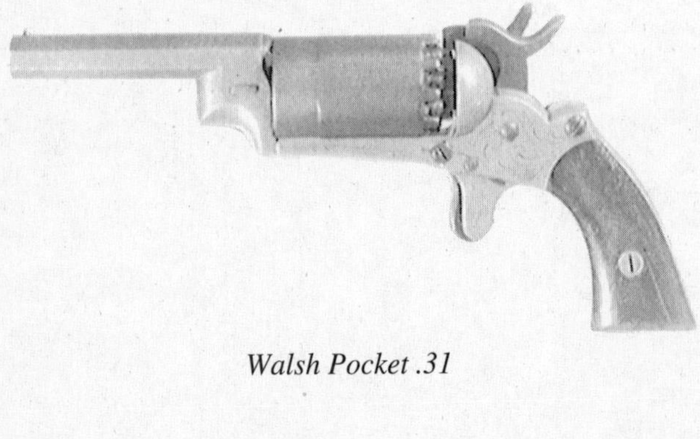

Walsh Pocket .31

WALSH, JAMES

Philadelphia, Pa., 1775–1779. See Kentucky Rifles and Pistols and U.S. Military.

WALTHER

First started in 1886 by Carl Walther in Zella Mehlis, Germany. After his death in 1915 the firm was operated by his sons Fritz, George, and Erich. Post–World War II production was in Ulm/Donau, West Germany. Also see German Military and Manurhin. The handsome book by Manfred Kersten, entitled *Walther Eine deutsche Legende* (1997), is a large-format, beautifully illustrated tribute to the unusual history of the family and of the company. The use of a Walther pistol by the fictional character James Bond has proven a boon to sales of the company's product line, as has the introduction of air pistols, made under license from manufacturers like Colt and Beretta, and in replication of models from their lines.

AIRGUNS

	Fair	V. Good	Excellent
Model CP-2 C02, .177 Caliber, Singleshot, Blue	$200	$500	$600
Model LGR Match, .177 Caliber, Singleshot, Blue	600	1250	1500
Model LGR Running Boar, .177 Caliber, Singleshot, Blue	500	1000	1250
Model LGR, .177 Caliber, Singleshot, Blue	400	800	1000
Model LP-3, .177 Caliber, Singleshot, Blue	150	375	475

TARGET PISTOLS

	Fair	V. Good	Excellent
Model GSP C, .22 Short, 5 Shot Clip, Target Pistol, *Modern*	500	1050	1100
Model GSP C, .22 Short, 5 Shot Clip, Target Pistol, with .22 L.R. Conversion Kit	350	750	1000
Model GSP, .22 L.R.R.F., 5 Shot Clip, Target Pistol, *Modern*	400	950	1200
Model OSP, .22 Short, Blue, Five Rounds Capacity, *Modern*	400	850	1100
Olympia Rapid Fire, .22 L.R.R.F., Target Pistol, *Modern*	350	750	900
Olympia Sport, .22 L.R.R.F., Target Pistol, *Modern*	350	600	850

HANDGUN, SELF-LOADING—PRE 1945

	Fair	V. Good	Excellent
ac40 (40 added), 9mm, Double Action, *Curio*	450	1200	1500
Model 1, .25 ACP, Blue, *Curio*	200	400	450

	Fair	V. Good	Excellent
Model 2, .25 ACP, Pop-Up Rear Sight, Blue, *Curio*	$250	$950	$1450
Model 3, .32 ACP, Blue, *Curio*	500	1250	1600
Model 4, .32 ACP, Blue, *Curio*	150	350	450
Model 5, .25 ACP, Solid Rib, Blue, *Curio*	150	300	350
Model 6, 9mm Luger, Blue, *Curio*	2000	4500	5750
Model 7, .25 ACP, Blue, *Curio*	275	450	625
Model 8, .25 ACP, Blue, *Curio*	200	375	500
Model 9, .25 ACP, Blue, *Curio*	200	400	500
Model HP, .30 Luger, Single Action, *Curio*	2000	4000	5500
Model HP, .30 Luger, Single Action, Wood Grips, *Curio*	2500	4500	6000
Model HP, 9mm, H Prefix Serial Number, *Curio*	600	1200	1750
Model HP, 9mm, Hi-Gloss Blue, *Curio*	500	1000	1200
Model HP, 9mm, Military, Blue with Eagle/359 on Right Slide, *Curio*	500	1000	1200
Model HP, 9mm, Military, Blue, *Curio*	400	800	1000
Model HP, Commercial Finish, 9mm Luger, Double Action, Lightweight, *Curio*	1600	3500	4250
Model P38, 9mm, *Curio*	600	1200	1500
P-38 ac-45 Zero Series, 9mm, Double Action, Military, *Curio*	400	800	1000
P-38, "480," 9mm, Double Action, Military, *Curio*	600	1300	2250
P-38, 1st, Model Zero Series, 9mm, Double Action, *Curio*	1600	3500	4250
P-38, 2nd, Model Zero Series, 9mm, Double Action, Military, *Curio*	900	2200	3250
P-38, 3rd, Model Zero Series, 9mm, Double Action, Military, *Curio*	500	900	1200
P-38, ac No Date, 9mm, Double Action, Military, *Curio*	2200	5000	6500
P-38, ac-40, 9mm, Double Action, Military, *Curio*	450	1200	1500
P-38, ac-41 Military Finish, 9mm, Double Action, Military, *Curio*	250	500	650
P-38, ac-41, 9mm, Double Action, Military, *Curio*	400	800	1000
P-38, ac-42, 9mm, Double Action, Military, *Curio*	250	450	650
P-38, ac-43 Double Line, 9mm, Double Action, Military, *Curio*	200	400	500
P-38, ac-43 Police, 9mm, Double Action, Military, *Curio*	1000	2500	3250
P-38, ac-43 WaA 135, 9mm, Double Action, Military, *Curio*	450	900	1250
P-38, ac-43, Single Line, 9mm, Double Action, Military, *Curio*	225	500	700
P-38, ac-44 WaA140 Frame, 9mm, Double Action, Military, *Curio*	200	425	500
P-38, ac-44 Police, 9mm, Double Action, Military, *Curio*	1100	2500	3000
P-38, ac-44, 9mm, Double Action, Military, *Curio*	250	500	600
P-38, ac-45 Mismatch, 9mm, Double Action, Military, *Curio*	$150	$300	$375
P-38, ac-45, 9mm, Double Action, Military, *Curio*	250	500	600
P-38, byf-42, 9mm, Double Action, Military, *Curio*	300	650	800
P-38, byf-43 Police, 9mm, Double Action, Military, *Curio*	500	1000	1500
P-38, byf-43, 9mm, Double Action, Military, *Curio*	300	500	600
P-38, byf-44 police F Dual T, 9mm, Double Action, Military, *Curio*	500	1000	1500
P-38, byf-44 Police L Dual T, 9mm, Double Action, Military, *Curio*	1100	1800	2500
P-38, byf-44 Police L, 9mm, Double Action, Military, *Curio*	500	1000	1500
P-38, byf-44, 9mm, Double Action, Military, *Curio*	300	500	600
P-38, crq Zero Series, 9mm, Double Action, Military, *Curio*	450	600	750
P-38, crq, 9mm, A or B Prefix, *Curio*	300	500	600
P-38, crq, 9mm, Double Action, Military, *Curio*	275	450	500
P-38, svw-45 French, 9mm, Double Action, Military, *Curio*	200	500	600
P-38, svw-45 Police, 9mm, Double Action, Military, *Curio*	1000	2500	3250
P-38, svw-45, 9mm, Double Action, Military, *Curio*	300	700	800
P-38, svw-46 French, 9mm, Double Action, Military, *Curio*	200	400	500
PP "A.F. Stoeger, Inc., New York," .32 ACP, Double Action, Pre-War, High-Polish Finish, *Curio*	500	1250	1650
PP "Chas A. Heyer & Co., Nairobi," .32 ACP, Double Action, Pre-War, High-Polish Finish, *Curio*			Rare
PP (Early) 90 Degree Safety, .32 ACP, Double Action, Pre-War, Commercial, High-Polish Finish, *Curio*	300	700	775
PP (Early) Bottom Magazine, .380 ACP, Double Action, Pre-War, Commercial, High-Polish Finish, *Curio*	400	800	900
PP AC Police F, .32 ACP, Double Action, Pre-War, Nazi-Proofed, *Curio*	300	700	775
PP AC Waffenamt, .32 ACP, Double Action, Pre-War, Nazi-Proofed, *Curio*	200	450	500
PP AC, .32 ACP, Double Action, Nazi-Proofed, *Curio*	125	350	400
PP Bottom Magazine Release, .32 ACP, Double Action, Pre-War, Commercial, High-Polish Finish, *Curio*	400	850	1000
PP Bottom Magazine Release, .32 ACP, Double Action, Pre-War, Commercial, High-Polish Finish, Lightweight, *Curio*			Rare
PP Czech, .32 ACP, Double Action, Pre-War, Commercial, High-Polish Finish, *Curio*	400	800	950

	Fair	V. Good	Excellent
PP NSKK, .32 ACP, Double Action, Pre-War, High-Polish Finish, Nazi-Proofed, *Curio*	$900	$2000	$2650
PP PDM, .32 ACP, Double Action, Pre-War, High-Polish Finish, *Curio*	300	750	900
PP Persian, .380 ACP, Double Action, Pre-War, Commercial, High-Polish Finish, *Curio*	900	1800	2200
PP Police C, .32 ACP, Double Action, Pre-War, High-Polish Finish, Nazi-Proofed, *Curio*	450	900	1200
PP Police C, .32 ACP, Double Action, Pre-War, Nazi-Proofed, *Curio*	350	725	850
PP Police F, .32 ACP, Double Action, Pre-War, Nazi-Proofed, *Curio*	300	600	700
PP RFV, .32 ACP, Double Action, Pre-War, High-Polish, *Curio*	300	600	700
PP RJ, .32 ACP, Double Action, Pre-War, High-Polish Finish, *Curio*	300	650	750
PP SA, .32 ACP, Double Action, Pre-War, High-Polish Finish, *Curio*	600	1250	1550
PP Verchromt, .32 ACP, Double Action, Pre-War, Commercial, *Curio*	600	1250	1550
PP Verchromt, .380 ACP, Double Action, Pre-War, Commercial, *Curio*	`900	1800	2350
PP Waffenamt, .32 ACP, Double Action, Pre-War, High-Polish Finish, Nazi-Proofed, *Curio*	200	450	500
PP Waffenamt, .32 ACP, Double Action, Pre-War, Nazi-Proofed, *Curio*	200	400	450
PP Waffenamt, .380 ACP, Double Action, Pre-War, High-Polish Finish, Nazi-Proofed, *Curio*	400	850	1100
PP with Lanyard Loop, .32 ACP, Double Action, Pre-War, Commercial, High-Polish Finish, Nazi-Proofed, *Modern*	200	450	500
PP, .22 L.R.R.F., Double Action, Pre-War, Commercial, Nickel Plated, *Curio*			Rare
PP, .22 L.R.R.F., Double Action, Pre-War, Commercial, Nickel Plated, Nazi-Proofed, *Curio*			Rare
PP, .22 L.R.R.F., Double Action, Pre-War, Commercial, High-Polish Finish, *Curio*	300	750	900
PP, .22 L.R.R.F., Double Action, Pre-War, Commercial, High-Polish Finish, Nazi-Proofed, *Curio*	300	750	900
PP, .25 ACP, Double Action, Pre-War, Commercial, High-Polish Finish, *Curio*	1400	3000	3500
PP, .32 ACP, Double Action, Pre-War, Commercial, High-Polished Finish, *Curio*	200	400	450
PP, .32 ACP, Double Action, Pre-War, Commercial, High-Polished Finish, Nazi-Proofed, *Curio*	200	400	450
PP, .32 ACP, Double Action, Pre-War, Commercial, Lightweight, High-Polish Finish, *Curio*	$300	$600	$725
PP, .32 ACP, Double Action, Pre-War, Commercial, Nazi-Proofed, *Curio*	150	325	375
PP, .32 ACP, Double Action, Pre-War, Commercial, Nickel Plated, Nazi-Proofed, *Curio*			Rare
PP, .32 ACP, Double Action, Pre-War, Commercial, Nickel Plated, *Curio*			Rare
PP, .32 ACP, Double Action, Pre-War, Nazi-Proofed, Lightweight, High-Polish Finish, *Curio*	300	600	675
PP, .32 ACP, Double Action, Pre-War, Nazi-Proofed, Lightweight, *Curio*	200	400	450
PP, .380 ACP, Double Action, Pre-War, Commercial, High-Polish Finish, *Curio*	400	800	900
PP, .380 ACP, Double Action, Pre-War, Commercial, High-Polish Finish, Nazi-Proofed, *Curio*	400	800	900
PP, .380 ACP, Double Action, Pre-War, Commercial, Nickel Plated, *Curio*			Rare
PP, .380 ACP, Double Action, Pre-War, Commercial, Nickel Plated, Nazi-Proofed, *Curio*			Rare
PPK "Cas A. Heyer & Co., Nairobi," .32 ACP, Double Action, Pre-War, High-Polish Finish, *Curio*			Rare
PPK "Stoeger," .32 ACP, Double Action, Pre-War, High-Polish Finish, *Curio*			Rare
PPK (Early) 90 Degree Safety, .32 ACP, Double Action, Pre-War, Commercial, High-Polish Finish, *Curio*	250	550	600
PPK Czech, .32 ACP, Double Action, Pre-War, Commercial, High-Polish Finish, *Curio*	400	850	1050
PPK DRP, .32 ACP, Double Action, Pre-War, High-Polish Finish, *Curio*	400	850	950
PPK Party Leader, .32 ACP, Double Action, Pre-War, High-Polish Finish, *Curio*	900	2250	2500
PPK PDM, .32 ACP, Double Action, Pre-War, High-Polish Finish, Lightweight, *Curio*	600	1350	1500
PPK Police C, .32 ACP, Double Action, Pre-War, High-Polish Finish, Nazi-Proofed, *Curio*	300	675	750
PPK Police C, .32 ACP, Double Action, Pre-War, Nazi-Proofed, *Curio*	250	550	600
PPK Police F, .32 ACP, Double Action, Pre-War, Nazi-Proofed, *Curio*	400	800	900

	Fair	V. Good	Excellent
PPK RFV, *Curio*	$400	$850	$1050
PPK RZM, .32 ACP, Double Action, Pre-War, High-Polish Finish, *Curio*	400	850	1000
PPK Verchromt, .32 ACP, Double Action, Pre-War, Commercial, *Curio*	800	1800	2200
PPK Verchromt, .380 ACP, Double Action, Pre-War, High-Polish Finish, Curio	900	2000	2350
PPK Waffenamt, .32 ACP, Double Action, Pre-War, High-Polish Finish, Nazi-Proofed, *Curio*	400	875	1100
PPK Waffenamt, .32 ACP, Double Action, Pre-War, Nazi-Proofed, *Curio*	350	750	900
PPK, .22 L.R.R.F., Double Action, Pre-War, Commercial, High-Polish Finish, *Curio*	500	1000	1250
PPK, .22 L.R.R.F., Double Action, Pre-War, Commercial, High-Polish Finish, Nazi-Proofed, *Curio*	500	1000	1250
PPK, .25 ACP, Double Action, Pre-War, Commercial, High-Polish Finish, *Curio*	2500	4500	6000
PPK, .32 ACP, Double Action, Pre-War, Commercial, High-Polish Finish, *Curio*	225	475	525
PPK, .32 ACP, Double Action, Pre-War, Commercial, High-Polish Finish, Nazi-Proofed, *Curio*	225	475	525
PPK, .32 ACP, Double Action, Pre-War, Commercial, Lightweight, High-Polish Finish, *Curio*	300	650	750
PPK, .32 ACP, Double Action, Pre-War, Commercial, Nazi-Proofed, *Curio*	200	450	550
PPK, .32 ACP, Double Action, Pre-War, Nazi-Proofed, Lightweight, High-Polish Finish, *Curio*	300	650	750
PPK, .32 ACP, Double Action, Pre-War, Nazi-Proofed, Lightweight, *Curio*	250	550	650
PPK, .380 ACP, Double Action, Pre-War, Commercial, High-Polish Finish, *Curio*	900	1800	2250
PPK, .380 ACP, Double Action, Pre-War, Commercial, High-Polish Finish, Nazi-Proofed, *Curio*	900	1800	2250
PPK, .380 ACP, Double Action, Pre-War, Commercial, Nickel Plated, *Curio*			Rare
PPK, .380 ACP, Double Action, Pre-War, Commercial, Nickel Plated, Nazi-Proofed, *Curio*			Rare

HANDGUN, SELF-LOADING—POSTWAR

	Fair	V. Good	Excellent
P-1, 9mm, Double Action, Alloy Frame, *Modern*	150	350	450
P-38, .22 L.R.R.F., Double Action, *Modern*	300	600	700
P-38, .30 Luger, Double Action, Blue, *Modern*	350	700	850
P-38, 9mm, Double Action, *Modern*	$200	$500	$600
P-38-IV (P-4), 9mm, Double Action, *Modern*	200	450	500
P-38k, 9mm, Double Action, Short Barrel, *Modern*	400	700	800
P-5, 9mm, Interarms, Double Action, Blue, *Modern*	250	550	700
PP Super, 9 × 18mm, Clip Fed, Blue, *Modern*	200	500	650
PP, .22 L.R.R.F., Double Action, *Modern*	250	500	650
PP, .32 ACP, Double Action, Blue, *Modern*	200	450	600
PP, .380 ACP, Double Action, Blue, *Modern*	250	500	650
PPK, .22 L.R.R.F., Double Action, Lightweight, Post-War, *Modern*	300	600	700
PPK, .22 L.R.R.F., Double Action, Post-War, *Modern*	300	650	750
PPK, .32 ACP, Double Action, Lightweight, Post-War, *Modern*	200	425	500
PPK, .32 ACP, Double Action, Post-War, *Modern*	200	450	525
PPK, .380 ACP, Double Action, *Modern*	300	600	700
PPK/S, .22 L.R.R.F., Double Action, *Modern*	250	450	550
PPK/S, .32 ACP, Double Action, Blue, *Modern*	150	300	400
PPK/S, .380 ACP, Double Action, Blue, *Modern*	250	450	550
PPK/S, .380 ACP, Double Action, Blue, Seven Rounds Capacity, *Modern*	200	400	500
PPK/S, .380 ACP, Double Action, Stainless Steel, Seven Rounds Capacity, *Modern*	200	400	500
TPH, .22 L.R.R.F., Double Action, Clip-Fed, *Modern*	250	500	650
TPH, .22 L.R.R.F., Double Action, Clip-Fed, German Manuf., *Modern*	200	400	575
TPH, .25 ACP, Double Action, Clip-Fed, *Modern*	175	350	400
TPH, .25 ACP, Double Action, Clip-Fed, German Manuf., *Modern*	175	375	400

HANDGUN, SELF-LOADING—WALTHER MARK II

	Fair	V. Good	Excellent
PP Mark II "Manurhin," .22 L.R.R.F., Double Action, High-Polish Finish, Blue, *Curio*	150	350	425
PP Mark II "Manurhin," .32 ACP, Double Action, High-Polish Finish, Blue, *Curio*	150	300	375
PP Mark II "Manurhin," .380 ACP, Double Action, High-Polish Finish, Blue, *Curio*	150	300	400
PPK Mark II "Manurhin," .22 L.R.R.F., Double Action, High-Polish Finish, Blue, *Curio*	225	500	550

	Fair	V. Good	Excellent
PPK Mark II "Manurhin," .22 L.R.R.F., Double Action, High-Polish Finish, Blue, Lightweight, *Curio*	$225	$500	$600
PPK Mark II "Manurhin," .32 ACP, Double Action, High-Polish Finish, Blue, Curio	150	375	450
PPK Mark II "Manurhin," .32 ACP, Double Action, High-Polish Finish, Blue, Lightweight, *Curio*	200	450	550
PPK Mark II "Manurhin," .380 ACP, Double Action, High-Polish Finish, Blue, *Curio*	250	500	550

RIFLE, BOLT ACTION

	Fair	V. Good	Excellent
KKJ, .22 Hornet, 5 Shot Clip, Open Rear Sight, Checkered Stock, *Modern*	250	500	700
KKJ, .22 Hornet, 5 Shot Clip, Open Rear Sight, Checkered Stock, Set Trigger, *Modern*	300	650	850
KKJ, .22 L.R.R.F., 5 Shot Clip, Open Rear Sight, Checkered Stock, *Modern*	200	400	500
KKJ, .22 L.R.R.F., 5 Shot Clip, Open Rear Sight, Checkered Stock, Set Trigger, *Modern*	200	450	600
KKJ, .22 WMR, 5 Shot Clip, Open Rear Sight, Checkered Stock, *Modern*	250	500	700
KKJ, .22 WMR, 5 Shot Clip, Open Rear Sight, Checkered Stock, Set Trigger, *Modern*	300	650	850
KKM International Match, .22 L.R.R.F., Singleshot, Target Stock, with Accessories, *Modern*	300	600	800
KKM-S Silhouette, .22 L.R., Singleshot, Blue, *Modern*	300	650	850
Model B, Various Caliber, Checkered Stock, Mauser Action, Set Triggers, *Modern*	150	350	425
Model GX-1, .22 L.R., Singleshot, Blue, *Modern*	600	1200	1500
Model KKW, .22 L.R.R.F., Pre-WW2, Singleshot, Tangent Sights, Military Style Stock, *Modern*	150	350	500
Model V "Meisterbushe," Singleshot, Pistol-Grip Stock, Target Sights, *Modern*	150	350	450
Model V, Singleshot, Sporting Rifle, Open Rear Sight, *Modern*	150	300	375
Moving Target, .22 L.R.R.F., Singleshot, Target Stock, with Accessories, *Modern*	225	550	700
Olympic, .22 L.R.R.F., Singleshot, Target Stock, with Accessories, *Modern*	350	750	950
Prone "400," .22 L.R.R.F., Singleshot, Target Stock, with Accessories, *Modern*	225	550	650
Running Boar, .22 L.R., Singleshot, Blue, *Modern*	300	650	900
U.I.T.-E. Universal Match, .22 L.R., Singleshot, Blue, *Modern*	$400	$950	$1200
UIT Match, .22 L.R.R.F., Singleshot, Target Stock, with Accessories, *Modern*	350	750	1000
UIT Special, .22 L.R.R.F., Singleshot, Target Stock, with Accessories, *Modern*	450	900	1200

RIFLE, SELF-LOADING

	Fair	V. Good	Excellent
Model 1, Clip Fed, Carbine, *Modern*	150	300	375
Model 2, .22 L.R.R.F., Clip Fed, *Modern*	175	375	475

SHOTGUN, DOUBLE BARREL, SIDE-BY-SIDE

	Fair	V. Good	Excellent
Model S.F., 12 or 16 Gauges, Checkered Stock, Cheekpiece, Double Triggers, Sling Swivels, *Modern*	175	375	475
Model S.F.D., 12 or 16 Gauges, Checkered Stock, Cheekpiece, Double Triggers, Sling Swivels, *Modern*	250	500	600

WAMO

Wamo Mfg. Co., San Gabriel, Calif.

HANDGUN, SINGLESHOT

	Fair	V. Good	Excellent
Powermaster, .22 L.R.R.F., Target Pistol, *Modern*	75	100	125

WARNANT

L. & J. Warnant Freres, Hognee, Belgium.

HANDGUN, REVOLVER

	Fair	V. Good	Excellent
.32 S & W, Double Action, Folding Trigger, Break Top, *Curio*	50	75	100
.38 S & W, Double Action, Folding Trigger, Break Top, *Curio*	50	100	125

HANDGUN, SELF-LOADING

	Fair	V. Good	Excellent
6.35mm, Clip Fed, Blue, *Curio*	75	175	225

HANDGUN, SINGLESHOT

	Fair	V. Good	Excellent
Traff, 6mm R.F., Spur Trigger, Parlor Pistol, *Curio*	50	100	125
Traff, 9mm R.F., Spur Trigger, Parlor Pistol, *Curio*	50	100	125

RIFLE, SINGLESHOT

	Fair	V. Good	Excellent
Amelung, Various Rimfires, Checkered Stock, Set Triggers, Parlor Rifle, *Curio*	50	75	100
Amelung, Various Rimfires, Plain, Parlor Rifle, *Curio*	25	50	75

WARNER

Warner Arms Corp., Brooklyn, N.Y., formed about 1912, moved to Norwich, Conn., in 1913, and in 1917 merged and became Davis-Warner Arms Corp., Assonet, Mass., out of business about 1919. See also Schwarzlose.

	Fair	*V. Good*	*Excellent*
SELF-LOADING			
Infallable, .32 ACP, Clip Fed, *Modern*	$100	$275	$300
Revolver, .32 CAL., 5-Shot, *Modern*	50	125	150

WARREN ARMS CORP.

Belgium, c. 1900.

SHOTGUN, DOUBLE BARREL, SIDE-BY-SIDE			
Various Gauges, Hammerless, Damascus Barrel, *Modern*	50	150	175
Various Gauges, Hammerless, Steel Barrel, *Modern*	75	175	200
Various Gauges, Outside Hammers, Damascus Barrel, *Modern*	100	200	300
Various Gauges, Outside Hammers, Steel Barrel, *Modern*	100	200	300
SHOTGUN, SINGLESHOT			
Various Gauges, Hammer, Steel Barrel, *Modern*	25	50	75

WATSON BROS.

London, England, 1885–1931.

RIFLE, BOLT ACTION			
.303 British, Express Sights, Sporting Rifle, Checkered Stock, *Modern* ...	300	625	950
RIFLE, DOUBLE BARREL, SIDE-BY-SIDE			
.450/.400 N.E. 3", Double Trigger, Recoil Pad, Plain, Cased, *Modern*	2000	4000	6000

WATTERS, JOHN

Carlisle, Pa., 1778–1785. See Kentucky Rifles.

WEATHERBY

South Gate, Calif., 1945 to date. Designer, sportsman, ballistician and gunmaker Roy E. Weatherby planted the seed for his future fame and fortune while experimenting with high performance cartridges of his own design in 1937. The company he founded in 1945 made its reputation from an exclusive series of hunting rifles and high velocity ammunition, built to demanding standards for the discriminating outdoorsman and adventurer. Weatherby's experiments were in the designs of cartridge cases, capacities of powders, and calibers of the projectiles. The theories of this dedicated rifleman and ballistician were based on bullet speed being more important to the sportsman than bullet size and weight. The "one shot kill" became his goal. Extensive testing and experimentation revealed that fast-traveling bullets follow a trajectory flatter and of greater power. When striking their prey, the projectiles create extraordinary hydrostatic shock. The first Weatherby magnum high velocity cartridge was available to the public in 1945, built on such actions as the Mauser, Springfield Model 1903, the Enfield, and the Winchester Model 70. Beginning in the 1950s Weatherbys were built on the FN action, but the designer's goal was to build rifles on actions of his own design. Accordingly in 1958 he introduced the Weatherby Mark V, described as "a truly innovative mechanical design with nine locking lugs instead of the usual two, a streamlined enclosed bolt sleeve and a counterbored bolt face to receive and totally enclose the cartridge case head." The new rifle offered several features: "a hammer-forged barrel, fluted bolt body with three gas escape ports, and a high-luster epoxy stock finish." Many experienced hunters regarded the new rifle as the finest available for its price in the world. Weatherby's Mark V is built in the following calibers of the inventor's own design: .224 W.M. Varmintmaster (with a scaled down action, having six locking lugs), .240 W.M., .257 W.M., .270 W.M., 7 mm W.M., .30-06 Mark V, .300 W.M. (one of the world's finest sporting rifle cartridges), .340 W.M., .378 W.M., and the .460 W.M. Weatherby later developed a sophisticated over-and-under shotgun, as well as a special series of rifle, known as the Vanguard. This bolt-action series features a construction described by the factory as "rugged," with the quality and several details of the Mark V series. The shotguns are the Athena and the Orion, available initially in 12 and 20 gauges, but soon offered in 28 and .410 as well. In the mid 1990s, Weatherby brought out a competitive shotgun—the Athena Master—for skeet shooting. Billed as the "most versatile, and beautiful shotgun ever made," the Athena Master is fitted with double sets of barrels in 12, 20, 28, and .410 gauges! Weatherby prides itself on the excellence of its stock wood, usually selected from blanks of Northern California walnut. These carefully selected, thoroughly seasoned, and finely built stocks are a hallmark of Weatherby rifles and shotguns. The company also rests its reputation on the "consistent performance, durability and value" of its products. In 1989 Weatherby added its first cartridge to the original list of nine: the .416 Weatherby. The .416 was developed to offer a further choice for big game hunters, between the .378 and the .460. The company also refined the Vanguard group of bolt-actions, and added the Classic II model, featuring traditional styling, and such detailing as oil-finished stocks. The Vanguard Classics' appearance combined English elegance with American strength and durability. The result was a rifle series in distinct contrast to the original California style of Weatherby bolt-actions. Among other details of the Vanguard Classics are the hammer-forged barrels, the matte blue finish, and individual inletting and hand-bedding to the barreled actions. Still another innovation was the firm's addition of the Mark XXII self-loading .22 long rifle repeater (with singleshot selector system), "Weatherguard" synthetic stocks, and the development of a line of accessories—cases, slings, caps, jewelry, loading dies, and the famous lucite cartridge display block.

	Fair	*V. Good*	*Excellent*
HANDGUN, SINGLESHOT			
Mk. V. Silhouette, Various Calibers, Thumbhole Target Stock, Target Sights, *Modern*	$800	$1750	$2000
RIFLE, BOLT ACTION			
Deluxe, .378 Wby. Mag., Magnum, Checkered Stock, *Modern*	400	850	950

	Fair	V. Good	Excellent
Deluxe, Various Calibers, Checkered Stock, *Modern*	$400	$800	$900
Deluxe, Various Calibers, Magnum, Checkered Stock, *Modern*	400	825	925
For German Manufacture, Add 30%–50%			
Mark V Crown Custom, Various Calibers, 24" or 26" Barrel, Right Hand Only, *Modern*	1400	3000	3500
Mark V Fibermark, Various Calibers, Fiberglass, Right Hand Only, *Modern*	350	750	850
Mark V Lazermark, Various Calibers, Carved Stock (Carved with Laser Beam), *Modern*	425	850	1100
Mark V, .378 Wby. Mag., Checkered Stock, *Modern*	450	900	1100
Mark V, .460 Wby. Mag., Checkered Stock, *Modern*	500	1000	1250
Mark V, Various Calibers, Checkered Stock, *Modern*	325	650	750
Mark V, Various Calibers, Varmint, Checkered Stock, *Modern*	400	850	950

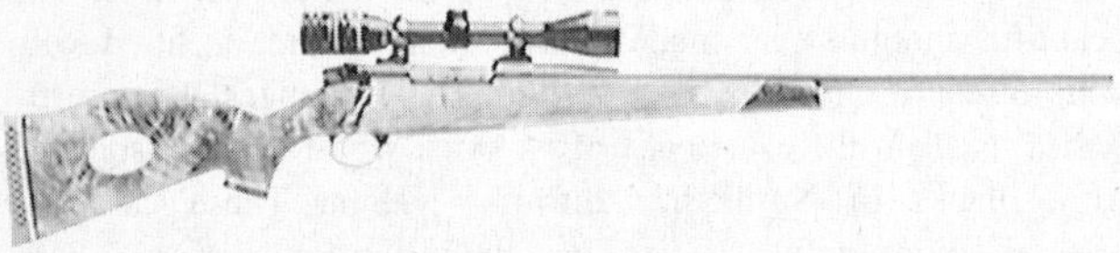

Weatherby Mark V

	Fair	V. Good	Excellent
Vanguard, Various Calibers, Checkered Stock, *Modern*	200	400	450

RIFLE, SELF-LOADING

	Fair	V. Good	Excellent
Mark XXII, .22 L.R.R.F., Clip Fed, Checkered Stock, *Modern*	150	300	325
Mark XXII, .22 L.R.R.F., Tube Feed, Checkered Stock, *Modern*	150	325	350
Model M-82, Various Gauges, Gas Operated, Various Barrel Lengths, *Modern*	200	400	450

SHOTGUN, DOUBLE BARREL, OVER-UNDER

	Fair	V. Good	Excellent
Athena Skeet Grade, 12 Gauge, Single Selective Trigger, 26" Barrels, *Modern*	600	1250	1500
Athena Trap Grade, 12 Gauge, Single Selective Trigger, 30" Barrels, *Modern*	$500	$1000	$1250
Orion 20 Field Grade, 20 Gauge, Single Selective Trigger, 26" or 28" Barrel, *Modern*	350	775	850
Orion Field Grade, 12 Gauge, Single Selective Trigger, 26" or 28" Barrel, *Modern*	350	775	800
Orion Skeet Grade, 12 Gauge, Single Selective Trigger, 26" Barrels, *Modern*	350	750	825
Orion Trap Grade, 12 Gauge, Single Selective Trigger, 30" or 32" Barrel, *Modern*	350	750	825
Regency, 12 Gauge, Trap Grade, Vent Rib, Checkered Stock, Engraved, Single Selective Trigger, *Modern*	325	675	750
Regency, Field Grade, 12 and 20 Gauges, Vent Rib, Checkered Stock, Engraved, Single Selective Trigger, *Modern*	350	725	775

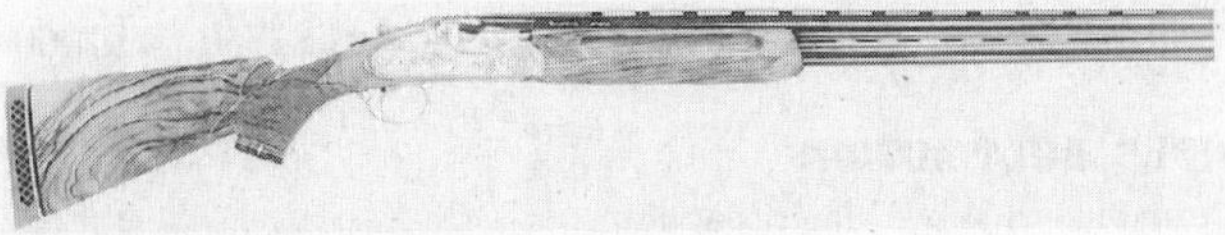

Weatherby Athena

SHOTGUN, SELF-LOADING

	Fair	V. Good	Excellent
Centurion, 12 Gauge, Field Grade, Vent Rib, Checkered Stock, *Modern*	100	225	275
Centurion, 12 Gauge, Trap Grade, Checkered Stock, Vent Rib, *Modern*	100	200	250
Centurion Deluxe, 12 Gauge, Checkered Stock, Vent Rib, Light Engraving, Fancy Wood, *Modern*	125	250	300

SHOTGUN, SLIDE ACTION

	Fair	V. Good	Excellent
Model M-92, 12 Gauge, Vent Rib, Three Sheel Mag., *Modern*	100	225	275
Patrician, 12 Gauge, Field Grade, Checkered Stock, Vent Rib, *Modern*	100	200	225
Patrician, 12 Gauge, Trap Grade, Checkered Stock, Vent Rib, *Modern*	100	225	250
Patrician, Deluxe, 12 Gauge, Checkered Stock, Light Engraving, Fancy Wood, Vent Rib, *Modern*	100	225	275

WEAVER, CRYPRET

Pa., c. 1818. See Kentucky Rifles.

WEBLEY & SCOTT LTD.

Located in Birmingham, England, operating as P. Webley & Son, 1860–1897; Webley & Scott Revolver & Arms Co., 1898–1906; Webley & Scott, 1906–1979.

HANDGUN, REVOLVER

	Fair	V. Good	Excellent
#1, .577 Eley, Solid Frame, Double Action, Blue, *Curio*	2000	4500	5500

	Fair	V. Good	Excellent
British Bulldog, Various Calibers, Solid Frame, Double Action, *Curio*	$100	$300	$350
Tower Bulldog, Various Calibers, Solid Frame, Double Action, *Curio*	100	275	325
Webley Kaufman, .45 Colt, Top Break, Square Butt, Commercial, *Antique*	300	600	800
Webley MK 1, .455 Revolver Mk 1, Top Break, Round Butt, Military, *Antique*	125	225	250
Webley MK 1*, .455 Revolver Mk 1, Top Break, Round Butt, Military, *Antique*	100	200	225
Webley MK 1 Navy,** .455 Revolver Mk 1, Top Break, Round Butt, Military, *Modern*	100	200	225
Webley MK 2, .455 Revolver Mk 1, Top Break, Round Butt, Military, *Antique*	100	225	250
Webley MK 2*, .455 Revolver Mk 1, Top Break, Round Butt, Military, *Curio*	100	225	250
Webley MK 2,** .455 Revolver Mk 1, Top Break, Round Butt, Military, *Curio*	100	225	250
Webley MK 3, .455 Revolver Mk 1, Top Break, Round Butt, Military, *Curio*	100	250	275
Webley MK 4, .455 Revolver Mk 1, Top Break, Round Butt, Military, *Curio*	100	200	250
Webley MK 5, .455 Revolver Mk 1, Top Break, Round Butt, Military, *Curio*	100	225	275
Webley MK 6, .455 Revolver Mk 1, Top Break, Square Butt, Military, *Curio*	150	300	350
Webley MK 6, Detachable Buttstock Only	150	300	350
Webley Mk III M & P, .38 S & W, Top Break, Square Butt, Commercial, *Modern*	125	250	300
Webley Mk IV, .38 S & W, Top Break, Square Butt, Military, *Curio*	100	225	275
Webley Mk VI, .22 L.R.R.F., Top Break, Square Butt, Commercial, *Modern*	200	400	475
Webley R I C, .455 Revolver Mk 1, Solid Frame, Square Butt, Commercial, *Antique*	100	225	250
Webley-Green, .455 Revolver Mk 1, Top Break, Square Butt, Commercial, Target Pistol, *Antique*	250	550	600
Webley-Green, .476 Enfield Mk 3, Top Break, Square Butt, Commercial, Target Pistol, *Antique*	350	800	900

HANDGUN, SELF-LOADING

	Fair	V. Good	Excellent
Model 1904, .455 Webley Auto., Clip Fed, Grip Safety, Hammer, *Curio*	300	650	750
Model 1906, .25 ACP, Clip Fed, Hammer, *Modern*	$100	$225	$250
Model 1909 M & P, 9mm Browning Long, Clip Fed, Hammer, *Curio*	200	400	450
Model 1909 M & P, 9mm Browning Long, South African Police, Clip Fed, Hammer, *Curio*	250	500	550
Model 1909, .25 ACP, Clip Fed, Hammerless, *Modern*	100	225	250
Model 1909, 9mm, Clip Fed, Hammerless, *Modern*	200	400	450
Model 1911 Metro Police, .32 ACP, Clip Fed, Hammer, *Modern*	300	625	700
Model 1911 Metro Police, .380 ACP, Clip Fed, Hammer, *Modern*	350	700	800
Model 1912, .455 Caliber, Clip Fed, Hammerless, *Curio*	200	400	450
Model 1913 Mk 1 #2, .455 Webley Auto., Clip Fed, Grip Safety, Adjustable Sights, Hammer, *Curio*	400	950	1200
Model 1913 Mk 1, .455 Webley Auto., Clip Fed, Grip Safety, Military, Hammer, *Curio*	900	2000	2250
Model 1913, .38 ACP, Clip Fed, Hammerless, *Curio*	500	1000	1250

SHOTGUN, DOUBLE BARREL, SIDE-BY-SIDE

	Fair	V. Good	Excellent
Model 700, 12 and 20 Gauges, Box Lock, Hammerless, Checkered Stock, Light Engraving, Single Trigger, *Modern*	700	1450	1600
Model 701, 12 and 20 Gauges, Box Lock, Hammerless, Checkered Stock, Fancy Engraving, Double Trigger, *Modern*	900	2000	2500
Model 701, 12 and 20 Gauges, Box Lock, Hammerless, Checkered Stock, Fancy Engraving, Single Trigger, *Modern*	1000	2200	2600
Model 702, 12 and 20 Gauges, Box Lock, Hammerless, Checkered Stock, Engraved, Double Trigger, *Modern*	800	1750	2200
Model 702, 12 and 20 Gauges, Box Lock, Hammerless, Checkered Stock, Engraved, Single Trigger, *Modern*	800	1800	2250

WELSHANTZ, DAVID

York, Pa., 1780–1783. See Kentucky Rifles, U.S. Military.

WELSHANTZ, JACOB

York, Pa., 1777–1792. See Kentucky Rifles, U.S. Military.

WELSHANTZ, JOSEPH

York, Pa., 1779–1983. See Kentucky Rifles, U.S. Military.

WESSON & HARRINGTON

Worcester, Mass., 1871–1874. Succeeded by Harrington and Richardson.

HANDGUN, REVOLVER

	Fair	V. Good	Excellent
.22 Short R.F., 7 Shot, Spur Trigger, Solid Frame, Single Action, *Antique*	$75	$150	$175
.32 Short R.F., 5 Shot, Spur Trigger, Solid Frame, Single Action, *Antique*	75	150	175
.38 Short R.F., 5 Shot, Spur Trigger, Solid Frame, Single Action, *Antique*	75	175	200

DAN WESSON ARMS

Monson, Mass., since 1970. A direct descendant of Daniel B. Wesson, Dan Wesson was a talented designer and marketer and created a most unusual line of revolvers, the main feature of which was interchangeability of barrels and cylinders, allowing for a shooting system with multiple calibers for a lesser price, built on the same frame. Among the admirers of Wesson, and a friend as well, was a contemporary well known in his own right as a designer and marketer, one William B. Ruger Sr. Quite rare are engraved Dan Wesson revolvers, a few of which were embellished by A. A. White Engravers, Inc., in the early 1970s. These will demand a premium, depending on coverage. Some were done by Alvin White himself, and will be so signed.

HANDGUN, REVOLVER

10", 15-2 $20.00–$40.00; 15-2H $35.00–$55.00; 15-2V $35.00–$55.00; 15-2VH $40.00–$70.00; 44-V $55.00–$85.00; 44-VH; 715 $35.00–$55.00; 715V $45.00–$65.00; 715VH $50.00–$80.00; 744V $60.00–$100.00; 44-VH $70.00–$110.00
12", 15-2 $50.00–$80.00; 15-2VH $75.00–$110.00; 715 $75.00–$110.00; 715V $80.00–$120.00; 715VH $95.00–$140.00
15", 15-2 $75.00–$110.00; 15-2H $95.00–$135.00; 15-2V $95.00–$135.00; 15-2VH $120.00–$160.00; 715 $80.00–$120.00; 715V $95.00–$140.00; 715VH $100.00–$155.00
Extra Barrel Assemblies, Add:

	Fair	V. Good	Excellent
Model 11, .357 Magnum, Double Action, 3-Barrel Set, Nickel Plated, *Modern*	150	300	400
Model 11, .357 Magnum, Double Action, 3-Barrel Set, Satin Blue, *Modern*	150	300	400
Model 11, .357 Magnum, Various Barrel Lengths, Nickel Plated, Double Action, *Modern*	75	150	225
Model 11, .357 Magnum, Various Barrel Lengths, Satin Blue, Double Action, *Modern*	100	150	200
Model 11, .38 Special, Various Barrel Lengths, Nickel Plated, Double Action, *Modern*	75	125	200
Model 11, .38 Special, Various Barrel Lengths, Satin Blue, Double Action, Modern	75	150	175
Model 12, .357 Magnum, 3-Barrel Set, Satin Blue, Adjustable Sights, *Modern*	$150	$300	$400
Model 12, .357 Magnum, Various Barrel Lengths, Double Action, Blue, Adjustable Sights, *Modern*	100	200	250
Model 12, .357 Magnum, Various Barrel Lengths, Double Action, Nickel Plated, Adjustable Sights, *Modern*	100	175	300
Model 12, .38 Special, Various Barrel Lengths, Double Action, Blue, Adjustable Sights, *Modern*	50	125	150
Model 12, .38 Special, Various Barrel Lengths, Double Action, Nickel Plated, Adjustable Sights, *Modern*	50	125	175
Model 14, .357 Magnum, Double Action, 3-Barrel Set, Nickel Plated, *Modern*	150	300	400
Model 14, .357 Magnum, Double Action, 3-Barrel Set, Satin Blue, *Modern*	175	325	425
Model 14, .357 Magnum, Various Barrel Lengths, Double Action, Satin Blue, *Modern*	100	175	225
Model 14, .357 Magnum, Various Barrel Lengths, Double Action, Nickel Plated, *Modern*	100	125	175
Model 14, .38 Special, Various Barrel Lengths, Double Action, Satin Blue, *Modern*	50	100	150
Model 14, .38 Special, Various Barrel Lengths, Double Action, Nickel Plated, *Modern*	50	100	150
Model 14-2, .357 Magnum, Double Action, 4-Barrel Set, Blue, *Modern*	200	350	450
Model 14-2, .357 Magnum, Various Barrel Lengths, Double Action, Satin Blue, *Modern*	100	125	150
Model 14-2B, .357 Magnum, Double Action, 4-Barrel Set, Brite Blue, *Modern*	200	350	450
Model 14-2B, .357 Magnum, Various Barrel Lengths, Double Action, Brite Blue, *Modern*	50	100	150
Model 15, .357 Magnum, Double Action, 3-Barrel Set, Satin Blue, Adjustable Sights, *Modern*	175	300	400
Model 15, .357 Magnum, Double Action, 3-Barrel Set, Blue, Adjustable Sights, *Modern*	150	300	400
Model 15, .357 Magnum, Various Barrel Lengths, Double Action, Nickel Plated, Adjustable Sights, *Modern*	100	200	275
Model 15, .357 Magnum, Various Barrel Lengths, Double Action, Satin Blue, Adjustable Sights, *Modern*	100	200	225
Model 15, .357 Magnum, Various Barrel Lengths, Double Action, Blue, Adjustable Sights, *Modern*	100	200	250

	Fair	*V. Good*	*Excellent*
Model 15, .38 Special, Various Barrel Lengths, Double Action, Nickel Plated, Adjustable Sights, *Modern*	$100	$175	$250
Model 15, .38 Special, Various Barrel Lengths, Double Action, Satin Blue, Adjustable Sights, *Modern*	75	150	200
Model 15, .38 Special, Various Barrel Lengths, Double Action, Blue, Adjustable Sights, *Modern*	75	175	225
Model 15-2, .357 Magnum or .22 L.R.R.F., Double Action, 4-Barrel Set, Blue, Adjustable Sights, *Modern*	200	300	400
Model 15-2, .357 Magnum or .22 L.R.R.F., Various Barrel Lengths, Double Action, Blue, Adjustable Sights, *Modern*	75	150	200
Model 15-2H, .357 Magnum or .22 L.R.R.F., Double Action, 4-Barrel Set, Blue, Adjustable Sights, Heavy Barrel, *Modern*	200	300	400
Model 15-2H, .357 Magnum or .22 L.R.R.F., Various Barrel Lengths, Double Action, Blue, Adjustable Sights, Heavy Barrel, *Modern*	75	150	225
Model 15-2V, .357 Magnum or .22 L.R.R.F., Double Action, 4-Barrel Set, Blue, Adjustable Sights, Vent Rib, *Modern*	250	400	500
Model 15-2V, *Modern*	75	150	225
Model 15-2VH, .357 Magnum or .22 L.R.R.F., Double Action, 4-Barrel, Vent Rib, *Modern*	225	400	500
Model 15-2VH, .357 Magnum or .22 L.R.R.F., Various Barrel Lengths, Double Action, Adjustable Sights, Heavy Barrel, Vent Rib, *Modern*	100	200	275
Model 44-V, .44 Magnum, Double Action, 4-Barrel Set, Blue, Adjustable Sights, Vent Rib, *Modern*	200	400	500
Model 44-V, .44 Magnum, Various Barrel Lengths, Double Action, Blue, Adjustable Sights, Vent Rib, *Modern*	200	400	500
Model 44-VH, .44 Magnum, Double Action, 4-Barrel Set, Blue, Adjustable Sights, Heavy Barrel, Vent Rib, *Modern*	300	600	800
Model 44-VH, .44 Magnum, Various Barrel Lengths, Double Action, Adjustable Sights, Heavy Barrel, Vent Rib, *Modern*	200	450	500
Model 714, .357 Magnum, Double Action, 4-Barrel Set, Stainless Steel, Fixed Sights, *Modern*	200	400	500
Model 714, .357 Magnum, Various Barrel Lengths, Double Action, Stainless Steel, Fixed Sights, *Modern*	100	200	250
Model 715-2, .357 Magnum, Double Action, 4-Barrel Set, Stainless Steel, Adjustable Sights, *Modern*	200	400	500
Model 715-2, .357 Magnum, Various Barrel Lengths, Double Action, Stainless Steel, Adjustable Sights, *Modern*	$150	$225	$275
Model 715-2V, .357 Magnum, Double Action, 4-Barrel Set, Stainless Steel, Adjustable Sights, Vent Rib, *Modern*	200	400	500
Model 715-2V, .357 Magnum, Various Barrel Lengths, Double Action, Stainless Steel, Adjustable Sights, Vent Rib, *Modern*	150	275	350
Model 715-2VH, .357 Magnum, Double Action, 4-Barrel Set, Stainless Steel, Adjustable Sights, Vent Rib, Heavy Barrel, *Modern*	200	400	500
Model 744-V, .44 Magnum, Double Action, 4-Barrel Set, Stainless, Adjustable Sights, Vent Rib, *Modern*	300	500	600
Model 744-V, .44 Magnum, Various Barrel Lengths, Double Action, Stainless, Adjustable Sights, Vent Rib, *Modern*	200	300	400
Model 744-VH, .44 Magnum, Various Barrel Lengths, Double Action, Adjustable Sights, Stainless, Heavy Barrel, Vent Rib, *Modern*	300	650	700
Model 744-VH, .44 Magnum, Various Barrel Lengths, Double Action, Adjustable Sights, Stainless, Heavy Barrel, Vent Rib, *Modern*	200	400	500

Others:, 15-2 $20.00–$40.00; 15-2H $35.00–$55.00; 15-2V $35.00–$55.00; 15-2VH $40.00–$70.00; 44-V $55.00–$85.00; 44-VH; 715 $35.00–$55.00; 715V $45.00–$65.00; 715VH $50.00–$80.00; 744-V $60.00–$100.00; 44-VH $70.00–$110.00

WESSON, FRANK

Worcester, Mass., 1854 to 1865. 1865–1875 at Springfield, Mass. Also see U.S. Military, Wesson & Harrington, Harrington & Richardson.

HANDGUN, DOUBLE BARREL, OVER-UNDER

	Fair	*V. Good*	*Excellent*
Vest Pocket, .22 Short, Twist Barrel, Spur Trigger, *Antique*	350	700	1000
Vest Pocket, .32 Short, Twist Barrel, Spur Trigger, *Antique*	250	500	600
Vest Pocket, .41 Short, Twist Barrel, Spur Trigger, with Knife, *Antique*	500	1100	1500

HANDGUN, SINGLESHOT

	Fair	*V. Good*	*Excellent*
Model 1859, .22 Short, Tip-Up Barrel, Spur Trigger, *Antique*	200	400	500
Model 1859, .32 R.F., Tip-Up Barrel, Spur Trigger, *Antique*	200	450	600
Model 1859, .39 R.F., Tip-Up Barrel, Spur Trigger, *Antique*	200	450	600
Model 1862 Pocket Rifle, Various Calibers, Medium Frame, Spur Trigger, Target Sights, Detachable Stock, *Antique*	250	500	550

	Fair	V. Good	Excellent
Model 1862, .22 Short, Tip-Up Barrel, Spur Trigger, *Antique*	$100	$250	$300
Model 1862, .30 R.F., Tip-Up Barrel, Spur Trigger, *Antique*	200	450	600
Model 1862, .32 R.F., Tip-Up Barrel, Spur Trigger, *Antique*	200	450	600
Model 1870 Pocket Rifle, .22 Short, Small Frame, Spur Trigger, Target Sights, Detachable Stock, *Antique*	200	400	450
Model 1870 Pocket Rifle, Various Calibers, Large Frame, Spur Trigger, Target Sights, Detachable Stock, *Antique*	350	725	850
Model 1870 Pocket Rifle, Various Calibers, Medium Frame, Spur Trigger, Target Sights, Detachable Stock, *Antique*	200	400	500

RIFLE, SINGLESHOT

.32 Long R.F., Two-Trigger, Tip-Up, *Antique*	250	500	550

WESTERN ARMS CO.

HANDGUN, REVOLVER

.32 Long.F., 5 Shot, Folding Trigger, Double Action, *Antique*	50	75	100

WESTERN FIELD

Trade name for Montgomery Ward.

RIFLE, BOLT ACTION

Model 56 Buckhorn, .22 L.R.R.F., 5 Shot Clip, Open Rear Sight, *Modern*	25	50	75
Model 724, .30-06 Springfield, Checkered Stock, Full-Stocked, *Modern*	75	125	175
Model 732, .30-06 Springfield, Checkered Stock, Recoil Pad, *Modern*	75	125	175
Model 734, 7mm Rem. Mag., Checkered Stock, Recoil Pad, *Modern*	75	125	175
Model 765, .30-06 Springfield, Checkered Stock, *Modern*	50	100	150
Model 770, *Modern*	75	125	175
Model 78, Various Calibers, Checkered Stock, Sling Swivels, *Modern*	75	125	175
Model 780, Various Calibers, Checkered Stock, Sling Swivels, *Modern*	75	150	175
Model 815, .22 L.R.R.F., Singleshot, *Modern*	20	40	50
Model 822, .22 WMR, Clip Fed, *Modern*	20	40	50
Model 83, .22 L.R.R.F., Singleshot, Open Rear Sight, Takedown, *Modern*	20	40	50
Model 830, .22 L.R.R.F., Clip Fed, *Modern*	$20	$40	$50
Model 832, .22 L.R.R.F., Clip Fed, Checkered Stock, *Modern*	20	40	50
Model 84, *Modern*	20	40	50
Model 840, .22 WMR, Clip Fed, *Modern*	25	50	75
Model 852, .22 L.R.R.F., Clip Fed, *Modern*	20	40	50
Model 86, .22 L.R.R.F., Tube Feed, Takedown, Open Rear Sight, *Modern*	20	40	50
Modl 842, .22 L.R.R.F., Tube Feed, *Modern*	20	40	50

RIFLE, LEVER ACTION

Model 72, .30–30 Win., Pistol Grip Stock, Plain, Tube Feed, *Modern*	75	100	125
Model 72C, .30–30 Win., Straight Grip, Plain, Tube Feed, *Modern*	75	100	125
Model 79, .30–30 Win., Pistol Grip Stock, Plain, Tube Feed, *Modern*	75	100	125
Model 865, .22 L.R.R.F., Tube Feed, Sling Swivels, *Modern*	25	50	75
Model 895, .22 L.R.R.F., Tube Feed, Carbine, *Modern*	25	50	75

RIFLE, SELF-LOADING

Model 808, .22 L.R.R.F., Tube Feed, *Modern*	20	40	50
Model 828, .22 L.R.R.F., Clip Fed, Checkered Stock, *Modern*	25	50	75
Model 836, .22 L.R.R.F., Tube Feed, *Modern*	25	50	75
Model 846, .22 L.R.R.F., Tube Feed, *Modern*	25	50	75
Model 850, .22 L.R.R.F., Clip Fed, *Modern*	25	50	75
Model 880, .22 L.R.R.F., Tube Feed, *Modern*	50	50	50
Model M-1, .30 Carbine, Clip Fed, *Modern*	100	125	150

SHOTGUN, BOLT ACTION

Model 150, .410 Ga., Clip Fed, *Modern*	20	40	50
Model 172-5, 12 and 20 Gauges, Magnum, Clip Fed, Adjustable Choke, *Modern*	25	50	75

SHOTGUN, DOUBLE BARREL, SIDE-BY-SIDE

12 and 20 Gauges, Single Trigger, Hammerless, Checkered Stock, *Modern*	50	125	150
Long-Range, Various Gauges, Double Trigger, Hammerless, *Modern*	50	150	175
Long-Range, Various Gauges, Single Trigger, Hammerless, *Modern*	75	175	200
Model 330, Various Gauges, Hammerless, Checkered Stock, *Modern*	50	125	150

	Fair	V. Good	Excellent
Model 5151, Various Gauges, Hammerless, Steel Barrel, *Modern*	$50	$125	$150
Various Gauges, Hammerless, Plain, *Modern*	50	100	125

SHOTGUN, SELF-LOADING

	Fair	V. Good	Excellent
Model 60, 12 Ga., Takedown, Plain Barrel, Checkered Stock, *Modern*	75	125	150
Model 600, 12 Ga., Takedown, Vent Rib, Checkered Stock, *Modern*	75	125	150

SHOTGUN, SINGLESHOT

	Fair	V. Good	Excellent
Model 100, Various Gauges, Hammerless, Adjustable Choke, *Modern*	20	40	50
Trap, 12 Ga., Hammer, Solid Rib, Checkered Stock, *Modern*	50	125	150

SHOTGUN, SLIDE ACTION

	Fair	V. Good	Excellent
Model 500, .410 Ga., Plain, Takedown, *Modern*	75	100	125
Model 502, .410 Ga., Checkered Stock, Light Engraving, Takedown, Vent Rib, *Modern*	75	125	150
Model 520, 12 Ga., Takedown, *Modern*	75	100	125
Model 550, 12 and 20 Gauges, Checkered Stock, Light Engraving, Vent Rib, Takedown, *Modern*	75	125	150
Model 550, 12 and 20 Gauges, Checkered Stock, Light Engraving, Vent Rib, Takedown, Adjustable Choke, *Modern*	75	125	150
Model 550, 12 and 20 Gauges, Plain, Takedown, *Modern*	75	100	125
Model 620, Various Gauges, Takedown, *Modern*	75	125	150

WESTLEY RICHARDS

Birmingham, England. Since 1812.

RIFLE, BOLT ACTION

	Fair	V. Good	Excellent
Stalker, Various Calibers, Express Sights, Fancy Wood, Fancy Checkering, Repeater, *Modern*	4000	8000	10000

RIFLE, DOUBLE BARREL, SIDE-BY-SIDE

	Fair	V. Good	Excellent
Best Quality, Various Calibers, Sidelock, Double Trigger, Fancy Engraving, Fancy Checkering, Express Sights, *Modern*	12000	27000	35000

SHOTGUN, DOUBLE BARREL, OVER-UNDER

	Fair	V. Good	Excellent
Owundo, 12 Ga., Sidelock, Single Selective Trigger, Selective Ejector, Fancy Engraving, Fancy Checkering, *Modern*	4500	10000	15000

SHOTGUN, DOUBLE BARREL, SIDE-BY-SIDE

	Fair	V. Good	Excellent
10 Ga. Pinfire, Engraved, Carbine, *Antique*	$400	$850	$950
Best, Pigeon, 12 Ga. Mag. 3", Sidelock, Hammerless, Fancy Engraving, Fancy Checkering, Double Trigger, *Modern*	7000	17500	22000
Best, Pigeon, 12 Ga. Mag. 3", Sidelock, Hammerless, Fancy Engraving, Fancy Checkering, Single Selective Trigger, *Modern*	8000	18500	22500
Best Quality, Various Gauges, Box Lock, Hammerless, Fancy Engraving, Fancy Checkering, Single Selective Trigger, *Modern*	3000	7000	8500
Best Quality, Various Gauges, Sidelock, Hammerless, Fancy Engraving, Fancy Checkering, Double Trigger, *Modern*	7000	17500	27500
Best Quality, Various Gauges, Sidelock, Hammerless, Fancy Engraving, Fancy Checkering, Single Selective Trigger, *Modern*	8000	20000	25000
Best Quality, Various Gauges, Sidelock, Hammerless, Fancy Engraving, Fancy Checkering, Double Trigger, *Modern*	4500	10000	13500
Deluxe Quality, Various Gauges, Box Lock, Hammerless, Fancy Engraving, Fancy Checkering, Double Trigger, *Modern*	3500	7000	9000
Deluxe Quality, Various Gauges, Box Lock, Hammerless, Fancy Engraving, Fancy Checkering, Single Selective Trigger, *Modern*	4000	8000	10000
Deluxe Quality, Various Gauges, Sidelock, Hammerless, Fancy Engraving, Fancy Checkering, Double Trigger, *Modern*	5500	13000	16500
Deluxe Quality, Various Gauges, Sidelock, Hammerless, Fancy Engraving, Fancy Checkering, Single Selective Trigger, *Modern*	6500	14000	18500
Model E, Various Gauges, Box Lock, Hammerless, Engraved, Double Trigger, Selective Ejector, *Modern*	2200	5000	6000
Model E, Various Gauges, Box Lock, Hammerless, Engraved, Double Trigger, *Modern*	1600	4000	4750
Model E Pigeon, 12 Ga. Mag. 3", Box Lock, Hammerless, Engraved, Double Trigger, Selective Ejector, *Modern*	1800	4000	5000
Model E Pigeon, 12 Ga. Mag. 3", Box Lock, Hammerless, Engraved, Double Trigger, *Modern*	1800	4250	5250

410 ga. add 50%
28 ga. add 30%

	Fair	V. Good	Excellent
SHOTGUN, SINGLESHOT			
12 Ga., Trap Grade, Vent Rib, Fancy Engraving, Fancy Checkering, Hammerless, *Modern*	$1200	$4000	$5500
12 Ga., Vent Rib, Plain, Monte Carlo Stock, Trap Grade, *Modern*	1200	2500	3000

WESTON, EDWARD

Sussex, England, 1800–1835.

	Fair	V. Good	Excellent
HANDGUN, FLINTLOCK			
.67, Pair, Dueling Pistols, Octagon Barrel, Silver Furniture, Plain, *Antique*	1800	4000	5500

WHEEL LOCK EXAMPLES

	Fair	V. Good	Excellent
COMBINATION WEAPON, PISTOL			
German, 1500s War-Hammer, All Metal, *Antique*	4500	12000	15000
HANDGUN, WHEEL LOCK			
Augsburg, Late 1500s, Ball Pommel, Engraved, Ornate, *Antique*	8000	18000	22500

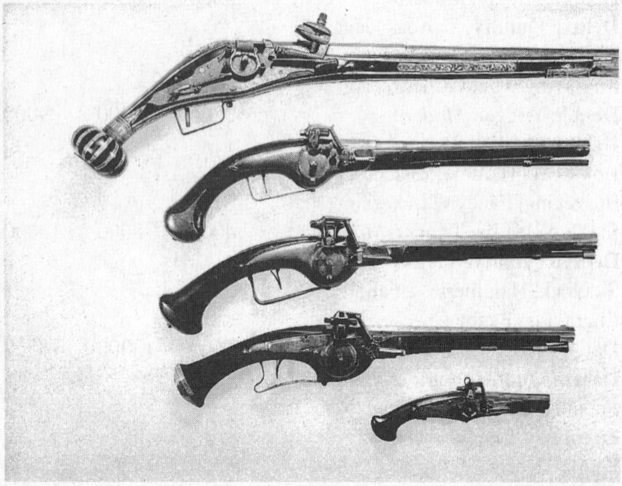

Wheel lock pistols, from the top, *German 16th-century ball-butt; military pistol with 14½" part round, part octagonal barrel; another military, perhaps English; French of c. 1700 with ebony stock and chased silver butt cap, ferrules, and forend mount; miniature-size pistol of only 9" overall length, one of smallest military wheel locks made.*

	Fair	V. Good	Excellent
Brescian, Mid-1600s, Military, Fish-Tail Butt, Plain, *Antique*	750	2000	3000
Embellished Original, Ornate, *Antique*	1450	2500	4000
Enclosed Lock German, Mid 1600s, Engraved, Holster Pistol, *Antique*	2200	3000	4250
Enclosed Lock, Late 1600s, Military, Plain, *Antique*	$750	$1500	$2750
English, Mid 1600s, Military, Holster Pistol, Plain, *Antique*	750	1500	2750
English, Mid 1600s, Ornate, *Antique*	8000	18000	23500
Franch, Early 1600s, Military, Silver Inlays, *Antique*	1400	2500	3600
German Puffer, Late 1500s, Horn Inlays, Ball Pommel, *Antique*	3000	8000	11500
German Style, Reproduction, Engraved, Inlays, High Quality, *Antique*	800	1400	2200
German, 1600, Dagger-Handle Butt, Military, Plain, *Antique*	1200	2500	3250
German, Late 1500s, Carved, Horn Inlays, Ball Pommel, Flattened, *Antique*	7000	14500	18000
German, Mid-1500s, Horn Inlays, Dagger-Handle Butt, Gold and Silver Damascened, Ornate, *Antique*	9000	20000	25000
German, Mid-1600s, Military, Fish-Tail Butt, Plain, *Antique*	625	1250	2000
Italian, 1500s, Dagger-Handle, External Mechanism, *Antique*	4500	15000	18500
Late 1500s Odd Butt, all Metal, Engraved, Ornate, *Antique*	4000	9000	12500
Old Reproduction, High Quality, *Antique*	600	1200	1800
Pair Brescian, Mid-1600s, Inlays, Engraved, Ornate, Fish-Tail Butt, *Antique*	9000	18000	26500
Pair Dutch, Mid-1600s, Holster Pistol, Gold Damascened, Inlays, Ornate, *Antique*	9000	18000	26500
Pair Saxon, Late 1500s, Ball Pommel, Inlays, Engraved, *Antique*	12000	24000	32500
Pair Saxon, Late 1500s, Ball Pommel, Light Ornamentation, *Antique*	4500	12000	15000
Pair Saxon, Late 1500s, Ball Pommel, Medium Ornamentation, *Antique*	8000	18000	22500
Saxon, Dated 1579, Horn Inlays, Engraved, Ball Pommel, *Antique*	3000	7000	10000
Saxon, Double Barrel, Over-Under, Inlays, Ornate, Ball Pommel, *Antique*	11000	24000	32500
Saxon, Late 1500s, Ball Pommel, Checkered Stock, Military, Plain, *Antique*	2000	5000	7500
RIFLE, WHEELLOCK			
Brandenburg 1620, Cavalry Rifle, Military, *Antique*	3000	7000	9500

WHIPPET

Made by Stevens Arms.

	Fair	V. Good	Excellent
SHOTGUN, SINGLESHOT			
Model 94A, Various Gauges, Hammer, Automatic Ejector, *Modern*	25	50	75

WHITE POWDER WONDER

Made by Stevens Arms.

SHOTGUN, SINGLESHOT

	Fair	V. Good	Excellent
Model 90, Various Gauges, Takedown, Automatic Ejector, Plain, Hammer, *Modern*	$25	$50	$75

WHITE STAR

c. 1880.

HANDGUN, REVOLVER

	Fair	V. Good	Excellent
.32 Short R.F., 5 Shot, Spur Trigger, Solid Frame, Single Action, *Antique*	75	150	175

WHITE, ROLLIN ARMS CO.

Hartford, Conn., 1849–1858; Lowell, Mass., 1864–1892.

HANDGUN, REVOLVER

	Fair	V. Good	Excellent
.22 Short R.F., 7 Shot, Spur Trigger, Tip-Up, *Antique*	150	425	600

HANDGUN, SINGLESHOT

	Fair	V. Good	Excellent
SS Pocket, .32 Cal., no Triggerguard, *Antique*	200	500	700

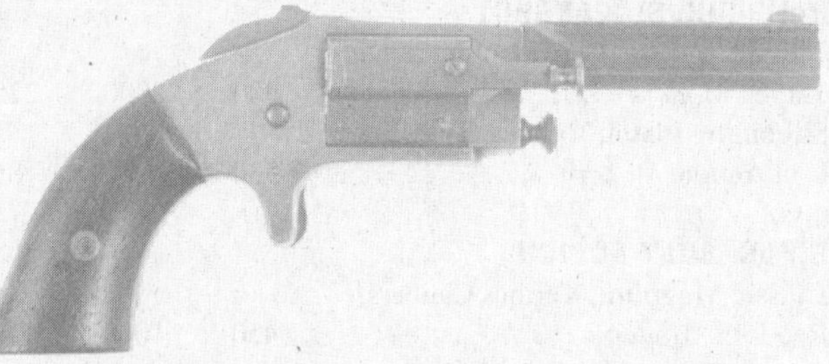

Rollin White Singleshot Pocket Pistol, .32 Caliber

WHITNEY ARMS CO.

New Haven, Conn., 1866–1876, also see U.S. Military.

HANDGUN, PERCUSSION

	Fair	V. Good	Excellent
Eagle Navy, .36, 6 Shot, Colt 1851 Type, *Antique*	700	1500	1850
Hooded Cylinder, .28, 6 Shot, Hammer, *Antique*	900	2000	2350
New Pocket Model, .28, 6 Shot, Single Action, *Antique*	300	625	800
Pocket Model, .31, 5 Shot, Single Action, *Antique*	300	675	850
Whitney Navy, .36, 6 Shot, *Antique*	500	750	1250
Whitney-Beals Walking Beam Pocket Revolver, .31 6 Shot, *Antique*	500	1000	1350
Whitney-Beals, .31, Ring Trigger, 7 Shot, *Antique*	1100	2500	3500

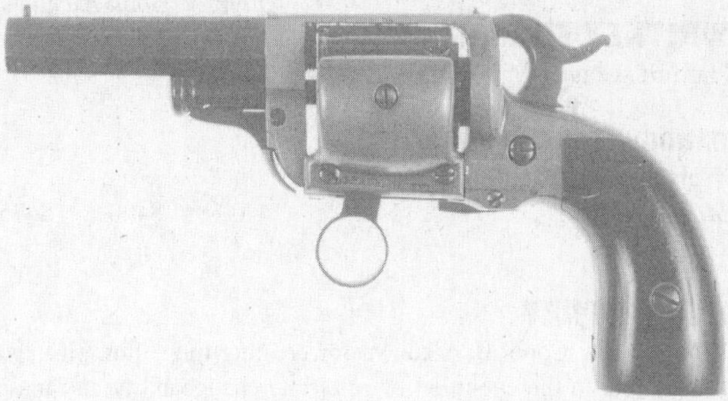

Whitney-Beals Walking Beam Pocket Revolver, .31 Caliber

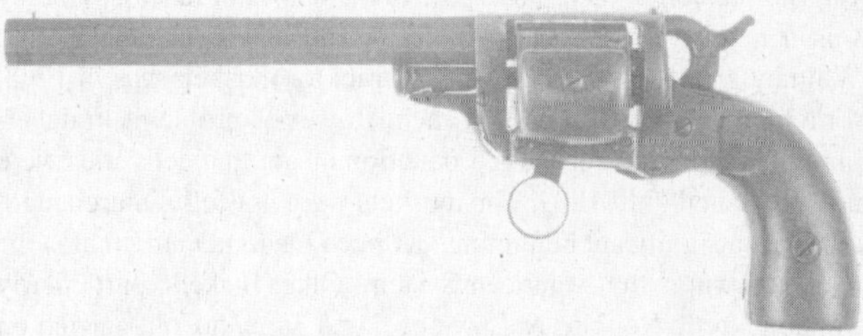

Whitney-Beals Standard Revolver, .31 Caliber

HANDGUN, REVOLVER

	Fair	V. Good	Excellent
.22 Short R.F., 7 Shot, Spur Trigger, Solid Frame, Single Action, *Antique*	$100	$275	$325
.32 Short R.F., 5 or 6 Shots, Spur Trigger, Solid Frame, Single Action, *Antique*	100	225	275
.38 Short R.F., 5 Shot, Spur Trigger, Solid Frame, Single Action, *Antique*	100	275	325

RIFLE, LEVER ACTION

	Fair	V. Good	Excellent
Kennedy, Various Calibers, Tube Feed, Plain, *Antique*	600	1250	1750
Model 1886, Various Calibers, Tube Feed, Plain, *Antique*	700	1750	2350

RIFLE, SINGLESHOT

	Fair	V. Good	Excellent
Phoenix, Various Calibers, Carbine, Hammer, *Antique*	800	1750	2000
Phoenix, Various Calibers, Rifle, Hammer, *Antique*	900	2000	2350
Rolling Block, Various Calibers, Carbine, *Antique*	400	1000	1350
Rolling Block, Various Calibers, Rifle, *Antique*	400	900	1150
Whitney-Howard, .44 R.F., Carbine, Lever Action, *Antique*	600	1200	1500
Whitney-Howard, .44 R.F., Rifle, Lever Action, *Antique*	500	1000	1350

SHOTGUN, DOUBLE BARREL, SIDE-BY-SIDE

	Fair	V. Good	Excellent
12 Ga., Damascus Barrel, Outside Hammers, *Antique*	100	550	750

WHITNEY FIREARMS CO.

Hartford, Conn., 1955–1962.

HANDGUN, SINGLESHOT

	Fair	V. Good	Excellent
Wolverine, .22 L.R.R.F., Blue, *Modern*	$200	$400	$475

ELI WHITNEY

Whitneyville, Conn. Best known for creating the cotton gin, and for his role in the evolution of parts interchangeability and mass production, Eli Whitney (1765–1826) is one of the most renowned of all American inventors and entrepreneurs. Though the concept of parts interchangeability appears first to have come to America via Thomas Jefferson (while U.S. Ambassador to France), Whitney was a nearly, though not completely, unsuccessful practitioner. Whitney's first U.S government contract for muskets was in 1798, for a total of 10,000, at $13.40 each. However, problems in developing his programs for mass production meant that deliveries were not completed until 1809. The muskets were not fully interchangeable, but a significant beginning had been made toward what came to be known as the American System. Other makers, particularly Simeon North, Robbins & Lawrence, and Samuel Colt, carried on to pioneer a system which came to be copied, and admired, by enlightened manufacturers worldwide. Long before Henry Ford, the American firearms industry established true parts interchangeability and mass production, often with government support and with assistance from the national armories at Springfield and Harpers Ferry. Other federal contracts were awarded to Whitney, whose armory facilities were set up in a town, fittingly called Whitneyville. From 1812 to 1824, 33,000 more muskets were contracted from the Whitney Armory by the federal governments, and several thousand more from the states for militia units: the New York and Connecticut Contract Pre-1812 Muskets, U.S. and Massachusetts Contract 1812 Muskets, 1822 U.S. Contract Musket, South Carolina Contract 1816 Musket, Composite 1816 Musket, and the 1816 Massachusetts Percussion Conversion. Only military arms are believed to have been manufactured by the Whitney family, during the founder's lifetime. Following Whitney's death, January 8, 1826, the Armory carried on under direction of nephews Philos and Eli Whitney Blake, who in turn were succeeded by Eli Whitney, Jr. (1842). Among the firm's later production were 17,600 Model 1841 "Mississippi Rifles" (through 1855), 15,001 rifled-muskets, and approximately 11,214 revolvers in the Civil War period. A little known fact is that the Walker Colt revolvers were manufactured by the Whitney Armory, on contract for Samuel Colt. Many of the parts had been subcontracted, with final assembly at Whitneyville. Whitney and Colt had a profit-sharing agreement, and Colt retained ownership of machinery built or purchased for the Walker production. Unfortunately, Eli Whitney, Jr. lacked the inventive genius and business skills of his father. Attempts at re-servicing surplus firearms, buying out parts from such firms as the Robbins & Lawrence factory, and other schemes, proved largely unsuccessful. Following the Civil War Whitney greatly expanded the company's product line, even including rolling block and hinged-breech singleshot rifles, lever-action repeating rifles, and a double-barreled shotgun. Approximately 30,000 breechloading rimfire metallic cartridge revolvers were made, from 1871–79. Some of the longarm products were manufactured for other inventors. The firearms industry was highly competitive, especially following the Civil War, and Whitney, suffering business losses, began seeking a buyer for the Armory as early as 1883. In 1888 the Winchester Repeating Arms Co. bought the Whitney Armory, moving much of the machinery to New Haven, and selling out remaining stocks of firearms. Today the Whitney Armory site is occupied by the Eli Whitney Museum of Invention, founded by the late Merrill K. Lindsay. Among surviving buildings are the Whitney barn and employee dormitory, the water turbine–powered electric works, a blacksmith/foundry site, the reproduction Towne-patent covered bridge, and a factory building serving as museum offices, exhibit space (including the Anthony D. Darling Memorial Firearms Gallery), and workshops.

WHITNEYVILLE ARMORY

See Whitney Arms Co.

WHITWORTH

Made in England, imported by Interarms.

RIFLE, BOLT ACTION

	Fair	V. Good	Excellent
Express, Various Calibers, Checkered Stock, *Modern*	$250	$550	$800

WICHITA ARMS CO.

HANDGUN, SINGLESHOT

	Fair	V. Good	Excellent
Classic, Various Calibers, Singleshot, Target, *Modern*	900	2000	2250
Silhouette Pistol, Various Calibers, Bolt Action, *Modern*	350	750	850

RIFLE, BOLT ACTION

	Fair	V. Good	Excellent
Classic Magnum, Various Calibers, Repeater, *Modern*	450	1000	1250
Classic Silhouette, Various Calibers, Singleshot, Target, *Modern*	550	1250	1500
Classic Varmint, Various Calibers, Repeater, Target, *Modern*	600	1250	1500

WICKLIFFE

Triple-S Development, Wickliffe, Ohio. (Discontinued).

RIFLE, SINGLESHOT

	Fair	V. Good	Excellent
Deluxe, Various Calibers, Falling Block, *Modern*	150	350	400
Standard, Various Calibers, Falling Block, *Modern*	150	300	350
Stinger Deluxe, Various Calibers, Falling Block, *Modern*	150	350	400
Stinger Standard, Various Calibers, Falling Block, *Modern*	150	300	350
Traditional 1st, Various Calibers, Falling Block, Modern	150	300	350

WIDE AWAKE
Made by Hood Fire Arms, Norwich, Conn., c. 1875.

HANDGUN, REVOLVER

	Fair	V. Good	Excellent
.32 Short R.F., 5 Shot, Spur Trigger, Solid Frame, Single Action, *Antique*	$75	$150	$175

WILKINSON ARMS
Parma, Idaho.

HANDGUN, SELF-LOADING

	Fair	V. Good	Excellent
Linda, 9mm Luger, Clip Fed, Blue, *Modern*	125	250	300

WILKINSON ARMS
South El Monte, Calif., c. 1976.

HANDGUN, SELF-LOADING

	Fair	V. Good	Excellent
Diane, .25 ACP, Clip Fed, Blue, *Modern*	50	100	125

WILKINSON ARMS CO.
Made in Belgium for Richmond Hardware Co., Richmond, Va., c. 1900.

SHOTGUN, DOUBLE BARREL, SIDE-BY-SIDE

	Fair	V. Good	Excellent
Various Gauges, Hammerless, Damascus Barrel, *Modern*	50	150	175
Various Gauges, Outside Hammers, Steel Barrel, *Modern*	50	175	200
Various Gauges, Hammerless, Steel Barrel, *Modern*	50	175	200
Various Gauges, Outside Hammers, Damascus Barrel, *Modern*	50	150	175

SHOTGUN, SINGLESHOT

	Fair	V. Good	Excellent
Various Gauges, Hammer, Steel Barrel, *Modern*	25	50	75

WILLIAMS, FREDERICK
Birmingham, England, 1893–1929.

SHOTGUN, DOUBLE BARREL, SIDE-BY-SIDE

	Fair	V. Good	Excellent
Gga., Damascus Barrel, Outside Hammers, Checkered Stock, Engraved, *Antique*	200	400	550

WILLIAMSON, DAVID
Brooklyn, N.Y., and Greenville, N.J., 1864–1874. Also see Moore's Patent Firearms, Co.

HANDGUN, SINGLESHOT

	Fair	V. Good	Excellent
.41 Short R.F., Derringer, Nickel Plated, *Antique*	200	400	450

WILLIS, RICHARD
Lancaster, Pa., c. 1776. See Kentucky Rifles and Pistols.

WILMONT ARMS CO.
Belgium, c. 1900.

SHOTGUN, DOUBLE BARREL, SIDE-BY-SIDE

	Fair	V. Good	Excellent
Various Gauges, Hammerless, Damascus Barrel, *Modern*	$50	$150	$175
Various Gauges, Outside Hammer, Steel Barrel, *Modern*	100	225	325
Various Gauges, Hammerless, Steel Barrel, *Modern*	50	175	200
Various Gauges, Outside Hammer, Damascus Barrel, *Modern*	100	225	300

SHOTGUN, SINGLESHOT

	Fair	V. Good	Excellent
Various Gauges, Hammer, Steel Barrel, *Modern*	25	50	75

WILSON, R.
London, England, 1720–1750.

SHOTGUN, FLINTLOCK

	Fair	V. Good	Excellent
Fowling, 9 Ga., Queen Anne Style, Half-Stock, *Antique*	600	1250	1750

WILTSHIRE ARMS CO.
Belgium, c. 1900.

SHOTGUN, DOUBLE BARREL, SIDE-BY-SIDE

	Fair	V. Good	Excellent
Various Gauges, Hammerless, Damascus barrel, *Modern*	50	150	175
Various Gauges, Outside Hammers, Steel Barrel, *Modern*	50	175	200
Various Gauges, Hammerless, Steel Barrel, *Modern*	50	175	200
Various Gauges, Outside Hammers, Damascus Barrel, *Modern*	50	150	175

SHOTGUN, SINGLESHOT

	Fair	V. Good	Excellent
Various Gauges, Hammer, Steel Barrel, *Modern*	25	50	75

WINCHESTER REPEATING ARMS CO.

WINCHESTER AND ITS PREDECESSOR ARMS
The company's complex history began with the Jennings Rifle and has continued with numerous upward and downward movements through today's split identity: the Winchester Division of Olin (makers of ammunition only), and the U.S. Repeating Arms Co. (established 1981; makers of firearms).

THE NEW HAVEN ARMS CO. AND ITS PREDECESSOR FIRMS
With its roots as far back as 1849, Winchester is the world's oldest manufacturer of lever-action repeating firearms. Early models

which led up to the Winchester were the Hunt, Jennings, Volcanic, and Henry Rifle, and the succession of companies evolving concurrently with these products were Smith & Wesson, the Volcanic Repeating Arms Co., and the New Haven Arms Co. In the early years of development the fortunes of what became Winchester and what became Smith & Wesson were one and the same, in Norwich, Connecticut. Many would argue that it was the Winchester that won the West, and rifles of that make were the most sought after of repeating longarms in the saga of the Great American West. At its peak during World War II, Winchester was the largest gun and cartridge maker in the world with over 61,000 employees (including Western Cartridge Co.). In ammunition alone, Winchester remains the world's largest. The marque is recognized as one of history's most famous brand names.

THE VOLCANIC RIFLES AND PISTOLS

One of the most sought after of all firearms from the genre Winchester is the Volcanic. Built originally as the Smith & Wesson Volcanic, these arms were lever-action, constructed first in Norwich, Connecticut, and then in New Haven. Site of manufacture will be revealed by barrel markings. Lucky Winchester employees after World War II were offered unfired New Haven Volcanics which still remained unsold, left over from the 1850s! At that time specimens were made available at prices far below what they were sold for when originally produced. Old-time employee Harry Sefried remembers when these guns were sold from stock, and was one of the fortunate purchasers.

THE HENRY RIFLE

One of the most notable of all the early Winchester predecessor arms, the Henry Rifle was the first of the product line to prove practical and successful. Inventor, gunmaker, mechanic, and New Haven Arms Co. plant superintendent B. Tyler Henry was involved with lever-action repeating arms since as early as 1857. Henry was granted a patent in October of 1860 covering his new rifle with a rimfire metallic cartridge, replacing the impractical self-contained leader, powder, and primer projectile used in the Volcanic series. The new rimfire ammunition was vital to making the new Henry Rifle a practical firearm. In fact, the cartridge bore an H headstamp, in Henry's honor, and the rifle was named in his honor as well. Financial backing by O. F. Winchester was instrumental in the tooling up for manufacture of the Henry. Business was given a boost by demands of the Civil War, and the first Henrys were in field use by the middle of 1862. Although U.S. government orders were relatively few, private orders were instrumental in making the Henry the first successful lever-action firearm. Approximately 14,000 were produced, from 1860 to 1866.

Variations

Iron-Frame Henrys: Serial numbered from 1 to approximately 400; blue frames, with rounded-style buttplate and no lever latch.*

Early Brass Frame Rifles: Similar to Iron Frame, though some with lever latch; serial range 1 to approximately 1500.

Late Brass Frame Rifles: Heel of buttplate with pointed profile; lever latch present; serial range of most above approximately 2500. Some of these purchased by Union companies, especially from Illinois, Indiana, Kentucky, and Missouri.

U.S. Government Issue Rifles: Approximately 1731 (1862–65), with most in range 3000 to 4200. U.S. rifles with "C.G.C." inspector markings on barrel breech and stock.

*Possibly made for New Haven Arms by Colt's Pt. F. A. Mfg. Co.

THE MODEL 1866

Successor to the Henry was the Model 1866, the first Winchester to bear the name of the major stockholder and company president, O. F. Winchester himself. This was the arm known to Native Americans as "the yellow boy," due to its brass frame. Oliver F. Winchester, a New Haven shirtmaker and skilled businessman, had gradually increased his investments in the Volcanic operation. That struggling company evolved slowly for a few years, accumulating debt. But with the perfection of both a rimfire cartridge and a lever-action firearm, the reception given the Henry Rifle finally rewarded Winchester's entrepreneurial courage. Henry sales were followed quickly thereafter by the Model 1866—which reached over 170,000 by 1898. Even more popular was the Model 1873, with a total production run of over 720,000.

MODEL 1873 LEVER ACTION

The Winchester Model 1873 was designed with mechanical ingenuity and made with advanced manufacturing techniques—such as mass production—decades before Henry Ford and the automobile. Further, this classic Winchester was graceful and handsome in line and form. The Model 1873 was first offered in the new .44-40 cartridge and was built in carbine, rifle, and musket configurations. This model played a vital role in Winchester's emergence as the predominant maker of longarms and ammunition in America. A feature of the new rifle was a reloading tool, a design patented by the major stockholder's son William Wirt Winchester. Genuine American frontier hero and world class show business superstar William F. "Buffalo Bill" Cody wrote of the '73: "I have been using and have thoroughly tested your latest improved rifle. Allow me to say that I have tried and used nearly every kind of a gun made in the United States, and for general hunting, or Indian fighting, I pronounce your improved Winchester *the boss.*" Researching Winchester factory shipping ledgers allows for identifying the original features of most Model 1873s. However, although this data reveals when a '73 came to the shipping department and when it left, the records rarely indicate the destination. The number of variations of the '73—in barrels, sights, magazines, finishes, stocks, engraving, and various mechanical and physical configurations—is substantial. Trying to "own them all" is a virtual impossibility to the collector who wants to have each and every variant. Most glamorous and appealing of the variations of the Model 1873 was the One of One Thousand and One of One Hundred series. These special rifles helped capture for Winchester an image of prestige, quality, and performance. Only 133 Model 1873 One of One Thousands were made, and only eight One of One Hundreds. Each had a specially selected barrel, tested for extreme accuracy. The barrel breeches were engraved with the designations 1 of 1000 or 1 of 100, in numerals or spelled out in script letters. A similar series was built in the Model 1876, totaling fifty-one One of One Thousands and seven One of One Hundreds. Judging from a variety of sources, including period photographs, documents, and surviving firearms, the patrons of the Model 1873 comprised a broad spectrum from the expectable—ranchers and cowboys—to a litany of some of the most colorful characters of the late 19th and early 20th centuries: William F. "Buffalo Bill" Cody, Annie Oakley, Pawnee Bill Lilly, Doc Carver "Champion Rifle Shot of the World," and any number of other Wild West show personalities; frontier lawmen like Pat Garrett, numerous Texas Rangers; outlaws like Billy the Kid; stagecoach and express guards; and sportsmen like the indomitable Theodore Roosevelt, the best-known Winchester devotee of all time. Hollywood has long played a role in the immortalization of the '73: The One of One Thousand series inspired the only Hollywood Western movie name for a specific model of Winchester—*Winchester '73*, starring James Stewart (1950). Gene Autry, Roy Rogers, Burt Lancaster, Kirk Douglas, Steve McQueen, Clint Eastwood, and Kevin Costner, to name a few, have all used '73 models in films or on television. With its handsome lines and captivating history and romance, more collectors and Wild West enthusiasts are attracted to the Model 1873 than to any other Winchester. Not only did its production total exceed most lever-action Winchesters, the models' popularity is reflected in its use in Western films and television productions, in endless fictional and factual books of the West, in historic photographs, and in the proliferation of modern replicas. Manufacture was from 1873 to 1919, and sales from inventory continued through c. 1925; the total made was in excess of 720,610. Calibers were .44-40, .38-40, and .32-20, with a special variation (lacking loading gate aperture on the sideplate) in .22 rimfire.

Variations

Early First Model: From serial 1 to about 28000; dust cover (an innovation of the Model 1873) with guide grooves at front of frame; separately secured oval thumbrest motif on dust cover; two screws located above trigger on frame

Late First Model: Serial range of about 28000 to 31000; similar type dust cover with oval checkered thumbrest; trigger pin under two frame screws, over trigger.

Second Model: Serial range of about 31000 to 90000; center rail mount for dust cover at rear of frame; checkered oval thumbrest panel later replaced by serrated style edges.

Third Model: Serial range of about 90000 to end of production; dust cover rail mounting now integral with frame; two frame screws and pin near trigger no longer present.

JOHN M. BROWNING AND WINCHESTER

Thanks to the long-time association between John Browning and Winchester, a string of rifle and shotgun designs were developed, entering into manufacture such recognizable rifle models as the 1879 single-shot and the lever-action 1886, 1892, 1894, and 1895, plus miscellaneous pump-action rifles and shotguns, a bolt-action rifle, and a lever-action shotgun. Oliver F. Winchester's son-in-law, Thomas G. Bennett, contracted with John Browning for the 1879 single-shot, following up with arrangements for manufacture of what became an unequaled product line. So prolific was Browning that Winchester's policy was to purchase rights to every design which he offered, to avoid other firms having access to the brilliant inventor's output. Over three quarters of Browning's designs never entered into manufacture; those that did, however, served as the basis for the Winchester line from the middle of the 1880s well into the 20th century. With a production run of over a century, and a total made in excess of six million, the Model 1894 holds the record as the most popular lever-action rifle ever made, and the most popular arms design sold to Winchester by Browning. Inspired by the adoption of smokeless powder late in the 19th century, John Browning created the Model 1894 soon after his design of the Model 1892. The profile of the 1894 was strikingly similar to the 1892, which used a vertical bolt locking system. A flat plate which pivots at the bottom of the breech is the most visible distinguishing feature of the Model 94 from the Model 92. In announcing the new rifle, Winchester noted: "We believe that no repeating rifle system ever made will appeal to the eye and understanding of the rifleman as this will and that use will continue to warrant first impressions." This prophetic statement is borne out by the fact that the Model 94 is the company's all-time best-selling centerfire rifle, of any model or configuration. In the long production run of the Model 1894 no major design changes have been made other than the introduction of side ejection (1983), the hammer block system (1984), the cross-bolt hammer stop (1992), as well as adoption of the .22 rimfire Model 9422 (1972) and of the .375 Winchester Big Bore Model 94 (1979). The .22 and .375 rifles have their own serial number ranges. Although initially marketed in the blackpowder cartridges of .32-40 and .38-55, the Model 1894 was the first lever-action repeating rifle to be made and marketed specifically for ammunition using smokeless powder. The new chamberings were .25-35 Winchester and .30–30 Winchester. The latter became the all-time classic of deer-hunting cartridges, as did the rifle which to this day utilizes that cartridge more than any other: the equally classic deer rifle, the Model 94. Two other variations of the Model 1894 were the Models 55 and 64. The Model 55 was built from 1924 through 1932, with a total of more than 20,500. The Model 64 was marketed from 1933 to 1957, and over 66,700 were made. At the same time the '94 remained in production in the carbine version only. These offspring were outlived by the venerable '94, whose immortality seems assured. Production of the Model 1894 continued from 1894 to date, with total production exceeding six million by 1997.

Model 1894 Variations (basic types, numerous variants over the years)

Rifle: 26" octagonal barrel; case hardened hammer, lever, trigger, buttplate.

Rifle: Blued finish.

Rifle: Blued finish, with round barrel.

Extra Light Weight Rifle: Barrel lengths from 22" to 26"; rapid taper round barrel, shotgun buttplate on straight buttstock.

Takedown Model Rifle: Dismantling system mounted at muzzle end of magazine tube.

Carbine: 20" round barrel; made with or without saddle ring on left side of frame through 1925; carbine sights; shotgun buttplate.

Trapper's Model Carbine: Barrels at lengths of 14", 16", and 18"; saddle ring may not be present.

Numerous variations in markings and finishes in a number of commemorative configurations based on the Model 94 (see Commemoratives listing).

Model 55 rifle

Model 64 rifle

RIFLE, BOLT ACTION

	Fair	*V. Good*	*Excellent*
Hotchkiss 1st Model Fancy, .45-70 Gov't, Sporting Rifle, *Antique*	$800	$2000	$2650
Hotchkiss 1st Model, .40-65 Win., Sporting Rifle, *Antique*	500	1200	1600
Hotchkiss 1st Model, .45-70 Government, Carbine, *Antique*	500	1000	1250
Hotchkiss 1st Model, .45-70 Government, Military, Carbine, *Antique*	500	1000	1250
Hotchkiss 1st Model, .45-70 Government, Military, Rifle, *Antique*	900	2200	2650
Hotchkiss 2nd Model, .45-70 Government, Military, Rifle, *Antique*	600	1200	1600

	Fair	V. Good	Excellent
Hotchkiss 2nd Model, .45-70 Government, Navy Rifle, *Antique*	$600	$1200	$1500
Hotchkiss 2nd Model, .45-70 Government, Sporting Rifle, *Antique*	600	1200	1500
Hotchkiss 3rd Model, .45-70 Government, Military, Carbine, *Antique*	600	1200	1500
Hotchkiss 3rd Model, .45-70 Government, Military, Rifle, *Antique*	600	1200	1500
Lee Straight-Pull, 6mm Lee Navy, Musket, *Antique*	400	1000	1250
Lee Straight-Pull, 6mm Lee Navy, Sporting Rifle, *Antique*	350	700	900
M121 Deluxe, .22 L.R.R.F., Singleshot, *Modern*	50	100	175
M121, .22 L.R.R.F., Singleshot, *Modern*	75	100	150
M121-Y, .22 L.R.R.F., Singleshot, *Modern*	75	100	150
M131, .22 L.R.R.F., Clip Fed, Open Rear Sight, *Modern*	50	100	150
M135, .22 WMR, Clip Fed, *Modern*	50	100	150
M141, .22 WMR, Tube Feed, *Modern*	50	125	175
M145, .22 WMR, Tube Feed, *Modern*	50	125	175
M1900, .22 Long R.F., Singleshot, *Modern*	300	600	700
M1902, Various Rimfires, Singleshot, *Curio*	75	200	250
M1904, Various Rimfires, Singleshot, *Curio*	75	175	250
M43 Special Grade, Various Calibers, *Modern*	250	525	600
M43, Various Calibers, Sporting Rifle, *Modern*	200	475	550
M47, .22 L.R.R.F., Singleshot, *Modern*	100	200	250
M52 International Prone, .22 L.R.R.F., *Modern*	300	600	650
M52 International, .22 L.R.R.F., *Modern*	300	625	700
M52 Slow-Lock, .22 L.R.R.F., *Modern*	200	450	500
M52 Speed-Lock, .22 L.R.R.F., *Modern*	200	400	450
M52 Sporting, .22 L.R.R.F., Rifle, *Modern*	1000	2200	2650
M52, .22 L.R.R.F., Heavy Barrel, *Modern*	250	525	600
M52-B, .22 L.R.R.F., *Modern*	225	450	525
M52-B, .22 L.R.R.F., Bull Gun, *Modern*	250	575	625
M52-B, .22 L.R.R.F., Heavy Barrel, *Modern*	225	550	600
M52-B, .22 L.R.R.F., Sporting Rifle, *Modern*	1000	2200	2500

	Fair	V. Good	Excellent
M52-C, .22 L.R.R.F., *Modern*	$250	$550	$600
M52-C, .22 L.R.R.F., Bull Gun, *Modern*	250	575	650
M52-C, .22 L.R.R.F., Standard Target, *Modern*	250	550	600
M52-D, .22 L.R.R.F., *Modern*	225	475	525
M54, Various Calibers, Sporting Rifle, *Modern*	250	500	700
M54 Match, Various Calibers, Sniper Rifle, *Modern*	300	675	750
M54 National Match, Various Calibers, *Modern*	350	750	850
M54 Super Grade, Various Calibers, *Modern*	400	900	1200
M54 Target, Various Calibers, *Modern*	250	550	600
M54, .270 Win., Carbine, *Curio*	300	600	750
M54, .30-06 Springfield, Sniper Rifle, *Modern*	350	750	850
M54, Various Calibers, Carbine, *Modern*	300	650	750
M56, .22 L.R.R.F., Sporting Rifle, *Modern*	200	450	500
M57, Various Rimfires, Target, *Modern*	225	450	500
M58, .22 L.R.R.F., Singleshot, *Modern*	125	250	275
M59, .22 L.R.R.F., Singleshot, *Modern*	150	375	425
M60, .22 L.R.R.F., Singleshot, *Modern*	100	200	250
M60-A, .22 L.R.R.F., Target, Singleshot, *Modern*	125	325	400
M67 Boy's Rifle, Various Rimfires, Singleshot, *Modern*	75	150	250
M67, Various Rimfires, Singleshot, *Modern*	50	100	150
M68, Various Rimfires, Singleshot, *Modern*	75	125	150
M69 Match, .22 L.R.R.F., Clip Fed, *Modern*	100	200	250
M69 Target, .22 L.R.R.F., Clip Fed, *Modern*	100	200	250
M69, .22 L.R.R.F., Clip Fed, *Modern*	100	200	250
M70 Action Only, Various Calibers, Pre '64, *Modern*	150	300	350
M70 African, .458 Win. Mag., Pre '64, *Modern*	1200	3000	3750
M70 Alaskan, Various Calibers, Pre '64, Checkered Stock, *Modern*	800	1500	1700
M70 Barreled Action Only, Various Calibers, Pre '64, *Modern*	250	475	550
M70 Bull Gun, Various Calibers, Pre '64, Checkered Stock, *Modern*	600	1250	1500
M70 Carbine, Various Calibers, Pre '64, Checkered Stock, *Modern*	600	1250	1500
M70 Featherweight Sporter Grade, Various Calibers, Pre '64, Checkered Stock, *Modern*	700	1500	1750

	Fair	V. Good	Excellent
M70 Featherweight, Various Calibers, Pre '64, Checkered Stock, *Modern*	$400	$775	$900
M70 National Match, .30-06 Springfield, Pre '64, *Modern*	450	900	1100
M70 Target, Various Calibers, Pre '64, Checkered Stock, *Modern*	500	900	1100
M70 Varmint, Various Calibers, Pre '64, Checkered Stock, *Modern*	400	900	1100
M70 Westerner, Various Calibers, Pre '64, Checkered Stock, *Modern*	350	650	800
M70, For Mint Unfired, Pre '64, Add 25%			
M70, for Pre-War, Add 25%–50%			
M72, .22 L.R.R.F., Tube Feed, *Modern*	100	225	275
M75 Target, .22 L.R.R.F., Clip Fed, *Modern*	200	450	500
M75, .22 L.R.R.F., Sporting Rifle, Clip Fed, *Modern*	300	625	700
M99 Thumb Trigger, Various Rimfires, Singleshot, *Modern*	450	1000	1250
Model 52 I.M. Kenyon, .22 L.R.R.F., Post '64, Heavy Barrel, Target Stock, *Modern*	200	450	500
Model 52 I.M., .22 L.R.R.F., Post '64, Heavy Barrel, Target Stock, *Modern*	200	425	475
Model 52 I.M.I.S.U., .22 L.R.R.F., Post '64, Heavy Barrel, Target Stock, *Modern*	250	525	575
Model 52 International Prone, .22 L.R.R.F., Post '64, Heavy Barrel, Target Stock, *Modern*	200	425	475
Model 52D, .22 L.R.R.F., Post '64, Heavy Barrel, Target Stock, *Modern*	250	500	550
Model 677, Various Calibers, Post '64, Scope Mounted, *Modern*	250	500	600
Model 70 African, .458 Win. Mag., Post '64, Checkered Stock, Open Rear Sight, Magnum Action, *Modern*	300	600	675
Model 70 International Match, .308 Win., Post '64, Checkered Stock, Target Stock, *Modern*	250	575	650
Model 70 Standard, Various Calibers, Post '64, Checkered Stock, Open Rear Sight, *Modern*	150	275	325
Model 70 Target, Various Calibers, Post '64, Checkered Stock, Target Stock, *Modern*	200	475	525
Model 70 Varmint, Various Calibers, Post '64, Checkered Stock, Heavy Barrel, *Modern*	150	300	350
Model 70, Various Calibers, Pre '64, Checkered Stock, Open Rear Sight, Magnum Action, *Modern*	300	600	750
Model 70A Police, Various Calibers, Post '64, *Modern*	125	250	300
Model 70A Standard, Various Calibers, Post '64, *Modern*	100	225	275

	Fair	V. Good	Excellent
Model 70A, Various Calibers, Post '64, Magnum Action, *Modern*	$150	$300	$350
Model 70XTR Featherweight, Various Calibers, No Sights, *Modern*	175	350	400
Model 70XTR Featherweight, Various Calibers, with Sights, *Modern*	200	400	450
Model 70XTR Super Express Magnum, .375 H&H, *Modern*	250	500	575
Model 70XTR Super Express Magnum, .458 Win., *Modern*	250	525	600
Model XTR Ranger, Various Calibers, No Scope, *Modern*	150	275	325
Model XTR Sporter, Various Calibers, *Modern*	150	325	375
Model XTR Varmint, Various Calibers, *Modern*	150	325	375

RIFLE, LEVER ACTION

	Fair	V. Good	Excellent
Henry, .44 Henry, Brass Frame, Military, Rifle, *Antique*	15000	50000	60000
Henry, .44 Henry, Brass Frame, Rifle, *Antique*	9000	40000	50000
Henry, .44 Henry, Iron Frame, Rifle, *Antique*	20000	60000	75000
M1866 Improved Henry, .44 Henry, Carbine, *Antique*	4000	12000	15000
M1866 Improved Henry, .44 Henry, Rifle, *Antique*	3500	12000	15000
M1866, .44 Henry, Rifle, *Antique*	6000	17500	22500

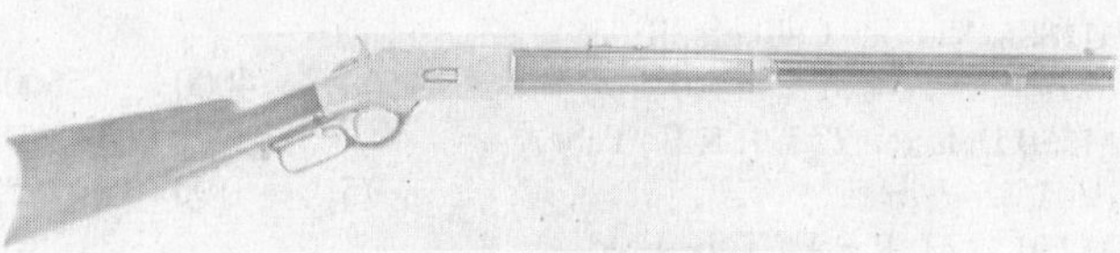

Winchester M1866

	Fair	V. Good	Excellent
M1873 1 of 1,000, Various Calibers, Rifle, *Antique*	25000	100000	125000
M1873, For Deluxe, Add $500.00–$750.00			
M1873, For Extra Fancy Deluxe, Add $5000.00–$7500.00			
M1873, under #525,299, Various Calibers, Carbine, *Antique*	1250	4000	5500
M1873, under #525,299, Various Calibers, Musket, *Antique*	1000	1750	2750
M1873, under #525,299, Various Calibers, Rifle, *Antique*	1000	3000	4250
M1873, Various Calibers, Carbine, Curio	1500	4000	5250
M1873, Various Calibers, Musket, *Curio*	1500	4000	5250

Winchester M1873

	Fair	V. Good	Excellent
M1873, Various Calibers, Rifle, *Curio*	$875	$4000	$5500
M1876 RCMP, Various Calibers, Carbine, *Antique*	3000	8000	9500
M1876, For Deluxe, Add $550.00–$750.00			
M1876, For Extra Fancy Deluxe, Add $5000.00–$7500.00			
M1876, Various Calibers, Carbine, *Antique*	2000	5000	7500
M1876, Various Calibers, Musket, *Antique*	4000	9000	11000
M1876, Various Calibers, Octagon Barrel, Rifle, *Antique*	2000	7000	8500
M1876, Various Calibers, Round Barrel, Rifle, *Antique*	2000	6000	7500
M1886, For Deluxe, Add $400.00-$750.00			
M1886, For Extra Fancy Deluxe, Add $3500.00-$5000.00			
M1886, under #118,433, Various Calibers, Carbine, *Antique*	3500	10000	12500
M1886, under #118,433, Various Calibers, Musket, *Antique*	6000	12000	15000
M1886, under #118,433, Various Calibers, Rifle, *Antique*	1500	4000	5500
M1886, Various Calibers, Carbine, *Curio*	4000	8000	9500
M1886, Various Calibers, Musket, *Curio*	5000	9000	10500
M1886, Various Calibers, Rifle, *Curio*	1500	4000	5500
M250 Deluxe, .22 L.R.R.F., Tube Feed, *Modern*	75	100	125
M250, .22 L.R.R.F., Tube Feed, *Modern*	50	75	100
M255 Deluxe, .22 WMR, Tube Feed, *Modern*	100	125	150
M255, .22 WMR, Tube Feed, *Modern*	75	100	125
M53, Various Calibers, *Modern*	900	2000	2500
M55, Various Calibers, *Modern*	450	1000	1250
M64 Deer Rifle, Various Calibers, Pre '64, *Modern*	700	1200	1500
M64, .219 Zipper, Pre '64, *Modern*	600	1750	2000
M64, .30–30 Win., Late Model, *Modern*	150	300	350
M64, Various Calibers, Pre '64, *Modern*	600	900	1200
M65, .218 Bee, *Modern*	1200	2500	3000
M65, Various Calibers, *Modern*	1200	2000	2500
M71 Special, .348 Win., Tube Feed, *Modern*	550	750	950
M71, .348 Win., Tube Feed, *Modern*	400	725	800
M92, For Takedown, Add $150.00-$275.00			
M92, under #103316, Various Calibers, Carbine, *Antique*	800	1750	2150
M92, under #103316, Various Calibers, Musket, *Antique*	4000	8500	9500
M92, under #103316, Various Calibers, Rifle, *Antique*	$700	$1800	$2150
M92, Various Calibers, Carbine, *Curio*	800	2000	2350
M92, Various Calibers, Musket, *Curio*	3500	7500	8500
M92, Various Calibers, Rifle, *Curio*	750	1800	2000
M92 44/40 cal. Add 25%			
M94 Standard, .30–30 Win., *Modern*	100	175	250

Winchester M94XTR Big Bore

	Fair	V. Good	Excellent
M94 Trapper, .30–30 Win., Pre '64, *Curio*	1000	2000	3750
M94, .30–30 Win., Carbine, Late Model, *Modern*	100	200	250
M94, .44 Magnum, Carbine, *Modern*	100	225	275
M94, under #50,000 Various Calibers, Carbine, *Antique*	900	2500	3000
M94, under #50,000 Various Calibers, Rifle, *Antique*	800	2000	2500
M94, Various Calibers, Carbine, Pre '64, *Modern*	300	600	700
M94, Various Calibers, Carbine, Pre-War, *Curio with Saddle Ring*	800	1800	2000
M94, Various Calibers, Rifle, Pre-War, *Curio*	900	1750	2000
M94, Various Calibers, Rifle, Takedown, Pre-War, *Curio*	800	2000	2250
M94XTR Big Bore, .375 Win., *Modern*	125	200	275
M94XTR, .30–30 Win., *Modern*	100	175	250
M95, For Takedown, Add $100.00–$200.00			
M95, under #19,477, Various Calibers, Carbine, *Antique*	700	1500	2250
M95, under #19,477, Various Calibers, Rifle, Antique	900	2000	2500
M95, Various Calibers, Carbine, *Curio*	800	2000	2500
M95, Various Calibers, Musket, *Curio*	500	1200	1500
M95, Various Calibers, Rifle, *Curio*	800	1800	2100
M95 in 405 Win. cal. Add 25%			
Model 9422, .22 L.R.R.F., Tube Feed, *Modern*	100	200	250
Model 9422M, .22 WMR, Tube Feed, *Modern*	125	250	275
Model 9422MXTR, .22 WMR, Tube Feed, *Modern*	125	300	325
Model 9422XTR, .22 L.R.R.F., Tube Feed, *Modern*	125	275	300

RIFLE, SELF-LOADING

	Fair	V. Good	Excellent
M100, Various Calibers, Clip Fed, *Modern*	$200	$400	$450
M100, Various Calibers, Clip Fed, Carbine, *Modern*	250	500	550
M190, .22 L.R.R.F., Tube Feed, *Modern*	75	100	125
M1903, .22 Win. Auto R.F., Tube Feed, *Curio*	150	350	400
M1905, Various Calibers, Clip Fed, *Curio*	200	500	550
M1907 Police, .351 Win. Self-Loading, Clip Fed, *Curio*	200	400	450
M1907, .351 Win. Self-Loading, Clip Fed, *Curio*	175	350	400
M1910, .401 Win. Self-Loading, Clip Fed, *Curio*	225	550	650
M290 Deluxe, .22 L.R.R.F., Tube Feed, *Modern*	75	125	150
M490 Deluxe, .22 L.R.R.F., Clip Fed, Monte Carlo Stock, *Modern*	100	200	225
M55 Automatic, .22 L.R.R.F., *Modern*	75	125	150
M63, .22 L.R.R.F., Tube Feed, *Modern*	200	400	550
M74, .22 L.R.R.F., Clip Fed, *Modern*	75	150	175
M77, .22 L.R.R.F., Clip Fed, *Modern*	75	125	150
M77, .22 L.R.R.F., Tube Feed, *Modern*	75	150	175

RIFLE, SINGLESHOT

	Fair	V. Good	Excellent
High-Wall, Various Calibers, Musket, *Curio*	1200	3000	3750
High-Wall, Various Calibers, Schutzen Rifle, *Curio*	3000	7000	8000
High-Wall, Various Calibers, Schutzen Style Rifle, *Curio*	3000	7000	7750
High-Wall, Various Calibers, Sporting Rifle, *Curio*	1500	3500	4250
Low-Wall, .22 Long R.F., Carbine, *Curio*	2000	4500	5250
Low-Wall, Various Calibers, Sporting Rifle, Curio	900	2000	2750
Model 310, .22 L.R.R.F., Bolt Action, *Modern*	75	150	175
Winder, .22 Long R.F., Musket, *Curio*	300	700	800

RIFLE, SLIDE ACTION

	Fair	V. Good	Excellent
M1890, under #64,521, Various Rimfires, Case Hardened, *Antique*	900	3000	3750
M1890, Various Rimfires, *Curio*	300	700	900
M1906, .22 L.R.R.F., Tube Feed, Hammer, *Modern*	250	600	700
M270, .22 L.R.R.F., Tube Feed, *Modern*	50	75	100
M270 Deluxe, .22 L.R.R.F., Tube Feed, *Modern*	75	100	125
M275, .22 WMR, Tube Feed, *Modern*	75	100	125
M275 Deluxe, .22 WMR, Tube Feed, *Modern*	$75	$125	$150
M61, .22 L.R.R.F., Tube Feed, *Modern*	200	425	475
M61, Various Rimfires, Tube Feed, Octagon Barrel, *Modern*	300	850	1000
M61 Magnum, .22 WMR, Tube Feed, *Modern*	300	550	600
M62, .22 L.R.R.F., Tube Feed, Hammer, *Modern*	200	400	450
M62 Gallery, .22 Short R.F., Tube Feed, Hammer, *Modern*	200	500	600

SHOTGUN, BOLT ACTION

	Fair	V. Good	Excellent
Model 36, 9mm Shotshell, Takedown, Singleshot, *Curio*	200	425	475
Model 41, .410 Ga., Takedown, Singleshot, *Modern*	150	300	350
Model 41, .410 Ga., Takedown, Singleshot, Checkered Stock, *Modern*	175	325	375

SHOTGUN, DOUBLE BARREL, OVER-UNDER

	Fair	V. Good	Excellent
Model 101 Pigeon 3 Barrel Set, Various Gauges, Skeet Grade, Single Trigger, Automatic Ejector, Checkered Stock, Engraved, *Modern*	900	2500	3000
Model 101 Magnum, 12 Ga. 3", Single Trigger, Automatic Ejector, Engraved, *Modern*	350	700	900
Model 101 Pigeon, 12 and 20 Gauges, Skeet Grade, Checkered Stock, Single Trigger, Automatic Ejector, Engraved, *Modern*	500	1000	1250
Model 101 Pigeon, 12 Ga., Trap Grade, Monte Carlo Stock, Single Trigger, Automatic Ejector, Engraved, *Modern*	600	1350	1600
Model 101 Pigeon, 12 Ga., Trap Grade, Single Trigger, Automatic Ejector, Engraved, *Modern*	600	1250	1500
Model 101, 12 Ga. Mag. 3", Trap Grade, Single Trigger, Automatic Ejector, Checkered Stock, Engraved, *Modern*	300	675	750
Model 101, 12 Ga., Field Grade, Single Trigger, Automatic Ejector, Engraved, *Modern*	400	800	900
Model 101, 12 Ga., Trap Grade, Monte Carlo Stock, Single Trigger, Automatic Ejector, Engraved, *Modern*	400	850	1000
Model 101, 12 Ga., Trap Grade, Single Trigger, Automatic Ejector, Checkered Stock, Engraved, *Modern*	400	800	950
Model 101, Various Gauges, Featherweight, Single Trigger, Automatic Ejector, Checkered Stock, Engraved, *Modern*	400	850	950

	Fair	V. Good	Excellent
Model 101, Various Gauges, Skeet Grade, Single Trigger, Automatic Ejector, Checkered Stock, Engraved, *Modern*	$350	$700	$800
Model 96, 12 and 20 Gauges, Field Grade, Checkered Stock, Vent Rib, *Modern*	250	575	625
Model 96, 12 and 20 Gauges, Skeet Grade, Checkered Stock, Vent Rib, *Modern*	300	600	650
Model 96, 12 Ga., Trap Grade, Checkered Stock, Vent Rib, *Modern*	250	500	550
Model 96, 12 Ga., Trap Grade, Monte Carlo Stock, Vent Rib, *Modern*	250	550	600

SHOTGUN, DOUBLE BARREL, SIDE-BY-SIDE

	Fair	V. Good	Excellent
Model 21 Custom, 12 Ga., Hammerless, Single Selective Trigger, Selective Ejector, Fancy Engraving, Fancy Checkering, *Modern*	3000	6750	9500
Model 21 Custom, 20 Ga., Hammerless, Single Selective Trigger, Selective Ejector, Fancy Checkering, Fancy Engraving, *Modern*	4500	7500	10500
Model 21 Duck, 12 Ga. Mag. 3", Hammerless, Single Selective Trigger, Selective Ejector, Raised Matted Rib, *Modern*	1200	2500	3000
Model 21 Duck, 12 Ga. Mag. 3", Hammerless, Single Selective Trigger, Selective Ejector, Vent Rib, *Modern*	1500	3500	5000

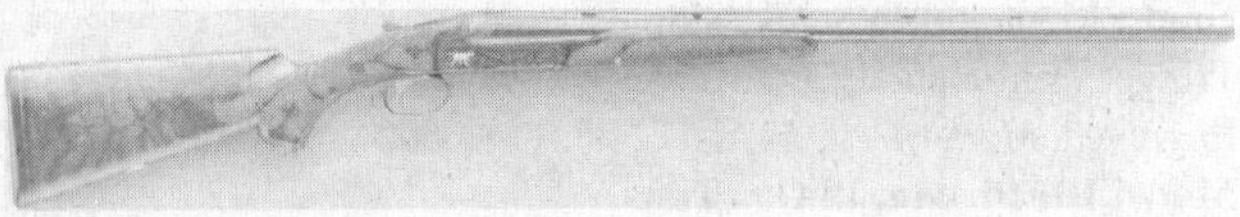

Winchester Model 21 Grand American

	Fair	V. Good	Excellent
Model 21 Grand American, 12 Ga., Hammerless, Single Selective Trigger, Selective Ejector, Fancy Engraving, Fancy Checkering, *Modern*	6500	12500	17500
Model 21 Grand American, 20 Ga., Hammerless, Single Selective Trigger, Selective Ejector, Fancy Checkering, Fancy Engraving, *Modern*	8000	15000	19500
Model 21 Pigeon, 12 Ga., Hammerless, Single Selective Trigger, Selective Ejector, Fancy Engraving, Fancy Checkering, *Modern*	4000	8000	10000
Model 21 Pigeon, 20 Ga., Hammerless, Single Selective Trigger, Selective Ejector, Fancy Engraving, Fancy Checkering, *Modern*	7000	10000	12500
Model 21, .410 Ga., Checkered Stock, Fancy Wood, *Modern*	$12000	$20000	$25000
Model 21, 12 and 16 Gauges, Field Grade, Double Trigger, Automatic Ejector, Hammerless, *Modern*	800	1800	2000
Model 21, 12 and 16 Gauges, Field Grade, Single Selective Trigger, Automatic Ejector, Hammerless, *Modern*	1200	3250	3500
Model 21, 12 and 16 Gauges, Skeet Grade, Hammerless, Single Selective Trigger, Selective Ejector, Vent Rib, *Modern*	1500	3500	4000
Model 21, 12 Ga., Trap Grade, Hammerless, Single Selective Trigger, Selective Ejector, Raised Matted Rib, *Modern*	1200	2750	3000
Model 21, 20 Ga., Field Grade, Double Trigger, Automatic Ejector, Hammerless, *Modern*	1000	1750	2000
Model 21, 20 Ga., Field Grade, Single Selective Trigger, Automatic Ejector, Hammerless, *Modern*	1500	3000	3500
Model 21, 20 Ga., Skeet Grade, Hammerless, Single Selective Trigger, Selective Ejector, Vent Rib, *Modern*	2500	4500	4750
Model 21, 20 Ga., Skeet Grade, Hammerless, Single Selective Trigger, Selective Ejector, Raised Matted Rib, *Modern*	2500	4250	4750
Model 21, For Extra Barrels, Add 25%–30%			
Model 21, For Vent Rib, Add $400.00–$600.00			
Model 23 English, 12 or 20 Gauges, Hammerless, Single Trigger, Selective Ejector, Fancy Checkering, Engraved, *Modern*	400	850	1000
Model 23 Grand European, 12 Ga., Hammerless, Single Selective Trigger, Selective Ejector, Fancy Engraving, Fancy Checkering, *Modern*	600	1250	1450
Model 23 Pigeon, 12 or 20 Gauges, Hammerless, Single Trigger, Selective Ejector, Engraved, Fancy Checkering, *Modern*	400	900	1050

Winchester Model 23 Pigeon

	Fair	V. Good	Excellent
Model 24, Various Gauges, Double Trigger, Automatic Ejector, *Modern*	200	450	500

SHOTGUN, LEVER ACTION

	Fair	V. Good	Excellent
1901, 10 Ga., 2⅞", Tube Feed, Plain, *Curio*	500	1000	1350

	Fair	V. Good	Excellent
M 1887, 10 Ga., $2^{7}/_{8}$", Tube Feed, Plain, *Curio*	$700	$1750	$2000
M 1887, Deluxe Grade, 10 Ga., $2^{7}/_{8}$", Tube Feed, Checkered Stock, Damascus barrel, *Curio*	900	2650	3250
M 1887, Deluxe Grade, 12 ga. *Antique*	900	2350	2750
M 1887, 12ga., *Antique*	700	1500	1750

SHOTGUN, SELF-LOADING

	Fair	V. Good	Excellent
Model 1400 Deer, 12 Ga., Open Sights, Slug Gun, *Modern*	125	225	250
Model 1400 Field, 12 and 20 Gauges, Winchoke, *Modern*	100	225	275
Model 1400 Field, 12 and 20 Gauges, Winchoke, Vent Rib, *Modern*	125	250	300

Winchester Model 1400

	Fair	V. Good	Excellent
Model 1400 Skeet, 12 and 20 Gauges, Vent Rib, *Modern*	150	300	350
Model 1400 Trap, 12 Ga., Monte Carlo Stock, Vent Rib, *Modern*	150	325	375
Model 1400 Trap, 12 Ga., Vent Rib, *Modern*	150	300	350
Model 1400 Trap, 12 Ga., Vent Rib, Recoil Reducer, *Modern*	175	375	425
Model 1500, 12 or 20 Gauges, Field Grade, Plain, *Modern*	100	225	275
Model 1500, 12 or 20 Gauges, Field Grade, Vent Rib, *Modern*	125	250	300
Model 1911, 12 Ga., Takedown, Checkered Stock, *Modern*	175	375	425
Model 1911, 12 Ga., Takedown, Plain, *Modern*	150	350	400
Model 40, 12 Ga., Takedown, Field Grade, *Modern*	175	375	425
Model 40, 12 Ga., Takedown, Skeet Grade, *Modern*	200	425	475
Model 50, 12 and 20 Gauges, Field Grade, Plain Barrel, Checkered Stock, *Modern*	150	300	350
Model 50, 12 and 20 Gauges, Field Grade, Vent Rib, Checkered Stock, *Modern*	175	400	500
Model 50, 12 and 20 Gauges, Skeet Grade, Vent Rib, Checkered Stock, *Modern*	250	500	600
Model 50, 12 Ga., Trap Grade, Vent Rib, Monte Carlo Stock, *Modern*	200	400	500

SHOTGUN, SINGLESHOT

	Fair	V. Good	Excellent
Model 101, 12 Ga., Trap Grade, Vent Rib, *Modern*	400	850	1000
Model 20, .410 Ga., $2^{1}/_{2}$", Takedown, Hammer, Checkered Stock, *Modern*	$150	$325	$400
Model 37A, For Red Letter, Add 25%-40%			
Model 37A, .410 Ga., Takedown, Automatic Ejector, Plain Barrel, *Modern*	100	175	250
Model 37A, 12 Ga., Takedown, Automatic Ejector, Plain Barrel, *Modern*	100	125	150
Model 37A, 16 Ga., Takedown, Automatic Ejector, Plain Barrel, *Modern*	100	125	150
Model 37A, 20 Ga., Takedown, Automatic Ejector, Plain Barrel, *Modern*	100	125	150
Model 37A, 28 Ga., Takedown, Automatic Ejector, Plain Barrel, *Modern*	75	150	250

SHOTGUN, SLIDE ACTION

	Fair	V. Good	Excellent
Model 12, 12 Ga., Post '64, Trap Grade, Checkered Stock, *Modern*	250	550	600
Model 12, 12 Ga., Post '64, Trap Gun, Monte Carlo Stock, *Modern*	250	575	625
Model 12, 12 Ga., Pre '64, Takedown, Trap Grade, Raised Matted Rib, *Modern*	300	675	900
Model 12, 12 Ga., Pre '64, Takedown, Trap Grade, Vent Rib, *Modern*	300	725	1200
Model 12, 12 Ga., Pre '64, Takedown, Trap Grade, Vent Rib, Monte Carlo Stock, *Modern*	350	775	1200
Model 12, 12 Ga., Pre-War, Takedown, Riot Gun, *Curio*	400	800	900
Model 12, 12 Ga., Pre-War, Takedown, Vent Rib, *Curio*	300	700	900
Model 12, Featherweight, Various Gauges, Pre '64, Takedown, *Modern*	250	400	550
Model 12, Heavy Duck, 12 Ga. Mag. 3", Pre '64, Takedown, Vent Rib, *Modern*	300	600	700
Model 12, Heavy Duck, 12 Ga. Mag. 3", Pre '64, Takedown, Raised Matted Rib, *Modern*	300	550	650
Model 12, Pigeon Grade, 12 Ga., Pre '64, Takedown, Trap Grade, Vent Rib, *Modern*	800	1500	1750
Model 12, Pigeon Grade, 12 Ga., Pre '64, Takedown, Trap Grade, Raised Matted Rib, *Modern*	800	1450	1650
Model 12, Pigeon Grade, 12 Ga., Various Gauges, Pre '64, Takedown, Skeet Choke, Raised Matted Rib, *Modern*	800	1400	1550
Model 12, Pigeon Grade, Various Gauges, Pre '64, Takedown, Skeet Choke, Vent Rib, *Modern*	700	1400	1600

	Fair	V. Good	Excellent
Model 12, Pigeon Grade, Various Gauges, Pre '64, Takedown, Skeet Choke, Plain Barrel, *Modern*	$400	$800	$900
Model 12, Pigeon Grade, Various Gauges, Pre '64, Takedown, Plain Barrel, *Modern*	400	1000	1500
Model 12, Pigeon Grade, Various Gauges, Pre '64, Takedown, Vent Rib, *Modern*	700	1550	1900
Model 12, Standard, Various Gauges, Pre '64, Takedown, *Modern*	300	600	700
Model 12, Super Pigeon, 12 Ga., Post '64, Takedown, Vent Rib, Engraved, Checkered Stock, *Modern*	800	2000	2500
Model 12, Various Gauges, Pre '64, Takedown, Raised Matted Rib, *Modern*	225	600	700
Model 12, Various Gauges, Pre '64, Takedown, Skeet Grade, Raised Matted Rib, *Modern*	350	1000	1200
Model 12, Various Gauges, Pre '64, Takedown, Skeet Grade, Vent Rib, *Modern*	800	1500	1600
Model 12, Various Gauges, Pre '64, Takedown, Skeet Grade, Plain Barrel, *Modern*	400	800	900
Model 1200, For Recoil Reducer, Add $50.00-$75.00			
Model 1200 Deer, 12 Ga., Open Sights, *Modern*	100	150	200
Model 1200 Defender, 12 Ga., *Modern*	75	125	250
Model 1200 Field, 12 and 20 Gauges, *Modern*	100	150	200
Model 1200 Field, 12 and 20 Gauges, Adjustable Choke, *Modern*	150	200	250
Model 1200 Field, 12 and 20 Gauges, Adjustable Choke, Vent Rib, *Modern*	175	225	275
Model 1200 Field, 12 and 20 Gauges, Vent Rib, *Modern*	125	175	225
Model 1200 Field, 12 Ga. Mag. 3", *Modern*	150	175	200
Model 1200 Field, 12 Ga. Mag. 3", Vent Rib, *Modern*	125	175	225
Model 1200 Police Stainless, 12 Ga., *Modern*	150	200	250
Model 1300, 12 or 20 Gauges, Plain Barrel, *Modern*	200	250	300
Model 1300, 12 or 20 Gauges, Plain Barrel, Winchoke, *Modern*	250	300	350
Model 1300, 12 or 20 Gauges, Vent Rib, *Modern*	225	275	325
Model 1300, 12 or 20 Gauges, Vent Rib, Winchoke, *Modern*	275	325	375
Model 1300 Deer, 12 Ga., Open Sights, *Modern*	225	275	325
Model 25, 12 Ga., Solid Frame, Plain Barrel, *Modern*	150	300	500

	Fair	V. Good	Excellent
Model 42, .410 Ga., Field Grade, Takedown, *Modern*	$400	$750	$850
Model 42, .410 Ga., Field Grade, Takedown, Raised Matted Rib, *Modern*	500	800	1000
Model 42, .420 Ga., Skeet Grade, Takedown, Raised Matted Rib, *Modern*	800	1500	1750
Model 42 Deluxe, .410 Ga., Takedown, Vent Rib, Fancy Checkering, Fancy Wood, *Modern*	900	2000	2500
Model 97, 12 Ga., Solid Frame, Plain, *Modern*	250	500	650
Model 97, 12 Ga., Solid Frame, Riot Gun, *Modern*	250	500	650
Model 97, 12 Ga., Takedown, Plain, *Modern*	250	550	700
Model 97, 12 Ga., Takedown, Riot Gun, *Modern*	300	600	750
Model 97, 16 Ga., Solid Frame, Plain, *Modern*	250	550	650
Model 97, 16 Ga., Takedown, Plain, *Modern*	300	600	750
Model 97 Pigeon, 12 Ga., Takedown, Checkered, *Modern*	900	2000	2750
Model 97 Tournament, 12 Ga., Takedown, Checkered Stock, *Modern*	600	1200	1650
Model 97 Trap, 12 Ga., Takedown, Checkered Stock, *Modern*	500	1000	1350
Model 97 Trench, 12 Ga., Solid Frame, Riot Gun, Military, *Curio*	700	1500	1950
Model 97 Trench, 12 Ga., Solid Frame, Riot Gun, Military, with Bayonet, *Curio*	800	1600	1950

WINFIELD ARMS CO.

Made by Crescent, c. 1900. See Crescent Fire Arms Co., Shotgun, Double Barrel, Side-by-Side; Shotgun, Singleshot.

WINFIELD ARMS CO.

Made by Norwich Falls Pistol Co., c. 1880.

HANDGUN, REVOLVER

	Fair	V. Good	Excellent
.32 Short R.F., 5 Shot, Spur Trigger, Solid Frame, Single Action, *Antique*	75	150	175

WINGERT, RICHARD

Lancaster, Pa., 1775–1777. See Kentucky Rifles, U.S. Military.

WINOCA ARMS CO.

Made by Crescent for Jacobi Hardware Co., Philadelphia, Pa. See Crescent Fire Arms Co., Shotgun, Double Barrel, Side-by-Side; Shotgun, Singleshot.

WINSLOW ARMS CO.

Established in Venice, Fla., in 1962, moved to Osprey, Fla. in 1976, and is now in Camden, S.C.

RIFLE, BOLT ACTION

For Left-Hand Act, Add $70.00–$100.00

	Fair	V. Good	Excellent
Commander, Various Calibers, Fancy Checkering, Inlays, *Modern*	$250	$500	$550
Crown, Various Gauges, Carved, Fancy Wood, Inlays, *Modern*	500	1250	1500
Emperor, Various Gauges, Carved, Fancy Engraving, Ornate, Fancy Wood, Inlays, *Modern*	3000	6000	6500
Imperial, Various Gauges, Carved, Engraved, Fancy Wood, Inlays, *Modern*	2200	3500	3750
Regal, Various Calibers, Fancy Checkering, Inlays, *Modern*	300	600	650
Regent, Various Calibers, Inlays, Carved, Fancy Wood, *Modern*	350	725	775
Regimental, Various Calibers, Carved, Inlays, *Modern*	400	850	1000
Royal, Various Calibers, Carved, Fancy Wood, Inlays, *Modern*	700	1500	1750

WITHERS, MICHAEL

Lancaster, Pa., 1774–1805. See Kentucky Rifles, U.S. Military.

WITTES HDW. CO.

Made by Stevens Arms.

SHOTGUN, DOUBLE BARREL, SIDE-BY-SIDE

	Fair	V. Good	Excellent
Model 311, Various Gauges, Hammerless, Steel Barrel, *Modern*	75	150	175

SHOTGUN, SINGLESHOT

	Fair	V. Good	Excellent
Model 90, Various Gauges, Takedown, Automatic Ejector, Plain, Hammer, *Modern*	25	50	75
Model 94, Various Gauges, Takedown, Automatic Ejector, Plain, Hammer, *Modern*	25	50	75

WOGDON

London, England & Dublin, Ireland, 1760–1797.

HANDGUN, FLINTLOCK

	Fair	V. Good	Excellent
.56, Officers, Holster Pistol, Flared, Octagon Barrel, Steel Furniture, Engraved, High Quality, *Antique*	900	2500	3250

WOLF

Spain, c. 1900.

HANDGUN, SELF-LOADING

	Fair	V. Good	Excellent
7.65mm, Clip Fed, *Modern*	50	100	125

WOLF, A. W.

Suhl, Germany, c. 1930.

SHOTGUN, DOUBLE BARREL, SIDE-BY-SIDE

	Fair	V. Good	Excellent
12 Ga., Engraved, Platinium Inlays, Ivory Inlays, Ornate, Cased, *Modern*	$3000	$6000	$7000

WOLFHEIMER, PHILIP

Lancaster, Pa., c. 1774. See Kentucky Rifles.

WOLVERINE ARMS CO.

Made by Crescent for Fletcher Hardware Co., c. 1900. See Crescent Fire Arms Co., Shotgun, Double Barrel, Side-by-Side; Shotgun, Singleshot.

WOODWARD, JAMES & SONS

London, England.

SHOTGUN, DOUBLE BARREL, OVER-UNDER

	Fair	V. Good	Excellent
Best Quality, Various Gauges, Sidelock, Automatic Ejector, Double Trigger, Fancy Engraving, Fancy Checkering, *Modern*	8000	22500	30000
Best Quality, Various Gauges, Sidelock, Automatic Ejector, Single Trigger, Fancy Engraving, Fancy Checkering, *Modern*	9000	22000	28500

410 ga. Add 100%
28 ga. Add 75%

SHOTGUN, DOUBLE BARREL, SIDE-BY-SIDE

	Fair	V. Good	Excellent
Best Quality, Various Gauges, Sidelock, Automatic Ejector, Double Trigger, Fancy Engraving, Fancy Checkering, *Modern*	8000	17500	23500
Best Quality, Various Gauges, Sidelock, Automatic Ejector, Single Trigger, Fancy Engraving, Fancy Checkering, *Modern*	8500	18500	25000

410 ga. Add 100%
28 ga. Add 75%

SHOTGUN, SINGLESHOT

	Fair	V. Good	Excellent
12 Ga., Trap Grade, Vent Rib, Hammerless, Fancy Engraving, Fancy Checkering, *Modern*	3000	7000	9500

WORTHINGTON ARMS

Made by Stevens Arms.

SHOTGUN, DOUBLE BARREL, SIDE-BY-SIDE

	Fair	V. Good	Excellent
M 315, Various Gauges, Hammerless, Steel Barrel, *Modern*	100	150	175
Model 215, 12 and 16 Gauges, Outside Hammers, Steel Barrel, *Modern*	100	150	175

WORTHINGTON ARMS CO.

Made by Crescent for Geo. Worthington Co., Cleveland, Ohio. See Crescent Fire Arms Co., Shotgun, Double Barrel, Side-by-Side; Shotgun, Singleshot.

WORTHINGTON, GEORGE

Made by Stevens Arms.

SHOTGUN, DOUBLE BARREL, SIDE-BY-SIDE

	Fair	V. Good	Excellent
M 315, Various Gauges, Hammerless, Steel Barrel, *Modern*	$100	$150	$175
Model 215, 12 and 16 Gauges, Outside Hammers, Steel Barrel, *Modern*	$75	$125	$150
Model 311, Various Gauges, Hammerless, Steel Barrel, *Modern*	100	150	175

WUETHRICH

W. Wuethrich, Werkzeugbau, Lutzelfluh, Switzerland.

RIFLE, SINGLESHOT

	Fair	V. Good	Excellent
Falling Block, Various Calibers, Engraved, Fancy Wood, Scope Mounted, *Modern*	500	1000	1350

Y

YATO
Hamada Arsenal, Japan.

HANDGUN, SELF-LOADING

	Fair	V. Good	Excellent
Yato, .32 ACP, Clip Fed, Military, *Curio*	$900	$2000	$2200
Yato, .32 ACP, Clip Fed, Pre-War, *Curio*	1100	2500	3000

YDEAL
Made by Francisco Arizmendi, Eibar, Spain.

HANDGUN, SELF-LOADING

	Fair	V. Good	Excellent
6.35mm, Clip Fed, Blue, *Curio*	50	100	125
7.65mm, Clip Fed, Blue, *Curio*	50	125	150

YOU BET
Made by Hopkins & Allen, c. 1880.

HANDGUN, REVOLVER

	Fair	V. Good	Excellent
.22 Short R.F., 7 Shot, Spur Trigger, Solid Frame, Single Action, *Antique*	$75	$150	$175

YOUNG AMERICA
See Harrington & Richardson Arms Co.

YOUNG, HENRY
Easton, Pa., 1774–1780. See Kentucky Rifles.

YOUNG, JOHN
Easton, Pa., 1775–1788. See Kentucky Rifles, U.S. Military.

Z

	Fair	V. Good	Excellent

Z

Ceska Zbrojovka, Prague, Czechoslovakia.

HANDGUN, SELF-LOADING

Vest Pocket, 6.35mm, Clip Fed, *Modern*	$50	$100	$125

ZABALA

Zabala Hermanos, Eibar, Spain.

SHOTGUN, DOUBLE BARREL, SIDE-BY-SIDE

12 Ga., Boxlock, Checkered Stock, Double Triggers, *Modern*	50	100	125

ZANOTTI

Brescia, Italy. 1625–Date.

HANDGUN, FLINTLOCK

Brescia Style, .50, Carved Stock, Engraved, Reproduction, *Antique*	75	125	150

ZARAGOZA

Zaragoza, Mexico.

HANDGUN, SELF-LOADING

Corla, Type 1, .22 L.R.R.F., Colt System, Clip Fed, Blue, *Modern*	250	575	650
Corla Type 2, .22 L.R.R.F., Colt System, Blue, *Modern*	200	400	450

ZASTAVA ARMS

Zavodi Crvena Zastava, Kragujevac, Yugoslavia. Also see Mark X.

HANDGUN, SELF-LOADING

Model 65, 9mm Luger, Clip Fed, Blue, *Modern*	150	325	375
Model 67, .32 ACP, Clip Fed, Blue, *Modern*	125	225	275

ZEHNA

Made by E. Zehner Waffenfabrik, Suhl, Germany, 1919–1928.

HANDGUN, SELF-LOADING

	Fair	V. Good	Excellent
Vest Pocket, 6.35mm, Clip Fed, Blue, *Curio*	150	300	350
Vest Pocket, 6.35mm, Under #5,000, Clip Fed, Blue, *Curio*	$125	$250	$300

ZEPHYR

Tradename of A. F. Stoeger.

SHOTGUN, DOUBLE BARREL, SIDE-BY-SIDE

Sterlingworth II, Various Gauges, Checkered Stock, Sidelock, Double Triggers, Light Engraving, *Modern*	250	575	650
Woodlander II, Various Gauges, Checkered Stock, Boxlock, Double Triggers, Light Engraving, *Modern*	200	425	475

410 ga. Add 25%

ZOLI, ANGELO

Brescia, Italy.

RIFLE, PERCUSSION

.50 Hawkin, Brass Furniture, Reproduction, *Antique*	100	150	175

SHOTGUN, DOUBLE BARREL, OVER-UNDER

Angel, 12 and 20 Gauges, Field Grade, Single Selective Trigger, Engraved, Checkered Stock, *Modern*	300	675	800
Angel, 12 Ga., Trap Grade, Single Selective Trigger, Engraved, Checkered Stock, *Modern*	350	700	850
Condor, 12 and 20 Gauges, Single Selective Trigger, Field Grade, Checkered Stock, Engraved, *Modern*	300	600	725
Condor, 12 Ga., Trap Grade, Single Selective Trigger, Engraved, Checkered Stock, *Modern*	300	625	750
Monte Carlo, 12 and 20 Gauges, Field Grade, Single Selective Trigger, Engraved, Checkered Stock, *Modern*	350	750	900
Monte Carlo, 12 Ga., Trap Grade, Single Selective Trigger, Engraved, Checkered Stock, *Modern*	350	775	925

ZOLI, ANTONIO

Gardone, Val Trompia, Italy.

	Fair	V. Good	Excellent
SHOTGUN, DOUBLE BARREL, OVER-UNDER			
Golden Snipe, 12 and 20 Gauges, Skeet Grade, Single Trigger, Automatic Ejector, Engraved, Checkered Stock, *Modern*	$200	$450	$550
Golden Snipe, 12 and 20 Gauges, Vent Rib, Single Trigger, Automatic Ejector, Engraved, Checkered Stock, *Modern*	150	350	450
Golden Snipe, 12 Ga., Trap Grade, Single Trigger, Automatic Ejector, Engraved, Checkered Stock, *Modern*	200	450	550
Silver Snipe, 12 and 20 Gauges, Skeet Grade, Single Trigger, Vent Rib, Engraved, Checkered Stock, *Modern*	200	450	550
Silver Snipe, 12 and 20 Gauges, Vent Rib, Single Trigger, Engraved, Checkered Stock, *Modern*	200	425	500
Silver Snipe, 12 Ga., Trap Grade, Single Trigger, Vent Rib, Engraved, Checkered Stock, *Modern*	200	450	500

	Fair	V. Good	Excellent
SHOTGUN, DOUBLE BARREL, SIDE-BY-SIDE			
Silver Hawk, 12 and 20 Gauges, Double Trigger, Engraved, Checkered Stock, *Modern*	$200	$400	$500

ZONDA

Hispano Argentina Fab. de Automiviles, Buenos Aires, Argentina.

HANDGUN, SINGLESHOT			
.22 L.R.R.F., Blue, *Modern*	100	225	275

ZULAICA

M. Zulaica y Cia., Eibar, Spain.

HANDGUN, SELF-LOADING			
Royal, .32 ACP, Clip Fed, Blue, Military, *Curio*	50	150	175
AUTOMATIC, REVOLVER			
.22 L.R.R.F., Zig-Zag Cylinder, Blue, *Curio*	300	650	750

Appendix I: Bibliography

The organization of this listing of important reference works has been devised to allow the formation of a master library for the ultimate arms collecting enthusiast. Rather than place these titles in various sections of the *Price Guide,* under specific entries in the database (e.g., Colt, Remington, S & W, Winchester), the author felt that organizing the listing by broader categories would be more useful. Further, it allows for copying these pages, and carrying them along to gun shows. A number of books are available at these shows, and dealers are usually comfortable with trading or discounts, though generally only for quantity purchases. One of the great pleasures of collecting is building a strong reference library, an unending and vital process.

The hundreds, and sometimes thousands, of books, magazines, and catalogues and other source materials that one can collect are a constant source of pleasure, and necessary in attempting to master the extraordinary world of firearms. For reference value alone, a library is the cheapest, most useful and important component of a collector or dealer's repertoire. This writer would be lost without his library, even though a great deal of my work requires original research, in previously unpublished sources.

The author's longtime friend Peter Buxtun maintains up-to-date files on the broad spectrum of collectors' arms and armor, and these thorough records, as in the past, have proven useful in updating the Bibliography. The Buxtun Archive features a collection of articles removed from thousands of magazines, and other sources, over more than thirty-five years of collecting. The amount of material unearthed through this impressive collection was quite substantial; consider the fact that in the firearms world alone there must be over 175 publications on the subject worldwide. Even Poland and Russia now have firearms magazines, and the leading Russian publication already has 100,000 subscribers!

One can never have too many books, or subscribe to too many firearms magazines, or accumulate too many articles, auction catalogues, or other records on the subjects of your collecting and/or dealing interests.

And if space is a consideration, there are many ways to lick that. Any good bookstore will have source works on how to turn space into the most efficient storage imaginable. In the author's West Coast apartment there is very little space, but he has adapted book shelving, a desk and computer complex, and closets, to the extent that he still has room for more books, and more reference materials, as he toils on manuscripts like this one, into the wee hours of every morning he is there.

GENERAL TITLES

See also List of Gun Magazines
Antal, Laslo. *Competitive Pistol Shooting.* 1989.
Gates, Elgin T. *The Gun Digest Book of Metallic Silhouette Shooting.* 1988.
Hounshell, David A. *From the American System to Mass Production, 1800–1932.* 1984.
Mace, Boyd. *The Accurate Varmint Rifle.* 1991.
Matunas, Edward A. *Shooting.* 1986.
Meadows, Edward Scott. *U.S. Military Automatic Pistols 1894–1920.* 1993.
Mullen, John. *The Gun Report Subject Index June, 1955–May, 1990.* 1993.
Ota, Mitchell A. *Pin Shooting: A Complete Guide.* 1992.
Simpson, Layne. *The Custom Government Model Pistol.* 1992.
Stone, George Cameron. *A Glossary of the Construction, Decoration and Use of Arms and Armor in All Countries and in All Times.* 1934.
Taylerson, A.W.F. *Revolving Arms.* 1967.
———. *The Revolver 1865–1888.* 1966.
———. *The Revolver 1899–1914.* 1970.
———. and R.A.N. Andrews, J. Firth. *The Revolver 1818–1865.* 1968.
Wilson, R. L., and Ian V. Hogg. *Textbook of Automatic Pistols.* 1975.
Yuryev, A. A. *Competitive Shooting.* 1985.

Videos

The History Channel. *The Story of the Gun.* Two parts, two hours each.
The History Channel. *Tales of the Gun,* numerous hour-long segments, as discussed in *The Year in Review,* 2nd and 3rd editions of *The Official Price Guide to Gun Collecting.*

Accessories

Stroebel, Nick. *Old Gunsights: A Collector's Guide, 1850–1965.* 1999.

Air Rifles and Pistols

Galan, J. I. *Air Gun Digest.* Various editions.

Allen, Ethan, Allen & Thurber, Allen & Wheelock (et al.)

Thomas, H. H. *The Story of Allen & Wheelock Firearms.* 1965.

Blackpowder

Adler, Dennis. *Colt Blackpowder Reproductions & Replicas: A Collector's and Shooter's Guide.* 1998.
Brockway, William R. *Recreating the Double Barrel Muzzle-Loading Shotgun.* 1985.
Buchele, William, et al. *Recreating the American Longrifle.* 1983.
Cline, Walter M. *The Muzzle-Loading Rifle, Then and Now.* 1991. Reprint.
Fadala, Sam. *The Complete Black Powder Handbook.* 1990.
——— and Dale Storey. *Black Powder Hobby Gunsmithing.* 1994.
Kirkland, Turner. *Dixie Gun Works Catalogue.* An annual publication numbering over 720 pages. The book for 2000 is no. 149, with Harry Carey Jr. saluted on cover and inside cover.

Catalogues

In addition to original catalogues and numerous reprints on the market, two books of special interest are:

Saterlee, L.D. *Fourteen Old Gun Catalogues for the Collector, Volume 2.* 1962.
———. *Ten Old Gun Catalogues, Volume 1.* 1962.

Civil War

GENERAL

Coates, Earl J. and Dean S. Thomas. *An Introduction to Civil War Small Arms.* 1990.
Coggins, Jack. *Arms & Equipment of the Civil War.* 1983.
Edwards, William B. *Civil War Guns.* 1962.
Lord, Francis. *Civil War Collector's Encyclopedia.* 1963.
Johnson, Paul D. *Civil War Cartridge Boxes of the Union Infantryman.* 1998.

CONFEDERATE

Albaugh, William A., III and Edward N. Simmons. *Confederate Arms.* 1993.

——— and Hugh Benet. *Confederate Handguns.* 1993.

Albaugh, William A. *The Original Confederate Colt.* 1993.

———. *The Confederate Brass-Framed Colt and Whitney.* 1993.

———. *Tyler, Texas C.S.A.* 1958.

Forgett, Valmore J., and Alain and Marie-Antoinette Serpette. *LeMat: The Man, the Gun.* 1999.

Fuller, Claud E. and Richard Steuart. *Firearms of the Confederacy.*

Gary, William A. *Confederate Revolvers.* 1987.

Hill, Richard Taylor, and William Edward Anthony. *Confederate Longarms and Pistols: A Pictorial Study.* 1978.

Murphy, Dr. J. *Confederate Carbines and Musketoons.* 1986.

———. *Confederate Rifles and Muskets.* 1995.

Wiggins, Gary. *Dance & Brothers: Texas Gunmakers of the Confederacy.* 1986.

UNION

Marcot, Roy M. *Civil War Chief of Sharpshooters Hiram Berdan, Military Commander and Firearms Inventor.* 1990.

See also numerous titles on gunmakers, e.g., Colt, Remington, Spencer, Sharps, Smith & Wesson, and others commonly used by Union forces.

Colonial, Revolutionary War, and War of 1812

Brown, M. L. *Firearms in Colonial America, The Impact on History and Technology, 1492–1792.* 1980.

Moore, Warren. *Weapons of the American Revolution and Accouterments.* 1967.

Neumann, George C. and Frank Kravic. *Collector's Illustrated Encyclopedia of the American Revolution.* 1989.

Peterson, Harold L. *Arms and Armor in Colonial America 1526–1783.* 1956.

Colt

Bady, Donald B. *Colt Automatic Pistols.* 1974.

Beinfeld, Wallace, ed. *Armsmear.* Reprint of 1866 edition; the first Colt book.

Brunner, Dr. John W. *Colt Pocket Hammerless Pistols.* Williamstown, New Jersey: Phillips Publications, 1997.

Clawson, Charles W. *Colt 45 Service Pistol Models of 1911 and 1911A1: Complete Military History, Development and Production, 1900 Through 1945.* 1993.

Cochran, Keith. *Colt Peacemaker Encyclopedia.* 1986. Vol. II, 1992.

Condry, Ken and Larry Jones. *The Colt Commemoratives 1961–1986.* 1989.

Edwards, William B. *The Story of Colt's Revolver: The Biography of Col. Samuel Colt.* 1957.

Ezell, Edward C. and R. Blake Stevens. *The Black Rifle, M16 Retrospective.* 1987.

Garton, George. *Colt's S.A.A. Post War Models.* 1987.

Goddard, William H. D. *The Government Models: The Development of the Colt Model of 1911.* 1988.

Graham, Ron, John A. Kopec, and C. Kenneth Moore. *A Study of the Colt Single Action Army Revolver.* 1976; revised edition, 1979.

Grant, Ellsworth. *The Colt Armory: A History of Colt's Manufacturing Company.* 1995.

Greeley, Horace IV. *The Colt U.S. General Officers' Pistols.* 1990.

Haven, Charles T., and Frank A Belden. *A History of the Colt Revolver.* 1940.

Houze, Herbert G. *Colt Rifles & Muskets from 1847 to 1870.* 1996.

Hughes, David R. *The History and Development of the M16 Rifle and Its Cartridge.* 1990.

Kopec, John A. *Colt Cavalry and Artillery Revolvers: A Continuing Study.* 1994.

Maxwell, Samuel L., Sr. *The Colt-Burgess Magazine Rifle.* 1985.

Moore, C. Kenneth. *Colt Revolvers and the U.S. Navy 1865–1889.* 1987.

———. *Colt Single Action Army Revolvers, U.S. Alterations.* 1998.

———. *Colt Single Action Army Revolvers and the London Agency.* 1990.

Parsons, John E. *The Peacemaker and Its Rivals.* 1950.

———. *Sam Colt's Own Record 1847.* 1992. Reprint.

Rapley, Robin J. *Colt Percussion Accouterments 1834–1873.* 1994.

Rosa, Joseph G. *Colonel Colt London.* London: Arms and Armour Press, 1976.

Sellers, Frank. *Colts from the William M. Locke Collection.* 1996.

Serven, James E. *Colt Firearms from 1836.* Various editions since 1954.

Shelden, Douglas C. *A Collector's Guide to Colt's .38 Automatic Pistols,* 1987.

Sheldon, Douglas G. *Colt's Super .38: The Production History from 1929 Through 1971.* 1999.

Shumaker, P. L. *Colt's Variations of the Old Model Pocket Pistol 1848–1872.* 1957.

———. *Colt Revolvers and the Tower of London.* 1988.

Swayze, Nathan L. *'51 Colt Navies.* 1993.

Ulrich, Arthur A. *A Century of Achievement.* Originally published 1936; reprint edition from Wolfe Publishing Co., 1992, under title: *Colt's 100th Anniversary Firearms Manual 1836–1936: A Century of Achievement.*

Whittington, Lt. Col. Robert D. *The Colt Whitneyville-Walker Pistol.* 1984.

Wilkerson, Don. *The Post-War Colt Single-Action Revolver.* 1980.

———. *Colt's Single Action Army Revolver Pre-War Post-War Model.* 1991.

———. *Colt's Double-Action Revolver Model of 1878.* 1998.

Wilson, R. L. *Colt: An American Legend.* 1985. Official history of Colt firearms with detailed serial-number tables. *The Colt Heritage* (1979), a smaller edition by approximately 84 pages.

———. *Fine Colts: The Dr. Joseph A. Murphy Collection,* 1999.

———. *The Book of Colt Engraving* (1974), *Colt Engraving* (1982), *The Colt Engraving Book* (2000, in two volumes).

———. *The Book of Colt Firearms.* Considered the standard reference in the Colt field. 1971 and 1993.

———. *The Arms Collection of Colonel Colt.* 1963.

———. *Colt's Dates of Manufacture 1837–1978.* Detailed serial numbers by year; tables for all models of Colt handguns and long arms. 1985.

———. *Colt Commemorative Firearms.* 1969 and 1974 editions.

———. *Evolution of the Colt.* 1967.

———. *The Book of Colt Engraving* (1972), *Colt Engraving* (1982), *The Colt Engraving Book* (2000).

———. *The Colt Heritage.* 1979.

———. *Fine Colts. The Dr. Joseph A. Murphy Collection.* 1999.

———. *Samuel Colt Presents.* Hartford, Connecticut: Wadsworth Atheneum, 1961.

———, and R. E. Hable. *Colt Pistols.* 1976.

———, and Philip R. Phillips. *Paterson Colt Pistol Variations.* Dallas. 1979.

———, and Janet Zapata. *The Arms of Tiffany.* Work in progress.

Videos

Son of a Gun or How Sam Colt Changed America. Hour-long video by BBC-TV, presenting history of Colonel Colt and the influence of Colt firearms on history.

Colt Firearms Legends. Narrated by Mel Torme, script by R. L. Wilson. Hour-long video done as companion to *Son of a Gun.*

Combat Handguns

Karwan, Chuck. *Combat Handgunnery.* Various editions, annual.

Taylor, Chuck. *The Complete Book of Combat Handgunning.* 1982.

Thompson, Leroy and Rene Smeets. *Great Combat Handguns.* 1993.

Custom Rifle Makers

Hughes, Steven Dodd. *Custom Rifles in Black and White.*
Simmons, Dick. *Custom Built Rifles, Their Design & Production.*
Warner, Ken, ed. *The Gun Digest Review of Custom Guns.* 1980.

Derringers

Kirkland, Turner. *Southern Derringers of the Mississippi Valley.* 1971.
Parsons, John E. *Henry Deringer's Pocket Pistol.* 1952.
Wilson, R. L. and L. D. Eberhart. *The Deringer in America. Volume I: The Percussion Period.* 1985. *Volume II: The Cartridge Period.* 1993.

Engraving, Stockmaking, and Fine Guns

Abbiatico, Mario. *Modern Firearms Engraving.* 1980.
———. *Incisione delle Armi Sportive.* 1982.
Austyn, Christopher. *Gun Engraving.* 1998.
Bleile, C. Roger. *American Engravers.* 1980. Study of contemporary engravers.
———, Gianoberto Lupi, and Franco Vaccari. *Grandi Incisioni su Armi d'Oggi.* 1977.
Grancsay, Stephen V. *Master French Gunsmiths' Designs of the Mid-Seventeenth Century.* 1950.
———. *Master French Gunsmiths' Designs.* 1970.
Gusler, Wallace B. and James D. Lavin. *Decorated Firearms 1540–1870.* 1977.
Harris, Dr. Fredric A. *Firearms Engraving as Decorative Art.* 1989.
Kennedy, Monte. *Checkering and Carving of Gun Stocks.* 1962.
Meek, James B. *The Art of Engraving.* 1973.
Nobili, Marco E. *Il Grande Libro Delle Incisioni.* 1989. Preface by Firmo Fracassi.
Prudhomme, E. C. *Gun Engraving Review.* 1961.
Turpin, Tom. *Custom Firearms Engraving: The Techniques and Treasures of the World's Greatest Artists.* 1999.
Wesbrook, Dave. *Professional Stockmaking.* 1994.
Wilson, R. L. *Steel Canvas: The Art of American Arms.* 1995. Decorative arms from the 1500s to modern times, primarily American, but including decorated European arms as well.
———. *L. D. Nimschke: Firearms Engraver.* 1965. Original engraver's record book and several pictured firearms of one of the 19th century's leading arms engravers.

Gatling Gun

Berk, Joseph. *The Gatling Gun: 19th Century Machine Gun to 21st Century Vulcan.* 1991.
Stephenson, E. Frank, Jr. *Gatling: A Photographic Remembrance.* 1994.
Toppel, Donald R. and Paul Wahl. *The Gatling Gun.* 1965.

Griffin & Howe

Howe, James Virgil. *The Modern Gunsmith.* 1934–41. (Deals with a number of makers, including Griffin & Howe.)

Handguns

GENERAL

Arnold A. *Shoot a Handgun.* 1993.
Baker, William Clyde, III. *The American Pocket Pistol 1848–1898.* 1970.
Comus, Steve. *The Gun Digest Book of 9mm Handguns.* 1993.
Cumming, Robert. *Christie's Guide to Collecting: Up-to-Date Information and Practical Advice on Becoming a Collector, Looking After a Collection, Buying and Selling.* 1984.
Gould, A. C. *Modern American Pistols and Revolvers.* 1988.
Konig, Klaus-Peter, and Martin Hugo. *9mm Parabellums: The History & Development of the World's 9mm Pistols & Ammunition.* 1993.
Leatherdale, Frank and Paul. *Successful Pistol Shooting.* 1988.
McGivern, Ed. *Fast and Fancy Revolver Shooting.* 1984.
Morrison, Gregory Boyce. *The Modern Technique of the Pistol.* 1991.
Shaw, John. *Shoot to Win.* 1985.
Swiggett, Hal. *Handguns '95.* 1995 and later editions, with identification by year.

AUTOMATICS

Bruch, Gordon. *Webley & Scott Automatic Pistols.* 1992.
Grennell, Dean A. *The Gun Digest Book of the .45.* 1989.
Hoffschmidt, E. J. *Know Your .45 Auto Pistols—Models 1911 & A1.* 1974.
Kasler, Peter Alan. *Glock: The New Wave in Combat Handguns.* 1993.
Ramos, J. M. *.45 ACP Super Guns.* 1991.
Wilson, R. K. *Textbook of Automatic Pistols.* 1990.

Revolvers

GENERAL

Keith, Elmer. *Sixguns.* 1992.
Numerous other titles under makers' names.

PERCUSSION

Smith, Samuel E., and Frank Sellers. *American Percussion Revolvers.* 1971.
Winant, Lewis. *Early Percussion Firearms.* 1959.

METALLIC CARTRIDGES

Brown, Taylor. *James Reid and His Catskill Knuckledusters.* 1990.
Phelps, Art. *The Story of Merwin, Hulbert & Co. Firearms.* 1991.
Sell, DeWitt, Ph.D. *Handguns Americana.* 1972.
Numerous other titles under makers' names.

"SATURDAY NIGHT SPECIALS"

Goforth, W. E. "Bill." *Iver Johnson's Arms & Cycle Works Handguns, 1871–1964.* 1991.
Webster, Donald B., Jr. *Suicide Specials.* 1958.

High Standard

Dance, Tom. *High Standard: A Collector's Guide to the Hamden & Hartford Target Pistols.* 1991.
Petty, Charles E. *High Standard Automatic Pistols 1932–1950.* 1989.

Holsters

Bianchi, John. *Blue Steel and Gunleather.* 1978.
Rattenbury, Richard. *Packing Iron.* 1993.

Kentucky Rifles and Pistols

Chandler, Roy F., and James B. Whisker, *Behold the Longrifle.* 1993.
Dillin, Captain John G. W. *The Kentucky Rifle.* 1993 (reprint).
Dresslar, Jim (David Wesbrook, photography). *Folk Art of Early America: The Engraved Powder Horn.* 1996.
Guthman, William H. *Drums A'beating Trumpets Sounding.* 1993.
Kauffmann, Henry. *The Pennsylvania-Kentucky Rifle.* 1960.
Kentucky Rifle Association. *Kentucky Rifles and Pistols 1756–1850.* 1976.
Kindig, Joe, Jr. *Thoughts on the Kentucky Rifle in Its Golden Age.* 1984.
Shumway, George. *Rifles of Colonial America, Vols. 1 and II.* 1980.

REGIONAL MAKERS

Bivens, John. *Longrifles of North Carolina.* 1988.
Harriger, Russell H. *Longrifles of Pennsylvania, Volume 1, Jefferson, Clarion & Elk Counties.* 1984.
Hartzler, Daniel D. *Arms Makers of Maryland.* 1975.

Hutslar, Donald A. *Gunsmiths of Ohio—18th & 19th Centuries: Volume 1, Biographical Data.* 1973.

Lewis, Michael H. *The Gunsmiths of Manhattan, 1625–1900: A Checklist of Tradesmen.* 1991.

Shumway, George. *George Schreyer, Sr. and Jr., Gunmakers of Hanover, Pennsylvania.* 1990.

———. *Pennsylvania Longrifles of Note.* 1977.

Lever-Action Rifles

Jamieson, G. Scott. *Bullard Arms.* Ontario, Canada: The Boston Mills Press, 1989.

Maxwell, Samuel L., Sr. *Lever-Action Magazine Rifles Derived from the Patents of Andrew Burgess.* 1976.

See also under manufacturers, e.g., Winchester, Marlin, Remington.

Machine Guns

Chinn, Colonel George M. *The Machine Gun.* Four volumes: Vol. 1 (1951), Vol. II (1952), Vol. III (1953), Vol. IV (1955).

Helmer, William J. *The Gun That Made the Twenties Roar.* 1977. (The Thompson submachine gun.)

Hill, Tracie L. *Thompson: The American Legend: The First Submachine Gun.* 1996.

Truby, J. David. *The Lewis Gun.* 1988.

Wardman, Wayne. *The Owen Gun.* 1991.

Manhattan

Nutter, Waldo E. *Manhattan Firearms.* 1958.

Wilson, R. L. *The Guns of Manhattan.* Work in progress.

Marlin

Brophy, Lt. Col. William S., USAR, Ret. *Marlin Firearms: A History of the Guns and the Company That Made Them.* 1989.

Military

General

Bazelon, Bruce S. and William F. McGuinn. *A Directory of American Military Goods Dealers & Makers 1785–1915, Combined Edition.* 1999.

Frey, Steve. *Imported Military Firearms 1866–1899.* 1999

MUZZLE-LOADING

Bazelon, and McGuinn. *A Directory of American Military Goods Dealers and Makers 1785–1915.* 1990.

Brophy, William S. *Krag Rifles.* 1980.

Dorsey, R. Stephen. *Indian War Cartridge Pouches, Boxes and Carbine Boots.* 1993.

Gluckman, Arcaidi. *United States Martial Pistols and Revolvers.* 1956.

———. *Identifying United States Muskets, Rifles and Carbines.* 1965.

Hicks, James. *U.S. Firearms 1776–1956, Notes on U.S. Ordnance, Vol. I.* 1957.

———. *Ordnance Correspondence, Vol. II.* 1940.

Huntington, R. T. *Hall's Breechloaders.*

Jordan, John W. *The Eagle on U.S. Firearms.* 1992.

Lewis, Berkeley R. *Small Arms and Ammunition in the United States Service.* 1956.

Lewis, Jack. *The Gun Digest Book of Assault Rifles.* Various editions; annual.

Madis, George. *U.S. Military Arms Dates of Manufacture from 1795.* 1989.

Moller, George D. *American Military Shoulder Arms: Volume I, Colonial and Revolutionary War Arms.* 1993.

———. *American Military Shoulder Arms: Volume 2, From the 1790s to the End of the Flintlock Period.* 1994.

———. *Massachusetts Military Shoulder Arms 1784–1877.* 1989.

North, S. and R. North. *Simeon North: First Official Pistol Maker of the United States.* 1972.

Pitman, Brigadier General John. *The Pitman Notes on U.S. Martial Small Arms and Ammunition, 1776–1933, Volume 2, Revolvers and Automatic Pistols.* 1990.

———. *U.S. Breech-Loading Rifles and Carbines, Cal. 45.* 1992. (Trapdoor rifles, muskets, carbines.)

Reilly, Robert M. *United States Martial Flintlocks.* 1986.

———. *U.S. Military Small Arms 1816–1865.* 1983.

Smith, Samuel E. and Edwin W. Bitter. *Historic Pistols: The American Martial Flintlock 1760–1845.* 1986.

METALLIC CARTRIDGE

Canfield, Bruce N. *A Collector's Guide to the M1 Garand and the M1 Carbine.*

———. *A Collector's Guide to the '03 Springfield,* 1989.

———. *A Collector's Guide to U.S. Combat Shotguns.* 1992.

Crossman, Captain E. C. *Military and Sporting Rifle Shooting.* 1988. Reprint.

Duff, Scott A. *The M1 Garand: World War 2.* 1990.

———. *The M1 Garand: Post World War.* 1993.

Gander, Terry. *Guerrilla Warfare Weapons.* 1990.

Hatcher, Major-General J. S. *The Book of the Garand.* 1977.

Pyle, Billy. *The Gas Trap Garand.* 1999.

Ramos, J. M. *World's Deadliest Rimfire Battleguns.* 1990.

Russell, A. L. *Illustrated Handbook of Rifle Shooting.* 1992.

Ruth, Larry. *M1 Carbine.* 1987.

———. *War Baby!: The U.S. Caliber 30 Carbine, Volume I.* 1992.

———. *War Baby Comes Home: The U.S. Caliber 30 Carbine, Volume 2.* 1993.

Stevens, R. Blake. *U.S. Rifle M14—From John Garand to the M21.* 1991.

Swearengen, Thomas F. *The World's Fighting Shotguns.* 1979.

NAVAL

Gilkerson, William. *Boarders Away, Volume II: Firearms of the Age of Fighting Sail.* 1993.

Winter, Frederick R. *U.S. Naval Handguns, 1808–1911.* 1990.

New England

Achtermeier, William O. *Rhode Island Arms Makers & Gunsmiths 1643–1883.* 1980.

Deyrup, Felicia Johnson. *Arms Makers of the Connecticut Valley.* 1948.

Lindsay, Merrill K. *The New England Gun.* 1975.

Logan, Herschel C. *Underhammer Guns.* 1965.

Oddities

Frost, H. Gorden. *Blades and Barrels.* 1972.

Winans, Lewis. *Firearms Curiosa.* 1955.

Patents

British Patent Office. *Patents for Inventions, Class 119 (Small Arms), 1855–1930.* 1993. Seven volumes.

Stockbridge, V. D. *Digest of U.S. Patents Relating to Breech Loading and Magazine Small Arms, 1836–1873.* Reprint.

Pepperbox Firearms

Dunlap, Jack. *American British & Continental Pepperbox Firearms.* 1964.

Winant, Lewis. *Pepperbox Firearms.* 1952.

Plains Rifles

Baird, John D. *Fifteen Years in the Hawken Lode.* 1976.
———. *Hawken Rifles, The Mountain Man's Choice.* 1976.
Hanson, Charles E., Jr. *The Hawken Rifle: Its Place in History.* 1979.
———. *The Northwest Gun.* 1976.
———. *The Plains Rifle.* 1989.
Roberts, Ned H. *The Muzzle-Loading Cap Lock Rifle.* 1991.
Russell, Carl P. *Firearms, Traps, & Tools of the Mountain Men.* 1967.
———. *Guns of the Early Frontiers.* 1957.

Remington

Karr, Charles Lee, Jr. and Caroll Robbins Karr. *Remington Handguns.* 1956.
Lacy, John F. *The Remington 700.* 1990.
Layman, George. *The Military Remington Rolling Block Rifle.* 1992.
Madaus, Howard M. and Simeon Stoddard. *The Guns of Remington Historic Firearms Spanning Two Centuries.* 1997. Photographed by Paul Goodwin.
Marcot, Roy M. *Remington, America's Oldest Gunmaker, The Official Authorized History of Remington Arms Company.* 1998.
Peterson, Harold L. *The Remington Historical Treasury of American Guns.* 1966.

Ruger (Sturm, Ruger & Co., Inc.)

Dougan, John C. *Compliments of Col. Ruger: A Study of Factory Engraved Single Action Revolvers.* 1992.
———. *Know Your Ruger Single-Action Revolvers 1953–63.* 1981.
———. *Know Your Ruger Single-Actions: The Second Decade 1963–73.* 1989.
Hiddleson, Chad. *Encyclopedia of Ruger Rimfire Self-Loading Pistols: 1949–1992.* 1993.
Long, Duncan. *The Ruger "P" Models.* 1993.
———. *The Ruger .22 Automatic Pistol, Standard/Mark I/Mark II Series.* 1989.
Lueders, Hugo A., ed. by Don Findley. *Ruger Automatic Pistols and Single Action Revolvers.* 1993.
Roberts, Joseph Jr. *Ruger.* 1991 (Compilation of miscellaneous articles in *The American Rifleman*, regarding Ruger firearms and William B. Ruger.)
Wilson, R. L. *Ruger & His Guns.* New York: Simon & Schuster, Inc., 1996.

Sharps

Bailey, DeWitt. *The Model 1874 Sharps.*
Hopkins, Richard E. *Military Sharps Rifles & Carbines, Vol. I.* 1967.
Sellers, Frank. *Sharps Firearms.* 1982.
Smith, Winston O. *The Sharps Rifle.* 1965.

Shotguns

GENERAL

Barnes, Mike. *The Complete Clay Shot.* 1993.
Brister, Bob. *Shotgunning: The Art and the Science.* 1976.
Butler, David F. *The American Shotgun.* 1973.
Conley, Frank F. *The American Single Barrel Trap Gun.* 1989.
Croft, Peter. *Clay Shooting.* 1990.
Davies, Ken. *The Better Shot.* 1992.
Hinman, Bob. *The Golden Age of Shotgunning.* 1982.
McIntosh, Michael. *Best Guns.* 1989.
Meyer, Jerry. *Clay Target Handbook.* 1993.
Wallack, L. R. *American Shotgun Design and Performance.* 1977.
Zutz, Don. *The Double Shotgun.* 1985.
———. *Shotgunning Trends in Transition.* 1990.

BROWNING

Browning, V. *A History of Browning Guns from 1831.* 1986.
Desert Publications. *Browning Hi-Power Pistols.* 1982.

FOX

McIntosh, Michael. *A. H. Fox: The Finest Gun in the World.* 1994.

ITHACA

Snyder, Walter Claude. *The Ithaca Gun Company from the Beginning.* 1991.
———. *Ithaca Featherlight Repeaters . . . The Best Gun Going. A Complete History of the Ithaca Model 37 and the Model 87.* 1998.

L. C. SMITH

Brophy, Lt. Col. William S. *L. C. Smith Shotguns.* 1979.

LEFEVER

Elliot, Robert W., and Jim Cobb. *Lefever: Guns of Lasting Fame.* 1986.

PARKER & BROS.

Baer, Larry L. *The Parker Gun.* 1980.
Muderlak, Ed. *Parker the Old Reliable.* 1948.

Single-Shot Rifles

Cleveland, H. W. S. *Hints to Riflemen.* 1864.
deHaas, Frank. *A Potpourri of Single Shot Rifles & Actions.* 1993.
———. *More Single Shot Rifles and Actions.* 1989.
Delisse, Frank and Mark. *Single-Shot Actions, Their Design and Construction.* 1991.
Grant, James J. *Single Shot Rifles.* 1947.
———. *Boy's Single Shot Rifles.* 1967.
———. *More Single Shot Rifles.* 1959.
———. *Single Shot Rifle Finale.* 1992.
Kelver, Gerald O. *Reloading Tools, Sights and Telescopes for Single Shot Rifles.* 1982.
Layman, George J. *A Guide to the Maynard Breechloader.* 1993.

Smith & Wesson

Jinks, Roy G. *Artistry in Arms.* 1991. Book accompanying worldwide tour of S&W firearms.
———. *The History of Smith & Wesson: No Thing of Importance Will Come Without Effort.* 1977. Revised 1988.
———, and Robert J. Neal. *Smith & Wesson 1857–1945.* 1975.
Parsons, John E. *Smith & Wesson Revolvers.* 1957.

Spencer

Marcot, Roy M. *Spencer Repeating Firearms.* 1983.

Sporting Rifles

deHaas, Frank. *Bolt Action Rifles.* 1984.
Fadala, Sam. *Legendary Sporting Rifles.* 1992.
———. *Rifle Guide.* 1993.
Fremantle, T. F. *The Book of the Rifle.* 1988. Reprint.
Keith, Elmer. *Big Game Rifles and Cartridges.* 1984. Reprint.
———. *Keith's Rifles for Large Game.* 1986.
McIntosh, Michael. *The Big-Bore Rifle.* 1990.
O'Connor, Jack. *The Big Game Rifle.* 1994. Reprint.
Truesdell, S. R. *The Rifle: Its Development for Big-Game Hunting.* 1992.

Springfield Armory

Brophy, Lt. Colonel William S. *The Springfield 1903 Rifles.* 1985.
———. *Arsenal of Freedom, The Springfield Armory, 1890–1948: A Year-by-Year Account Drawn from Official Records.* 1991.
Crossman, Edward C. and Roy F. Dunlap. *The Book of the Springfield.* 1990.
Fuller, Claude. *Springfield Shoulder Arms 1795–1865.* 1986.
Poyer, Joe and Craig Riesch. *The .45–70 Springfield.* 1991.
Waite, M. D. and B. D. Ernst. *The Trapdoor Springfield.* 1983.

Stevens Arms & Tool Co.

Cope, Kenneth L. *Stevens Pistols and Pocket Rifles.* 1992.

Target Rifles and Handguns

Fadala, Sam. *The Book of the Twenty-Two: The All American Caliber.* 1989.
Johnson, Rick. *Rifleman's Handbook: A Shooter's Guide to Rifles, Reloading & Results.* 1990. An NRA publication.
Parish, David. *Successful Rifle Shooting.* 1993.
Smith, Roy M. *The Story of Pope's Barrels.* 1993.

Underhammer Guns

Logan, Herschel C. *Underhammer Guns.* 1965.

Weatherby

Gresham, Grits and Tom. *Weatherby: The Man, The Gun, The Legend.* 1992.

Whitney

Fuller, Claud E. *The Whitney Firearms.* 1946.

Winchester Repeating Arms Co., Its Predecessors and Successors

Butler, David F. *Winchester Model 1873.*
Campbell, John. *The Winchester Single-Shot: A History and Analysis.* 1995.
Canfield, Bruce. *A Collector's Guide to Winchester in the Service.* 1991.
Fadala, Sam. *Winchester's .30–30, Model 94.* 1986.
Henshaw, Thomas E. *The History of Winchester Firearms 1866–1992.* Sixth edition. 1993.
Houze, Herbert G. *Winchester Repeating Arms Company: Its History & Development from 1865 to 1981.* 1995.
———. *Winchester Bolt Action Military & Sporting Rifles, 1877 to 1937.* 1998.
———. *To the Dreams of Youth: The .22 Caliber Single Shot Winchester Rifle.* 1993.
Madis, George. *The Winchester Book.* Various editions since 1961.
———. *Winchester Dates of Manufacture 1849–1984.* 1984.
———. *The Winchester Handbook.* 1981.
———. *The Winchester Model Twelve.* 1982.
McDowell, R. Bruce. *Evolution of the Winchester from the 1847 Hunt, the Jennings, Smith-Jennings, Smith & Wesson, "Volcanic," Henry Rifle, and Beyond.* 1985.
Parsons, John E. *The First Winchester.* 1955.
Pirkle, Arthur. *Winchester Lever Action Repeating Firearms, Volume 3: The Models of 1894 and 1895.* 1998.
Poyer, Joseph. *U.S. Winchester Trench and Riot Guns and Other U.S. Military Combat Shotguns.* 1992.
Renneberg, Robert C. *The Winchester Model 94: The First 100 Years.* 1991.
Rule, Roger C. *A Catalogue Collection of 20th Century Winchester Repeating Arms Co.* 1984.
Schwing, Ned. *Winchester Slide-Action Rifles, Volume 1: Model 1890 & 1906.* 1992.
———. *Winchester Slide-Action Rifles, Volume 2: Model 61 & Model 62.* 1993.
———. *The Winchester Model 42.* 1990.
———. *Winchester's Finest, The Model 21.* 1990.
Stadt, Ronald W. *Winchester Shotguns and Shotshells.* 1984.
Watrous, George. *A History of Winchester Firearms, 1866–1966.*
Williamson, Clyde "Snooky." *Winchester Lever Legacy.* 1988.
Williamson, Harold F. *Winchester: The Gun That Won the West.* 1961.
Wilson, R. L. *Winchester: An American Legend.* 1991.
———. *Winchester Engraving.* 1991.
———. *Winchester: The Golden Age of American Gunmaking and the Winchester 1 of 1000.* 1983.

GENERAL SUBJECTS

Ammunition

Barnes, Frank. *Cartridges of the World.* Various editions.
Dixon, W. B. *European Sporting Cartridges.* 1998.
Erlmeier, Hans A. and Jakob H. Brandt. *Manual of Pistol and Revolver Cartridges, Vol. 2, Centerfire U.S. and British Calibers.* 1981.
Hatcher, Julian. *Hatcher's Notebook.* 1992.
Hoyen, George A. *The History and Development of Small Arms Ammunition, Volumes 1 and 2.* 1991. (Volume 1 deals with military longarms and early machine guns and their ammunition, period of the 18th and 19th centuries.)
———. *The History and Development of Small Arms Ammunition (British Sporting Rifle) Volume 3.* 1991.
Huon, Jean. *Military Rifle & Machine Gun Cartridges.* 1990.
Iverson, Dick. *Encyclopedia and Price Guide of American Paper Shotshells.* 1991.
———. *The Shotshell in the United States.* 1988.
Keith, Elmer. *Sixgun Cartridges and Loads.* 1984.
Kent, Daniel W. *German 7.9mm Military Ammunition.* 1991.
Matthews, Paul A. *Loading the Black Powder Rifle Cartridge.* 1993.
Suydam, Charles R. *The American Cartridge.* 1986.
Wolfe Publishing Co. *Big Bore Rifles and Cartridges.* 1991.
Various authors. *Wildcat Cartridges, Volume I.* 1992. By writers for *Handloader* and *Rifle* magazines.
Various authors. *Wildcat Cartridges, Volume II.* 1992. By writers for *Handloader* and *Rifle* magazines.

HAND-LOADING

Bell, Bob. *Handloader's Digest.* Various editions, annual.
Grennell, Dean A. *The Gun Digest Book of Handgun Reloading.* 1987.
Sharpe, Philip B. *Complete Guide to Handloading.*
Whelen, Colonel Townshend. *Why Not Load Your Own?* 1957.

Children

Lindsay, Merrill. *The Lure of Antique Arms.* 1976.
Rees, Clair F. *Beginner's Guide to Guns and Shooting.* 1988.

Encyclopedic Volumes

Amber, John T. *Gun Digest.* Various editions. See also later editions, edited by Ken Warner.
Brownell, Bob. *The Encyclopedia of Modern Firearms, Volume 1.* 1959.
Grennell, Dean A. *Handgun Digest.* Various editions.
Murtz, Harold A. *The Gun Digest Book of Exploded Long Gun Drawings.*
———. *The Gun Digest Book of Exploded Handgun Drawings.* 1992.

National Rifle Association. *Firearms Assembly 3: The NRA Guide to Rifles and Shotguns.* 1980.
———. *Firearms Assembly 4: The NRA Guide to Pistols and Revolvers.* 1980.
Peterson, Harold L. *Encyclopedia of Firearms.* 1964.
Petzal, David E. *The Encyclopedia of Sporting Firearms.* 1992.
Rice, F. Philip. *Outdoor Life Gun Data Book.* 1987.
Steindler, R. A. *Steindler's New Firearms Dictionary.* 1985.
Warner, *Gun Digest.* Various editions, annual (see also *Gun Digest* published under editorship of John T. Amber).
Wood, J. B. *Firearms Assembly/Disassembly, Part I: Automatic Pistols.* 1990.
———. *Firearms Assembly/Disassembly, Part I: Revolvers.* 1990.
———. *Firearms Assembly/Disassembly, Part I: Rimfire Rifles.* 1994.
———. *Firearms Assembly/Disassembly, Part I: Centerfire Rifles.* 1991.
———. *Firearms Assembly/Disassembly, Part I: Shotguns.* 1992.
———. *Firearms Assembly/Disassembly, Part I: Law Enforcement Weapons.* 1981.

Fakes

Edgerly, Harold. *The Revolving-Cylinder Colt Pistol Story from 1839 to 1847.*
Peterson, Harold L. *How Do You Know It's Old?* 1975.

Gun Legislation and Gun Laws

Bureau of Alcohol, Tobacco and Firearms. Book of regulations; available free of charge from any BATF office, and occasionally obtainable from displays by BATF agents at firearms shows.
Gottlieb, Alan. *The Gun Grabbers.* 1988.
Greenwood, Colin. *Firearms Control: A Study of Armed Crime and Firearms Control in England and Wales.* 1972.
Halbrook, Stephen P. *A Right to Bear Arms.* 1989.
———. *That Every Man Be Armed: The Evolution of a Constitutional Right.* 1984.
Kates, Don, ed. *Restricting Handguns: The Liberal Skeptics Speak Out.* 1979.
———, ed. *Firearms and Violence.* 1984.
———, ed. *The Great American Gun Debate.* 1997.
Kukla, Robert J. *Gun Control: A Written Record of Efforts to Eliminate the Private Possession of Firearms in America.* 1973.
Lott, John R. Jr. *More Guns Less Crime.* 1998.
Quigley, Paxton. *Armed and Female.* 1989. Various editions.
Sturm, Ruger & Co., Inc. *Firearms Ownership in America—Our Responsibility for the Future.* 1995.
Wright, James D., Peter H. Rossi, Kathleen Daly. *Under the Gun: Weapons, Crime and Violence in America.* 1983.

Gunmaker Lists

Sellers, Frank. *American Gunsmiths.* 1983.
Bacyk, T., D. Bacyk and T. Rowe. *Gun Powder Cans & Kegs.* 1998.
Kempers, R.T.W. *Eprouvettes: A Comprehensive Study of Early Devices for the Testing of Gunpowder.* 1999.

Gunpowder

Bacyk, T., D. Bacyk and T. Rowe. *Gun Powder Cans & Kegs.* 1998.
Kempers, R.T.W. *Eprouvettes: A Comprehensive Study of Early Devices for the Testing of Gunpowder.* 1999.

Gunsmithing, Gunmaking

Angier, R. H. *Firearms Bluing and Browning.*
Brownell, Bob. *Gunsmith Kinks.* 1969.
———. *Gunsmith Kinks 2.* 1983.
Brownell, Frank. *Gunsmith Kinks 3.* 1993.
Dunlap, Foy F. *Gunsmithing.* 1990.
Handloader and *Rifle* magazines, editors of. *Gunsmithing Tips and Projects.* 1992.
Matunas, Edward A. *Practical Gunsmithing.* 1989.
Mitchell, Jack. *The Gun Digest Book of Pistolsmithing.* 1980.
———. *The Gun Digest Book of Riflesmithing.* 1982.
Nonte, George C., Jr. *Pistolsmithing.* 1974.
Raynor, Ken and Brad Fenton. *The NRA Gunsmithing Guide—Updated.* 1984.
Stelle, J. P. and William B. Harrison. *The Gunsmith's Manual.* 1982.
Traister, John E. *First Book of Gunsmithing.* 1981.
———. *Gunsmithing at Home.* 1985.
Walker, Ralph. *The Gun Digest Book of Shotgun Gunsmithing.* 1983.

Guns of the West

Cunningham, Eugene. *Triggernometry.* 1970.
duMont, John S. *Custer Battle Guns.* 1988.
Garavaglia, Louis A. and Charles G. Worman. *Firearms of the American West 1803–1865.* 1984.
Kieft, Gary. *Beyond the Wild Bunch: The Fast-Growing Sport of Cowboy Action Shooting.* 1999.
———. *Firearms of the American West 1866–1894.* 1985.
Markham, George. *Guns of the Wild West.* 1993.
Rattenbury, Richard and Thomas E. Hall. *Sights West: Selections from the Winchester Museum Collection.* 1981.
Rosa, Joseph G. *The West from Lewis and Clark to Wounded Knee: The Turbulent Story of the Settling of Frontier America.* 1994.
———. *The Gunfighter, Man or Myth?* 1969.
———, and Robin May. *Buffalo Bill and the Wild West.* 1992.
Schreiner, Charles III, et al. *A Pictorial History of the Texas Rangers.* 1969.
Serven, James E. *Conquering the Frontiers: Stories of American Pioneers and the Guns Which Helped Them Establish a New Life.* 1974.
Wilson, R. L. *The Peacemakers: Arms and Adventure in the American West.* 1992.

Video

A & E Network. *The Guns That Tamed the West.* 1995.
Bar H Productions, *A Complete Guide & Introduction to the Exciting Sport of Cowboy Action Shooting* and *The Top Shooters Guide to Cowboy Action Shooting, Part II, Quicken the Pace.*

Hunting

Aitken, Russell Barnett. *Great Game Animals of the World.* 1974.
Atwater, Sally and Judith Schnell. *Ruffed Grouse.* 1989.
Batten, John H. *The Formidable Game.* 1983.
Bell, W.D.M. *Karamojo Bell.* 1990.
———. *The Wanderings of an Elephant Hunter.* 1990.
Bland, Dwain. *Turkey Hunter's Digest.* 1986.
Boddington, Craig. *Campfires and Game Trails: Hunting North American Big Game.* 1985.
———. *Safari Rifles: Double Magazine Rifles and Cartridges for African Hunting.* 1990.
Boone & Crockett Club. *Records of Hunting North American Big Game.* Various editions.
Buckingham, Nash. *"Mr. Buck": The Autobiography of Nash Buckingham.* 1990.
Bull, Bartle. *Safari: A Chronicle of Adventure.* 1989.
Cadieux, Charles L. *Pronghorn, North America's Unique Antelope.* 1986.
Capstick, Peter. *Death in the Long Grass.* 1977. (One of several books of African safari adventure by a former Wall Street banker who became a professional hunter in Africa.)
Corbett, Jim. *The Jim Corbett Collection.* 1991.
Cottar, Charles. *Cottar: The Exception Was the Rule.* 1999.
Elliott, Brook. *The Complete Smoothbore Hunter.* 1986.
Elman, Robert. *1001 Hunting Tips.* 1983.
———, and George Peper. *Hunting America's Game Animals and Birds.* 1975.
Fergus, Jim. *A Hunter's Road.* 1992.

Fish, Chet, ed. *The Outdoor Life Bear Book.* 1983.
Foster, William Harnden. *New England Grouse Shooting.* 1983.
Gassett, Jose Ortega y. *Meditations on Hunting.* 1985.
Gates, Elgin T. *Trophy Hunter in Asia.* 1982.
Grinnell, George Bird. *American Duck Shooting.* 1991 (reprint).
Halls, Lowell K. *White-Tailed Deer: Ecology and Management.* 1984.
Hemingway, Ernest. *Green Hills of Africa.* (First published 1935; reflects Hemingway's fascination with safari hunting.)
Huggler, Tom. *Quail Hunting in America.* 1987.
Karsnitz, Jim and Vivian. *Sporting Collectibles.* 1992.
Laycock, George. *The Hunters and the Hunted.* 1990.
Levinson, John M. and Somers G. Headley. *Shorebirds: The Birds, The Hunters, The Decoys.* 1991.
Madsen, John, et al. *The Outdoor Life Deer Hunter's Encyclopedia.* 1985.
Mellon, James. *African Hunter.* 1988. (The definitive book on African hunting.)
Morris, David. *Hunting Trophy Whitetails.* 1993.
National Muzzle Loading Rifle Association. *The North American Big Game Muzzleloading Record Book.* 1992.
O'Connor, Jack. *Sheep and Sheep Hunting.* 1992.
Patterson, J. H. *Man-Eaters of Tsavo.* 1986.
Reiger, George. *The Wildfowler's Quest.* 1989.
———. *The Wings of Dawn.* 1989. (Waterfowl hunting, including history thereof.)
Rikhoff, Jim. *Fair Chase.* 1984.
Roosevelt, Theodore. *Ranch Life and the Hunting Trail.*
———, and George Bird Grinnell, et al. *Hunting in Many Lands.*
Ruark, Robert. *The Old Man and the Boy and The Old Man Grows Older.* 1989. Reprint.
———. *Horn of the Hunter.* 1987. Reprint.
———. *Use Enough Gun.* 1992. Reprint.
Rue, Leonard Lee, III. *Whitetails.* 1991.
Sheehan, Laurence. *The Sporting Life: A Passion for Hunting and Fishing.* 1992.
Smith, Steven. *Hunting Ducks and Geese.* 1984.
———. *Hunting Upland Game Birds.* 1987.
van Zwoll, Wayne. *Elk Rifles, Cartridges and Hunting Tactics.* 1992.
Waterman, Charles F. *The Hunter's World.* 1983.
Wegner, Dr. Robert. *Deer and Deer Hunting: The Serious Hunter's Guide.* 1984. Followed by *Deer and Deer Hunting Book 2* and *Deer and Deer Hunting Book 3.*
———. *Wegner's Bibliography on Deer and Deer Hunting.* 1993.
Wildlife Management Institute. *Big Game of North America, Ecology and Management.* 1983.
Wilson, R. L. *Theodore Roosevelt Outdoorsman.* 1971 and 1994.
Woolner, Frank. *Timberdoodle.* 1987. (A woodcock hunting classic.)
Wooters, John. *Hunting Trophy Deer.* 1983.
Vettier, Jacques. *Big Game Hunting in Asia, Africa, and Elsewhere.* 1993.
Zumbo, Jim and Robert Elman, ed. *All-American Deer Hunter's Guide.* 1983.

Video

In the Blood. Feature film documents two African safaris: the first led by President Roosevelt in 1909, the second by his grandson nearly 80 years later. Proof of the key role of hunting in the conservation of wildlife.

HUNTING WITH HANDGUNS

Boothroyd, Geoffrey. *The Handgun.* 1989.
Kelly, Larry and J. D. Jones. *Hunting for Handgunners.* 1990.

Identification and/or Values

Fjestad, Steven. *Blue Book of Gun Values.* 20th edition. 1999.
Flayderman, Norm. *Flayderman's Guide to Antique American Firearms and Their Values.* Various editions.
Herr, Eugene. *Der Neue Stockel.* International listing of gunmakers from 1400 through 1900; in three volumes: 1978, 1979, 1982.
Quertermous, Russell and Steve. *Modern Guns: Identification & Values.* 1992.
Schroeder, Joe. *The Gun Digest Book of Modern Gun Values.* Various editions, annual.
Schwing, Ned. *Standard Catalog of Firearms.* Various editions, annual.

Law Enforcement

Askins, Charles, Jr. *Unrepentant Sinner.* 1985.
Ferguson, Tom. *Modern Law Enforcement Weapons & Tactics.* 1991.
FitzGerald, J. H. *Shooting.* 1993.
Jordan, William H. *No Second Place Winner.* 1962.
Keith, Elmer. *Hell, I Was There!* 1979.

Military

George, Lieutenant Colonel John. *Shots Fired in Anger.* 1991.
Hesketh-Prichard, Major H. *Sniping in France.* 1993.
Hogg, Ian V. *Military Small Arms of the 20th Century, 6th Edition.* 1991.
———. *Small Arms: Pistols and Rifles.* 1994.
———. *Pistols of the World.* 1992. Various editions.
Hunnicutt, Robert W., ed. *Self-Loading Rifles: Data and Comment.* 1988.
McBride, H.W. *A Rifleman Went to War.* 1987.
Stevens, R. Blake and Edward C. Ezell. *The SPIW: Deadliest Weapon That Never Was.* 1985.
Walter, John. *Rifles of the World.* 1993.
Weeks, John. *World War 2 Small Arms.* 1989.
Articles from *The American Rifleman, Guns & Ammo,* and various other periodicals.

Miniatures

Brown, Arthur, Joel Morrow, and David Hall, *The Art of Miniature Firearms Centuries of Craftsmanship,* Miniature Arms Society. 1999.
Keeble, K. Corey. *From the Kingdom of Lilliput: The Miniature Firearms of David Kucer* combined with *The Making of Miniatures,* by David Kucer. 1994.
Lindsay, Merrill. *Miniature Firearms.*

Auction-House and Dealer Catalogues

Bourne, Richard A., Co. *The Remington Collection of Karl F. Moldenhauer.* October 20, 1980.
Dexter, F. Theodore. *Thirty-Five Years Scrap Book of Antique Arms.* Vols. 1 and 2.
Finer, Peter. *Peter Finer.* Lavish book presenting arms and armor, with detailed, scholarly descriptions and illustrations. The series begun c. 1995, and issued approximately every one or two years.
Francis Bannerman Sons. Eightieth-anniversary hardbound catalogue.
Martin, Greg. *The Estate of Richard C. Marohn, M.D.* San Francisco: Butterfield & Butterfield, October 16, 1996. (Catalogue of the Marohn Collection, including artifacts, documents and memorabilia of L. D. Nimschke, and of the Young family of engravers.)
———. Miscellaneous auction catalogues including the John R. Woods Collection (October 22, 1991), the Warren Anderson Collection (March 23 and July 14, 1992), the Press Collection (various dates), the Lowenstein Collection (July 24, 1996), and the George R. Repaire Collection (April 14, 1997).
U.S. Cartridge Co. *Illustrated Catalogue of United States Cartridge Company's Collection of Firearms.* c. 1905.
Wilson, R. L., Peter Hawkins, Christopher Brunker. *Colt/Christie's Auction of Fine and Rare Firearms.* October 7, 1981.

GENERAL REFERENCE

Amber, John T. (ed.). *Gun Digest.* Annual first appeared in 1947. (Amber was succeeded by Ken Warner, c. 1979.)

Fjestad, Steven. *Blue Book of Gun Values,* various editions (20 as of 1999).

Flayderman, Norm. *Flayderman's Guide to Antique American Firearms . . . and Their Values.* Various editions, annual.

———, ed. *Illustrated Catalogue of Arms and Military Goods.* New Milford, Conn.: N. Flayderman & Co., 1961. Reprint edition of the 1864 Schuyler, Hartley & Graham company catalogue.

Hand, R. A. *A Bookman's Guide to Hunting, Shooting, Angling and Related Subjects.* 1991.

Hayward, John F. *The Art of the Gunmaker.* 1962–63. Two volumes.

———. *One Hundred Great Guns.* 1967.

Held, Robert. *The Age of Firearms.* Various editions since 1957.

Houze, Herbert G. *The Sumptuous Flaske.* 1989.

Logan, Herschel C. *From Hand Cannon to Automatic.* 1944.

Murtz, Harold A. *Gun Digest Treasury.* Various editions. (Earlier editions edited by John T. Amber.)

———. *Guns Illustrated.* Various editions, annual.

O'Connor, Jack. *Complete Book of Shooting: Rifles and Shotguns, Handguns.* 1983.

Peterson, Harold L. *Treasury of the Gun.* 1962.

———, and Robert Elman. *The Great Guns.* 1971.

Pollard, H.B.C., ed. by Claude Blair. *A History of Firearms.* 1983.

Pope, Dudley. *Guns: An Illustrated History of Artillery.* 1971.

Rattenbury, Richard. *Packing Iron: A Survey of Military and Civilian Gunleather on the Western Frontier.* 1993.

Riling, Ray. *The Powder Flask Book.* 1953.

———. *Guns and Shooting, A Selected Bibliography.* 1982.

Schroeder, Joseph J. *Gun Collector's Digest.* Various editions, annual.

Sellers, Frank. *American Gunsmiths.* 1983.

———. *The William M. Locke Collection.* 1973.

Sheldon, Lawrence P. *California Gunsmiths 1846–1900.* 1977.

Stoeger. *Shooter's Bible.* Various editions, annual.

———. *Gun Trader's Guide.* Various editions.

Tanner, Hans. *Guns of the World.* 1977.

Tappan, Mel. *Survival Guns.* 1993.

Tarassuk, Leonid. *Antique European and American Firearms at the Hermitage Museum.* 1971.

Traister, John. *How to Buy and Sell Used Guns.* 1984.

van Zwoll, Wayne. *America's Great Gunmakers.* 1992.

Warner, Ken, ed. *Gun Digest.* Various editions, annual.

Weil, Robert. *Contemporary Makers of Muzzle Loading Firearms.* 1980.

Wilkerson, Frederick. *Small Arms.* 1966.

Wilson, R. L. with Greg Martin. *Buffalo Bill's Wild West, An American Legend.* 1998.

OTHER COUNTRIES

General

Gaier, Claude. *Les Plus Belles Gravures d'Armes de Chasse.* 1998 (French text).

Joly, Eric. *Legendary Sporting Guns Shotguns and Rifles.* 1999.

Walter, John. *Guns of the First World War, Rifles, Handguns and Ammunition from the Text Book of Small Arms, 1909.* 1991.

Australia

Skennerton, Ian D. *Australian Military Rifles & Bayonets.* 1988.

———. *Australian Service Machine Guns.* 1989.

———. *9mm Austen Mk 1 & Owen Mk 1 SMG.* SAIS #3. 1993.

——— and D. Balmer. *S.L.R.—Australia's FN FAL.* 1989.

Britain

Blackmore, Howard L. *Gunmakers of London 1350–1850.* 1986.

Bruce, Gordon and Christien Reinhart. *Webley Revolvers.* 1988.

George, J. N. *English Pistols and Revolvers.* 1979; first published 1938.

Glendenning, *British Pistols and Guns 1640–1840.*

Grancsay, Stephen V. and Clay P. Bedford. *Early Firearms of Great Britain and Ireland from the Collection of Clay P. Bedford.* 1971.

Jackson, H. J. and C. E. Whitelaw. *European Hand Firearms of the Sixteenth, Seventeenth, and Eighteenth Centuries.* 1923.

Markham, George. *Guns of the Empire.* 1991.

———. *Guns of the Elite.* 1987. (Special Forces arms, from 1940.)

Munson, H. Lee. *Mortimer, The Gunmakers, 1753–1923.* 1992.

Pam, David. *The Royal Small Arms Factory: Enfield & Its Workers.* 1998.

Royal Armouries Museum. *Royal Armouries Yearbook,* published annually from 1996.

Skennerton, Ian D. *British Small Arms of WW2.* 1988.

———. *Lee-Enfield Story.* 1992.

———. *The British Sniper.* 1984.

———. *.303 Rifle No. 1, S.M.L.E. SAIS #1.* 1993.

———. *.303 Rifle No. 4, SAIS #2.* 1993.

———. *.303 Rifle No. 5 Mk 1, S.M.L.E. SAIS #4.* 1993.

———. *.303 Bren Light Machine Gun. SAIS #5.* 1993.

———. *British Service Sword & Lance Patterns. SAIS #6.* 1993.

———. *.303 Lee-Metford & Lee-Enfield Rifles & Carbines. SAIS #7.* 1997.

———. *Vickers Machine Gun Mk. 1. SAIS #8.* 1997.

———. *.455 Webley Revolvers. SAIS #9* 1997.

——— and P. Laidler. *.303 No. 4 (T) Sniper Rifle.* 1992.

——— and R. Richardson. *British & Commonwealth Bayonets.* 1986.

——— and G. Stamps. *.380 Enfield Revolver.* 1992.

Tate, Douglas. *British Gun Engraving.* 2000.

GAME GUNS

Akehurst, Richard. *Game Guns & Rifles: Percussion to Hammerless Ejector in Britain.* 1993.

Baxter, D. R. *Blunderbusses.* 1970.

Boothroyd, Geoffrey, and Susan Boothroyd. *The British Over-and-Under Shotgun.* 1996.

Rogers, H.C.B. *Weapons of the British Soldier.* 1972.

Shore, Captain C. *With British Snipers to the Reich.* 1988.

REVOLVERS

Chamberlain, W.H.J. and A.W.F. Taylerson. *Revolvers of the British Services 1854–1954.* 1982.

———. *Adams' Revolvers.* 1976.

Wilkinson, Frederick. *The Illustrated Book of Pistols.* 1979.

SPORTING ARMS

Austyn, Christopher. *Modern Sporting Guns.* 1996.

———. *Classic Sporting Rifles.* 1997.

———. *Gun Engraving.* 1998.

Kirton, Jonathan G. *The British Falling Block Breechloading Rifle from 1865.* 1985, 1997 editions.

Winfer, Walter G. *British Single Shot Rifles, Volume I: Alexander Henry.* 1998.

———. *British Single Shot Rifles, Volume 2: Gibbs Farquharson.* 1998.

———. *British Single Shot Rifles, Volume 3: W. J. Jeffery and the Trade Farquharsons with Notes on the Development of Jeffery's Nitro Cartridges.* 1998.

Scotland

Kelvin, Martin. *The Scottish Pistol: Its History, Manufacture and Design.* 1996.
Whitelaw, C. E., ed. by S. Barter-Bailey. *Scottish Arms Makers.* 1977.

Belgium

Gaier, Claude. *Liege Firearms.* 1985.
Nobili, Marco E. *Lebeau-Courally Guns & Rifles Maker Since 1865.* 1999.
Stevens, R. Blake. *UK and Commonwealth FALS.* 1987.

Canada

Phillips, Roger F., and Donald J. Klancher. *Arms and Accouterments of the Mounted Police 1873–1973.* 1982.

Czechoslovakia

Ramos, J. M. *The CZ-75 Family: The Ultimate Combat Handgun.* 1990.
Berger, R. J. *Know Your Czechoslovakian Pistols.* 1989.

Denmark

Hoff, A. *The Rasmussen Revolving Gun.*

France

Hicks, Major James E. *French Military Weapons, 1717–1938.* 1973.
Medlin, Eugene and Jean Huon. *Military Handguns of France 1858–1958.* 1993.

Germany

Datig, Fred A. *German Military Pistols 1904–1930.* 1990.
Dugelby, Thomas B. and R. Blake Stevens. *Death from Above: The German FG42 Paratrooper Rifle.* 1990.
Gotz, Hans Dieter. *German Military Rifles and Machine Pistols, 1871–1945.* 1990.
Markham, George. *Guns of the Reich.* 1989.
Quarrie, Bruce. *Weapons of the Waffen-SS.* 1991.
Speed, Jon. *Mauser Smallbores: Sporting, Target & Training Rifles.* 1999.
———. *Mauser: Original Oberndorf Sporting Rifles.* 1997.
Whittington, Robert. *German Pistols and Holsters 1934–1945, Vol. 2.* 1990.
———. *German Pistols and Holsters, 1934–1945, Volume 4.* 1991.

LUGERS

Bender, Eugene J. *Luger Holsters and Accessories of the 20th Century.* 1993.
Datig, Fred A. *The Luger Pistol: Its History & Development from 1893 to 1947; Monograph IV: The Swiss Variations 1897–1947.* 1992.
Gibson, Randall. *The Krieghoff Parabellum.* 1988.
Gortz, Joachim and John Walter. *The Navy Luger.* 1988.
Jones, Harry E. *Luger Variations.* 1975.
Kenyon, Charles, Jr. *Lugers at Random.* 1990.
———. *Luger: The Multi-National Pistol.* 1991.
McFarland, David J. *The P-08 Parabellum Luger Automatic Pistol.* 1982.

MAUSER

Belford & Dunlap. *The Mauser Self-Loading Pistol.*
Berger, R. J. *Know Your Broomhandle Mausers.* 1985.
Kuhnhausen, Jerry. *The Mauser M91 Through M98 Bolt Actions: A Shop Manual.* 1991.
Law, Richard D. *The German K98k Rifle, 1934–1945: The Backbone of the Wehrmacht.* 1993.
Olsen, Ludwig. *Mauser Bolt Rifles.* 1976.
Smith, Walter H. B. *Mauser Rifles and Pistols.* 1990.

WALTHER

Gangarosa, Gene, Jr. *P-38 Automatic Pistol.* 1993.
Hoffschmidt, E. J. *Know Your Walther P-38 Pistols.* 1974.
———. *Know Your Walther PP & PPK Pistols.* 1975.
Kersten, Manfred. *Walther Eine Deutsche Legende.* 1997. (In German, with English translation planned for 1998–99.)
Long, Duncan. *Powerhouse Pistols—The Colt 1911 and Browning Hi-Power Source.* 1989.
Nonte, Major George C. *Walther P-38 Pistol.* 1982.
———. *Pistol & Revolver Guide.* 1975.
———. *Pistol Guide.* 1991.
———. *Revolver Guide.* 1991.
Rankin, James L. *Walther Models PP and PPK, 1929–1945.* 1974.
———. *Walther, Volume II, Engraved, Presentation and Standard Models.* 1977.
———. *Walther, Volume III, 1908–1980.* 1981.

Holland

The following set of six volumes represents the most extraordinary single tribute to one nation's gunmaking by a single individual: collector and arms authority Henk L. Visser of The Hague, Netherlands. This lifetime achievement is a masterpiece of scholarship, richly illustrated, and magnificent in every respect.

Kist, J. B. *Dutch Muskets and Pistols.* 1974.
Puype, J. P. *The Visser Collection: Arms of the Netherlands in the Collection of H. L. Visser, Volume 1, Catalogue of Firearms, Swords and Related Objects.* 1996. Part 1, catalogue nos. 1–243; Part 2, catalogue nos. 244–495; Part 3, catalogue nos. 496–758.
Roth, R. *The Visser Collection: Arms of the Netherlands in the Collection of H. L. Visser, Volume II, Ordnance: Cannon, Mortars, Swivel-Guns, Muzzle- and Breech-Loaders,* 1996.
Visser, H. L., and D. W. Bailey (eds.). *Aspects of Dutch Gunmaking.* 1997.
E. A. Yablonskaya, et. al., ed. by M. N. Larchenko. *Dutch Guns in Russia in the Moscow Kremlin Armoury, Moscow Historical Museum, Hermitage St. Petersburg, Gatchina Palace Museum.* 1996.

Italy

di Carpegna, Nolfo. *Brescian Firearms.* 1997.
Held, Robert and Marco Morin. *Beretta: The World's Oldest Industrial Dynasty.* 1980.
Nobili, Marco E. *Fucili d'Autore The Best Guns.* 1999. Various editions have been produced since 1991, presenting detailed text and illustrations on best quality guns, primarily from Val Trompia, Italy. The 1999 edition is over 840 pages in length.
———. *Il Grande Libro delle Incisioni.* 1994 (various editions since 1989).
Smith, Steve, and Laurie Morrow. *The Italian Gun.* 1998.
Wilson, R. L. *The World of Beretta: An International Legend.* 2000.
Wood, J. B. *Beretta Automatic Pistols.* 1985.

Japan

Honeycutt, Fred L. Jr. *Military Pistols of Japan.* 1991.
———. *Military Rifles of Japan, 4th Edition.* 1989.
Leithe, Frederick E. *Japanese Handguns.* 1985.

Russia

Datig, Fred A. *Soviet Russian Postwar Military Pistols and Cartridges.* 1988.
———. *Soviet Russian Tokarev "TT" Pistols and Cartridges 1929–1953.* 1993.

Ezell, Edward, Ph.D. *The AK47 Story.* 1988.
Remling, John. *A Collector's Guide to Tokarev Pistols.* 1984.
Walter, John. *Kalashnikov Machine Pistols, Assault Rifles and Machine-Guns, 1945 to the Present.* 1999.

Spain and Portugal

Antaris, Leonardo M. *Astra Automatic Pistols.* 1989.
Lavin, James. *Spanish Firearms.*

Sweden

Wennberg, Kaa. *European Firearms in Swedish Castles.* 1986.

Appendix 2: Booksellers*

Dan Antrim, Bookseller
PO Box 675
Devon PA 19333

Blacksmith Corp.
830 N. Road No. 1 E.
PO Box 1752
Chino Valley AZ 85323

Blacktail Mountain Books
42 First Ave. W.
Kalispell MT 59901

Blue Book Publications
3009 34th Ave. S., #175
Minneapolis MN 55425

Braverman Arms Co.
912 Penn Ave.
Pittsburgh PA 15221

Brownell's Inc.
200 S. Front St.
Montezuma IA 50171

Cape Outfitters
599 County Rd. 206
Cape Girardeau MO 63701

Clark's Brothers
Rte. 5, Box 100
Warrenton VA 22186

Dick's Gun Room
3010 State Rd.
Cuyahoga Falls OH 44223

Dixie Gun Works
PO Box 130
Union City TN 38261

Bert Garber (BSG Books)
305 Bent Tree Court
Covington, LA 70433

Golden Age Arms Co.
115 E. High St.
Ashley OH 43003

Greenhill Books/Lionel Leventhal Ltd
Park House, 1 Russell Gardens
London NW11 9NN
England

Guidon Books
7117 Main St.
Scottsdale AZ 85251

Gullivers, Inc.
2918 Vine St., #270
Hays KS 67601

Guncraft Books
10737 Dutchtown Rd.
Knoxville TN 37932

Gunnerman Books
PO Box 214292
Auburn Hills MI 48321

Heritage/VSP Gun Books
PO Box 887
McCall ID 83638

Holland & Holland, Ltd
50 E. 57th St.
New York NY 10022

Hungry Horse Books
4605 Hwy. 93 S.
Whitefish MT 59937

I.D.S.A. Books
PO Box 1457
Piqua OH 45356

Intersports
Royal Publications, Inc.
790 W. Tennessee Ave.
Denver CO 80223

Jaqua's Fine Guns
900 E. Bigelow Ave.
Findlay OH 45840

Krause Publications
700 E. State St.
Iola WI 54990

Little John's Antique Arms, Inc.
1740 W. LaVeta
Orange CA 92668

Little Professor Book Center
22174 Michigan Ave.
Dearborn MI 48124

Little Professor Book Center
101 Boardman-Canfield Rd.
Boardman OH 44512

J. Martin Bookseller
PO Drawer AP
Beckley WV 25802

J. Millet & Co.
PO Box 6506
Santa Ana CA 92706

Navy Arms Co., Inc.
689 Bergen Blvd.
Ridgefield NJ 07657

Old Western Scrounger, Inc.
12924 Hwy. A-12
Montague CA 96064

Old West Gun Room
3509 Carlson Blvd.
El Cerrito CA 94530

Outdoorsman's Bookstore
Llangorse
Brecon
Powys
LD3 7UE England

Pahaska Books
8436 Samra Dr.
West Hills Ca 91304

Gerald Pettinger Books
Rte. 2, Box 125
Russell IA 50238

Pioneer Guns
5228 Montgomery Rd.
Cincinnati OH 45212

Potomac Arms Corp.
PO Box 35
Alexandria VA 22313

R & R Books
4447 East Lake Rd.
Livonia NY 14487

Rettig's Frontier Ohio
16 N. 3rd St., PO Box 122
Waterville OH 43566–1411

Martin B. Retting, Inc.
11029 Washington Blvd.
Culver City CA 90230

Rich's Cigar Store, Inc.
801 SW Alder St.
Portland OR 97205

Ray Riling Arms Books
6844 Gorsten St, PO Box 18925
Philadelphia PA 19119

*Should this list have any omissions, booksellers are invited to contact the author for inclusion.

Rutgers Book Center
127 Raritan Ave.
Highland Park NJ 08904

S & S Firearms
74–11 Myrtle Ave.
Glendale NY 11385

Safari Press, Inc.
15621 Chemical Lane, Building B
Huntington Beach CA 92649

Shooting Gallery Books
53 Blue Spruce Lane
Ballston Lake NY 12019

George Shumway
3900 Deep Run Lane
York PA 17402

Stoeger Industries
5 Mansard Court
Wayne NJ 07470

Trophy Room Books
Box 3041
Agoura CA 91301

Ken Trotman Arms Books
135 Ditton Walk
Unit 11
Cambridge England CB5 8PY

M.C. Wiest
10737 Dutchtown Rd.
Knoxville TN 37932

Wilderness Adventures
PO Box 627
Gallatin Gateway MT 59730

Appendix 3: Auction Houses

Butterfield & Butterfield, Inc.
220 San Bruno Ave.
San Francisco CA 94103

Christie's
8 King St.
London England

Christie's East
219 E. 67th St.
New York NY 10021

David Condon, Inc.
109 E. Washington St.
Middleburg VA 22117

Pete de Coux (Ammunition and Related Items)
235 Oak St., Box 8
Butler PA 16001

J.C. Devine, Inc.
PO Box 413
20 South St.
Milford NH 03055

Dunnings
755 Church Rd.
Elgin IL 60123

Faintich Auction Services, Inc.
10902 St. Charles Rock Rd.
St. Louis MO 63074

Fischer Galleries
Haldenstrasse 19
Lucerne Switzerland 6006

Wm. "Pete" Harvey
1270 Rte. 28A
PO Box 280
Cataumet MA 02534

James D. Julia, Inc.
Rt. 201, Skowhegan Rd.
PO Box 830
Fairfield ME 04937

Little John's Auction Service, Inc.
1740 W. La Veta
Orange CA 92868

Rock Island Auction Co. (Richard S. Ellis, Consultant)
1050 36th Ave.
Moline IL 61265

Sotheby's
1334 York Ave.
New York NY 10021

Supica's Old Town Station, Ltd.
PO Box 15351
Lenexa KS 66285

Wallis & Wallis
West Street Auction Galleries
Lewes, Sussex BN7 2NJ
England

Weller & Dufty
141 Bromsgrove St.
Birmingham
W. Midlands B5 GRQ
England

Western Reserve Auction Comp.
5900 S.O.M. Center Rd.
Bldg. 12, Suite 275
Willoughby OH 44094

Witherell's Americana Auctions
3620 West Island Court
Elk Grove CA 95758

Appendix 4: Arms Dealers

PROFESSIONAL ANTIQUE-ARMS DEALERS

Ackerman & Co.
16 Cortez St.
Westfield MA 01085

Ahlman Guns
Rte. 1, Box 20
Morristown MN 55052

Mike D'Ambria
PO Box 177107
San Diego CA 92177

American Heritage Investment, Inc.
1574 Pennwood Circle N.
Clearwater FL 34616

American Ordnance Preservation Association, Ltd.
311 Millbank Rd.
Bryn Mawr PA 19010

Dale C. Anderson
4 W. Confederate Ave.
Gettysburg PA 17325

Antique Arms Co.
1110 Cleveland Ave.
Monett MO 65708

Antique & Modern Firearms, Inc.
2263 Nicholasville Rd.
Lexington KY 40503

James O. Aplan Antiques & Art
HC 80
Box 793-25
Piedmont SD 57769

The Armoury, Inc.
Rte. 202, Box 2340
New Preston CT 06777

Knox Baldwin
PO Box 262
Brentwood TN 37024

Bedlan's
1318 E. St. Box 244
Fairbury NE 68352

Bell Consulting, Inc.
PO Box 579
Lady Lake FL 32158-0579

Bellinger's Military Antiques
Box 76371
Atlanta GA 30358

Robert B. Berryman
PO Box 143
Mt. Home TX 78058

William Boggs
1816 Riverside Drive Circle
Columbus OH 43212

Andrew Bottomley
The Coach House
Huddersfield Rd.
Holmfirth
W. Yorkshire England HD7 2TT

Bernard Braverman
1183 St. Vincent
Monroeville PA 15046

British Antiques
PO Box 7
Latham NY 12110

Buckskin Machine Works
3235 S. 358th St.
Auburn WA 98001

David Buehn
16881 Bolero Lane
Huntington Beach CA 92649

Buffalo Arms
123 S. Third, Suite 6
Sandpoint ID 83864

Cannon's Guns
Box 1036
320 Main St.
Polson MT 59860

Douglas R. Carlson
PO Box 71035
Des Moines IA 50325

Larry Carpenter (Old West Catalogue)
Box 1173
Kingsport TN 37662

Jim Chambers Flintlocks Ltd.
Rte. 1, Box 513-A
Candler NC 28715

Cherry's
3402-A W. Wendover Ave.
Greensboro NC 27435-0307

Chuck's Gun Shop
PO Box 597
Waldo FL 32694

Cole's Gun Works
Old Bank Building
Rte. 4, Box 250
Moyock NC 27958

Collectors Arms International, Inc.
John Jones
Box 425
Haymarket VA 20168

Collector's Firearms
Mike Clark
3301 Fondren
Houston TX 77042

Richard Cowles
Box 1629
Silver City NM 88062

D & D Gunsmiths, Ltd.
363 E. Elmwood
Troy MI 48083

David's Firearms, Ltd.
PO Box 6039
Falmouth ME 04105

Delhi Gun House
1374 Kashmere Gate
Delhi India

Dixie Gun Works, Inc.
PO Box 130
Gun Powder Lane
Union City TN 38261

Dixon Muzzleloading Shop, Inc.
RD 1, Box 175
Kempton PA 19529

Charles E. Duffy
Williams Lane
West Hurley NY 12491

Peter Dyson & Son Ltd.
29–31 Church St.
Honley Huddersfield
W. Yorkshire England HD7 2AH

Ed's Gun House
Rt. 1, Box 62
Minnesota City MN 55959

Richard S. Ellis
1000 36th Ave.
Moline IL 61265

Elmira Arms Co., Inc.
1128 Broadway
Elmira NY 14904

Enguix Import-Export
Alpujarras 58
Alzira
Valencia Spain 46600

Erickson's Frontier & Western Antiques
PO Box 9483
Fargo ND 58106

Floyd Everhart
PO Box 129
New Paris OH 45347

William Fagan
22952 15 Mile Rd.
Clinton Township MI 48035

Jeff Faintich
10902 St. Charles Rock Rd.
St. Louis MO 63074

Peter Finer, Ltd.
The Old Rectory
Ilmington, Shipston-on-Stour
Warwickshire England CV 36 4JQ

Jack First, Inc.
1201 Turbine Dr.
Rapid City SD 57701

Marshall F. Fish
Rte. 22 North, PO Box 2439
Westport NY 12993

N. Flayderman & Co., Inc.
PO Box 2446
Ft. Lauderdale FL 33303

Val Forgett (Navy Arms Co.)
689 Bergen Blvd.
Ridgefield NJ 07657

Chet Fulmer's Antique Firearms
PO Box 792, Rte. 2
Buffalo Lake
Detroit Lakes MN 56501

Herb Glass, Sr., and Jr.
Bullville NY 10915

James Goergen
Rte. 2, Box 182
Austin MN 55912

Golden Age Arms Co.
115 E. High St.
Ashley OH 43003
Will Gorges
Civil War Antiques
2100 Trent Blvd.
New Bern NC 28560

Great Northern Guns, Inc.
Joseph Andreis
2920 Tudor Rd.
Anchorage AL 99507

Leon E. "Bud" Greenwald
2553 S. Quitman St.
Denver CO 80219

The Gun Room
1121 Burlington
Muncie IN 47302

The Gun Room
127 Raritan Ave.
Highland Park NJ 08904

The Gun Works
247 South 2nd
Springfield OR 97477

Guncraft Sports, Inc.
10737 Dutchtown Rd.
Knoxville TN 37932

Guthman Americana
PO Box 392
Westport CT 06881

Thomas Haas
Guns Unlimited
RR 2, Ponderosa Ranch
Spencer IN 47460

Hansen & Co.
244 Old Post Rd.
Southport CT 06490

Wm. "Pete" Harvey
1270 Rte. 28A
PO Box 280
Cataumet MA 02534

Historical Investors Group
60 Harvest Moon Rd.
Easton CT 06612

The Horse Soldier
PO Box 184
Cashtown PA 17310

Investment Arms
PO Box 40253
Molrose Station
Nashville TN 37204

Jeb Klitzke
Main St.
Ransom KS 67572

Michael and Carol Kokin
Sherwood's Spirit of America
Santa Fe NM

Martin Lane Historical Americana, Inc.
205 W. Houston St.
New York NY 10010

Larry's Gun Room
105 N. 8th St.
Beresford SD 57004

Tom Lewis
PO Box 1748
Evergreen CO 80439

Liberty Antique Gunworks
19 Key St. PO Box 183
Eastport ME 04631

Little John's Antique Arms, Inc.
1740 W. La Veta
Orange CA 92868

Lock's Philadelphia Gun Exchange
6700 Rowland Ave.
Philadelphia PA 19149

Log Cabin Sport Shop
8010 Lafayette Rd.
Lodi OH 44254

Mitch Luksich
PO Box 1527
Sonoma CA 95476

Jack Malloy
PO Box 276
Wye Mills MD 21679

R.J. Maroni & Son, Inc.
Box 43325
Upper Montclair NJ 07043

Greg Martin
PO Box 330011
San Francisco CA 94133

Martin's Gun Shop
937 S. Sheridan Blvd.
Lakewood CO 80226

George E. Mathews & Son, Inc.
10224 S. Paramount Blvd.
Downey CA 90241

Ray Meibaum
Box 524
Florissant MO 63033

John A. Mendez
PO Box 620984
Orlando FL 32862

LeRoy Merz
Rt. 1—Nirschl Addition #2
Fergus Falls MN 56537

Damon Mills
718 Spring Valley Rd.
Montgomery AL 36116
Model Investments, Inc.
1032 26th St.
West Palm Beach FL 33407

Montana Outfitters (Lewis E. Yearout)
308 Riverview Dr. E.
Great Falls MT 59404

Walt Moreau
PO Box 14764
San Francisco CA 94114

Mountain Bear Rifle Works, Inc.
100 B Ruritan Rd.
Sterling VA 20164

Museum of Historical Arms
2750 Coral Way, Suite 204
Miami FL 33145

Muzzleloaders, Etcetera, Inc.
9901 Lyndale Ave. S.
Bloomington MN 55420

N.C. Ordnance Co.
PO Box 3254
Wilson NC 27895

Ray Petry
PO Box 385
Unionville PA 19375

Ron Peterson Guns
4418 Central South East
Albuquerque NM 87108

Pioneer Guns
5228 Montgomery Rd.
Norwood OH 45212

Pony Express Sport Shop, Inc.
16606 Schoenbom St.
North Hills CA 91343

Powder Horn Antiques
Robert N. Mandel, Marlene M. Mandel
PO Box 4196
Ft. Lauderdale FL 33338-4196

W.R. Powell
PO Box 186
Roanoke TX 76262

Brian Radcliffe
229 N. Main St.
Cheboygan MI 49721

Rare Arms Co.
PO Box 6107
Plymouth MI 48170

Martin B. Retting, Inc.
11029 Washington
Culver City CA 90232

Dick Reyes
PO Box 3296
Carson City NV 89702

Tommy Rholes
PO Box 638
Van TX 75790

Steve Rogers (Civil War)
PO Box 6595
Ithaca NY 14851

S & S Firearms
74-11 Myrtle Ave.
Glendale NY 11385

Frank Sellers
Crane Brook Rd.
Alstead NH 03602

Charles Semmer
7885 Cyd Dr.
Denver CO 80221

Ralph E. Shattuck (specializing in German Lugers)
19044 N. 98th Lane
Peoria AZ 85382

Michael Simens
13104 Lake Shore Blvd.
Bratenahl OH 44108

Simmons Gun Company
PO Box 495
Leichhardt
NSW 2040 Australia

Simpson Ltd. (Lugers)
140 S. Seminary St.
Galesburg IL 61401

C.W. Slagle
PO Box 4185
Scottsdale AZ 85261

Paul Sorrell
PO Box 7918
Beaumont TX 77726

Steve's House of Guns
Rte. 1
Minnesota City MN 55959

Stott's Creek Armory
RR 1, Box 70
Morgantown IN 46160

Victor W. Strawbridge
6 Pineview Dr.
Dover NH 03820

Jim Supica
Old Town Station
PO Box 15351
Lenexa KS 66285

Sweeney's Emporium
PO Box 936
Shawnee Mission KS 66201

David W. Taylor (Civil War)
Box 87
Sylvania OH 43560

Vintage Arms, Inc.
6003 Saddle Horse
Fairfax VA 22030

Mike Wamsher
17732 W. 67th St.
Shawnee KS 66217

Paul Weisberg
Rt. 30, PO Box 581
Schoharie NY 12157

Tom Wibberley
11001 Lincoln Ave.
Hagerstown MD 21740

M.C. Wiest
10737 Dutchtown Rd.
Knoxville TN 37932

Dean Williams
1304 140th St.
Spirit Lake IA 51360

The Winchester Sutler, Inc.
270 Shadow Brook Lane
Winchester VA 22603

Michael Zomber Co.
11050 Washington Blvd.
Culver City CA 90232

DEALERS PRIMARILY IN HIGH-GRADE MODERN AND VINTAGE SPORTING ARMS, SOME OF WHOM ALSO HANDLE ANTIQUE ARMS*

Albemarle Arms Co.
Mahlon G. Kelly/Thierry Duguet
Box 288, Rt. 250 West
Ivy VA 22945

Bill Birkbeck
Route 112 Box 7
Conway NH 03818

Thomas Bland & Sons
PO Box 363
Benton PA 17814

*There is an association of collectors and arms dealers, organized for membership of professionals and active collectors; membership is by application and invitation: Collector Arms Dealers Association (CADA), PO Box 427, Thomson IL 61285.

Cabela's
812–13th Ave.
Sidney NE 69160

Cape Outfitters
599 County Rd. 206
Cape Girardeau MO 63701

Herschel Chadick
Chadick's Ltd.
PO Box 100
Terrell TX 75160

Champlin Firearms, Inc.
PO Box 3191
Woodring Airport
Enid OK 73701

Classic Guns, Inc.
Frank S. Wood
3230 Medlock Bridge Rd., Suite 110
Norcross GA 30092

Colonial Gun Shop
143 Boone Square St.
Hillsborough NC 27278

Lewis Drake & Associates
305 South 8th St.
Murray KY 42071

Tony Galazan
PO Box 1692
New Britain CT 06051

Griffin & Howe, Inc.
36 W. 44th St., Suite 1011
New York NY 10036

Hallowell & Co.
340 W. Putnam Ave.
Greenwich CT 06830

Imperial Russian Armory, Inc. (Miniatures)
Joel Morrow
10547 South Post Oak
Houston TX 77035

Lefever Arms Co., Inc.
6234 Stokes
Lee Center Rd.
Lee Center NY 13363

Gary Herman (Safari Outfitters)
Route 44, Washington Hollow Plaza
R.D. 1, Box 2
Salt Point NY 12578

Holland & Holland, Ltd.
50 E. 57th St.
NY NY 10022

Jacqua's Fine Guns
900 E. Bigelow Ave.
Findlay OH 45840

William Larkin Moore & Co.
8727 E. Via de Commencio, Suite A
Scottsdale AZ 85258

New England Arms Co.
Box 278
Lawrence Lane
Kittery Point ME 03905

The Orvis Co.
Rt. 7
Manchester VT 05254

Allen B. Postel
Postel Gun Sales
214 S.E. 2nd
Ames IA 50010

Quality Arms
PO Box 19477
Houston TX 77224

Specialty Firearms
Brian Radcliffe
229 N. Main St.
Cheboygan MI 49721

Thad Scott Fine Guns, Inc.
PO Box 412
Indianola MS 38751

Wingshooting Adventures
0-1845 West Leonard
Grand Rapids MI 49544

*Note: there is an association of collectors and arms dealers, which professionals and active collectors may be able to join. Membership is by application and invitation: CADA (Collector Arms Dealers Association), PO Box 427, Thomson, IL 61285.

Appendix 5: Arms Collectors' Organizations

NATIONAL ORGANIZATIONS

BY MAKE AND TYPE

Automatic Pistol Collectors Association, National
PO Box 15738
Tower Grove Station
St. Louis MO 63163

Auto Collectors Association–Utah, Inc.
PO Box 514
Centerville UT 84104

Auto Weapons Association, Inc., Oregon
PO Box 83929
Portland OR 97283

Bayonet Collectors, The Society of
PO Box 234
East Islip NY 11730

Browning Collectors Association
2749 Keith Dr.
Villa Ridge MO 63089

Cartridge Collectors Association, International
PO Box 5297
Ormond Beach FL 32174

Colt Collectors Association
25000 Highland Way
Los Gatos CA 95030

Deringer Collectors, National Association
PO Box 20572
San Jose CA 95160

Deringer Collectors Association
500 East Old 66
Shamrock TX 79079

Egyptian Collectors Association, Inc.
PO Box 45
Burnt Prairie IL 62820

Finnish Arms & Militaria Collectors Association
PO Box 2988
Jackson MS 39207-2988

Garand Collectors Association
PO Box 181
Richmond KY 40475

Glock Collectors Association
PO Box 840
Park Hills MO 63601-0840

Golden Eagle Collectors Association
11144 State Creek Road
Grass Valley CA 95945

Harrington & Richardson Gun Collectors Association
330 S.W. 27th Ave., Suite 603
Miami FL 33135

High Standard Collectors' Association
540 W. 92nd St.
Indianapolis IN 46260

Hopkins & Allen Arms and Memorabilia Society
1309 Pamela Circle
Delphos OH 45833

International Ammunition Association, Inc.
8 Hillock Lane
Chadds Ford PA 19317-9705

Kentucky Rifle Association
844 Round Hill Rd.
Winchester VA 22602

Longrifles Collectors Association of Ohio
Rt. No. 1, Box 168-A
Beverly OH 45715

Mannlicher Collectors Association
PO Box 7144
Salem OR 97303

Marlin Firearms Collectors Association
407 Lincoln Building
44 Main St.
Champaign IL 61820

Miniature Arms Collectors/Makers Society, Ltd.
4910 Kilburn Ave.
Rockford IL 61101

M1 Carbine Collectors Association
PO Box 4895
Stateline NV 89449

Mossberg Collectors Association, National
PO Box 487
Festus MO 63028

Muzzle Loading Rifle Association, National
PO Box 67
Friendship IN 47021

Remington Society of America
11900 N. Brinton Rd.
Lake MI 48632

Ruger Collectors Association
PO Box 240
Greens Farms CT 06436

Sako Collectors Association
1725 Woodhill Lane
Bedford TX 76021

Scheutzen Society, Southern California
34657 Ave. E
Yucaipa CA 92399

Sharps Collectors Association
PO Box 6451
Phoenix AZ 85005

Single Shot Rifle Association, American
709 Carolyn Dr.
Delphos OH 45833

Smith & Wesson Arms Collectors Association
PO Box 24
Great Bend KS 67530

Thompson/Center Association
PO Box 792
Northboro MA 01532

Weatherby Collectors Association, Inc.
PO Box 888
Ozark MO 65721

The Winchester Arms Collectors Association
PO Box 230
Brownsbord TX 75756-0230

The Winchester Club of America
3070 South Wyandot
Englewood CO 80110

NATIONAL ORGANIZATIONS OTHER THAN BY MANUFACTURER OR TYPE

American Custom Gunmakers Guild
PO Box 812
Burlington IA 52601

American Pistolsmiths Guild
PO Box 67
Louisville TN 37777

American Society of Arms Collectors
PO Box 2567
Waxahachie TX 75165

Benchrest Shooters Association, Englishtown
64 Cooke Ave.
Carteret NJ 07008

Blackpowder Hunting Association, International
PO Box 1180
Glenrock WY 82637

Boone & Crockett Club
250 Station Dr.
Missoula MT 59801

Buckskinners, National Association of
1981 E. 94th Ave.
Thornton CO 80229

Citizens Committee for the Right to Keep and Bear Arms
Liberty Park
12500 NE Tenth Place
Bellevue WA 98005

Collector Arms Dealer Association (CADA)
PO Box 427
Thomson IL 61285

Continental Arms Collectors Association, Inc.
1126 Co. Rt. 20
Oswego NY 13126

Ducks Unlimited, Inc.
One Waterfowl Way
Memphis TN 38120

Federally Licensed Firearms Dealers, National Association of
2455 E. Sunrise
Ft. Lauderdale FL 33304

Fifty Caliber Shooters Association
11469 Olive Street Rd.
Suite 50
St. Louis MO 63141

Firearms Coalition
PO Box 6537
Silver Spring MD 20906

Firearms Engravers Guild of America
332 Vine St.
Oregon City OR 97045

Foundation for North American Wild Sheep
720 Allen Ave.
Cody WY 82414

Gun Owners Civil Rights Alliance
PO Box 131254
St. Paul MN 55113

Gun Owners of America
8001 Forbes Place, Suite 102
Springfield VA 22151

Handgun Hunters International
PO Box 357 MAG
Bloomingdale OH 43910

Handgun Metallic Silhouette Association, International (IHMSA)
PO Box 5038
Meriden CT 06450

Handloading Association, International
6471 Airpark Dr.
Prescott AZ 86301

Hunter Education Association
PO Box 525
Draper UT 84020

Jews for the Preservation of Firearms Ownership
2872 South Wentworth Ave.
Milwaukee WI 53207

Mule Deer Foundation
1005 Terminal Way, Ste. 110
Reno NV 89502

National Alliance of Stocking Gun Dealers
PO Box 187
Havelock NC 28532

National Association to Keep and Bear Arms
PO Box 78336
Seattle WA 98178

National Firearms Association
PO Box 160038
Austin TX 78716

National Foundation for Firearms Education
Mark K. Benenson, President
185 Madison Ave.
New York NY 10016

National Rifle Association of America
11250 Waples Mill Rd.
Fairfax VA 22030

National Shooting Sports Foundation
Flintlock Ridge Office Center
11 Mile Hill Rd.
Newtown CT 06470

National Skeet Shooting Association
PO Box 680007
San Antonio TX 78268

National Sporting Clays Association
PO Box 680007
San Antonio TX 78268

National Wild Turkey Federation
PO Box 530
Edgefield SC 29824

New England Antique Arms Society
Jim Mountain, (978) 827-6709
www.NEASS.org

North American Hunting Club
PO Box 3401
Minnetonka MN 55343
North-South Skirmish Association
204 W. Holly Ave.
Sterling VA 20164

Quail Unlimited
Rte. No. 3, PO Box 29B
Edgefield SC 29824

Rocky Mountain Elk Foundation
PO Box 8249
Missoula MT 59807

Safari Club International
4800 West Gates Pass Rd.
Tucson AZ 85745

Second Amendment Foundation
James Madison Building
12500 N.E. 10th Place
Bellevue WA 98005

Sporting Arms and Ammunition Institute
Flintlock Ridge Office Center
11 Mile Hill Rd.
Newton CT 06470

Sporting Clays of America
9 Mott Ave., Suite 103
Norwalk CT 06850

U.S. Practical Shooting Association (IPSC)
PO Box 811
Sedro Woolley WA 98284

U.S. Revolver Association
40 Larchmont Ave.
Taunton MA 02780

The Varmint Hunters Association
PO Box 759
Pierre SD 57501

The Wildcatters
PO Box 170
Greenville WI 54942

The Women's Shooting Sports Foundation
1505 Highway 6 South
Suite 101
Houston TX 77077

ORGANIZATIONS BY STATE

Alabama

Alabama Gun Collectors Association
PO Box 70965
Tuscaloosa AL 35407

Alaska

Alaska Gun Collectors Association
PO Box 111496
Anchorage AK 99511

Arizona

Arizona Arms Association
PO Box 46464
Phoenix AZ 85063

Arkansas

Arkansas Gun Cartridge Collector's Club, Inc.
PO Box 1015
Little Rock AR 72203-1015

Ark La Tex Gun Collectors Association, Inc.
9601 Blom Blvd.
Shreveport LA 71118

California

California Rifle & Pistol Association
12062 Valley View St., Suite 107
Garden Grove CA 92645

California Waterfowl Association
4630 Northgate Blvd., #150
Sacramento CA 95834

Far West Arms Collectors, Inc.
9460 Wilshire Blvd.
5th Floor
Beverly Hills CA 90212

Greater California Arms & Collectors Association
8291 Carburton St.
Long Beach CA 90808

Los Angeles Gun and Cartridge Collectors Association
20810 Amie Ave., Apartment No. 9
Torrance CA 90503

San Bernardino Valley Arms Collectors
18710 Cajon Blvd.
San Bernardino CA 92407

Santa Barbara Historical Arms Collectors Association
PO Box 6291
Santa Barbara CA 93160

San Fernando Valley Arms Collectors Association
PO Box 65
North Hollywood CA 91603

San Gabriel Valley Arms Collectors
1140 Daveric Dr.
Pasadena CA 91107-1740

San Luis Obispo Historical Arms Society
PO Box 3554
San Luis Obispo CA 93403

Southern California Arms Collectors Association
PO Box 7432
Thousand Oaks CA 91359-7432

Colorado

Colorado Gun Collectors Association
3267 Lowell Blvd.
Denver CO 80211

Connecticut

Stratford Gun Collector's Association, Inc.
PO Box 132
Fairfield CT 06430

Ye Connecticut Gun Guild
602 Park Rd.
West Hartford CT 06107

Delaware

Delaware Antique Arms Collectors Association, Inc.
PO Box 3512
Greenville DE 19807

Delaware Weapons Association
97 Johnson Rd.
Bangor PA 18013

Forks/Delaware Weapons Association
97 Johnson Rd.
Bangor PA 18013

Florida

Florida Gun Collectors Association
PO Box 10
Safety Harbor FL 34695

Northern Florida Arms Collectors Association, Inc.
7003 SW 46th Ave.
Gainsville FL 32608

Palm Beach Gun Collector's Association
6304 Silver Moon Lane
Greenacres FL 33463-3811

Tampa Bay Arms Collectors Association
PO Box 41666
St. Petersburg FL 33743-1666

United Sportsmen of Florida
PO Box 6565
Tallahassee FL 32314

Georgia

Georgia Arms Collectors Association
PO Box 277
Alpharetta GA 30239

Southeastern Antique Arms Collectors
PO Box 1104
Alpharetta GA 30239

Hawaii

Hawaii Historic Arms Association
PO Box 1733
Honolulu HI 96806

Illinois

Central Illinois Gun Collectors Association
PO Box 875
Jacksonville IL 62651

Illinois Gun Collectors Association
Rt. 1, PO Box 371
Kankakee IL 60901

Illinois State Rifle Association
PO Box 637
Chatsworth IL 60921

Kankakee Gun Collectors Association
347 S. Cleveland
Bradley IL 60915

Mississippi Valley Gun and Cartridge Collectors Association
PO Box 61
Port Byron IL 61275

Orville Dunham Antique Gun Collectors
4040 E. Cerro Gordo
Decatur IL 62521

Sauk Trail Gun Collectors
PO Box 1113
Milan IL 61264

Wabash Valley Gun Collectors Association
2601 Willow Rd.
Urbana IL 61801

Indiana

Indiana State Rifle and Pistol Association
PO Box 552
Chesterton IN 46304

Midwest Gun Traders, Inc.
1823 Frenchmans Xing
Ft. Wayne IN 46824

Northern Indiana Gun Collectors Association, Inc.
PO Box 898
Dowagiac MI 49047

Southern Indiana Gun Collectors Association
309 W. Monroe St.
Boonville IN 47601

Iowa

Beaver Creek Plainsmen
PO Box 298
Bondurant IA 50035

Central States Gun Collectors Association
633 3rd St., SE
Mason City IA 50401

Kansas

Chisholm Trail Antique Gun Association
1906 Richmond
Wichita KS 67203

Kansas Cartridge Collectors Association
Box 84
Plainville KS 67663

Kentucky

Kentuckiana Arms Collectors Association
7520 Greenlawn Rd.
Louisville KY 40242

Kentucky Gun Collectors Association
6607 Thoreau Village
Utica KY 42376

Louisiana

Ark-La-Tex Gun Collectors
9601 Blom Blvd.
Shreveport LA 71118

Bayou Gun Club
PO Box 313
Arabi LA 70032

Pelican Arms Collectors Association
PO Box 747
Clinton LA 70722

Washitaw River Renegades
PO Box 256
Main St.
Grayson LA 71435

Maryland

Baltimore Antique Arms Association
1034 Main St.
Darlington MD 21304

Eastern Shore Arms Collectors, Inc.
PO Box 1836
Easton MD 21601

Maryland Arms Collectors Association
Box 525
14917 York Rd.
Sparks MD 21152

Potomac Arms Collectors Association
PO Box 1812
Wheaton MD 20915

Massachusetts

Bay Colony Weapons Collectors
PO Box 111
Hingham MA 02043

Massachusetts Arms Collectors
PO Box 31
North Carver MA 02355

Michigan

Boardman Valley Collectors Guild
County Rd. 600
Manton MI 49663

Huron Gun Collector's Association
1694 Wismer
Ypsilanti MI 48198

Michigan Antique Arms Collectors
PO Box 1824
Warren MI 48090-1824

Pioneer Gun Club
8532 Schmeid Rd.
Vestaburg MI 48891

Minnesota

Minnesota Rifle and Revolver Association
10 Pheasant Lane
North Oaks MN 55127

Minnesota Weapons Collectors Association
PO Box 138
Mapleton MN 56065-0138

Zumbro Valley Arms Collectors
4138 32nd St. SE
Rochester MN 55904

Mississippi

Mississippi Gun Collectors Association
PO Box 16323
Hattiesburg MS 39402

Missouri

Mineral Belt Gun Collectors Association
1110 Cleveland Ave.
Monett MO 65708

Missouri Arms Collectors Association
634 Scottsdale Rd.
St. Louis MO 63122-1109

Missouri Valley Arms Collectors Association
8906 Bellview
Kansas City MO 64114

St. Louis Antique Arms Association, Inc.
3303 North Lindberch
St. Ann MO 63074-3307

Montana

Montana Arms Collectors Association
1516 21st Ave. S.
Great Falls MT 59405

Northwest Montana Arms Collectors Association
PO Box 653
Kalispell MT 59901

Weapons Collectors Society of Montana
3100 Bancroft
Missoula MT 59801

New Hampshire

New Hampshire Arms Collectors
Route 28, PO Box 44
Windham NH 03087

New Jersey

Civil War Round Table of North New Jersey
124 Conover Lane
Red Bank NJ 07701

Fort Lee Arms Collectors, Inc.
415 Beveridge Rd.
Ridgewood NJ 07450

Jersey Shore Antique Arms Collectors
PO Box 100
Bayville NJ 08721

New Jersey Arms Collectors Club
230 Valley Rd.
Montclair NJ 07042

South Jersey Arms Collectors
6 Georgetown Rd.
Glassboro NJ 08028

New Mexico

New Mexico Gun Collectors Association
PO Box 13687
Albuquerque NM 87192

New York

Empire State Arms Collector's Association, Inc.
PO Box 20488
Rochester NY 14602-0488

Iroquois Arms Collectors Association
2816 Mckoon Ave.
Niagra Falls NY 14305

Long Island Antique Gun Collectors Association
112 Fernwood Ave.
Oakdale NY 11769

Mid-State Arms Collectors
24 S. Mountain Terrace
Binghamton NY 13903

New York State Arms Collectors Association, Inc.
24 S. Mountain Terrace
Binghamton NY 13903

North Eastern Arms Collectors Association
331 Netherland Ave.
Staten Island NY 10303

Westchester Collectors Club
54 Farm View Rd.
Pt. Washington NY 11050

North Carolina

North Carolina Gun Collectors Association
PO Box 23570
Charlotte NC 28227-0272

North Dakota

Dakota Territory Gun Collectors Association, Inc.
1012 14th Ave. West
Watertown ND 58078

Ohio

Maumee Valley Gun Collectors Association
1427 Cass Rd.
Maumee OH 43537

Ohio Gun Collectors Association
PO Box 9007
Maumee OH 43537-9007

The Stark Gun Collectors
5666 Waynesburg Dr.
Waynesburg OH 44688

Tri-State Gun Collectors
709 Carolyn Dr.
Delphos OH 45833

Oklahoma

Indian Territory Gun Collectors Association
PO Box 33201
Tulsa OK 74153-1201

Oregon

Oregon Arms Collectors Association
PO Box 8986
Portland OR 97207-8986

Oregon Cartridge Collectors Association
52 Northwest 2nd
Gresham OR 97030

Western Sportsmen & Arms Collectors
PO Box 20733
Keizer OR 97307

Williamette Valley Arms Collectors Association
PO Box 5191
Eugene OR 97405

Pennsylvania

Central Penn Antique Arms Association
PO Box 914
Mechanicsburg PA 17055

Lancaster Muzzle Loading Rifle Association
779 Prospect Rd.
Columbia PA 17512

Pennsylvania Antique Arms Collectors Association
PO Box 63
Media PA 19063

Pennsylvania Gun Collectors Association
5209 Norma Dr.
Pittsburgh PA 15236

Presque Isle Gun Collectors Association
156 East 37th St.
Erie PA 16504

South Carolina

South Carolina Arms Collector's Association
403 Wilton St.
Greenville SC 29609

South Carolina Shooting Association
PO Box 12658
Columbia SC 29211

South Dakota

Dakota Territory Gun Collectors Association
Castlewood SD 57223

Tennessee

Memphis Antique Weapons Association
2444 Yesteroaks Dr.
Germantown TN 38139

Smoky Mountain Gun Collectors Association
8609 Kingston Pike
Knoxville TN 37933

Tennessee Gun Collectors Association
3556 Pleasant Valley Rd.
Nashville TN 37204

Tennessee Military Association
PO Box 1006
Brentwood TN 37024

Texas

Alamo Arms Collectors Association
9215 Havelock
San Antonio TX 78250-2229

Austin Gun Collectors Association
c/o McBride's Guns
2915 San Gabriel
Austin TX

Dallas Arms Collectors Association, Inc.
PO Box 704
Desoto TX 75123

Houston Gun Collectors Association
PO Box 741429
Houston TX 77274

Paso Del Norte Gun Collectors, Inc.
PO Box 31613
El Paso TX 79930

Pioneer Gun Collectors Association
4500 South Georgia
Amarillo TX 79110

Texas Cartridge Collectors Association
5606 Duxbury
Houston TX 77035

Texas Gun Collectors Association
PO Box 273
Portland TX 78374

Texas State Rifle Association
PO Drawer 710549
Dallas TX 75371

Utah

Utah Gun Collectors Association
PO Box 711161
Salt Lake City UT 84121

Virginia

Shenandoah Valley Gun Collector's Association
PO Box 288
Winchester VA 22601

Virginia Arms Collectors Association
c/o American Historical Foundation
1142 W. Grace St.
Richmond VA 23220

Virginia Gun Collectors Association, Inc.
RR 1, Box 365
Waterford VA 22190-9512

Washington

Arms Collectors of Southwest Washington
PO Box 2622
Vancouver WA 98668

Washington Arms Collectors, Inc.
PO Box 389
Renton WA 98057

Wisconsin

Central Wisconsin Gun Collectors Association
PO Box 2184
Oshkosh WI 54903

Great Lakes Arms Collectors Association
2913 Woodridge Lane
Waukesha WI 53188

Indianhead Firearms Association
RR #9 Box 186
Chippewa Falls WI 54729

Wisconsin Gun Collectors Association
PO Box 181
Sussex WI 53089

Wyoming

Wyoming Weapons Collectors
PO Box 284
Laramie WY 82070

INTERNATIONAL

Australia

Sporting Shooters Association of Australia
PO Box 2066
Kent Town, SA 5071
Australia

Canada

Canadian Historical Arms Society
PO Box 901
Edmonton, Alberta, Canada T5J 2L8

National Firearms Association
PO Box 1779
Edmonton, Alberta, Canada T5J 2PI

Tri-County Antique Arms Fair
PO Box 122
RR No. 1
North Lancaster, Ontario, Canada KOC 120

England

Arms and Armour Society
E.J.B. Greenwood
Field House
Upper Dicker
Halisham, East Sussex BN27 3PY
England

Historical Breechloading Smallarms Association
D. J. Penn M.A.
Imperial War Museum
Lambeth Road
London SE 1 6HZ
England

National Rifle Association
Bisley Camp
Brookwood, Woking
Surrey GU24 OPB
England

France

Syndicat National de l'Arquebue serie du Commerce de l'Arme Historique
B.P. No. 3
78110 Le Vesinet
France

Germany

Bund Deutscher Sportschutzen e.v. (BDS)
Borsigallee 10, 53125
Bonn 1
Germany

New Zealand

New Zealand Deerstalkers Association
Michael Watt
PO Box 6514
Wellington, New Zealand

South Africa

Historical Firearms Society of South Africa
PO Box 145
5 Newlands
Republic of South Africa

SAGA (S.A. Gunowners' Association)
PO Box 35204
Northway 4065
Republic of South Africa

ABOUT THE AUTHOR

R. L. WILSON is a freelance consultant and author in the broad fields of firearms and engraving. His career began with intern positions at the Royal Armouries, H.M. Tower of London, and the Corcoran Gallery of Art as well as at the Wadsworth Atheneum, where he was appointed Curator of Firearms at the age of twenty-three. He has served on advisory boards or as consultant to The Metropolitan Museum of Art, the U.S. Marshals Service, Colt's Manufacturing Company, Inc., the Winchester Museum (now termed Cody Firearms Museum, Buffalo Bill Historical Center), the U.S. Society of Arms and Armour, Tiffany & Co., and the Autry Museum of Western Heritage.

The most published author in the history of arms collecting, Wilson's career began with *Samuel Colt Presents,* a 314-page publication of the Wadsworth Atheneum (1961), based on the loan exhibition of the same title, which he organized.

Wilson was born in Minnesota, the son, nephew, and grandson of Presbyterian ministers. He studied history and art as a scholarship student at Carleton College, Northfield, Minnesota. A longtime resident of Connecticut, he is the author of approximately 34 books and more than 250 articles on firearms and engraving subjects. Keenly interested in museums and historic houses since childhood, Wilson has visited over 750 such institutions over the years, ranging from artistic, historical, and natural science themes, to country houses and gardens.

In addition to writing books and articles, he is consultant on American arms to Christie's, for whom he was active in organizing the Colt/Christie's sale of October 1981 and The Metropolitan Museum of Art, Arms and Armor Department benefit auction of October 1985, as well as nearly twenty other sales, several of them milestones in the history of arms collecting, setting record prices for American firearms and launching the current popularity of the firearms auction venue.

Publishers of Wilson's books include Random House, Simon & Schuster, Crown/House of Collectibles, Abbeville Press, the Buffalo Bill Historical Center, and the Wadsworth Atheneum. His articles have appeared in numerous publications, including most of the popular firearms-related magazines, as well as *Audubon, Sports Afield, True,* the French art magazine *L'Oeil,* and the hardcover automobile magazine, *Ferrarisima.*

Wilson has been the subject of (or noted in) articles in a variety of newspapers and magazines, including *The New York Times, The Washington Post, The Wall Street Journal, USA Today, M, The Chicago Tribune, Newsday, BusinessWeek, The Houston Chronicle, Esquire, Art and Antiques, Robb Report, Forbes, Connoisseur, Forbes FYI, Vanity Fair,* and *Town & Country.* For Christmas 1999, *The Today Show*'s Gene Shalit featured *Buffalo Bill's Wild West.*

Wilson's book *The Colt Heritage* is the only firearms-related work ever nominated for the American Book Awards (1979). That title, later reissued in an expanded edition as *Colt: An American Legend* (both titles recognized as the official history of Colt firearms), was hailed by publisher/author Michael Korda as "a classic . . . the most beautiful book on firearms ever published and a milestone in modern book design and production." In promotion of the *Legend* book, Abbeville Press organized a two-week, seven-city author's tour during which Wilson made over thirty-five radio and television appearances, newspaper interviews, and bookstore signings. Over 180,000 copies of these two Colt titles are in print, in four languages.

These Colt titles began a series of firearms books of like style and design, on a variety of subjects. Next in the series was *Winchester: An American Legend,* appearing in 1991 (50,000 copies in the first edition)—the official history of Winchester firearms and ammunition. *The Peacemakers: Arms and Adventure in the American West* appeared in 1992 and was honored with a Wrangler in the National Cowboy Hall of Fame's annual Western Heritage Awards program (1993). In 1999, *Buffalo Bill's Wild West* was also honored with a Wrangler, the Western Americana equivalent of winning an Oscar.

Colt: An American Legend, Winchester: An American Legend, The Peacemakers, and *Buffalo Bill's Wild West* have been published in foreign language editions, generally in Italian, French, and German. Their oblong format, clean design, and thorough scholarship have set high standards for quality in the publication of firearms books and have garnered a following among book collectors.

Nineteen ninety-six marked the publication of Wilson's *Ruger and His Guns: a History of the Man, the Company and Their Firearms,* the official history of Sturm, Ruger & Co., and its founder, William B. Ruger Sr. *Buffalo Bill's Wild West* joined the series in the fall of 1998. His next title in the oblong format is *The World of Beretta: An International Legend,* due in the fall of 2000. This official volume on the historic Italian gunmaker appears simultaneously in an unprecedented five languages. It will be the seventh in Wilson's series of oblong, specially designed books on firearms.

Appearing in the fall of 1999 was *Fine Colts: The Dr. Joseph A. Murphy Collection,* followed in the fall of 2000 by the more than 900-page opus in two volumes: *The Colt Engraving Book.*

Wilson has appeared frequently on radio and television, and these national and international programs include: A&E's *The Story of the Gun* and *The Guns That Tamed the West;* numerous episodes in the History Channel's phenomenally successful series *Tales of the Gun;* on the Discovery Channel's *Gunpower* and *The Gunfighters;* the PBS Frontline documentary *Gunfight USA;* CNN's *Pinnacle* (on William B. Ruger Sr.); *Business Unusual* (on Beretta); and a CNN profile. Other appearances include CNN's *Business Day; Good Morning Australia; The Barry Gray Show* (New York); documentaries on Channel 4 (London) and Japan Broadcasting TV; and the BBC documentaries *The Gun Industry in America* and *Son of a Gun or How Sam Colt Changed America.*

Wilson was scriptwriter for the Sony video presentation *Colt Firearms Legends* (narrated by Mel Tormé). In the $2.25 million feature-length film and video on conservation, hunting, and the African safari, *In the Blood,* Wilson was one of the "stars," as well as co-executive producer. As president of Castle View Productions, he produced *Mille Miglia: The Most Beautiful Race in the World* (1995). He is presently assisting in a video project on Annie Oakley, produced and directed by documentary filmmaker Riva Freifeld, and appeared in yet another documentary on the Mille Miglia (the 1999 event, in which he competed as navigator in a 1927 Type 43 Bugatti).

An appraiser of rare firearms, Wilson's clients have included P. R. Phillips, Gene Autry, Monte Hale, Mel Tormé, various members of the Lilly, Ford, Mellon, and Deering families, the Sagamore Hill Historic Site, the Theodore Roosevelt National Park, the Autry Museum of Western Heritage, the Art Institute of Chicago, the Buffalo Bill Museum, the Wadsworth Atheneum, the National Cowboy Hall of Fame, the Texas Ranger Museum, and the Colt company. He was a consultant to the Wadsworth Atheneum on the lavish exhibition, *Sam and Elizabeth: Legend and Legacy of Colt's Empire* (September 1996 to March 1997).

In collaboration with George A. Strichman, late Chairman of the Board of Colt Industries, Wilson organized the Colt Industries Museum Collection (1972–85), as well as Chairman Strichman's own 170-piece Colt collection. Both arms groups are now featured exhibits at the Autry Museum of Western Heritage.

Wilson is past president (1989–1995) of The Armor and Arms Club of New York (founded in 1921) and is currently an Honorary Director of the Texas Gun Collectors Association. He has also served on the board of directors of the National Firearms Museum in Fairfax, Virginia, and is currently on the board of the Eli Whitney Museum in New Haven, Connecticut. He has spoken on fine guns and related subjects to The Connecticut Historical Society, the Boone and Crockett Club, the Australian Arms Collectors Society, the Houston Museum of Fine Arts, The Armor and Arms Club of New York, The Rotary Club of Brescia (Italy), The Mzuri-Safari Foundation, The New York/Tri-State Chapter of Safari Club International, and other groups.

In connection with *Buffalo Bill's Wild West,* Wilson and coauthor Greg Martin (with collector Michael Del Castello) assisted in producing the Royal Armouries Museum major blockbuster exhibition of "Buffalo Bill's Wild West" at that institution's $100 million site in Leeds, England. Following the initial presentation in the summer of 1999, the collection was featured in special loan exhibitions at the Autry Museum of Western Heritage (Los Angeles; spring 2000) and the Tennessee State Museum (Nashville; fall 2000). The Denver Museum will exhibit the collection in the spring of 2001.

Still another project is an exhibition, book, and video, *The Arms of Tiffany & Co.,* in collaboration with former Tiffany & Co. archivist Janet Zapata. Other current projects include *Firesticks and Tomahawks* and *The Guns of Manhattan*—both part of his history of firearms series.

A keen sportsman, Wilson has pursued game shooting in England, Scotland, France, Spain, Belgium, Italy, Australia, India, Africa, and extensively in the Western Hemisphere, including three trips to Alaska. He has been on nine African safaris, and is a member of the historic Camp Fire Club of America (founded in 1897). He is also a member of a number of other firearms and conservation organizations as well as a life member of the National Rifle Association.

The R. L. Wilson Educational Endowment has been established with the nonprofit NRA Foundation, a fund that continues to grow annually. He is also a donor to the National Firearms Museum and the sponsor of a special display on "The Shot Heard Round the World."

Wilson was appointed Chairman of the National Foundation for Firearms Education, headquartered in New York City. Among members of the Foundation board are Michael Korda, Roy Innis (Chairman of CORE), Les Line (conservationist, former Editor, *Aubudon Magazine*), and President Mark K. Benenson (former Chairman, Amnesty International, USA).

In 1972 Wilson became chairman of the U.S. office of the Tarassuk Appeal, devoting six solid months in that year and in 1973, promoting efforts to win exit visas from the Soviet Union for Dr. and Mrs. Leonid Tarassuk, their two children, and Tarassuk's mother. Nearly two years later the Tarassuks were finally allowed to leave, the campaign in the U.S. and Europe having been instrumental in gaining their freedom.

A devoted student of automobile racing, Wilson has attended numerous Formula 1, Indy Car, and endurance events including the LeMans 24 Hours, the Grand Prix of Monaco, and the Indianapolis 500 and has visited several museum and private automobile collections throughout Europe and North America. He has participated in such competitions as Italy's Mille Miglia (1993, '94, '95, '97, '98, '99, and 2000), the Tour de France (1996), and the American U.S. Express, popularly known as the "Cannonball." He is a graduate of the three-day single-seater race car course and the two-day advanced single-seater course of the Jim Russell Driving School at Laguna Seca, California, and a graduate of the three-day single-seater course of the Skip Barber School at Bridgehampton, New York.

Since the late 1970s Wilson has been researching a lavishly illustrated book on the North American Racing Team and on the celebrated race driver and Ferrari importer, Luigi Chinetti, and his son, race driver, Ferrari importer, and automobile designer, Luigi Chinetti Jr.

"Larry Wilson's contributions to the study, collecting, and appreciation of Colt firearms and history have no parallel."

—George A. Strichman, Chairman Emeritus, Colt Industries

"R. L. Wilson has examined, handled, and written about more fine and historical guns than anyone in the entire history of firearms." —Mel Tormé

Books by the Author Which Can Be Ordered Directly from R. L. WILSON BOOKS

P.O. BOX 430, HADLYME, CONNECTICUT 06439, U.S.A.
FAX: 860 526 9514
E-MAIL: WILSONBOOK @ AOL.COM
WEB SITE: WILSONBOOKS.COM

***NEW—THE OFFICIAL R. L. WILSON PRICE GUIDE TO GUN COLLECTING, 3rd Edition.** The most comprehensive book ever published on gun collecting, with in-depth commentary on the entire world of arms collecting, and featuring a history of the "world's greatest hobby," and virtually everything anyone would want or need to know about this most captivating field. Over 220 illustrations, covering the entire spectrum of arms collecting, and including over 32,000 gun value figures, selected reference books, the world of gun shows, cataloguing, buying, selling, trading, and much, much more. **$22.95.** Special limited edition of 500 copies, **$40.** 1st Edition—a few copies left, **$25**; limited edition, **$40.** Second Edition—a few copies left, @**$25**; limited edition, **$40.**

****NEW*—FINE COLTS The Dr. Joseph A. Murphy Collection.** This lavish new work covers exquisite deluxe and rare Colt arms from Paterson and other percussion revolvers to the cartridge period and up through modern times. The Dr. Murphy collection serves as the ideal source for reviewing the captivating story of deluxe and engraved colt arms. Over 250 richly detailed illustrations, most in color. Detailed text on Colt engraving. Hardcover, in vertical format, 9" × 12", 264 pages. Limited edition of 3,000 signed and numbered copies, **$100.00.**

****NEW*—THE COLT ENGRAVING BOOK,** R. L. Wilson. This third edition from the original texts of 1974 and 1982 has been fine-tuned and expanded dramatically, and is by far the most complete and illuminating. VERTICAL format, so this work joins the author's *The Book of Colt Firearms,* and *Fine Colts* as companion volumes. Over 1,200 illustrations, more than ⅔ in color. More than *900 pages, in two volumes.* Each volume at **$175, for a total of $350.** Each volume is numbered and signed, and in a limited edition of 3,000.

BUFFALO BILL'S WILD WEST, R. L. Wilson with Greg Martin, featuring the collection of Michael Del Castello, with treasures from the Buffalo Bill Museum, Buffalo Bill Historical Center (Cody, Wyoming), and the Autry Museum of Western Heritage (Los Angeles). Over 340 pages, over 225 color plates and 160 B&W illustrations. Winner of the Wrangler from the National Cowboy Hall of Fame Western Heritage Awards, 1999, as "[a] unique volume. . . . the most spectacular, lavish and detailed illustrated tribute ever to Buffalo Bill and his Wild West show-business originals." Sixth in author's oblong format "History of American Firearms" books. Photos by Peter Beard and Douglas Sandberg. **$60.** *Author's special limited edition of 500 copies,* **$85.**

***NEW*—THE WORLD OF BERETTA An International Legend.** 358 pages; over 250 illustrations, most in color, including spectacular collages by Peter Beard. History of the oldest industrial dynasty in the world, and the oldest gunmaker. Published on the 475th anniversary of Beretta. Standard edition **$65**; author's own numbered, limited edition of 500 copies **$85**. Leatherbound edition, numbered, limited to 1,000, **$250.00**.

***Special 50th Anniversary Edition*—RUGER & His Guns: A History of the Man, the Company and Their Firearms,** R. L. Wilson, photos by Peter Beard and G. Allan Brown. The story of the Sam Colt of our time, and his dedication to firearms. Official history, profusely illustrated and including Colts, Winchesters, Remington, S&W, fine U.S. and British single shot rifles, double rifles, and more. Fifth in the "History of American Firearms" books. 368 pages; over 2,000 illustrations, **$65.00**. *Author's own numbered, limited edition, of 500 copies,* **$85.00**.

COLT, AN AMERICAN LEGEND, R. L. Wilson. Over 400 color plates, over 110 black & white. Official history of Colt firearms with detailed serial number tables. All-time bestselling book on Colt firearms. Standard edition, **$40.00**. *Numbered, limited edition, of 500 copies,* **$65.00**.

STEEL CANVAS: THE ART OF AMERICAN ARMS, R. L. Wilson, photos by Peter Beard, G. Allan Brown, *et. al.* For the first time, a comprehensive, panoramic tribute to fine American arms, their European predecessors, and contemporary arms of the finest quality. Foreword by William R. Chaney, Chairman of the Board, Tiffany & Co. Featured are leading gunmakers from the Kentucky rifle to Colt, Winchester, Remington, Sharps, Marlin, Deringer, and many, many more. This extraordinary compilation of fine guns from the 1700s to modern times includes richly decorated European arms as well. Over 325 color plates and 165 B&W. 1995. **$65.00.** *Special limited edition of 500 copies, numbered and signed by the author,* **$85.00**. **Special leatherbound edition, numbered, limited to 1,000. Only a handful of copies remaining: $250.**

THE PEACEMAKERS: ARMS AND ADVENTURE IN THE AMERICAN WEST, R. L. Wilson, photos by Peter Beard, G. Allan Brown, *et. al.* A unique pictorial celebration of the West, lavishly illustrated and unsurpassed in its authenticity: a collector's item for anyone interested in America's colorful past. From the Lewis & Clark Expedition to today's Western films and videos, the arms and adventurers who made the Colt, the Winchester, and many other marques into American gun legends. Over 325 color plates, over 225 B&W. Standard reference. 1992. **$65.00.** *Special limited edition of 500 copies, numbered and signed by the author,* **$85.00**.

THE BOOK OF COLT FIREARMS, R. L. Wilson. 1993 re-edition of the 1971 work, considered the standard reference in the Colt field. Improvements and changes made over the original work, including introduction detailing how book was created. **$150.00** *Special limited edition of 500 copies, numbered, signed by the author,* **$175.00**.

COLT PISTOLS, R. E. Hable and R. L. Wilson. Lavish presentation of the Hable Collection of Colt firearms. This is the most elaborate book on Colt handguns ever published, and covers production from the 1830s to the late 1970s. Profuse color illus., limited edition, with slip case. Out of print. **$150.00.**

SON OF A GUN or How Sam Colt Changed America, hour-long video by BBC-TV, presenting history of Colonel Colt and the influence of Colt firearms on history. Appearances by Mel Tormé, Greg Martin, and R. L. Wilson. **$30.00.**

COLT FIREARMS LEGENDS, narrated by Mel Tormé, script by R. L. Wilson. Hour-long video done as companion to *Son of a Gun*. Shows over $25,000,000 worth of fine and rare Colt firearms. Rated best collector oriented gun video done to date. **$30.00.**

IN THE BLOOD. Feature film by the director of *Pumping Iron*. Starring Robin Hurt, Tyssen Butler, President Theodore Roosevelt, Greg Martin, and R. L. Wilson. Gripping tale of hunter and hunted. Documents two African safaris: the first led by President Roosevelt in 1909, the second by his grandson nearly 80 years later. Features TR's Holland & Holland rifle. Intense, powerful, provocative, breathtaking; and proof of the key role of hunting in the conservation of wildlife. **$39.95.**

COLT'S DATES OF MANUFACTURE 1836–1978, R. L. Wilson. Detailed serial numbers by year. Tables for all models of Colt handguns and long arms. **$10.00.**

L. D. NIMSCHKE FIREARMS ENGRAVER, R. L. Wilson. Large format. Unique pictorial record of engraving impressions and gun photographs revealing the work of one of America's foremost arms embellishers; active 1850–1904. Numerous prints and photographs of deluxe guns of Lt. Col. George Armstrong Custer, cowboys and ranchers, kings and queens and more. Second edition. **$100.00.** New edition planned for fall 2001.

THE RUSSIAN COLTS, Dr. Leonid Tarassuk and R. L. Wilson. Published on occasion of a loan exhibition of presentation Colt revolvers by The Hermitage Museum, St. Petersburg, to The Metropolitan Museum of Art. With details on all other known gold inlaid percussion Colts. Profusely illustrated. 32 pages. **$25.00.**

WINCHESTER: AN AMERICAN LEGEND, R. L. Wilson. Official history of Winchester arms and ammunition, issued in conjunction with Winchester's 125th anniversary. Companion book to **Colt: An American Legend**. Featuring color photography by G. Allan Brown. Detailed appendix tables. Random House, 1991. Over 300 color plates, over 160 B&W. Standard edition, **$65.00.** *Special limited edition of 500 copies, numbered and signed by the author.* **$85.00.**

WINCHESTER ENGRAVING, R. L. Wilson. Only book devoted to Winchester arms embellishment, from the Jennings, Volcanic and Henry on up to modern times. Over 500 pages, 100 color plates and 700 B&W. **$115.00.**

THE DERINGER IN AMERICA, Vol. 1 (Percussion period), L. D. Eberhart & R. L. Wilson. Standard reference on the deringer, c. 1830–1870, with exhaustive detail on all known makers. 28 color plates and over 400 B&W plates. 8½" × 11" format. **$65.00.** *Serial #'d edition, signed and limited to 500 copies,* **$95.00**.

THE DERINGER IN AMERICA, Vol. 2 (Cartridge period), L. D. Eberhart & R.L. Wilson. Standard reference on the deringer, c. 1860–early 20th century. Covers over 75 makers of cartridge pistols, as well as an updating of percussion deringers missed in volume 1. Like vol. 1, presents voluminous information not found in any other book. Same 8½" × 11" format, special color section and over 500 B&W illus. Colt, Remington, Sharps, and much, much more. **$65.00.** *Serial #'d edition, signed and limited to 500 copies,* **$95.00**.

THE COLT HERITAGE POSTER with cover and eight dramatic color shots from **THE COLT HERITAGE** book, published in 1979. Rare memento of classic Colt book. Signed by the author, **$15.00**.

PATERSON COLT PISTOL VARIATIONS, P. R. Phillips and R. L. Wilson. Only publication on the rarest of all Colt arms. Over 100 B&W and color illus., with detailed text. 232 pp. 8½" × 11". Out of print; only a few copies remaining. **$60.00.**

COLT: The Making of an American Legend, William Hosley, published in documenting the exhibition held at the Wadsworth Atheneum, 1996, by University of Massachusetts Press. A fresh and original look at the Colt legend in American and European history, with guns and other artifacts from the collection of Colonel and Mrs. Samuel Colt. **$35.00.**

NOTE: The author has more than ten books in various stages of completion. **THE ARMS OF TIFFANY, ARROWS AND FIRESTICKS The Arms of the American Indian**, and **THE GUNS OF MANHATTAN** are but three of the titles. He is collecting photographs and information on arms subjects continually and appreciates hearing from collectors and other sources for his ever-expanding pictorial archives on arms and armor.

NOTE: Books, articles, or videos ordered from this list will be sent via UPS or parcel post insured. Please add $5 per title for postage & handling in the U.S. Please add $12 for first title for International orders, and $6 per additional title. Check or money order, or Mastercard/Visa. Should you wish books by RLW inscribed, please so indicate on order.

LOAD UP WITH *THE OFFICIAL®* *GUIDE TO GUNMARKS*, THE *BEST* IDENTIFICATION GUIDE ON THE MARKET !

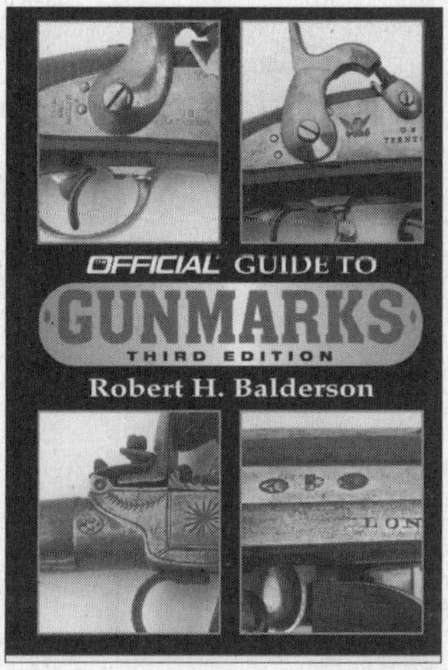

- Over 1,500 gunmarks illustrated and indexed for easy reference
- Proof and inspection marks from the late nineteenth century to date, indicating country of origin, date of manufacture, and the test performed to qualify the gun
- Includes Military Acceptance marks
- Alphabetical listing of trade names and codes for guns without trademarks
- Special section on the *Waffenamt* numerical system used by the Germans during World War II

HOUSE OF COLLECTIBLES

SERVING COLLECTORS FOR MORE THAN THIRTY-FIVE YEARS

ORDER FORM

❑ YES. Please send me *The Official® Guide to Gunmarks,* 676-60039-5.
My price direct from the publisher is just $15.00 plus $3.00 shipping and handling. If not satisfied, I may return this book at the end of 30 days for a prompt refund.

Name ____________________

Address ____________________

City ____________ State ________ Zip ________

❑ Check enclosed for $__________* (payable to House of Collectibles).

❑ Charge my

❑ VISA ❑ MasterCard ❑ American Express ❑ Discover

Credit Card Number *Expiration Date* *Signature (required)*

* Please add applicable sales tax.

HOUSE OF COLLECTIBLES
299 Park Avenue, New York, NY 10171

ALLOW AT LEAST 4 WEEKS FOR DELIVERY.